Margaret Thatcher

CHARLES MOORE

Margaret Thatcher

*The Authorized Biography:
Single-volume Centenary Edition*

Edited by Daniel J. Collings

ALLEN LANE
an imprint of
PENGUIN BOOKS

ALLEN LANE

UK | USA | Canada | Ireland | Australia
India | New Zealand | South Africa

Allen Lane is part of the Penguin Random House group of companies whose addresses can be found at global.penguinrandomhouse.com

Penguin Random House UK
One Embassy Gardens, 8 Viaduct Gardens, London SW11 7BW

penguin.co.uk

First published in Great Britain by Allen Lane 2025

002

Copyright © Charles Moore, 2025

Material in this volume was adapted from:

Margaret Thatcher: The Authorized Biography, Volume One: Not For Turning
Margaret Thatcher: The Authorized Biography, Volume Two: Everything She Wants
Margaret Thatcher: The Authorized Biography, Volume Three: Herself Alone

Penguin Random House values and supports copyright. Copyright fuels creativity, encourages diverse voices, promotes freedom of expression and supports a vibrant culture. Thank you for purchasing an authorized edition of this book and for respecting intellectual property laws by not reproducing, scanning or distributing any part of it by any means without permission. You are supporting authors and enabling Penguin Random House to continue to publish books for everyone. No part of this book may be used or reproduced in any manner for the purpose of training artificial intelligence technologies or systems. In accordance with Article 4(3) of the DSM Directive 2019/790, Penguin Random House expressly reserves this work from the text and data mining exception.

The moral right of the author has been asserted

Set in 10.2/13.5 pt Sabon LT Std
Typeset by Six Red Marbles UK, Thetford, Norfolk
Printed and bound in Great Britain by Clays Ltd, Elcograf S.p.A.

The authorized representative in the EEA is Penguin Random House Ireland, Morrison Chambers, 32 Nassau Street, Dublin D02 YH68

A CIP catalogue record for this book is available from the British Library

ISBN: 978–0–241–68767–3

Penguin Random House is committed to a sustainable future for our business, our readers and our planet. This book is made from Forest Stewardship Council® certified paper.

To Patrick Gillachrist Moore
and in memory of Julian Seymour (1945–2025)

Contents

List of Illustrations	xi
Preface	1
1. From Grantham to Oxford 'Mahogany and child'	9
2. Becoming Mrs Thatcher 'What a pity such a charming girl should be lost to politics!'	35
3. Member, minister, milksnatcher 'The Most Unpopular Woman in Britain'	67
4. Who dares wins: leadership challenge 'Heath will murder you'	102
5. The Iron Lady 'It *is* a moral struggle'	128
6. Labour isn't working 'There's only one chance for women'	156
7. Downing Street 'They thought she was a sort of right-wing baboon'	179
8. Not for turning 'They are all against me, Robert. I can feel it'	207
9. Russia … and Reagan 'The only European leader I know with balls'	236
10. Hunger in Ireland 'The lady behind the veil'	250
11. The 1981 Budget 'We've got to move fast to save her'	267
12. The Falklands 'I don't think anyone else but you could have done it'	281

13. Landslide, 1983 — 325
    'I live in a big house called 10 Downing Street. I'm going to live there for a long time'

14. Reagan plays her false — 349
    'If I were there Margaret, I'd throw my hat in the door before I came in'

15. The enemy within — 377
    'If anyone has won, it has been the miners who stayed at work'

16. Sales of the century — 398
    'Privatization was thought to be a pipe dream. Now it is a reality'

17. The coming of Gorbachev — 414
    'For heaven's sake, try and find me a young Russian'

18. Irish agreement; Brighton bomb — 444
    'The day I was not meant to see'

19. Poll tax; Single European Act — 463
    'How dare they! We saved all their necks in the war'

20. The death-knell of monetarism — 489
    'She's a moral coward when it comes to dealing with people'

21. Helicopter crash — 505
    'Her hands were not entirely clean'

22. That Bloody Woman — 527
    'We are in danger of a major disaster'

23. Against Queen and Commonwealth — 545
    'Blacks and their families out of work? *Moral?* Poof!'

24. To Moscow — 562
    'The light is coming from the West'

25. What they saw in her — 583
    'Mrs Thatcher is the point at which all snobberies meet'

26. The last victory, 1987 — 599
    'There's a woman who will never fight another election'

27. Bourgeois triumphalism — 614
    'What's to stop us?'

28. Schools, AIDS and health 635
'Do we <u>have</u> to do the section on Risky Sex?'

29. The shadow of Lawson 651
'You can't buck the markets'

30. Bush turns away 676
'I respect her. I like her. But I'm the President of the United States!'

31. Secrets and lies 706
'They're as bad as Nazis'

32. Ten years, then an ambush 729
'No resignations yet, I see!'

33. Unfinished business 758
'The proposals are bold . . . Please go ahead indicating my full support'

34. God; climate; South Africa 775
'No generation has a freehold on this earth'

35. The Wall falls; Germany rises 802
'Toad is at the wheel'

36. Trouble at home 838
'I'd never seen her flailing before'

37. 'No. No. No.' 856
'She was determined to have the fight'

38. Downfall 877
'But it's a coup'

39. The lioness in winter 912
'The Almighty had shaped her to be prime minister, but not to do anything else'

40. The light fades 945
'Good night, Margaret. Sleep well'

Epilogue 964
Acknowledgements 973
Index 975

This volume is published without endnotes. Readers seeking source citations will find them at the parallel point in the original three-volume edition of the biography.

Biographical notes for many of those appearing in the text can be found in the Index.

List of Illustrations

1. Margaret Roberts with her father, c. 1927. (© *Manchester Daily Express*/Science & Society Picture Library)
2. Margaret Roberts's mother, Beatrice Stephenson, as a young woman. (© Lady Thatcher. Reproduced with permission from www.margaretthatcher.org, the website of the Margaret Thatcher Foundation)
3. Exterior of the Roberts family shop in Grantham. (© *Manchester Daily Express*/Science & Society Picture Library)
4. Margaret Roberts among the girls who matriculated at Somerville College, Oxford, 1943. (With permission of the Principal and Fellows of Somerville College, © Gillman and Soame)
5. Tony Bray as an army officer, probably 1946. (By kind permission of Tony Bray)
6. Margaret the scientist at J. Lyons, 1950. (© Chris Ware/Keystone Features/Getty Images)
7. Margaret Roberts's first election address, Dartford, 1950. (Oxford, Bodleian Library, Conservative Party Archive, Shelfmark: PUB 229/9/5)
8. Robert Henderson, Buckingham Palace, 1947. (By kind permission of Mark McLaren)
9. Margaret Roberts with handbag at a Dartford fête, 1951. (© Ullsteinbild/Topfoto)
10. Letter from Margaret to Muriel, 1951. (By kind permission of Andrew Cullen)
11. Denis and Margaret's wedding reception, December 1951. (© Alpha Press)
12. Married love, 1957. (By kind permission of Jane Cullen)
13. Seeing Mark and Carol off to school, 1959. (© Barratt's/S&G Barratts/EMPICS Archive)
14. Mrs Thatcher in front of Big Ben, 1961. (© Popperfoto/Getty Images)
15. Margaret plays the piano to her family, June 1970. (© Ian Showell/Keystone/Hulton Archive/Getty Images)
16. With a portrait of Ted Heath, 1973. (© Paul Delmar/Getty Images)
17. 'My cupboard is not a hoard in any sense of the word.' 'Maggie' the housewife, December 1974. (© *Daily Mail*/Rex Features)
18. With her family after the second ballot, February 1975. (© Trinity Mirror/Mirrorpix/Alamy)

LIST OF ILLUSTRATIONS

19. The first meeting between Mrs Thatcher and Ronald Reagan, April 1975. (© PA/PA Archive/Press Association Images)
20. With Peter Morrison, Isle of Islay, August 1978. (By kind permission of Dame Mary Morrison)
21. At a Conservative local government conference, March 1979. (© PA/PA Archive/Press Association Images)
22. 'Where there is despair, may we bring hope.' Mrs Thatcher enters 10 Downing Street as Prime Minister, May 1979. (© PA/PA Archive/Press Association Images)
23. In the uniform of the UDR, South Armagh, August 1979. (© PA/PA Archive/Press Association Images)
24. Listening to Ted Heath at the party conference, Blackpool, October 1981. (© Bill Cross/*Daily Mail*/Rex Features)
25. With Denis at Chequers, 1980. (© Richard Slade/Camera Press)
26. With Admiral Lord Lewin, St Paul's Cathedral, October 1982. (© PA/PA Archive/Press Association Images)
27. With Airey Neave. (© Rex Features)
28. Bernard Ingham, Mrs Thatcher's press spokesman. (© Topfoto)
29. With Harold Macmillan, 1979 (© Keystone/Getty Images)
30. Keith Joseph at the Conservative Party conference, 1980. (© Keystone/Getty Images)
31. Denis Thatcher listening to his wife during the election campaign, 1983. (© John Downing/Getty Images)
32. Canvassing the voters of Salisbury, 1983. (© Harry Kerr/*The Times*/News Syndication)
33. Celebrating the election victory with Cecil Parkinson, 10 June 1983. (© Homer Sykes/Alamy)
34. Police face the picket line outside Orgreave Coking Plant, June 1984. (© PA Photos)
35. Helping to decorate Carol's new flat, 1984. (© Scope Features)
36. Cutting Mark's birthday cake, Imlau, 1985. (© Churchill Archives Centre, Cambridge: THCR 8/1/103)
37. Greeting Ronald and Nancy Reagan during the London Economic Summit, June 1984. (© News Syndication)
38. Mrs Thatcher during the European Economic Community summit in Fontainebleau, June 1984. (© AP/PA Photo)
39. The Thatchers and Cynthia Crawford leaving the Grand Hotel in Brighton, 12 October 1984. (© John Downing/Getty Images)
40. Bomb damage to the exterior of the Grand Hotel. (© ANL/Rex Shutterstock)

41. Meeting Deng Xiaoping in Beijing, 1984. (© Pierre-Antoinne Donnet/ AFP/Getty Images)
42. With Ronald Reagan in a golf cart at Camp David, 1984. (© AP/PA Photos)
43. Clowning with the press on the return flight from Washington. (© Mirrorpix)
44. With Garret FitzGerald, during the signing of the Anglo-Irish Agreement, November 1985. (© Corbis/Reuters)
45. Mrs Thatcher at home doing her boxes, 1983. (© Herbie Knott/Rex Shutterstock)
46. Michael Heseltine, 1986. (© *Daily Mail*/Rex Shutterstock)
47. With Prince Bandar of Saudi Arabia, 1984. (© PA/Topfoto)
48. With King Fahd of Saudi Arabia, 1987. (© Tim Graham/Getty Images)
49. The Thatchers on holiday in Imlau, August 1984. (© Churchill Archives Centre, Cambridge: THCR 8/1/103)
50. The Thatchers on holiday in Cornwall, August 1986. (© *Daily Mail*/ Rex Shutterstock)
51. With François Mitterrand at Canterbury Cathedral, February 1986. (© Peter Jordan/Getty Images)
52. Receiving the Queen at Downing Street, 1985. (© Brian Harris/ Alamy)
53. Nigel Lawson. (© Brian Harris/Rex Shutterstock)
54. Kelvin MacKenzie and Rupert Murdoch, January 1986. (© PA Photos)
55. Visiting workers' housing in Moscow, March 1987. (© Steve Back/ Rex Shutterstock)
56. With Gorbachev at the Kremlin. (© Boris Yurchenko/AP/PA Photos)
57. Campaigning in Finchley, 1987. (© *The Times*/News Syndication)
58. Celebrating the election victory with Norman Tebbit, 1987. (© Fox Photos/Getty Images)
59. Mrs Thatcher visiting Thornaby, Middlesbrough, 12 September 1987. (© Peter Reimann/Mirrorpix/Getty Images)
60. Meeting Mikhail Gorbachev at RAF Brize Norton, 7 December 1987. (© Ken Lennox/Mirrorpix)
61. With Lech Wałęsa, Gdańsk, 4 November 1988. (© Wojtek Laski/Getty Images)
62. At Downing Street, 1990. (© John Downing/Getty Images)
63. Charles Powell at the door of 10 Downing Street, during Gorbachev's visit, 6 April 1989. (© Ken Towner/Associated Newspapers/ Shutterstock)
64. Michael Thatcher, with Mrs Thatcher and his parents, Mark and Diane Thatcher, May 1989. (© PA/TopFoto)

65. Visiting Her Majesty Queen Elizabeth II, Balmoral, *c.*1983. (© by courtesy of Andrew Parker Bowles)
66. With Geoffrey Howe at the G7 summit, Paris, July 1989. (© The Churchill Archives Centre, Cambridge: THCR 8/1/154. Copyright unknown)
67. John Major and Kenneth Baker at the Conservative Party conference, Blackpool, 12 October 1989. (© Howard Walker/Mirrorpix)
68. Listening to Nigel Lawson's speech at the Conservative Party conference, Blackpool, 12 October 1989. (© Paul Smith/Mirrorpix)
69. With George Bush and Helmut Kohl at the G7 summit, Paris, 14 July 1989. (© Süddeutsche Zeitung/Alamy)
70. Arriving for a meeting with George Bush at Camp David, 24 November 1989. (© George H.W. Bush Presidential Library and Museum)
71. Mrs Thatcher with the Cabinet, July 1990. (© Crown Copyright)
72. With Nelson Mandela, 4 July 1990. (© AP/TopFoto)
73. With Douglas Hurd during the CSCE conference, Paris, 20 November 1990. (© The Churchill Archives Centre, Cambridge: THCR 8/1/173. Copyright unknown)
74. Making her final speech in the House of Commons, 22 November 1990. (© Parliament.uk. All Rights Reserved)
75. Speaking on the steps of 10 Downing Street for the last time as Prime Minister, 28 November 1990. (© Theodore Wood/Camera Press, London)
76. Shedding a tear, 28 November 1990. (© Ken Lennox/Mirrorpix)
77. Announcing she will leave the House of Commons at the next general election, 17 Great College Street, 28 June 1991. (© the *Sun*/Shutterstock)
78. Among the US Marine Corps after the Gulf War, March 1991. (© Collection of Alexandra Warfield Davis. Copyright unknown)
79. Visiting the Reagans, Rancho del Cielo, Santa Ynez, California, 7 February 1993. (© Ronald Reagan Presidential Foundation/The Churchill Archives Centre, Cambridge: THCR 8/1/221)
80. Signing copies of her memoirs, Hong Kong, April 1995. (© Mark Ralston/*South China Morning Post*/Getty Images)
81. The Thatchers with their grandchildren, Michael and Amanda, 1994. (© Thatcher Family collection)
82. Seated in the House of Lords for the state opening of Parliament, 21 June 2001. (© Shutterstock)
83. At Denis's memorial service, the Guards Chapel, London, 30 October 2003. (© Ian Waldie/Getty Images)

84. Welcoming the Queen to her 80th birthday party, the Mandarin Oriental Hyde Park, 13 October 2005. PA/TopFoto
85. Viewing the casket of President Reagan on Air Force One, June 2004. (© Pete Souza for the Ronald Reagan Presidential Foundation)
86. With Sir John Major at the Garter service, St George's Chapel, Windsor, 18 June 2007. (© Leon Neal/AFP/Getty Images)
87. Received by Gordon Brown, 10 Downing Street, 13 September 2007. (© Alessandro Abbonizio/AFP/Getty Images)
88. With Crawfie, Venice, 2008. (© by courtesy of Romilly, Lady McAlpine)
89. With pensioners at the Royal Hospital, Chelsea, 14 February 2008. (© Shutterstock)
90. Mourners at Lady Thatcher's funeral at St Paul's Cathedral, 17 April 2013. (© Nils Jorgensen/Shutterstock)

Preface

This book appears just before the centenary of its subject's birth. Margaret Hilda Roberts was born over her father's grocer's shop in Grantham on 13 October 1925. The Baroness Thatcher, LG, OM, died in the Ritz Hotel, London, on 8 April 2013. This book is the story of the woman, brought up in that provincial setting, who became, after Winston Churchill, the most important British political leader of the twentieth century. She remains the most famous and consequential elected woman in human history.

The single volume here published is the final iteration of a long process. It began in 1997, when Lady Thatcher, having left office in 1990 and then written her memoirs, needed to decide how her personal political papers should best be preserved for posterity. After her unprecedented continuous eleven and a half years in office and a work rate matched by no prime minister before or since, the quantity of material was vast. Having been refused an honorary degree by her own university, Oxford, while she was Prime Minister, Lady Thatcher decided to offer the papers to Churchill College, Cambridge, the best modern British political archive. Under the rules then prevailing, most of the papers could not be released to the public at that time.

Friends advised Lady Thatcher, however, that someone – indeed, many people – would want to write her biography. They suggested that she choose a writer with whom she had a good relationship as her authorized biographer, granting him immediate access to the papers. For reasons she never explained, she chose me. Our acquaintance, which was friendly but not intimate, had begun in her middle years as Prime Minister, arising from my work as Editor of *The Spectator*, and grown closer after she left office. At the time she offered me the task I was Editor of *The Daily Telegraph*.

She stipulated that I should be allowed to see all her papers in Churchill College and she would grant me interviews for the book. In addition, she issued a general invitation to family, friends, colleagues, former civil servants and staff and world leaders to cooperate with my inquiries. This was invaluable, because until then many of them had been discouraged from speaking, especially by Civil Service rules of confidentiality, which the then Cabinet Secretary, Sir Richard Wilson, now agreed to waive. This resulted in interviews, sometimes multiple ones, with roughly 600 people. Lady Thatcher also sought and gained Sir Richard's permission for me to see all those government papers not yet released, most of which were held, pending their eventual transfer to the National Archives at Kew, in the Treasury. I was also able to access numerous records abroad, especially the United States, many of which had never been made public before. Although Lady Thatcher commissioned me to write the book, she did not pay me. It was up to me to take her offer to possible publishers. I accepted the contract offered by Penguin Books.

Lady Thatcher's other conditions were that she would not be allowed to read my manuscript and that it could not appear in her lifetime. Otherwise, she feared, people would assume she had tried to control the book. That would gravely damage its claims to independence and the proper freedom of historical inquiry. I am eternally grateful to her and her advisers that she set these conditions without me having to ask for them: if I had asked and she had said no, a tricky tussle might have ensued. I had feared that she might indeed try to control the project. As it turned out, she was interestingly uninterested in it. I think her attitude was, 'I did it: someone else can write about it.' She had considerable egotism, but little petty vanity. Although often self-critical, she was rarely introspective: she had little desire to examine her own life and motivations, which made my task more of a journey of discovery than it might otherwise have been. Temperamentally, she was always more inclined to look forward than back. This makes her an unusual biographical subject. After reading the first volume of my book, the late novelist Hilary Mantel wrote to tell me that she had been 'utterly gripped' by it, because 'I am also "working with" a character (in the shape of Thomas Cromwell [the subject of her great *Wolf Hall* trilogy]) who is clever and complex but doesn't spend time in introspection: who really lives in the present moment, like a Test batsman facing fast bowling.'

A consequence of the conditions attached to my work was that I could not know how long I had to write the book. Lady Thatcher was seventy-one when she approached me, and in good health. A few years later she suffered a notable decline in her mental powers, particularly at the time of the death of her husband, Denis, in 2003. It was then that I decided to leave the editorship of the *Telegraph* to make more time for the work. As it turned out, Lady Thatcher was to live for a further decade, by which time my first volume was ready for publication. I can recall correcting the final page of the final proof on a journey to London. By an eerie coincidence, the moment I got off the train, I was informed that she had died.

In its original form the book appeared in three volumes, the second following in 2015, the final volume in 2019. The length of the book is explained by the circumstances described above – first, because Mrs Thatcher, as Prime Minister, was unbelievably busy and uniquely long-lasting and, second, because it was my task, as the first person to study the great majority of the papers and to talk to almost all the dramatis personae, to give a full account to the world of what they revealed. Mrs Thatcher was very much a prime minister – perhaps the last of the kind – who governed primarily through studying the papers in her red boxes and issuing written memos, drafted by her private office, in response. She did not practise what was later called 'sofa government' and in her time there were no emails or mobile phones, let alone WhatsApp group chats or viral posts on social media. Even her television and radio appearances, though she realized how important they were, were sparingly used. She governed through paper and through the House of Commons. It is only by reading the papers she read, and especially the comments which she scrawled over so many of them, that one can fully understand what she was about.

In 2023, with Covid-19 at last out of the way and all three volumes long since launched, Stuart Proffitt, my outstanding editor at Penguin, suggested a single-volume version of the book. I never doubted his commercial judgement but I was, at first, a bit resistant. Authors like to believe that all their words are precious, and I was keen to ensure that the rich detail of Mrs Thatcher's story should not be lost. I also liked – and still like – the fact that the space afforded by three volumes allowed some of the context of the exciting times in which she thrived to be set before the reader and to give scholars confidence that they could depend on the book for study. A further pleasure of the three volumes is that they have room for political and cultural atmosphere. This includes the uniqueness, as it was at the time, of a woman in charge of a man's world. It made everything excitingly different, and I think it stimulated her.

But when, with the vital and tireless help of Daniel Collings, I embarked on the task of cutting and reshaping my own words, getting rid of 60 per cent of them, I found the process more rewarding than I had expected. In every sentence one hunts down redundancy and works as hard as possible for clarity. I had to try to apply to my own work the sort of discipline which Mrs Thatcher herself always applied to her task of governing, sifting the difference between what mattered and what did not, trying to maintain the aim and avoid distraction.

On the whole, Mrs Thatcher emerges well from this exercise. When the barnacles are scraped off and a way cut through the seaweed, it becomes more evident that the governments she led were not usually, at least by twenty-first-century standards, adrift. Rather than being swept hither and thither by the tides of public opinion, held back by the drag anchor of bureaucracy, or trying vainly to ride the waves of what Harold Macmillan called 'events, dear boy, events', they were sustained with a sense of purpose which came, to a very large degree, from her. Putting aside my role as author and imagining myself as a general reader, I think I would enjoy this tale crisply told. This book aims to capture the essence of Margaret Thatcher. Because it is for that general reader, it is shorn of the endnotes and bibliography which are part of the full service provided by the three volumes. It contains minor updates and revisions but has not identified any previously undiscovered body of evidence.

Over the nearly thirty years since I began this task, I have seen the reputation of Margaret Thatcher undergo a great many changes. In the early years of my work she was still, for many on the left, the wicked witch of privilege who had 'torn the heart out of communities' (particularly mining villages). At the same time, however, as was cogently explained to me for the book by Tony Blair, her first Labour successor as Prime Minister, she was of great use to his party as a model in how to lead a reforming government which would confront vested interests and ruthlessly marginalize political opponents. Although no Thatcherite, Sir Tony remains one of her strongest admirers.

After the Labour landslide of July 2024, Sir Keir Starmer's new Labour government, the first for fourteen years, quickly became mired in a series of mistakes, economic and presentational, which showed its inexperience. After about six months it was Blairites, displaying the toughness they had learnt from Mrs Thatcher, who came back in to bring focus to Labour. At the time of writing it is too early to say whether this will ultimately work, but it is possible to discern a sort of apostolic succession of political leadership, with Starmer learning from Blair learning from Thatcher. Despite their disagreement with her politics, her example remains the yardstick by which many Labour politicians judge their own success. (The same is, obviously, true of all Conservative leaders.)

Labour's use of Thatcher-inspired statecraft has been especially noticeable in the handling of Britain's relationship with the United States. Nothing could replicate the longevity and closeness of Mrs Thatcher's ties to Ronald Reagan (which lasted his entire eight years in the White House), but the lessons were learnt, with both Bill Clinton and George W. Bush. In the era of Donald Trump's second presidency, Sir Keir allowed himself to be guided in Trump-handling by Blairites like Lord Mandelson and Jonathan Powell (brother of Mrs Thatcher's closest civil servant, Charles). They coached him in the pragmatic management needed when there is potential strain in the relationship with Britain's most powerful ally. For the first time since his victory the year before, Sir Keir began to acquire something of a statesmanlike aura.

With Trump's second presidency, the world order in which Mrs Thatcher was so powerful passes firmly into history. The global context for Margaret Thatcher was the Cold War struggle against Soviet Communism and the related need, as she and Reagan saw it, to revive the free-market economies of the West. Both these aims were, broadly speaking, achieved, and although not always well maintained by the succeeding generation, they remained the basis of Western policy until the beginning of 2025. It is an irony that the moves away from these assumptions are being led by a Republican President who seems to prefer the Russian regime of Vladimir Putin to those of his country's allies. One tries to imagine President Trump meeting Prime Minister Thatcher and to guess which of these two formidable characters would have prevailed.

In the economic sphere, Trump, though a devout believer in the importance of business, repudiates Thatcher/Reagan free-trade doctrines and proclaims the virtues of protectionism (without attacking their progenitors by name). More generally, he does not seem to subscribe to the Thatcher/Reagan vision of an outgoing set of Western values which challenges tyranny and welcomes strong allies and new recruits. He expresses personal fondness for Britain, but his doctrine of America First leaves little room for concepts such as Mrs Thatcher's unity of the English-speaking peoples or America's concern at the end of the 1980s to establish 'Europe, whole and free'.

At present, conservatives and economic liberals all over the world are uncertain and divided about how to respond to these changes. They also agonize about the conflict between established orders and 'populism'. If, as seems likely, they will eventually wish to fight back against Trumpian isolationism, the story of Mrs Thatcher, America's most consistent external friend since 1945, will be a source for inspiration.

Another great change in the twenty-first century, to which Donald Trump's re-election was an angry reaction, is a loss of self-confidence among leading Western democracies on a scale not seen since the 1930s. The rise of Islamist terrorism since 11 September 2001, preceded and, even more, followed by growing mass immigration from the Muslim world, has created unease. At much the same time, the assumption that economic growth can be assured by globalism and low interest rates has been kicked away by the financial crisis of 2008–9, the after-effects of Covid-19 and the energy crisis created by Putin's invasion of Ukraine. The incapacity of governments to deliver or even preside over growing prosperity has created a lack of faith in ruling elites not unlike the one which enabled Mrs Thatcher to rise to power in the 1970s.

That loss of faith is not only economic, but also cultural. The mood is that nothing effective or admirable can be expected from our leaders. The symptoms include – on the left – a 'decolonizing' rejection of a white imperial past and, on the right, a narrative of betrayal of the nation by globalized elites. Margaret Thatcher began her rise to power after her predecessor as Conservative leader, Edward Heath, lost the February 1974 election. Asking voters the question, 'Who governs Britain?', he failed to get the clear answer he wanted. Between 1979 and 1990 she succeeded, for better and for worse, in proving that *she* governed Britain. This set an extraordinarily powerful example of which all her successors, of both parties, have been envious. Part of the reason why Britain, in 2016, voted for Brexit – the largest single vote (17.4 million) for one side ever cast in British history – was the sense that we were not being allowed to govern ourselves. (Indeed, that was the principal motivation behind Lady Thatcher's private support for leaving the European Union in her post-office years.) Resentment at this sense of powerlessness is a feature not only of Britain today but of all the Western world, and it helps to explain the appeal of Trump in the United States.

In her time, Mrs Thatcher strongly identified with and represented the impatience of ordinary voters with tired elites of both parties. She had considerable natural sympathy with those who wish to make the best of their chances in life and she wished to spread those chances more widely. She remained, however, a legitimist – never challenging the underlying structure of the constitutional order, the monarchy, Parliament, the judges, the traditional impartiality of the Civil Service, even the position of the Established Church. Although in many ways an economic revolutionary and what is nowadays called a 'disruptor', she was also profoundly respectable, both in personal dealings and in cultural attitudes. Even at the time, she seemed positively old-fashioned in this respect. Today, she seems from another age entirely.

And yet her disruptive power remains striking. It lay not only in her ideas of economic choice and personal liberty, but also in her sex. Without revealing her hand too often, she revelled in the thought that a woman could outwit the men, outwork them and beat them at their own game – the control of money, war and power. She truly believed that women, because of their importance in the home and family, were better grounded than men in the economic and emotional realities of life, and she was determined to bring that advantage to bear upon the male-dominated public sphere. In the hundreds of talks I have given about Mrs Thatcher, in a good many countries, the theme raised by audiences (especially, of course, by women) even more often than the nature of her conservative beliefs is her character and achievements as a woman. It is because of this, above all, that the Iron Lady became in her lifetime and will probably always remain a myth and an icon.

Charles Moore
Etchingham, August 2025

I
From Grantham to Oxford
'Mahogany and child'

Phoebe Stephenson took her granddaughter, Muriel Roberts, upstairs. Through the bedroom door came the cry of a newborn baby. 'Can you hear something?' Phoebe asked the four-year-old Muriel. 'I said "no",' Muriel recalled more than seventy years later, 'I *could* hear something but I wouldn't say so.' With this lack of fanfare, on 13 October 1925, the future Margaret Thatcher came into the world.

She was born Margaret Hilda Roberts, in the house of her parents Alfred Roberts and his wife Beatrice Stephenson – 1 North Parade, Grantham, Lincolnshire. They lived above the shop, a grocery that Alfred had bought in 1919. Muriel was Margaret's only sister. The Robertses had no sons.

Alfred Roberts had left school at thirteen to make a living, but he longed for education, and acquired it by voracious reading and study. He had risen through the retail trade and was also a local preacher in the Methodist church. In one of his sermons, delivered after the Second World War, Roberts reflected on 'The neglected length of mahogany counter' and what might be made of it: 'what a thing of beauty it became when the craftsman contributed all his skill of polishing. But the beauty was there, just waiting to be revealed.' Roberts went on to offer an example of a neglected child, given new life and love by foster parents: 'The child was gloriously beautiful, a most lovable disposition, and infectious cheerfulness. These things were there all the time but only when someone made their full contribution did they become part of human experience.' When Alfred Roberts's younger child had made her 'full contribution' to her country, she reread these notes, in preparation for her memoirs, and linked the two stories. Adding a note, she wrote: 'Mahogany and child'.

The mahogany counter across which Margaret sometimes served customers was always beautifully polished. 'If you get it from Roberts's ... you get – THE BEST' boasted an advertisement in the *Grantham Almanack* in 1925. Margaret herself lovingly recalled: 'Behind the counter there were three rows of splendid mahogany spice drawers with sparkling brass handles, and on top of these stood large, black, lacquered tea canisters ... Wonderful aromas of spices, coffee and smoked hams would waft through the house.'

The shop stood on a corner between the richer and poorer districts of Grantham. As well as being a high-class provision merchant, Roberts's was also a post office and therefore served the clients of the early welfare state. Poverty and bourgeois comfort lived in close proximity. Seventy years later, Margaret remembered a widow in black entering the shop with two young children: 'She asked if she could have three small oranges for the price of two because she had to be so careful.' As Margaret explained, 'Life was not something we did not know about. We were right in it.'

The Robertses saw it as their duty to help where they could. Every Thursday afternoon, Beatrice Roberts would have a 'big bake', giving out loaves to 'people we knew' who were in need, with the act of charity carefully obscured: 'Mother's had a big bake and she wondered whether you would like this.'* Alfred Roberts's shop prospered, and not long before Margaret's birth he added a second. Although never rich, Roberts established a secure and respected business, the base from which to serve the town as councillor, Rotarian and Methodist.

The base was quite austere. When Margaret lived there the house had no garden, no hot water, and an outside lavatory. 'I remember having a dream', she said later, 'that the one thing I really wanted was to live in a nice house, you know, a house with more things than we had.'

Home life was strict. It was dominated by work and by religion, ensuring that Margaret was never idle. As her daughter Carol put it, 'She never experienced nothingness.' Sundays saw almost continuous religious activity: preaching for Alfred Roberts and church services and Sunday school for the rest of the family. Roberts often brought visiting speakers home. It seems to have been meeting Methodist missionaries from India that inspired Margaret's ambition. After listening to them, she remembered, 'I wanted to be an Indian civil servant, because I thought that India was a remarkable place and I would love to be ... a cog in the wheel of this great empire.' Margaret appreciated and even enjoyed many aspects of Methodism. She participated fully in the musical life, playing the piano (like her mother) and, at eighteen, learning the organ. She also enjoyed the conversation on public questions in the shop parlour to which Methodists repaired after the Sunday evening service. 'Father taught me to like what

---

* This was a traditional form of charity. In George Eliot's *Silas Marner*, Dolly Winthrop, the wheelwright's wife, brings poor Marner some lard-cakes, imprinted with the initials of Jesus, giving the excuse that she has had a baking day and that the cakes are more than she needs.

he called "discussion",' she recalled. Her father's sermon notes are full of precepts one can almost hear her own lips speaking: 'There is no promise of ease for the faithful servant of the Cross,' or 'God wants no faint hearts for His ambassadors'. 'We were Methodist and Methodist means method,' Margaret told one biographer. She always loved method.

She also studied her father's speaking technique. 'Have something to say. Say it as clearly as you can. That is the only secret of style,' he wrote in his sermon notes, quoting Matthew Arnold. That was her view too. She admired Alfred's methods, but also observed with a critical eye. 'Sometimes I'd say, "Pa, that was your sermon voice, your sermonizing voice" and then it would be a bit lighter.'

Margaret rarely criticized her upbringing but conceded that the family's religious life set them 'a little bit apart'. She greatly enjoyed visiting her schoolfriend Jean Farmer, whose father was a builder at Fulbeck, ten miles outside Grantham, where the atmosphere was freer and more joyful. Margaret's elder sister Muriel was harsher about the girls' upbringing. 'It was all church, church, church,' she said. 'We had an uncle every Christmas who sent us religious books. Oh God how we hated it. You weren't allowed to play games. That really is bigoted, isn't it?' Alfred Roberts once said: 'I'll never put my foot inside a Catholic church.' Such attitudes were not at all uncommon, but the Robertses made their daughters feel them more than most families. When Margaret had children of her own, Beatrice Roberts protested when they were taken to the Church of England rather than to Methodist services.*

The Roberts girls laid the blame for restriction and narrowness squarely on their mother.† Margaret described herself in *Who's Who* as 'd of late Alfred Roberts', with no mention of her mother. Roberts's surviving letters (all post-war) show love for both his daughters, though sprinkled with small reproaches to Margaret for not paying him enough attention. In everything he did he tried to advance his girls. During the war he asked a friend, the Anglican Canon Goodrich, to coach Margaret for her university entrance exam. 'My great wish', he said, 'is to get Margaret into Oxford.' This was not the action of a paterfamilias who wished to keep his

---

* Margaret was always vague about the sacramental aspect of religion. When the present author asked her, at the baptism of Oliver Letwin's twins (to one of whom she stood godmother), about the baptism of her own twins, she said perplexingly, 'Oh well, they were christened, but they didn't have the water.'

† Margaret, in later life, would brook few criticisms of her father. She was, it appears, unaware of his reputation for a wandering eye, and worse, with women. Kenneth Wallace was the son of the Robertses' dentist. His wife used to say, 'I wouldn't trust that man an inch. If he had half a chance, he'd have his hand up my skirt.' According to Wallace's sister, Mary, Roberts 'touched women in a way completely uncalled for'.

daughter tied to hearth and home. 'He wanted me to have what he hadn't had,' said Margaret.

In Muriel's view, Beatrice Roberts was 'a bigoted Methodist... Margaret and I weren't close to her ... Mother didn't exist in Margaret's mind.' Margaret always expressed herself more charitably, but tended to speak of Beatrice, if at all, in a subsidiary role. She later explained this by recourse to her beloved Rudyard Kipling and the poem 'The Sons of Martha': 'Mary was the one who listened at the feet of Jesus and always was interested in what was going on and Martha was the one who always went, "Now is there enough to eat?" "Do you want fresh clothes?" "Would you like to lie down?" This was my mother.'

It is telling that Margaret retained the Kipling version, because his poem portrays the Sons of Martha as the people in life who make sure that God's work is actually done, seeing things through to the end without pretension:

> Not as a ladder from earth to Heaven, not as a witness to any creed,
> But simple service simply given to his own kind in their common need.

There is nothing Margaret Thatcher admired more than 'simple service simply given'. She believed that was what her mother contributed.

But she did not like it much at the time. The letters she wrote to Muriel in the 1940s mention their mother often, but almost always in passing and usually in connection with some prohibition. One example was her desire for a maroon leather handbag: 'I haven't told Mummy or Daddy about this as I am sure that Mummy at any rate would think it very extravagant.' In 1944, after her first summer at Oxford, she went with Beatrice to see *Now, Voyager*: 'I have never liked Bette Davis but nevertheless I thought she was simply marvellous.' Mrs Roberts had demurred: 'I think she would have preferred it to end happily ever after sort of style.' The implication was that Margaret felt more intellectually sophisticated than her mother. Perhaps Beatrice Roberts's reservations are not so surprising, since the film concerns a daughter's defiance which so shocks her overbearing mother that she dies of a heart attack. 'I loved her dearly,' Margaret said later, 'but after I was fifteen we had nothing more to say to each other.'

In fact, the mother's influence was never expunged from her daughter's character. Margaret Thatcher was always more a Martha than a Mary: she loved domestic labour. Beatrice Stephenson, a professional seamstress before she met Alfred Roberts, had taught her daughters her craft, lessons Margaret did not forget. One contemporary at the Bar remembered Margaret's own children wearing duffel coats lined with their old nursery curtains. In her surviving letters to Muriel, clothes (often illustrated by rough drawings) are a far more common subject than politics. Even in her pomp, Margaret liked to remember human need – for food, comfort, praise or consolation, though not, unless heavily prompted, for sleep. Fussing around people was her favoured way of showing affection and concern: she loved to be practical. She might leave her husband each morning to go and run the country, but not before she had cooked his breakfast. All this was the legacy of Beatrice Roberts.

In later life, Margaret felt she had been unappreciative of her mother. Unlike with her father, whom she believed to be the greatest positive influence in her life, she found it difficult to find words to convey her belated appreciation. In the end, she said simply: 'I don't think I thanked my mother enough, because you don't realize.'

The Grantham in which Alfred Roberts became an increasingly important figure was a modestly successful market town. The Belvoir Hunt, the foxhound pack of the Duke of Rutland, always met in Grantham on Boxing Day. Roberts would take his daughters along. The young Margaret enjoyed her rural walks, picking rosehips on Hall's Hill or visiting friends like Jean Farmer, but she and her family were really town mice. It was always towns, preferably cities, which allured her.

The most powerful local man – and the biggest landowner – was Lord Brownlow, whose family, the Custs, were seated at Belton, just outside Grantham. According to Muriel, Caroline Cust, Lord Brownlow's daughter, used to 'rave' about Margaret. The Brownlows were the first of several grandees who looked favourably on her and whom she, in turn, admired. When she became Prime Minister, Mrs Thatcher arranged with the then Lord Brownlow to borrow Belton silver for use in Downing Street.*

The approach of war led to strong economic growth for Grantham. The town benefited from its position on the main road and rail links between London, the North East and Scotland. From 1934, new factories were built at the rate of about one a year. War itself brought the armed services to Grantham, which boasted four RAF bases locally. Margaret's letters to Muriel about wartime dances always mention the hordes of flight

---

* There was a popular theory in circulation that Margaret Thatcher had Cust blood. The story was that Margaret's grandmother, Phoebe Stephenson, had been a maid at Belton (a fact never established). She was seduced, the theory goes on, by Harry Cust, a famous womanizer and, in all probability, the true father of Lady Diana Cooper. Her maiden name was Crust – almost Cust – and her granddaughter supposedly had 'Cust eyes'. Caroline Cust, later the Hon. Mrs Caroline Partridge, believed in the theory, though in her view Cust was Margaret's father, not her grandfather. This is impossible, since Harry Cust died eight years before Margaret was born. There is no evidence for the theory and its details don't add up. It was widely believed, however, in grand Tory circles. When the present biographer put the theory to Margaret Thatcher, she answered, with a certain pride: 'Blue eyes aren't the preserve of the aristocracy.'

lieutenants eager to mark her card. Grantham provided the national headquarters for Bomber Command and from October 1943 there was a large USAAF presence in the town. This created tension because US servicemen were paid five times more than their British counterparts and were accused of immorality with local girls. Such problems of war led Roberts to unbend his Sabbatarian principles, defying his fellow Methodists by supporting the Sunday opening of cinemas for the troops. He believed it was better for them to have entertainment than to have nothing. To Margaret, this showed pragmatism and independence of mind.

Alfred Roberts began his career in local council politics well before the war, sitting as an Independent Ratepayer from 1927. Although Margaret was evasive on the point, Muriel insisted that their father was originally a Liberal, albeit wedded to the convention of the time that national party allegiance should be kept out of local government. In the early 1930s, Roberts supported the Conservative-dominated National Government, but avoided a clear party allegiance. When Margaret was chosen as prospective parliamentary candidate for Dartford in 1949, he broke the habit of a lifetime by speaking at a party political meeting, in her support.

Before and during the war, ideology did not intrude much into council affairs. But since only Labour defied the convention about political identification, it is fair to say that Labour was always Roberts's political opponent. In the 1935 general election he threw his growing influence behind the Conservative candidate, Sir Victor Warrender. This gave Margaret her first taste of politics. She helped fold Warrender's election addresses into envelopes and on polling day acted as a runner, taking information about who had voted from the tellers at the polling station to the Conservative committee rooms to verify that their canvass had turned out to vote. 'I don't know why I was so staunchly Conservative,' she once said of her early political allegiance, 'I think it was the idea of my father that you can get on somehow.' But she immediately took to Warrender: 'He had a presence, a natural presence. He had ... a good overcoat. Good, not flashy. He was rather a handsome man. When he spoke, you listened.' As so often in later life, she was susceptible to good-looking men, to elegant clothes, to what used to be called an air of breeding.*

In forming his views on the international scene, Alfred Roberts relied heavily on Rotary, that worldwide movement composed largely of

---

* The two corresponded in warm terms in the 1970s, and when Mrs Thatcher was Prime Minister she often stayed at Schloss Freudenberg near Zug in Switzerland, the home of Lady Glover. One man to whom she made a pilgrimage at his family's home in Gstaad was the by then extremely old Victor Warrender. A witness says that their meeting was touching: Mrs Thatcher thanked him for being the foundation of her political ambition.

businessmen and dedicated to social improvement and charitable endeavour. A founder member of Grantham Rotary, in 1935 Roberts became its president. The organization's approach to politics was deliberately uncomplicated. It called for people to sink their political differences in the wider public interest. Margaret said that her family first realized that there was something wrong with Hitler 'when we heard that he had suppressed Rotary'. She saw the wider world through Rotarian eyes.

For Roberts, those same Rotarian eyes which favoured reconciliation over confrontation, paired with his Methodism, made him sympathetic to appeasing Hitler. He supported Neville Chamberlain, Prime Minister from 1937, and about as perfectly Rotarian a figure as ever reached 10 Downing Street. 'Appeasement' was not then a dirty word, but one used by the appeasers themselves; they believed that peace could be preserved by talking. Margaret Thatcher, later famous for her dislike of appeasing dictators, approached the subject of her father's support for Chamberlain rather obliquely. Chamberlain, she later insisted, 'was a very honourable man ... he knew that in 1938 he must gain time to get us ready'.

Once war came in September 1939, however, any hesitations were cast aside and Alfred Roberts became a more important figure in Grantham. He was one of three councillors appointed to the emergency committee which exercised the powers of the full council. In February 1943 the council appointed him an alderman, a mark of local distinction. Roberts, aged fifty, was probably the youngest Grantham man ever chosen for the office. The circumstances in which he lost it, more than ten years later, were to make a profound impression upon his daughter. Just after the war ended, Roberts accepted the mayoralty of Grantham.* At home until her departure for Oxford in October 1943, Margaret witnessed her father's endless public spiritedness, a life which, because of war, shrank the sphere of private pleasures even smaller. Duty, work, patriotism – and the sense of an enemy – dominated.

It was Alfred's daughters who, indirectly, put his Rotarian principles to the test. As teenagers both girls had a foreign penfriend, arranged through their school. Muriel's was an Austrian called Edith Mühlbauer, who was Jewish. In 1939, to escape the Nazis, Edith's parents pleaded with Roberts to take their daughter in. He agreed. Unfortunately, generous though the Robertses were, Edith was not terribly happy with them. 'We didn't have a proper bathroom in those days,' said Margaret; 'she was used to better things.' As if to protect her from possible threat, Edith's Jewishness was

---

* Roberts had, in fact, been offered this in 1940, but had refused due to a lack of time.

not mentioned, but it seems to have contributed to the provincial Robertses' sense that she was rather apart from them. Edith also didn't like the Robertses' Sunday afternoon walk into the fields beyond Grantham: 'She said, "It'll ruin my shoes."'

Alfred Roberts, it seems, was shocked by Edith's sophistication and her tendency, thought dangerous in teenage girls, to wear make-up. Edith told Mary Wallace, the daughter of the Robertses' dentist, that she found 1 North Parade a 'repressive household'. She was 'patently unhappy' there and seems to have stayed for no more than a fortnight. As Muriel recalled, 'Daddy . . . went round to all Rotarians in turn persuading them to have Edith . . . I sometimes think he regretted having got her over.' Edith was much happier in the larger and less provincial home of the Wallaces, with whom she stayed for the best part of a year before settling in Brazil.

The story of Edith shows Alfred Roberts in an interesting light – a man determined to live by his principles, but also stern and forbidding. Perhaps it was easier to admire him than to live with him. Margaret, several years younger than Edith, was shocked above all by one feature she related of her life in Vienna: 'She said that Jewish women were being made to scrub the streets.'

What was Margaret's education, and how did it form her? There is an oft-told story about a prize she won at the age of nine. When the head congratulated her on her luck, Margaret retorted, 'I wasn't lucky. I deserved it.' The tale is sometimes taken to indicate big-headedness or arrogance, but it shows the young Margaret's literal-mindedness.* She had not been lucky; she *had* deserved it, so she felt bound to say so.

In 1936, Margaret won a scholarship to Kesteven and Grantham Girls' School (KGGS), the best girls' school in the area. Founded in 1910, it was a fee-paying grammar school, which when Margaret arrived that September had some 330 pupils, including Muriel, who was not a scholarship girl. Social backgrounds varied from the prosperous or highly educated (top managers in the engineering firms, the Anglican clergy) to daughters of poor families who had got in on their wits. Financially, the Robertses probably stood slightly below the middle of the school; socially, because of Alfred's growing role in the town, rather higher.

Margaret was placed in the B Stream because there were too many scholarship girls to accommodate in the A Stream. This fostered the slight

---

* Literal-mindedness was a quality that Margaret Thatcher observed in herself. In her memoirs she says, 'I was perplexed by the metaphorical element of phrases like "Look before you leap". I thought it would be far better to say "Look before you cross" . . .'

but definite sense of separation from her peers that many felt Margaret showed. It also threw her together with Jean Farmer, the builder's daughter, and the two became firm friends. Jean was an easy-going, popular girl, known, in the parlance of the time, as a 'scream'. Margaret's demand that she be allowed Sundays as free and jolly as those of the Farmers gave rise to Alfred Roberts's famous response: 'Margaret, never do things just because other people do them. Make up your own mind what you are going to do and persuade people to go your way.' Margaret both kicked against such injunctions and imbibed them. She resented what her father taught, but generally believed he was right.

Jean liked Margaret without reservation. She described her as 'a very pleasant, happy, fun-loving girl', even 'happy-go-lucky', a 'slightly plump' child who was 'polite, hard-working and joined in everything'. Jean did not regard Margaret as a genius, but she did note her 'marvellous powers of concentration' and one of her most famous characteristics as Prime Minister: 'she didn't need as much sleep as we did.' Jean's parents were particularly fond of Margaret and kept up a correspondence in later years. 'It seems a long time since I was "home" in Lincolnshire,' Margaret wrote in March 1974, following the Tory defeat in the general election a month earlier. 'In some ways I think they were happier and fuller days than those I live now.'

Another of Margaret's friends was Shirley Walsh (later Ellis), a pretty girl on whose doorstep Margaret would arrive every morning ('she was always early') so that they could walk to school together. When they were a bit older, Margaret and Shirley both worked at Toc H, the mission for servicemen, on a Saturday serving in the forces' canteen. In Shirley's view, Margaret 'was never disdainful of her schoolfriends or peers' and had a good sense of humour – 'She didn't instigate, but she joined in.' Writing to Muriel about a bus trip back from a hockey match, Margaret showed the dry wit which stayed with her as an adult. The vehicle, she explained, was so crowded that the girls had to sit on sacks of potatoes 'which by the time we arrived at North Witham were just about cooked and mashed'.

Although all her contemporaries attest to a seriousness in Margaret which made her stand out, she pursued the usual interests of a teenage girl, including tennis and hockey. More striking, and more at odds with her upbringing, was a strong interest in glamour, both in fashion and films. The latter receives mention in almost every letter to Muriel. Films in Grantham were made more acceptable to Margaret's parents by the fact that one cinema, the Picture House, was owned by the Campbells, who were Roberts's customers and fellow Rotarians. Their daughter, Judy, was a very beautiful woman who became a well-known actress and the first to popularize the song 'A Nightingale Sang In Berkeley Square'.* Margaret knew Judy a little and greatly admired her. She had a particular fondness for the films of Ginger Rogers, which led Jim Allen, Grantham's leading local historian of Margaret Thatcher, to ask her in old age if the reason she liked Rogers was her portrayal of a woman succeeding in a man's world in *Kitty Foyle*. 'No, it wasn't,' replied Lady Thatcher, 'I always wished I could have danced like her.'

By Margaret's account, the 'biggest excitement of my early years' was her only pre-war trip to London, aged twelve. Her hosts, the Revd Mr Skinner and his wife – he being a Methodist family friend who would later marry her and Denis – showed her the London sights, including 10 Downing Street, but for Margaret the 'high point' was seeing Sigmund Romberg's famous musical *The Desert Song*. 'For three hours I lived in another world, swept away as was the heroine by the daring Red Shadow.' Touchingly, she writes that the Skinners' 'kindness had given me a glimpse of, in Talleyrand's words, "*la douceur de la vie*"'. For all her subsequent fame, she seldom had time to savour this indefinable quality, but when she did, she loved it. She also thrived on the excitement of places that mattered: even the soot of London's buildings lent a 'dark, imposing magnificence which constantly reminded me that I was at the centre of the world'. Except in political allegiance, the centre was always where she wanted to be.

Apart from films, the other way to bring glamour to unexciting Grantham was through clothes. Margaret constantly sought elegance and quality in what she wore, no easy task in wartime. Her correspondence with Muriel includes regular requests for material, nylons, buttons and so on. On 30 July 1944, just after the abortive Bomb Plot by German officers against Hitler, she writes to Muriel of having 'bought two underwear sets that I am very pleased with. I got a white Kayser set and a pink rather dainty set of some other make. I also got pink uplift bras . . .' She then chose 'a Vogue pattern for a frock. I think there will be just sufficient material over to make a small berry [she meant beret] shaped hat of the kind that are in fashion now . . .' For her birthday in 1941, her father gave Margaret a pound to buy a powder bowl, 'telling me to bring back the change'. Eschewing the one she really wanted ('green, very large and cut glass'), she found a nice but plain example for 10 shillings (50p) ('just ordinary glass with a little gold paint round the top').

---

* Judy Campbell was also the mother of Jane Birkin, equally famous for a very different sort of love song, 'Je t'aime . . . moi non plus', in the late 1960s. Jane's daughter, Charlotte Gainsbourg, starred in the painfully explicit film *Nymphomaniac* early in the twenty-first century.

Margaret always exhibited a practical approach, whether to price or to friendship. Lorna Smith, a schoolfriend, remembered her as 'quiet, hard-working, poised, calm and self-confident. Some people found her slightly irritating, and even rather conceited, but I fear there was an element of envy there! For myself, I found her pleasant and helpful.' What marked Margaret out was her sense of purpose. As Shirley Ellis put it, 'She always stood out because teenage girls don't know where they're going. She did.'

This purposefulness was accompanied by a fondness for simple moral precepts. In the 1930s, schoolgirls kept 'autograph books', in which they would collect the signatures of friends and little improving remarks or quotations. On 23 March 1937, the eleven-year-old Margaret Roberts wrote in a friend's autograph book:

> Tis easy enough to be pleasant,
> When life goes by with a song.
> But the one worth while
> Is the one that can smile
> When everything goes dead wrong.

Precepts, once learnt, had also to be proclaimed. Margaret's first public performances were recitations, and she favoured such poetry – well-known passages of Longfellow, Tennyson, Whitman or Kipling – as made its moral meaning plain. It was partly for these exercises that she began the first of several elocution courses which were to punctuate her career. From these, not from any later, political attempt to improve her social standing, sprang the cut-glass voice for which Margaret was later to be criticized.

The lessons produced results. In 1937, Margaret won the silver medal at the Grantham eisteddfod for her recitation of John Drinkwater's 'Moonlit Apples' and Walter de la Mare's 'The Travellers'. Though not a literary girl, Margaret was easily stirred by the high sentiments of poetry. 'I loved language and rhythm,' she recalled, 'Kipling was our hero.' She adored what were then the 'obvious' anthologies . To her first serious boyfriend she gave Palgrave's *Golden Treasury*. To the man whom, before Denis, she most nearly married she sent the complete works of Shakespeare. She extended these feelings to the Authorized Version of the Bible, singling out Isaiah, the Gospels and the Acts of the Apostles: 'There is no greater English literature.' Her choice of Acts is worth noting – it is the most important book in the Scriptures about the propagation of a message to the world. To the end of her life, she retained the words of scores of classic English hymns. At Denis's funeral in July 2003, when her anguish and mental confusion were such that she was not sure whether it was her husband's or her father's coffin in front of her, she was seen to sing all the hymns, word-perfect, without looking at the service sheet.

In the summer of 1941, Margaret sat the School Certificate exams (the rough equivalent of GCSEs). Writing to her sister, she confessed she'd found the pace intense, requiring 'a terrific amount of swotting'. Geography was the worst: her paper 'on the British Isles and one continent was very disappointing. For one continent we did America and the questions on it were not at all bad, but out of the three on the British Isles there was only one we could touch.' All of them involved knowledge of Scotland and Ireland. 'Unfortunately we had not touched island [sic] and had had precisely two lessons on Scotland . . .' Even at the age of fifteen, the map of her future political sympathies was clear. England and America understood, Scotland little studied, Ireland *terra incognita* and Continental Europe not even mentioned.

In September, Margaret reported to Muriel that she had received distinctions (the top grade) in chemistry, arithmetic and algebra, and credits in all other subjects except for life drawing, in which she managed only a lowly pass. No other girl managed three distinctions. Indeed, eleven out of forty failed. Some girls now stayed in a lower form to retake, while others, including Margaret, set their sights on university.

With the ready nostalgia of the very young, Margaret lamented the changes: 'Life in 6 Lower is not half as nice as life in form Va. Our crowd have broken up of course . . . there is nothing to hold us together.' In V Lower there had been fifty-three girls. After Christmas 1941 there would be only four – Margaret, Madeline Edwards, Jean Farmer and Lorna Smith, who was new. Of Margaret's intimates, only Jean Farmer survived in the same class.

Margaret was not greatly impressed with all of the teaching staff: 'The history mistress is very disappointing. She is quite middle-aged and very dowdy in dress.' Margaret reserved a specially tart comment for the headmistress, Miss Dorothy Gillies, about her handling of the exam results: 'There was no message of congratulation (or sympathy) from the Head, just a blunt "Pass" or "Fail".' Setting her shoulder to the wheel of work, she shared her thoughts with her sister: 'Daddy does not like the idea of medical at all, but I am taking Biology, Chemistry and Maths main with French subsid. The next idea on the list is to go to University and take a science degree then sit for a Civil Service exam for posts abroad. A degree is necessary for this for a woman. Of course I shan't be able to go to University at all unless I get a scholarship.' Already, the fifteen-year-old Margaret Roberts shows herself clear, confident, ambitious, diligent, clever and slightly acidulous.

In this letter there is no direct mention of the war, which impinges only in small ways – a note of the rare availability of salmon salad, news that the evacuated Camden School for Girls was sharing KGGS's facilities, the increasing age of the teaching staff. The war, which formed so many of her beliefs and her idea of her country, was seen at the time as merely the backdrop to school life.

Lorna Smith, arriving as a shy new girl in the Lower Sixth in September 1941, felt that Margaret was not as striking as some of her peers: 'she nevertheless had even features, a clear complexion, intelligent grey-blue eyes, a very good figure and legs, and a sharp intellect. She radiated quiet confidence.' Although Margaret said she was going to be a scientist, she told Lorna 'she was also interested, like her father, in politics, and would perhaps try for Parliament one day. "Imagine – an MP!" I said, admiringly. "Perhaps you could <u>even</u> be Prime Minister!" She waved away the idea, but she was looking both dreamy and purposeful.'

Discussion of politics, though, was a rarity at KGGS. The school's prevailing allegiance was vaguely Conservative, but debates were more likely to centre on religion than politics. The girls were idealistic, said Rita Hind, herself one of them: it was 'a very moral period'. As Margaret put it, 'There were more important things to do than boys.' It was a time of aspiration and a love of education. No one remembered Margaret debating political issues, though all remembered her interest in the subject. Lorna Smith recalled many schoolgirl discussions about faith, not least a surreal conversation with Margaret just before Christmas in 1942. 'She remarked that, really, she didn't think she could believe in angels. "Oh, why?" I asked, wondering what Ald. Roberts would think. "Well," she replied, "I have worked it out scientifically that in order to fly, an angel would need a six-foot-long breastbone to bear the weight of its wings."' Lorna added, perhaps superfluously, 'Margaret could be very earnest at times.'

KGGS was competitive, at least in its higher academic echelons, no one more so than Margaret. Even the good-natured Lorna Smith found her pride rather tiresome. She recalled feeling 'slightly miffed' when, in July 1942, Margaret reported 'rather boastfully, that our form-mistress had said that all our geography results were extremely disappointing – except hers'. Her faults, in the eyes of her contemporaries, concerned her tendency to come top, to be right and to rub it in. Madeline Edwards and Margaret Goodrich recalled her irritating habit of asking the first, well-informed question of any visiting speaker, even when she was a little fourth-form girl ('We'd look at one another and say, "She's at it again,"' said Madeline). The less competitive girls, however, such as Lorna, Jean and Shirley, found Margaret less oppressive.

Margaret was not considered an intellectual genius, but she was at the top of the class, became a prefect and consistently earned good reports. As early as Christmas 1936, she is recorded as having 'worked steadily and well throughout the term. She has definite ability, and her cheeriness makes her a very pleasant member of her form. Her behaviour is excellent.' After promotion to the A Stream, she continued to come top every year except one, in which she came second. When Margaret applied to Oxford, Miss Gillies, who had a scratchy relationship with her pupil, nevertheless provided a reference calling her 'a very logical thinker' with 'very clear mind'.

Margaret accepted and admired the ethos of KGGS, as both pupil and alumna. Visiting in 1986 to open the Roberts Hall in memory of her father, who had been, for almost forty years, first a governor and then chairman of the governors, she declared: 'I would not have been in No. 10 but for this school.' When she accepted a peerage she took her title from her school, not from her town, becoming Baroness Thatcher of Kesteven.

Margaret's relationship with KGGS, as with Grantham itself, was probably more ambiguous. Much of this can be put down to her difficulties with the headmistress. Her first headmistress at KGGS was Miss Gladys Williams, whom Margaret loved: she was always much influenced in her feelings about women (and, indeed, about men) by their manners, elegant appearance and demeanour, and Miss Williams impressed her for these reasons.* In 1939, Miss Williams retired. Her successor, Miss Gillies, was very different. More of a scholar than Miss Williams, she also had much more of a temper. 'She was a fiery Scot,' said Rita Hind. Madeline Edwards remembers her hurling books and shouting at the girls, 'You're all suet puddings!' She and Margaret did not get on. Margaret considered her ungracious, while Miss Gillies thought Margaret needed taking down a peg.

Their main disagreement concerned Margaret's application for Oxford. By the time of School Certificate, Margaret began to make plans for university, choosing science as her likely subject because, as she later said, 'Science was the way of the future.' She consulted Harold Marks, a master at the boys' grammar school in Grantham, whom her father had arranged to act as occasional private tutor, and followed his suggestion of switching to geography. She buckled down also to biology ('I never dreamt there was so much inside a worm before. One of the toughest jobs is to find

---

* Most of the young Margaret's harshest comments are reserved for those who make nothing of their appearance and exhibit sourness or slatternliness. In a letter to Muriel written in December 1941 she describes the school hockey team's visit to a match in Melton: 'Their gym mistress was an awful old irritable thing. She had a spotty complexion, lank, greasy hair – eton-cropped, wore glasses and dowdy clothes. She found fault with everything possible and actually coached her own side while refereeing.'

the ovary . . .') and told Muriel she would 'take Latin to help with Biology, and also because you must have it for entrance to most universities'.

Her studies went well and in 1942, before she had taken Higher Certificate (the equivalent of the modern A-Level), she was offered places at Nottingham University and Bedford College, London. But when the idea of Oxford grew in the minds of Margaret and her father, this, along with the extra Latin teaching required, was resisted by Miss Gillies, allegedly provoking Margaret to say, 'You're thwarting my ambition.' According to Muriel, Margaret earned her Latin School Certificate only after coaching from Harold Marks. Margaret never forgot what she considered to have been Miss Gillies's obstruction.

When Margaret sat the scholarship for Somerville College, Oxford, in 1943, she narrowly missed out, being instead awarded an ordinary place for the autumn of 1944. This required her to return to KGGS for a year to avoid being called up for the services. Because women did not take part in combat, there was no stigma of 'draft-dodging' against girls, but Margaret nonetheless felt 'a little bit guilty'.

KGGS began Michaelmas term of 1943 with two head girls for the first time – Madeline Edwards and Margaret Roberts. Margaret's first taste of supreme authority did not last long. Three weeks into the school term, a girl who had been accepted by Somerville dropped out and the college offered an immediate place to Margaret. She accepted and vaulted suddenly into another world.

Margaret was apprehensive about Oxford. She had never before been away from home for more than a few days. Wartime made the separation greater. She was the first woman in her family to go to university, and the first of either sex to go to Oxford. Before going up, she consulted Mary Wallace and Margaret Goodrich, the only other people she knew there.

Margaret, recalled Mary Wallace, was 'very keen to do the right thing', and, as so often in her later career, expressed this in an anxiety about 'what sort of clothes to wear'. In Margaret Goodrich's view, 'Oxford was a big jump for her.' When she and her father first visited Margaret at Somerville they found her lonely and disconsolate, toasting a teacake by a fire that was rationed to one scuttle of coal per week. Margaret herself admitted that she felt 'shy and ill-at-ease'. She sometimes walked alone round Christ Church Meadow. In doing so, she felt she was fulfilling C. S. Lewis's injunction in *Christian Behaviour* (1944) to set aside time for solitary thought, but one may guess that her isolation was not entirely voluntary.

Without a scholarship, Margaret was dependent on her father and various small college bursaries. While her parents did their best, sending small sums and cakes baked by her mother, she was always short. Her lack of funds contributed to Margaret's sense of adversity and to the impression she created: her contemporaries recalled her appearance as 'brown', both in hair and clothes, and somehow in personality. Rachel Willink, one of only two women before Margaret to become President of the Oxford University Conservative Association (OUCA), remembered her as someone who 'hadn't got the style' to 'make up' for her background: those who had known Margaret at Oxford later found it 'a thing out of nature' that 'that rather humourless mouse' had been so astonishingly successful. According to Mary Wallace, also an officer of OUCA, Margaret was 'merely tolerated' by the club's grandees as 'someone who could be relied on to do the donkey work' – a 'slogger', without star quality.

The surviving letters from Margaret's time at Oxford, almost all to Muriel, dwell on clothes and the difficulty of affording them. Brownness recurs. In September 1944, she wrote of visiting Bond Street, London, for the first time ('though I didn't tell Mummy'). She had bought brown court shoes to match her brown handbag and wanted a similarly coloured 'fairly plain frock' to have 'a completely brown-fawn rig-out'. She fell in love with an 'absolutely stunning' gown before discovering, 'to my open-mouthed dismay', that it cost £20. She settled instead on 'a fairly plain little frock with a peter pan collar, two little pockets on the bodice and two to match on the skirt' for £3 16s. Even this price was high for Margaret, but the 'elderly' assistant persuaded her it was 'superb value for money' (always the way to Margaret's heart). 'I'll try to smuggle it home next time to show you without Mummy seeing.'

When the present author asked Lady Thatcher what she thought of her looks as a young woman, she answered, 'Oh, I never thought I was good-looking. I thought I was slightly overweight.' This anxiety was reflected in her letters: 'I still weigh about 10st 4lbs,' she wrote to Muriel (the nurse). 'Can you recommend . . . anything from the medical point of view for reduction of the area of the seat and control of the tummy muscles – oh and also reduction and uplift of bust?' Her weight reached 10 stone 10 pounds, quite a lot for a twenty-year-old girl of 5 foot 5 inches.*

But if Margaret was disparaged as a slightly podgy, frumpy person in Oxford's grander circles, she faced almost the opposite problem within her

---

* Her anxiety about her weight was to persist. In October 1974, Mrs Thatcher told the BBC's *Any Questions?*: 'Oh, I've tried to lose weight . . . If I didn't, I'd just get enormous. I lose half a stone every year and promptly put it back on . . . but I do think people should look after their weight. You know, one Labour politician in Parliament said to me, "If politicians can't have enough self-discipline over what they eat, how can you expect them to have enough self-discipline over their political lives?"'

own college. Betty Spice recalled that she had difficulty fitting in with her fellow grammar-school girls. Her voice was 'not natural'. She was 'pretty, in a baby-doll sort of way', but 'You couldn't get close to her. She didn't want us because we were only grammar-school girls. She was interested in making her way with people who would help her.' According to another exact contemporary, Jean Southerst, 'Her voice, elocution-trained, was regarded as affected, and her preoccupation with her appearance caused amusement.'

Despite this, Margaret won respect. Even Betty Spice records that she was 'an honest person' and that she quite enjoyed being teased about possible boyfriends ('She would blush from the neck upwards'). Jean Southerst recalled that 'her room in college was always open for pleasant evenings for gossip, poetry reading (I owe her much for that) and partaking of the excellent coffee and cakes etc., which, as a grocer's daughter, made her a very popular hostess!' She impressed as someone who would do what she promised and who 'had a clear idea of what she wanted to attain'. And Margaret happily took part in Oxford jollifications. After her third-year exams, she saw the film *Quiet Wedding* with friends: 'It's an absolute scream,' she wrote to Muriel, 'I laughed more than I have for months.' 'Did I tell you', she added, 'that seven of the men failed?'

The prevailing expectation among Somerville undergraduates was of work involving educational or public service. The privilege of a woman's education at a great university had to be repaid. Margaret herself believed devoutly in worthiness and public service, but she came to apply these beliefs in a way which many Somervillians did not like and with a success of which some, perhaps, were jealous. Betty Spice said, 'We're not proud of Margaret. We found it a bit galling that she became prime minister, and that she married Denis and got his money and then had the twins in one go.' Something similar applies to many Somerville dons, particularly those under the influence of Janet Vaughan, the Principal from 1945 and a progressive who regarded being a Conservative as a mental defect. 'She stood out,' she commented, 'there weren't many Conservatives about then . . . We used to entertain a good deal at weekends, but she didn't get invited. She had nothing to contribute, you see.' The truth is that most of Margaret's Somerville contemporaries did not know her terribly well, and were not strongly attracted by what they did know.

Mrs Thatcher always spoke well of Somerville. Partly because of her warm respect for Daphne Park, Principal of Somerville from 1980 to 1989, she maintained an interest in the place throughout her years as Prime Minister. But it is also true that she kept no close friends from Somerville days.

*

Part of Margaret's relative isolation at Somerville derives from the fact that she was one of only five women in the whole year studying chemistry. Long hours in the labs and at lectures kept her away from her fellow Somervillians. Margaret did not particularly enjoy life in the lab: 'I was much more interested in the theory.' She was fortunate, though, that in Dorothy Hodgkin Somerville had one of the most distinguished chemists in the world. Mrs Hodgkin, who later won the Nobel Prize, was, in the words of Margaret's fellow chemist Betty Spice, a 'brilliant chemist, but an awful tutor'. Nonetheless, Margaret greatly admired her and elected to add a year of research to her degree to complete a thesis under Mrs Hodgkin's supervision.*

How good a scientist was Margaret Roberts? She certainly had a serious interest and worked hard throughout, perhaps too hard. At the end of her third year, she had to sit some of her exams in the sanatorium. She never admitted as much, but there is evidence that she was suffering from nervous exhaustion brought on by overwork. After four years, she was awarded a respectable second-class degree. 'I came to rate her as good,' wrote Professor Hodgkin. 'One could always rely on her producing a sensible, well-read essay and yet there was something that some people had that she hadn't quite got.'

It was true, too, as Dorothy Hodgkin also said, that 'she was not absolutely devoted' to chemistry. While at Oxford, she developed a growing interest in the law. In her memoirs she recalls lunching with her father and his friend Norman Winning, a King's Counsel. 'At one point I blurted out: "I wish I could be a lawyer; but all I know about is chemistry and I can't change what I'm reading at Oxford now."' Winning explained that unless she stayed on for a second degree, in law (something she could not afford), she would have to get a job in or near London and study for the Bar in the evenings. She took this advice to heart: writing to Muriel in the summer of 1947, she notes that a potential job at ICI, six hours from London, would be 'an awful disadvantage for the Bar Exams'. Her interest in law was real, but the certainty that she could afford to start a legal career came later, with the financial security that Denis Thatcher brought her.

In later years, Margaret Thatcher discerned a pattern in her youthful

---

* In later years, this respect was tempered slightly by Hodgkin's membership of the anti-nuclear Pugwash group of scientists considered by many to have been extremely credulous in their attitude to the Soviet Union. She used to write to Mrs Thatcher to put the case against cruise missiles and warn her not to listen too much to Soviet dissidents. Mrs Thatcher remained affectionate towards her, but thought her views naive. Having received her at Chequers in 1983, she said to her fellow guest Daphne Park, 'Is it possible to educate Dorothy a bit more on the issue of Russia?'

interests: 'As a Methodist in Grantham, I learnt the laws of God. When I read chemistry at Oxford, I learnt the laws of science, which derive from the laws of God, and when I studied for the Bar, I learnt the laws of man.' This was sincere but underplays the extent to which she saw all her main occupations, the law not the least, as instrumental to a political career. Politics was her obsession, her dream. As soon as she went up to Oxford, she joined OUCA and threw herself into its activities. Hers was not, at this stage, a strong engagement with political ideas and beliefs, nor yet the undergraduate love of politicking. It was simply a determination to engage in political life and to do it as well as she possibly could.

War had the curious effect of making Oxford less actively political than at many other periods, notably the 1930s. The Oxford Union, the centre of university political debate, allowed only men to take part and so many were away in the forces.* The overriding need to win the war also dampened the tendency to quarrel. Contemporaries remember that, although the progress of the war was constantly discussed in casual mealtime conversations, controversial issues were not. According to Amy Wootten, typical Somerville table talk would move between war news to its small consequences – 'They've got bananas in a shop in the High' – to the ordinary gossip of the day. Political awareness was quite low.† Reflecting this atmosphere, Margaret's letters from Oxford contain scarcely a single expression of political views and next to nothing about current political events. Politics, when it occurs, is presented as an activity requiring hard work but opening up social opportunities and giving pleasure. It is something to be done, not something to be debated.

Conservatism at Oxford towards the end of the war was not spoiling for a fight. It did not, for instance, warn of the dangers of too uncritical an association with Stalin or cry out in protest at the growth of the welfare state.‡ In common with almost all her fellow Conservatives, Margaret had a belief in the capacity of Whitehall men to run the country in a humane and orderly way. She admired the White Paper on Full Employment, directly influenced by John Maynard Keynes, which appeared in

* Even when she was President of OUCA, Margaret could attend Union debates only in the gallery, and then only if she was given guest tickets by a member.
† Wootten, in fact, was under the misapprehension that Margaret was a Liberal, just because her two fellow chemists were.
‡ When working on her memoirs in the 1990s, Mrs Thatcher recalled reading Friedrich von Hayek's *The Road to Serfdom*, which was published in 1944. But there is a sense that this memory is dredged up rather than strongly felt. She herself admitted that 'I cannot claim that I fully grasped the implications of Hayek's little masterpiece at the time.'

1944, and she credited 'Winston', as she always in later life referred to Churchill,* with wisdom in creating the Ministry for Reconstruction and Development. She liked the fact that the wartime economy was 'an economy with a purpose' which gave almost everyone a job. She said that she didn't feel she was a 'right-wing Tory': 'Fairness is a big streak in the British character,' a streak which was satisfied by rationing. She said that what she wanted was 'a freer society, which produced a large part of the power that made Britain great'.

The end of the war in Europe in May 1945 and the general election in July hardened politics up. Margaret took part in the campaign – mostly, since it was held on 5 July,† in Grantham. She served as warm-up speaker for the Conservative candidate, Squadron Leader Worth, as he toured the surrounding villages night after night. She remembered these occasions quite self-critically: 'I wasn't terribly good at keeping going. My training had been scientific. Therefore I spoke in short sentences ... machine-gun style,' but her readiness to do so showed precocious courage.

One such performance drew the attention of the *Sleaford Gazette*. As the paper reported, she insisted that restoring prosperity to Britain required re-establishing trade with Europe. She spoke also of Germany: 'Miss Roberts said that once in her lifetime, twice in many people's time, and three times in the lives of some people, Germany had plunged the world into war. Germany must be disarmed and brought to justice.'‡ Much of her speech was in praise of Churchill, but she ended with the theme that most fired her imagination: 'Miss Roberts was very fervent in her determination to stand by the Empire. It was the most important community of peoples the world has ever known ... The Empire must never be liquidated.'

There is something laughable, perhaps, about the nineteen-year-old alderman's daughter thus laying down the law for the world, but also something astonishing and impressive. Soon afterwards, Muriel received a letter from Liz Barrington, an old nursing friend, 'overjoyed' to hear of Margaret's 'marvellous effort at election speaking. You have a very clever sister ... I wonder where she will eventually end up? Maybe I shall be able to say, "Oh yes I have the pleasure of knowing that young lady" in days to come ...'

---

* Mrs Thatcher was often criticized for referring to Churchill thus, as if she were presuming acquaintance with the great man. It seems more likely that she was repeating the usage of fellow Young Conservatives, rather as the equivalents, in her time, would call her 'Maggie', without pretending that they knew her.
† Because of the need to collect votes from servicemen abroad the result was not declared until 26 July.
‡ In the 1990s she would use an uncannily similar formulation about the frequency with which Germany had caused war, although sometimes replacing 'Germany' with 'Continental Europe'.

When the votes were counted, Clement Attlee's Labour Party was swept into office by a landslide. In Grantham, Denis Kendall, a flamboyant Independent, held his seat against the Tory challenge. For Margaret, the results were a shock. Sixty years later, she said that the loss of Winston Churchill was 'really quite shattering'. It ended her experience, until then continuous in her entire political memory, of Tory dominance. As it was to do even more markedly in 1974, defeat galvanized her.

The Oxford to which she returned in October 1945 was changed in atmosphere – by the atom bombs and subsequent Allied victory in the Far East, by the Labour election victory and by the presence of undergraduates who had fought. She had returned to what she called 'a more mature Oxford' which benefited from being 'more cross-generational'. Now an officer in OUCA, Margaret joined its policy subcommittee with Stanley Moss, an undergraduate who returned injured from the war, and Michael Kinchin-Smith. Their report, produced that term, contains notes of what later became familiar Thatcher tunes such as 'Individual enterprise is the mainspring of all progress.' But the toughest comments refer to the Conservative Party itself: 'a reorientation of conservatism within the framework of the 20th century state such as that carried out by Peel will be necessary if the party is to avoid annihilation.' The section labelled 'Policy' begins:

> Conservative policy has come to mean in the eyes of the public little more than a series of administrative solutions to particular problems, correlated in certain fields by a few unreasoning prejudices and the selfish interests of the monied classes. If this extremely damaging view is to be refuted it is essential that the relation between overall policy and the various solutions be shown and that the latter be demonstrably free from any suspicion of compromise between national and sectional interests.

Rereading the pamphlet fifty years later, Lady Thatcher jibbed at a few passages, including a proposed redistribution of wealth, but in general she accepted that these had been her thoughts. They were scarcely revolutionary, but they did represent a fiercer, more rebellious and more socially mobile Conservatism than had expressed itself in wartime. It was a Conservatism which understood it had to fight for its existence.

In October 1946, Margaret became President of OUCA and went for the first time to the party conference in Blackpool. By the standards of Tory conferences of that era, the mood from the floor was rebellious. She identified with such feelings. 'I had the sense', she later wrote, 'that the Party leadership – with the notable exception of the Party Leader [Churchill] – had arrived at Blackpool prepared to reconcile itself and Conservatism to the permanence of socialism in Britain . . . This was decidedly not what the rank and file wanted to hear ... My instincts were with the rank and file.' It should not be thought, however, that Margaret's meritocratic, 'rank and file' political beliefs excluded her from the Oxford Tory mainstream. However genuine her political convictions, she also saw OUCA as a form of social advancement, the opening of the door upon a more civilized world.

One of the chief embodiments of this world was Edward Boyle. Neither handsome nor self-confident, Boyle was nevertheless a very appealing figure to Margaret. An Etonian at Christ Church who had already inherited a baronetcy, he was a man of intellectual refinement and gentle good manners. Boyle was generally seen as a future Conservative prime minister and, said one contemporary, 'brilliant in a way you couldn't quite fathom'. Boyle's influence over Margaret was not so much ideological as moral.* She considered that he had 'a great mind. He never had a mean or trifling thought.' She did not share his form of unworldliness, but she loved him for it, and for his lack of snobbery towards her.

Margaret's letters to Muriel highlight the pleasure she derived from her OUCA friendships and the prestige of her OUCA work. In October 1946, she writes to ask Muriel to lend her pearls and her black dinner frock because she has two OUCA dinners in quick succession. The following May, when Muriel's birthday is approaching, she writes to tell her sister that she has found her '<u>sheer</u> silk stockings – fully fashioned ... (<u>not</u> black market)'. She also mentions a visit to Cambridge for a Conservative (Balfour Club) dinner, after which 'at about midnight – we unmoored a punt and went on the river. (I did not wear my black velvet frock thank goodness.)'. It is clear, too, that OUCA was offering more informal pleasures. 'Neil and Roger have been round to tea etc. several times,' she writes in January 1947. 'Two evenings we have been out "on the razzle" and have had the most hilarious time.'

'Roger' was Roger Gray, from the Queen's College, a handsome war veteran who had just become president of the Oxford Union and as such was probably the best-known undergraduate in the university. 'Neil' was Neil Findlay, from Worcester College, unpolitical, but a great friend and wartime comrade of Roger Gray and, like him, fond of parties and drinking.† Both men appealed more to Margaret than she did to them. Roger, apparently, 'found her rather hard work' and sometimes, after a few drinks, would poke her chest and say, 'Is it marble, Margaret?' It was not. Margaret

---

* Boyle later moved to the left of the Conservative Party, but in the 1940s was closer in politics to Margaret.

† Roger Gray, who died in the 1990s, went on to a career at the Bar where he ended up as a recorder of the Crown Court. Friends believed that his undoubted brilliance was dimmed by his heavy drinking. Findlay became an executive in the paper industry.

was smitten with Neil, a fact of which he was half aware. According to Neil, Margaret was attracted towards people with greater social presence, and they didn't always respond. He felt a little sorry for her.

Margaret saw OUCA as her best way of overcoming any handicap. In May 1947, writing to Muriel to discuss her sister's forthcoming visit to Oxford, she presented a rather sparse social calendar. Edward Boyle had 'asked us to lunch one day – if he remembers', she added tartly. She also hoped to 'wangle a meeting with Roger and/or Neil'. The problem, though, is that 'OUCA activities for the term finish with a garden party tomorrow and I'm otherwise powerless to ask them round. I'll just have to rely on their dropping in which they do on very rare occasions.' Despite four successful years at the university, she remained in a position of traditional, womanly weakness. Besides, she was still smarting from the loss of an earlier, more serious love.

It seems highly unlikely that Margaret ever had any boyfriends in Grantham. There is no doubt, however, that she was a carefully dressed young woman whom many considered attractive. Contemporaries remembered her rosy cheeks and elegant legs. Kenneth Wallace, of Grantham, enjoyed her fluent and intelligent conversation. As she started to go to parties in Grantham towards the end of the war, men, often servicemen, asked her to dance. Some pressed their suit quite strongly. In August 1944, she attended a dance at the Grantham tennis club and, as she told Muriel, 'settled down with a Flight-Lieutenant aged about 40!!!! Or rather he had settled down with me.' At the turn of the year she went to a dance in Corby, near Grantham:

> To my horror I recognised one of them – the bald one – as the [same] Flight-Lieutenant ... My heart sank when I saw him walking across the floor to ask me for the first dance ... He was unfortunately rather difficult to get rid of. He wanted me to go to the pictures with him. I told him instantly that I was going back to Oxford for an electioneering course ... I don't want to go around with a man of his age,* and when I vaguely mentioned the fact at home Daddy said, 'No, of course not!' in a very final tone.

Unmentioned here, though referred to elsewhere in the letter, is that Margaret already had a boyfriend. His name was Tony Bray.

Tony, an army cadet, had arrived in Oxford in October 1944 to pursue a six-month course combining military training with lectures on the 'general

---

* Yet all but one of the men who were to attract Margaret's serious interest were considerably older than she.

sciences'. Of solidly bourgeois stock, he was short and not particularly good-looking, but, by his own account sixty years later, 'not half bad as a dancer'. Born in 1926, he was a little younger than Margaret. The two had met through OUCA that autumn. Margaret seemed to Tony 'very thoughtful and a very good conversationalist'. He was also impressed with her enthusiasm for politics – 'Not many girls were like that' – and, like Tony, she was 'a genuine, old-fashioned Conservative'. He was also taken with her appearance: 'She was a plump, attractive girl in a well-built way.' She 'dressed elegantly, though not in a top stylish way'. He felt also that she had 'a degree of loneliness' which was part of 'the reason we got on'.

Over tea in one another's rooms, Margaret and Tony quickly became close. He found her serious, and 'a bit blue-stocking', but liked that she read a great deal and loved music. She took him to the St Matthew Passion in which, as a member of the Bach Choir, she was performing. Tony respected her because 'she held her thoughts very sincerely'. Shortly before Christmas 1944, Margaret arrived at a birthday party for Margaret Goodrich clutching a carnation which, as the latter recalled, 'seemed very precious to her'. This was from Tony. At roughly the same time, she gave him Palgrave's *Golden Treasury*. It was his impression from the way Margaret kissed that she had had no boyfriend before, but she showed a delight in physical intimacy. They followed the rules of those days, however, and never slept together.

Gradually, Tony noticed how stretched Margaret was financially: she was 'not ashamed of her background' but was reticent about it. He also noticed something else: 'She was a person who, though not apparently sociable, enjoyed socializing . . . she astonished herself how much she could relax and be relaxed.' They had fun together. This pleasure, and the heightened sense of life's possibilities that comes through first love, can be found in Margaret's letters to Muriel. On 25 March 1945, she wrote breathlessly of attending the Randolph Ball with Tony. The evening had begun with dinner at the Crown and Thistle in Abingdon: 'We had a marvellous time . . . I managed to borrow a glorious royal blue velvet cloak which match [*sic*] the blue frock perfectly.' Tony presented her with a spray of eight carnations 'sent for me from London so with the front part of my hair piled up on top Jean and Mary said I looked simply smashing. I felt absolutely on top of the world as we walked through the lounge at the Crown and Thistle and everyone looked up and stared.'

When they reached the Randolph Hotel at a quarter to nine, 'Things were in full swing . . . The floor was simply packed so from the point of view of dancing it wasn't terrifically marvellous. The Duchess of Marlborough arrived soon after we did and seemed very nice . . . Altogether it was the best and biggest ball I've ever been to.' Asked about it sixty years later, Tony remembered buying the carnations from Moyses Stevens. When reminded of Margaret's blue dress he suddenly broke down in tears, saying: 'It was a very special evening.'

Once term had ended, Tony whisked her off for a day in London which included lunch at the Dorchester ('It is not the acme of hotels it is reported to be'), a matinée performance of Strauss's *A Night in Venice* at the Cambridge Theatre and finally a tea dance at the Piccadilly Hotel. For Margaret, who had known so few worldly pleasures, it was heady stuff.

It also, in her mind, betokened something quite serious. In the same March letter to Muriel she reported that Tony was coming to stay with their parents: 'I do hope everything will be all right.' This would not have happened if she had seen her relationship with Tony as some passing fancy; and her parents, themselves serious-minded, would have regarded it as a potentially very significant occasion.

Such thoughts crossed Tony's mind and worried him. In old age, he recalled that he and Margaret never discussed marriage, and that he, with his legal training, was wary of doing so because of the threat, still lingering from Victorian times, of an action for breach of promise. He thought of their relationship as 'just a boy and girl who thoroughly enjoyed each other's company'. Margaret, perhaps, thought it meant rather more. Visiting Grantham, Tony found Alfred Roberts 'slightly austere' and 'totally correct', a good, chapel-going man; Beatrice was 'very proper' and 'motherly'. Tony and the Roberts family all attended the Methodist church together. It was not a riotous weekend.

It also marked a moment of parting. Tony's six-month course at Oxford had come to an end and his full military training began in April in Dorset. The next year Tony was posted to Germany after being commissioned in the Royal Inniskilling Dragoon Guards. He sent Margaret a photograph of himself in military uniform, which he inscribed to her. But later that year his replies to Margaret's letters began to peter out and eventually stopped altogether. Margaret became so distressed that she wrote to Tony's mother, whom she had never met, to ask what had happened to him. The answer was nothing very much. Tony had simply decided that the relationship should be allowed to 'fizzle out'.

As Tony later explained, the austere seriousness of Margaret's background had unnerved him. He wanted fun and had found it with a Dorset girl called Prudence, whom he describes as 'vivacious, outgoing and attractive'. Aged barely twenty, he was not looking for commitment.

What of Margaret herself? When asked by the present author, she replied with the understandable untruth that she had had no boyfriends before Denis. When later asked specifically about Tony, she acknowledged the circumstances described above but would not be drawn further. So, in her last two years at university, Margaret had an absent and eventually an ex-boyfriend who was refusing to communicate with her. When Tony faded away she formed her unrequited crush on Neil Findlay. She was successful at Oxford academically and rose to the top of Conservative politics there, making the contacts that would stand her in good stead. But when she went out into the world of work in the summer of 1947, she was, as she had been when she first arrived at the university, fundamentally alone.

2
Becoming Mrs Thatcher

'What a pity such a charming girl should be lost to politics!'

In the late summer of 1947, Margaret began work as a research chemist at BX Plastics in Manningtree, Essex. She saw the job as necessary, no more. It paid her £350 a year (the equivalent male employee earned £400), sufficient to live on, but not to save from. Manningtree was close enough to London for her to keep in touch with politics and to contemplate reading for the Bar.

Taking the company bus every morning from her digs in Colchester, Margaret felt that life, compared with Oxford, was rather dull. She lodged at 168 Maldon Road, the home of a young widow called Enid Macaulay. Occasionally she went to the 'flicks' (her word) with a fellow lodger, Teddy West, but he '<u>doesn't dance</u>', she complained to Muriel. West soon developed a girlfriend who, Margaret reported Mrs Macaulay as saying, was 'as common as muck – thoroughly tarty, but she's got hold of him and is trying to rush the affair as soon as possible . . .' Margaret's indignation suggests that she found Teddy West quite attractive.

Lack of money was a constant preoccupation. The rent, which began at two guineas (£2.10) per week, soon went up to £2 10s (£2.50), which Margaret found 'more than a little worrying'. Every expense had to be carefully weighed. 'Not going to Oxford this weekend,' she wrote to Muriel, 'I decided to buy a really nice undie-set to go under my turquoise chiffon blouse . . . [it] cost £5-5-0.* I'll not have to spend anything else for the rest of the month!' Because she could not afford a perm, she changed her hairstyle – 'am now wearing it in a big doughnut bun at the back'. When

---

* It is worth noting how much more expensive such items were in those days. The modern equivalent would cost less than £60. The five guineas Margaret paid represented over £150 in today's money.

she asked her father for money for a tweed suit, she wrote to him at the shop in North Parade* to avoid her less indulgent mother.†

In this pinched world, it was politics, as in the past, that provided Margaret with acceptance and excitement: 'If Methodists aren't very friendly, Conservatives are,' she told Muriel. 'Someone learned of my being here in Colchester and the word has gone round like wildfire.' Through these connections she met Brian Harrison, a Cambridge graduate 'with a small estate of 1500 acres' in Essex and further family lands in Australia. A veteran of the war in the Far East, he was a leading light in the 39–45 Group, an organization of Essex Tories with war experience. With her taste for older, soldierly men, Margaret warmed to the tall, sporting, kindly Harrison and to his group. Harrison, who was to become Conservative MP for Maldon in 1955, remembered Margaret with affection as 'an attractive girl . . . very very clued up', good company and a good dancer. She was 'ambitious', he said, 'but intelligent enough to hide it'.

Harrison was also chairman of the Colchester Young Conservatives. By the spring of 1948, Margaret had become a leading figure among their ranks. As ever, her appearance mattered intensely to her. In May, she told Muriel about a weekend political school she had attended: 'competition for the best dressed woman' had been 'fiercely contested by Jean Murphy and I [sic] . . . I turned up in my black two-piece and black hat on Saturday – she wasn't wearing a hat that day – but on Sunday she turned out in a floral dress, fox fur and straw boater with strands of veiling tied under the chin – I didn't like the hat myself and definitely thought it too much with a fur . . . I think I won the day both days.' Serious as Margaret was about her politics, she also saw the Tories as her social theatre. She went to the Derby with them ('don't tell parents!') and to the Boat Race. 'The only chance I get to wear my best black clothes these days is at Conservative meetings of some sort!' Her two-piece, she told Muriel, 'caused quite a stir in the digs and complimentary comments came from all sides except Mr West, who said not a word, to my annoyance!'.

Her political outings in Colchester included a talk to the Young Conservatives on 'Science in the Modern World' and participation in a Brains Trust of rising Conservatives including 'Brig. Powell (the Conservative Central Office authority on housing)', her first recorded encounter with Enoch Powell, the man who, many believe, cleared the intellectual path

---

* By this time, the Roberts family no longer lived above the shop, but had graduated to a house of their own.
† Margaret's mother was one victim of this shortage of money: 'I shan't be able to afford a birthday present for Mummy so shall just send a card,' she told Muriel.

for what came to be called Thatcherism. Life was opening up. 'I shall be awfully sorry when the time comes to leave Colchester,' she told her sister.

There was another reason for Margaret's improved self-esteem. On 17 February 1948, she informed Muriel that she had heard, unexpectedly, from Tony Bray: 'The letter was very weird and sentimental . . . I shall write back and tell him to let sleeping dogs lie. Don't tell parents about this.' Back from Germany, Tony was doing a full honours degree at his old college in Oxford. His letter had been, he said fifty-six years later, sincere: 'I was serious. I wasn't just being gallant.' Despite her words about letting sleeping dogs lie, Margaret agreed to meet him in Oxford 'more to let him see how I've changed than to see him!'. Afterwards, on 18 May, she confided in her sister that she had 'left out or not made clear' several points when writing to her parents about the Oxford trip. These were:

> 1. That I was staying with the Mandelbergs [Oxford Conservative friends]. I thought Pop might think I had a very expensive weekend at a hotel and maybe stump up . . .
> 2. That I met Tony Bray again once or twice over the weekend . . . Strangely enough I found him extremely easy to get on with. There was no embarrassment whatsoever . . . The only direct reference I had of times past was when he said quite steadily – 'you only realise what you had when you've lost it – and you know what I'm referring to.'

Punting with Tony on the Saturday afternoon, Margaret continued, she had finally received 'a full-blooded apology'. Tony had expected to be away in the army for at least three years and felt, 'he couldn't "ask me to hang on" all that time, but he didn't want to kill the feeling between us by writing and saying let's finish':

> He now realised that his very inaction must have killed anything there was between us and that in any case it was quite apallingly [sic] rude not to have written . . . I did not comment on the apology – he assured me he had not been infatuated with anyone else (I, of course, didn't mention Prudence). It all sounded to me as if it were partly true and partly false . . .
> . . . No mention was made of any future arrangements for which I was truly thankful – for it just wouldn't have been 'on' for me . . . he's a weird-looking chap to cart around the place! By the way, he didn't know I had been President of OUCA . . . he was immensely impressed.

Margaret did not maintain her resolve about making no future 'arrangements'. In early September she told her sister that, once again, her letter to her parents had been untruthful. 'In point of fact I was not meeting a "crowd of old college cronies" in London yesterday, but Tony.' The couple went on to see *Carissima* at the Palace, where they had 'absolutely dead central seats' in the stalls and dined at Kettner's ('quite a fashionable West End restaurant'). 'I was wearing my blue frock and little blue hat, little fur jacket with all wine accessories. And I forgot to mention he presented me with a spray of pink roses!' 'I really enjoyed the evening very much,' Margaret concluded, '– though I wouldn't dream of re-striking up the association with Tony.'

Nonetheless, the association did continue, in some form, into 1949. They met again in Oxford and, that February, Tony sent Margaret a Valentine. That proved the last mention of Tony Bray in Margaret's correspondence. As Tony later explained, although he was fond of Margaret, he realized that she was embarking on a serious political career, which was not something he was looking for in a woman. The renewed relationship with Margaret came to an end in 1949, and in June 1950 he became engaged. He telephoned Margaret and received 'polite congratulations: she didn't wax lyrical'. He did not invite her to his wedding – 'It would have been the kiss of death.'

For her part, Margaret, probably more excited by Tony than she would explicitly admit, even to Muriel, did not want to be hurt again.* In the winter of 1948 she wrote to Muriel, who by this time had a boyfriend called Ken: 'I don't know that your "male" problem is the same as mine – you seem infinitely more successful with them than I do with his Colchester counterpart!' The 'Colchester counterpart' is obviously a generic type of man that Margaret feels she cannot find, but may also have been a reference to David Papillon, a leading Young Conservative in Colchester, much liked and admired. Margaret records her excitement when Papillon sent her a Christmas card or asked her to a party. What she failed to realize was that Papillon was homosexual. Throughout her life, she remained innocent about such things. Margaret was clearly looking for other men while Tony Bray was still on the scene and feeling a little wistful about not finding them. For now, her self-confidence rested heavily on the approval and attention of others. While her confidence grew as her career prospered, in the winter of 1948 she still felt a little fragile.

Tony Bray had been right to detect a hardening of Margaret's seriousness about a political career. In October 1948, she attended the Conservative

---

* When asked about Tony Bray in 2004, Lady Thatcher said she remembered the royal-blue cloak she had worn to their dinner before the Randolph Ball. When reminded that Tony had got back in touch with her on returning from the army, regretting his neglect of her while he had been away in the army, she said, echoing his apology to her in Oxford, 'It's no good thinking over the chances you missed,' and would not be drawn further on the subject.

Party conference in Llandudno as a representative of the Oxford Conservative Graduates' Association. Margaret did not expect this to produce any specific development in her career. In August, indeed, she had applied to the Colonial Office in pursuit of her childhood ambition of working as a civil servant in the Empire and also put her name on the Overseas Scientific and Technical Register. Such appointments would have kept her out of politics. While the conference itself proved a damp squib, it provided the chance for the twenty-three-year-old Margaret to become reacquainted with an old Oxford mentor and friend, John Grant, a director of Blackwell's the booksellers, and a man she looked up to: 'we had a long discussion over personal and political affairs and a job for me,' she told Muriel. 'We went on talking until 2:30 a.m.'

Grant now gave Margaret the introduction which was to launch her political career. That weekend, he urged John Miller, chairman of Dartford Conservative Association, to consider adopting her as their parliamentary candidate. Dartford, a Kent town on the eastern fringes of London, was a strong Labour seat and an industrial stronghold. Miller was sceptical. 'I don't think a woman would do at all,' he told Grant. Over lunch, however, Margaret made a very favourable impression. On 31 January 1949 she was chosen as the prospective Conservative candidate for Dartford, defeating the four men on the shortlist. Ken Tisdell, a Young Conservative, recalled her as 'streets ahead of anyone else'. Dartford Conservatives, languishing in a safe Labour seat, were looking for a fighter and were prepared to take risks. For them, it was a positive advantage that Margaret was a woman, and a young woman at that.

Conservative Central Office put an enthusiastic stamp on Dartford's choice. The day after her selection, Margaret saw Beryl Cook, the party's area agent, who reported at once to Central Office, 'I was tremendously impressed and think that she is a winner.' She also saw Marjorie Maxse, the party's women's chairman, who added that her 'platform knowledge and speaking ability were far above those of the other candidates'. 'She wants', added Miss Maxse, 'a salary of £500 a year and would like a job in some big chemical firm like the [sic] ICI ... She is particularly keen on Empire subjects as well as ordinary bread-and-butter politics.'

The references Margaret provided for Central Office included one from Lord Balfour of Inchrye, a former Air Minister. 'A grand young candidate,' he wrote laconically. 'Speaks well. Good-looking. Keen, knows her subjects. Watch and encourage.' John Grant's reference declared Margaret 'responsible for the resurgence of OUCA after the war, despite the fact that she is considerably younger than the men she was leading'. His 'despite' might better have been replaced with 'because of', since it was precisely with older men that Margaret could lead most successfully. The fullest reference came from Margaret's Grantham neighbour, Susan Brace, who recalled her 'surprising interest in politics' even as a child: 'I was astonished at her grasp of affairs and her facility in communicating her views ... For some years I served on the local Town Council with her father, who is exceptionally intelligent and able. Altogether her "background" is that of "public service" at its best, coupled with a very superior intellect and the anxiety to work hard for principles in which she believes.'

For Margaret, her selection for Dartford was an even greater moment than her entry into Oxford. It revealed the extent of her political talents, threw her into the combat she always enjoyed and set her on the course of her life. It led to her marriage, and it made her intensely happy. In that moment, her thoughts turned, as so often, to clothes. After her selection, she wrote to Muriel: 'Hope Mummy will get my housecoat done as soon as possible though I know she is very busy but if I am going down to stay with various officials in the constituency, I shall have to look nice from skin outwards and from head to heel the whole 24 hours.' She also noted eagerly all the reactions to her Dartford selection, especially from David Papillon: 'I gather he is saying ... what a pity such a charming girl should be lost to politics! She'll find it very heavy-going, wonder if she'll stay the course. The what a pity such a charming girl lost to politics – such an unnatural life, should have stayed at home, sentiments have been re-echoed and in a way, I suppose they are complimentary.' Margaret liked to bank such praise, but if she herself felt the qualms about a political career for a woman that so many voiced, she never recorded them.

Margaret's Dartford adoption meeting, when she would be formally proclaimed as the candidate, was called for 28 February 1949. She had a new haircut but not, to avoid expense, a perm. Shortly before the great day, however, another significant event, unrelated to Dartford, took place. Margaret, as she told Muriel, had dined with 'a Scotch farmer who has a place around these parts'. After they met at Brian Harrison's 39–45 Group, the farmer had been in hot pursuit:

> Eventually I said yes and we dined at the George. He's about 35 and has a kind of naïveté that only Scotsman [sic] can have. I expected to be bored to tears but in fact he was really rather sweet with quite a sense of humour. He practically presented his credentials to me. His farm is worth £25,000, he has 3,000 £1 shares of ICI now standing at 47/-. . . And being a Scotman [sic] he left a ninepenny tip for the waiter. I could have fallen through the floor. That's how people with money keep it!

Her suitor was pressing: 'He drove me home in his present rather old car – and got quite ardent on the way! I said I couldn't possibly fix another definite date so he's going to 'phone me! The funniest part is that although I have been introduced to him twice, I can never catch his name and still don't know it!'

Before Margaret had found out the name of her Scottish farmer, Dartford had welcomed its new Conservative candidate. At the adoption, the chairman praised Margaret and revealed, perhaps tactlessly, that four prominent local businessmen had been sounded out but declined the candidacy. Then Margaret spoke. 'She stressed', recorded the *Erith Observer*, 'that Imperial Preference* was still the cornerstone of Conservatism.' She was identifying with pre-war bourgeois right-wing views, rather than with the free-trade principles she would later embrace, in a way that showed independence from the party leadership. She also declared, as she was so often to do in later years, that 'The Government should do what any good housewife would do if money was short – look at their accounts and see what was wrong.'

The meeting, she wrote to Muriel, 'was a thrilling affair'. 'People who had come to be very critical were all won over by the end of the evening. They gave me a lovely bouquet of pink carnations, blue irises, blue grape hyacinths and prunus blossom.' Drinks followed, after which, 'a director of a small paint company in the constituency ... a Major Thatcher, who has a flat in London (age about 36, plenty of money) ... drove me back to town at midnight. As one would expect he is a perfect gentleman. Not a very attractive creature – very reserved but quite nice. He's not very fond of meeting "people" ... We arrived back at Liverpool St at about 1 am and packed me into the milk train which left at 3.40. Altogether it was a thrilling evening.'

The 'small paint company' was the Atlas Preservative Company, the family business of Denis Thatcher, who was its general manager. As an old boy of a minor public school (Mill Hill), a former officer mentioned in despatches, and with his own prosperous firm, Denis was socially a cut above Margaret. He was also quite active in the Dartford Conservative Association. Indeed, he was one of the four local businessmen first approached to be the parliamentary candidate. Denis had refused. If he had accepted, he would presumably never have met Margaret and there would not have been a prime minister called Mrs Thatcher. Even before he met her, he had made way for her.

---

* That is, free trade within the Empire, and tariffs outside it.

According to Denis, a business colleague had invited him for the night of the adoption meeting saying, 'Come to dinner: I want you to meet a very pretty girl,' without revealing who she was. When Denis arrived, he said to himself, 'Good God, it's the candidate!' He thought Margaret was 'a nice-looking young woman, a bit overweight'. Driving her to the station allowed him to get to know her better. They arrived at 1 a.m. It is unclear whether Denis stayed talking to her for the full two hours forty minutes before the milk train left. If he did (as her phrase 'packed me into the milk train' suggests), it would explain how she had formed what was, for her, an unusually full first impression.

Back in Colchester, her romance, if that is the right word, was developing. 'My Scottie farmer met me off the train,' she told Muriel: 'I'm afraid he's got it rather badly ... His name, by the way, is William Cullen.' She invited Muriel to come and meet him. Margaret's motives here were interesting. 'Went to the flicks yesterday with my farmer friend,' she had written four days earlier, 'and got him all primed up to meet you sometime. I showed him the snapshot of you and I [*sic*] together – and he said he could scarcely tell the difference so I should think we could easily substitute me for you. When can you come down for a weekend?' She seemed to be searching for a husband for herself and for her sister, and to be thinking of the man who was chasing her in the latter role.

Dartford was a heavily industrial seat with a strong trade union presence. The Labour majority of 20,000 was considered unassailable. The young Margaret Roberts, however, set out cheerfully to assail it. In her certainty that Labour's policies could not work, she was closer to the party's grass-roots than to the patrician leadership of her party, which, after 1945, was in a defeatist frame of mind. She understood small business and the aspirations of young lower-middle-class people like herself born with no great advantages. They worried that Labour's tax, controls and nationalization would deny them the post-war opportunities they had hoped for and were ready for a fight.

During her time in Dartford, membership of her association rose a remarkable 37 per cent to 3,160. Several hundred were Young Conservatives, virtually all of whom identified with and admired Margaret. These people – bank clerks and bank managers, solicitors' secretaries, employees of local businesses – saw in their smartly dressed, polite and keen young candidate a slightly grander or idealized version of themselves. While Margaret was regarded as 'upper-class educationally', they also considered her 'one of us in a way'. As one Dartford Conservative recalled, all were struck by her 'perfect manners' and her genuine gratitude. Edward Heath, by contrast, who sat for the neighbouring seat of Bexley, and who was also young and of similar social origins to Margaret, treated the Young Conservatives as 'the lowest of the low'. Margaret was 'plump, smart, pretty, loved hats, lovely skin'; and yet 'always knew the price of everything'. They also admired the fight in her – 'I was amazed how brave she was.' Pat Luker, a close associate from Margaret's second Dartford campaign, put it thus: 'I think she was really, truly English. Everything was for the good of the country, the English people.' Note that the word 'English' rather than 'British' is used. Although always Unionist in theory, Margaret Thatcher saw her country through a very English prism.

As Margaret quickly got to grips with the constituency, her Labour opponent, the sitting Member, Norman Dodds, made the mistake of underestimating her and perhaps patronizing her because of her sex. As Margaret told Muriel, their first meeting occurred at a dance, when she and Dodds were 'dragged out into the middle of the ballroom': 'I wore my black velvet frock with long white gloves, pearls, and long drop pearl ear-rings. Mr Dodds said he was very sorry I was an opponent! He then publicly asked me for the next dance and the M.C. said what did I request. I said a Tango. They said which one. I said "Jealousy"! We danced the whole dance – the only couple on the floor.' As the press took pictures, 'I said "we were in tune when dancing" and Mr Dodds said "in perfect harmony". I imagine the report will make front page news next week!' It did.

Dodds had unwisely challenged Margaret to a public debate, an opportunity she seized in late November. Through detailed attacks on the policies of the Labour government, including the recent devaluation of the pound,* Margaret proved her mettle and her knowledge. She continued in the strong vein of her adoption speech as she campaigned in the constituency, speaking out against Communism and calling for a recovery of personal responsibility: 'In wartime there was a slogan "It all depends on me." People seem to have forgotten that, and they think it depends on the other person.' She offered women what would nowadays be called empowerment: 'Don't be scared of the high language of economists and Cabinet ministers, but think of politics at our own household level.'

Margaret accepted the prevailing consensus about what later came to be called the welfare state. But she pointed out that the National Health Service and social security would be of 'no use if the country goes bankrupt'.

---

* She called for a new policy by which 'the pound can look the dollar in the face and not in the bootlaces'.

Perhaps the candidate's strongest appeal, made much stronger by her youth and sex, was a stirring call for a recovery of national greatness. Writing in the local press, she declared that 'Women are intensely patriotic, and the loss of Britain's prestige under the present Government weighs heavily on their minds.' Perhaps Margaret was simply projecting her own feelings on to her sex, but if so, it was a projection to which many responded enthusiastically.

Margaret's Dartford candidacy required a rearrangement of her life. With the help of the Tory Party Chairman, Lord Woolton, she secured a new job as a research chemist at J. Lyons and Co., the food company, in Hammersmith.* By July she was lodging in Dartford, catching the 7.10 train to London and returning on the 6.08 to an evening's political work in the constituency. The expense was worrying, and the burden of work would have crushed many a spirit, but Margaret found the whole thing exhilarating, not least the clothes: 'Mrs Prole [a milliner in Colchester] has made me a smaller black velvet hat with a white ostrich feather on it and it looks very charming,' she told Muriel. 'Not so dressy as the green cock feathers – much more a hat for any occasion.'

There remained the matter of 'Scottie'. Back in Colchester, Willie Cullen continued to court Margaret. 'He is awfully sweet,' she wrote to Muriel, 'I am getting quite fond of him.' But Margaret was strengthening her idea of herself as matchmaker, aware that Muriel's own romance had faded. 'You had better come down here some other weekend to meet the current boyfriend,' she wrote. 'By the way, he will never become your brother-in-law though I have high hopes that he may be mine one day!' On 8 April, only a few weeks after the relationship had begun, Margaret introduced Muriel to Willie Cullen.

The original flirtation continued, perhaps a merry diversion for Margaret, perhaps more serious for Willie. He took her to the Caledonian Ball in March and then to the races at Newmarket, at which he won an enormous sum. For Margaret the event was memorable for a different reason: 'SAW PRINCESS ELIZABETH' she wrote excitedly afterwards of the woman whose eighth Prime Minister she would eventually become, 'AND SHE SAW ME!' Willie persevered. One of his presents seemed particularly well suited: 'William has given me a very nice black-calf handbag,' Margaret wrote

---

* As with everything she did, Margaret was conscientious and put her work to use. Before long, she was talking to the Dartford Rotary Ladies Day about food research – 'Another recent problem concerned sandwiches which were to be eaten at 20,000ft in the air,' read a surreal report in the local paper.

to Muriel. 'It's not an awfully expensive one as my conscience wouldn't let me do that – but I chose a very nice one at £7-3s. We had my initials put on as well and it looks awfully nice ... I quite loftily say it's not "very expensive" – it's about twice as much as you or I would pay ... I'll have to hang on to William for a while longer now!' There is the humorous heartlessness of youth in this, a Margaret who plays with men and enjoys it. In the same letter, she mentioned that she was going to the North Kent Rotary Ball 'with a chap called Denis Thatcher* ... He's all right – but is most unpopular with his men. He's far too belligerent in dealing with them and they naturally don't like it.'

Willie Cullen introduced Margaret to his family. In May, after dining at Foulton Hall, Cullen's farm, she shared her impressions with Muriel:

> The wives were typical wives – they know of domestic matters and nothing else. I stayed with the men after supper talking about many other things and when William suggested that maybe we ought to 'join the ladies' David [Macaulay, a local farmer] said in rather contemptuous fashion 'Why, – they don't talk politics or anything else in there.' And that's how they regard their wives. And indeed when we did join the ladies for half-an-hour or so much later, conversation flagged entirely.

What is visible here is not only Margaret's lifelong preference for male company, but a presentiment that she could not be happy as a farmer's wife.†

When Muriel came down again to see Willie he took her, with Margaret, to meet his mother. Margaret gave her sister very particular instructions about what to wear: 'I expect you'll have your highwayman coat on, but don't come too exotic underneath. We must be as nice as possible to make Mrs Cullen feel at her ease.' Perhaps because the Roberts sisters avoided being 'exotic underneath', the meeting seems to have been a success. Willie liked Muriel more and more, as was intended. Indeed, he seemed to fit in with Margaret's master plan more readily than was pleasing to her. That July, Willie told Margaret that he would call on the Robertses in Grantham en route to Glasgow. Muriel was at home with her parents, and Margaret was not. 'I hope to goodness he doesn't give Daddy the impression of being a prospective son-in-law,' Margaret wrote to Muriel, 'it would scare Pop out of his wits at the moment. Anyway, I can't see it ever coming off.'

---

* Margaret appears to have forgotten that she had mentioned Denis to Muriel a few weeks before.
† When she next visited Foulton, she reported that 'the sitting-room looks smaller in daylight'.

The visit took place and was repeated on Willie's return journey south. As Margaret wrote to Muriel, 'he told me he could have stayed much longer!':

> Daddy's only comment to me was 'He seems a sensible sort of chap . . . whoever you want to marry it will be all right by me, my dear.' . . . I shan't marry Bill for though very fond of him I am not in love with him and a marriage between us would falter after 2 or 3 months. We have completely different outlooks, and quite different sorts of friends. While I get on all right with his, he would feel out of water with mine.

What Margaret was saying, with a mature delicacy, was that her ambitions were higher than anything that the hard-working plain Scottish farmer could satisfy.

Over the autumn and winter of 1949, the relationship between Margaret and Willie Cullen continued to cool as that between him and Muriel warmed. That October, while politicking in Dartford, Margaret met someone else. Robert Henderson was the medical superintendent at the Southern Hospital. 'He's a most unusual chap,' she scribbled to Muriel. '. . . He's over 40, so he'd do quite nicely for you! He said I was to 'phone whenever I felt fed up with politics, but of course I shan't.' 'William says he hasn't heard from you yet,' she chided. 'Do write to him as quickly as possible.' She added that she had teased Willie about her new-found friend: 'he wrote back and said I was giving him a hint to get out'. And she referred again to Denis Thatcher, who was taking her to dinner and the theatre that night. This letter is notable for referring to three of only four men (Tony Bray being the other) who were ever important in the affairs of Margaret's heart. Margaret was toying with them. When she finally came to choose, she would do so with the utmost seriousness, but she was not above enjoying the game.

What happened over the next two months is partially obscure. One way or another, Willie Cullen did 'take the hint to get out'. The process of being gently dumped by Margaret and pushed towards Muriel involved a good deal of negotiation, but with no apparent falling-out between the sisters. In January 1950, Margaret informed Muriel that she and Willie would meet in London 'to talk over the various aspects of "we three" and it will then be broken off between he and I [sic], for good and all'. In fact, as Margaret noted in a postscript, the meeting did not take place because Willie rang her instead. 'I told him from henceforth that I would "in law" only be taking a sisterly interest in future. He seemed quite satisfied and is quite pleased with "future prospects".'

Once 'we three' were rearranged, Margaret was keen to get everything settled. On 14 February 1950, Muriel's engagement to Willie was announced in the *Daily Telegraph*,* shortly before the general election, which had been called for 23 February. That same day Margaret sent Muriel a typed letter finalizing arrangements for the couple to visit her on election day. ('You will be coming to the Count with me on Thursday night, so bring a smart hat.') In her own hand, Margaret added: 'So glad the announcement is in today's *Telegraph*, one feels it gives the stamp of finality to the whole affair. Gather you're having diamonds in your ring, a plum coloured corduroy suit to go away in and a blue gown for the ceremony . . . The campaign goes fairly well – we are having packed meetings.'

After the election, Margaret, the only bridesmaid at the wedding in April, threw herself into its every detail. Muriel must have a headdress with a veil 'otherwise folks won't know bride from bridesmaid. I'll just have a little draped cap.' She made suggestions about flowers and gloves and drew a sketch of the frock, of her own design, which she proposed to wear. She implored Muriel to ensure that Willie took 'the right clothes to Paris' for their honeymoon. All Margaret's interventions were well meant, but her sister would not have been human if she did not sometimes feel irritated to be told what to do, almost to have had her marriage arranged, by an unmarried woman four years her junior. Her marriage to Willie Cullen proved long and successful (he died in 1998), but as Andrew Cullen, one of Muriel and Willie's two sons, said: 'Dad did hold a soft spot for Auntie Margaret.' In old age Muriel described her relationship with her sister with characteristic briskness: 'She [Margaret] says, "I consider my sister my best friend." All she means by that is that I told her what I thought.' 'The Robertses are not very good at feelings,' said Muriel's daughter, Jane. 'They deal with facts and reality.'

Although Margaret never really had any intention of marrying Willie Cullen, what probably precipitated the break was the arrival on the scene of Robert Henderson. Forty-seven when Margaret first met him (just over twice her age), he had risen from being the son of an Aberdeenshire blacksmith to enjoy a distinguished medical career.† Physically, he resembled Denis Thatcher, although he was shorter and considered better-looking.

---

* A minor family row ensued about this announcement. Alfred Roberts had placed the notice and described himself in it as 'Ald.', short for Alderman. Muriel was upset by this and continued to be so more than fifty years later, feeling that it turned her wedding into a municipal announcement. Margaret concurred, perhaps for the slightly different reason that local government titles are not grand enough to parade on social occasions. 'I agree with you that it was quite wrong. I raised my eyebrows at the time.'

† He was best known for having devised his own version of a tank respirator he had seen in America for the treatment of patients who could not breathe. During the war, this 'iron lung', as it was known, was manufactured and distributed to hospitals throughout Britain and the Empire. It saved many lives.

He was canny with money – '£100 would go for ever' – and a supporter, though not actively involved, of the Conservatives. He liked women. In 1949, he was still unmarried.

In Margaret's letters to Muriel, Robert Henderson is the only boyfriend who is invariably referred to with respect, sometimes even with tenderness. Having described her parting with Willie Cullen, Margaret explains she had met Robert afterwards: 'He said he thought I looked flat and miserable and I ought to go out for a little while on my first night back. Wasn't it sweet of him?' She was self-mockingly nervous, however, of her chances. He had spent Christmas, she said, with a rich family who had 'five daughters of marriageable age . . . The prospects don't look very hopeful do they!?' Later in January 1950, however, she wrote of a 'wonderful party' with Robert, given by a friend of his who was 'consultant epidemiologist to the Royal family'. 'I think we are both getting very fond of one another,' she added, '– in fact more than that. I hope so.'

The entertainments became more glamorous and more intimate. 'By the way,' Margaret wrote to Muriel, 'after Polling day Robert and I are dining and dancing at the Berkeley . . . On Saturday I'm going down to Eastbourne for the weekend. Robert is coming to join me on the Sunday staying overnight and he will drive me back on the Monday. Needless to say I'm looking forward to it tremendously.' This was perhaps as near as Margaret ever came to enjoying a naughty weekend.

True to Margaret's intense dislike of other people knowing about her private life, she mentioned Robert to no one in Dartford, yet their relationship deepened, and was to continue almost until she left Dartford for good.

In her election address for the general election of 23 February 1950, Margaret Roberts spoke in her own distinctive voice. The 'first task' of a new Conservative government, she said, would be 'setting the finances of the nation in order'. She praised the 'small shopkeepers' – 'such men and women are part of the strength and backbone of England' – reaffirmed her support for Imperial Preference and declared that 'A separate house for every family is our aim.'

In a newspaper article, Margaret spelt out her vision of Britain and the crisis caused by socialism. She argued that Britain's global reputation had fallen low under Labour, which had failed to join in resisting Communism, but that 'The world needs her.' Margaret then challenged the voters: 'Are YOU going to let this proud island race, who at one time would never accept charity, drift on from crisis to crisis . . . ? Or do you believe in sound finance . . . ?' Quoting 'a young unknown engineer from one of the Dominions',* who had written to her asking what had happened to the sturdy British love of freedom, she made a passionate plea: 'It was not a Government that built up the skill and craft of this country – the woollen goods, the beautiful china, and the precision engineering, which have made their way into the markets of the world. It was private individuals who patiently persevered, building up their businesses bit by bit.' The British spirit had to be rediscovered: 'Do you want it to perish for a soulless Socialist system, or to live to recreate a glorious Britain? YOU WILL DECIDE.' Throughout her career, Margaret Thatcher was to diverge very little from the substance and the tone of this article. It is, perhaps, the first clear text of Thatcherism. As with Thatcherism when fully formed, the emotional force is not a doctrine about economic liberty – strong though that is – but a romantic belief in the greatness of her country.

With such powerful beliefs, and a precocious confidence in her powers of expressing them, Margaret Roberts fought the campaign with gusto. Believing that the candidate should be immediately identifiable, she invested in a hat with a black and white ribbon, to which she added a 'bit of blue inside the bow' and alternated two suits. She threw herself into the campaign, speaking outside factory gates to the all-male workers in defiance of trade union officials, and addressing huge public meetings night after night – 'heckling suited me a treat'. The campaign went extremely well, but, as she recalled more than forty years later, 'I have never felt so tired in any election since.' The result was:

Norman Dodds (Labour)	38,128
Miss M. H. Roberts (Conservative)	24,490
A. H. Giles (Liberal)	5,011
Labour majority	13,638

Margaret had knocked 6,000 off Dodds's majority, doing much better than the average Tory candidate. Nationally, Labour clung on to power by an overall majority of six, which made a second election highly probable. Margaret allowed her supporters no rest. 'You sign on for next time tomorrow morning,' she told them after the count. 'Dartford', she assured her association a few days later, 'will certainly have first refusal of my services as a candidate in the next election.' They did not refuse. In fact, Margaret did secretly consider an alternative. South Hammersmith Conservatives, fighting a Labour seat with a smaller majority than Dartford's,

---

* This was the name for nations such as Australia, Canada and New Zealand, which came later to be referred to as 'the white Commonwealth' and, later still, as 'the old Commonwealth'.

approached her. She confided this to Muriel: 'their 2,000 adverse majority is even more solid than Dartford's 13,000. I don't feel it would be worth changing under those circumstances.' Her devotion to Dartford was qualified by her ambition.

With her second candidacy assured, Margaret began reading for the Bar. Even she quailed slightly at the labour involved. 'My goodness there's a lot of work to be done and it will come terribly expensive,' she wrote to Muriel. With the help of David Renton, the Conservative MP for Huntingdonshire, who had a family connection with Dartford, she was admitted to Lincoln's Inn that August.

The relationship with Robert Henderson continued, although it began to show signs of difficulty. He was proving circumspect about introducing Margaret to his friends: 'whether it will ever come to anything I very much doubt,' she told Muriel in March, 'for he thinks the difference between our ages very great'. Through Robert, Margaret learnt more about the medical and nursing professions and how they had been affected by Labour's introduction of the National Health Service in 1948. Although never opposed to universal care free at the point of use, she believed strongly that the way in which it was introduced worked against the freedom of individual hospitals and submitted doctors and nurses to unnecessary and overcentralized control. She watched Robert gradually surrendering some of his mastery of the huge Southern Hospital. She did not like it.

As she began reading for the Bar, Margaret searched for lodgings in London. This was not easy. In June, she lived briefly in a tiny flat in Westminster Palace Gardens. She told Muriel she had 'loved' the experience: 'It isn't nearly so strenuous as travelling up from Dartford daily and its [sic] nice not to be questioned by an enquiring landlord and landlady.'* From it, she sallied forth to be the youth speaker offering a vote of thanks to Winston Churchill at a party rally at the Albert Hall on 7 June 1950, the only time she was to meet the great wartime Prime Minister: 'The Winston meeting went off quite well. I was absolutely terrified of the enormous audience but got through all right. Everyone was very flattering about it.'

The following year, 1951, Margaret found a more permanent place to live: 101 St George's Square Mews in Pimlico. This brought her joy, in part because she was at last living in the middle of things: 'It was a great thrill to come to London. In Grantham it was like swimming in a very

---

* Margaret had been unhappy with her landlords in Dartford, the Woollcotts. Lacking children of their own, they had come to lavish attention on Margaret that she, as someone who guarded her privacy fiercely, resented. The situation was such that Robert Henderson had taken to meeting Margaret at the end of the street rather than at her house.

small pool: you keep bumping into the sides.' For Muriel, she described in enormous detail the decorative and domestic arrangements. By this time, her sister had given birth to her first child, Morton, and Margaret includes brief and brisk references to the baby – 'So glad to hear that you are home again and that the infant is making good progress. Hope the vomiting soon clears up' – but she quickly returns to the subject of her own homemaking, lamenting the absence of a bath and complaining that the sideboard has woodworm and so on. Margaret evinces no desire to see the newborn baby, or her sister, who had been quite ill after the birth. When she does suggest a visit, it is because she wishes to take advantage of the Cullens' farm: 'I am practically out of eggs and they are my main diet at the moment – scrambled eggs on toast!'*

Alfred Roberts helped Margaret with her move. Yet tension arose, in part because he felt unthanked, but also because he feared that Margaret's Dartford friend, Mary Rohan, a Roman Catholic, was exercising a malign influence. 'I should be grieved beyond measure if the R/Cs got hold of Margaret,' he wrote to Muriel:

> As you know, I have left you both free in regard to religion, as a parent must and does who trusts his children, but R/C is Spiritual Totalitarianism with all its damning intolerance for others. Margaret has been very hard at times and apparently ungrateful for all I've done, altho that hasn't & wouldn't stop me from doing all I could for either of you. But truthfully it has kept me poor, and I was beginning to rejoice that she would soon be well established & independant [*sic*] when she had got through the law business. Now comes this worry . . .

There is no evidence that Roberts's anxieties were justified.† As Muriel recalled: 'I just wrote back and said, "Don't be silly. It would take more than Mary or anyone else to influence Margaret."' But she did feel that, at times, Margaret failed to notice the sacrifices her parents made to help her rise in the world.

One of Margaret's chief motives in getting and beautifying the flat was to impress Robert Henderson, whose attention she continually worried might drift elsewhere. She was determined to entertain him royally. While she also (separately) invited Denis for a drink, an evening with Robert

---

* That month, Margaret managed to pass her driving test, arranged by her father in Grantham. Because she had two outstanding driving lessons paid for when she passed, she went ahead and had them all the same.
† Margaret became increasingly sympathetic to the Catholic Church in later life, but her strong Christianity was never of a Catholic, sacramental or even churchy kind. At no point in her life was Margaret about to 'pope'.

required more elaborate treatment: 'Last time he came I cooked a slap-up dinner, four courses just to show him! But I can't rise to that every time.' The last surviving references to Robert Henderson in Margaret's correspondence date from May 1951. On 25 September, Alfred Roberts wrote to Muriel with news he felt she would find 'surprising': Margaret and Denis Thatcher were to be engaged:

> As I told you, I met Dennis [sic] on the Sunday I left you and heard from Margaret that he had asked her to marry him and that she was considering it but wanted to see me first . . . He has been taking Margaret about the place to various functions for almost two years but his proposal was unexpected. The Robert business upset Margaret very much but that will pass. Dennis has had an unfortunate experience. He was married during the war, but after only about five weekends' leave spent with his wife she left him. She is now Lady Hicks,* it appears the title did the damage. I told Margaret she could disregard this as he was in no way at fault and actually he is an exceedingly nice fellow also of course <u>very</u> comfortably situated financially.

What had happened? Margaret's letters are reliably more tender towards Robert than towards Denis. Indeed, she told Muriel, after going to the play *His Excellency* with Denis, 'I can't say I really ever enjoy going out for the evening with him. He has not got a very prepossessing personality.' Robert Henderson died in 1999 aged ninety-seven, but his widow, Josie, recalled that he explained it thus: 'Denis had more money and more future and from then on, he [Robert] didn't stand a chance . . . He understood that Denis was a much better catch.' This cannot be the whole story, however, since it does not explain the fact that the two men ran in parallel for two years of Margaret's life with Denis, who met her before Robert, coming second in the race until the late summer of 1951. Part of the answer may lie in the age gap of twenty-four years. In later life, at the suggestion that Robert had perhaps hoped that she would be the future Mrs Henderson, Lady Thatcher replied: 'I wouldn't disagree with that, but he was so much older.' If the decision was as cut and dried as that, however, why did Alfred Roberts think that his daughter had been 'upset very much' by it? On the other hand, it seems highly unlikely that Robert and Margaret parted on poor terms. Unlike with Tony Bray, she maintained friendly, though not close, relations with him for the rest of his life.†

What of Denis Thatcher? Having suffered deeply in the collapse of

---

* Actually she was Lady Hickman.
† It was to Robert Henderson that Margaret turned when considering where she might have the infant Mark circumcised (an operation then quite common on grounds of hygiene), feeling he would be 'wonderfully looked after' at the Southern Hospital. The fact that Margaret

his first marriage, and not being an impulsive man, he did not rush. His admiration for the pretty, intelligent and spirited girl he had met on the night of her adoption meeting slowly grew. Denis recognized Margaret as someone with a powerful mind and character 'different from any other young woman I'd ever met in my life'. He liked her ability to recite poetry. 'Let's have a go,' he said to himself, and in the late summer of 1951 he did, proposing after dinner in his flat. The key difference between Denis and Robert, from Margaret's point of view, was that Denis asked her to marry him, and Robert did not.

As Denis put it nearly fifty years later, 'She didn't leap at it.' The proposal was a surprise and came at a time when her feelings about Robert Henderson were probably not fully resolved. So she went away and pondered his offer: 'Things last better that way,' she said years later. She admired Denis the ex-soldier, echoing the centurion in the Gospel, as 'obviously someone who had known authority'. She was pleased to have a man who shared her political interests with a good job and a flat in Chelsea. He was a passport to the Home Counties respectability that she sought. She seems to have intuited, if not actually discussed with Denis, his acceptance of her political ambitions, which was exceptional for a man of that generation. His financial and moral support would allow her to qualify for the Bar. She was worried by the fact of his divorce, but also believed him when he said that 'he really meant it this time'. She wanted the security of marriage and children: she liked the age difference of eleven years. She accepted him.

The couple drove up to Grantham to see the Robertses. The meeting was amicable. Denis found Margaret's parents to be 'sweet people', with 'old man Roberts' 'very quiet spoken and well read', but a bit 'straitlaced', and Mrs Roberts 'very quiet, very typical of a wife'. The conversation was, Denis remembered, 'A bit sticky. Eventually Margaret says, "Father, Denis does like a drink." Very long faces, long hunt through the house; finally blow dust off bottle of sherry.' Relations between Denis and Margaret's parents were to go on as they began – correct but never close. He felt that, although they had always done their best, Margaret had not had 'all that happy a childhood': 'It was work, work, work, all her life.' Among other things, Denis provided the pleasure principle that her upbringing had lacked. He too was a hard worker, but he enjoyed life, and he would help her enjoy it.

In the extremely short term, however, Denis's proposal presented Margaret with a problem. She did not want it known until after the coming

---

was prepared to put her son's manhood almost literally in the hands of her former boyfriend suggests a high level of trust.

general election. In those days, wedlock generally signalled an end to a woman's career. Denis's divorce, a far more controversial issue then than now, posed an additional concern. Although Denis was blameless – his wife having taken up with a baronet called Sir Howard Hickman while Denis was serving in the army abroad – talk of divorce would not have helped Margaret's campaign.

So, for the course of October's election campaign, Margaret's office was sworn to secrecy. Only on the eve of poll was the engagement put out to the press, unbeknown to Margaret. In later years, she believed it had been done by Beryl Cook to attract some last-minute votes. This irritated her.

Between the two elections, the tone of politics changed. The Korean War, which began in June 1950, brought home the reality of the Communist threat and raised the spectre of a wider war. On Communism, Margaret knew where she stood. In a speech in Dartford in September, she warned that: 'If Germany were to become another Korea tonight, every one of us would shake in our shoes.' 'The only thing that allowed Britain time to negotiate', she added, 'was her atomic superiority.'* In her New Year message in the *Dartford Chronicle* she wrote, 'We must firstly *believe* in the Western way of life and serve it steadfastly. Secondly we must build up our fighting strength to be prepared to defend our ideals, for aggressive nations understand only the threat of force.'†

During this time, Margaret grew in stature as a candidate. W. F. Deedes, a Kent candidate (at Ashford) in 1951, noted her impact at the Conservative Prospective Parliamentary Candidates' Association meetings. 'Once she opened her mouth the rest of us began to look rather second-rate.' Through the association, she met present and future leading lights of the party, notably the Colditz hero Airey Neave, whose support in the leadership battle in 1975 would ensure her victory. She was becoming part of a Tory social network – at that time still dominated by the well-off, the ex-military and the landed Etonians – which she enjoyed and which would serve her well.

Unable to maintain his party's tiny majority in Parliament, Attlee called

---

* Britain, under the Attlee government, had decided to develop a nuclear bomb. However, it did not test a device until 1952.
† The idea of Britain as a strong nation alone and brave had religious echoes in Margaret's mind, deriving from the biblical idea of the righteous remnant. At the Dartford Free Church Federal Council annual meeting, she chose the text from Genesis in which Abraham pleads with God to spare the righteous from the destruction of Sodom and Gomorrah. Applying this to our age, she declared that 'it depended on the few men of the Battle of Britain to save civilisation from immediate doom'. Throughout her career, the story of 1940 was the myth (by which is not meant untruth) which most dominated her imagination.

a general election for 25 October 1951. Margaret stood in Dartford for the second time. The issue of Communism and the threat to peace was still running strongly. 'Britain ...' she said in her election address, 'must be strong, strong in arms, and strong in faith in her own way of life. The greatest hope for peace lies in friendship and co-operation with the United States of America.'

The campaign was hard-fought and boisterous. Denis did his part, appearing in his Jaguar and helping his secret fiancée canvass. Chairing one of Margaret's public meetings, he declared: 'She has unlimited beauty, brains and charm, three qualities which we can do with in the House of Commons.' Whenever Margaret was heckled, Denis became very upset and had to be held back from intervening. This time, she had a straight fight with Dodds, with no Liberal candidate. The result was:

Norman Dodds (Labour)	40,094
Miss M. H. Roberts (Conservative)	27,760
Labour majority	12,334

She had cut Dodds's majority by a further 1,300. Countrywide, Labour received more votes than the Conservatives, but the votes stacked up too heavily in safe Labour areas, allowing the Conservatives to gain more seats. Under Churchill, they returned to power for the first time since the war, with an overall majority of seventeen, but Margaret Roberts went off to get married.

The wedding took place on 13 December 1951 in Wesley's Chapel, City Road, London. The bride remembered it as 'a cold and foggy December day'. As befitted the weather – and perhaps her slightly uneasy status marrying a divorced man – she did not wear white, but a velvet dress of sapphire-blue, modelled on the black velvet dress she had cherished at Oxford, and a striking hat, in the manner of Gainsborough's portrait of Georgiana, Duchess of Devonshire, clinging to the back of her head with ostrich feathers cascading down the right-hand side. The photograph shows a sparkling, happy and pretty young woman, with a bridegroom who looks – and was – older and shyer. The couple were married to the strains of 'Lead Us, Heavenly Father, Lead Us', whose words proved prophetic as the marriage successfully carried the couple for more than half a century 'o'er the world's tempestuous sea'. About fifty people attended, and the reception was held at the Carlton Gardens home of Alfred Bossom, the MP for Maidstone and one of Margaret's earliest patrons.

The Thatchers spent their wedding night in the Savoy Hotel in London, thence to Estoril in Portugal by flying boat. After a few days, they crossed to Funchal (Madeira's capital city), and another Savoy Hotel, where they spent Christmas. On Christmas Eve, Margaret sent Muriel a postcard: 'Funchal really goes gay at Christmas... We change for dinner every night and dine and dance either here or at Reids hotel... You can get pure silk shirts made to measure for £3 each & nylon socks for 15/- a pair so it is indeed a paradise for men buying clothes.'

Back home, Mrs Thatcher enjoyed newly married life. She had improved social status, a husband she liked and respected, and a comfortable mansion-block flat which she set about redecorating with her customary domestic energy. In her memoirs, she waxes lyrical about this period, 'the reawakening of normal happy life after the trials of war-time and the petty indignities of post-war austerity'. But, for her, there was to be no slackening of pace, no exile from the great world to the kitchen. Following the death of King George VI (on 6 February 1952), she penned an article for the *Sunday Graphic* entitled 'Wake up, women'. 'If as many earnestly pray,' she wrote, 'the accession of Elizabeth II can help to remove the last shreds of prejudice against women aspiring to the highest places, then a new era for women will indeed be at hand.' She regretted that 'The term "career woman" has unfortunately come to imply in many minds a "hard" woman devoid of all feminine characteristics.' She traced this prejudice: 'Far too often, I regret to say it comes from our own sex.' In her view, 'The idea that the family suffers is ... quite mistaken.' She praised various current women role models, and asked: 'Why not a woman Chancellor – or Foreign Secretary?'

As she had made clear on leaving Dartford, Margaret Roberts had 'no intention of leaving politics' but her immediate preoccupation was the law. Her first exams took place in May 1952. She was called to the Bar on 9 February 1954, but in between came motherhood. Her pregnancy proved difficult and exhausting. Although her baby was expected on 29 September 1953, on 14 August she went into Queen Charlotte's Hospital in London after experiencing labour pains. The next day the doctors broke the news that she was carrying twins, a fact of which she had been unaware. They were born by caesarean section then and there, a girl, Carol Jane,* and a boy, Mark. Each weighed 4 pounds. At that time, hospitals did not permit fathers to be present during births, but Denis, watching the England v Australia Test match at the Oval, did not even know it was happening.

According to Carol, Denis's reaction to the first sight of his children was

---

* It took some time to agree on Carol's name. When she came out of hospital more than a month later because of her low weight and an infection, Margaret still wrote of her to Muriel as 'the little girl twin'.

to exclaim: 'My God, they look like rabbits. Put them back.'* Mrs Thatcher, herself, was not someone who considered motherhood her vocation in life. She was pleased to have twins, mainly because it meant that she need not get pregnant again. By her own account, she was almost frightened by the emotional impact of the birth, the miracle of life sharpened by the perils of prematurity – 'Oddly enough, the very depth of the relief and happiness at having brought Mark and Carol into the world made me uneasy' – and she realized that she must keep her career plans constantly in mind: 'I needed a career because, quite simply, that was the sort of person I was.' She decided to go ahead and sit her Bar finals on 1 December. Politics she placed on hold, but only temporarily. She told the Party Vice-Chairman she would 'not consider a candidacy for at least six months. The household needs considerable reorganisation and a reliable nurse must be found before I can feel free to pursue such other activities with the necessary fervour.'

An Austrian nurse, Gerda, was followed by Barbara, a nanny from Kent who stayed for five years. Barbara credited Denis for remembering to wave to the twins through the nursery window as he left each morning for work, whereas 'Mrs Thatcher, whose mind was already on the job, would forget.' But Denis was not an involved father. 'Mr Thatcher left parenting to Mrs Thatcher and me.' Just after the twins came home for the first time, Denis was briefly away, and there was a gap in domestic help. 'We have several outstanding bits of entertaining to do,' Margaret told Muriel, 'but as I shall be on my own all day and all night doing 3-hourly feeds throughout the 24 hours with 2 bairns that will have to wait.'†

Driven and career-oriented though she was, Mrs Thatcher remained a concerned and conscientious mother. Her letters to Muriel, now more sporadic, show a woman attentive, in a slightly uninquiring and practical way, to the needs of her children. At five months, she reported that Mark had a 'tummy bug' – 'I slept in the nursery as I should have been about all night and probably have woken Denis.' A year later, she congratulated Muriel on the birth of her daughter. The twins, she said, were 'in the pink' and had just had '2 little friends round': 'Having made all the cakes and scones the night before I left Nannie to get on with it. With three nannies I should only have cramped their style.'

---

* In the 1990s, when staying with friends where the Thatchers were fellow guests, the present author's wife, also a parent of twins, sought to engage Denis on the subject. What had been his first thought, she asked him, on the discovery that he had two babies? 'I just wished the little buggers had been drowned at birth' was his reply.
† The sixth-floor flat at Swan Court was quite unsuited to young children. When the twins were three, Denis solved this by renting the flat next door so that 'I could slam the door on all three of them.'

Although it was not in Mrs Thatcher's nature to subject her children or indeed the rest of her life to close emotional analysis, the correspondence discloses small judgements scarcely considered as they are made, yet still significant. 'Mark can ride a fairy cycle and is very anxious to have one,' she told Muriel in July 1958, but the price of £12 was high and 'we'd have to get two and that would be too much of an item this year'. In September 1960, by this time an MP, she noted that Nanny would be away for six weeks: 'It will be very difficult but I shall have to try to get more time off. I don't want to upset the children by having a new person in for a short time.' And when the twins first go to school, together, Mrs Thatcher notes: 'They seem to be enjoying school but doing a tremendous amount of painting there.' The 'but' in that sentence is characteristic.

Mrs Thatcher was, in truth, frightened of the boredom she associated with the life of a housewife. Interviewed shortly before being first elected to Parliament, she declared: 'I should vegetate if I were left at the kitchen sink all day. The twins are at school and in any case I have a full-time nanny ... I don't think the family suffers at all through my political ambitions.' In old age, however, she came to worry that the family had suffered far too much.* 'I have no right to complain,' Carol remembered. 'But I don't think our childhood was a very important part of her life, to be honest.'

With Margaret's marriage to Denis came a growing separation, though never an estrangement, from her sister Muriel and from her parents. She kept in reasonably close touch with Muriel, but it is clear – indeed, implicit in her decision not to marry Willie Cullen – that there was a social gulf between Margaret and her sister's family, a gulf which would put her father more on Muriel's side of the fence than on hers. This tension expressed itself over a name. When Muriel gave birth to her daughter in January 1955, the Cullens considered calling her Agnes after Willie's unmarried sister. To Margaret, the very Scottish 'Agnes' was anathema: 'You used to like "Penelope" and "Nicola" – have either of those come up for consideration? For heaven's sake let <u>one</u> of your children have an English name as England is the country of William's <u>choice</u> as distinct from that of his birth.' Luckily for Mrs Thatcher's feelings, Muriel and Willie settled on plain, English Jane.

But Mrs Thatcher was now moving into a world which was more that of Penelope or Nicola, a combination of professional Chelsea and

---

* Denis Thatcher was also, in later life, afflicted by a sense of guilt about the way the twins were brought up. He told the present author that he should have spent more time with them. Business frequently took him abroad for almost the whole of the summer. He delegated a good deal of the twins' upbringing to their nanny, Abbey. 'Teach the children some manners,' he instructed her.

semi-suburban, highly Conservative Kent. Her life in London, while certainly not grand or fashionable, had some pretensions to elegance. She and Denis enjoyed shows, opera and films. They bought good-quality furniture and clothes, while always very careful about price.* They gave cocktail parties and buffet suppers and, of course, attended Conservative balls ('Mrs Anthony Eden received us. Really she is a most colourless personality').† More Denis's world than the one she had been brought up in, she was very keen to be a part of it. One Saturday, Margaret watched Denis referee rugby at the military academy at Sandhurst: 'what impressed me most was the young chaps who go there. Saturday afternoon was naturally off-duty time but we didn't see so much as even one person slouching. They held themselves as if in military uniform and went about their business in a most impressive way.'

Pursuing their *haut-bourgeois* dream and the needs of the twins for more space, the Thatchers moved, before Christmas 1957, to Farnborough in Kent. Their new house, for which they paid £6,600, was called Dormers. After six years in Chelsea, it took a while to settle in but gave the twins their nearest approximation to a permanent home. Margaret herself literally put down roots: she 'became manic about gardening' and grew 'dahlias the size of dinner-plates'. It was a long way – on the whole a pleasantly long way – from life above the grocer's shop in Grantham.

By the time of the move, Mrs Thatcher was a practising barrister. Having passed her Bar finals on 1 December 1953, at the suggestion of John Senter QC, a leading light in Conservative legal circles, she obtained pupillage with Fred Lawton (later, as Sir Fred, an Appeal Court judge). Lawton was one of the most remarkable and best-liked lawyers of his generation, whose extensive common-law practice offered her experience in civil as well as criminal cases. The fee for pupillage was £50 for six months, plus five guineas for the clerk. 'As I am costing Denis that much,' Mrs Thatcher wrote to Muriel, 'I shall just have to go about in rags when my present clothes drop off me!'

Pupillage was hard to obtain for a woman because barristers' clerks feared they would earn them less money. Fred Lawton, however, soon came to consider Mrs Thatcher 'the best pupil I had ever had'. He felt 'she had a feeling for the law' and was 'fascinated by the human aspects

---

* She bought a summer coat from Peter Jones, for example, which, because it had been worn by a mannequin, was reduced from 12 guineas (£12 60 pence) to 79s 6d (£3 97.5 pence).
† This is a very typical Mrs Thatcher judgement of another woman. In fact, Clarissa Eden was well known for her beauty, intelligence and strong character.

of the kind of work I did'.* Lawton considered that she could have been a highly successful QC, 'but I don't think she would have been the first woman Law Lord, because she hadn't got that depth of mental capacity'. Her only shortcoming was that she never established a good relationship with Lawton's clerk, Stanley Hopkins, who came to Lawton and said: 'I wish you'd tell that pupil of yours that I'm not the chambers boy who carries books.'†

Mrs Thatcher perfected in her legal work the accuracy and meticulousness which she was to display in her political career. But her feeling about the law went deeper. She saw the law, even more than democracy, as the shibboleth that distinguished free from unfree societies. And in her mind, the rule of law had found better expression in Britain than almost anywhere else. Fred Lawton put it thus: 'we all grew up I'm afraid with the jingoistic attitude that British law is best. It was something with which you never argued.' According to English law, Lawton explained, 'a statute is to be construed by the words used in it and by nothing else . . . The Continental view is that statutes . . . are to be construed according to the purpose for which they were passed . . . Well, this was all foreign, strange to us in the 1950s.' It remained foreign to Mrs Thatcher for the whole of her life. She saw such wide-ranging law as a usurpation of the work of politicians, and its universal claims as contrary to national independence.

It is doubtful, however, whether Mrs Thatcher gave a great deal of thought to such doctrines at the time. After a year with Lawton she concluded that, much as she enjoyed the work, the lifestyle, which included frequent travel at short notice, was incompatible with her duties as the mother of young children. Influenced by John Senter, she shifted to tax law.

Tax meant doing pupillage in Chancery, and so she moved to the chambers of John, later Lord, Brightman. As usual, there was resistance to a woman. It would have made sense for her to use the room of Norman Daynes, an elderly QC who was very seldom present, but he had declared, 'Brightman, on no account is a woman ever going to sit in my room,' so she sat with Brightman in his own room. According to Lady Brightman, this arrangement gave rise to jokes: 'My husband's colleagues teased me about her looks.' As was to prove so important in her political career, Mrs Thatcher benefited from the rarity of women, particularly attractive

---

* Mrs Thatcher liked even the most trivial cases. 'I had to go to Cambridge Assizes last Friday,' she wrote to Muriel in May 1955, 'and thoroughly enjoyed it. It was a case about onion seeds!'
† While Hopkins had never been friendly to the idea of women pupils, according to Lawton, 'a rather randy Welshman' in the chambers was friendly to the idea for the wrong reasons. He made a pass at her: 'I gather she dealt with it very firmly.'

women, at the Bar. Without the slightest hint of impropriety, she made it clear that she sought and enjoyed the company of clever, older men. The Bar consisted of little else, and many of them responded enthusiastically.

As Mrs Thatcher well knew from the beginning, the Bar was a good entrée to politics, and many barristers were politically engaged. She joined the Inns of Court Conservative and Unionist Association, whose secretary, Pamela Thomas, got her on to its tax committee. Other Conservative barristers at that time included Patrick Jenkin, later one of her Cabinet ministers, and Geoffrey Howe, her eventual nemesis. According to Pamela Thomas, Mrs Thatcher was a 'tip-top lawyer', but her political ambitions were clear – she wanted to be Chancellor of the Exchequer. Thomas recalled her being much distressed by the collapse of the Suez adventure, when Britain, France and Israel attacked President Nasser's Egypt in 1956 after Nasser had seized the Suez Canal. In her memoirs, Mrs Thatcher identified Nasser's political (though not military) victory in Suez as the moment when 'the British political class . . . went from believing that Britain could do anything to an almost neurotic belief that Britain could do nothing'. It was lack of US support, permitting a run on the pound, which had forced Eden to withdraw. Britain, she concluded, should never again get on the wrong side of America in any great enterprise.

For Mrs Thatcher, politics never really went away. In June 1952, she visited her patron and admirer Beryl Cook. Reporting to John Hare at Conservative Central Office, Cook wrote: 'To quote her own words – "It's no use; I must face it: I don't like being left out of the political stream."' Denis, Mrs Thatcher had explained, was very supportive: 'now that she is married to a man who is comfortably off she will not have the financial worries she had while she was at Dartford'. 'Politics', said Miss Cook, 'is in her blood.' A week later, Hare himself met Mrs Thatcher at Central Office: 'she struck me as being a woman of immense personality and charm with a brain quite clearly above the average. I did my best to warn her of the horrors of life in the House of Commons especially in so far as this life affects the home. Nothing I said deterred her.'

Since there was never, truly, a point when Mrs Thatcher laid aside political ambition, there may be no need to explain the timing of her attempted return to the fray. But it did coincide with the abrupt end of her father's political career. Alfred Roberts had been made an alderman of Grantham in 1943. In 1952, emboldened by electoral success, the Labour-controlled council refused to renew his term, seeking its own majority on the aldermanic bench. This provoked outcry. Grantham aldermen had never before been removed for party political reasons, and Roberts, such a respected figure, was considered a particularly unsuitable victim.

According to Muriel Cullen, her father 'was upset because he really loved Grantham'. When Roberts was voted off, he said, 'It is now almost nine years since I took up these robes in honour, and now I trust in honour I lay them down.' As he spoke, he pulled off his robes and laid them on the table in front of him. 'No medals,' he said quietly. 'No honours, but an inward sense of satisfaction. May God bless Grantham forever.'

The incident had a profound effect on Roberts's younger daughter. As she spoke of it, in a 1985 television interview, tears came into her eyes, and she had to pause for a moment. 'I thought my father's example there was so wonderful,' she said later. 'So hurtful but so wonderful, and so dignified.'

While the arrival of the twins prevented Mrs Thatcher from going forward in politics quite as fast as she had hoped, it did nothing to quench 'the necessary fervour'. When the Conservative-held seat of Orpington became vacant in late 1954, it seemed too good a chance to miss. Orpington was close to Dartford, but much more Conservative, the heartland of the Tory suburban Kent to which marriage to Denis had introduced her. Although shortlisted, she failed to prevail. This brought her closer than ever, before or since, to departing the political scene. Writing to Hare on 3 January 1955, Mrs Thatcher declared that Orpington had been 'the only political temptation left for the next 10 years'. Now she wished to have her name withdrawn from the candidates' list. Hare wrote back, urging her to reconsider if a winnable seat came up, but she replied that she had 'quite made up my mind to pursue law to the exclusion of politics'. The ten years' self-denial, however, turned out to be thirteen months. On 28 February 1956, Mrs Thatcher wrote to Donald Kaberry, the new Vice-Chairman of the party responsible for candidates, once again using the word 'temptation' – the 'temptation to return to active politics' – to which she promptly succumbed. Over the following year, she tried for several seats and flogged around the speaking circuit. 'I spoke at a women's afternoon meeting in North Kensington on Tuesday,' she wrote to Muriel. 'It went very well indeed – but what is the use of it's [*sic*] going well in a bad constituency?' Her best chance seemed to be at Maidstone, where her benefactor Alfred Bossom was stepping down. In March 1958, she reached the shortlist of three, but again fell short. The report from the area agent explains why:

> Mrs Thatcher . . . was asked about her ability to cope as a Member, having in mind the fact that she had a husband and a small family, and I do not think

her reply did her a lot of good. She spoke of having an excellent nanny and that as a Member she would have the mornings free (quite ignoring the fact that Members have committees in the mornings). She also spoke of having the weekends free, and made no reference to spending time in Maidstone at the weekends.* She did say she would have to give up the Bar.

It was all very discouraging. On her merits, Mrs Thatcher seemed to do well every time, only to lose because of her sex. And then came Finchley.

On 3 July, she mentioned her latest prospect to Muriel: 'Once again I have been shortlisted for a "safe" constituency. This time it is Finchley, which has a Conservative majority of 12,000. Three of us are on the final list† and we have to go down on Monday evening 14th July for the final selection. I expect the usual prejudice against women will prevail and that I shall probably come the inevitable "close second".'

On the night, the 'usual prejudice' was certainly present. John Tiplady, a postman who later became chairman of the Finchley Association, went along with his wife, who said she would never vote for a woman. Some, particularly women, stuck by that view, but others, including Tiplady, were won over. As Mrs Thatcher rather flirtatiously wrote to Donald Kaberry afterwards, 'I wore the outfit you said I was to wear: the black coat dress with brown trim and small black hat'. Tiplady noted her 'striking appearance', which he contrasted favourably with that of her rival, Thomas Langton, a local man and holder of the Military Cross. One local businessman present whispered to Tiplady, 'We're looking at a future Prime Minister of England.' The absence of Mrs Thatcher's husband, still on business in Africa, made a notable contrast with the presence of the wives of the three men, but not one that necessarily harmed Margaret. There was something exciting about this good-looking, well-dressed thirty-two-year-old woman all alone and speaking with such force. In the first round, she came top, with Langton only one vote behind. In the play-off between the two of them, she won by forty-six votes to forty-three. That, at least, was the declared result. But Bertie Blatch, the constituency chairman responsible for counting the votes, told his son Haden that night: 'She didn't actually win. The man did, but I thought, "He's got a silver spoon in his mouth. He'll get another seat." So I "lost" two of his votes and gave them

---

* Mrs Thatcher consistently avoided making any commitment to having to live in any constituency which might select her. There was a limit to what could be imposed on Denis and the twins.
† In fact, it turned out to be a shortlist of four. One candidate, the war hero C. M. Woodhouse, had dropped out between rounds because he had been selected for Oxford, and so the executive committee, rather than allowing the contest to be between only two, inserted the next two candidates down. If anything, this made Mrs Thatcher's task easier, since two of the four were known to be slightly below par.

to her.' If so, Mrs Thatcher (unknowingly) won her way to Parliament through fraud. The absent, uncontactable Denis learnt of her victory by chance: 'I'd had a lot to drink and I staggered aboard the plane. I had to change in Kano and on the seat was the *Evening Standard* . . . there was this tiny little paragraph announcing that Margaret Thatcher had been adopted as Conservative candidate for Finchley. I've always said that it was bloody lucky that I was away because it was a close-run thing and if they'd taken one look at me they would have said, "We don't want this pair."' The *Standard* headline which Denis saw said 'Tories Choose Beauty'.

It was customary for the association's executive to endorse the chosen candidate unanimously, but in Mrs Thatcher's case it did not. Five members, unreconciled to selecting a woman, withheld their support even at her adoption meeting on 31 July. This did little to take the shine off the occasion. 'The Conservatives of Finchley and Friern Barnet', declared the *Finchley Press*, which, being owned by the Conservative chairman, Bertie Blatch, knew which side its bread was buttered, 'have armed themselves with a new weapon – a clever woman.' 'Clad in restrained black and gold and with a small black hat' (the same outfit as at the selection?), the new candidate had given a 'clear-cut appraisal of the Middle East situation, weighed up Russia's propagandist moves with the skill of a housewife measuring the ingredients in a familiar recipe, pinpointed Nasser as the fly in the mixing bowl'.

The Middle East bulked larger in Finchley than in most British electoral contests because the constituency had a substantial Jewish vote. At the time of Mrs Thatcher's selection, the Liberals had benefited from a row about attempts to block the admission of Jews to Finchley Golf Club, for which some Conservatives, among others, were blamed. Reflecting anti-Semitic feeling in the Conservative Association, the outgoing MP, Sir John Crowder, is supposed to have complained that Conservative Central Office was trying to impose a choice on the constituency between 'a bloody Jew and a bloody woman'. Not long after she had been adopted, Mrs Thatcher sought to mend the fences. As she informed Central Office on 17 September 1958, she was concerned that those of 'Jewish faith have allied themselves to Liberalism . . . we are naturally apprehensive and are now making great efforts to further the Conservative cause'.

Through her Finchley experience, Mrs Thatcher conceived a strong admiration for Jewish values. Jews, she later declared, are 'one of the most scholarly races'. She was attracted, too, by their very active sense of community – 'My, they were good citizens' – which expressed itself in 'not just talking, but doing and giving'. And she liked their entrepreneurial virtues, seeing Jews as 'natural traders' who managed 'positively to get on by their own efforts'. She approached them without the prejudices which existed in some sections of her party, and they responded warmly.

Anyone can see, in retrospect, that Mrs Thatcher was bound to hold Finchley for the Conservatives at the next election. This moderately prosperous, *petit-bourgeois*, owner-occupied, suburban constituency was a safe Tory seat, and ideally suited for its chosen candidate. Besides, since Harold Macmillan had replaced Eden as Prime Minister in January 1957 and set his course on expansionary policies, the political wind had been blowing in the party's favour. On 20 July 1957 Macmillan declared, famously: 'most of our people have never had it so good'. This was true. The average real pay for industrial workers had risen by 20 per cent since the Tory victory in 1951. Although this approach struck a chord in the country, some in the Conservative Party were deeply alarmed by growing public spending, which they feared would lead to inflation. In January 1958, Macmillan's Treasury team, led by the Chancellor, Peter Thorneycroft, and including Enoch Powell, resigned in protest. Macmillan dismissed the resignations as 'little local difficulties', and got away with it. As the 1959 election drew near, the headline rate of inflation remained below 3 per cent. Macmillan's political approach to public spending seemed vindicated.

One of Mrs Thatcher's best political gifts, born of a surprising lack of self-confidence and a female conscientiousness, was never to take anything for granted. If her party risked complacency, she did not. She campaigned ferociously hard, fulfilling 130 requests to speak since her adoption. She was happy enough to join in the boasts about ever-growing spending, but nevertheless put down a few markers of her own. At a public meeting in Friern Barnet on 3 April 1959, she noted that, despite the increase in material prosperity, there seemed to be little moral advance. 'If one desires above all to build a responsible society of responsible citizens,' she asked, 'how can Parliament bring it about?' To the small extent that it could, firm standards and the pursuit of excellence were the keys. At her election adoption meeting on 21 September, she emphasized the simple verity which was so often to stand her in such good stead: 'The whole of our future at home and abroad depends on our having a solvent society.' Although Macmillan paid only formal obeisance to this doctrine, there was nothing dangerously unorthodox in the views of the thirty-three-year-old parliamentary candidate. Instead, she stood out because she was already a bit of a star – through her sex, her looks, her dynamism and her air of being, true blue though she was, something new for the Tory Party, a persuasive meritocrat.

At the count on 8 October, rigid with nerves, Mrs Thatcher heard that she had increased the Conservative majority from 12,825 to 16,260, winning well over half of the votes cast. The result was:

Mrs Margaret Thatcher (Conservative)	29,697
Eric Deakins (Labour)	13,437
Ivan Spence (Liberal)	12,260
Conservative majority	16,260

The national result – a Conservative majority of 107 – was the party's best since the war. Margaret Thatcher reached Parliament at a peak in her party's fortunes from which it could only decline.

3
Member, minister, milksnatcher
'The Most Unpopular Woman in Britain'

The new Member of Parliament who walked up the steps of the House of Commons with her characteristically short, brisk stride gave every air of outward confidence. She was greeted by her secretary, Paddi Victor Smith. Mrs Thatcher was 'very pretty, well groomed', recalled Victor Smith, who was 'surprised right from the start at how together she was'.* Mrs Thatcher probably felt less poised than she looked. Despite her electoral success and the security provided by her marriage, she remained an outsider. Although loyal to her family, she found her lower-middle-class roots a little embarrassing: 'Would you believe it,' she wrote to Muriel shortly after the 1959 election, 'Uncle Harold [her father's brother] turned up on election day. Visited two committee rooms, got himself into the count and then, as he hadn't arranged any transport back, I had to take him on to a party with me before driving him back to town.'

Three days later, the girls' father wrote to Muriel. 'We, so far, have only received a short letter from Margaret,' he began, rather sadly, 'but she says she is completely inundated with correspondence.' Harold's decision to visit Margaret 'without previous indication to anyone ... has upset me very much'. Alfred continued: 'as kindly and reasonably as possible I have told him he mustn't obtrude'. He had also had cause to write to his sister, Frances Garland, whose husband Charlie had presented himself at the Thatchers' house without warning: 'Frances has written a nasty letter in reply, but I will put up with that if it saves Margaret and Denis future trouble. Why do they want to cash in on Margaret's success in this pushing way.'

Harold Roberts's unannounced presence on Margaret's great day was awkward, a scene reminiscent of Pip's reunion with his simple

---

* This impression of neatness and competence never went away. When, later, she visited Mrs Thatcher at Dormers, Paddi Victor Smith noted that 'all her clothes were beautifully hung in plastic bags' and that she seemed to possess early prototypes of the freezer bags that are common today.

brother-in-law Joe Gargery in Dickens's *Great Expectations*. Being a conscientious woman, Mrs Thatcher looked after Harold that night, but being also an upwardly mobile one, she devoutly wished he wasn't there.

In the Commons, while Mrs Thatcher's social origins do not seem to have been much held against her, her sex was more of an issue. One of only twelve women Conservative MPs, and considerably the most attractive, she found herself treated with a studied politesse which she liked, but which, she perfectly well understood, was intended to restrict the scope of her political career. When she entered the House, unwritten conventions indicated that any speech by a woman Member be described as 'charming', whether or not it had been. Margaret could undoubtedly deploy charm, but the word did no justice to her abilities or to her ambition. In her first appearance on BBC Radio's *Any Questions?*, in January 1960, she had to answer questions about the working week for wives ('it's not the hours you put in, it's what you put into the hours that counts') and to give advice on looking for a husband ('Look for a husband who is kind. I think it is quite a rare virtue in men.').*

The new Member for Finchley was not part of any gang or club, and never had any taste for trying to form one with members of her own sex. Like most MPs at that time, Mrs Thatcher had no office of her own in Parliament. Unlike most, she did not find her way to the Smoking Room or other drinking haunts, but worked in the 'Lady Members' Room'. Financially, everything was on a shoestring: Members had to buy their own postage stamps and pay their secretaries themselves. Paddi Victor Smith recalled Mrs Thatcher as 'a fairly exacting boss. She paid quite well and expected a good day's work.'† Sometimes she would take Paddi with her to the hairdresser and dictate to her while under the dryer.

Hard work, as always, was Mrs Thatcher's sovereign remedy for every difficulty. By chance, the opportunity for a serious tranche of it arose almost at once. In the ballot for Private Members' Bills at the beginning of the parliamentary session, she came second. These Bills allowed legislation to be introduced from the back benches and represented an opportunity for Members to make a name for themselves. Her maiden speech in the House,

---

* In the same month, a London paper asked her for tips on getting children to save: 'My six-year-old twins always managed to get the coins out of their money boxes or to break them open. So each now has a savings box which cannot possibly be opened by anybody but the banking authorities.'

† Mrs Thatcher paid Miss Victor Smith over the going rate to secure her exclusive services.

unlike most others, would now need to be substantive and legislative. From the beginning, she was serious.

Mrs Thatcher had some difficulty over her choice of subject, but eventually settled on the admission of the press to the meetings of local government. This issue was not chosen at random. It had become the subject of political controversy over the past year when several Labour councils had voted to exclude the press from some proceedings.* The Conservative manifesto for the 1959 election had promised action, a pledge Margaret now took up with zeal.

The 'first purpose' of the Bill, she said in her maiden speech, was to make sure that the public knew how their money was being spent; but, in reality, she was galvanized by a political motive, the dislike of trade union power and its municipal alliance with socialism. She may also have been thinking of the politics in her own backyard, where the Liberal Party posed the greatest threat. With the Tories in Finchley accused of deciding everything in 'secret' committee meetings, it did no harm for their new Member of Parliament to put herself on the side of openness. It also helped in her long campaign to recover Jewish support from the Liberals.†

If Mrs Thatcher expected plain sailing, however, she was quickly disabused. On 9 December, Henry Brooke, the Minister of Housing and Local Government, minuted the Cabinet Home Affairs Committee: 'Mrs Thatcher's Bill, coming at this moment, presents us with something of a problem.' Brooke wished to honour the party's manifesto pledge but considered her Bill 'wrong' to offer 'such wide-ranging rights to the press'. A legislative remedy might stir up unnecessary conflict between local and central government. The government preferred a code of conduct. The solution, the committee agreed, was 'to prepare and hand to Mrs Thatcher a Bill which the government could accept'. In other words, to co-opt her.

But the understanding, if such it was, soon ran into difficulties. A memo from an official, dated 7 January 1960, reported on an exhausting session with Mrs Thatcher and the parliamentary draftsman, John Fiennes:

> Mrs Thatcher wanted the Bill strengthened in ways which seemed to indicate that she was expecting a much more drastic Bill than we have had in mind. Some of her remarks suggested, moreover, that she would not put much conviction into opposing amendments which in her view would strengthen the

---

* In Liverpool, for example, because a local paper had produced a blackleg edition during a print strike, its journalists had been voted out of the council chamber.
† Much later, she was rewarded by the defection of one of the leading Jewish Liberal councillors to the Tory ranks.

Bill ... Mrs Thatcher ... is obsessed with the minority of the councils who might act irresponsibly, whereas we have had in mind the great majority of local authorities whose relations with the press are basically satisfactory ... [she] clearly holds a low opinion of local authorities, their members and officials.

Tension rose. Mrs Thatcher, noted Dame Evelyn Sharp, the ministry's Permanent Secretary, 'seems to be going back on the clear understanding which I thought we had reached with her'. In this tussle between civil servants who wanted the Bill to achieve very little, and Mrs Thatcher, who wanted it to do what it purported to do, one can see, in miniature, the character of a thousand future disagreements between her and officials.*

Margaret Thatcher rose for the first time in the House of Commons on 5 February 1960 and moved the second reading of her Bill. W. F. Deedes, the Member for Ashford, noticed that she had turned herself out particularly well for the occasion. She wore 'a patterned gown. The dominant note was chestnut.' He noted also how economically she used her notes. Her speech, essentially a defence of the public's right to know how their local representatives were spending public money, was learnt pretty well by heart and delivered with great self-confidence.

Because Private Members' Bills were, by convention, debated on a Friday, the House was often thinly attended as MPs returned to their constituencies. With her customary thoroughness, though, Mrs Thatcher had written individually to 250 of her backbench Conservative colleagues ('I have always believed in the impact of a personal, handwritten letter – even from someone you barely know') asking them to attend and vote. Many did. Her Bill was carried overwhelmingly, by 152 votes to 39. The Labour MP Charlie Pannell,† opposing the Bill, nevertheless praised Mrs Thatcher's 'rather beautiful maiden speech'.‡ For the government, Henry Brooke said that Mrs Thatcher's 'fluency' had achieved the unusual feat of making a parliamentary reputation on a Friday: 'no words of mine can be too high praise for the brilliance of the speech'. He stood at a distance from the Bill, however: he preferred a code of conduct to law. As so often in the key moments of her early political career, her husband was not there to see it: Denis was on a business trip to the Middle East.

---

* Mrs Thatcher's technique in the negotiations, Brooke noted shrewdly, 'is to say she must have much more than she really expects to get!'.
† Pannell had been the Labour Mayor of Dartford when Margaret Roberts had been a candidate there. He was now MP for Leeds West and her friendly parliamentary 'pair'.
‡ There is probably a sexist joke (or gallant compliment) hiding in the phrase, with the words 'rather beautiful' governing the word 'maiden' rather than the word 'speech'.

Her speech produced an immediate rash of press attention. 'Fame and Margaret Thatcher made friends,' said the *Sunday Dispatch*, manoeuvring her into betraying her ambition even as she disclaimed it: 'I couldn't even consider a Cabinet post until my twins are older.' Later in the month she was writing in the *Evening News*, however, under the headline 'I SAY A WIFE CAN DO TWO JOBS'. A few days later, she talked about her children to the *Daily Express*. Margaret's hopes for her son and daughter were not very different: she wanted both to have a good education and a worthwhile career. 'If money were short,' she went on, revealing her absolute assumption that her children would have a private education, 'and I had to choose between educating my son or my daughter, I would choose entirely on merit. (Except that my husband would probably insist that Mark went to his old school.)'* But she added that a boy can regulate the course of his life via his career more than a girl, because 'To her there is one great unknown factor – marriage.'

Back in Parliament, Mrs Thatcher's Bill wended a tortuous way through committee, its provisions weakened with government acquiescence. Becoming law at the end of October, it probably did not make a vast difference to the conduct of council business, but it founded Margaret Thatcher's parliamentary reputation. On *Any Questions?* that November, Mrs Thatcher showed some self-awareness when asked about what form her eccentricity might take if she had any: 'Extreme bad temper,' she replied. 'Sacking everyone through inefficiency and doing everything myself. And it would probably be done a great deal better and a great deal quicker, but I should be miserable as a result.'

In April 1961, Mrs Thatcher returned to the headlines as one of only three women MPs to vote in favour of birching. In the debates on the Criminal Justice Bill that February she had argued that 'the true purpose of punishment' should be 'the protection of the community', but this had been eroded by 'our desire for the humanitarian reform of offenders'. 'I do not agree', she said, 'that crime is a symptom of mental disease.' In her view, some criminals had become 'so hardened, vicious and amoral that a much more curative element is needed'. She did not like corporal punishment, but it was 'the only alternative readily available to beat the crime wave in the coming years'.

Mrs Thatcher's stance had considerable appeal to the Conservative rank and file, but of this she was wary. 'I do not in any way seek either publicity or promotion by way of rebellion,' she declared, 'but I do not think that can stop one from holding sincere views in this matter.' This was the

---

* In the event, this did not happen. Denis had been to Mill Hill; Mark went to Harrow.

only occasion in her entire Commons career when Margaret Thatcher voted against the line of her own party. It is quite possible, since the whips sought always to balance opinion, that her promotion to ministerial rank was hastened by this signal that she stood slightly on the right of the party and was prepared to say so.

From the summer of 1959, the health of Margaret's mother began to fail. 'Time is getting on with us now,' Alfred wrote to Muriel a year later. In September he told her about her mother's difficult nights: 'Mummy is having another rest in bed today,' but the doctor 'says she's getting better and nothing to worry about'. By the time of his next surviving letter, written on 16 December 1960, Beatrice had died.

There is no mention of her mother's death or illness in any of Mrs Thatcher's correspondence (though what survives is certainly incomplete). There is also no record of her seeing her mother after August 1960. The only sign of strain, though there could easily have been other causes, was that she fainted in the Commons on 24 November. Throughout her career, she was inclined to faint because of low blood pressure. The *Yorkshire Post*, the only paper to have reported the incident, attributed it to overwork.

Beatrice Roberts died in Grantham on 7 December. The family sent out a printed card thanking people for their condolences, in the names of Alfred, Muriel and Margaret. The day before, the *Liverpool Daily Post* published a chirpy piece by Margaret about family and political work. The woman in politics, she wrote, 'must have a complete fascination for the subject . . . charm is not enough!' and she recounted how her children always came to Westminster at half term: 'their greatest joy is to climb Big Ben'. The article reads strangely in the (unmentioned) context of her mother's final illness.

Margaret and Denis invited the widowed Alfred Roberts to spend his first Christmas alone with them. From Dormers, he complained to Muriel that he still felt lonely: 'every one is busy on their different jobs and engagements'. Margaret's version, written to Muriel after Christmas, betrayed growing impatience: 'Re Pop* – he is <u>determined</u> to stay with us both as long as possible. He told Abi† that he dreads the thought of going home . . . He is eating the most enormous meals and doing absolutely nothing.' With the return of Parliament, Margaret decided to act: 'I shall <u>have</u> to shunt Pop off on Saturday 14th Jan,' she wrote to Muriel '. . . Will this be all right with you?'

After he returned from Essex to Grantham, the widowed Alfred Roberts

---

* Margaret's familiar address of her father varied. In later life she would always refer to him as 'Father', but when he was alive he was very occasionally 'Pop', quite often 'Father', but mostly 'Daddy'. He was never 'Dad'.

† This refers to Abbey, by this time the twins' nanny.

wrote a series of bleak letters to his elder daughter. Not for the first time, he felt sorry for himself, and a little neglected by his younger daughter. 'Have had a short letter from Margaret,' he wrote on 1 March, 'but no enquiries as to how I am getting on ... She seems frantically busy of course.'

It would be wrong to say that Mrs Thatcher was undutiful in her behaviour to her father. She had him to stay on other occasions and in June she, Denis and Mark took him to the Test match. She also kept up a correspondence. In September 1961, for example, she reports that they have been burgled at Dormers ('I was disturbed [by the sound of their entry] but told myself not to be so silly and that I was imagining things'), losing their jars of sixpences, the twins' birthday money and jodhpur boots. The following midsummer, Margaret proudly boasts that she has been with Denis to a Buckingham Palace cocktail party. 'The Queen', she writes with a touch of unconscious self-application, 'has a much stronger personality than most people realise and she is certainly not overshadowed by the Duke of Edinburgh.' But what the whole correspondence – father to elder daughter, Margaret to Muriel, younger daughter to father – suggests is a woman so busy and so keen to get on that family problems do not engage her imagination. From November 1965, such problems eased after Alfred Roberts married Cissie Hubbard, the widow of a local farmer, and his loneliness ceased to be a problem for his daughters.

On 9 October 1961 the Prime Minister, Harold Macmillan, reshuffled his government. 'Mrs Thatcher, a clever young woman MP, and Monty Woodhouse are the newcomers,' he wrote in his diary.* She was not only the first of the new intake to be promoted, but also the youngest woman ever to have been made a minister, and the first with a young family on appointment. Her job was Parliamentary Under-Secretary at the Ministry of Pensions and National Insurance (MPNI). Her salary was £3,250 a year. As had become usual in these important junctures of her life, Denis was away – in Africa – and found out only after the news became public.

When Mrs Thatcher saw the Prime Minister, she wore, by her own account, 'my best outfit, this time, sapphire blue'. The party took full propaganda advantage by putting her on the platform at the annual conference in Brighton on the potentially unlucky Friday 13 October, her thirty-sixth birthday. She emerged, she recalled, 'from a royal blue car

---

* Macmillan had been less impressed with Mrs Thatcher when she was first elected: 'The trouble is that none of the women MPs have a real brain,' he wrote in his diary in late October 1959. 'I can think of none (at present) who could be a Minister.'

and wearing a royal blue dress and hat'. None of this sartorial excitement meant that the party leadership had grand plans for Mrs Thatcher. Her very junior post was one of the few which were, in effect, reserved for women, partly because much of the work concerned pensions for widows. As Mrs Thatcher recalled, women MPs at that time always ended up with 'the welfare thing, either a welfare or education or social services job'. The MPNI post did not interest the men who aspired to run the Conservative Party. It was an unpolitical, detailed job concerned with the nuts and bolts of the welfare state. Few people thought it mattered much. Despite her preference for a man's job, especially an economic one, Mrs Thatcher gradually learnt that it did. It taught her how welfare worked, and did not work, and why government spent so much money.

Her new minister, John Boyd-Carpenter, had assumed that her appointment was, as he put it, 'just one of Macmillan's gimmicks', but 'I soon found how wrong I had been to harbour such doubts. With her quick trained barrister's brain, she mastered quickly the intricacies of National Insurance. And despite the fact that ... she always looked as if she had spent the morning with the coiffeur and the afternoon with the couturier, she worked long and productive hours in the ministry.' On her arrival she also met the Permanent Secretary, Sir Eric Bowyer, a famously stern Glaswegian. 'She's very able,' Bowyer told Boyd-Carpenter. 'She will go a long way.' The minister nodded grim agreement: 'She's trouble. What can we do to keep her busy?' The answer was a study of the role of women in the benefits and National Insurance system. Her paper has not survived, but, according to Michael Partridge, Bowyer's private secretary, it was an impressive piece of work which foreshadowed the equalizing of the employment, pension and taxation rights of women which Mrs Thatcher was to put into practice in the 1980s. It seems strange in the twenty-first century that such a study was considered a dead end.

Mrs Thatcher's day-to-day duties, however, concerned detail, not policy. She was called upon regularly to defend her department in the Commons. Two Labour reactions to the new young minister were noticeable. The first was what would now be considered a sexist appreciation of her charms. Willie Hamilton, for example, later famous as an anti-monarchist, said during a Commons debate, 'We appreciate the honourable Lady's statistics, but we do not like her figures – in the plural.' She seems to have been happy to play up to this banter. In another debate Mrs Thatcher declared, perhaps by accident, 'I have got a really red-hot figure.' When several Members shouted, 'Hear, hear,' she came back: 'I am very glad that I am not wearing a red dress today. To continue, I have a bang up-to-the-minute figure.' The other reaction was a respect for her debating abilities which shaded into exasperation at her lawyerly tendency to argue a case cleverly but without apparent human feeling. Debating a Labour motion complaining that benefits had not kept up with inflation, the Labour MP John Mendelson accused Mrs Thatcher of 'making a long speech on the tragic position of many of our old people without making any reference whatsoever to her real experience of how they live'. The notion of Margaret Thatcher's heartlessness was born.

In reply to such attacks, Mrs Thatcher was generally polite, but never conceded any ground, sometimes fighting back fiercely. 'The honourable Member will forgive me if occasionally I say "Nonsense" to him,' she told a frequent adversary, Douglas Houghton. '. . . Nevertheless, I meant it.' Boyd-Carpenter recalled how she not only stood up to Richard Crossman on the floor of the House of Commons but, for all his formidable intellectual qualities, scored off him again and again by the quick and adroit use of facts and figures. As Crossman noted in his diary: 'She is tough, able and competent.'

Mrs Thatcher later wrote that, on assuming her duties at MPNI, her 'first step was to re-read the original Beveridge Report'. This report, produced by the economist William Beveridge for Churchill's wartime coalition in November 1942, had become a landmark reform of the post-war era.* Mrs Thatcher accepted its essential recommendation: establishing a scheme of National Insurance that provided, in return for contributions, benefits up to subsistence level paid out regardless of means. Beveridge had argued that his plan could not work without the avoidance of mass unemployment (hence the drive for the 1944 White Paper), and without reasonable 'free' health care (whence sprung the National Health Service). Here lay what Mrs Thatcher regarded as a sensible, though in some respects flawed, blueprint for the welfare state. In fact, more strenuously than most, she sought to apply the spirit of the report – that need be answered, but idleness discouraged and independence not crushed. 'The Beveridge Report never meant to oust the voluntary principle,' she said in later years. This was true. She was and remained in favour of a basic state pension, and she agreed with Beveridge's idea that National Insurance should be exactly

---

* The two comparable reforms of this era were R. A. Butler's Education Act of 1944, which developed the split system of grammar school and secondary modern, and the 1944 White Paper on Employment Policy, heavily influenced by Keynes, which for the first time made it the government's responsibility to manage the economy in order to maintain 'a high and stable level of employment' (soon interpreted as full employment). During her career, Margaret Thatcher was to wrestle unhappily with the first and break almost completely – though she carried it everywhere with her in her handbag – with the second.

that, rather than tax by another name. Her attitude to questions of welfare was never one of pure free-marketry or devil-take-the-hindmost. It was more old-fashioned, more influenced by the war, surprisingly confident that government was fit for the task. She wanted the state to help the unfortunate, and always believed that there was no full private substitute for this, but she always feared two things – that the 'shirkers' would benefit at the expense of the workers, and that the cost, if not carefully controlled, would produce national ruin.*

Mrs Thatcher spent three years at MPNI, ending only with the general election of October 1964. She enjoyed the work, discovering her appetite for detail, and finding scope for her combative qualities. Unlike Tory grandees, she received an education in the engine room of government rather than the officers' mess, which would serve her well. She admired the senior officials with whom she worked, and they admired her too, though, as Clive Bossom, her parliamentary private secretary (PPS)† in 1961, put it, 'they did not love her'. One night, Bossom witnessed her going through a pile of letters presented for her signature. As she read them, she ripped each one at the top of the page. 'I'm not sending these off,' she said, 'they're double Dutch.' Bossom also heard the official's response, out of Mrs Thatcher's hearing: 'Bloody woman. Her job is to sign them, not read them.'

The government machine in which Margaret Thatcher was a minor cog nearly derailed. As early as 1960, inflation and the growth of government spending stoked the demand for higher wages, leading to the 'pay pause' for public employees, the first shadow of an incomes policy. Economic growth slowed. In 1963, France vetoed Britain's bid to join the European Economic Community (or 'the Common Market') and the government was shaken by the Profumo affair.‡ As his government started to totter, Macmillan himself fell ill. On 10 October he resigned in dramatic fashion, just as his party's annual conference met in Blackpool.

In this sequence of events, Margaret Thatcher played virtually no part.

---

* Although conservative in moral questions, Mrs Thatcher maintained throughout her career a dislike of laying down the law about marital and sexual behaviour and using the tax and benefit system punitively in this context. This was apparent during her time at MPNI. Opening a home for unmarried mothers and babies in her constituency, she declared that 'It is our job to help and not to sit in judgment.'

† The parliamentary private secretary is an MP who is bag-carrier for a minister. His is not a ministerial job, and is unpaid, but is often the first rung on the ministerial ladder. Bossom was the son of Margaret's patron, Alfred.

‡ This scandal forced the resignation of the Minister of War, John Profumo, after he lied to the House about his relationship with Christine Keeler, a model and showgirl alleged to have been also involved with the Soviet naval attaché.

Her public pronouncements were loyal, but her distinct set of views was beginning to emerge, not wholly at one with the top of the government. Before she became a minister, Mrs Thatcher had called for the separate taxation of working women, noting that the current means of controlling public expenditure were inadequate. She also favoured financial stringency: 'You would think you were not bringing up your child properly if you said "yes" to everything they asked for. What sort of government would that be?' Concerning trade unions, she rejected the extreme caution of most ministerial pronouncements: 'We are approaching a time when trade union laws ought to be revised.' She also defended, against considerable protest from Jewish constituents, the right of Sir Oswald Mosley, the fascist orator, to hold a rally in Trafalgar Square. 'If Mosley's meetings are banned,' she told Finchley Tories, 'it means any meeting which the Communists do not like could be banned.'

Her greater concern, however, seemed to be a sense that Macmillan's leadership was beginning to falter, and perhaps a mild dislike of his rather patronizing manner towards her. In July 1963, hosting Finchley Conservative women for tea on the terrace of the House of Commons, she dropped strong hints about her admiration for R. A. Butler, praising his 'terrific capacity for work'. In the same month, Macmillan's PPS, Knox Cunningham, included Mrs Thatcher on a list of four junior ministers who were 'not in full support'. When the leadership crisis broke in October 1963, she initially favoured Butler over Quintin Hailsham as Macmillan's successor.

Under the prevailing system, Conservative leaders were not elected, but 'emerged' from an informal process of consultation. At the chaotic Blackpool party conference it was Lord Home, the Foreign Secretary, who began to emerge. When Mrs Thatcher saw the party whips after the conference and her thirty-eighth birthday, she told them that she preferred RAB, but 'I was then asked my view of Alec [Lord Home]. "Is it constitutionally possible?" I asked.* Assured that it was, I did not hesitate. I replied: "Then I am strongly in favour of Alec."' Although Mrs Thatcher's view would have made no difference, Macmillan did what she wanted and advised the Queen to send for Home.

Mrs Thatcher had then, and retained, a very high regard for the man who, on ceasing to be the 14th Earl of Home, became known as Sir Alec Douglas-Home. She always referred to him as 'Alec' and respected his judgement, his thoughtfulness and his personal goodness. His problem,

---

* Home was then a Member of the House of Lords, from which it was no longer considered possible to lead the party. In fact, this was not an insuperable objection since the law had just been changed to permit heirs to seats in the Lords to disclaim them.

as she put it later, was that he was not someone 'the populace could take to. Television isn't kind to some people.' She was disappointed not to be promoted by the new Prime Minister, but, as she wrote to her father in November 1963, 'I feel certain we shall be happy under the new administration. Home is a much more approachable person than Harold Mac ever was.' Home was someone whose birth might cause him to look down on her, and yet didn't. He was her ideal of a gentleman.*

Douglas-Home's premiership lasted for less than a year: its chief purpose was to enable Conservative recovery in time for the general election. In this, Mrs Thatcher played an energetic, though not important, part. She loyally supported the government's record, including measures, such as the establishment of the National Economic Development Council and selective government help to industry, which she was later to decry. When the government, led on the subject by Ted Heath, set out to abolish most of the remaining price controls known as Resale Price Maintenance, Mrs Thatcher supported it, not with the arguments of free-market theory but with reference to her father's attitudes: 'When small shopkeepers write and say: "I'm afraid it will put us out of business," I can only say that my father would have said the same thing 10 years ago. But Resale Price Maintenance has virtually gone from the grocery trade, and opportunities for small shops have increased.'† The grocer's daughter believed in letting business get the rewards of hard work, and was always opposed to heavy state control, but her wartime experience inclined her to think that the state could play a useful role in setting some economic priorities. When she later came to overturn the post-war economic consensus, she did so because she believed it had failed, not because she had never believed in it.

With the general election called for 15 October 1964, the Conservative candidate in Finchley fought a vigorous election, conventional enough in its treatment of the issues. She began the campaign on economic prosperity and ended it by attacking nationalization and Labour's defence policies. One close observer, Bernard Donoughue, recorded that Mrs Thatcher was 'formidable', with a high recognition factor and the ability to answer questions with 'a barrage of official statistics'. Her face was 'very well made', he recalled over forty years later, 'almost Japanese' in its perfection of form: 'No one would have thought "I'm not sure if I can trust her."' He particularly remembered one public meeting on a wet night. Mrs Thatcher

---

* Home was tolerant of her faults. After she became leader in 1975 he would say, 'Undeniably, she is a bossy woman. It's sometimes necessary to stand up for yourself.'
† Privately, she was highly critical of this campaign. 'Resale Price Maintenance lost us the election,' she said thirty years later. 'It was right, but you don't do it in the last year. Every single little grocer was right against it.'

'came in like one of the Valkyrie, rolled her raincoat up and tossed it over her shoulder to a man without looking at him'. It was Donoughue's first sight of Denis.

Mrs Thatcher retained her seat. The result was:

Mrs Margaret Thatcher (Conservative)	24,591
John Pardoe (Liberal)	15,789
Albert Tomlinson (Labour)	12,408
Conservative majority	8,802

Her majority was nearly halved, and the Liberals did better than in most of the country, Labour worse. But it was no disaster.* Nationally, the Tories did better than expected. They lost office, but Harold Wilson formed the first Labour government for thirteen years with an overall majority of only four. Mrs Thatcher began her first experience of Opposition.

Mrs Thatcher found the loss of a job and of power very difficult. 'I hated opposition,' she recalled. 'I was not a natural attacker.' This remark reveals a startling lack of self-knowledge, since attacking was one of her best things. But her dislike of Opposition was genuine enough. Her own standing in the Conservative Party was secure, but it was scarcely restorative to her spirits to be made the Shadow spokesman for the ministry – pensions – which she had previously helped to run. In her analysis of the Tory defeat, which she developed gradually through the 1960s, she would find the seed of the views which came to full flower ten years later.

Her immediate anxieties were more personal than political. Approaching his fiftieth birthday, Denis had the nearest thing that a no-nonsense, unself-pitying man can get to a midlife crisis: 'I was working like nobody's worked before,' he recalled, '. . . I was probably drinking a bit too much anyway.' He was worried about his company, Atlas, particularly with his family's money tied up in company shares. 'It seemed to me that the whole depended on the life of one man.' The doctor told him that he must rest completely. In the autumn of 1964, Denis took a boat to South Africa. He stayed there for more than two months before returning, much restored. In 1965 he sold his company to Castrol, who immediately employed him. Thus he obtained a capital sum, and a good job.†

In later years, Denis would always deny that this crisis had anything to do with Margaret's political career but, according to Carol Thatcher,

---

* Donoughue noted that a survey of Jews shortly before the election had suggested proportions of six Labour to three Conservative to one Liberal, but that Mrs Thatcher's campaign altered the proportions in her party's favour to 2:2:1.
† In due course a further takeover gave Denis a new and even better job, at Burmah Oil.

friends believed that Margaret's absorption in it had left him feeling isolated. She believed that, as well as being 'genuinely knackered', 'he didn't like every aspect of being married to a politician'. He may even have contemplated divorce. In Carol's judgement, Denis had not yet achieved a satisfactory role in relation to his wife's career: 'He came into his own later on.'

Denis recalled Margaret as 'very worried' around this time. 'She didn't show it, but I think she said it to one or two of her closer friends.' The episode goes unmentioned in her memoirs, but she herself later recalled: 'Eventually, everything came out all right, but for a time your world is upside down. Denis worried because if things matter to you, you don't take them lightly. It was a very worrying time . . . I am very glad to have come through it.' Mrs Thatcher would not be drawn further, but it seems reasonable to surmise that, when Denis left for South Africa, she had no certainty that he would ever return to her. If this had been the end of her marriage, her world would, indeed, have been 'upside down'. She would have been alone, without her husband's support and affection, with two children, not enough money, and a career which, given the attitudes of the time, would certainly have suffered. When she said, 'I am very glad to have come through it,' she was implying that she might not have done so. It was the worst personal crisis of her married life. When Denis returned, the strain caught up with her and, uncharacteristically, she fell seriously ill, going down with pneumonia. She was unable to attend Winston Churchill's lying-in-state in January 1965 and had to watch his funeral on television at home.

Denis's change of job, and the greater financial security it brought, allowed the Thatchers to move house. They sold Dormers and bought a flat, 34 Westminster Gardens, Marsham Street, one of the functional London mansion blocks favoured by MPs, at the beginning of 1966. This ended Margaret's wearisome commute from Farnborough. To avoid losing touch with Kent, they also acquired The Mount, a large, comfortable, rather ugly 'stockbroker Tudor' house, handsomely situated above the village of Lamberhurst. Denis later remembered their arrival, shortly before Christmas 1966: 'Woke up. Lovely morning. Sun shining. I said: "Come on, love. Let's go to church." Do you know, the vicar was anti-South Africa and anti-Rhodesia! Came out. Said "Thanks very much, padre." Never went back!' Despite this ecclesiastical disappointment, Denis found other pleasures in Lamberhurst. With a golf course visible from the house, he began to play the game seriously for the first time.

Margaret, meanwhile, pursued her strong interest in buying antiques. In the 1950s she had lost a tiepin with two sapphires mounted upon it, a present from Denis, and since then had preferred spending money (though not much)* on furniture and, above all, porcelain. Her strong homemaking instinct had greater rein than before, and she felt relief that the financial and marital worries of 1964 were in the past. Following the Labour landslide of 1966, it was Denis's turn to comfort her, rather than the other way round. He bought her an eternity ring, she recalled, 'because I was down in the dumps', which she wore for the rest of her life.

In July 1965, Alec Douglas-Home agreed, under some pressure, to step down as party leader. This greatly surprised and upset Mrs Thatcher, who had known nothing of the plotting. She was grateful to Home for his kindness, and perhaps intuited that she would experience less of this quality from a successor from her own generation.

For the first time ever, the Leader of the Conservative Party would be chosen via a ballot of its MPs. The candidates were Reginald Maudling, Edward Heath and Enoch Powell, none from the patrician background of the Macmillan/Home era. Although Powell was to prove by far the greatest influence on Mrs Thatcher, he was too much of a maverick to be a serious contender. That left Maudling and Heath, both of whom Mrs Thatcher knew. Initially she leaned towards Maudling but, although charming, he was not really her type, being fat, lazy and, as Chancellor, a natural overspender. Keith Joseph, already the senior Conservative to whom she was closest, soon brought her over to Heath. He told her: 'Ted has a passion to get Britain right,' a phrase which she was dutifully to use about him in public for years afterwards. She instinctively disliked Heath's gauche manners, especially with women, but she respected his political seriousness and liked his father, a down-to-earth character from a lower-middle-class small-business background quite like her own.† After a campaign of less than a week, Heath won by 150 votes to Maudling's 133; Powell received 15 votes.

The new leader's first assignment for the MP from Finchley was Shadow spokesman on housing and land. In the six years of Opposition, Mrs Thatcher held six Shadow posts. The first three were as a junior spokesman – for pensions, then housing and land, then Treasury affairs – the second three in the Shadow Cabinet – dealing with fuel and power,

---

* To the end of her days, she remembered her extravagance in paying £66 in the mid-1950s for a lacquered cabinet with mirrors. Long after her memory for the details of political events had faded, she remained minutely accurate about what she had collected, where she had bought it and what she had spent on it.
† She later felt that Ted Heath had abandoned his father's common sense in favour of a more pompous, clubby Tory milieu.

transport and finally education. From these differing experiences some common characteristics emerge. The first is that she could absorb almost any amount of detail and argue it through late-night sittings. At a time when a politician's reputation depended on performance in Parliament, Mrs Thatcher repeatedly impressed with her combativeness and her industry. She was not yet a star, but she was a worker and a fighter in a party slightly short of both. She was given the opportunity to stretch beyond the subjects traditionally handed to women MPs, and she took it eagerly. When, for example, she savaged the government's Selective Employment Tax in parliamentary debate on 5 May 1966, an admittedly partial Iain Macleod declared that this was the only 'triumph' he could ever remember a woman scoring in the House of Commons.

The second noticeable characteristic is that Mrs Thatcher took advantage of every brief to pursue a common political theme. She could see the onrush of socialism and set out to resist it without apology. Her own 'Thatcherite' ideology had not fully developed, but her temperamental aversion to retreat and compromise came to the fore. Untiringly, she preached a gospel of economic freedom and opposition to the creeping power of the state. In 1965, one finds her deploying what was to become a favourite phrase: 'Every Labour government we have had has foundered on money and they have always succeeded in running out of other people's money.' Like most front-rank politicians, Mrs Thatcher wasted little emotional energy on ill feeling towards her political opponents. She liked Harold Wilson, for example, describing him as 'very wily but very kind'. But her hatred for socialist doctrines was genuine, and it provided the necessary energy to develop and advance her strong views.

In April 1966, after only six months, Heath moved Mrs Thatcher into the area she had always most desired, economic affairs. As Deputy Treasury Shadow her boss was Iain Macleod, who, to her pleasure, 'chose me to do the hard work'. Two weeks into the job, she found herself debating Labour's proposed Selective Employment Tax in Parliament, up against Jack Diamond, the Chief Secretary to the Treasury. This payroll tax sought to take money from some industries, mainly services, and redistribute it to others, mainly manufacturers. Its process was astonishingly complicated, collecting, as Mrs Thatcher later worked out, £1,130 million and then handing back £890 million of it within industry. 'I really think that the right hon. Gentleman needs a woman at the Treasury,' she declared in her first debate. 'This is just sheer stupidity. If my chief had come to me and put up a cockeyed scheme like that, I should have asked him if he was feeling all right.' Mrs Thatcher attacked the idea of permanent subsidies that lay behind the Bill: 'The Chancellor will be very popular with inefficient industries, but I do not wish to be popular with inefficient industries. I would rather be popular with the efficient ... The inefficient ... ought to go out of business.' Such words were notably bold, strongly against the grain of the times.

Throughout the summer of 1966, Mrs Thatcher attacked. She used the voice of the plain-speaking housewife: 'So once more the married woman who goes to the butcher, grocer and dry cleaner and then, when she is finished and wishes for a little pleasure, to the hairdressers, will find that prices are going up.' Her agenda was a feminist one. She attacked discrimination against married women in taxation, assaulted the system by which estate duty was charged to widows, and supported an amendment to give tax relief on maintenance payments to divorced or deserted mothers. Later in the year, she ridiculed the government's growing attempt to regulate prices and incomes, using women's clothing as an example. 'One cannot control the price of a garment which has a mini-skirt in July, but a skirt four inches below the knee in January. I doubt very much that the President of the Board of Trade [Douglas Jay] would even notice the difference.'* Such aggressive, if almost flirtatious, rhetoric was deployed to drive forward an essentially radical approach to taxation. Not only was Mrs Thatcher saying that tax was too high,† she was also questioning the wisdom of those who tried to run the British economy. More radical still, she was saying that women, through work, motherhood and marriage, understood more about the effects of taxation and inflation than the men who inflicted both. By implication, she was challenging the established order in both parties.

It was part of her skill in charming her party that her male colleagues mostly enjoyed her approach. At the highest levels, however, suspicions were aroused that the rise of Margaret Thatcher might threaten male peace and tranquillity. According to Jim Prior, Heath resisted promoting her to the 'statutory woman' slot in the Shadow Cabinet after Labour's landslide in the 1966 general election. 'Willie agrees she's much the most able,' Heath said of William Whitelaw, the Chief Whip, 'but he says that once she's there we'll never be able to get rid of her.'

Although Mrs Thatcher, kept out of the Shadow Cabinet for the time being, naturally chafed at the 'statutory woman' role, she also understood how to take advantage of it. BBC Radio's *Any Questions?*, then the most influential current affairs discussion programme, was always in search of

---

* She was wrong there. Jay was known to have a marked interest in short skirts.
† Income tax had now reached a top rate of 19 shillings and 3 pence, there being 20 shillings in the pound.

a woman to enliven the panel, and could rely on her to do so. Through media appearances she established a marked public persona, never missing an opportunity to speak up for her sex, often to the disparagement of the male. Asked whether judging a woman's intelligence by her legs could be applied to a man (a typical question of the programme in that period), she replied: 'I really only ever look at a man's head to see whether he's intelligent, and so often the answer is that he's not, that one doesn't need to look any farther.' She knew exactly how far to go in referring questions about female advancement to herself. To a question about equal pay, she focused on equal opportunity: 'There is an awful tendency in Britain to think of women as making excellent Number Twos, but not to give them the top job.' Another panellist cut in to suggest the possibility of a woman prime minister. Mrs Thatcher: 'Well, I wasn't quite thinking at that level.'

When it came to the hotly argued moral and social questions of the 1960s, Mrs Thatcher found her sex an advantage, giving her stronger, more practical ground in any dispute. She always liked to refer to the individual example or experience which she found persuasive. Her support for the legalization of abortion, for example, came from the suffering she had observed of a severely handicapped child of Bertie Blatch, her constituency chairman in Finchley. The boy, she remembered, had often asked his parents 'Why me?', and this led her to believe that abortion of those with severe genetic defects was the kindest course. Her backing of the liberalization of the laws against homosexual acts derived from cases she had seen as a barrister, which she considered a humiliating intrusion into privacy. On the other hand, her experience as a mother made her instinctively hostile to the permissive society presided over by Wilson's government. She supported Mary Whitehouse's condemnation of pornography and said that the 'average woman' feared sexual licence and drugs for her children.

Only once in this period, at the Conservative Party conference in Brighton on 10 October 1969, did Mrs Thatcher agree to take a prominent party platform to put forward her views on women's questions.* Her opening was typical: 'I think it was Socrates who said long, long ago that when woman is made equal to man she becomes his superior, and I would not dissent from anyone as wise as Socrates.'

Coming out of the 1964 general election with a parliamentary majority of just four, which itself soon dwindled, Harold Wilson found governing almost impossible. After he called a snap election for 31 March 1966, the

---

* The organizers wanted a leading woman to promote the new policy document *A Fair Share for the Fair Sex*, an embarrassing title about which she publicly complained.

electorate rewarded him with a majority of ninety-eight. Mrs Thatcher's own election efforts in Finchley had gone well. She had campaigned against Labour's desire to 'increase the power of the State at the expense of the subject' and called for a review of trade union law. She tapped into the economic anxieties of her constituents: 'Inflation means cheating the thrifty out of part of their savings.' Concerning the question of British entry into the European Economic Community, she suggested 'Europe' could become a world power, an idea she was later to deride. But even now a hint of suspicion underlay her Europeanism: 'I don't like the idea of a Europe without us there, directing and guiding its powers.'

The Liberal vote, nationally and in Finchley, fell sharply, so that Mrs Thatcher, though winning fewer votes than last time, increased her majority by 662. The results were:

Mrs Margaret Thatcher (Conservative)	23,968
Mrs Yvonne Sieve (Labour)	14,504
F. Davis (Liberal)	13,070
Conservative majority	9,464

Although the Labour victory was huge, economic problems closed in upon Harold Wilson's government. Inflation, wage rises, high government spending, low government revenues and an unfavourable balance of payments bore down upon the administration, resulting, in November 1967, in the devaluation of the pound from its fixed rate of $2.80 to one of $2.40.* Mrs Thatcher was moved from her Shadow Treasury brief in the month before the final collapse, but from the 1966 election until then she had a ringside seat, and she used it effectively to heap obloquy on Labour's head.

She had always believed that nationalization, high taxes and government interference were bad. Now she saw the car crash she had predicted happening before her eyes. She was not frightened of seizing the moral high ground: 'Members of the Government have talked about social justice,' she told the Commons in April 1967. 'There are many ways in which one can be socially unjust. One of them is to take away too high a proportion of anyone's income.' At the Conservative Party conference in Brighton that October she went further:

> freedom has been gained in this country – not by great abstract campaigns, but through the objections of ordinary men and women to having their money taken from them by the State. In the early days, people banded together and said to the then Government, 'You shall not take our money before you have

---

* General de Gaulle rubbed salt in the wound by again refusing British entry to the EEC, nine days after devaluation.

redressed our grievances.' It was their money, their wealth, which was the source of their independence against the Government. This is crucial.

On 10 October 1967, ten days before her speech, Edward Heath at last gave Mrs Thatcher the recognition due to her talent and promoted her to the Shadow Cabinet, as Shadow Minister for Fuel and Power.* She still had no access to the confidences of the leadership, nor notable influence on its ideology, nor an independent power base. Yet it was clear she was formidable.

Once in the Shadow Cabinet, Mrs Thatcher began to show signs of developing an overall, publicly argued political position of her own. Her first big opportunity to present this came when she delivered the Conservative Political Centre Lecture in October 1968. The person asked to give this prestigious lecture was marked out as a coming man, so this was Heath's way of saying that Mrs Thatcher was a coming woman. Rejecting his suggestion that she speak on the subject of women's rights, she chose instead the all-embracing title 'What's wrong with politics?'

Recognizing the lecture's importance, both intellectually and politically, Mrs Thatcher delivered it in a gold brocade coat-dress, deliberately chosen to attract the greatest possible attention. Although at times plodding in style, her speech laid out many of the main beliefs that animated her, most of which would come to matter more.

'I believe', she said, 'that the great mistake of the last few years has been for the government to provide or to legislate for almost everything.' In this, the Tories were not guiltless. In the early 1960s, she argued, as 'growth' became the key political word, the contest between the parties centred too much on economics, not enough on people. Those who promised the most through governmental agency seemed the most attractive, leading to national plans and then prices and incomes policy to control inflation. But, said Mrs Thatcher, governments could not run prices or incomes: 'we have too little regard for the essential role of government which is control of the money supply and the management of demand'. Governments had been paying for expenditure by 'printing the money'. Enter, for the first time, Thatcher the monetarist. 'There is nothing wrong with people wanting larger incomes,' she continued, but the 'condition precedent' was 'hard work'. If people could keep more of what they earned they could contribute

---

* She was up against a minister, Dick Marsh, whom she knew from her Dartford days. It indicates something of where she stood in the political firmament that, earlier in the year, a *Sunday Times* 'Spot the Prime Minister' magazine feature about rising political talent had given Mrs Thatcher's odds as 1,000–1, whereas Marsh was favourite at 5–1.

more to the general good, she said, conjuring an image of which she would never tire: 'The Good Samaritan had to have the money to help, otherwise he too would have had to pass by on the other side.'

She ended with a call to Conservatives to break the consensus. She repeated the words of 'a young undergraduate', who 'came to me and said, "I had no idea there was such a clear alternative." He found the idea challenging and infinitely more effective than one in which everyone virtually expects their MP or the Government to solve their problems. The Conservative creed has never offered a life of ease without effort.' Here the voice of Alderman Roberts in the pulpit was coming through. 'Democracy is not for such people. Self-government is for those men and women who have learned to govern themselves.'

While there was certainly nothing disloyal in anything Mrs Thatcher said, it was politically an artful performance. Her speech tapped into a growing unease about Heath's approach: his technocratic leadership having failed to offer an alternative account of economics or, indeed, of the purpose of government itself. It marked her out as a person of combative conviction. It also positioned her carefully in the rows within the party over its most controversial figure, Enoch Powell.

Earlier in the year, a dramatic speech by Powell on immigration had finally forced Heath's hand. 'We must be mad, literally mad, as a nation to be permitting the annual inflow of some 50,000 dependants,' Powell had declared in Birmingham on 20 April. '... As I look ahead, I am filled with foreboding. Like the Roman, I seem to see "the River Tiber foaming with much blood".'

Margaret had admired Powell since first meeting him in the late 1940s. They were not personally close but were on friendly terms, the two couples dining together occasionally. Always impressed by intellectual attainment, and surprisingly humble about what she considered her own lack of it, Mrs Thatcher was in awe of Powell's brain ('His intellect was second to none') and drawn to his arguments. It was Powell who had long attacked centrism and corporatism. He had developed what came to be called monetarism and ridiculed the idea that prices and incomes policies could control inflation. On the Sunday morning when Powell's immigration speech was reported in the newspapers, Heath rang round Shadow Cabinet colleagues to tell them he proposed to sack him. By her account, Mrs Thatcher replied, 'Ted, I wouldn't heighten what he said too much.' But Heath replied: 'No, no. Most people think he must go.' Go he did, never to return to the front bench.

In the ensuing months Mrs Thatcher contrived, without any disloyalty, to make it clear in party circles that she was quite sympathetic to Powell. In her CPC Lecture she prayed his name in aid to point out the limits of private provision. Hospitals, she argued, were something the state could provide and the citizen could not, and she quoted Powell's ten-year hospital plan as Minister of Health to that effect. This was cunning: the leadership could not complain, and yet a link to the great rebel had been made. As the general election of 1970 approached, Mrs Thatcher continued quietly to maintain the Powell connection. During the campaign itself Powell made a series of speeches about the 'hidden enemy within' – the leftist agitators, who were trying to stop the South African cricket tour in Britain because of their opposition to apartheid. When the Home Secretary, James Callaghan, finally decided to stop the tour, Powell denounced him, feverishly comparing his capitulation to the sinking of *Repulse* and *Prince of Wales* in 1941. Heath's office privately described the speech as 'fascist', but Mrs Thatcher told the journalist Andrew Alexander, 'I agree with every word.' Powell's phrase 'the enemy within' was one that, when she became Prime Minister, she did not forget.

Like most British people of her generation, except for those who had served in the forces, Margaret Thatcher had seen little of the world.* In the period 1964–70, her growing seniority in the party, and the freedom offered by Opposition, allowed her to travel more. In June 1965 she spent eight days in Israel, the natural result of Jewish connections in Finchley. She toured the country and admired the purposeful activity everywhere. 'They don't pay people for being idle in Israel,' she reported, rather implying that, nearer home, they did. She reinforced her uncomplicated belief that Israel was a good country which wanted peace with its neighbours: 'Israel holds out the hand of friendship to all who will accept.'

By far her longest and most important visits, however, were to the United States. The first, courtesy of the State Department's International Visitor Program,† began in February 1967 and lasted for nearly six weeks. Denis was unable to spare so much time from his business, so Mrs Thatcher travelled alone. Her trip began in Washington DC where, given the political orientation of the State Department, she was steered towards people to the left of her own views. Among others she met Senator Joseph Clark, a liberal Democrat who attacked President Johnson's record in Vietnam, and Margaret Chase Smith, the first ever woman to be elected to both the House of Representatives and the Senate. No record survives of her meetings.

---

* She first visited Continental Europe on her honeymoon, and her subsequent visits had largely been confined to skiing holidays there.
† This was a large-scale scheme to give prominent non-US citizens an extended opportunity to get to know the country. The programme paid all travel expenses and a per-diem living allowance of $25.

But according to John Campbell's biography, 'she did not always know how to behave': 'A senior [British] Treasury official serving in Washington was horrified by the way she lectured the Director of the IMF, Pierre-Paul Schweitzer – a languid, cigarette-smoking French intellectual of the type she had probably never encountered before – on subjects he knew far more about than she did – and altogether behaved "like a bull in a china shop".'*

As she went around the country, Mrs Thatcher won better reports. One of her hosts recorded that she was 'undoubtedly one of the most delightful and competent visitors we have had. She has charmed and impressed local sponsors from coast to coast.' In Houston, the NASA manned-spacecraft centre, with its wealth of cutting-edge technology, enthused her more than anything else in the entire trip. She then flew to San Francisco, sending a card to her sister Muriel inscribed 'This is the most beautiful of them all.' Back east, she met the great economist Paul Samuelson, who was working on the control of inflation at MIT. She finished in New York City, whence she flew to Albany to meet the state Governor, Nelson Rockefeller, later Gerald Ford's Vice-President.

As she travelled, Mrs Thatcher gave speeches and interviews. The *Houston Post*, with a byline from the 'Women's staff', began: 'A gracious lady member of British Parliament pulled on velvet gloves when quizzed Wednesday about English trade with North Vietnam.' Mrs Thatcher defended this trade. She was asked if the Common Market would bring ruin to Britain. '"Nothing will bring ruin to Great Britain," Mrs Thatcher replied briskly.' She said that sterling's weakness was caused by excessive public spending, but the *Houston Post* described her as one 'who approves of the Keynes theory of economics because "we've found none better"'. Almost nothing indicated much of the political figure that she would become.

Mrs Thatcher's own feelings about her visit were uncomplicatedly positive. Despite her position in British politics, she behaved more like an energetic tourist than a politician dealing with professional counterparts. She was receptive and charming and was charmed and well received in return. She enjoyed American courtesy, American warmth and American technology, business know-how and political culture. In her memoirs she wrote, 'The excitement which I felt has never really subsided.' This was the simple truth. She loved America, felt at ease there and wanted to go back.†

---

* It seems reasonable to assume that this Treasury official was Douglas Wass, as he was the only such official present at the lunch with Schweitzer. Wass was Permanent Secretary at the Treasury when Mrs Thatcher came into office in 1979, and was believed to have taken an equally dim view of her economic policy.

† In March 1969 she did just that, returning to the USA at the request of the English-Speaking Union (ESU), a non-political association dedicated to strengthening links among

She also drew political lessons from her trip. From that time on, her speeches began to cite American examples, often contrasting them favourably with the situation in Britain. Above all, she noticed the contrast between a society with bearable tax rates and free markets and the alternative: 'The maximum rate of tax on personal incomes in the United Kingdom is 91.25 per cent ... and for a married couple with two small children it starts at an income of £18,900. The same marginal rate in the United States ... is 60 per cent, and it does not start until an income of £77,000.'

When she paid her first visit to the Soviet Union in 1969, therefore, Mrs Thatcher had a clear standard of superpower comparison. Although an official guest, as Opposition transport spokesman, of the Soviet government, she paid her own fare to make herself less beholden to her hosts. She visited the Kremlin, where, when her hosts asked her if NATO had become irrelevant, she replied 'Certainly not.' She went to Moscow University and to GUM, the huge Moscow department store with 'pathetically little in it'. In Moscow her interpreter showed her a sculpture of a man beating a sword into a ploughshare. 'That's communism,' he told her. 'It's not, you know,' she replied. 'It's the Bible.' Visiting a palace on the outskirts of Leningrad (as St Petersburg was then called), she fell into conversation with an attendant. She asked him where his family was.

'In America.'

'Wouldn't they like to come back?'

'Oh, no, no, no.'

As she boarded the plane for home, she remembered thinking to herself, 'Oh, the relief!'

When Heath made Mrs Thatcher Shadow Education Minister on 21 October 1969, he was pitching her into an area where Conservative principles seemed to conflict with what many real live Conservatives wanted. The difficulty lay in the comprehensivization of secondary schools, by then happening fast. The introduction of 'comprehensives' abolished selection at the age of eleven and got rid of the 1944 division between grammar schools, attended by the more intellectually able, and secondary moderns, which educated the less academic majority. It was natural, in principle, for Conservatives to favour the continued existence of grammar schools. They represented excellence, allowed parental choice, and were the best ladder

---

English-speaking people around the world, who invited her to deliver a series of lectures. Her texts do not survive, but the reaction was clear and summed up neatly by one of her American hosts: 'She came, She saw, She conquered!'

of advancement ever devised for bright children from poor backgrounds. In practice, the situation was more complicated. Less than a fifth of all children attended grammar schools. The big objection was that children could be 'branded a failure' at the age of eleven. Many Conservative voters had children who had failed or, they expected, would fail the 'eleven-plus', the examination which determined entry to secondary school at that age. So support for the comprehensive alternative was considerable. In June 1966, for example, the Shadow Cabinet discussed an NOP poll which showed 65 per cent of the public in favour, and Conservative voters split exactly in half on the issue.

There was a further complication. Under R. A. Butler's 1944 Education Act, esteemed by both parties, the provision of schools was to be determined locally, with the national government limited to providing funding. So it was local authorities who made the running. The first comprehensive experiment, in 1957, was conducted by Leicestershire County Council, which was Conservative-controlled. The Labour Party developed a fiercely ideological commitment to comprehensives and translated this into central government pressure, but even without this the trend to comprehensivization was considered unstoppable. By the time Mrs Thatcher took up her position, almost a quarter of children were in comprehensives, and all but about thirty of the 163 education authorities had submitted plans to comprehensivize.

Of Mrs Thatcher's own views there was never any doubt. 'I am a firm believer in grammar schools,' she declared in 1967. 'For many years now they have been the ladder from the bottom to the top.' But by the time she took up her post, a general election was expected within the year, which left little time to rethink the subject. Mrs Thatcher thus decided to be the loyal executant of the existing policy. It was not a question, she told the press, of comprehensives 'versus' grammars: what she was against was 'imposing' comprehensives. Under Labour, Circular 10/66 had tied grants for new school-building to the progress of a council's schemes for comprehensives. In resisting this, the Tory fight had become more a defence of the independence of local government than a stand on the quality of education.

Mrs Thatcher's slightly precarious stance was eased by the fact that the Labour government introduced legislation compelling the introduction of comprehensives but was unable to pass it before the election. This atmosphere of ideological zeal mixed with incompetence allowed her to promote her criticisms of the comprehensive ideal without opposing the whole process. She could assault Labour's absolutism, and also its motives:

'I think that the Labour Party must hate the middle class, because every time the worst they can say about a school ... is that a large proportion of the middle class get through there.'

On 10 February 1970, Alfred Roberts died, aged seventy-seven, shortly after listening to his daughter's appearance on BBC Radio's women's discussion programme *Petticoat Line*.* He had been ill for some time with emphysema, which had led to weakness in his heart. In his last months, feeling sorrowful and neglected, he lamented that 'I never hear anything from Margaret either by letter or by phone.' Margaret did visit him in his last illness: Carol remembered her being 'very tearful' about the state of his health, but her mother was not with him when he died. She was in London, receiving a delegation from the anti-comprehensive group, the National Education Association. Two days later, she spoke in the Commons debate on the second reading of the ill-fated Education Bill.

Alfred's funeral took place in Grantham on 16 February. Although Muriel recalled that her sister did not attend ('of course she didn't go, did she? She'd got something on'), this was not true.† Margaret was present at the church service, although not the cremation that followed. Most likely she took the train back to London in order – as her diaries suggest – to keep her appointments for the following day. It was typical of Margaret's attitude to her father when he was alive to behave correctly but perfunctorily, sometimes with a touch of impatience. In later years, perhaps feeling some guilt about this, she celebrated his influence and his memory. In 1970, she was in too much of a hurry.‡

From the beginning of 1970, the Conservatives felt they should be ready for a general election. Conscious that the party's policies still lacked final form, Ted Heath convened the Shadow Cabinet at the Selsdon Park Hotel in Croydon, beginning on 30 January. While Harold Wilson invented a figure called 'Selsdon Man' who, he claimed, had emerged from the conference as the hard-hatted, free-market, devil-take-the-hindmost spirit of Heath's Toryism, Selsdon was more a talking shop than the moment at

---

* The title says much about attitudes of the time.
† Muriel did recall her sister attending the reading of their father's will, which took place immediately before the funeral. Cissie Hubbard invited Muriel and Margaret to pick any bits of furniture, antiques and pictures that they wanted. In Muriel's recollection, Margaret simply said: 'I want something that was my mother's.'
‡ On 18 October 1970, by which time she was Education Secretary, Mrs Thatcher attended a memorial service at Finkin Street Church in Grantham at which a lectern was dedicated in memory of Alfred Roberts. At the ceremony, according to Muriel Cullen, her sister complained to her: 'They don't know how to treat a Cabinet minister, do they?' Muriel replied, 'This service isn't for you.'

which the party 'lurched to the right'. Most of Mrs Thatcher's interventions concerned her own area. She warned against singling out teachers for a battle over public-sector productivity. Forbidden by Heath from any general discussion of education policy, she engaged in only one set-to with him and colleagues. It concerned the proposal for an independent university, favoured by free-marketeers and those worried by the trends in higher education, led by Max Beloff, an academic and Oxford contemporary of Heath's. The minutes show Mrs Thatcher asking, 'Can I make a speech giving it a fair wind?' Worried about the cost, Heath said that the backers should 'put their own money in it, keep educational standards – but don't want it to come to State for money'. When Mrs Thatcher stressed that, without the guarantee of a Royal Charter, the proposed university would struggle to raise money, Heath blanched: 'Not committing myself to a Royal Charter. Wouldn't trust Max Beloff for a minute.* Already got too many universities.'

On 18 May 1970, Wilson called a general election for 18 June. The Conservative manifesto, *A Better Tomorrow*, emphasized practicality. Launching it, Heath promised to change 'the whole style of government'. Mrs Thatcher was lined up to appear in party political broadcasts, but came across as stiff and unnatural in a pilot and so was withdrawn. She spent most of the campaign, which she expected the Conservatives to lose, in Finchley, focusing on economic woes, law and order and – coding her criticism of mass immigration – conserving 'our British character'. To the confusion of the opinion polls, the Conservatives won the election with an overall majority of thirty-one. The Finchley result was as follows:

Mrs Margaret Thatcher (Conservative)	25,480
Michael Freeman (Labour)	14,295
G. Mitchell (Liberal)	7,614
Conservative majority	11,185

Both Mrs Thatcher's vote and her majority were up. Hearing late that night on the car radio that the Conservatives were winning, the Thatchers, who were driving to Lamberhurst, turned round and went to the *Daily Telegraph* party at the Savoy.

Margaret Thatcher accepted her first Cabinet post, as Edward Heath's Secretary of State for Education and Science, on 20 June 1970. Although she often referred to her background as a scientist, she made very little

---

* Beloff had come from the left and at this time was in the Liberal Party, moving fast to the right.

of the fact that she had, briefly, been a teacher. In 1944, during Oxford's long summer vacation, she had worked at Grantham's Central School for Boys for almost three months.* Still aged only eighteen, she taught science, but also maths, and, under protest, other things too. 'School has not gone down any too well this past week,' she wrote to Muriel. 'We are working terrifically hard . . . I have a set of <u>English essays</u> to mark this weekend as well as some algebra and physics and I've never seen such appalling tripe in all my life.' She also had to take the boys for swimming lessons at the Grantham baths: 'We . . . stay on the bank and try to teach them by yelling at them what they are doing wrong. I don't think it is a very satisfactory method personally, but still I don't think I'd like to appear in front of them in a bathing costume with my present figure.'

Margaret did not relish her experience as a teacher.† She wrote to Muriel of her relief when she finished the school week on Friday evening, 'It was like being released to freedom once more.' The school, however, was enthusiastic: 'Mr Thorpe [the headmaster] was awfully nice the last day and thanked me . . . all in front of the school who clapped wildly for what seemed like ages.' She added, untruthfully, 'I was quite glad when the ceremony was over.'

No doubt it was wise of Mrs Thatcher not to dwell in later life on her experience as a teacher: such a short stint would never have stood comparison with the work of people who had given their life to the profession. But those few weeks gave her a respect for the hardships that teachers endure and reinforced her belief in making sure that children learn things properly. She always approached education with an odd mixture of feelings – a solemn conviction that it was overwhelmingly important for civilization and for the individual, combined with a certain impatience. Carol remembered that Mrs Thatcher, generally quite indulgent as a mother, would upbraid her children strongly if they received bad reports from school: 'I'd twigged before the Russians that she was the Iron Lady.'

The Department of Education and Science (DES) did not stand high in the Whitehall pecking order. Many DES officials, including the Permanent

---

* A reorganization of the Lincolnshire schools' academic year to allow pupils more time to help with the potato harvest in the autumn left considerable overlap between term time and Oxford's vacation. Margaret taught for almost two months of the summer term and three weeks of the subsequent Michaelmas term.
† In addition to her formal duties, Margaret coached David, a would-be naval cadet, for his maths exams. 'I'm afraid he's not a very smart kid at all,' she told Muriel, '. . . he still doesn't know his tables properly and nothing I can do for him can ever make up for that. I think teaching him has been the hardest earned £2-2s I've ever had or hope to have in my life.'

Secretary, Sir William Pile, would have preferred to be in other government departments. In part, this reflected the cultural assumption that education was a 'woman's subject', unworthy of the attention of men whose job it was to rule. More, it arose from the department's lack of power. Pile's predecessor described its work as 'like steering a boat with a rubber tiller'. Virtually everything in education was delegated, or mediated, universities receiving their money via the University Grants Committee and schools through local education authorities.

So Mrs Thatcher's new department produced money – for school-building and for teachers' salaries in particular – but not ideas. She later claimed to have protested at this to Pile when she arrived: 'I'm worried about the *content* in schools,' she remembered saying, 'rather than the structure.' But she did not try to change the balance of power. Indeed, her most immediately controversial policy – scrapping the Labour Circulars 10/65 and 10/66 which tried to force comprehensivization – took its stand on the familiar principle of local independence rather than any objection to comprehensives in principle.

Mrs Thatcher withdrew the Labour Circulars at once, informing her officials on her first working day (Monday 22 June) and making the public announcement on 30 June. For this speed she was criticized. Unions and local authorities complained of the lack of consultation. Worse, from Mrs Thatcher's point of view, 10 Downing Street indicated displeasure at her failure to discuss the matter in Cabinet first. In his introductory remarks at his very first Cabinet meeting, Heath urged ministers, 'Don't be rushed into hasty decisions of policy.' His Education Secretary had just rushed into one the day before. The feeling was that she was getting above herself. Mrs Thatcher, however, believed she was simply doing what the manifesto had promised. This pledge required no legislation and so it should happen at once.

Circular 10/70, as her new policy was called, offered more a change of tone than a reform of huge importance. The comprehensivization of schools was too far advanced to be stopped. On the day when Mrs Thatcher took office there were 1,137 comprehensive schools in England and Wales. When she left it in March 1974 she had approved 3,286 comprehensive schemes and rejected only 326; she had saved ninety-four grammar schools. All that 10/70 ensured was that no local authority was compelled to go comprehensive. It did not give Mrs Thatcher new powers to shape education.

There were successes. Mrs Thatcher prevented the compulsory comprehensivization of Birmingham, in train when she arrived in office, and helped save nearly half of Birmingham's grammar schools. In general, however, the policy did not please enough people enough. Particularly awkward were Conservative authorities which wanted to go comprehensive. 'Look at who fought me,' she would lament in later years. In June 1971, in her own constituency, Mrs Thatcher blocked several parts of Barnet Council's plan to go comprehensive.* The normally loyal *Finchley Press* reported the local teachers as 'staggered': Vic Usher, Conservative chairman of the council's education committee and usually friendly to Mrs Thatcher, expressed his 'tremendous disappointment'.

Perhaps the most disappointed was Mrs Thatcher herself. Although she genuinely believed it was a bad idea that central government should decree the nature of every school in the country, she had little practical faith in the capacity of local authorities to make the right decisions. This was noticed. *The Times Educational Supplement*, the voice of the educational establishment, complained that she continued 'to hide behind the autonomy of the local authorities . . . when it suits her, but as soon as they use their autonomy in a way she does not like, out comes the big stick'. As for alternative policy solutions, she lacked the official support, the intellectual preparation and the political clout to produce any of her own. In essence, she found herself presiding over a vast change of educational structure whose egalitarian principles she opposed, but which she was powerless to reverse.

Her frustration was fed by isolation. At the DES she was not among friends. In her memoirs she describes the prevailing atmosphere there as 'self-righteously socialist'. After Bill Pile and his wife had come to lunch in Lamberhurst, she was irritated not to receive a thank-you letter from Pile's left-wing wife. Irritated, but not surprised: 'What do you expect?' she complained to an official. 'She's Communist Party. She's CP.' She saw Communist influence in the National Union of Teachers (NUT), a subject she raised in Cabinet, and was shocked by what she considered the crony relationship between the NUT and DES officials.

Mrs Thatcher's directly political accusations against her department were somewhat unfair. This was no Labour bastion. Officials had found Ted Short, her Labour predecessor, pedantic, prickly and slow-witted. They rejoiced in the shift to someone obviously more intelligent and determined: 'You came out from a conversation with her feeling that you'd had three very hard sets of tennis,' said one senior official. There was, nevertheless, a cultural gap, some of which may have related to her sex. Pile, said a fellow senior official, 'never missed a chance to slag her off behind her back'. It

---

* This had been supported by 86 per cent of some 28,000 responses to a consultation on the subject.

was not only that she was a woman, but such a carefully turned out, utterly Tory woman. John Banks, her first private secretary, found her 'difficult to relate to' because of her 'mannerized [sic] style of talking to civil servants'. It struck officials, partly with amusement and partly with irritation, that Mrs Thatcher had never for a second considered sending her own children to state schools.* One day, Mrs Thatcher and Banks were driving past Pimlico Comprehensive in London, then a new and famous school. He said he might send his son there. 'Oh, John,' said Mrs Thatcher, 'you couldn't think of sending your child to that glasshouse.' As John Hedger, another of her private secretaries, put it, 'The department respected her enormously, but were bothered by her prejudices.' She in turn was irritated by the opposite prejudices among her officials. She remembered calling in one chief inspector of schools and saying: 'You're absolutely against grammar schools. They're being made to feel guilty but they're doing well ... They need a bit of praise from people like you,' and she accused public-school-educated officials like Banks (Eton) of acting out of feelings of guilt induced by their privilege. Most of her officials resisted change, especially from a woman, new to the Cabinet and from outside their own tribe, whose own ideas on the subject, while markedly different from their own, were not fully formed.† This edgy relationship with her own department helps explain the fiasco which made her a household name for the first time and came quite close to aborting her political career.

One of the first acts of the Heath government was to inaugurate a review of all public spending. Mrs Thatcher immediately applied herself to this with the literal-mindedness in which, contrary to widespread belief, there always lurked an element of deliberate self-parody. 'The PM says we must take extreme care with spending,' she intoned in the direction of her Permanent Secretary as he walked back to his tobacco-stained office, 'so therefore there will be no redecoration here without permission from *me*.'

But Mrs Thatcher did fight her department's corner. At a time when school rolls were rising and almost the only power she had was her ability to spend, she was determined to increase the DES budget. Her tactic

---

* The twins were by this time sixth-formers. Carol, now at St Paul's, found it particularly difficult that her mother was Education Secretary while she was being educated.
† At this time a series of education 'Black Papers', published by academics, teachers and writers, including the novelist Kingsley Amis, who were worried about the trends in progressive education, caused a great stir. Mrs Thatcher was sympathetic to the Black Papers and gave their authors a friendly hearing, but there is little evidence that she tried to apply much of their thought to her action in government. The prevailing orthodoxy was strong in the opposite direction, and she did not feel ready to defy it.

was to accept short-term cuts in exchange for long-term growth, and cuts in non-educational aspects in favour of increases in truly educational spending. When the Chief Secretary to the Treasury, Maurice Macmillan, proposed abolishing the long-standing provision of free milk for health reasons to all primary-school pupils,* Mrs Thatcher was not unsympathetic. Nonetheless, she opposed complete withdrawal as 'too drastic a step [that] would arouse more public antagonism than the saving justifies'. Macmillan resisted, but as Mrs Thatcher reported to the Cabinet on 29 September, eventually agreed to her insistence on retaining school milk for infants. When the Chancellor of the Exchequer, Anthony Barber, announced his public spending package in late October, Mrs Thatcher was judged to have done well. In addition to the promise to increase spending on primary-school buildings, she had contrived to save the Open University, an invention of Harold Wilson's which most Tories disliked but which she believed would be 'a means of getting good teaching on television' and extend educational opportunity. This was a considerable achievement for an entirely untried Cabinet minister.

Problems, however, grew. The political danger in the reduction in free milk became more apparent because this change required new legislation. The original hope was that the milk cuts would be inconspicuous in wider legislation led by Keith Joseph's Department of Health and Social Security. When this was rejected for lack of parliamentary time, the DES had to forge ahead alone. By the parliamentary debate on the second reading on 14 June 1971, opposition had grown sufficiently that Ted Short felt able to call the legislation 'mean, squalid and unworthy of a great country'. Nutrition experts, social workers, the NUT, the Child Poverty Action Group all pitched in against Mrs Thatcher. Here was a subject on which everyone could easily have an opinion and where the case for the cut, however reasonable, could never seem attractive.† The *Sun* asked, 'Is Mrs Thatcher human?' At the Labour Party conference that September, a floor speaker coined the phrase 'Mrs Thatcher, milksnatcher'. This soon became the only thing most of the public knew about her.

All this fuss was peculiarly painful to Mrs Thatcher. It was her first experience of being hated for her public work. It cut her to the quick

---

* In an earlier economy measure the previous Labour government had abolished milk for secondary-school pupils.

† Perhaps the only people who, for the most part, did not share the outrage were the children themselves. The bottles of milk supplied at elevenses were unpopular with pupils because few schools had the necessary refrigeration in those days and the milk, delivered early and often sitting for hours in crates beside radiators, was warm and semi-separated. The present author's generation felt liberated from the age of compulsory milk.

that people should think that she – a mother – could be indifferent to the health of children. She felt the great unfairness of it all and realized, to her mortification, that she had allowed the press to develop a public character for her which was unattractive and damaging to her career. An early sign came with a BBC *Panorama* documentary which aired in July 1970. The programme depicted Mrs Thatcher as an aggressively middle-class Tory woman, able, but fundamentally unsympathetic and in favour of privilege. One sequence showed her in the chemistry class of a London comprehensive in which pupils were learning about sulphur in food-making. 'Particularly on breakfast spoons,' Mrs Thatcher chips in, 'if they're silver, they go brown and Mother has to clean them. So these days we tend to use stainless steel, don't we?' Few, if any, of the pupils would have seen any silver at home. What Mrs Thatcher recalled as 'a wretched little film' was wonderful propaganda for the left. It helped to set a media and therefore a public mood against her. Protests followed her across the country. Students waited for her train at station platforms and charged up to bang on her window. Officials remembered how this frightened her and were touched by such human frailty.* By November, the *Sun* marked her down as 'The Most Unpopular Woman in Britain'.

Mrs Thatcher found the whole experience almost unbearable. 'Why, why? Why are you doing it?' she asked during an interview with the *Guardian*, an uncharacteristic outburst of self-pity. For strength she drew on Denis, and on the conviction that the policy was, in essence, right: 'The idea that most people couldn't pay a small amount for their children's milk was to me utterly ridiculous ... And it showed up those who were using it not really about school milk, but to try to get me out of Education.' In later years Mrs Thatcher gained a reputation for physical and psychological stamina, but that toughness had to be acquired by bitter experience. People who knew her in the 1970s often remarked how tired she seemed, and how upset by attack. 'Milk' was her first big test, and she did not pass it easily. Unbeknown to her, Ted Heath discussed sacking her with colleagues. The Chief Whip, Francis Pym, told him that he could not dismiss the only woman in his Cabinet. Heath dropped the notion.

---

* One of the threats made to Mrs Thatcher was nastier still. A man approached her at a meeting and said that he was from the Angry Brigade, a minor terrorist grouping of the period, and she would be blown up in twenty minutes. He was lying, but she had to start thinking about the threat of terrorism for the first time. From the period of the milk dispute, and for the rest of her life, she was subject to the attention of extremists and mobs of protesters. This probably did her more political good than harm, but it was a heavy personal burden for her and her family to have to bear. In February 1972 she raised the matter in Cabinet, asking if government ministers were insured against terrorist attack.

The last straw came just before Christmas 1971. Mrs Thatcher learnt that the milk Circular the department had put out contained a loophole which threatened to defeat its entire purpose. Pile wrote to her to 'apologise unreservedly' for the mistake. 'It adds a further embarrassment in an area which is already causing you much trouble.' So angry was she that at the office Christmas party, to which she had brought Pile a present, she turned and whispered to an official: 'Put that Christmas present away. I cannot give it to him now.' Fortunately for Mrs Thatcher, the correction of the Circular went out without publicity, and the defiance of the milk edict mysteriously melted away. By 9 January 1972, Britain was embroiled in the first of the Heath government's miners' strikes and the media had lost interest in milk.

At this point, Ted Heath, showing a concern for which Mrs Thatcher always remained grateful, took matters in hand. Politically she was in a vulnerable position, but instead of sacking her Heath backed her. At a meeting at Chequers on 12 January, he effected a reconciliation between his Secretary of State and her officials. Heath had been impressed by Mrs Thatcher's tenacity, culminating in her victory in Cabinet over funds for school-building in June 1971, getting more money for her department. They now agreed, in essence, to take the heat out of education and to put money into it. Mrs Thatcher would concentrate on popular areas – more primary schools, further education, more polytechnics, raising the school leaving age, an expansion of nursery education and a White Paper to set out the bright future.

Following the Chequers meeting, Heath praised Mrs Thatcher in Parliament. She used his support for what is nowadays called a relaunch. A spate of press interviews presented her as someone who had learnt from her ordeal and bounced back. 'I'm afraid I'll be remembered for milk,' she told the *Liverpool Daily Post*. 'But I'd like to be remembered as the Minister who actually, actually did raise the school leaving age instead of just talking about it,' and she added, 'I must confess the record really is pretty impressive. I think the Prime Minister thinks so too.' The school leaving age was raised from fifteen to sixteen with effect from September 1973. By May 1972 she was giving hints about the expansion of nursery schools. She was effective in her fight with the Treasury – officials remembered that 'it was almost literally true that Tony Barber [the Chancellor of the Exchequer] walked backwards when he saw her coming'.

As a political tactic, Mrs Thatcher's readiness to shut up and spend worked well. The educational interest groups were placated, and it became known that she was persistent in arguing the case for better pay for teachers in Cabinet. The department began to feel at ease once more. A White Paper was duly produced: a Sir Humphrey's dream, it created new work for officials for years to come and projected an almost 50 per cent rise in expenditure over the coming decade. On 30 November 1972, Heath praised it to his Cabinet colleagues as 'the most important White Paper [on the subject] since 1944', but stressed they should make clear that it was 'concerned with the structure, not with the content of education'. So Mrs Thatcher's urgings about content had got precisely nowhere. As she said at the press conference to launch the White Paper on 6 December, 'there is little that can be accomplished in education without money,' and really money was all that it was about.*

After the milk row, Mrs Thatcher's emollient tactic had ensured her political survival, but the price – the loss of her distinctive voice – was high. She told the *Illustrated London News* how pleased she was that the atmosphere in primary schools was 'much better . . . much more progressive', whereas in private she complained to inspectors that such education was 'all rag dolls and rolling on the floor'. For the first and almost the only time in her political career, Mrs Thatcher started to face more attacks from the right than from the left. She gave interviews and made speeches designed to show that her Tory heart remained in the right place. But, on the whole, she became bland, the loyal, careful and strictly departmental spokesman of a government that found itself in growing trouble. Over the course of 1973, as economic prospects darkened, it became clear that the extra spending proposed in her White Paper was no longer viable.

On 13 November, action by the National Union of Mineworkers led the government to proclaim a state of emergency. One consequent cut planned was of heating in schools. After Mrs Thatcher got wind of this, on the BBC's *Today* programme, she went straight round to the Department of Trade and Industry to complain. Within twelve hours the order was stopped. Mrs Thatcher was at pains to reveal this decisive intervention to the world. If the equivalent to the milk row was looming, she wanted this time to be on the right side of the fence.

---

* The White Paper identified five areas – nursery education, school-building, staffing standards in schools, teacher-training and higher education – where expenditure 'will continue to increase substantially in real terms over the coming decade'.

4
Who dares wins: leadership challenge

'Heath will murder you'

In the June 1970 general election, the Conservatives had been elected on a manifesto informed by free-market liberal economics. As they put it baldly: 'We utterly reject the philosophy of compulsory wage control.' Instead, the introduction of a new Industrial Relations Act would permit a return to free collective bargaining (that is, unregulated pay negotiation between management and trade unions). The manifesto was equally firm in its condemnation of inflation, which it attributed to 'Labour's damaging policies of high taxation and devaluation'. Government spending had risen from 44 per cent of Gross Domestic Product in 1964 to 50 per cent in 1969. That drift, the Tories had argued, had to stop. The Conservatives who won in 1970 were committed to a smaller state and a freer economy. They failed, and their failure created the conditions for Margaret Thatcher to become their leader.

By far the biggest difficulty confronting Edward Heath's government was industrial relations. Union leaders who had seen off Harold Wilson's efforts at reform in 1969 were not going to make it easier for a Tory prime minister. They flexed their muscles. As soon as the Tories gained office there was a dock strike, which was settled only at a very high price. That December, regular power cuts began as power station employees worked to rule. Ailing industry also took its toll. In February 1971, the aero-engine company Rolls-Royce informed the government it was insolvent. Heath rescued the company in the interests of national defence. Then came news that Upper Clyde Shipbuilders, a partly government-backed conglomerate on which depended 15,000 mainly Scottish jobs, was going to apply for liquidation. Initially Heath refused to consider a bailout, but after protests posed a threat to public order, in October the Cabinet agreed to a rescue.

The government was also immersed in its most significant industrial dispute, and with its most symbolically important foe. In July 1971, the National Union of Mineworkers had demanded a wage increase of 45 per cent. This was rejected and so, on 9 January 1972, the first national miners' strike for nearly fifty years began. Aggressive union picketing prevented the movement of coal stocks and oil to power stations. Matters came to a head on 10 February, when violent pickets, led by the rising star of the hard left in the NUM, Arthur Scargill, defied the police to force the closure of Saltley coke depot in Birmingham. Heath recalled Saltley as 'the most vivid, direct and terrifying challenge to the rule of law that I could ever recall emerging from within our own country', and it came at a time when the shortage of power, which had already put much of industry on a three-day week,* threatened a total blackout. 'Until Saltley,' said Mrs Thatcher later, 'Ted gave a strong lead and made up his mind. Then he made up his mind the other way.' Heath now invited the judge Lord Wilberforce to conduct a hurried inquiry, which led to a punishingly generous settlement.

From this Heath concluded that there had, after all, to be an 'industrial strategy'. On 21 March 1972, Anthony Barber, Chancellor since the early death of Iain Macleod, presented a reflationary Budget to Parliament. The Industry Bill followed in May, allowing ministers to use public money to 'back winners' in industry, with a bias in favour of depressed regions. Tony Benn, a champion of the left, greeted this warmly from the Labour benches as 'spadework for socialism'. In June, after a run on the pound, the government allowed sterling to float freely, confirming its decline. On 6 November, Heath announced that he would impose a ninety-day freeze on wages, prices, rents and dividends. Although this was framed as an emergency measure, it was clear that the government had broken with the principles of a free economy. There was no general revolt in the party, but that autumn Tory backbenchers elected Edward du Cann, a long-standing opponent of Heath, as Chairman of the 1922 Committee.† The crisis measures were well received at first. But for the rest of Heath's time in office, the emergency deepened and the distance from the intentions of 1970 grew.

In after years, critics of Mrs Thatcher attacked her acquiescence in changes which she later so decisively repudiated. Heath himself took some pleasure in pointing out that she 'didn't argue a great deal in Cabinet'. She had a somewhat uneasy conscience. 'Should I have resigned?' she wrote in

---

* This was not *the* 'three-day week', a formal arrangement imposed by the government from 1 January 1974.
† The 1922 Committee consists of all Conservative Members of Parliament. Its Executive is drawn from the back benches. Its private meetings provide a forum for backbenchers and the chance to discuss matters with frontbenchers. At that time, its Chairman commanded great prestige and was considered a counterbalance to the power of the Prime Minister.

her memoirs. 'Perhaps so. But those of us who disliked what was happening had not yet either fully analysed the situation or worked out an alternative approach.' In fact, there is no evidence that she even considered resigning.

In June 1973, in a confidential cable to the State Department, the US Ambassador in London, Walter Annenberg, assessed Mrs Thatcher as a 'strong supporter of Heath'. He judged her performance as 'solid, respectable and unspectacular. She has not sought to introduce radical remedies to deal with Britain's problems in education and science . . . it is most doubtful that she could, or does, realistically expect to lead her party.' Annenberg's cable accompanied a memo from Dirk Gleysteen, an Embassy official, which offered a gossipy account of a recent lunch with Mrs Thatcher. Of Geoffrey Howe, Gleysteen recorded, 'Mrs Thatcher obviously respects and thinks highly of him but said he is "too willing to compromise".' 'She said Michael Haseltine [sic] [her nemesis twenty years later] had everything it took in politics except brains.' She reserved her highest praise for Keith Joseph, for whom she had 'tremendous admiration. She said that he could handle any ministry and she was confident that he has been marked for higher responsibility.' Parts of this report indicate that Mrs Thatcher is a woman of her own views ('slightly to the right-of-center', said Annenberg). Nothing suggests serious revolt against the direction of the government.

Records show that Mrs Thatcher maintained a fairly consistent position in Cabinet – though not an important one, because of her non-economic brief and her lack of seniority. Almost all her broader interventions demonstrated opposition to corporatism, union power and wage and price control.* Cecil Parkinson, who had entered Parliament in a by-election in 1970, remembered her taking him aside in 1973 and saying, 'Look, I'm fighting all these incomes policies and statutory controls in Cabinet, but I need people outside Cabinet to speak up.' She intensely disliked the idea that inflation was a price worth paying for economic growth and social peace. She always remembered a conversation in the rose garden at Chequers with Robin Butler, then a young official. He told her, she recalled, 'If we can't beat inflation, we've got to learn to live with it.' Mrs Thatcher replied emphatically, 'Robin. No. No!' Ten years later, when she interviewed Butler for the post of principal private secretary, she reminded him of the incident: 'You said inflation was endemic. I've never heard a more shocking remark from a young man.'

It is not hard to understand why Mrs Thatcher, and others who felt

---

* Seated on the same side of the table as Heath, but as far away from him as it was possible to sit, Mrs Thatcher sometimes found difficulty in getting attention, and on one occasion the Cabinet Secretary, Burke Trend, actually records her intervention as 'not heard' (though he heard it himself).

dissatisfaction with the Heath government, nevertheless went along with it. Having defied expectations and won the 1970 election, Heath was highly successful in establishing himself in public respect, though not affection. He was also surprisingly good at forging a loyal team and making traditional Cabinet government work.* Years later, Mrs Thatcher paid him a backhanded compliment: 'I was impressed by the lead Ted gave in Cabinet. If I'd have done it, I'd have been called bossy.'

Heath's flagship Industrial Relations Bill, finally enacted in August 1971, established the right to join or not to join a trade union and provided that future collective agreements should be legally enforceable. But it foundered on the refusal of the unions to play by its rules. The new National Industrial Relations Court (NIRC) created by the Act found that unions, rather than their individual members, were legally responsible for those members' actions, but this ruling was overturned in the Appeal Court. This left the NIRC to pursue individual members instead, plenty of whom were only too happy to be arrested for their cause. In July, five dockers who defied an order from the NIRC to stop obstructing container lorries in Hackney were arrested and detained in Pentonville prison, quickly becoming the 'Pentonville Five'. There were sympathy stoppages across industry and also a national dock strike. The TUC voted for a one-day general strike and broke off the tripartite talks which Heath had begun.

The Law Lords subsequently overturned the Appeal Court's ruling, paving the way for the release of the Pentonville Five. This saved the government from out-and-out confrontation, but not from humiliation. The attempt to give a legal framework to labour relations was dead. Given the push of inflation and the power of the unions, another way towards industrial sanity had to be found. By a logic which the Heath government did not like, but could no longer resist, that was a prices and incomes policy. When the Counter-Inflation (Temporary Measures) Bill came before the House, Enoch Powell was the only Conservative to vote against it. The U-turn was complete.

Even more than she was worried by the change of economic policy, Mrs Thatcher was shocked by the unions' challenge to the rule of law. In a speech on 29 July 1972, she linked, in terms of moral obliquity, the defiance of the Industrial Relations Act with the sectarian disorders in Northern Ireland which had led Heath to impose direct rule from Westminster in

---

* Mrs Thatcher later complained that his Cabinet was much reduced in importance after the first year in government, and there is some truth in this, particularly over economic policy. But the records show many lively discussions, even towards the end of the administration.

March. The lesson she learnt was that labour law had to be framed differently: 'Never, never, never put a trade unionist in prison for going on strike' and 'Never go for the person; go for the funds.'

At first, the prices and incomes policy, with its Stage 1 and Stage 2, was reasonably orderly, and the short-term economic growth caused by Barber's expansionary policies anaesthetized the wounds. But many saw that a battle could not be indefinitely delayed. In his private diary on 15 February 1973, the senior and disgruntled Conservative backbencher Airey Neave used a phrase which was soon to acquire public resonance: 'Who governs Britain?' Gradually, the tide of public opinion turned against the Conservatives. In July, a surge of support for the Liberals gave them amazing by-election victories in Ripon and the Isle of Ely. Late in the same month, growing inflation forced Barber into dramatic rises in the Minimum Lending Rate (MLR) which went from 7.75 per cent to 11.5 per cent. In late August, the twenty-year-old Carol Thatcher wrote to her aunt Muriel succinctly summing up her mother's predicament: 'I think Education and the prospect of losing her seat to the Liberals at the next election is driving Mum round the bend ... don't write here* – everything goes to Dept Ed. for metal detecting and bomb checks – bloody Irish.'

Stage 2 of the prices and incomes policy had given workers a pay rise. Stage 3, announced on 6 October, sought to identify – and later address – pay grievances between different groups of workers. But the onset of the Yom Kippur War, just days later, gave new power to the NUM. As global oil prices skyrocketed, the government became ever more reliant on coal. Heath's efforts to placate the miners with the promise of Stage 3 came to naught. An overtime ban, with an immediate effect on output, began on 12 November. The government duly declared another state of emergency. As negotiations wore on, Heath received the entire NUM Executive at No. 10. At this meeting he asked Mick McGahey, the Scottish miners' leader and a Communist, what he wanted. McGahey replied, 'I want to see the end of your government.' The Last Battle approached.

Seeing the strength of support for the government's position in the opinion polls, William Waldegrave, now head of Heath's political office, advised the Prime Minister to exploit the crisis and go for a 'Who governs Britain?' election. Heath, however, was doubtful. He shared the anxiety of senior Tories such as Lord Carrington and Ian Gilmour, who feared letting 'the genie of social revenge out of the bottle'. He also feared, rightly, that an early election would bring down his recently achieved Sunningdale

---

* The Thatcher home in Flood Street, Chelsea. They moved here in 1972 after selling The Mount, although they continued in Lamberhurst at weekends, renting a flat in Scotney Castle.

power-sharing agreement in Northern Ireland. He was not ready to grasp the nettle. Mrs Thatcher recalled going to a party in Lamberhurst shortly before Christmas at which everyone was urging the government to fight: 'Go on, you show 'em this time.' Tory supporters were waiting for a lead.

On 1 January 1974, Airey Neave wrote in his diary, 'The next few weeks may decide the future of the parliamentary system.' On the same day, the government imposed a three-day week to avoid power cuts. Heath continued to dither, putting his hopes in yet another meeting with the TUC. Mrs Thatcher's patience was wearing thin. In Cabinet she agreed to 'one last heave but with miners and not TUC. Can't go on being a puppet government.' The NUM called a strike for 9 February. On 7 February, Heath announced a general election for the 28th. Mrs Thatcher told Cabinet colleagues it 'will be a bitter election but at the same time the most idealistic'.

Although the logic of his electoral decision dictated otherwise, Heath still disliked the idea of a fight about 'Who governs Britain?' He did not want a head-on collision with the miners. He announced, even as he launched his election campaign, that he would refer their claim to the Pay Board and abide by its view, making people ask why an election was needed at all.

For Heath, the campaign was unhappy. New retail price figures showed inflation running at 20 per cent per annum, emblematic of the government's economic failure. At the outset, Enoch Powell had declared that he would not stand again as a Conservative Party candidate because the government had betrayed its manifesto promises. Two weeks later he called on his supporters to vote Labour because of its opposition to membership of the EEC.*

For his part, Harold Wilson, fighting his fourth election as Labour leader, seemed jaded. His party avoided offering any answers to the economic crisis, but this did not matter much. It was Heath who had submitted an unsatisfactory record to the electorate, Heath who was causing all this bother. 'I'm like Baldwin,' Wilson said to Bernard Donoughue, who was to run his Policy Unit after the election, 'I'm here to give people a quiet life.'

Mrs Thatcher, like most of her party, believed that the Conservatives would win. 'There was a feeling that we were being tough,' she later recalled, 'and that that was a good thing.' Although she played no prominent part in the campaign, in Finchley she focused on the dangers from inflation and, more uncompromisingly than Heath, on the problem with the miners: 'The coal industry is nationalized,' she declared. 'You own

---

* In Powell's stronghold of the West Midlands, enough of his followers duly did so. Given that the margin of defeat proved so small, it could fairly be said that it was Powell who turned Heath out.

it ... This election is a ballot of all the owners of the industry.' In her only national broadcast of the campaign, a BBC *Election Call* programme, Mrs Thatcher dismissed the idea of a nation-saving coalition of all the talents: 'I think it's a false assumption that if you get a government of all the best brains, the best brains will agree what to do.' And in her only full press interview she presented herself as doughty: 'I get *very* wild with people who don't realise that underneath all this' – she taps a gold suit button – 'there's a bit of tough steel that's me.'

By mid-morning on polling day, Mrs Thatcher was worried. She didn't like the way so many people on normally apathetic non-Tory council estates in Finchley were turning up to vote. Her fears were justified. Her own majority was almost halved.

Mrs Margaret Thatcher (Conservative)	18,180
Martin O'Connor (Labour)	12,202
Laurence Brass (Liberal)	11,221
Conservative majority	5,978

The national result gave the Conservatives a larger share of the vote than Labour, but four fewer seats. The Liberals, with an astonishing 6 million votes (almost 20 per cent of the whole), pulled the Tories down, although their gain of seats was tiny. Labour won 301 seats, the Conservatives 297, the Liberals 14. No party had an overall majority in the Commons.

Heath tried to cling to power. As convention dictated, the Queen allowed him to try to form a new government. After overtures to the Ulster Unionists came to nothing, Heath and those closest to him, such as Carrington and Prior (Whitelaw being ill), favoured an anti-socialist coalition with the Liberals. This appalled Mrs Thatcher. At Cabinet, on 1 March, for the first time in three and a half years, she let rip. She protested at any accommodation with the Liberals: 'But 5 m. Lib. votes are non-Liberal. They are ours, and if we coalesce we lose them for ever. And don't sell constitution for a mess of pottage.' Recorded by the Cabinet Secretary Sir John Hunt as one voice speaking together, she and Keith Joseph said: 'We must keep our integrity.' 'What wd effect on parly party be of dabbling with electoral reform?' asked Mrs Thatcher. 'We must accept consequences of election and offer patriotic opposition to Labour,' said Joseph. The Cabinet disagreed and Heath courted Jeremy Thorpe, the Liberal leader, but without success.* On 4 March, Heath resigned and the Queen asked Harold Wilson to form his third Labour administration.

---

* It is a reflection on the more gentlemanly mores of the time that throughout the campaign of February 1974 the Conservatives were in possession of information about the homosexual

Unusually for a Secretary of State for Education, the department gave a farewell party for Mrs Thatcher: they had grown quite fond of her by the end. In a newspaper interview she declared breezily: 'It is easier for a woman than a man to give up power because you are not so lost. I can fill the time by spring-cleaning the house.' But her later memory of her reaction was almost the opposite: 'I can't tell you how lost I felt.'

Tory disappointment was deep. Heath, Airey Neave recorded, 'is much deflated. He was also, one remembers, a bad Leader of the Opposition.' The plotting against him was pretty well instantaneous. On 13 March, Neave joined a dinner attended by Whitelaw, who, he noted, was 'drinking a fair amount of whisky'. 'Willie wants Ted Heath's job but would not be my choice, though I thought so a few weeks ago.' Other names thrown up in conversation among leading Tories included Robert Carr, Mrs Thatcher, Du Cann and Geoffrey Howe. None of these excited enthusiasm, but the basic problem remained. 'His [Heath's] leadership is bad and he and his Cabinet have been wrong about everything for the last 3½ months,' Neave wrote a day later. On 18 March he added: 'the knives are really out for Heath'.

By late May, the unhappiness neared breaking point. The 1922 Executive, to which Neave and other rebels had now been elected, seriously discussed a coordinated revolt. Heath was able to maintain his position, however, partly because of the disunity of his opponents, but more because, with Labour lacking an overall majority, an election seemed imminent. With no appetite for an intra-party fight in such circumstances, the 1922 Executive 'decided to keep the leadership question "on ice"'.

Heath might have maintained his position better if he had incorporated critical voices into his new Shadow Cabinet. His instinct, though, was to surround himself with those closest to him. He made the crucial decision to deny Keith Joseph his ambition to become Shadow Chancellor, handing the post instead to the loyal but unexciting Robert Carr. To prevent Joseph leaving the Shadow Cabinet and so causing public division, Heath granted him a position without portfolio, with an emphasis on economic questions, allowing him to range over the whole field of ideas. This was dangerous. He also permitted Joseph to set up his own think tank. This was fatal. The declared purpose of the think tank was to study the workings of the market economy, particularly abroad. Thus the Centre for Policy

---

scandal involving Jeremy Thorpe which was later to bring him down. Lord Carrington, the Party Chairman, ordered that it be locked away and not used. It is hard to imagine such a policy being followed today.

Studies (CPS) was born. Putting in Adam Ridley, the Deputy Director of the Conservative Research Department, as his spy on the board, Heath thought all was well. He was wrong. The CPS gave Joseph the platform and back-up he needed to launch a full intellectual critique of the Heath years. In May, Mrs Thatcher, the only potential rebel whom Heath had promoted (to Shadow Environment Secretary), joined the CPS as Joseph's Vice-Chairman.

It was largely through Joseph and the CPS that Mrs Thatcher's interest in the power of conservative ideas rekindled. For the first time, she began to question the basis of her party's policies. As she did so, she began to think more boldly. She never possessed the intellectual's spirit of free inquiry, impracticality or love of paradox. Instead she was motivated by moral earnestness and her desire to achieve certain right results. But ideas and the men – almost all of them were men – who purveyed them excited her. Now she plunged into Keynes (whose *Economic Consequences of the Peace* she admired much more than the demand-management theories of the Keynesians which she so often attacked), Milton Friedman, Frédéric Bastiat, the mid-nineteenth-century French free-trader, Arthur Koestler and much more. The Institute of Economic Affairs (IEA), presided over by Ralph Harris and Arthur Seldon, provided an intellectual forum for the development of free-market ideas, then outside the mainstream of political discourse. Mrs Thatcher devoured its pamphlets.*

The CPS gave Mrs Thatcher the context, sense of direction and camaraderie she sought. She helped it set up shop in Wilfred Street, even assisting with wiring up the electric plugs. Simon Webley, one of the CPS's moving spirits, remembered her holding up the wires and exclaiming, 'The brown one is supposed to be the live one. That is absolutely ridiculous. Brown is for earth.' For her the CPS was the chance to 'get back to the north star', to find the words for what she knew she believed but which the Heath years had suppressed.

For new ideas, Mrs Thatcher relied on Joseph and Alfred Sherman. Throughout her career she maintained deep admiration and affection for Joseph. His gentlemanly public-spiritedness, his sometimes tortured courtesy, his Jewishness, his enthusiasm for policy all endeared him to her. So did the fact that, from her earliest days in Parliament, Joseph had encouraged her rise. In Heath's Cabinet the two had been drawn closer by a growing, not fully articulated unease. After the defeat of February 1974 their feelings burst out, like a forbidden love at last permitted to express itself.

---

* She also enjoyed the writings of liberal economists such as Graham Hutton, Brian Griffiths and Douglas Hague.

Sherman was a very different character. An ex-Communist and former machine-gunner for the anti-Franco Republicans in the Spanish Civil War, he maintained a Marxist rigour of thought after his conversion to the right, and a Leninist capacity to identify virtually everyone else as the enemy. He took pride in 'thinking the unthinkable'. Having persuaded Joseph of the virtue of market solutions at the time of the Selsdon conference (see p. 92), by February 1974 he had found in Joseph a repentant sinner desperate to atone. He told him how to do so. 'Alfred Sherman was a genius,' Mrs Thatcher remembered. She linked his Jewishness with that of Joseph as part of their combined virtue and declared: 'We owe them so much.'

Over the summer and autumn of 1974, Joseph used a series of speeches to diverge significantly from Heath's economic approach. At Preston on 5 September 1974 he gave the fullest airing yet to the theory of monetarism and its application to the political crisis. Worried about what Joseph might say, Heath asked Mrs Thatcher and Geoffrey Howe to inspect the text and prevent trouble. They made no decisive alterations.

'Inflation is threatening to destroy our society,' Joseph began, warning of 'the processes of despair and disintegration which ultimately invite dictatorship'. Inflation, he argued, was caused by excessive increases in the supply of money, something which governments had the means to control. 'Monetarism', he said, was not the answer to everything, but rather 'a pre-essential for everything else we need and want to do'. The most devastating and, for Heath, embarrassing part of the speech was Joseph's admission of collective and repeated error by Conservative as well as Labour governments in ignoring this pre-essential. Governments had believed that a bit of inflation would help unemployment, economic growth and the funding of the social services, but it had turned out to be a 'mortal threat to all three'. The 'menacing tensions' created by inflation 'cannot be cured by incomes policy', Joseph insisted, but by government bearing down upon the excessive supply of money.

Joseph flagellated himself harder than anyone else, but his argument undermined the economic basis on which Heath had governed the country, had lost the previous election, and was about to fight the next. Its effect was to raise the standard of revolt for a battle which could be fought only after the next general election.*

In the Shadow Cabinet, Margaret Thatcher, along with the much more low-key Geoffrey Howe, were the only two who supported Joseph's

---

* Ever the practical politician as well as the true believer, Mrs Thatcher, though she agreed with every word of Joseph's Preston speech, said a few months afterwards that it had been a straightforward minus for the party in the October election.

rethink. But she trod cautiously, saying things like 'I think we should give careful attention to what Keith is saying' rather than arguing for a complete break with the past. Partly because an election seemed imminent, Mrs Thatcher made few public expressions of dissent. Yet she was increasingly singled out as a rising star. A newspaper interview in June 1974 described her as 'currently the person whose name is rustling along the corridors of power as someone who could supplant Ted Heath as Tory Party leader'; but she was careful not to promote herself excessively, and even in private gave no indication of wanting Heath's job.

In giving Mrs Thatcher the subject of the environment, which included housing and local taxation, Heath put her at the centre of his strategy for the coming election, although he still excluded her from his inner circle. As Alison Ward, her secretary, remembered it, 'Ted piled more and more on her because he resented her, but she did better and better.' Heath had come to believe that he had lost the February election because his government had not given the middle classes enough of what they wanted. He now intended to win them back with a fairly shameless electoral pitch, centred on housing and local property taxes ('the rates').

In one sense, Mrs Thatcher was happy to oblige. Housing was one of her interests, and she identified absolutely with the bourgeois aspiration to own one's own home. In another, she was chary of what Heath wanted. She was happy to put forward certain reforms, such as a lump sum for first-time buyers to match their own savings, but fought shy of bolder measures. In particular, she worried that a commitment to hold mortgages to a particular rate would prove irresponsibly expensive.

Similarly, on council rates Mrs Thatcher was cautious. She spoke publicly of interim rate relief, a central government power to cap local council spending and an investigation of the possibility of local income tax, but went no further. None of this satisfied Heath. On 1 August he summoned her back from holiday in Lamberhurst and prevailed on her to accept that a mortgage rate 'below 10 per cent' could be promised. At the end of the month he pushed her into a specific promise of 9.5 per cent. Heath also pressed her to promise the abolition of domestic rates in the next Parliament. This she reluctantly did, though no one knew what the replacement would be.

It is typical of Mrs Thatcher's political professionalism that, despite her resentment at being strong-armed, she made the most of the policies she had not wanted. She announced these eye-catching initiatives at a press conference on 28 August, which was followed that evening by a party political broadcast. With a voice-over that said, 'For the first time someone has gone back to basics,' Mrs Thatcher repeated her promise to cut the mortgage rate to 9.5 per cent and attacked domestic rates because they 'often have nothing to do with what you can afford to pay or with the services you receive'. Whatever new system the Tories brought in would be 'based on what you can afford'. Her performance made a strong impression. On 8 September, the Conservative manifesto for the expected general election leaked. This revealed that Mrs Thatcher had made one more policy concession. She had consented to offer a 'right to buy' to all council house tenants, with a discount equal to a third of the market price. The Tories would 'place a duty on every council to sell homes on these terms'.

On 18 September 1974, Harold Wilson called a general election for 10 October. Partly because the Conservatives were anxious to preserve a studied vagueness and moderation in their economic approach, Mrs Thatcher's specific policy promises were almost the only important ones of the campaign. She fought it with gusto and without embarrassment, strongly promoting the middle-class interests which Heath regretted having neglected when in office. It was the first campaign in which party strategists made her nationally prominent. She profited from this, proving herself combative, persuasive and much better than people had expected on television. As election day approached, Mrs Thatcher was one of those chosen to present the culminating party political broadcast. Her pledges, she said, were 'firm, unshakeable, categorical'. She delivered such lines well, and they rattled the Labour Party. Bernard Donoughue recorded in his diary: 'The only new issue is Thatcher's 9½ percent mortgage commitment, and everybody is frightened of that.'

But there was another reason why Mrs Thatcher's were almost the only concrete Conservative promises of the campaign. Heath had decided to push the notion of 'national unity', which implied coalition. He therefore wanted as few policies as possible which would quarrel with this aim. Such talk greatly annoyed Mrs Thatcher. As in the aftermath of the February election, she was intensely suspicious of any deal with the Liberals. She believed that the answer to the national crisis was not the forging of a national consensus round the old, wrong policies but a bold leap for new, right ones. On the BBC's *Any Questions?* in the last week of the campaign, she maintained the party line that a government of national unity might be a good thing, but went out of her way to say that she 'could never sit in the same government with Michael Foot or Anthony Wedgwood Benn, because they believe in nationalizing the lot'.

The day before her BBC appearance Heath had told her he wanted to push for a 'government of national unity' and asked her to be ready to drop her housing and rates pledges on air. Having been marched up to the top of the hill on these subjects by Heath himself, Mrs Thatcher was not going to be marched down again. 'I was absolutely fed up,' she remembered. 'I wasn't going to say: "I'm going to become half-socialist."' So on *Any Questions?* she stuck to her guns.

There was a fundamental problem with the 'government of national unity' idea. Who was going to lead it? Heath naturally thought that he would, but polls showed that the public regarded him, more than any other leading politician, as divisive. The Tory campaign therefore ended in incoherence. Wilson was able to present the 'national unity' idea as a 'Con trick'. The Labour Party increased its majority to forty-two over the Conservatives, though its overall majority in the Commons was only three. In Finchley, Mrs Thatcher's majority fell by 2,000:

Mrs Margaret Thatcher (Conservative)	16,498
Martin O'Connor (Labour)	12,587
Laurence Brass (Liberal)	7,384
Mrs Janet Godfrey (National Front)	993
Conservative majority	3,911

'I was now in no doubt', Mrs Thatcher recalled, 'that Ted should go.'

Even before the October defeat, plans for Heath's departure had been inconclusively debated across the party. On 7 August 1974, Sara Morrison, Heath's only close female adviser and as loyal to him as anyone, had spoken privately to Airey Neave: 'She agreed that E. Heath has to go if we lose. She favours Ian Gilmour but accepts W. Whitelaw interim. She rules out Margaret. Robert Carr can't decide "whether he wants a boiled or a fried egg". Keith Joseph is played out.' On the day of the result, Morrison tried to get Heath to resign. So did Lord Carrington and Jim Prior. None succeeded. The problem, as Carrington succinctly put it, was 'Ted'. Heath continued to believe that he alone was fit to be national leader when, as he expected, the economic crisis demanded a coalition government. He clung on, and his unhappy close supporters stayed loyal, but the Tory Party began to move against him.

On Monday 14 October the Executive of the 1922 Committee met. As Neave recorded it, 'All thought Heath should go, but varied when.' After Du Cann reported this sentiment to Heath, his camp counter-attacked. The Chief Whip, Humphrey Atkins, told the left-wing but anti-Heath MP Nigel Fisher that the Executive of the '22 would be rejected *en bloc* in the coming elections to be held on 7 November. Heath now refused to meet the Executive until after these elections. For Neave, a period of anxiety and gloom ensued. On the train to Brighton he noted his disgust at 'the vulgar, sleek, first-class passengers. I wonder if they realised that the country is on the verge of revolution.'*

When the full 1922 Committee met on 31 October, Edward du Cann was cheered and only two speakers supported Heath: nineteen opposed him. One backbencher, Kenneth Lewis, struck home with his deadly phrase that the leadership was 'a leasehold, not a freehold'. 'Anyone but he [Heath] would resign after this meeting,' wrote Neave. Heath still refused. On 7 November the entire anti-Heath 1922 Executive was re-elected, despite the whips. Emboldened, its members drafted a letter to Heath calling for an early contest. Part of the difficulty was that the 1965 rules for the election of the leader made no provision for a challenge to an incumbent. Under pressure, Heath agreed to a review of the electoral system, overseen by Lord Home, the leader whom Heath, though not by direct challenge, had displaced.

It was now expected that there would be a leadership election in February 1975. Much less certain, though, was who, apart from Heath, would be a candidate. Neave cast rather desperately around for an alternative. In the course of 1974, his diary shows he looked with favour often on Du Cann, quite often on Margaret Thatcher, sometimes on Whitelaw, sometimes on Joseph, occasionally on Gilmour. Like most Conservative MPs, he was following no strong ideological line. He was simply searching for a credible replacement for Heath.

If Mrs Thatcher's own account is to be believed, she had no thought, in the wake of the October election, of challenging for the party leadership herself, but gave her wholehearted backing to Keith Joseph. While this loyalty was real, she is over-innocent about her attitude. During 1974, growing numbers had begun to notice her abilities. Some had told her so. One omen, auspicious at a time when the Morrison family was credited with preternatural powers of understanding the Tory psyche, was a visit paid her by Peter Morrison, at that time a new MP, in August 1974. He passed on and endorsed the view of his father, Lord Margadale, who had chaired the 1922 Committee in the 1950s and 1960s: 'Mark my words, Mrs Thatcher is going to be the next Leader of the Conservative party.'†

---

* The sense of Britain on the verge of collapse was widespread. Bernard Donoughue spent August in France. On his return he wrote in his diary: 'From abroad I could see England a little clearer. It looked in a terrible mess. Falling apart socially as well as economically. Seems very frail compared to France, which is becoming a giant again.'

† Margadale had stated this view to a large lunch at his Scottish house on the island of Islay as early as 1972: 'Mrs Thatcher is going to be the next leader of the Conservative Party and so

The press began to take notice. Everyone agreed that Mrs Thatcher had had a good campaign in October 1974. On polling day, the *Sun* singled her out as the only Tory to have done so. She began to test the water. On 20 October, in an artful interview in the *Sunday Express*, she insisted that 'my only wish is to further the Conservative Party and the philosophy upon which it is founded'.* She phrased her sympathy for Heath in a way that contrasted him unfavourably with herself: 'All this is so wretched for him ... And unlike me he hasn't a family around him from whom to draw strength.'† She then answered, quite specifically, whether she would stand: 'If that time comes and people thought I was that woman, I would accept the challenge and do the job – as I have tried to do everything in my life – to the utmost of my ability.' These were not the remarks of a person who had not given the leadership a moment's thought.

In private, Mrs Thatcher was explicit on the point. On 15 October Fred Silvester, a disillusioned Heathite MP, wrote to encourage her to stand for the leadership. In her reply, she was frank: 'If the contest were to come immediately, I wouldn't stand a chance. If later, I may ... At present the country contains too much prejudice to accept a woman but with the sort of discussion that is now taking place through the media, it may change.'

Nevertheless, Mrs Thatcher's working assumption remained that Joseph would challenge Heath and that she would back him. But then, on 19 October, came Joseph's speech in Edgbaston. The problem, in an otherwise thoughtful address, came when Joseph highlighted demographic trends that he found dismaying. 'A high and rising proportion of children are being born to mothers least fitted to bring children into the world,' he declared. '... Some are of low intelligence, most of low educational attainment ... They are producing problem children ...' Joseph appeared to argue that such young women should be much more vigorously encouraged to use contraceptives.

For reasons unknown, Joseph had not followed his usual practice of running drafts past Mrs Thatcher and other colleagues. The first that Mrs Thatcher knew of the speech was when she picked up the *Evening Standard* at Waterloo station. 'SIR KEITH IN "STOP BABIES" SENSATION'

---

she should be.' When he made the remark all those present considered it 'very extraordinary'.
* References to Tory 'philosophy' were coded attacks on Heath, because he was thought to have abandoned it.
† It is possible that Mrs Thatcher was also ambitious enough to be dropping a hint, at a time when such things were considered a source of shame, that Heath was homosexual. Many believed that he was. W. F. Deedes noted a private conversation with Mrs Thatcher in 1976: 'M. seems convinced TH is a homosexual. (Women have more accurate instincts than we.) I said charitably: "an instinct sublimated in boats!".'

said the headline. She knew at once that this was trouble. Joseph might, perhaps, have survived the original mauling if he had been ready to rebut the attacks but, characteristically, he instead began to apologize. As Joseph faded, more looked to Mrs Thatcher. In an interview on 3 November, she acknowledged that she was receiving many letters from the public urging her to stand. Joseph himself appears to have understood the way things were going. Shortly after the Edgbaston speech he told Cecil Parkinson: 'I think Margaret could become the standard-bearer.'

As uncertainty over the leadership persisted, Heath announced changes to his Shadow Cabinet. The press had spoken of Mrs Thatcher as a possible Shadow Chancellor, but he offered her the almost humiliating post of number-two Treasury spokesman (though with a Shadow Cabinet seat) under Robert Carr. Rather than grumbling, however, she set to work with a will. On 12 November, the Chancellor, Denis Healey, introduced a full-scale Budget which invented Capital Transfer Tax and imposed a new tax on North Sea oil. In the Commons, two days later she teased Healey for allowing public-sector borrowing to rise by £6 billion since his last Budget in March. By tackling this only now, he was opting for sacrifice by instalments when the people would have accepted the full thing there and then: 'The people were ready. The Chancellor was not. He and they will regret it.' Airey Neave judged it a 'brilliant speech': Mrs Thatcher had been 'amusing and increased her reputation'. As more urged her to stand, she demurred. 'The party isn't ready for a woman,' she told Fergus Montgomery, her PPS, 'and the press would crucify me.'

On 21 November, Keith Joseph visited Mrs Thatcher at his request. As she recalled in her memoirs, Joseph said, 'I am sorry, I just can't run. Ever since I made that speech the press have been outside the house. They have been merciless. Helen [his wife] can't take it and I have decided that I just can't stand.' 'His mind was quite made up,' Mrs Thatcher went on. 'I was on the edge of despair. We just could not abandon the Party and the country to Ted's brand of politics. I heard myself saying: "Look, Keith, if you're not going to stand, I will, because someone who represents our viewpoint *has* to stand."' Joseph promised his support. Remembering the occasion, Mrs Thatcher used to say that she had been 'really rather shocked ... he [Joseph] really was the leader'.*

It may be doubted, however, whether Mrs Thatcher was either surprised or upset. What she 'heard myself saying' was what she had been ready to say before the meeting began. She had, the day before, informed Humphrey

---

* Characteristically, Mrs Thatcher shifted blame for Joseph's failure to grasp his opportunity on to his wife: 'I *was* surprised. I thought Helen would be 100 per cent behind him.'

Atkins of Joseph's decision not to stand and of her decision that she should, indeed must.* She knew she was better suited for the task than Joseph. By the time they met, her mind was made up. She genuinely loved and admired Joseph, but she understood his character quite well enough to know he was no leader. Although she said it was 'a tragedy that he never became prime minister', she added, in the same breath, that he 'would have agonized over every decision'. When the working hypothesis of a Joseph candidacy collapsed, there was more relief than dismay.

In Mrs Thatcher's account, she went home to Flood Street that night and told Denis of her decision. 'You must be out of your mind,' he said. 'You haven't got a hope.' His own version is more coloured, but to the same effect: 'I did suck my teeth a bit. "Heath will murder you," I told her.'

It did not follow from her brave decision to stand that Mrs Thatcher's way now lay clear. Many regarded her candidacy as nothing more than a chance to prepare the ground for a challenge by someone more serious, or for malcontents to let off steam. Visiting the Conservative Research Department, R. A. Butler said to Chris Patten, the Director: 'We don't need to take this Thatcher business seriously, do we?' The *Economist*, jaunty in its erroneous confidence, described her as 'precisely the sort of candidate who ought to be able to stand, and lose, harmlessly'. Plenty of Tory MPs looked on the contest with ribaldry. At the 1922 Committee on 28 November, one said that it was a two-horse race:

> A Member: You mean one filly.
> Another Member: And a gelding.

Mrs Thatcher was extremely worried by the exile she feared would follow if she failed, and by the reaction of Heath himself. When Peter Morrison offered his support, before she had announced her candidacy, she said, 'You must understand, I have no chance.'

Events moved quite fast. On 24 November she was interviewed for the *Daily Mail*. Explaining her decision to stand, she said: 'The party has got to be given a choice.' The *Mail* presented her as 'Thoroughly Modern Maggie', the 'candidate of change', and praised her 'guts and honesty'. On the next day she called on her leader in his room in the Commons. The meeting was short. Mrs Thatcher remembered Heath saying, 'You'll lose,' to which she

---

* According to Fred Silvester, who had just been appointed a junior whip, Mrs Thatcher told him on the evening of 17 November that she had just informed the Chief Whip of her intention to stand.

added, 'That remark gave a certain zest to my competitive spirit.' In his own memoirs Heath says, 'I thanked her.' The atmosphere was not warm.

On the day of this interview, Airey Neave had spent a good deal of time on the telephone to Edward du Cann, 'who has still not decided whether to stand'. He was becoming irritated by Du Cann's hesitation, and worries about his chiaroscuro business career were growing.* At the same time, Neave noted cautiously, 'it is going to be fairly hard to "sell" Margaret Thatcher'. Such efforts were not made any easier when, four days later, she suffered the first dirty-tricks story of the campaign.

On 28 November, the newspapers were full of an interview she had given before the general election and before she was a candidate for the leadership (a fact the reports did not make clear) to an obscure magazine called *Pre-Retirement Choice*. In discussing preparations for retirement (Denis was approaching sixty), Mrs Thatcher had spoken about the effects of inflation on housekeeping. 'I, for the first time in my life,' she said, 'have started steadily buying things like tinned food.' Following her mother's wartime example, she went on, she was collecting 'the expensive proteins: ham, tongue, salmon, mackerel, sardines. They will last for years.' She noted that honey, 30 pence the previous year, now cost 40 pence: 'It's interesting to mark the prices on the jars as you buy it and you can see how the prices go up.'

After Heath's team eagerly drew this to the media's attention, Mrs Thatcher was accused of the unpatriotic vice of 'hoarding' (a term still resonant from wartime). The attacks came thick and fast. For a short time it looked as though her whole campaign could be blown off course.

All this upset her. It brought back memories of her ordeal over school milk and emphasized once again how women politicians were attacked more personally than male ones. It showed her what she later called 'the blackness of the official Tory Party'. She quickly rallied, however, saying, 'They [the press] are never going to do to me what they've just done to Keith.' To fight back, she invited the press in to look at her larder in Flood Street. The *Daily Express* printed a full inventory:

Eight pounds of granulated sugar,
One pound of icing sugar ('for Christmas'),

---

* On 26 November, Neave recorded: 'Cecil Parkinson told me that the Whips had heard via J. Selwyn Gummer that Shirley Williams (of all people) had said the Labour Party had a "dossier" on Edward du Cann and his City connections. They hoped he was going to stand so they could make use of it.' The Heath camp also hoped that Du Cann would be a challenger, Neave noted the next day, because they 'all knew that he had such a dubious financial record as to make him an easy target'.

Six jars of jam,
Six jars of marmalade,
Six jars of honey,
Six tins of salmon ('to make salmon mousse'),
Four 1lb cans of corned beef,
Four 1lb cans of ham,
Two 1lb cans of tongue,
One tin of mackerel,
Four tins of sardines,
Two 1lb jars of Bovril,
Twenty tins of various fruits,
'One or two' tins of vegetables, 'but we don't really like them from a tin'.

This domestic setting gave Mrs Thatcher the chance to show the public how much she differed from the old Tory establishment. Neave felt reassured: 'Many housewives think she is taking a sensible precaution.' When Denis Healey shouted a jibe about hoarding at her across the floor of the House, Mrs Thatcher responded in kind, referring to his several comfortable properties: 'I am not as successful as the Chancellor at hoarding houses.' Her 'housewife' economics had been used against her, but she had turned the attack to her advantage.

In mid-December, Home's review suggested significant changes to the leadership contest rules, in effect lowering the barrier for a challenge to Heath.* This was 'Alec's revenge'. The committee's recommendations could not be voted on and implemented until the new year, so the exact date of the contest remained uncertain. Equally uncertain were the identities of the likely challengers. Du Cann's indecision continued into January 1975. In the uncomfortable position of having promised to back both candidates, Neave flitted between the two, trying desperately to ascertain Du Cann's intentions.

'Not too happy about E. Du Cann,' he wrote on Christmas Day, 'since his bank, Keyser Ullmann, is clearly in difficulties. I plan to ring him in a week's time to discover whether he has decided to stand. If not, we must back Margaret.' A meeting between the two potential challengers in the

---

* There were two main changes: both, as it turned out, were to have notable effects on Mrs Thatcher's later career. The first was that it should be possible to challenge a sitting leader once every parliamentary session (in practice, usually once a year). The second was that, to win on the first ballot, the leading candidate needed an absolute majority plus a margin of 15 per cent over his nearest rival of all eligible voters (the 1965 rules had required a margin of 15 per cent only of votes cast).

new year did nothing to resolve the situation. Mrs Thatcher felt that Du Cann remained 'undecided', while Du Cann told Neave that he thought her 'naïve but admired her character'. Du Cann suggested a head count of their respective supporters to clarify matters. Neave put the idea to Mrs Thatcher over lunch at Flood Street on 9 January. 'A very nice house,' he recorded, 'a bit too tidy, and everything wrapped in cellophane. However M looked well, rather fatter and in good form.' Mrs Thatcher agreed to the idea of a head count, but the issue soon became moot. Five days later Du Cann finally decided not to stand. The following evening, Neave agreed to 'chair a new group to support Margaret Thatcher'.

A meeting was held in the Commons to discuss organization, but even at this late stage 'Several "anti-women" voices' were raised. 'Afterwards I spoke to Fergus Montgomery,' noted Neave, 'who has been running Margaret Thatcher's "organisation" (which hardly exists) and arranged with W. Shelton to hold a meeting to discuss "identification" of her supporters on Monday at 9 p.m.' The next day, 16 January, the 1922 Committee approved the Home committee's recommended change of rules.

A further complication entered Neave's calculations: 'Having told me that he would not stand, Hugh Fraser has now changed his mind. He would certainly take votes off Margaret and Heath but what would it avail?' The answer was very little. Fraser, a charming, romantic man, and a long-standing backbench critic of Heath, was not considered a serious candidate and so Neave carried on regardless. On Sunday 19 January he shared the names of Du Cann's supporters with Mrs Thatcher: 'She said I should consult Keith Joseph who would back her. This means that supporters of Joseph, Thatcher and Du Cann are now united.' The following evening, Neave and Shelton met to seal the pact. 'So the balloon has gone up,' wrote Neave. 'The Campaign group is formed of people of all shades of thought in the party.'

Neave had not been exaggerating when he said that Mrs Thatcher's campaign team hardly existed. Before the Neave alliance, her only two known lieutenants had been William Shelton and Fergus Montgomery, neither of whom stood high in parliamentary seniority or reputation. As Montgomery himself put it, 'We were useless.' The third man helping Mrs Thatcher from the start was not in the Commons. He was Gordon Reece, the public relations guru who advised the Conservatives on their party political broadcasts. He had long admired the 'clearness with which she saw things' and after the October 1974 defeat had told her there was a 'unique opportunity for a woman leader'. He now did all he could to seize it. Mrs Thatcher also benefited from the support of Peter Morrison, although, since he had entered the Commons only in February 1974 his sway was limited. With this ragtag bunch Neave set about convincing his parliamentary colleagues to back Mrs Thatcher.

The key constituency was the 'knights of the shires'. These men, the mainly rural, mainly gentry backbone of the Conservative parliamentary party, came mostly from public schools. Many had served in the Second World War. They tended to share a rather regimental, officers' mess attitude to the party and a strong, though vague, patriotism much more powerful than any definite ideology. They considered the habits of politics those of a club. By the autumn of 1974, many of them believed that Heath had let down the regiment, weakened the spirit of the club and offended their patriotism. They felt overlooked and were distressed that his policies had failed to prevent socialism taking a grip of the country they loved. Mrs Thatcher admired the values of this club – she had more or less married into it – but was not herself part of it: 'I was conscious of being a woman and being of a different social background, although they never made me feel it.' It would not have occurred to most of the knights of the shires, unprompted, that a woman could lead the Conservative Party, but when the proposition arose they were surprisingly unworried by it. Some were softened by Mrs Thatcher's sex appeal, and a larger number took to her character. Her parliamentary performance and the manner of her challenge convinced them that she had the quality they admired above everything else – courage.

In the debate on the second reading of the Finance Bill, on 17 December, Mrs Thatcher railed against Denis Healey's inflation and delighted Conservative troops with her attack on his proposals for capital taxes: 'a capital transfer tax does not redistribute wealth, nor does a wealth tax. They concentrate wealth in the hands of the Government, which is the very opposite of distribution.' From 15 January to 11 February 1975, including the days of both leadership ballots, Mrs Thatcher spoke in twelve Finance Bill committee debates, often very late at night, and almost always to good effect. She combined an astonishing mastery of the technical facts with a sure sense of the emotions aroused among voters by tax, inflation and economic mismanagement. On 22 January, she reiterated her attacks on a grander scale. Healey responded by accusing her of 'a defiant reassertion of birth and privilege . . . She emerged in this debate as La Pasionaria* of privilege.' Mrs Thatcher was equal to this: 'I wish I could say that the Chancellor of the Exchequer had done himself less than justice. Unfortunately, I

---

* This was a reference to the eloquent Communist orator and broadcaster in the Spanish Civil War.

can only say that I believe he has done himself justice. Some Chancellors are macro-economic. Other Chancellors are fiscal. This one is just plain cheap.' She emphasized that she was born 'with no privilege at all'. Her combativeness against the able and aggressive Healey won her much admiration.

Airey Neave, whose mindset was similar to that of the men he was trying to win over, knew how to turn this to good electoral effect. As campaign manager, he saw it as his task to keep Mrs Thatcher out of the fray of intrigue. With Shelton as the guardian of what turned out to be highly accurate lists, Neave, who loved skulduggery and backstairs work, sidled up to people in the corridors and the Smoking Room and told broken-down backbenchers that Mrs Thatcher admired them. One trick he used on John Farr, a typical example of the genre, was to say, 'Margaret assumes you must have turned down a job offer from Ted.' Farr: 'Why?' Neave: 'Oh, because you so obviously should have one if you want it.' Neave also cultivated his acquaintance with Humphrey Atkins, the Chief Whip, supposedly neutral in the contest, but actually inclined towards Mrs Thatcher.

The Thatcher campaign was greatly assisted by Heath's pitiful effort at campaigning. The Tory Party, he told Bernard Weatherill, the Deputy Chief Whip, consists of 'shits, bloody shits and fucking shits', and he was not entirely successful at concealing this belief from colleagues whose votes he wanted. Those close to Heath believed that his natural awkwardness was exacerbated by Mrs Thatcher's sex. He was so surprised at being challenged by a woman, and found it so distasteful, that he could not quite work out how to deal with it. 'It's a matter of opinion', he told Sara Morrison, 'whether you think she's a woman or not,' but if Mrs Thatcher had not been he would have found it much easier.

Although the only electorate in the contest was parliamentary, the attitudes of MPs would obviously be affected by public opinion and the media. Gordon Reece attended to this aspect. Since the aim was to pick up the widest range of the disaffected, he wanted a negative campaign in the first stage and 'nothing on policy at all'. Mrs Thatcher needed to look like a winner and 'This was quite a tall order,' he later noted, 'particularly as she was not at this stage good at either communicating with people, or on television.' For two months Mrs Thatcher gave no press or broadcast interviews whatsoever, breaking her silence only a week before the first ballot. Staying away from policy, she spoke to ITN and then Michael Cockerell for the BBC's *Midweek*, which aired footage of her having her hair done.

On the same day, in the *Daily Telegraph*,* Mrs Thatcher offered her

---

* The position of the *Daily Telegraph* at this time reflected that of the Conservative Party. Officially, the paper supported Ted Heath's continuation in office, a line maintained by the

campaign's nearest thing to a manifesto. Under the headline 'My Kind of Tory Party', the piece, drafted chiefly by Angus Maude, began with the premise that the Conservatives had 'failed the people'. There were two lessons of this failure – that inflation was 'the worst enemy' and that the preoccupation with macroeconomics should not 'blind us to the day-to-day problems of ordinary people'. There was nothing wrong with defending what people called 'middle-class values': 'This is not a fight for "privilege"; it is a fight for freedom – freedom for *every* citizen.' She continued her attack on Capital Transfer Tax and said that those who did not respect private property should 'become a socialist and have done with it'. The message was reinforced in a speech to her constituents in Finchley the next day in which she warned that, because her party had failed to defend its ideals 'explicitly and toughly enough' in the past, 'Britain is set on a course towards inevitable Socialist mediocrity'.

Mrs Thatcher put herself more in the front line in the last week because of her team's growing confidence. As early as 21 January 1975, Neave told her that, by their count, she had taken the lead. He released this to the media and, on 23 January, it led the BBC *Today* programme. 'This has caused a sensation,' wrote Neave, 'and sent the establishment into a flat spin.' On Sunday 26 January, Neave spoke to George Clark of *The Times*: 'I said Margaret was in a "strong position" on the first ballot ... She has 112 pledges and Heath less than 80 but this must be too optimistic. It is essential to give out no figures.'*

As the campaign entered its closing phase, the 'establishment' which

---

proprietor, Lord Hartwell, and strongly pushed by his wife, Pamela. But the majority of the staff who concerned themselves with these matters – the Deputy Editor Colin Welch and leader writers such as T. E. Utley, Frank Johnson and John O'Sullivan, as well as Alfred Sherman, who worked part-time at the paper – were fierce critics of Heath and had led the way in attacking the U-turn when he was in office. W. F. Deedes, who left Parliament at the October 1974 election, was made Editor immediately after it, but not with immediate effect. The day before his appointment was announced Deedes dined with Heath, who enlisted him in his plan to try to cling on. In a private memo he sent to his predecessor, Maurice Green, the next day, Deedes set out Heath's reasoning, and his own view that 'Labour would be swift to exploit the appearance of Heath being Shanghai'd by an ungrateful party ... Therefore he owes it to his own party ... to take his time.' Deedes took up his position as Editor at the beginning of 1975, shortly before the contest was held. He saw it as the paper's role to hold the ring in the Tory Party. The *Daily Telegraph* therefore endorsed Heath, but, pre-Deedes, it had prepared the intellectual ground for Mrs Thatcher.

* According to Bernard Donoughue, at this time Joe Haines, Harold Wilson's press secretary, suggested providing Mrs Thatcher with a police escort – 'to help her subtly in the leadership contest with Heath because Joe said he wanted Heath beaten: "He is still the most dangerous." HW [Harold Wilson] agreed at first and then wavered – he said he feared Thatcher as well, especially as a woman.'

Mrs Thatcher had decided to take on pulled out all the stops. Lord Home announced his support for Heath. The constituency chairmen, generally more supportive of the central power than the rank and file beneath them, declared heavily for Heath too. Even the battered rank and file, according to a poll in the *Daily Express* published on 3 February, backed Heath: 70 per cent of Conservative voters said they preferred him to any rival. His campaign managers put it about that Ted was winning, hoping that this momentum would frighten off opposition. At this, Neave altered his tactics. He understood that many inclining to Mrs Thatcher did so not because they wanted her to be leader, but because they sought a second ballot in which other candidates could stand. Neave wanted to encourage such voters. On 1 February, *The Times* endorsed Whitelaw, even though he was not yet a candidate. Neave promptly put it about, though his numbers told him otherwise, that 'Margaret is doing well, but not quite well enough.'*
The tactic worked. Faced with the prospect of yet more Heath, several men with no time for Mrs Thatcher voted for her. Amid such machinations, the challenger herself remained calm, almost detached. Following Neave's advice, she got on with the Finance Bill. Those close to her at that time were impressed. Joan Hall, who helped with her campaign, thought that Mrs Thatcher understood she was riding a tide: 'She was above all ordinary mortals,' waiting quietly for whatever fate held in store.

The first ballot took place on 4 February. Shelton's final canvass had suggested 124 votes for Mrs Thatcher and 122 for Heath. In fact, this underestimated his candidate's support. Among votes cast on the spot the two leading candidates were neck and neck, but the postal votes pulled Mrs Thatcher ahead: she got 130 votes, Heath 119, Fraser 16.†

It has often been reported that when Ted Heath heard the news of his defeat he said, 'We got it all wrong,' implying a mismanaged campaign. William Waldegrave, who was present, remembered it differently. Heath said, 'So it's all gone wrong then,' by which he meant that something had fundamentally changed, and that the politics which Heath stood for had lost. 'He thought he'd lost the Apostolic Succession.'

---

* On the night before the ballot, Neave privately briefed the *Evening Standard* that Heath's figures were higher than he really thought they were. The paper's first edition duly ran with the story. Bill Shelton was instructed to buy extra copies for the Commons Smoking and Tea Rooms for the supporters of alternative successors to Heath, such as Whitelaw or Prior, to peruse.
† There were six abstentions and five spoilt ballot papers. Canvass records suggest, though he has never confirmed this, that one of these abstentions was Michael Heseltine. Another was certainly Jim Prior, a Heath supporter, whose train arrived too late for him to vote.

The Thatcher camp, which had retained discipline throughout, now suffered a lapse of taste. On the night of the result, Neave gave a party with champagne in his flat, and the television cameras were allowed in – a mistake since there was, as yet, no final winner. It looked as though they were rubbing Heath's nose in his defeat. Denis was filmed grinning toothily and making one of his very few public utterances. Asked for his reaction, he said, 'Delighted! Terribly proud, naturally. Wouldn't you be?' Due to the astonishing demands of her parliamentary timetable, Mrs Thatcher then returned, after dinner with the Neaves, to the Commons for further debate of the committee stage of the Finance Bill. She was not able to go home until 2.30 in the morning.

Under the rules, Mrs Thatcher had not won outright. There would be a second ballot, and perhaps a third. Heath at last faced the inevitable and resigned. With hindsight, it is easy to see that Mrs Thatcher's victory on the second ballot was now almost assured. She had the momentum, the press excitement and the prestige which came from having had the courage to challenge. But that was not how she saw things at the time. It seemed perfectly possible that the party, having screwed itself up to get rid of Heath, would turn ungratefully upon its chosen assassin.* Many agreed with Reggie Maudling, who bumped into Kenneth Baker in the hours after the result of the first ballot and told him: 'This is the darkest day in the history of the Tory Party: they've all gone absolutely mad.' Willie Whitelaw declared his candidacy on the night of Heath's defeat and Mrs Thatcher always maintained in later years that she thought he would beat her.† John Peyton, Jim Prior and Geoffrey Howe also entered the fray. Only Howe perturbed her. She had told Neave that Howe would be almost the only member of the Shadow Cabinet apart from Joseph to support her. In fact, he had voted for Heath. 'I didn't have the wit to realize it at the time,' Mrs Thatcher remembered, 'but he had far more naked ambition than I'd thought.'

Whitelaw quickly couched his appeal as one of unity and moderation. Mrs Thatcher's campaign therefore moved towards the centre, denying she was a monetarist or necessarily opposed to incomes policy. She spoke up,

---

* Heath himself may have hoped for this effect: at a Buckingham Palace reception he told the Editor of the *Economist*, Andrew Knight: 'Gangsters! She's a gangster. They're all gangsters!'
† Whitelaw immediately picked up the support of the third candidate, Hugh Fraser. His wife, Lady Antonia, recorded in her diary of 4 February that Hugh would have had twenty more votes 'if people had not been frightened of Ted's publicity and thought they should vote for Margaret to catch him'. On the Chief Whip's instructions, Fraser went off to see the defeated Heath: 'Ted was sitting behind his desk looking very fat. Like a pathetic whale,' said Hugh. 'I wanted to hug him. I did manage to get him in a sort of embrace.'

too, to quash rumours that she was anti-European. To attract centrist votes an approach was made to Prior, hinting that, if he dropped his candidacy, he could become Mrs Thatcher's deputy leader. He turned this down.

The only set-piece public appearance before the second ballot was provided by the Young Conservatives conference in Eastbourne.* Mrs Thatcher and Whitelaw paraded together on the seafront for the cameras, and he offered her a public kiss with the unintentionally hilarious justification to the press that they had done it often before 'and it is perfectly genuine and normal and right to do so'. At a question-and-answer session, Whitelaw's performance was considered lacklustre. Mrs Thatcher, campaigning more obviously, delivered a platform speech: 'I believe we should judge people on merit and not on background. I believe the person who is prepared to work hardest should get the greatest rewards and keep them after tax; that we should back the workers not the shirkers . . .' She received sixty-seven seconds of applause. In the next morning's *Sunday Express* she declared, 'We may not have a Churchill now [subtly hinting that they might soon be getting one] – but the instincts and traditions on which Churchill founded his appeal to the nation to fight and to survive are very far from dead.' 'The party will unite itself,' she said. 'What *I* want to do is to unite the country.' Against all this, Whitelaw's television stunt, in which he was filmed drying the dishes at home in his cardigan, was not powerful.

On Tuesday 11 February 1975, the second ballot took place. The result was 146 votes for Mrs Thatcher, 79 for Whitelaw, 19 apiece for Prior and Howe, 11 for Peyton and two spoilt papers. She had therefore won outright, without needing a third ballot. She sat with Fergus Montgomery in Airey Neave's small room in an attic corridor of the Commons. She remembered Neave opening the door softly and saying, 'so quietly', 'I have to tell you you are the new Leader of the Opposition.'

---

* After a fierce row, Gordon Reece managed to persuade Mrs Thatcher not to go on *Panorama* for a debate with the other four candidates. She had wanted to prove she was not frightened just because she was a woman, but Reece's argument that 'The dragon in shallow water is the sport of shrimps' prevailed.

5
The Iron Lady
'It is a moral struggle'

Meeting the press immediately after her victory, Mrs Thatcher said: 'To me it is like a dream that the next name in the line after Harold Macmillan, Sir Alec Douglas-Home, Edward Heath, is Margaret Thatcher.' The fact that her election did indeed seem like a dream was a large part of her problem.

It is hard to exaggerate the sheer strangeness, as it seemed at the time, of the event. Geoffrey Howe recalled her addressing the 1922 Committee two days after her election: 'She was flanked only by the all-male officers of the Committee. Suddenly she looked very beautiful and very frail as the half-dozen knights of the shires towered over her. It was a moving, almost feudal, occasion. Tears came to my eyes.' The oldest, grandest, in many people's eyes the stuffiest political party in the world had chosen a leader whose combination of class, inexperience and sex would previously have ruled her out. It was not obvious that it had really meant to do so, or that it was confident of its choice. Apart from anything else, the instant change in verbal and visual style produced by a woman leader was bewildering. What was the issue on which she had won, the press asked? 'I like to think it was merit,' she answered. 'Could you expand on that?' they asked. 'No, it doesn't need expansion. You chaps don't like short answers, or direct answers. Men like long, rambly, waffly answers.' On the BBC's *Midweek*, she described her reaction to the news of her victory. With an intense, almost sensual expression she said, 'I almost wept when they told me. I *did* weep.' Would her 'dream' – which, for her establishment opponents, was a nightmare – turn out to be waking reality, or would it vanish in the cold light of normal politics?

Mrs Thatcher's most delicate question was what to do with Ted Heath. In her campaign she had promised to offer him a place in her Shadow Cabinet, but naturally hoped he would refuse. Seeking to appear polite, and to settle the matter without delay, she called on Heath at home the morning after her victory. 'He was like a bird who's broken its wing,' Mrs

Thatcher remembered. She intended to offer him his choice of post in the Shadow Cabinet. In fact, as Tim Kitson, Heath's PPS who was there to make the coffee, recalled: 'Ted made it quite clear that he wouldn't take a job, and therefore she didn't actually offer him one.' The meeting was over so quickly that the coffee had not even arrived. Heath withdrew without ceremony. Thus began his self-exclusion from contact with his successor which became known as 'the incredible sulk', and lasted, with one or two tiny deviations, until his death in 2005.

Willie Whitelaw, the good soldier, accepted the post of deputy leader, although reportedly on the condition that Keith Joseph not be made Shadow Chancellor. Joseph wanted the Shadow Chancellorship or nothing, but Mrs Thatcher convinced him to become her number three, in charge of policy and research. Howe became Shadow Chancellor. The prominent Heathites, Robert Carr and Peter Walker, were removed, but there was no general purge. Jim Prior took on employment and Francis Pym agriculture. Ian Gilmour was promoted to Shadow Home Secretary, and Mrs Thatcher brought back Reggie Maudling, making him Shadow Foreign Secretary. Airey Neave, at his request, was made Shadow Secretary for Northern Ireland. Keen to have the backing of the party's elder statesmen, she kept Lords Hailsham and Carrington in the team, the first without portfolio and the second as Shadow Leader of the Lords, and accepted Willie Whitelaw's suggestion that his cousin, Lord Thorneycroft, become Party Chairman.

Of the twenty-four in Mrs Thatcher's Shadow Cabinet, perhaps four – Neave, Joseph, Angus Maude and Sally Oppenheim – had voted for her in the second ballot and only two of these – Neave and Joseph – had been her leading supporters. In a memo that April, the founder-director of the Centre for Policy Studies, Nigel Vinson, questioned the need for the CPS's continued existence 'now that the Tory Party is in the hands of true believers'. But it wasn't. She did not feel nearly secure enough yet to make sure that it would be.

Nor was her own entourage, at the beginning, a source of strength. The limitations of her PPSs, William Shelton and Fergus Montgomery, were well known.* As Willie Whitelaw wrote to Robert Carr, 'it is now becoming clear that her cohorts have a. little talent and b. have no idea at all about running a party'. Although she would not have phrased it thus, Mrs Thatcher did not really dissent. Within a fortnight of the leadership

---

* An additional concern came with growing private rumours that Montgomery had been involved in the homosexual scandal involving the Soviet spy John Vassall in the early 1960s. His exposure was feared.

election, Neave, titular head of her private office, had recruited Richard Ryder, a journalist on the *Daily Telegraph*, to run the operation day to day. Mrs Thatcher hired Caroline Stephens as her diary secretary and retained Alison Ward as her secretary.

In reshaping all these arrangements, Mrs Thatcher demonstrated the caution that, for all her courage, was an important part of her character. Although she was to acquire a reputation as the scourge of the Tory grandees, she was by nature deferential to social systems. She took pains to observe the proprieties. She was, for example, always worried by matters of dress and protocol. Not long after becoming leader, she was invited to dinner with the Carringtons at their house in Ovington Square. Since the dinner was formal, Mrs Thatcher became filled with anxiety about whether she should wear gloves, and would not rest until her office had telephoned Lady Carrington for guidance. Writing to the Queen for the first time as leader, she got in a tizz about how to end the letter. Caroline Stephens advised her simply to write 'yours sincerely', an error which prompted Sir Martin Charteris, the Queen's private secretary, to tell Caroline ('very sweetly') the proper form, and ask her to convey it to her boss.*

The party grandees were carefully watched by Mrs Thatcher's team for how well they treated her. Lord Carrington did pretty well. Willie Whitelaw 'behaved beautifully to her face though he would make snide comments behind her back'. Christopher Soames, at that time a European Commissioner, was considered 'top of the list of snobs'. The old establishment watched the new leader with a mixture of fascination, admiration, repugnance and bemusement. Even those with benign intentions encountered the problem, compounded by her sex, class and personality, that she found it hard to relax in their company. There was a cultural gulf. Chris Patten, retained as Director of the Conservative Research Department, though himself of what the grandees would have considered humble birth, sided culturally and politically with them. He and his colleagues used to refer to their leader by her starchy Victorian second name, 'Hilda', or sometimes 'Milksnatcher'.

Yet Margaret Thatcher was no little girl lost. She had something that compensated for all these disadvantages: a burning sense of mission. On the day of her election she had declared, 'You don't exist as a party unless you have a clear philosophy and a clear message.' She was confident that she could supply both. The propagation of ideas was one of her greatest strengths. On 20 February 1975 she called for more forthright leadership,

---

* The proper form is (with slight variants) 'I remain, Your Majesty's obedient servant'.

'more emphasis on principle'. On 25 March she enthused the Federation of Conservative Students by telling them that 'This Party of ours has been on the defensive for too long.' 'If we can win the battle of ideas, then the war will already be half won.' Her readiness for this battle sustained her, won support from outside her party and riveted public attention upon her.

Strictly speaking, Mrs Thatcher was ill-equipped for intellectual combat. Despite her brisk efficiency, she did not have an intellectually orderly mind; nor did she have an original one. 'She wasn't a woman of ideas,' said Alfred Sherman, who during this period supplied many of them. 'She was a woman of beliefs, and beliefs are better than ideas.' John Hoskyns, an independent businessman, first met her in August 1976. He was impressed by her belief that 'something simply had to be done'. 'I don't think she had any idea what to do, but she had a patriotic impulse and a sense of shame about what had happened to our country.' He was struck by her combination of 'insecurity, sense of destiny and reckless courage'.

From the first, these qualities constituted a style of leadership and created the space for ideas to come forward, many of which emerged from Keith Joseph and Alfred Sherman via the Centre for Policy Studies. Thus it was with *Notes Towards the Definition of Policy*, a self-lacerating and explosive paper that Joseph placed before the new Shadow Cabinet. It began with an attack on the post-war Conservative embrace of consensus of which he had, he admitted frankly, been a keen supporter. The party had been guilty of 'subordinating the rule of law to the avoidance of conflict'. He advocated an approach to economic policy that recognized 'the threat to the nation which came from economic weakness, the threat of the Soviet Union from without and from Communist subversion within'. 'If we lose independence, we lose all,' said Joseph, and 'already we are being disarmed by inflation.' Both the money supply and public spending must be controlled and price increases must be permitted. He accepted that, in the current climate, denationalization might not be practicable, but argued that a legal framework for trade union activity 'will come one day'. The Tories should get rid of regional subsidies, try to arrest the decline of the family because 'the family ... is the sole reliable transmitter of attitudes and culture', and consider introducing education and health vouchers.*

This startling paper furnished the main elements of what came to be called Thatcherism, both in specific policy and in general psychological terms. Yet Joseph imbued it with a dark and gloomy tone. Mrs Thatcher's natural tone was much more optimistic. She knew how to inspire hope

---

* Joseph also suggested considering decriminalizing drugs (a revolutionary suggestion for a Conservative at that time) and the introduction of a Bill of Rights.

as well as fear. It was one of the qualities which made her a much better natural leader than Joseph.

The Joseph paper caused consternation in the Shadow Cabinet. Lord Hailsham kept a private record of proceedings:

> Reggie [Maudling]: I do NOT agree with ONE little bit.
> Gilmour: Up to 1970 consensus was a *Conservative* consensus, not a Labour one.
> Howe: 1970 manifesto was a *departure* from consensus. It does not differ from the present document. What we failed to do was to explain it and present it properly.
> Margaret: Ian, do you believe in capitalism?
> Ian: That is almost blasphemy. I don't believe in Socialism.
> Keith: The hundred years of relative decline (since the Great Exhibition) is objectively demonstrable . . .
> Pym: Society is moving more left. There must be continuity – which means a broad measure of agreement – The Keith paper is a recipe for disaster.
> Heseltine: On TV we don't look like anyone people know.
> WW [Whitelaw]: The most fatal thing in politics is to try and look different from what we are. People always complain that I look very large on TV. What wd they say if I appeared in a bathing dress?

Hailsham concluded, deadpan, 'There was hardly a dull moment.'

There was, to use Mrs Thatcher's least favourite word, no consensus about the analysis, and therefore no agreement about possible solutions. Part of her difficulty was that the political situation did not present obvious, immediate opportunities. When wages and prices were shooting up (the Retail Price Index [RPI] for June 1975 recorded an annual inflation rate of 26 per cent), it could be made to seem unpatriotic to oppose a policy to keep them down. The language of emergency weighed more heavily with the public than the seemingly abstract ideas of monetary control and free collective bargaining.

The first big political campaign of Mrs Thatcher's leadership, the referendum on continuing Britain's membership of the European Economic Community, also offered her few opportunities. Like most senior Conservatives, Mrs Thatcher supported a 'yes' vote on 5 June. But, not pretending to expertise in the subject, she yielded the ground to Ted Heath.* At the 'yes' campaign launch on 16 April 1975 she sat next to him on the platform:

---

* Although Heath refused her offer to lead the Conservative contribution to the 'yes' campaign, it was he who made the most prominent Tory speeches on the subject.

'Naturally,' she said, 'it's with some temerity that the pupil speaks before the master.' Heath did not respond with similar generosity.

Mrs Thatcher never bought the more visionary version of Europeanism. She rejected a federal Europe, favouring instead 'closer co-operation'; but she defended membership on the grounds that British loss of sovereignty was largely 'technical'. She strongly subscribed to the prevailing Tory view that the EEC could become a bulwark against Communism. The convincing endorsement of continuing membership by nearly two-thirds of those voting did her no harm politically, and no good. But the campaign helped restore Ted Heath's reputation, rekindling the idea that he might return. Because the 'yes' campaign had been a cross-party affair, it provided a possible model for a coalition of national unity to deal with the economic crisis. Such a coalition would have been the end of Margaret Thatcher.

With the help of Gordon Reece, seconded to her office from May 1975, Mrs Thatcher began to rethink her party's electoral strategy. As Reece wrote in an unpublished memoir, she understood that 'the middle class divide was breaking down' and so concentrated on 'the voters who had the greatest need or ambition to improve their lives. Priority was given to women in Labour-voting households, the people who actually spent the family budget ... Secondly priority was given to skilled and semi-skilled workers, those who had the best opportunity to benefit from increasing prosperity. And thirdly to first-time voters, people who would not just hope for a better life but vote for one.' In Reece's view, 'The people we had to reach would read the *Mirror*, increasingly the *Sun*, the *Express*, the *Mail*, the *People*, the *News of the World*, they would watch *Coronation Street*, Jimmy Savile, *Top of the Pops*, they listened to Jimmy Young on the wireless. And any aspiring Prime Minister had better go to them, and not expect them to come to her.'

Mrs Thatcher, who aspired passionately to be prime minister, acted upon this advice.* Bearing in mind her target of women who managed the family budget, she frequently spoke as a woman who did just that, relating her own experience to that of the entire nation as it struggled with inflation. She had the gift of direct speech, free of jargon, and the actressy side to her character made her extremely effective in walkabouts and factory visits. Yet she was not a natural with the media. Her parliamentary and legal training had left her ill-suited to television.† She was also intensely serious and

---

* She spoke to Jean Rook in the *Daily Express* and to *Woman's Own*; she appeared on *Woman's Hour* on Radio 4 and *The Jimmy Young Show* on Radio 2. After she appeared on Jimmy Savile's *Jim'll Fix It* in December 1976, the two struck up a friendly acquaintance. In doing so she was unaware of the allegations of child abuse that disgraced Savile after his death.
† Parliament was not yet televised or even, until 1978, broadcast on the radio.

high-minded, and touchingly cut off from the coarser aspects of daily life. When, for example, the Conservatives gained Woolwich West in the June 1975 by-election, she flashed a 'V for victory' sign to the cameras. To the dismay of Reece, she did the sign the wrong way round, turning it into the well-known obscene gesture. So great was her innocence that 'Even when we had explained it, she still didn't really understand what she had done.'

Reece was effective with Mrs Thatcher in part because he himself was in accord with the moral and ideological thrust of what became known as Thatcherism and believed in her character as the vehicle for advancing it. But his success also rested on her remarkable humility and professionalism. 'Gordon Reece taught me', she said later, 'that television is a conversation, not a lecture,' though this was not a lesson she invariably remembered. He told her to get up close to the microphone to sound more 'sexy, confidential and reasonable'. Reece was frank about other changes too. He told her that her clothes were too fussy; her hats should go; she wore too much jewellery for television; her hair was too frizzy for a potential prime minister. She must also flatter Fleet Street editors. Mrs Thatcher never forgot her lessons from Reece, and repeated them as essential truths. She would say, 'You must wear plain, tailored clothes on television' in the same tone of voice as she would say, 'You must have liberty – and not just liberty, but law-based liberty.'

Mrs Thatcher chose to make the first highly controversial speech of her leadership on the Cold War. In 1975, the buzzword of the Western elites towards the Soviet Union was détente. Through the Helsinki talks, culminating in a 'Final Act' in August 1975, the Western allies sought to trade an acceptance of the Soviet domination of Eastern Europe for the improvement of human rights in the Soviet bloc. The process, initiated by President Richard Nixon, had broad support on both sides of the Atlantic. It was considered maverick right-wing to question it. Mrs Thatcher, however, chose to do so, asking Robert Conquest, the historian of Stalin's purges, to draft her speech. She wanted to know whether the Soviets had the long-term aim of getting rid of Western democracy – 'The answer was yes,' he told her – and whether the Soviet Union was, in the long term, viable – 'The answer was no.'

On 26 July 1975, Mrs Thatcher delivered her speech to the Chelsea Conservative Association. It was wrong to pretend, she declared, as the Helsinki Final Act approached, that there was 'peace and trust' between East and West: 'Throughout this decade of détente, the armed forces of the Soviet Union have increased, are increasing and show no signs of diminishing.' Unless NATO maintained its conventional forces, Soviet aggression would leave the allies with the appalling choice of either surrender or 'early use of nuclear weapons'. This language was strong enough, but what really separated Mrs Thatcher's approach from the orthodoxy was its definition of the Soviet threat. She saw the Soviet Union as, by its nature, an attack on the West. The Soviets were 'arrayed against every principle for which we stand'. She held up the recently exiled Soviet novelist Alexander Solzhenitsyn as the model of truth-telling against Communist lies. Her test of whether peace was really coming closer was whether there was any advance in 'the free movement of people and of ideas'.

Mrs Thatcher pointedly did not consult her Shadow Foreign Secretary, Reggie Maudling, before her speech: 'I knew that all I would receive were obstruction and warnings.' Instead she took heart from discussions with Lord Home, who also offered careful comments on the draft.* Chelsea marked Margaret Thatcher's first major public pronouncement on the state of the world. It set a standard of clarity and controversy which she was to maintain.

One of Mrs Thatcher's earliest decisions was to visit the United States.† There was a conscious desire, by putting her on the world stage, to establish her as somebody of substance ahead of her first party conference as leader in early October. This was linked with her ideological interest in the American language of freedom and liberty which she wanted to reinject into British political debate. She also wanted to repair ties to American politicians, which had fallen victim to Heath's obsession with Britain's EEC entry and his personal anti-Americanism.‡

On 18 February 1975, shortly before announcing her Shadow Cabinet, Mrs Thatcher had breakfast with the American Secretary of State, Henry Kissinger, at Claridge's. Kissinger remembered: 'I found her totally different from other politicians. Every other politician I knew said that in order to win elections you had to win the centre. Her position was that you have to articulate your position as clearly as you can and the centre

---

* Of all the Tory leaders between Churchill and Mrs Thatcher, Home was the most robust in his dislike of Soviet Communism.
† Her first foreign visit, out of deference to the recent EEC referendum, had been to West Germany, where she had met and been impressed by the then Chancellor Helmut Schmidt, and also met the Christian Democrat leader Helmut Kohl. She decided at once that Kohl was 'the German equivalent of Ted Heath', a view which was to have important and malign consequences.
‡ In a briefing document, prepared for Ford for his meeting with Edward Heath in September 1974, Henry Kissinger did not mince his words: 'Heath is a doctrinaire person, Gaullist in his outlook, and the only anti-American UK Prime Minister in many years. He is a complex, sensitive man who tends to sulk.'

will come over to you ... I was always very taken with her. You could say she seduced me ... But I thought she might never get elected with those views.' As Kissinger told President Ford at the time: 'Soames may be a big Conservative leader sometime. I don't think Margaret Thatcher will last.'

On 9 April, Mrs Thatcher sat down with another visiting American dignitary in her Commons office. His name was Ronald Reagan. Although this was their first *tête-à-tête*, Reagan had come to her attention some years earlier. Back in 1969, Denis had attended a meeting at the Institute of Directors in London addressed by Reagan, then Governor of California, and had come home full of praise for him. Her meeting with Reagan, planned for forty-five minutes, doubled that time. 'I was immediately won over by his charm, directness and sense of humour,' she later wrote. Reagan recalled: 'It was evident from our first words that we were soul mates when it came to reducing government and expanding freedom.' In one of his weekly radio commentaries, Reagan noted speculation that Britain could go to the polls that autumn: 'If so, Britain may get its first woman Prime Minister in its more-than-900-year history. Mrs. Margaret Thatcher, the new leader of the Conservative Party, is a woman of charm and poise and also strength. The British like their politicians to stand for something and she does.' 'That evening,' recalled one of his aides, 'Reagan was still going on and on about this wonderful woman he'd met.' They were not to see one another again until 1978, but their staffs stayed in touch. The seeds of future friendship had been sown.

Ahead of her US visit, the Foreign Office urged Mrs Thatcher to give American audiences an upbeat account of the state of Britain. An article in the *Wall Street Journal* entitled 'Goodbye, Great Britain, it was nice knowing you' attracted much notice. Indeed, Mrs Thatcher quoted it when addressing Scottish Conservatives over the summer. 'It is to Britain that journalists now come, following the scent of economic and political decay.'* Writing to her press secretary, one Foreign Office official suggested 'Mrs Thatcher will no doubt wish to underline the positive side of the picture (relatively low level of unemployment, improved balance of payments, firm action to grasp the nettle of inflation etc).' Beside these suggestions, Mrs Thatcher wrote two large question marks. She certainly wanted to embrace the potential of her country, but she had no desire to talk up the achievements of the Labour government.

---

* Private discussion was equally gloomy. In a conversation with President Gerald Ford in January, Henry Kissinger told him that 'Britain is a tragedy – it has sunk to begging, borrowing, stealing until North Sea oil comes in ...'

Mrs Thatcher arrived in New York on 13 September 1975. Two days later, in her first full speech, entitled 'Let Our Children Grow Tall', she offered a fierce and full expression of her belief that 'The pursuit of equality is itself a mirage.' Candid about the failings of British economic management, she argued that it was essential to create wealth before giving so much attention to its distribution. 'Let our children grow tall,' she declared, 'and some taller than others if they have the ability to do so.' 'You'll be the next PM,' shouted out one of the guests, to general applause.

Back in Britain, the speech nearly turned to disaster after an early draft, released by Conservative Central Office, suggested that government spending on kidney machines should be limited.* Reece, ringing around Fleet Street, killed the story just in time: Larry Lamb, the Editor of the *Sun*, had prepared a front-page headline 'Let 'Em Die, Says Maggie'. Even without the kidney machines, her fighting words caused controversy at home. The Foreign Secretary, Jim Callaghan, criticized her 'argumentative passages'. Ministers complained privately to the Foreign Office and a British Embassy official briefed against her unattributably in Washington. Mrs Thatcher was unrepentant, however: 'It's no part of my job', she told *The Times*, 'to be a propagandist for a socialist society.' Overall, the general impression created in New York was highly favourable, one of pleasant surprise. 'The most operative word is lady,' the *New York Times* quoted one luncheon guest as saying. 'Here is this little blonde, blue-eyed woman in this pale peach dress with baby blonde hair. She is a flower among thorns. But it's no little girl act either. She is just plain well-informed and extremely articulate.'

Mrs Thatcher was much happier discussing her views rather than her sex. Before an interview with Barbara Walters, Walters warned her that she 'might have to ask some questions about how it felt to be a woman in such a high post, much as she disliked that kind of question'. Mrs Thatcher shook her head: 'Isn't it too bad that there aren't more women around who feel as we do . . .'

On 17 September, Mrs Thatcher flew to Washington. Within twenty-four hours she met Kissinger, the Defense Secretary James Schlesinger, the Treasury Secretary Bill Simon and President Ford, as well as members of both Houses of Congress. General Brent Scowcroft, present at her meeting with Ford, remembered Mrs Thatcher as 'very warm, very friendly, very composed . . . my overall impression was "nice lady"'. Mrs Thatcher was similarly gratified and similarly unexcited. 'She was pleased to have met

---

* Reece believed that Central Office, who refused to withdraw what it had circulated, had acted with unfriendly intent.

Ford,' recalled one of her entourage, 'but more due to his position than the substance of their discussions.'

Other encounters, however, were more rapturous. 'To my great surprise,' recalled James Schlesinger, 'in came this striking woman singing the praises of what was then called the Schlesinger doctrine.* She didn't know much about it, but she was very eager to learn. We talked about our strategic nuclear forces for perhaps an hour and a half.' At the Treasury, Bill Simon collected the same flattering impression of a soulmate-cum-disciple who was keen to learn. 'Your dedication and knowledge made a deep impression,' he wrote to her afterwards, commending her for her 'courage in pursuing the policies necessary to bring inflation under control'.

The following night Mrs Thatcher sat next to Alan Greenspan, the future Chairman of the Federal Reserve Board, at a dinner given for her by Mrs Kay Graham,† proprietor of the *Washington Post*:

> the very first thing she said to me was 'So, Dr Greenspan, why is it that we in Britain don't have an M2?' She was referring to a monetary aggregate that was not then used in Britain for technical reasons. This, of course, was not the first question I was expecting... I found our conversation startling. She had a level of understanding of the way the world worked that most people in the political realm are unable to acquire. And it was a view that I would agree with. She believed in free-market discipline...

Mrs Thatcher was not only networking, she was searching for allies who would help validate the ideological and political change she sought at home.

During the rest of her trip Mrs Thatcher made three more set-piece speeches. To the National Press Club in Washington she spoke darkly of Britain's plight and put it in the context of political and cultural struggles across the world. She worried that the Western allies were 'losing confidence in ourselves and in our case'. Marxism was 'the negation of human dignity', and it was the duty of the United States and Britain to 'revive belief in freedom under the law'. She also explicitly linked her own life and beliefs with the story of America: 'I was not brought up to prosperity. Hard work

---

* The Schlesinger doctrine was an attempt to strengthen nuclear deterrence through laying out the level and scope of US nuclear retaliation in the event of acts of Soviet aggression of varying magnitudes.

† Such a dinner was, itself, was a mark of Washington respectability. But Mrs Graham was never much of a friend to Mrs Thatcher. At a lunch given shortly afterwards in London by Lady Hartwell, wife of the owner of the *Daily Telegraph* (also no fan of Mrs Thatcher), Mrs Graham provoked fierce argument by declaring: 'I think she's just a vulgar fishwife.'

was the only way ... It is a moral struggle ... the puritan morality of the founders of America.' In Chicago she focused on economics. 'Inflation', she declared, 'is a pernicious evil capable of destroying any society built on a value system where freedom is paramount.' All this led the *Guardian* to conclude she had 'broken decisively with the Disraelian Tory tradition of pragmatism ... the Conservative Party is now launched on a crusade in the cause of reaction; the Tories have been taken over by the extremists'. Mrs Thatcher would not, of course, have agreed about the extremism, but she was not sorry to have stirred up attention.

Her trip did much to boost her own confidence and solidify her position before the party conference. It also offered a glimpse of what was to come. Her last set-piece speech, in Toronto, Canada, took to task the phrase most emblematic of post-war Tory centrism: 'It is often said that politics is the art of the possible. The danger of such a phrase is that we may deem impossible things which would be possible, indeed desirable, if only we had more courage, more insight.' She was beginning to develop her unique contribution to British politics – the art of the impossible.

Between her election in February 1975 and the party conference in October, Mrs Thatcher had gradually built up the entourage she needed. Having brought back Gordon Reece, in June she chose Alistair McAlpine as Party Treasurer, with the instruction, born of her wariness of the party machine: 'You work for me.' Young, hospitable, short, tubby and eccentric, McAlpine was extremely well connected, both with traditional sources of Tory funding and with more raffish and arty worlds of which Mrs Thatcher knew almost nothing. With her approval, he began to build up a group of powerful businessmen sympathetic to her cause.*

Mrs Thatcher also sought what she termed a 'wordsmith'. She needed someone who could supply material in her tone of voice, capture her essence and at the same time loosen her up a bit. Enter Ronald Millar, a playwright and screenwriter who could be found most nights at the Theatre Royal, Haymarket. At their first meeting, Millar suggested a quotation for her first party political broadcast as leader: 'You cannot strengthen the weak by weakening the strong. You cannot bring about prosperity by discouraging thrift ...'† Mrs Thatcher listened in silence. She then reached slowly and dramatically for her handbag and produced

---

* These included Sir Frank McFadzean of Beechams, Michael Richardson, at that time at the stockbrokers Cazenove's and later to be important to her at Rothschild's, and Sir Marcus Sieff and Sir Derek Rayner of Marks and Spencer.
† Millar wrongly attributed these words to Abraham Lincoln. The true author was one William Boetcker, writing some seventy-five years later.

a piece of yellowing paper containing the same lines. 'It goes wherever I go,' she told him. Forever afterwards, Mrs Thatcher had faith in Millar. Like many of her most trusted associates, he was an unlikely companion. Humorous, camp, silk-dressing-gowned, slightly seedy, he was from the world of Noël Coward, not of Westminster. It says a good deal for the surprising broadmindedness of her taste that Mrs Thatcher got on so well with people like Reece, McAlpine and Millar. Though extremely correct, she was never stuffy.*

Mrs Thatcher's first party conference speech as leader, she well knew, would be the most important speech of her career so far. The days beforehand were tense and chaotic. After laborious hours of laying out endlessly retyped texts on the floor of her hotel room, Mrs Thatcher remained unsatisfied. So Ronnie Millar was summoned up to Blackpool. It was only at 4.30 in the morning of Friday 10 October, the day of delivery, that she considered herself ready and went to bed.

Mrs Thatcher looked well on the platform that Friday afternoon, three days before her fiftieth birthday. She wore a peacock-blue dress, tie collar and a slim-fitting turquoise coat. On the top of her script she had written, as she often did at this time: 'Relax. Low Speaking Voice. Not too slow.' She addressed head-on the complaint that she had criticized Britain while in America. She had criticized socialism, she said – 'Britain and Socialism are not the same thing.' She painted a gloomy picture of the economic situation but, as so often, gave it a moral rather than a technocratic context. 'What kind of people are we?' she asked:

> Let me give you my vision: a man's right to work as he will, to spend what he earns, to own property, to have the state as servant and not as master – these are the British inheritance ... We must get private enterprise back on the road to recovery, not merely to give people more of their own money to spend as they choose, but to have more money to help the old and the sick and the handicapped ... We are coming, I think, to yet another turning point in our long history. We can go on as we have been going and continue down. Or we can stop and – with a decisive act of will – we can say 'Enough'.

The ensuing standing ovation was the genuine reaction of long-disheartened troops hearing their own innermost beliefs expressed with

---

* There were limits, however, to Mrs Thatcher's tolerance. Patrick Cosgrave, the Political Editor of the *Spectator*, had been one of the first to tip her for the top. He also wrote one of her early biographies. Cosgrave was brilliant, but seldom sober, and had allegedly been sick on Mrs Thatcher's shoes (with her inside them). In any event, he ceased to be part of her inner circle, although he listed himself in *Who's Who* as 'Special Adviser to The Rt Hon. Margaret Thatcher 1975–9'.

vigour and optimism. A Marplan poll now gave the Conservatives 54 per cent support, compared to 31 per cent for Labour. For the first time, she felt secure in her leadership.

At this time, family life was changing too. Denis, now sixty, retired from Burmah Oil in May 1975. Although busy with non-executive directorships, he became more important in his wife's political counsels. Having sold The Mount, the Thatchers moved into the old dower flat in Scotney Castle, also in Lamberhurst, that October. They enjoyed Scotney, but Margaret's job ensured they lived, mostly, in Flood Street, Chelsea. With the twins, aged twenty-two, based at home, this was not easy. Carol, without enthusiasm, was completing her training as a solicitor. Mark, who had greatly upset his parents four years earlier by refusing a place at Keble College, Oxford, in favour of having fun in South Africa, was failing to obtain his qualifications as an accountant. Short of time and always inclined to look indulgently on her son, Mrs Thatcher was considered by some who worked with her to be 'the ultimate chequebook mum'.* In Carol's view, after her Grantham upbringing, 'which had control as its middle name', her mother erred too far the other way.

The Thatchers enjoyed a friendly relationship with their neighbour, Sue Mastriforte. Deserted by her husband, Ms Mastriforte had been left to bring up her children with very little money. This shocked Mrs Thatcher, who was kind and tactful in giving her food, gifts and sometimes small sums. She also paid her to do some of her shopping and look after her house. In Ms Mastriforte's mind, Carol did not enjoy her mother's eminence: 'I think Carol would have liked a suburban mother with a pinny . . . baking cakes all day.' Carol sometimes felt neglected, becoming overweight and suffering Mrs Thatcher's criticism for dressing frumpily. But, in Ms Mastriforte's view, 'Margaret was fairer than Carol gave her credit' and certainly cared for her welfare. To her, Denis and Margaret seemed 'a very close couple'; the fact that she was Conservative leader made him 'ten feet tall with pride'.

In November 1975 Mrs Thatcher was given police protection, which was to remain with her for the rest of her life.† This separated her from anything that could be described as normality. But Bob Kingston, her Special Branch officer who stayed until the mid-1990s, was struck by how

---

* Denis used to exclaim, despairingly: 'The boy's a financial alcoholic!'
† This came after the IRA murdered Ross McWhirter, a Thatcher supporter and a leading light in founding the National Association for Freedom, publicly launched soon after his death, which tried to combat trade union power.

'remarkably easy' Mrs Thatcher was and how friendly. 'In twenty years, she never once raised her voice to me.'

In the autumn of 1975, Mrs Thatcher tried to capitalize on her conference success. In the Commons this was hard to do. In the eyes of Harold Wilson's senior policy adviser, Bernard Donoughue, she seemed 'petrified' when facing the Prime Minister, 'like a rabbit in front of a stoat'. With advice,* her performance improved, but during her first year as leader there was no occasion on which she won control of the House. Although well prepared and sharp in argument, she lacked the confident spontaneity required. This was bad for the morale of her MPs, particularly as Heath remained an effective and baleful presence. In October, she replaced William Shelton as PPS with the well-connected Adam Butler, son of RAB, and, after Christmas, exchanged poor Fergus Montgomery for the more able, though not more popular, John Stanley. Her parliamentary position was improving incrementally, but she had no palpable hits of which she could boast.

Mrs Thatcher was much more successful in her public preaching role, which allowed her to project her combative personality. In Kensington town hall, on 19 January 1976, she returned with incendiary effect to the subject she had raised in Chelsea the previous July. The Labour government, she warned, was 'dismantling our defences at a moment when the strategic threat to Britain and her allies from an expansionist power is graver than at any moment since the end of the last war'. The Russians were 'bent on world dominance' and, in Central Europe, Warsaw Pact forces now massively outnumbered those of NATO. So she had been right, she insisted, to warn about the illusions of Helsinki. Her remedy lay not only in rearming, but also in 'a reasoned and vigorous defence of the Western concept of rights and liberties'. Much of Britain's decline had been brought about by socialism. The Conservatives faced 'the vital task of shaking the British public out of a long sleep'.

This was a powerful speech, but Mrs Thatcher could not have known how lucky she would be in the reaction. Intending a sexist comparison with Bismarck, the nineteenth-century 'Iron Chancellor' of Germany, the Red Army's newspaper *Red Star* satirically described her as 'the Iron Lady'. Speaking to her own Conservative Association in Finchley, she seized this opportunity: 'I stand before you tonight in my Red Star chiffon evening gown, my face softly made up and my fair hair gently waved, the Iron

---

* Most notably from a group of young MPs known as the Gang of Four. They were Nigel Lawson, Norman Tebbit, Geoffrey Pattie and George Gardiner.

Lady of the Western world. A Cold War warrior . . . Yes, I *am* an iron lady, after all it wasn't a bad thing to be an iron duke; yes, if that's how they wish to interpret my defence of values and freedoms fundamental to our way of life.'

It is hard to think of a neater way of placing herself where she wanted to be – a wholly feminine but strong woman, a figure respected by her enemies, a patriotic leader in the tradition of the Duke of Wellington ('the Iron Duke'), a defender of the nation and its values. Thanks to her opponents, she had graduated to being a global figure with a sobriquet that marked her out – the Iron Lady.

On 16 March 1976, Harold Wilson suddenly resigned as Prime Minister. Watching the tributes at Prime Minister's Questions that afternoon, Bernard Donoughue recorded: 'Heath was superb. But Thatcher got it wrong again, graceless, with some snide petty points and a call for a general election, which clearly embarrassed many people on her own side.' As attention shifted to the Labour leadership contest, Mrs Thatcher was left looking irrelevant and somehow uninteresting. On 5 April, Jim Callaghan emerged victorious. Labour MPs had preferred the only candidate without an Oxford degree over Michael Foot, the main choice of the left.

This was a bad result for Mrs Thatcher. If Foot had won, her excoriations of socialism would immediately have resonated. With Jim Callaghan, the Red wolf wore more effective sheep's clothing than ever before. Callaghan was an unquestionably patriotic product of the respectable working class. A tall man, who deployed what Mrs Thatcher well described as 'avuncular flannel', Callaghan treated her at the despatch box with a condescension which suited the heavily male House. In an early exchange, Mrs Thatcher claimed that 'his only policy is to put Britain deeper in the red, to keep the red flag flying here'. Callaghan replied: 'I still have hopes that one day Question Time will be a serious period, without Members just thinking up clever phrases in advance and then shouting them across the Dispatch Box . . . I am sure that one day the right honourable Lady will understand these things a little better.' Throughout his time as Prime Minister, Callaghan had a higher personal popularity rating with the public than she did.

Two days after Callaghan became leader, Labour lost its overall Commons majority. As the Liberals and the minor parties propped up Callaghan's premiership, Mrs Thatcher struggled to keep her troops in permanent readiness for a war which might still be three years away – the end of the legal life of the Parliament. With most Commons votes so finely balanced, parliamentary chaos became frequent. In May 1976, Labour's

Bill to nationalize the shipbuilding and aircraft industry was carried in dubious circumstances.* After left-wing Labour MPs started to sing 'The Red Flag' in the Chamber, Michael Heseltine, the Conservative industry spokesman, grabbed the Mace, which symbolizes the delegated authority of the Crown, and waved it aloft. Mrs Thatcher seems quite to have enjoyed the kerfuffle and did not reprimand Heseltine. She suspended all parliamentary cooperation until Callaghan agreed to a second vote on the Bill, which he did four weeks later.†

Even the nation's economic plight was not pure advantage to the Tories. In the debate on the Budget, the day after Callaghan became Prime Minister, Mrs Thatcher turned in her most effective parliamentary performance yet as leader. She pointed out that when Healey had presented his Budget a year before, the pound had been worth $2.37; now it was worth $1.87. The size of the deficit now 'dominates everything the Chancellor can do'.‡ The 'influenza' was recession: the 'cancer' was 'the underlying structural problem, that we are living beyond our means'. In September, a new sterling crisis forced Healey to approach the International Monetary Fund (IMF) for $3.9 billion, a loan that came with strings, requiring deep cuts in public expenditure. For the next fifteen years, the memory of Labour going 'cap in hand' – as it was always expressed – to the IMF became a standard feature of Tory propaganda.

Although these humiliations proved the Conservatives right, they also changed the political atmosphere, bringing back talk of national unity, a coalition government even.§ Against the rhetoric of pulling together, Mrs Thatcher's message that incomes policies could not work seemed to strike the wrong note. At the same time, the Labour government became more visibly responsible. In response to the IMF crisis, Healey produced the 'stern, decisive measures' which Mrs Thatcher had demanded. At the Labour Party conference, taking place in the middle of that crisis, Callaghan declared that the option of borrowing and spending one's way out of economic trouble 'no longer exists'. The era of 'cuts' really began with this

---

* Because the Speaker had declared it 'hybrid' (that is, a mix of general provisions and those applying to specific businesses), the Bill should have followed a special procedure, which it did not. The Tories further alleged it was carried only after the government whips induced one of their MPs to break his pair (the informal arrangement whereby MPs from opposing parties coordinate their absences from particular votes).
† By this time Callaghan had the votes to ensure the Bill's passage.
‡ The Public Sector Borrowing Requirement stood at £12 billion.
§ The possibility of a coalition government was touted by Harold Macmillan, who secretly imagined himself, aged eighty-two, at its head. Mrs Thatcher recalled visiting him at this time at the house of his son, Maurice. She said she heard the old man asking his son, 'Has the call come?' – meaning was there a move to ask him to lead a national government.

speech. As the man to lead the nation soberly through a crisis, Callaghan looked convincing, even if the crisis had been of his own government's making.

In her party conference speech in Brighton the following week, Mrs Thatcher was therefore, in her own words, 'almost neurotically cautious about the need for responsibility and caution'. John Gummer, who often helped draft her conference speeches, wearily recalled that 'What she liked best was being defiant, so it was one's job to find something for her to be defiant about.' In October 1976, that something was not to be found. To support Callaghan without boosting him, Mrs Thatcher took a stand which appeared to eschew party advantage in the national interest. She spoke of the virtues of 'a generally agreed basis for wage bargaining', while not seeking confrontation with the unions: 'the confrontation that matters to us is confrontation with rising prices, with rising unemployment, with rising debts'. As a piece of political positioning, the speech did its work. *The Times* tried to wrap her to its establishment heart: 'Mrs Thatcher has moved with characteristic caution on to the middle ground of politics.' But in the hall it fell rather flat. In her memoirs Mrs Thatcher acknowledged its comparative failure. She had conceded more than she liked to the consensual wing of the party.

In his speech to conference, Ted Heath had offered Mrs Thatcher somewhat grudging support. The text which bound them in uneasy unity was a document called *The Right Approach*. As Chris Patten, its chief drafter, put it, this represented 'a treaty' between the Heathite and Thatcherite strands of Conservatism. Like all good treaties, it offered comfort to both sides. In rhetorical terms, the centrist voice (Patten's) dominated. *The Right Approach* talked repeatedly of 'a return to common sense' and warned against being 'too dogmatic'. In substance, however, it was almost Thatcherite enough for Mrs Thatcher. The key section, entitled 'Bringing the Economy into Balance' ('balance' here appealing to Heathites as suggesting moderation and to Thatcherites as implying a balanced budget), identified control of the money supply as 'a key feature of economic policy, though by no means the only one', while public spending cuts were deemed 'essential'. Once borrowing had been successfully reined in, the tax burden would be reduced.

In only two areas was the caution arising from internal disagreement visible. The first concerned trade union reform. While individual rights against the closed shop would be better protected, the Conservatives did 'not intend to introduce a major round of new industrial relations legislation'. This was less than Thatcherites sought, but represented broad agreement that discretion was the better part of valour: the wounds of the Heath Industrial Relations Act were still raw. In the second, related area of incomes policy, *The Right Approach*'s need for compromise reduced it almost to nonsense. Experience suggests, the paper declared, that restraint in pay bargaining is not best achieved by an incomes policy, nonetheless, 'The same experience demonstrates the unwisdom of flatly and permanently rejecting the idea.' This aside, Mrs Thatcher was well pleased with the treaty-drafting. *The Right Approach* even produced a phrase later falsely attributed to her: 'The facts of life invariably *do* turn out to be Conservative.'

Mrs Thatcher had the great advantage that her favoured battleground was economic. Her critics within the party were weak on economics. Although many grandees instinctively disliked her direction, they did not have the knowledge to mount a resistance based on clear argument. Of those assigned economy-related posts in the Shadow Cabinet, only Jim Prior, at Employment, represented a block on the analysis of Keith Joseph and the passion of Margaret Thatcher. He was the only man brave enough to raise serious objections. Her remaining Shadow Cabinet critics took refuge in the general, pragmatic hope that 'events would modify her views'.

On the Thatcher side of the argument were ranged an intellectually impressive but politically less experienced group of mainly younger men. They included David Howell, Nigel Lawson, Nicholas Ridley, John Nott, John Biffen, Ian Gow, Cecil Parkinson, Norman Lamont and Jock Bruce-Gardyne. All possessed considerable brainpower and applied it to develop a new approach to policy that would bring greater freedom to the economy.

Mrs Thatcher also sought economic advice beyond politicians. She complained that at the Conservative Research Department, supposedly the party's intellectual powerhouse, 'there was nobody in the room with a single idea that was worth having'. As Chris Patten remembered ruefully, Mrs Thatcher would study the work of the policy groups, but 'You'd know that she was also seeing a crazed Swiss professor.' Through Keith Joseph, Alfred Sherman and the Centre for Policy Studies, and to a lesser but significant extent through Arthur Seldon, Ralph Harris and the Institute of Economic Affairs, she met a steady stream of economic and political thinkers, of whom Friedrich von Hayek and Milton Friedman were the most famous. She took as her watchword Solzhenitsyn's dictum that 'it is part of the business of the artist and the philosopher to light up the politician's path'. The path which she most wanted illuminated was that which led to greater freedom, under the rule of law. She would pull Hayek's *Constitution of Liberty* out of her handbag, declaring '*This* is what we believe.' And she loved to invoke the authority of great thinkers as part of her campaign of public evangelizing.* On the recommendation of others, she would set herself homework. 'I have just embarked on holiday reading,' she wrote to Adam Butler. 'But after Dostoevsky's *The Possessed* and Koestler's *Darkness at Noon* am none too cheerful!' She amazed the novelist and journalist Jilly Cooper by telling her that during the broiling summer of 1976 she had read the entire 845 pages of Kipling's *Collected Poems*.

Mrs Thatcher had no less an appetite for drier economic study. By the time she met Alan Walters in America in September 1977, she had read his *Money in Boom and Slump*. She also studied Douglas Hague's *A Textbook of Economic Theory*. Hague had first advised her in the late 1960s. A fellow Methodist, he reminded her of the famous advice of John Wesley – 'Get all you can; save all you can; give all you can' – and she deployed it in public argument. He would prove important later in persuading Mrs Thatcher to lift exchange controls. She also received more technical advice from Gordon Pepper, a senior partner at Greenwell's, the stockbrokers. Pepper helped deepen her suspicion of the Bank of England and its prevailing doctrines. She did not take to Gordon Richardson, the Governor, describing him as 'a peacock of a man'.

An important subsection of what might be called 'Intellectuals for Margaret' was composed of converts from socialism. Woodrow Wyatt, a journalist and former Labour MP, was one. Brian Walden, considered the most eloquent of his generation of Labour MPs, but disillusioned by the rise of the left, was another. Walden left Parliament in 1977 to take up a career as a television interviewer. His interviews with Mrs Thatcher became famous for their personal rapport and his perceptiveness about the elemental force of Thatcherism.

Alfred Sherman, himself originally from the extreme left, made it his business to cultivate defectors, with Mrs Thatcher's enthusiastic support. One such was Hugh Thomas, the historian of the Spanish Civil War, whom Mrs Thatcher drew on for advice on foreign policy, particularly the Communist threat in southern Africa.† 'She was interested to know

---

* During the Opposition years Mrs Thatcher's speeches referred admiringly to, among many others, Karl Popper, Bastiat, Keynes, Burke, Schumpeter, Tocqueville, Alfred Marshall, C. S. Lewis, Adam Smith and Rudyard Kipling. In preparing more substantial speeches she supplemented these authorities with current thinkers and commentators. A typical example, a speech in January 1977 entitled 'The Will-o'-the-wisp of the Classless Society', drew on articles by Shirley Robin Letwin, P. T. Bauer, Milton Friedman, Samuel Brittan, Robert Skidelsky, Hayek, Alan Walters and Paul Johnson.

† Other distinguished historians and thinkers roped in by Mrs Thatcher included Leonard Schapiro, Michael Howard and Isaiah Berlin – all three of whom also advised the Liberal Party at the time. From them she sought ideas about the nature and danger of Soviet Communism.

how historians saw things,' he recalled, 'though she hadn't done much background reading.'

Hugh Thomas, in turn, was influential with his old friend Paul Johnson (though Johnson claimed that the process worked more the other way). From 1975, Johnson talked to her sometimes about policy ('She was completely at sea') and about history, ideas and what books she should read.* Although a strong Thatcherite, he considered Mrs Thatcher 'the most ignorant politician of her level that I'd come across until I met Tony Blair'. 'I always liked her,' he said, 'but she always bored me a bit.'

Johnson's support was particularly valuable through his prolific journalism, notably in the *Daily Mail* and the *Spectator*. He was one of many newspaper journalists whose support helped change the conversation of the chattering classes. Others included John O'Sullivan, Frank Johnson and T. E. Utley, all of the *Daily Telegraph*. Samuel Brittan, the main economic commentator of the *Financial Times*, was her chief economic guru in the press. His weekly column was the only piece of journalism which she read without fail. These writers contributed to an exciting feeling that the collectivist tide was receding and at last, as Hugh Thomas put it, 'everything was possible'.

A similar excitement pervaded the Conservative Philosophy Group, an informal society set up by Hugh Fraser and Jonathan Aitken, which mingled politicians with writers and thinkers. Through this group, Mrs Thatcher met Edward Norman, the Dean of Peterhouse, Cambridge. At one meeting, Norman predicted that the issue of nuclear weapons would soon reappear as a great moral struggle. He argued it was a worthy object of policy for the West to resist the philosophical materialism of Soviet Communism. 'I agree with Dr Norman,' Mrs Thatcher announced: 'We must defend Christian values with the ATOM BOMB.' As the great CND battles of the early 1980s took hold,† she consulted Norman on the ethics of this debate and in her search for Christian justifications for capitalism. These last had long been active in her mind. 'Choice is the essence of ethics,' she told the Zurich Economic Society in March 1977, and 'The economic results [of the Western way of life] are better because the moral philosophy is superior.'

This quest for the Christian roots of her beliefs, particularly of her economic doctrines, gave depth to Mrs Thatcher's approach to the national crisis. She always had strong personal Christian values, focused on duty

---

* Johnson persuaded her to read David Watkin's *Morality and Architecture*. 'She said she found it hard going,' he recalled.

† Mrs Thatcher was much impressed that Norman's prediction in this regard had held true. Later she referred to him as a 'prophet'.

to God and ethics. Alfred Roberts had believed in what Gladstone called 'effort, honest manful effort', and it was a combination of Gladstonian economic views of retrenchment and reform with Methodism which animated Mrs Thatcher.* 'It is noteworthy', she told the bankers of Zurich, 'that the Victorian era – the heyday of free enterprise in Britain – was also the era of the rise of selflessness and benefaction.' She wanted, said Norman, to 'resuscitate a world we had lost' and she 'ransacked' Christian thought for intellectual backing.

The fruits can be seen in the Iain Macleod Memorial Lecture, drafted by Sherman, which Mrs Thatcher delivered in the summer of 1977. Conservatism, she declared, was 'part of the living flesh of British life' and rested on the idea that man is individual, social and spiritual, all at once. Far from being the antithesis of care for others, self-interest worked with it because 'man is a social creature, born into family, clan, community, nation, brought up in mutual dependence ... "Love your neighbour as yourself" expresses this.' She never wavered in this belief: it is what she meant ten years later when she declared 'There is no such thing as society.'

The following year, from the pulpit of St Lawrence Jewry in the City of London, she was more explicit about religion. 'I never thought that Christianity equipped me with a political philosophy,' she said, 'but I thought it did equip me with standards to which political actions must, in the end, be referred.' The relief of poverty and suffering was a religious duty, but not one necessarily best performed by the state, she declared, taking her favourite example: 'I wonder whether the State services would have done as much for the man who fell among thieves as the Good Samaritan did for him?'

Some intellectuals fell in love with Mrs Thatcher. John Vaizey, an educationalist, wrote to her to tell her how interesting her voice was to listen to. The historian David Dilks was struck by her 'directness, quickness on the point, anxiety to listen to a wide range of views, conscious exploitation of feminine charm, and a certain motherly quality'. Some, however, thought her naive. Edward Norman, though an admirer, recalled that she had 'no real sense of intellectual inquiry' and 'an extraordinarily intelligent, but unformed mind'. Some simply doubted she was up to the task. After their first meeting, in 1978, Milton Friedman told Ralph Harris that he had found Mrs Thatcher 'a very attractive and interesting lady. Whether

---

* Denis Thatcher believed that some of what people thought of as his wife's 'right-wingery' actually came from her religious upbringing: 'She can't find a sustainable argument that people should be paid for not doing any work.'

she really has the capacities that Britain so badly needs at this time, I must confess, seems to me a very open question.'

But all shared a certain wonderment at the phenomenon of a party leader in search of ideas. Mrs Thatcher's energy made her critics look dingy and negative. Chris Patten was one of them. As he put it, 'the most fundamental aspect of her leadership ... was that she believed she was engaged in a battle of ideas': 'Even though I was running the Conservative Party's Research Department, interested in ideas, I was much more used to an approach to politics that saw things in a less intellectually confrontational way. I happen to think she was right. But I remember the first time she said to me, "We have to win the battle of ideas in British politics," I thought, "This is a bit rum."'

This ferment of ideas would have been of little use, however, without anyone to relate it to actual policies. Here the most important person was Geoffrey Howe, whom Richard Ryder saw as the 'tapestry master of Thatcherism'. One of the few senior politicians to be what is nowadays called a policy wonk, Howe spawned a vast amount of detailed rethinking. With Keith Joseph, Nigel Lawson and the tax expert Arthur Cockfield, he plotted a free-market path for a future Conservative government. His approach was cautious, but dogged. He shared most of Joseph's aims, but was concerned about 'too breakneck a pace'. He favoured 'not-so-benign neglect of harmful institutions' over 'theatrical reform'.

Mrs Thatcher, however, had certain reservations about Howe. Since he stood against her in the leadership election, she harboured a growing suspicion that he was ambitious for her job. She had uneasy relations with Howe's wife, Elspeth, too much on the left and perhaps, being of grander class origin, too socially confident a woman to appeal to Mrs Thatcher. Many years later, Denis Thatcher would refer to Elspeth Howe as 'that bitch of a wife'.* Lady Howe liked to quote John Biffen's image that she and Mrs Thatcher were 'like two wasps in a jam-jar'.

Mrs Thatcher was irritated by Howe's quiet, almost inaudible voice, his tendency to be long-winded and his slightly pudgy, soft, bespectacled demeanour. He was never dashing, and she liked dash. Howe saw his own role as the patient antidote to her 'reluctance to think ahead'. But

---

* Mrs Thatcher was annoyed by Lady Howe's decision to serve as Deputy Chairman of the Equal Opportunities Commission in 1975. She had opposed the sex equality legislation that had created the commission and now feared that Lady Howe's actions might compromise Conservative positions. When she raised this indirectly with Geoffrey Howe, he half-acknowledged the problem while still defending his wife. On this and other issues, Howe's refusal to come down clearly on one side infuriated Mrs Thatcher (and his wife).

his patience made her impatient. Howe had not been her first choice as Shadow Chancellor and she doubted, unfairly, that he could be relied upon in the fight to come. In Opposition she made repeated half-hearted attempts to move him, but Howe resisted, even as he did more than any other politician to prepare the Conservatives to rescue the British economy. 'We all thought Geoffrey Howe was great,' recalled Norman Strauss, one of the most radical thinkers of the Thatcher project. 'He seemed to have the greatest understanding of what we were about.'

All these tensions, personal and ideological, tactical and strategic, were at their tautest over incomes policy and trade unions. Talking to Ted Heath in March 1977, the journalist Hugo Young recorded, 'The note of contempt for Thatcher and her team remains unabated. If they get in, Ted says, "They wouldn't know what to do" about the unions and economic policy. But they would be driven, he says, to a form of incomes policy. "But they would have wasted all this time . . . Why won't people learn the lessons of the past?"' The Thatcherite idea that it was the government's job to control the money supply and the employers' job to settle wages with employees seemed simultaneously too radical to understand and too old-fashioned to countenance.

For the Heathites, the issue went back to the 1930s, which had taught the Conservatives to fear unemployment above all things. They believed in an incomes policy as an earnest that the government would act to prevent economic hardship. The problem was that, by a slim margin, voters tended to favour Labour on this issue because it could 'get on with the unions'. To someone like Prior, it followed that the Conservatives risked permanent exclusion from power unless they could convince voters that they had a friendly working relationship with trade union bosses. That required reaching an agreement about pay and prices to 'control' inflation.

Mrs Thatcher did not agree with this. Her nature revolted against the idea that trade union leaders should have anything to do with deciding economic policy, or even general wage levels. Since she did not believe that inflation was caused by wage rises, she was sure that prices and incomes policies could not cure anything. Yet she shared Prior's political anxieties. She had seen how the Heath Industrial Relations Act had collapsed. Although she had no temperamental aversion to a fight with the unions, she certainly had no desire to lose one. She therefore heeded Prior, and other cautious voices, notably Willie Whitelaw's, while trying to push the argument on.

The process was necessary but painful. In the summer of 1976, Prior produced a Shadow Cabinet paper on employment policy. Mrs Thatcher's copy shows her tetchy reaction. When he floats the idea of a 'deal' allowing some secondary picketing in return for limiting picket numbers, she writes, 'Why?' She was instinctively more attracted to Joseph's suggestion that blame should be laid where blame was due: 'Trades unions and the Labour Party are the manifestations of the same purposes,' Joseph wrote in December 1976. 'Their common aim has become to usurp political and economic power.' He proposed educating the public that the medicine required would take 'at least five years' and would involve confronting the unions.

Hating confrontation, but wanting real reform, Geoffrey Howe searched for a middle way. His Economic Reconstruction Group duly advocated a version of German 'Concerted Action'. 'I disagree most strongly with this paper,' Mrs Thatcher scribbled. 'We are trying to cut down advisory bodies and requests for statistics – not multiply them.' Howe sent her an explanatory paper by a German economist about how Concerted Action would work. 'This paper frightens me to death even more,' she wrote. 'We really must avoid some of this terrible jargon [for Mrs Thatcher, an attack on 'jargon' was often a disguised attack on substance]. Also we should recognise that this German talking shop works because it consists of Germans.'

In public Mrs Thatcher held the line, trying to take a stand against mandatory incomes policy, but not returning to free collective bargaining too suddenly. But she was impatient about the crablike progress.

The problem of union power took particularly contentious form in 1977 because of a bitter industrial dispute at Grunwick, a photographic processing plant in north-west London. By the summer, huge and often violent pickets descended upon Grunwick in what had become a battle over union efforts to impose a closed shop.* The struggle brought home the street power of the left. As the Labour government stood back from condemning the violence, there was the sense, as with the Saltley coke depot under Heath, that neither government nor police had the power or will to impose order.

Mrs Thatcher was shocked by Grunwick, and everyone knew where her sympathies lay. But the Conservatives, though condemning violence and lawlessness, kept their distance. In part this was because of doubts about the business practices of Grunwick's owner, but it was also true that

---

* The row was not originally about union membership but the dismissal of a number of workers. Some of those dismissed had then joined the APEX trade union which demanded 'recognition' from Grunwick and the reinstatement of the sacked workers. A court upheld the legality of the dismissals, and a secret ballot at Grunwick showed that 80 per cent of those working at the plant did not want to join any union. If APEX prevailed, it was expected to impose a closed shop on the Grunwick plant.

a great many businessmen in large companies favoured the closed shop. They told the Conservatives that they found it simpler to negotiate with only one group of people.

This irritated Mrs Thatcher, who considered such people spineless, but it also inclined her to listen more to Jim Prior about the need to move slowly. In September 1977, while she was visiting the United States, an inquiry by Lord Scarman into the Grunwick dispute came out in favour of the unions. In her absence, Keith Joseph condemned Scarman and appeared to call for the outlawing of the closed shop. But Mrs Thatcher stuck with Prior's more cautious approach. 'We do not like the closed shop,' she told a press conference she had hoped would be about her meeting with President Jimmy Carter. 'But because I do not like it, and think it is against the freedom of the individual, does not necessarily mean that I can pass legislation about it.' In an interview with Brian Walden on *Weekend World* the following Sunday she offered the arresting idea that, should a Conservative government again be confronted by the miners, she would put the issue to a referendum,* because 'all of the people of this country are shareholders in miners'. She was reaching over the heads of trade union leaders to claim rank-and-file trade unionists for her side. But it was, in essence, a different way of asking the 'Who governs Britain?' question that had caused the Heath government so much grief. The idea went nowhere.

Perhaps burnt by internal disagreement publicly displayed, Mrs Thatcher became increasingly protective of Prior's exclusive right to pronounce on trade union matters. In January 1978, Geoffrey Howe sent her a draft of a speech he proposed to make about the unions. Her notes on it are almost the angriest she penned while Leader of the Opposition. When Howe wrote, 'These questions do not involve any special criticism of trade unions,' Mrs Thatcher wrote, 'Ha, ha!' When he advocated change 'step by step', she wrote 'Why.' '<u>Too defensive</u>,' she scrawled, '– If you can only be defensive – leave it alone!' 'Geoffrey – This is <u>not</u> your subject. Why go on with it – the press will crucify you for this . . . It would be better if Jim Prior said these things.' Howe's text was not delivered.

Mrs Thatcher was also under pressure from those arguing for a more radical approach. Their number included Hoskyns and Norman Strauss, who had come into her orbit through Keith Joseph. Their earlier efforts, in August 1976, to advise on her party conference speech had not been a success. In his diary, Hoskyns recorded sitting with Margaret and Denis in Flood Street with Mrs Thatcher 'defensively holding forth, lecturing us on things we were quite well aware of. I showed slight irritation once &

---

* This idea had not been squared with any of her colleagues in advance.

Mr T looked at me, stunned that I shouldn't be party to the inevitable mild sycophancy which makes her feel she's so much more remarkable than she is. She is a limited, pedantic bore, with no lateral grasp, very little humour.'* Hoskyns and Strauss persisted, however. Their aim was to get it into Tory heads that to bring about the economic change required, the unions must be confronted.

The result was a process known as Stepping Stones. Its first report, in November 1977, aimed both to unstitch the unions in public debate and to get the Tories to make explicit commitments to trade union reform to gain a mandate for government. Mrs Thatcher endorsed the report, which Hoskyns considered the 'turning-point'. 'Margaret's key contribution is guts and determination and a complete lack of the self-importance and pomposity which would make it so hard for many politicians to take advice of this kind,' he wrote afterwards, but added: 'She is quite limited intellectually . . . she is unaware of the fact that other people's intelligence may be superior to her own.'

A battle then ensued with Prior, Thorneycroft, Gilmour and Patten most opposed. Their opposition was ideological, but also tactical. In February 1978, Patten tried to push Stepping Stones to one side: 'The authors of "Stepping Stones" have described their political strategy in terms of painstakingly building a model of St Paul's with matchsticks. I would use a different metaphor. A successful strategy is like an artillery bombardment with half a dozen properly targeted heavy guns.' Stepping Stones should therefore be confined to an 'up-market campaign' 'without interfering with any of our other plans'. Patten's 'heavy guns' would aim at tax, law and order, housing, education and other matters. On the unions, they were silent.

As Patten's paper approached, Hoskyns confided his fears to his diary: 'the breathtaking vision and innovation which the situation calls for is [*sic*] not going to come from Thatcher – of that I am almost certain. Alfred has been warning of a "putsch" against her from Prior, Whitelaw, Gilmour – but this seems unlikely . . . Pym is seen as the successor . . . it seems a preposterous fear. But there's no doubt she does not lead and manage her Shadow Cabinet.'

Had Hoskyns witnessed the meeting of the steering committee on 30 January 1978, he would have been even more depressed. Suggesting that the

---

* The evening was not helped by the fact that, at one point, a cat stroked Norman Strauss's leg and then Mrs Thatcher's. She started, apparently thinking for a second that Strauss had been stroking her leg, and was then embarrassed.

Stepping Stones paper contained 'too much detail',* Mrs Thatcher insisted that Prior would lead on union reform. When John Davies (Maudling's replacement as Shadow Foreign Secretary) 'argued that if we told the truth about the unions we should certainly lose the election, Mrs Thatcher acknowledged this could not be the centrepiece of our strategy'. Shortly after this, Hoskyns and Strauss tried to persuade Mrs Thatcher to sack Prior. She naturally refused, but 'was not too put out by it. I think she sees Jim as a disaster in the context of any really intelligent and resolute plan for recovery ... Now he's in a very strong position and, with an election pending, she can do nothing.'

As the election expected in October 1978 approached, the Tories fought themselves to a stalemate. Mrs Thatcher's heart was with Joseph, Stepping Stones and taking on the unions. But her head was with those who argued that a fuzzier, more cautious approach was electorally necessary. As late as 22 August, Neave said privately that it had taken eighteen months' work to persuade Mrs Thatcher to accept the Prior approach. She was trapped in moderation.

---

* So frank were these minutes that Mrs Thatcher took the unusual step of asking Richard Ryder to lock them in the safe.

6

Labour isn't working

'There's only one chance for women'

Even as she struggled over policy, Mrs Thatcher grew into her role as leader. In the autumn of 1977, she joined all her Tory predecessors at the memorial service for Arnold Ashdown, a party treasurer. Ashdown was Jewish, and so all the men, as well as Mrs Thatcher, wore hats. In appearance each leader fulfilled his popular caricature. Harold Macmillan wore an Edwardian silk top hat; Alec Home the more modest Homburg customary in his youth. Ted Heath forgot that a hat was needed and had to borrow a paper yarmulke from the organizers. Mrs Thatcher stole the show, striking all in black topped by a hat with a very large brim. Already she was achieving a presence on the public stage.

For all her inexperience and social insecurity, Mrs Thatcher displayed the conspicuousness and panache which are inseparable from leadership. This was partly because of the uniqueness of her sex, but it also owed much to her appearance and force of character. No one else in her party, with the partial exception of Heath, could rival the hold on the popular imagination she was beginning to exert. She liked being noticed; she liked leading. Michael Portillo, as a young employee of the Conservative Research Department, recalled meeting her one morning during the 1976 Cambridge by-election campaign. As she leapt out of the car, she flashed her eyes at him and said, 'Take me to the battle!' Although it was a semi-comic moment, it also impressed him deeply: 'She had a thing about needing to look and play the part of leader.'

No leader can play the part of future prime minister without a presence on the international stage. After her 1975 visit to the United States she toured European capitals, the Middle East, China* and Australasia. Following the

---

* Mrs Thatcher's first visit to Communist China, in April 1977, was not politically eventful, but it made an impression. Because of extreme Chinese hostility to the Soviet Union at that time, she was welcomed with some pomp by the party leadership. She gave a reception for which the invitation read:

victory of the Democrat Jimmy Carter over Gerald Ford in the 1976 US presidential election, she decided to return to America. Carter's ascent to the presidency had been marginally unhelpful to her cause. She had few links to the Democrats and mistrusted his rather starry-eyed belief that the hearts of dictators could be changed if the West expressed its sincere desire for peace.

In May 1977, before her visit that September, she met Carter for a twenty-minute courtesy call at Winfield House, the American Ambassador's residence in London. Zbigniew Brzezinski, Carter's National Security Advisor, recorded in his diary: 'She impressed me as a shrewd and forceful politician. She amused me by mentioning . . . that she had read several of my books . . . Perhaps she would have done better to have read Carter's book. She didn't mention this at all(!).' The *New York Times* reported: 'Brimming with self-confidence, she told Mr Carter that her party would win the election no matter when it came.' This desire to convince people that she was the Prime Minister in waiting drove much of Mrs Thatcher's second visit to the USA as leader. 'I'm the next government,' she told a group of American journalists, 'I think I should meet your Cabinet.'

As the visit approached, the White House got cold feet. Suggesting that the President should not spend his time meeting Opposition leaders, Brzezinski advised Carter to 'plead a heavy schedule' and pass her off to the Vice-President. Carter's aides may also have had ideological objections and certainly did not want to upset James Callaghan, to whom they were close. Only an intervention from Peter Jay, the British Ambassador, secured a presidential meeting.*

Mrs Thatcher flew first to New York City. Media interest in her was less than in 1975, and a fighting speech to the British-American Chamber of

---

Margaret Thatcher
At Home
In the Great Hall of the People

But she did not feel at home at all. John Gerson, the official who accompanied her, recalled that 'To say she was open-minded would be an insult. She understood they *were* Communist, and she hated Communism.' In background conversation with journalists, she predicted that 'the spark of human spirit' would be the undoing of China and would eventually make India a more successful country. In public she described the Chinese approach as 'wholly alien to us. They have a correct view, and they hand down that correct view . . . Fortunately, we don't have a correct view.' She was accompanied by Douglas Hurd, who had served as a diplomat in China before entering politics. After visiting the Great Wall, she asked him, 'Did I get to the top quicker than Ted?'

* Mrs Thatcher actually benefited from the fact that Peter Jay, the new British Ambassador in Washington, was Callaghan's son-in-law. Given his 'unusual connections' with the Labour government, Jay felt he should 'lean over backwards' to help her.

Commerce was not extensively reported. At a dinner given by NBC she nearly fainted because of a combination of heat, exhaustion and a lifelong tendency to low blood pressure. As Caroline Stephens, accompanying her, recorded, 'she should really play the grande dame more and demand to sit down if she feels faint. But she is too polite and socially insecure.'

The next stop was Houston, Texas, where the English-Speaking Union organized a dinner, though organized is scarcely the right word. Caroline Stephens recorded: 'No hairdresser for MT (as ordered); no one to press her dress (as ordered) and just to crown it MT got locked in the bathroom . . . these setbacks did not amuse MT and she became distinctly irritated . . .'

Declaring the 'common heritage' of British and American ideas to be under attack, her speech was the preaching to the converted at which Mrs Thatcher always excelled. Christian values, she warned, would be undermined without a properly functioning free economy. 'Keynes . . . is reputed to have said: "In the long run, we are all dead." But in the long run, our children and their children will live; let it be in freedom.' Roy Fox, the Consul-General in Houston, was struck by the speech's power: 'They loved her more and more as the minutes ticked away. Her message could have been a bible for the Republican Party.' A slightly more equivocal compliment came from the man who introduced her at the dinner, one George H. W. Bush. He said Mrs Thatcher was 'a bright lady . . . frighteningly bright'. The future President's nervous praise foreshadowed their later interactions.

As for the serious politics of her visit, it was the future of Rhodesia (modern Zimbabwe) which gave her the greatest trouble. Ever since Ian Smith's white minority government had unilaterally declared independence from Britain in 1965, the former colony had been a thorn in the side of successive British governments. Britain and America had now put forward a joint plan to transition Smith's government to majority rule, but a major difficulty concerned the composition of the country's security forces. Carter had suggested that the existing (largely white) Rhodesian security forces should disband in favour of a new army 'based on the liberation armies' currently fighting the guerrilla war against Smith. This was a non-starter with Smith and the neighbouring white government of South Africa. Mrs Thatcher had warned publicly that such a move 'could introduce a destabilising factor', a view she repeated when she met Cyrus Vance, the Secretary of State, in Washington the day before meeting Carter. 'She is strongly opposed to including any black "terrorists" in the Rhodesian Army – which she likened to the British Army accepting elements of the

Irish Republican Army,' Vance reported. 'I hope they are not giving support to Smith,' Carter wrote in the margin.

Her meeting with the President was not easy. As Walter Mondale, the Vice-President, recalled, she declared that 'the US approach was all wrong': 'Rhodesia, she insisted, needed to be given a chance to work itself out. Carter didn't say anything, but I knew him well. There was a blood vessel in his neck that used to throb when he got irritated. And when Margaret Thatcher got onto the subject of Rhodesia it started to throb with a vengeance. It wasn't the fact that she disagreed with him, but . . . the way she did it. She was imperious.'

At the ensuing press conference Mrs Thatcher naturally avoided any impression of disagreement, but some discomfort lingered. Friendly Americans felt it too. Henry Kissinger gave her dinner in Washington: 'it seemed to me she felt snubbed by the Carter administration,' he recalled. She consoled herself by meeting the staunchly conservative Senator Jesse Helms and with what Caroline Stephens called 'private and disturbingly rightwing meetings'.

A combination of unspoken tension with Carter's people and the party rows about the closed shop back home proved too much for Mrs Thatcher. Before flying home on 14 September, at the British Embassy she became caught up in an argument with the press. As Peter Jay recalled: 'She got very angry. She gave a real hectoring speech . . . And then suddenly, she stood up and walked out. I followed her as the dutiful host . . . And then I saw – she was in tears – tears of rage I think, partly. I had to give her several whiskies to restore equilibrium.' Although the *Guardian* reported, following White House private briefing, that her attitude to Rhodesia had made the Carter administration 'uneasy', there had been no public breach. She had gone down well in New York, and a storm in Houston, but she knew that her Washington visit had not been politically successful. As she returned to her party's divisions about trade unions, she had reason to feel dispirited.

Throughout her time as Leader of the Opposition, Mrs Thatcher knew she was on probation with her party. Operating in a hung Parliament, she proved a skilled party manager. She listened to the Chief Whip, Humphrey Atkins, and to Willie Whitelaw, and was endlessly patient with the grass-roots and backbenchers. Setting aside those issues – chiefly economic – which she regarded as key to national recovery, she usually treated other matters more with an eye to party unity than to doctrinal purity.

Rhodesia is a case in point. In March 1978, Ian Smith reached an 'internal settlement' for a form of majority rule with elements of the black population, led by Bishop Abel Muzorewa. The agreement was immediately denounced by Robert Mugabe and Joshua Nkomo, the main black leaders fighting the civil war, and by the 'international community'. To many Conservatives, however, resisting what they saw as the persecution of 'our kith and kin' in Rhodesia, Smith's preparedness to make a deal seemed laudable. They thought the party leadership should support it. These sentiments, strongly backed by Denis, who knew the region well, were Mrs Thatcher's own. Echoing Lord Randolph Churchill's famous inflammatory comment about Ulster ninety years earlier, she told an *ad hoc* party policy meeting that if Marxist Mugabe were allowed to come to power, 'The whites will fight, and the whites will be right.' But when pressure grew for the Conservatives to nail their colours to the Smith-Muzorewa mast, she became cautious.

As the Conservatives' annual party conference approached, party representatives tabled an amendment supporting the unilateral lifting of sanctions against Rhodesia. Lord Carrington resisted this strongly, insisting that it would prevent a Tory government being a 'bridge between the various parties'. Initially Mrs Thatcher held back, but after revolt broke out at the conference she accepted Carrington's position. When the renewal of sanctions came to the vote in the Commons, the frontbench decision to abstain caused the largest Tory rebellion since the Second World War, with 114 Conservatives disobeying the whip. Mrs Thatcher later claimed that she would rather have opposed the renewal but, with a general election approaching, felt it 'better to have a full-scale backbench revolt than to lose members of the Shadow Cabinet'. She used a technique which would often serve her well – to indicate her sympathy with grass-roots feeling while giving the party establishment most of what it wanted.

Rhodesia evoked strong emotions in Tory breasts, but it was a much easier issue for Mrs Thatcher than devolution for Scotland. At first, pushed by her leading Scottish MPs,* she maintained the devolutionist position inherited from Ted Heath. *The Right Approach* spoke of 'a directly elected Scottish assembly, acting as another chamber of the UK Parliament'. But the policy began to shift, for several reasons.

The first was that most English and Welsh Tory MPs felt increasingly uncomfortable with anything which might break up the Union. The second was that those Tories who did support devolution – such as Ian Gilmour, Francis Pym and Alick Buchanan-Smith, the Shadow Scottish

---

* In the October 1974 election Tory representation in Scotland had fallen to sixteen MPs, its lowest since the introduction of universal suffrage.

Secretary – tended also to be those who were attracted by 'national' or coalition government and proportional representation. All this was anathema to Mrs Thatcher, and aroused her suspicion of the motives of those who promoted it.

She contemplated the question with quite a cold eye. Although an instinctive Unionist, she was conscious of waning Tory support in Scotland. Visiting three times in her first seven months, she sought to work out whether devolution was an electoral plus or minus north of the border. This was hard to do, because her Scottish party was divided into bitter factions. Broadly speaking, the more upper-class and rural elements, which dominated the party hierarchy, were pro-devolution, and the more urban and working-class elements were anti. During 1976 tensions grew. Rather than rejecting the principle of devolution, the party tried to unite by opposing Labour's specific plans,* but once the government produced a Bill the strain became intolerable. Buchanan-Smith's pro-devolution faction was adamant that its members should vote for the second reading of the Bill, but the Shadow Cabinet disagreed. He and his juniors, including the young Malcolm Rifkind, threatened to resign their frontbench posts. Mrs Thatcher did almost everything in her power to stop them. After she met the troubled Scots, Rifkind recorded:

> Margaret stated categorically that she was not prepared to contemplate our mass resignations and that some compromise must be found ... If we went she would have to appoint antis like Teddy Taylor as Scottish front-bench spokesman and this would be impossible ... She remarked, laughingly, that if we had to resign, she would appoint us again the following day if necessary!

She promised that a Tory government would put its own proposals for a Scottish assembly before Parliament. Rifkind and Buchanan-Smith resigned nonetheless, but others were dissuaded. In desperation, as she had warned Rifkind, she appointed Teddy Taylor Shadow Scottish Secretary.† In the parliamentary vote, twenty-seven Conservatives, including Heath, abstained and five voted with the government. A comparable number of Labour MPs rebelled against their whip the other way. The Bill advanced,

---

* This was possible because the Tories favoured a directly elected assembly tied to the Westminster legislative system, whereas Labour sought a separate Scottish parliament with its own executive.

† Taylor, a tough and eccentric working-class Glaswegian whose seat in that city depended on high Scottish Nationalist support taking Labour votes, remembered that Mrs Thatcher told him: 'I want you to destroy the SNP.' Taylor was more than willing to try, but replied: 'If we do that, I'll destroy my seat too.' His prediction was correct. The Conservatives gained seven Scottish seats from the SNP in the 1979 general election. The only one they lost was his, to Labour.

but there now emerged a more satisfactory situation for Mrs Thatcher. Pro-devolution Tories felt they had been politely treated; anti-devolutionists knew things were going their way; all felt freer to unite against Labour. Callaghan ploughed on, holding referendums in Scotland and Wales in March 1979. Neither vote reached the threshold required to enact devolution.* The resulting strains with the Nationalist parties caused the Labour government to fall later that month.

As for the Conservatives, they had opposed the government's Bill without rejecting the principle of devolution and campaigned, low-key, for a 'no' vote. Their eventual May 1979 manifesto confined itself to promising 'discussions about the future government of Scotland'. At that election, the Tories won a net gain of six seats in Scotland. Given the strange parliamentary predicament and the divisions Mrs Thatcher faced, this outcome was impressive. She had demonstrated the qualities which her opponents claimed she lacked – tact, the ability to listen, and a good measure of cunning.

There was another matter, of greater long-term significance, which called for Mrs Thatcher's political management. Over the summer of 1978, the EEC agreed to create the European Monetary System (EMS). This would begin on 1 January 1979. Britain now had to decide whether to participate in its most important element, the Exchange Rate Mechanism (ERM).

The Conservatives were relieved that the decision fell to Callaghan, whose party was beset by divisions on Europe. But the Tories nevertheless needed a line. The party establishment was clear. The Heathites, who had taken Britain into the EEC, remained intent on developing the project. At the other end of the spectrum, the consistently Powellite Eurosceptic John Biffen attacked the ERM publicly as a strengthening of the Franco-German axis. In October 1978, Nigel Lawson and Geoffrey Howe wrote separately to Mrs Thatcher. Lawson sought to steer a course between 'Eurofanatics and Europhobes' and advocated that 'we should avoid committing ourselves to any firm position on the EMS† for as long as possible ... it is a hideously complex and awkward issue, both economically and (more important) politically'. While a case might be made for the ERM's fixed exchange rate to buttress a tight monetary and fiscal policy, the associated conditions might render the EEC 'so unpopular as to make support of continuing EEC membership political suicide'. But, by not joining, Britain would 'risk abdicating for good the leadership of Europe'. Lawson coolly

---

* The Bill was hampered by an amendment carried by Labour rebels, which prescribed a threshold of 40 per cent of the electorate voting 'yes' before devolution could be enacted. In neither vote was this threshold reached. Wales, indeed, voted 'no' outright.
† Politicians at the time often referred to joining the EMS when they meant the ERM.

added his best recipe – a quick collapse of the system so that 'we could propose some alternative and more sensible framework for European economic convergence'. Any undertaking to join the ERM, he warned, 'would gratuitously split the party'.

Geoffrey Howe, by contrast, was unequivocal. The Tories, he said, should 'pronounce in favour' of the ERM for 'providing greater currency stability and encouraging convergence of economic policies'. He went on: 'The political case for this conclusion is a strong one: the alternative means surrendering the direction of the EEC ... to the Franco-German high table.'

Mrs Thatcher's attitude is clearly discernible from her annotations to Howe's letter. Against his claims about currency stability and economic convergence she wrote 'Why?' Beside his proposition about the Franco-German high table she wrote simply 'No.' Jim Callaghan's decision, that December, to reject British ERM entry let the Conservatives off the hook. But this early skirmish perfectly foreshadows – in tone, content, personalities, even choice of words – the matter which was to cause such extreme bitterness and division in Mrs Thatcher's later Cabinets. She was already suspicious of the project of European integration, but surrounded by senior colleagues who disagreed with her.

To set the terms of policy discussion, Mrs Thatcher would often express opinions more trenchant than those of her colleagues. On the ERM these remained private. On immigration they did not. Ever since Enoch Powell's 1968 'Rivers of Blood' speech, the issue had been toxic in Conservative politics, but public feeling against immigration (and continuing wide working-class support for Powell) was real enough. Indeed, it regrew as Labour relaxed controls.*

In early 1978, with the Conservative lead in the polls vanishing, Mrs Thatcher sensed an opportunity. According to Richard Ryder, 'She felt hemmed in on incomes policy, so she thought she would take a free hit on immigration.' In an interview broadcast on 30 January she noted that there would probably be 4 million Pakistani and New Commonwealth immigrants in Britain by 2000. This was 'an awful lot', she said, and British people feared that they 'might be rather swamped by people with a different culture ... We are a British nation, with British characteristics.'

---

* In 1977, Roy Jenkins, the former Labour Home Secretary responsible for much of the relaxation, temporarily left British politics to become President of the European Commission. Immigration dominated the campaign for the by-election that followed in his former seat of Stechford. It led to a dramatic gain for the Tories, but the virulently anti-immigration National Front won 8.1 per cent of the vote.

There was widespread outrage in the broadsheet press and at Westminster, and widespread approval in the country. Willie Whitelaw told Roy Jenkins 'how absolutely ghastly life was with that awful woman, how he was thinking of resigning,' but, characteristically, continued much as before. In private, Chris Patten expressed the perturbation of the liberal wing of the party. 'Just imagine', he told Michael Portillo, 'if she'd said we were being swamped by Jewish people.' In Parliament the excitable Labour MP Andrew Faulds was ordered by the Speaker to 'control himself' in his attacks on Mrs Thatcher. Faulds shouted back: 'With that bloody woman in the House, how can you expect it?' His phrase 'that bloody woman' was taken up by many critics, often abbreviated to 'TBW'.

Mrs Thatcher's remarks were significant not for any change in policy – most Tories agreed that immigration controls should be strengthened – but for her choice of language.* In standing up against the chattering classes, she almost enjoyed being 'TBW'. On immigration she felt that a politician must attend to people's legitimate fears: voters were entitled to greater certainty about numbers and commitments.† The Conservatives now shot up in the opinion polls to an eleven-point lead over Labour. In February they won the Ilford North by-election. All this fuelled Mrs Thatcher's growing belief that 'I must trust my own judgement in crucial matters, rather than necessarily hope to persuade my colleagues in advance; for I could expect that somewhere out in the country there would be a following and perhaps a majority for me.'

In the spring of 1978, the Tories selected Saatchi & Saatchi as their advertising agency for the next election. Given that the Saatchi brothers, Maurice and Charles, had no previous political involvement it was a bold choice, which came at the urging of Gordon Reece. Tim Bell, their chairman, thought it a bad idea. There was no money in it, he said, and much

---

* An interesting example of Mrs Thatcher's personal attitude to immigrants was noted by the young Michael Portillo when, as a member of the Research Department, he attended part of a Shadow Cabinet meeting in the summer of 1976. In the middle of a discussion on immigration the division bell rang. Mrs Thatcher asked what the vote was about and was told that it was about giving Sikhs special exemption from wearing crash helmets on their motorbikes, so that they could keep their turbans on. Carrington made some *sotto voce* remark about the piquancy of this vote at this precise moment. Mrs Thatcher said sharply, 'What did you say?' Carrington said, 'It was a joke, Margaret,' and explained. She replied, 'Well, it's not very funny. These people fought for us in the war.'

† Mrs Thatcher used the experience to reiterate her belief that the National Front, far from being the authentic, or even the perverted, voice of the patriotic right, was 'a socialist front', concerned to bring about a siege economy and state control. She was interested in the fact that the word 'Nazi' was short for National Socialist, and felt that the socialist aspect was dangerously ignored.

aggravation, but he was overruled and became the link man with Reece. Alistair McAlpine, the Treasurer, shocked Saatchis by saying: 'If we win the election, we'll pay you. Otherwise not.' But he was one of the most enthusiastic for their work. He would go round to rich donors with a sheaf of Saatchi suggestions for election campaign posters and ask, 'Which one of these would you like to pay for?'

Reece, Bell and McAlpine formed a team within Conservative Central Office unconstrained by the party bureaucracy. As Reece recalled it, 'we were engaged in a great crusade'. They were also (in Bell's words) 'in love' with Margaret Thatcher. Their emotional loyalty was to her, not to the Tory Party. This gave an edge to their work.

The Saatchi-Reece strategy, however, was not to focus public attention on their heroine. Bell told Thorneycroft that Mrs Thatcher was 'hard to sell' because she looked too much like people's idea of a Tory wife, and the image of a Tory wife supporting her husband was incompatible with the image of a leader. Instead, Saatchis seized upon the old saw that 'oppositions don't win elections; governments lose them'. People in general were saying how ghastly everything was, so the Conservatives should say so too. They recommended striking at what had traditionally been Labour's strongest points. Unemployment, which had hit 1.5 million in 1977, was an obvious example. With the slogan 'Labour isn't working' they created a poster showing an old-fashioned dole queue snaking into the distance. Although sparingly put up, the poster was heavily trailed to selected newspapers. Denis Healey raged against it, ensuring acres of free publicity. It marked the beginning of the Conservatives' rhetorical conquest of Labour.*

Mrs Thatcher had little natural feel for what made a good election poster, though she often offered small, practical comments. She also raised common-sense objections on grounds of taste or comprehensibility and required every joke to be laboriously explained. Jeremy Sinclair, the Creative Director of Saatchis, remembered that 'she'd cross it all out, rewrite it, and end up pretty much where we'd started'. Her first reaction to the 'Labour isn't working' poster was to complain because 'the largest word on it is "Labour"', but, Bell remembered, she was quickly won over 'because she saw it was hurtful [to Labour], and she liked that'.

Mrs Thatcher was quite humble in areas of which she had little knowledge. She trusted Reece and liked the people, notably Bell, whom he brought in. As early as 1972, when she was a Cabinet minister, Reece had helped her with her voice. He bumped into Laurence Olivier on a train and

---

* Variations on the theme followed later: 'Educashun isn't working' said a poster of a boy writing those misspelt words on a blackboard.

asked the great actor's advice. Olivier lent her the services of Kate Fleming, the National Theatre's voice coach, to make her sound less shrill. Mrs Thatcher had submitted to this uncomplainingly. She now allowed Saatchis to make party political broadcasts untraditional, stylish and funny, though these were not natural Margaret Thatcher characteristics. She also warmly supported campaigns aimed at those without a strong interest in politics. Advertisements were placed in women's magazines, which said: 'Do this quiz to find out if you're Labour or Conservative.' After questions about different policies, the quiz ended:

> Which of these people is more likely to know what it's like to do the family shopping?
> a. James Callaghan
> b. Your husband
> c. Mrs Thatcher

Cultivation of the popular newspapers was part of the same strategy: Mrs Thatcher flattered Larry Lamb, Editor of the *Sun*,* and placed great faith in the power of the paper's leading articles which appeared on page two, opposite the famous page-three girls. On one occasion, arguing with her advisers, Mrs Thatcher alighted on two leaders in that day's *Sun* which vigorously confirmed her prejudices. 'There,' she cried, spreading the paper before them. 'What do you think of those two?' The young aides found themselves staring at a large pair of breasts and almost suffocated with suppressed laughter. Mrs Thatcher, of course, failed to notice the source of their mirth.† Gordon Reece also drew on his own friendships with editors. When the *Mail* got hold of the previously unknown story of Denis's first marriage, Reece exploited his relationship with David English, the paper's editor, to ensure that the piece was written in a friendly manner. Indeed, English wrote it himself.‡ Reece's skill unlocked in a correct and almost

---

* When, in May 1978, the circulation of Rupert Murdoch's right-wing *Sun* surpassed the Labour-supporting *Daily Mirror* for the first time, Mrs Thatcher sent the paper a message of congratulation.

† Mrs Thatcher always had to have *double entendres* explained, and she came to dread uttering them by mistake. She saw them as a specifically male thing which would always remain a mystery to her. Once she wanted to use the word 'blackball' in a speech, and her advisers tried to prevent her without quite having the courage to tell her why. Eventually, Adam Butler solved the problem by saying, 'Doesn't it sound a bit too clubby, Margaret?' Perhaps the best-known example was her statement in a 1984 television interview that she was 'always on the job'.

‡ It says something about the difference between Mrs Thatcher's successful management of her public image and her uneasy management of her children that the fact of the first marriage had been unknown to Mark and Carol. Carol was in Australia as the story broke and it fell to Alison Ward to inform her about it. Mark remembered the incident as very distressing.

inhibited woman the showbiz, populist, communicative gifts which lurked within. Her ability thus to master the media made life far more difficult for rivals and opponents.

Working on the assumption of an autumn 1978 election, the Conservatives drew up their manifesto. The process made all factions anxious, and the cautious tended to prevail over the bold. Mrs Thatcher was wary of too many promises. At a Shadow Cabinet meeting on 31 July she warned that 'because a large number of nuggets were being inserted, we were in danger of losing our credibility on the reduction of expenditure. She proposed that the next manifesto draft put the main emphasis on a few central objectives on which everything else depended: (a) the cutting of taxes and (b) strengthening internal and external defence.' But the same meeting went on to agree that 'We should not pick a fight with the unions on a minor issue by a crude commitment on strikers' benefits.' Mrs Thatcher was torn between prudence and conviction.

In a private interview given to the political scientists David Butler and Dennis Kavanagh on 9 August, she revealed she had tidied her desk and was ready for 10 Downing Street. She had no time for any government of national unity, or for proportional representation, the method of voting likely to bring such a coalition about. In the Shadow Cabinet, Carrington, she said, 'was always articulating his doubts and uncertainties and this made her impatient. She said to people like him: I know what. You tell me how.' That last sentence could stand as a summary of her approach throughout her years of Opposition. She warned that, in office, it would take a huge amount of time to 'unscramble socialism'. Against those colleagues who still supported wage controls, Mrs Thatcher said that the worst thing about the Heath government's incomes policy had been that it 'undermined respect for the rule of law'. In this private interview, more than in public utterances, Mrs Thatcher articulated the robust views for which she would later become famous.

The full manifesto draft emerged at the end of August 1978. Despite 'Labour isn't working', the foreword failed to mention jobs as a priority until Mrs Thatcher wrote it in herself. The longing, felt so strongly by Butskellites,* to be seen to be 'striking a balance' governed much of the document. 'We will be even-handed in our approach to industrial problems,' said the draft. 'We shall not undertake any sweeping changes in the law on industrial relations.' Mrs Thatcher went to work. She deleted the

---

* The word, meaning moderates of all parties, was created by amalgamating the surnames of R. A. Butler and Hugh Gaitskell.

suggestion that union reforms must come from within the union movement, and where the draft said the closed shop could be retained when a 'massive majority' voted for it she wrote caustically, 'i.e. no rights for minorities'. 'Need for more emphasis on left wing drift of Labour,' she scrawled. Against a tentative section on pay she wrote, 'This paragraph is pathetic.' Where the draft wanted Members of the European Parliament to 'have the authority to halt the flow of unnecessary legislation', Mrs Thatcher, ever alert against increasing the EEC's constitutional powers, crossed out 'have the authority to halt' and substituted 'should deter'. Yet she could only do so much. Even with the leader's injections of vim, the document which the Conservatives planned to offer the electorate was bland.

On 7 September 1978, Jim Callaghan announced that there would not be an autumn election. It was a surprising decision which wrongfooted everyone, including, perhaps, himself. That summer, inflation had fallen below 10 per cent, while a 5 per cent norm for pay increases held out the promise of orderly management. Yet Callaghan decided to wait, gambling on beating inflation by the following summer.

Touring the Midlands, Mrs Thatcher was deflated by Callaghan's announcement, although she knew, rationally, that it did not damage Tory chances. She had been so girded for battle that it hurt to lay down her armour. Exhausted, but conscientious as ever, she stayed up talking to the travelling press late into the night. At last Denis pushed his way into the crowded room and said, 'Come on, woman. Bedtime.' She meekly followed.

The short-term effect of Callaghan's decision was to help Labour. Gallup, which had recorded a 7 per cent Tory lead in September, returned a 5 per cent Labour lead the next month. The Tories duly obliged their opponents with another public split about pay policy.

The immediate cause was Ted Heath. Early in the year, strenuous attempts had been made to improve his relations with Mrs Thatcher, but to little effect. Matters had, in fact, deteriorated after Heath believed, mistakenly, that the Chief Whip had suggested that Mrs Thatcher would welcome him joining the Shadow Cabinet. Discovering this was not the case, Heath chose to take offence. At the party conference in October he made a speech described by *The Times* as 'stuffy and charmless' and spoke out on television. 'Free collective bargaining produces massive inflation,' he said, and if Callaghan 'says he is going to the country and expresses the view that we cannot have another roaring inflation or another free-for-all, I would say I agree with that'.

With opinion polls showing that the public preferred the Heath-Callaghan view about pay to the free-for-all which she was thought to advocate, Mrs Thatcher was embarrassed. But she was also determined not to get trapped into committing to an incomes policy. Privately, she rejected the idea that the country could be run by a pact between unions and government. 'Sovereignty of Govt has to be reasserted,' she said, according to notes of a conversation with Bill Deedes. In her party conference speech, which the dispirited rank and file considered slightly weak, she allowed scope for differences without conceding her position: 'We believe in realistic, responsible collective bargaining, free from government interference.' Later that month, Labour held Berwick and East Lothian, its best by-election result in that Parliament. Heath had appeared on the hustings and reiterated his support for an incomes policy. An NOP poll in November showed a Tory lead of 3 per cent which rose to 14 per cent if Heath were leader. The Tories felt stuck.

On 13 December the government lost a vote in Parliament to impose sanctions against employers which had broken the 5 per cent pay limit. A vote of confidence followed, which the government won. Mrs Thatcher failed to rise to the occasion: 'She sped on as if nobody else was in the House,' Bernard Donoughue recorded, 'and very soon people were chatting on the back benches or leaving for tea – because she does not involve them.' Afterwards, Callaghan told Donoughue that Mrs Thatcher didn't realize that a large part of success in Parliament came from treating it as a form of show business, but added that 'she was good when provoked'.*

On the last day of the year, the Thatchers gave a lunch party at Scotney Castle amid heavy snow. She told Bill Deedes that she had 'just endured the worst two months of her time as Leader'. But Britain's difficulties were to prove her opportunity. The public-sector unions had already rejected Stage 3 of the government's pay policy. On 3 January 1979, a strike by lorry drivers began. In Downing Street Callaghan grumbled that things were 'all falling apart'. Soon afterwards he flew off to the sunny Caribbean island of Guadeloupe for an international conference. Images of him there in shirtsleeves, when the British winter was beastly cold, roused feeling against him. Stepping off the plane back home, with disputes under way in road haulage and railways, and approaching in coal, gas, electricity, local authorities and the Civil Service, he appeared complacent about Britain's plight. 'Crisis? What Crisis?' was the splash headline in the *Sun*. Callaghan never uttered these words, but they stuck.

To take advantage of changing circumstances, Mrs Thatcher was persuaded to change her tone. As what was being called the 'Winter of

---

* Mrs Thatcher was aware of this tendency in herself. She told the *Observer* in an interview conducted nine days later, 'This animal, if attacked, defends itself.'

Discontent' deepened, it had become obvious to Mrs Thatcher's advisers – not just the centrist Chris Patten, but also the loyalist Gordon Reece, Tim Bell, T. E. Utley and Ronnie Millar – that conciliation would be more electorally popular, and much more lethal to Callaghan, than partisan aggression. Mrs Thatcher was intensely suspicious.* To Tim Bell, who literally went down on his knees to plead with her, she said: 'You're going to try to sell me a One Nation Tory message, aren't you?' Her advisers persuaded her, however, that it was a matter of tone, not principle: they were going to turn her into a statesman and make the government look like the party of Opposition refusing to come together for the greater good of the country. Gordon Reece cunningly added the bait that she would put herself on the right side of public opinion and so force Jim Prior to endorse all the main trade union reforms she wanted.†

Mrs Thatcher, although grumpy, conceded. As always, once she had agreed to something she threw herself into it with gusto and professionalism. In her party political broadcast on 17 January she declared: 'it is our country, the whole nation, that faces this crisis . . . This is no time to put party before country.' There had to be changes in the law and she offered parliamentary cooperation to the government if it would ban secondary picketing and provide for postal and secret ballots in strike votes and union elections. The broadcast was artfully constructed to remind viewers of Labour's responsibility for the problem while reaching out to Labour in the name of national unity. 'We have to learn again to be one nation,' she concluded, suppressing her dislike of the phrase, 'or one day we shall be no nation.'

The broadcast succeeded in turning the pressure on to Callaghan. She knew that the precariousness of his parliamentary and trade union position made it impossible to grant what she asked, and yet that most voters would see her offer as reasonable. By now the Winter of Discontent involved innumerable industrial disputes across the country. There was even a time in Liverpool when the dead went unburied. The day after Mrs Thatcher's broadcast, the Cabinet debated whether to call a state of emergency (they decided not to): 'Afterwards', Donoghue recorded, Callaghan said 'with a straight face: "How do you announce that the Government's Pay Policy has completely collapsed?"' Suddenly there was a sense that the main point of Labour government – that it could achieve industrial harmony – had vanished.

---

* She had made her preference clear in a letter to Hugh Thomas on 10 January: 'If I have one resolution for the New Year', she wrote, 'it is that I should not depart from my convictions by one iota – nor should I fear the reaction of the so-called Liberal Establishment to what I have to say.' What her advisers were suggesting was not quite in this spirit.

† Reece and Bell filled her room in the House of Commons, from which her broadcast took place, with flowers to make her feel that she had not lost the argument.

At last the Conservatives felt emboldened, having discovered, almost by accident, a way of sounding both tough and non-partisan. Mrs Thatcher warmed to her themes. On *The Jimmy Young Show* on BBC Radio 2, as rubbish accumulated in the streets and the power station workers and dockers were demanding 15 per cent pay rises, she spoke of the nation's 'spiritual crisis'. And she adopted the rhetoric of battle, against which, earlier, she had been cautioned: 'If someone is confronting our essential liberties, if someone is inflicting injury, harm and damage on the sick, my God, I will confront them.' She drove home her point that the rule of law was under threat, explicitly disagreeing with Arthur Scargill, not yet the Leader of the National Union of Mineworkers but already its leading firebrand: 'There can be no liberties unless the law is enforced. That is my great quarrel with Scargill.' An opinion poll in the *Daily Express* on 6 February put the Conservatives 19 per cent ahead of Labour.

The last few weeks of the Labour government were dominated by parliamentary arithmetic. After the devolution referendums on 1 March, Callaghan could no longer rely on the Nationalists to prop up his government. So the Tories tabled a vote of confidence, designed to bring down the government. In the debate itself, Mrs Thatcher did not speak very well. Concerned only to win the vote, she did not want to give any hostages to fortune. Callaghan performed rather more effectively, but the numbers were against him. The final vote was 310 for the government and 311 against.* Callaghan duly asked the Queen for a dissolution of Parliament.

Callaghan chose the last possible date for a general election now open to him – 3 May. He wanted time to divert attention from Labour's problems and on to Mrs Thatcher herself: 'She is the dominant personality of the campaign,' he told Donoughue. 'If we win, it will be because people cannot take her.' For this reason he broke with precedent and offered to join her in a televised debate.† Mrs Thatcher was keen to accept. She was terrified of being considered terrified, particularly being terrified 'as a woman'. Yet she was advised strongly against by voices as diverse as Willie Whitelaw, Lord Thorneycroft, Gordon Reece and everyone at Saatchis.‡ They believed a

---

* Michael Foot, the Leader of the House, wound up for the government in a brilliant speech of partisan denunciation. Denis Thatcher was 'under the Gallery' watching it, and got furious at Foot's jibes. He had had a drink or two, and kept saying 'Rubbish' until rebuked by a doorkeeper.
† Until then it had been traditional for the incumbent to refuse the invitation to a television debate between the party leaders. None took place until the general election of 2010.
‡ Reece was so worried that Mrs Thatcher would agree to the debate that he hid the first invitation from her and refused it on her behalf. A second letter arrived, however, and she challenged Reece about not being shown the first. Reece remembered: 'All the moisture in my

debate would be make-or-break for Mrs Thatcher, but not for Callaghan, a much better-known quantity: with the Conservatives ahead, why take the risk? There was also a view that, even if she had won the debate, the sight of a woman humiliating a man would have unsettled male voters. As Thorneycroft put it, 'many men would have resented it. They would have said, "That's my wife" and it wouldn't have been a good thing.'

Reece, who was desperate to focus the election on the Winter of Discontent, greeted Mrs Thatcher's decision not to debate with relief. The Conservatives now redrafted their manifesto. 'I think the existing draft will have to be radically changed,' wrote Mrs Thatcher, 'consequent on recent events and on much more robust union policy. But the general approach of limited objectives first (i.e. tax cuts etc. to encourage wealth creation) remains. In my view the average person ... wants "tax cuts and order".' The revised version failed to impress: 'Have read through this with considerable dismay,' she scribbled in March. Against the line 'Our economic weakness has been partly caused by failure to accept that the interests of all classes within the nation are ultimately the same,' she wrote, 'No it hasn't – it isn't.' Beside the assertion 'Nor can we go on, year after year, tearing ourselves apart in increasingly bitter and calamitous industrial disputes,' she noted. 'The chances are we shall for quite a time.'

Mrs Thatcher was irritated by the consensual tone which still crept in. Where the draft promised a 'moderates' charter' for trade union reform she scrawled, 'Don't be "moderate" in the defence of liberty or the rule of law. It is the way to lose both.' Throughout, she sought to toughen everything up. Yet her natural caution also showed through. Whenever a commitment seemed too specific she wrote, 'Hostage!' or 'hostage to fortune'.

Despite the ferocity of Mrs Thatcher's assault, the final product was not rabid in tone. Indeed, her foreword now began with a rejection of dogma: 'For me, the heart of politics is not political theory, it is people and how they want to live their lives.' Her party's manifesto was based 'above all on liberty of the people under the law'. She evoked an almost wartime sense of solidarity: 'The things we have in common as a nation far outnumber those that set us apart.' On trade unions, the sentence she had questioned about 'tearing ourselves apart' stayed. Pay policies were condemned and three specific reforms proposed – the removal of immunities from secondary picketing, a proper ballot about a closed shop and the right of individual

---

mouth dried up because the row was so terrible.' Mrs Thatcher said, 'Gordon, you'd better go home.' In the early hours of the morning, Reece, by this time drunk, rang Tim Bell and said, 'It's all over. My career is finished,' but Bell advised him simply to return to work the next day and say nothing. He did so, and, somehow or other, his view prevailed.

appeal against membership, and secret and postal ballots, publicly funded, for union elections and strike votes.

On taxes, the manifesto declared, 'We shall cut income tax at all levels to reward hard work,' but offered no specific rates. Such cuts would 'take priority for the time being over the abolition of the domestic rating system'. There would be cuts in public spending, but the document was deliberately vague about where these would fall. *Sotto voce*, the manifesto explained that income tax cuts could not be paid for without a 'switch to some extent from taxes on earnings to taxes on spending'. Nationalization was denounced, but denationalization not strongly proclaimed.* There would be better police pay, firmer immigration controls and higher defence spending. On Europe, the manifesto called for a 'single voice' in foreign policy. 'National payments into the budget should be more closely related to ability to pay,' it added, a low-key harbinger of a row to come. By the admittedly modest standards of the genre, the Conservative manifesto read well. It set out a scale of priorities. It was reticent, but not dishonest, about the need for spending cuts and for an increase in VAT. It expressed a sense of urgency without lapsing into extremism, and offered a clear difference from Labour's message of reassurance.

As is customary, the party had begun discussions with the Civil Service of how this might be translated into government. Mrs Thatcher herself had seen Sir Ian Bancroft, head of the Home Civil Service. Kenneth Stowe, who, as Callaghan's principal private secretary, would be hers for the transition, talked to Bernard Donoughue about this process; 'Ken says she gives the impression of wanting to run the whole show herself. It is clear that the Civil Service is viewing the prospect of her arriving with some dismay.'

On 30 March, the Tory campaign was shaken by a front-page story in the *Mirror*. The paper printed a letter received by a Mrs Evelyn Collingwood, who had complained to Mrs Thatcher about the state of her council house. The letter (sent 'at Mrs Thatcher's request') pulled no punches: 'I hope you will not think me too blunt if I say that it may well be that your council accommodation is unsatisfactory, but considering the fact that you have been unable to buy your own accommodation you are lucky to have been given something, which the rest of us are paying for out of our taxes.'

Written by Matthew Parris, a young member of the Conservative Research Department, these words had never been cleared with Mrs Thatcher. But in the media frenzy this mattered little. The story resonated

---

* Only shipbuilding and aerospace were specifically marked for denationalization; it was also promised that shares in the National Freight Corporation would be sold off.

because it seemed to confirm the widespread fear that Mrs Thatcher was a divisive figure, the fierce spokesman of her own class, trampling on those below her.

This story, however, was eclipsed by much darker news. That same morning Airey Neave was murdered by a car bomb planted by the Irish National Liberation Army, an Irish Republican splinter group, as he attempted to leave the House of Commons car park.* In Opposition, Mrs Thatcher had devoted little personal attention to Northern Ireland, trusting Neave to develop the right policies himself. His death brought out her strongest native feeling on the subject – her hatred of giving any sort of victory to terrorists. 'Some devils got him,' she told the BBC. 'They must never, never, never be allowed to triumph.' It sounds callous to say it, but Mrs Thatcher's campaign benefited from Neave's murder, not only because it diverted attention from Matthew Parris's letter. Such terrible occasions brought out both her natural human warmth and her attachment to certain simple principles. On 2 April, paying tribute to the man who, more than any other MP, had won her the leadership, she said: 'Airey's death diminishes us, but it will enhance our resolve that the God-given freedoms in which he believed, and which are the foundation of our parliamentary democracy, will in the end triumph over the acts of evil men.' For the public, Neave's death subliminally deepened the idea that Mrs Thatcher stood for something important. Alistair McAlpine noted, at Neave's funeral, a sense that 'This was definitely the moment, the feeling that this was her hour.'

The campaign was slow to start. Aware of Callaghan's tactic of trying to get Mrs Thatcher to make mistakes, Reece kept her quiet. At the manifesto launch on 11 April, Mrs Thatcher was cautious. She promised – though she hated it – to honour the findings of the Pay Comparability Commission, chaired by Professor Hugh Clegg, and stressed there could be no sudden end to industrial subsidy. She pushed aside arguments about the distribution of the 'national cake': the point was to create more cake 'before we can decide how the extra shall be sliced up'.

Mrs Thatcher's more emotional speeches – disparaged by Patten as 'hot-gospelling' – were confined to ticket-only rallies across the country.

---

* Republicans were keen to murder Neave, chiefly because he was close to Mrs Thatcher, but also because his approach to Northern Ireland was nearer to integrationist moderate Unionism than had been the policy under Heath. From their point of view his murder was worthwhile, since from then on the anti-Unionist search for 'power-sharing' dominated Tory thinking, even though Mrs Thatcher herself never much cared for it. Republicans believed that power-sharing – the division of the spoils between Unionists and Nationalists – gave them more chance of ultimate success in Northern Ireland than did the integration of the province with the rest of the United Kingdom.

In Cardiff on 16 April she delivered one of her classic self-descriptions: 'in politics I've learnt something that you in Wales are born knowing. It's this: if you've got a message, preach it! [*applause*] The Old Testament prophets didn't go out into the highways saying, "Brothers, I want consensus." They said, "This is my faith and my vision! This is what I passionately believe!" And they preached it.' This refusal of consensus was something which Callaghan tried to exploit, but it also helped her dominate the debate.

The Reece plan aimed to get Mrs Thatcher on the early evening television news watched by women and in the local papers reporting favourably the leader's visit to their area, rather than the national ones trying to take apart every word she said. He got her out of London, lock-stitching clothes in Leicester, for example, and, famously, cuddling a calf on a farm in Suffolk for thirteen minutes to get the right camera angles. Back then such techniques were novelties, the more novel because they were being performed by the first woman to lead a British political party. She was blonde, 5 foot 5, size 14 and 9½ stone:* she was different, and she was bursting with energy.

Frank Johnson captured this when she visited the Cadbury chocolate factory in the marginal constituency of Birmingham, Selly Oak. Inevitably, he wrote in the *Daily Telegraph*, she was 'urged to try chocolate packing herself': 'The problem, of course, would be to stop her. Maniacally, she would raid the hazel crispy clusters and shove them in passing boxes ... What a scene! The genius at Conservative Central Office who thought it up must get a knighthood.'†

An added reason for such stunts was that Mrs Thatcher was very good at them. Interviewed during the campaign, she was surprisingly frank about how she played everything for the camera. In a passage in which her manner now seems almost comically flirtatious, she explained the incident with the calf: 'The press say, "Look, we don't want just another photograph

---

* Mrs Thatcher found it hard to keep her weight down, and for two weeks of the campaign she subjected herself to a diet, aimed at losing 20 lb, which she checked against a daily sheet of instructions. This began: 'Abstain from everything not included in the diet and be sure to eat what is assigned rather than do without. NO EATING BETWEEN MEALS.' The diet involved eating twenty-eight eggs per week, grapefruit for breakfast (with 'black coffee or clear tea'), steak and salad. By the time she entered No. 10, she did look more slender.

† He did. Reece became Sir Gordon in 1986. In his opinion, however, Mrs Thatcher was slow in realizing his full importance. In 1981 she offered him the CBE. He wrote back, with icy anger: 'It is my view that with the exception of yourself, no member of the Conservative Party contributed more effectively to the result of the 1979 election than I did ... Not that such services demand a knighthood ... But I respectfully suggest that that or nothing were the alternatives ... I am conscious of the honourable estate of the CBE. In the circumstances I would prefer not to accept it.'

of you, with a hundred, uh, bullocks looking in *superb* condition." There was a beautiful calf, and after all, we had 70 or 80 cameramen around with us. They have to do their job . . .' It was important to consider, she said, 'what you're like in three dimensions'. She emphasized that she had to get everything right because 'There's only one chance for women. 'Tis the law of life.' This determination brought out her showman's flair and contrasted with Callaghan, good performer though he was, who by this time (he was sixty-seven and had held all the main offices of state) had too little to prove.

Nevertheless, Mrs Thatcher's campaign was not strikingly successful. The press soon got to work on those areas of tax and spending which the Conservatives did not want to talk about. Would the Tories break the link between earnings and pensions? Yes, but they were reluctant to say so. Would they double VAT? Callaghan havered about driving this point home because he feared that if Labour won he too would have to increase VAT, but towards the end of April Labour started to push much harder on tax and prices.*

After two weeks, the Conservative campaign seemed to stall. The Gallup poll on 25 April showed the gap between the parties, which had stood at 10 per cent when the campaign began, down to 5 per cent. That night, over dinner with colleagues, Mrs Thatcher learnt that Peter Thorneycroft wanted her to share a platform with Ted Heath to show unity and rescue centrist votes. As Michael Dobbs recalled, a furious row ensued. 'No, I won't have it,' said Mrs Thatcher and she stormed out in tears, to be comforted by Carol. In Dobbs's view, they were tears of frustration at men telling her she wasn't good enough. Her sense of upset persisted, exacerbated by her tiredness. Two days later she snapped at unsympathetic journalists. Her manner – and her voice – showed signs of strain. Her organizers cancelled a speech and walkabout that day. A MORI poll the following morning brought the Tory lead down to 3 per cent and gave Callaghan his biggest lead yet as the 'best PM' – 19 per cent ahead of Mrs Thatcher.

Looking back, one can see that these Tory jitters failed to consider the underlying situation. As Callaghan said privately during the campaign, 'It does not matter what you say or do. There is a shift in what the public wants

---

* Michael Portillo, whose job it was to brief Mrs Thatcher on the contents of the press every morning of the campaign, remembered drafting an answer which said: 'We won't double VAT, or anything like.' When Geoffrey Howe crossed out 'or anything like', he realized for the first time how big were the tax changes contemplated. Agreement about the near-doubling of VAT had been secretly reached by Howe, Lord Cockfield and Nigel Lawson without the involvement of Mrs Thatcher. As a result, she could say in an election broadcast that the VAT increase would be 'Not a lot, but a little' (27 April) without actually lying.

and what it approves. I suspect there is now such a sea-change – and it is for Mrs Thatcher.' In this sense, although she made some tonal mistakes, Mrs Thatcher was right about the almost prophetic message of change in her campaign. She stood for something which she presented as necessary, and which she contrived to make seem both attractively new and reassuringly old-fashioned. On 30 April, five days before polling day, her performance on a television programme called *The Granada 500* epitomized this. Presented with the 'woman' question, Mrs Thatcher inserted a comparison with Queen Elizabeth I, without sounding vainglorious. On the unions, she sided with the majority against 'the few destroyers' and declared, 'Someone's got to tackle this problem.' On capital punishment, she reiterated her personal support for hanging, while explaining that it could not be party policy. On immigration, answering an immigrant worried about proposed tightening of the rules so that fiancés would not automatically be admitted, she made no concessions and won big applause from the audience. The overall impression was of a woman in touch with the anxieties of 'lower-middle' England and ready to do something about them. It was this England that had really lost faith in Labour and was ready to turn.

That same day, Mrs Thatcher gave the final Conservative election broadcast, the first in which she alone spoke. The hoarseness in her voice could be detected, but she looked fresh and elegant, indeed almost too immaculate, beside a bowl of daffodils. Her message was of a great country gone wrong, which it was not yet quite too late to put right. As if the tune from the patriotic hymn 'I Vow to Thee, My Country' were playing in the background, she said, 'there's another Britain which may not make the daily news' of 'thoughtful people, oh, tantalisingly slow to act yet marvellously determined when they do': 'may this land of ours, which we love so much, find dignity and greatness and peace again'. Critics, attacking the broadcast as artificial,* missed how genuine it was. As Mrs Thatcher put it the following day, 'there is one thing stronger than armies, and that is an idea whose time has come'.†

In the month after the election, in a private interview, Nigel Lawson said something so blindingly obvious that its importance tended to be neglected by those used to the politics of Harold Wilson: 'A key to understanding Mrs Thatcher was that she actually said what she believed.' Brian Walden, listening to her more carefully than most, understood this: 'Mrs Thatcher was saying something *quite* different,' he commented, 'but didn't

---

* Bernard Donoughue castigated the broadcast as 'completely artificial, all sugary, an attempt by Mrs Thatcher to imitate the Queen's Christmas broadcast'.
† She was quoting, without attribution, Victor Hugo.

want to be seen to be *too* different … This election *was* about a woman who believes in inequality, passionately, who isn't Keynesian, who is *not* worried about dole queues.' In his view, if interviewers had wanted to find the truth, they should have asked her, 'Mrs Thatcher, do you believe in a more unequal society?'

On polling day Mrs Thatcher voted in Chelsea, Denis in Lamberhurst. Just before midnight she and Denis arrived at Barnet town hall for her count. By this time the early results were showing that she would be Prime Minister, but, with her usual combination of caution and a respect for form, she refused to claim victory until it had been arithmetically achieved, which meant 318 Conservative seats.

In Finchley the result was:

Mrs Margaret Thatcher (Conservative)	20,918
Richard May (Labour)	13,040
Anthony Paterson (Liberal)	5,254
William Verity (National Front)	534
Mrs Elizabeth Lloyd (Independent Democrat)	86
Conservative majority	7,878

Her majority had nearly doubled since October 1974.

Nationally, the Conservatives won 339 seats to Labour's 269: an overall majority of forty-three.* The swing to the Tories was 5.1 per cent, the biggest swing either way since 1945. It was bigger in the South and Midlands than in the North and Scotland, and notably bigger among 'lower-middle' England. The Conservative share of the vote was just under 44 per cent (13,897,690 votes).

Mrs Thatcher drove to Central Office, arriving at about 4 a.m. She was still not admitting victory, but Michael Dobbs, in the car with her, noticed that, as they passed Buckingham Palace, the escort of two cars suddenly gained three more cars and a motorcycle. This, he considered, was 'the moment of power'. Shortly after victory became certain, at 2.45 that afternoon, Mrs Thatcher drove to Buckingham Palace to kiss hands† with the Queen. 'Good luck, Prime Minister,' Alistair McAlpine shouted after her as she left. 'Don't call me that yet,' she said, with constitutional correctness.

---

* There were twelve Ulster seats, all but two of them Unionist, eleven Liberal ones, two Scottish and two Welsh Nationalists.
† Hands are not actually kissed.

7
Downing Street

'They thought she was a sort of right-wing baboon'

Margaret Thatcher arrived at Buckingham Palace shortly before 3 p.m. on 4 May 1979, accompanied by Denis. The first woman Prime Minister wore a blue outfit with a pleated skirt which Cynthia Crawford, her assistant who had helped her choose it, considered 'very dainty'. After her audience of the Queen, the Thatchers were driven to Downing Street, where a cheering crowd awaited them. The Prime Minister was advised to sit immediately behind the driver so that she could get out without the waiting press and photographers seeing her legs first.

In front of the famous door, Mrs Thatcher promised to 'strive unceasingly to try to fulfil the trust and confidence that the British people have placed in me and the things in which I believe'. Then she quoted 'some words of St Francis of Assisi which I think are really just particularly apt at the moment. "Where there is discord, may we bring harmony. Where there is error, may we bring truth. Where there is doubt, may we bring faith. And where there is despair, may we bring hope."'* These words had come, at the last minute, from Ronnie Millar. They were to be used against her in later years by those who accused her of sowing more discord than ever. Even at the time, they seemed a little pious. 'I thought she'd gone mad,' said Michael Dobbs, listening from the hall of No. 10. But the divisions of the nation were then causing the greatest public anguish. The new Prime Minister had to address them. Although she knew a fight might come, she was not spoiling for one.

Before she went inside, a reporter asked Mrs Thatcher about her father: 'I just owe almost everything to my own father,' she replied. 'He brought me up to believe all the things I do believe . . .' Then she pushed through the door to be greeted by the assembled staff, roughly seventy-strong. Dobbs, part of a tiny group of party men accompanying her, surveyed the ranks of waiting career civil servants. He decided 'it was an uneven contest'.

---

* They were not, in fact, the words of St Francis, but a nineteenth-century follower.

The introductions completed, Ken Stowe, whom she had inherited as principal private secretary from Callaghan, led Mrs Thatcher to the Cabinet Room. 'Ken,' she said, 'what do I do now?' 'You might want to speak to John Hunt [the Cabinet Secretary], Prime Minister,' said Stowe. 'You've got to form an administration.' Stowe and his colleagues were heartened to find Mrs Thatcher turning to them for help. She had a temperamental and ideological suspicion of the Civil Service; her time at Education had made her angry about how officialdom could frustrate her aims. So Stowe and his colleagues had not expected her to be sympathetic. Bryan Cartledge, her foreign affairs private secretary, recalled that an atmosphere of 'Lib-Labbery' prevailed among No. 10 officials, and a fear of Mrs Thatcher's 'general stridency'. At lunchtime on the day he left office, Jim Callaghan offered his closest Downing Street assistants a modest and melancholy farewell meal of cottage pie. The civil servants present had fully expected to be the victims of the fierce new broom which would begin sweeping that afternoon. That night, however, they found themselves in the State Dining Room with the new Prime Minister, huddled by the fireplace once again eating cottage pie. Mrs Thatcher had no plans to get rid of anyone.

In fact, in this area she had almost no plans at all. She never showed much interest in how to organize matters and control appointments. She did not believe that the bureaucracy should be reshaped from top to bottom, rather that it should be re-galvanized. The private office she inherited was touched and 'astonished that she accepted us without any question'.* She understood the importance of the men who made the machine work and would support them so long as they made it work for her. After a few months of governing she looked up from her desk at Clive Whitmore, who had replaced Stowe in June, and said: 'Clive, I'd be able to run this Government much better if I didn't have ministers, only permanent secretaries.'

Mrs Thatcher's chief method of exerting her will over the machine was not institutional but personal. She used every remark, memo and meeting to challenge existing habits and preach incessantly the main aims of her administration.† The ritual of Prime Minister's Questions in Parlia-

---

* The officials were less enamoured of Mark Thatcher, who accompanied his mother as she entered No. 10 that day. Turning to one, he asked how many people were employed there. 'About seventy,' he was told. 'Hmm, would make a nice little business,' he said.

† Just five days after her election victory, for example, Mrs Thatcher directed her private secretary to inform the Foreign Office of her dissatisfaction with the 'wordy generalisations and the re-statement of facts or conclusions which are, or should be, well known' in the briefing documents provided to date. 'The Prime Minister, who is a quick reader, is fully prepared to tackle long briefs when necessary; but she would like their content to be pithy and concisely expressed.'

ment (every Tuesday and Thursday that the House was sitting) made her familiarize herself with the work of all departments. She would be briefed early in the morning about likely questions, and then, over a light lunch which everyone ate holding plates on their knees, would rehearse possible answers. Armed with a book of about forty 'subject notes', she would take her place in the Commons at 3.10 for the fifteen-minute contest. She did well out of the combination of the parliamentary political joust and the twice-weekly cramming of facts. Her strongest form of self-criticism, she herself recalled in old age, was provoked 'whenever I had not prepared thoroughly enough for something'.

Her other method of control, used much more rarely, was to visit different departments to see what they were up to. These were memorably demanding occasions. In an outing to the Department of Employment she started arguing with a rising star called Donald Derx, who was so nettled by her hectoring that he said, 'Prime Minister, do you want to know the facts or not?' As a result of this incident, it was said, Derx's career stalled.* Visits like this ensured that Mrs Thatcher was feared. From first to last, for eleven and a half years, she sent tremors through Whitehall.

At the same time, Mrs Thatcher's unworldly vagueness, even weakness, about who should do which job caused immediate confusion. Adam Ridley, her main economic adviser in the Conservative Research Department in Opposition, fully expected to take charge of the No. 10 Policy Unit. But Mrs Thatcher had decided, even before the election, that the more radical John Hoskyns should have the job. 'You spark her,' Denis had told Hoskyns, while Adam Ridley 'cannot see the wood for the trees'. She failed, however, to communicate her intentions. So Ridley arrived at No. 10 raring to go, only to be told his services were not required.† More surprising, she did not have much idea about what the Policy Unit should do. It always had to generate its own momentum. Tim Lankester, her first economic private secretary, felt 'she wasn't very interested in strategy'. From the other side of the official fence, Hoskyns thought the same. The most missionary of all modern prime ministers never sat down to define or implement her mission.

In such a hurry to get on with her self-appointed task of rebuilding the British economy, Mrs Thatcher grabbed whatever tools lay to hand. One such body was the Central Policy Review Staff, the 'Think Tank' founded

---

* Mrs Thatcher's visits also helped her identify young talent for herself. At a better-starred visit to the Ministry of Defence, she marked out Clive Whitmore, making him her principal private secretary soon thereafter,
† A place was found for Ridley as special adviser to Geoffrey Howe.

by Ted Heath. Its purpose was to think, as people did not then put it, 'outside the box' and investigate longer-term policy. At first she could not see the point of it. Dr John Ashworth, the Chief Scientist, who worked within the CPRS, asked to see her shortly after she had arrived at No. 10. As he entered, the Prime Minister said: 'Who are you?' 'I am your Chief Scientist,' Ashworth replied. 'Oh,' said Mrs Thatcher, 'do I want one of those?' He explained his work, including the almost unstudied subject of climate change. She stared at him: 'Are you standing there and seriously telling me that my government should worry about the *weather*?'* She also told Ashworth she had no need for a minister for science: 'I'm a scientist. I shall be my own Minister for Science.'

Fighting talk aside, Mrs Thatcher quickly realized that, her Policy Unit being so small and staffed by people without experience of the workings of government, she needed experts to help with progress-chasing. After a bit, the two organizations made common cause. What virtually all her advisers recognized was that Mrs Thatcher was not, in the normal managerial sense, much good at running things. In Ashworth's view: 'She hated muddle, but she also caused it, because she did not really appreciate how bureaucracies need sharp lines.' She did not know how the machine worked and, as Hoskyns put it, 'My worry was that she didn't know what she didn't know.'

In forming her first Cabinet, Mrs Thatcher displayed a similar tendency not to want to upset the institutional applecart. Her appointments sought political balance more than ideological affinity. She turned first to Willie Whitelaw, whose loyalty she rewarded with the post of Home Secretary and, in effect, though not in formal title, Deputy Prime Minister. Her friend Hector Laing once praised Whitelaw for his 'low cunning and lovable dimness'. Mrs Thatcher laughed and said: 'I'm not very good at either.' But cunning, lovability and at least the appearance of dimness were essential characteristics in the Tory tribe, so Whitelaw was indispensable. Filling the hole left by the death of Airey Neave, Humphrey Atkins accepted, reluctantly, the post of Northern Ireland Secretary. Michael Jopling succeeded Atkins as Chief Whip. Keeping her promise to Whitelaw never to make Keith Joseph Chancellor, she appointed Geoffrey Howe. Her relations with Howe were not easy, but she was not seriously reluctant to give him the job for which, she could not deny, he was well qualified. Joseph became Secretary of State for Industry.

It was only in economic portfolios that Mrs Thatcher appointed her

---

* Much later, however, Mrs Thatcher would be the first head of a front-rank government to make a major speech on climate change.

ideological soulmates. As well as Howe and Joseph, she made John Nott, one of the most original free-market economists in Opposition, Trade Secretary and put John Biffen, as Chief Secretary to the Treasury, in charge of public spending control. She had great respect for Biffen's intellect and assumed that his opposition to the Heath U-turn proved he was at one with her. As became clear later, however, Biffen, more Powellite than Thatcherite, was not really 'on board'. To coordinate economic policy and steer it through Cabinet, these ministers – Howe, Joseph, Nott and Biffen – established a secret breakfast with Mrs Thatcher every Thursday. As Employment Secretary, Jim Prior was the only Heathite with an economic job. Although Mrs Thatcher did not personally dislike him ('Jim's a jolly, red-faced Englishman'), she disliked his belief that trade unions should be appeased. She appointed him for the sake of party unity.

In her other appointments, Mrs Thatcher's chief concern was to construct a government which reflected the party's balance of power and experience. For Foreign Secretary she chose Lord Carrington. Extremely senior and yet, because he sat in the House of Lords, no threat to her job, he had the relevant experience, contacts and prestige. Ian Gilmour joined him as Foreign Office spokesman in the Commons and in the Cabinet as Lord Privy Seal. Following similar principles, she appointed the veteran Lord Hailsham as Lord Chancellor, Francis Pym as Defence Secretary and Christopher Soames as Leader of the Lords. Norman St John-Stevas became Leader of the House of Commons and the rebellious Peter Walker was marginalized in Agriculture.

Mrs Thatcher appointed no women to her first Cabinet. Of the six most senior men, all were older than she, and only two (Howe and Joseph) agreed with her economic strategy. Most of the older men, who had fought in the Second World War,* had difficulty taking their new Prime Minister seriously. They did not conspire against her, but neither did they think it likely that she would survive. She felt patronized and was conscious of being in a minority.

The only hitch came when Michael Heseltine refused Energy, insisting on the Environment portfolio he had been shadowing. Mrs Thatcher gave in at once. This early skirmish foreshadowed the difficult relationship to come. 'I don't like one-to-one confrontations with Michael,' she said to one official. The Energy job was given instead to David Howell, an early free-marketeer. When the Cabinet was complete, it was a reasonable balance of the forces and talents available.

There was one important deliberate omission – Ted Heath himself.

---

* Whitelaw, Carrington and Pym had been decorated with the Military Cross.

Although few expected Mrs Thatcher to offer him a Cabinet post – she felt he 'would never have been able to take orders from a woman' – Heath took this very badly. Matters were made worse by Carrington's well-meaning suggestion that he be offered the ambassadorship in Washington. 'She's trying to get me out of the bloody House,' Heath complained, and wrote her a curt letter of rejection. News of his refusal leaked. From then on, Heath's hostility would prove absolute.

Mrs Thatcher left it to her new Chief Whip, Jopling, to propose appointments to junior ministerial posts. 'She named a few as "my people",' he recalled, 'but gave no impression of political bias; she saw it all in terms of talent.' On the Sunday after her victory, he discussed this with her and Whitelaw over lunch in No. 10. It was, he discovered, her first sight of the flat which she and Denis were to inhabit for more than eleven years.

The flat, at the top of the house, was small and almost poky, but it suited Mrs Thatcher. She liked the idea of 'living over the shop', as in her Grantham childhood. Security was greater, and she hoped her children could come and see her easily.* Denis paid rent to the government of £3,000 per year for the flat; Mrs Thatcher paid for its redecoration and also for the redecoration of her first-floor study in No. 10, banishing the sage-green wallpaper which she disliked. Due to the remarkable strictness of government rules, the Thatchers were provided with no domestic help. Since Denis held old-fashioned views on such matters, it fell to Mrs Thatcher to procure, generally with the help of Caroline Stephens and more junior secretaries, food and cook it. Denis was known to hurry home from drinks with chums after ringing No. 10 – 'She says if I don't come now dinner will be cold, and by that she means it will have *got* cold.' Lack of time meant that more wholesome convenience foods – fish pie from Marks and Spencer, for example – were consumed in large quantities. She herself usually ate quite heartily but without much attention, treating food as fuel. She drank plentiful quantities of Famous Grouse whisky with ginger ale, but was never drunk. Denis, recalled one observer, 'was on the Gordon's'.

David Wolfson served as the unpaid chief of staff of Mrs Thatcher's political office. His business links gave her comfort, and so did his money. Cynthia Crawford (always known as 'Crawfie'), who would become increasingly important in the smooth running of Mrs Thatcher's life, was paid for by Wolfson. Mrs Thatcher also brought into No. 10 the highly

---

* In practice, there were problems. Mark had to leave for the United States in 1984 when press criticism of him for exploiting his relationship with his mother for commercial gain became too great. Carol liked bringing friends to the flat at the weekend. One boyfriend, a journalist without security clearance, was brought along, after which the rules were tightened.

trusted personal staff she had used in opposition. Richard Ryder ran the political office. Caroline Stephens, who was to marry Ryder in 1981, remained diary secretary. Alison Ward came as constituency secretary. Tessa Jardine-Paterson, a political secretary, remembered that she and her colleagues saw it as part of their jobs to rustle up drinks and even meals for Mrs Thatcher. They felt perfectly happy to do so because she herself was so unsnooty, often plunging her hands into the sink to wash up with the words 'It's much easier to do it yourself.' Although an egotist, Mrs Thatcher was almost always extremely considerate towards staff and their families. 'It was a great mistake to tell the Prime Minister that one of your children had got measles or something, because she'd go on talking about it for some days afterwards . . .'

In 1979, there were no computers in Downing Street and Mrs Thatcher drew heavily on the career secretaries and typists, traditionally known as the 'Garden Room girls' because they worked in the basement rooms overlooking the garden. According to Jane Parsons, who ran the Garden Room when the Thatchers arrived and had worked for every prime minister since Attlee and Churchill, the whole enterprise felt like 'a cosy family unit and the PM was head of the family'. While some prime ministers, notably Heath and Wilson, had been stand-offish about this ethos, the Thatchers loved it. Denis said, 'I'll do whatever you want me to do so long as it doesn't coincide with rugger.'* Mrs Thatcher would 'bounce' into the Garden Room to see what was going on. On one occasion, she came across a letter from a small florist in Wandsworth who said his business was being undermined by supermarket flower sales. From then on, she placed all her flower orders with him. She liked to watch her own office in action. A private secretary was at his desk one day having a losing argument with the Treasury on the telephone. As he put down the receiver, he said, 'S***! F***!' Only then did he notice the Prime Minister beside him, her eyes shining with pleasure. 'Temper! Temper!' she said.

This cosiness extended to the Thatchers' life at Chequers, the large Buckinghamshire country house that serves as a retreat for the British Prime Minister. There, as in London, Mrs Thatcher quickly established a mixture of formality – she and Denis always dressed smartly – with friendliness towards those working for her. The duty private secretary stayed in an estate cottage. A nervous Michael Pattison, on his first weekend in the role,

---

* If an occasion did clash with rugby matters, Denis was not pleased. In November, after Caroline Stephens had written to him to enlist him for the state banquet for the President of Indonesia, Denis replied, reluctantly agreeing to go: 'J.C. [Jesus Christ] What I do for the Party! . . . The same evening I was going to probably the best Rugby Football Dinner this year . . . All the chums will be there.'

came with his young family. Over drinks before Sunday lunch, his two-year-old daughter climbed over Mrs Thatcher on the sofa and removed one of her earrings.* 'She met with a very soft response,' he remembered. For anyone who had experienced the Heath days, such a scene was unimaginable (even allowing for the fact that Heath would not have worn earrings).

The first woman Prime Minister had needs previously unknown in Downing Street. The private office was uneasy about putting the word 'hairdresser' into the diary, fearing it detracted from the dignity of the office, so with the help of Caroline Stephens the phrase 'Carmen rollers' was agreed as code. Strict government rules prevented the acceptance of personal presents of any substantial value, but Mrs Thatcher was allowed to take such gifts on loan. She wore British clothes on these terms, and the many jewels which Arab potentates pressed upon her. Care was taken to record which frock she wore at which occasion, and dresses were given nicknames for easy recognition.† One with red and white circles on it, for example, was called 'Balloons'.

Mrs Thatcher had frequently to be reminded of the symbolic importance of her role as the leading elected representative of her sex. To help reduce public expenditure, John Hunt and John Ashworth told her she must choose between cutting the National Council for Women and a scientific body, the Advisory Council for Applied Research and Development (ACARD). Without hesitation, Mrs Thatcher, the scientist, said: 'Can't get rid of ACARD. Better get rid of the other one.' Ashworth pointed out that it might look bad for the first woman Prime Minister to ditch the National Council for Women. The result, which the two officials in this *Yes, Prime Minister* game had intended, was that both quangos survived.

Probably the most important member of Mrs Thatcher's personal entourage was her parliamentary private secretary (PPS). As Prime Minister she settled on Ian Gow, the MP for Eastbourne. Although Gow had supported his friend Geoffrey Howe's 1975 leadership bid, he had later served as PPS to Airey Neave. After Neave's assassination, his move to Mrs Thatcher came naturally. Gow's friendship with Howe became an advantage, helping communication between No. 10 and the Treasury. Gow was completely, chivalrously committed to Mrs Thatcher, whom he was the first to describe

---

* Mrs Thatcher's ears were never pierced. In her generation, it was often considered gypsyish to have pierced ears. According to John Ashworth, if she became excited while wearing earrings, her lobes would become engorged; occasionally, under the pressure, an earring would pop off.
† Mrs Thatcher's clothes were looked after, in the early days, by Lady (Guinevere) Tilney, who was known, slightly mockingly, as the 'Mistress of the Robes'. Crawfie later succeeded to this informal title.

as 'The Lady'. 'I shall love her', he declared to the less enamoured Howe, 'till the day I die.'* He saw his job, normally considered a stepping stone to higher things, as the great task of his life.

Gow's chief role as PPS was to keep open the links between the Prime Minister and her parliamentary party, links which had broken, with such disastrous results, under Ted Heath. His method was a huge amount of controlled but sustained drinking with Members of Parliament. 'Cars run on petrol,' he would say, 'I run on alcohol.' Gow devoted endless hours to listening to MPs' complaints. 'X is unhappy and needs to be loved,' he would tell the diary secretary. 'Please get him in to see Margaret.' Known half-affectionately as 'Supergrass', he would attend the meetings of Conservative backbench committees and report to Mrs Thatcher. Building on her own remarkable tendency to criticize 'the government' as if she, as Prime Minister, had nothing to do with it, Gow was not above concerting parliamentary resistance to proposals from Cabinet colleagues which she did not like. This sometimes caused unnecessary trouble. But Gow was the most useful sort of aide – the one who knows his principal's mind so completely that he does not need to ask her permission before he acts. No one did more to help Mrs Thatcher survive the potential political crises of her early years.

This cohesive personal team had to cope with the astonishing demands of their boss's routine. Mrs Thatcher would rise at about 6 a.m. and listen to BBC radio.† Overnight she would have demolished two or sometimes three of the previous evening's red boxes. After 8.30 she would descend to her study and begin a day of meetings. She took virtually no exercise, except for going up and down the stairs to the flat. These journeys were required, among other things, to use the lavatory, because there was none for a woman near her study, though her staff noted her ability, like the Queen, never to seem to need to 'go'. She allowed herself no leisure. In the evening she would often take her shoes off, tuck her legs beneath her on

---

* A significant factor in Mrs Thatcher's political success was that quite large numbers of men fell for her. The Scottish genealogist Sir Iain Moncreiffe of that Ilk was the only man known to have made an indecent suggestion to her while she was Prime Minister, but many harboured a romantic devotion which teetered on the edge of the sexual. Sir Hector (later Lord) Laing, the Chairman of United Biscuits, would send her notes which he requested be placed under her pillow. Kingsley Amis, the novelist, described Mrs Thatcher as 'one of the best-looking women I had ever met . . . The fact that it is not a sensual or sexy beauty does not make it a less sexual beauty, and that sexuality is still, I think, an underrated factor in her appeal (or repellence).' Brian Walden reported David Owen as saying to him: 'The whiff of that perfume, the sweet smell of whisky. By God, Brian, she's appealing beyond belief.' Alan Clark, when asked by the present author about the nature of his proclaimed love for Mrs Thatcher, said: 'I don't want actual penetration – just a massive snog.'
† First she listened to the news on the BBC World Service and then to Radio 4's *Today* programme.

the sofa and chat – always shop – over a glass of weak whisky.* This would continue until one or two in the morning. The hardest task for her entourage was to make her go to bed. Although she had immense stamina, she was not as invincible as she believed. She got tired. When that happened, she talked more and achieved less.

The global impact of Margaret Thatcher was immediate and enormous, because she was, after Golda Meir of Israel, the first elected woman leader in the Western world. Yet Mrs Thatcher gave extraordinarily little thought to media relations. Charles Anson, a No. 10 press officer when she arrived, noticed an 'absolutely instant' change in the level of interest from all over the world.† But in Anson's view she showed 'very little interest in how she was projected'. She did not really read the newspapers herself, beyond a cursory glance at Denis's *Daily Telegraph*. It was hard to persuade her to pay much attention to what they were saying.

In those days there was no twenty-four-hour news cycle and Mrs Thatcher's main public communications were in Parliament and through set-piece speeches. In this, as in so much else, she conformed to existing rules.‡ Her first press secretary was Henry James, a former civil servant with no party background. When, in November 1979, James returned to Vickers, from which he had been seconded, Mrs Thatcher appointed Bernard Ingham to succeed him. A former Labour supporter and government information officer, Ingham was a naturally combative man. Perhaps excessively proud of his Yorkshire common sense, he was strongly in sympathy with the changes Mrs Thatcher was trying to make in British society. Conscious of the need to make the Prime Minister attend to how she was being reported, he developed, early on, a daily press digest of about five pages and, as he recalled, 'sat down with her while we read it to make sure she *did* read it' most mornings at 9. This briefing became her window on the world. Mrs Thatcher paid attention to the *Daily Telegraph* since it was the main line to her natural supporters, and also to the *Sun*, whose

---

* Sometimes Denis would join her, with rather more to drink. On one evening he came in when she was composing a big speech about Rhodesia. He offered a few comments to which she paid no attention and then went up to the flat. About half an hour later, the ceiling of the room in which Mrs Thatcher was sitting shook with a tremendous crash. 'Oh,' she said. 'That must be Denis. I think he must have fallen out of a broom cupboard.' She made no attempt to find out what had happened.

† Her arrival in office led to a rash of questions on subjects that had never come up before, like whether there was a women's lavatory near the Cabinet Room.

‡ Once inside No. 10, Mrs Thatcher ignored Gordon Reece's advice to give more television interviews and crossly stamped on his request that her image be used for merchandising in aid of the party: 'No permission to be given on any goods of any kind. Don't mind a straight photograph.'

importance in winning working-class voters over from Labour she readily acknowledged.* But 'The real problem', Ingham remembered, 'was that she was not in touch.' When, on occasion, he suggested she might usefully read the 'leader' (anonymous editorial comment) in a particular paper, he discovered she did not know where the leader page was.

Ingham considered her 'unprofessional in not thinking about presentation enough'. Too often he would be told about government decisions only minutes before he had to brief the lobby. What he also noticed at once, however, were her gifts as a public performer. She was very concerned about her physical appearance and, when going on television, 'indulged herself with the make-up girl . . . She was an actress who could turn on a tremendous performance when it had to be turned on.' While not media-minded, she was a media star.

The first foreign politician to ring Mrs Thatcher to congratulate her on her victory on 4 May 1979 was Ronald Reagan. But at that stage the ex-Governor of California counted for little in the official mind. The Downing Street switchboard did not put him through. President Jimmy Carter, eager to counter speculation that he had been hoping for a Labour win, called later on. He and Mrs Thatcher spoke for only two minutes.

When she and Reagan managed to speak a few days later, his enthusiasm was undiminished. He was confident in their relationship, having seen her for a second time in London the previous November. 'They sparked,' said Richard Allen, who witnessed the encounter. In one of his weekly radio broadcasts, Reagan, now campaigning once again for the Republican presidential nomination, cheered her on from the sidelines:

> I couldn't be happier than I am over England's new Prime Minister. It has been my privilege to meet and have two lengthy audiences with Margaret Thatcher and I've been rooting for her to become Prime Minister since our first meeting.
>
> If anyone can remind England of the greatness she knew during those dangerous days in WWII when alone and unafraid her people fought the Battle of Britain it will be the Prime Minister the English press has already nicknamed 'Maggie'.

There was no comparable rapture in the chancelleries of Europe, but there was certainly keen interest. Most were quite pleased by the return of the

---

* In October 1979 the *Sun* asked Mrs Thatcher for a message of congratulation on the tenth anniversary of its Murdoch revamp. Ingham, who was still three days short of formally starting his job, recommended against, complaining of the 'somewhat flimsy basis'. Mrs Thatcher, however, scribbled: 'The *Sun* is a friend! Will do.'

Tories, then regarded as the more Europhile of the two parties. Honouring an arrangement with the previous government, the first foreign leader to visit No. 10 was Helmut Schmidt, the Chancellor of West Germany.* 'Why's he coming?' Mrs Thatcher complained to John Hunt. 'I didn't ask for it.' But the visit, a week after her victory, was a success. Schmidt was staggered by Mrs Thatcher's mastery of her brief. In her speech over dinner, she was admiring of German economic success. On the EEC she spoke warmly but realistically, complaining that Britain paid the 'lion's share' of the bill for wasteful agricultural surpluses.

Her remarks on EEC subjects were conditioned by the fact that, eleven days after winning one election, she had to start fighting another. For the first time, direct elections were held for the European Assembly.† In her one speech of the campaign she maintained the party's pro-European orthodoxy, but expressed it to fit with her other preoccupations. The EEC, she argued, should promote freedom, both in economic terms and against Soviet tyranny. Without beating an anti-Brussels drum, she stressed that Britain's contribution to the European budget was 'manifestly unjust'. On 7 June the Conservatives won sixty seats against the Labour Party's seventeen.

The first journey abroad of Mrs Thatcher's premiership was to France, to meet President Valéry Giscard d'Estaing. Although both were leaders of the centre-right, this was not a success. As Bryan Cartledge recalled, 'Giscard was insufferable towards her.' She later, in private conversation, described Giscard as 'very [long, disdainful pause] *noble*'. Giscard recalled their Elysée encounter thus: 'When our children were young, my family, being rather snobbish, employed an English nanny. She was very correct, very tidy, with a very neat hairdo. She was efficient, religious, always opening the windows, especially when the children were ill; rather tiresome. When I met Mrs Thatcher, I thought "She is exactly the same, *exactly* the same!"'

Giscard also hosted the EEC Council of Ministers in Strasbourg on 21–22 June. This provided Mrs Thatcher's first formal chance to express her dissatisfaction with Britain's EEC budget contribution. Although only the seventh richest member state (per head of population), Britain paid, after Germany, the largest net contribution. The summit proved, in the words of Clive Whitmore, 'quite an eye-opener for her'. Although Giscard had indicated privately to Mrs Thatcher that he would agree to a proper discussion of the budgetary problem on the first day, he then sought to relegate it to dinner. This would have made it vaguer, because no officials would

---

* Jack Lynch, the Irish Taoiseach, however, slipped in an unscheduled meeting just before Schmidt.
† Although this remained its formal title, it was, by now, becoming known as the European Parliament. Mrs Thatcher, wary of its pretensions, preferred 'Assembly'.

have been present, and would have kept it out of the communiqué. So Mrs Thatcher said 'No'. Her efforts were rewarded with a communiqué that mandated the European Commission to come up with proposals to solve the budget problem in time for the next summit, in Dublin that autumn. But she was angry at the attempt to circumvent her. As crowds gathered to watch her go off to dinner in the ambassadorial Rolls-Royce, she turned to Cartledge and asked: 'Do I really have to go through with this?' Ever afterwards, Mrs Thatcher disliked the process and style by which the EEC did its business. 'She was hostile to the European Community from the beginning,' Giscard considered.

From 29 to 30 June, Mrs Thatcher attended her first G7 summit, in Tokyo. The agenda included inflation and the growing energy crisis, aggravated by the Islamist revolution in Iran earlier that year which had reduced the world supply of oil.* Mrs Thatcher approached Tokyo with the native suspicion she brought to summitry.† She was particularly impatient of the Japanese fondness for platitudinous communiqués. She wanted a focus on energy problems and opposed any attempt to reflate the world economy. The Japanese, to whom the idea of a woman prime minister was fascinatingly alien, devised a special security plan. Every other national leader was assigned twenty male karate experts to protect them. The Japanese proposed twenty 'karate ladies' to guard Mrs Thatcher. The Cabinet Secretary had to intervene: because Mrs Thatcher was attending 'as Prime Minister and not as a woman *per se*', he told the Japanese, she would have 'no objection' to being attended by twenty 'karate gentlemen'.

At the last-minute invitation of the Kremlin, Mrs Thatcher broke her flight at Moscow airport, where she was given an impromptu supper by the Soviet Prime Minister, Alexei Kosygin. This was her first encounter with the Soviet leadership. By her own account, she gave Kosygin a talking-to about the plight of the Vietnamese Boat People – victims, she told him, of Communism. 'It was very plain speaking from a prime minister, not wrapped up at all in diplomatic nicety,' recalled Whitmore, 'but to be fair, Kosygin was not knocked sideways but gave as good as he got.' Although Mrs Thatcher felt no affection for her Soviet interlocutor, and vice versa, both leaders rather enjoyed their verbal joust.

---

* As a result of the oil shock, British power stations had switched to coal rather than oil. This concerned Mrs Thatcher because it threatened the government's ability to build up coal stocks at power stations as a hedge against possible trouble from the miners.
† She told Bryan Cartledge, who accompanied her, to count the size of the respective national delegations, in the hope that Britain's would be the smallest, and was annoyed to discover that the Canadian was smaller still.

Mrs Thatcher was pleased with Tokyo, partly because she was the centre of vast media attention. 'She relished being the new girl,' said Cartledge, who felt that negotiation 'came entirely naturally to her'. She proved unafraid of cutting through the summit hierarchy. Unlike other leaders, she would visit the 'sherpas' (the summit officials) and harangue them directly on points of detail. In her opening statement at the summit she spoke succinctly and without notes. She painted a gloomy picture of the consequences of high oil prices but pleaded with colleagues to 'let the price mechanism work in full', while pushing for more nuclear energy.* She stuck to her opposition to reflation. While the Seven were gathered in Tokyo, the price of Saudi oil rose from $14.54 to $18 a barrel. Their collective impotence was emphasized.

In the margins of Tokyo, Mrs Thatcher met Jimmy Carter for the first time as Prime Minister. That May, Zbigniew Brzezinski had told Carter that their ambassador in London considered the new Prime Minister 'a cooler, wiser, more pragmatic person now than the Opposition Leader you met in May, 1977 or the dogmatic lady who visited you in Washington that fall'. 'I agree,' Carter wrote in the margin. Nevertheless, Brzezinski continued, 'it will take patience to deal with Mrs Thatcher's hard-driving nature and her tendency to hector'. The most pressing and immediately difficult issue they had to discuss was Rhodesia.

Under the 'internal settlement' devised by the Rhodesian Prime Minister, Ian Smith, multiracial elections, albeit entrenching disproportionate white power, had taken place in April 1979. After the black radical parties, including Robert Mugabe's Patriotic Front, boycotted the elections, a government emerged led by Bishop Muzorewa, the more accommodating black candidate favoured by Smith. The Carter administration and Callaghan's government had refused to recognize the elections, wanting Rhodesia isolated until a more inclusive settlement was reached. Mrs Thatcher, however, had promised to await a report into the elections she had commissioned from Lord Boyd, the former Colonial Secretary. The implication was that, if Boyd pronounced the elections fair, she would recognize the new government's legitimacy. This caused much upset in Washington. Lord Carrington, unsympathetic to the internal settlement, recalled the Carter administration as 'pretty unpleasant . . . they thought

* One reason she advanced in favour of nuclear energy was ecological. People who were concerned about the environment, she said in a pre-summit interview, 'should also be worried about the effect of constantly burning more coal and oil because that can create a band of carbon dioxide round the earth which could itself have very damaging ecological effects'.

she was a sort of right-wing baboon . . . They were pressing rather hard not to recognize Muzorewa, and I think that was rather counterproductive.'

In mid-May, Boyd concluded that the elections had been as free and fair as possible. Carter's people held their breath. Yet Mrs Thatcher held back. In Parliament on 15 May, she stressed she wanted 'a return to legality in conditions that secure wide international recognition'. Carrington duly sent Lord Harlech, the former British Ambassador to Washington, off to tour the 'front-line' African states and get their views. As Carrington recalled, what 'really persuaded' Mrs Thatcher not to recognize the internal settlement 'was that no one was going to support her . . . And there might have been sanctions against us . . . Lord Harlech came back reporting all this. Which of course is why I sent him. She respected his conclusions.'

Mrs Thatcher now had to be convinced of a new course. Robin Renwick, head of the Foreign Office's Rhodesia department, devised a radical plan which he hoped might appeal. Britain would intervene directly in Rhodesia to reach a new, internationally acceptable internal settlement. Elections, open to all, would follow, which Britain would supervise. 'Since it wasn't what she was expecting,' Renwick recalled, 'she was impressed by it.' But Mrs Thatcher did not hurry to make up her mind. She needed a position for the Commonwealth Heads of Government Meeting (CHOGM) in Lusaka that August, but until then she havered.

On 12 July, in London, she told Kurt Waldheim, the United Nations Secretary-General, that the Western world should support Muzorewa: 'if the West were to follow a policy which preferred bullets to ballots, there was no hope . . . When Lord Carrington interjected that some changes like a reduction of the white presence in parliament and Government should be achieved, the Prime Minister said: "Poor Peter always has to pick up the pieces when I have made my statements."' This report vividly conveys Mrs Thatcher's perennial hostility to dealing with anyone she considered a terrorist* and her habit of expressing herself with what, for diplomats, was almost unbearable directness. But it also contains a hint of another of her characteristics – a readiness to give in, protesting, to people whose knowledge she respected. She worried that she was 'being conned by aristos', but she almost enjoyed the process.

On 25 July, Mrs Thatcher finally made a statement to the Commons along the lines that the Foreign Office sought. She promised that Britain would take charge and make firm proposals for broadly acceptable

---

* At that time, roughly 500 people per week were being killed in the Rhodesian civil war; 1,000 whites per week were leaving the country.

constitutional arrangements for Rhodesian independence. Then it was on to Lusaka, arriving on 30 July. Knowing little of the region, she feared for her own safety. Carrington recalled asking her why she had brought dark glasses: 'Margaret answered very clearly, "I am absolutely certain that when I land at Lusaka they are going to throw acid in my face." ... I laughed. "... They're more likely to cheer you." Margaret stared at me, "I don't believe you."' It was on that flight that Cartledge noticed how well Mrs Thatcher got on with Carrington. The Foreign Secretary had successfully developed the ability to tease her. He could 'make her throw her head right back with laughter'. Since virtually everyone else was too terrified of Mrs Thatcher to attempt such a thing, Carrington gained a particular standing in her eyes, and a freedom to do what he wanted.*

Mrs Thatcher was also worried by the presence of the Queen in Lusaka. In her capacity as the head of the Commonwealth, the Queen might, in theory, find herself at odds with her own, British government. Mrs Thatcher's attitude to the monarch was compounded of constitutional correctness, old-fashioned deference and a certain unease, probably related to the fact that both were women, and neither had much experience of working with women at a high level. She worried she would either upstage the Queen or be overshadowed by her. Caroline Stephens used to remind new private secretaries that Mrs Thatcher was 'a very ordinary woman'. It was a strange thing to say about someone so clearly *extra*ordinary, but it was also true. She was anxious about meeting the Queen in the way that most ordinary citizens would be, worrying about what to wear, when to curtsey and being on time.† She needed frequent reassurance.

In fact, the Queen left Lusaka soon after the opening formalities. Her initial presence made life easier for Mrs Thatcher since the respect felt for the Queen by the Commonwealth leaders rubbed off on her. Mrs Thatcher was charmed by Kenneth Kaunda, the Zambian President, even dancing with him after dinner.‡ She told the conference that it was Britain's responsibility to help Rhodesia reach an acceptable settlement through a constitutional conference. The Commonwealth gave its support. Carrington was delighted: 'She did terribly well at Lusaka. She really was

---

* Carrington had a genuine respect and affection for Mrs Thatcher, but he was also driven mad by what he saw as her stubbornness and lack of realism. One day, climbing the stairs to her study, he turned to Clive Whitmore and said: 'Clive, if I have any more trouble from this f***ing stupid, petit-bourgeois woman, I'm going to go.'

† When she attended the first meeting of the new Privy Council at Buckingham Palace after her victory in 1979, Mrs Thatcher arrived without her own officials – as is customary for Privy Council gatherings – and so worried by lateness that she was forty-five minutes early.

‡ Cartledge had discovered that Kaunda was, like Mrs Thatcher, the parent of twins. It is auspicious, in African culture, to have twins. This helped.

brilliant ... I think she thought they were a lot of savages. When they turned up and Kaunda was a smooth old guy and they were all very agreeable, I think she thawed a bit.'

Mrs Thatcher had a clear understanding of the nature of her success at Lusaka. When Sir Anthony Parsons, Britain's UN Ambassador, congratulated her, she replied: 'Well, Tony, you know how it is, you people convinced me, but when it came to doing it in public, I think I did it a great deal better than you could have done.' A conference was called at Lancaster House in London for September. There were rumblings on the right at the party conference in October, but nothing unmanageable. For the first but by no means the last time, Mrs Thatcher was able to force something upon her party which they would have found unpalatable coming from almost anyone else.

On her first day in office, Mrs Thatcher received briefs on the state of the British economy. These documents were relentlessly gloomy. The Treasury predicted that the Retail Price Index inflation would rise to an annual rate of 10–11 per cent during 1979 and that the Public Sector Borrowing Requirement (PSBR) would rise from £8.5 billion to £10 billion. This increase would result chiefly from the public-sector pay settlements proposed by Professor Clegg's Comparability Commission which, during the campaign, Mrs Thatcher had reluctantly promised to implement. John Hunt reminded her of the vast range of public employees whose pay she would shortly have to settle, and that 'close behind [the Budget] in terms of time, and ahead in terms both of intrinsic importance and inherent difficulty, is the development ... of a strategy for public expenditure'. The overall picture for the short term, he warned, is 'a rising rate of inflation and slow growth, leading to continued uncertainty and instability'.

In a way, it helped Mrs Thatcher that things were so bad. Only disaster had led voters to reject the soothing approach of Jim Callaghan. Only disaster would incline them to accept the nasty medicine the strict new nurse was offering. At the election the Conservatives had won a decent mandate for radical economic change. But there was an enormous gulf between the seriousness of the situation and the practical readiness of the new government to do something about it. From the moment she first sat at her desk, she feared that events might run away from her. She began immediately to scribble with frantic energy over the briefs she received.* In the margins she would express her feelings with some violence: 'No!!', or

---

* Civil servants quickly came to recognize that Mrs Thatcher's repeated underscoring of a passage with straight lines signified approval. A wavy line meant the opposite.

'No' (underlined three times), or even, as was much later to become famous in another context, 'No. No. No.' On 4 May, Hunt asked her to confirm that 'comparability (properly carried out) is the key to establishing public sector pay'. 'No,' she wrote, ignoring her commitment to honour the Clegg Commission. When Hunt drafted a memorandum for Cabinet discussion on pay and cash limits, she wrote: 'Discussion on this paper in Cabinet would be <u>futile</u> – and on any other paper which raises such enormous questions and supplies so few answers! It would weaken our hand – not strengthen it. <u>Delete from Agenda</u>.' She dreaded using the Cabinet as a place where people, especially people who did not agree with her, could merely air opinions: she wanted the focus on action.

Over the future of Clegg, Mrs Thatcher was determined to avoid further commitment. She saw the basic principle of comparability – the idea that wages could be determined by comparing them with those of other workers rather than being based on productivity and affordability – as financially ruinous. When Clegg refused her request to add considerations of efficiency and overmanning to his remit, her concerns that his recommendations would produce inflationary settlements were confirmed. His commission clung to life because of the fear of industrial disruption from winding it down too quickly. Its abolition was announced in August 1980.

Pursuing the subject of pay, Jim Prior urged early talks between government and TUC and, separately, government and CBI, to consider 'objectives'. Beside this Mrs Thatcher wrote '<u>No</u>.' What she called this 'flimsy paper' was removed from the Cabinet agenda. As discussion moved to the Cabinet's E Committee, a paper by Howe fared little better. He urged that the government await the completion of the Clegg round in August before determining the level of funding for local authorities, a course that would constrain the government's choices. He also canvassed some kind of economic and industrial forum, to which the Tories were vaguely committed and sought 'informal contacts' with union leaders, seeking Cabinet endorsement of his principles. 'There aren't any <u>principles</u> in those paras,' wrote Mrs Thatcher crossly. 'This is a very poor paper and we can only charitably assume that the Treasury is "otherwise occupied" at the present . . . we certainly cannot wait until Clegg has finished all his work.'

The matter in which the Treasury was 'otherwise occupied' was the Chancellor's first Budget, due on 12 June.* Before that, however, there had to be

---

* Mrs Thatcher was determined not to repeat the mistake of the Heath government, which, coming into office in June 1970, had waited until the customary time the following spring before presenting its first Budget. The same applied to public spending, which the government was determined to cut even though the spending year had already begun.

the Queen's Speech, announcing the legislative programme. The problem was that the government did not yet have an agreed strategy. On his first day, the new Trade Secretary, John Nott, wrote to Mrs Thatcher to urge immediate abolition of the Price Commission, a statutory body whose attempt to control prices contradicted Thatcherite principles. Though Mrs Thatcher did not put it in so many words, she worried about the sudden effect on the RPI. She told Nott she favoured 'metamorphosis rather than extinction' because she did not wish to jeopardize the 'two main purposes of our strategy: i. to restore incentives by direct tax cuts and consequently to tolerate indirect tax increases and ii. to establish credibility and authority by the necessary amendments to trade union law'.

This version of her own strategy was strangely partial, leaving out the attack on inflation and on public spending. She did not prevail. Keith Joseph intervened in support of Nott and immediate abolition was agreed at E Committee on 14 May. In her memoirs Mrs Thatcher writes, 'Perhaps the first time our opponents truly realised that the Government's rhetorical commitment to the market would be matched by practical action was the day we announced abolition.' This is correct, but at the time she had come close to preventing it.

At the State Opening of Parliament, Mrs Thatcher, in a white hat, set a new tone of smartness. She was even seen brushing specks of scurf from Norman St John-Stevas's collar. On 15 May, she led the debate on the Loyal Address in the Commons. In political terms, her words were combative. This had been, she said, 'a watershed election': a clear choice had been made in favour of the individual and against government. As well as abolishing the Price Commission, she promised a Bill to give tenants the right to buy their council houses. She foreshadowed the Assisted Places Scheme, which would pay for talented state school pupils to be educated in independent schools. There was the hint of compromise about the future of Rhodesia, and a hint of confrontation over the EEC budget.

The most controversial measure was a Bill to reform some trade union practices but, reflecting Prior's continuing influence, this was not very radical. It sought to restrict picketing to the place of work, gave individuals the right of appeal against closed-shop membership and made public funds available for postal ballots for union elections. While signalling a direction of travel, it would not be enough to establish the 'credibility and authority' which her strategy sought.

In the run-up to the Budget, Howe brought Mrs Thatcher worse and worse news. The Callaghan government's pre-election spree of borrowing and spending was now playing havoc with monetary control. By 6 June, sterling

M3 (the measure of all coins, notes and bank deposits, now the Treasury's preferred measure of money supply) was growing at an annual rate of 13.1 per cent and would be higher still that month. The government's target was 7–11 per cent. Concerned that inflation would inevitably rise, Howe reported that Gordon Richardson, the Governor of the Bank of England, advised a 2 per cent increase in the Minimum Lending Rate to 14 per cent. This was bound to put up mortgage rates to 13 per cent. The rise should take effect the following day, Howe insisted, to avoid it becoming involved in the Budget.

Mrs Thatcher was presented with a dilemma which was to trouble her repeatedly. In those days, control of interest rates rested, in effect, with the Chancellor, consulting with the Prime Minister. Such decisions were inevitably political, as well as economic. Approaching such issues, Mrs Thatcher had an innate distrust of the Bank of England for its Keynesian approach, and she was particularly suspicious of Richardson.* She once asked John Ashworth, the government's Chief Scientist, 'What do you think of Gordon?' 'Gordon who?' said Ashworth. 'Oh, you know, that fool who runs the Bank of England.'† While no one was stronger than she on the need to beat inflation, no one was more conscious of the effect of high interest rates on what she called 'our people'. The most consistent of threads in the economic history of Margaret Thatcher was her initial objection to any interest rate rise. She saw penalizing young people on or approaching the housing ladder as a sure way to crush the aspirations which she wished, for reasons of belief and of party politics, to foster.

In early June, Mrs Thatcher resisted Howe's demand for an immediate rise in rates, suggesting he wait until the Budget the following week. Furthermore, her private secretary minuted, she 'was doubtful whether a full 2 per cent was needed'. She asked for a reconsideration. Howe held fast. He and Richardson took the view that the government must send the right signals: 'given our commitment to monetary targets,' Howe argued, 'our first use of a monetary policy instrument should be effective and unequivocal'. With great reluctance she accepted his judgement, while making it clear she thought 2 per cent a mistake.

Mrs Thatcher was perfecting her technique of permitting a decision but distancing herself from it. Noting press reports that mortgage rates

---

* Richardson was an intellectual who preferred expressing himself in indirect and apparently inconclusive ways which irritated her. He was also a handsome man, but one who did not treat her as if she were an attractive woman – a fatal combination in her eyes.

† Monetarists such as Tim Congdon and Hayek himself had, in fact, floated the idea of surrendering political control of interest rates, but Mrs Thatcher never contemplated passing authority to Richardson.

might now go up (the inevitable consequence of raising interest rates), she wrote to Howe affecting great shock, saying: 'This <u>must</u> <u>not</u> happen.' She suggested a temporary subsidy to stave off a rise. While this was not forthcoming, the intervention showed her readiness, for political reasons, to diverge from the market stringencies on which, in principle, she insisted.

As the first Budget was prepared, Mrs Thatcher also complained that the Treasury 'was not nearly tough enough' on public expenditure. She wanted a PSBR of £7.5 billion, rather than the £8.5–10 billion projected. She was less robust, however, about the tax plans, being 'extremely perturbed at the prospect of having to increase VAT from 8 per cent to 15. This would mean a sudden jump in the RPI of at least 3 per cent. The result could be catastrophic for the next pay round.' As Howe later pointed out, she was displaying 'the ambivalence she often showed when the time came to move from the level of high principle and evangelism to practical politics'. He pushed back. To demonstrate the government's long-term determination, he told her, he wanted to cut income tax from 33 to 30 per cent at the basic rate and from 83 per cent to 60 per cent at the top rate. This could be paid for only by a 15 per cent rate of VAT.

In her constant battle between her cautious and radical instincts, Mrs Thatcher now edged towards caution. Was it really wise, she wondered, to try to cut income tax so much, so quickly? But Howe stood firm: 'This Budget provides our only opportunity to make a radical switch from direct to indirect taxation and thus honour the commitment on which our credibility depends.' Reluctantly, Mrs Thatcher accepted Howe's plans. They also agreed that the PSBR must be below £8.5 billion, a slippage from the originally desired £7.5 billion which they would quickly rue.

Howe could see, more clearly than Mrs Thatcher, that a new Conservative government had to signal a new view about what tax was for, emphasizing incentive and choice. It even, as Brian Walden had noted, had to suggest the benefits that came from inequality. If Mrs Thatcher's first Budget had not been bold about tax, her later ones would almost certainly have been more cautious still. The impetus for change would have faltered.

The Budget Howe introduced on 12 June included all the major tax changes he had wanted. In the past, increases in the state pension had been linked to the rise in prices or earnings, 'whichever is the greater'. Henceforth they were to be linked to prices alone. Since wages tended to outstrip prices without compensating improvements in productivity, this change was huge in its long-term effect. So was the decision to begin lifting exchange controls. For the first time in a generation, large-scale foreign investment in the UK private sector became a serious proposition, as did new British investment abroad.

Everyone could see the radical change that Howe's first Budget represented, and it was acclaimed or reviled accordingly. Prior later described the Budget as an 'enormous shock'. He vented his anger by protesting privately at the resulting increases in the RPI. For an anti-monetarist like Prior who believed that wage increases, not the quantity of money, caused inflation, the Budget was a great error. The real problem, however, was not the price increases, politically uncomfortable though they were,* but whether the course charted by the Chancellor could be sustained. Would the government really be able to contain public spending enough to reduce taxes without yet more borrowing? Mrs Thatcher sensed she had missed her first chance to be really tough on spending. At the party she gave to celebrate the Budget, she said to Robin Butler, then a Treasury civil servant, 'I asked for too little, didn't I?'

John Hoskyns worried that Mrs Thatcher had not settled on an overarching strategy. He remembered observing in her what General Sir Alan Brooke had observed in Winston Churchill: 'I despair of getting the Prime Minister to understand the connection between different theatres of war.' 'She *was* very remarkable, but like Churchill she had no strategic sense in the executive meaning of the word.' On the day of the Budget, he sent Mrs Thatcher a paper entitled 'Government Strategy' which sought a 'coherent approach to the task of turning round the British economy'. His concept for the first term was what he called Stabilization – getting the economy on an even keel of zero inflation, market pay systems and a stable, competitive exchange rate. From Stabilization could come Rebuilding, a greater reduction of the government's percentage of GDP, a freed-up labour market, a switch of talent to the private sector. Rebuilding without Stabilization would be 'like trying to pitch a tent in the middle of a landslide'. Perhaps the most important single thing, said Hoskyns, was to change the role of trade unions. Reverting to the earlier Stepping Stones papers, he urged that the 'union debate' be 'started properly: We need to force unions to address their members in the language of the real world.'

Mrs Thatcher drew a large black arrow pointing to this last sentence, showing that she approved of it. But her response to his broader suggestions was muted. She disliked the word 'stabilization', believing that it was 'a stagnation-type word' condemning the country to no growth. She had a habit of seizing on particular words and wrestling with them. Sometimes this was extremely effective. At other times, as with Hoskyns, she got the

---

* Most of these increases, as Geoffrey Howe had successfully persuaded Mrs Thatcher, would drop out of the RPI after a year because they would not be repeated. They were not, in the proper sense, inflationary.

wrong end of the stick. Instead of settling upon a strategy, as Hoskyns urged, she preferred to jump about, latching on to one phrase, rejecting another, contradicting sometimes herself and, much more often, everyone else. Such methods drove some of those working with her to distraction, but to others, such as Richard Ryder, this flexibility was evidence that 'she was a brilliant, intuitive, instinctive politician' rather than a doctrinaire one. Even Hoskyns conceded that only she had the stomach for the fight, pursuing his war analogy: 'Without Churchill i.e. her, we'd have surrendered in the first few months.'

There was only one area of political combat where the battle proved surprisingly easy – the sale of council houses. So popular was this policy that Michael Heseltine, whose department implemented the policy, considered it 'next to the "Winter of Discontent" itself . . . the single most important contributory factor' in the 1979 election victory. As well as the principal political and social purpose of bestowing the freedom of ownership on more people, the policy also helped the Treasury. Council house sales would not only yield revenue, but also remove large numbers from future council housing provision: the 'giveaway' was also a cut. Not surprisingly, perhaps, the social and financial objectives were in partial conflict. Heseltine at Environment wanted the largest possible number of council house sales. The Treasury wanted the largest sums of money.

For her part, Mrs Thatcher behaved as prime ministers are conventionally supposed to do, promoting the policy while trying to reconcile differing departments. She warmly supported the right to buy, and constantly deployed it as part of wider themes of freedom and opportunity. She also agitated for other measures which would spread private owner-occupation. But she did not become heavily engaged in the detail. The Housing Bill that established the right to buy offered a discount of the purchase price, based on length of tenure.* It also empowered the government to intervene if, as was correctly predicted, hostile councils tried to find ways of impeding it.

By the end of Mrs Thatcher's first administration, half a million families were living in council houses which they had bought, mainly under the right to buy. The policy had its disadvantages. The most notable were the gradual build-up of a housing shortage and the stoking, for the future, of a housing bubble. But it worked extraordinarily well in its stated aims. It also produced huge political loyalty to Mrs Thatcher, often from people who had never voted Conservative before. By 1983 it would become

---

* This began at 33 per cent of the market value and rose to 50 per cent at the maximum.

commonplace for people, mainly from the upper working class, to declare 'Maggie got me my house.'

The overall economic situation followed no such steady course. The biggest factor preventing the Hoskyns Stabilization was public spending. As Mrs Thatcher reminded the Cabinet, there were 'inherited promises' on pay, the Tories' own promises of increases in police and army pay and to exempt the National Health Service from cuts. Then there were the cash-hungry nationalized industries. Then there was local government. And what should be done about central government, where the pay settlement for the non-industrial Civil Service, reached before the election, exceeded the funds available? When the Cabinet met, Mrs Thatcher reported that the high forecasts for the PSBR meant cuts would have to be £500–600 million greater than already sketched out.

Energy price increases were seen as a possible cover for price rises in the nationalized industries to recover the cost of broken cash limits. 'The right course', the Cabinet minutes recorded with frank dishonesty, 'might be to seek very large price increases immediately, and attribute this to the inefficiency of the industry.' On 31 May the Cabinet agreed spending reductions and immediate large sales of public-sector assets to balance the books, but stipulated that the assets be sold 'in a way which would secure the best possible spread of ownership'.

Immediately, however, the implications of the cuts became clearer and the demands greater. By July, Howe told Mrs Thatcher that cuts of £5.5 billion would be needed to reduce public spending to the level of 1977–8 (the agreed target). But to prevent tax rises, cuts of £6.5 billion would be required. Mrs Thatcher backed the higher figure. In her zeal, she considered no economy too small. Thinking that the Garden Room needed better equipment, Kenneth Stowe had ordered thirty-two new typewriters. One day Mrs Thatcher entered No. 10 to find these objects in packing cases, just delivered. 'What's going on?' she cried. Eventually she allowed Stowe to keep three. The other twenty-nine had to go back.

Just as the spending figures were proving worse than had been thought, some Cabinet ministers, led by Jim Prior, started saying the policy was already too tough. John Hunt recommended that Mrs Thatcher 'bring this issue to a head' at Cabinet on 12 July. Following this advice, she deployed the unorthodox style of chairmanship for which she was already known, announcing the conclusion of the meeting at its beginning: 'Unless we go for this, we'll be taking a larger proportion of national revenue and have no scope for further tax reductions.' There was a fierce debate in which, as the official minutes put it, 'it was suggested that the Government faced the most serious dilemma in economic policy of any post-war Government'. Mrs

Thatcher, haunted more by past Tory failure than by anything Labour had done, begged colleagues to support the Chancellor: 'Remember the Barber spending spree,' she cried. Cuts, retorted Prior, with some support, would lead to 'massive redundancies' and would be worse politically than putting up taxes. He warned of 'severe depression'. Using the time-honoured official formula for expressing both sides, the minutes added: 'Against this, it was argued strongly that no one had faulted the Chancellor's analysis of the economic prospects.'

Mrs Thatcher had no intention of trimming in Prior's direction, but the battle against spending increases was still not successful enough. Cabinet ministers returned from holiday in September to a stern Treasury memo warning that the government's economic strategy was contingent on 'substantial reductions in the inherited expenditure plans ... Our ability to face up to this issue will be seen as the crucial test of our determination to stick to our announced policies, and will thus play a vital part in affecting expectations.'* For all this, the public spending plans for 1980–81 presented to the Commons on 1 November were £500 million short of the reduction sought.

As well as the question of how much to cut, there was the problem of how to achieve it. An enormous amount of public spending was attributable to local government. Some was paid for by the local rates, but 61 per cent came from central government through the Rate Support Grant (RSG). If the government reduced the RSG, rates, which fell mainly on Tory-voting homeowners and on businesses, would have to rise. Michael Heseltine, the Environment Secretary, argued that they must keep rates down: 'This would fit in with our economic strategy and the attack on inflation and would be seen as not incompatible with our longer term intention to abolish domestic rating.' To achieve this, he argued, the RSG should remain constant. Mrs Thatcher reluctantly saw the force of this argument. Worried about the effects on Conservative shire counties, she gave in.

Although she supported the Treasury in Cabinet discussions, Mrs Thatcher was also increasingly displeased with it as political pressure on her grew. So irritated was she by John Biffen's feebleness under fire that Howe brought in Nigel Lawson, Financial Secretary to the Treasury, to assist the beleaguered Chief Secretary. She sensed a lack of focus and was

---

* The reference to 'inherited plans' was intended to remind ministers that they were not being asked for actual, aggregate cuts, but this distinction between cuts in planned increases and genuine cuts in spending totals was one which the public never readily understood. The general view was that the Thatcher government was engaging in 'cuts'. There was to be no year in which public spending fell under Mrs Thatcher, although it did decrease as a proportion of GDP.

irritated by Howe's prolixity: 'We are getting far too many "woolly" papers from the Treasury,' she wrote in mid-September.

Mrs Thatcher was also annoyed with Biffen's desire to include the government's unemployment assumptions in the public spending White Paper. She was conscious of the political embarrassment they would cause and considered the 1.65 million projected unemployed for 1980–81 'unduly pessimistic'. When Biffen, a strong Parliamentarian, insisted, she gave in, but her enthusiasm for him had now markedly diminished.

The public spending White Paper, published on 1 November, was not badly received in the Commons, but the broader mood was restive. At Prime Minister's Questions that day, the veteran Labour MP Douglas Jay, father of the journalist Peter, asked Mrs Thatcher: 'As this Government have been in office for six months and as, according to the CBI, business confidence is falling, industrial production is falling, investment is falling and the pound is falling, does the Prime Minister feel that her policies are yielding results?' Mrs Thatcher struggled to respond. She was aware that, after six months in office, her government had little economic progress to show. Three weeks earlier she had cautioned her party's annual conference that results would come slowly. 'We have to think in terms of several Parliaments,' she had declared.

One exception came a week before the White Paper was published. On 23 October, Howe announced the complete lifting of exchange controls. In the interests of market secrecy, this had not been put to an amazed, though, except for Michael Heseltine, supportive Cabinet until the last moment. Mrs Thatcher, originally cautious about acting too fast, had eventually been persuaded that the controls had to be lifted before the sale of government-owned BP shares. When she agreed, she said to Howe, 'On your own head be it, Geoffrey . . . if anything goes wrong,' a remark which Howe interpreted, surely wrongly, as a joke. She used a similar form of words when she told Carrington she would accept his Rhodesian proposals. It was her way of keeping a political escape route. As so often, her radicalism was tempered by her instinct for survival.

The lifting of controls was a bold step. Ever since the war, British governments had believed they must control the movements of money in and out of the country to prevent a collapse of sterling.* When the day of currency freedom dawned, there was no collapse but rather, if anything, the opposite problem. The British economy, particularly the City of London,

---

* British tourists going on holiday had to register the currency they took with them: in the 1960s the maximum was £50 per head.

at last had the opportunity to compete globally. In time this would pay rich dividends, but in the short term it did little for the economic situation, which continued to deteriorate. Less than a week after the White Paper's publication, the money supply target was heavily exceeded. The stated spending targets were not tough enough to convince the markets that the future was going to be different: with annual inflation hitting 16 per cent, the purchasers of government debt 'went on strike' and a funding crisis ensued. On 5 November, Howe told Mrs Thatcher that, with a further fiscal package 'unthinkable', to bring the growth of the money supply within the target range they would have to raise the MLR once again. He warned that inflation was unlikely to fall below 14 or 15 per cent by the end of 1980. Declaring herself 'most unhappy', she asked: 'How could this be so if the Government were pursuing a tight monetary policy?' It was a question to which more and more people would demand an answer in the coming months.

Mrs Thatcher had little choice but to agree with her Chancellor. On 15 November interest rates went up by 3 per cent to 17 per cent. This punitive increase, the highest nominal level in British history, was designed to be so big as to brook no market doubt. In Cabinet Jim Prior pronounced himself 'disappointed and shocked', but Mrs Thatcher pointed out acidly that 'It wouldn't be 17 per cent if we got our expenditure down.' In a characteristic formulation, Howe told the Cabinet he was trying to keep things 'as un-unpleasant as possible'. Events were proving him right that – the famous phrase was, in fact, his, not Mrs Thatcher's[*] – 'There is no alternative.'

Two arguments about the government's economic policy were now being conducted at once, but separately. The first, much the noisier, was that between Howe, Mrs Thatcher and their allies on the one hand and the Keynesians, Heathites and Labour on the other. This concerned whether the policy, often characterized as cruel and 'doctrinaire', was destroying British jobs and prosperity. The second, much the more important for the economic future, was between those who agreed about the essential thrust of the policy but criticized its implementation. Mrs Thatcher was confident that Prior and co. were wrong, but it was they who had more political capacity to break her. By this time, adapting a public-school usage, Mrs Thatcher's opponents within the Conservative Party were becoming known as 'Wets', with her supporters inevitably becoming 'Dries'. She knew that if she were forced to adopt a Wet position she

---

[*] The phrase first gained currency in the course of 1978. It was sometimes shortened to the acronym TINA and became a nickname for Mrs Thatcher.

would catch her political death of it. It was among the Dries, therefore, that real debate took place.

However appalling the political and economic pressures became in these years, there was never panic about the direction of economic policy. The world beyond Downing Street expected a U-turn, having seen one with Heath. Those within knew this would not happen. What they feared was simply that events would overtake Mrs Thatcher and electoral unpopularity or a party coup would bring her down. The challenge, as she told the *New York Times* on 9 November, was 'Can we get far enough by the next election to show that it – our program – is working?'

8
Not for turning
'They are all against me, Robert. I can feel it'

The sense of courage in adversity, of one woman battling against heavy odds, was intrinsic to Mrs Thatcher's style of leadership and to her popular appeal. This leadership was quickly evident not only in economic matters, but in the wider range of challenges she faced as Prime Minister.

On 27 August 1979, Lord Mountbatten, the Queen's cousin and the last Viceroy of India, was murdered, with three others, while sailing near his home in the Irish Republic. The IRA were responsible. On the same day, eighteen British soldiers were killed in an IRA booby trap at Warrenpoint in Northern Ireland. Two days later Mrs Thatcher visited the province. In Crossmaglen, she put on the uniform of a 'Greenfinch', the female members of the Ulster Defence Regiment, the only regiment of the British Army permanently serving in Northern Ireland. The commanding officer presented her with an epaulette of the Queen's Own Highlanders which had belonged to Colonel David Blair, the most senior soldier killed at Warrenpoint: 'This, Prime Minister, is all that is left of Colonel Blair.' She wept. Her instinctive solidarity with the British security forces was strong, deep and always vividly expressed.

In a different sphere, the new Prime Minister also had to contend with the unravelling of a fifteen-year cover-up. Ever since the defections of Guy Burgess and Donald Maclean to the Soviet Union in the 1950s and that of Kim Philby in 1963, there had been a hunt for the so-called 'Fourth Man' of the Cambridge spy ring. This was Anthony Blunt. Blunt had spied for the Soviet Union from 1940 to 1945 while working for the British Security Service (MI5). A distinguished art historian, he later became Surveyor of the Queen's Pictures. In the autumn of 1979 Andrew Boyle published a book called *The Climate of Treason*, which dropped heavy hints about Blunt. Boyle challenged the government to identify him.

The position was a difficult one because, in 1964, Blunt had accepted an offer of immunity from prosecution in return for a confession.* Given Blunt's royal connection, it would be damaging if it became known that the government and the Palace had agreed to cover up his treachery. MI5 advised against any prime ministerial intervention, but the Attorney-General, Sir Michael Havers, noted that if Blunt were not named by the government he would be free to sue for libel if others named him. This would be intolerable. Mrs Thatcher, new to all this, listened carefully. Her straightforward instinct was that 'he had betrayed his country', and there was now no reason to protect him. That November she named Blunt in the Commons, calling his behaviour 'contemptible and repugnant'. Buckingham Palace announced that Blunt would be stripped of his knighthood. The story was covered feverishly in the press and the optics favoured Mrs Thatcher. It looked as if she would have nothing to do with the corrupt and weak old ways of doing things. Many jumped to the conclusion that she would inaugurate a new era of transparency in the security services. They would be sorely disappointed.

Nothing did more than the long row over the EEC budget to bring out the qualities which made Mrs Thatcher so impressive to her admirers and so irritating to her detractors. When Bryan Cartledge departed as her foreign affairs private secretary in September 1979, she wrote him a remarkably frank thank-you letter: 'I get more and more disillusioned with the EEC. We are going to have a real fight over the budget and by one means or another we have to get our way. We need the money.' These few words summarize her approach. She wanted a fight; she wanted the money; and she found the whole EEC set-up uncongenial. While not systematically anti-European, Mrs Thatcher was frustrated, and jealous of encroachments upon British sovereignty. The attitudes of her main European counterparts brought out her combative instincts. Although agreeing with officials that her government must show itself friendlier to Europe after the fraught Wilson-Callaghan years, she did not like most of the suggested ways of doing so.

One was joining, or promising soon to join, the Exchange Rate Mechanism. On the day she reached No. 10, John Hunt had sent her a memo advocating 'an open-minded approach to the concept of a zone of monetary stability in Europe'. She wrote: 'I doubt whether this can be achieved

---

* There was little possibility of prosecuting Blunt because the conclusive evidence had come from the American traitor Michael Straight and was not of the sort that could be presented in court.

by a currency system. Indeed it can't – unless all of the underlying policies of each country are right.' Lord Carrington shared Hunt's view. 'I despair of FO memos,' she wrote on one of them. 'This is jabberwocky to me. What is it supposed to mean.' Over the summer and autumn, Roy Jenkins, the Commission President, pushed for British ERM membership but she resisted. In October the government privately decided that it was the wrong time for Britain to join.

Although her European attitudes gave the Foreign Office the vapours, they were popular in the country and caused her little political difficulty in her own party. Bernard Ingham told an off-the-record lobby briefing that, while he had voted to join the EEC, 'I am sure like millions of others, I didn't vote to go in to be fleeced.' He was annoyed to find these words quoted in print, attributed to Mrs Thatcher herself, but they probably reflected the prevailing mood among Tory supporters and did his boss no harm. Nor was she arraigned by the Opposition. The Labour rank and file, though not the leadership, remained anti-EEC. On her own side, a newly elected MP by the name of John Major put down an Early Day Motion congratulating her on her tough negotiating stance.

In the autumn Mrs Thatcher returned to the attack on Britain's budgetary contribution. At her party's conference in Blackpool she spoke of the 'appalling prospect' of paying out £1 billion net per annum to Brussels.* In a formal address in Luxembourg later that October, she was fierce about the 'manifest inequity' of the budget problem: 'I cannot play Sister Bountiful to the Community while my own electorate are being asked to forgo improvements in the fields of health, education, welfare and the rest.' Her vision of the EEC was already one that no other European leader would have advanced. It was to link the EEC and NATO in liberty. Away with 'grey uniformity': the point of the whole thing, she believed, was to advance in 'the struggle between liberty and tyranny'. Asked, in an interview, about a United States of Europe, she said: 'That has never, I believe, been the practical intention.'

For most of those leading the project, however, that was indeed the intention. 'The Commission *was* trying to create a United States of Europe,' said Michael Jenkins, who worked there with Roy Jenkins, 'with a common currency and a constitution.' Most relevant Foreign Office officials were of like mind. They included Michael Butler, the United Kingdom's Ambassador to the EEC from 1979, David Hannay, who ran European Community affairs for the Foreign Office at the same time, and Sir Michael Palliser,

---

* The net contribution five years earlier had been £16 million.

the Permanent Under-Secretary. Many British ministers, too, saw 'Europe' as an unquestionably 'good thing'. When they met at European councils, Roy Jenkins and Ian Gilmour, who were great friends, would 'wring their hands' about Mrs Thatcher.

Even before the battle of the budget, Mrs Thatcher lacked the instinctive sympathy with mainland Europe which, for much of the British elite, was a mark of being civilized. Michael Palliser first met her in 1975. He found her 'exceptionally ignorant, but with some deep-rooted prejudices' which did not alter over the years. One such was that the French were preternaturally cunning. 'They are cleverer than us,' she told him. 'They will run rings round us.'*

This gulf between Mrs Thatcher and her European counterparts had roots of quasi-theological significance. Her insistence that the British contribution was unfair offended against the European doctrine that 'own resources' – the percentage of VAT receipts voted to the Community by the member states – belonged absolutely to the EEC. To them, Mrs Thatcher's talk of 'our money', or sometimes 'my money', was anathema. Going against the grain only increased her determination. The need to fight if everyone else seemed to disagree with her was deeply ingrained in her character. As she told Ingham: 'My father taught me to "dare to be a Daniel".'

At the European Council in Dublin on 29 November 1979, Mrs Thatcher brought matters to a head. Her government's position, going in, was to settle for a reduction in Britain's net contribution of between three-quarters and two-thirds so long as 'the solution was as long as the problem', not one-off. There was little disagreement among ministers about this. Even the government's most committed Europhiles could see that Britain was being set up. If necessary, Mrs Thatcher would accept isolation at Dublin and warn, as Howe had proposed, that unless she got satisfaction she 'would not thereafter be able to facilitate the operation of the Community'. Shortly before the summit, Roy Jenkins had called on Mrs Thatcher. Seeking to calm the waters, he said she should avoid building up a 'head of steam' about the budget question. She 'said that there was already an uncontrollable head of steam'. When Jenkins predicted she would not get what she wanted at Dublin she warned there would be 'no movement in the Community' unless she prevailed.

Mrs Thatcher now went to war. She refused all prepared texts for her

---

* It is interesting that the French believed the same thing, in reverse. 'It was dangerous for us. The British are cleverer than we are, and what they wanted was not legitimate,' Giscard d'Estaing told the present author, speaking of the EEC budget negotiations.

opening statement, preferring to extemporize and thus speak more vigorously. At the heads of government dinner she kept them all at table for four hours. 'I want my money back,' she kept repeating. Schmidt pretended to fall asleep and Giscard was alleged, though he denied this to the author, to have read a newspaper. Mrs Thatcher's performance was, according to Carrington, 'a rant'. Giscard agreed: 'It was unpleasant, because it wasn't a conversation. It was a repetition.' Britain was offered £350 million in rebate. Arguing that the full £1 billion contribution be rebated, Mrs Thatcher scornfully dismissed it as 'a third of a loaf'. She resented being ganged up against. As she scribbled during the summit, 'we thought we had joined an equitable system'. She considered the Continental approach un-British: 'What I would not accept was the attitude that fairness did not seem to enter into the equation.' The negotiations had been 'totally unsatisfactory', she told the press afterwards: 'all we are doing is asking for our own money back.'

While Mrs Thatcher's behaviour annoyed the European leaders, even Euro-enthusiasts like Michael Butler believed that her stance was essentially correct: the other heads of government 'were always pretending to be outraged by what she said'. The budget mechanism *was* inequitable, and the nations – the majority – which benefited tried hard to avoid surrendering their advantage. More than 70 per cent of the Community budget went on the Common Agricultural Policy (CAP), a policy essentially designed for France's benefit. Strikingly little of it benefited Britain. Giscard told a close associate that 'we must keep on bashing the British steak to make it tender'. Given domestic opinion, Mrs Thatcher had to fight. Her style of doing so did her more political good than harm.

A special summit in Luxembourg in April 1980 to resolve the issue made little headway, but Carrington got wind of the desire to settle. He started working on Mrs Thatcher, planting the idea of a three-year deal, pending a longer-term solution. When he first broached this she declared herself 'so horrified' that she saw little point in meeting to discuss it: 'I feel as if the FCO [Foreign and Commonwealth Office] is going to cancel out all my own efforts.' Carrington pushed ahead, though not without much storming from Mrs Thatcher. After one meeting in the Cabinet Room he got up to leave, still arguing, and without looking where he was going. He knocked into one of the Doric pillars. 'My God,' he exclaimed, 'I've hit another immoveable obstacle.'

On 30 May, in Brussels, Carrington and Ian Gilmour reached a provisional deal. It included two-thirds off the net contribution for the next three years, with a longer-term settlement to be reached by 1981. 'I am convinced that this is the limit of what we can negotiate,' Carrington telegraphed Mrs Thatcher. The Continental press helped his cause: 'all the French media are presenting the Brussels proposals as a great victory for you and a defeat for France,' Whitmore told her. Mrs Thatcher remained highly suspicious. When Carrington and Gilmour flew to Chequers, she gave them a hard time. She did not like the figures; possibly she did not like the feeling that the wind had been taken out of her sails. '"I'll resign," she said,' recalled Carrington. '"No," I said, "I'll resign."' No one resigned. On Monday 2 June the Cabinet endorsed the deal, but noted that it gave the United Kingdom 'less than would be ideally desirable'.

The perceived success of Mrs Thatcher's first big European battle won her admirers at home and even, more grudgingly, abroad. Yet the budget row contained the seeds of problems which were to become toxic by the end of the 1980s. The experience confirmed Mrs Thatcher's resentment at the way the EEC worked. Again and again, she would scribble exclamations of exasperation on memos charting the negotiations ('The more I read the more appalled I become'). On a memo about EEC rules on how refunds should be approved, she wrote: 'No – the procedure is ridiculous. Its whole purpose is to demean Britain.' Through a series of unpleasant surprises, she discovered that more powers had been ceded than she had realized. She found it hard to resolve the conundrum of all EEC negotiation: how much should a matter of principle, such as national independence, be sacrificed for a specific, material advantage or for the Foreign Office concept of 'influence'?

In the quieter months after the Brussels deal, John Nott, the Trade Secretary, wrote her a thoughtful note about future strategy. In his view, recent negotiations had come close to the crucial objective of reforming the CAP, 'but we lost the opportunity when we accepted a temporary settlement'. Mrs Thatcher underlined these words twice and put three ticks beside them. Nott had captured her sense that any victory, however good in specifics, was always bought by the longer-term sacrifice of Britain's interests.

Shortly after the Dublin summit in November 1979, Mrs Thatcher prepared to visit the United States. Her instinctive sympathy with America was as ingrained as her instinctive distance from Continental Europe. She hoped her cordial relationship with Ronald Reagan might bear fruit in the 1980 presidential contest, but for now she had to work with Jimmy Carter. The two respected but did not particularly like one another; disagreeing especially on how to deal with the Soviet Union. There was also a question for both about how much effort should be put into their relationship. The US administration thought that Britain no longer mattered much. A CIA report for Carter assessed that 'The "special relationship" between the

United States and the United Kingdom, finally, has lost much of its meaning.' For her part, Mrs Thatcher was conscious of Carter's weakness. On 4 November the US Embassy in Teheran was occupied by Islamic extremists and the staff taken hostage. Efforts to secure their release consumed the remainder of the Carter presidency and so, recalled Jim Rentschler, a National Security Council staffer, the Anglo-American relationship 'was largely left to the bureaucracy to manage'.

In her December visit, Mrs Thatcher was concerned above all to make a favourable impression and establish herself as a player on the Washington stage. At the British Embassy on the night of her arrival, 16 December, the Ambassador, Sir Nicholas Henderson (commonly known as 'Nicko'), noted with surprise and pleasure how much she listened to Carrington. The party discussed whether Britain should support the United States in seeking Chapter Seven powers (which could include sanctions or even the use of military force) from the United Nations Security Council over the hostage-taking in Iran. Mrs Thatcher, concerned about British interests in Iran, was doubtful. It was Carrington who urged her on: 'Leaning forward on the sofa, Peter Carrington said, "Margaret, you have got to say, yes."'

The next morning, the Prime Minister was received in solitary splendour on the White House lawn, with military honours. She immediately praised Carter's handling of the hostage crisis: 'At times like this, you are entitled to look to your friends for support. We are your friends. We do support you. And we shall support you.'* She offered Carter her backing over Chapter Seven: 'No other course of action was thinkable.' When she confirmed this to the waiting press, the impact was immediate: 'Warm Words on a Wintry Day; Thatcher Vows to Back Iran Sanctions' headlined the *Washington Post*.

At lunch at the British Embassy, Mrs Thatcher was able to announce, impromptu, that a constitutional settlement for Rhodesia had just been initialled at Lancaster House. 'The Margaret Thatcher who arrived yesterday for her first American visit as Prime Minister is being received as the most effective British statesman (she would scorn "stateswoman") since Harold Macmillan, the fabled Supermac,' judged the *New York Times*. That afternoon she went to Capitol Hill, where her reception was almost rapturous.† Over dinner at the White House that night, Carter applied a quotation from *Pickwick Papers* to Mrs Thatcher: 'She knows what's

---

* This warm, humanizing reference to 'friendship' had been written into the speech by Mrs Thatcher personally, replacing the cooler and rather wooden language provided by the Foreign Office.

† Henderson recorded that one senior Senator told him three times how marvellous she had been and said: '"I do not recall any visitor to the USA who has made such an impact." I asked

what, she does.' There was a faint feeling that the President found this quality irritating.

The following morning, in New York, Mrs Thatcher told the Foreign Policy Association that 'Self-questioning is essential to the health of any society. But we perhaps have carried it too far and carried to extremes of course it causes paralysis. The time has come when the West – above all Europe and the United States – must begin to substitute action for introspection.' Without being guilty of any diplomatic incorrectness, she was filling a gap in the West which many Americans felt had been created by Carter's vacillation. Even within the administration, Mrs Thatcher appealed to people who felt that their own country's leadership was lacking. Jim Rentschler recalled: 'Bob Blackwill [a colleague on the National Security Council staff] came out of a meeting that included both Carter and Thatcher: "In that room there was one giant and one pigmy," he said, "and the giant was female."'

The Lancaster House Agreement over Rhodesia was not really Mrs Thatcher's doing. She felt little natural warmth towards the process, indeed a fierce distaste towards Joshua Nkomo and even more towards Robert Mugabe, and left the negotiations to her Foreign Secretary, who briefed her each night. As her foreign affairs private secretary, Michael Alexander, recalled: 'Her role was to be rather extreme, to criticize all the participants all the time* ... "I won't have it; I won't do it" and "Absolutely not!" ... Peter would then go back to Lancaster House and say that the Prime Minister was giving him a hard time and that the participants had better agree to whatever he proposed "for fear of something worse".' Mrs Thatcher also sent regular updates to President Carter. Carter felt the pressure from black activists in the Democratic Party, who feared that the white minority would find a way to thwart genuine majority rule: they were unfriendly towards the British.

American cooperation was sometimes required, however. The most important occasion came in December when Carrington sent Lord Soames, the designated Governor of Rhodesia for the transitional period to independence, to Salisbury before a ceasefire had been agreed. Privately, Soames expected 50 per cent casualties among the 350 servicemen who accompanied him. In the event, though there was some factional violence, his troops were largely unmolested. To show international support for this bold move,

---

whether he was referring to visitors to Congress. "No," he replied, "I mean any visitor anywhere to the United States."'

* Alexander noted that he did not keep a record of these discussions: 'they would not have done her reputation much good!'

Britain wanted sanctions lifted immediately. When the Americans hesitated Mrs Thatcher wrote to Carter, asking him, in effect, to overrule his State Department. He agreed at once.

Although Mrs Thatcher was prudent and, where Carter was concerned, persuasive in advancing the Lancaster House process, her scepticism continued. From her time in Opposition she had maintained links with Jesse Helms, the right-wing Senator from North Carolina whose unbending anti-Communism and segregationalism placed him in Ian Smith's corner. When, in September, his staff came to London to try and stiffen Smith against a settlement, Mrs Thatcher received one of them, John Carbaugh, at No. 10. Carbaugh recalled: 'I said, "Mrs Thatcher, Peter Carrington is not serving you well." She said, "That is not for you to decide."' The fact that she saw Carbaugh at all is evidence of her alertness to the right-wing threat to Lancaster House, perhaps of her sympathy for it. Looking back, Carrington summed up her attitude:

> I don't think that Margaret, in her heart of hearts, was ever convinced about the process – in the sense that if it had gone wrong . . . [here Carrington made a throat-slitting gesture and laughed] she wouldn't have taken the can . . . She was supportive, but it was rather reluctant support: 'My mind tells me that this is the right thing to do, but my instinct tells me you're a pig.'

What happened much later in Zimbabwe, when Robert Mugabe, from the mid-1990s, began the repression and impoverishment of his country, was to confirm Mrs Thatcher's pessimism. Yet her task, on coming into office, was essentially to get out of a problem which had consumed vast amounts of British government time for no clear benefit. The course she chose, under Carrington's direction, was bold. By the standards which it set itself, the Lancaster House Agreement was an astonishing success, and Mrs Thatcher showed the flexibility and opportunism that leadership requires by letting it happen.

But the Rhodesian settlement never made her happy. As she stood in the hall of No. 10 on 21 December 1979 to leave to put her initials to the Lancaster House Agreement, Mrs Thatcher had a last-minute attack of anger. She turned to Clive Whitmore and said, 'I am not going to shake the hands of terrorists.' Whitmore held out her coat and said, 'Put this on, Prime Minister. We're going to Lancaster House.' She did so, but with an ill grace.

Mrs Thatcher ended 1979 in an odd position. While some critics branded her rigid, dogmatic and unfeeling, a much greater problem, for her economic policy, was the suspicion that she was infirm of purpose.

The idea known as 'monetarism' was not an innovation of Mrs Thatcher's government. Denis Healey, the Labour Chancellor, had himself pursued monetary control after the intervention of the IMF in 1976, making a political calculation that inflation was even more unpopular than unemployment. Mrs Thatcher, however, saw monetarism as a matter of principle as well as of expedience. The problem was that, with British decline now an orthodoxy, people were sceptical that a new Conservative government could succeed where Labour had failed.

To demonstrate seriousness of intent, it was not enough to increase interest rates by fearsome amounts, as had happened in November 1979. Monetarist theory dictated that governments and central banks adhere to strict monetary rules. In the phrase of Nigel Lawson, the approach's keenest advocate, 'Rules rule, OK?' Instead of the 'letters of intent' which the IMF had extracted, under virtual coercion, from the previous government, there should be free-will declarations of financial objectives with target dates. As well as delivering economic benefits, such rules were intended to produce political ones, helping to explain the absence of jam today by indicating jam tomorrow. They could show how, if public borrowing fell, there would be room for tax cuts and – just as important – how, if it didn't, there wouldn't. The name devised for the set of rules was the Medium-Term Financial Strategy (MTFS).

Initially, this made Mrs Thatcher nervous. She referred to plans of this sort disparagingly as 'numbers marching across the page'. Her real concern was that the MTFS would leave no room for political flexibility. That was, in a sense, the point. As Howe told her, it would put a straitjacket on big-spending ministers and, he added cunningly, help bring down interest rates, Mrs Thatcher's perennial desire. Slowly but surely, she came round. The MTFS was agreed by the pre-Budget Cabinet in March 1980 without much fuss. It was remarkable that the Wets did not take a stand against the new strategy. It defied their desire to improve demand in the economy, setting a course to which they were opposed. Perhaps they continued to believe that such plans had little meaning. Perhaps they hoped that for Mrs Thatcher – to reverse Mr Micawber's remark – something would turn down.

Mrs Thatcher had, in fact, tried hard to avoid any economic debate in Cabinet that would have given potential rebels an opportunity. From November 1979, economic policy was driven by an 'Inner Group', which included Howe, Joseph, Nott, Biffen, David Howell, Patrick Jenkin and Willie Whitelaw. Prior and Francis Pym, the Defence Secretary, were deliberately kept in the dark. When Howe circulated his pre-Budget paper only to the Inner Group, Robert Armstrong, who had succeeded John Hunt as

Cabinet Secretary, protested to the Prime Minister: 'I think it is wrong that Ministers should be asked to take far-reaching policy decisions, involving major political issues, on the basis of two or three lines in the Chancellor's annual Public Expenditure paper.' The word 'wrong' was a big one for a Cabinet Secretary to use. Mrs Thatcher scribbled: 'They don't. They <u>ought</u> to <u>know</u> their departments and what is going on.' A general economic discussion in Cabinet was postponed until after the Budget, giving Howe sufficient room to advance the MTFS. Under this approach, as he outlined in the Budget, the growth of sterling M3* would fall by 1 per cent annually, reaching growth of 4–8 per cent in 1983–4. The PSBR (nowadays called the budget deficit) would fall from 4 per cent of GDP in 1980–81 to 1.5 per cent in 1983–4. The MTFS did not, in itself, change the policy, but it did formalize the position and hold the government to its course. The monetarist government now had a monetarist strategy.

But, as Keith Joseph had long before said, 'Monetarism is not enough.' Sound money was a necessary but not a sufficient condition of recovery. John Hoskyns saw economic recovery as having three legs – the attack on inflation, the ending of indexing and other privileges of the state sector and curbing the trade unions. The MTFS had been introduced, but little else had happened. The stool had only one leg to stand on.

The sharpest internal disagreement concerned the trade union leg. In the early days, Mrs Thatcher had allowed Prior's cautious approach to govern the first Employment Bill. By the end of 1979, however, the state of industrial relations had become more desperate. On 13 December, the Court of Appeal sided with the unions over the scope of their legal immunity. The court ruled, in effect, that the law afforded no protection to firms dragged into an industrial dispute with which they were not concerned. In early January 1980 the steelworkers' union, the ISTC, called a strike over its pay claim against the British Steel Corporation (BSC) and quickly spread the strike to otherwise unrelated private-sector steel producers. On 28 January, Hoskyns wrote to Mrs Thatcher: 'The only way to penalise unions is to attack their funds. Never go after the individual . . .' Unions were 'financial enterprises which operate on a no-risk basis'. The government must stand firm in the steel strike, he insisted, and act immediately to remove union immunities.

A struggle now raged. Prior insisted that removing immunities would be a terrible mistake, while Howe told her that unless the Conservatives

---

* M3 was the broad measure of money (or 'monetary aggregate') favoured by the government; it included cash and bank deposits.

did just that, 'we might as well not have fought (and won) the last General Election'. Mrs Thatcher shared Howe's sentiment. If the law on immunities were not changed, she wrote privately to the businessman Hector Laing in February,* 'we should be telling the law-abiding citizen that we prefer to strengthen the powers of those who inflict injury rather than to help those who suffer from it. That course is not open to anyone who fought the last election on the Conservative manifesto, and it is therefore not open to me.'

Immunity, she told Laing, should be confined to the primary action, and common-law remedies restored to the victims of secondary action. Now was the time to act:

> For obvious reasons I have not been able to put this view publicly yet . . . a lot of industrialists share it and would go much further. Some want a new criminal offence of 'unlawful picketing'. I would prefer to see what we can do through the civil law.
>
> You quoted a saying to me. Let me counter with another famous quotation: 'Our doubts are traitors / And make us lose the good we oft might win / By fearing to attempt.' *Measure for Measure.*

In government, however, there was little sense of urgency. On 13 February 1980, E Committee agreed that 'trade union immunities should eventually be considered' and a Green Paper prepared. With Prior in no hurry, it seemed they would endure another winter without the necessary legislation in place.

Just four days later, on Sunday 17 February, Mrs Thatcher confronted the news that a mass picket at Hadfields, the private steelworks in Sheffield, organized by Arthur Scargill, the militant hero of Heath's Saltley humiliation (see p. 103), had succeeded. Angry at her government's impotence, she rang Willie Whitelaw. 'The Government could not sit aside and do nothing': there should be a one-clause Bill that week to prevent such picketing.

Throughout the day, telephone calls ricocheted back and forth. Joseph passed on Lord Hailsham's suggestion that a charge of unlawful affray be brought against Scargill. To this Mrs Thatcher replied: 'It might suit Mr Scargill very well to be charged.' The new picketing clause she sought would follow the safer route of allowing injunctions to be taken out. At 10.45, Whitelaw warned her about the state of the Sheerness steelworks, also threatened with mass picketing. The Chief Constable of Kent was 'quite determined to keep Sheerness working: he hoped that Ministers would support him though he feared they would not'. Mrs Thatcher

---

* Laing, Chairman of United Biscuits, was a great admirer of Mrs Thatcher, but also a good friend of Jim Prior. He had written to her to urge she follow Prior's 'step by step' approach.

repeated her desire for a civil law remedy. The Bill she proposed would allow the Sheerness steelworks to seek an injunction against the pickets.

During this hectic, semi-coherent day Mrs Thatcher was deeply alarmed: she feared she was suffering her own Saltley. Here was the fate of Ted Heath staring her in the face. Thanks to Prior, her government had not provided itself or employers or, she worried, the police with the legal powers necessary to prevent this.* A few days later, she was asked about comments made by Prior critical of British Steel's management which had leaked. 'I think it was a mistake,' she said, 'and Jim Prior was very, very sorry indeed for it, and very apologetic. But you don't just sack a chap for one mistake.' The fact that she spoke about sacking him at all reflected her state of mind.

As it turned out, the militants' victory at Hadfields did not signal a wider war between government and unions. The failure to achieve a similar success at Sheerness was important. When it became clear that, breaking with past practice, the government had no intention of intervening, the steelworkers' union sought a way out. Even though they secured a high pay award, the political winner, on points, was the government. In April a Scottish-American businessman called Ian MacGregor was appointed, at Prior's recommendation, to take over as BSC Chairman. Mrs Thatcher referred to him in public as a 'mighty man', a favourite phrase of Denis's. His task was to turn BSC into a functioning business.

Even bigger, and therefore even more disastrous, than British Steel was British Leyland. Leyland was chiefly an unsuccessful volume car-maker in which the government owned the controlling share. It employed 160,000 people when Mrs Thatcher came into office (with a similar number directly dependent on the company's existence). Although parts of the company, such as Land Rover and Jaguar, held promise, extensive trade union problems kept productivity so low that Leyland survived only through vast government subsidies.† Unsurprisingly, Mrs Thatcher was not well disposed to the company. In early 1979, while still Leader of the Opposition, she had been to lunch with its dynamic Chairman, Sir Michael Edwardes, and his board. As he recalled: 'She said, "Well, why should I give you any money?"' As Prime Minister she continued to ask this question but never felt she received a satisfactory answer.

All Mrs Thatcher's inclinations were that BL should close or be broken

---

* Despite Mrs Thatcher's anxiety, a special meeting of E the next day agreed that a separate Bill about picketing would not be brought forward, but the Attorney-General would remind the Commons about the criminal law on picketing.
† Leyland could not compete effectively with other car manufacturers. Its UK market share, 33 per cent in 1974, had fallen to 20 per cent by 1979.

up and its workable bits sold off. The political difficulty was twofold. How could she introduce economic reality without job losses which would cause the Conservatives to lose every seat in the West Midlands? How, also, could she support Michael Edwardes's tough approach to industrial relations and at the same time pull the plug?

In October 1979, 87.2 per cent of Leyland's workforce voted to back a new BL 'Recovery Plan' put forward by Edwardes. This would require another £300 million from the government in 1980. As John Hoskyns identified for Mrs Thatcher, this posed a dilemma. 'The BL ballot', he wrote, 'was seen as the workers putting their faith in good managers instead of politically motivated union activists. To reward Edwardes's efforts and his work-force backing with closure would seem to be a deliberate blow against everything the Government is trying to encourage.' Shortly before Christmas, Mrs Thatcher agreed to the extra £300 million. The condition was Edwardes's acceptance that the Recovery Plan would be abandoned – resulting in total closure – if thrown off course by strikes.

Just as Mrs Thatcher wanted to get away from 'beer and sandwiches at No. 10', by which trade unions helped make government policy, so she wanted an almost equally arm's-length relationship with the heads of nationalized industries. She therefore had no substantive meeting with Edwardes until, at Keith Joseph's prompting, she gave dinner to the BL board on 21 May 1980. There Edwardes expressed confidence in the company's future, but, given the damaging exchange rate, demanded another £500 million over the next three or four years. Mrs Thatcher's manner, he recalled, was 'somewhat reminiscent of the Spanish Inquisition'. At first, saying she was 'very disturbed', she resisted, but over the course of the evening he sensed her opposition softening.*

In December 1980, however, Joseph reported that BL's demand for 1981–3, £130 million in the 1980 Corporate Plan, was now £1,140 million. Mrs Thatcher peppered Joseph's document with exclamation marks and wrote, in reference to Jaguar and Land Rover, 'Sell off.' It fell to E Committee, in January 1981, to resolve the issue. Robert Armstrong, conscious of Mrs Thatcher's politically precarious position, urged her not to 'show your hand in the discussion. I believe that serious consequences would ensue if the decision was to continue financial support ... and it

---

* Edwardes recalled that the key moment came after dinner when they moved to the drawing room: 'Suddenly she turned everything on its head ... She turned to Geoffrey Howe and said, "Geoffrey, how much have we got in the contingency fund?" Geoffrey said, "Do you think it is proper for them to know?" "Get on with it. Tell Michael how much is in there," she said. There was actually two or three billion in it.' Edwardes considered this the indication of support he was looking for.

then came out (as I fear it might) that that decision had been taken against your advice.' He was warning her about the leaky habits of far from loyal Cabinet colleagues.

In the end, the extra money was agreed, but the company was also put on a path towards winding down what was unsustainable and selling off what was not. This compromise did not please Mrs Thatcher. Indeed, the capitulation to BL's demands was seen by many Thatcherites as a tremendous disaster. At the Centre for Policy Studies, Alfred Sherman turned the framed photograph of Keith Joseph to the wall.

On 19 June 1980, John Hoskyns sent the Prime Minister a cautionary note. 'Experience of past Governments', he wrote, 'suggests a tendency to drift into what the historians later recognise as the crucial period with little or no idea of what they are doing. We are now moving into what could be the first, and critical, six months of a make-or-break year. The thinking must be done before the uproar begins.' This was a hint of the exasperation Hoskyns felt at her lack of strategy, but she herself felt exasperated. These feelings had come to a head the previous month.

On entering No. 10, Mrs Thatcher had appointed Sir Derek Rayner, formerly of Marks and Spencer, to investigate waste in government and spur Civil Service reform.* Few past prime ministers had shown interest in such matters, but for her it was a continuing preoccupation. It fitted, said Clive Priestley, Rayner's deputy, with her 'womanly theme of good household management', and with her suspicion that the Civil Service conspired to frustrate the aims of elected governments. Faced with incomprehension from colleagues and senior officials, Mrs Thatcher had proposed a meeting with the permanent secretaries so that she might enthuse them with the task. Sensing trouble, Willie Whitelaw argued that a dinner would be more congenial. This was duly arranged at No. 10 for 6 May.

Six days before the dinner, Iranian Arab terrorists stormed the Iranian Embassy in Princes Gate, taking the occupants hostage. Fruitless negotiations followed and on 5 May a dead body was thrown on to the street.† Whitelaw, who, as Home Secretary, was the minister responsible, sought Mrs Thatcher's agreement to mobilize the Special Air Service (SAS) to rescue the hostages. 'Yes, go in,' she said. During the crisis Mrs Thatcher

---

* As well as seeking out waste, the 'Rayner Scrutiny' worked to alter the belief at the top of the Civil Service that brains alone mattered, and encourage the idea that results mattered too. It wished to import notions of management from the private sector, including reviews of performance with good officials rewarded and bad ones punished.
† It later turned out that the body was of a hostage killed earlier, but at the time it looked as if it was the first of many, designed to ratchet up the crisis.

visited the Cabinet 'war room' from which operations were being conducted. On her first two visits, according to John Chilcot, Whitelaw's private secretary, she was 'frankly dreadful', trying to dominate the occasion without really being on top of the detail. The third was much more successful. 'She was very good,' judged Sir Peter de la Billière, the Director of the SAS. 'She simply set the overall direction of policy and delegated it to Whitelaw to execute.' That afternoon the world watched as hooded gunmen leapt in through the windows of the Embassy. All the surviving hostages were rescued. One terrorist was captured and the other four were killed. The public reaction was immensely favourable. The SAS, previously little known, became a household word for heroism. Although the person in charge was Whitelaw, not Mrs Thatcher, the incident added to her reputation for dash and decisiveness. Ever afterwards, the fantasy of Mrs Thatcher dressed in black combat kit and swinging into buildings with a gun in her hand became a staple of newspaper cartoonists.

The very next day, Mrs Thatcher gave her dinner for the permanent secretaries. Elated by the success of the Princes Gate siege, she was painfully conscious of what Clive Priestley remembered as the contrast between 'the boys in black and the men in grey'. The evening was not a success. 'Her speech was, "You and I can beat the system." They effectively replied, "We *are* the system."' At one point, Sir Frank Cooper, from the Ministry of Defence, left the room. 'Where's Frank gone?' someone asked. 'He's gone to get the SAS,' was the *sotto voce* reply. Mrs Thatcher whispered to Armstrong: 'They are all against me, Robert. I can *feel* it.'

In later years Mrs Thatcher liked to say, 'That meeting is etched on my soul.' She felt beleaguered and – which she disliked even more – patronized and whinged at. It made her wonder whether she would ever be able to wrench the country round to face reality.

Although there was not yet the 'uproar' of which John Hoskyns had warned, in the early months of 1980 the grumbling grew louder. In February, Ian Gilmour made a speech setting out with remarkable frankness (though not mentioning Mrs Thatcher by name) the basic Wet disagreement with her approach. 'In the Conservative view, economic liberalism à la Professor Hayek, because of its starkness and its failure to create a sense of community, is not a safeguard to political freedom but a threat to it.' He warned, in effect, that such a programme risked electoral defeat. As Gilmour later admitted, he was close to breaching the doctrine of collective Cabinet responsibility. His justification was that Mrs Thatcher had herself already departed from a collective approach, making economic policy through a 'secretive monetarist clique'. In truth, Gilmour and his allies felt emboldened because they believed she was almost bound to fail.

Faced with this challenge, Mrs Thatcher did not publicly rebut the criticism or attack Gilmour directly.* The Wets concluded, probably correctly at that moment, that she did not have the power to slap them down. They began to increase their resistance to those measures – union reforms, pay stringencies and above all spending cuts – which would implement Mrs Thatcher's intentions.

At the same time, people essentially sympathetic to her aims were also becoming more alarmed. In February 1980, Milton Friedman called on Mrs Thatcher at No. 10. He was strongly supportive of the central thrust of the government's policies, but he worried that the chosen method of controlling the money supply was wrong.† Mrs Thatcher gathered a small, senior group, including Nigel Lawson, Geoffrey Howe, Ian Gilmour and Gordon Richardson, to meet Friedman, and matters were discussed in broad, almost philosophical terms. At one point, after Friedman had uttered a piece of wisdom, Mrs Thatcher swept the gathering with her finger, saying, 'Now, we all believe that, don't we?' Her finger stopped when it reached Gilmour and lingered, accusingly.

As he explained publicly that July to the Commons Treasury Select Committee, Friedman disagreed with the government's reliance on fiscal policy and interest rates to control the money supply. His critique was based on two points: first, fiscal policy affects money supply only indirectly and at best has a blunt, second-order effect on inflation. And second, interest rates do not control the money supply. Instead, interest rates reflect the prevailing supply and demand for money. In Friedman's view, these difficulties could be avoided by targeting the monetary base (known as M0), a much narrower monetary aggregate than the M3 measure favoured by the government. This could be controlled by the central bank printing less money. In Friedman's view, M0 was both easier to manage and more directly correlated with inflation than M3.

This long-running argument was technical. Some close to Mrs Thatcher criticized her for bothering her head with a matter which she did not fully

---

* When asked specifically about Gilmour's speech in a television interview, Mrs Thatcher said only that all his speeches were 'very scintillating' and that there was 'something in it for everybody'.
† Lawson noted that Friedman 'has been concerned recently lest the Bank of England should be intervening too heavily on the foreign exchange markets. He has always stressed the incompatibility between pursuing targets for the money supply and the exchange rate.' This incompatibility would, years later, be the chief criticism aimed at Lawson himself.

understand. Its political importance, however, which grew in 1980, was that, just as the government was being attacked for its harsh 'monetarism' and just as Britain moved into sharp recession, its chosen measure of money supply, M3, exploded. Interest rates were punitive. So were exchange rates. At the end of March 1980, two weeks after approval of the MTFS, Howe told the Cabinet that 'The money supply seems to be coming under control.' In fact, M3 grew at 19.4 per cent in the target period of 1980 to 1981. In the face of this, a narrower, more controllable monetary aggregate had obvious appeal.

Through the summer of 1980, Mrs Thatcher and her Treasury ministers began to fight a fiercer battle with the spending departments. Failing to get her way in private, Mrs Thatcher increased, if anything, the passion of her public rhetoric. It was one of her unusual and effective political techniques that she almost always ignored Denis Healey's 'First Law of Holes': 'If you are in a hole, stop digging.' She dug furiously. 'Ministers, Treasury knights, and civil servants', she said provocatively in a speech that June, 'can never understand budgeting by cash' (as opposed to volume), but cash limits were 'something which every woman knows'. 'There will be no U-turns along this road,' she added. John Hoskyns's diary for 28 May recorded the mood: 'David [Wolfson] v. despairing about Margaret at present. Reads papers superficially, treats colleagues very badly, still overexcited by being PM, will not sit down and think about key issues. Prior and Co . . . biding their time for a forced U-turn when she will have to resign.'

At E Committee on 17 June, Mrs Thatcher opened with a little speech indicative of her state of mind and of her idea of chairmanship. As Robert Armstrong noted it, she said:

> Indicators of output down, earnings up.
> We have nothing to distribute.
> If we go on like this in the public sector, we shall be redistributing wealth from the private sector to the public sector.
> Resentment against public-sector wage increases enormous.
> Devaluing savings to give public sector increases.

In early July, Mrs Thatcher agreed that Terry Burns, the Treasury's chief economic adviser, should give a presentation to the Cabinet to illustrate both the gravity of the crisis and the necessity of the government's monetary policies. Burns pointed out early signs that the inflation rate was beginning to fall. He impressed Hoskyns: 'Terry's presentation did the trick, made colleagues realise just how much historical evidence was on the side of monetarism and how little alternative there was to our policies.'

But, to the more hierarchically minded members of the Cabinet and the mandarinate, there was something irritating about being lectured by a man still in his thirties. Douglas Wass, Permanent Secretary at the Treasury, recalled that Burns gave 'a child's guide to the economy ... I don't know what good it did'.

In the subsequent discussion political anxiety centred on unemployment, which Prior feared would reach 2.6 million in 1982.* He argued for more measures to help the young unemployed. Peter Walker warned that there would be 'no British industry to recover', and Nicholas Edwards, the Welsh Secretary, who was by no means a paid-up Wet, worried about a sustained downturn and called for more flexibility over interest rates. This gave Howe his cue to tell the meeting that he would announce a 1 per cent cut in interest rates that day. There was so little reaction that Mrs Thatcher said: 'Did everyone hear that?' Someone, probably Prior, said: 'It's a mistake. People will think it's just because of this meeting.'

The following week the Cabinet reconvened for a sterner discussion of public spending. On 10 July, Howe waved in front of colleagues the *Financial Times* report that 40 per cent of the year's PSBR had already been used up in three months. The Treasury sought further cuts. Jim Prior reacted angrily. 'Is this right in a recession?' 'An increase in PSBR', he added heretically, 'will not necessarily put up [interest] rates.' Mrs Thatcher fell back on the bluntness which did not endear her to colleagues: 'We never get the reductions in consumption ... People, including you, won't make the cuts.' This ill-tempered meeting was the last full discussion of economics and public spending before the House rose for the summer recess

As a parting shot before she went on holiday in August, Mrs Thatcher deployed a phrase for which, in another context, she would become famous. Would she relax the squeeze, asked her interviewer, Hugo Young? 'No, no, no!' she cried. And she went on: 'Deep in their instincts ... they [the British people] find what I am saying and doing right ... if I give up, we will lose.' She told an American interviewer: 'If we had ever looked at Dunkirk as a kind of balance sheet, as sometimes I am asked to look economically at this country, well I don't think we would have gone on at that time. If you looked at it as a matter of the spirit of the people then it is totally different.'

One who wanted her to give up her policies was her first Prime Minister, Harold Macmillan. After visiting her at Chequers in August, he followed up with a memorandum calling for 'powerful reflationary measures' and urging a return to '"consensus" politics, sneered at by some, but the essence

---

* The figure hit 2 million at the end of August 1980, and reached Prior's prediction for 1982 in June 1981. It hit three million in January 1982.

of Tory democracy'.* His message, put bluntly, was that Mrs Thatcher was completely wrong. The memo also contained the implication, which was sustaining the Wets, that her policies were bound to fail. There is no record that she replied to it.

Mrs Thatcher always disliked holidays. She found their break with what she called 'rhythm' unsettling. Once, when Education Secretary, she and Denis went on holiday to Corsica for ten days. After four days, her secretary Alison Ward was surprised to receive a telephone call: 'Hello, dear. We're at Heathrow.' 'Oh,' said Alison, 'has something dreadful happened?' 'Oh no, dear. We've done Corsica.' In the summer of 1980 she went to stay with Sir Douglas and Lady Glover at Schloss Freudenberg in Switzerland.† There was little to do there except admire the magnificent views and walk, which Mrs Thatcher always did in a skirt, up the nearest mountain. But Lady Glover would scour Switzerland and neighbouring countries for people of sufficient brainpower and eminence to come to daily lunches and dinners with the Thatchers. In 1980 Mrs Thatcher met Karl Brunner, the Swiss-born, American-based monetarist economist at one such lunch and, at another, Fritz Leutwiler, the President of the Swiss National Bank. They echoed Friedman's concerns over her government's reliance on sterling M3 and suggested that the Bank of England was mishandling the money supply.

Mrs Thatcher came steaming back from the Alps, furious at what she had heard. Wishing to arraign the Bank of England, she called for the Governor and his deputy, only to find that both were on holiday. This did not improve her temper. Despite opposition from both Bank and Treasury, she became ever more convinced of the need for narrower monetary base control.‡ From across the Atlantic Professor Alan Walters, whom she had first met in Opposition, agreed. In January 1981 she made him her

---

* 'The so-called "money supply" policy', Macmillan wrote, 'may be useful as a guide to what is happening just as a speedometer is in a car; but like the speedometer it cannot make the machine go faster or slower.' Macmillan liked comparisons between Mrs Thatcher and driving. Once a visitor to his country house, Birch Grove, said, 'I've got a new kind of car. It says things to me like "Now fasten your seatbelt" in a Japanese voice.' 'Ah yes,' said Macmillan, 'a Mrs Thatcher type of car.'

† Douglas Glover had been a long-standing backbench Conservative MP. His wife, Eleanor, was the rich and clever widow of a Swiss industrialist.

‡ On the question of narrower monetary base control, Mrs Thatcher found a sympathizer within the Treasury machine, Peter Middleton, who oversaw the detail of monetary policy. Covertly, he produced an agenda for Mrs Thatcher to use with the Treasury when arguing for the targeting of M0. 'Peter Middleton would be most grateful if you could avoid waving this piece of paper around', minuted her private secretary. 'He has not admitted to the Chancellor or Treasury colleagues that he has produced it.'

economic adviser in Downing Street. Having read Hoskyns's economic briefing papers, Walters told him: 'These things still haven't been done? I keep wondering whether it's already too late.'

It might have been too late if Mrs Thatcher had lost the support of her party, but this had not happened. To cultivate the grass-roots, she threw herself into preparing her speech for the party's annual conference at Brighton in October 1980. By 6 October, John Hoskyns noted she was 'obviously in a panic'. On 9 October, the day before the speech, she calmed down a little:

> Ian [Gow] and Clive [Whitmore] beginning to handle Margaret more firmly, Denis showing a more robust impatience – 'Honestly, love, we're not trying to write the Old Testament' ... We had a laugh about something while Margaret was still in the bedroom, changing. Sure enough, Clive told us this went down badly and she said to Caroline [Stephens], 'Make sure they keep their noses to the grindstone.'

When she spoke the following day, Mrs Thatcher acknowledged unemployment as a 'human tragedy'. To tackle this, she insisted, the fight against inflation had to be won. Then she addressed the unspoken fear – or, depending on point of view, hope – that the government would change course, as it had done under Heath: 'To those waiting with bated breath for that favourite media catchphrase, the "U" turn, I have only one thing to say, "You turn if you want to. The lady's not for turning."' The phrase stuck.*
'The punchline worked perfectly,' recorded Hoskyns, 'and she delivered it just right ... Prolonged laughter and applause.'

Mrs Thatcher also took heart from the state of her opponents. Five days after her speech, Jim Callaghan resigned as Labour leader. On 10 November he was replaced by Michael Foot, the most left-wing of the candidates. With the leaders of Labour's social democratic right looking to a future outside the party,† there could be little doubt that Labour would split.

Within the government, though, the pounding got ever harder. At a meeting on 12 November, preparing for the Chancellor's Autumn Statement, Howe and Mrs Thatcher agreed to cut interest rates by 2 per cent to 14 per cent. They were, however, deeply concerned by the deteriorating financial position of the nationalized industries, which, as she put it, 'had undermined

---

* This was a characteristic Ronnie Millar wordplay, adapting the title of the by then unfashionable romantic comedy *The Lady's Not for Burning* by Christopher Fry.
† They were Shirley Williams, David Owen and Bill Rodgers. They had also enlisted Roy Jenkins, across the water in Brussels.

the Government's whole public expenditure strategy'. They felt that the next Budget would probably have to be even more restrictive.

The Cabinet, however, was not agreeable to further stringency. The Wets still believed that, ultimately, Mrs Thatcher would be forced to reverse course: 'she is mad to cut off so many possibilities,' Francis Pym told Hugo Young. 'Why the hell does she keep on saying that she's not for turning, etc. etc.?' In her memoirs, Mrs Thatcher says that, on 30 October, the Cabinet agreed in principle to further cuts in public spending for 1981–2. Yet this 'agreement' was not what it seemed. Armstrong's Cabinet notebook shows several ministers, notably Prior, Walker, Pym and Soames, jibbing at Whitelaw's proposal of a 2 per cent cut across the board. 'I don't think we are agreeing the same thing,' protested Prior. The Wets felt supported by the CBI, whose annual conference had just backed Prior's 'softly, softly' approach to union reform and promised a 'bare-knuckle fight' with the government over interest rates.

On 13 November, Howe told Cabinet colleagues that they should save money by breaking the indexing of benefits to inflation. Prior warned of social unrest: 'If we believe in One Nation, we can't do it.' Instead the Cabinet agreed to increase employees' National Insurance contributions by 1 per cent. Some of these arguments leaked, and newspapers began to run articles about division and loss of confidence. Peter Jenkins, in the *Guardian*, wrote of the 'dawning of disbelief' in Thatcherism and claimed that Mrs Thatcher had lost confidence in her Chancellor. Matters deteriorated after Howe's Autumn Statement was badly received.* 'By the end of 1980,' Mrs Thatcher later wrote, 'I began to feel that we risked forfeiting the public's confidence in our economic strategy.'

Just before Christmas, Brian Griffiths, the prominent academic economist and future head of the Policy Unit, went to see Mrs Thatcher. He later shared his experience with Bill Deedes. Griffiths, Deedes recorded, was met by Geoffrey Howe, who 'begged BG not to be too critical': '"She's in a very odd mood..." Hour with PM. Twice, says BG, near to tears. What had gone wrong? Speechless on the Governor of the Bank of England ... Clearly feels that Chancellor has lost grip.' Mrs Thatcher was badly rattled, and doubtful of her lieutenants.

It was Howe, though, who gave the fairest assessment of the situation. 'You will be disconcerted, as I was,' he wrote to Mrs Thatcher on 31 December, 'to find the transatlantic commentators referring to "Thatcherisation"

---

* Because Howe omitted to mention the automatic increases in National Insurance payments caused by the rise of wage levels he was accused of dishonesty. This led to general outrage and broader attacks on the direction of policy.

as a condition to be avoided, if possible!', but he went on to say, with a touch of flattery, that there was an underlying strength in the government's position: 'the Thatcher factor. People do have a sense that this Government – more particularly you . . . is possessed of a tenacity, which might just work, if only its [*sic*] sustained . . .' Bernard Ingham sent her the annual prediction of the venerable soothsaying publication *Old Moore's Almanack*:

> There are rare moments in history when one man or woman can, almost alone, shape the future of the nation. Now is such a moment. Margaret Thatcher is such a woman. The compelling pattern of her fate is so intimately interwoven with the present destiny of the UK that it is impossible to imagine that she will pass from power before her mission to heal and reinvigorate Britain is complete.

Howe, Ingham and Old Moore were on to something. 'Thatcherism' was never a philosophy, but a disposition of mind and character embodied in a highly unusual woman.

Brooding over Christmas, Mrs Thatcher planned a reshuffle. The smallness of the changes, announced on 5 January 1981, demonstrated the weakness of her position. Francis Pym, whose largely successful resistance to defence cuts had annoyed her, was moved to replace Norman St John-Stevas as Leader of the House and put in charge of policy presentation, an extraordinary choice given his own scepticism about that policy. John Nott replaced Pym at Defence. John Biffen, who had proved weak in the spending negotiations, replaced Nott at Trade, and was in turn replaced by Leon Brittan, a close ally of Howe. Mrs Thatcher had shifted the centre of gravity only very slightly in her favour.

Searching for proper financial control of the nationalized industries, Mrs Thatcher and Geoffrey Howe did not intend to spare the coal industry. Back in May 1979 she had summoned Willie Whitelaw and Sir Robert Wade-Gery, the Deputy Secretary to the Cabinet, and announced: 'The last Conservative Government was destroyed by the miners' strike. We'll have another one, and we'll win. And you, Willie, will do it.' Whitelaw chaired the Civil Contingencies Unit, which tried to draw up the strategic principles and practical measures. Most important was the accumulation of coal stocks, not only at pitheads but at power stations, to allow the country to weather a strike.* The immediate problem, however, was to get any department to

---

* The unit also realized that if there was to be a strike it should begin in the spring and it should be over pit closures, which tended to divide miners, rather than over pay, which tended to unite them.

listen. As Wade-Gery remembered it, people said, 'The woman's mad. You can't win miners' strikes. All you can do is buy them off.'

There was a further problem. While it might make political sense to pile up the coal, it made no immediate financial sense. Without an agreed overall strategy, the Treasury sought to run down coal production to save money. In June, officials predicted that, by the turn of the year, stocks of five to six weeks would have been built up. They added, though, that the 'survival period depends on the extent of picketing outside the industry itself and, if there is secondary picketing, the extent of stockholdings that are vulnerable to picketing'. The state of the law did not inspire confidence. As for contingencies, 'No plan involving servicemen is now considered practicable.'

In September 1980, the Energy Secretary, David Howell, presented his Strategy for Coal to E Committee. He saw a growth of coal production 'as supplies of other fossil fuels decline', but believed that this could come from low-cost pits and that many existing high-cost pits should be closed. Mrs Thatcher wrote: '<u>Thin</u> – what I don't find in these papers is any attempt to <u>cut</u> the <u>costs</u> of production. That is what private industry would have to do.' But she did not oppose the idea of pit closures. Nor did she, at this point, indicate any anxiety about industrial unrest.

On 29 January 1981, Mrs Thatcher backed the National Coal Board's proposed closures. Twenty-three pits were to be closed, though rumour quickly raised this number to fifty. With the famed 'triple alliance' between railwaymen, steelworkers and miners in place, a national strike against these closures seemed possible. Bernard Ingham, stepping briefly outside his normal tasks, counselled Mrs Thatcher that the NCB was doing too much, too quickly, and that Joe Gormley, the moderate miners' leader, would be forced to act toughly 'to protect his flank against Scargill'. Ingham feared that the public would like the idea of 'defending one's livelihood' and would therefore be sympathetic to the miners.

The end was not long in coming. On 16 and 18 February, Mrs Thatcher had meetings with David Howell at which it became clear that coal stocks could not withstand a strike. As Howell remembered, she held up a copy of the *Evening Standard* with the words 'That's that, then, isn't it?' The headline proclaimed, 'Government dithers'. 'Bring it to an end, David,' she said, 'make the necessary concessions.' Without Cabinet discussion, she decided to give in. 'She *was* right to cut and run,' said Howell, because 'we just weren't ready'.

With grim relish, Ingham's press digest on 18 February quoted virtually every headline about the U-turn – '"Surrender to King Coal". *Express*. "You've won, lads". *D. Star*' and so on. And he informed his boss of the

Sun's judgement: 'for the first time since you came to power your credibility at stake'. The government's concessions cost £400–500 million and contributed to the myth that the miners were invincible. Remembering what had happened to Heath, many people believed that the next confrontation would result in the fall of the Tory government.

It was a timely distraction from the government's woes that on 24 February 1981 the engagement was announced between the Prince of Wales and Lady Diana Spencer.

The next day, Mrs Thatcher flew to the United States as the guest of the new President, Ronald Reagan. The day after his inauguration, on 20 January 1981, he had taken a call from her. Declaring herself 'thrilled' by his inauguration speech, she said: 'The newspapers are saying mostly that President Reagan must avoid Mrs Thatcher's mistakes [about economic policy] so I must brief you on the mistakes.' Reagan replied genially, 'I don't think I have to worry about that,' and commiserated on the 'uphill battle' she was fighting in her own country:

> Mrs Thatcher: Well you know it makes it worth it because you are fighting for the things we are fighting for ...
> Reagan: We'll lend strength to each other.
> Mrs Thatcher: We will.

Reagan invited Mrs Thatcher to Washington at the end of February. She would be his first visiting European head of government and he instructed his aides to 'make the visit special'. Its aim, as Secretary of State Alexander Haig briefed Reagan, was to 'demonstrate publicly and privately that Thatcher is the major Western leader most attuned to your views on East–West and security issues'. But the situation was more difficult for Mrs Thatcher than those warm words made it sound. Many Americans, even Reagan supporters, were coming to the view that the Thatcher economic experiment was going wrong.

Critics came from different camps. Supply-siders disliked Mrs Thatcher's failure to cut the overall burden of taxes. 'I'm not sure she was as committed as Ronald Reagan was to the idea that if you get taxes low enough you are going to generate increased tax revenues by virtue of increased economic growth,' recalled James Baker, then Reagan's Chief of Staff. To Bernard Ingham the difference was almost one of temperament:

> I think she probably felt that Reagan was never more wayward than over economic management. She used to worry intensely about the huge propensity

for spending and refusal to tax ... She said that he believed that it would all come right in the end. That was the sunny disposition ... to which she was not entitled, being a British politician who'd seen 35 years of post-war mismanagement. She was constantly worried about the budget deficit.

But even those sympathetic to monetarism were critical. Beryl Sprinkel, Under-Secretary for Monetary Affairs, briefed Reagan's Treasury Secretary, Don Regan, on Mrs Thatcher's failure to cut government spending and how the money supply (M3) was 'soaring', despite a commitment to its tight control.* The State Department's briefing said a core objective for the visit would be to 'Exchange views with Thatcher on her experience, in part to learn from British mistakes.'

The new President himself ignored all these difficulties. 'You know what I want to do in the United States is what Margaret Thatcher has started to do in the United Kingdom,' Reagan had said privately during his election campaign, 'to get the government off the backs of the people.' He was not interested in technical disagreements. According to Paul Volcker, Chairman of the Federal Reserve Board, Reagan 'had a few basic convictions. Fortunately one of these convictions was that inflation was a bad thing.' This worked to Mrs Thatcher's advantage.

Reagan's briefing from Richard Allen, his National Security Advisor, began with an exordium about the relationship between the two leaders which could read equally well as its epitaph:

> Your reunion with British Prime Minister Margaret Thatcher ... will dramatise something rare in the exchanges between US and West European leaders these past few years: a meeting of minds which encompasses not only philosophical affinities, similar economic outlooks, and a common allegiance to the idea of revitalized defense efforts, but also a tough, pragmatic determination to do something about them.

In Allen's view, the visit should demonstrate that the two leaders had taken the measure of the difficulties they faced but were undaunted: 'Sleeves-rolled-up, sobriety-with-optimism is the main message you should be getting across with this visit; politically it can prove an especially effective chord both at home and abroad.'

At the White House, on 26 February, Reagan welcomed her, declaring: 'we share laws and literature, blood, and moral fibre'. Mrs Thatcher, in

---

* Sprinkel noted, however, that Mrs Thatcher's government had the same principal economic objectives as the Reagan administration: 'So far results have been mixed but I am confident that the lady will not turn, and that if she can hang on politically somewhat longer as I believe is the probable case, she will make further progress.'

turn, proclaimed that 'we, in Britain, stand with you. America's successes will be our successes. Your problems will be our problems, and when you look for friends we will be there.' The private reception was equally warm, which encouraged her to be frank. In his diary Reagan recorded that she 'Expressed regret that she tried to reduce govt. spending a step at a time & was defeated in each attempt. Said she should have done it our way – an entire package – all or nothing.'

On the same day, however, Don Regan told a Congressional committee that Mrs Thatcher had failed to control the money supply, produced 'an explosive inflationary surge' and kept taxes too high. Here was a clear effort to distance the administration's policy from their guest of honour.

Fortunately for Mrs Thatcher, the warmth of Reagan's reception overwhelmed such criticism. A grand dinner at the White House was followed the next evening by a reciprocal affair at the British Embassy. Taking advantage of the Reagan team's inexperience, Nicko Henderson, the wily British Ambassador, had got Dick Allen to promise that the President would attend. By the time Reagan's people realized this violated the convention that only the Vice-President attended return dinners, Henderson had sent out the invitations. Reagan came with a good grace.

In her speech that night, Mrs Thatcher added some words about the 'two o'clock in the morning courage' which leaders require when faced with lonely decisions. This greatly pleased Reagan, who replied that she herself had already shown such courage 'on too many occasions to name'. The only disappointment for Mrs Thatcher was that the Reagans left without dancing to the band. When Henderson asked her to dance, 'Mrs T accepted my offer without complication or inhibition, and, once we were well launched on the floor, confessed to me that that was what she had been wanting to do all evening. She loved dancing, something, so I found out, she did extremely well.' She was most reluctant to go to bed, threatening a different sort of 'two o'clock courage' by going off to see the floodlit Washington monuments, 'but Denis put his foot down, crying, "bed"'.

Both sides rejoiced at the visit. 'It was a great success,' Henderson remembered. 'They saw completely eye to eye.' 'I believe a real friendship exists between the P.M. her family & us,' Reagan wrote in his diary. The essence of this friendship was simple and effective. They believed the same things, and they both wanted to work actively to bring them about. They also had compatible, though utterly different, temperaments – he the relaxed, almost lazy generalist who charmed everyone with his easy-going ways, she the hyperactive, zealous, intensely knowledgeable leader who injected energy into all her doings but also displayed what Reagan considered to be the elegance of a typical, gracious English lady. Not only did they share a moral outlook, but their personal chemistry was undeniable. In Robin Butler's view, 'He treated her in a very courteous and sort of slightly flirtatious way, to which she responded.'

Yet, for all her enthusiasm and affection, Mrs Thatcher was not blind to Reagan's limitations. Carrington recalled that after she left the meeting in the Oval Office she pointed at her head and said, 'Peter, there's nothing there.'* What she came to realize was that Reagan's strengths and mental abilities were very different to her own, but she never lost her underlying admiration for him. To her typed thank-you letter to Reagan she added, in her own hand: 'We shall never have a happier visit.' She felt she had a powerful friend. She knew that he would help in the struggles ahead. Her pleasure and gratitude were genuine.

As John Hoskyns reminded Mrs Thatcher in November 1980, she had herself spoken of the need for a 'shock package'. Without fundamental reform the UK economy would remain 'simply unmanageable'. To stress that time was running out he sent her a copy of Peter Jenkins's article about the 'dawning of disbelief' in Thatcherism. 'On the one side,' Hoskyns argued, 'we can start to move increasingly towards what is "politically possible" but simply inadequate for solving the problem. On the other, we will have to find ways of doing things which appear to be "politically impossible", but which are essential if we are to have the slightest chance of getting back onto our strategic course.'

Events in the ensuing months appeared to drive the government ever further from that course. The capitulations to the miners, to BL and to other nationalized industries, the growing mutterings from the Wets and the continuing rise in both public spending and unemployment all seemed to force the government down the narrowing path of what was 'politically possible' against which Hoskyns had warned.

Yet there were two reasons why the situation was not quite as bad for Mrs Thatcher as most people believed. The first was political. On 25 January 1981, Labour veterans Roy Jenkins, Shirley Williams, David Owen and Bill Rodgers produced their Limehouse Declaration, announcing 'the need for a realignment of British politics'. A new political party was expected by the summer. The immediate result was a collapse in Labour's opinion poll lead, which fell from 16 per cent over the Conservatives to 2 per cent.

---

* As Carrington recalled it, Mrs Thatcher's reaction came after Reagan had said '"Well of course, the South Africans are whites and they fought for us during the war. The blacks are black and are Communists." I think even Margaret thought this was rather a simplification.'

As public attention focused on Labour extremism and the weakness of Michael Foot's leadership, Mrs Thatcher reaped the rewards.

The second factor which helped Mrs Thatcher survive was that her core team did not doubt their direction of travel. There was, despite everything, a belief in the leader. She drove them on. As Andrew Duguid, in the Policy Unit, recalled: 'Force of personality was the most striking thing about her – almost too powerful for easy rational discussion to take place.' The very impossibility of some of Mrs Thatcher's demands and moods fostered a camaraderie among her close associates. Some of her womanly qualities inspired a loyal affection. When times were particularly rough, Ian Gow would say, 'Our girl's tired this evening,' and the inner circle would feel the urge to protect her.

At a Chequers seminar on 17 January to discuss Hoskyns's latest strategy paper, Howe warned that public expenditure 'is continuing to "run away from us" and we can't see any end to it'. 'As we spoke,' Hoskyns recorded, 'Margaret said, "We should really have taken some of these measures a year ago."' 'It now looked as if we were heading', he later recalled, 'for a replay of the sort of crisis that had overwhelmed Denis Healey and the Labour Government in 1976 ... With the Budget due on 10 March we had less than eight weeks to break out of the box. If we failed, we were finished.'

9
Russia ... and Reagan
'The only European leader I know with balls'

For Mrs Thatcher, economic policy was only part of the struggle to restore the strength and freedom of the Western way of life. The global backdrop to all her efforts was the weakness of the West. The Cold War dominated everything. She wanted to make sure that Britain could fight it properly.

Within days of Mrs Thatcher becoming Prime Minister, her Foreign Secretary, Lord Carrington, recommended that the Queen send a message to Leonid Brezhnev congratulating him on his 're-election' as Chairman of the Praesidium of the Supreme Soviet. 'Please not,' Mrs Thatcher wrote, 'Some election.* Let the Foreign Secretary write or send a message through our Ambassador. Not the Queen.' As was often her way, she was using a small thing to make a bigger point. Since her 'Iron Lady' speech in 1976, her suspicion of *détente* had only strengthened. She believed that the Soviets were working hard, both politically and militarily, to achieve world mastery, and that the West should not bargain with them unless from strength. But she also believed that alliance disunity was the prize which the Soviet Union sought most. She had to tread carefully to bring her allies with her.

In refining her ideas, Mrs Thatcher drew on two, often opposing sources. The first were what Carrington called her 'gurus'. Of these the most important was Robert Conquest. 'Now that the battle has begun,' she wrote to him in June 1979, 'I shall need your encouragement more than ever before.' Conquest foresaw 'enormous danger' in the years ahead. What worried him most was 'the erosion of Western sense and nerve', caused chiefly, he believed, by the weak character of President Carter. 'I feel the real urgency',

---

* The post, needless to say, had not been contested.

he wrote to her that August, 'to stiffen up Washington,' a sentiment which Mrs Thatcher underlined.

She also drew on Hugh Thomas, who assembled other experts, such as the military historian Michael Howard, Elie Kedourie and Leonard Schapiro.* Part of Mrs Thatcher's hold over the intellectuals was her female allure. In 1983, after a party at which she met several writers, Conquest reported to Ian Gow a comment from the novelist Anthony Powell: 'He says that afterwards "I did some market research as to whether people find her as attractive as I do and all, including Vidia [Naipaul], were in complete agreement."' Philip Larkin, the poet, was similarly smitten: 'Very few people are both right and beautiful.'

Before the 1979 election, Conquest floated the idea that Mrs Thatcher appoint him Ambassador to the UN. Believing that the Civil Service should not be supplanted at the public expense, she rejected this notion. They continued to correspond after Conquest left for Stanford University in America, but for advice on a daily basis she relied on the Civil Service. Often this worked well. She reposed trust in Bryan Cartledge, her first foreign affairs private secretary and, from September 1979, his successor Michael Alexander. Alexander was one of the Foreign Office's greatest experts on East–West relations, and a man of formidable intellect. His views sometimes hewed too closely to Foreign Office orthodoxy for her taste, but she respected him.

When Carrington invited Mrs Thatcher to meet the Foreign Office gurus, including Rodric Braithwaite and Christopher Mallaby, she said, 'Oh, they don't know anything about Russia at all.' When she came, however, she was impressed by the knowledge displayed. After Mallaby laid out the serious difficulties facing the Soviet Union she replied, 'if it's like that, the Soviet Union can't survive, can it?' The officials politely demurred: 'The germs of change are at work inside Soviet society ... But it will not easily happen while the Soviet Communist Party and its apparatus of repression are still intact.' How then should Britain deal with a hostile Soviet Union whose power was beyond question, but whose long-term future was uncertain? The Foreign Office had put its eggs in the basket of détente several years

---

* Thomas also fortified her decision to rely on these outside advisers. Past prime ministers, he told her, had used 'irregulars' (Churchill's word) to counter official advice: Churchill, for example, as recorded by Sir John Colville, 'had no love for the Foreign Office [since] he suspected them of pursuing their own policy irrespective of what the Government might wish, and he mistrusted their judgment'.

earlier. Many officials were 'deeply hostile' to Mrs Thatcher on the subject, considering her rhetoric provocative.*

Mrs Thatcher was always far more willing than the Foreign Office to draw attention to the Soviet Union's failure to live up to its promises. The continued suppression of Soviet dissidents, in defiance of the Helsinki Accords, provided an important example. She regarded human rights abuses as symptoms of the disease of Soviet totalitarianism and wished to publicize them. The Foreign Office tended to regard the subject as an irritating distraction.

Whatever the Soviet Union's long-term prognosis, Mrs Thatcher was determined to challenge Moscow. As Carrington put it, 'I don't think she thought there was any point in negotiations. The aim was to win the Cold War really . . . they were dangerous wicked people.' The very title – 'Managing Russia' – of the analytical paper which the Foreign Office presented to Mrs Thatcher illustrated the problem. She did not want to 'manage' the Soviet Union but to defeat it.

The Carter administration noticed the change. 'Tories are far less convinced than Labor that détente works to the West's advantage,' Zbigniew Brzezinski warned Carter when Mrs Thatcher came to office. Writing to congratulate her on her election victory, Carter stressed the overwhelming importance he attached to the ratification of his Strategic Arms Limitation Treaty with the Soviets. Under SALT II, both sides agreed to broad and equal limits on strategic offensive nuclear weapons systems. Mrs Thatcher, who mistrusted the treaty, scribbled, 'We shall have to send quite a long and frank reply.' She worried that the deal could see Britain's own nuclear capacity bargained away, and that focusing on limiting nuclear weapons would discourage the increase in Western nuclear capacity she thought essential.

In her view, the growing Soviet nuclear arsenal threatened the system of deterrence which had kept the post-war peace in Europe.† As the Soviets deployed new intermediate-range missiles (SS-20s), she felt that NATO must field an equivalent. This meant stationing US Pershing II missiles and ground-launched Cruise missiles (GLCMs) – collectively known as Intermediate Nuclear Forces (INF) – in Europe. Such deployment was hugely

---

* Foreign Office officials were sensitive to Soviet criticism in this regard, so much so that, on one occasion, when Moscow objected to the West's oft-stated desire to negotiate from a 'position of strength', Mallaby suggested to a colleague that it might be 'preferable if Ministers said that we wish to negotiate on equal terms'. Such Foreign Office timidity infuriated Mrs Thatcher.
† This was a concern she had discussed at length with Ronald Reagan during their meeting in November 1978.

controversial, especially in West Germany, with its strong movement for unilateral nuclear disarmament.

Mrs Thatcher's reply to Carter's letter urged him to 'strike the right balance' between SALT II ratification and making public opinion understand NATO's need to 'maintain and modernise its nuclear forces'. There had to be 'concrete decisions' on INF modernization and deployment by the end of the year. Receiving the West German Chancellor, Helmut Schmidt, in Downing Street a week after coming into office, she was heartened to hear that Germany would accept INF on its soil, so long as other non-nuclear European powers agreed to do so. Despite growing protests from the left, she was determined Britain should play its part. In September, the Cabinet agreed that Britain would accept 144 of the 464 GLCMs planned for Europe.*

Mrs Thatcher's tone, both at home and abroad, marked a clear break with the conciliation of the Labour years. She injected a sense of urgency. 'We in Europe have unrivalled freedom,' she told her party conference in October 1979, 'but we must never take it for granted. The dangers to it are greater now than they have ever been since 1945. The threat of the Soviet Union is ever present. It is growing continually.'

Mrs Thatcher wanted to be frank with the enemy. When she met the Soviet Prime Minister Kosygin at Moscow airport en route to the Tokyo G7 in June, Kosygin insisted that 'the Soviet Union was a peace-loving country which did not produce all the massive armaments which the Prime Minister attributed to them ... The Prime Minister told Mr Kosygin that he should not be so modest. Nobody who had seen the Soviet tanks and missiles which were paraded through Red Square would underestimate the Soviet Union's capacity.'

On Christmas Day 1979, the Soviets invaded Afghanistan. Writing to Brezhnev in protest, Mrs Thatcher declared herself 'profoundly disturbed'. Her anger was real enough, but 'disturbed' was not really the right word. The invasion fitted with her expectations of Soviet behaviour. As Robert Conquest wrote: 'For anyone with an ounce of sense, there is no lesson to be learnt from the Afghan events: they merely confirm, in dramatic fashion, what ... should have been known to all of those concerned with Western policy. For the time being, those who have been dangerously in error about Soviet motivations and intentions have been shocked into facing reality' (Mrs Thatcher's underlinings). With the enemy in plain view, Mrs Thatcher felt vindicated, and her blood was up. Her arguments were now listened

---

* A further sixteen were later accepted, at West Germany's request.

to more carefully, and the case for deploying INF in Europe became easier to make. President Carter was one of those whom Conquest described as 'shocked into facing reality'. He suspended efforts to ratify SALT II and imposed an embargo on grain sales to the Soviet Union. Mrs Thatcher was keen to help him wake up the West. But with no clear idea herself of how to respond, she merely told the Foreign Office to make sure that the 'enormity of the act' of invasion 'was not lost to sight'.

The most obvious way of ostracizing the Soviet Union was to boycott the Olympic Games in Moscow that summer, an idea encouraged by the United States. Mrs Thatcher backed a boycott, but felt it was not the government's role to forbid athletes to take part. She wanted instead to persuade. Britain's vocal support pleased the Americans. As Brzezinski recalled: 'All things considered we were very happy with their actions. Far more so than most European nations.' Yet try as she might, Mrs Thatcher proved unable to persuade the British Olympic Committee to accept the boycott.* In the end, some British athletes, encouraged by their official bodies, went to Moscow. Others, following Mrs Thatcher's urging, stayed at home. The Games were not a great success, but nor was the boycott.

Much the same no-score draw was achieved by short-term Western reaction to the invasion in general. The Russians had made a mistake, in both propaganda and military terms, from which Soviet Communism never fully recovered. Yet the West's response was largely ineffective.† Mrs Thatcher failed in her attempt to implement Carter's request for an emergency NATO summit on Afghanistan but, fearing this would only highlight disunity, her heart was not really in it. Such fears came to the fore in June, when President Giscard welcomed the withdrawal of some Soviet military units from Afghanistan and proposed France as the intermediary between the West and the Soviets. Michael Alexander noted that Giscard had been very prompt in circulating this message. Mrs Thatcher scribbled: 'Yes – he is – half way to Neville Chamberlain.'

---

* Further embarrassment was caused because the Queen's husband, the Duke of Edinburgh, President of the International Equestrian Federation (FEI), had originally expected to go to Moscow. In April, he became caught up in a press statement decrying the pressure for a boycott. Writing personally to Mrs Thatcher, Prince Philip apologized, stressing his own view that international federations should not become involved in political issues. 'Alas,' she replied, rather tartly, 'everything in connection with the USSR has a political flavour. That, unfortunately, is the problem.' Prince Philip did not go to Moscow.
† Although the West's immediate response had little impact, certain decisions with huge and controversial consequences were made at this time – the arming of Afghan mujahidin resistance to the Soviets, and a much greater Western support for increasing the military power of President Zia's Islamist regime in Pakistan (about which Mrs Thatcher professed herself 'a little unhappy').

More broadly, she felt sure that the argument was coming her way. As she told her party conference that autumn:

> Long before we came into office, and therefore long before the invasion of Afghanistan, I was pointing to the threat from the East. I was accused of scaremongering. But events have more than justified my words. Soviet Marxism is ideologically, politically and morally bankrupt. But militarily the Soviet Union is a powerful and growing threat ... there are those who say that by speaking out we are complicating East–West relations, that we are endangering détente. But the real danger would lie in keeping silent. Détente is indivisible and it is a two-way process.

What she still lacked was a powerful ally who shared her world view. This was changing. That July, Ronald Reagan was about to receive the Republican nomination for the 1980 US presidential election. His political guru, Stuart Spencer, asked him: 'Why are you doing this, Ron? Why do you want to be President?' 'Without a moment's hesitation Reagan answered, "To end the Cold War."'

While Reagan's election in November thrilled Mrs Thatcher, it alarmed British officials. They were concerned, in Christopher Mallaby's words, by the prospect of 'a very hard-line, perhaps a crude, policy towards the Soviet Union', but it was this 'crude' or, as she would have said, principled approach which attracted Mrs Thatcher. Carrington summed it up: 'I think that in many ways Reagan and Thatcher were exactly the same. She was basically extremely hostile towards the Soviets ... she believed it really was an evil empire.'

The 'evil empire' was, of course, Reagan's own phrase, first used later, in March 1983. The slogan, calculated to make diplomats blanch, reflected the moral tone which both Reagan and Mrs Thatcher employed in describing the Soviet Union. In his first press conference as President, Reagan declared that 'the only morality [the Soviets] recognise is what will further their cause, meaning they reserve unto themselves the right to commit any crime, to lie, to cheat ...' On the same day, 29 January 1981, in London Mrs Thatcher attacked the dishonesty with which the Soviets conducted détente, which earned her a personal letter of thanks from Reagan. Privately he referred to Mrs Thatcher as 'the only European leader I know with balls'.

When Brezhnev issued a surprise invitation to a superpower summit shortly after Reagan took office, Mrs Thatcher helped reinforce caution. Visiting Washington in February, she told Reagan that 'when you sup with the devil you must have a long spoon. In fact you had better have a whole lot of long spoons.' Speaking in New York, she developed her line. Her criticisms of the Soviet Union – 'what is there in the Soviet system to admire?

Material prosperity? It does not produce it. Spiritual satisfaction? It denies it' – were so harsh as to drive Carrington out of town to avoid attending. But in fact she restated the position which she and Reagan shared, that dialogue should be explored when the time was right, but that 'military balance' must first be established.

The Foreign Office was pursuing a different line. In January, informed that Carrington intended to negotiate a new Cultural Agreement with the Soviet Union, Mrs Thatcher expressed her dismay. 'They will gain from it – we shall lose. So much for Afghanistan.' In March she told Carrington she was 'very worried indeed' by his plan to visit Moscow to establish better Soviet contacts. 'Can we not keep contacts to meetings in the margins of international fora.' One dark evening, she was standing at the door of No. 10, staring up at the bulk of the Foreign Office opposite. 'Look at that,' she said to an official, 'the place that keeps the light out of Downing Street.'

Mrs Thatcher devoted her main energies to restoring the military balance. In her mind, INF deployment was the key. Although she disliked the idea of INF negotiations with the Soviets, she realized the best way of persuading European allies to accept these missiles was the strategy of 'dual track', linking deployment to a US commitment to pursue such negotiations. With Reagan's arrival, she found herself having to uphold the plan agreed with Carter in the face of criticism from her new friends in Washington. Those in the administration who knew Europe well, such as Al Haig, the new Secretary of State, agreed with Mrs Thatcher and argued forcefully in favour of dual track. More hawkish members of the administration resisted the idea of any negotiation with the Soviets.

Mrs Thatcher understood how many Reaganites wanted to change the whole approach towards the Soviet Union. She did too. But being geographically, if not mentally, a European, she worried about the alliance splitting. This left her playing – surprisingly well – the unaccustomed role of bridge-builder. She thus stood with Haig in opposition to the administration's hawks. As Haig remembered, her support was 'an invaluable help to me within the Administration'. After strong British lobbying, the State Department succeeded in inserting support for dual track into the President's public remarks during Mrs Thatcher's visit to Washington in February 1981. At the end of April, Haig urged Reagan to move ahead with this approach. He prayed in aid all the main European players: 'The British remain our most reliable ally, the French by far the most robust. However, both Mrs Thatcher and Giscard are deeply concerned that we take into account the situation in the FRG. Mrs Thatcher almost pleaded with me in London that we take care not to isolate Chancellor Schmidt, whom she described as "a really good friend of the US".' History does not usually write down Mrs Thatcher as a healer of alliance wounds but so, at this stage, she was. Reagan decided to proceed with the dual-track approach.

If negotiations were to take place, however, what would be their aim? Against Haig's wishes, Reagan approved a stance known as the zero option.* Under this approach, the US would consider only an agreement that led to the complete withdrawal of all existing Soviet intermediate forces from the European theatre in return for NATO agreement *not* to deploy American INF. Advocates of the zero option called it laudably ambitious; critics considered it an effort to sabotage the negotiations. In November 1981, when Mrs Thatcher commended it to the Commons, Michael Foot needled her, claiming that a zero option was more in tune with Labour's call for a nuclear-free Europe. The difference, which she pointed out, was that Reagan was proposing zero missiles on both sides whereas Foot advocated a unilateral Western zero.

Mrs Thatcher's true feelings were more complicated. She went along with the zero option, but only, as she later admitted, 'in the hope that the Soviets would never accept'. Here lay a real difference with Reagan. As Ken Adelman, later Director of the US Arms Control and Disarmament Agency, put it: 'Thatcher was always very good on zero INF, as long as the zero proposal wasn't going to go anywhere. She was less excited about it going anywhere than Reagan was. He, however, was thrilled.' Mrs Thatcher believed in the doctrine of nuclear deterrence. She considered that world war was prevented by the capacity of the West to frighten the East with its nuclear arsenal, which therefore must remain large and credible. She wanted INF missiles not only to match the SS-20s but to deter a Soviet conventional attack. Reagan was just as keen to defeat Soviet totalitarianism, but wanted to abolish nuclear weapons. He considered them immoral, and a cause of instability more than of peace. This difference was to bulk large in his efforts during the Gorbachev era – and cause Mrs Thatcher considerable distress. In the early 1980s, however, President and Prime Minister were at one in wishing to reassert the power of the West against the Soviet Union. The zero option, as a tactic, helped.

On coming into office, Mrs Thatcher had immediately set about finding a replacement for Britain's ageing Polaris submarine-based nuclear missiles

---

* This idea originated with Richard Perle. As he explained: 'I certainly believed that it was a lot less likely that we would get the agreement than the easier-to-reach agreements that would favour the Soviets. But, if we got it, it would be very useful. And since I wasn't all that eager for an agreement and certainly an agreement for agreement's sake, it made perfect sense to go for the harder but more useful.'

which, in practice, meant procuring the US Trident missile. After considerable foot-dragging from President Carter, who, said one US official, viewed the idea 'rather sceptically', the Americans agreed, in June 1980, to let Britain have Trident, albeit on fairly expensive terms.

With the advent of Reagan, the situation changed. In August 1981, the new administration offered Britain a more powerful and more expensive version of Trident ('D5') that it had decided to develop. John Nott, the Defence Secretary, was keen to accept but, as he later recalled, 'the difficulty was money'. There was a certain irony in American control over the supply of what was supposed to be Britain's independent nuclear deterrent. As Robin Butler put it, 'It wasn't entirely satisfactory to [Mrs Thatcher] that we had to be so dependent. We were always just a little worried about if we ever actually needed the thing whether the Americans would allow us to make it work.' Many, even in the Conservative Party, were unconvinced that Britain should commit so much money to Trident.* But for Mrs Thatcher, as for Nott and Carrington, there was no alternative. As Carrington noted: 'Failure to acquire TRIDENT would have left the French as the only nuclear power in Europe. This would be intolerable.' With Cabinet approval, the deal was pushed through the bureaucracies quickly at an impressively advantageous price for Britain.† As Mrs Thatcher wrote to Reagan: 'I can think of no way in which our two countries could more powerfully have illustrated our common resolution in defence of freedom and our unique ability to reinforce each others [*sic*] efforts.'

Mrs Thatcher followed developments in Poland with great interest.‡ Although internationally recognized as being within the Soviet sphere, Poland was showing stirring signs of change. Ever since the election of Karol Wojtyła as Pope John Paul II in 1978, any moral authority still clinging to Communism in Eastern Europe had withered. When the Polish Pope

---

* In early 1981, John Nott warned Mrs Thatcher that 'two-thirds of the Party and two-thirds of the Cabinet were opposed'.

† The USA was required by law to charge R&D costs on the sale of Trident, unless the deal could be considered in the US national interest. Reagan officials agreed it was in the national interest for Britain to maintain a stronger naval capability than was proposed by Nott's forthcoming defence cuts. So in exchange for a waiver of Trident R&D costs, Britain promised to keep more of its surface ships. 'So one could say', recalled Richard Perle, then an assistant secretary at the Pentagon, 'that we ended up subsidizing the Royal Navy.'

‡ Mrs Thatcher's personal affection for the Polish cause was strong. When she came into office, a dispute arose about ministerial attendance in London at the annual commemoration of the Katyn massacre in 1940 in which Soviet troops had massacred 4,000 Polish officers. Fearing the wrath of the Soviet bloc, the Foreign Office counselled against representation. Mrs Thatcher, who had sent Airey Neave on her behalf to the ceremony before she came into office, replied: 'I do not agree ... that is why Airey Neave attended last year.'

returned to visit his own country the following year, millions attended his speeches and Masses, with the authorities powerless to prevent them. The rebel trade union Solidarity, under the leadership of Lech Wałęsa, organized widespread resistance of industrial (and later agricultural) workers to the Communist government, notably through strikes in the Gdańsk shipyards.

Mrs Thatcher was naturally thrilled. In 1980 and 1981, however, concerns grew that the Soviets might intervene. On 13 December 1981, General Jaruzelski, Poland's Prime Minister since February, imposed martial law. Mrs Thatcher was not exactly surprised but, in common with her European allies, she was not quite sure how to react. President Reagan, however, took a forceful view. 'Dear Maggie,'* he wrote six days later, warning of the possibility of direct Soviet intervention, 'This may well be a watershed in the political history of mankind – a challenge to tyranny from within.' He wanted a strong, shared allied response. The following morning, on the telephone to Mrs Thatcher, Carrington was dismissive and she seemed to agree, calling it 'simply an internal situation'. When Carrington opined that Reagan wanted to take it out on the Russians, she answered, 'it seems a bit absurd if the Russians aren't actually in the front line'. She replied in uncharacteristically weak terms to Reagan, saying this was a 'complex and difficult situation', avoiding commitments.

Reagan, however, was determined to act. Before the end of the year, his administration took a series of measures which included sanctions preventing the export of oil and gas equipment to the USSR. Part of the early Reagan credo was that the Soviet Union should be beaten into economic submission. The Reaganites had been horrified by Carter's acquiescence, in 1978, in the agreement between West Germany and the Soviet Union to build a gas pipeline across western Siberia. By supplying natural gas to Europe, Reagan believed that the Russians would make energy an instrument of their foreign policy. It would also earn them hard currency.† In July 1981 the administration decided to prevent construction of the pipeline. 'The Soviets have spoken as plainly as Hitler did in "Mein Kampf",' Reagan told an NSC meeting. 'They have spoken world domination – at what point do we dig in our heels?'

Finding little support for blocking the pipeline, Reagan raged against

---

* In early correspondence, Reagan had addressed Mrs Thatcher as 'Madam Prime Minister', graduating to 'Dear Margaret' in early August 1981. The attempt to reach an even greater level of intimacy through moving to 'Maggie' (first seen in October 1981) no doubt led to wry smiles in No. 10, since she disliked the moniker. Realizing the error, Reagan reverted to 'Dear Margaret' for their subsequent correspondence.
† Both these fears would much later prove well grounded after Vladimir Putin ordered Russia to invade Ukraine in February 2022.

'those "Chicken Littles" in Europe'. The 'Chicken Littles' were duly furious, partly because they wanted the pipeline, partly because they disliked the unilateralism and partly because they felt that America was imposing hardship which it was not applying to itself. Mrs Thatcher had more sympathy with Reagan's aims than did most Europeans.* But she respected British commercial interests – hundreds of British jobs hinged on the Scottish firm John Brown Engineering supplying turbines for the pipeline – and she was alarmed at the prospect of alliance disunity. In late January 1982, she saw Al Haig, who shared her fears. The French and Germans, she said, would not agree to what America wanted. 'We should not do the Russians' job for them' by causing a split. Haig encouraged her to write personally to the President about this because he (Reagan) had a 'great respect' for her.

Mrs Thatcher despatched a letter to Reagan that same day. 'We risk losing the prize if we act hastily or out of step,' she told him. She was referring to the plans to deploy INF weapons, which depended on alliance unity. Her words seemed to have some effect. At an NSC meeting in February, Reagan explained that he had assumed that the construction of the pipeline depended predominantly on firms based in the United States rather than in Europe. 'Now', he continued, 'Maggie Thatcher has made me realise that I have been wrong.'

On 2 April 1982, Argentina invaded the British colony of the Falkland Islands, leaving Mrs Thatcher with very little time for anything else (see p. 265). Yet it was now that, from her point of view, the debate in Washington over the Soviet Union took a turn for the worse. Encouraged by William Clark, his new National Security Advisor, Reagan reverted to his idea of economic aggression against the Russians. 'Why can't we just lean on the Soviets until they go broke?' he asked at an NSC meeting in March. 'That's the direction we're going to go.'† The administration now sought to delay the pipeline's construction, increasing costs for the Soviets and providing time to develop alternative European gas reserves.

In June, President Reagan made a formal visit to Britain. Initially he had not planned to make a speech, which disappointed Mrs Thatcher, who

---

* Mrs Thatcher was familiar with the idea of defeating the Soviet Union by economic means. At the end of 1980, Hugh Thomas and Leonard Schapiro had furnished her with a paper called 'A Western policy towards the Soviet economy', which advocated 'economic warfare' to exploit Soviet weakness. She told Thomas she was attracted to the idea but did not feel in a position to accept it.

† In May, Reagan signed a top-secret policy document – NSDD 32 – which sought to 'contain and reverse the expansion of Soviet control and military presence throughout the world ... and weaken the Soviet alliance system by forcing the USSR to bear the brunt of its economic shortcomings'.

had hoped for a rhetorical blast against the unilateralists. She therefore proposed, privately, that he address both Houses of Parliament. But after the White House leaked this a mighty row broke out: such an invitation was rightly the prerogative of Parliament, which had not been consulted. Mrs Thatcher was forced to abandon the idea. After the White House again suggested it might be better for Reagan not to speak at all, a compromise emerged whereby he would address Parliament's less grand Royal Gallery. The White House was informed that Mrs Thatcher 'personally would be very disappointed' if the President turned this down. Reagan bowed to her wishes.

The White House now became enchanted with the whole idea of the visit. Reagan was particularly excited by the suggestion that he ride with the Queen in Windsor Great Park.* This expectation of pleasure and amity was helpful in winning Reagan's support for British military action over the Falkland Islands (the culmination of Britain's efforts to retake the colony), but the dispute over the pipeline was a different matter.

Immediately before his visit to Britain, Reagan attended the G7 summit in Versailles, at which there was hope he might bring the pipeline sanctions to an end. This proved misplaced. Listening to his hardliners, Reagan was now considering *extending* the sanctions unless the Europeans agreed to tough limits on credit for the Soviet Union. They refused and the summit ended without agreement.

In London, on 7 June 1982, Reagan delivered his much-anticipated speech before the Royal Gallery. 'From Stettin on the Baltic to Varna on the Black Sea', he declared (consciously echoing Winston Churchill's 1946 'Iron Curtain' speech at Fulton, Missouri), there had been no free elections in thirty years. The speech set out in classic form Reagan's governing idea. The Soviet state, inspired by that 'barbarous assault on the human spirit called Marxism-Leninism', was collapsing under the weight of its own contradictions. He called for a 'crusade for freedom' to consign Marxism-Leninism to the 'ash-heap of history'. In a passage on which he had personally insisted, Reagan linked British troops in the Falklands with his wider cause: they had been fighting for 'the belief that armed aggression must not be allowed to succeed'.†

Mrs Thatcher was thrilled. The Royal Gallery speech, and the visit, were

---

* During a discussion about what gift should be presented to Reagan, Judge Clark opined that the President could 'always use more leather'. An English saddle and bridle were duly agreed.
† Reagan's people also took great care with the visuals. For the first time in Britain, a transparent Perspex autocue system was used, making it look as if Reagan were speaking off the cuff or reciting from memory. Jim Hooley, part of the President's advance team, recalled: 'We wanted the guys in the really cool uniforms [that is, Beefeaters] in the photo when Reagan

extremely important in making manifest the unity with America which she sought and the more vigorous advancement of Western values which she espoused. The speech also complemented the attitude to peace which, bolstered by the Falklands, she was developing. She saw peace not as merely avoiding war, but as a tougher and more durable thing – 'peace with freedom and justice'.

Nothing, however, did the trick on the pipeline. Angered by the failure at Versailles, Reagan decided to extend the sanctions extraterritorially, increasing the headache for many non-US firms trying to honour their Soviet contracts. As Clive Whitmore recalled, this decision, announced without consultation, made Mrs Thatcher 'very, very angry'.

When she visited Reagan in Washington on 23 June, the atmosphere was strained. Usually Mrs Thatcher took care to avoid direct confrontation with Reagan, picking instead on his advisers. 'She would turn to the relevant Secretary or official and say "Bill, how could you ever go in that direction?"' recalled Judge Clark. 'The President would sit there with a catbird smile and roll his eyes as if to say, "Yes, Bill, how *could* you ever have done such a thing?"' This time, however, her ire reached beyond Reagan's aides. As the State Department's Thomas Niles recalled, she told the President his actions were 'just unacceptable ... our companies cannot be put under US law'. Reagan's talking points, Niles continued, 'essentially had him saying, "Look Margaret, we've talked to your company John Brown and they told us that this doesn't bother them" ... That was the point at which she really went ballistic ... "Put down your pencils," she said, and banged the table. I'll never forget it. And she said to the President, "Ron, you talk to your companies and I'll talk to mine."'

This exchange brought Mrs Thatcher up against the limits of her relationship with Reagan just when it seemed to be going so well. 'I think this really did come as a bit of a blow for her,' recalled Whitmore. 'She was unable to make the good old personal relationship work in such a way that she could enlighten him.' She also noted that Reagan had nothing like her grasp of the detail. 'And so she began to take the view that well, maybe he ... was a bear of very little brain. It was disappointing for her. You felt a significant change in her mood after the visit ... The scales fell from her eyes.'

Mrs Thatcher continued to press Reagan on the pipeline over the summer. According to NSC staffer Roger Robinson, 'The President felt the pressure of his relationship with Mrs Thatcher.' But what really broke

---

was speaking. Our counterparts were looking bemused, but we kept saying "couldn't they be just a little closer?"'

the impasse was Reagan's decision to replace Secretary of State Al Haig with George Shultz at the end of June. As a new appointee Shultz had considerable freedom of manoeuvre. He also understood the wider context which worried Mrs Thatcher so much: 'I had it very much in mind that the following year was going to be the year of missile deployment in Europe. We couldn't afford to go into that year with this dispute in the air, so we got it settled.' A face-saving solution was agreed and on 13 November Reagan announced that the sanctions would be lifted.* The hawks stressed the delay to the pipeline and the additional costs imposed on the Soviets. The private view in the British Embassy, however, was that the Americans had suffered a great defeat. Mrs Thatcher was delighted. 'I am pleased that we have all been able to reach agreement on a common approach to the handling of East/West relations,' she wrote to Reagan, 'particularly at a time when we must be seen to be standing together.'

The pipeline episode disproved the accusation that Mrs Thatcher was the poodle of the United States. She argued her case with tenacity and, after ten months of wrangling, prevailed. But the row showed Mrs Thatcher that, even with her prestige so high after the Falklands victory, she could not expect an easy ride.

Three days before Reagan announced the lifting of sanctions, Leonid Brezhnev, the President of the Soviet Union, died. The Foreign Office sent Mrs Thatcher a draft letter of condolence. In her own hand she deleted anything suggestive of grief and added the sentence, 'The consequences of his death will be felt far beyond the frontiers of his own country.' It was intended as an optimistic prophecy, not a funerary platitude. She was hoping for change.

---

* In return for the lifting of American sanctions, the allies agreed to develop a series of security-minded East–West economic policies. There would be a review of energy alternatives for Western Europe and no new Soviet gas supply contracts signed.

10

Hunger in Ireland

'The lady behind the veil'

On becoming Prime Minister, Mrs Thatcher did not have a policy towards Northern Ireland. It had died with Airey Neave just as the election campaign began. 'I'd never thought of anyone else for Northern Ireland,' she said later. '... He understood the "Irish factor". He'd studied it.' Given that her first Northern Ireland Secretary, Humphrey Atkins, knew nothing about the subject, it fell to Mrs Thatcher to give a lead, but she herself did not know much either.

More important, she had little feel for the problem. She did not go so far as Denis, who had an English, saloon-bar impatience with the whole thing: 'If the Irish want to kill each other that does seem to me to be their business.' Although in principle a strong Unionist, Mrs Thatcher possessed what Robert Armstrong called 'a very English Englishness', and little natural rapport with the people whose cause she favoured. 'Airey was a convinced Unionist,' she said later, 'and, in a way, so was I, because they had been jolly loyal to us.' She always thought of the people of Northern Ireland, even the Unionist population, as 'they', quite separate from 'us'.

In addition she found the Irish, on both sides, irritating, disliking their prolixity and what she saw as their unreliability. 'You don't expect anything decent to come from an Irishman,' she said in private, and only half in jest. In retirement, she once called Nationalists in the North 'traitors' because of their wish for a united Ireland. Then she stopped herself: 'No, no. I shouldn't say that. That is not the right word.' But she never worked out what the right word was. While she treated Northern Ireland with care and attention, it was a subject which, though she would not have put it so, she wished would go away.

Since the suspension of the Unionist-dominated Stormont Parliament in 1972, and despite the failure of the short-lived 'Sunningdale' Agreement in

1974,* the prevailing orthodoxy was that the province should be governed by different rules from those prevailing in Westminster. Devolution with 'power-sharing', which ensured places in government for both sides of the community, was considered sacred as an aim of British policy, regardless of party, even if, because of conflict, it was usually suspended in favour of direct rule. In this context, the approach bequeathed by Neave in the Conservative manifesto of 1979 contained a certain ambiguity: 'In the absence of devolved government, we will seek to establish one or more elected regional councils with a wide range of powers over local services.'† In these words, Unionists sensed that the province might once again govern itself, at least in local matters, without a return to Stormont or the imposition of Whitehall's 'power-sharing' model and involvement of the Irish Republic. In fact, the manifesto was carefully non-committal: while it said nothing about a return to power-sharing devolution, it did not veto the idea.

Coming into office, Mrs Thatcher found no expectation among her civil servants that attention should be paid to the manifesto. On her first day, the Cabinet Secretary, John Hunt, told her that a 'new initiative' was widely expected and that 'Expectations are also high in Dublin and the United States.'‡ She put her wiggly line of doubt under the words 'new initiative' (the phrase invariably referred to some form of power-sharing devolution and/or an 'Irish dimension') and 'Dublin'.

When Jack Lynch, the Taoiseach (Irish Prime Minister), paid Mrs Thatcher a courtesy call on 10 May he warned against what he called 'the late Airey Neave's ideas on Regional Councils'. The nationalist Social Democratic and Labour Party (SDLP), whom Dublin wished to encourage, regarded power-sharing as the *sine qua non* for their participation in Northern Ireland politics. On the other side, Ian Paisley's sectarian

---

* The Sunningdale Agreement, signed at the end of 1973, led to the creation of a short-lived power-sharing Executive headed by Brian Faulkner, previously the Unionist Prime Minister in the Stormont Parliament, and the moderate Nationalist leader Gerry Fitt. This caused a split within Unionism; the Executive collapsed after the Loyalist Ulster Workers' Council called a general strike in May 1974 and direct rule was restored.

† Airey Neave was a famously secretive man, and his attitude to Northern Ireland will forever be disputed. Some believed that he had become a convinced integrationist, arguing that the province should be administered as other parts of the United Kingdom: a position to which some Unionist leaders were sympathetic. Others thought, however, that he was more pragmatic, and, seeing how power-sharing had collapsed in 1974, was simply taking things cautiously.

‡ The Irish-American lobby did its part to raise these expectations and put pressure on President Carter accordingly. 'I am sure that a personal expression of interest by you to Mrs. Thatcher will encourage the new Government to pursue a political solution more vigorously,' Tip O'Neill, the Speaker of the House of Representatives, wrote to Carter in June. The President promptly obliged by telephoning her.

Democratic Unionists railed against power-sharing but sensed opportunity in the devolutionist agenda. Having topped the poll in the 1979 European elections in Northern Ireland, Paisley told Mrs Thatcher he considered himself 'the leader of Ulster'. As he challenged his Unionist rivals, the right sort of devolution could serve him well.

Mrs Thatcher's senior Cabinet colleagues were personally committed to some version of power-sharing and a greater role for the Republic. The Home Secretary, Willie Whitelaw, Northern Ireland Secretary under Ted Heath, was chairman of the ministerial group on policy in Northern Ireland. As an architect of the Sunningdale Agreement he was never going to depart from that paradigm.

In short, almost everyone involved was against anything resembling the policy orphaned by the death of Neave. The only exceptions to this were the 'Official' Unionists. Led by Jim Molyneaux and backed by Enoch Powell's intellectual rigour, the Ulster Unionist Party (UUP) was the largest political party in Northern Ireland. They had allies in the Tory Party, of whom by far the most important was Ian Gow. The only other exception was Mrs Thatcher herself, and although she knew what she did not like, she lacked a coherent policy of her own.

Not until 27 August 1979, with the IRA's assassination of Lord Mountbatten and the deadly attack at Warrenpoint (see p. 207), did Mrs Thatcher's attention swivel to Northern Ireland. These atrocities strengthened her conviction of the need for strong security measures and to put much greater pressure on the Republic to prevent terrorism. It was 'harbouring known murderers', she angrily told a meeting of senior ministers. She wanted 'leverage' to force their extradition. With typically energetic sympathy, she wrote letters to every family of the murdered soldiers, each one different and all in her own hand. No prime minister had ever thought of doing this before. It was a custom she was to maintain. It reminded her, after each death, of the human cost of Ulster's tragedy.*

A second meeting with Jack Lynch took place during his visit to London for Lord Mountbatten's funeral. When she pressed an unreceptive Lynch

---

* Mrs Thatcher never ceased to pay close attention to the victims of terrorism and to be strongly affected by their suffering. In October 1981 the IRA blew up the dismounting Tower of London Guard near Chelsea Barracks, wounding twenty-three Irish Guardsmen and killing two civilians. The commanding officer, Robert Corbett, recounted Mrs Thatcher's visit to the injured the following day: 'When she saw how terribly injured many of them were she turned to one side so deeply affected that I had to take her out of the ward for a brief moment. She was in tears.' Weeks later she invited Corbett and his wife to No. 10. 'The most striking thing about her was that she knew precisely the state of health and progress of each of those injured soldiers.'

to do more about security, matters became heated. Backed by an unusually hawkish Carrington, she warned him that 'she would be unable to restrain public opinion in this country' if they were 'unable to point to anything new [on security] that would be done'. The Irish delegation were taken aback. According to Dermot Nally, a senior official, 'One of the ministers made the remark that "You may not like the idea but some people have a quantity of sympathy with the men of violence." That made her furious. "Are you condoning murder?" She nearly had to be held back. The meeting with Lynch was not a success.'

To achieve improved security, it was argued that an effort must be made towards political conciliation. In October, Humphrey Atkins announced an initiative to have all the parties in Northern Ireland come together and consider how to bring about devolution. Declining to take part, the Official Unionists now evoked the name of Airey Neave. As Ian Gow reported to Mrs Thatcher, Molyneaux was insisting that, in return for his party's support in the confidence vote that brought down the Labour government in March 1979, he had been promised (echoing the manifesto) one or more elected regional councils in Northern Ireland. Gow insisted Neave had told him nothing of this: 'Nevertheless, it is, of course, correct to say that the policy on which you and Airey had agreed for Ulster had been [given] the broad assent of the Official Unionists.'

In March 1980, Mrs Thatcher was forced to confront this revelation, after Enoch Powell raised it with Kenneth Stowe, now Permanent Under-Secretary at the Northern Ireland Office, and asked to see the Prime Minister. As Stowe recorded: 'I was struck by the stark clarity and precise terms in which Mr Powell referred to his agreement with Mr Neave. I was also struck by the fact that he seemed not to assume that the secretary of state was a party to, or even aware of this agreement, but plainly indicated that the PM was, hence his decision that he must go to see her.' Mrs Thatcher insisted she had known nothing about it.

When Mrs Thatcher met Powell on 1 May, he attacked the Atkins proposals but, oddly, made no mention of the Neave promise. Without proof of Neave's commitment, she decided to press on with the Atkins plan regardless.* This undermined trust between Official Unionism and her government. From then on, Unionists tended to conclude either that Mrs Thatcher herself was deceiving them or – more often, because they admired her personally for her robust attitude to terrorism – that she was not fully master in her own

---

* She was inclined to do so not only by the general institutional push for devolution, but by the belief in some official circles that Ian Paisley might, after all, prove more predisposed to a deal than his granite rhetoric suggested.

house. Moderate Unionism was sidelined, and Paisleyism, which prospered whenever 'sell-out' and 'betrayal' were suspected, continued to grow.

In the first half of 1980, as the Atkins initiative stuttered on, the British government – though not Mrs Thatcher herself – became still more interested in dealing directly with Dublin. Under considerable pressure, she agreed to invite Charles Haughey, who had become Taoiseach in December 1979, for lunch at No. 10. When they met on 21 May, Haughey presented her with a Georgian silver teapot and tea-strainer on which were inscribed the words she had declaimed on her first day in Downing Street: 'Where there is disharmony, let there be peace.' It was intended to prick her conscience. Haughey came away proclaiming a 'great admiration' for Mrs Thatcher, whom he considered to be 'a woman of her word'. For her part, Mrs Thatcher had been quite charmed, but conceded nothing of importance. As one official put it later: 'The PM liked being led up the garden path by Haughey, but didn't like the garden when she got there.'

During the next month, drafts of Atkins's proposals circulated, which included ideas from the 'garden' into which Haughey had sought to lead her. The draft reformulated the British 'guarantee' to Northern Ireland, which Haughey so much disliked, as 'Northern Ireland will not cease to be part of the United Kingdom without the consent of the majority of the people.' Mrs Thatcher noted, 'Wholly written in the negative i.e. as if it is truly wanting Ulster to go.' Commenting on the draft, Gow wrote: '. . . WE MUST NOT FRAME OUR PROPOSALS TO PLEASE THE REPUBLIC.' Mrs Thatcher was sensitive to possible ramifications for other parts of the Kingdom. Responding to a proposed advisory council of Northern Ireland, she scribbled, 'leading to a Council of Scotland?'. Finding allies in Cabinet, she insisted on substantial redrafting to remove the draft's 'negative features [and] avoid the impression that the Government's longer-term policy was to give Northern Ireland away'.

The revised Atkins proposals were published on 2 July 1980 to decidedly mixed reviews. When politics resumed in the autumn, political initiatives were pushed aside by dramatic events.

It was part of the IRA's self-characterization as an army that its men, if convicted, should be treated as prisoners of war. For this very reason, British governments resisted. On 10 October 1980, in pursuit of 'special-category' status setting them aside from common criminals,* the Republican inmates

---

* In 1976, the Labour government had righted a grave political error of the Heath government and removed 'special-category status' from all new terrorist prisoners.

in the Maze prison announced a hunger strike, to begin on 27 October. On 23 October, Charles Haughey warned Mrs Thatcher of 'serious repercussions for the security situation in Ireland' if the strike went ahead. On the same day, the Cabinet decided that the prisoners should, after all, be allowed to wear 'civilian-type clothes' rather than the existing prison uniform.* As Mrs Thatcher told the Cabinet, 'I am concerned to get us into the most reasonable position before the start, and stick to it.' She also stated that she did not want to lose Haughey's security cooperation.

This concession angered Unionists and Tory backbenchers but failed to prevent the strike, in which seven prisoners took part. Mrs Thatcher now toughened up. 'We cannot make any concessions,' she scribbled in early November, but then, referring mentally to the concessions already made, added: 'When will the new issue clothing be ready?'

In early December, pressed by Haughey, Mrs Thatcher said she would be prepared to 'dress up' the concessions already on offer. Haughey suggested Britain should talk 'quietly and unobtrusively' to the strikers through the prison chaplains. This was dangerous territory for Mrs Thatcher, who was fearful of linking political movement with any concessions to terrorists. But British officialdom was, in fact, 'quietly and unobtrusively' moving even faster than Haughey was demanding. In the mid-1970s, an SIS officer named Michael Oatley had maintained contact with the IRA through a Londonderry businessman called Brendan Duddy.† At the beginning of December 1980, Duddy reactivated this link. He told the officer that Gerry Adams and Martin McGuinness, now prominent figures in the Provisionals, wanted the hunger strike stopped. To save face, however, they needed some sign of movement from the government. Ken Stowe duly drew up a list of possible gestures, to be passed back through the Oatley/Duddy channel. As Stowe recalled, Mrs Thatcher endorsed the plan, 'fully aware that it involved dealing with Sinn Fein [the political arm of the IRA]'. 'I didn't deal directly with the PIRA leadership,'‡ she insisted later, '. . . never, never in my life.' This was technically true, but disingenuous.

---

* 'Civilian-type' clothes were different from 'civilian' clothes because the former, though not uniform in style, were issued by the prison authorities rather than the personal property of the prisoners. This point, it was argued, allowed control to be maintained.
† Brendan Duddy (1936–2017) had first acted as an intermediary in 1972 and was involved as a backchannel before and during the Provisional IRA's 1975 ceasefire. He was again active in the early 1990s and in 1993 he communicated the IRA's offer of a ceasefire to the British government. Oatley was not his only contact during these years. The link through Duddy and his British contact was known to the IRA as the 'Mountain Climber'.
‡ The Provisional IRA was formed out of the split in the IRA in 1969. The Official IRA effectively forswore violence. PIRA supported it. Mrs Thatcher sometimes referred to the PIRA, but the term 'IRA' was commonly used to refer to the Provisionals.

On 18 December, the prisoners ended their strike. Atkins then announced a series of 'humanitarian' concessions and had to fend off charges of a deal.* While the strike's collapse was a victory for Mrs Thatcher, the prisoners took the government's insistence that these limited concessions were unconnected to the strike as evidence of bad faith. The IRA also now understood, however, that Mrs Thatcher would take part in what was, in effect, negotiation. They pocketed this knowledge and bided their time.

Mrs Thatcher was fortunate that the failure of the hunger strike burnished her reputation for toughness, because her summit with Charles Haughey ten days earlier had caused outrage among Unionists. This was the first prime-minister-led bilateral delegation of British ministers to Dublin since Partition – as so often in Irish matters, occasions which she regarded as practical were seen by the Republic as mightily symbolic. After she arrived early at Dublin Castle, the old seat of British power, one official took her on an impromptu tour during which she seized upon a plaque in the Irish language: 'What does that say?' she demanded. As the official recalled:

> a worker, who was fixing a light switch, turned and said, 'I'll tell you what it is, ma'am. That's the sign that says this is where youse took James Connolly† before youse took him out and shot him.' She said, 'Oh, very interesting,' and they marched on. It was the best possible introduction to a meeting with Charlie Haughey because Charlie would have to explain that in Ireland the wounds of history were still very open.

The meeting itself went well enough. Mrs Thatcher rejected Haughey's request for a conference to review 'the totality of our relationship', but agreed to the idea of 'joint studies' which might develop 'new structures' of cooperation. She declared herself pleased with security cooperation. Before lunch, Haughey had invited Mrs Thatcher to sit on the throne once occupied by Queen Victoria. She 'firmly' declined, but suggested Haughey might do so. 'Both laughed.' After she left, one of Haughey's officials turned to him and told him he could now sit on the throne with impunity: 'Sure after today aren't you the King of Ireland?' Haughey duly sat on the throne and jokingly told the company to kneel in front of him.

Mrs Thatcher was not happy that Haughey was happy. His success, she believed, had been bought at her expense. The trouble lay in the

---

* The concessions were 'humanitarian' in that they were applicable to all prisoners in Northern Ireland, not just terrorist ones. They included greater freedom to wear 'civilian-type' clothing, more recreation and free association at weekends.
† James Connolly was the Socialist Republican trade union leader and commander of the Dublin Brigade in the 1916 Rising.

communiqué. It announced that when the leaders next met, they would discuss 'the totality of relationships within these islands', with the Joint Studies commissioned 'for this purpose'. There was uproar from Unionists, who thought this gave Dublin a role in deciding the future of the province. Mrs Thatcher had not understood the incendiary implication of the phrase 'the totality of relationships'. Her officials almost certainly did but had not warned her. 'Ever after that', she recalled, 'I was wary.'

The situation was made much worse by the Irish Foreign Minister, Brian Lenihan, who sought to exploit the newly established institutional structures: 'As far as we are concerned, everything is on the table,' he told BBC Radio Ulster. The following March (1981) he suggested that a federal structure for the whole of Ireland might emerge from Anglo-Irish discussions. At the European Council in Maastricht that same month, Mrs Thatcher told Haughey that Lenihan's outbursts 'might well have "undone" everything'. Haughey admitted that the whole thing was a 'mess'. Dermot Nally remembered Mrs Thatcher's vitriol: '"I said nothing about the constitution, nothing whatsoever was said." She went on and on and on ... This destroyed her belief in the idea that she could reach agreement with Haughey. It destroyed her faith in him.'

The process, however, was not destroyed. The Joint Studies gave British and Irish officials a framework of regular contact. In a masterly piece of mandarin handling, Robert Armstrong persuaded Mrs Thatcher to allow the Cabinet Office, which he oversaw, to take charge of the Joint Studies. Armstrong had long had a personal interest in the Irish question. As Ted Heath's principal private secretary, he had been intimately involved in the Sunningdale Agreement. This experience – power-sharing and some sort of Irish dimension – remained his mental model. From the Sunningdale era, Armstrong had established a good relationship with Dermot Nally, who, from 1980, was his equivalent in Dublin. To a man of Armstrong's elite, administrative mind, the future of Northern Ireland was better handled as an intergovernmental affair than by the inhabitants of the province. Sympathetic to a united Ireland, Armstrong wanted the Unionists kept at bay. As a loyal, able and professional civil servant he was always careful to protect Mrs Thatcher's position, but he was also trying to push her towards his view of Ireland.

Once the Joint Studies were agreed at Dublin, Armstrong and his deputy, Robert Wade-Gery, sought to move the political situation forward. Wade-Gery regularly held secret meetings with officials in the Taoiseach's office. Such contacts were not forbidden, but their full content was not known to the Prime Minister. Wade-Gery recalled that they were 'very gingerly' beginning to talk about what would eventually, in 1985, become the Anglo-Irish Agreement.

As the plans for the Joint Studies developed, Mrs Thatcher did what she could to challenge their assumptions. But when Ian Gow suggested the studies include a review of the Irish Constitution's claim to Northern Ireland* she was uneasy. As she told Enoch Powell, were she to 'raise the constitutional issue with the Irish Government, it would then seek to raise the constitutional position of Northern Ireland within the United Kingdom, and that was something [she] would never agree to discuss'.† The one issue which Unionists were prepared to discuss was thus ruled out of order by Mrs Thatcher.

In March 1981, Wade-Gery reported that the Irish government wanted an Anglo-Irish Council to emerge from the Joint Studies, and a joint parliamentary forum too. Their 'eventual objective was a federal Ireland'. Mrs Thatcher was deeply perturbed. When the Joint Studies papers were presented in late April, she finally exploded:

> This is the most alarming set of papers on the UK/Irish situation I have read. They reveal starkly a total difference of approach. We are trying to achieve increasing cooperation and reconciliation between our two countries ... They are using every study as a step towards takeover. If these papers go ahead to publication ... I am not prepared to go along with the studies. The Irish view would incur such mistrust, hostility and downright anger in the North that it would set Anglo–Irish relations back for years and do untold harm to many innocent people if the Protestant paramilitary groups reacted. It is no longer a question of changing the wording of a few sentences. We are at the heart of the matter.

All over the studies, sometimes four times on the same page, she wrote 'NO', and, *in extremis*, 'NO!'‡ She strongly disliked the whole vision but offered no alternative.

It is remarkable that Mrs Thatcher devoted such close attention to this large and often tedious bundle of documents. The Joint Studies process coincided

---

* Articles Two and Three of the 1937 Irish Constitution laid claim to the 'whole island' as the national territory. The wording was eventually amended following the Belfast (Good Friday) Agreement of 1998.
† Powell took a different view: 'He said that if he was contemplating lending his lawn mower to his next door neighbour, when his next door neighbour was claiming that the lawn mower was his, and not Mr Powell's, he, Mr Powell, would find it difficult to continue discussions as to whether he, Mr Powell, should lend the lawn mower to his neighbour.' The analogy is, untypically for Powell, inexact. The dispute was over the ownership not of the lawn mower but, as it were, of the lawn.
‡ When British officials suggested that the word 'Council' should be conceded in order to keep Irish goodwill, she wrote, 'What about our good will?' To the Irish suggestion that their citizens should sit on juries and hold elected office in the North, she wrote: 'This is monstrous.'

with the economic and political crisis which followed the 1981 Budget and the Brixton riots in April. In Northern Ireland itself, a second and much more formidable hunger strike was by now in progress. On the day of her angry note on the Joint Studies, she knew that the first hunger striker, Bobby Sands, was on the point of death.

Early in January 1981, Mrs Thatcher had been informed that the hard men in the Maze were plotting a second hunger strike. Atkins told her the strike was about political status and that the prisoners sought at least one death. On 1 March, Sands, leader of the IRA prisoners in the Maze, began the strike himself. Four days later, Mrs Thatcher reiterated her simple position: 'There is no such thing as political murder, political bombing or political violence. There is only criminal murder, criminal bombing and criminal violence. We will not compromise on this. There will be no political status.' On the same day, Frank Maguire, the Republican MP for Fermanagh and South Tyrone, died. Sands, from his prison bed, became a candidate to succeed him. The SDLP decided not to contest the seat and on 9 April Sands was elected. This gave the IRA a huge propaganda boost.

Mrs Thatcher came under immense pressure. At home in mainland Britain, and among Unionists, there was almost complete support for resistance to the hunger strike. In the rest of the world, the opposite was the case. In the Republic, the United States and the EEC, calls for a way out grew louder.* On 22 April, Armstrong reported that Nally had passed on Haughey's concern that if Sands died soon, 'The whole areas [sic] would go up in flames.' A record of a telephone conversation with Humphrey Atkins at this time, however, shows that she was prepared for Sands's death and others too:

> The Prime Minister: But there are two or three others behind him [Sands] aren't there Humphrey?
> Secretary of State for Northern Ireland: Yes ... I think there is bound to be a weak link later.
> The Prime Minister: Yes I think they will be getting worried after all if one died and then a second one died then a third one died and nothing happened.
> Secretary of State for Northern Ireland: Yes it doesn't look very attractive.

---

* Despite plenty of criticism for Mrs Thatcher's stance in the US Congress, President Reagan and his close advisers never joined this chorus. 'We do not wish to place any pressure on Britain regarding the situation there,' the National Security Advisor Richard Allen wrote to Reagan in May 1981. 'It is up to Mrs Thatcher's government to work with its own citizens in Northern Ireland and with the government of the Irish Republic.'

The situation was not, in Atkins's inadequate phrase, very attractive to either side. On 5 May 1981, Sands died. Thirty thousand people attended his funeral in Belfast. In death, Sands became a world figure. Streets were named after him in Paris and Teheran. Haughey urged Mrs Thatcher to give ground, fearing the political rise of Sinn Fein. On 12 May, a second hunger striker, Francis Hughes, died. John Hume begged Mrs Thatcher to make concessions on clothing and free association, lest his SDLP be 'swept away' politically by the disturbances. Michael Foot came to see her with similar anxieties. She dismissed them all. 'Foot', she said, was 'giving notice that he was "a push-over".'

Throughout this tense time Robert Armstrong was firm against concessions to the prisoners, but called for 'long-term political development'. He warned the Prime Minister of the dangers of another Bloody Sunday (the rioting in Londonderry in 1972 when thirteen people were killed by British soldiers). On 27 May, the General Officer Commanding Northern Ireland, General Sir Richard Lawson, and the Chief Constable of the RUC, Jack Hermon, told Mrs Thatcher that the alienation of the Catholic population was now a greater challenge than the security problem. They advised concessions to 'dispel the impression of inflexibility'. Humphrey Atkins warned her they were losing not only the Catholics but 'the sympathy of world opinion'. He pushed for more 'political development'. Armstrong, however, was silkily dismissive, suggesting she keep 'at the back of your mind the possibility that you may wish to appoint a new Secretary of State before long'. He knew that a Cabinet reshuffle was imminent.

In June, the members of the Irish Commission for Justice and Peace (ICJP)* suggested they might help bring the hunger strike to an end. From 23 June, Michael Alison, the NIO Minister responsible for prisons, began to meet them. At the same time, Brendan 'Bik' McFarlane, the IRA leader in the Maze, told Gerry Adams that he was worried by the opinion of the strikers' families: 'If Brits don't meet with Commission and forward a very watery offer, can we cope with the families i.e. prevent their disintegration if we refuse . . . It appears that they [the British] are not interested in simply undermining us, but completely annihilating us . . . They are insane – at least Maggie is anyway.' But 'Maggie' was not insane, nor bent on annihilation. She was perplexed, even confused, about tactics.

Unwilling to make concessions, Mrs Thatcher agreed to entertain the suggestion of the new Taoiseach, Garret FitzGerald, that the ICJP might

---

* This was a body set up by the Irish Catholic hierarchy primarily concerned with aid to Third World countries.

play a greater role.* The commissioners, it was suggested, would be allowed into the Maze to repeat the government's message and, without negotiating, return with the prisoners' reply. Mrs Thatcher, though sceptical, was persuaded by colleagues to allow the plan to go ahead. In his meetings with the ICJP, Alison referred to 'the lady behind the veil' as the final, exacting arbiter of his position. The Commission understood him to be referring to Mrs Thatcher, but Alison later claimed that this was only a symbolic way of explaining that he was not the ultimate authority. On 4 July, Mrs Thatcher agreed with Alison that the Commission would tell the prisoners they must end the strike unconditionally, but in the knowledge that the government was under a moral 'obligation to move forward' on the areas of clothing, free association and prison work. The ICJP thought this was an 'about-face' on clothing which might bring a result.

On 4 and 5 July, as the death of the next hunger striker, Joe McDonnell, seemed imminent, the ICJP went into the Maze. The proposals which they brought appeared that they might satisfy the strikers, but difficulties arose after the IRA soured on the ICJP. Again using Brendan Duddy as an intermediary,† they made their concerns clear to the British. Fearing the appearance of 'sell-out' or a double-cross, they wanted parcels of clothes to be ready immediately after the strike ended and sought to approve the British statement after the strike's end in advance. Mrs Thatcher was shown the draft of the message which would be sent through the channel, toughening it up on work and association. She also approved the following: 'If the reply we receive is unsatisfactory and there is subsequently any public reference to this exchange we shall deny it took place.' There can be no doubt, therefore, that Mrs Thatcher went against her public protestations about not negotiating with terrorists, and actively did so, though at a remove. 'The lady behind the veil' had weakened.

On 7 July, the government passed its proposed statement to the IRA, who immediately objected. The government sought to 'elaborate' the statement overnight, but at 5.40 in the morning Joe McDonnell, the next hunger striker, died. Any chance of ending the strike evaporated.

In the endgame, Adams and his associates had mishandled matters. Their problem was that the political success caused by the hunger strike seemed too great to risk ending unless they could claim an unambiguous

---

* FitzGerald had come into office, replacing Charles Haughey, on 30 June 1981.
† This time Michael Oatley was not involved, but since the 1980 hunger strike Duddy had instead been in contact with a British official he called 'Tom'. During the key period of activity in July 1981, Duddy spoke to his British and Republican contacts for hours at a time either in person or on the telephone. Duddy was referred to in the Prime Minister's papers by the codename 'Soon'.

victory. So they missed their big chance to deal.* The British were also blamed, of course, above all for intransigence. In an angry letter to Mrs Thatcher in this vein, Garret FitzGerald called future cross-border cooperation into question. When Carrington worried that relations with the Republic and the United States 'were now at serious risk', Mrs Thatcher allowed the International Committee of the Red Cross into the Maze. But she refused his suggestion that the prisoners should be surreptitiously fed intravenously with glucose in their drips. Force-feeding, she believed, 'was almost a violence against the person', and if people wanted to kill themselves, they should be discouraged but not prevented. In Britain public opinion remained solidly behind her.

The IRA's grip on the prisoners, most of whose families naturally did not want them to die, was beginning to weaken. On 31 July, the family of Paddy Quinn, who had been on hunger strike for forty-seven days, intervened to save his life. But on 20 August the tenth hunger striker died.† With each death there were protests and renewed rioting, but each time the public attention was less. Mrs Thatcher's government was winning, at least in the sense that no one now believed that she would give in to the IRA. Garret FitzGerald quietened down over the summer. He realized that his public criticisms of the British government undermined his aspirations for a change in the relationship between the Republic and the United Kingdom. He now publicly floated his idea that the Irish Constitution's claim to Northern Ireland should be amended.

On 14 September 1981, Mrs Thatcher reshuffled her Cabinet, replacing Humphrey Atkins with Jim Prior. Prior had fought hard against moving to Northern Ireland, which did not endear him to the Unionist population. But the fact that she gave Prior quite a free hand in his new job clarified the decision-making process. On 17 September, he visited the Maze prison. Later that month, he agreed to meet the Catholic Primate, Cardinal Tomás O'Fiaich, and Father Denis Faul, one of the prison chaplains, to discuss a way forward. As he later recalled, 'The quid pro quo for ending the hunger strike was to allow prisoners to wear their own dress and I thought on balance this was a small price to pay.'

---

* In 2005 the former prisoner Richard O'Rawe revealed that the prison leadership, including McFarlane, had wanted to accept the British offer but that their decision had been overruled by the Republican leadership outside the prison, specifically by a committee which included Gerry Adams. O'Rawe alleged that the Sinn Fein leadership wanted to delay the ending of the hunger strike for political gain. There is a bitter debate within the Republican movement about where responsibility lay.

† This happened to be polling day for the second Fermanagh by-election. This time Owen Carron, who had been Bobby Sands's agent in the first by-election, proved victorious.

An understanding was at hand. On 2 October, Prior promised a statement on 'the development of the prison system'. The hunger strike ended the next day. Prior's statement on 6 October duly made clear that prisoners would have more freedom of association, in choice of work and in what clothes they wore, and better recovery of remission. These changes went slightly further than the concessions which had been the subject of negotiation in July, but did not differ in principle from the terms that Mrs Thatcher had been prepared to offer. No changes were implemented before the hunger strike had ended.

Who won the hunger strike? Mrs Thatcher certainly emerged from it with her reputation for determination and courage enhanced. This helped her greatly with Unionist opinion and made her politically much more formidable. The IRA had expected that she would be forced to make concessions, perhaps because she was a woman, but they had been proved wrong. On the other hand, the temporary electoral success that accrued to Sinn Fein because of the strike led to the strategy of 'a ballot box in one hand and an Armalite in the other'.* The more favourable prison regime that emerged allowed the IRA to act freely within the Maze. It is also true that, as a sort of trade-off for her toughness, Mrs Thatcher came under even greater pressure to move towards political development. Most damaging to her reputation, had it been known, and to her own conscience, was that she did, in effect, negotiate with terrorists. She never quite admitted this, even privately, but it was so.

Mrs Thatcher felt sad about the hunger strike. She admired the strikers' courage, describing them as 'poor devils' who knew that 'if they didn't go on strike they'd be shot . . . What a waste! What a terrible waste of human life!' As a result of the hunger strike, though she did not immediately know this, she went to the top of the IRA's death list. In public she never complained about the inevitable fear, but she did feel it, both for herself and for her family: 'you walk into a crowd', she said later '– it's always absolutely terrifying. Or if someone hands you something – look at Rajiv Gandhi – hidden in flowers.'

On 6 November 1981, just over two months after the hunger strike ended, Mrs Thatcher and Garret FitzGerald held a summit in London. In the preparation, she protested about the name of the Anglo-Irish Council proposed by the Joint Studies, insisting it be called the Anglo-Irish Intergovernmental Council. She was alert to anything which might imply any jurisdiction by

---

* This was articulated by Danny Morrison at Sinn Fein's Ard Fheis (annual conference) at the end of October.

the Republic in the affairs of Northern Ireland. She particularly resisted FitzGerald's desire for a rephrasing of the British guarantee to Northern Ireland in what he called a 'more positive' – by which he meant a more Nationalist – form. Rather desperate, Michael Alexander reminded her that 'The improved relationship between London and Dublin is an achievement of yours which you want to preserve and build upon.' In fact, she constantly resented what she had herself agreed. Meeting FitzGerald in 1983, she read out the phrase 'the Anglo-Irish Intergovernmental Council' 'in tones of contempt'. 'What's that?' she asked. 'Margaret, you invented it,' said FitzGerald.

The summit itself, however, laid the foundations for a good working relationship. At the top of the draft communiqué she wrote out the adjectives she would use to describe the meeting: 'Friendly, constructive, practical'. But, after her experience at Dublin, she was extremely anxious about the wording of the communiqué, and sought the advice of Ian Gow (Gow reminded her: 'We both remember what the Foreign Office did to us last time!').* In the Commons, she made much of the fact that FitzGerald had publicly accepted the principle of consent in relation to the North. But she was assailed by Unionists who feared the implications of the new Council and the Joint Studies. 'Northern Ireland is part of the United Kingdom,' she declared, 'as much as my constituency is.'†

Towards the end of the year, Prior threw his weight behind devolution and tried to sell the idea to Mrs Thatcher. She remained unconvinced, her concerns amplified by Ian Gow: 'To seek to combine Republicans and Unionists in the same power-sharing Executive is as absurd as asking Pétain and De Gaulle to sit in the same Cabinet in 1940.' Prior's plans were 'moving in fundamentally the wrong direction', he told her in March 1982, and 'doomed to failure'.

Prior's proposals were much disputed within the government. The White Paper that eventually emerged proposed a role for the Republic, via the Council and its inter-parliamentary arm, in the affairs of Northern Ireland. Gow told Mrs Thatcher this would be 'gravely damaging' – should it become law, he would have to resign. This left her in a quandary. She pretty much agreed with Gow, but was warned by Armstrong, probably

---

* Mrs Thatcher rejected a draft which said that the British government would 'support' movement to a United Ireland if the majority in the North so wished and replaced it with the word 'accept'.

† This was altered, in mythology, to a claim that Ulster was 'as British as Finchley', but this was not quite what she was saying. She was not asserting that Northern Ireland and north London were culturally the same. Rather, she was defending the constitutional position and the rights of the people protected by it.

correctly, that Prior's 'personal position' would be 'very difficult' if his proposals were rejected. Aware that most of the Cabinet tended to side with Prior, she felt she had to let the Bill go ahead. Somehow, she squared Ian Gow. On 2 April, he wrote to her: 'The die is now cast, but you understand, and <u>thank</u> you for understanding, how difficult my position is. I cannot forget Airey.'

The day after the Cabinet had agreed the Prior Bill, Argentina invaded the Falkland Islands. Mrs Thatcher was now preoccupied, so Prior made much of the running. Facing a revolt from Unionist Tories, the whips decided to guillotine the Bill. Prior recalled his chief's reaction: 'She turned to me and said, "Thank God I am going to be in the United States and am not going to have to vote for it."' In the event, twenty-six Conservative backbenchers voted against the guillotine motion. Mrs Thatcher probably had it in her power to block the Bill, but she chose not to do so. It was enough for her purposes to indicate her displeasure.

The Falklands also had the effect of freezing Anglo–Irish relations. Charles Haughey, who believed that Mrs Thatcher's behaviour during the hunger strikes had lost him the 1981 election, had returned to power in March. He saw the Falklands as the chance for revenge. Ireland now became by far the least friendly Western European country to the British cause. Sean Aylward, Haughey's private secretary, explained: 'it was a combination of substantial sympathy in Ireland for the Argentinian position and the smouldering resentment of the way in which the Thatcher government had influenced the hunger strikes ... Retrospectively, there is no question that it was a mistake because it simply wasn't understood in England and we lost a lot of friends too.' At the end of May, Haughey told the British Ambassador in Dublin that the 'spirit of the Anglo-Irish Initiative' was 'quite dead' because of the failure to consult Dublin.

Unlike her officials, Mrs Thatcher did not mind that the Irish government had withdrawn from political partnership. But she minded very much indeed that the Irish had tried to impede British victory in the Falklands. In August, she tired of Armstrong's efforts to persuade her to re-engage. 'Certainly I have no intention of having further bilateral meetings with the Taoiseach,' she scribbled on his memo. Her patience with the whole subject of Ireland, never strong, was temporarily exhausted.

Over drinks with officials in early December, Mrs Thatcher was in a more reflective mood. She discussed Ireland with David Goodall, Deputy Secretary to the Cabinet and a Roman Catholic of Irish descent with a long-standing commitment to Anglo-Irish rapprochement. Rather boldly, he told her it was a 'scandal' that British troops, triumphant in the Falklands, were still being lost in anger within the United Kingdom, in Northern

Ireland. The Prime Minister and he talked about Irishness. 'I am completely English,' said Mrs Thatcher stoutly. 'I'm not,' said Goodall; 'both my grandfathers were Irish.' 'Actually,' said the Prime Minister reflectively, 'my great-grandmother was a Sullivan,* so I'm one-sixteenth Irish.' She mused a little. 'If we get back [after the next general election],' she said, 'I should like to do something about Ireland.'

---

* In fact she was an O'Sullivan. The descent was on her father's side. She is believed to have been descended from Colonel Sir John William O'Sullivan, Quarter-Master General to Prince Charles Edward Stuart (Bonnie Prince Charlie) in the rising of 1745.

11
The 1981 Budget
'We've got to move fast to save her'

The Chequers seminar of 17 January 1981 had left Mrs Thatcher in no doubt as to the desperate state of the economy. With the Budget due in fewer than eight weeks, debate turned urgently to the severe measures required to bring the PSBR under control. Such talk, recalled Terry Burns, made her 'quite nervous'. She seemed tired and cross: when she appeared not to remember a late-night meeting, Hoskyns noted in his diary: 'Oh dear! I think she'd had one or two drinks on an empty stomach.'

On 10 February, with the PSBR forecast at £13 billion and rising, Alan Walters warned the Prime Minister that failure to bring borrowing under control 'may lead to a funding crisis, but it certainly will lead to high interest rates, retaining high exchange rates and yet another squeeze on the private sector. This outcome must be avoided – it would be a quite impossible scenario for the approach to an election.' He called for 'painful decisions now'. Hoskyns agreed. He told Mrs Thatcher that the Budget offered a choice between 'underkill' and 'overkill'. Overkill would require tax increases. Underkill, aimed at better growth and lower unemployment, would be politically popular, but would lead to

> a mid-summer funding crisis, with a desperate attempt at further cuts, splits in Cabinet, trivial savings to show for it, and finally a further rise in MLR and then the exchange rate. This will lead to yet lower activity, higher unemployment and PSBR, which will no longer be reversible before the election. The credibility of MTFS and of Geoffrey himself will be destroyed and our own position undermined.

Hoskyns added to Mrs Thatcher's anxieties by sending her work by the Swiss economist Jürg Niehans about the damage done by the high exchange rate. Niehans, though sympathetic to monetarism, argued that the shock administered by the government's monetary squeeze had been too great.* If this continued, Niehans told Hoskyns, 'you won't just have a recession; you'll have a slump'.

David Wolfson noted that at each meeting of Chancellor and Prime Minister the PSBR kept expanding. To the implication that she must rein this in by whatever means necessary Mrs Thatcher replied, 'Are you sure you're right, because if not, my prime ministerial term is going to be pretty short.' On 13 February, Walters advocated holding the PSBR to £10 billion by raising the basic rate of income tax. Howe argued for £11.5 billion, and he and Mrs Thatcher united against a tax rise. 'Alan was the economist,' she later wrote. 'But Geoffrey and I were politicians. Geoffrey rightly observed that introducing what would be represented as a deflationary budget at the time of the deepest recession since the 1930s would be difficult enough; doing so via an increase in the basic rate would be a political nightmare.'

Mrs Thatcher later claimed she had supported Howe against tax rises 'without much conviction', but few noticed this lack of conviction at the time. As Alan Walters recalled, 'she screamed at me: "You're just an academic and you don't know what the political implications are."' He replied that she would be politically ruined by the collapse of financial markets and referred (knowing this would sting her) to the fiasco of Edward Heath's 'dash for growth'. Walters, Hoskyns and Wolfson began to speak of resigning simultaneously if their Budget advice was not taken.

The following week, Mrs Thatcher held fast. On 20 February, two days after the humiliating climbdown over pit closures (see p. 230), Hoskyns warned her that the PSBR would now expand further, reiterating that the 'overkill' Budget would be the 'turning-point'. She wrote 'sharp comments' on his note. Hoskyns feared their relationship was close to breakdown. But, just when all seemed dark, on 24 February he recorded an 'amazing volte-face by Margaret. She started swinging back, in a budget bilateral with Geoffrey and Douglas Wass, to the need for a smaller PSBR and perhaps to raise income tax . . . as they start to leave, she says words to the effect, "if there's a funding crisis then you (Geoffrey) are for the chop".' The official record shows that Mrs Thatcher doubted interest rates could be

---

* Niehans believed that Sterling M3 figures gave a misleading picture: money supply targets would be better expressed in terms of the monetary base, which had been ruthlessly held down. The Treasury, with its MTFS, had been pursuing the 'gradualist' approach advocated by Milton Friedman. But the markets' perception of what was happening had produced a high exchange rate, thus precipitating the crisis advocated as a necessary shock by Friedrich von Hayek. David Willetts, then private secretary to Nigel Lawson, remembered: 'Though we were trying to do Friedman, we were actually doing Hayek.'

reduced without a PSBR of around £10.5 billion. 'From a political standpoint, she thought it might now be possible to justify a 1p increase in the basic income tax rate on account of the increased spending on the NCB and BSC.' When Howe resisted, Mrs Thatcher said she was 'prepared to accept his political judgement', but her point about the lower PSBR stood.

Calling on Mrs Thatcher the next morning, Alan Walters found her packing hats for her visit to the United States the following day. She told him she had ordered Howe to take £3.5 billion off the PSBR. Walters said, 'Are you sure?' Mrs Thatcher replied: 'Of course I'm sure. That's what you want, isn't it?' Perhaps because she then left for America, it was not immediately clear that a decision had been made. Hoskyns, Walters and Wolfson prepared a note of resignation for when, as they still expected, their Budget advice was not taken. In fact, she had come round to their way of thinking and persuaded Howe to accept it. It would have spoken ill of her political judgement if she had rushed into a contractionary Budget without protest. Nevertheless, the orchestration in favour of a tough Budget by her Downing Street advisers made the difference. 'It was Walters she really listened to,' said Terry Burns: he had a 'disarming way of being absolutely sure he was right'. She, in turn, 'did strengthen the backbone of the Treasury'. Before the 1981 Budget, Mrs Thatcher had been forced to confront the possibility that she might fail dishonourably by abandoning what she believed. Walters, and other close advisers, helped keep her on the straight and narrow.

Geoffrey Howe presented his Budget to Parliament on 10 March 1981. By then, the Treasury forecast for the PSBR had risen to £14.5 billion (6 per cent of GDP).* Howe's tax increases were designed to reduce it to £10.5 billion. Child benefit and one-parent-family benefit were indexed, but the decision not to index tax thresholds brought £2 billion.† Alcohol, tobacco and car and petrol duties all rose, and a once-for-all levy on banks' non-interest-bearing deposits brought £400 million. Interest rates were to come down by 2 per cent to 12 per cent.‡

---

* To illustrate how bad the situation was, it should be borne in mind that, for the next thirty years, a deficit of 3 per cent of GDP was considered the maximum desirable.
† This was Howe's solution to the problem of generating substantial revenue without raising the rate of income tax.
‡ Howe also announced that, in future, public spending would be controlled in cash rather than volume terms (i.e. instead of departments agreeing on what they needed to purchase and then finding the money, they would first negotiate the money and then buy what they could afford). This made the controls on spending tougher than in the past, but also more predictable and therefore easier to handle. If departments knew their cash limits in advance, they were less likely to find themselves confronted with the 'in-year' cuts that they detested.

Knowing that his Budget was more controversial than usual, Howe shared it the day before with his most senior colleagues, seeing Whitelaw, Carrington, Prior and Pym individually. This was unusual because, by convention, the Budget is not considered a collective Cabinet decision but the prerogative of the Chancellor, in consultation with the Prime Minister. None was thrilled, but only Prior expressed clear hostility, telling Howe that it was 'pretty disastrous'. The following morning, Prior, Peter Walker and Ian Gilmour, the three most dissident Wets, met and debated resignation. They decided against, recalled Walker, 'because of the effect on sterling'. Prior, in retrospect, considered their decision, or rather indecision, feeble: 'We were wet in the true sense of the word.'

Presenting his Budget to the Cabinet, Howe received a gloomy reception. Keith Joseph offered strong support, but the Wets expressed disappointment and concern. Even Whitelaw, his criticism shaded by loyalty, said there was an 'enormous need for hope'. Lord Carrington criticized the failure to discuss such a consequential Budget beforehand. All Mrs Thatcher could say was that they should unite behind the Chancellor.

'The Budget is not well received,' began Bernard Ingham's daily press digest the following day. 'Howe It Hurts' screamed the *Sun*. The next day, telling tales out of school, Ingham warned Mrs Thatcher that, in briefing the press, Francis Pym had 'rather deftly applied public pressure for a pre-Budget discussion in Cabinet of economic strategy'. The idea of forcing such a discussion 'is not merely being nursed by a few Ministers', warned Ingham, 'it is beginning to take off'.* There was now clear and semi-concerted opposition within the Cabinet. Moves were afoot, clothed in demands for changes in process, to isolate the Prime Minister.

At the same time, the ranks of Mrs Thatcher's trusted associates had thinned out. Richard Ryder had left to stand for Parliament at the next election, Gordon Reece was working in the USA and Alistair McAlpine had been temporarily pushed out as Party Treasurer by Lord Thorneycroft. As Hoskyns noted in his diary, Ronnie Millar was deeply worried: 'He said that Gordon had heard in the US that Kissinger says his friends in the Cabinet (Carrington?) say she'll be out within a year. He feels we've got to move fast to save her.'

At this moment, in Ingham's words, '364 economists cook up round-robin to condemn your economic policies'. This was probably helpful. The 364 signatories to the letter, published in *The Times*, included five former

---

* The next day, Ingham's digest noted, '*Guardian* says many Ministers and backbenchers are openly discussing possibility of Palace revolution in summer when Government is told to change policies.' Fortunately for Mrs Thatcher, the mood on the back benches, though hardly rapturous, was not as mutinous as the *Guardian* reported.

chief economic advisers to the government. It dismissed the government's approach as having 'no basis in economic theory' and posing a threat to 'social and political stability': 'The time has come to reject monetarist policies and consider which alternative offers the best hope of sustained recovery.'

Whatever their distaste for the government's policies, the public were not particularly likely to be impressed by economists, nor to think that 364 of them were better than one. Their timing, as Nigel Lawson put it in his memoirs, proved 'exquisite'. Output touched its lowest point in the quarter that ended on the day when the letter was published. In the eight years from 1981 to 1989, real GDP growth averaged 3.2 per cent, whereas there were sixteen months of negative growth during 1980 and 1981. Although no one knew it at the time, the economy had turned the corner.*

Not that confidence and calm returned quickly. At the end of March, the Civil Service unions began a 'selective' strike. The day when industrial production turned up for the first time in ten months was also the day when serious rioting broke out. Anti-police riots by mainly black youths in Brixton, south London, on 13 April injured 150 police amid widespread looting. Mrs Thatcher came out strongly, saying there was 'no excuse' for the riots and that government money had already been 'poured into' Lambeth to little effect. The public were deeply shocked by the scale of the violence and were disposed, unlike the metropolitan elites, to blame it on the people who had rioted. But it was natural that Mrs Thatcher's critics should see the disturbances as a response to growing unemployment. Wets could claim that their prophecies of tears in the social fabric had come true.

Mrs Thatcher was extremely wary of demands for Cabinet discussions of economic strategy. She was seized of the danger of leaks and feared being ambushed and outnumbered. Nonetheless, a meeting was arranged and a paper for discussion drafted by Howe. This set out the growth in public spending since 1979 and concluded that, unless the policy changed, 'we shall enter the election with the overall tax burden much heavier than the one we inherited. Not only politically, but also economically, that is not tolerable.' On his draft, Mrs Thatcher added the one area of proposed reform which was common ground between her and the Wets: 'Plans to train and occupy young people.' In best mandarin style, Robert Armstrong

---

* From the first quarter of 1983 the number of people employed began to rise, and from the third quarter of 1986 the number of unemployed began to fall. Alan Walters's prediction that the inflation rate would fall to 5 per cent in 1982 was over-optimistic, but the rate for 1983 was 4.6 per cent. As for the PSBR, its eventual outturn was £8.5 billion, £2 billion better than budgeted for.

advised that she may 'want to agree in the Cabinet the line to be taken with the press – and to invite them to resist the temptation to embroider it'.

At the meeting, on 17 June, Prior led the charge: 'I see solution not in cutting public expenditure but in getting growth.' Walker, Carrington, Pym and others also expressed unhappiness. Even Willie Whitelaw allowed himself to say, 'I fear the effects of unemployment on crime are very serious.' The next day's press carried excited accounts of how Mrs Thatcher had seen off the rebels ('Maggie Crushes Jobs Revolt by Wets'). Ingham, it seemed, had done some embroidering of his own. The press now began to write Mrs Thatcher up as a successfully ruthless politician. On the following day, the rate of inflation fell to 11.7 per cent, and on 24 June Mrs Thatcher trounced Michael Foot in a debate on unemployment.

But the sense of crisis grew. New riots broke out in Southall, west London, on 4 July and spread elsewhere, including Moss Side in Manchester and the Toxteth area of Liverpool. Mrs Thatcher's response was tough. 'The law must be upheld,' she said. 'People must be protected.' She denied the link between unemployment and rioting. But the fact that she tacked this on to a party political broadcast, rather than addressing the shocking events in a fuller setting, showed her uncertainty in handling the crisis. It was alleged that Mrs Thatcher's private reaction to the rioting was to exclaim, 'Those poor shopkeepers!' To some this seemed laughable, almost contemptible. In fact, such sentiments mirrored a feeling in the country. Her problem was that she did not seem to have the situation in hand. On 10 July there was rioting in twelve cities, the most extensive yet.

Mrs Thatcher now asked for the return of the Riot Act, which, once read out at the scene of a disturbance, had given extensive powers to the police to arrest, disperse and even open fire. There were several calls for intervention, on the model of Harold Macmillan, who had sent Lord Hailsham as special minister for the depressed North-East in the early 1960s. Mrs Thatcher was unconvinced: Labour authorities had created problems with 'horrible housing, high rise etc.' and 'We have a whole generation brought up on 5 hours a day of TV.' Heseltine again demanded a Hailsham-style minister, with the unspoken implication that he was the man for the job. Mrs Thatcher asked for time to think.

On 13 July she visited Liverpool, where, as Ingham's press digest put it, she was 'pelted with tomatoes and toilet rolls; most [newspapers] feature your 10 most worrying days since you took office'. Three days later she agreed to send Heseltine to Liverpool to see what could be done.*

---

* Mrs Thatcher insisted this was not a 'special ministerial appointment' but a 'pilot, prototype scheme'. Eventually, and reluctantly, she gave Heseltine a more lasting role, earning him

That same day, the Conservatives lost their deposit in the Warrington by-election. But the main story was the success of the SDP, who came tantalizingly close to winning the previously safe Labour seat on a swing of 13.3 per cent. On polling day the inflation rate was announced as 11.3 per cent, the lowest since Mrs Thatcher took office.

The Cabinet met on 23 July to discuss the public expenditure survey for 1981. Mrs Thatcher had just returned from the G7 summit in Ottawa, where the final communiqué had pleased her by stressing the need 'urgently to reduce public borrowing'. In private, she had told President Reagan how worried she was about the effect of high US interest rates on Britain, but had resisted French and German attempts to gang up on him. She felt protective towards the President, who had only recently reappeared in public after having been shot by a would-be assassin on 30 March. As the summit began, Reagan, and Reagan alone, received a very public kiss on the cheek from Mrs Thatcher. Over dinner with his fellow world leaders, the President tried to explain his own economic approach but was criticized, if not ridiculed, from all sides. As he later recalled, the only person who came to his defence was Margaret Thatcher: 'she leaned over to me and patted my elbow and said, "Don't worry about it, Ronnie, it's just boys being boys."' She stored up much goodwill. Mrs Thatcher told the Cabinet it had been 'quite the best economic conference the Government could have had'.*

The Cabinet, however, wanted a showdown. Fresh from his Liverpudlian experience, Michael Heseltine took up the charge. Attacking Howe's plans for cuts of £5 billion, he called instead for a pay freeze, which would leave '£5 billion at our disposal'. What was he proposing, cried Mrs Thatcher, a pay freeze, a pensions freeze, a social security freeze? 'I want the maximum of that package I can get,' said Heseltine, whose use of the first person singular left her uneasy about his motives. Ever conscious of the terrible Heath example, she said, 'it must not get out of this room that a pay freeze is being talked about'.

All the Cabinet critics pitched in. Even John Nott and John Biffen, intellectually committed to 'monetarism', sided with the Wets. Only Joseph backed the Treasury team. Woundingly, the Lord Chancellor, Lord Hailsham, drew a comparison with the American President at the beginning of the Great Depression, Herbert Hoover. 'Hoover succeeded in destroying the Republican Party,' said Hailsham; 'we are in danger of destroying

---

the moniker 'Minister for Merseyside'. His visits there, calling for more intervention, made a great splash.

* Mrs Thatcher was sufficiently impressed, and perhaps intrigued, by President Reagan that, when she noticed he had left an assortment of doodled heads and faces at the summit table, she took them home as a souvenir. Today they survive among her personal papers.

our own.' Howe hit back that the 1980s were not like the 1930s because inflation was 'still rampant'. Mrs Thatcher insisted they must not repeat the disastrous Barber boom. 'The most frightening thing I've heard is that we should abandon policy of keeping inflation down. OK for people with muscle . . . The rest would see savings being confiscated.' She concluded, 'We must not get to a pocket money society [her phrase for a socialist, high-tax economy]. That's the end of us.'

Mrs Thatcher was very upset by the Cabinet arguments, especially Hailsham's Hoover comparison. The press reported the split and some mentioned Francis Pym as an alternative leader. On 29 July, the Prince of Wales married Lady Diana Spencer amid scenes of general happiness not witnessed since the Coronation. The wedding, Ingham wrote, had been a 'national tonic'. Just days later, however, an opinion poll gave an SDP-Liberal Alliance 45 per cent, Labour 29 per cent and the Conservatives 25 per cent. It was time for the recess, which could work to Mrs Thatcher's advantage.

The summer had shown that Mrs Thatcher could not govern with her existing team. She railed against the Wets in private, calling them 'dumb bunnies'. While Whitelaw and Michael Jopling, the Chief Whip, leant to the 'moderate' tendency in the party, both had been 'outraged' by the challenge to her authority in the Cabinet of 23 July. They insisted that a Cabinet that did not support her was 'intolerable'. A reshuffle was needed.

By this time, Mrs Thatcher was sufficiently shaken by recent events to envisage her own political mortality. 'I could always scrub floors,' she told her private secretary. She also thought seriously of getting rid of Howe. Clive Whitmore, however, told her she could not distance herself from her Chancellor's economic decisions: 'If Geoffrey Howe goes, you've got to go.' Jopling felt she did not really want to remove Howe, but was suspicious of him because he was 'instinctively on the moderate side'. While she was right in sensing this, the chief strength in her precarious position came from the fact that no one could drive a wedge between her and her Chancellor: to do so herself would have been fatal.

Her doubts about Howe were part of a wider problem, produced by stress, that she was almost as irritated with her allies as with her opponents, and they with her. In August, Hoskyns settled down to what he called a 'blockbuster' memo to his boss. To avoid her dismissing it as 'just me being disagreeable', he got David Wolfson and Ronnie Millar to add their names.* Hoskyns wanted Millar because, for Mrs Thatcher, he was 'that

---

* Since the paper mentions the merits of Millar by name, however, the pretence that he was one of its authors cannot have fooled Mrs Thatcher.

rare thing, a trusted friend who wanted her to succeed and was therefore prepared to tell her things she did not want to hear'. The fact that Wolfson, so close an associate, joined the effort is also striking. Entitled 'Your Political Survival', the paper was put into the Prime Minister's red box as she went on holiday on 20 August.

The 'blockbuster' was quite possibly the bluntest official document ever seen in Downing Street. While recognizing that 'things in the economy are better than people realise', it warned that internal revolt now threatened Mrs Thatcher's position. 'Your own credibility and prestige are draining away very fast,' wrote Hoskyns. The most likely outcome was 'you as another failed Tory prime minister sitting with Heath', but she might be simply thrown out before the next election. He then listed her faults. 'You lack management competence.' 'Your own leadership style is wrong.' He warmed to his theme: 'You bully your weaker colleagues. You criticise colleagues in front of each other and in front of their officials. They can't answer back without appearing disrespectful, in front of others, to a woman and to a Prime Minister. You abuse that situation.' 'The result', the next paragraph was headed, 'is an unhappy ship.' To survive, 'you have an absolute duty to change the way you operate'.

The Hoskyns memo called for Mrs Thatcher to 'Lead by Encouragement, not by Criticism'. She needed to give credit to others: 'Say "we" and not "I".'* Hoskyns wanted a new Party Chairman and a thoroughgoing reshuffle. She should restore her public image and cut her diary commitments: 'To be frank, I believe you fill your diary because it's a good way to avoid having to do the unpleasant strategic thinking ... which you don't enjoy and which is not your forte.' He concluded: 'it will be no comfort to you, to us, or to the Country as a whole if you go into the history books with the prize for the "Best Loser"'.

In Hoskyns's view, the 'blockbuster' failed: 'Two or three weeks later she hissed at me, out of the corner of her mouth ... "I got your letter. No one has ever written like that to a prime minister before."' He felt she had 'never experienced advice of this kind', which left their working relationship 'undoubtedly damaged'. They never talked about the memo again. Hoskyns believed she was beginning to suffer the isolation of high office: 'the seeds of her downfall were being sown'. This may be right, but surely underplays the simple fact that almost no human being, particularly one under intense strain, can be expected to take such brutal criticism easily.

---

* It is possible that Mrs Thatcher followed this advice too closely. She became notoriously shy of using the word 'I', sometimes slipping into a 'royal we', as, famously, when she said, speaking in public after the birth of her first grandchild: 'We have become a grandmother.'

His 'blockbuster' is testimony to how very trying Mrs Thatcher could be, even – perhaps particularly – to her friends. It is evidence, too, of the sense of crisis that summer.

Without ever acknowledging the justice of the criticism, Mrs Thatcher acted in its spirit. In late August, she planned a Cabinet reshuffle with Hoskyns, Wolfson and Gow. Most importantly, Jim Prior would be replaced at Employment by Norman Tebbit, and offered Northern Ireland. Cecil Parkinson would succeed Thorneycroft as Chairman. At his own request, Keith Joseph would move from Industry to Education. David Howell would move to Transport, with Nigel Lawson taking his job at Energy. Christopher Soames and Ian Gilmour would be out.

Prior heard what was afoot, however, and decided to resist. In an ill-tempered meeting with Mrs Thatcher on 2 September, he again rejected reform of trade union immunities. She told him his ideas were 'far too modest'. The meeting ended in impasse. Many thought she was not in a strong enough position to move Prior, but the political situation was starting to shift. The emergence of the SDP, vigorously opposed to trade union political power, meant the Tories no longer held the monopoly of anti-union votes. Prior's caution might lead his party to be outflanked: his position was weaker than he imagined.

The reshuffle took place on 14 September. Prior accepted Northern Ireland, with the sop that he could remain on E Committee. Christopher Soames was replaced as Leader in the Lords by Janet Young, an old friend of Mrs Thatcher and the first and last woman ever appointed to her Cabinet.* Gilmour wrote to Mrs Thatcher, in the normally courteous exchange of letters when a minister departs: 'You asked for my resignation ... this was, in view of our disagreements, neither surprising nor unwelcome.' But of course it *was* unwelcome. The Wets looked much less dignified sacked than they would have looked if they had resigned on principle; and there was something in their sense of affront at being sacked by a woman which was haughty. Mrs Thatcher still lacked a majority of true believers in her Cabinet, but in Tebbit, Parkinson and Lawson she had a new generation of active, clever, enthusiastic supporters. Equally important, she had proved that she could sack the grandees without the heavens falling.

There was no obvious or immediate improvement, however, in Mrs Thatcher's fortunes. Interest rates, which rose 2 percentage points on the day of

---

* Christopher Soames reportedly complained to friends that he would have sacked his gamekeeper with more courtesy than Mrs Thatcher had shown him, though why one should expect gamekeepers to be shown less courtesy than Lord Soames in matters of employment was not clear.

the reshuffle, added a further 2 points on 1 October to reach an agonizing 16 per cent.* Private polling for the Conservatives showed that if a Social Democratic Alliance came into being, 40 per cent of voters would support it. Only 16 per cent would support the Conservatives.

Ted Heath chose the run-up to the October party conference to launch his fiercest and most direct attack on the government's economic policy yet. Decrying the rise in unemployment, he called for 'a return to consensus politics', membership of the ERM and the reintroduction of exchange controls. Mrs Thatcher hit back. Consensus, she said, was 'the process of abandoning all beliefs, principles, values and policies in search of something in which no one believes, but to which no one objects'. As was almost always the case, Heath's intervention was useful to Mrs Thatcher. It made the dispute look personal, and so the party faithful naturally rallied to the leader.

In the same week, representatives of the younger generation of mainly centrist Conservative MPs (known as the 'Blue Chips') produced a pamphlet called *Changing Gear*, which politely but clearly put down a marker against the trend of Mrs Thatcher's policies. Led by Chris Patten and William Waldegrave, they were ambitious young men who included most of the brightest and best-connected of the 1979 intake.† The fact that, in Patten's phrase, 'we asked one question too many' was an ill omen for Mrs Thatcher.

Imbued with the spirit of the Macmillan era, the pamphlet's epigraph deployed two-edged words from the old man himself, praising Mrs Thatcher as 'a Prime Minister of courage, who I hope will not be led away from the old tradition of consensus'. At its core, the pamphlet was a criticism of the social effects of Thatcherism by people who believed that the Conservatives would lose the next election. Howe recognized its importance: the arguments, he told Mrs Thatcher, were chiefly about tone and flexibility: 'we must heed them'.

At the party conference Heath continued to assail the government, while almost every leading Wet made speeches of what the press called 'coded' criticism. The rank and file, though, were with Mrs Thatcher and the revolt did not take off. The most notable platform speech came from the

---

* At the time of the second interest rate rise on 1 October, Geoffrey and Elspeth Howe were staying with the Hendersons at the British Embassy in Washington. By chance, Roy Jenkins, an old friend of Nicko Henderson, and Ian Gilmour were staying too. Henderson gave dinner to Jenkins and Gilmour himself, while arranging for the Howes and their entourage to have dinner in their room, an untypically gauche decision which indicated a bet about who was likely to be in, who out. Elspeth Howe said to the company: 'Insurrection is being plotted downstairs.'
† Other members included Lord Cranborne, John Patten, Tristan Garel-Jones and Richard Needham. Soon afterwards, it was joined by John Major. In time, this left-leaning group formed a grand, almost aristocratic network.

new Employment Secretary, Norman Tebbit. Speaking in the tone of slight menace which made him a compelling orator, he said that he had grown up with an unemployed father in the 1930s: 'He didn't riot. He got on his bike and looked for work.' Forever afterwards known as the 'on your bike' speech, this became an object of hatred to the left and an encapsulation of the Thatcherite approach to work. It cemented the perception of Tebbit as the bootboy of Thatcherism.

In John Hoskyns's view, Mrs Thatcher offered the conference 'the most boring and anti-climactic speech I ever heard her make'. Drafts by Hoskyns and Millar were superseded by 'large chunks of "wallpaper" . . . and even worse stuff from [John Selwyn] Gummer' which, Hoskyns moaned in his diary, 'commend themselves to Margaret, who has no taste or judgment whatsoever'. There were acknowledgements of the pain of unemployment, and 'the dignity which comes from work'. Overall, the speech tried to marry a conciliatory tone with the tough message of persistence in the face of economic difficulty. This left the audience in Blackpool somewhat reassured, but not inspired. Ingham's press digest reported the 'shortest standing ovation any leader has received for years'. The press confidently predicted a leadership challenge.

On 20 October, the Cabinet reconvened to discuss Howe's proposed public spending savings of £3.5 billion. Many colleagues were unsympathetic. Michael Heseltine said he would rather increase borrowing than make such cuts. Prior, Biffen, Carrington and Walker all attacked Howe's plans. Francis Pym warned: 'We haven't produced a ray of light; and we are asking people to make sacrifices without hope.' This time, however, it was not only Keith Joseph who supported the Chancellor. Patrick Jenkin, now at Industry, and the new boys, Parkinson, Lawson and Tebbit, all backed Howe. The Cabinet agreed to set up a small *ad hoc* group under Willie Whitelaw to work through the options for cuts, but, as so often, disagreements leaked. Mrs Thatcher angrily told the Cabinet that 'If anyone here is doing things which result in leaks to the press, the honourable course is to resign.' Ill feeling persisted.

But the spirit of innovation also strengthened. At Employment, Tebbit was ready to take the step which Prior had refused – an end to the immunity of trade union funds from claims for damages. Other changes included periodic ballots to weaken, though not abolish, the closed shop. The essence of the proposals reached the statute book by December 1982. The end of the unique legal privileges of trade unions was eventually to prove decisive. As Prior later conceded: 'Tebbit was right rather than me.'

As autumn turned into winter, there was no dramatic improvement in the economy or in Mrs Thatcher's political position. Speaking to the

Lord Mayor's Banquet in November, she insisted that the trough of the recession had been passed in the middle of the year. But the small signs of recovery remained invisible to most. At the end of November, Shirley Williams won the Crosby by-election for the SDP with a majority of over 5,000, taking the seat from the Conservatives. In December a Gallup poll gave 50.5 per cent to the SDP and Liberals in alliance, 23.5 per cent to Labour and 23 per cent to the Tories. Unemployment hit 3 million for the first time at the end of January 1982. Despite the failure of critics to mount the leadership challenge which, under the rules, had to happen in November, Mrs Thatcher did not feel secure. The night before the Chancellor's Autumn Statement on public spending on 2 December she burst in, unannounced, on the late-night meeting Howe was holding with officials. John Kerr, Howe's private secretary, remembered her as 'quite full of whisky'. In front of everyone she berated Howe for his proposed speech. 'If this is the best you can do,' Howe recorded her saying, 'then I'd better send you to hospital and deliver the statement myself.'

Inevitably, the Autumn Statement proved unpopular. To avoid certain cuts, employees' National Insurance contributions rose by a further 1 per cent, council house rents and prescription charges rose, and most social security benefits went up by less than the rate of inflation. Discontent on the Conservative back benches followed, but the revolt proved half-hearted.* Weakened in Cabinet, the Wets began to realize that it was too late to change course before the next election. Some sort of truce was needed for the party to survive: '*Telegraph* says the Chancellor is determined last week's announcement will be the last unpalatable one before the Election,' reported Ingham's digest. That was about the sum of it.

Besides, the political situation was calculated to make Tories stick together. That November, Michael Foot's approval rating as Leader of the Opposition fell to 16 per cent, the lowest Gallup had ever recorded.† In early December Arthur Scargill was elected President of the National Union of Mineworkers, a victory hailed publicly by Tony Benn as giving 'fresh hopes for battles inside and outside of Parliament'. In the same month martial law was declared in Poland, with dozens killed. The world watched anxiously to see if the Soviets would launch a full-on invasion. Not for the first time, the sense of threat helped Mrs Thatcher rally people to her side.

---

* Fourteen Conservative MPs abstained in the vote.
† Foot's difficulty in appealing to the public became clear beyond doubt at the Cenotaph Remembrance Day ceremony that November after he appeared wearing a mouldy-looking donkey jacket and laid his wreath with, as the *Daily Telegraph* put it, 'all the reverent dignity of a tramp inspecting a cigarette end'. For many, this seemed to confirm the idea that Foot could never conceivably be prime minister.

Early in 1982 Mrs Thatcher also revealed, which people had been inclined to forget, that she was a human being after all. Taking part in the Paris–Dakar motor rally, Mark Thatcher got stuck in the Sahara Desert in Algeria, his whereabouts unknown for four days. 'Algerian report suggests kidnap,' said Ingham's digest with brutal directness. Mrs Thatcher was distraught. Very unusually for her, she cancelled some engagements. Besieged by reporters, she could not keep back tears. This was the only time that anyone working with Mrs Thatcher could remember when private events made normal work impossible. The popular papers said she had touched 'the hearts and compassion of the people' and that people now warmed to her 'as a woman and a mother'.

Denis flew out to Algeria and with adroit courtesy, which Mrs Thatcher never forgot, President Mitterrand of France put his military at her disposal. After thirty-one hours of air searches, Mark was discovered and flown home safe and well. His adventure left the government £1,191 out of pocket. The Foreign Office intended to pick up the bill, but Mrs Thatcher insisted on paying herself. 'We can therefore say that *no* extra cost has fallen on the British taxpayer,' she scribbled. 'To who [*sic*] do I make out the cheque?' It was left to Carol to provide a slightly critical note. In the tabloids, Ingham reported, she 'says she hopes Mark stops racing because the Prime Minister could do without this additional hassle'.

When the Cabinet met for its first discussion of Budget ideas on 28 January, contention had mysteriously vanished. Even Prior declared: 'I think we are just about out of recession.' Nigel Lawson encapsulated the Dry narrative of economic recovery: 'This Budget should be different from last year's Budget; because of last year's Budget, it can be.' When the Budget came, on 9 March, Howe could boast that, for the first time in his Chancellorship, the PSBR had come in below the forecast, and so interest rates had already dropped 3 percentage points from their autumn high of 16 per cent. He increased income tax thresholds above inflation and cut the National Insurance surcharge by 1.5 per cent.

The Budget was well received in the press and by Conservative MPs. Although tremendous economic difficulties remained, the sting of the controversy in 1981 was drawn. A Thatcherite recovery – or at any rate, a recovery with Mrs Thatcher firmly in charge – had begun, weeks before the news from the South Atlantic which was to convulse British politics.

12

The Falklands

'I don't think anyone else but you could have done it'

Early in the morning of Friday 2 April 1982, Argentine forces invaded the Falkland Islands, a British colony in the South Atlantic. The prospect of imminent invasion had become clear only on 31 March, and as late as 5 p.m., London time, the following day intelligence reports contained no definitive evidence of an impending attack. A week earlier, Argentina had not yet decided to invade. A month earlier, there had been no obvious crisis. At 9.25 a.m., Falklands time (12.25 p.m. in London), on the day of the invasion the British Governor ordered the small contingent of Royal Marines defending Government House in the capital, Port Stanley, to surrender. Argentine troops made them lie on the ground to be photographed. The Argentine flag flew over Port Stanley. The humiliation of Britain was sudden and complete. Unless it could be reversed, Mrs Thatcher could not expect to survive as Prime Minister.

How could such a thing have happened? The origins of the Falkland Islands dispute dated from their discovery by Europeans. A Royal Navy captain was the first person to land on the islands, in 1690, and named them after Lord Falkland, First Lord of the Admiralty. The French and then the Spanish established settlements, the latter expelling the British. When Argentina became independent of Spain in 1816, it considered itself the heir to all Spanish claims, including Las Malvinas, as they always called the islands.* In 1833, however, the British reoccupied them, and have been there ever since. Despite this, Argentina regarded the Malvinas as part of its title deeds. In a country which, in 1982, was ruled by an unpopular military oligarchy, this was the only issue guaranteed to produce emotional unity. As the 150th anniversary of British rule approached, the junta grabbed the moment to right the seeming wrong.

---

* Las Malvinas was a Spanish version of the name Les Malouines (because of a supposed resemblance to St Malo in Brittany), reflecting the fact that France had occupied the islands.

This coincided with a particularly weak British position. With only 1,800 inhabitants, 8,000 miles from Britain, and little apparent strategic significance, the islands needed economic development, but this was difficult without the help of Argentina, just 300 miles away. To the British Foreign Office, the Falklands impeded good relations with Latin America. Not long after Mrs Thatcher came into office, the Foreign Secretary, Lord Carrington, offered a solution. He resisted the idea, arising from a report by Lord Shackleton,* of a 'Fortress Falklands' policy of economic development regardless of Argentina. Instead he advocated a form of 'leaseback', by which sovereignty was ceded to Argentina in return for continuing British administration and way of life.

Mrs Thatcher's immediate reaction was hostile: 'I cannot possibly agree to the line the Foreign Secretary is proposing. Nor would it get through the H of C – let alone the Parliamentary Party.' The islanders, she wrote, 'must not be pressured into agreeing'. When the Foreign Office produced a detailed memo for the Cabinet's Overseas and Defence Committee (OD) she was even more suspicious. Alongside the statement that 'the Argentine claim is not just a matter of law but of national honour and machismo,' she commented: 'According to the Foreign Office our national honour doesn't seem to matter!?' 'Please don't deal with this before the Rhodesian issue is finished,' she added, fearing rebellion from the Tory right. When the matter returned to OD in January 1980, Carrington had managed to push his case. While concerned not to 'foreshadow a surrender of sovereignty', Mrs Thatcher agreed to 'general and exploratory' talks with Argentina. Nicholas Ridley, the relevant junior minister at the Foreign Office, duly opened channels. By August the principle of leaseback, with ninety-nine years as the probable extent of the lease, was hypothetically agreed.

At a meeting of OD on 7 November, Mrs Thatcher expressed her doubts. 'This would be very difficult: surrender of sovereignty,' Robert Armstrong noted her saying. She later recalled reacting angrily to Ridley's claim that Britain could not defend the Falklands: 'We could bomb Buenos Aires if nothing else.' 'It was just an instinctive reaction,' she added. 'It was not recorded.' What *was* recorded was her view that 'We can't afford to defend them. We are yielding to threats.' She urged Ridley to work on backbenchers and said: 'Our fallback is that we do nothing without consent of the islanders.'

---

* Lord Shackleton, son of the Antarctic explorer Ernest Shackleton, was asked by Harold Wilson's government to produce a comprehensive survey of the Falklands. His report, published in 1977, called for major new investment and development of the islands.

Consent was not forthcoming. Later that month Ridley visited the islands, but found few converts to the leaseback idea. On 2 December, in the Commons, his proposals were fiercely attacked, as Mrs Thatcher had privately predicted, by MPs on all sides for betraying the Falklanders. On 7 January 1981, the Falklands Councillors – the islands' elected representatives – gave a hostile view of leaseback and advocated a freeze to the sovereignty dispute. This provoked borderline contempt from the Foreign Office. The islanders were 'simple people and they clung to simple ideas', declared Michael Palliser. With leaseback shelved, there was impasse in the negotiations. In July, the Joint Intelligence Committee (JIC)* warned that if Argentina felt it would not get a peaceful transfer of sovereignty 'a full-scale invasion cannot be discounted'.

This uneasy situation coincided with pressures on public spending at home. That January Mrs Thatcher had appointed John Nott as Defence Secretary, instructing him to make the cuts that his predecessor, Francis Pym, had resisted. Britain's commitment to NATO meant that defence cuts had to be found outside of Europe. One victim was the ice patrol ship HMS *Endurance*, the only Royal Navy vessel regularly in service in the South Atlantic. Its withdrawal, for 1982, was announced in June. The Foreign Office objected, but Mrs Thatcher had little sympathy. As late as March 1982 she told Richard Luce, who had replaced Nicholas Ridley at the Foreign Office, that '*Endurance* was no good; it just went "pop, pop, pop".' By sentencing *Endurance* to death Britain had signalled a lack of will to defend the islands.

Early in December 1981, a new junta had grabbed power in Argentina, led by General Leopoldo Galtieri. It quickly seized upon the Malvinas issue. In early March 1982, Argentina broke off talks with Britain, insisting on prompt British recognition of Argentine sovereignty. On the telegram from the British Embassy in Buenos Aires reporting this Mrs Thatcher wrote, 'We must make contingency plans.' As Lawrence Freedman puts it in his official history of the Falklands War, Mrs Thatcher's request 'does not appear to have reached any part of the intelligence community'.

The prevailing view remained that Argentina would not actually attack the Falklands. The Reagan administration had established better relations with Argentina – a fact which emboldened the junta. On 12 March, Thomas Enders, the Assistant Secretary of State for Inter-American Affairs, assured

---

* The JIC is the Whitehall body responsible for directing the national intelligence organizations on behalf of the Cabinet.

the British that Argentina was not contemplating 'anything drastic'.* On 19 March, Anthony Williams, British Ambassador in Buenos Aires, wrote to Luce dismissing the idea of an Argentine attack: 'we know the current team to be much too intelligent to do anything so silly'. In fact, Argentina's 'current team' was about to do something very silly indeed.

On 18 March 1982, Argentine scrap metal dealers had landed on the British dependency of South Georgia, governed from the Falklands Islands, and raised the Argentine flag. Rex Hunt, the Governor, ordered them to leave. On 21 March the condemned but still functioning *Endurance* was despatched for South Georgia, with the strong agreement of Mrs Thatcher. While Richard Luce promised 'firm action', Tory backbenchers were suspicious, even of Mrs Thatcher. When Alan Clark, the maverick MP on the right, told colleagues that she would surely sympathize with those, including himself, who 'think Imperially', Nick Budgen replied: 'Don't bet on that, Alan. She is governed only by what the Americans want. At heart she is just a vulgar, middle-class Reaganite.'

On 25 March, at Cabinet the Lord Chancellor, Lord Hailsham, pressed for robust action: 'We said we're going to remove them.' But Carrington shied away: 'No – that they must go.' The meeting concluded that 'if the Argentines thereafter threatened military action, Britain would face an almost impossible task in seeking to defend the Islands at such long range'. The next day, unknown to Mrs Thatcher, the junta ordered the invasion of the Falklands to proceed. That same day, the Ministry of Defence presented her with hastily prepared contingency plans. Deterring Argentine aggression would require a substantial Royal Navy flotilla. While sufficient to ward off any invasion, 'if faced with Argentine occupation on arrival there would be no certainty that such a force would be able to *retake* the dependency'. 'You can imagine that turned a knife in my heart,' Mrs Thatcher later recalled. Her great concern was that to take such action would provoke the very thing that she was trying to forestall, i.e. an invasion, which would then become a fait accompli. She rejected the plan. Instead, on 29 March, she and Carrington agreed to send a submarine to the South Atlantic. Carrington then left for a planned visit to Israel. Neither he nor

---

* There is no evidence that Enders or anyone else associated with the Reagan administration had any advance knowledge of the Argentine invasion, but some close to Mrs Thatcher saw connections nonetheless. 'It is hard not to believe that some Argentinean Generals let their US counterpart have some inkling as to what was being planned in March,' Hugh Thomas wrote to her later in April. 'Surely Dr Costa Méndez must have winked, at least, at Assistant Secretary of State Enders, after the latter's recent visit to Buenos Aires.' Reviewing the letter with felt pen in hand, Mrs Thatcher scored no fewer than four lines under 'Enders'.

Mrs Thatcher thought Argentina was about to invade. In the Commons the following day, Luce said that, if an invasion came, Britain would defend the Falklands 'to the best of our ability': 'I knew deep down how dangerously empty these words had become.'*

It was not until the early evening of Wednesday 31 March 1982 that an intercept provided London with 'the first clear indication' that Argentina would invade the Falklands on Friday. This news broke with Whitehall surprisingly empty. Carrington was in Israel. The Chief of the Defence Staff (CDS), Admiral Sir Terence Lewin, the Chief of the General Staff, General Sir Edwin Bramall, and the Commander-in-Chief Fleet, Admiral Sir John Fieldhouse, were all overseas. These absences may have added to the confusion, but from Mrs Thatcher's vantage point they may also have made a positive difference in what now transpired.

Mrs Thatcher was in her room in the Commons in the early evening with Richard Luce and officials when John Nott brought her the intelligence report of the invasion. She later described Nott's announcement as 'the worst ... moment of my life'. The atmosphere in the room was gloomy and confused. The priority was drafting an urgent message asking President Reagan to intervene. The sense of impotence left Mrs Thatcher disheartened. Nott said he thought recapture all but impossible. Doubts about the chance of recapture were also held by some service chiefs, notably Bramall, so the balance of expert knowledge was against her. John Coles, her foreign affairs private secretary, recalled the exchange between Defence Secretary and Prime Minister: 'Mrs Thatcher: "You'll have to take them back." Nott: "We can't." Mrs Thatcher: "You'll have to."' She had the will, but not yet the way.

Another man who had received the intelligence report was Henry Leach, the First Sea Lord, who now sought out Nott in the Commons. When he reached the Prime Minister's office he found 'an aura of complete gloom. No one was talking. They were patently floundering.' Both Leach and Mrs Thatcher, who was always impressed by a uniform, were conscious that he was the only serviceman in the room. It was the admiral, not the Prime Minister, who took the initiative. Leach asked for political clearance to assemble a task force. As he remembered it, 'No one uttered a word.' 'What does that mean?' she asked eventually. He explained, and pointed out that

---

* The government was embarrassed, in the questions on Luce's statement, when Jim Callaghan revealed to the House that in 1977, when there had been some trouble with Argentina, he had ordered British ships to stand 400 miles off the Falklands, ready to protect them if necessary. It has subsequently emerged that Argentina did not know of this action at the time, so Callaghan's revelation held no lessons about deterrence, but the House did not know this.

everything was in short supply, but not impossibly so. Recent defence cuts went unmentioned, but the consciousness of these was palpable. This gave Leach the moral advantage. 'How long will it take to assemble the Task Force?' asked Mrs Thatcher. 'Three days,' said Leach. 'How long to get there?' 'Three weeks.' 'Three weeks!' exclaimed the Prime Minister, innocent of geography and of the sea. 'Surely you mean three days.' 'No, I don't.'

'Can we do it?' asked Mrs Thatcher with piercing urgency. 'We can, Prime Minister,' said Leach, 'and, though it is not my place to say this, we must.' 'Why do you say that?' 'Because if we don't do it, if we pussyfoot . . . we'll be living in a totally different country whose word will count for little.' At this, Leach remembered, she gave a sort of half-smile, as if it was what she had wanted to hear. By the time he left the meeting, Leach had full authority to assemble the Task Force.

The meeting of 31 March has acquired mythical status in the history of the Falklands War, and rightly so. Leach gave Mrs Thatcher 'tremendous heart', according to Clive Whitmore, and it was heart that she needed most. Diplomacy was in ruins; defeat, in the imminent invasion, was certain. Her country's honour, her government and her career might all be lost in a matter of days. Her instincts told her to fight, but she could not do so in defiance of all expert advice. Leach gave her the countervailing expertise she needed.

The next morning, Thursday, April Fools' Day, the Cabinet met and wrung its hands. Mrs Thatcher was disappointed by a 'very flabby reply' from US Secretary of State Al Haig to Carrington's request for help. Much rested therefore on the results of her own appeal to Reagan. Difficulties with America soon became a recurring theme. They caused neuralgia in Whitehall because of the collective memory of the disaster in 1956 when the United States had decided not to support the Anglo-French occupation of the Suez Canal. The result had been the fall of Anthony Eden, the Prime Minister, and the end of Britain's standing as an imperial power. On this day, however, President Reagan did his best. He rang the Argentine President, but Galtieri at first refused to take the call. When they did speak, later that evening, Galtieri rejected the President's good offices. After he refused to give an assurance that there would be no landing the next day, Reagan warned that Mrs Thatcher would retake the islands by force and that, if she did so, the USA would back her. After Nicko Henderson, the British Ambassador in Washington, was informed of this unsuccessful conversation he called the Prime Minister. Waking her up at 4 a.m., he found her 'not at all in a bellicose mood, but in a very sombre one, understanding full well the dangers that lay ahead'.

In the morning of 2 April, the Cabinet was told that the invasion was imminent and was bound to succeed. Mrs Thatcher explained the plans for the Task Force and said the government could announce that 'we have put people on immediate notice to sail'. Geoffrey Howe thought this a bad idea because it would 'give [the] impression that we are in a position to reverse or reconquer. We ought to convey the opposite impression.' Nigel Lawson, however, thought that people would be passionately engaged: 'Public opinion won't regard this as a faraway island.'

Once the invasion was a known fact, the Cabinet met for a second time. They now faced a crucial decision. As Mrs Thatcher put it: 'We have to decide whether to tell the fleet to sail, and say so in the House tomorrow.' (It had been agreed that, as had not happened since the Suez crisis, the House should sit on a Saturday.) Carrington said: 'I rather doubt whether our speeches are credible if we don't tell the force to sail.' Mrs Thatcher asked the opinion of each Cabinet minister in turn. Only one, John Biffen – 'a little runt of a man' in the view of Henry Leach – was brave enough to say he was against the despatch of the Task Force.

As Luce admitted, this proved 'a very bad day for the Foreign Office'. A memorandum written by the Foreign Office's John Weston left Mrs Thatcher furious. Pessimistic about securing allies to retake the Falklands, it declared that even if Britain got the islands back they would be difficult to hold. Anyway, it went on, 'Unless the 1,800 islanders were manifestly being subjected to inhumane treatment by Argentine occupying forces, it would be hard to persuade people that the game was worth the candle.' As Mrs Thatcher put it in her memoirs, such Foreign Office advice 'summed up the flexibility of principle characteristic of that department'. The draft it supplied for her Commons speech on Saturday fared little better. So appalled was she that she had Coles and Whitmore rewrite it overnight. In drafting the aims of the Task Force, they settled upon calling for the 'restoration of British administration'.* Mrs Thatcher was under great strain. At one point she realized that all the GMT hours in the draft had been wrongly computed against Argentine time. 'She almost visibly collapsed,' remembered John Coles, 'Whitmore calmed her down beautifully.'

In a broadcast to the Argentine people that night, General Galtieri explained that the British 'lack of goodwill' in negotiations had made the invasion necessary.† 'Glory to the great Argentine people,' he exclaimed.

---

* At first they proposed the restoration of 'British sovereignty', but decided it was more accurate (since sovereignty had not been removed by the invasion) to use the phrase 'British administration'.
† From Argentina's point of view, it must indeed have seemed that negotiations in which the British always happily held out the possibility of conceding sovereignty and yet never did so were a dishonest game.

'May this be God's will.' In letting the invasion build up, Britain had failed to understand the mentality of a military dictatorship. But Argentina had made the greater error: it did not understand the powerful interaction between the sympathy due to the islanders, who saw themselves as British, and the power of the British Parliament when roused.

Parliament met on Saturday 3 April 1982 in a state of high emotion, stirred up by a furious press. Carrington and others were right that the government could not survive the wrath of MPs if it were not able to announce that the fleet would be ready to sail on Monday. Mrs Thatcher opened the debate. Alan Clark recorded that she spoke at first 'very slowly but didactically' but later, when being barracked, 'She changed gear and gabbled.' She was not derailed, but failed to rouse her own benches. Her position, however, was clear: 'I must tell the House that the Falkland Islands and their dependencies remain British territory. No aggression and no invasion can alter that simple fact. It is the Government's objective to see that the islands are freed from occupation and are returned to British administration at the earliest possible moment.' These words bound her from the beginning, as she intended they should.

The Labour leader, Michael Foot, attacked the government's unpreparedness but accepted the Task Force. It was Enoch Powell, understanding Mrs Thatcher's mentality, who issued the most arresting challenge. She was known as 'the Iron Lady', he said. 'In the next week or two this House, the nation and the right honourable Lady herself will learn of what metal she is made.' In his diary, Alan Clark noted 'how low she held her head, how *knotted* with pain and apprehension she seemed as he [Powell] pronounced his famous judgment'. It was this sense of being put to the test, by Parliament, nation and her own conscience, which stuck with her.

John Nott, who wound up for the government, delivered what Mrs Thatcher recalled as a 'lousy speech', in which he attacked Labour as part of his self-justification. This party politics went down very badly. Both Nott and Carrington then had to appear before an impromptu meeting of the 1922 Committee proposed by the Chief Whip, Michael Jopling. Jopling remembered the backbenchers 'baying for blood'. Ian Gow scribbled Mrs Thatcher a note of proceedings. His written record slips into capital letters at moments of high stress:

PACKED MEETING.
<u>Buck</u>. MOST DISTURBING. MOST WORRYING ... <u>Hogg</u>. MUST RECOVER SOVEREIGNTY. Unless we do Party will not hold loyalty ... <u>Stokes</u>. Working men appalled at what has happened ... smell of

appeasement about the FO ... <u>Waller</u>. They should resign. <u>Colvin</u>. NO RESIGNATIONS NOW ... <u>Lord Onslow</u>. SINK THE WHOLE FLEET. <u>Aitken</u>. DECLARE WAR AS FLEET SAILS. *

Carrington, never easy with the parliamentary party, was badly shaken. So was Nott. Both edged towards resignation.† On Sunday, rumours spread of a hostile leading article planned for *The Times* the following morning. With the Foreign Office having failed either to foresee or to avert the invasion, there was a sense that Carrington must fall on his sword. Mrs Thatcher, however, was most reluctant to see him go. Apart from anything else, she felt exposed.

On Monday morning, with *The Times* just as tough as rumoured, Carrington resigned. Luce and Humphrey Atkins followed.‡ John Nott begged to be allowed to go too. Mrs Thatcher refused, saying she 'could not possibly accept when the Task Force was on the ocean'. The true reason, however, was political: she feared that losing the only remaining Cabinet minister involved in the debacle would leave her own position vulnerable.

When Carrington saw Mrs Thatcher to tell her his decision, he recalled she 'behaved with the greatest possible kindness' and explained she would replace him with Francis Pym. 'Margaret, you mustn't do that,' said Carrington. 'You hate him. It'll all end in tears.' 'I know,' she replied, 'but he's the only one with the experience.' This was true enough.§ The additional – and most unwelcome – reason why Mrs Thatcher felt she had to promote Pym was that he was now the favourite to succeed her. Even before the Falklands crisis, she was on probation with the party. Pym had positioned himself in case 'anything should happen to her'. He could not now be overlooked for promotion. Nonetheless, Carrington was right about their personal relationship. With his hunched, anxious demeanour, Pym held

---

* By no means all Conservative MPs were as robust as those who spoke up at the 1922 meeting. Three days later, Jopling drew up a report of backbenchers' attitudes. It mentioned several, including Julian Critchley and Chris Patten, who felt that an attempt at recapture was too dangerous ('the military difficulties are insurmountable'), Ian Gilmour, who said, 'It will make Suez look like common sense', and Kenneth Clarke, whose view was summarized as 'Hopes nobody thinks we are going to fight the Argentinians. We should blow up a few ships but nothing more.'
† That weekend, Carrington asked Lord Home what he should do. Face to face, Home tried to persuade him that he should stay, but when Carrington left the drawing room to go to the lavatory, Lady Home met him in the passage and told him: 'Alec says if he were in your position, he wouldn't have any hesitation about going.'
‡ As Lord Privy Seal, Atkins spoke for the Foreign Office in the Commons. This was necessary because the Foreign Secretary was a member of the House of Lords.
§ Like Carrington, and Willie Whitelaw, Pym had won the MC in the Second World War. As Leader of the House, and a former Chief Whip, he could bring to this new job a deep knowledge of the Commons from which Carrington had been absolutely disqualified.

little appeal for Mrs Thatcher. He was one of those men, quite common in his generation, who hated arguing with a woman. As Antony Acland, now Permanent Under-Secretary at the Foreign Office, recalled, he quailed when she came at him 'with her hair glued up and her eyes flashing'. Their encounters were 'slightly like the Mad Hatter's tea party. There she was opposite and Francis was the dormouse, who had snuck into the tea party and was getting smaller and smaller and smaller.'*

That afternoon, the leaders of the Tory tribe attended the memorial service of R. A. Butler in St Margaret's, Westminster. Combined with Carrington's resignation, it provided the funeral rites for a certain sort of whiggish Conservatism. Butler had spoken of politics as 'the art of the possible'. Now, both in her economic policies and in the Falklands crisis, Mrs Thatcher was attempting the art of the impossible.

That day, and the next, with bands playing and families weeping, the initial Task Force set sail from Portsmouth, led by the aircraft carriers *Invincible* and *Hermes*.† Among those on board *Invincible* was the Queen's second son, Prince Andrew, a helicopter pilot. Fearing hostage-taking and political problems, Mrs Thatcher had opposed his participation, but the Palace insisted he go. It was to an earlier queen that she turned for inspiration as the fleet sailed. Asked whether she would resign if the enterprise failed, she replied 'Failure? Do you remember what Queen Victoria once said? "Failure – the possibilities do not exist."' As the fleet began its journey, François Mitterrand mused to his adviser Jacques Attali about Mrs Thatcher: 'Do I admire her ... or envy her?'

Although the Foreign Office had probably never been at such a low ebb, by this time one of its number had already secured the most lasting diplomatic success of the war. As soon as the invasion had become imminent, Anthony Parsons, Britain's Permanent Representative at the United Nations, had called an emergency meeting of the Security Council. He tabled a resolution condemning Argentina, even though it seemed unlikely that Britain could muster the nine votes required. Overruling his cautious officials, Luce authorized Parsons's action.

The Security Council met in the evening of Saturday 3 April. Earlier that evening, Mrs Thatcher had received a most encouraging telephone call from President Mitterrand, who told her: 'I quite realise that Britain is quite big enough to find its own solutions to this problem. But it's important you should realise that others share your opposition to this kind of aggression.'

---

* In the original, the dormouse does not, in fact, get smaller. He simply gets put into the teapot.
† The Task Force also included the assault ship *Fearless* and eleven frigates and destroyers.

His message showed the solidarity of one nation with far-flung possessions for another and gave her hope for support from the EEC. It also helped form a personal bond with the socialist French President that transcended their considerable ideological divide.* With Britain just one vote short in the Security Council, at Parsons's urging Mrs Thatcher appealed personally to King Hussein of Jordan for his country's support.† This the King promptly granted. Security Council Resolution 502 called for the 'immediate withdrawal' of Argentine forces and instructed the governments to seek 'a diplomatic solution to their differences and to respect fully the purposes and principles of the Charter of the United Nations'. These purposes and principles included Article 51, the right of self-defence, on which Britain could now rest to justify armed response. It was a triumph which, Parsons well knew, could not be improved upon, and Mrs Thatcher brandished it from then onwards to the greatest effect. Parsons was the Henry Leach of diplomacy, hurrying forward with a clear solution while others dithered. Mrs Thatcher loved him for it.

As she worked to put her government on a war footing, Mrs Thatcher sought advice. Frank Cooper, Permanent Secretary at the Ministry of Defence, advised her to avoid a situation in which the Chancellor of the Exchequer could pull the plug on financial grounds – as Harold Macmillan, then the Chancellor, had done to Eden over Suez, getting himself made Prime Minister in the process. She should replicate the successful wartime arrangements instituted by Winston Churchill. On 6 April, Harold Macmillan visited Mrs Thatcher and confirmed this. It would, he told her, be 'fatal' to mix any 'economic committee' with the 'campaign committee'. Mrs Thatcher, who had already noticed that Geoffrey Howe harped more than she liked on the need for peace, duly excluded him from the War Cabinet.‡

Known officially as the South Atlantic subcommittee to OD or OD(SA), the War Cabinet met at least once a day during the conflict. It was chaired by the Prime Minister and its members were Whitelaw, Pym, Nott and Cecil Parkinson, brought in partly to handle press relations, but also to balance a potentially defeatist axis of Whitelaw and Pym. Mrs Thatcher warned Parkinson there would be 'no room for fainthearts'. The words echoed one of her father's sermons, 'God wants no fainthearts for His ambassadors.' The War Cabinet was serviced by Armstrong and Wade-Gery and attended

---

* Jacques Attali, who acted as interpreter for the conversation, recalled that whenever Mrs Thatcher was reminded of the call in later times, tears would come into her eyes.
† Jordan being, at that time, one of the non-permanent members of the Security Council.
‡ Howe always maintained that he accepted this decision happily, but according to his private secretary, John Kerr, 'he *was* upset'.

by Lewin, the Chief of the Defence Staff, and the Attorney-General, Sir Michael Havers.

The majority of those at this most senior level had served in the armed forces. It was an important compensation to Mrs Thatcher, who, of course, had not, that Denis had fought in the Second World War. She would turn to him in the most difficult moments and he sometimes broke his self-imposed general rule and 'offered advice without being asked'. Beyond Denis, however, she had no soulmate with whom to share the burdens of war. Parkinson was loyal, but lacked relevant experience. Perhaps her closest political companion was Ian Gow. Passionately loyal and seized of the romance of the situation, he gave her great comfort, but was not in any position of command or of policy-making.* During her long-running economic battles she had worked closely with the Treasury team, but for the Falklands crisis she had nothing comparable. 'I'm jolly well realising that I need a department,' she complained later to Tony Parsons, '. . . I have to rely on third-hand hearsay and I don't like it.' While served ably by her private secretaries Clive Whitmore and John Coles, Mrs Thatcher did not run policy through them as she was later to do with Coles's successor, Charles Powell. So, in a crisis about which, she admitted to Whitmore, she knew very little, she was almost alone.

The disadvantages of her ignorance were clear. 'Couldn't we put up a smokescreen?' she suggested one day as a remedy for Argentine air attack. 'There were titters round the Cabinet Room,' Coles recalled. There were also a few 'Churchill moments' when she would suddenly propose something dramatic and impractical like the occupation of Tierra del Fuego. But on balance her lack of knowledge helped. It gave her the humility which she was often, in other matters, accused of lacking, and encouraged her to listen to colleagues with military experience.† She also turned to her naval and military commanders for moral support. She particularly admired John Fieldhouse and, above all, Lewin himself. According to Coles, Lewin 'exuded calm, confidence, experience and a charm to which she was not immune'. She came to rely on his judgement more than on anyone else's. This ensured that the needs of the armed services came

---

* Shortly after the Task Force had sailed, Gow sent Mrs Thatcher a handwritten letter about the 'loneliness of your task'. There were 'many of us', he said, 'who, whatever the future holds in store, will be forever thankful for having had the privilege of trying to help the finest chief, the most resolute and far sighted leader and the kindest and most considerate friend that any man could hope to serve'.

† Mrs Thatcher's lack of knowledge meant she was almost incapable of reading naval charts. Michael Havers, who had served in the RNVR, understood these charts well. He and she would spread them out on the floor and she would firmly point out the Falkland Islands in quite the wrong place. He would then find them for her.

first. The key to success, as Denis advised her, was, 'Get the Chiefs, give them clear objectives and then get out of the way.' According to Philip Goodhart, a junior defence minister and former soldier, 'She wouldn't have done it if she'd been a man and if she'd been in the armed forces during the war. Then she'd have been aware how dreadfully wrong everything was likely to go.'

When the War Cabinet met for the first time on Wednesday 7 April 1982 there was pressure to decide on a Maritime Exclusion Zone (MEZ) round the Falkland Islands within which Britain would have authorized itself to attack all Argentine shipping. This was resisted by Francis Pym lest it prejudice the imminent visit of the US Secretary of State, Al Haig, who hoped to find a peaceful resolution to the conflict. After long argument, Mrs Thatcher later wrote, 'eventually through patient persistence the rest of us managed to overcome Francis' objections. It was a pattern to be repeated many times.'

In the Commons that afternoon, Nott announced the 200-nautical-mile MEZ, to be imposed from midnight on 11 April, when the first submarine would be ready. In her later, private account of the conflict* Mrs Thatcher stressed that 'at <u>no time</u> during the Falklands operation did we say we would take action <u>until</u> we were in a position to do it . . . I was determined that we should never put ourselves in a position where "bluff could be called".' For the first time, the House noticed possible differences between Prime Minister and Foreign Secretary. For his part, the Shadow Foreign Secretary, Denis Healey, started to qualify Labour support for the use of force. It was becoming easier to see how the Opposition would undermine the government when things started to go wrong.

The biggest immediate problem, however, was America. As by far Britain's most important ally, the United States was essential in securing international support. The Americans were also vital logistically, partly because they used the British colony of Ascension Island in the middle of the Atlantic as a military base: Ascension was the only stopping point from which the Task Force could operate effectively. The Americans could deny or supply Britain with crucial satellite information, intelligence, technology and military hardware. Active American support was all but a necessity, and active American opposition would certainly be fatal.

Mrs Thatcher had assumed American backing would be wholehearted.

---

* Mrs Thatcher wrote her account of the war over the Easter of 1983, relying on her memory and the minutes of the War Cabinet for reference. She kept this so secret that no one, not even her private secretaries, knew about it at the time. Her motive, she said many years later, was the thought 'I'll damn well write some of this down for posterity.'

'She just felt that this was such an act of naked aggression – unprovoked and unnecessary – that there could not be any question that the Americans would take our view,' recalled Clive Whitmore. In terms of American public opinion, her instinct was correct, but she was disappointed by the reaction of the US administration. Reagan's team were deeply divided. On one hand, Jeane Kirkpatrick, America's UN Ambassador, was the most articulate believer in the Reagan administration's strategy of getting close to Latin America to resist the Communist threat there. She opposed anything that might damage relations with Argentina. On the other hand, at the Pentagon, whose world view centred on the NATO alliance, the main players were firmly pro-British. John Lehman, the Secretary of the Navy, and his boss, Caspar Weinberger, the Defense Secretary, did everything they could for Britain from the first: 'Weinberger believed very, very strongly in the Anglo-American alliance,' recalled one of his officials. 'It was clear that to him this was the bedrock of how to deal with the Soviets and ensure that the West eventually won the Cold War.'

The State Department, meanwhile, was divided between its Latin American and European departments. In terms of personal sympathy, Al Haig, the former NATO Supreme Allied Commander in Europe, was pro-British. The European camp argued that, should Mrs Thatcher not prevail, her government would fall and plans to deploy INF missiles on British soil would be in jeopardy. For all this, Haig was conscious of the danger to the United States' position in Latin America and fancied himself as an 'honest broker' between the two countries. Haig's mercurial and somewhat self-aggrandizing personality complicated matters. According to Bud McFarlane of the NSC staff, 'There were suspicions among the senior White House staff of Secretary Haig's actions being motivated in part by his political ambitions.'

Questioned by reporters on 5 April, President Reagan stressed the USA was friends with both Britain and Argentina. He sought a peaceful resolution 'with no forceful action or no bloodshed'. On 7 April, Reagan attended a meeting with all the US principals. Haig laid out his plan to shuttle between London and Buenos Aires to seek a diplomatic solution. 'There will not be a war in the South Atlantic,' he declared. According to Jim Rentschler, taking minutes, Reagan said, 'It seems to me that we have an opportunity to do some good here. The main thing we have to do is to get these two brawlers out of the bar room.' Supported by Weinberger, he authorized Haig to try his mission. The President, dressed in blue blazer and polo shirt, was ready to take off for his Easter holiday in Barbados. But Jeane Kirkpatrick cut in, urging him to 'keep our neutrality in this and not be seen to be favouring the British'. This provoked an impassioned intervention from Bobby Ray Inman, the Deputy Director of the CIA. America had to stick with 'the links of language, law, culture, mother country', insisted Inman, not to mention the 'unparalleled co-operation we have with them [the British] in every military and intelligence chapter'. Now visibly eager to go on holiday, Reagan turned to Kirkpatrick. 'Look,' he said, 'I would love to stay friends with Argentina, but I think our first loyalty, our first order of business if worst comes to worst, is to side with the Brits.' On this basis, Haig set off for London.

Before Haig arrived, Mrs Thatcher wrote, 'we made it clear [in public] that he was coming as a friend and not as a mediator,' but this was not how he saw matters. When he arrived at Downing Street on 8 April, she sought to set the mood by showing him and his party portraits of Nelson and Wellington: 'very appropriate,' Rentschler recorded her saying, 'considering the subject on our minds!' She then told Haig she had been 'rather disturbed' by Reagan's public proclamation of friendship with both countries. 'Mr Haig said that the Prime Minister would well know where the President really stood,' but he 'had to be cautious' about 'profile'. Haig then sought agreement to getting the Argentines off the islands without total loss of face: it was 'important to avoid a priori judgments about sovereignty'. Couldn't there be some sort of interim administration? Mrs Thatcher was unimpressed. Rentschler recorded the scene:

> High color is in her cheeks, a note of rising indignation in her voice, she leans across the polished table and flatly rejects what she calls the 'wooliness' of our ... face-saving ploy for Galtieri: 'I am pledged ... to restore British administration. I did not dispatch a fleet to install some nebulous arrangement which would have no authority whatsoever. Interim authority! – to do what? I beg you, I beg you to remember that in 1938 Neville Chamberlain sat at this same table discussing an arrangement which sounds very much like the one you are asking me to accept ... We in Britain simply refuse to reward aggression – that is the lesson we have learned from 1938.'

Poor Haig was rather battered, but he detected a deeper truth: 'Mrs Thatcher needed this. We – the US and Britain – needed it, to be perceived to be trying to get a peaceful solution.' Despite her irritation with Haig, she did not dissent. She knew that to retain support internationally – and domestically – a diplomatic effort was essential. As was often her way, she secretly registered the need for certain concessions while arguing flat out against them. On 11 April she was presented with the draft 'line to take' for government spokesmen. It said, 'There can be no negotiation about the future status of the Falkland Islands until the Argentine forces have withdrawn and British administration has been restored.' Despite her tough talk, she took her pen and crossed out 'and British administration has been restored'.

On leaving London for Buenos Aires, Haig cabled Reagan: 'The Prime Minister has the bit in her teeth ... She is clearly prepared to use force, though she admits a preference for a diplomatic solution. She is rigid in her insistence on a return to the status quo ante, and indeed seemingly determined that any solution involve some retribution.' He told the President that if he made progress with the Argentinians, it 'may then be necessary for me to ask you to apply unusual pressure on Thatcher'. If 'the Argentines offer very little ... it may be necessary to apply even greater pressure on the British if we are to head off hostilities'. As was often the case with Haig, however, his line was not entirely clear. In a second cable to the President, he first declared that Mrs Thatcher's principle that aggression should not pay was vital for the USA: 'That said, the consequences of hostilities would be devastating ... the Soviets might even establish a foothold in the southern cone.' So Mrs Thatcher must get her way, and yet fighting must be avoided: this did not reflect reality.

Reagan stuck to his line of seeking a peaceful solution while in the end favouring Mrs Thatcher, but he was detached, almost cynical, in his approach. On 16 April, the journalist Jack Anderson published the tape of an illicitly intercepted call in which Reagan asked Haig about a possible British attack: 'That submarine of theirs, do you think it's apt to go ahead with retribution and sink anything within the 200 miles, and would that be enough to vindicate them?' This report, which Mrs Thatcher was informed by Nicko Henderson was authentic, distressed her.

Fortunately for Mrs Thatcher, the Haig party, inhospitably received, had a miserable time in Buenos Aires. Haig cabled Reagan that, after 'nearly twelve hours of gruelling and emotion-filled talks' with Galtieri and the Foreign Minister, Nicanor Costa Méndez, he had extracted a new formulation he thought worth taking to London. As he left Buenos Aires, however, Haig was handed a paper by Costa Méndez which retreated from earlier concessions. Because Costa Méndez called these his 'personal thoughts', Haig put them aside and continued to London.

On the morning of 12 April, Haig told Mrs Thatcher that Galtieri had warned him that Cuba had offered Argentina all possible help 'with the full support of the Soviet Union' and that the Soviets were prepared to sink British vessels. He then served up the first of many versions of essentially the same dish. His seven points included mutual withdrawal of troops, a US-UK-Argentine 'commission' and the restoration of 'traditional local administration', but with Argentine representation and no return of the British Governor; a final settlement would have to be achieved by 31 December that year.

The War Cabinet was not disposed to reject the proposals out of hand. The problem, however, as Mrs Thatcher recorded, was that 'Galtieri wanted the Task Force to turn back the moment an agreement was signed.' This she could not accept, although she conceded that the Task Force might move more slowly. She even agreed to drop the word 'interim' when referring to the proposed joint administration, seeing the point of the vagueness to which she was constitutionally averse. She accepted that 'it might be worth making big concessions if Argentine withdrawal could be guaranteed'.

That morning, however, everything changed. Argentina suddenly insisted that the 'personal thoughts' which Costa Méndez had handed Haig were the official Argentine position. Earlier concessions were off the table. 'What a sad thing!' Mrs Thatcher told Haig. As she later recalled: 'The condition for withdrawal was that they keep the spoils of invasion.'

Al Haig was, Mrs Thatcher said, 'very depressed'. She could now have insisted there was nothing left to talk about, and all negotiations should therefore end. She did not do so. She realized that less friendly actors might seek to step into Haig's shoes and remained acutely aware of the demands of public opinion. Haig agreed to continue his efforts.

Mrs Thatcher was impressed by the level of international support accumulated since the invasion. First, covertly, had come Chile, whose own dispute with Argentina over the Beagle Channel had made it hypersensitive to Argentine aggression.* Most Commonwealth countries, notably those of the Old Commonwealth, also fell in quickly behind Britain. On 10 April, the EEC had voted to impose a total four-week ban on Argentine imports. Pleasantly surprised, Mrs Thatcher was conscious this goodwill should not be presumed upon. At home, she came to understand that continuing the diplomatic process until the Task Force reached its destination would placate her party's 'wetter' members, and disable the Opposition, without enraging her natural supporters. John Nott summed up the emerging role of Haig: he was 'polite, charming, a frightful nuisance, but he filled this great long vacuum'.

On 14 April, it became clear just how annoying, from the British point of view, Haig could be. The *Washington Post*, under the front-page headline 'US Aiding British Fleet in Atlantic', reported the extent of US assistance.

---

* Even before the invasion was complete, Chile had offered Britain the use of its ports. From then on, intelligence and logistical cooperation was constant. By 6 April it had offered the services of its air force and navy, authorized by the dictator, General Augusto Pinochet.

After Argentina threatened to break off negotiations, Haig rang Mrs Thatcher. He proposed to put out a statement denying the story and saying that there would be no help to Britain 'beyond the customary patterns of co-operation . . . British use of facilities on the UK island of Ascension has been restricted accordingly.' She was furious. 'What I'm saying, Al, is for Pete's sake, get that use of Ascension Island out of your statement, because it's our island and we can't exactly invade our island.' 'Of course not,' said Haig meekly, 'I will take that out.'

Mrs Thatcher was only partially aware of how true the story in the *Washington Post* was. Almost from the first day, through the good offices of the Pentagon, the United States had been providing secret assistance to Britain. Weinberger, confident in Reagan's tacit support, acted at first without telling the President directly. When, days into the crisis, Weinberger raised the issue, Reagan's response was simple: 'Give Maggie everything she needs to get on with it.' Weinberger happily complied.* He would soon become one of Mrs Thatcher's lifelong heroes.

On 15 April, Al Haig returned to Buenos Aires, where he found the Argentinians in no mood to compromise. Indeed, the proposals he extracted offered so little promise that he saw no point in heading once more to London and so returned, instead, to Washington. The War Cabinet, realizing Britain could not be blamed, swiftly rejected the text which Haig had passed on, believing that this long game was now over. Exhausted though he was, however, Haig was not yet finished. He now invited Pym to Washington on 22–23 April for a final round of discussion. Mrs Thatcher was uneasy, but the War Cabinet agreed that Pym should go, bearing counter-proposals to those last offered by Argentina, which Britain had already rejected.

While Haig flew back and forth, the Task Force moved steadily onwards. The War Cabinet increasingly concerned itself with the military reality. On 15 April, the 'window' of two to three weeks in May, when a landing 'without terrible casualties' would be possible, was emphasized. Mrs Thatcher recalled that her political colleagues appeared 'somewhat stunned'. 'I remember saying everyone must look confident as they left.' The following

---

* According to the Pentagon's Dov Zakheim, 'Weinberger wanted to ensure that Britain had whatever it needed . . . He wanted to know what had happened to each request.' Britain also benefited from the endeavours of the US National Security Agency (NSA), who had broken the code for Argentina's military communication. As Jim Rentschler recalled, 'they were able to pass the data to the British in real time, so they got it even before those in the Falklands. It then leaked out that this was happening so the Argentines changed the code. But the NSA broke it again in just twenty-four hours.'

day, the War Cabinet was asked to agree the repossession of South Georgia and associated Rules of Engagement (ROE).* Mrs Thatcher pushed the idea: while not a military necessity, retaking South Georgia would right the wrong of the first Argentine aggression and demonstrate serious intent. On 19 April the War Cabinet decided that, regardless of the Haig process, the attack on South Georgia should proceed.

When Haig was informed of this hugely secret plan, to Britain's dismay he declared that, to avoid the charge of UK-US collusion, he would have to give Argentina advance notice. Nicko Henderson managed to dissuade him, but Haig warned he would publicly criticize Britain for using force. It was against this tense background that Pym flew into Washington.

On the morning of Saturday 24 April, Pym returned blearily to London. In her own account Mrs Thatcher wrote: 'This was one of the most crucial days in the Falklands story and a critical one for me personally.' Pym came bearing new proposals from Haig. In her view, this plan 'was a complete sell-out'. It would, she wrote on the master copy, create 'Merger [of the Falklands] with Argentina' and, by mentioning only 'due regard for the rights of the islanders' rather than the paramountcy of their wishes, it would have 'signed away all possibility of [their] staying with us'. As she recalled: 'I repeated to Francis that we could not accept [Haig's terms]. He said he thought we should accept them. We were at loggerheads.'

The War Cabinet was due to meet at 6.15 that night. Despite her objections, Mrs Thatcher recalled, Pym submitted a paper 'recommending acceptance of the Haig terms ... A former Defence Secretary and present Foreign Secretary of Britain recommended peace at that price. Had it gone through the committee I could not have stayed.' To bolster her position, she spoke to Whitelaw beforehand: 'As always, he backed my judgement.' At the meeting Pym presented his case, then Mrs Thatcher, who had spent the day in meticulous preparation, went through 'clause by clause' comparing draft with draft. She got the support of most in the room. Rather than outvote Pym, John Nott suggested a procedural way forward. Instead of commenting on the draft, they would have Haig put it first to the Argentinians. The War Cabinet recognized this as risky but considered it 'virtually impossible' that Argentina would agree to withdraw. Once Buenos Aires rejected the Haig proposal, the United States would have to come down on

---

* The War Cabinet also debated whether Britain should bomb enemy aircraft on the Argentine mainland. The OD(SA) minutes record: 'Although there was in reality no intention of attacking the Argentine mainland, there might be some military advantage in the Argentinians being afraid of that.'

Britain's side. As Mrs Thatcher put it in her private memoir: 'So the crisis passed, the crisis of Britain's honour.'*

Why, exactly, was Mrs Thatcher so beside herself about the text which Francis Pym brought back from Washington? In her memoirs she makes much of differences between it and earlier plans. Most importantly, the text effectively ruled out a return to the *status quo ante*. She was bound to be dissatisfied. But she had made concessions in the past and – as will be seen – in future negotiations she would countenance concessions just as damaging as those proposed by Pym. The contents of the Haig-Pym plan do not fully explain the intensity of her reaction.

Part of the explanation is surely that the agreement was concluded by the Foreign Secretary alone, and abroad. In general, as with the negotiations over the EEC budget, she tended to become jumpy when a minister went abroad on his own on an important mission. The prospect of Pym agreeing a plan with the unreliable Haig would have seemed particularly toxic. She was frightened that a political rival would return with a 'peace' deal which would ditch her, lose the Falklands and gain him her job.

But there was an even stronger reason for Mrs Thatcher's high emotion. On Thursday 22 April, Lewin and Nott had brought her disturbing news. In appalling weather, two British helicopters had crashed while attempting to rescue Special Forces trapped on a glacier in South Georgia. Lewin and Nott did not know whether lives – as many as seventeen were at stake – had been lost. At this, Mrs Thatcher wept. Clive Whitmore said to her quietly, 'There's going to be a lot more of this.' 'My heart was heavy,' she remembered. '. . . Was the task that we had set ourselves impossible.' She went on: 'Just as I reached the bottom of the staircase Clive came rushing out of the office.' A third helicopter had managed to save all the men: 'I went out walking on air. Nothing else in the world mattered – the men <u>were safe</u>.'

Years later, Mrs Thatcher described the day of the South Georgia rescue as 'one of the most terrifying I can remember'. This was her first experience of sending men into situations in which they might die. Her natural, maternal human sympathy and her ardour for British servicemen's welfare made her acutely sensitive to this. She was also conscious of political danger: if the first bold strike, urged on by her, had ended in fiasco and tragedy, how long would public support last? Two days later, with this overcome, but

---

* Mrs Thatcher chose not to quote this powerful phrase in her published memoir. It was typical of her caution that, when writing her memoirs, she needed a good deal of persuasion to include an explicit account of this dramatic day. She worried that she might be unfair to Pym, even that she might be libelling him. She was also in a constant state of anxiety about revealing private conversations such as these.

South Georgia not yet retaken, Mrs Thatcher was naturally impatient with the demands of diplomacy. The idea that the government might nullify the efforts of British troops even as they were going in to recapture a British possession took on a peculiar horror in her mind. She had given instructions that the War Cabinet should not be fully informed of the near-disaster in South Georgia: while these emotions seethed within her, their cause was unknown to Francis Pym.

In the afternoon of Sunday 25 April, Mrs Thatcher was informed that British forces had regained South Georgia, capturing the Argentine submarine *Santa Fe*. That evening she saw the Queen at Windsor: 'It was so wonderful to be able personally to give her the news that one of her islands had been restored to her.' Back in Downing Street, Prime Minister and Defence Secretary emerged together and Nott made a statement. He read out the message from the victorious HMS *Antrim*: 'Be pleased to inform Her Majesty that the White Ensign flies alongside the Union Flag in Grytviken South Georgia. God Save The Queen.' The press tried to get a reaction from Nott. Mrs Thatcher intervened: 'Just rejoice at that news and congratulate our forces and the Marines.' 'Are we going to war with Argentina, Mrs Thatcher?' asked a reporter. By this time, she and Nott were turning back towards the front door. 'Rejoice,' she said again, and passed through the door. Her words were represented as triumphalist. Denis Healey later described Mrs Thatcher as 'glorying in slaughter'. In fact, South Georgia had been recaptured without loss of life on either side and this, she considered, merited rejoicing. Besides, fortune, which on Thursday had seemed so doubtful, had now favoured the British cause: 'It had indeed been an eventful weekend. One went from near despair to confident reassurance.'

The retaking of South Georgia naturally strengthened Mrs Thatcher's position. She had championed it, against military doubts. Now, through courage, skill and a good deal of luck, British forces had prevailed. An opinion poll for the *Economist* showed a rise in public satisfaction with the government's handling of the situation from 60 per cent to 76 per cent. Henceforth the military impetus became ever harder to stop. The War Cabinet agreed a Total Exclusion Zone (TEZ) round the Falklands, including aircraft as well as ships. The aim was to legitimize all attacks which British forces might wish to carry out and to impose a blockade.

But military advance also made the handling of negotiations even more delicate. On *Panorama*, Mrs Thatcher pointed out that the timing of negotiations was tight because 'I have to keep in mind the interests of our boys.' As the Haig mission faltered, Michael Foot started to make great play with the possible peace-making intervention of the new United Nations Secretary-General, Javier Pérez de Cuéllar. She leant ever more clearly the other way: 'I had to say in the House over and over again that no military steps were being held up because of negotiations. And they never were.' This was not always strictly true,* but Mrs Thatcher did increasingly regard negotiation as a delaying tactic contrary to Britain's interests.

The recapture of South Georgia had naturally enraged the Argentines. Despite the demand for a definitive answer to Haig's proposals by midnight on 27 April, none was forthcoming. When the full Cabinet met on the morning of 29 April, Haig was still permitting Argentine delay. The Cabinet was very unhappy. Hailsham argued that 'US have to understand that they are in danger of undermining US–UK relationship ... they are playing along just as they did at Suez.' Nott urged the Cabinet to leave the ball in Argentina's court. The Cabinet agreed that the Prime Minister, without formally rejecting the proposals, should tell the President that they were unacceptable, and that Argentina's failure to reply by the deadline amounted to a rejection.

Mrs Thatcher wrote to Reagan accordingly. She also reminded him of his administration's promise of public support for Britain: 'I cannot conceal from you how deeply let down I and my colleagues would feel if under these circumstances the US were not now to give us its full support.' Aware of the state of opinion at home† and concerned about growing hostility to the United States in Britain, Reagan decided to keep his promise. On 29 April, having finally received Argentina's rejection of Haig's plan, he wrote to Mrs Thatcher confirming that the USA would side with Britain: 'We will leave no doubt that Her Majesty's Government worked with us in good faith and was left with no choice but to proceed with military action based on the right of self-defence.'

In her manuscript account she wrote: 'The President, Al Haig and we believe Mr Weinberger were magnificent ... From then on he, Haig and Weinberger couldn't do enough for us.' What was lost in the retelling was the rest of Reagan's letter, in which he said it was 'as important as ever that we preserve the ground for a negotiated solution' and reminded her of the need to find a 'mutually acceptable framework for peace'. Here was a clear signal that American support did not automatically endorse British

---

* There were also earlier examples of actions not taken because of the pressure of diplomacy. According to Admiral Sir Henry Leach, a request to sink the Argentine carrier, the *25 de Mayo*, was refused because it would have interfered with the progress of the Haig shuttle.

† That day, 29 April, the Senate passed by seventy-nine votes to one (the one being Jesse Helms) a resolution calling for the implementation of Resolution 502 'to achieve full withdrawal of Argentine forces from the Falkland Islands'.

use of force. This was unwelcome to Mrs Thatcher. She tried to exclude it from her mind and, later, from her memory.

The next day, Haig announced the cautious tilt towards Britain, which included materiel support and economic measures against Argentina, such as the suspension of all military exports. US sanctions on Argentina were less harsh than those imposed by the EEC. Even now, Reagan implied a certain disdain for the whole business: 'we must remember that the aggression was on the part of Argentina', the President told reporters, 'in this dispute over the sovereignty of that little ice-cold bunch of land down there'. On 2 May he sent a message to South and Central American leaders sympathetic to the Argentine cause: 'no American believes that colonisation by any European power is to be accepted in this hemisphere'. This made Mrs Thatcher so angry that when the American Ambassador came to lunch at Chequers the following weekend, she tore out part of the telegram she had received reporting Reagan's message and thrust it into his hand.

She was nonetheless immensely relieved by the Argentine rejection and the consequent American shift. As Cecil Parkinson remembered: 'She said, "I will never, ever, ever take a chance like that again ... if the Argentinians had said yes we would have been in one hell of a mess." It was a gamble and it worked.' As it turned out, Mrs Thatcher would take some other, equally big chances in the weeks ahead.

On Friday 30 April, Mrs Thatcher addressed a huge crowd in Mid Bedfordshire. Her speech was imperial in tone. She invoked her beloved Kipling and spoke of 'might, right and majesty'. She praised the British monarchy and declared, 'We still have the right, and we're not half bad when it comes to the might either.' Citing Dean Acheson's endlessly repeated quotation that Britain had lost an empire and not found a role, she declared: 'I believe Britain has now found a role. It is in upholding international law and teaching the nations of the world how to live.' These were large, almost hubristic claims to make,* but they fitted the mood of her audience and her own inner feelings: 'It was a very emotional time,' she later wrote, 'Britain was being tested ... yet no one had any doubt we could ... win through. The responsibilities on one's shoulders were enormous.' The same night, Britain attacked the Falklands for the first time. A Vulcan bomber bombed the runway at Port Stanley, while the Royal Navy despatched nine Sea Harriers to attack other targets. In a broadcast which became an

---

* Perhaps sensing this, General Galtieri broadcast to his nation the following day, speaking of 'the British empire' and, paying an unintended compliment, complaining of 'the unspeakable boldness of the invader'.

emblem of both accurate war reporting and good news, the BBC's Brian Hanrahan reported: 'I counted them all out and I counted them all back.' All returned safely to base. The knowledge that British aircraft could reach the Falklands was of immense propaganda and military importance.

During the night of 1–2 May, intercepts picked up Argentine naval plans. The Task Force Commander, Rear Admiral John 'Sandy' Woodward, on board the carrier *Hermes*, was alarmed. He knew that an Argentine group led by Argentina's only aircraft carrier, the 25 *de Mayo*, was seeking to attack the British fleet, and he feared that the *Belgrano*, a light cruiser, was leading a pincer movement to effect this. It was a given that the loss of the two British carriers – perhaps the loss of only one – would deprive the Task Force of the necessary air-cover and prove fatal to the British cause. On 30 April, the War Cabinet had changed the ROE to allow the Task Force to attack the Argentine carrier even if outside the TEZ. To date, however, it had evaded detection. The *Belgrano*, on the other hand, was being successfully shadowed by the submarine *Conqueror*. Under the existing ROE, so long as the cruiser stayed just outside the TEZ, she would remain safe from attack. Frustrated that he could do no more to thwart the impending Argentine pincer movement, Woodward escalated the issue: the Chiefs of Staff agreed to ask the War Cabinet to extend the altered ROE to all Argentine ships, submarines and auxiliaries outside the TEZ.

On the morning of Sunday 2 May, Lewin and Fieldhouse brought this urgent request to Mrs Thatcher at Chequers. She quickly assembled all those members of the War Cabinet on hand – including Whitelaw, Nott, Parkinson, Havers and Antony Acland (Francis Pym was in Washington), as well as the two admirals – in the small white drawing room. Clive Whitmore remembered that 'the issues were presented in stark and simple terms'. As always, Mrs Thatcher was very careful about legality but there was no dissent. The *Belgrano* was considered a threat. It was agreed that the ROE should be extended, with the general purpose of allowing the British fleet the freedom of action which the Argentines had given themselves, and the specific and immediate purpose of allowing *Conqueror* to attack the *Belgrano*.

That night, at 1857Z (the 'Z' denotes GMT), *Conqueror* torpedoed the *Belgrano*. The submarine withdrew quickly, evading counter-attacks. The remaining Argentine vessels were deliberately left unmolested,* but made

---

* The British decision not to attack the Argentine destroyers after hitting the *Belgrano* annoyed Admiral Woodward: 'each of them is likely to return with four Exocet,' he cabled to Fieldhouse. '. . . I request early political recognition that there is a war going on down here.'

1 (*Left*) 'I just owe almost everything to my father': Margaret with her father, Alfred Roberts, *c.* 1927.

2 (*Above*) Beatrice Stephenson as a young woman. 'After I was fifteen we had nothing more to say to each other', Margaret remembered sorrowfully.

3 The family grocery shop, North Parade, Grantham. 'If you get it from Roberts's ... you get – THE BEST'.

4 The girls who matriculated at Somerville College, Oxford, in 1943. Margaret Roberts is third from left, back row.

5 Tony Bray in the uniform of the 5th Royal Inniskilling Dragoon Guards, probably in 1946: 'a cavalry regiment, green trousers, all the rest of it'.

6 (*Above left*) Margaret the scientist, working for J. Lyons, the food company. This picture was published at the beginning of the 1950 general election campaign: she was the youngest candidate for any party.

7 (*Above right*) Margaret's first ever election address in Dartford, 1950. She cut the Labour majority by 6,000.

8 (*Above left*) Robert Henderson outside Buckingham Palace after being invested with the CBE in 1947 for his services to medicine. 'I think we are both getting very fond of each other,' Margaret wrote, '– in fact more than that.' On the left is his younger sister, Ada.

9 (*Above right*) The power of the handbag: Margaret Roberts, as candidate, queues for the autograph of the actress Patricia Dainton at a Dartford fête in 1951. The bag with her initials on it was given to her by Willie Cullen.

I forgot to tell you that William has given me a very nice black-calf handbag. It's not an awfully expensive one as my conscience wouldn't let me do that — but I chose a very nice one at £7-3. We had my initials put on as well and it looks awfully nice. It's a flat one with a clasp — see sketch — in a plain calf. I am very pleased with it indeed. Of course I quite loftily say it's not

initials on the flap.

'very expensive' — it's about twice as much as you or I would pay. But compared to some of the others (£10-£20) it's quite reasonable. I'll have to hang on with William for a while longer now!

I should like as many bundles as possible as I have so much to pack up. I haven't heard any further news about digs yet.

Glad to hear that crisps are in production. Hope they pay dividends.

Love
Margaret

10 The story of the bag: Margaret tells Muriel why she will 'have to hang on with William for a while longer now!'

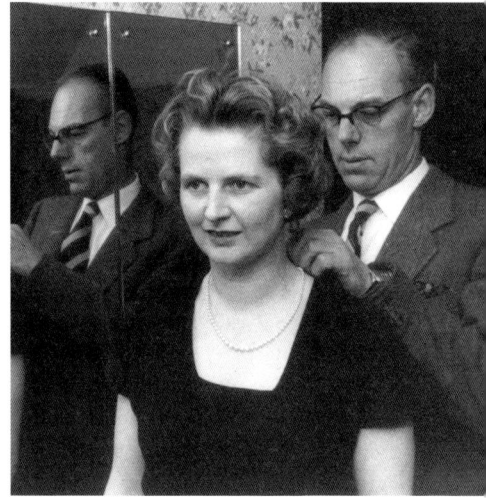

11 (*Above left*) Margaret and Denis cut the cake at their wedding reception at 5 Carlton Gardens, the house of Sir Alfred Bossom, 13 December 1951. Her hat was modelled on that of Georgiana, Duchess of Devonshire, in Gainsborough's portrait.

12 (*Above right*) Married love: Denis fastens his wife's necklace at Dormers, Farnborough, Kent, where they moved just before Christmas 1957.

13 (*Above left*) Waving them away: Mark and Carol leave Dormers for school, 1959. Mrs Thatcher is not taking them to school herself.

14 (*Above right*) In October 1961, Mrs Thatcher was one of the first of her parliamentary intake to achieve ministerial office, as Parliamentary Under-secretary at the Ministry of Pensions and National Insurance. She is reading the parliamentary order paper.

(*Above left*) Mother in the Cabinet: Margaret plays to her family in their house, The Mount, Lamberhurst, after the Conservative election victory of June 1970.

(*Above right*) With a portrait of Ted Heath in 1973. Her part in his downfall was yet to come.

(*Above left*) 'My cupboard is not a hoard in any sense of the word': 'Maggie' the housewife fends off accusations of hoarding by showing her larder to the cameras during the leadership challenge to Heath, December 1974.

(*Above right*) Wife, mother, Leader: the Thatchers celebrate her victory in the second ballot, 11 February 1975, outside the house of William Shelton, one of her campaign managers.

19 (*Above left*) Friendship off the cuff: The first meeting between Mrs Thatcher and Ronald Reagan, April 1975. From their rapport when both were out of office much later success flowed.

20 (*Above right*) Never off duty: Mrs Thatcher consults her watch while on holiday with the Morrison family on the isle of Islay in August 1978. Beside her is Peter Morrison, who would become her parliamentary private secretary at the end of her time in office. She is dressed more for work than for the Scottish islands: she could never see the point of holiday

21 (*Above left*) The famous Saatchi poster often supposed to have appeared during the election campaign of May 1979 was actually launched in the late summer of 1978. Here Mrs Thatcher speaks vehemently above it at a local government conference in March 197

22 (*Above right*) 'Where there is despair, may we bring hope': Mrs Thatcher enters 10 Downing Street for the first time as prime minister, 4 May 1979. To the extreme left is the broadcaster Jon Snow.

3 (*Above left*) On the front line: Mrs Thatcher in the uniform of the Ulster Defence Regiment, visits 'bandit county' in South Armagh, Northern Ireland, after the murders of Lord Mountbatten and of eighteen British soldiers at Warrenpoint, 19 August 1979. Her appearances in uniform had a great impact.

4 (*Above right*) Mrs Thatcher listens with displeasure as Ted Heath furiously attacks government policies at the party conference of October 1981. The vehemence of his attack probably made ministerial rebellion against her more difficult.

5 (*Above left*) Margaret and Denis at Chequers. 'I am glad that Chequers played quite a part in the Falklands story,' she wrote, 'Winston had used it quite a lot during World War II.'

6 (*Above right*) At the Falklands Commemoration Service at St Paul's Cathedral, October 1982, Mrs Thatcher is standing with Admiral Lord Lewin, Chief of the Defence Staff, whom she trusted and admired. She was outraged at attempts by the St Paul's clergy to avoid giving thanks for the Falklands victory.

27 (*Above left*) With Airey Neave, soldier, man of secrets, queenmaker, assassination victim

28 (*Above right*) Bernard Ingham, Mrs Thatcher's blunt but wily press spokesman. He sometimes seemed to know her thoughts before she did.

29 (*Above left*) At the feet of Harold Macmillan. But he had no time for her economic policies, and she knew it.

30 (*Above right*) Keith Joseph, Mrs Thatcher's dearest political friend and the man who made way for her to be leader. She loved him, but could be rude to him for his lack of political sense.

no immediate attempt to rescue survivors, who took to the life rafts. In total, 321 men of the *Belgrano* died.

'Gotcha', roared the *Sun* headline of the following day, and although this was later used as an example of jingoistic callousness, it did reflect widespread popular reaction. Public opinion was acutely conscious of the danger to the lives of British servicemen and correspondingly relieved when any threat was removed. In the Commons the next day, Nott suggested the *Belgrano* had been closing in on the Task Force when attacked. When it emerged that it had been moving away from the TEZ,* opponents began to suspect a cover-up.

Critics charged that the ship had been sunk in order to destroy the US-Peruvian 'peace process', but the War Cabinet had no knowledge of the Peruvian proposals when it took the decision. The military effect of the sinking was to prevent the Argentine fleet from daring to break through the TEZ for the rest of the war. The immediate political effect was to alter international opinion. Ireland pronounced itself 'appalled' and demanded a meeting of the UN Security Council to call for a ceasefire. There was highly unfavourable reaction even from more supportive EEC states, including France and Germany. To a world which until then had regarded the Falklands crisis as a comic opera, the scale of the loss of life was horrifying.

No one reacted with more frenzied activity than Al Haig, who had developed a new set of peace proposals, presented as an initiative from President Belaúnde of Peru. Pushing this so-called 'Peruvian Plan', Haig told Nicko Henderson the British should propose a ceasefire. 'I told him', Henderson reported to London, that 'we were not in a mood to rush to an Armistice just because the Argentines were losing hands down.' That day Haig rang Henderson three times, urging swift acceptance of his proposals. He later denied 'putting any pressure on Britain', but Mrs Thatcher resented his actions. 'The devil! Al Haig!', she complained in private. As Haig fretted, Caspar Weinberger now made the British an offer so generous that it seemed embarrassing: he proposed to make an American aircraft carrier available to provide a mobile runway. Despite its gratitude, Britain refused.

Late in the evening of 4 May, John Nott informed MPs that, earlier that day, the destroyer HMS *Sheffield* had been hit by an Exocet missile. Fires had broken out and spread fast, forcing the ship to be abandoned. It emerged that twenty crewmen had died and twenty-six had been wounded:

---

* At 0811Z, the *Belgrano* had turned west because the Argentine Commander Allara had concluded that a lack of wind meant that his carrier could not launch Skyhawks against the British. This change of course had no effect on Woodward's intentions, since a ship moving away from him one day could be expected to return the next.

'So many suffered such bad burns,' Mrs Thatcher later recalled.* The Prime Minister took the news very hard. After Nott's statement she sat in her Commons room, with Willie Whitelaw, in tears. 'Don't let anyone in,' Whitelaw told her detective, Barry Strevens, as he left. 'She wants to be alone.'

Throughout the crisis, Clive Whitmore had reminded Mrs Thatcher that she needed to make a private calculation, grim though it was, of how many British deaths the government could sustain. She refused, but was interested in his answer. He told her a maximum of 1,000. When the news of *Sheffield* broke, Mrs Thatcher understood that the public would need all possible reassurance. She rejected Parkinson's offer to go on television, saying: 'No, no, they'll never believe a politician, CDS must do it.' So Lewin himself spoke to reporters at Northwood: 'It was the only time during the Falklands that I appeared on TV.'

The crisis had progressed, noted a CIA memo, from its 'comic opera stage into the grim business of killing'. As Jim Rentschler analysed matters from the NSC perspective: 'The stance of these two disputants increasingly resembles that of a couple of staggering streetfighters, spastically-swinging at each other while blinded into fury by the flow of their own blood.' Haig wrote almost desperately to Francis Pym, warning that the British sticking points with his Peruvian Plan would inevitably lead to Argentine rejection. Reagan was now persuaded he must intervene personally with Mrs Thatcher. Rather than using the telephone, where her greater grasp of detail tended to wrongfoot him, he approved the following letter:

> Dear Margaret
> The decisions I made last Friday [the tilt of 30 April] were aimed at putting you in the strongest possible position to achieve a peaceful settlement in line with the basic principles and values to which we are both committed. I believe there is now a chance to realize that aim, and that we must seize it before more lives are lost.

Reiterating that Pym's answers to Haig's 'formulations' would not work with Buenos Aires, Reagan went on:

---

* In this case, the decision was made to tell the world about the loss of *Sheffield* before the next of kin had been informed about casualties. Mrs Thatcher hated this but thought it better than keeping people in doubt about which ship had been hit, particularly as Argentina often put out false statements which caused even more alarm uncorrected.

I urge you to agree to have these ideas proposed by us and Peru as soon as possible ... This, I am convinced, is now our best hope.

Sincerely,
Ron

Mrs Thatcher summoned an emergency meeting of the full Cabinet, the first such since 2 April, for the morning of 5 May. She circulated the US-Peruvian proposals. Pym suggested that Argentina probably would not accept, but it 'would be acceptable to us' if it did. A long debate followed. Patrick Jenkin said that 'what happened yesterday' (the sinking of *Sheffield*) meant that Britain had to offer a ceasefire. Several others disagreed and the Chief Whip, Michael Jopling, warned that Conservative MPs would see British efforts to negotiate as a climbdown after the loss of *Sheffield*. Whitelaw argued that, should they refuse the proposals, 'We'll lose [the] Americans,' and might lose in the Commons. He recommended acceptance, sticking in a few 'unfundamental changes' which would improve Britain's position.

It was the Prime Minister herself who pushed colleagues towards acceptance. She agreed that the Peruvian Plan 'compromises principles': 'I fear we can't get wishes of people and self-determination ... [but] If we can get something different on local administration, exclusion of South Georgia,* guarantee from US, then worth it.' When Jopling warned of the danger of leaks about a divided Cabinet, she demurred: it was 'not a basically divided Cabinet', and – to counter the undercurrent which most worried her – she added, '*Sheffield* not a fatal moment'. Britain would accept the plan, noted the official minutes, because otherwise 'she would be severely criticised by international opinion, which was already moving against her'. Far from scuppering the US-Peruvian proposals, the sinking of the *Belgrano* (followed by the loss of *Sheffield*) forced Mrs Thatcher to be seen to accept them.

After Cabinet, the Prime Minister replied to the US President. Unlike Reagan's slightly chilly letter, hers was more personal: 'I am writing to you separately because I think you are the only person who will understand the significance of what I am saying.' She had, she said, always tried 'to stay loyal to the United States', but she feared that the US suggestions would compromise the democracy and freedom of the Falklanders. That said, she

---

* The government was anxious to establish that the 'dependent territories' such as the reoccupied South Georgia were not necessarily to be covered by the same agreement as the Falkland Islands.

made clear she would accede to Reagan's request, subject only to what Whitelaw had called 'unfundamental changes'.* 'In a word,' Judge Clark told Reagan, 'Maggie accepts the proposal.'

In her memoirs, Mrs Thatcher says that she was 'deeply unhappy about the US/Peruvian proposals' and stresses the modifications she pressed for. She records that her original letter to Reagan had to be redrafted because it 'revealed perhaps too much of my frustration'. This is true, but grossly understates the facts. Her first draft, written in her own hand, was a personal letter from Margaret to Ron, half begging, half defiant – a cry of wounded friendship. In it, she bluntly rejected Reagan's claim that his suggestions were 'faithful to the basic principles we must protect' – 'alas they are not'. She went on:

> Before this aggression, the Falklands were a democratic country, with liberty and a just law. After the proposed settlement, the one thing they cannot have is the only way of life they want. Perhaps you will now see why I feel so deeply about this. That our traditional friendship, to which I still loyally adhere, should have brought me and those I represent into conflict with fundamental democratic principles sounds impossible while you are at the White House and I am at No. 10.

If she had sent this message, she would have forced the President to choose a side. In the end, she did not dare.

In her memoirs, Mrs Thatcher cannot quite bring herself to say that she did, though with qualifications, approve the plan which she so much disliked. She accepted what she had avoided accepting with Haig's ideas in April, and what, at that time, she had described as 'the crisis of Britain's honour'. The 'Peruvian' proposals, by her own admission, would have removed the self-governing and self-determining rights of the Falkland Islanders. Was this, after British blood had been shed, honourable?

Most of those close to Mrs Thatcher claim she accepted the Peruvian proposals in perfect confidence that Argentina would reject them. She was indeed highly doubtful that Argentina would make a genuine deal. However, she was acting now not only out of calculation, but out of desperation. With international sympathy for Britain fading, Reagan's intervention convinced her that she had to make concessions. So she

---

* The settlement proposed 'did not provide unambiguously for the right of self-determination', she told Reagan, therefore she wanted the interim administration at least to consult with the locally elected representatives. 'It is not too much to ask,' she wrote, '– and I do not think you will turn it down.'

conceded.* She may have been tactically correct to do so, but it troubled her conscience.

As before, it was General Galtieri who got Mrs Thatcher out of her immediate difficulty. Late on 5 May, Argentina rejected the US-Peruvian proposals. Argentine attention shifted to the UN, where they sought a resolution for a ceasefire without withdrawal. As the efforts of Secretary-General Javier Pérez de Cuéllar came to the fore, the resourceful Anthony Parsons was ready. As early as 3 May, he cabled Pym to say that they would soon need to 'fill the diplomatic vacuum'. He proposed to reply to Pérez de Cuéllar's recent aide-memoire, inviting him to 'refine his ideas'. Sure enough, as Haig bowed out, offers of help, mostly unwelcome, poured in from around the world.† At home, the discontent expressed by Cardinals Hume and Gray, the leaders of the Roman Catholic Church in England and Scotland respectively, caused Mrs Thatcher anxiety because the proposed visit of Pope John Paul II to Britain, the first by any pope in history, planned for the end of the month, now hung in the balance. The handling of Britain's cause was not becoming any easier.‡

As Parsons had correctly calculated, British readiness to deal with Pérez de Cuéllar enabled the Secretary-General to persuade the Irish not to press their case for a ceasefire resolution. With Argentina trying to force Britain to break off UN negotiations, the best response was to spin them out. Possible texts flew back and forth. Mrs Thatcher telephoned Anthony Parsons in New York. 'I feel a little bit remote,' she told him. Referring to the sinking of the *Belgrano*, she felt that 'perhaps ... we did not make the best impression last weekend'; now she wanted to appear as willing as possible: Pérez de Cuéllar was 'probably the only person who can sort something out between us. Are you with me?' Even now, she was still contemplating the possibility of a deal with Argentina. She told Parsons how deeply she felt

---

* It is worth noting that in her letter to Reagan she did clearly acknowledge and plan for the possibility of Argentine acceptance. The letter ended: 'Assuming that they [the Haig proposals] are accepted by Argentines, then during the negotiation period that will follow we shall have to fight fiercely for the rights of the Falklanders who have been so loyal to everything in which you and we believe.'

† The King of Spain, for example, called for a ceasefire and proposed his good offices to the Secretary-General. The President of Mexico suggested to Mrs Thatcher that he set up a meeting between her and General Galtieri.

‡ One unwelcome solution to the Falklands problem was proposed at this time by Mrs Thatcher's economic adviser, Alan Walters. He sent her a memo suggesting a plebiscite on the islands which would offer £50,000 per head in return for Argentine sovereignty, or continuing British sovereignty and no money. Mrs Thatcher remembered it as 'a rat's way out'.

about restoring self-determination and freedom for the islanders, and yet, she said, 'it is going to be the most awful waste of young life if we really do have to go and take those islands'.* Her opponents often accused Mrs Thatcher of lacking human concern, but, as these words suggest, she felt this keenly.

On 9 May, Argentina suddenly suggested that recognizing its sovereignty over the Falklands was not, after all, a precondition of negotiations. This shift would prove short-lived: just a week later this new language was dropped. But, at least for a few days, Argentina appeared to be making the running. Mrs Kirkpatrick ensured that President Reagan was made aware of what she considered a crucial concession. At the same time, President Figueiredo of Brazil alarmed Reagan with the suggestion that the British were on the verge of striking mainland Argentina. This combination of pressures persuaded Reagan to telephone Mrs Thatcher.

The call, on Thursday 13 May, came when Mrs Thatcher was feeling particularly unreceptive: 'If anything my views are hardening,' she had written on a Foreign Office note the day before, 'because I think much of the compromise texts will be totally unacceptable to our people.' On the day of Reagan's call, the leading article in the *Daily Telegraph* attacked the suggestions coming from Pym and the Foreign Office: 'The idea that men went to the bottom of the ocean so that diplomats could go peacefully to their beds would provoke fury.' 'Some "populars"', Ingham warned her, '. . . feel there is a smell of Munich in the air.' At Prime Minister's Questions, Mrs Thatcher took a more robust approach than Pym, who had suggested earlier that the British government had an 'open mind' on sovereignty. The difference did not go unnoticed and, as she remembered it, Pym's 'weaker line was not liked'.

Reagan opened their call by saying that, after her grilling in Parliament, 'He thought she might like to hear a friendly voice.' This attempt to placate her fell flat. She told him she was sick of Argentine game-playing. It was not true the two sides were close. Hinting he could facilitate an informal backchannel negotiation with Galtieri, Reagan asked if she would 'hold off military action'. Mrs Thatcher would have none of it. Britain would not delay, because time was running out. Reagan ventured he 'had been under the impression that the Argentines had conceded the main points'. She said tartly that this was 'not the case'. The Falkland Islanders 'were a loyal, true and thrifty people' who wanted to 'live their own lives . . . The two greatest democracies must surely protect that wish.' The President

---

* When writing her memoirs ten years later, Mrs Thatcher argued with her assistants that her phrase about the 'awful waste of young life' should be taken out, lest it upset the families of those who had died. In the end she backed down, and the words appeared.

replied that he 'could not quarrel with these arguments'. He retired hurt. Noting the call in his diary, he wrote: '[I] don't think I persuaded her against further military action.'*

Mrs Thatcher was acutely aware of what Admiral Woodward called 'the tyranny of our timetable' – the fact that the South Atlantic winter would make naval action impossible by late June. While the Task Force would be ready to attempt to land on the Falklands from 16 May, Mrs Thatcher also had to consider world opinion. She was persuaded, against her instincts, to put together one final compromise negotiating package to convince the world of British reasonableness.

On Sunday 16 May, the War Cabinet met at Chequers, with Parsons and Henderson attending in person. Although complicit in the process – working out Britain's final negotiating position for presentation to Argentina on a take-or-leave-it basis – Mrs Thatcher was also resentful of having to go through it at all. She therefore took it out on her colleagues. As Nicko Henderson recorded: 'The PM veered the whole time towards being uncompromising, so that the rest of us, and in particular the FCO participants, constantly found themselves under attack for being wet, ready to sell out, unsupportive of British interests, etc.' Parsons bore the brunt, but his self-confidence and sense of humour won the Prime Minister over: 'He curled his feet under the chair, saying to her "I'm getting out of the way because you're going to kick me."'†

Gradually, he and Henderson pulled Mrs Thatcher along. The text they agreed contained several important compromises, or, as Mrs Thatcher preferred to think of it, put forward 'a very reasonable offer'. It abandoned resumed British administration in favour of a UN administrator supervising a mutual withdrawal. Self-determination was not mentioned,‡ and the UN would be charged with conducting negotiations about sovereignty which, given Argentine intransigence, were not likely to go Britain's way. The deadline for Argentina's response would be 19 May. This would allow just enough time for the expected rejection before the planned British assault.

When the meeting ended, Parsons wanted to be sure Mrs Thatcher understood just how much had been conceded, so he took her aside. The

---

* Mrs Thatcher felt that she knew where to place the blame: 'Mrs Kirkpatrick's behaviour had been very vexing and thoroughly anti-British.'

† Parsons was one of very few officials who would stand up to Mrs Thatcher. On one occasion during the conflict, she asked him for his view but then interrupted him almost immediately. 'First, you have to shut up,' Parsons responded, 'then you have to listen to me and then you have to give what I say some consideration.'

‡ The plan did, however, include references to Article 73 of the UN Charter which mentions 'developing self-government'.

concessions made, he said, 'take us a long way from our original negotiating position . . . you are content with what I'm taking back to New York?' 'Yes, I am content,' she replied, 'I understand the full implications of it. You go ahead and do your stuff.' The War Cabinet had gone as far as it felt it should, perhaps further. As Parsons said to Pérez de Cuéllar the following day, there could be no substantive alteration of the offer because 'The existing draft would already be extremely difficult to defend in Parliament.' It did not feel like it at the time, but the day at Chequers proved a successful, and for the Prime Minister a rare, exercise in compromise and consensus.

Britain's show of willingness certainly helped the diplomacy. The EEC voted to extend sanctions, though allowing dissenters such as Ireland to opt out. Pérez de Cuéllar professed himself delighted with Britain's flexibility and presented the final offer to Argentina. On the morning of 18 May, awaiting a response, the War Cabinet met to make the key decision – whether to authorize the military repossession of the Falkland Islands. Mrs Thatcher was advised to nail down the positions of each of the Chiefs of Staff and ministers and to record individual replies. If the casualties turned out to be 'controversially high or if the operation fails', her Cabinet Office briefing advised, 'no one should be able to argue that the Chiefs were bullied by the politicians into undertaking it against their better judgment'.

At the meeting the Chiefs showed shades of difference, but all endorsed the plan.* As Mrs Thatcher later wrote, the anxieties were clear, and common to all present: 'We should be vulnerable on landing, had we enough air cover [question mark missing].' The meeting noted there would be tremendous pressure for a ceasefire once the troops had landed. They would need to hurry to secure the whole of the Falklands before they could be held hostage to politics and diplomacy. The attack would take place by night, and 'we could stop it until late Thursday'.

Mrs Thatcher went to bed at 2 a.m. on the night of 18–19 May and rose at 6.30. A telegram from Parsons reported that Argentina had in effect rejected the British final offer and Pérez de Cuéllar accepted this as a fact. At 9.30, the War Cabinet agreed she should place the British draft before Parliament the following day.† Notice of Argentina's rejection would be

---

* Bramall, the Chief of the General Staff, and always the least optimistic of the group, warned that air superiority was 'one of the modern principles of war; and it had not yet been achieved.' He was, recalled Michael Palliser, 'really very worried that it might not work'.

† Pérez de Cuéllar then made a last-minute bid to avert hostilities by announcing he had produced a paper of his own. Both Haig and Pym thought Britain should respond positively, but the War Cabinet, meeting on the morning of 20 May, decided that the military operation would go ahead as planned.

published at lunchtime. To the full Cabinet, Mrs Thatcher reported this rejection and that the authority for landing had been given two days before. No one jibbed at the idea of landing. Armstrong noted Mrs Thatcher's summing up: 'All agreed. This is the most difficult time we have ever faced. Our job to stick together, and keep up morale. Total confidence in Task Force and every good wish.'

In Parliament that afternoon Mrs Thatcher set out the British proposals, explaining that, because of Argentine rejection, they were off the table. The decision to publish these paid off. Those who had been arguing for a negotiated settlement were forced to admit that the British suggestions were reasonable. Those who had not wanted Britain to make concessions now felt relieved that they had gone. Mrs Thatcher did not say that a British landing was imminent, but this was understood. All she said was 'Difficult days lie ahead,' but 'our cause is just'.

That night, Pérez de Cuéllar ended his peace efforts. Looking back, even Jeane Kirkpatrick believed that the fault 'was almost entirely Argentine from start to finish. I tried to persuade them as they went into the quicksand . . . They dug themselves deeper and deeper.'

On 21 May 1982, British troops began to land at San Carlos Bay.

As with the recapture of South Georgia, the start of actual operations left Mrs Thatcher superfluous to requirements. On the day of the landing, a Friday, she kept a speaking engagement in her constituency. At her constituency office she learnt 'in concealed language' that 'events had happened but no more news . . . Then it was given on TV and the emotion at a reception at Woodhouse School that night was overwhelming. The Union Jack was flying in San Carlos Bay. We had returned to the Falklands. My heart was full but desperately anxious about casualties.' She returned to Downing Street, where cheering crowds had gathered. There John Nott informed her that HMS *Argonaut* and HMS *Brilliant* had been badly damaged by air attack and the frigate HMS *Ardent* had been lost, with twenty-two men dead. At 2025Z hours, Nott issued a statement saying: 'British forces have now established a firm bridgehead on the Falklands.' Five thousand men had landed. It was, wrote Admiral Woodward, 'one of the most successful landings in military history'.

This was true, but the protracted business of unloading gave many more opportunities for Argentina to attack. Mrs Thatcher was in a fever of impotent anxiety. 'You couldn't find me some decisions to take, could you?' she asked Robert Wade-Gery, 'I find all this waiting around very difficult.' On the Saturday 22 May, she visited Northwood. This did not please Admiral Fieldhouse, despite his excellent relations with the Prime

Minister. 'Keep that woman away,' he said to Wade-Gery, 'I've got a war to fight.' Mrs Thatcher was sufficiently worried by the Argentine air attacks to ask Fieldhouse, 'Can we still win?'*

Favoured by clear weather, the skilful Argentine pilots began numerous daring attacks on the British forces, climaxing on 24 and 25 May. It fell to the Sea Harriers to repel them, armed with Sidewinder missiles, supplied, thanks to Weinberger, by the United States.† Without the Sidewinders, Mrs Thatcher wrote, 'we could not have retaken the Falklands'. On 25 May, Argentina's Independence Day,‡ the Argentine air force launched their most successful attacks of the war. First that evening came news that the destroyer HMS *Coventry* had been bombed and was sinking. It later turned out that nineteen men had died. Then Mrs Thatcher learnt that the *Atlantic Conveyor*, carrying nineteen Harriers and the helicopters intended to transport troops to Port Stanley, had been hit. There was even a report from Argentina that *Invincible* had been struck. That night Denis Thatcher found his wife sitting on the end of their bed, weeping: 'Oh no, oh no! Another ship! All my young men!' He sat down beside her and said, 'That's what war's like, love. I've been in one. I know.'

Early the next morning, Mrs Thatcher was informed that most of the crews of both stricken vessels had been rescued. The Harriers were also safe, though not the helicopters, eight of which were lost. There had been no strike against *Invincible*. She had gone to bed that night not knowing any of these things, and worrying, too, that 'somewhere east of the Falklands was the QEII carrying 3,500 troops': 'Perhaps this was the worst night of all . . . we learned the deep sorrows of war.'

Deep sorrow only strengthened Mrs Thatcher's resolve. She now suggested Britain attack Argentine ships within their own waters and even launch raids on the Argentine mainland. Although 'visibly uncomfortable at having to disagree with her', the Attorney-General, Michael Havers, told her that this would be contrary to international law. The idea was not pursued. World opinion reacted adversely to the land war. From New

---

* In writing her memoirs, she did not want such a strong expression of doubt recorded. Instead, she quoted herself as saying, 'How long can we go on taking this sort of punishment?'

† After the official US tilt towards Britain on 30 April, the supply of US arms and materiel increased considerably. It included not just the Sidewinders, but also helicopter engines, thousands of tonnes of airstrip matting, Stinger ground-to-air missiles, assistance in ship repair and much more. 'I think the full extent of our assistance has never been fully documented,' recalled the Pentagon's Richard Perle. 'There was *matériel* support on a massive scale.'

‡ In a vain attempt to maintain friendly relations with Argentina, President Reagan sent Galtieri a congratulatory telegram to mark Independence Day. This displeased him, since it seemed hypocritical, and enraged Mrs Thatcher.

York, Parsons reported that 'The elastic of our support, even from our close friends (with the exception of the Old Commonwealth) is stretching very thin.' Speaking of his 'deep anguish', Pope John Paul II, whose visit to Britain the following week remained in the balance, called for a ceasefire. Mrs Thatcher replied that his anguish 'finds immediate echo here in London', but that the conflict was Argentina's fault.* On 24 May, Al Haig saw Henderson. Praying in aid Winston Churchill, Haig pushed for Britain to show 'magnanimity'. Henderson, however, pointed out that 'Churchill was talking about magnanimity once victory had been achieved,' not while British forces still risked life and limb. Henderson also deployed a sensitive argument: 'I reminded Haig how often he had assured me that this would not be another Suez. If the US Government now took action which would have the effect of trying to bring our forces to a halt before their mission was accomplished, the charge of another Suez would be raised.'

Haig continued, nonetheless, to churn out new ideas for a settlement. Mrs Thatcher felt compelled to look at these politely but, with British troops landed, she was no longer willing to concede anything substantial. Henderson was worried by her reaction, lest it provoke the Americans. 'Mrs T has not yet consigned me to the Tower,' he later wrote, 'but I am told that her voice drops two dangerous decibels when she goes through my telegrams during inner Cabinet meetings. How much lower would it sink in patient but intolerant wrath if I included in my messages all Haig's pleas that she should ... even before we have overcome the Argentinian garrison, show magnanimity.'

On 26 May, Pym informed Haig that the ideas they had discussed previously 'were just not political starters now'. Haig now began to bow to reality: 'We should conserve our leverage with Mrs. Thatcher until it can be used to produce results,' he advised Reagan, 'i.e., when the islands are effectively in British hands.' Jeane Kirkpatrick, however, refused to accept this. Finding allies among the President's political staff, who feared that Reagan's upcoming trip to Britain and Europe would be tarnished if the fighting continued, she urged that he call Mrs Thatcher in the name of peace. He did so at 11 p.m. UK time on Monday 31 May.

The President began with flattery to make his point: 'Your impressive military advance could maybe change the diplomatic options ...', but Mrs Thatcher did not give him much of a chance. British troops, she said, were

---

* The idea that the Pope might not visit distressed Mrs Thatcher: 'After all the eager and detailed preparation of our Roman Catholics and the keen anticipation of many other people to see this good man who was such a courageous leader, I very much wanted the visit to go ahead.' Her solution was to take politics out of it, making the visit purely pastoral. This solution was accepted, and the Pope reached English soil on 28 May.

only 'a third of the way' to reconquest. She would not countenance any premature settlement: 'I didn't lose some of my finest ships and some of my finest lives to leave quietly under a ceasefire.' Reagan was interrupted repeatedly by her flow and found himself reduced to the occasional 'yes', 'Well ...' or 'Margaret, I ...' How would the President feel, she asked, 'supposing Alaska were invaded'? Reagan suggested that such a situation might not be entirely analogous. 'More or less so,' she snapped. 'Ron ... I'm not handing over the island now ... after we've lost some of our finest young men.' 'Well, Margaret, I know that I've intruded,' he said, 'and I know how ...' Mrs Thatcher cut him short yet again: 'You haven't intruded at all, and I'm glad you telephoned.'

In the White House there was much consternation. Jim Rentschler noted the 'disastrous' exchange in which Reagan 'came off sounding like even more of a wimp than Jimmy Carter'. Mrs Thatcher also chose to be angry. She rang Henderson and said that she was 'dismayed' by Reagan's attitude and wanted Henderson to tell the President so. 'It is pure Haigism,' she said. 'This phrase', Henderson noted, 'was uttered in the most withering tone, the speaker no doubt aware of the openness of the line.' Mrs Thatcher was deploying her indignation with calculation. 'I don't recall her being all that angry with Reagan personally over this,' said Whitmore. 'She understood that he was ... straddling still an administration that was pulling in different directions.' In Whitmore's view, she felt confident that 'she could count on their support in the final analysis'.

Given the course of the fighting in the ten days after the Task Force landed, it was scarcely surprising that Mrs Thatcher hardened her attitude to any deal. The combination of painful losses and military success fired up her passions. Would-be peacemakers must understand that nothing should prejudice the success of the Task Force or unnecessarily endanger servicemen's lives. What applied to diplomats and foreign leaders also applied to the media. Mrs Thatcher was outraged that the BBC seemed neutral between Britain and Argentina.* This she more than once criticized in Parliament. 'My concern was always the safety of our forces,' she later wrote. 'Theirs was news.' Luckily for her, most of Fleet Street, though not the broadcast media, was extremely sympathetic to her cause.

Once the Task Force was landed, Mrs Thatcher worked to strengthen her broad moral and political arguments for what it was doing. Speaking to

---

* Mrs Thatcher shared the fury among the Task Force at the BBC's decision, when British troops were preparing to attack the Argentine forces at Goose Green, to broadcast that the 2nd Battalion the Parachute Regiment were within five miles of nearby Darwin. 'Can there ever have been an army which had to fight its battles against media reporting like that?' she later wrote.

the Conservative Women's Conference on 26 May, she deployed the phrase of Harry Truman which would become her Cold War mantra – she wanted not mere peace, but 'peace with freedom and justice'. For the *Washington Post* she took from the Falklands experience a renewed idea of the British character: 'If you ask a person here what he would associate with Britain ... he would say "We are a free country".'

At the conference, Mrs Thatcher also used a phrase which betrayed the problem on her mind. There was, she said, 'no question of pressing the Force Commander to move forward prematurely'. But there was just such pressure. It was imperative that growing international calls for a ceasefire be superseded by swift British victory. The War Cabinet also believed that a pause following the landings would dismay domestic opinion. It therefore urgently wanted visible gains. An attack on the Argentine garrison at Goose Green seemed to fit the bill.

On 26 May, Fieldhouse sent Brigadier Julian Thompson, Commander of the Landing Force, a signal making the political dimension of the risk of a ceasefire explicit and ordering that he 'do all you can to bring the Darwin/Goose Green operation to a successful conclusion with Union Jack seen to be flying in Darwin'. Thompson, though, worried about moving outside the air defence umbrella now established at the beachhead and felt his logistical difficulties were not understood at Northwood.* This was not a classic row between politicians demanding a propaganda victory and generals sticking to military priorities. Cecil Parkinson recalled that 'There was a feeling that Julian Thompson "had better get a bloody move on", but it wasn't the politicians who said this, it was the Chiefs.' The War Cabinet minutes of 27 May record Mrs Thatcher declaring that 'it was most important to make the earliest possible progress with the operations on land'. The top brass, translating her inclination into specific action, decided upon Goose Green.

The battle of Goose Green, which went through the night of 27 May, was fierce. When the Argentines finally surrendered they had lost forty-five men. The British lost sixteen, including Colonel 'H' Jones, commanding 2 Para, who had led the assault. In later analyses, debate over the necessity of the battle never went away. Denis Thatcher, for example, believed that '"H" Jones should never have been killed.' Mrs Thatcher was deeply troubled by his death, more so, thought Robert Armstrong, than by any other disaster of the war except the loss of *Sheffield*. While Goose Green was not a battle on which the defeat of Argentina directly depended, it certainly

---

* One complication was that, because of the loss of the helicopters in the *Atlantic Conveyor*, British troops would have to advance towards Port Stanley on foot.

produced a clear victory and an example of astonishing heroism in 'H' Jones, who was posthumously awarded the Victoria Cross. Congratulating Jones's successor as commanding officer, Major Chris Keeble, Fieldhouse said, 'You have kindled a flame in land operations which will lead to the raising of the Union Jack in Port Stanley.' This was correct. There was now no real doubt that Britain would win the war.

One last diplomatic minuet remained – the G7 economic summit in Versailles. It coincided with the UN Security Council debate over a ceasefire resolution. When Reagan met Mrs Thatcher *tête-à-tête* before the summit began, he no longer had any stomach for challenging her over the Falklands.* He sympathized with Britain's position and wanted to avoid the sharp end of her tongue. Mulling Versailles over with Henderson the following week, Haig 'said that we were rapidly losing international support'. Henderson asked whether Reagan had made this clear to Mrs Thatcher in their private talk. 'He regretted that he did not think that he had done so. I said it was hopeless my telling Mrs Thatcher that the US government felt strongly the need for Britain to show magnanimity towards the Argentinians ... if the President himself said nothing about it.'†

Reagan's acceptance encouraged the same at Versailles. President Mitterrand, the summit host, had, apart from the Old Commonwealth prime ministers, been the most consistently supportive foreign leader. He issued a declaration at the summit's close: 'we wished to make a point of affirming our full solidarity with Great Britain whose national interests and national pride have been violated ... Great Britain's rights must be preserved.' This marked the end of efforts to persuade Britain to stop short of Port Stanley. Mitterrand had been, to use one of Mrs Thatcher's favourite words, staunch. Early in the conflict he had personally insisted on providing Britain with the means to counter the threat from the Exocet missiles which France had sold to Argentina. Mitterrand's tone and manner had also pleased her: 'He treated her as a great leader of a great country.'‡

The atmosphere at the UN was less friendly. To block the ceasefire

---

* Before leaving Washington, Reagan had refused to send a message to Mrs Thatcher, drafted by the State Department, calling for a ceasefire short of complete surrender and abridging the rights of the islanders to decide their own future.

† On 8 June, Robert Armstrong wrote to John Coles with information that American support, especially that of President Reagan personally, was not as absolute as Mrs Thatcher, at her Versailles debriefing, had conveyed to her officials. It extended only to the complete cessation of hostilities and did not necessarily endorse what Britain intended to do next. Whitmore wrote on it, 'Sir Robert Armstrong and I were inclined <u>not</u> to show this to the Prime Minister.'

‡ On a personal level, there was an element of flirtation in the relationship, which Mrs Thatcher recognized and enjoyed. 'Well, Prime Minister, that went rather well,' suggested

THE FALKLANDS 319

resolution, at the Security Council meeting of 4 June, Britain would be forced to use its veto. Haig had left instructions for the United States to do the same, but changed his mind at the last minute. This came too late for Mrs Kirkpatrick, who had just joined Parsons in vetoing the resolution. But then, as Parsons recorded, she 'astonishingly stated that she had been asked by her government to say that if it were possible to change a vote once cast the US would like to change its vote from a veto to an abstention'. Britain was furious at American behaviour, yet benefited from its sheer oddness; as Pym cabled to Mrs Thatcher at Versailles, Mrs Kirkpatrick's performance 'excited much more media attention than our veto'. At Versailles the next day, just before luncheon, a reporter asked Reagan about the UN vote. Mrs Thatcher was watching: 'Poor Ron – he knew nothing about it <u>to my amazement</u> . . .' The interviewer then asked for her reaction: 'I wasn't going to have a row on the media so merely said I didn't give interviews over lunch!'*

Reagan's visit to Britain began on Monday 7 June. There was no whisper of disagreement over the Falklands. In his set-piece speech to MPs and peers in Parliament's Royal Gallery, Reagan linked the Falklands to his 'crusade for freedom' that would lead the West to victory in the Cold War:

> On distant islands in the South Atlantic young men are fighting for Britain. And yes, voices have been raised protesting their sacrifice for lumps of rock and earth so far away. But those young men aren't fighting for mere real estate. They fight for a cause – for the belief that armed aggression must not be allowed to succeed, that the people must participate in the decisions of government – the decisions of government under the rule of law.†

This was the only part of his speech which attracted applause. As British troops prepared for the final assault, Mrs Thatcher could not have asked for clearer public support.

That same day, Mrs Thatcher received grim news. Two ships, *Sir Galahad* and *Sir Tristram*, had been hit by Argentine air attack as they unloaded their troops at Port Pleasant in the Falklands. Forty-nine men were killed, including thirty-nine Welsh Guards. Mrs Thatcher visited Northwood the next day: 'we all felt – <u>how</u> many more'. At Fieldhouse's request, she reluctantly

---

Robert Armstrong after Mitterrand's first presidential visit to the UK in September 1981. 'Yes, I suppose it did,' she replied. And then she paused. 'He likes women, you know.'
* The blame for Reagan's ignorance lies with Haig, who had kept knowledge of the UN vote from both the President and Judge Clark to maximize his own room for manoeuvre.
† Reagan had, himself, written this passage into the speech, against the advice of the State Department.

overruled John Nott and agreed to hold back casualty details from the public, though informing the next of kin, to make Argentina believe that the losses had been greater than they really were and that the assault on Stanley would be seriously hampered. As she later put it: 'Surprise was vital.'

As British troops conducted their remarkable 'yomp' on foot across East Falkland towards the capital, Mrs Thatcher again had little to do. Characteristically, she busied herself with the details of the Sovereign's Birthday Parade (Trooping the Colour). There was a debate about whether 'Last Post' and 'Reveille' should be sounded for those lost in the Falklands, but the Queen thought this 'might encourage "hysteria"'. She proposed a moment of silence at the beginning of proceedings. Mrs Thatcher agreed. Early in the morning of Saturday 12 June, the day of Trooping the Colour, Mrs Thatcher was informed that HMS *Glamorgan* had been hit by a land-based Exocet. Thirteen men were killed. 'It is impossible to describe the depth of feeling,' she later wrote. For the ceremony, it 'poured with rain and somehow that seemed fitting although unpleasant for the Guards. I wore black – there was so much to mourn.' Just as all seemed bleak, however, came the news she had been waiting for. Shortly before 1 p.m., 'we heard that all the objectives had been achieved'. Victory was at hand.

It took two more days for the reconquest to be complete. At 0200Z on 15 June, General Moore signalled to London that he had received the Argentine surrender: 'The Falkland Islands are once more under the government desired by their inhabitants. God Save the Queen.' In the course of the war, 255 British servicemen had died, 649 Argentines* and three Falkland Islanders.

With the news widely reported, crowds gathered in Downing Street. Mrs Thatcher, punctilious as she usually was about sharing news with Parliament first, went across to the Commons. At 10.14 p.m. she stated that large numbers of Argentine soldiers had thrown down their weapons. 'They are reported to be flying white flags over Port Stanley.'† Surrender negotiations were now in progress, she explained: 'it was important in that she used the phrase, " ... negotiate a *surrender*" (not a ceasefire),' wrote Alan Clark. 'Trust her. She has led from the front all the way.' 'The House cheered,' Mrs Thatcher recalled. In her Commons room afterwards, colleagues gathered: 'I don't think anyone else but you could have done it,' said Willie Whitelaw, proposing a toast. 'And she wept, out of sheer relief,' remembered Antony Acland. 'Denis put his arm round her, and said: "Well done. Have a drink."'

---

* There is some dispute about the exact figure for Argentine deaths.
† It seems unlikely that Argentine flags of surrender were, in fact, flying. The only known example of a white flag that day was flown by a civilian anxious to indicate that there was no longer any need for a British attack.

At midnight she went home, among crowds singing 'Rule, Britannia', with whom she mingled:

> Downing Street was full of people, young people. It was their generation who had done it . . . As I went to sleep very late that night I felt an enormous burden had been lifted from my shoulders . . . It was a miracle wrought by ordinary men and women with extraordinary qualities. Forever bold, forever brave, forever remembered.

At Prime Minister's Questions three days later, Enoch Powell rose to offer an answer to his earlier question about the metal of which Mrs Thatcher was made: 'the substance under test consisted of ferrous matter of the highest quality . . . it is of exceptional tensile strength, is highly resistant to wear and tear and to stress, and may be used with advantage for all national purposes'. The joke was laboured, but the compliment gave Mrs Thatcher great pleasure. She had indeed proved herself the Iron Lady.

Thanks to total victory and, as she saw it, the rightness of the cause, Mrs Thatcher now felt no need to entertain a new constitutional status for the Falklands. 'There was no prospect of negotiating anything for the moment,' she told Pérez de Cuéllar on 14 June, 'nor did she think there would be for some time.' Her approach was to implement the spirit of the Shackleton Report, without seeking international assistance. The 'Fortress Falklands' policy, which the Foreign Office had always sought to avoid, came into being. As a result of the Malvinas debacle, Galtieri's government fell and Argentina eventually returned to democratic rule.

The Falklands victory had many consequences for Mrs Thatcher. The most obvious was the transformation of political fortune. Although she had already come through the worst of her unpopularity before Argentina invaded, only a few far-sighted supporters had judged her likely to win the next general election. Within Mrs Thatcher's own party, her critics had believed that the Falklands, like a rerun of Suez, would bring her down. The opposite happened. The Falklands War established her personal mastery of the political scene and convinced people of her special gifts of leadership.*
The loneliness of command in those eleven weeks made her unassailable.

It was not mere flattery to say that only she could have done it – it was widely believed and is probably true. Within the armed services there had

---

* As the war progressed, the producers of *Anyone for Denis?*, the satirical West End revue based on *Private Eye*'s fictitious 'Dear Bill' letters supposedly written by Denis, brought the show to an end.

been a feeling that, despite a catalogue of post-war affronts to British power, things would be different this time. In Julian Thompson's view, it was clear that Mrs Thatcher 'was a different kettle of fish'. John Coles, who had entered her private office with the usual somewhat anti-Thatcher prejudices of the Foreign Office, 'became a very great admirer because of her extraordinary courage and clarity'. In this he was typical of most who worked with her. As Clive Whitmore put it, 'She led as well as could possibly be expected.'

The Falklands War brought out Mrs Thatcher's best qualities – not only the well-known ones of courage, conviction and resolution, but also her less advertised ones of caution and careful study. She did not allow her desire for victory to overwhelm the need to be pragmatic and diplomatic. Because she knew nothing about war, she approached the subject modestly. She trusted her military leaders to do their job. Even in the Foreign Office, she recognized and relied on the talents of individuals such as Nicko Henderson and Anthony Parsons. The war also proved her to be utterly genuine. In private and public, she cared passionately for the cause and for the people involved. In this, her sex was important. She was the first female war leader with executive power in the British Isles since Elizabeth I, and the first ever in a democratic age. She felt a maternal, almost a romantic, identification with the men she was sending into battle, and they responded with a chivalrous devotion to her as a woman and as an embodiment of national spirit. The Falklands was a great occasion, and she rose to it.

From the Falklands crisis Mrs Thatcher derived the self-confidence which, in some ways, she had previously lacked. Rather as Britain standing alone in 1940 had been the sustaining myth for Winston Churchill, Mrs Thatcher's solitary leadership during the Falklands became for her the talisman of what she could do. In her mind, it helped to create the dangerous idea that she acted best when she acted alone. But it also renewed her belief that her efforts to transform her country accorded with the underlying character of the British people. As she told a Conservative rally in early July: 'We have ceased to be a nation in retreat. We have instead a new-found confidence – born in the economic battles at home and tested and found true 8,000 miles away . . . Britain found herself again in the South Atlantic and will not look back from the victory she has won.' Mrs Thatcher's idea of what had been achieved fitted her unusual mindset, which was both conservative and revolutionary. She saw herself as restoring an inherent British greatness which had been battered by imperial decline. At the same time, she believed she was bringing about enormous change.

The Falklands set the standard by which she judged individuals. Anyone who had been 'staunch' in the war was in her good books for evermore.

As well as the armed services, her list of heroes included – forgetting the wobbles – Ronald Reagan and Caspar Weinberger, President Mitterrand, President Pinochet, Robert Muldoon of New Zealand, King Hussein of Jordan, Rex Hunt, the Governor of the Falklands, and David Owen of the SDP.* Her villains included the Irish, the United Nations (though not Pérez de Cuéllar personally), Francis Pym, Jeane Kirkpatrick and Denis Healey.†

The world, in turn, revised its estimation of her. The Americans were deeply impressed. In the middle of the Cold War, her Falklands rhetoric about free people standing up to aggression resonated. Her achievement in successfully projecting force halfway across the world also caused the Soviet Union to revise its estimation of the will and capacity of the West.

All over the world, Margaret Thatcher now became a figure of legend, the embodiment of strong leadership, more famous, perhaps, than any other political leader of the time. On the day of victory, Alan Clark bumped into Ian Gow in the Commons. '"The Prime Minister has complete freedom of action now," I said, "no other Leader has enjoyed such freedom since Churchill, and even with him it did not last very long." I suppose he may have thought that I was referring to freedom of choice in making appointments, but I was not, really, I meant freedom in imposing domestic, foreign and defence policies.' Clark was right. No transformation in modern British history had been swifter, or more complete. She now had command of the whole field.

It fitted Mrs Thatcher's deep gratitude to the armed services and her sense of reverence and romance that there should be a service of thanksgiving for victory, and other public celebrations. In all this, however, she was sensitive to accusations of hubris. This made her genuinely reluctant to push herself forward. For the proposed service, for example, she wrote to John Coles: 'It would be much more appropriate for CDS or CinC Fleet to read the lesson. If I did, it would be misinterpreted and leave a <u>bad taste</u>. <u>No politician</u> in my view!'

The discussion of the service itself was fraught. As Mrs Thatcher recorded, 'It was as much as we could do to persuade the Church authorities to allow anyone who had taken part in the Falklands campaign to take part in the service . . .' This was true. Many religious leaders had opposed the war and were deeply uncomfortable. Some clerics suggested they would not take part if members of the armed forces read the lessons. Furious,

---

* The British Antarctic Survey, who had advised her on the terrain, became such favourites that not only did she ensure they received more government money, but she also listened to them when, years later, they warned of the damage to the ozone layer caused by pollution.
† Michael Foot, by contrast, she considered to have been basically patriotic.

Mrs Thatcher 'threatened to make this known in parliament and therefore publicly'. When it was reported to her that the Dean of Saint Paul's wanted the Lord's Prayer in Spanish 'her eyes widened in absolute horror', and at the suggestion that it should be a service of reconciliation rather than thanksgiving she struck the table a tremendous blow and exclaimed scornfully, 'A service of reconciliation!' 'All Christians stay away,' whispered Clive Whitmore *sotto voce*.

For the service, at the end of July, Mrs Thatcher arrived 'looking absolutely like a thundercloud'. Although it had been agreed that servicemen would read biblical passages, she remained concerned that the armed services might be denied proper thanks and consequent spiritual comfort. It was the Queen who put her finger on the problem. 'I don't think you should ever leave a Christian service feeling sad,' she said to the Archbishop of Canterbury afterwards. 'The service was not well arranged for that reason.' Mrs Thatcher herself summed it up: 'The Thanksgiving part was virtually dropped from the Service. But because of the presence of the Queen and all the Royal Family – the superb pageantry of the military band – trumpeters, the service was a great comfort to the bereaved and that mattered more than anything else.'

The secular celebrations were less awkward. On 12 October, 1,250 representatives of the Task Force marched to Guildhall, with a fly-past of helicopters and aircraft. Then there was lunch inside. When Mrs Thatcher rose to speak from the high table at which she sat with the top brass, 'Before she could say anything,' recalled Julian Thompson, 'there was a standing ovation from the floor, started by the boys. The other politicians couldn't believe what was happening. When Mrs Thatcher had quietened everyone down, she said "It is I who should be down there, thanking you."' The night before, at No. 10, she gave dinner for 120 of those most involved in the Falklands victory. In her speech after dinner she quoted the Duke of Wellington: 'There is no such thing as a little war for a great nation.' 'She spoke like Queen Elizabeth I,' remembered David Goodall. 'She *looked* like Queen Elizabeth I!'

So many people had been invited to the dinner that there was no room for spouses, who were instead invited for post-dinner drinks in the drawing rooms. Because all the main players in the Falklands crisis had been men, Mrs Thatcher was the only woman at dinner. After the toasts which followed her speech, the Prime Minister rose in her seat again and said, 'Gentlemen, shall we join the ladies?' It may well have been the happiest moment of her life.

13
Landslide, 1983

*'I live in a big house called 10 Downing Street. I'm
going to live there for a long time'*

By October 1982, Margaret Thatcher had led her country continuously for longer than any of her major Western counterparts. In little more than three years, she had moved from ingénue of international politics to doyenne. The Falklands victory ensured this transformation was swift and dramatic. She felt that her beliefs were being vindicated, and that she was entitled, more than ever, to export them.

Within ten days of her Falklands triumph on 14 June, Mrs Thatcher was addressing the UN General Assembly in New York, expounding her doctrine of 'peace with freedom and justice' rather than 'peace at any price'. She boldly described the nuclear deterrent as a 'priceless achievement' because it made such peace possible. At her party's conference on 8 October, she made clear that freedom and justice were not just the guarantors of the carve-up between West and East, but dynamic forces opposed by 'political systems *evil* enough to seek to enslave the whole world'. She saw freedom everywhere on the march. Citing her government's privatizations, Mrs Thatcher claimed that 'already we have done more to roll back the frontiers of socialism than any previous Conservative Government'. Her battles, at home and abroad, had the same purpose, and she was winning them.

Mrs Thatcher's dealings with her ministers reflected her new dominance. David Goodall, a Cabinet Office official, bore witness during the summer of 1982:

> In Cabinet, Mrs Thatcher's authority seemed absolute, and her manner that of a headmistress dealing with recalcitrant staff ... she came across as though she were 'everyone's mother in a bad temper'. 'WHO authorised this memorandum?' she demanded ... waving a paper indignantly before her. Silence. 'WHO authorised it?' Eventually, the Secretary of State for Wales ... poked

his head cautiously round the Cabinet Secretary (Robert Armstrong) and said, 'I did, Prime Minister.' Pause. 'But I cleared it with the Chancellor of the Exchequer.' Geoffrey Howe simply studied his papers. 'And with the Foreign Secretary.' Francis Pym remained similarly silent. 'Well, it should NEVER have been issued.'

Mrs Thatcher had always had a tendency to hector, but in the past this had been restrained by the weakness of her political position. Now this restraint was lessened. In Goodall's experience, although 'acerbic in argument', she was never 'actually rude to officials'. But her personality would change dramatically depending on the setting:

> at a meeting there is something actually repellent about the poisoned smile and didactic way in which she reiterates her points. In informal conversation, she sheds her scaly covering, her smile becomes normal, her femininity apparent and one can argue with her in a friendly, even bantering way. But it is still extraordinarily difficult to find a point of entry to put a case counter to the one she is making.

Mrs Thatcher's refusal to provide that easy 'point of entry' was essential to her way of working. Given that she was radical, always kicking against the pricks of bureaucracy and inertia, she could not have maintained momentum if she had made life easy for nay-sayers. But her methods did store up resentment from Cabinet colleagues, even her political allies.

A common complaint from Tory critics was that Mrs Thatcher was not really a conservative at all. The Wets saw her as a 'nineteenth-century liberal', a doctrinaire free-marketeer who reduced the subtleties of human society to the dry facts of a balance sheet. This was never the case. She was, in fact, rather historically minded, although her sense of history was more romantic than accurate. She was also much more specifically British and less austerely theoretical than her critics alleged. Thatcherism was more a vision than a doctrine. She carried in her head a picture of her country derived from its past greatness, energetically projected on to its future. From her earliest political declarations as a young candidate in Dartford, this vision had been present; now it became more explicit.

In late 1982, showing the writer Sir Laurens van der Post around 10 Downing Street for a television programme, Mrs Thatcher revealed how her choice of pictures and decorations was influenced by her self-identification with the high points of Britain's greatness. She pointed out the Chinese Chippendale table which had belonged to Clive of India,

Pitt the Younger's desk and the portraits of Nelson and Wellington.* In acknowledgement of her background, she was building up 'a little scientific gallery' with pictures or busts of Humphry Davy, Joseph Priestley and Grantham's most famous son, Isaac Newton. In the Cabinet Room, she pointed out, she sat in 'Winston's chair'. Against this backdrop, van der Post drew her out. 'Would you have been a Roundhead or a Cavalier?' he inquired. 'Oh, no slightest shadow,' replied the woman often accused of being a puritan, '. . . I'd have been a Cavalier, a Royalist.'†

In material not broadcast, Mrs Thatcher reverted to her childhood fascination with India, in whose civil service she had aspired to work. She said that the British record there had been blemished by the colour bar, but all the same 'we taught what was right and we upheld what was right', and it was the Lord Chief Justice Lord Mansfield who had, as she quoted, 'let the black go' in a famous eighteenth-century court case (*Somerset* vs *Stewart*, 1772), signalling the end of slavery. The Empire had stood for 'incorruptible law – the incorruptible military – the incorruptible civil servants'. Referring to the common law, she praised Blackstone and Coke – 'fantastically courageous men . . . who said to the king: "No. These things do not come from a king . . . these rights come from God, and you are not entitled to set them aside."' Much of civilization, she slightly grudgingly admitted, came from Continental Europe, 'And yet the law came from us.'

A critic of Mrs Thatcher's historical assertions could easily have mocked her odd mixture of Liberal imperialism and the Tory bloody-mindedness of Lord Salisbury. He could have laughed at her romantic schoolgirl's idea of a national past teeming with great men and great ideas. But she had her answer for such people. They were, she declared in November 1982, part of the 'army of professional belittlers'. She had been criticized for preaching 'the parables of the parlour. But I do not repent: those parables would have saved many a financier from failure and many a country from crisis.' What some saw as grand simplicities were for her passionate declarations of belief.

In January 1983, Brian Walden suggested she was proposing 'an approval of what I would call Victorian values'. Mrs Thatcher grabbed the

---

* She told van der Post that she had been thinking of Wellington 'very much because I was very upset at the people who lost their lives in the Falklands . . . he walked around the battlefield [of Waterloo] totally and utterly sickened and grief-stricken by it'.
† When Woodrow Wyatt raised the Cavalier or Roundhead question with Mrs Thatcher in private, however, at lunch at Chequers in 1986, she said she 'must be a bit of a Puritan, particularly as she doesn't draw her full salary as Prime Minister but now they've bought [their house in] Dulwich she rather wishes she had . . . "I'm a Cavalier," says Denis.'

phrase: 'Oh exactly. Very much so. Those were the values when our country became great, but not only did our country become great internationally, also so much advance was made in this country.' The phrase stuck. To her critics it stood for inequality and evoked poverty, workhouses and other horrors. What she sought to capture, however, was the Victorian spirit of improvement and reliance on community and voluntary organizations. As she put it, 'as our people prospered, so they used their independence and initiative to prosper others, not compulsion by the State'. This was what she so admired.*

The world's heightened expectations of Mrs Thatcher, and her own rhetoric about the British commitment to freedom, were soon put to the test by the issue of Hong Kong. This prosperous, capitalist port was a British colony which had flourished despite the hostility of neighbouring Communist China. The island of Hong Kong itself had belonged to Britain absolutely since 1842, but the surrounding New Territories were rented from China. China, however, rejected Britain's rights over both freehold and leasehold. From 1997, when Britain's lease expired, it wanted the whole place back.

Emotionally, though not physically, ethnically or economically, Hong Kong resembled the Falklands: most of its people were pro-British and dreaded the rule of the country which laid claim to it. But, unlike in the Falklands, there was a lease set to expire and the overwhelming might, in the last resort, of the People's Liberation Army. Early in her premiership, Mrs Thatcher seemed little moved by the issue. As late as January 1982 she had underlined approvingly a report from Sir Percy Cradock, the British Ambassador in Peking† and the most important Foreign Office 'China hand', which noted that 'a willingness to cede sovereignty . . . will be essential to an [sic] satisfactory settlement'. No mention was made of the people of Hong Kong.‡ It suited both Communist China and the Foreign Office that the people's wishes should not be the decisive factor in the territory's future. Mrs Thatcher disliked both these entities, but until the second half of 1982 she did not get in their way.

---

* In a letter to John Evans, MP, dated 5 May 1983, Mrs Thatcher explained that when she spoke of Victorian values 'I mean respect for the individual, thrift, initiative, a sense of personal responsibility, respect for others and their property, and all the other values that characterised the best of the Victorian era.'

† At this time, the Chinese capital was always referred to in government in its Europeanized 'Wade-Giles' version – Peking. Gradually, from the 1980s, people in the West started to use the 'Pinyin' rendering – Beijing.

‡ 'Hong Kong people' was the phrase for the colony's inhabitants preferred to 'Hong Kong citizens' because it avoided the question of whether their status was British, Chinese or something in between. Since the British Nationality Act of 1981, they had lacked right of abode in the UK.

Immediately after the Falklands victory, however, with a visit to China planned for September, she focused on the issue. With her elevation of the rule of law over diplomacy, she paid attention to the treaties with China, questioning the Foreign Office's idea that these should be discarded just because the Chinese demanded it. Her hope, at this stage, was that Britain's freehold on Hong Kong island might be retained even if the New Territories were to revert to China. At a meeting on 28 July with Cradock, Antony Acland, Edward Youde, the new Governor of Hong Kong, and Francis Pym, the Foreign Secretary, she worried that China had 'a fundamental lack of comprehension' of what was needed to maintain confidence in Hong Kong. Cradock retorted that the Chinese were determined to assert their sovereignty regardless. Mrs Thatcher, however, sought to park the sovereignty question and discuss administrative arrangements to perpetuate the current free-market system after 1997. What she could not do, she insisted, 'particularly in the light of the recent Falkland Islands problem, was simply to announce that we had conceded sovereignty over Hong Kong.' The meeting agreed that her visit's minimum objective should be talks about the future of Hong Kong without prejudicial public statements.

As John Coles put it, Mrs Thatcher had 'a very strong feeling in her mind that it was inconsistent to hand over British territory'. This caused tension with the Foreign Office. In early September, as the visit to China approached, she told Youde and leading Hong Kong people that her 'instinct was to concede nothing until it was clear we could obtain precisely what we wanted'. This led Cradock to express 'serious reservations'. It was important, he warned Pym, to 'make a bow to the Chinese position on sovereignty' or risk 'the complete failure of the visit'.

Mrs Thatcher arrived in Peking on 22 September. Her trip proved particularly arduous because she had recently endured an operation on her varicose veins. Meeting the Chinese premier Zhao Ziyang, she sought to evade the sovereignty question: 'Confidence in Hong Kong,' she insisted, 'and thus its continued prosperity, depend on British administration.' Zhao told her bluntly that the return of sovereignty to China could not be delayed after 1997. If necessary, sovereignty would take precedence over prosperity.

On 24 September, Mrs Thatcher met Deng Xiaoping. Those present felt an air of unease as the two formidable individuals confronted one another. Robin Butler remembered a 'great diatribe' by Deng, with Mrs Thatcher being 'pretty equally aggressive'. While she spoke, Deng started hawking and expectorating into the spittoon which was uncomfortably near to her: 'She moved her legs. It threw her.' She spoke of her 'duty, which she felt deeply ... to reach a result acceptable to the people of Hong Kong'.

She reminded him of the validity of existing treaties 'in international law', which must be changed only by agreement, and proposed talks about continued British administration after 1997. Deng flatly refused. Sovereignty would return to China in 1997. 'That was certain.' It was a precondition of any agreement.

'After two and a half hours,' according to Butler, 'it all seemed disastrous,' but, discussing a communiqué, a form of words provided by Cradock which said nothing about sovereignty made quick progress. The statement said both sides wished to secure 'the stability and prosperity of Hong Kong' and agreed to start talks. To British surprise, 'Deng snapped his fingers in approval.'* As she left, Mrs Thatcher stumbled on the steps of the Great Hall of the People, which, according to Chinese superstition, was an ill omen.

She flew on to Hong Kong – the first visit there by a British prime minister in office – where she pledged to speak 'for Britain's moral responsibility and duty to the people of Hong Kong'. Hong Kong people were pleased by her visit, but extremely anxious. China's public comments were tough. Within ten days of Mrs Thatcher leaving China, the Hong Kong stock market had fallen 25 per cent. Nonetheless, as Cradock acknowledged, her visit to China did 'secure our main objective' – the agreement to begin talks.

A war of nerves ensued. The Chinese put out belligerent propaganda and prevaricated about starting talks. But Mrs Thatcher held firm. In November she gave dinner to Henry Kissinger at No. 10. 'That whole evening was her fighting the idea of giving Hong Kong up at all,' he recalled. 'And then seeing various levels of retreat.' Having just visited the Chinese leadership, Kissinger reported they 'were not angry with the Prime Minister. They respected her and did not regard her as hostile.' The best tactic, he told her, was to avoid demands about sovereignty and focus on administration. A month later, Kissinger wrote to her saying the Chinese would welcome informal talks. But Mrs Thatcher remained unhappy. The Chinese ideas, she replied, 'still fall a long way short of a really satisfactory package'. They wanted an 'autonomous, capitalist-style Hong Kong under China's control', but without any guarantee of future freedom, prosperity and stability. At the end of 1982, she discreetly sought an assessment

---

* It showed how the Chinese government wished to make life uncomfortable for Mrs Thatcher that, as she gave the 'return' banquet to her hosts in the Great Hall of the People that evening, most of the leadership did not attend, but caroused with the North Korean dictator, Kim Il Sung, in another part of the building. The British team were also ill-treated by being given inferior accommodation. Only Denis Thatcher overcame this indignity by complaining so loudly (in the apparent privacy of his own room) that he did not have a gin and tonic that the eavesdroppers arranged for some to be supplied.

from the Chiefs of Staff about reinforcing and defending Hong Kong. The unsurprising verdict was that it could not be militarily defended for long.

China's refusal to engage in talks until its sovereignty was conceded divided the British side. Mrs Thatcher characteristically sought ways of entrenching public support for her approach: 'Perhaps we should now develop the democratic structure [in Hong Kong] as though it were our aim to achieve independence or self-government.' Equally in character, the Foreign Office was anxious to prevent Hong Kong people having a say. In February 1983, Francis Pym warned there might be no alternative to 'Chinese recovery both of sovereignty and administrative control after 1997'. Therefore, he wrote, 'we must not allow our consideration for the "wishes of the people" to develop into acceptance of the paramountcy of [their] will'. He advocated 'the avoidance of unhelpful or unrealistic commitments ... in particular, the acceptance of responsibility with no power to fulfil it'.

Ill disposed to Pym at the best of times, Mrs Thatcher exploded: 'It is not a question of new acceptance of responsibility,' she scribbled, 'WE HAVE IT ALREADY BY VIRTUE OF THE TREATIES.' 'This paper is pathetic,' she wrote, '– it is a recipe for a sell-out. There are other possibilities.' She now proposed dual sovereignty after 1997 whereby the two countries ran the place together.*

As so often when she argued most strenuously, Mrs Thatcher knew she was in a tight spot. On 10 March 1983 she wrote a secret letter to Zhao Ziyang, which Percy Cradock, who devised it, called 'the first finesse'. While, strictly speaking, her letter did not concede anything, it acknowledged that Chinese sovereignty would be recognized if agreement could be reached on administrative arrangements acceptable to Parliament and the people of Hong Kong. Zhao, in his reply, deliberately misinterpreted this as agreement to the recovery of sovereignty by China as 'the premise and basis for further talks'. But he also declared the way open for negotiations. Then came the general election.

The Foreign Office saw the process described above as a year's work in getting Mrs Thatcher to make the inevitable concessions over sovereignty. There is something in this. As time passed, she did end up tacitly accepting many of Cradock's arguments. But there is a counter-case to be made. According to John Gerson, at the time one of the government's greatest China experts, she understood something which the Foreign Office sinologists did not. She had a clear sense of the evil of the regime. People like

---

* Under this arrangement, China would get back the New Territories while Britain kept Hong Kong proper.

Cradock, in Gerson's view, tended to see the nastiness of the Communists as a reason for concessions: 'It became a mantra that "This is a question of sovereignty for the Chinese," at which point the Foreign Office always wanted to give in to them.' Mrs Thatcher's opposite reaction – to harden up – gave the Chinese pause. 'She went without knowing what her final objective would be and brilliantly left them not knowing what theirs was.' Her treatment of Deng as an equal when they met was 'completely baffling for the Chinese. It made them say: "Hang on! They've just squashed the Argies. They have got Polaris. Perhaps they *won't* give Hong Kong back."' In this view, if Mrs Thatcher had behaved according to diplomatic norms the Chinese would have won hands down. By being bolder she achieved 'seismic uncertainty'. Because of her stubbornness, both parties had time to adjust and discuss. Luckily, China *was* changing. Mrs Thatcher's 'unreasonableness' made real negotiation possible as conventional diplomatic behaviour would not have done.

The arrival of Helmut Kohl as Chancellor of West Germany in October 1982 seemed good news for Mrs Thatcher. The Social Democratic Party (SPD) of his predecessor, Helmut Schmidt, was split over the deployment of INF missiles. Kohl's conservative Christian Democrats were considered more reliable allies. Kohl, who, though already Chancellor, had yet to win an election, believed that her prestige could assist him politically.

Once in power, Kohl communicated his desire to visit Mrs Thatcher. He wished, reported the British Ambassador in Bonn, to 'lay the basis for an effective personal dialogue with the Prime Minister'. Flatteringly, Kohl sought 'advice on how to handle his discussions with President Reagan'. She was happy to help. Kohl, John Coles briefed her, was keen on a public presentation of friendship: he suggested a photocall outside 10 Downing Street, 'emphasising a meeting of minds'.

When the two leaders met in Downing Street on 19 October, they were mostly in accord. Kohl told her he was 'resolved' to accept US missiles on German soil and determined to be 'full friends and partners of the United States'. This inclined her to agree with some of Kohl's criticisms of President Reagan's aggressive approach. 'She had the clear impression that the Americans now recognised that the action which they had taken over the [Siberian gas] pipeline was a mistake and were looking for a way out.'

In a recent address to the Bundestag, Kohl had called for 'progress towards the unification of Europe', so Mrs Thatcher was well aware that he did not share her vision in this regard. There was, however, no set-to about the European Community in their meeting. With the press afterwards, Mrs Thatcher used the approved phrase about 'a true meeting of minds'. Kohl agreed but was also open about his goal of realizing 'the unification of Europe in the course of this decade'. She could not say later that she had not been warned.

Now it was her turn to visit Kohl. In Berlin, on 29 October, Mrs Thatcher was greeted by enthusiastic crowds who 'told her that they were heartened by her actions in the Falklands'. As she contemplated the Berlin Wall for the first time, tears came into her eyes. 'I think it's even worse than I imagined,' she told reporters. 'I laid flowers. There was one young girl [shot trying to escape to the West], she was only 18 . . .' The 'lesson of Poland' under Soviet-backed martial law, she said, was that 'pitiless ideology only survives because it is maintained by force': eventually it would be overcome by popular anger. 'One day,' she concluded, 'liberty will dawn on the other side of the wall.'

Already, relations between Mrs Thatcher and Kohl were not particularly cordial. She found him boring, long-winded and intellectually inferior. With his great girth, ponderous manner and unglamorous looks, Kohl was not her type of man. Besides, as a child of the Second World War, she had a prejudice against his nationality which his demeanour brought out. Once, she took the present author aside, as if to share a confidence. 'You know the trouble with Helmut Kohl?' she asked, '– He's a *German.*' At this stage, however, none of this surfaced. Kohl saw her visit as 'a gesture of friendship and solidarity with the Germans'.

By early 1983, the struggle over INF deployment was coming to a head. With no breakthrough in arms control talks with the Soviets, American missiles were due to arrive in Europe later that year. Successful deployment promised to hand the West a significant victory in the Cold War. But the Campaign for Nuclear Disarmament (CND), with covert Soviet backing, stirred up opposition across Europe. Mrs Thatcher was particularly alarmed by the strength of neutralism in Germany. Refusal to accept the missiles on German soil, the policy of the opposition SPD, would probably be fatal to the whole enterprise. At Chequers on 4 February she told Kohl she 'wished to do all we could presentationally to help'.* 'We are the true disarmers,' she said, standing with Kohl at the press conference that followed, 'in that we stand for all-sided disarmament, but on a basis of balance.' Whatever their inner thoughts, the two leaders had become close allies.

As she prepared for her next election, Mrs Thatcher sought help from her friend Ronald Reagan. Privately, the Americans were horrified at the

---

* Thinking about the date that deployment might begin purely in terms of electoral politics, Mrs Thatcher told Kohl she favoured November 1983. This implied she was considering going to the polls in or before October.

prospect of Michael Foot's unilateralist Labour Party taking power. In early 1983 an opportunity to help Mrs Thatcher – and thus hinder Foot – arose. In Britain there was growing public concern over the possibility of the Americans deciding unilaterally to launch their missiles from British soil. Mrs Thatcher knew that the 1952 Truman-Churchill agreement provided the British Prime Minister with a veto over the use of US nuclear weapons based in Britain, but because this remained secret, her ability to reassure the public was constrained.*

In mid-April she despatched the British Ambassador in Washington, Oliver Wright, to see Reagan. 'Mrs Thatcher will be asking for your approval in saying more openly that she has a veto over the use of those weapons,' Judge Clark, the National Security Advisor, warned the President. Expert opinion in Washington was deeply opposed. Theoretically, any veto weakened the deterrent effect of deployed missiles because it made it less likely that they would be launched. More important, the Americans feared similar demands from less reliable allies. By appealing directly to Reagan, Mrs Thatcher circumvented these concerns. 'We were all worried that anything Margaret Thatcher asked for, Ronald Reagan would want us to give her,' recalled one NSC staffer. Sure enough, Reagan authorized her to tell Parliament that 'no nuclear weapon would be fired or launched from British territory without the agreement of the British Prime Minister'. Thus she persuaded the President to overrule official caution and overturn forty years of precedent. She had asserted a principle central to Britain's national interest and gained valuable ammunition for the coming election.

In domestic politics, the question of the election date coloured all decisions. Mrs Thatcher's natural inclination was to press on with reform, but its timing carried electoral risks. Despite the gradual improvement in the British economy, the problems of public spending remained severe. In January 1982 unemployment had risen above 3 million for the first time. On 15 July, armed with the latest sluggish growth figures, Geoffrey Howe warned the Cabinet that the progress of recovery was 'hesitant and patchy'. Mrs Thatcher sought tight control of spending, not least because the next Budget would be the last chance for pre-election tax cuts. The critics, meanwhile, focused on unemployment, which Michael Heseltine insisted would be the 'crucial issue' at the next election. Unlike the previous summer, the Cabinet did not fail outright to agree a strategy, but scepticism was strong.

* It was noted, in Cabinet committee, that in the highly unlikely event that the President failed to make good on this commitment, British personnel could 'take action which would make it virtually impossible for the Americans to launch their weapons'.

That summer, the 'Think Tank' (the Central Policy Review Staff) offered its own suggestions for tackling public spending. Under the directorship of John Sparrow, it had shed its Heathite origins and now proposed such dramatic changes as an end to the state funding of higher education (to be replaced by student loans), education vouchers for schools, the de-indexing of all social security payments and replacing the National Health Service (NHS) with a system of private health insurance.

After the Think Tank paper was circulated at Cabinet on 9 September, a storm of protest erupted. Speaking for many, Peter Walker said that such things were 'for party matters, not Whitehall'. Mrs Thatcher hit back (as abbreviated by Armstrong): 'Are you saying not in Cab.? That is astonishing.' She felt that the ideas in the report should be 'pursued': 'We must not duck them.' Regretting that the paper had been circulated, Walker said: 'I have no doubt that it will leak.' He then leaked it himself to the *Economist*. Outrage followed. The government, it was claimed, was trying to abolish the welfare state. Although Mrs Thatcher later wrote that she was 'horrified' by the paper, this was not so. Its suggestions reflected her direction of travel. Nothing about them upset her, except for the political embarrassment they caused.

The fiasco had two consequences. The first was the end of the Think Tank. Even before the leak, Mrs Thatcher had come to resent that it did not work directly for her, and wanted to wind it up. She had been persuaded to stay her hand, but the leak hardened her views. It was duly abolished after the 1983 election. Meanwhile, the role of the Policy Unit, which did work exclusively for Mrs Thatcher, grew. Under Ferdinand Mount, who had replaced John Hoskyns as Director, the unit became more capable of giving form to her often inchoate ideas and projecting them across Whitehall. As Mount recalled, their aim was to enlist Mrs Thatcher's 'angry will . . . If we could catch her enthusiasm she would immediately run with it and haul in the relevant minister and carpet him. He would glare at us.' The unit produced crisp, clear memos developing specific policy issues along Thatcherite lines. These usually avoided the grand ideological sweep which, if leaked, could cause such mayhem.

Mrs Thatcher also sought independent advice on foreign affairs. In August 1982, with her Falklands experience in mind, she suggested a full, separate foreign affairs and security policy unit. She wanted Sir Anthony Parsons to head it. This caused fury in the Foreign Office. Pym, Armstrong reported, feared it would be 'very damaging to the morale of the diplomatic service (already bruised)' and 'be seen as a "slap in the face" for himself'. Mrs Thatcher maintained her position – 'I have made a firm decision.' Discussing it with Pym, on 18 October, proved disagreeable. He accepted she should have advice, 'but not in a form which would create divisions between her and himself. He was already disturbed by reports of such divisions.' With an ill grace, he accepted Parsons's appointment but, when the story leaked, had what Ferdinand Mount remembered as 'a complete hissy fit'. He told Mrs Thatcher her staff were leaking against him. She denied slighting her Foreign Secretary, but the fact remained that she did have a low opinion of Pym and made little effort to conceal it. The appointment of Parsons did not fulfil Pym's fears. He was, by and large, a 'Foreign Office man' and his genial, well-informed presence helped make Mrs Thatcher less jumpy about what the Foreign Office might be up to.

The second consequence of the CPRS leak, however, was bad for Mrs Thatcher. The impetus for reforming government spending was gravely slowed. As the annual party conference approached, fears that the government wished to abolish the NHS ran wild. At Cabinet on 30 September, Willie Whitelaw intoned (as abbreviated by Armstrong): 'Grave political danger abt NHS, following CPRS paper. The PM alone can kill it.' When Mrs Thatcher addressed the conference, she had to box herself in: 'Let me make one thing absolutely clear. The National Health Service is safe with us,' she declared, before renewing her commitment to healthcare for all, regardless of ability to pay.

Before the general election the following June, Mrs Thatcher made no further speeches about the social policy areas covered in the CPRS report. Frequently criticized for trying 'to dismantle the welfare state', she was, in truth, more open to the opposite charge that she shied away from serious reform. The effects of this hesitation would be visible throughout her time in office.

Not that policy work on all these subjects abruptly ceased. In November 1982, Keith Joseph produced a report on education vouchers. This long-standing, market-minded idea was that parents should be offered state-funded vouchers covering a school education redeemable at the school of their choice. Joseph, however, had not put this into practice. The plan he presented offered vouchers only for parents who wished to send their children to independent schools.* Even getting this far, Ferdinand Mount told Mrs Thatcher, had been a 'tremendous struggle': 'At every step, the opposition of the bureaucracy has been fierce and unremitting. We are facing nearly 40 years of fossilised prejudice.' Nonetheless,

---

* In framing it thus Joseph was, in effect, proposing an expansion of the existing Assisted Places Scheme offering funding for some pupils to attend independent schools, rather than comprehensive reform.

he argued that Joseph had to think bigger: *every* parent should receive a voucher. Mrs Thatcher agreed. Joseph revised his draft accordingly, but now suggested that most parents who used the voucher would have to pay something themselves towards their children's education. 'In many ways,' Mount commented, 'the latest draft is worse than the first. It is obviously politically dangerous. I also think it is both unjust and unnecessary.' On 8 March, Mrs Thatcher rejected Joseph's efforts: it now became clear that nothing would be ready in time for the election. Joseph was the intellectual driving force of Thatcherism, but he was also, by character, a Hamlet. So education reform was 'sicklied o'er with the pale cast of thought'. A key moment was missed.

The choice of election date also affected the progress of privatization. Privatization policy had taken shape only gradually and was still, even by 1982, far from settled. In Opposition Mrs Thatcher had favoured denationalization, but considered the subject too dangerous to pursue. A seventh of the British workforce was employed by nationalized industries. She feared the claim that privatization would produce mass unemployment and the possibility of an unstoppable wave of strikes in those industries brought to market. In addition, the state of most nationalized industries was considered too parlous for them to find a buyer. So cautious was she that the word 'privatization' had not even appeared in the 1979 Conservative manifesto.*

In office, the Treasury, more than Mrs Thatcher, pushed the subject forward. The most pressing reason was the need for money. In November 1979, £290 million was raised from selling part of the government's remaining 51 per cent stake in BP.† The sale of council houses, following the 1980 Housing Act, though never described as such, was another early form of privatization. Its success in spreading popular ownership showed that such an approach could reap political rewards.

Gradually, progress was made. The focus, for now, was on asset sales, including shares in British Aerospace (BAe) and the sale of Cable and Wireless and Amersham International.‡ In October 1981 Nigel Lawson, the Energy Secretary, announced the privatization of the entire oil-producing

---

* The only sell-offs mentioned in the manifesto were those of the recently nationalized shipbuilding and aircraft industries, and the sale of shares in the National Freight Corporation.
† A precedent for such a sale had been set by the Labour government, desperate for money, in 1977.
‡ These offerings proved widely popular: Cable and Wireless was oversubscribed 5.6 times and Amersham International twenty-four times. The underpricing sent out a clear message that there was money to be made in privatizations.

business of the British National Oil Corporation (BNOC). Arguing his case, Lawson enunciated the general doctrine: 'No industry should remain under State ownership unless there is a positive and overwhelming case for it so doing.' The sale of Britoil (the company hived off from BNOC) brought in £549 million just over a year later, the largest sum raised to date.

By the end of 1981, privatization had become a major aim of the Thatcher government, rather than a mere scramble for cash. Increasingly, ministers tried to weigh the desire to maximize proceeds against other claims – wider share ownership, employee share ownership, greater management efficiency and more competition.

Privatization eventually became Mrs Thatcher's best-known global export, but she was not yet its cheerleader. Lawson believed she 'went along with it initially entirely because of the money it could raise'. Others considered her driven by her desire for wider share ownership. But privatization was for her, at first at least, more a solution to a problem than a grand ideological principle. According to Oliver Letwin, that problem was 'getting the industries concerned to run properly and getting rid of their subsidy'. In the case of natural monopolies, such as water, she started from the proposition that they would be better regulated by government, and 'had no strong feeling that these citadels should be stormed'. According to Peter Gregson, working at the Department of Trade and then at the Cabinet Office, there was 'not a lot of "We must forge ahead with this" from Mrs Thatcher; more, "I hope they know what they're doing"'.

By far the most important first-term test of privatization came with British Telecom (BT). This gigantic monopoly, spun out of the Post Office, controlled almost all the telephones in Britain. The entire company, employing nearly 250,000 people, was unionized. There was a desperate need for modernization,* but no prospect of the Treasury authorizing the necessary expenditure because of the hit to the PSBR. So the search for new money was on.

In July 1981, Keith Joseph persuaded Mrs Thatcher that BT should be privatized, a decision then endorsed by the Treasury. But when, from September, his successor Patrick Jenkin sought to push ahead, she seemed less certain. 'It's a monopoly,' she said. 'At least if it's in the public sector, we have control of it.' She advised breaking it up, a position Jenkin opposed

---

* In 1981 there was a waiting list of a quarter of a million people for a new phone line, and no promise from BT of a date by which each line could be installed. Towards the end of his first year, George Jefferson, BT's Chairman and Chief Executive, went to tea with Gordon Richardson, the Governor of the Bank of England: 'He told me that, unless I could rapidly improve telecom services in the City, it was almost certain that the City would lose its position as major financial centre.'

because of how long this would take. The Treasury, ever keen on maximum proceeds, wanted the company sold whole.

Despite Mrs Thatcher's misgivings about monopoly, after Jenkin announced the plans for BT to the Commons on 19 July 1982 she was anxious to push ahead and blocked an attempt to refer BT to the Monopolies and Mergers Commission. At the party conference in October she highlighted the privatization, adapting Dr Johnson's famous remark about the effect on a man of knowing that he will be hanged: 'Depend on it,' she said, 'when you know you are going to be privatised in a fortnight it concentrates the mind wonderfully.' She was noting one of the most striking effects of privatization – that the mere prospect of it changed the behaviour of everyone involved. There was insufficient time to pass the necessary legislation before the 1983 general election, but should the Conservatives be returned for a second term it was certain to be reintroduced. None of the biggest and most controversial privatizations had yet taken place, but the way now lay open.

Few subjects were more fraught for Mrs Thatcher's first government than local government spending and the domestic rates. She had been pitched into this area in 1974 when, as Ted Heath's Environment spokesman, she had promised publicly to abolish the rates. The problem, then and afterwards, was what to put in their place. Domestic rates were extremely unpopular, particularly with likely Conservative voters. Because they were a tax on property, they were payable only by householders. This meant that fewer than half of the 35 million local electors in England were liable for them, or, because of various rebates, paid them in full. They therefore bore disproportionately on those who did pay. Militant Labour councils, using their rate-raising power, were only too happy to make that disproportion even greater. How could more accountability be brought to the system of local taxation?

In 1982 the Cabinet subcommittee MISC 79, chaired by Willie Whitelaw, considered the problem, without success. A memo from the Environment Secretary, Michael Heseltine, ruled out a local income tax (incompatible with the government's overall taxation policy) and a local sales tax (too complex and unaccountable). This left a poll tax (so described). Imposing a tax on every voter would offer more accountability. But it would do nothing to address what Heseltine called the 'main complaint about rates ... that the means of taxpayers are not fairly judged'. Unable to see a path through, MISC 79 ruled out the abolition of the domestic rates for the time being.

At this time, local government in the metropolitan areas suffered – or, according to taste, benefited – from an extra layer of government. The idea was growing that the 'mets' and the Greater London Council (the GLC), which harboured the greatest groupings of Labour councillors keen to make difficulty for the government, could be abolished. Heseltine urged caution. The Conservatives must not, he told Mrs Thatcher, 'forget our fundamental beliefs about the constitutional role of local government'. Ferdinand Mount admitted that the abolition of the mets and the GLC was 'superficially attractive', but shied away from another 'commitment whose virtues and defects are not fully explored, as in the case of the promise to abolish the rates'. 'Can it be right', he continued, 'to dispense with some kind of directly elected council for Greater London which speaks for all citizens who regard themselves as Londoners?'

With time running short to come up with something eye-catching for the next election, at the turn of the year Whitelaw reported that his committee lukewarmly recommended abolishing the mets and the GLC. He added it had failed to agree on a plan to impose direct control over rates and spending: the problems, he warned the Cabinet, 'were intractable'. On 3 May, when asked about the rates in an interview, Mrs Thatcher replied: 'The first thing you always have to look at in politics is – "I know what I want to get away from, but what am I going to put in its place?"' Government indecision was almost final, waiting until the moment when the election was called.

The Conservatives were almost bound to win the general election of 1983. The Falklands effect was too strong and the Labour Party, under the leadership of Michael Foot, too weak for any other result to be likely. Even without the Falklands, there had been some Tory recovery. From the week before the Falklands crisis broke, the Conservatives were continuously ahead of Labour in the polls. But, to the woman who had to pick the date of the election, matters were not so obvious.*

Mrs Thatcher had always said that the restoration of Britain would take two or even three terms of Conservative government. 'If we lose, we lose it all,' she told Ferdinand Mount. She worried that settling upon the wrong election date would be fatal. This decision, hers alone, made her extremely tetchy. She understood that trying for a snap election after the Falklands, after scarcely three years in government, would have been seen

---

* Under the British unwritten Constitution, the sitting prime minister has the right to ask the sovereign for the dissolution of Parliament at any point up to the moment when the Parliament's statutory five years are complete.

as opportunist and punished accordingly. Originally, she favoured running the full five years, but by 1983 came to focus on a potential election that October.*

One factor which affected her calculations more than most realized was the inquiry into the invasion of the Falklands she had established under Lord Franks. Mrs Thatcher genuinely feared that Franks might find against her and, if so, recalled Robin Butler, 'she thought she'd be done for'. In fact, the inquiry's report, which she saw on Christmas Eve 1982, found that the invasion 'could not have been foreseen' and the government could not be blamed. In the new year she celebrated by visiting the Falklands, for the first time, in conditions of great secrecy, in part out of fear that Argentina might try to intercept her aircraft.† She was warmly received, although Butler recalled she 'was disillusioned with the locals, whose lethargy shocked her, and fell asleep in their company'. On the other hand, she 'was very happy with the military and behaved like a young filly'. Once she had returned to Britain, election speculation grew. It was becoming harder to get on with the business of government.

Although Labour's weakness was well known, Conservative electoral calculations also had to include a factor which, as a deliberate tactic, Mrs Thatcher hardly ever mentioned in public – the centrist SDP-Liberal Alliance. Moderate Tories fretted that the party needed to tack to the centre to block this new force.‡ In fact the SDP, formed in revolt against the unions' dominance of Labour, also posed a challenge on the right. During 1982, they began to attack the Tories for not going far enough to tackle the unions. That October, Norman Tebbit, the hardline Employment Secretary, warned that the SDP was now making the 'political levy' – the system by which union members automatically paid money to the Labour Party – 'a matter of public debate'. This was difficult, he noted, because any debate over the funding of political parties would focus on the Tories' business

---

* Mrs Thatcher always wanted to keep open the option to go early, however. In September 1982 she wrote to President Reagan, who was at that time proposing to hold the G7 economic summit in Williamsburg on 11 June 1983. She told him that the date was difficult for her, without explaining why. The first draft, not sent, even pretended that she could not come to the United States because of the Sovereign's Birthday Parade ceremony in London. The President, always anxious to help her electorally, took the hint and replied that, because of her anxiety, 'we left the timing vague'.
† The Cabinet Secretary, Robert Armstrong, was authorized to turn her plane round should news of her visit break. She was recognized during her stopover on Ascension Island, and Armstrong endured a sleepless night waiting for the dreaded leak, but the news held until she arrived.
‡ For a background interview in November 1982, Chris Patten, the rising young hope of the Tory Wets, declared he thought 'the Tory party was completely off the rails under Margaret' and he wanted 'people of principle to put out public markers that they dissented'.

donors. The same month, Ferdinand Mount, though generally more moderate than Tebbit, criticized him in a fierce memorandum to Mrs Thatcher, warning of 'complacency and timidity' in trade union reform. 'I agree,' she wrote. Both strike ballots and changes to the political levy were included in a Green Paper Tebbit published in March 1983, but in a conciliatory form that allowed unions to resolve the issues themselves. The SDP made politics more multidimensional when most Conservatives, including Mrs Thatcher, were happy with straightforwardly bashing the left.

The Bermondsey by-election of February 1983 boded ill for the Conservatives. After the Liberals took the seat from Labour, with the largest swing in by-election history (44 per cent), concerns arose that the SDP-Liberal Alliance could overtake Labour nationally, with frighteningly unpredictable electoral results. But the Darlington by-election in March was considered the key barometer of Tory fortunes. If Labour lost, the party likely would ditch Foot and veer suddenly towards electability. In the event, Labour narrowly held the seat from the Conservatives, with the SDP failing to break through. This result was satisfactory for the Tories.

Even now, Mrs Thatcher hung back. To make it difficult for her to go to the country, Denis Healey heckled her in the Commons for wanting to 'cut and run'. Becoming heated, she accused him of fearing an election and let slip a touch of the Lincolnshire dialect which her education had ironed out of her: 'Frightened? Frit? Could not take it? Cannot stand it? If I were going to cut and run, I should have gone after the Falklands. Frightened! Right now inflation is lower than it has been for thirteen years – a record which the right hon. Gentleman could not begin to touch.' Without quite meaning to, she was campaigning already.

Good results in the local elections on 5 May removed the last obvious objection to going to the polls. The manifesto was ready; so were the troops. But Mrs Thatcher was not. Summarizing the weekend's news coverage, Bernard Ingham advised her that 'there is only one topic: the election . . . and <u>when</u> (and whether) an announcement will be made'. On this note she scribbled '<u>Calm Down</u>.' That Sunday, she held a meeting at Chequers to consider election possibilities with Whitelaw, Cecil Parkinson, the Party Chairman, and his Vice-Chairman, Michael Spicer, Howe (in charge of the manifesto), Tebbit, the Chief Whip, Michael Jopling, her PPS, Ian Gow, and various advisers.

With polls heavily favouring the Tories, it was obvious to all that an election should be called – to all, that is, except Mrs Thatcher. She was, perhaps, 'frit'. She produced arguments against each date suggested, while fretting about the unseemliness of 'going early'. The meeting finished without any decision, but Parkinson, Jopling and Gow stayed to supper. As the discussion continued, attention focused on early June, but still she held back.* As Parkinson explained: 'Her resistance to an idea is a technique meaning "Persuade me."' It was also, as Jopling observed, a way of shifting responsibility: 'She was saying, "If this is what you want to do, do it, but don't blame me if it all goes wrong."' After the supper guests had left, Mount heard Mrs Thatcher say to Denis: 'I'm not sure it's the right thing to do at all. I shall sleep on it.' But Denis lost patience: 'You can't do that, Margaret. They've all gone back to town saying it's going to be the 9th ... The horses have bolted.' So 9 June it was.

As soon as the election was called, there was a surge in favour of the Conservatives: one poll suggested a twenty-one-point lead over Labour. Mrs Thatcher had less to do with the manifesto, which was launched on 18 May, than in 1979. Now that she had an actual record on which to fight, it mattered less. Its tone mostly reflected the more 'small-c' conservative and less radical side of her party's nature. In her foreword, Mrs Thatcher spoke not of revolution but of recovery. Britain had renewed its 'confidence and self-respect'. The task was 'to defend Britain's traditional liberties and distinctive way of life'.

The document was quite short and its specific promises were few. Trade union members would be given the right to ballot for election to their governing bodies, with the legal immunity of unions withdrawn if a strike were called without a secret ballot. On unemployment, the manifesto promoted the enormous Youth Training Scheme to ensure that every school-leaver not in further education would be in work or training. Health was presented in terms of extra money spent and higher numbers employed.† Pledges on tax were studiously vague, and modest. The only eye-catching announcements were promises to sell off BT, Rolls-Royce and British Airways‡ and to abolish the GLC and the metropolitan counties.

This was a well-constructed document, creating the space for widespread reform without alarming people with strident language or dangerous detail. The Labour manifesto by contrast pledged to renationalize industries, end the sale of council houses, get out of the European Community and disarm

---

* Mrs Thatcher tried one last, futile way of avoiding the issue. The Queen, she objected, would not be available at short notice to grant a dissolution. Ian Gow slipped out of the room and returned to say that he had spoken to the Palace, and the Queen would be happy to see the Prime Minister at noon the following day. 'If looks could kill, she'd have killed him.'
† The Conservative claim was that only £7.75 billion had been spent on the National Health Service in 1979, compared with £15.5 billion in 1983.
‡ The manifesto named other nationalized industries that would be sold off in part, including British Steel and British Leyland.

unilaterally. The Labour MP Gerald Kaufman famously described it as 'the longest suicide note in history'. Mrs Thatcher carried it with her always and quoted from it gleefully.*

The Conservative manifesto launch set the tone of the campaign. Fizzing with energy, Mrs Thatcher said the choice at the election was 'absolutely stark in philosophical terms': did Britain want greater liberty and a smaller public sector, or a return to state socialism? Although Cabinet ministers sat on the platform and Geoffrey Howe also spoke, she dominated the show. The media enjoyed the confidence and theatricality of her daily press conferences. The political scientist David Butler, who attended them, noted privately, halfway through the campaign, that Mrs Thatcher sounded 'as though she was completely on top of her situation and on top of all her colleagues.† People laughed at her, but admiringly.' The pleasure the press took in these occasions emanated in their favourable coverage.

From the campaign's perspective, the best thing, once the press conferences had set the day's agenda, was to get Mrs Thatcher away from London, charging up and down the country campaigning. This suited her temperament. As Stephen Sherbourne saw it: 'It's a shooting war, and she's a foot soldier. She's not the general back at HQ. She's in the front line.' Except for a few set-piece speeches, her purpose there was not to make political arguments but to be seen in a good light.

This succeeded. In *The Times*, Frank Johnson noted that: 'having her as Prime Minister seems to be part of the natural order of things'. Mrs Thatcher was nonetheless highly unpopular in some areas, and was followed around the country by a tiny mob from the Socialist Workers Party trying to disrupt her every word. She relished the chance to respond to hecklers and, she later recalled, 'was thrilled to bits' when they showed up. Their efforts probably enhanced her standing. For the most part, she was photographed from favourable angles in pleasant places. In the Isle of

---

* Much as she loved attacking Labour, Mrs Thatcher drew the line at anything personal against Michael Foot. A proposed advertisement by Saatchi & Saatchi showed a picture of the sixty-nine-year-old Foot, with his familiar walking stick, over the line 'As a pensioner, he'd be better off with the Conservatives.' Mrs Thatcher was 'appalled'. Tim Bell, presenting the advertisement for Saatchis, recalled that she 'threw me out of the office'.

† At the first press conference, asked about the Falklands, Francis Pym started talking about 'further sensible conversations' with Argentina. Mrs Thatcher cut across him: 'No I'm sorry, I thought you [the press] were going to misunderstand that. The Foreign Secretary said quite clearly on commercial links ... but not on sovereignty.' In fact, the Foreign Secretary had said no such thing, and his discomfiture at the general laughter was visible. The next day, Pym rashly declared that a landslide victory for the Conservatives would not be healthy. Publicly, Mrs Thatcher put this down to 'a natural ... ex-Chief Whip's caution. You know there's a club of Chief Whips. They're very unusual people.' It was apparent that Pym's political career was drawing peacefully to its close.

Wight, for example, she swept up the beach at the prow of a hovercraft, as if she were the figurehead of Britannia on a man-o'-war. At a Finchley supermarket she went on one of her manic pretend shopping trips, but forgot to take any money, and so Carol, accompanying her, had to pay. Michael Foot, meanwhile, had a much harder time. There was no discernible pattern to his outings. Wandering about with his walking stick and his dog, Foot was an endearing figure to many voters, but not remotely a prime ministerial one.

In these circumstances, attacks on Mrs Thatcher which, in more normal times, might well have struck home, failed. This was particularly true of the Falklands, a subject on which she wisely said little. Labour's rising star, Neil Kinnock, hitting back at a heckler who shouted that Mrs Thatcher had 'guts', said it was 'a pity that people had to leave theirs on the ground at Goose Green in order to prove it'.* These remarks damaged only Labour. The party's activists reported that voters 'really admired' her over the Falklands: 'Labour was now seen as the unpatriotic party.'

The Conservatives could not push this line directly in relation to the Falklands, but they could and did in relation to nuclear weapons. Especially among working-class voters, the idea that, through disarming unilaterally, Labour would leave Britain undefended rendered it unfit for government. 'Patriotism' had been 'restored to our vocabulary', Mrs Thatcher declared. Even more importantly, it had become linked, for the first time in modern British politics, with only one party.

In the middle of the campaign came the G7 economic summit at Williamsburg. Mrs Thatcher had agonized constantly about whether she dared be abroad at such a time.† Reagan encouraged her to come, but his aide, Michael Deaver, passed on the President's private thought that 'Hell, the main thing is to get her re-elected.' If she did come, said Deaver, there would be excellent photo opportunities. She decided to go.

Although her friend President Reagan was the host, Mrs Thatcher harboured serious worries that the summit might endorse economic policies

---

* It was over the Falklands, however, that Mrs Thatcher suffered a rare embarrassment during the campaign. In a BBC television phone-in she was asked by Mrs Diana Gould, a member of the public, about the sinking of the *Belgrano*. Mrs Gould appeared to catch her out about the direction which the ship had been taking when she was torpedoed. Mrs Thatcher was flustered. The interview 'really made me jolly cross', she later recalled; 'they had no idea what it was like to be in charge'. Even on the *Belgrano*, however, it was the view of her advisers that the subject was 'a total plus' for Mrs Thatcher with the electorate.
† In one discussion with officials, in which she protested that she could not go, she declared: 'I'll send somebody else.' 'Mr Pym?' presumed an official. Mrs Thatcher looked horrified. 'No, no, not him,' she said. 'I'll send Mike [Michael Scholar, her Treasury private secretary].'

that undermined her own, thus making her more vulnerable electorally. Preparatory meetings of the summit 'sherpas' focused on 'promoting greater stability in exchange rates' and strengthening the machinery for international financial cooperation. 'I do <u>not</u> like the way this is developing,' she scribbled. '... We are in danger of becoming committed to something <u>fundamentally unsound</u> just for the sake of saying something in a communiqué.'

When Mrs Thatcher expressed these concerns to Reagan's team, they agreed to try to lower expectations of what the summit would say. The Americans were also looking for a statement at Williamsburg backing INF deployment in the autumn. Mrs Thatcher was cautious. Naturally she wanted a statement, but she knew that if the Europeans fell out over it one of her best electoral advantages would collapse.

Behind the scenes, the summit was not easy. By the morning of Sunday 29 May the leaders had a draft communiqué that Mrs Thatcher pronounced 'excellent'. François Mitterrand, however, objected to the declaration's endorsement of NATO policy, though not to that policy's content.* The Canadian Prime Minister, Pierre Trudeau, meanwhile declared that the statement was sending 'the wrong message, utterly and tragically wrong'. Instead of endorsing INF deployment, it should offer 'something about mutual trust'.

Mrs Thatcher pointed out that she was fighting, and Kohl had recently fought, a general election on this issue: Trudeau's words were 'utterly devastating and could only give comfort to the Soviet Union'. Reagan urged his fellow leaders to accept the proposed declaration. There would be 'a barrage of headlines' if they failed to agree, and besides, the strategy would work: 'The Soviet Union were at full economic stretch ... faced with the possibility of an arms race, the Soviet Union would pull back.'

After a few changes to please Mitterrand, Reagan won the day. Mrs Thatcher returned to London well pleased. On economics, the summit had resisted coordination mechanisms for economic policy and pushed for lower interest rates. On defence, it had endorsed INF deployment. She was delighted not only by the substance, but by Reagan's skill and charm at Williamsburg. 'The President was wonderful,' she told Parkinson. 'He had done his homework.'

On 2 June, a Harris poll put the Conservatives on 46 per cent, Labour on 28 per cent and the Alliance on 24 per cent. Forty-six per cent of those

---

* Mitterrand's objection was based on France's special position outside the NATO command structure.

backing the Tories attributed their support to Mrs Thatcher's leadership; only 31 per cent mentioned the party's policies.

As the election campaign progressed, Mrs Thatcher was vindicated in her then unfashionable view that the SDP-Liberal Alliance was far less formidable than her party had feared. This, alongside Labour's travails and her success at Williamsburg, led her to cast aside some of her habitual caution.* Arriving at Manchester airport on 1 June, she approached a small boy riding in a ten-pence-a-ride miniature aeroplane. 'My name's Margaret Thatcher,' she announced, 'and I live in a big house called 10 Downing Street. I'm going to live there for a long time.' There were now no serious dangers for the Conservative campaign. Mrs Thatcher felt sufficiently confident to spare the party's coffers by ordering Cecil Parkinson to cancel the three-page newspaper advertisements planned for the last Sunday of the campaign.

It has become historical orthodoxy that Mrs Thatcher dominated the 1983 election campaign. This is true, in the sense that her personality, energy and record were the focus of attention, but only in the last party political broadcast, two days before polling, did she take centre stage. By now, consistently strong polls had stilled fears that she might put off floating voters and the broadcast spoke of the things achieved 'because of one woman'. When that woman herself appeared in a grey-blue suit against a background of roses, she held out 'the certainty of liberty' and 'the chance of property ownership'. Voters should ask themselves, she said, 'who would best defend our freedom, our way of life, and the much loved land in which we live'.

On 27 May, with less than two weeks of the campaign remaining, David Butler interviewed Cecil Parkinson. The Party Chairman, he felt, 'showed extraordinary anxiety for someone who was 15 per cent ahead in the polls ... why he should have been under such strain I can't imagine'. At Saatchi & Saatchi, there was confusion as to why a certain poster kept being rejected by Central Office. It showed a newborn baby held by a midwife, and boasted of the government's increase in nurses and midwives under the slogan 'Even labour's better under the Conservatives'.

The explanation was tragi-comic. On polling day, Mrs Thatcher summoned Parkinson to No. 10 to discuss his future. 'I'd thought of Foreign

---

* Even so, Mrs Thatcher was reluctant to finalize plans for her likely return to Downing Street for a second term. 'Let's not count chickens,' she scribbled on a note from Bernard Ingham and Robin Butler outlining media planning for 10 June. 'We can always make arrangements quickly.'

Secretary,' she told him. 'Foreign Secretary for two or three years, then Chancellor; then it's up to you.' Plucking up the courage to tell her something he had withheld during the campaign, Parkinson confessed that he had made his former secretary, Sara Keays, pregnant. Mrs Thatcher's reaction surprised him: 'What's that got to do with anything?' she asked. 'They tell me Anthony Eden leapt into bed with any good-looking woman. You can sort this out.' Parkinson was unconvinced. Mrs Thatcher pointed out that 'If the successful party Chairman isn't in government, everyone will be asking why.' They resolved that Parkinson should become head of a new department combining the Ministries of Trade and of Industry. The job was important but did not have such a high profile. They did not discuss what would happen about Miss Keays's pregnancy.

As usual, Mrs Thatcher spent election night at her Finchley count. Her result, which saw her majority rise to 9,314, was:

Mrs M. Thatcher (Conservative)	19,616
L. Spigel (Labour)	10,302
M. Joachim (SDP-Liberal Alliance)	7,763
(Eight minor party candidates)	736

While the Conservative national vote had fallen by nearly 700,000 to 13,012,316, the Labour vote had collapsed from 11.5 million to 8,456,934. Voters had deserted Labour in droves in favour of the Alliance, who received 25.4 per cent of the total vote. Labour had only 27.6 per cent. The Conservatives had 42.4 per cent. They won 397 seats, Labour 209 and the Alliance 23. The Tories had an overall majority of 144, the largest for either party since the Labour landslide of 1945.

There were scenes of jubilation in Central Office and Mrs Thatcher, arriving shortly before 4 a.m., had Parkinson join her at the window to acknowledge the cheers in Smith Square. To Peter Cropper, head of the Conservative Research Department, the moment of victory was ambiguous: 'She really did start walking on water. It was wonderful in a way. But the triumphalism horrified me.'

14

Reagan plays her false

'If I were there Margaret, I'd throw my hat in the door before I came in'

After her landslide victory on 9 June 1983, Mrs Thatcher received a note from her private office setting out the historical scale of her triumph. She had just become the first leader of any party to serve a full term and then increase her majority, and the first Conservative Prime Minister to win two elections in a row.* Her victorious margin (over 4.5 million votes) was the greatest since 1931. Only two years earlier, most people had believed she could not win another election. Now her enemies – inside and outside her party – lay prostrate before her.

Mrs Thatcher herself did not pause to reflect on this favourable situation. She was simply relieved and, as always, eager to get on with her work. The scale of her success was a problem in itself, as Bernard Ingham, writing to her before the result, warned it would be: she should not 'under-estimate the British capacity to reject success' and should 'play down expectations and prepare people for a quiet life'. Stephen Sherbourne, appointed to revive Mrs Thatcher's political office, recalled the atmosphere as he entered No. 10: 'It was as if I was in a very well-run country house and the couple had gone away for a three-week cruise, and everything was working just as before ... There was no discussion about what we were going to do. It was just straight down to business.'

Mrs Thatcher reshuffled her Cabinet. 'I'm not a good butcher,' she told the BBC, 'but have had to learn to carve the joint,' implying that this traditionally male role was not to her taste. The most important change was to make Nigel Lawson, the greatest exponent of her free-market philosophy, Chancellor of the Exchequer. The economic doctrines of Thatcherism – tax cuts, privatization, deregulation and tax reform, as

---

* The last time the Conservatives had increased their majority was in 1959, when Mrs Thatcher was first elected to Parliament. 'I imagine that you must have felt much as I do after your great triumph in 1959,' she wrote to Harold Macmillan. 'There is so much to do.'

well as strong monetary controls – having been tested in adversity, could now be boldly applied in what was beginning to look like prosperity. Early in this glad, confident morning, Michael Scholar, Mrs Thatcher's Treasury private secretary, recalled arriving, to his shame, forty minutes late to a meeting between Prime Minister and Chancellor at Chequers to discuss public spending cuts. He braced himself for the wrath of his boss, but instead found the two 'sitting there wreathed in smiles'. 'Don't worry, Michael,' she told him, 'Nigel and I have fixed the whole thing – it's all done.' It was evident that they felt 'very pleased with one another'.

Mrs Thatcher was able to build most of the rest of her Cabinet as she wanted it. John Wakeham, whom she saw as 'another of my boys', became her new Chief Whip. As previously agreed, instead of Foreign Secretary, Cecil Parkinson took on the newly created post of Secretary of State for Trade and Industry. This upset Norman Tebbit, who had been wanting to move on from Employment and hoping for a version of this job. But Mrs Thatcher intended no insult. She was braced for a major battle with the unions and considered Tebbit the best person to fight it. Tebbit was irritated, nonetheless, that his old friend Parkinson was ahead of him.* This marked the beginning of increasingly fractious relations between Mrs Thatcher and her toughest public defender.

It was a mark of how power had shifted that Mrs Thatcher was able to remove Francis Pym from her government with ease. Feeling slightly guilty, she sought to engineer the Speakership of the Commons for him, but without success. Pym preferred the freedom of the back benches, which was exactly what she did not want him to have. He quickly became a focus for discontented Tory MPs. In his stead, she appointed Geoffrey Howe as Foreign Secretary, believing that, with his preference for negotiation and discussion (the Foreign Office's 'two stars in the firmament') over making decisions, he was well suited to it.

Willie Whitelaw presented Mrs Thatcher with a delicate situation. She wanted to remove him from the Home Office, where his moderate approach sat ill with her tougher instincts, but she regarded him, in her words, as 'quite simply, indispensable to me in Cabinet'. Understanding that he 'could sometimes sway colleagues when I could not', she wanted to keep him by her side as Leader of the House of Lords. Whitelaw, however, was loath to leave the Commons, so she flattered him by reviving

---

* The Tebbit–Parkinson relationship went back to their days together as young Conservative activists in Hemel Hempstead in the early 1960s. As upwardly mobile, ambitious young men, they felt rivalry as well as friendship.

the dormant right to create hereditary peers, making him a viscount. This readiness to put the clock back was evidence of the romantic, high Tory streak in her nature. She also emphasized his role as Deputy Prime Minister, an office 'unknown to the constitution' but useful in establishing hierarchy.* He accepted. She thus had to jettison the existing Leader of the Lords, Lady Young. Characteristically, Mrs Thatcher seems to have been unworried that she was removing the only other woman in the Cabinet. There would never be another, so long as she was Prime Minister.

The new Home Secretary was Leon Brittan, promoted from the junior Cabinet post of Chief Secretary to the Treasury. This proved the most controversial of her appointments. Lacking the traditional seniority for the Home Office (one of the three 'great offices of state'), he was seen as a creature of Mrs Thatcher. This was unfair, not least because, with his strongly pro-European opinions and liberal social views, he was a Thatcherite only in strictly economic matters.† Contained in the grumbling was a submerged element of anti-Semitism: it was all very well for Jews to take 'clever' ministries to do with money, but in matters of law and order the Tory Party preferred someone 'more English'. Lawson and Joseph (who stayed on at Education) were also Jewish, leading Harold Macmillan, in 1986, to joke privately that there were now 'more Estonians than Etonians' in the Cabinet. Mrs Thatcher's sympathy with Jews reflected her anti-establishment instincts and her belief that conservatism was a creed of opportunity. She did, however, come to accept that she had promoted Brittan too fast. 'If I had my time again,' she recalled, 'I would know that people who are excellent lawyers, excellent at taking a brief, aren't much good at . . . deciding a line to take.' She seemed to forget she was a lawyer herself.

Among the Cabinet ministers who fundamentally disagreed with Mrs Thatcher's approach, only three survived – Michael Heseltine at Defence, Jim Prior in Northern Ireland, and Peter Walker, whom she promoted from Agriculture to Energy, expecting coming confrontations in the coal industry. She respected Walker's talents. Besides, as she later recalled, he 'would

---

* In Britain, unless there is a coalition government, the title of 'Deputy Prime Minister' is given to a Cabinet minister as recognition of seniority in the governing party. It is not unusual for the position to be vacant. There are no required official duties, and no automatic rights of succession.
† Brittan was a member of the so-called 'Cambridge mafia' who had been at the university together in the late 1950s and early 1960s. Other mafiosi included Norman Fowler, Kenneth Clarke, John Selwyn Gummer, Michael Howard and Norman Lamont, most of them on the left of the party. These men owed their political careers to Mrs Thatcher, although they were not necessarily Thatcherites.

have been a deadly enemy on the backbenches'. The reshuffle also brought Alan Clark into government as a junior minister at the Department of Employment.* Clark now gave a lunch to discuss 'What the Government Should be Doing with Its Huge New Mandate'. He noted how reserved his colleagues were in talking about the 'broad canvas': 'I fear that we all still suffer from a lack of confidence . . . when we win something we can barely believe our eyes. There is no follow-through.' This was a good summation of traditional male Tory psychology, a state of mind which Mrs Thatcher never shared and always fought.

After four extraordinarily successful years as Mrs Thatcher's parliamentary private secretary, Ian Gow was promoted to Minister of Housing. This did her serious damage. Throughout her first term he had advanced her causes, protected her from her own innocence about the motivations of colleagues and helped keep relations with Howe in tolerable repair. With Gow absent, and Howe translated to the more distant role of Foreign Secretary, there was no one to prevent the two drifting apart.

Gow's successor was Michael Alison. Except for the fact that both Alison and Gow were utterly loyal to Mrs Thatcher, their characters could scarcely have been more different. An earnest convert to evangelical Christianity, Alison was, in the view of Stephen Sherbourne, 'not that interested in politics' and therefore 'not really suited to the job'. So godly was he that there were moments, sometimes during preparations for Prime Minister's Questions, when he slipped off to prayer meetings from which he could not be fished out.

Mrs Thatcher benefited from Alison's religious perspective and sought his advice on Church-and-state and moral issues and on Church appointments.† His daughter Rosie felt that Alison served Mrs Thatcher almost like a private priest. This gave her solace and did something to mitigate the atmosphere of intrigue which tends to surround the 'court' of any prime

---

* This came about only after John Wakeham got wind that Clark was planning to set up a 'Shadow Cabinet' to keep the government up to the mark with right-wing policies. To head this off, Wakeham urged that he be made a junior minister. Mrs Thatcher, who had a soft spot for Clark, agreed. He ended up as Under-Secretary of State at the Department of Employment (a role of great unimportance) because Norman Tebbit was the only Cabinet minister who agreed to take him. Tebbit said, 'I don't really mind who my junior ministers are, so long as they keep out of my hair.'
† In his own prayers, Alison would seek divine guidance about which passages of Scripture would be most suitable for the Prime Minister. He would then read them to her on long car journeys, as well as improving books such as *The Screwtape Letters* by C. S. Lewis.

minister. But in terms of party political management Alison was almost useless, too good for the world in which his job forced him to move.*

As Mrs Thatcher's connection with opinion in Parliament and party now weakened, so the role of No. 10 in the direction of policy grew. As she closed down the CPRS, her Policy Unit, under Ferdinand Mount, expanded.† Mount saw its role as making sure Mrs Thatcher's ideas and wishes provided 'a course of injections into the Whitehall bloodstream'. It now became central to the projection of her will throughout government.

This was to have two consequences. The first was that ministers became annoyed at what they saw as *lèse-majesté*. By his own account, Norman Tebbit was so infuriated to find Mrs Thatcher quoting against him from a unit briefing about the motor industry that he told her, 'Prime Minister, you have done me the honour of making me, as secretary of state, your principal adviser on this matter. I would be grateful, therefore, if you would take my advice. Good day.' He then walked out. Tebbit's anger at not being master in his own house resembled that which Francis Pym had felt about the appointment of Anthony Parsons or which Nigel Lawson later exhibited about Alan Walters. The second consequence was that, much more than before, policy action could be driven forward from No. 10. The trend would help to Thatcherize the government, but also increased resentment against her. Traditionally, the system of British government gives considerable departmental autonomy to Cabinet ministers, with the Prime Minister acting more as executive chairman than supreme commander. This works well in terms of breeding capable decision-makers and ensuring a degree of harmony across government. It works badly in terms of driving overall mission. Mrs Thatcher understood the theory, but was irritated by the practice. She wanted to get on, and she saw Cabinet ministers as getting in the way. This tension helps explain both her successes and her failures.

On 17 June, Mrs Thatcher flew to Stuttgart for a European Council meeting. With Britain's budgetary contribution still unresolved, she gave and received the usual hard pounding. It had been 'v. difficult', she told the Cabinet, but 'We owe a fantastic amount to Kohl [the Germans held the

---

* On one occasion, Matthew Parris came to see Mrs Thatcher on behalf of Tory MPs like himself who wanted her to take gay rights more seriously. After he plucked up the courage to tell her that he was himself homosexual, Mrs Thatcher's only reaction was to say 'There, dear ... That must have been very hard to say.' Being a politician, Parris naturally assumed that when Alison asked him for the names of the other MPs for whom he spoke, he wanted the information to use against the men later. In fact, Alison told his secretary, he had asked for the names so that he could pray for them.

† John Redwood continued his role in the unit. Additions included Oliver Letwin from Keith Joseph's office and David Willetts from the Civil Service (where he had earlier been Nigel Lawson's private secretary).

EEC presidency]. I don't know how he bettered Mitterrand, but he did.' Thanks to Kohl's chairmanship, she won agreement for another year of temporary rebate for Britain, pending permanent settlement. She suggested that Britain would eventually consider increasing the Community's 'own resources' (the percentage of taxes permitted to it by member states), but only if fair budgetary mechanisms and controls on the Common Agricultural Policy were agreed first. 'What I am really afraid of is next year,' she told the Cabinet. 'It will be very rough.'

She was also persuaded to sign the Solemn Declaration on European Union, which sought 'an ever closer union of the peoples and Member States of the European Union'.* The customary Foreign Office approach, in which specific, detailed gains were considered more important than issues of principle, prevailed. As Mrs Thatcher later explained, 'the document had no legal force'. As so often with these windy European generalizations, however, the declaration was as solemn as its name: it intended to move towards something deeper than anything she ever wanted. This would come back and hit her two years later.

In parliamentary affairs, Mrs Thatcher faced two thorny difficulties – the Speakership and MPs' pay. The first was of her own making. Her efforts to steer the job towards Pym had alienated the most likely candidate, Jack Weatherill, and offended many MPs because, constitutionally speaking, the appointment was their prerogative. She then tried to rally support for Humphrey Atkins, whom she favoured over the more independently minded Weatherill. The House responded by electing Weatherill unopposed. She began the new Parliament with a botched attempt to manipulate it.

Further resentment built over the matter of MPs' pay, where Mrs Thatcher resisted Lord Plowden's recommendation of an increase in salary from £14,510 to £19,000 a year. Her suggestion of a 4 per cent rise was in turn rejected, with MPs deciding to accept Plowden (plus a bit extra), albeit phased in over several years.† Given her calls for public-sector wage restraint, she probably had to resist the demands, but her approach added to the ill will among her parliamentary colleagues.‡

---

* This marked a change from the original Treaty of Rome, which had spoken only of the 'peoples' being in ever-closer union.
† As compensation for the lack of jam today, various allowances were made more generous – a slightly surreptitious means of handing out money which would eventually, in the twenty-first century, attain the proportions of a scandal.
‡ Mrs Thatcher volunteered, as she had done since 1979, to take only the standard Cabinet minister's salary of £40,000 a year, forgoing the extra £10,000 to which she was entitled. Such self-sacrifice probably made her even less popular with her ministers, who would have felt the implied reproach. Others pointed out that since her husband was quite rich, she could afford

On 13 July the House voted on the return of capital punishment, which had been suspended since 1965. The subject was always treated as a matter of conscience and therefore unwhipped.* But now, with such an overwhelming Conservative majority, it seemed possible that 'the rope' – always anathema to the 'chattering classes', but always strongly supported in opinion polls – could at last return. Mrs Thatcher's long-standing support for the death penalty had helped her in the party and with many potential Conservative voters. But whereas Margaret, the battling housewife, could rage against detestable crimes and call for the ultimate deterrent, Mrs Thatcher, the Prime Minister, knew that bringing back capital punishment would be a legislative and political nightmare, setting her colleagues against one another. By letting it be known she did not think the vote would go her way, she helped fellow Tories vote against her wishes without seeming disloyal. The Commons duly rejected the death penalty by a majority of 145. In practical terms, this was probably what Mrs Thatcher wanted.

By July, the talk was of Mrs Thatcher's 'banana skins' and 'lack of direction'. While most issues were more atmospheric than substantive, difficulties with the economy were tangible. The need to win a general election had, as always, weakened the public finances. At Cabinet on 7 July, Nigel Lawson warned that the PSBR was 'substantially higher than forecast for last 6 months'. Tax now took 38.75 per cent of GDP whereas, in Labour's last year, it had been only 34.75 per cent. More than £1 billion was needed off the PSBR, so the Chancellor demanded spending cuts and an increase in what he called 'the disposals programme'.† Lawson immediately encountered resistance. Michael Heseltine complained that 'everyone will say there were secret plans'. It was agreed that the Chancellor would return to Cabinet a fortnight later to present his ideas in full.

All those concerned with the long-term economic strategy now begged Mrs Thatcher to stand firm. 'This is the one non-repeatable opportunity to roll back public spending,' Alan Walters told her. 'If a Tory majority of 144 cannot do it, then there is little hope for Britain.' Analysing the present discontents, Bernard Ingham told Mrs Thatcher that the lobby journalists considered the defeat of capital punishment to have shown her 'in a less resolute light', but the questions over public spending were

---

it. There was some truth in this, though it is worth pointing out that Denis and Margaret kept their finances entirely separate, and he did not pay any of her bills.

* It is traditional in Parliament not to impose a whip on votes which are deemed a matter of conscience, such as abortion, fox-hunting, euthanasia.

† Lawson favoured the Treasury word 'disposals', rather than 'privatization', indicating his department's overwhelming concern for how much money could be raised rather than what would happen to the industries sold.

'more damaging'. The sense that the Chancellor had been 'less than frank' could damage her because 'potentially at least your priceless assets with the electorate – integrity and resolution – may have been compromised'. So the media would be watching the coming public-expenditure Cabinet for evidence that 'rising damp in the Cabinet has become a surge' and the markets would want 'reassurance that the Government really is determined to keep on top of spending and exercise restraint as a way of life'. Mrs Thatcher underlined this passage vigorously.

At the public-spending Cabinet on 21 July, Heseltine renewed his objections, joined by others, including Norman Fowler at the Department of Health and Social Security. 'For the first time, it was absolutely explicit that the whole purpose was to cut spending to make room for tax cuts,' recalled Fowler. 'The old One Nation thing was swept aside. We hadn't remotely gone into the election saying this. For me, this was a major torpedo.' Lawson, however, stressed that he was merely insisting ministers stick to spending totals already agreed. Mrs Thatcher backed him strongly. For now, ministers agreed, but Heseltine called for a collective discussion of longer-term plans – just what Mrs Thatcher wanted to avoid.

By his own account, Lawson was having to adopt a more cautious stance than he would have liked. The panic caused by the CPRS leak the previous year had made it impossible to advance tax cuts through actual reductions in public spending. The best he could do was to aim for 'a slower rate of growth for public spending than the sustainable growth rate of the economy as a whole, with the result that public spending would steadily decline as a share of GDP'. For all the radicalism of the Thatcher years, total public spending was never cut. The frontiers of the state were indeed rolled back from interference in economic activity, but in terms of money spent they ceded surprisingly little ground.

On 28 July came further angst, after the by-election in Penrith and the Border caused by Whitelaw's elevation to the Lords saw the Tory majority cut from 15,421 to 552. At this time, Mrs Thatcher herself was not quite on her top form. John Coles, her foreign affairs private secretary, noticed a decline in her energy (though, by ordinary standards, it was 'still prodigious'). One reason, obviously, was fatigue after the campaign, but there was something else. A couple of days after the 1983 victory she told Coles, 'I have not long to go.' He was very surprised, given the scale of her victory, and asked why. 'My party', she replied, 'won't want me to lead them into the next election – and I don't blame them.'

This was an important part of Mrs Thatcher's psychology which hindsight has obscured. In 1983 she knew that, well before the next general election, she would have served longer as party leader than any since Winston Churchill. Having herself brought about Heath's downfall, she understood how colleagues could rebel. She did not feel much more secure than before her landslide victory: she was right not to. Possibly related to the strain caused by hard work, she was also suffering from a physical ailment. Shortly after the Penrith by-election she was diagnosed with a detached retina in her right eye and, on 3 August, admitted to a private hospital in Windsor for an operation. Perhaps because of her air of invulnerability, most of those close to Mrs Thatcher did not take the moment as seriously as they should have done. Robin Butler recalled talking to her about the arrangements made necessary by her treatment, before realizing, guiltily and too late, that 'what she really wanted me to say was "Poor you"'.

To convalesce, Mrs Thatcher and her husband went to stay with Lady Glover at Schloss Freudenberg. For once, she was forced to have a bit of real rest.* She was inundated with more than 1,000 letters from well-wishers which she answered on her return from Switzerland. Ferdinand Mount sent a postcard: 'We have been trekking across Tuscany where P. Shore, R. Hattersley & N. Kinnock are all said to be on holiday. Luckily, so far we have only seen S. Botticelli & L. da Vinci.' Thanking Cecil Parkinson for his note, she added, 'We shall need to have a great new drive in September–October.' She still had every expectation of keeping her favourite minister.

During the recess, Parkinson became increasingly worried that the pregnancy of his former secretary, Sara Keays, would become public knowledge. Reluctantly, Mrs Thatcher accepted his advice that it would be prudent to replace him as Party Chairman, even before the party conference that October. Her choice to succeed him was John Selwyn Gummer, a junior minister at the Department of Employment. In Gummer, whom she knew well because he often helped with her speeches,† Mrs Thatcher saw a youngish man who could perform well on television and counter David Steel, David Owen and Neil Kinnock, the forty-one-year-old favourite to succeed Michael Foot as leader at the coming Labour Party conference. In her eyes, Gummer had the additional advantage of being securely married.

Nevertheless, Gummer was a controversial and eccentric choice. He

---

* Mrs Thatcher did, however, on 5 August (while still in hospital), sign a personal minute to all Cabinet ministers, urging them to work out with the Chief Secretary the longer-term trends in public expenditure.
† Mrs Thatcher also liked Gummer's interventions at the General Synod of the Church of England, where he was one of the few members who defended the government on moral, social and nuclear issues.

lacked the seniority expected in a Party Chairman, so more seasoned colleagues felt affronted. Norman Tebbit, Gummer's departmental boss, 'came steaming into Downing Street, very angry', and told Mrs Thatcher that he 'wasn't having it'. His protest was in vain, but understandable. As was obvious to those working for her, the godly combination of Gummer and Michael Alison would prove a poor imitation of the worldlier Parkinson and Gow. It also created a void in her life. Parkinson was the sort of man who greeted her by saying things like 'You're looking wonderful today, Margaret.' It is unimaginable that Gummer, fourteen years her junior, could have attempted such a thing.

In early October, the satirical magazine *Private Eye* referred to Parkinson's 'marital difficulties', noting that his 'fun-loving secretary Ms Keays is expecting a baby in three months' time'. It also falsely suggested she was having an affair with another Conservative MP, Marcus Fox. Using its jokey euphemism for illicit sexual relations, the *Eye* said that Miss Keays 'had only recently returned from exploring the jungles of Uganda' with Fox. Robin Butler immediately showed this to Mrs Thatcher. 'Oh, that's really libellous,' she exclaimed. At a meeting of ministers she waved the magazine about: 'Robin's shown me this. I know it's untrue. Marcus told me he's never visited Africa.' It fell to Butler to explain what the phrase meant, while Cabinet colleagues tried to contain their mirth.

On 5 October, Parkinson's affair finally became public. As she had done throughout, Mrs Thatcher stood by Parkinson. Bernard Ingham informed her the Sunday newspapers were trying to keep the story going. Would there be 'less talk of Victorian values' now, they asked? Was it true that 'the Government is running into early trouble and that you are running out of luck'?

Parkinson's fate now lay in the hands of the party conference at Blackpool. The Tory rank and file, taking their tone from the leader, clapped whenever Parkinson's name was mentioned in speeches. The grandees were more tepid. The final straw came late at night on Thursday 13 October, Mrs Thatcher's fifty-eighth birthday.* She was working on her set-piece speech when, around 11 p.m., Butler learnt that in tomorrow's *The Times* Miss Keays would denounce Parkinson and reveal exactly how often he had promised her marriage during their affair. 'I've had it, haven't I?' said Parkinson after Butler broke the news to him. Parkinson recalled Mrs Thatcher's characteristic reluctance to make the key decision herself. 'It's up to you,' she said. He resigned.

---

* Mrs Thatcher downplayed her birthday celebrations, refusing to have a cake presented to her in the conference hall.

The loss of Parkinson was a serious blow to Mrs Thatcher. He understood her politics and was uniquely good at handling her productively. She 'adored the Cecil type of flattery' – now she was like a queen who had lost her most loyal and dashing knight. As well as making her government look ill-starred, Parkinson's departure exposed her more clearly to the possibility of eventual challenge. In his stead she promoted Norman Tebbit to the DTI, replacing him at Employment with Tom King and bringing her close ideological ally, Nicholas Ridley, into the Cabinet at Transport. This left Tebbit the acknowledged leading figure on the right to succeed her. He himself considered Michael Heseltine his only rival. Those surrounding Mrs Thatcher felt that this new status left Tebbit surprisingly touchy and awkward.

Tebbit did not, in later life, deny his ambition. At the DTI, he was second only to the Chancellorship in carrying out the Thatcher revolution, transforming the supply side of British business and presiding over the bulk of the privatizations. In comparison, Heseltine, at Defence, lingered in impotent eminence. After he had succeeded Parkinson, Tebbit soon found that 'Relations with Margaret became quite bad across the waterfront.' In part they disagreed over industrial policy, but, in Tebbit's view, it was also 'a case of "Uneasy lies the head that wears the crown".' Following Parkinson's resignation, Ingham's press digest quoted the *Sun*: 'Mr Tebbit is now just a heartbeat away from Tory leadership.'

For all this, Mrs Thatcher was not deflected from her essential purpose. The scale of her victory had finally convinced the Civil Service that, as Ferdinand Mount put it, 'This lot has an ongoing future: we must bend with its wind and learn its language.' The global effect was similar. 'Thatcherism works' was the simple headline of a *Washington Post* piece by Alan Walters. This was a message that the world was now ready to hear. The concept of Thatcherism was simultaneously vague – in the sense that it had no agreed sacred text or statement of principles – and strong. It was opposed to big government, high taxes and high deficits, the political power of trade unions, and Communism. It was in favour of individual opportunity and choice, free markets, strict monetary control, nuclear weapons and a vigorous NATO alliance. Thatcherism saw conservatism as a dynamic and creative force, the best way of advancing the prosperity and security of the many.

Things really had changed. As Ronnie Millar wrote to Mrs Thatcher after the election: 'I see poor old Foot keeps saying Labour lost because they failed to get their message across. Not so. They lost because they got their message across all too clearly – and the people cared not for it. Let's hope Kinnock takes over, because then the message will be virtually the same – and so will the people's answer. Which means, dear, you will have to go on forever.'

In late June 1983, Ferdinand Mount wrote to Mrs Thatcher to point out how lucky the Tories had been that unemployment had not been a greater issue in the general election. They would not be so lucky again. He proposed a mixture of measures – some, like 'interim retirement benefit' for workers over sixty, to massage the headline figure down; others, like attacking benefit traps and excessive employment protection, to let new jobs grow. The orthodox view was that jobs had to be 'saved'. Mrs Thatcher believed that many old jobs were bound to go: but was the economy free enough to create new ones?

In early September, Mrs Thatcher met ministers at Chequers to consider the government's next steps towards 'creating a more prosperous and enterprising British economy and thus reversing the growth in unemployment'. This very formulation provided part of the answer: successful employment would come from successful enterprise. Topics ranged over portable pensions, further reductions in union power, taxation and employment, housing and labour mobility and much more.

Alan Walters took rough notes. His summaries of Mrs Thatcher's interventions show how she jumped between subjects: 'Wage-related pension burden', 'Defence exp – cannot go on increasing it', 'Orders from Mexico and Brazil for ships', 'L'pool [Liverpool] had more money and made things worse', 'DES dreadful – portrait of Lenin in one room', 'keyboard skills'. Nigel Lawson's recorded interventions, reflecting his more orderly mind, tended to concentrate on tax reform. Although the conversations were almost absurdly wide-ranging, they produced an effect rather like an orchestra in its first rehearsal of a new symphony. Those taking part were serious about getting the music right.*

In her speech to the party conference the following month, Mrs Thatcher tried to advance her economic radicalism as a unifying idea. 'We have created the new common ground,' she said, echoing Keith Joseph's 1975 phrase urging the party to pursue policies with broad appeal rather than tacking to the political centre. The people had utterly rejected state socialism and understood that 'There is no such thing as public money; there is only taxpayers' money.' Lawson would ensure those taxes would be lower: 'Further action there will be.'

---

* There was actual music at Chequers as well. Michael Scholar soothed Mrs Thatcher by playing Bach, Mozart, Schubert and Schumann on the Steinway piano that Ted Heath had installed when Prime Minister.

Before Christmas that year, Ferdinand Mount left the Policy Unit, feeling a little jaded by his 'holiday from irony' under Mrs Thatcher. John Redwood, his successor, was a very different character, more trained in economic questions and much more strictly committed to the Thatcher political project. In his first memo, Redwood told her she had the opportunity to dominate the popular ground of British politics: 'Your personal authority and commitment to . . . restoring individual freedom, responsibility and choice can be used to define what people want, and to find practical ways of giving it to them. Many of the things this Government wants to do . . . have wide appeal far beyond the bounds of the Conservative Party.'

Redwood's message was that while her government dominated the economic agenda, it still seemed uncertain about the social one. It was time to remedy this. 'The work I am initiating', he told her, was designed '. . . to write the concerns and views of your Government into the grammar book of politics.' The metaphor was a good one. The strict, energetic, innovative schoolmistress was indeed teaching a new grammar. Even the unruliest pupils were having to learn it.

Concerning the future of Hong Kong, Mrs Thatcher's smashing election victory did not seem to strengthen her hand with the world's largest dictatorship. After nine months of hostile Chinese pressure, confidence trembled. The week after the election, she told Geoffrey Howe that she still hoped China could be persuaded to accept 'little more than titular sovereignty' over Hong Kong. Taking his new office's line, Howe worried about making any settlement conditional on being 'acceptable to the people of Hong Kong'. Mrs Thatcher retorted that she could not recommend the transfer of sovereignty if it were unacceptable to them. This exchange summed up a difference at the heart of the government.

Nevertheless, the difference worked, on the whole, creatively. Although not directly involved in the negotiations, Mrs Thatcher, as Howe put it, was 'marvellous as a card off-stage'. She reminded Cradock of Jorkins in Charles Dickens's *David Copperfield*. Jorkins is the largely absent business partner of nice Mr Spenlow, who 'finds it convenient to turn him [Jorkins] into a hard man, an ogre, to whom he can attribute refusals of any inconvenient request'. 'We operated', Cradock went on, 'on the same principle . . . with the difference that our Jorkins, in London, needed no invention.' In the view of Charles Powell, who succeeded Coles as her foreign affairs private secretary the following summer, her 'original ridiculously unobtainable goals' made it possible for Britain to get more than anyone would otherwise have dared. '"If the Chinese think you're being difficult," she told the Foreign Office, "just tell them who can be really, really difficult." She was a tiger kept in a cage.'

Mrs Thatcher's other crucial role was in maintaining the confidence of the people of Hong Kong. To the Foreign Office, China was a subject only diplomats understood. Cradock felt little need to inform, let alone involve, Hong Kong people. Mrs Thatcher took a different view. She understood more clearly than colleagues that the confidence in capitalist Hong Kong which everyone, even the Chinese Communists, wished to maintain depended much more on whether Hong Kong people believed in the future than on whether Britain and China could get all the sub-clauses right. She was the closest Hong Kong people had to a political champion.

At every turn in the negotiations, Mrs Thatcher could be found pleading these people's cause. In December 1983, as Cradock pressed harder for her to concede that no link of authority between Britain and Hong Kong after 1997 would survive, she wrote, 'The most difficult thing is acceptability to the people of Hong Kong.' Throughout, she spent hours listening to the 'Unofficials' (or EXCO) – the non-governmental advisers to the Governor who, as much as anyone, represented Hong Kong opinion. Mrs Thatcher would sympathize with their woes and offer reassurance that the government would not abandon them. Without these sessions, it is doubtful whether their nerve would have held.

Early in 1984, China applied maximum pressure. It insisted on Deng's inflexible deadline for agreement – September 1984, demanding a Joint Liaison Group to help China prepare for the handover be set up in the colony itself. Hong Kong people feared it would become 'an organ of power'. At an emotional meeting in London with the Unofficials in early April, S. Y. Chung, the head of EXCO, warned Mrs Thatcher that the colony 'would become ungovernable long before 1997'. Later that month, visiting Hong Kong, Geoffrey Howe announced publicly that the British administrative link would be broken entirely in 1997. This was, he later recalled, 'the most anxious moment of my life'.

Unlike Cradock, Mrs Thatcher agreed strongly with Chung that 'To transfer land was one thing. To transfer people was another.' That she, the great Cold Warrior, might end up delivering a free people to Communism was an unbearable thought. That she, the Falklands victor, should fail to help a pro-British colony was, if anything, even worse. But, however tempted, she never gave up on the negotiations. She reluctantly accepted Cradock's analysis that China was determined to win the full outward form of sovereignty and power but would be flexible about almost everything else. His metaphor was of a house. China must have the house but had few ideas about how to furnish it: that was Britain's chance to make a difference. She therefore overruled the Unofficials' objections and agreed Britain should try to meet the Chinese deadline.

Howe and Cradock arrived in Peking in late July, ready to reach an agreement. The Chinese now encapsulated what they wanted for Hong Kong in their formula – first conceived in relation to Taiwan – of 'One Country, Two Systems'. Cradock considered this 'the moment of truth'. With Howe's agreement, he cabled 'Jorkins' in London to urge acceptance. She gave 'encouragement, but not *carte blanche*'. Now that the Chinese believed they had won on sovereignty, questions that had stalled for years were suddenly settled.

As Cradock explained to Mrs Thatcher, Britain could develop the Basic Law by which Hong Kong would be ordered, while Deng should be flattered with 'undue credit' for the idea of One Country, Two Systems. The Chinese had won the house, but the British were ready to furnish it. With a generosity rare in her dealings with the Foreign Office, she wrote: 'Thank you – many congratulations to you both [that is, Howe and Cradock] – it was an excellent result – progress beyond all expectations.' When Mrs Thatcher saw the Unofficials the following month, Chung told her that he could commend the Agreement to the people of Hong Kong 'in good conscience'. She thanked him. That phrase, she said, had 'very deep significance' for her.

Mrs Thatcher agreed to fly to Peking for the signing of the Agreement – known as the Joint Declaration. On 18 December 1984, the day before the signing, she met Deng in the Great Hall of the People. He had grown old and deaf, and, Charles Powell recalled, 'There was a lot of shouting at him down an ear trumpet.' Deng told her that the Agreement had 'historic significance' and that China would honour it. Following Cradock's advice, she praised 'One Country, Two Systems' as a 'stroke of genius'. She asked why he had agreed to a precious feature of the deal, which was that One Country, Two Systems would last for at least fifty years from 1997. He answered that it was because China 'hoped to approach the economic level of advanced countries by the end of that time'.* Charles Powell considered her 'actually rather impressed' by Deng. 'He dominated the others, who were plainly in thrall to him. Did she warm to him as a human being? No. He was a Communist and a tyrant.'

After this meeting, Mrs Thatcher signed the Hong Kong Agreement in what she described as 'a spirit of pride and of optimism'. The next day, she

---

* In fact, China was to achieve this early in the twenty-first century, roughly forty years ahead of schedule – at least as measured by total output rather than per capita.

flew to sell it to the anxious but mostly welcoming people of the colony she had just agreed to hand over. Huge difficulties remained. No one could really know how China, emerging under Deng from utter totalitarianism, would behave. Mrs Thatcher had not got anything like what she had set out to attain in 1982. Those on the conciliatory side of the argument – notably Cradock and Howe – were therefore the more pleased.

In Powell's view, Mrs Thatcher was 'never really happy' with the final outcome. It was, nonetheless, 'a remarkable agreement given that the Chinese could just have walked into Hong Kong'. According to EXCO's Lydia Dunn, Mrs Thatcher was 'perhaps alone among the British team in understanding that Hong Kong was a human issue, not just a diplomatic one. Those in EXCO were convinced of her genuine empathy and thus trusted her. This helped to overcome . . . suspicion of the so-called "British sell-out".' Her 'instinctual sympathy' for Hong Kong people and their dilemma made a crucial difference.

In her memoirs, written before the handover and after the trauma of Tiananmen Square in 1989, Mrs Thatcher devoted little space to the Agreement, perhaps worrying that everything might yet go wrong. Indeed, in due course it did. In 2020, China imposed Hong Kong's National Security Law, effectively undermining One Country, Two Systems with less than half its fifty-year period expired. Her work put off the evil day, but did not save free Hong Kong.

By winning the 1983 general election, Mrs Thatcher had also won a mandate for the deployment of US cruise missiles on British soil. Unilateral nuclear disarmament had been clearly offered to the electorate by the Labour Party, and clearly defeated. Mrs Thatcher's triumph – electoral, international and, in her view, moral – gave her the space to reflect. Calling to offer his congratulations, a delighted President Reagan declared her victory 'a shot in the arm for all of us who have a kind of solid philosophy worldwide'. She replied that 'she believed the result would strengthen the Western alliance and might encourage the Soviet Union to show more flexibility in disarmament negotiations'.

Although a hawk in Soviet relations, Mrs Thatcher was no absolutist. Even before her election victory, she had indicated an interest in negotiation. In July 1982 she had received the former US President Richard Nixon, whose foreign policy expertise she respected. 'The Soviets will listen to you before they listen to us . . .' Nixon told her. 'With your credentials, you can bring a new realism into East–West relations.' On the death of the long-time Soviet leader Leonid Brezhnev in November 1982, she and Reagan agreed they should now 'make it clear to the new Soviet leaders that a more constructive East/West relationship is available if they are willing to adopt a new approach'.

In March 1983, Mrs Thatcher had met József Marjai, the Hungarian Deputy Prime Minister, in London. 'The biggest problem we have in Hungary', he told her, 'is to convince the Hungarian people that the government has no money of its own.' 'Her eyes lit up,' recalled Malcolm Rifkind, the junior Foreign Office minister in charge of relations with the Soviet Union and Eastern Europe,* who was present. 'But that's what I'm always saying in this country!' She became readier to recognize that not all Communists were necessarily alike.

Following her election victory, she requested a seminar of experts on the Soviet Union to be held at Chequers. In Britain and America, there was a similar desire to work out how to bargain from strength. But while Reagan and Thatcher were as one in their hatred of Communism and their belief in the Western way of life, they did not agree about how best to defend it. She did not share Reagan's strong personal antipathy to nuclear weapons. He was always seeking to supersede the dominant post-war nuclear doctrine of Mutually Assured Destruction (MAD).† On 23 March 1983, the President told a startled world he might have found it. Through what was known as the Strategic Defense Initiative (SDI) – often referred to, usually derisively, as Star Wars – Reagan announced that the USA would develop a defensive missile shield which would make MAD obsolete. The reaction was a mixture of mockery that the notion was fanciful and wouldn't work and fear that it wasn't and would. The Russians considered SDI a brazen attempt to undermine the Anti-Ballistic Missile (ABM) Treaty‡ and exempt the United States from deterrence: if the USA could block Soviet missiles, then it could launch a first strike with impunity.

Mrs Thatcher later gave the impression she had welcomed SDI. She boasted that her scientific education, contrasted with 'laid back generalists

---

* The fact that Rifkind, a Parliamentary Under-Secretary, and therefore on the lowest rung of the ministerial ladder, had this large role shows how little importance British officialdom ascribed to East–West links at that time.
† For Reagan, a biblical Christian, a nuclear holocaust carried significant scriptural connotations. '[S]ome day people are going to ask why we didn't do something now about getting rid of nuclear weapons,' he once told his national security team. 'You know I've been reading my Bible and the description of Armageddon talks about destruction, I believe, of many cities and we absolutely need to avoid that.'
‡ The ABM Treaty between the USA and the USSR placed strict limits on developing defences against nuclear-armed ballistic missiles. 'Strategic ballistic missiles' were considered the most potent nuclear weapons due to their rapid speed and ability to deliver a devastating payload anywhere in the world. 'Cruise missiles' travelled more slowly and had lesser ranges. The term 'Intermediate Nuclear Forces' (INF) covered non-strategic, land-based ballistic (e.g. Pershing) and cruise missiles with a range of 300 to 3,400 miles.

from the Foreign Office', enabled her to run with the concept. But, as Robert Armstrong recalled, this very scientific education led her to be 'dubious about the practicality ... I think she instinctively doubted whether it would be as effective as Reagan seemed to think.' Her immediate reaction was to emphasize that SDI was a programme of research, not deployment. This enabled her to play down the prospect of deployment and her broader disagreement with Reagan about nuclear weapons. She never departed from the view that nuclear deterrence had kept the peace since 1945: any talk of abolishing nuclear weapons risked making Europe 'safe for conventional war'. The threat to Britain's independent deterrent was also real. For if the Soviets too could develop a shield sufficient to defend against Britain's very limited nuclear arsenal, then its *raison d'etre* would vanish overnight. She did not make a public fuss, but she never abandoned these points. They would bulk large later.

The Chequers seminar on 8 September 1983 was carefully prepared by Foreign Office officials. It was their greatest opportunity to influence the Prime Minister's thinking. Beforehand, the FCO argued that 'the time is ripe for a more active policy towards the Soviet Union'. Mrs Thatcher doubly underlined 'ripe' and 'more active policy', but scribbled 'by whom?'. She remained deeply wary of the FCO's intentions. In a cross reply to suggestions about possible attendees, she wrote: 'This is NOT the way I want it. I am not interested in gathering in every junior minister, nor everyone who has ever dealt with the subject at the FO ... I want also some people who have really studied Russia – the Russian mind – and who have had some experience of living there. More than half the people on the list know less than I do.'

Above all, Mrs Thatcher wanted to hear from experts from outside the government machine. The final list of invitees was not, in fact, displeasing to the Foreign Office,* but as the seminar approached, events appeared to conspire against the supporters of engagement. On 1 September, the Soviets shot down a South Korean civilian airliner (KAL 007), which had accidentally strayed into their airspace. All 269 on board were killed. Hawks in Washington insisted the West should break off all contact with Moscow. But Mrs

---

* The eight academics present were Ronald Amann (Birmingham University), Archie Brown (Oxford University), the Rev. Michael Bourdeaux, Christopher Donnelly (Royal Military Academy, Sandhurst), Michael Kaser (Oxford University), Professor Alec Nove (Glasgow University), Alex Pravda (Reading University) and George Schöpflin (LSE). On the government side, Mrs Thatcher was accompanied by Geoffrey Howe, Michael Heseltine and Malcolm Rifkind as well as Hugh Thomas (then Chairman of the Centre for Policy Studies and an informal adviser to her on foreign affairs) and a range of officials.

Thatcher kept her options open, refraining from immediate comment while backing sanctions by the allies. Howe wrote to her arguing that, far from showing that dialogue with the Soviets was impossible, the atrocity demonstrated 'how dangerous is the state of affairs where the two superpowers talk to each other more across the floor of the United Nations than they do on the Hot Line'. At the seminar itself, Archie Brown, one of the academics present, noted what happened when Howe tried to make a similar point:

> just before lunch Sir Geoffrey Howe finally got in a question he had had his mouth open to put half a dozen times which was whether the rhetoric in which Western comment on the Soviet Union's actions was couched made any difference ... Mrs Thatcher butted in to say but, of course, we must condemn them in the strongest possible terms when they do something like shooting down the Korean airliner. She then announced that we should adjourn for a pre-lunch drink.

At the seminar, Mrs Thatcher hewed to a tough line, questioning the value of negotiations. She felt that the Soviets would use negotiations only to pursue military superiority. But she did listen to the experts, whose drift was that Britain should, indeed, engage with the Soviet leadership. She accepted this more readily from them than she did from the Foreign Office.

At the Chequers seminar, Mrs Thatcher heard the name of Mikhail Gorbachev for the first time. Archie Brown told her that Gorbachev was not only a likely successor to the ailing Yuri Andropov (who had replaced Brezhnev), but also the best choice from both the Soviet and Western points of view. As Brown recalled: 'Mrs Thatcher turned to Sir Geoffrey Howe ... and said: "Should we not invite Mr Gorbachev to Britain?" Howe concurred.'* An important seed had been planted.

All through the meeting, the Foreign Office officials were anxiously pushing the Prime Minister towards dialogue. At first, as one official recorded, she made 'a great show of reluctance about accepting the present lack of channels to Moscow damaged our interests ... She agreed in the end that once the KAL crisis had died down there should be an improvement in links with the Russians so long as they did not involve herself and it was understood that she had the right to veto these talks if they went too far.' The Chequers seminar marked no dramatic reversal of Mrs Thatcher's approach, but the Foreign Office was correct to see it as

---

* There is some dispute among those claiming the credit for first noticing Gorbachev in Britain. Rodric Braithwaite, later British Ambassador to the Soviet Union, has said: 'Archie Brown believes that he was the first person to notice Gorbachev, but people in the Foreign Office at the time disagree. They say that everybody noticed Gorbachev at the same time.' Nonetheless, Brown may well have been the first to draw Gorbachev to Mrs Thatcher's attention.

pushing her further down its preferred path. As the official record put it, 'the aim should be to build up contacts slowly over the next few years', with the possibility of arranging for 'senior members of the Politbureau, particularly potential successors to Andropov, to visit London'.

On 29 September, Mrs Thatcher visited Reagan in Washington. Giving the President a preview of her speech that evening to the Winston Churchill Foundation, she stressed she would 'be emphasising that we must deal with the Soviets from strength', but she felt it might be time to engage. 'While she would not say so this evening, we must, she stressed, strive to establish normal relations ... The President replied that he shared her views.' Reagan, too, was beginning to explore engagement with the Soviets. Shultz noted that the President always had 'a great deal of confidence in her judgement'. Reagan would say, 'Well, I see this is the cable that has come from the Foreign Office, but what does Margaret really think?' On this occasion, her instincts reinforced his own.

Her speech that evening contained plenty of strong anti-Soviet words that the press happily reported: 'Their creed is barren of conscience, immune to the promptings of good and evil.' But Mrs Thatcher later complained that 'no-one took any notice of the part that I thought they would fall upon'. By this she meant her point that 'We have to deal with the Soviet Union ... We live on the same planet and we have to go on sharing it. We stand ready therefore – if and when the circumstances are right – to talk to the Soviet leadership.'

Secure in Reagan's support, she felt emboldened to make her readiness for dialogue more public. At the Conservative Party conference in October, hours after Cecil Parkinson's resignation, she repeated her words about talking to the Soviets once the circumstances were right, 'But such exchanges must be hard-headed. We do not want the word "dialogue" to become suspect in the way the word "détente" now is.'

The Soviet reaction was negative. According to Oleg Gordievsky, a KGB officer recruited by SIS* as a double agent, the Soviet leadership disliked Mrs Thatcher as much as she disliked them. They felt that 'A Labour government would always be much better for the Soviet Union.' Once she came into office, their 'hatred and respect for her grew ... The general attitude was that she was the Iron Lady. She's an imperialist. She's an American lackey ... there was not much of a belief that she would change.'

There was also a more specific, dangerous anxiety, which Gordievsky's

---

* The British Secret Intelligence Service (SIS) is often referred to as MI6 even though this name is formally obsolete.

clandestine work for Britain revealed. The Soviets were becoming increasingly worried that the West might launch a pre-emptive nuclear strike. Soviet paranoia came to focus on a NATO 'command post' exercise, known as ABLE ARCHER, planned for November 1983, which would simulate a gradually escalating conflict with the Soviets. Because of Gordievsky's warnings, recalled Geoffrey Howe, 'NATO deliberately changed some aspects of the exercise so as to leave the Soviets in no doubt that it was only an exercise.'* Moscow, however, remained deeply suspicious. Britain's intelligence analysts later concluded that 'we cannot discount the possibility that at least some Soviet officials/officers may have misinterpreted Able Archer 83 . . . as posing a real threat'.

If Soviet paranoia was indeed genuine, what should be done about it? Rodric Braithwaite, one of the Foreign Office Russia 'doves', recalled that 'What Gordievsky made clear was that the rhetoric that she and Reagan were using was terrifying.' Always someone who believed in the value of intelligence, Mrs Thatcher was strongly impressed with Gordievsky's reporting, and worried by what it conveyed. In the view of John Scarlett, then Gordievsky's SIS case officer and much later the head of the Service, the Soviet reaction to ABLE ARCHER had a wider, slower influence on policy: 'It is possible that this set off a train of thought that Cold War stability wasn't so stable. We were misjudging the mentality and psychology of the rather old Soviet leadership.'† That train of thought led naturally to an interest in a fuller conversation with that leadership. It fitted with the Chequers conclusions.

Just as she was seeking a better understanding of her Soviet enemies, Mrs Thatcher was confronted with a nasty shock from her American friends. At 7.15 p.m. on 24 October 1983 the Prime Minister was presented with a cable from President Reagan. He said he was now so worried about the political turmoil on the tiny Caribbean island of Grenada that he was 'giving serious consideration' to a request from the Organization of Eastern Caribbean States (OECS) for military assistance. Reagan sought her thoughts and pledged to inform her 'in advance' on whatever course of action he chose to pursue. Mrs Thatcher, as she later wrote, was 'strongly against intervention'. As she left for a farewell dinner for the outgoing US Ambassador, John Louis, she asked for a reply to be drafted accordingly. She hoped to extract some explanation from the guest of honour, but when

---

* Originally the plan had been for Western leaders, including Mrs Thatcher, to take part in ABLE ARCHER. In the event, only officials participated.
† It was considered important, in this context, that Andropov had never travelled outside the Soviet bloc, and therefore found it hard to imagine life in the West.

the ladies 'retired' after dinner, the Prime Minister, now increasingly 'edgy', was forced to make small talk with the wives while the men lingered over port and brandy. 'Oh, I do wish they would come out!' she exclaimed. When they finally emerged, she buttonholed the Ambassador, only to discover he knew less than she did.

Returning to No. 10 shortly after 11 p.m., Mrs Thatcher found a second message from Reagan waiting, informing her he had decided to take military action. He was invading without the consultation he had promised little more than three hours earlier. 'We were both dumbfounded,' recalled Geoffrey Howe. 'What on earth were we to make of a relationship, special or otherwise, in which a message requesting the benefit of our advice was so quickly succeeded by another which made it brutally clear that that advice was being treated as of no consequence whatsoever?'

The Americans had long been worried about Communist subversion in Grenada, a former British colony that retained the Queen as head of state after independence. On 13 October 1983, hardliners in the Marxist government of Maurice Bishop, led by the military commander General Hudson Austin, overthrew their leader, who was executed six days later. The Americans had been concerned by a growing Cuban presence on the island. According to Bud McFarlane, who had succeeded Judge Clark as National Security Advisor, Reagan saw the coup as 'a strategic move by the Soviet Union' aimed at subverting the entire region. A more immediate concern was the fate of the 1,000 US medical students based on the island, who might be taken hostage. The Americans drew up contingency plans to rescue the students. In reality, though, as Lawrence Eagleburger, a senior State Department official, put it, the students were the pretext. The real aim was to 'get rid of that son of a bitch [General Austin] before the Cubans got any further embedded'.

The British, recalled Howe, 'were aware of the long-standing US concern with Communists on Grenada, but we didn't really take it very seriously'. So when, on 21 October, the Americans sought a view from the Foreign Office about direct intervention, they were, in the words of Robin Renwick, Head of Chancery at the Embassy in Washington, 'heavily brushed off'. As Renwick saw it, this ensured the British were 'excluded from US planning'.

On the same day, 21 October, Mrs Thatcher received reports that Tom Adams, the Prime Minister of Barbados, was trying to arrange 'a multi-national intervention' in Grenada, involving the Americans, various Caribbean states and 'a British contribution'. Mrs Thatcher put her wiggly line of disapproval under the last phrase. At the idea that 'American troops' and 'the SAS' might be involved, she wrote: 'This seems most unwise' (underlined three times).

In the early hours of Saturday 22 October, Reagan received – and granted – a formal request for 'assistance' from the OECS. In Washington at 9 a.m. local time on the Saturday, the Special Situations Group (SSG), chaired by the Deputy National Security Advisor, John Poindexter, met to plan the invasion. According to Poindexter, consultation with the British 'wasn't a big deal to us', but informing Mrs Thatcher was discussed and it was agreed to 'notify her at the last minute'. Duane Clarridge of the CIA, who was present, explained the reasoning: 'We anticipated that Mrs Thatcher would be unhappy. We ... didn't want to give her any room for manoeuvre, either publicly or privately.'

There is no record of an explicit order by Reagan or Shultz to keep Mrs Thatcher unsighted, but both were complicit. Ken Adelman recalled hosting a dinner for Sir Anthony Kershaw, the Chairman of the House of Commons Foreign Affairs Committee, who visited Reagan in Washington shortly after the invasion. As Adelman told the story, Kershaw repeatedly asked the President why he had not consulted Mrs Thatcher earlier. Eventually Reagan 'took off his glasses, which showed he was a little angry, and said, "Because I didn't want her to say no."'

At Chequers that weekend, Mrs Thatcher followed the situation closely. Informed that Geoffrey Howe, from Athens, had authorized HMS *Antrim* to depart in the direction of Grenada, she rang Richard Luce, deputizing for Howe. '"What are you doing sending ships?" she demanded. "We don't want a war!"' She calmed down only when Luce explained to her that the ship was approaching the island (keeping below the horizon) to be ready to rescue British citizens. As Luce recalled, she said 'she was "fearful of being dragged into an unwarranted conflict"' and of embarrassment that might be caused to the Queen.

On the same day, Mrs Thatcher had learnt of the OECS request for military assistance. CARICOM, the wider and more powerful organization of Caribbean states, had taken a cautious line, urging a diplomatic solution. She also knew that Grenada's Governor-General, Paul Scoon, had that morning assured Buckingham Palace 'that there was no threat to himself or to Lady Scoon, and that they were both in good form'. In the circumstances, it did not seem wise to agree to the OECS request. The British government chose inaction, masterly or otherwise.

On the Sunday morning, 23 October, events in Lebanon provided a sudden and tragic distraction. The US Marine barracks in Beirut, part of a multinational peacekeeping force, were destroyed by a truck bomb. The eventual death toll was 241. This terrible development obviously made it harder for Mrs Thatcher, if she was still so minded, to get in touch with Washington about Grenada. For an America which had not seen full-scale military action since Vietnam, the combination of this attack with the perceived threat in Grenada was a powerful spur to action. It helped brush aside any remaining doubt about acting over Grenada.

On the morning of 24 October, Mrs Thatcher chaired a meeting of OD at which Howe, as much in the dark as anyone, reported that the USA was not planning military action. That afternoon, he reassured the Commons that the government was 'keeping in the closest possible touch' with the Americans. Asked by Denis Healey whether the United States intended to invade, he replied simply: 'I know of no such intention.'

That same day, the Americans put into action the plan developed by the SSG to notify Mrs Thatcher 'at the last minute'. The first of two Reagan messages, suggesting consultation, was cabled at 14.47 EST (6.47 p.m. UK time), almost exactly as planned. The second, which arrived before she had returned from dinner, was that the invasion was going ahead. There had been no consultation at all.*

Mrs Thatcher was seriously affronted: 'She didn't see how the invasion of sovereign territory could be right,' recalled John Coles. She was also mortified that a country of which the Queen was head of state was to be invaded. Above all, she was shocked by the duplicity of the Americans. At half past midnight, she replied to Reagan's second cable, expressing her 'gravest concern' at his decision. Invasion without agreement or consultation, she said, would undermine her case that America could be trusted to behave with restraint. She reminded him that, in the next few days, she would have to persuade Parliament to accept 'the siting of cruise missiles in this country': 'I cannot conceal that I am deeply disturbed by your latest communication. You asked for my advice. I have set it out and hope that even at this late stage you will take it into account before events are irrevocable.'

Mrs Thatcher was now persuaded, with some reluctance, to call Reagan. She shied away because she did not want a row, but accepted it would be helpful, when explaining events the next day, to be able to say she had spoken to the President. Her words to Reagan were not angry ones and the call lasted only three minutes. Robin Butler, who listened in, confirmed that it had 'barely any substance at all. Reagan was very reluctant to come to the telephone. When he did eventually . . . I can only describe his tone of voice as one of a naughty schoolboy who had been caught out doing something

---

* Archival evidence suggests that, when US officials were preparing to send Reagan's first cable, they already had a final draft of the second one in front of them: 'send via CABO at 1500,' an official wrote on a note covering a draft of the first cable, '2nd cable later'.

he shouldn't have been.' Recording the main points, Coles noted that Mrs Thatcher urged Reagan 'to consider her [cabled] reply very carefully indeed. The President undertook to do so but said, "We are already at zero."'

As Mike Deaver recalled, when Reagan hung up he said 'She's not going to be with us.' 'I could tell, knowing him, the pain for him of the conversation . . . He said, "But we have to go forward." . . . It was clear from when he hung up and his shoulders kind of sagged that he was disappointed not to have his friends with him.'

Much later that evening, Reagan sent a third message to Mrs Thatcher, conciliatory in tone but firm in content, insisting that invasion was 'the lesser of two risks'. Two hours later, US forces began their assault on Grenada.

Although the Americans had not intended to humiliate Mrs Thatcher, they deliberately misled her. It took time for the full import of this to sink in. As she had predicted, critics used the invasion to question US reliability over cruise missiles. Her claims to a close relationship with the President were widely ridiculed. 'Reagan's midnight snub for Maggie', said the *Sun*, '– stunning humiliation'. On 26 October she felt the embarrassment of her position when she saw the Queen for her usual weekly audience. Foreign Office officials noted she 'understood that the Queen was upset and Mrs Thatcher was very disturbed by this'. The full extent of British dismay was now conveyed to Reagan. He 'felt badly about it', recalled Jim Baker, Deputy Chief of Staff, and was advised to telephone Mrs Thatcher to 'kiss and make up'.

Reaching her on 26 October, during the emergency Commons debate on the invasion, Reagan attempted to disarm the Prime Minister with a line which could have come from one of his 1940s movies. 'If I were there Margaret,' he said, 'I'd throw my hat in the door before I came in.' 'There's no need to do that,' she replied primly. Reagan attributed his reluctance to consult her earlier to the need for absolute secrecy. He assured her that all was 'going beautifully' in the operation, though some fighting continued. He praised Eugenia Charles, the Prime Minister of Dominica, and Tom Adams of Barbados: 'They all feel – and dating from the days when they were under the Crown – she [Miss Charles] used the expression: kith and kin. I don't know if that's one of our expressions or one of yours.' 'It's one of ours,' said Mrs Thatcher. 'Well,' said President Reagan gallantly, 'we still use it here. We still have the heritage . . .' He was making a play for her sense of British cultural hegemony. 'There's a lot of work to do yet, Ron . . .' she warned. 'And it will be very tricky.' When he apologized for 'any embarrassment that we caused you', she chose not to engage. Soon afterwards she told him she must return to the Commons debate. 'Go get 'em. Eat 'em alive,' Reagan urged her. 'Goodbye,' she replied and hung up abruptly.*

Mrs Thatcher had not yet forgiven Reagan and she was, as usual on the telephone, guarded in her responses. Nonetheless, she was somewhat mollified; and he, hearing no renewal of her earlier concerns, was greatly bucked up.

Discussing Grenada in Cabinet on Thursday 27 October, Mrs Thatcher defended the USA against more sceptical colleagues. 'I am not surprised that US told as few people as possible,' she insisted, stressing that the Americans were 'entitled to see things in a different perspective'. Her one strong criticism was about the wider effects of the crisis. She feared that the invasion would undermine 'US/NATO lore that NATO is only defensive' and that only the Soviets launched military action against independent nations. In Prime Minister's Questions that afternoon, Mrs Thatcher maintained her protective public attitude. 'We stand by the United States,' she told Neil Kinnock. 'And will continue to do so in the larger alliances.' She was trying to bury the hatchet.

That was on the Thursday. On the following Sunday 30 October, she dug the hatchet up again and waved it in the air. As a guest on the BBC World Service international phone-in, she was asked whether US help during the Falklands meant that her government had a duty to support America over Grenada. This hit a nerve. In the Falklands, she said,

> Britain went to get its own territory back . . . That has no parallel whatsoever with Grenada . . . I am totally and utterly against Communism and terrorism. But . . . if you are pronouncing a new law that wherever Communism reigns against the will of the people . . . there the United States shall enter, then we are going to have really terrible wars in the world . . . the West has defensive forces in order to defend our own way of life and when things happen in other countries which we don't like, we don't just march in.

It was a classic statement of her approach to armed conflict, national sovereignty and the rule of law, eloquently expressed.

It was also exasperating for the Americans, because it reopened the whole issue. Bud McFarlane fired off a cable of protest to Robert Armstrong, expressing 'profound disappointment'. He singled out Mrs Thatcher's remarks about marching into other countries as 'unusually harsh': the

---

* In 2014, the audiotape of this call was released by the Reagan Library. In it Reagan's tone is one of embarrassed, gallant conciliation, like that of a suspect boyfriend. Mrs Thatcher's is one of correct and chilly politeness.

airing of public differences could 'only serve to diminish British–American solidarity which has served our mutual interests so well'. He was sending this message, he said, to 'clear the air'.* But Mrs Thatcher was unwilling to let the matter drop. When Armstrong sought to send a conciliatory response, she insisted he toughen it up.

Why was Mrs Thatcher so annoyed, more so as time passed? Normal explanations must play a part. In early November, a *Sunday Times* poll suggested that a little over a third of those asked believed she was good in a crisis, down from almost two-thirds before the Grenada episode. The press and Opposition jibes that she was the humiliated poodle of the President obviously had to be countered. But to understand the depth of her feeling, one must look to her character, and perhaps her sex.

Ever since Ronald Reagan had become President, Mrs Thatcher had tried to forge an Anglo-American friendship and had succeeded beyond expectation. She liked Reagan for his gentlemanly charm, his courtesy to her as a woman, but above all because he inspired her trust. In her mind, there was no greater virtue than trust. Over Grenada, she could not avoid concluding that the President had betrayed that trust. Her suspicions seemed confirmed by a report from Robin Renwick, which had reached her shortly before her World Service broadcast. It concluded that Reagan had decided to invade as early as 22 October. In these circumstances, she considered Reagan's cables and flattering words dishonest. His emollient call had, one might say, rubbed sugar in her wounds.

And so Mrs Thatcher, who always invested strong personal feeling in her relationships, and was susceptible to charming, well-dressed men who flattered her, was as disappointed as a two-timed girlfriend. 'My relations with President Reagan will never be the same again,' she told one official. She felt she had been made a fool of. In this sense, her World Service outburst was uncalculated, a natural expression of pique. One might conjecture that President Reagan, also fulfilling the stereotype of his sex, felt as deflated as does any professional charmer when his arts fail. It was surprising – and lucky for both sides – that the press did not pursue this rift much further. It had the potential to do real harm.

The bureaucracies of both countries now struggled to get the relationship back on track. At Chequers on 7 November, Mrs Thatcher vented her irritation with Kenneth Dam, the Deputy Secretary of State. In Dam's view,

---

* Strongly worded as this message was, the final draft had been toned down. An earlier draft had been more personal, suggesting Mrs Thatcher's attitude had put at risk 'the solidarity which our respective heads of state have worked so hard to foster'.

the conversation 'ended on a very cordial note. She had just been blowing off a huge head of steam.' In her Mansion House speech on 14 November she reiterated alliance solidarity – 'it is the strength and resolution of the Western alliance which keeps the peace today' – but she remained grumpy.

It was the historian Hugh Thomas, her informal adviser, who provided the most thoughtful summary of her problem, parts of which Mrs Thatcher underlined. He counselled against 'drawing up a general indictment' of the US administration over Grenada '<u>unless</u> there is some alternative general underpinning of our foreign policy <u>with which you wish to experiment</u>'. She herself had ruled out greater European defence collaboration, he wrote, so what alternative was there? She should try to 'make a new start' with the Americans after Christmas:

> You have such a fine reputation over there. Those of us who look to you to provide us with the kind of direction that de Gaulle gave France have always pointed out that yr strength, in comparison with the general, is that you do accept the essential part that the US has had since 1945. All US officials & politicians . . . except you from their general moans about European defeatism. You can surely rebuild on the basis of those facts.

This letter was well expressed because it played on Mrs Thatcher's temptation to define her national leadership by cutting loose from America, only to dismiss it. Although she never admitted that she had gone too far in her wrath over Grenada, she knew that Thomas's argument was right.

That November, the Russians had responded to INF deployment by walking out of the Geneva negotiations. Having demonstrated Western strength, Mrs Thatcher was conscious of the need for dialogue. It was in this spirit that she began 1984.

15

The enemy within

'If anyone has won, it has been the miners who stayed at work'

In her first term, Mrs Thatcher had tried to avoid direct confrontations with the trade unions. In her second term, she began to believe she could finally prevail. While she saw confrontation with the National Union of Mineworkers (NUM) as almost inevitable, the ground for her first battle concerned trade union power in a separate area, but one close to her heart – national security.

The Government Communications Headquarters (GCHQ) at Cheltenham was, for technological reasons, an ever more important part of Britain's intelligence capacity and intelligence cooperation with the United States. GCHQ's operations were secret, but its staff were members of the general Civil Service, free to join trade unions. The Security Service (MI5) and the Secret Intelligence Service (SIS), by contrast, stood apart from the general Civil Service. Their staff were permitted neither to join a union nor to strike.

The union presence at GCHQ worried Mrs Thatcher. During the 1981 Civil Service strike, the unions had deliberately targeted GCHQ. The Director, Sir Brian Tovey, told staff that the strikes meant the services were losing confidence in GCHQ's ability to provide early warning of Soviet intentions. He added that the US National Security Agency (NSA) was also alarmed. If this continued, he told Mrs Thatcher, the Americans would 'insist on supplying personnel' to man British stations.

Mrs Thatcher was furious with the Civil Service unions. 'There was a sense of betrayal,' recalled Robert Armstrong. 'She never forgave them.' She was a passionate believer in national security and in the importance of the Anglo–American relationship. To avoid future strikes she resolved, supported by the management of GCHQ, to ban union membership at Cheltenham. This was no easy matter. To justify GCHQ's exclusion from the general Civil Service (and the removal of union rights), it would be necessary to 'avow' its secret SIGINT (signals intelligence) activities. Avowal would, however, have knock-on consequences for SIS, which was, at that time, totally secret. This gave Mrs Thatcher pause. She felt conflicted between her desire to delay avowal and her desire to ban unions.

The case of Geoffrey Prime, a GCHQ employee convicted of passing secrets to the Soviet Union, changed matters. In November 1982, explaining this case to Parliament, Mrs Thatcher effectively avowed GCHQ's work. Under these changed circumstances, she asked Armstrong to move ahead with a union ban. He was, recalled Lord Gowrie, then Civil Service Minister, 'very iffy about the whole thing', but neither he nor anyone else advised Mrs Thatcher against banning unions at GCHQ. On 25 January 1984, Geoffrey Howe* announced the union ban to the Commons, explaining that each employee would be offered £1,000 in compensation. Because of the demands of secrecy, GCHQ staff and the unions had been told only minutes beforehand. Armstrong reported to Mrs Thatcher the 'outrage' among the trade unions, who 'protested bitterly' at not being consulted sooner. They described the £1,000 as a 'bribe'.

In GCHQ itself, while there was anger at the ban, many employees swiftly accepted the money.† Tony Comer, then a young GCHQ employee and later the official historian of the organization, recalled that significant numbers appreciated the benefits of trade union membership, but were nevertheless 'uncomfortable with the danger of their work in GCHQ being compromised to support somebody else's agenda'. The press and public reaction was mostly negative. Some thought the measure a slur on the loyalty of trade unions. Many more simply thought it was being mishandled.

Discussions with the unions followed. Armstrong found them 'desperate ... They would go to almost any lengths to keep their foot in the door.' After they offered significant concessions, including no-strike agreements, he advised Mrs Thatcher that 'There is a case for giving the unions a chance.' She disagreed. When, at Armstrong's request, she received the union leaders, she told them, politely, that she 'did not doubt the dedication of individual staff', but she gave no ground on the 'inherent conflict of loyalty' created by the needs of national security on the one hand and the nature of the trade union structure on the other.‡

---

* Howe made the statement because the Foreign Office was the lead department responsible for GCHQ.
† In the first twenty-four hours, 460 employees accepted the new status and the money, and only two rejected it. Twenty-four hours later the number of acceptances had doubled and that of rejections had halved (since one of the two who had refused changed his mind).
‡ There is no reason to doubt that Mrs Thatcher's admiration for the majority of the GCHQ staff was genuine. In early April, just after the Queen had visited Jordan, she wrote to Peter

Geoffrey Howe later described the GCHQ saga as an example of 'one of Margaret's most tragic failings: her inability to appreciate, still less accommodate, somebody else's patriotism'. In his negotiations, Armstrong believed he achieved '97 per cent' of what Mrs Thatcher wanted, but 'She wanted to get the unions out of GCHQ hook, line and sinker. She wanted everything.' Numerically at least, she nearly got it. By 2 March, 6,616 employees, almost 95 per cent of the Cheltenham staff, had accepted the new arrangements and only 45 had refused. GCHQ would henceforth have a staff association, without any right to industrial action or exterior trade union link. Once GCHQ's funding had been transferred to the 'secret vote', hidden from public gaze, it was easier to provide its staff with better pay and conditions. As Mrs Thatcher later recalled, 'I saw to it that they did a damn sight better with the staff association than they had ever done with a Trade Union.'

Throughout the almost year-long processes of consultation and the judicial review which the government eventually won in December, Mrs Thatcher resisted any compromise. In this she was strongly supported by her principal private secretary, Robin Butler, who, in Gowrie's phrase, was 'hawkier than thou'. As Butler himself put it: 'I probably thought Robert was too chummy with the Civil Service unions.' But Butler was also conscious of wider accusations of drift. 'If you are not resolute about this,' he wrote to Mrs Thatcher, 'it will be taken as proof positive that you are not as resolute in your second Administration as you were in your first.' If she weakened now, 'the unions will have the Government over a barrel'. Butler was surely right. If she had blinked, she would also have disabled herself for the much bigger battles to come. The fact that an ambitious civil servant could see this showed how Mrs Thatcher really had got the better of establishment doubters. Butler understood how she was changing everything.

Six weeks after announcing the GCHQ union ban, Mrs Thatcher found herself engaged in another battle over industrial relations. This would prove the most titanic struggle with a single trade union ever known in Britain.

In 1981, facing the threat of a strike by the NUM, Mrs Thatcher had surrendered at once (see p. 230). With the government ill-prepared to resist, this had been the right move, but, as Butler put it, 'She reckoned she

---

Marychurch, who had succeeded Tovey as the GCHQ Director, to thank them for monitoring threats to the monarch and for the 'devotion and professionalism' they had shown through this time of 'personal difficulties and anxieties'.

couldn't cut and run again.' Mrs Thatcher did not know how or when a national coal strike would come. All she knew was that it would be decisive for her premiership. And so, unusually for a woman who tended to act more by instinct than strategy, she started to plan.

What mattered most was called 'endurance': there had to be enough coal to survive a complete shutdown of production. The coal would need to be stockpiled at both pitheads and power stations and transported as needed. This, in turn, demanded trade union laws which restricted the ability of pickets to block coal movement, and police with enough authority and resources to enforce both these and the common law. The target for endurance was at least six months. From July 1981, Peter Gregson, at the Cabinet Office, chaired an 'official group' on strike preparation with this in mind.*

Mrs Thatcher had also begun the necessary political preparation. In 1981 she replaced David Howell as Energy Secretary with her rising star, Nigel Lawson. According to Lawson, her brief to him was 'succinct': '"Nigel," she said, "we mustn't have a coal strike."' As Gregson explained: 'We were *never* spoiling for a fight. We wanted as much time as possible.' In November 1981, over 70 per cent of NUM members voted for the left-wing extremist Arthur Scargill to succeed the moderate Joe Gormley as their President. Scargill's political opposition to the Tory government was absolute. An attack was therefore expected.

It is surprising that the build-up of coal stocks passed almost unnoticed. 'I was astonished we got away with it,' recalled Gregson. 'Everyone could see these mountains of coal at the power stations. Why didn't Scargill stop it?' The extra production, however, was good news for ordinary miners because it helped to keep otherwise threatened pits open. In July 1983, Armstrong reported to Mrs Thatcher that, by November, power station endurance would be six months. The government gave thought to human resilience as well. To bolster the Central Electricity Generating Board (CEGB), Mrs Thatcher strongly supported Lawson's choice of Sir Walter Marshall as the new Chairman. She admired Marshall's credentials as a scientist and his fierce commitment to the development of nuclear power which, if fully pursued, would supersede dependence on coal forever. As Chairman of the National Coal Board, an even more crucial post, Lawson chose Ian MacGregor, the controversial (and also elderly) Scottish American whom Keith Joseph had appointed in 1980 to turn round British Steel. MacGregor took up his post in September 1983. The other important

---

* As a young private secretary to Edward Heath, Gregson had witnessed and felt 'deep depression' at the first capitulation to the NUM in 1972.

replacement was for Lawson himself, once he became Chancellor after the election. Mrs Thatcher settled on Peter Walker, the chief remaining Wet in government. She mistrusted Walker but also had a high regard for his abilities. He had intended to refuse office, but when she offered him Energy he realized that if he refused she would say, 'Faced with Scargill, he went.' So he accepted.

By the autumn of 1983, then, Gregson could advise Mrs Thatcher that stocks at power stations had almost reached physical capacity. It was time to push ahead with efforts to put the industry on an economic footing. How to achieve this was a matter for the newly arrived Ian MacGregor, who, Peter Walker reported, believed the future of coal industry could be 'bright indeed'. He wanted continued investment in new, low-cost capacity to be 'presented to the workforce as a quid pro quo for closures'. He felt that a further seventy-five pits could close by 1985, reducing manpower from 202,000 to 138,000.*

As the MacGregor package developed, Mrs Thatcher's chief concern was to be ready for a strike. The first rumbles were felt on 31 October 1983, when the NUM began an overtime ban over the current pay offer and rumours of pit closures. Only on 6 March 1984 did MacGregor confirm the loss of 20,000 jobs that year, prompting a series of wildcat strikes. Two days later, the NUM executive declared strikes in Yorkshire and Scotland official. In a move that would assume tremendous significance, its Rule 43, which demanded a ballot before any national strike, was not invoked.

Mrs Thatcher wanted to show that her government's approach was different. She told the Cabinet the dispute 'was strictly between the NCB and the National Union of Mineworkers and the Government should neither intervene nor comment ... The Home Secretary should continue to ensure the law was upheld.' There was sense in this doctrine. Many of

---

* Critics, such as the BBC's former industrial correspondent Nicholas Jones, have seized upon the record of this meeting as evidence of a 'secret plan to destroy the British coal industry', proving that, as Scargill claimed, the government had a secret 'hit list' of over seventy pits earmarked for closure. This document does not provide evidence of a government 'hit list'. What it does record is MacGregor's insistence, reported by Walker, that there be 'no closure list, but a pit by pit procedure'. The seventy-five-pit figure was merely MacGregor's early suggestion, which left ministers unconvinced. There 'would be considerable problems in all this', Walker concluded, and no decisions were taken. The policy was settled only at a meeting on 19 January 1984. This time there was no talk of a specific number of pit closures, but ministers focused on reducing manpower. MacGregor proposed to accelerate workforce reductions over the next two years from 28,000 to 45,000, aided by a generous redundancy scheme. Mrs Thatcher summed up by saying that 'the objective of a more accelerated run-down of coal capacity was accepted', as were the terms of the enhanced redundancy package. The policy was to put the industry on a sustainable footing, not to destroy it.

the Heath-era disasters had come too much from intervention by politicians. On the other hand, the doctrine of non-intervention was a fiction. The government was paying for the NCB's enormous losses and was ultimately responsible for public order and for ensuring energy supply. If everything went wrong, the government would fall. It was therefore inextricably involved.

Mrs Thatcher had to face this contradiction the very next day. Visiting her at No. 10, Ian MacGregor warned that flying NUM pickets from Yorkshire were preventing men in Nottinghamshire from going to work, while the police did nothing. He emphasized Arthur Scargill's political purposes. This, then, was Mrs Thatcher's first real test: where miners wished to continue working, could pits be kept open in the face of intimidation from those on strike elsewhere? Would the law be upheld? According to Andrew Turnbull, her private secretary, her response was 'a great explosion'. The Prime Minister was 'deeply disturbed' that the disasters of the 1970s might be recurring. 'The events at Saltley cokeworks* were being repeated,' she declared. It was essential to 'stiffen the resolve of the Chief Constables'. She ordered Leon Brittan, the Home Secretary, to urge the head of the Association of Chief Police Officers (ACPO) 'to tell the police that they must allow people to get to work rather than just maintaining order'.

Later that day, an uneasy Brittan reported that he 'had gone to the limit of what the Home Secretary could do while respecting the constitutional independence of Police Forces'. Although the Home Secretary could not issue operational orders to the police, there was precedent for police forces stopping flying pickets out of area.† The principles of 'mutual aid' were also well established between police forces. What the chief constables needed to know was that they would get the political and financial backing required. Understanding this, Brittan had asked his Permanent Secretary, Brian Cubbon, to communicate as much to the chief constables. Cubbon sent them all what he called 'a stiffening letter'. He also got in touch with the Chief Constable of Nottinghamshire to encourage him.‡

---

* The confrontation at the Saltley cokeworks in 1972 had proved a turning point in the struggle between Edward Heath and the NUM. Arthur Scargill, then a leader of the Yorkshire miners, had succeeded, by mass picketing, in forcing the police to turn away coking lorries. Shortly afterwards, the government, as Heath's political secretary, Douglas Hurd, wrote in his diary, ended up 'wandering vainly all over the battlefield looking for someone to surrender to'. The miners won their fight over pay, and Scargill took much of the glory.
† This had been done during the dispute over Eddie Shah's union-busting newspapers the previous year, when police in Bedford had interdicted pickets heading for Shah's offices in Manchester.
‡ The chief constables needed money too to defray the extra costs. As the dispute went on, they would get most of what they demanded via special subventions from the Home Office.

These efforts had an immediate effect. On Monday 19 March, Andrew Turnbull reported that forty-four pits were working, compared with only eleven the previous Friday. Commenting to Mrs Thatcher in retrospect, Turnbull argued that her reaction that day had been crucial: 'you galvanised the Home Secretary, who in turn galvanised the police into keeping the entrances to the pits open . . . <u>If that first battle had been lost, the rest would have been academic</u>.' She underlined his last sentence approvingly.

The strike retained the same essential character throughout. The NUM always refused a national ballot, and Nottinghamshire and a few other areas, often under heavy police protection, went on working. At the lowest point, 20 per cent of normal national coal production was maintained, and at the highest point – towards the end – 50 per cent. Since government calculations of endurance had assumed zero production, this was all gain from Mrs Thatcher's point of view. Looking back, one might see the strike as a war of attrition which – given the coal stocks built up – the government was bound to win. This was not so. At any moment it was possible that trade union solidarity, NUM violence, legal disaster, Coal Board mishandling of negotiations or a loss of political nerve would produce defeat, and most probably a Heath-like end to her premiership.

As in a war, the picture could change dramatically each day, and on several fronts. Downing Street staff studied what was called the 'Daily Coal Report'* with almost as much anxiety as they had devoted to the Falklands conflict. Instead of names like Bluff Cove and Goose Green, they became familiar with pits like Shirebrook and Bilston Glen. The endurance required was not only that of coal stocks but of will, concentration and morale. Scargill's failure to call a national ballot meant that the war was also internecine. Once the violent picketing had started, Mrs Thatcher was quick to tell the public: 'This is not a dispute between miners and Government. This is a dispute between miners and miners.' This line never failed her.

Also as in wars, there was a debate about command. MISC 101 was the rough equivalent of a war cabinet. Ian MacGregor and the Coal Board were solely responsible for dealing with the NUM. The Department of Energy dealt with the Coal Board. It followed that it was not considered appropriate for Mrs Thatcher to meet MacGregor regularly. For a line into the Coal Board, she relied on Walker. While these arrangements made theoretical sense, they could never satisfy Mrs Thatcher's congenital anxiety to understand the detail; nor could they allay her suspicion of Walker.

---

* This document, supplied to ministers and officials, listed statistics of tonnes produced, pits operating and miners working, injuries to police, legal actions proposed, and so on.

According to Butler, she feared that Walker and MacGregor would 'do a fudge, like Pym and the Foreign Office in the Falklands had tried to do' and 'solve' the strike on terms she would consider utterly unacceptable.

In these circumstances, Mrs Thatcher liked to draw on other sources. One was her Policy Unit, run by John Redwood.* Another was Bernard Ingham, one of the few close to her who knew the trade unions well, having been labour correspondent of the *Guardian* in the 1970s. He maintained informal links with union leaders and helped interpret union behaviour to her. He could also make up for the inadequacies of the NCB's press department, a growing factor as the strike continued.

Once it became clear the working miners were to be central figures in the drama, the government wanted to know much more about them. Mrs Thatcher thought these men 'in many ways chimed with her view of the world'. They seemed to represent everything she most admired: they wanted to work, they resisted left-wing union militancy and they faced intimidation and violence bravely. To understand them better, she drew on her third and most eccentric source of advice: a man called David Hart.

Hart was the sort of insider/outsider for whom Mrs Thatcher had a soft spot. 'She liked dangerous people, and he was one of them,' observed one official. Intermittently rich, Hart was a Cold Warrior with several good contacts inside the Reagan administration. He helped raise money to allow the working miners to organize and fight Scargill and the NUM in court.† Mrs Thatcher listened to Hart's mixture of fantastical self-promotion and genuine knowledge and flair despite the efforts of staff, who thought him too disreputable, to keep him at bay.‡

As soon as the strike began, Hart visited the pit areas, sometimes in a chauffeur-driven Mercedes, to find out what was happening. From these forays he would send Mrs Thatcher vivid despatches. In April 1984, for example, he contrasted his visit to Nottinghamshire miners with his experience of a Scargill rally in Sheffield, where he 'could not escape thoughts of Nuremberg . . . The stink of fascism.' He warned her that although the Notts miners were 'very angry with Scargill' for trying to coerce them, if

---

* Particularly through David Pascall and Peter Warry, and Redwood himself, the Policy Unit tried to maintain the aim of getting a slimmed-down, well-functioning coal industry to emerge from the dispute, rather than seeing a settlement as automatically desirable.

† Hart persuaded the British-based American billionaire and philanthropist John Paul Getty, for example, to provide large sums to the working miners.

‡ At the party conference in 1983, Hart sought to change the draft of her speech at a late stage. Mrs Thatcher told Stephen Sherbourne that 'I've just seen David Hart, and he's got marvellous ideas for the speech.' 'I was horrified,' Sherbourne recalled. 'I opened my door on to the detectives in the hotel corridor and said, "If a man called David Hart comes looking for me, I'm not here." "I *am* David Hart," said the man in the suit.'

they were given the ballot they demanded they might vote for a strike. Mrs Thatcher read such reports carefully: 'He did have some real intelligence,' she later recalled.

After the opening salvoes of the strike, the next crisis came when the question of a national ballot returned to the fore. On 19 April, Scargill persuaded the NUM to reduce the threshold required to strike from 55 per cent of those voting to 50 per cent. This made the government extremely nervous. A yes vote on a national strike would not only halt production, but also, by legitimizing the strike, build pressure on other unions to act 'in sympathy'. Power station stocks would last until the end of September, but supplies were dropping and the public would 'go soft' if the dispute started to hurt them. Yet even now Scargill avoided calling a national ballot. Insufficiently confident of victory, he trusted in his ability to use mass picketing to coerce where he could not persuade. At Cabinet on 3 May, Brittan reported that Scargill had 'taken personal charge' of the NUM tactics, trying to hit individual pits hard to achieve 'the maximum surprise'. Walker was nevertheless able to tell colleagues that the production and movement of coal now stood at its highest since the strike had begun.

Violence now intensified. But the more Scargill's Yorkshire-based vanguard turned up to tell their Nottinghamshire neighbours what to do, the more Notts' loyalty to the central union waned. In May, fighting broke out when Scargill supporters, mainly from Yorkshire, demonstrated in Mansfield in Nottinghamshire. This left 90–100 police injured but did little to stop the Notts men working. Such violence only hardened Mrs Thatcher's attitude to any possible settlement and renewed her anxieties about the Coal Board's readiness to settle. It was lucky for her that Scargill rendered possible concessions by the NCB impossible by sticking to his position that no pit should ever be closed for economic reasons. A less extreme union leader would have worked out the differences between the Coal Board, the Department and 10 Downing Street and exploited them.

Scargill saw himself in an ideological and heroic role. At the end of May, trying to replicate his 1972 success at Saltley, he began a series of mass pickets designed to stop coke* being moved from the British Steel coking works in Orgreave, South Yorkshire. On 29 May, there was grave violence, with darts and bricks thrown at police and sixty-nine people injured. Mrs Thatcher reacted with horror. Speaking at Banbury Cattle Market the following day, using the repetition which, in her, was usually a sign of vehemence, she attacked what she called 'an attempt to substitute the rule of the mob for the rule of law . . . it must not succeed. It must not succeed.'

---

* In this context, 'coke' is the term for the high-carbon fuel derived from coal.

As trouble continued at Orgreave, Mrs Thatcher wanted British Steel to use the law against the NUM. Turnbull tried hard to discourage this. For him, as for several working closely with her, Mrs Thatcher's enthusiasm for invoking her own government's laws against the NUM was one of her 'reckless ideas'.* Here was a rare instance in which Walker and Norman Tebbit, the Trade and Industry Secretary, agreed, albeit as a matter of tactics. Their line was: 'Keep the temperature down and don't give the unions any pretext.' Mrs Thatcher 'railed against this but took the advice'. It was better, she later wrote, to show 'it was the basic criminal law of the country which was being flouted by the pickets and their leaders, rather than "Thatcher's laws"'.

Mrs Thatcher was less ready to listen to anything that smacked to her of appeasement. While the picketing of Orgreave continued, there were talks between the Coal Board and the NUM. After Walker reported MacGregor's belief that the talks 'had begun to move towards a satisfactory discussion of the issues', Downing Street became agitated. But once again, talks foundered on Scargill's refusal to budge. Turnbull expressed and fanned his principal's anxieties: 'What is surprising is not the outrageous nature of Mr Scargill's demands but the fact that it was reported to you last Friday that Mr MacGregor was detecting signs of realism.'

On 18 June, the climactic 'Battle of Orgreave' took place. The pickets, estimated at between 5,000- and 10,000-strong, confronted about 5,000 police. Despite a fierce contest,† they never succeeded in preventing the lorries loaded with coke from leaving the plant. Orgreave looked, Andrew Turnbull recalled, 'like the Wars of the Roses' and it carried the implication of civil war which goes with that comparison. For the majority of the public it confirmed a growing view that the NUM, and Scargill in particular, were committed to unjustified violence.‡ More important still, Orgreave proved that the police now had the numbers, the equipment and the will to prevail. In the last full week in June, 1,400 miners returned to work, bringing the total working to 53,000. While this was not a seismic numerical change, the attempt to break the will of the working miners

---

* Mrs Thatcher also fantasized about 'snatch squads', organized by members of local rugby clubs, or even involving the army, to go in to picketed mineheads to get the coal out, but these notions were not pursued.
† Twenty-eight police officers, and many more pickets, were injured and ninety-three arrests were made.
‡ Orgreave nevertheless quickly became a talismanic name in the legends of trade unionism. It was later the subject of the Dire Straits song 'Iron Hand' (1991) and was re-enacted for Channel 4 television in 2001. To this day, the left continues to demand an inquiry into the events of Orgreave.

had failed. Scargill at Orgreave exorcized for Mrs Thatcher the demon of Scargill at Saltley twelve years earlier.

It did not automatically follow, however, that the government would win. Key trade unions might combine successfully against it. And if public opinion came to see Mrs Thatcher's desire to defeat Scargill as personal and vindictive, it would turn against her. If, on the other hand, she conceded too much, she risked alienating working miners and her natural allies. Conservative supporters could not understand why the trade union laws which they had warmly backed were being shunned, and they hated the police being made to endure so much violence. Many were puzzled why Mrs Thatcher seemed to hold back. As Ronnie Millar wrote to her in July: 'I am sure the country is just waiting for you to take this gentleman [Scargill] apart.' There was a genuine dilemma about handling.

On 9 July, the government's position deteriorated significantly after a dock strike broke out almost without warning. That the leadership of the Transport and General Workers' Union were close to the NUM was no coincidence. 'The extreme Left', wrote John Redwood, 'is mounting a major extra-parliamentary challenge to the Government on a number of fronts . . . There is only one thing worse than presiding over industrial chaos,' he went on, in a passage which Mrs Thatcher underlined, 'and that is giving in to the use of industrial muscle for unreasonable ends.' Any 'fudged formula' on closures 'is defeat', said Redwood. There had to be a return to the 'war of attrition'.

The government's priority now was to keep the docks working at all costs. On 15 July, the use of troops was considered but rejected:* the fact that such plans were discussed at all shows how precarious the government's position had become. It was made worse when, that same day, judicial review of the union ban at GCHQ found the government had acted beyond its powers. Robin Butler recalled Mrs Thatcher's response: 'She said to me: "We'll appeal, of course, but if we go down, we'll have to accept this. The law is the law." I admired her very much that this was her first reaction. Think of how defeat on this issue would have helped the miners.'

So uncomfortable did the situation appear that President Reagan tried to raise her spirits.† 'I have thought often of you with considerable empathy,' he wrote, noting her struggles with the miners' and dockworkers' unions:

---

* The Ministry of Defence estimated that 2,800 troops could move 1,000 tonnes (fifty lorries) a day. Ministers feared this 'far too low' to make much of a difference. The adverse publicity from deploying troops was not worth the small gains on offer.
† It was highly usual for a foreign ally, even one as close as President Reagan, to write with words of encouragement for a purely domestic political difficulty.

'I'm confident as ever that you and your Government will come out of this well.' It was, perhaps, a good omen. That same day, 18 July, Mrs Thatcher's sky began to brighten. First, NCB talks with the NUM broke down over the closure of uneconomic pits. 'I have to say I was enormously relieved,' wrote Mrs Thatcher in her memoirs. The following day the dock strike collapsed for lack of support from TGWU members.

The war of attrition with the NUM resumed, but Mrs Thatcher felt easier. She had been reassured by the trusted Walter Marshall that, on current trends, endurance would last until June 1985. She had also been spurred on by advice from Walker, normally more cautious than she, that the government should encourage two Nottinghamshire miners who were bringing a legal case against the NUM. She had constantly been advised that any association with the working miners, whom she so admired, would 'undermine their position', so the prospect of the court case cheered her up.

Throughout the miners' strike, Mrs Thatcher had no doubt over Scargill's broader aims. Ever since the 1970s, she had agreed with those who saw a serious, semi-organized attempt by the extreme left to subvert British parliamentary democracy. Fear of this informed her attitudes on many issues – détente, local government, education policy, police reform, the Labour Party, intelligence, sanctions against South Africa, IRA terrorism and trade union militancy itself. The miners' strike was part of this wider phenomenon. Scargill's approach paralleled that of many Labour activists in local government, notably members of the Militant Tendency, such as Derek Hatton in Liverpool and Ken Livingstone, the Leader of the GLC. As the strike proceeded, so did the government's legislation to abolish the GLC and the metropolitan counties. 'I was up to my neck with Scargill,' recalled Livingstone. 'We broadly merged the miners' strike and the GLC campaign.' Scargill's local government allies thus did what they could to help the striking miners, providing them (sometimes illegally) with council funds or seeking to punish the police for tackling mass pickets.* The fact that Scargill had publicly spoken of overthrowing the elected government allowed Mrs Thatcher to have some of the strikers' activities monitored by the Security Service. Stella Rimington, later head of the service, classified Scargill as 'an unaffiliated subversive'.

For Mrs Thatcher, all this showed what would happen to Britain if her policies did not prevail. When she addressed backbenchers at the traditional

---

* In South Yorkshire, for example, scene of the Orgreave battles, the left-wing police authority tried to have the Chief Constable suspended.

'end of term' meeting of the 1922 Committee before the summer recess, the night after the NUM-NCB talks collapsed, she was fired up.* Her manuscript notes capture the occasion. The relevant passage began:

> Since Office
> Enemy without – beaten him
> & strong in defence
> Enemy within –
> Miners' leaders.
> Liverpool & some local authorities
> – just as dangerous
> in a way more difficult to fight
> But just as dangerous to liberty
> Scar across the face of our country.

Her speech was noisily applauded by the traditional banging of desks;† but not all Tory MPs liked its tone. Critics seized upon the phrase 'the enemy within' as the epitome of her divisive approach.‡ Although she had spoken only of the miners' *leaders* (and the left-wing local authorities) as being the enemy within, this was quickly misrepresented as her description of all miners. It would be used against her forever afterwards.

What she actually said was not far from a statement of plain fact. The main miners' leaders were proud of being the enemy of the government and were declaredly set on bringing it down. They consistently refused their members the national strike ballot which their constitution demanded. And they did, by means of violence and intimidation, try to prevent other miners from working. In addition, some, especially Scargill himself, were in alliance with revolutionary elements and, as later events were to show, in contact with foreign regimes hostile to Britain. They *were* the enemy within.

Mrs Thatcher was emboldened to speak out by the agony of the Labour Party. From the start of the dispute, Labour had been torn between its hereditary, instinctive loyalty to trade unions – especially miners, especially

---

* The occasion is always a private one, but details of her speech quickly leaked.
† Clapping being, by convention, forbidden in the Palace of Westminster.
‡ Chris Collins of the Margaret Thatcher Foundation has pointed out that the phrase 'enemy within' would have been familiar to Mrs Thatcher because of her Methodist background. The words are used, for example, in Wesley's Sermon 13, *On Sin in Believers*, and also in a number of Methodist hymns. In more recent times, the Labour Prime Minister Clement Attlee had spoken of an 'enemy within' when warning about Communist infiltration of the trade unions. Twenty years later, Enoch Powell referred to a 'hidden enemy within' to describe leftist agitators undermining British democracy. Mrs Thatcher was well aware of Powell's speech: she had endorsed his sentiments at the time. She presumably remembered Attlee's as well.

against Tory governments – and its anxiety about the circumstances of the strike. Neil Kinnock had favoured a national ballot, and had publicly said so, but somewhat obliquely.

Mrs Thatcher played on Kinnock's difficulties. Prime Minister's Questions, which should have provided good moments for Kinnock to arraign her over the strike, were often the other way round. Despite the provocation of her 'enemy within' speech, Kinnock did not raise it or the miners' strike with her before the summer recess. This visible evasiveness emboldened her. In a no-confidence debate on 31 July, she accused him of 'appeasement' because he refused to call for a ballot. Her parliamentary victory over Kinnock that day, so soon after the crisis of the dock strike had loomed, put heart into her MPs as they left for their summer break.

For her customary but always unwelcome summer holidays, Mrs Thatcher went once again to stay with Lady Glover at Schloss Freudenberg in Switzerland. At the end of August, Peter Gregson was up a tree in his garden, tending to his apples, when the telephone rang. 'She's coming back!' wailed an official from No. 10. 'She'll be here by lunchtime. She's worried it's all going wrong. Come and reassure her.' Gregson did so. It turned out that she had no specific anxiety, just her perpetual fear of being out of touch.

Mrs Thatcher was right to be anxious. The miners' return to work had slowed since July, and the season of conferences produced a plethora of peace plans. On 3 September came news that further talks were being arranged between the NCB and the NUM. MacGregor even suggested the NUM 'was taking "a more realistic" approach', words which Mrs Thatcher marked with her squiggle of scepticism. Deeply suspicious, she told Walker and MacGregor that a line had to be drawn – 'the NCB could make no further concessions on the principle of closing uneconomic pits'. But talks and meetings continued. In early September, the press got wind of a secret meeting between the NCB and the NUM. Arriving, MacGregor pretended to hide from the media by covering his face with a green plastic bag. The resulting bizarre pictures contributed to Downing Street's growing dismay about his conduct of the dispute.

A NCB mishandling now brought about what Turnbull considered 'the single most dangerous moment' of the entire strike. In the completely unionized world of coal mining there were other, smaller unions as well as the mighty NUM. Mine safety was overseen by the elaborately named National Association of Colliery Overseers, Deputies and Shotfirers (NACODS). If their members refused to work, pits would be legally obliged to close. In the middle of August, seemingly without thought for the possible consequences, the NCB issued a circular ordering NACODS members to cross picket lines, on pain of losing pay. Their leaders, who were more sympathetic to Scargill than most of their members, seized the moment and called a strike ballot for 28 September.

This mess confirmed Downing Street's fears about the NCB's dispute management. MacGregor seemed too fierce against NACODS, too wobbly about the NUM. The new Bishop of Durham, Dr David Jenkins, a left-wing theological radical, caused a stir by declaring that neither side must win a victory. He proposed that MacGregor should withdraw from his chairmanship and Scargill from his 'absolute demands': 'The withdrawal of an imported elderly American to leave a reconciling opportunity for some local product is surely neither dishonourable nor improper.' Few took the Bishop's specific suggestion seriously, but its focus on MacGregor's shortcomings was part of a trend which was difficult from Mrs Thatcher's point of view. With a sense of intransigence on both sides, people cast around for compromises.

Scargill, Robin Butler warned in a memo, had 'made headway' with his argument that putting pressure on the NCB and the government was 'the best way of finishing the dispute quickly'. Mrs Thatcher was increasingly worried that MacGregor might yield. Even David Hart told her that the NCB Chairman was 'an acute business negotiator who has not yet fully understood that he has been cast in the greater role of statesman ... He has his "wets" as you had yours. He is more likely to give in to them.' 'This', Hart warned her, 'is the greatest danger for you.' 'Most people,' Butler's memo continued, 'including those in the unions, desperately want to see Scargill defeated but may be beginning to doubt that we have the means of doing it.' Two days later NACODS members voted overwhelmingly to strike.

The NACODS leaders demanded not only the withdrawal of the NCB's circular – a wish easily granted – but also a system of independent, binding arbitration before any pit closure. They would start a strike on 8 October – the day before the opening of the Conservative Party conference – unless they got their way. They were persuaded to delay this date, but as the Tories converged on Brighton, the threat still hung in the air. The political atmosphere was one of extreme unease.

The Conservative Party conference at Brighton in 1984 is remembered for the IRA bombing of the Grand Hotel on Friday 12 October. Mrs Thatcher survived unscathed, but five people were killed and many others were injured, some very seriously. Public sympathy, at a low ebb when she arrived in Brighton, switched at once to Mrs Thatcher's side. This dramatic change in circumstances led her to tone down parts of her conference speech. While she pruned the most partisan elements, what she ended up saying about the miners' strike was still combative. She even linked, by implication, the terrorism she and her party had just experienced with the extremism of Arthur Scargill and his supporters. She spoke of 'the emergence of an organized revolutionary minority' prepared to exploit industrial disputes, and the threat of violence which lay behind their demands. She concluded: 'The nation faces what is probably the most testing crisis of our time, the battle between the extremists and the rest . . . This nation will meet that challenge. Democracy will prevail.' The extremists at the top of people's minds were now, of course, the IRA, but she meant Scargill and his militants too.

As befits the self-absorption of industrial disputes, the miners' strike continued as if no bomb had gone off. Barely rested from her ordeal, on the Sunday after the bombing Mrs Thatcher told MacGregor that the government could not accept the binding independent colliery review body on which NACODS were insisting. Ministers privately agreed that 'if necessary, the possibility of a strike by NACODS should be faced'. The expected strike date was 25 October.

The government was now seriously alarmed. It did not trust MacGregor to handle the negotiations right. Noting his own telephone conversation with Mrs Thatcher on 14 October, David Hart recorded: 'MAC SELLS PASS SANS REALISING WTHR THRU OLD AGE OR TOTAL LACK POLITICAL AWARENESS I DON'T KNO.' The government knew it had to make the ultimate decisions about NACODS, but was nervous of getting in deeper.

Mrs Thatcher was also – unusually in the history of the strike – embarrassed in Parliament. At Prime Minister's Questions on 23 October, Neil Kinnock accused her of having a 'hit list' for closures and of blocking attempts at a reasonable settlement. Wanting neither to give in nor to provoke NACODS, she sought refuge in bland, procedural language. She looked both weak and obstructive at the same time. But the next day, lacking support from their members, the NACODS executive decided to call off the strike. This was, as the government's Daily Coal Report gloated in a rather un-Whitehall way, 'a massive blow to Scargill'. NACODS had been the NUM's last hope of shutting down the pits altogether.

With the NACODS threat gone, the legal net tightened on the NUM. While Mrs Thatcher had reluctantly refrained from relying on new 'Tory laws' during the dispute, others had used this legislation to bring various actions against the NUM. At the end of September, the High Court upheld an attempt by two working miners to have the strike declared unlawful. Scargill was personally fined £1,000 for contempt of court and the union £200,000. On 25 October, the NUM's assets were sequestrated. Eventually, £8 million of NUM money was found hidden in Dublin, Luxembourg and Zurich. Defiance of the court might be popular with enthusiastic strikers, but it drove the NUM into the position of an impoverished outlaw, and into the arms of dangerous friends.

On 28 October the *Sunday Times* revealed that with Scargill's backing, Roger Windsor, the Chief Executive of the NUM, had visited Libya to solicit money to support the strike from the country's dictator, Colonel Muammar Gaddafi. Later, the paper established that $200,000 reached the NUM from this source. Given the nature of Gaddafi's regime, which was known to supply arms to the IRA, this revelation was extraordinarily damaging. British intelligence had known what Scargill was up to and how money was being moved. Mrs Thatcher was aware of this, and of helpful covert leaks. On 5 November, Robert Armstrong informed Robin Butler that 'Steps are being taken to prompt journalistic inquiries' about the NUM's connection with the Soviet Union and the Eastern bloc. The press duly reported that Scargill himself had solicited money from the Soviets, with $1.4 million authorized to be paid across. It would have been hard for anti-Scargill propagandists to have constructed a less favourable picture than the truth. Here was the miners' leader consorting secretly with the enemies of his country – the enemy within and the enemy without.

As the NUM's position became more compromised, the working miners gained confidence. Mrs Thatcher discovered she could best show her support by treating the issue in a humanitarian rather than a political way. This she did by corresponding with, and receiving delegations from, the wives of working miners. In September she had met a group of three such wives, who told her about intimidation, the need for transfers from troubled areas when the strike finished, the unhelpfulness of the BBC to their cause and the support for the NUM among some NCB managers. Mrs Thatcher's manuscript notes of the meeting reveal her strong reaction:

Fear
Threat
Hands knees – rocks
... Totally disillusioned
... NUM 'slush fund'
Danger to life.
Churches – money to miners
Hoax 999 ...
... Picketing – outside home

Such stories fed Mrs Thatcher's indignation against the strikers and her solidarity with those who defied them. All through the dispute there were violent attacks on working miners and their families, such as the wife of a working miner who was held down by youths in Nuneaton while others scraped her face with a Brillo pad (to remove the 'scab'). Perhaps because of her sex, Mrs Thatcher was more conscious of the suffering of the families concerned than were her male colleagues. Her attitude to the strike was governed not only by her determination that the NUM should lose, but also by her desire that the working miners should win.

On 30 November, the violence reached a dreadful climax. An attack on a taxi, carrying a miner to work, led to the death of the driver, David Wilkie. 'I have said', Bernard Ingham wrote to Mrs Thatcher, 'that you are horrified and utterly condemn this murderous activity.' Even Arthur Scargill, who had previously avoided any criticism of violence, was forced to condemn this attack.* Until then, violence had been on the rise as the strikers became more desperate. Now the fight went out of them.

Once the NACODS strike was called off, more miners began to return to work. By 7 November, 72,000 men were working, roughly 30,000 more than at the beginning of the strike. A further 6,000 returned over the next week. The government now realized it would almost certainly win. 'Ministers', said the Cabinet minutes for 15 November, 'should avoid any appearance of gloating over the continuing return to work.' On 13 November, Harold Macmillan, elevated by Mrs Thatcher to the House of Lords as the Earl of Stockton, made his maiden speech there, at the age of ninety. Lamenting the coal conflict, he declared that the miners were 'the best men in the world. They beat the Kaiser's army and they beat Hitler's army. They never gave in.' Whether or not Macmillan was right in his history, it was already perceptible that the miners were not going to beat Margaret Thatcher.

Desperate to avoid a humiliating defeat for the unions, the TUC began to search for a deal. Mrs Thatcher, however, was determined to maintain her bottom line. As she told Walker on 13 December, 'nothing should be agreed which would undercut the position of the working miners,' and it was 'essential to prevent the NUM from claiming that the programme of pit closures had been withdrawn'.

In February 1985, in a characteristically highly coloured missive, David Hart summed up the situation in terms that were probably not displeasing to Mrs Thatcher, who underlined parts of it: 'Like the snow, the last few weeks of the dispute must be endured bravely. We are on the brink of a great victory. If we don't throw it away at the last moment. Much greater

---

* Scargill did so on a platform shared by Neil Kinnock, and when he uttered the word 'condemn' Kinnock leapt up to applaud. As Kinnock recalled, 'I and Stan Orme [a member of his Shadow Cabinet] jumped up at once to clap it,' in order to make Scargill's condemnation as unqualified as possible. Kinnock's actions meant that Scargill's full words were drowned out. What he actually said was that he condemned such attacks when they happened 'away from picket lines'.

than the Falklands because <u>the enemy within is so much harder to conquer</u>.' He was also, it seems, the first person to set out to her on paper 'the most likely' way the strike would end. 'The NUM will lead its men back to work with no settlement,' he foretold. 'It is the best option for us ... an unequivocally clear victory,' which would prove 'the utter pointlessness of the strike'.

Hart's prediction proved correct. On 3 March 1985, a special delegate conference of the NUM voted to return to work without a settlement. Scargill promised that 'guerrilla warfare' would continue. Men went back to the pits, some marching to the music of colliery bands. On 8 March, the Daily Coal Report said that 97 per cent of miners were now not on strike: 'Because the situation has settled down coal reports will no longer be issued on a daily basis.' 'We shall miss you!' wrote Andrew Turnbull.

Mrs Thatcher had won the most important single victory of her career. She had vindicated trade union reform. She had laid the ghosts of the NUM defeats of Edward Heath and crushed the hard left in the person of Scargill. She had settled the awkward question of February 1974, 'Who governs Britain?' She did, as Prime Minister. Naturally she did not put it this way. 'If anyone has won,' she said outside 10 Downing Street, 'it has been the miners who stayed at work' and all those 'that have kept Britain going'.

The government's internal post-mortem was presented to Mrs Thatcher in late May. The economic loss directly attributable to the strike in 1984–5 was 1.25 per cent of GDP and public expenditure had increased by £2.5 billion because of it. Twenty-six civil cases were brought against the NUM and forty-seven injunctions granted; remedies under the 'Tory laws' were used as well as under the common law. In England and Wales, 1,390 police officers had been injured and 10,372 criminal charges brought. The report identified three main reasons for the defeat of the NUM: the provisions for endurance, the NUM's failure to get enough support from other unions and its own members, and the success of police 'mutual aid'.

By this stage, Mrs Thatcher's chief concern was to support the working miners. She wanted the government to '<u>instruct</u>' the Coal Board that working miners who requested a transfer to another pit (to escape retribution) should have one, expenses paid, and should not suffer financially for having worked through the strike.* She attended a secret dinner hosted by Woodrow Wyatt to meet the Nottinghamshire-based President of the Working

---

* Mrs Thatcher intervened with MacGregor, who, she felt, did not care enough about the issue in general to support the Fjaelberg family. Mrs Fjaelberg, one of the three wives who had visited No. 10, had been prominent in the working miners' wives group and wanted a transfer from Wales to Nottinghamshire because of harassment.

Miners' Committee, Colin Clarke, and leaders from other regions. They discussed how best to set up their own national union, which eventually, in December, became the Union of Democratic Mineworkers.

Mrs Thatcher was extremely sensitive in later years to what she considered the 'widespread belief that the Government had let the working miners down'. In a sense, this belief was correct. The let-down was not intentional: government documents throughout the strike show numerous suggestions for building a thriving coal industry. But none of this materialized. The economics proved damning. In Turnbull's retrospect, it was the collapse in the oil price to $10 a barrel in 1986 which finally discouraged serious efforts to maintain a big coal industry: 'You couldn't fight for the principle of economic pits and then keep uneconomic pits open because of a fondness for the working miners.' By the 1990s, Arthur Scargill's prediction that the coal industry would be destroyed had come true. But for his total resistance to the idea of an economic pit and the immense cost of his suicidal strike, this need not have happened.

The political and psychological situation for Mrs Thatcher after the end of the strike was a strained one. Even for the victors, there was melancholy. Millions who had no time for Scargill had nevertheless felt uneasy on behalf of the miners. There was also a problem of tone. Mrs Thatcher had won the key industrial relations battle of the post-war era, but she felt she could not say so publicly for fear of seeming triumphalist. By April, Bernard Ingham advised that 'we ought progressively to get over [that is, convey] the fact that the NUM lost'. Yet it was feared that Mrs Thatcher's reputation for being too confrontational would be exacerbated if she were to drive her victory home. There was sense in this view, but it underestimated the extent to which a failure to say something important in politics tends to be interpreted as weakness.

Besides, the miners' strike was not, in reality, an event which showed Mrs Thatcher's character in a bad light. She was not intemperate, as she often was in her EEC dealings, or vengeful, as she was accused of being over GCHQ, or uncollegiate with Cabinet ministers, or divisive of her party. Whatever her longing for dramatic interventions, she maintained personal and collective discipline throughout, listening carefully to Walker and usually erring on the side of caution. She was in charge but not embroiled. Even Ian MacGregor, with whom she had many disagreements, was in no doubt about her leadership. 'If you fight a war,' he told Tim Bell when it was all over, 'you want a great general. She was a great general.' Such points were not publicly made at the time. In some areas of policy – privatization, for example – Mrs Thatcher was given more personal credit than was due. For the conduct of the miners' strike, she was given too little.

Mrs Thatcher's most passionate feelings in the saga had been engaged by the cause of the working miners. Shortly after the strike ended, she wrote a remarkable letter to a Mrs Hackett, from Staffordshire, whose husband Terry had refused to strike and had met Mrs Thatcher at Woodrow Wyatt's dinner. Thanking Mrs Hackett for her courage and support for her husband, Mrs Thatcher set out what she thought about people like Terry Hackett:

> The miners who stood up for their right to work in the mining dispute were defending a fundamental privilege of a free people. We can be very proud of them. They withstood, and continue to withstand, the most extreme threats and intimidations with a courage which is an example to us all. The nation owes them a debt of gratitude.

Remarkably, Mrs Thatcher had the imagination to consider how a letter marked '10 Downing Street' might be received in the potentially hostile territory of a mining community. With an attention to detail hard to imagine in a male prime minister, she wrote a covering note which said: 'Please send in <u>Plain envelope</u>.'

16

Sales of the century

*'Privatization was thought to be a pipe dream.
Now it is a reality'*

With the sheer intensity and length of the miners' strike, one might assume that Mrs Thatcher's government had little energy remaining. This was not the case. Even as attention turned to the pits, it embarked on further major tax reform, and on privatization on a grand scale. Nigel Lawson's 1984 Budget, indeed, was delivered to Parliament on 13 March, the day after the miners' strike was called.

While not completely aligned over the Budget, No. 10 and No. 11 shared a sense of common purpose. Writing to Mrs Thatcher, John Redwood backed Lawson's plans to concentrate on reforming business taxation: 'This is the budget to be bold.' At the Department of Trade and Industry (DTI), Norman Tebbit also weighed in on Lawson's side, arguing, for example, the vital importance of getting rid of the job-damaging employers' National Insurance Surcharge (NIS) imposed by Labour. 'I had, to a reasonable extent, the confidence of the PM, and I had the friendship of Nigel,' he recalled. 'So I could sweet-talk them.' Jeffrey Sterling, special adviser to all Mrs Thatcher's DTI secretaries of state, considered that 'If Norman and Nigel worked together, they would nearly always succeed in persuading her.'

In this case, however, Mrs Thatcher did not need much persuasion. She was fervently in favour of reducing burdens on business and obstacles to job creation. She therefore supported her Chancellor over cutting corporation tax and abolishing the NIS. What really mattered to her was that income tax cuts were recognized as the ultimate, though not necessarily immediate, goal. This was the case. As Lawson explained, he planned to sequence his Budgets for electoral advantage: 'With a neutral Budget in 1984 and a large fiscal adjustment [partly due to asset sales] in prospect for 1985, this leaves room for desirable changes in personal taxation, provided we keep public expenditure flat.' She underlined the words 'provided' and 'flat' many times.

Under the British system, the Budget is reserved to the Chancellor in consultation with the Prime Minister. More jealous of his rights than Howe, Lawson did little to enlighten the Cabinet about his Budget thoughts, provoking irritation. In early February, John Biffen briefed lobby journalists that 'Cabinet this morning [9 February] had been one of the most bland, miserably disappointing and boring meetings he had ever been at ... no lively debate, just unctious [sic] self-satisfaction.' Biffen's outburst, which Ingham reported to Mrs Thatcher, was untypical of the Cabinet, but probably reflected some colleagues' feelings of exclusion.

As to Mrs Thatcher, Lawson preferred to conduct their Budget consultations through discussion after a Sunday-night supper in No. 11. This avoided leaks because, on such matters, Mrs Thatcher was utterly discreet. Lawson also believed that it relaxed her, but in fact it made her uneasy because she preferred serious government business to be done on paper. In due course, Lawson's preference for chat would become a means of avoiding important differences. Ahead of the 1984 Budget, however, their differences mostly worked to their shared advantage. She qualified his reforming zeal with her political sense of what she called 'our people'. She advised him, for example, against imposing a levy on consumer credit and passed on Ingham's concern that extending VAT to newspapers would only set Fleet Street against them. She urged the Chancellor not to spoil the 'wonderful reception' his 'wonderful Budget' would otherwise get. VAT was not extended to newspapers. Politically, if in no other sense, Mrs Thatcher and Ingham were undoubtedly right.

On 13 March 1984, Lawson addressed the House. 'This Budget will set the Government's course for this Parliament,' he began. His two themes were the further reduction of inflation and reform of business taxation, paving the way for tax cuts. Lawson set the PSBR, optimistically, at only £7.25 billion, though in the previous year it had hit £10 billion. It was his tax changes, however, which commanded the most attention. Amid a range of bold measures,* he laid out plans for a phased reduction in corporation tax, lowering the rate over several years from 52 per cent to 35 per cent. Share options were taken out of income tax altogether and the NIS ('this tax on jobs') abolished. He held income tax rates steady but raised their thresholds well above inflation.

All this Lawson accomplished in a crisp and confident speech. Reviews like 'A Star is Born' (the *Spectator*), 'a pyrotechnic display of economic and

---

* These included halving stamp duty, withdrawing all new life insurance premium relief and getting rid of the 'investment income surcharge', which taxed 'unearned' income at a higher rate.

financial skills' (*Guardian*), followed. A week later, Redwood judged that 'The Government has now regained momentum, thanks to a strong Tory radical Budget.' He told Mrs Thatcher Lawson had successfully advanced the radicals without alienating the consolidators. For her, it was a novel and pleasing experience to be presented with a Budget which was, in her view, right, but also popular. It was the first big achievement which made Lawson, in the word she was to use at a later, much less happy moment, 'unassailable'.

One important issue over which most radicals and consolidators could unite was privatization. The subject had been foreshadowed in the supposedly over-cautious 1983 manifesto. Big names had been named including BT, Rolls-Royce and British Airways (BA).* The Tories promised to 'seek other means' of encouraging competition and capital in the gas and energy industries, while noting that 'Merely to replace state monopolies with private ones would be to waste an historic opportunity.' There was a clear agenda.

In this area, it helped that Mrs Thatcher and Nigel Lawson were ideological soulmates. Her relationship with Geoffrey Howe as Chancellor, though vitally important and, broadly speaking, successful, had been forged rather by necessity than shared zeal. Lawson, younger than Howe, began as more of an acolyte than an equal to Mrs Thatcher. A proto-Thatcherite, he was a more systematic developer of her own ideas than she was herself.

David Pascall, who joined the Policy Unit from the Think Tank, immediately felt this sense of common purpose. The 'big push', as the unit saw it, was for a competition agenda, rolling back the state, spreading popular share ownership. Privatization was central. In Pascall's view, Mrs Thatcher had an 'abiding hatred' of the nationalized industries because of the amount of money they consumed, their appalling labour relations and their inability to raise capital for proper investment. She longed for 'decisions to be taken at a commercial and not a political level'. According to Peter Warry, who joined the Policy Unit in the summer of 1984, the DTI and, to a lesser extent, the Treasury 'were quite well captured by the nationalized industries'. Mrs Thatcher was not. She was often well informed about particular nationalized industries, especially the 'smokestack' ones. She was well advised, Warry believed, by Denis: 'She was very impressive. Sometimes she knew things I had not read.'

---

* Substantial parts of the British Steel Corporation, British Shipbuilders and British Leyland were also promised for sale.

Beyond the question of how much money privatization might raise (which remained central to Treasury thinking), Mrs Thatcher now also saw the issue in political, social and industrial terms. Redwood, who took over as head of the Policy Unit in late 1983, was, in his words, its 'guru on privatization'. Part of his job was liaison with John Moore, the Treasury junior minister chosen by Lawson to push privatization through. Telegenic, young and self-made, Moore was widely regarded as Mrs Thatcher's 'blue-eyed boy' of the time. He felt empowered by this, and by Lawson's own enthusiasm for privatization. He knew that timing was crucial. If the privatization programme did not get off to a flying start, too little would be accomplished by the next election. The Policy Unit felt the same way: 'If we did not push,' said Pascall, 'everyone else would water it down.' In this they had Mrs Thatcher's complete backing.

It did not follow that Mrs Thatcher was either the most expert or the most confident member of her own government where privatization was concerned. In Redwood's view, she was 'ready for it, but not an evangelist for it'. She liked to ask, 'That's all very well, but how do we do it?' David Willetts, who, at the Policy Unit, observed her methods closely, recalled that she was always 'very wary of grand strategy' and 'brilliant at moving between strategy and tactics'. She had a way, 'rather like a camera in a film, of drawing back to get a panning shot and then focusing right in on a tiny detail'.

Mrs Thatcher's landslide victory in June 1983 had naturally improved her confidence. Previous privatizations had been relatively easy – profitable companies which could be sold intact. Henceforth, as Lawson wrote to her in July, 'we are increasingly working in the heartland of the public trading sector, where we shall have to deal both with the giant utilities and unprofitable companies'. He called for a programme and timetable for each privatization. She swung into action.

Over the summer and autumn, Redwood and Moore toured government ministries only to be told: 'It's a political disaster.' 'We must accelerate the programme,' Lawson insisted come October, adding that the government was not paying enough attention to getting rid of monopolies – an implied criticism of Peter Walker, at the Department of Energy, who wanted neither gas nor electricity broken up. On cue, Ferdinand Mount (at this stage still running the Policy Unit) commended Lawson's paper to Mrs Thatcher: 'It is now essential for you to put your full authority behind the privatisation programme.' 'We cannot allow Peter Walker and others to get out of this exercise ...' The Policy Unit also considered the DTI submission on the car manufacturer British Leyland (BL) to be 'woefully inadequate'. Here the unnamed villain was Norman Tebbit, who was thought to be suffering from 'producer capture' in his love of British car production at a punitive rate of subsidy (estimated at £200 million in 1983).

Ministers felt the pressure. By mid-January 1984, Lawson was able to send Mrs Thatcher the full programme of privatizations, with dates. There were twenty-three enterprises mentioned – including all those promised in the manifesto plus, among others, the British Gas Corporation, the National Coal Board and Electricity. It was one of the most ambitious plans for legislation ever laid before a British Cabinet. At the Cabinet sub-committee meeting, recalled Moore, Mrs Thatcher stared at the wall-chart of what would be sold when and said: '"This is marvellous. Isn't it? Isn't it? Are there any questions?" There was complete and absolute silence. The chart became the policy.' According to Gerry Grimstone, an official overseeing privatization, her role now shifted to maintaining the pace: 'She never saw herself as the captain of the team, but as the coachman flogging the horses.' Redwood, he added, 'put metal in the whips'.* With such an extensive agenda, there were endless opportunities for officials to slow the pace, so the Thatcher lash was often needed.

British Telecom, about six times bigger in value than anything sold before, was the great test of the government's resolve. If it succeeded, the way would lie open for other sales. If not, significant change would become almost impossible. If the sale were not to flop, it was likely to err on the side of BT being sold as a monopoly. Mrs Thatcher had opposed this in the first term but been forced to back down. She understood that the more BT's monopoly was restricted, the less desirable the company would appear to investors and the less the sale would raise. As the Trade Minister, Lord Cockfield, put it to her: 'There is an inescapable conflict here between competition and the Treasury.'

Mrs Thatcher acknowledged this problem, which gave her an uneasy conscience. Her scribbled interventions on memos about privatizations often complained about monopoly and its bad effects on prices and competition. But she knew that something as complicated as privatization could be forever postponed if ministers let the best be the enemy of the good. Reluctantly, she accepted that BT would be sold intact.† A similar pragma-

---

* This description of the roles is more accurate than Lawson's somewhat *parti pris* view that she did little about privatization herself, but 'left me to get on with it'.

† As Cecil Parkinson, the new Trade and Industry Secretary, explained at the second reading of the post-election BT Bill, breaking up BT before offering it to the public 'would require a delay of many years in order to put BT's accounts into a form which would make piecemeal disposals possible'.

tism drove the notion that the reluctant senior executives of nationalized industries should be paid much more to take their businesses to market. When nationalizing health care in the 1940s, Aneurin Bevan had won over consultants by, as he later put it, having 'stuffed their mouths with gold'. Now the Thatcher government used a similar method to achieve the reverse effect across a range of industries.*

To guard against BT's monopoly power, the government turned to regulation. A state-owned agency, the Office of Telecommunications (OFTEL), was established. OFTEL insisted that future BT price rises must be less than the prevailing rate of inflation.† Privatized industries were thus expected to make substantial efficiency gains, ensuring the customer would get more for less. At the same time, the more efficiently the companies operated, the more profit they would make. Intended, initially, as a stopgap measure until sufficient competition developed, this became a regulatory price model for other privatizations. Mrs Thatcher liked that it would gradually help push the inflation rate down.

The BT sale was, at the time, the biggest single equity issue anywhere in the world, ever. Partly for this reason, only 51 per cent of the company would be sold in the first tranche. Redwood argued strongly that shares be offered to the general public, as a chance to begin to create the 'society of owners' of which Mrs Thatcher increasingly spoke. He told her, 'This is the new council house sales.' The involvement of retail investors was crucial for another reason. Without them, there were doubts in the City that there would be sufficient demand. As David Willetts recalled, 'It was only because we got personal investors in that we could sell so much.' This ensured Mrs Thatcher's close involvement, because it was 'politically out of the question to sell shares to the public and then see them collapse'.

A virtuous circle was created. The price of the shares must not be so low that they would be 'stagged' – sold on immediately after flotation for quick profits. Yet it was vital that it should not be so high that the public either shunned the sale or lost money on their investment. Buying shares had previously been an arcane procedure: the BT sale inaugurated a new age in which applications could be made simply by filling out forms in the newspapers. Numerous marketing incentives encouraged small investors, who were deliberately favoured in allocation of shares. All this paid off

---

* In the case of BT, the Chairman, Sir George Jefferson, saw his salary rise more than 70 per cent to £160,000 shortly after privatization.
† This was achieved through a formula, invented by Professor Stephen Littlechild, known as RPI – X. RPI was the Retail Price Index and X was the percentage decreed by OFTEL. X was eventually settled, after much argument, at 3 per cent.

handsomely. When the BT shares were offered for sale in November 1984, City institutions bought 45.8 per cent, the public 34 per cent, overseas investors 14 per cent and employees 3.8 per cent.* Defying the anathemas of their union, 95 per cent of BT employees bought shares. The total proceeds were £3.615 billion. About 2.15 million people bought BT shares, roughly the same as the total number of British citizens who had owned shares of any kind when Mrs Thatcher first came into office. 'Just a few years ago, in Britain, privatisation was thought to be a pipe dream,' Mrs Thatcher declared before the US Congress in February 1985. 'Now it is a reality and a popular one,' and, she could have added, the first of its kind in the world.

Each privatization was different. Mrs Thatcher intervened much more in some than in others. Unlike BT, companies like BL and BA were losing very large sums, often in politically controversial ways. It was these which excited her interest the most. The BA story is a good example of the thorny path that privatization often had to take, and of Mrs Thatcher's striking methods of getting her way.

In February 1981, the government had appointed Sir John King as BA's Chairman. He took the job on the understanding that he would be able to sell the company, which was expecting losses of £400 million over 1980–83. King was a ruthless, charming, buccaneering man with a gleam in his eye, an expert in most industries connected with wheels and wings, and the sort of individualistic and inspiring leader who endeared himself to Mrs Thatcher.†

King understood that the Chairman of BA had enormous influence over MPs by the simple device of giving them free flights. Through this, he built up a vital network of parliamentary support for his company's interests. He presented to Mrs Thatcher a characteristic puzzle of privatization. On the one hand, his flair and gumption made him exactly the kind of man she wanted to sort out a nationalized industry.‡ On the other, he had the great industrialist's natural desire to squash all rivals, fighting for every sort of privilege that government could confer. He would accomplish the

---

* Everyone applying for 400 shares or fewer got 100 per cent of what they sought. Those who had applied for 100,000 shares or more got nothing. This was controversial in the City but good for the popular perception of the sale's purpose.

† Babcock International, of which King became Chairman in 1970, had given a good deal of money to the Conservative Party. Behind the scenes, King helped organize a City-industrial Conservative fundraising link. He was a long-time associate of other Thatcher supporters in business, notably Lord Hanson and Sir Gordon White.

‡ King was known in the press – and she never complained of it – as 'Mrs Thatcher's favourite businessman'.

turnround of the company and the eventual sale which she wanted, but at a price.

In April 1982, King told Mrs Thatcher he needed two more years to make BA a successful airline. He demanded the right to pay private-sector-style salaries to recruit the people to do it. Lord Cockfield objected. BA was a massive loss-maker: overpaying managers would set a bad example in nationalized industries. But Mrs Thatcher overruled him. By September, however, appalled by BA's newly uncovered loss of £600 million, she seemed to reverse course: 'why any increase in pay?' she wrote. 'We cannot just agree to any request which private companies could not afford.' She now urged a pay cut, or least a freeze. This left Cockfield to defend BA's position: 'we cannot pick out BA to impose a pay freeze which we are not prepared to impose elsewhere'. 'Why not,' Mrs Thatcher scribbled angrily, 'when they are losing or have lost so much? ... I feel we have been bounced.'

Mrs Thatcher also began to realize that the fattening-up of BA for privatization would involve the starving of its main British rival, British Caledonian (BCal). Would this not damage the competition dear to her heart? While she often expressed anxiety about BCal's fate, she let herself be beaten down by the argument that BA's real competitors were foreign airlines and so BA privatization was 'light years away from the substitution of a private for a public monopoly'.*

Quite a different barrier, however, still stood in the way. At Cabinet on 1 August, ministers had been told that legal suits in the United States against BA might yet delay privatization. This issue proved astonishingly tough, but Mrs Thatcher proved even tougher.

In March 1982, the 'cheap and cheerful' Laker Airways had gone bust, following a price war with the big monopolistic carriers. The US Justice Department, rightly suspecting collusion between the airlines, was considering prosecuting BA under antitrust legislation. Civil suits also loomed. With this potentially ruinous threat hanging over BA, privatization seemed impossible. Mrs Thatcher went to war. While she had supported Freddie

---

* King lobbied hard against the reallocation of routes to small airlines by the Civil Aviation Authority (CAA). This divided the Cabinet. Mrs Thatcher summed up the problem in September. The CAA review of routes 'touched on important elements of the Government's philosophy – its wish to encourage competition and enterprise and to reduce the boundaries of the public sector', she said, but then, with an untypical admission of ambiguity, added: 'Some of these objectives were in conflict with one another.' By the end of 1984, and only after King had annoyed her by threatening resignation, a 'route swap' was agreed. This was favourable to BCal, but much less so than the changes originally proposed by the CAA. It cleared this particular block to privatization without seriously hurting BA. The deal was also ultimately fatal to BCal. The company was forced to sell out to BA for £251 million the year after privatization.

Laker's emancipating, no-frills, transatlantic service,* she could not stand the thought of BA privatization being indefinitely delayed, tantamount, given the demands of the political timetable, to being dropped. And so, in March 1983, she wrote to Reagan, asking him 'personally and urgently' to intervene and prevent any antitrust investigation. Reagan refused. Although technically possible, a presidential intervention would amount to interference in an accepted legal process. 'This gets us into Nixon territory,' administration officials complained to the British Embassy. 'You know how highly I value our personal relationship . . .' Reagan told Mrs Thatcher. 'However . . . I feel I do not have the latitude . . .'

Immediately after her 1983 election victory Mrs Thatcher retaliated, effectively banning British airlines from cooperating with the US investigation. Laker's liquidators challenged this in the English courts and in July 1984 the House of Lords found against BA's position, allowing the case to be tried in the United States. A US Grand Jury was now considering a range of indictments against BA and its employees.

Mrs Thatcher attacked on all levels. Ministers and messages were despatched to Washington. In London, days after Reagan's re-election in November 1984, she saw the US Ambassador, Charlie Price, who was left shaken: 'She confirmed our worst fears about how she and her senior Cabinet ministers will react to an indictment decision . . .' He urged the White House to persuade the Justice Department to alter course.

On 16 November, the Laker arguments were laid before the President. Reagan listened, recalled one witness, and then rendered his verdict: 'We live in a very dangerous world. We don't have any friends better than Margaret Thatcher. If this is important to her, even I, as a law and order man, am not going to proceed, in the interests of US national security.'

Mrs Thatcher had been expecting bad news, so when Allen Wallis, Reagan's Under-Secretary for Economic Affairs, visited her with the President's decision she was 'positively effusive. She said that she was "thrilled" . . . and underscored her euphoria with gestures and movements showing genuine appreciation.' Wallis explained that, in return, they expected the British to accept greater flexibility in pricing and capacity in transatlantic routes and pledge to abide by US antitrust law. Mrs Thatcher conceded none of this. Instead, the British now made a further demand. Before any concessions of their part, the US administration would have to seek British aviation's exemption from the so-called 'treble-damage provisions' which permitted

---

* Mrs Thatcher had praised Laker by name in her 1981 party conference speech. When the airline had started to go down, she had contemplated a rescue ('My passengers! My poor passengers!'), until she discovered that the cost might be open-ended ('Oh dear! An open-ended situation! I couldn't wish that on my poor taxpayers').

injured parties to sue for three times the value of the damage they had suffered. This went down like a lead balloon in Washington. As Charlie Price wrote to the President, the British 'thanked us when we quashed the indictments – but so far we have nothing in hand but a bag of air'. The issue now loomed uncomfortably ahead of Mrs Thatcher's visit to Camp David just before Christmas.

At Camp David, on 22 December 1984, President and Prime Minister spent the entire morning discussing East–West relations and SDI. When Reagan proposed lunch, Mrs Thatcher asked that they discuss civil aviation first, tirelessly making the familiar arguments. She thanked Reagan for dropping the Grand Jury but lamented that the treble-damages remedy hung over BA 'like a dark cloud': American action was 'denying her the ability to denationalize British Airways'. Reagan's tone was sympathetic, but he told her Congress would reject a proposal to waive treble damages. Over cocktails and then lunch, she refused to let the issue drop. 'She was absolutely fierce about it,' recalled George Shultz. No progress was made.

When one considers that, in the course of the previous six days, Mrs Thatcher had met Mikhail Gorbachev for the first time (see p. 417), flown to Peking to sign the Hong Kong Agreement, flown on to Hong Kong to sell it to the colony's people, and then flown to Washington via Honolulu; and when one further reflects that the Cold War issues at stake were so important and demanding, it is well nigh incredible that she could have summoned the energy to argue the BA–Laker case repeatedly with her hosts. Almost any other British leader would have let himself be overcome by boredom, good manners or sycophancy towards his powerful hosts. But Mrs Thatcher was impervious to boredom if she thought a point mattered, and almost never considered repetition a fault. 'One of her great strengths was her single-mindedness,' said Charles Powell, 'and her absolute refusal to see that there could be another side to any case.' Her hosts – much more interested in what she had to say about the world-historical issues of the Cold War and SDI – were impressed and exasperated in equal measure.

Realizing she could not prevail over treble damages, Mrs Thatcher sought an informal solution. In February 1985, she requested Reagan's help in agreeing a favourable settlement for BA out of court with Ex-Im Bank, its largest creditor. This duly came to pass and, that July, a broader private settlement was reached covering most of Laker's outstanding claims. Thanks, in considerable part, to Mrs Thatcher's relationship with President Reagan, the privatization of BA could take place.

The company was finally sold in February 1987. It was presented as a proud moment for popular capitalism, which it was. People were keen to own a bit of the country's now successful airline. The sale raised

£900 million and was underpriced, being eleven times oversubscribed. The whole process had taken seven years.

'The Treasury should be given encouragement to keep up the pressure on reluctant departments,' Redwood had written impatiently to Mrs Thatcher in July 1984. 'In particular, you should expect much more urgency from the Department of Energy in pursuing the ideas on British Gas.' Both Chancellor and Prime Minister had long wanted British Gas (BG) broken up and sold once BT was done. Yet the whole issue was proving extremely difficult.

The problem, from Mrs Thatcher's point of view, began with the Chairman of BG. Sir Denis Rooke was the classic nationalized industry chief of the rare successful sort. He was a bully and, according to Lawson, 'a megalomaniac' who believed that he alone understood his trade, 'treating Ministers and officials alike with a mixture of distrust, dislike and contempt'.* As Energy Secretary, Lawson had worked hard to, as he put it, 'weaken Rooke's empire' by announcing the privatizations of the oil-producing business of the British National Oil Corporation (later Britoil) and BG's offshore oil business, and by abolishing BG's statutory monopoly on the purchase of gas and control of the onshore gas pipeline grid.

Peter Walker, Lawson's successor at Energy after the 1983 election, however, regarded Rooke as 'the best nationalised industry chairman I met'. Although not adamantly opposed to privatization, Walker had little objection to BG's monopoly power. He agreed with Rooke that the company should be a 'national champion'. If sold, he believed, it must be sold whole. In principle, neither Lawson nor Mrs Thatcher accepted this, but principle could not be the only consideration. Ministers believed that Rooke had the capacity to undermine confidence in the privatization and so had to be handled with great care. Peter Gregson, Permanent Secretary of the Department of Energy from May 1985, remembered Mrs Thatcher 'sometimes sucking her teeth and saying how convenient it would be if we could get rid of Denis; but she saw that he was a force of nature'. As they humoured Rooke, Gregson noticed the Chairman gradually coming to see that something might be made of privatization 'so long as he could wield great power'.

Given the joint power of Mrs Thatcher and Lawson, it might, in ordinary circumstances, have been possible to overrule Rooke and Walker; but the circumstances were extreme. Discussions of BG privatization began before the miners' strike and finished after it. Mrs Thatcher felt she could not afford to fall out with Walker while the strike was in progress, or to

---

* Rooke had a famously short fuse and had to take pills to prevent himself shouting at people. These were reported to be ineffective.

punish him after its successful conclusion. Walker advised that gas privatization would be doable but that, in the context of the miners' strike, electricity would not. He insisted that the sale must be of a single entity.

At a meeting on 26 March 1985, with Lawson, Moore and Walker, Mrs Thatcher conceded this, so long as the utility was sold without delay. She later defended the decision as the only way to ensure the sale before the next election. This was true, but not the whole truth. More than he liked to admit, Lawson was – almost *ex officio* as Chancellor – keen on maximizing the proceeds. Mrs Thatcher was not immune to this either. After the success of the BT sale, she had said to officials, 'What can we do that's twice the size of BT?' The stronger the monopoly, after all, the higher the price.

While the need to press on was genuine, by Mrs Thatcher's high standards of due diligence there remained something negligent in the way BG was handled. The biggest problem was that the sale of a monopoly was not adequately compensated for by new regulation. Although the government legislated for a regulator, it did so cautiously, fearing further explosions from Sir Denis Rooke. The failure to regulate rigorously would give rise to many difficulties and produce disillusionment with the privatization of utilities.

Once the sale of BG whole was agreed, however, the full energy of the government could go into getting it right. Great attention was given to tight pricing, and a huge effort was made to sell as many shares as possible to the general public. The advertising company Young and Rubicam devised a famous campaign which got round the rules restricting the puffing of a stock by inventing an invisible character called Sid, who might, or might not, learn about the sale. The catchphrase – 'If you see Sid, tell him' – entered popular discourse.* The whole of BG (except for the government's 'golden share', which allowed state buyback in an emergency) was sold in November–December 1986. Its handling was a triumph for the new world begun only a few weeks earlier with the City's reform of the Stock Exchange (see below). The sale raised £5.434 billion.† Two million of the buyers had never bought shares, so this was a giant leap for popular ownership. Not coincidentally, it was also a good way of securing Conservative votes in the election pencilled in for the following year.

On 27 October 1986, the City of London experienced what was known as Big Bang. On a single day, all the reforms of the Stock Exchange were

* 'Sids' became the name for all ordinary buyers of privatization stocks, and 'Siddery' the sometimes disparaging term for trying to lure the buyers in.
† Over 4.5 million applications were received, which made BG the company with the largest number of shareholders in world history.

implemented at once. The phrase was apt, because the changes were indeed explosive, but the phenomenon had small beginnings.

At first, the question had seemed almost technical. In May 1979, Mrs Thatcher had inherited from the Labour government a commitment by the Office of Fair Trading (OFT) to investigate the Stock Exchange for restrictive practices.* In those days, the Exchange operated as a sort of old boys' club (heavily dominated and hereditarily filled by pupils educated at the major public schools) which did well by its members, but kept charges high and new entrants out. Because the Conservatives were regarded as the friends of the City establishment, it was widely assumed that the new government would reverse Labour's decision and exempt the Stock Exchange from the OFT's investigation. For precisely this reason, it was reluctant to do so.

It began to become clear, however, that the court case which would inevitably result if no deal were done would be disastrous for the Stock Exchange – and tricky for the government, since the Exchange was the market for raising government debt. Nicholas Goodison, its Chairman, recognizing that the unreformed Stock Exchange was turning London into a backwater, supported change.† In 1982, the turnover of equities in New York (which had introduced stock exchange reform in the mid-1970s) was more than fifteen times greater than that of London. The pressure to adapt or die was becoming unstoppable.

Once Mrs Thatcher had won her 1983 landslide victory, things moved very fast. Goodison asked Cecil Parkinson, at the DTI, to prevent the OFT case in return for a Stock Exchange promise to reform. Parkinson was supportive and found an ally in Nigel Lawson. As the main intellectual driver for the abolition of exchange controls in 1979, Lawson had intended that this would lead to the end of the Stock Exchange's restrictive practices. He agreed it would be better to avoid snarling up change in a court case. He helped Parkinson persuade doubting Cabinet colleagues.

Mrs Thatcher herself was not deeply engaged. She continued to worry that it looked bad for a Conservative government to interfere, seemingly in favour of the Stock Exchange, in a legal case. But she did have some strong, relevant prejudices which made her easy to win over. She had a

---

* The OFT estimated that there were more than eighty such practices, but there were three that mattered. Membership of the Stock Exchange was severely controlled, and excluded all foreign firms; the members of the Exchange operated on fixed commissions, and the 'single capacity' rule meant that brokers could not themselves trade in shares but must buy and sell shares for their clients via 'jobbers', who could.

† The only foreign equities traded in London at that time were South African gold stocks and a few Australian mining shares.

distaste for monopoly and doubted the positive economic contribution made by the City's club mentality. She often felt slighted by City men.* Parkinson recalled her returning from lunch at a big bank before her first victory in 1979. 'They had given her hell. She was very depressed. I said: "Don't worry; they'll vote for you, and they'll forget it." "They may," replied Margaret, "but I won't."'

As with privatization, Mrs Thatcher herself was not particularly quick to see exactly how City reform might serve her wider economic agenda, but advisers were more than ready to help her. John Redwood pressed upon her the links between such reform and privatization, deregulation, wider ownership, a mass market in shares, personal 'portable' pensions, the rejuvenated London Docklands† and a more competitive, internationalized Britain. It was, he argued, part of the 'massive enterprise revolution' which she sought. In July 1983, she agreed that the government would announce its intention to exempt the Stock Exchange, by law, from the Restrictive Practices Act, so long as it reformed itself within three years. As the *quid pro quo*, Parkinson also publicly promised that there would be a Financial Services Act to bring new law to the new world which Stock Exchange reform would create.

Within No. 10, Redwood now gave Mrs Thatcher the most guidance. When the Stock Exchange had set out its own detailed proposals in April 1984, he counselled her in favour of liberalization: 'You should not be too worried about the possibility of foreigners coming in and buying up the British financial system ... This is a perfectly healthy development.' She duly welcomed what her private office called 'the radicalism of the Exchange's consultative document, which fully justifies the decision to take the case from the OFT'.

In general, Mrs Thatcher was seeking to balance proper control of the risks involved with what she and Lawson regarded as inevitable change. In April 1986, with Big Bang fast approaching, Brian Griffiths (Redwood's successor as head of the Policy Unit) and David Willetts produced a report updating Mrs Thatcher on the whole subject. They worried particularly about how, in bad times, the new firms might be tempted to 'dump their losses on to the client'. They pointed out the Glass–Steagall Act of 1933 in the United States, which enforced the separation of clearing banks and

---

* That said, Mrs Thatcher did have some strong supporters in the Square Mile, including Michael Richardson at Rothschilds, who, when at Cazenove, had arranged for that organization to pay for her office as Leader of the Opposition.
† This was a project Mrs Thatcher and Michael Heseltine had begun in the first term.

investment banks,* and said: 'It is open to question as to whether we shall some day, after a nasty scandal, be forced in the same direction.' Mrs Thatcher marked this passage very heavily. The risk was acknowledged; but in a culture quite unused to regulation of this sort, such a level of legislative interference was considered undesirable.

To this day, controversy swirls about Mrs Thatcher's unlocking of capitalism. What is certain is that her innovations of privatization and financial reform changed the world. The City 'club' disappeared, and London became a centre for international markets and for banks as it had not been since before the First World War. It is a mark of the boldness of her government that, despite all the well-known disadvantages of nationalization, no one before her had really tried to unscramble the state grab for industrial power of the middle of the twentieth century. And it is a mark of the policy's success that no nation, once embarked on privatization, has yet seriously attempted to reverse it, except in cases of monopoly utilities. Privatization became, and remains, the greatest policy export ever invented in Britain (unless one can describe parliamentary democracy or the rule of law as a policy).† Mrs Thatcher does not deserve personal credit for inventing the policy, but only a government led by her could have seen it through. The world recognized this, more perhaps than did her fellow countrymen.

In November 1985, about a year before BG was sold, Harold Macmillan, by then ninety-one years old, gave a famous speech likening privatization to the unwilling sale of the contents of a once-noble house: 'First of all the Georgian silver goes, and then all that nice furniture that used to be in the saloon. Then the Canalettos go.' It was wittily done, but it revealed Macmillan's paternalism. In his mind, he – or his friends – had once owned the family silver, and now it was gone. Its departure was therefore a loss. Seen from a wider point of view, however, the silver had not been sold away. As Mrs Thatcher put it, she was 'selling the family silver back to the family' – that is, the nation. It was now better-polished and better-used. This was a gain.

---

* This law was later repealed under the Clinton administration, a decision which was afterwards considered a major factor in the onset of the 2008 financial crisis.
† Oliver Letwin, who joined Rothschilds after his time at the Policy Unit, found the world coming to London to discover what Mrs Thatcher's governments had achieved and ask how it could follow suit. In his ten years at Rothschilds, Letwin found himself advising the following countries on privatization: Canada, the United States, Colombia, Mexico, Chile, Honduras, Kenya, Tanzania, Congo (Brazzaville), Morocco, South Africa, Ivory Coast, Singapore, Malaysia, Australia, New Zealand, Spain, Italy, France, Ireland, Portugal, the Netherlands, Sweden, Finland, Ireland, Poland, the Czech Republic, Slovakia, Hungary, Moldova, Russia and even Cuba.

There was a radical transformation in the performance of almost all the companies privatized or opened up by the breaking of cartels. There were serious failings too. Some monopolies were not tackled. The failure to prohibit the emergence of so-called universal banking (the merging of commercial 'high street' banks with merchant, later called 'investment', banks) contributed to the disaster of the credit crunch in 2008. But it remains unimaginable that a Stock Exchange playing by the old rules could have survived, or that a nationalized BT with monopoly power could possibly have presided over the telecoms revolution.

The privatized companies were also now owned, in a real sense, by millions of people. The campaign for wider share ownership was by no means an unqualified success. Although there were 3 million private shareholders in Britain in 1979 and 11 million when Mrs Thatcher left office in 1990, most British people did not become serious long-term holders of equities. Nonetheless, Mrs Thatcher's slogan of 'every earner an owner' acquired some reality. Owner-occupied houses, shares, portable pensions, employee ownership, much greater opportunities to start companies with small initial outlay, and even the highly controversial loosening of controls on personal credit all helped create prosperity and greater financial freedom for classes of British citizens who had never known such things before. It was partly the success of privatization and the opening up of the City which emboldened Nigel Lawson, in 1986, to start Personal Equity Plans (PEPs) allowing owners of modest amounts of shares to shelter them wholly from tax. In the form of ISAs, they remain an important part of many people's provision for retirement. There is truth in the accusation that Mrs Thatcher's policies, especially when oversold in the Lawson boom of the late 1980s, encouraged people to 'get rich quick', but most of the achievements did not melt away. Besides, getting rich, quick or otherwise, is broadly speaking better for a country than getting poor slowly, which was the situation Mrs Thatcher's policies sought to remedy.

Nigel Lawson made the simple point that 'it has not sufficiently come out in most accounts that the great success of Mrs Thatcher on the economic front was the reform and transformation of the economy'. Economically, this mattered more than the later rows about interest rates and exchange rates. It is what made the difference.

17
The coming of Gorbachev
'For heaven's sake, try and find me a young Russian'

The year 1984 was symbolic in Western minds because of George Orwell's famous novel of that name. Although Orwell was on the left, he was much admired by many on the right, including Mrs Thatcher, for his vision of the evil of Soviet Communism. As the year itself approached, people asked whether Orwell's vision of a world in which freedom had been snuffed out had come to pass. They assessed the Cold War and wondered who was winning.

Mrs Thatcher, like her American allies, felt growing strength, but a sense that the onus now fell on them to make progress. The Soviets, having walked out of the arms control talks in Geneva in protest at INF deployment, offered little encouragement. Giving dinner to Henry Kissinger just before Christmas 1983, Mrs Thatcher complained, 'She could barely recall a situation where there was at once so much uncertainty and so little contact.' Following her Chequers seminar, she made it her business to seek out the next generation of Soviet leaders. The year 1984 was to mark dramatic success in this search. That January, President Reagan softened his rhetoric, calling publicly for dialogue with the Soviets. Mrs Thatcher welcomed this warmly. In private she told Reagan: 'I thought you struck exactly the right note and at the right time.'

On 2 February, she travelled to Hungary, her first visit to a Warsaw Pact country (other than her 1979 stopover at Moscow airport) as Prime Minister. She had settled on Hungary because it had greater economic freedom than other Soviet satellites. She was also aware that the Hungarian leader, János Kádár, could be the conduit for messages to Andropov. The Foreign Office urged her to stress that 'Britain is once again playing a significant role in East/West relations ... not least under the present Prime Minister because of our special relationship with the US.'

In this vein, Mrs Thatcher hastened to report her meeting to Reagan. Kádár had told her he 'believed the West could do business with the Soviet

Union', but he had also made clear the strict limits to the Hungarian experiment, not least on political freedom, and insisted such things could not change. 'It follows', she told Reagan, that '... we have to find a way of living side by side with the Communist system, repugnant as it is.'

On 9 February, the day her message landed on Reagan's desk, Andropov died. Two years earlier Mrs Thatcher had refused to attend Brezhnev's funeral, but she now made the trip to Moscow. There she met Andropov's successor, Konstantin Chernenko, widely regarded as an elderly stand-in until the successor from the next generation could emerge.* Chernenko, recalled Tony Bishop, who interpreted, spoke to her in 'a high-speed gabble and with the same stumbles, monotony and lack of coherence that we had heard in public ... it was, for her, like meeting an ailing member of her father's generation'. She left 'unimpressed'. On the plane home she made her frustration clear. 'For heaven's sake,' she exclaimed, 'try and find me a young Russian.'

The search now focused on Mikhail Gorbachev, who, under Chernenko, had become the *de facto* number two in the Soviet hierarchy. In mid-June an invitation was despatched suggesting Gorbachev lead a 'parliamentary' delegation to Britain.† For a long time it received no reply.

That September, Reagan took an important step towards dialogue by hosting Andrei Gromyko, the Soviet Foreign Minister, for talks at the White House. As Reagan explained to Mrs Thatcher, his 'primary aim' was 'to impress upon the Soviet Government my strong, personal desire to put our relations on a more positive track'. She wrote back the same day to 'wholeheartedly endorse' his approach.

In mid-October 1984, just after the Brighton bomb, Mrs Thatcher learnt that Gorbachev had accepted the invitation to visit Britain. On the confirmation letter, Powell wrote: 'Will you see him here [Downing Street]? Or invite him to your dacha?' She preferred her dacha, writing 'Lunch at Chequers'. She saved this news until she spoke in the Queen's Speech debate in Parliament on 6 November.

Gorbachev's acceptance worked well for Mrs Thatcher. Following the

---

* During the inevitable waiting around before the meeting, Mrs Thatcher turned down the offer of a rare behind-the-scenes tour of the Kremlin, insisting the time could be better spent studying her briefing papers. 'Do you think I've come here as a *tourist?*' said the woman who always preferred work over leisure.

† The invitation to lead such a delegation was an appropriate ruse because Gorbachev had assumed the honorific position of Chairman of the Foreign Affairs Committee of the Supreme Soviet and was therefore 'parliamentary'. It avoided difficulties in protocol that would have resulted had Mrs Thatcher invited Gorbachev to visit outright.

Reagan–Gromyko meeting, it showed that the rising generation of Soviet leaders saw Britain as the best place to explore Western attitudes. It also complemented Reagan's landslide victory in the presidential elections on 7 November. She exploited the moment. 'What a victory! I cannot tell you how delighted I am,' she wrote to him the next day. Noting she would be in Peking to sign the Hong Kong Agreement, she suggested stopping off to see him on 22 December on the way home. This took the White House by surprise. 'Frankly we on the staff were horrified,' recalled Jack Matlock, a senior NSC staffer. The President would be at Camp David that weekend: 'normally that was private time for the Reagans. They never invited outsiders to Camp David. But it went in to Reagan and he was delighted ... so it became almost a family visit in a way ...'

Although the friendship was genuine, Mrs Thatcher had no interest in a purely 'family' visit. She had two goals for Camp David. The first was finding the best way of supporting Reagan over SDI while persuading him to try to ease European concerns. The second was to report on her meeting with Gorbachev, which was to take place a few days earlier. The importance of the Gorbachev visit, and thus of the Camp David trip, was increased after Moscow proposed that Shultz and Gromyko meet in January 1985 to agree terms for a wide range of nuclear negotiations. It was the perfect moment to help shape the emerging US approach.

Preparing for Gorbachev's visit, Mrs Thatcher underlined parts of her Foreign Office briefing that described him as 'intelligent and confident', while noting there was 'nothing to suggest he is not a convinced communist or that he intends (or would be able) to make fundamental alterations to the system itself'. Her general objectives included 'to teach him something about how a Western democracy works and what a free market economy can achieve'. The 'specific' objectives were chiefly to emphasize 'the sincerity and willingness of the West in general and President Reagan' in wanting to negotiate over arms.

As to Russian goals, Gorbachev's visit was a 'dress rehearsal for his future diplomatic role', recalled his future spokesman, Andrei Grachev. 'Gorbachev singled out Thatcher as the shortest way to send a message to Washington.' Percy Cradock, who had succeeded Anthony Parsons as Mrs Thatcher's foreign policy adviser, tried to read Russian intentions for her: 'space [that is, SDI] will be the key ... In return for assurances on space they may be ready to negotiate on offensive missiles.' She must not let the Soviets drive a wedge between the British and the Americans: 'it encourages them to think that they can divide and rule'.

The British drew on their mole, Oleg Gordievsky. Ever since his warnings about ABLE ARCHER, Gordievsky had been well heeded in Whitehall. This was partly because Mrs Thatcher herself had a great respect for British intelligence.* For her, intelligence furnished information which diplomacy, in the Cold War freeze, was ill-equipped to provide. According to Sir Colin McColl, head of SIS from 1988, 'She thought of us in the same way as she thought of the armed forces – part of the national defence. That was wonderful ... We knew we had her support.'†

In the past, British agents recruited from the KGB had been valued chiefly for their counter-intelligence, but, as McColl put it, what excited Mrs Thatcher even more about Gordievsky was 'the value of his *political* information'. Gordievsky's despatches uniquely conveyed to her how the Soviet leadership reacted to Western phenomena and, indeed, to her. In Gordievsky's view, this allowed her to start thinking of the Russians 'not as robots but as human beings'. The main human being who started to feature in his reports was Mikhail Gorbachev.

Gordievsky's reporting also helped illuminate the extent to which Arthur Scargill had sought assistance from the Soviets during the miners' strike. Mrs Thatcher knew that Gorbachev himself had signed off the effort to provide the NUM with $1.4 million back in October.‡ Eager to discourage such activity, she sought advice on whether she should raise the matter with Gorbachev.

Gorbachev and his wife Raisa arrived at Chequers on Sunday 16 December 1984.§ No sooner had they sat down for lunch, recalled Tony Bishop, the British interpreter, than Mrs Thatcher 'deliberately and breathtakingly ... set about serially cross-examining [Gorbachev] about the inferiority of the Soviet centralised command system and the merits of free enterprise and competition'. The contemporary record bears this out. She asked him how people could possibly better themselves 'in a centralised and rigid economy'. Gorbachev said he understood that the British system was

---

* As Leader of the Opposition, Mrs Thatcher had benefited from Airey Neave's ties to this world. Neave had arranged for her to meet former intelligence officers, who tended to confirm her fears, which the Foreign Office liked to play down, about Soviet penetration of the West.
† One way in which she demonstrated this support was through visiting the offices of the intelligence services. During her first visit to SIS, early in her career as Prime Minister, she asked the man sitting next to her, 'Do you employ forgers?' He said they sometimes did. 'How do you know', she asked, 'whether their references are genuine?'
‡ In early November, MI5 reported that the Soviet Foreign Trade Bank had tried to pay approximately $1.2 million to the NUM via banks in Switzerland and London, but the operation had been abandoned when the Swiss bank had grown suspicious.
§ As well as Denis, Mrs Thatcher was joined by Whitelaw, Howe, Heseltine, Rifkind, Paul Channon (standing in at Trade and Industry on account of Norman Tebbit's Brighton bomb injuries) and, because Gorbachev had supervised agriculture for much of his career, the Minister of Agriculture, Michael Jopling.

different, but 'the Soviet system was superior'. He invited her to come and have a look for herself: 'She would see how Soviet people lived – joyfully.' Mrs Thatcher underlined this last word in the record, writing '!' beside it.

When Gorbachev refused to engage on the Soviet treatment of dissidents and of *refusnik** Jews in general, Mrs Thatcher switched to the miners' strike. There had been much intimidation and violence, she said, 'and even recently a murder'.† 'Communism', she went on, 'was synonymous with getting one's way by violence. Its slogan was: "Brothers – when you are free, you will do as you are told".' She said that people like Scargill and his Communist Vice-President, Mick McGahey, 'gave Soviet Communism a bad name'.

Gorbachev took this, rightly, as an attack on the Soviet Union. Did the Prime Minister really think, he asked, that his country could run a miners' strike? The NUM, Mrs Thatcher told him, were 'being helped with finance from outside'. Gorbachev stoutly and mendaciously denied this‡ and then went on the offensive: 'The Prime Minister should blame Britain and not foreign Communists for the situation. *Das Kapital* had been written in London.' Mrs Thatcher 'interjected that in a free society it was entirely possible to do so and get it published'. Gorbachev said that he was aware 'that the Prime Minister was capable of defending herself. But the Second Congress of the RSDRP§ had also been held in London.' Unquenchable, Mrs Thatcher asked Gorbachev 'when she might contemplate the holding of British Party Congresses in Moscow. Lenin had set a tragic example of resorting to violence when unable to win through the ballot box.' Equally defiant, Gorbachev told Mrs Thatcher to 'deal with realities'. 'He recalled that Mr Churchill, a "dyed in the wool anti-communist"', had wisely joined forces with the Soviets.

At one point, Gorbachev later recalled, the conversation became so heated that he 'caught Raisa's eye across the table, and her lips moved to say "It's over!", and for a moment I wondered if we should leave'. But suddenly Mrs Thatcher changed tone: 'The Prime Minister said that the difficult part of their discussion was now over.' Welcoming her remarks,

---

* *Refusnik* was the Russian word for Jews who wished to emigrate to Israel but were forbidden to do so by the authorities.
† She was referring to the killing of David Wilkie.
‡ 'The Soviet Union had transferred no funds to the NUM,' Gorbachev declared. The official British record then added: '(After a sideways glance from Mr Zamyatin [the Central Committee's chief of international propaganda, part of the Soviet delegation], he amended this to "as far as I am aware").'
§ The Second Congress of the Russian Social Democratic Labour Party met in Charlotte Street, London, in August 1903. At this congress, the party split. The Bolshevik faction, led by Lenin, was ultimately victorious in the Russian Revolution of 1917.

Gorbachev proposed a toast, celebrating the '"domestic ambience" and the good atmosphere prevailing around the table'.

This lunchtime conversation had been one of the most remarkable ever to have taken place across that table. It defied all diplomatic norms. It produced almost nothing but disagreement, its sharp tone exceeding all the usual Foreign Office euphemisms for rude and quarrelsome meetings, such as 'frank' or 'candid'. Yet the occasion was immediately recognized as a success by both sides. Gorbachev's Marxism, thought Mrs Thatcher, was standard stuff. 'But his personality could not have been more different from the wooden ventriloquism of the average Soviet *apparatchik*.' Gorbachev recalled paying a similar compliment: 'I told Mrs Thatcher: "I know you are a person of staunch beliefs ... This commands respect. But please consider that next to you is a person of your own ilk. And I can assure you that I am not under instructions from the Politburo to persuade you to join the Communist Party." After that statement she burst into a hearty laugh ...' The British side was struck by Gorbachev's physical vitality. 'He was so visibly not one of the older men,' recalled Powell, who noted 'this short, energetic man bouncing on the balls of his feet': 'I think everybody was caught by surprise. She certainly was.' Without overconfidence, Gorbachev was acting as the next Soviet leader.*

After lunch, from neighbouring armchairs in the sitting room, and joined only by Howe, Powell and Bishop on the British side, Mrs Thatcher and Gorbachev got down to a less argumentative discussion about arms control. Suggesting their goal should be 'to diminish hostility and the level of armaments', she boasted that Britain had a bigger influence with the United States than any other NATO member. When he met Gromyko at Geneva, George Shultz would be looking for balance, not unilateral advantage. She was worried that 'unless the two sides could agree on how to deal with the problem of weapons in outer space, there would be a new spiral in the arms race'.

Gorbachev replied more luridly, speaking of 'avoiding a holocaust'. It had been difficult for the Russians to contemplate returning to negotiations (at Geneva), he complained, because Reagan had allowed Soviet–US relations to languish. Mrs Thatcher came back with a staunch but nuanced defence. The Americans did not want to dominate the world, she said, blaming the freeze in relations on the Soviet invasion of Afghanistan. Reagan 'had wished only to restore America's confidence' and make her 'strong enough to defend her way of life'.

---

* Tony Bishop, the interpreter, noticed that Gorbachev's language was 'irreproachably sound' in Soviet terms, but used refreshing colloquialisms, such as '*chepukha* (nonsense/twaddle)'.

Then Mrs Thatcher took a risk. Reagan also 'had a dream', she said, 'expressed through the Strategic Defence Initiative, of being able to rid the world of nuclear weapons. Sadly, it was not a viable dream because the process of acquiring a ballistic missile defence would inevitably lead to a fresh twist in the arms race spiral . . . In any case, the knowledge of how to build nuclear weapons could not be disinvented.' Spotting the divergence on SDI, Gorbachev tried to flatter Mrs Thatcher's sense of British independence by quoting Lord Palmerston's dictum about England having no permanent friends, or permanent enemies, only permanent interests. He implied that Britain could be closer to Russia and less close to the United States. The point had been made. 'What we need now is a process,' said Gorbachev, suggesting that their dialogue should continue. This, according to Bishop, was 'music to the PM's ears'. Her efforts to engage with the Soviet Union appeared to be bearing fruit.

The post-lunch meeting so exceeded its allotted time that Gorbachev did not leave for London until six, nearly two hours late for a reception at the Soviet Embassy. Mrs Thatcher lingered briefly with her officials before exclaiming, '"Tomorrow it's China, and I haven't had my hair done!" She ran upstairs and was gone.'

By the end of her day with Gorbachev, noted Charles Powell, Mrs Thatcher 'felt very elated: this really was something new'. Tony Bishop felt he had witnessed 'something akin to a flirtation between two people with much to gain from and offer to each other: a flirtation that was pleasurable and stimulating but ultimately "safe" and platonic'.* After Gorbachev had left, Bernard Ingham asked Mrs Thatcher how he should brief the press. The phrase to describe Gorbachev that emerged, in conversation with Powell, was 'a man to do business with'. Ingham released this that night. She repeated it the next day.

Gorbachev himself took an almost identical view. He told Richard Luce, at the Speaker's dinner in his honour, that his preconceived ideas about Mrs Thatcher's attitude to the Soviet Union had been wrong: 'to his great pleasure, he had established a good understanding with her'. She had what he considered good ideas about each country defending its own

---

* Mrs Thatcher, who rarely had much time for the wives of her fellow world leaders, paid slightly beady attention to the well-dressed Mrs Gorbachev, studying a report from the Foreign Office official who accompanied Mrs Gorbachev on her shopping expeditions in London, underlining references to 'the jewelled drop-earrings' she bought for £750 at Mappin and Webb which revealed her 'as someone accustomed to living life on that level'. Mrs Thatcher was always alert to the fact that the Soviet leadership lived in conditions of privilege, whereas the Soviet people went without.

interests: 'On such a basis, people could do business.'* Soon afterwards, Gordievsky passed on enthusiastic feedback from Moscow. 'The phrase that Gorbachev always used [about the nuclear confrontation] was "We can't live like this."' The Thatcher meeting made him feel that both sides could move towards the change required. The visit also helped Gorbachev's standing domestically. Given Mrs Thatcher's reputation as a staunch anti-Communist, recalled Andrei Grachev, there was a feeling that if Gorbachev 'could make it in London, he could make it anywhere'.

Mrs Thatcher now had only one immediate problem – how would the Gorbachev visit go down in Washington? The day after the Chequers meeting, Powell informed the Foreign Office that, in reporting the meeting to NATO allies, 'Particular care should be taken in dealing with any suggestions that the Prime Minister distanced herself from President Reagan over the question of arms control in space.' The 'particular care' was required because that is exactly what she had done.

Washington was already buzzing with rumours that Mrs Thatcher had gone too far. According to the *Washington Post*, Reagan hoped that, at Camp David, she would 'get off the gee-whiz kick about the Kremlin's personable heir apparent ... What shook White House insiders was the juxtaposition of Thatcher's "can-do-business" pledge and Gorbachev's assertion that killing Star Wars is the precondition for serious arms control negotiations.' The US Ambassador, Charlie Price, summed up prevailing US sentiment: 'During my first year in London, I have met with the PM perhaps 15 times,' he wrote to Reagan. 'In every meeting, she does most of the talking. On SDI, it's time she did some listening.'

That week leading up to Christmas 1984 demonstrated just how prodigious were Mrs Thatcher's powers of mental and physical endurance. On 17 December, the day after seeing Gorbachev, she flew to Peking to sign the Hong Kong Agreement and thence to Hong Kong itself. She then headed for Washington for her Camp David meeting on Saturday 22 December. Her flight lasted twenty-four hours and included two stops and a twelve-hour time change. Mrs Thatcher refused the one bed the VC-10 had to offer. 'I'm going to stay awake for the 24 hours,' she told Robin Butler. 'And

---

* A curious incident indicates something of Gorbachev's own excitement about his British visit. On 19 December 1984, one of Mrs Thatcher's private secretaries reported that at five o'clock that afternoon Gorbachev and his entourage had passed Downing Street on their way from Parliament to the Soviet Embassy. He had suddenly 'expressed a wish to see the outside of No. 10'. Special Branch had negotiated with the policeman at the barrier '(without informing us)', and he had been let in and then allowed to enter the front hall. 'They were gone before any private secretary had reached the spot – reportedly in good humour.'

I'm going to study the ABM Treaty and Cap Weinberger's statements on the SDI.' And so she did. The plane touched down in Honolulu in the early hours to refuel. Learning that Pearl Harbor was within walking distance, she insisted on taking a look. 'Well, it's dark,' came the response. 'Ah,' she replied, 'but I have a torch in my handbag' (something she always carried after the Brighton bomb that October). So the party set off, recalled Butler, 'She in her high-heeled shoes and this admiral and this air force commander dragging along.' Her inspection complete, 'We got back on the plane and she resumed her study of the ABM Treaty and Cap Weinberger's speeches.'

Arriving at the Washington Embassy on 21 December, she ordered a briefing meeting at 11 p.m. She got up at six the next morning for hairdressing and further briefings, reaching Camp David, some 60 miles away, by helicopter at 10.30 a.m.

Mrs Thatcher began by meeting *tête-à-tête* with Reagan before moving into a wider gathering, including Shultz, Bud McFarlane – but not, significantly, Weinberger* – which continued into a working lunch. At the private meeting, she told Reagan that Gorbachev was 'an unusual Russian ... much less constrained, more charming, open to discussion and debate, and did not stick to prepared notes. His wife was equally charming. The Prime Minister noted that she often says to herself the more charming the adversary, the more dangerous.' She 'had emphasized to Gorbachev that it would be a futile effort to try to divide Great Britain from the US'.

Reagan, not Mrs Thatcher, then broached SDI. Soviet attacks on it, he suggested, were part of their propaganda preparations for the Geneva talks. He defended SDI as designed to 'strengthen deterrence'. He denied the USA was violating the ABM Treaty and drew attention to SDI's 'moral context': 'We must search for ways to build a more stable peace. Our goal is to reduce, and eventually eliminate nuclear weapons.' 'These remarks made me nervous,' Mrs Thatcher later wrote, but she kept her peace for the time being. She stressed she had told Gorbachev that 'Britain supports the SDI program', which was the truth but not the whole truth. She also reported that Gorbachev had asked her to 'tell your friend President Reagan not to go ahead with space weapons'. Without endorsing this, she wanted Reagan to understand the impact SDI had made on the Soviet leadership. As ever, she stressed the distinction between SDI research, which she supported wholeheartedly, and deployment, for which she 'foresaw grave difficulties'.

---

* 'Colin Powell [Weinberger's military assistant] tells me Cap is very desirous of attending,' one NSC staffer minuted McFarlane ahead of the meeting. This plea was deliberately ignored.

At the larger meeting, Mrs Thatcher went to the heart of her anxieties: 'If we reached a stage where [SDI] production looked possible we would have some serious ... decisions to take.' According to Powell, she found 'the depth of Reagan's anti-nuclear sentiments' very difficult to navigate: 'first, because she disagreed profoundly with it. Secondly, because it might cause her immense embarrassment in the UK in the debate with CND and Kinnock over unilateral disarmament.' 'Nuclear weapons', she told Reagan, 'have served not only to prevent a nuclear war, but they have also given us forty years of unprecedented peace in Europe.' She was deeply worried, she continued, 'about SDI's impact on deterrence. The wretched press has tried to make out that we have major differences. This is simply not true, but we do feel it is unwise to conclude where we will go on SDI, before the research programme is completed.' Besides, she doubted SDI's ultimate feasibility: 'Even if an SDI system proved 95 per cent successful ... over 60 million people would still die from those weapons that got through.'

All this had quite an impact. 'Reagan was taken aback,' said Bud McFarlane. '... This was the first time he had grasped that the person he respected above all others was making a very compelling case. It was passionate. He was very sobered by it.' He conceded that her points needed to be addressed, but stuck to his vision. The argument rumbled on until, just before lunch, Mrs Thatcher seized the moment. 'Put these points down, the points we've been discussing, on a bit of paper,' she said to Powell, 'and we can see if we can't get them agreed.' Powell soon returned with a draft statement. It had Mrs Thatcher saying, 'I told the President of my firm conviction that the SDI programme which at present is solely a research programme should go ahead.' Then it presented the four points of agreement. The first was that the USA and the West aimed for balance, not superiority. The second said that 'SDI-related testing and deployment would, in view of treaty obligations, be a matter for negotiation.' Point three stated that 'The overall aim should be to maintain, not undercut, deterrence.' The fourth point said that the aim of resumed US–Soviet arms control negotiations would be 'to achieve security with reduced levels of offensive systems on both sides'. Points one, three and four reflected American positions with which the British agreed. At no stage previously, however, had the Americans conceded that SDI was bound by treaty obligations. Point two was therefore an important reassurance for Mrs Thatcher and for allies more generally.

After she passed the draft to Reagan, he nodded his approval. At the request of American officials, Powell's description of SDI as 'solely' a research programme was dropped. For point two, the word 'testing' was removed, leaving only 'deployment' as 'a matter for negotiation'. Nonetheless, the Four Points were a triumph for Mrs Thatcher. Not only would they quell reports of differences with Reagan, but she now had an all-purpose form of words. As Powell put it, 'The Camp David points became the Bible. They were the basic text . . . a position which could command broad support in the alliance as well.'

The text also helped settle the bitter struggle within the administration over the direction of policy. As Shultz put it in his memoirs: 'It was an excellent statement: it differentiated between research and deployment of space-based defense and gave me some running room in Geneva . . . The argument coming from Cap [Weinberger] . . . that we should not be willing to discuss SDI in any way was bypassed.' As the State Department's Richard Burt put it: 'Nobody could come back and say "How could you have done this?" You'd just say, "The President and Mrs Thatcher did it."'

Mrs Thatcher's views on Gorbachev also aroused anxieties in Washington, even as they influenced the administration. While many feared she had been taken in or, as the *New York Times* put it, developed a 'schoolgirl crush on The Russian With A Smile', the Americans were deeply interested in her unique, first-hand account. As Reagan later recalled: 'She told me that Gorbachev was different from any of the other Kremlin leaders. She believed that there was a chance of an opening. Of course, she was proven exactly right.' Her views, and Reagan's willingness to listen to them, gave heart to those in the administration arguing for greater dialogue. And precisely because Mrs Thatcher was the only foreign leader whom Cold War hawks regarded as sound, 'her opinions', as Shultz put it, 'had weight even with those who were dubious about the merits of dialogue'. As Colin Powell, then serving as Weinberger's military assistant, later described it: 'Along comes Gorby – he's like none we've ever seen before – with his beautiful suits, his French ties and a stunning wife who is every bit as smart as he is. And the first statement he got of acceptability was from Margaret . . . The feeling was "Jesus, if dear old Margaret thinks there's something here we'd better take a look."'

In a single week, then, Mrs Thatcher had held profoundly important conversations with the likely future Soviet leader, contracted a treaty with Communist China, and persuaded the President of the United States to adopt a new public stance on arms control. As she got home for Christmas, her country's global influence rivalled anything Britain had enjoyed in the post-Suez era.

On 20 February 1985, Mrs Thatcher was back again in Washington to mark the 200th anniversary of US–UK diplomatic relations.* In her Joint Address to Congress, an honour not accorded to any British prime minister since Winston Churchill, she flattered her hosts by proclaiming the 'incalculable' debt 'the free people of Europe' owed to America. But when she invoked Churchill she did so to serve her argument. 'No-one understood the importance of deterrence more clearly than Winston Churchill,' she declared,

> when in his last speech [in 1952] to you he said: 'Be careful above all things not to let go of the atomic weapon until you are sure and more than sure that other means of preserving peace are in your hands.' Thirty-three years on, those weapons are still keeping the peace, but since then technology has moved on and if we are to maintain deterrence – as we must – it is essential that our research and capacity do not fall behind the work being done by the Soviet Union [applause]. That is why I firmly support President Reagan's decision to pursue research into defence against ballistic nuclear missiles – the Strategic Defence Initiative [applause].

Newspapers immediately took up her words as an endorsement of SDI, as she had intended; but she framed SDI as crucial for maintaining deterrence, not as the means to a nuclear-free world.

Since Camp David, the White House had made significant efforts to bind her in on SDI, both through a briefing from the SDI Program Director, General Jim Abrahamson, and through dangling the possibility of SDI research contracts for British companies. The fact remained, however, that her approach to SDI and nuclear weapons was still no closer to Reagan's. At a White House arms control 'seminar' during her visit, she tried to dissuade the President from attacking the morality of nuclear deterrence. To maintain public support for INF and Britain's independent deterrent, she said: 'We must not get into a situation where people were told that nuclear weapons were wicked, immoral and might soon be rendered unnecessary by the development of defensive systems.'

Reagan reminded her that SDI was 'designed to render obsolete a strategy based on the nuclear destruction of populations. It was not a bargaining chip.' Back she came with her belief that, for the foreseeable future, nuclear weapons would remain 'the essential deterrent of war'.

---

* The US government gave Mrs Thatcher replicas of a pair of silver candlesticks which had belonged to John Adams at the time when the Treaty of Paris established diplomatic links. 'The Prime Minister proposes that the candlesticks should stand on the Cabinet table with those already there,' wrote Charles Powell to the Foreign Office '(but don't tell anyone this until we have had a look at them and made sure that they are not an eyesore).'

Reagan did not argue with this. In their absolute determination to prevent the Soviets gaining the upper hand in the arms race, the two were at one.

Mrs Thatcher's public statement on departure spoke of 'a real meeting of minds'. But, in personal terms, the meeting was rather unsuccessful. She seemed ill at ease, which Powell attributed to the presence of Geoffrey Howe and Michael Heseltine: 'They attended the plenary session and had the impertinence to say something! Not what she wanted. She regarded herself as the only true spokesman of her government with the President.'* Her frustration and anxiety drove her to be repetitive and strident. Ken Adelman noticed Reagan 'kind of inhaling and ready ... to talk, and Margaret Thatcher says, "One minute Ronnie, I'm almost finished." And she goes on.' After the meeting broke up, Adelman observed someone saying to Reagan, '"Boy, she's not a very good listener, is she?" And Reagan, face lights up, turns to this person and says, "No, but she's a marvellous talker!"'

No sense of frustration at Mrs Thatcher's seminar performance, however, permeated the atmosphere at the British Embassy dinner that night. Ronald and Nancy Reagan insisted on attending† because, as McFarlane put it, 'This was family. That's the way he felt about it. Mrs Reagan too. They liked Denis. They liked the Prime Minister.‡ ... This was the person above all others whom he was privileged to know in his presidency and he was confident would have an enduring place in history. Any occasion that offered a chance to elevate the standing of Prime Minister Thatcher he would do.'

On 11 March 1985, just after the miners' strike had collapsed, the death of Konstantin Chernenko was announced in Moscow. Mikhail Gorbachev was proclaimed his successor. Mrs Thatcher resolved to attend Chernenko's funeral and later wrote a manuscript account of the visit.§ In it, she recalled

---

* George Shultz spotted this. An early draft of his memoirs contained a passage, removed before publication, noting that Mrs Thatcher had 'a wonderful Foreign Secretary, Sir Geoffrey Howe, who I saw a great deal of and came to admire. But Margaret Thatcher seemed to pay little attention to him ... I know that, if I had been in Geoffrey's shoes I simply wouldn't have stood for it.'

† In accepting Mrs Thatcher's invitation, the Reagans chose to ignore the general rule that the President did not dine out in foreign embassies.

‡ Possibly, the First Lady was not quite as close to Mrs Thatcher as her husband was. That evening, Mrs Reagan was seen to be irritated by her husband's desire to stay late and go on talking to Mrs Thatcher. In the view of Charlie Price, without their mutual admiration for Ronald Reagan, Mrs Reagan and Mrs Thatcher 'wouldn't ever have been close personal friends'.

§ The account, entitled 'Return to Moscow', was composed as soon as Mrs Thatcher returned to London. It was most unusual for her to record her experiences and it is not clear why she chose to do so on this occasion. Her account contains little political analysis, and ends without

how reading Gorbachev's acceptance speech on the plane to Moscow confirmed her impression from Chequers that 'even if he wished to change matters he wouldn't know how to, because a rigid Communist system was the only one he had ever known'.

Arriving in Moscow, Mrs Thatcher was struck by the lack of lights in the shops and the dirty streets. At the Ambassador's residence, the motherly Prime Minister presented the staff with 'masses of fresh vegetables and fruit and English cheese because that is what they wanted most'.

At the funeral the next day, she met Chernenko's family: 'some in tears and all deeply grieved ... Even the head of a communist country who has no sympathy for those who disagree, nevertheless has a family who sorrow for him.'

According to Tony Bishop, Mrs Thatcher 'acquired heroic status in the eyes of the Russian TV audience by standing, unflinching, on Red Square ... while the ceremonies slowly unrolled in an air temperature of minus 12'. The weather 'felt very raw', she wrote. 'I do not possess a fur coat so make myself as warm as possible in a wool coat and fur-lined boots.' As was often the case at parades, she was much taken with the soldiers – 'very fine young men, superbly tailored grey greatcoats, white gloves, black boots, grey fur hats. They didn't move a muscle.' 'The speeches began,' she went on. 'The voice and command of Mr Gorbachev in such striking contrast with the hesitancy and muffed words of Mr. Chernenko's a year previously.'

Her encounter with Gorbachev that evening, scheduled for fifteen minutes, lasted nearly an hour. Mrs Thatcher's speaking note, prepared by Charles Powell, sought to counter the Soviet belief that she had hardened her support for SDI: 'As I said to you at Chequers, it is a <u>dream</u> which he [Reagan] has: and like all dreams no one can know whether it is capable of being realised.' On this paper Mrs Thatcher wrote, 'New occasions teach new duties,' a quotation from one of her favourite hymns, by James Russell Lowell, which begins 'Once to every man and nation comes the moment to decide / ... for the good or evil side.'

Sure enough, Gorbachev launched into SDI almost at once. Mrs Thatcher, however, explained that the Camp David agreement had changed matters; it 'was the first time that the Americans had been persuaded to put publicly on record that any deployment would require negotiation'. Gorbachev sought an 'expanded dialogue'. Bishop noted that 'When Gromyko

---

recording her substantive conversation with Gorbachev. Perhaps she intended but failed to write up the entire trip. She noted her impressions with an almost schoolgirl innocence, rather like a 'What I did in the holidays' essay, an impression added to by her intermittent punctuation.

chipped in that this could perhaps best be done by exchange of messages, Gorbachev pointedly went on to say that . . . he had been impressed by his discussion with the Prime Minister . . . "We must continue to meet, talk to each other and exchange views."'

Mrs Thatcher turned on all possible charm. As the Russian interpreter, Sukhodrev, told Gorbachev's aide Anatoly Chernyaev: '[she] was all over him, charming him, fascinating him and he responded in kind. That's evidently the way she "does politics" and with the help of M. S. [Gorbachev] she wants to outflank the likes of Kohl and Mitterrand – even Reagan himself – in world affairs. And she likes to use her woman's wiles to play games with Gorbachev in particular.'

As an analysis of Mrs Thatcher's methods and mindset, this was perceptive, but she was certainly not so foolish as to try to cut out the Americans. Before seeing Gorbachev, she had met Vice-President George Bush, who was representing the USA at the funeral. Bush had confided that he would give Gorbachev a letter from Reagan suggesting the two men meet, his first proposal of a formal summit since he had entered the White House. George Shultz had told her that their focus on Gorbachev had originated with her.

There is no doubt that, in terms of Anglo–American relations and of wider prestige, Gorbachev's emergence as the Soviet leader greatly helped Mrs Thatcher. In Powell's view, 'she was investing hugely in him. She was like a hedge fund manager. She had decided that she was going to buy Gorbachevs and profit from them.' Gorbachev seemed equally keen. A couple of months later, the British Ambassador in Moscow reported that according to an official in Gorbachev's office: 'Mrs Thatcher had made a great impression on Gorbachev. He was always speaking about her . . . this was an instance where a personal relationship could have an effect upon the course of history.'

It was not necessarily easy, however, for Mrs Thatcher to sustain the personal relationship, or her prominent role, once she returned from Moscow. She had a fine line to tread. On the one hand, she might try to exercise a greater influence than she truly possessed, thereby irritating at least one of the two great powers; on the other, she might fail to develop her own strengths. After all, if she effected a successful introduction between Reagan and Gorbachev, she might find herself being asked to leave the party. To avoid these pitfalls, she would need to display the skills which, in theory, she disparaged – those of a diplomat. It did not help that her own Foreign Secretary now broke ranks.

Perhaps irritated by Mrs Thatcher's tendency to ignore him, just three days after Chernenko's funeral Howe gave a speech attacking SDI: even if it worked exactly as planned in stopping all ballistic missiles, it would not deal with the other sorts of nuclear weapons. He warned against 'creating a new Maginot Line* of the 21st century'. Howe's views were not, in themselves, completely at odds with Mrs Thatcher's, but expressing them publicly risked undermining the triumph of the Four Points.† American suspicions of British sincerity were naturally aroused.

Mrs Thatcher, too, was furious with Howe. *The Times*, whose Editor, Charles Douglas-Home, knew her mind, branded Howe's intervention 'mealy-mouthed, muddled in conception, negative, Luddite, ill-informed'. At the foot of a letter to Reagan following Chernenko's funeral, Mrs Thatcher added: 'I can assure you of our continuing support. Our position has <u>not</u> changed, <u>whatever</u> you may have heard or read.' In the end, the incident showed once again that it was Mrs Thatcher herself, rather than any minister, who was the architect of British policies. It therefore did her no harm in Washington.

As the Reagan administration continued to argue internally about the merits of engaging with the new Soviet leader, Mrs Thatcher's efforts helped reinforce the President's own instincts. As Henry Kissinger put it, 'Reagan was determined to have a meeting with the Soviet leader. Mrs Thatcher's views gave him the moral strength, the encouragement to do it. Shultz undoubtedly also wanted a meeting. So you can't say she shifted the debate from "no" to "yes". But on a continuum ... she pushed him closer to a meeting.' On 3 July, a Reagan–Gorbachev summit was announced for November, in Geneva.

By this time, American efforts to stoke Mrs Thatcher's enthusiasm for SDI were beginning to bear fruit. In late July, she returned to Washington. With Reagan convalescing from a second operation for cancer, she instead met officials, including the Defense Secretary, Caspar Weinberger, and General Abrahamson. Abrahamson's 'highly restricted' briefing on SDI increased her excitement. As he recalled: 'She was delightful. She asked very good questions that would range from the deterrence basis to how are we going to get there? She loved the latter. At the end of the briefing she said, "I would like for you to plan for us to meet at least three times a year. I want to hear about this."'

---

* The Maginot Line was France's means of defence against Germany in the 1930s which proved useless when Hitler went round the fortifications and entered France through Belgium in 1940.
† Howe's words were given added weight when it was reported that the speech had been approved by Mrs Thatcher beforehand. The truth was rather more complicated. On the way home from Moscow, Charles Powell had been asked to vet it. But, as he later recalled, 'I'm ashamed to say that two pages into it I dropped asleep and never read any more.' Nevertheless, he sent a *pro forma* letter to Howe saying that the Prime Minister had 'seen and approved' the speech. For this mistake Mrs Thatcher later dressed down Powell so severely he thought he might be sacked.

Weinberger and Abrahamson were only too happy to oblige. Back in London, Foreign Office officials ruefully realized what was happening. As one of them, John Weston, put it, the Americans were working to cut out 'the political blockages in the FCO' by going straight to the Prime Minister. Abrahamson, they felt, would 'fill her up with all this stuff until it was coming out of her ears'. 'She thought as a scientist she understood those things better than others,' Powell recalled. The Americans played on this. Although she was inclined to exaggerate her influence, the Abrahamson conversations were part of a wider process by which she was placed in a position of trust, thereby attaining far more political sway than any other non-US citizen.

With Weinberger, Mrs Thatcher insisted that Britain 'would not be fobbed off with a few small contracts' for SDI research; '... it should be clear that Britain was in a different category to other countries'. Weinberger answered drily that 'there might be some unenlightened people in Congress who failed to recognise this. The Prime Minister replied that it was the Administration's task to tell them.'* Weinberger also expressed caution about the upcoming summit, which he thought would bring no great developments. Mrs Thatcher thought this inadequate. Problems at the current negotiations made it 'all the more important to ensure that the summit itself was a success and gave them a fresh impetus'.

Ahead of the November summit, Mrs Thatcher's efforts to engage with the Soviet Union faced their stiffest test to date as she became embroiled in the most important espionage confrontation of her time. On 22 July 1985, Oleg Gordievsky, Britain's long-standing KGB mole, defected to the United Kingdom. In May, he had been recalled to Moscow and interrogated on suspicion of being a British agent.† Gordievsky did not confess. He escaped his KGB minders and was successfully 'exfiltrated' over the Finnish border.

To some in the British foreign policy establishment, including Bryan Cartledge, the British Ambassador in Moscow, Gordievsky was an irritating distraction, but Mrs Thatcher believed strongly in his importance and was passionately committed to his welfare. Despite the difficulties she knew the exfiltration would cause in her relationship with Gorbachev, she had authorized the plan. 'We never thought for a minute that Mrs T would stop us,' recalled Colin McColl, then deputy head of SIS. In August, during his

---

* Despite Mrs Thatcher's admonition, by 1990 British SDI research contracts totalled just $81.9 million, a tiny share of a multi-billion-dollar pie.
† It is still not known what prompted Moscow's suspicion. Some believe Aldrich Ames, a Soviet mole in the CIA, was the first to give Gordievsky away. Gordievsky, however, insisted his cover was blown by 'another, as yet unidentified source outside the British intelligence community'.

debrief in southern England, Gordievsky received a personal letter from Mrs Thatcher telling him to be cheerful and not give up hope that his wife and children would get back to him.* But she added: 'You know what kind of people we are dealing with.' He was impressed by this, because it proved to him that she was not starry-eyed about Gorbachev.

Moscow had been informed of Gordievsky's defection in mid-August. In early September, the British government prepared to make this public and simultaneously expel all those Soviet officials known to be spies, sparing only the KGB's security officer. There were twenty-five of them. Robert Armstrong reminded Mrs Thatcher that relations with the Soviet Union were bound to worsen, but 'it would not have been right or understandable to respond less vigorously'. As he had predicted, the Soviets hit back, expelling twenty-five British nationals, not all of whom were intelligence officers. Mrs Thatcher ordered the expulsion of six more Russians (overruling Howe, who wished to expel only four). Moscow again responded in kind.

Many feared the Gordievsky row would sink Mrs Thatcher's capacity to 'do business' with Gorbachev. From Moscow, Cartledge quoted a Central Committee member complaining that 'Your Prime Minister thinks she can treat us as if we were Argentina.' In the end, although the affair did cool relations and, as Gordievsky put it, 'give her a bloody nose' in her attitude to Gorbachev, it also enhanced Mrs Thatcher's reputation and the salience of Britain in the Cold War.

Mrs Thatcher chose 12 September 1985, the same day as the announcement of Gordievsky's defection, to send Reagan a long letter. As his summit with Gorbachev approached, her timing seemed intended to make clear that the 'engagement' show was still on the road. Gorbachev, she told him, was, as expected, proving 'a deft operator':

> He is playing Western public opinion skilfully ... And his performance is spoiled only by the arrogance which he cannot always conceal. His purpose is, of course, to set opinion in Europe against the United States, to give the impression that the Soviet Union is full of initiatives and original ideas while the United States is flat-footed and unimaginative.

She pushed for the USA to produce 'appealing proposals of its own'. The summit must be one of substance: 'I am troubled, in particular, by the notion which is gaining ground that you see the meeting as little more

---

* In all her subsequent meetings with Gorbachev Mrs Thatcher pleaded vigorously for the release of the Gordievsky family, and she constantly urged Reagan, in his meetings, to do the same. The Gordievskys were finally allowed to leave Russia for Britain in September 1991, nearly a year after Mrs Thatcher had left office.

than a "getting to know you session".' She urged Reagan to explain to Gorbachev the rationale behind SDI, hewing to the Camp David Four Points. She never suggested that the President offer to give up SDI, but she did recommend limiting its freedom of action as a sweetener for Soviet concessions. She also warned Reagan that, in her experience, any effort to raise human rights led to Gorbachev 'hitting back with allegedly bad features of life in the West'. The 'best tactic', she said, was to stress that, while the West did not seek to undermine the Soviet state, 'human rights in the Soviet Union are our business: not just because both East and West have committed themselves to them at Helsinki:* but also because justice at home is more likely to produce stability and responsible behaviour abroad'.

She ended by trying to instil a sense of urgency: 'I am convinced that we must stop Gorbachev's bandwagon from gaining too much speed before your meeting by making clear now that the US is utterly serious about making the maximum progress at Geneva.'

Reagan responded warmly and quickly. While he stressed he would do nothing to endanger the future of SDI, he endorsed her desire for real progress at the summit. In a separate letter, he congratulated her over the Gordievsky affair. 'I admire the strong action you took', he told her, agreeing they must balance 'intolerance of Soviet hostile international activities' with 'our desire to build a constructive relationship with the Soviet Union'.

The groundbreaking summit at Geneva was now just a month away. At the Conservative Party conference on 11 October, Mrs Thatcher offered the President her support: 'The West could not have a better or a braver champion.' The previous difficulties in her relationship with Gorbachev now seemed to evaporate. The Soviet leader chose her sixtieth birthday, two days later, to send his congratulations. He wanted their mutual understanding from their earlier discussions to 'remain in force'. Business could still be done.

At the same time as Mrs Thatcher was coaxing Reagan towards a different approach to the Soviet Union, she began modestly to attempt something similar in relation to the Middle East.

When she came to office, Mrs Thatcher had been chiefly motivated by two related views in her approach to the Arab–Israeli conflict. The first was her strong belief – reinforced by her Jewish connections in Finchley – that

---

* In return for a commitment to respect human rights within the Soviet bloc, the Helsinki Final Act (1975) had recognized Soviet domination of Eastern Europe. At the time, Mrs Thatcher had been suspicious of the deal, but she now intended to hold the Soviets to their part of the bargain.

the story of the Jewish nation was heroic and that Israel was pro-Western. The second was her hatred of terrorism, and therefore her extreme suspicion of the Palestine Liberation Organization, led by Yasser Arafat.

She quickly clashed with the long-standing Arabism of the Foreign Office. Lord Carrington, her first Foreign Secretary, embodied this. As early as August 1979, he had urged her to support a UN Security Council call for Palestinian self-determination. 'I will leave Lord Carrington a free hand in this,' she wrote, but noted her concern. The fact that the Palestinians might be considered as a people should not be 'the sole determinant of the way we vote', she went on. Should the Soviets succeed in subverting the Middle East's oil-producing states, 'There is only one nation there that would really stand & fight and that is Israel. If there is an ultimate East–West battle she will be our ally ... The problem with Israel at the moment is Begin [the Israeli Prime Minister]. Further – has anyone really thought through a new Palestinian "homeland"?'

Despite such concerns, Mrs Thatcher allowed herself to be dragged slowly in Carrington's direction. During her first six or seven years in office she constantly resisted moves to meet PLO representatives but, quite often, in the end, gave ground.* Luckily for the Foreign Office, her dislike of terrorism cut both ways. She was extremely ill-disposed to Menachem Begin, Israeli Prime Minister when she came into office, and his Likud successor, Yitzhak Shamir, because both had been involved in terrorist attacks on British forces during the British Mandate in Palestine which ended in 1948.†

In Israeli politics, therefore, Mrs Thatcher did not support the more right wing party but favoured the Labour Party of Shimon Peres, whom she liked. Her preferred interlocutors in the Middle East were Hosni Mubarak, President of Egypt following the assassination of Anwar Sadat in 1981, the rulers of Saudi Arabia, the Gulf States and Oman, and above all King Hussein of Jordan.

Unlike in areas of policy more central to her, such as the Cold War or trade union reform, in Middle East questions Mrs Thatcher had few

---

* Mrs Thatcher was, in fact, the first senior British politician to meet Yasser Arafat, but this was by mistake on her part, though not on his. He tapped her on the shoulder at the funeral of Marshal Tito in Belgrade in May 1980, and she shook hands with him politely before realizing who he was. Her dislike of Arafat was added to by the fact that he did not, in her view, shave properly. 'He *looks* like a terrorist!' she would exclaim.

† Begin had commanded Irgun, the organization which blew up the King David Hotel in Jerusalem in 1946, killing ninety-one people, many of them British soldiers. Shamir planned the assassination of Lord Moyne, the British Minister for Middle East Affairs in 1944. In discussions with the Canadian Prime Minister, Pierre Trudeau, in 1981, Mrs Thatcher described how Zionist terrorists in the 1940s had booby-trapped the bodies of two British soldiers, and broke down in tears.

'irregulars' to challenge official views. Her strong Jewish connections – most notably Keith Joseph and David Wolfson – kept her well in touch with Jewish feeling, as did her Finchley constituents. But none contributed sustained policy input. In Wolfson's opinion, Mrs Thatcher could be trusted by friends of Israel. In terms of her heart, this judgement was correct; it was perhaps not so true of her head.

As Mrs Thatcher's confidence grew, her views about the Middle East began to evolve. In 1981, after conversations with Crown Prince Fahd of Saudi Arabia and the rulers of Kuwait and Bahrain, she told Reagan of their 'grave disappointment with and alienation from the United States': 'I found this most upsetting but felt that I must let you know . . . Those to whom I talked argue that your Government is so wholly committed to Israel that it ignores the rightful claims of the Palestinians. It thereby creates acutely difficult problems for the moderate Arab leaders.' Increasingly, she tried to make herself the Western champion of these moderates, especially King Hussein.

Her focus on Hussein placed Mrs Thatcher in the mainstream of British policy. Jordan itself, and the Hashemite monarchy which ruled it, were creations of the British colonial era. The country's security was closely bound up with British protection. She was also very fond of the man himself. Hussein had been educated (like Mark Thatcher) at Harrow and, as an officer cadet, at Sandhurst. He was very pro-British. Like Mrs Thatcher, he maintained a courtly protocol without being haughty. He had man-of-action charm (he was an accomplished pilot), courage and a sense of honour, all of which she admired. He was extremely respectful towards her. According to John Coles, she was also 'intrigued' by his thoughts about leaders who, for her, were beyond the pale, such as Hafez Assad of Syria and Saddam Hussein of Iraq. For his part, Hussein understood her closeness to Reagan and saw her as his best conduit through the Washington labyrinth.

After winning the 1983 election, Mrs Thatcher reviewed her Middle East policy. From a meeting at Chequers in September emerged the conclusions that she should engage more with President Reagan on the subject, that the Gulf needed more attention and that 'the stability of Jordan was ever more important'. Her actions in the ensuing years usually followed these priorities.

In February 1985, an agreement between King Hussein and Arafat seemed to promise a turning point. For the first time, the PLO committed itself to working with Jordan for 'a just and peaceful settlement' of the Israel–Palestine dispute. Mrs Thatcher threw herself into supporting

Hussein's plan. She told Reagan that, 'under considerable pressure', Hussein was 'looking for evidence of your personal support for his initiative'. The next step, she argued, would be for the relevant US Assistant Secretary, Richard Murphy, to agree the membership of a Jordanian-Palestinian delegation which could be received in Washington, in order to put the Palestinians under pressure to negotiate along lines acceptable to the USA.

At first, everything seemed to go well. After what he called 'very fruitful talks' with Reagan, Hussein told Mrs Thatcher he planned to create a Jordanian-Palestinian delegation that included PLO representation. The inclusion of the PLO was hugely controversial, although Hussein insisted the delegation would publicly accept the key UN Security Council Resolutions 242 and 338, which acknowledged Israel's right to exist.* Seeking to build international legitimacy, Hussein wanted his delegation to be received by the British government. But Mrs Thatcher was wary of going out on a limb. She told Reagan what she had told the King. No British meeting should 'short-circuit' anything between the President and Hussein.

Charles Powell quickly reinforced her caution: a meeting in London 'is our high card and it is a great mistake to play it too early'. The nature of the delegation's PLO representation was crucial. Mrs Thatcher resolved that if the two PLO men involved would, while in London, publicly reject violence and sign up to Resolutions 242 and 338, she would permit Howe to receive them.

As the summer progressed, the White House became more nervous. They now insisted that Hussein's delegation remain entirely free of PLO representation. Reagan also told Hussein he would not authorize a meeting with Murphy without 'assurances of prompt and tangible movement towards direct negotiations' with Israel. Considering these new conditions unrealistic, Hussein refused them.

The American rejection came shortly before Mrs Thatcher's visit to Egypt and to Jordan, the first to the latter by any sitting British prime minister. When she met the King at the Nadwa Palace on 19 September, she found him in an emotional state. Everything had 'come to the end', he told her. It was unrealistic to expect to find a credible Palestinian who was not selected by the PLO. Moreover, 'direct and visible contacts with the Israelis' at this stage were simply impossible. Mrs Thatcher shared his mood. She would confront President Reagan with the 'enormity' of the

---

* These two resolutions, the first after the Six-Day War of 1967, the second after the Yom Kippur War of 1973, called on Israel to return to its 1967 borders, but also upheld the need for 'secure and recognised boundaries' of all states in the region to be respected.

consequences of the failure of Hussein's initiative, she told Hussein, and try to press ahead with it herself.

At dinner that evening in the British Ambassador's residence, the Jordanian Prime Minister, Zaid Rifai, darted between the table and the telephone, seeking a public commitment from the PLO-affiliated members of the proposed delegation to peaceful negotiations. As John Coles, by then Ambassador to Jordan recalled, 'When we sat down to dinner there was no agreement that the delegation would be received in London. By the coffee, there was.' Mrs Thatcher cabled Reagan immediately. She wanted, she began bluntly, 'to let you know how worried I am by the absence of progress following up King Hussein's peace initiative'. The British government, therefore, was now ready to meet the joint delegation in London, with the Palestinians represented by 'two well-known moderates' who would state their commitment to peaceful negotiation publicly.

Mrs Thatcher had, in Charles Powell's view, made 'a big concession'. She was, in effect, accepting that a senior British minister should meet the PLO. She did it for Hussein. 'She had stars in her eyes about the gallant little king.' Coles agreed, and indeed had intended this: 'If she hadn't paid a visit to Jordan,' he pondered later, 'I wonder if any of this would have happened.'

'Not welcome' was the headline of the leading article in Rupert Murdoch's *Sun*, which normally supported Mrs Thatcher ardently. Conservative Friends of Israel criticized her, as did Israel itself. The Americans were not pleased, although Richard Murphy 'felt hopeful that it might work'. But events conspired against her. Palestinian terrorists killed three Israelis in Cyprus, leading the Israelis to bomb the newly established PLO headquarters in Tunis. On 7 October, the Palestine Liberation Front (PLF) captured the cruise ship *Achille Lauro* and murdered a disabled American Jewish passenger.

After the delegation arrived in London on 13 October, one of the two Palestinians (Mayor Mohammed Milhem) now demanded the removal of any reference to Israel from his public remarks. 'This is clearly completely unacceptable,' Powell wrote to Mrs Thatcher: the meeting would not now take place at all. 'I am <u>deeply disappointed</u>,' she wrote to King Hussein. Her rather quixotic attempt to bring change in the Middle East had failed. In February of the following year, 1986, Hussein announced that he was giving up on the PLO altogether.

Mrs Thatcher's relations with the United States, or even with Israel, were not damaged by this adventure. Her goodwill was recognized. While, for the time being, her search for a solution to the Arab–Israeli conflict faded, her desire to support Peres was in part responsible for her decision to visit Israel in May 1986. She was warmly received. Speaking before the Knesset (the Israeli parliament), she maintained her position on Palestine, insisting that 'A future in which two classes of people have to co-exist with different rights and different standards is surely not one which Israel can accept.' She also met Palestinian leaders (but not PLO people), the first time a Western leader had done so during a visit to Israel. None of this impaired relations with Peres. Powell recalled 'driving back with her from the Negev towards Tel Aviv . . . with her and Peres on the back seat. They gradually fell asleep with her head resting on his shoulder. It was rather touching.' The British Ambassador to Israel reported that the warmth of Mrs Thatcher's welcome had been a 'personal triumph', with Anglo–Israeli relations at 'an all-time high'. But Mrs Thatcher's personal prestige in the region was greater than her power. Politically speaking, her visit to Israel changed little.

Trade featured heavily in Mrs Thatcher's dealings with the Arab and Muslim world, particularly sales of defence equipment. She was the most tireless saleswoman for British companies. 'Tell Treasury & Defence not to argue – just go and get the contract' was a typical injunction. Her attitude was simple, arguably simplistic: if countries wanted to be armed, better that the British should arm them. They would have better relationships with Britain and create more British jobs. This rule could apply even to potentially hostile countries.* She understood the importance of personal relationships in the Arab world and counter-intuited that her sex, far from being a disadvantage in that male-dominated environment, made her an object of fascination. She suffered from none of the traditional ruling-class British embarrassment about selling things hard.

The biggest pitch was to Saudi Arabia. In September 1983, Mrs Thatcher agreed that Britain should try to sell the Saudis Tornado combat aircraft. Initially, the British felt optimistic, but through conversations with Wafic Saïd, the Syrian-born *homme d'affaires* for many of the Saudi royal family's business dealings, they discovered that Prince Sultan, the Saudi Defence Minister, favoured a deal with the French. The only hope lay in Sultan's son, Prince Bandar, the Saudi Ambassador in Washington, who preferred the British. British officials now arranged for Saïd to meet Mrs Thatcher

---

* Customers, actual or potential, thus included allies like Jordan (which, not being an oil state, had little money), Egypt, the mostly rich Gulf states (Kuwait, Bahrain, Qatar, the UAE, Oman), with all of which Britain had historic connections, and then, much more problematically, Iraq and Iran (which were fighting each other) and Syria. Following the invasion of Lebanon in 1982, Britain had frozen its limited arms sales to Israel. By far the largest player in the market was Saudi Arabia.

informally. She was 'very angry' at the French advance, she told him. 'Have the Saudis misled me?' she asked. Saïd advised her to discuss the matter with Bandar.

Prince Bandar was an exceptional character. Appointed Ambassador to Washington at the age of only thirty-four, he was also a trained pilot, expert in military aircraft. He had perfected his flying skills at RAF Cranwell in Lincolnshire* before his days as a pilot were cut short by a car crash. Unlike his Francophile father, Bandar was extremely pro-British. He had little time for the French, who he felt were 'all like Inspector Clouseau'.

There was also a generational difference: 'Sultan was oldish, inscrutable,' recalled one MOD official, 'Bandar was open and Westernized, so we cultivated him.' As an expert, Bandar considered the Tornado superior to the Mirage. As a rising figure in Saudi court politics, he knew it would improve his influence if Saudi Arabia were to buy British rather than French. He also saw the matter strategically. In his view, 'Reagan, King Fahd and Mrs Thatcher had an informal meeting of the heart and agreement on the strategic outlook. We were all fighting Communism together.' He was also conscious that Fahd, four years Mrs Thatcher's senior, considered her a very beautiful woman: for that reason as well, the King was keen to do business with her.

Bandar called on Mrs Thatcher for the first time in December 1984. In Powell's view, she was impressed by the energetic and handsome young Prince. He was equally taken by the blonde stateswoman, who met him at the door of No. 10 and curtsied: 'I thought she'd slipped.' But her deference to his royal blood did not make her servile: 'She had such a powerful personality. She liked to give you a taste of it, to help you get to know her. She was a hell of a man!' Bandar presented her with a rock-crystal model of a bulldog with sapphire eyes in recognition, he told her, of the British fighting spirit. 'Isn't that a lovely present!' she said after he had left. 'Yes, Prime Minister,' said one official, 'but unfortunately that's a French bulldog.' 'If he buys aeroplanes from us, I don't care where he buys his bulldogs,' she exclaimed.

It was the beginning of a beautiful friendship. They began to meet frequently and privately, with only Charles Powell present.† With Bandar's encouragement, Mrs Thatcher started to write personal letters to King Fahd, commenting on world events and Middle Eastern affairs and reporting her

---

* Cranwell was the base with whose pilots the young Margaret had danced during the war.
† While in office, Mrs Thatcher had twenty-three meetings with Bandar, probably more than any other foreigner (apart from the US Ambassador, Charlie Price) who was not a head of government.

conversations with world leaders. Sometimes, Bandar himself would carry these messages by hand.*

In their first encounter, and in a longer meeting in early January 1985, Mrs Thatcher and Bandar discussed the prospects for the Tornado purchases and debated tactics. By Bandar's account, she greedily sucked up all information he had about what Saudi might want: 'Give me the numbers. And? And? And?' He informed her of Reagan's view that Congress would want to block the sale of US F-15 Strike fighter aircraft to his country.† This mattered because, thought Bandar, the Saudi purchase of French Mirages depended on the F-15 deal. These two planes together would give Saudi 'the right low–high airforce structure'. So if Congress rejected the sale, French prospects would dim. Mrs Thatcher saw considerable opportunity for Britain here. She knew that if Congress would not let Reagan sell his own country's aircraft to Saudi Arabia, he would much rather she, not President Mitterrand, get the benefit. Reagan privately advised King Fahd to buy British.

Invigorated by his Thatcher meetings, Bandar argued the British case to King Fahd. Both the Mirage and the Tornado are 'good aircraft', he argued, 'but the important question, Your Majesty, is, "Who do you trust – Mitterrand or Mrs Thatcher?" "Mrs Thatcher," he said. "Well," I said, "that solves the problem."' On 15 April, over dinner in Riyadh,‡ Fahd turned to her and said, 'Prime Minister, the deal is yours.'

The details were as laborious as the deal itself. There was a question whether BAc, already supplying Tornados to the RAF, would be able to produce the aircraft required in time. So committed to the deal was Mrs Thatcher that she ordered the first aeroplanes intended for the RAF to be sent to Saudi Arabia. The knowledge that this deal, formally signed in September, would be forthcoming probably helped her to act as boldly as she did in relation to Hussein's Jordanian-Palestinian initiative. She knew she stood high with non-militant Arabs and therefore had some advantage over the Americans. In September, Prince Sultan told her that King Fahd had wanted the contract because of his 'great respect for the Prime Minister': the deal should be considered a contribution to 'peace and stability'. He also noted that the prospect of a Jordanian-Palestinian meeting in London had been 'very well received in the Arab world'. In January 1986, the

---

* The typed correspondence survives, but a few of them, it seems, were handwritten. When King Fahd first received one of these, he was surprised. 'Does the lady not have someone to type letters for her?' he asked. It was pointed out to him that, in British culture, a handwritten letter was a mark of personal attention.
† Many in Congress considered such a sale incompatible with their strong support for Israel.
‡ Fahd had asked her to stop off for dinner as she returned from a Far East tour.

commercial terms were settled and the contract was named Al-Yamamah, the Arabic for a dove (of peace). Over more than twenty years, the deal is estimated to have amounted to £42 billion. It was, judged James Blyth, head of Procurement at the MOD, 'the biggest single deal anybody has ever done for the United Kingdom'.

Mrs Thatcher had now established for Britain a relationship both of trust and of profit with the most important oil state. Al-Yamamah would greatly assist her future diplomatic contacts and prove important in the first Gulf War. In Prince Bandar's view, 'Before her, no one really cared what Britain thought or did. In her time, all over the world, they asked: "What does Thatcher think? Where will Britain be?"'

Given the scale of her achievement, of which Mrs Thatcher was proud, it might seem surprising that she said almost nothing about it. In part, this reflected the extreme discretion she always exercised in such matters.* But there was another, more difficult reason, to do with her son.

Mark Thatcher was often accused of seeking to profit from his mother's position. In principle, this was not something Mrs Thatcher condoned. On one occasion, Carol recalled, 'she gave us both a little lecture about freebies. She was very against cashing in.' But the issue was not always so black and white. It arose in 1984 when the *Observer* newspaper revealed that Mark had been involved in a contract to build a university in Oman in 1981. The circumstances, the paper alleged, had been scandalous.

In November 1980, Mrs Thatcher had unwisely given her son, then aged twenty-seven, a handwritten letter of introduction to Sheikh Zayed, the President of the United Arab Emirates. At the same time, Mark acquired a consultancy with Cementation International, the Arab-world subsidiary of Trafalgar House.† Through Zayed's recommendation and because of whose son he was, Mark was granted an audience with the pro-British Sultan Qaboos of Oman. Eventually, Mark lobbied for Cementation to be given the contract to build the new university in Oman. After the Cementation bid succeeded, Mrs Thatcher stood accused of using her influence with the Sultan to get the contract for the firm for which Mark was working.

---

* In the twenty-first century, it was alleged that Al-Yamamah had been a highly corrupt contract, with large rake-offs for Saudi princes, including Bandar himself. If this was so, it is unlikely that Mrs Thatcher would have known about it, since no such arrangements would have been made with the British government. In those days, unlike today, the rules governing defence sales permitted the payment of agents. Indeed, sales in the Arab world could not be achieved without them.
† The Managing Director of this British construction conglomerate was Lord (Victor) Matthews, a close acquaintance of Mrs Thatcher.

The *Observer* story was not easy to shrug off, because it came in part from the ranks of officialdom. At issue was Mark's decision to join his mother unexpectedly during her official visit to Oman in April 1981. Ivor Lucas, the Ambassador in Oman, warned Whitehall that Mark's presence was 'a potential embarrassment'. This unease had only grown when, without warning, Mark had arrived to join Mrs Thatcher, Denis, Carol and others for a private lunch at the Sultan's perfume-filled Salalah summer palace on the beach. After lunch, Mrs Thatcher retired for a private *tête-à-tête* with the Sultan. During this, as she said publicly after the *Observer* story broke, 'I was advised to raise the matter of the whole university contract with the government of Oman. I did it. I believed in it very forcefully because I wanted the business to come to Britain.' She did not distinguish between British companies, she said: 'I bat for Britain.'*

The *Observer* story was not a knock-down blow. No iniquity was proved. Mark insisted he was doing nothing wrong: 'So what? I was at least working for a UK company. Dad always told me to take care only to work for UK companies. Would those who sought to criticize this have preferred me to work for a German or Cypriot company?' It is true, however, that Mark had close links to Brigadier Tim Landon, the Sultan's closest confidant, who sometimes came with Mark to see Mrs Thatcher at Chequers. Such connections were bound to make people suspect abuse of his mother's position. As Tim Lankester, one of her private secretaries, recalled, Mrs Thatcher 'really didn't understand conflicts of interest if they came under her category of batting for Britain'.

Clive Whitmore recalled quite often having to deal with problems of Mark 'trying to exploit his mother's name'. On one occasion the Chairman of BP came to see him, threatening to state publicly that Mark's activities with oil deals were endangering the company's established relationships. After Whitmore took the matter to Mrs Thatcher, she asked him to intercede with Mark: '"You cannot damage the reputation of your mother,"' Whitmore told him. '"It's got to stop." Mark accepted this.' The problem recurred in different forms, however, because, Whitmore believed, 'Mark was driven by greed and reluctant to pass up any opportunity.' A pattern developed in which Mrs Thatcher had 'an air of resignation about it all but was indulgent towards Mark. The rational PM knew well what he was up to. But the mother found it difficult to be tough with him.' Mark himself considered that Mrs Thatcher 'felt her maternal instinct with the

---

* Mrs Thatcher took her role in the promotion of British trade extremely seriously. During her visit, Lucas introduced her to staff in the defence attaché's office, explaining that they were responsible for the promotion of arms sales. 'Oh no, they aren't,' she replied loudly, 'they are so bad at it that I have to do the job for them.'

same fervour as she deployed her political arguments'. This was true, but she was much less adroit in working out how to act upon her maternal instinct successfully. Sometimes she would pass the task of reprimand to Denis, who would exclaim, 'The bloody young fool!' 'Denis did his best,' thought Whitmore, 'but was no more successful than his wife.

When the dimensions of the Al-Yamamah deal gradually emerged, allegations against Mark Thatcher began again. No wrong was ever proved. Nonetheless, there was pervasive unease about Mark's business dealings in areas where his mother's influence was high and about her reluctance to do anything decisive about them.

To be fair to Mark – which few were inclined to be – his attempts to pursue a business career were constantly harassed by a hostile press. After the 1984 Cementation story, Denis advised that Mark should leave the country, suggesting he go to the United States, where he had a work permit and employment offers that arose through his father's connections, not his mother's. 'I would have preferred to stay in England,' Mark recalled, and the whole thing was 'extraordinarily painful for my mother'. Nonetheless, in late 1984, Mark left Britain for Dallas, Texas.

Problems about his security cropped up almost immediately. *Irish American Voice*, the paper of IRA sympathizers in the United States, published his rough whereabouts. His mother was naturally upset. 'It is his flat that I am most worried about,' she wrote to her private office. 'There is <u>no</u> back way out and no means of getting help.' Fortunately, the American authorities were sympathetic. Mark was assured by Charlie Wick, a close Reagan associate, that 'The President is never going to allow himself to be put in a situation where he has to telephone your mother to say that her son has been injured on US soil.' So the American and British authorities shared the burden of protecting Mark. It was quite heavy work. One State Department official wrote drily to a colleague that Mark's sports car, 'a bright red Lotus [part of Mark's work was to promote the Lotus brand] was hardly the type of vehicle required to preserve or promote anonymity'. Letters flew back and forth complaining how hard it was to find Mark, especially when there were complications in his love life, and how rude he was when he was found.

After the American bombing of Libya from British air bases in April 1986, Mrs Thatcher became alarmed about Mark once more. 'I fear he may be a priority target,' she wrote to her private secretary, '– and so may <u>Carol</u> ... I thought the security people over there would <u>automatically</u> [underlined three times] think of giving him special protection but nothing has happened.' Then she turned to her daughter: 'Fortunately <u>Carol</u> has alarms in her house but I will ask my detectives if they can arrange for the local police to be especially watchful during the coming weeks. I will also remind her to <u>watch her car</u> for <u>explosives</u>.'

This letter was expressive not only of a mother's natural concern, but of guilt. Mrs Thatcher knew that her policies had increased the risk to her children. Despite Mrs Thatcher's apprehension, however, Carol steadfastly refused personal protection. She was following the example of her father, who declined to have permanent protection throughout the nearly thirty years it was accorded to his wife.

Mark trouble persisted. His Dallas neighbours complained about the disruption caused by his security, so he was asked to leave his apartment. Mark's difficulties calmed down only in December 1986 after he finally decided to buy a house in Dallas. He sought government money to have it made secure, reporting this would cost $25,000. 'May I first have a realistic estimate?' wrote Mrs Thatcher. 'The sums seem enormous – way beyond what I could reimburse.' A survey was duly conducted. As a British Embassy official reported, Mark's 'attitude was that the exercise should be done properly or not at all ... In Mr Thatcher's view there would be no difficulty in obtaining the necessary funds – he added that £160,000 had recently been spent on the Prime Minister's house.'

In the end, the cost was $61,618. Although Denis feared an outcry if British public funds were used, the Cabinet Office felt it could contribute up to $30,820. Mrs Thatcher accepted this gratefully: 'Mark's security is endangered because of my actions as Prime Minister and these safeguards are I believe justified.'

Effectively forbidden to live in Britain, Mark was at risk and experienced genuine difficulty. The trouble was, as one official put it, 'He was jolly hard to help.' Mrs Thatcher found this too. The supremely powerful, decisive and determined Prime Minister could never quite work out how to deal with her son.

18
Irish agreement; Brighton bomb
'The day I was not meant to see'

In late 1982, Mrs Thatcher told officials that, should she win the next election, she wanted to 'do something about Ireland'. She had, however, no idea what that 'something' might be. No political initiative in her early years had borne fruit. Enraged by the mischief, even malice, displayed by Charles Haughey's government during the Falklands War, she had frozen the tentative connections between London and Dublin. By December 1982, when Garret FitzGerald became Taoiseach for the second time, Anglo–Irish relations stood in a state of angry immobility.

FitzGerald was keen, despite the difficulties, to resume progress towards a settlement over Northern Ireland. One of his officials recommended a security-led approach: the Irish government should 'strike hard at the terrorists' – 'tougher action would be welcome to the British Government and would help to lay the basis for a resumption of an Anglo–Irish process'. This was a good reading of Mrs Thatcher's state of mind. For her, security came first, and she was perpetually, often justifiably, dissatisfied with the Republic's contribution.*

In her memoirs, Mrs Thatcher was rather unkind about FitzGerald, making sarcastic remarks about his loquacity and inability to understand Unionist fears.† This perhaps reflected her retrospective unease with the Anglo–Irish process. In office, she recognized FitzGerald's genuine desire for better relations and peace in Northern Ireland. His sincerity commanded her respect. In Robert Armstrong's view: 'She liked FitzGerald and

---

* Mrs Thatcher would sometimes put forward the idea of a fence, built all along the border, with what she called an 'access corridor'. No colleagues ever gave countenance to her notion.
† FitzGerald's quiet voice and rapid flow led Mrs Thatcher to remember him as an 'Irish Geoffrey Howe'. One of FitzGerald's officials recalled that 'before each meeting with Mrs Thatcher, I'd urge him to "speak slowly, speak slowly" . . . he'd start quite slowly and intelligibly, but then the ideas started to crowd in and he'd speed up'.

thought he was an honest, decent man. I think she felt motherly towards him: she wanted to stroke his curly hair.'

FitzGerald felt more urgency than she. His great fear was that Sinn Fein, the political wing of the IRA, might overtake the more moderate Nationalists of the SDLP, led by John Hume. This, he believed, would destabilize the Republic as well as the North. In May 1983, to bring the Nationalist parties together, he set up the New Ireland Forum.

Mrs Thatcher, suspicious of all-Ireland solutions, stood apart from FitzGerald's initiative. But she soon found that his agenda dominated discussion of Northern Ireland's future.* For her part, she had few sources of creative advice from the Unionist standpoint. After the election she had sent her closest Unionist associate, her PPS Ian Gow, off to become Minister of Housing, she had little personal relationship with the Ulster Unionist leader James Molyneaux and was uncomfortable with the 'arch-Unionist' Ian Paisley. Although she retained respect for Enoch Powell, she could not countenance his anti-American conspiracy theories.

Besides, Mrs Thatcher's Unionist instincts faced an even more formidable obstacle than Dublin – Robert Armstrong and his Cabinet Office colleagues, most notably David Goodall. As Cabinet Secretary, Armstrong took the lead in discussions with the Republic over Northern Ireland.† He and his counterpart in Dublin, Dermot Nally, shared a 'mutual respect and friendship'. The so-called 'Armstrong–Nally process' kept London/Dublin contacts alive in the most difficult days.‡ Both Armstrong and Goodall, a cerebral and almost saintly Roman Catholic of partially Anglo-Irish Protestant descent, were highly professional civil servants, but both harboured Irish Nationalist sympathies. 'Robert never definitely overstepped the mark,' said Charles Powell, 'but they were all going behind her back. Their meetings were principally to discuss how to handle her.'

---

* Sinn Fein performed less well than expected in the 1983 general election, receiving 13.4 per cent of the vote in Northern Ireland, in fourth place behind the SDLP (17.9 per cent). The election of Gerry Adams as MP for Belfast West, however, seemed to vindicate the 'Armalite and ballot box' strategy of younger Republicans. Adams became President of Sinn Fein later in the year.

† As discussed earlier, Mrs Thatcher had authorized this because she disliked the idea of the Foreign Office taking the lead in discussions about a part of the United Kingdom. In fact, Armstrong's views were even more 'green' (sympathetic to Irish Nationalism) than those of the Foreign Office. The Northern Ireland Office was only brought into the negotiations at a later stage.

‡ This process was formally known as the steering committee of the Anglo–Irish Intergovernmental Council. The two sides were so close that the Irish side even invented two ties, dark green for the Irish, maroon for the British, with the letters 'NA' (reflecting the Irish order of the two names) on them, and gave both to each side. Members of this unofficial club would wear them for reunions.

So, following Mrs Thatcher's 1983 election victory, it was Armstrong who urged her to get back on terms with the Republic. She was suspicious ('I don't like this at all'), but allowed him to move the process forward. Preparations began for a summit with the Taoiseach in November.

Irish officials now took the initiative. In September, FitzGerald's close adviser, Michael Lillis, floated to Goodall the idea that FitzGerald might support formal recognition of the Union in return for the 'participation of Irish security forces in operations in the North and of Irish judges in terrorist trials there'. They discussed the idea that the Republic would repeal Articles 2 and 3 of its 1937 Constitution which laid claim to Northern Ireland. This idea, without the reciprocal requirement to discuss Northern Ireland's British constitutional position that she had earlier rejected out of hand (see p. 258), was now dangled before her.*

Shortly before the November summit, FitzGerald himself followed up these ideas with Armstrong, who reported as much to the Prime Minister. Using a word which, did he but know it, was a red rag to Mrs Thatcher, who saw it as Marxist jargon, FitzGerald said that the minority in Northern Ireland suffered from 'alienation': 'What was needed was to create something upon which the loyalty of the minority in Northern Ireland could form.' The Irish might be prepared to state publicly that the Union would not, foreseeably, be overturned. In exchange, FitzGerald had suggested, 'the minority should be given law and order institutions on which it could focus confidence and loyalty'. Against this Mrs Thatcher drew her disapproving wiggles. On 2 November, she received a report that FitzGerald believed 'the main obstruction to progress on the issue of Northern Ireland did not take the form of constitutional restraints, but was the Prime Minister herself'.

The summit, on 7 November, was uneasy. 'It was electric the sensation that Mrs Thatcher exuded,' recalled Michael Lillis. When FitzGerald spoke of the 'alienation' of the Nationalist community, she cut him short: 'I do wish you would stop using that dreadful word, Garret.' FitzGerald spoke of the threat from Sinn Fein, and aired the New Ireland Forum's emerging suggestions of federation, confederation or joint sovereignty.† Mrs Thatcher said merely that 'she noted the Taoiseach's

---

* It was, perhaps, surprising that British officials set so much store by changing the 1937 Constitution. Articles 2 and 3 meant little in international law since, in 1925, the treaty between Ireland and Britain had recognized the partition of Ireland. If Articles 2 and 3 had significance, it was an emotional and political rather than a legal or practical one.

† All three Forum possibilities were unwelcome to Mrs Thatcher. FitzGerald recalled that she was particularly cautious about joint sovereignty because she wanted to be able to say truthfully afterwards that it had not been discussed.

concern', but after he left, the British team persuaded her to agree to develop a formal response to the Irish proposals. In what they called a 'basic equation', Britain would offer the Dublin government 'some form of political involvement in Northern Ireland in return for formal recognition of the Union'.

The year ended with several terrorist atrocities, including the IRA's bombing of Harrods, in which six people died. On balance, these helped FitzGerald's cause. Writing in *The Times*, he called for the two governments to fight terrorism 'together'. Mrs Thatcher publicly welcomed this. Privately, however, she was frustrated that more was not being done and occasionally threw out startling ideas. When she met ministers at Chequers in early 1984, David Goodall recalled her asking why those in Northern Ireland who did not wish for British rule could not be transferred to the Republic:

> After all, she said, the Irish were used to large scale movements of population. Only recently there had been a population transfer of some kind. At this point the silence round the fire became transfused with simple bafflement. After a pause, I asked if she could possibly be thinking of Cromwell. 'Cromwell: of course.' 'Well Prime Minister, Cromwell's policy was known as "To Hell or Connaught" and it left a scar on Anglo-Irish relations which still hasn't healed.' The idea of a population transfer was not pursued.*

As the pressure for negotiations mounted, on 16 February the Cabinet agreed to explore the evolving Anglo-Irish proposals secretly. Mrs Thatcher helped bring her cautious colleagues along. To those concerned that the Irish might not vote to amend Articles 2 and 3 and so matters would stand worse than before, she declared, 'You can't make it worse; you can't do nothing.'

On 2 May 1984, the New Ireland Forum published its report. It gave a highly unflattering account of the British role in Ireland and outlined three futures – the creation of a unitary Irish state, a federal or confederal Irish state, or some form of 'joint authority' over the province – all of which would have abolished or undermined the Union. While the Irish government favoured joint authority, Mrs Thatcher considered this 'really a form of joint sovereignty'. She rejected it out of hand. Once again, however, she did not prevent further negotiations.

---

* There was precedent for the idea of redrawing the Irish border. Mrs Thatcher was probably thinking of the Boundary Commission established after the Anglo-Irish Treaty of 1921 to determine whether areas with large Catholic populations should be transferred to the Free State. Although this came to nothing, she seems to have considered it a mistake not to allow troublesome townlands to be exchanged.

Mrs Thatcher was acutely aware of the need to keep relations with the United States, only recently recovered from the spat over Grenada, in good repair, particularly as President Reagan was to visit the Republic in June. According to William Clark, Reagan's National Security Advisor, the President did have 'to remind Mrs Thatcher . . . that his own life might go better, considering the Irish influence in the Congress, if London treated its counterparts in Dublin with a little more dignity . . . but in spite of his Irish name and his visit to his ancestral home, he didn't feel that strongly'. American pressure was gentle. But with the Irish government seeing the Forum report as an opportunity to influence American opinion, Mrs Thatcher realized the best way to give herself some cover was by being seen to be talking to Dublin.

Talks now focused on what Mrs Thatcher might agree to should the Irish do away with Articles 2 and 3. Rejecting Dublin's idea of a joint 'security force', British officials urged her to offer FitzGerald 'a means of exercising direct influence over the affairs of the province through institutionalised consultative arrangements about police and security matters'. Goodall thought this could be sold to FitzGerald as the first 'formal British acknowledgement of the Irish Government's right to a say in Northern Ireland's internal affairs'. She did not like the phrase 'right to a say', but did not jib at the essential deal being floated. That autumn, officials on both sides entered a 'mildly euphoric phase'. And then came Brighton.

On 11 October 1984, Mrs Thatcher worked late in her suite in Brighton's Grand Hotel, preparing her speech for her party's annual conference the next day. Denis had gone to bed, but Robin Butler was with her. As he recalled, around 2.50 in the morning 'there was this boom. I said, "There's a bomb. You ought to come away from the windows." "I must see if Denis is all right," said Mrs Thatcher,' and opened the door to the bedroom. She plunged into the darkness and emerged with her husband, in his pyjamas, dazed from sleep. The bathroom was badly damaged. If she had been in it, she would have been severely injured.

In a room across the corridor were several members of Mrs Thatcher's staff, enacting her changes to the speech. John Gummer, the Party Chairman, was with them. After the blast, he told everyone to lie on the floor. Then, gingerly, he crawled to the door and opened it. Oddly, the corridor lights were still working. He was surprised to be confronted by Mrs Thatcher, also on her hands and knees, and shoeless, on the other side of the door. She came into the room. 'That was meant for me,' she said. 'Are you all right, dears?' When Denis emerged, Bob Kingston, her detective, noticed he was rather shaken, but that she was calm and composed. Butler told them they must return to Downing Street at once, for the sake of her security. She said, 'I'm not leaving.'

Twenty minutes of confused debate followed. Leaving was considered risky because of fears of a second bomb, and of snipers. In fact there was only one bomb, which had been planted by an IRA operative, Patrick Magee,* several weeks earlier. This, of course, was not known at the time. Eventually, the police decided to take the Thatcher party to Brighton police station. They were escorted down the main stairs of the hotel by firemen, past the rubble that had fallen into the hall. 'The cement dust got in your mouth,' Mrs Thatcher remembered. She had 'dashed into the bedroom to get clothes for the next day – a navy suit, two blouses and shoes'. 'Don't worry, Prime Minister,' said Amanda Colvin, her diary secretary, 'I've got the speech,' the working assumption being that the conference would go on.† Mrs Thatcher's own secure car had been locked up for the night so David Wolfson drove her, Denis and Crawfie, her long-standing assistant.

When Mrs Thatcher left the hotel, she was not aware that anyone had died. In the days before mobile phones, emails and twenty-four-hour news there was an acute shortage of information. On the seafront, ministers, MPs and party representatives wandered around in a shocked state, some still in dinner jackets, others in their pyjamas. Sir Keith Joseph, resplendent in a Noël-Coward-style silk dressing-gown, conscientiously took his ministerial red box with him. Alistair McAlpine, the Tory Treasurer, rang the Chairman of Marks & Spencer and persuaded him to open his Brighton branch early so that the victims could reclothe themselves for the conference. At the police station, Mrs Thatcher spoke briefly to the BBC. 'The conference will go on,' she said. 'The conference will go on, as usual,' emphasizing those last two words.

At 4.40, the police drove the Thatchers to the nearby Lewes Police College. After saying prayers with Crawfie, Mrs Thatcher slept for about an hour and a half in her clothes. When she woke, Butler informed her that the bomb's effects had been much more serious than first supposed: rescuers were still trying to extricate the Chief Whip, John Wakeham, from beneath the debris. Crawfie turned on BBC breakfast television: 'Look!' she called out to Mrs Thatcher. 'They're getting Norman Tebbit out.' Tebbit, in his pyjamas, was trapped under rubble, and firemen were trying to work him

---

* Magee was given a life sentence for murder in 1986, but was released under the provisions of the Belfast Agreement in 1999.

† The saving of the speech much impressed Mrs Thatcher. She later wrote to Amanda Colvin's father, recalling that 'Amanda was absolutely marvellous throughout – cool, calm and very good-humoured. And, she & Tessa [Tessa Gaisman, Mrs Thatcher's Diary Secretary] remembered to bring out the speech. You can be very proud of her.'

free.* Although shocked, Mrs Thatcher insisted that the conference restart as planned: 'We must show that terrorism cannot defeat democracy. It's what they [the victims] would have wanted.'

The conference did start on time, and after lunch, as was customary, Mrs Thatcher delivered her speech. Dressed neatly and with her hair as well in place as ever, she denounced the 'inhuman' bomb as 'an attempt to cripple Her Majesty's democratically elected government ... the fact that we are gathered here now – shocked but composed and determined – is a sign not only that this attack has failed, but that all attempts to destroy democracy by terrorism will fail'. When she reached the end of her speech, the party faithful responded with a deafening standing ovation.

Mrs Thatcher and Denis visited the injured in hospital. John Wakeham was unconscious and Norman Tebbit scarcely able to speak, with 'his face so swollen that I could barely recognise him'. Tebbit's wife, Margaret, told her, 'Margaret, I can't feel a thing below my neck.' Mrs Thatcher also chatted to another survivor, Harvey Thomas, the conference organizer. 'She felt huge responsibility for all the deaths and injuries,' he recalled. 'It was this sense of loyalty.' Only at church, two days after leaving Brighton, did she give way to tears: 'As the sun came through the stained glass windows, I thought – "this is the day I was not meant to see" – And then I remembered my friends who cannot see it. I have never known such a blend of gratitude and sorrow.' Not long after the bomb, Denis gave his wife a watch with a note that said 'Every minute is precious.'

Five people died in the Brighton bomb and thirty-one were treated for injury.† Tebbit made a slow, and in the view of some, incomplete recovery. His wife was confined to a wheelchair until her death in 2020. Those close to Mrs Thatcher believed that, as well as being physically unscathed, she suffered no serious mental problems.‡ The main practical consequence was greater isolation from the public, as she was more intensely protected.§ The IRA statement claiming responsibility contained the famous and chilling

---

* For once in her life, Mrs Thatcher was grateful for the television cameras: their bright lights were trained on the ruins to help the firemen operate.

† The fatalities were Sir Anthony Berry MP, Eric Taylor, Lady (Jeanne) Shattock, Lady (Muriel) Maclean and Roberta Wakeham. Berry was killed by the force of the blast in the hotel room originally intended for Peter Walker, the Energy Secretary, who had decided to stay in London that night to deal with the NACODS dispute. It could therefore be said that the miners' strike saved Walker's life.

‡ There were a few small changes – from then on, Mrs Thatcher recalled, 'I always kept a torch beside my bed in a strange house.'

§ At the end of October a MORI poll gave Mrs Thatcher a popularity lead over Neil Kinnock of 18 per cent. This was put down to admiration for her courage during the Brighton bombing.

phrases: 'Today we were unlucky, but remember, we have only to be lucky once. You will have to be lucky always.'

Shortly after the bombing, Mrs Thatcher studied proposed speaking notes for her planned November meeting with FitzGerald. She was unhappy. 'The events of Thursday night at Brighton mean that we must go very slow on these talks if not stop them,' she scribbled. 'It could look as if we were bombed into making concessions to the Republic.' What seems extraordinary in retrospect, however, is how little the policy on Northern Ireland changed. No one suggested she seize the moment to insist on stronger security measures or rally the world against the IRA. Instead, after the slightest of pauses, the machinery of negotiation rolled on, almost as if nothing had happened. The only person trying seriously to slow it down was Mrs Thatcher.

Less than three weeks later, assassins murdered Indira Gandhi, the Prime Minister of India. This shocked Mrs Thatcher, who attended her funeral in Delhi.* While there, she reviewed suggestions from Geoffrey Howe for her upcoming summit with FitzGerald at Chequers.† Fired up, she objected to his proposal that a British government would endorse a pro-united Ireland vote in the North, or that the different communities should be 'reflected' in the institutions. 'It was no good talking to her about Ireland for quite a long time [after the bomb],' Powell noted. 'She would say, "If we appease them, it will be worse."'

Before the summit with FitzGerald, Mrs Thatcher complained to officials that the Irish were making 'a number of unacceptable demands': Dublin still did not understand that it could not have joint authority. She wondered 'whether the present talks could usefully continue'. Armstrong duly secured assurances from the Irish Ambassador, Noel Dorr, that this was not Dublin's 'bottom line', but this only made her suspicious. She guessed correctly that Armstrong had contrived Dorr's conciliatory message. Although it could be argued that Armstrong was helping clear up misunderstandings, it could also be said that he was trying to frustrate her intentions. As the Chequers summit approached, Dublin expected trouble:

---

* Although not close to Mrs Gandhi in political views, Mrs Thatcher had always liked and respected her as a leader. Both women were graduates of Somerville College, Oxford (though not contemporaries). Each had a fellow feeling for the only other woman in executive charge of an important country. They used to take comfort in private conversations about their difficulties with their children.

† Owing to the manifest threat, this was now to be held at Chequers rather than in Dublin. Arguing for the change of venue, Mrs Thatcher said: 'The IRA will probably get me in the end, but I don't see why I should offer myself on a plate.'

'We are aware of the enormous impact of both Brighton and the assassination of Mrs Gandhi ... The Prime Minister's cast of mind is strongly negative and this could create a real difficulty for the Taoiseach.'

The Chequers summit, on 18–19 November, saw heated discussion between Mrs Thatcher and FitzGerald. She questioned whether amending the Irish Constitution to recognize the border was realistic. If not, it would be better to work for less ambitious objectives, especially security cooperation. FitzGerald disagreed: without greater political progress, Sinn Fein would overtake the SDLP at the local elections the following May. He even warned of civil war, arguing that the minority could not identify with the local police. She responded that she was 'worried by the trend of the conversation. The Taoiseach seemed to be saying that he wanted a Republican enclave in Northern Ireland.' He replied angrily that 85,000 Catholics had been driven out of their homes in mixed areas – 'the biggest forced population move in Europe since World War Two'. She then raised a point which put the whole process in doubt. The structure of government in Northern Ireland, she said, had to be determined by the two communities, not through Anglo-Irish consultations. The prospect of devolved government gave the communities strong incentive to agree, she went on. 'But one had to ask oneself seriously: was the animosity so fundamental that agreement would never be attained?' In the end, all the two Prime Ministers could manage was a general expression of the need for progress.

In its combative frankness, the meeting was not unlike the famous one with Mikhail Gorbachev, also in Chequers, less than a month later. Mrs Thatcher ended the conversation positively. 'We like you,' she told FitzGerald. 'We're now tackling the problem in detail for the first time.' The parties broke up agreeing, as always, that Armstrong–Nally would continue.* There was no euphoria, but neither was there despair. It was Mrs Thatcher's press conference after FitzGerald left that caused the difficulties. Asked whether she had ruled out the recommendations of the Forum report, she answered with customary bluntness: 'a unified Ireland was one solution. That is out. A second solution was confederation of two states. That is out. A third solution was joint authority. That is out. That is

---

* Little noticed because of the heat of the prime ministerial discussions was that the British had made some concessions that were useful to Dublin. Devolution was no longer held out as the prelude to any Anglo–Irish deal, thus removing the Unionist power of 'veto' (a reference to the permanent Unionist majority in Northern Ireland). The right for the Irish government to be consulted in the formulation of policy in Northern Ireland, in return for amendment of their Constitution, remained on offer.

a derogation from sovereignty. We made that quite clear when the report was published. Northern Ireland is part of the United Kingdom.'

Strictly speaking, Mrs Thatcher was saying nothing new. By restating it, she was not attempting to embarrass FitzGerald. But her emphatic style and her love of repetition – 'out ... out ... out' – were too eloquent not to provoke a frenzy. The episode reinforced Irish doubts that FitzGerald was tough enough to deal with her. According to Michael Lillis, 'it nearly ended his leadership'. The Unionists were delighted. Robert Armstrong was in despair: 'I really thought "This is it."' The row escalated after the Taoiseach's private description of her words as 'gratuitously offensive' was widely reported.

FitzGerald then wrote Mrs Thatcher a pained but courteous letter, more in sorrow than in anger. He begged her to acknowledge the Forum report's virtue in recognizing the needs of Unionism and to admit the problem of 'alienation' of the minority, the concept she so much disliked. Armstrong suggested she might tell FitzGerald that she regretted if her manner at the press conference 'has created difficulties for him at home'. Mrs Thatcher, always acutely aware of the danger of apologies in politics, wrote 'Certainly NOT': 'The whole proposal is too contrived and apologetic. Why?' Such was the pressure from officials and ministers alike, however, that she bent slightly with the wind. On 29 November, she sent a more conciliatory letter to FitzGerald saying she shared his concern that her comments 'have been taken totally out of context'. In the margins of the Dublin European Council, on 3 December, the two Prime Ministers cleared the air. While she still refused to say anything nice about the Forum report, they parted amicably. Dermot Nally thought: 'She was feeling rather guilty about the damage she felt she had done ... When she came over she told him, "Garret, I am doing the best I can. I have been going around all day with a smile on my face."'

In retrospect, FitzGerald considered that Mrs Thatcher's 'out ... out ... out-burst' (as some wit called it) had actually helped convince his Cabinet just how great the difficulties were. Goodall agreed. The moment, he believed, had been 'a watershed'. Until then, the Irish had thought they would succeed in getting joint authority. After it, they knew they must settle for less. Mrs Thatcher's actions suggest she knew she had gone too far. She was never as strident on the subject again. An Anglo–Irish agreement became likelier.

It may not have been a complete coincidence that Mrs Thatcher's reconciliation with FitzGerald occurred in the same month as her visit to President Reagan. Before they met, Reagan had received a letter from Speaker Tip O'Neill asking him to 'encourage Mrs Thatcher to renew the Anglo–Irish dialogue over the Forum Report', citing strong Congressional support. Reagan always paid careful attention to O'Neill, whose help he needed for bipartisan purposes, but he was not minded to put pressure on her. When they met, she reassured him she was 'on good terms' with FitzGerald and they were 'making progress'. According to the US record, 'The President said making progress is important, and observed that there is great Congressional interest in this matter. Indeed, Tip O'Neill had sent him a personal letter, asking him to appeal to Mrs Thatcher to be reasonable and forthcoming.' By mentioning O'Neill's letter, but not endorsing it, Reagan fulfilled O'Neill's request but distanced himself from it.

When she addressed the US Congress two months later, in February 1985 (see p. 424), Mrs Thatcher emphasized the common front between Britain and the Republic: 'Garret FitzGerald and I will continue to consult together in the quest for stability and peace in Northern Ireland and we hope we will have your continued support for our joint efforts.' This was well received and made it harder for her to break out of the process of Anglo–Irish negotiation. Expectations were rising.

The greater sense of realism, post-Chequers, meant that the British were readier to accept that a referendum on revising Articles 2 and 3 was unlikely, and the Irish were less pressing about joint authority. But the Irish, to whom the whole business mattered more, proved more fertile than London with new ideas. The Republic wanted to alter what it saw as a Protestant bias in the RUC* and the Ulster Defence Regiment,† and promoted the idea of 'mixed' or 'joint' courts. Terrorist cases in Northern Ireland should be heard by a panel of judges, at least one of whom should be drawn from the Republic.‡ Another notion was an early release of some terrorists from prison. In the face of this, even Geoffrey Howe, of all senior ministers the most enthusiastic for an agreement, warned Mrs Thatcher that 'there is still a significant gap to be bridged'. On 24 April, the Cabinet subcommittee OD (I) met to discuss suggestions from Howe and Douglas Hurd, Northern Ireland Secretary since September, that a basis of agreement was 'now discernible'. In return for a consultative role in Northern Ireland, the Irish would make a 'constitutional declaration'

---

* The Royal Ulster Constabulary was established in 1922, as the successor in Northern Ireland of the Royal Irish Constabulary. It was later incorporated into the Police Service of Northern Ireland (PSNI) under reforms following the Belfast (Good Friday) Agreement.
† The UDR was a regiment of the British Army which was recruited locally during the Troubles in Northern Ireland. Its membership was overwhelmingly Protestant and failed to attract cross-community support. In 1992, it was merged into the newly formed Royal Irish Regiment.
‡ The status quo was that, because of the problems of intimidation in Northern Ireland, terrorist cases were heard by 'Diplock' courts, in which a judge, without a jury, sat alone.

about the status of Northern Ireland changing only by consent. Here was the 'basic equation' which both sides had long discussed. The proposed agreement, said Howe and Hurd, would bring Britain 'important gains on four fronts' – in dealings with the SDLP, with the Unionists, in security cooperation and in international image, especially in 'American goodwill'.

Including the Irish dimension would, it was believed, persuade the SDLP to participate in Northern Ireland's political institutions. Charles Powell told Mrs Thatcher she would need 'a firm undertaking from the Irish Government that John Hume and the SDLP will cooperate in moves towards devolution [after any agreement was signed]'. Unfortunately, the Irish government was in no position to give such an undertaking, so the main political premise was insecure. OD (I) nonetheless agreed that the British document be put to the Irish.

Mrs Thatcher still worried about the obvious asymmetry. As she pointed out to Hurd in June, the main British concession, '– a consultative role for the Republic – was incorporated in the agreement, but the potential benefits for the United Kingdom – improved security cooperation and SDLP participation – were not'. British fears about the Unionist reaction grew. They had been deliberately excluded from the process, whereas the SDLP had been kept informed by the Irish government. Armstrong argued that the Unionists were 'not affected' by the agreement in that the Union itself was not affected. Although worried, even Mrs Thatcher did not want to take them into her confidence. She knew the reaction she would encounter if she did, and the certainty of leaks. She also believed she could defend the Union perfectly well herself without tiresome Unionist leaders. As David Goodall put it, their exclusion was 'uncomfortable and indeed unfair'. It was bound to come back and bite the British government later.

Meeting FitzGerald at the Milan European Council at the end of June, Mrs Thatcher raised her fears about likely Unionist reaction. FitzGerald unwisely suggested that some judges in Northern Ireland did not agree with their own Lord Chief Justice, Lord Lowry, who had privately expressed his vehement opposition to joint courts a few days earlier. Mrs Thatcher brought him up smartly. These discussions, she said acidly, 'would run into acute difficulties if he purported to tell her about what went on in judges' meetings in part of the United Kingdom'. FitzGerald told her he was willing for the Republic to accede to the 1977 European Convention on the Suppression of Terrorism (ECST), which would facilitate the extradition of suspected terrorists,* but would not sign an agreement without joint

---

* This had both symbolic and practical importance, because the ECST sought to limit terrorists escaping extradition on the grounds that they had committed a 'political offence'.

courts. She refused anything beyond looking at the possibility of joint courts, repeating this 'with great emphasis'.

Now it was FitzGerald's turn to get passionate. 'Speaking with considerable emotion the Taoiseach said that he wanted the Prime Minister to understand that the Irish government and people did not want a role in Northern Ireland.' Driven by his fear of the rise of Sinn Fein, helped by Colonel Gaddafi of Libya, he spoke of the danger of Ireland 'coming under a hostile and sinister influence'. Then he made a personal appeal: 'He and the Prime Minister were the only two people able to reach an agreement.' They *must* do so.

On 25 July, the Cabinet approved the proposed Agreement with little dissent. According to Douglas Hurd, Norman Tebbit's intervention was crucial: 'He was not enthusiastic, but he dismissed the idea that we should change our policy because his wife had been crippled and he himself had been attacked. And that settled it.'

Although the two sides were now close, the ensuing period was extremely tense. There were fears of leaks, backslidings and Unionist sabotage. The Irish sought to attach more 'associated measures' to the Agreement. Mrs Thatcher wanted fewer. Pushing for concessions, Armstrong suggested she disclose to the Commons that terrorist prisoners would be released if there were 'a real and sustained reduction in the level of violence'. 'I am utterly astounded by this minute,' she wrote, refusing point-blank. Replying to Armstrong, Powell set out her criticisms sternly, but added a revealing gloss. She was saying, he wrote, that it would be 'counter-productive' to link the release of Irish prisoners to the Agreement: 'I interpret this to mean that she would not exclude some private assurance to the Irish government at a later stage.' There is no evidence that such a private assurance was given, but Powell's words suggest that, as during the hunger strikes, she may have been prepared to concede more behind the scenes than she admitted publicly.

Throughout the summer, no one was guiltier of backsliding than Mrs Thatcher herself, always anxious about what she might have conceded. 'Having read the Agreement again,' she wrote in late September, '– I fear it does <u>not</u> accurately convey our meaning. The fact is that this committee is no more than <u>consultative</u>. We have made it sound as if we have given the Republic some <u>authority</u> in our affairs. We haven't and we don't intend to.' Although the Irish role in Northern Ireland was only consultative, that word was avoided. Dublin could merely put forward 'views and proposals'.

In early September, Mrs Thatcher had reshuffled her Cabinet. Tom King now replaced Hurd at Northern Ireland. King asked her whether she was determined to push the Agreement through. 'Yes, I am,' she said. He was alarmed, when he took up the reins, to find how completely the Unionists were being ignored. On 27 September, he sent Mrs Thatcher a memo which Powell told her was 'a bit of a bombshell'. King warned that the draft Agreement 'strikes me as offering considerably more to the Irish than it does to us': they were getting 'an unprecedented foothold in the internal affairs of part of the United Kingdom'. Despite this, the Irish, wrote King in exasperation, were now saying they would not accede to the terrorism convention after all.

This stirred Mrs Thatcher. 'This could be the end of the agreement,' she wrote, 'no prospect of devolution.' She endorsed King's argument that the Agreement heavily favoured the Irish. For all this, she was not intending to cancel it. Although she liked King, he was no match for the more intellectual and experienced people like Howe and Armstrong, who now weighed in on the other side. Besides, as Powell saw it, she was 'far too far down the road to go back'. She saw King's warnings more as an opportunity to strengthen the British hand. At a meeting between Mrs Thatcher, Howe, King and Armstrong, it was agreed that they must secure Irish accession to the terrorism convention. Mrs Thatcher also insisted they must be able to make it 'crystal clear', in public, that 'the Irish Government would have no executive role in the North'. FitzGerald held fast on a firm commitment to the terrorism convention, but a compromise emerged in which the Irish 'intention' to accede echoed the British readiness to look at the 'possibility' of mixed courts. It was finally agreed that the Agreement would be signed on 15 November at Hillsborough Castle, the seat of British power in Northern Ireland.

At the end of October, the Agreement came to the Cabinet once more. This was the moment of real decision. Charles Powell reminded Mrs Thatcher of the rise of Unionist opposition, the weakening of security cooperation, the dilution of the Irish commitment to signing the ECST and the lack of any commitment from the SDLP. On the other hand, the Agreement was 'defensible': 'it concedes nothing significant, though we shall be honour-bound not to make this too obvious'. Failure to go ahead would disappoint the Americans. If the Cabinet chose not to go ahead, Powell suggested blaming the Republic's failure to accede to the ECST. But on 31 October, the Cabinet accepted the Anglo-Irish Agreement in principle, though inviting 'improvements'.

On 11 November, FitzGerald briefed the SDLP leaders on the full contents of the Agreement. The meeting ended with an emotional singing of the Irish national anthem. The mood in Ulster was quite different. Unionist newspapers and politicians sounded dire warnings. In Parliament, a day before the signing, Enoch Powell asked Mrs Thatcher, 'Does the right hon. Lady understand – if she does not yet understand she soon will – that the penalty for treachery is to fall into public contempt?' She replied that Powell's jibe was 'deeply offensive', and she meant it. But his words were telling all the same. They played on her biggest continuing anxiety about what she was doing.

Oddly, it was Bernard Ingham, normally keen that his boss should stand up to foreigners, who told her most clearly to put her heart into what was about to happen. Aware that her old friend Ian Gow was likely to quit, he urged her to 'deal firmly in public with those who resign'. 'The media', he went on, 'will be looking like hawks for signs of a lack of resolve.' At the press conference with FitzGerald, she might be asked, 'Is this a historic agreement . . . And if it doesn't mean much, why spend all the time and energy on getting it?' In her own mind, Mrs Thatcher did not have a confident answer to this question.

Early on Friday 15 November, Mrs Thatcher arrived at Hillsborough Castle via helicopter. Already, Ian Paisley and his crowd of supporters were gathering outside the gates to protest. Always soothed by domestic detail, she busied herself moving the flowers about and rearranging the furniture, making FitzGerald and Howe help her.* Then Ian Gow's letter of resignation arrived. The Agreement, he wrote, would 'prolong, and not diminish Ulster's agony'. She spoke to him at length on the telephone, but failed to dissuade him. The departure of such a close colleague on an issue of principle with which she instinctively sympathized made her even more anxious.

Those present noticed that her mood had changed. Watching from the Irish side, Michael Lillis observed 'the most intense tension': 'It sort of reminded me of the famous remark of Michael Collins [the Irish Republican leader] when he was leaving Downing Street in 1921 – "I have signed my death warrant" . . .' She signed nonetheless. The Taoiseach followed.

At the press conference, the protest of the Paisleyites beyond the gates was audible. Mrs Thatcher spoke first. She started with the rejection of violence and the mutual recognition of 'the validity of both traditions in Northern Ireland'. She placed only third in her order of priority the most controversial aspect – the intergovernmental conference which allowed the Irish government to put forward 'views and proposals' about the province. FitzGerald began with a few words in Irish, roughly translated as

* David Goodall recalled that Mrs Thatcher carefully 'checked [that] the picture on the wall behind the table at which she and the Taoiseach would sit [for the signing] had no overtly green or orange connotations' and was relieved that it was an eighteenth-century view of Windsor Castle.

'Nationalists of Northern Ireland, lift up your heads!'* Tom King considered this 'pretty insensitive', given that 'neither Margaret nor Geoffrey nor I had the slightest idea what he was saying'. Otherwise, FitzGerald stuck carefully to agreed lines. He spoke of himself and Mrs Thatcher coming to the negotiations 'with different historical perspectives and, as it were, different title deeds', but agreeing about the future. The press conference passed off peacefully.

The wider world welcomed the Anglo-Irish Agreement. President Reagan produced a statement, supported by Speaker O'Neill, offering US assistance and congratulating Mrs Thatcher and FitzGerald – 'my two good friends' – for their 'statesmanship, vision, and courage'. There was a wide welcome in the Commons too, which eventually voted for it by 473 votes to 47, though since the Labour Opposition praised the Agreement as a means of advancing a united Ireland, this was not wholly helpful to Mrs Thatcher.

The Agreement earned Garret FitzGerald his place in history but, as Mrs Thatcher told him in early December, 'You've got the glory and I've got the problems.' Among the Unionists, there was rage. Ian Paisley called for divine intervention to 'deal with the Prime Minister of our country'. 'O God,' he prayed, 'in wrath take vengeance upon this wicked, treacherous, lying woman.'†

The Almighty did not intervene as Paisley ordered Him, but He certainly did not hurry to Mrs Thatcher's aid either. All Unionist MPs resigned their parliamentary seats. Campaigning on the slogan 'ULSTER SAYS NO!', all but one won them back in the ensuing by-elections. A Unionist protest march descended on Maryfield, where the Anglo–Irish secretariat had been sited, and tore down the gates. But the security situation, though tense, never ran out of control.‡ On 3 March 1986 the Unionists ordered a 'Day of Action' in Northern Ireland: in effect, a general strike. It was widely observed.

Being the sort of person who, once she has decided something, does not budge, Mrs Thatcher was not moved by these protests, except to anger. 'I

---

* According to Michael Lillis, who drafted these words, the point FitzGerald was trying to convey was that this event should announce an end to the humiliation for successive generations of Nationalists.
† Mrs Thatcher, it appeared, did not take this to heart. Paisley might be a 'hardliner', she told President Reagan several months later, 'but not a terrorist; his bark is worse than his bite'.
‡ Mrs Thatcher received letters from wives and mothers of RUC officers who were worried about security. 'I can well understand the anguish you must feel as a mother of three police officers in the Royal Ulster Constabulary,' she replied to one, 'I have nothing but the deepest admiration for their courage and fortitude in carrying out their duties in the most difficult circumstances.'

was not prepared for the depths of the hostility,' she later recalled, 'but we get these things in Ireland.' However crossly she felt towards the Unionists, she did not feel correspondingly closer to the Nationalists. This left her effectively without allies. She had persuaded herself that the Agreement might promote devolution and stressed its provision for returning the powers gained by the Republic to a power-sharing government in Northern Ireland. None of this happened. Despite all the hopes, the SDLP did not take part in devolution or to urge its supporters to join the police or the UDR. A key premise of the Agreement fell away. Far from boosting the SDLP, the gradual effect was to strengthen the more extreme parties on both sides of the sectarian divide. In the summer of 1986, the Cabinet decided that the existing Northern Ireland Assembly was serving no useful purpose, and so no further elections were held. Far from regenerating the political life of the province, the Anglo-Irish Agreement produced stasis.

Worse, from Mrs Thatcher's point of view, was the failure of the Republic to deliver the security improvements which British officials had held up to her as the great prize. The trade-off between mixed courts and accession to the ECST fell to the ground.* Cross-border links between the RUC and the Garda Síochána (the Irish police) did not markedly improve, and she was particularly disappointed that greater intelligence cooperation did not result. As she later recalled: 'We received far better intelligence co-operation from virtually all other European countries than with the Republic.' Speaking in 2012, Michael Lillis accepted that, on security, 'we should have tried harder'. Mrs Thatcher was naturally inclined to ask whether the game was worth the candle. The scratchy chapter about the Agreement in her memoirs concluded with the words: 'In the light of this [negative] experience, it is surely time to consider an alternative approach.'

Was Mrs Thatcher too harsh in her retrospective judgement? People like Armstrong and Goodall thought so. They felt proud of their work, and admired her for the way in which, as they saw it, she had swallowed her prejudices to get the Agreement. They, and many others, saw it as the forerunner of the 'peace process' which reached its climax in the Good Friday Agreement of 1998.

In later years, Mrs Thatcher came to look upon the Anglo-Irish Agreement ever more unfavourably.† After all, it was she, more than any other

---

* The Republic did eventually ratify its accession to the ECST, but only after FitzGerald had lost office and eleven people had been killed in the Enniskillen Remembrance Day bombing of November 1987.

† This attitude found its final expression in her review of Simon Heffer's biography of Enoch Powell which appeared in 1998. 'On the matter of his [Powell's] objections to the 1985 Anglo-Irish Agreement,' she wrote, 'I now believe that his assessment was right.' She meant that

prime minister, who succeeded in overriding what pro-Nationalists called the Unionist 'veto'. She was not proud of this. Political change had been imposed on Northern Ireland from outside. In this sense, she began something which went against principles which she held dear. Charles Powell compared her regret at signing the Anglo-Irish Agreement to Queen Mary I of England's terrible sadness at the loss of Calais. 'Queen Mary spoke of having "Calais" inscribed on her heart. Mrs Thatcher will have "Anglo-Irish Agreement" inscribed on her heart.'

Where she did achieve something more positive, however, was in changing the attitudes of Irish and British governments to one another. The experience of the Thatcher–FitzGerald encounters was often bruising, but led, ultimately, to a permanent improvement in relations between their two nations. FitzGerald had been right that only he and she between them could strike a deal. She saw this and acted on it bravely. The Agreement was not the breakthrough of which FitzGerald dreamt, but it was a remarkable moment in the history of Britain and Ireland.

There is another way of looking at the story of the Anglo-Irish Agreement. Ignore, for a moment, the content, and instead study its methods. By doing so, one sees that the essential aim of both the British and Irish official machines was to persuade Mrs Thatcher into doing what she did not want to do. As FitzGerald recalled in retirement, 'Ultimately it was not a negotiation. Ultimately everybody was convinced that something should be done. "How do you persuade the Prime Minister?" was the question.' Geoffrey Howe, who in his memoirs wrote of the Taoiseach's 'statesmanship' in contrast to Mrs Thatcher's 'intemperance', took a similar view. Those involved in the Armstrong–Nally process were desperate for an agreement in a way that she never was. Between them, they created a structure which was bound to frustrate her instinctive beliefs.

As with many subjects – Rhodesia, Hong Kong, some aspects of the Cold War, the EEC – some of the cleverest men in the realm had real difficulty in understanding that the Prime Minister truly did not share their belief in internationalism and consensus or their instinctive aversion to asserting the claims of Britishness. They went to great lengths to oppose what they saw as her mistaken will. More often than not, they prevailed. It would be absurd, however, to argue that Mrs Thatcher was their prisoner, and paranoid to suggest that they cheated her. She was too formidable for that. As Charles Powell put it, 'They were all plotting to persuade her. She was

---

Powell's criticisms of the Agreement for its encroachment on British sovereignty were well founded.

tugged along. But she knew what it was about.' Why, then, did she do it? Surely because, although she never liked what was being proposed, she lacked the knowledge and backing to frame an alternative. She felt she had to do *something*. The subject did not matter to her so much that she was prepared to fight to what would certainly have been a bitter end.

19
Poll tax; Single European Act
'How dare they! We saved all their necks in the war'

Because Mrs Thatcher believed in property, she did not like property taxes. Her long quest to get rid of them came to fruition in her second term. The replacement, which she put into practice in her third term, proved the most unpopular domestic measure of her premiership. Although she adamantly refused to use the name, it became notorious as the 'poll tax'.

Mrs Thatcher had promised to abolish the rates, the property taxes that funded local government, as early as 1974. She disliked the rates levied on businesses because they were taxation without representation. She loathed domestic rates because, by targeting property owners, they broke the link between those voting and those paying the tax. Those who paid were often natural Conservative supporters. Left-wing councils, many of whose votes came from non-payers, could thus fund their profligacy almost with immunity.

Alongside the rates, local government spending was funded by the Rate Support Grant (RSG) provided by central government. By 1979, this accounted for over 60 per cent of local spending. Not only did the rates offer left-wing councils no incentive to curb their expenditure, but higher spending often led to higher grants from Whitehall. With lower government spending the responsibility of the Treasury, in financial terms, overspending could significantly increase the PSBR, undermining the government's broader discipline on public expenditure. Mrs Thatcher thus hated rates for both ideological and political reasons. It was her dream to abolish them.

The 1983 Tory manifesto, however, promised no such thing. Its pledges on local government were limited to legislation to 'curb excessive and irresponsible rate increases by high-spending councils' ('rate-capping') and the abolition of the Greater London Council and the metropolitan counties.*

---

* These overarching bodies – particularly the GLC – had relatively few duties: the real work was done by the London boroughs and the city councils.

More fundamental reform was not offered. 'I'd love to know what she wants to *do* with local government,' Terry Heiser, the Deputy Secretary at the Department of the Environment (which had responsibility for local government), said to Stephen Sherbourne shortly after the 1983 election victory. Sherbourne did not know the answer.

Nor, perhaps, did Mrs Thatcher herself. She focused on the lack of relationship between who votes and who pays. If only local government could be largely self-financing (as late as the early 1960s, central government had funded only about 35 per cent of its spending), and if only most voters understood the cost because they paid it, sanity would prevail, and Conservative votes would accumulate. These truths seemed so simple to her that she found the complications of reaching the happy state she sought intensely frustrating.

The manifesto policies on local government were scarcely more tractable to implement than the replacement of rates themselves. Except for a few bold reformers, mainly in London, Conservatives in local government were conservative. They were as proud as Labour about extracting money from Whitehall for local purposes and resisted reform accordingly. As for the GLC abolition, to many it just did not feel right. Much as they disliked Ken Livingstone, the charismatic and popular far-left Labour GLC leader, many Tories had constitutional objections. Others – more pragmatic and pessimistic – simply foresaw too much trouble from local government reform. This, in essence, was Willie Whitelaw's position. Before the 1983 election, Whitelaw had struggled with the issue with little success (see p. 339). From his new perch leading the House of Lords, he worried about the practicalities involved. Oliver Letwin, her main Policy Unit adviser on local government, recalled a meeting to discuss whether to send government commissioners into Liverpool, which was deliberately proposing to set an illegal budget. 'Well, Margaret,' said Whitelaw, 'of course you can send commissioners in. Of course you can. But how will you get them OUT?' His pragmatic argument prevailed in that case, but more generally it did not. Central government started to go in, often without safeguarding its passage back.

Whitelaw was so worried that he explicitly (though not, of course, publicly) opposed Mrs Thatcher's policy. In February 1984, shaken by his struggles to get the privatization of British Telecom through the Lords, he told her that he feared that the proposals for rate-capping and GLC abolition 'might be defective'. She listened – she always treated Whitelaw respectfully – but did not back down. Nonetheless, she tacitly acknowledged the amount of political and policy work still needed and began to rely more heavily on her Policy Unit to drive change through. According to her Treasury private secretary, Michael Scholar, she was 'in a bullying mood with ministers'.

Her mood was not improved by the growth of revolts against the proposed rate-capping. Liverpool's Labour City Council, now controlled by the hard-left Militant Tendency,* announced an unlawful budget plan, claiming that central government denied them the money they needed to fulfil their election promises. As they put it: 'It is better to break the law than break the poor.' Mrs Thatcher was determined to resist these actions, not only for the sake of financial control, but, more importantly, because she considered them part of the extra-parliamentary, semi-revolutionary opposition to her government that acquired sharp focus with the onset of the miners' strike in March 1984.

As for abolishing the GLC, Livingstone advanced his resistance under the slogan 'Say No To No Say'. The media consensus was that the government was being 'outspent, out-sloganised and out-advertised'. In June, it was defeated in the Lords on the 'Paving' Bill for GLC abolition. It looked bad for Mrs Thatcher that she was abolishing something for which people had voted and trying to remove from office those elected to it.† The arrangements to supersede the GLC had yet to be worked out. Bernard Ingham feared that the government was 'losing out with the public; that the devil has all the best tunes'.

Reconvening after her August break, Mrs Thatcher tried to grip the problem. In early September, Patrick Jenkin, the Environment Secretary, urged her to order a review of the whole system of local government finance. She was not terribly pleased, noting that from two previous reviews, 'only the most modest of mice had emerged'. John Redwood advised that it would be disastrous if yet another review recommended no change. 'Of all the options on offer,' he wrote, 'some kind of poll tax which is paid by every elector is the most likely to meet the requirements of accountability and visibility.' There is no evidence that Mrs Thatcher was immediately taken with this suggestion.

At a meeting of ministers in September, Nigel Lawson argued strongly

---

* The Militant Tendency was a long-standing Trotskyist entry group in the Labour movement. Although, from 1982, it was forbidden to affiliate to Labour, it played an important subversive role in the party, particularly in local government, for most of the 1980s. *Militant* was the name of its journal, allowing members to say, when challenged, '*Militant* is not an organization: it's a newspaper.' This, said Ken Livingstone, who, despite his own left-wing views, hated Militant's ideological rigidity, was 'always a lie'.

† Mrs Thatcher had originally sought to keep elected councillors in post after abolition, but had eventually let herself be persuaded by Patrick Jenkin's unpolitical arguments about efficiency.

against another review. As Chancellor, he disliked major tax reform not led by him. In his view, the focus should be on 'improving the working of existing arrangements where they were most inequitable'. Looking for the consensus which, despite her rhetoric, she often sought when in a tight spot, Mrs Thatcher allowed Jenkin his review, but – in a nod to Lawson – insisted it concentrate on 'serious inequities'. Jenkin could announce it at the upcoming party conference, but it should not be called a review – the preferred term was 'studies in the field' – and there should be no fanfare.

In the aftermath of the Brighton bomb, Jenkin's announcement was little noticed. The original draft of Mrs Thatcher's set-piece speech had planned to link local authority extremism to the violence and intimidation of the miners' strike. It warned of 'high spending Town Halls', where 'the new left seeks to use Councils to burst apart our carefully established programme for rational economic recovery', and directly quoted Livingstone and named Labour MPs who seemed to condone law-breaking and were ready to 'defy Parliament'. After the bomb, however, she cut this language, doing little more than reiterating the planned abolition of the GLC and the mets. But while the IRA's carnage had made her change her partisan tone, it strengthened, if anything, her determination to defeat what she saw as a coalition against freedom.*

At the end of October, those most closely involved in Jenkin's field studies – William Waldegrave, junior minister at the Department of the Environment, Terry Heiser, Letwin and Andrew Turnbull, Mrs Thatcher's Treasury private secretary – gathered at Chequers to give her a 'teach-in' (the phrase used) on local government finance. Waldegrave persuaded her to set up an independent team to propose solutions, headed by Lord Rothschild, formerly head of Heath's Central Policy Review Staff. Rothschild's involvement, Waldegrave hoped, would provide the clout which, as a junior minister, he lacked.† Mrs Thatcher 'liked Victor being a scientist', Waldegrave recalled, 'and she liked him being a Rothschild'. She invited Rothschild to give the 'whole vexed subject of local government finance ... a really fresh look': 'We need sharp advice from the outside.' Rothschild accepted. He loved what is nowadays called 'thinking outside the box'. Always excited by bright ideas, Letwin was delighted by the Rothschild

---

* Indeed, in her Carlton Lecture at the end of November, Mrs Thatcher advanced points she had removed from her Brighton speech: 'At the one end of the spectrum are the terrorist gangs within our borders, and the terrorist states which finance them and arm them. At the other are the Hard Left operating inside our system, conspiring to use union power and the apparatus of local government to break, defy and subvert the law.'

† Waldegrave had worked for Rothschild at the CPRS and was fond of him. He had, at one time, been engaged to marry Rothschild's daughter Victoria.

world in which clever people bathed difficult problems in the light of reason. Mrs Thatcher relied heavily on the twenty-eight-year-old Letwin. 'Because I was learning on the job,' he recalled, 'so was she.'

The politics of local government now grew hotter. In mid-November, Letwin warned her that 'The rate-capping revolt is just about to begin in earnest; but there has not yet been a clear statement of Government policy. Experience with the miners' strike shows that a clear line needs to be established from the start.' The tactic he urged was 'brinkmanship': 'If services break down, do nothing for as long as possible, explaining constantly that the council has the remedy in its own hands'.*

On New Year's Day 1985, Lord Rothschild wrote Mrs Thatcher a typically challenging letter complaining of the 'complexity of the arrangements' in local government finance. 'Has the time not come for the Prime Minister to say "Stop it"? ... A new and ruthless broom is needed.' It was exactly as a new broom, and a ruthless one at that, that 'Maggie', the housewife-superstar, liked to see herself. Kenneth Baker, much more political than his senior, Patrick Jenkin, also pushed a message of urgency. Originally a Heathite, he had started to prosper under Mrs Thatcher because of two qualities which she liked: as Sherbourne put it, he was 'hugely enthusiastic and positive' about whatever he was doing, and he 'carried his ministerial responsibilities lightly'. He and Waldegrave, Sherbourne continued, were 'terribly keen to curry favour with the Prime Minister'. Baker's way of doing this was to incite her to battle. Tapping into what he called her 'Grantham-speak', he warned that the hard left 'really do hope that the Government can be brought down by widespread action in the inner cities'. Local government policy must be set within this political context.

At the same time, a northern front opened up. Because of its different legal framework, Scotland was now compelled to have a rating revaluation.† In February 1985, Mrs Thatcher was warned this would lead to a 170 per cent increase in domestic rateable values: only 20 per cent of Scottish householders, most of whom were Conservatives, were liable to pay full rates. Horrified by the political implications, she sought delay. But, as the Scottish Secretary, George Younger, explained, this was not in her power. The 'only course', he claimed, was for the Treasury to hand over £64 million, allowing Scottish councils to halve the domestic rate increases. The Treasury resisted, and eventually Younger was forced to

---

* This approach became known as the doctrine of 'quarter past twelve'.
† England and Wales were overdue for such a revaluation, but were freer, in law, to postpone. Michael Heseltine, as Environment Secretary, had done this. So had Patrick Jenkin, at Mrs Thatcher's insistence.

settle for £38.5 million. The politics looked awful for the Scottish Tories. Mrs Thatcher was exasperated that this crisis had broken without warning. 'It is pretty pathetic,' she wrote on a begging letter from Younger, referring to the money from the Treasury, 'but Scotland must carry the can for not remedying the situation in time.' She understood, however, that she would have to carry the can elsewhere in the United Kingdom if the broader problem could not be remedied fast. This lent urgency to the upcoming meeting of the Waldegrave–Rothschild studies team. She was yearning for a big idea. Rothschild and his band of bright young brains wanted to oblige. Even more important, perhaps, was Willie Whitelaw. Sensing looming disaster in the wake of revaluation, he now cast aside his habitual dislike of radical reform. The man normally most likely to persuade Mrs Thatcher to hold back was ardent for change.*

The meeting was held at Chequers on Sunday 31 March 1985. The most significant absentee was Nigel Lawson. 'William [Waldegrave] has done a first-rate job,' Redwood and Letwin minuted Mrs Thatcher beforehand. They agreed with him that 'rates should be replaced by [a] poll tax'. While raising plenty of questions, they argued strongly that she should seize the moment: 'We believe that this review offers the only real hope of winning back the confidence of the Party. We also believe that it offers the prospect of a lasting change for the better in local Government. After years of half-remedies, you should now attempt a fundamental reform on the lines proposed.'

At the meeting, Waldegrave explained that the proposed solution included 'abolishing domestic rates and replacing them with a local residents' or community charge,† falling equally on all adults in each local area. This would achieve the objective of accountability 'better than any alternative tax'. There would need to be rebates for those on low incomes, 'but not such as to insulate them from increases in the community charge by high-spending councils'. The likely cost of the charge per head per year was guessed to be £50. Some remembered him ending with a flourish: 'So, Prime Minister, you will have succeeded in abolishing the rates.' Mrs Thatcher was 'purring at all this', recalled Letwin. She had 'a weak spot for Fellows of All Souls'.‡

---

* Whitelaw was greatly respected by both officials and ministers for his shrewdness. This led Cabinet committee colleagues to disbelieve his self-deprecation when he told them he did not understand the complex system of rates and grants in Scotland. They gradually realized that he was telling the truth. Whitelaw was not alone in his incomprehension.

† The word 'charge' was favoured by supporters of reform, including Mrs Thatcher, because it reflected the costs of local government to those who used its services, rather than being a 'tax' for general purposes. Nigel Lawson regarded this argument as 'completely bogus'.

‡ Waldegrave had been a Fellow of All Souls College, Oxford, since 1971.

Robin Butler remembered this meeting as 'the decisive moment'. Mrs Thatcher formally summed up in favour of reform. The aim now was to produce 'a predominantly White Paper with some green edges' in early autumn if the Cabinet agreed.* 'Some material' would be slipped to George Younger so he could give a little comfort to the annual Scottish Conservative Party conference in May.

Mrs Thatcher wrote to Lord Rothschild to thank him: 'I think we have the best opportunity for a long time to find a lasting solution to this perennial but increasingly acute problem.' She asked him to 'keep a fatherly eye on the infant's development'.

There had been little political discussion at Chequers of the war with the hard left, but the hopeful mood was closely related to the collapse of the miners' strike. Very shortly after this, the GLC decided not to set an illegal rate. It seemed that the left was crumbling. Having achieved what no previous Conservative prime minister had managed, Mrs Thatcher had become very difficult for colleagues to gainsay.

Shortly after the Chequers meeting, Rothschild wrote to Butler: 'The community charge is, I believe, a winner. But I am nervous lest it is accidentally or deliberately misinterpreted, for example: "Tories hit the poor once again . . ."' The question was whether the charge could 'avoid hardships and still collect what is necessary'. 'Only the figures', he went on, 'can provide the answers . . . and as, for some reason beyond my comprehension, they do not exist, they will have to be got.'

Rothschild had put his finger on a key point which was to dog the development of the poll tax. Without figures, it was impossible to calculate who would gain and who would lose. On such calculations would hang the success of the entire policy. Yet because the change was so complete, coming up with accurate figures proved all but impossible. In May, officials at the Department of the Environment predicted that 7,450,000 people would lose from the proposed reforms and that 9,250,000 would gain. Given the natural propensity of losers to make much more noise than those who gain, this figure was immediately recognized as dangerous.† Redwood and Letwin warned Mrs Thatcher that unless such problems could be 'sorted out this reform is unattractive'. Yet how *could* they be? The Cabinet Office

---

* A Green Paper is the Whitehall phrase for an official document which sets out government plans for a piece of legislation in an early version, offering them for consultation. A White Paper is the final version of the plans before they take actual legislative form.
† The calculations suggested that people living in inner London or parts of the northern industrial areas would suffer the most, especially those earning between £5,000 and £12,000 per year, the middle-income bracket at that time.

now estimated the poll tax at an average of £160 per year, over three times the figure imagined just six weeks earlier.

Nigel Lawson now warned of the 'horrifying picture' emerging from the data. 'A pensioner couple in inner London', he wrote, 'could find themselves paying 22 per cent of their net income in poll tax, whereas a better off couple in the suburbs would pay only 1 per cent.' Worse, local authorities 'would seize the opportunity to bump up their spending and revenue and blame it all on the imposition by the government of an alien system of taxation'. In brief, he considered the poll tax proposal 'completely unworkable and politically catastrophic'. He felt accountability could be improved by limiting rate rebates rather than by inventing a new tax.

It is a puzzle that Lawson's objections – trenchant even by his standards – should not have made more impact.* For the man in charge of the nation's money to be so opposed to a new tax was a big thing. At Mrs Thatcher's request, he worked up his own reform of rates which suggested basing them on capital values rather than putative rental ones, but did not throw himself into the fight. Since local tax reform bore no relation to his own reforms, he was, he said later, 'very happy' if it was 'not getting anywhere'.

Lawson felt he 'had no personal reason for arguing' about the poll tax and, as he began to fall out with Mrs Thatcher over broader aspects of economic policy (see Chapter 20), could not afford to open up another front. Those involved believed that if she had felt able to trust Lawson, many errors would have been avoided. For her part, Mrs Thatcher was acutely conscious that this was a tax issue – the only one, in fact – where she did not have to defer to the Treasury. Although she naturally listened to Lawson attentively, this was her subject, not his.

This policy debate played out against growing political desperation in Scotland. George Younger was now determined to push ahead with the poll tax at the Scottish Party Conference in May. Stephen Sherbourne advised Mrs Thatcher against his haste, primarily because there was still no agreement on what form the poll tax might take. Although sympathetic to this, she did authorize Younger to tell the conference that 'the status quo is not an option'. The political impetus was now becoming hard to stop. The desperately unpopular rate revaluation bearing down on Scotland could not be delayed indefinitely for England and Wales. A nationwide poll tax looked ever more likely.

Over the summer of 1985, there was some success in the government's rate-capping battles against councils controlled by the extreme left. In early

---

* The press did later run some stories that the Chancellor did not support the poll tax. But they did not attract much attention. Internal discipline kept the disagreement subterranean.

September, Liverpool, having failed to frighten the government into intervening by operating a 'deficit budget', found itself obliged to put its entire council staff on three months' notice. Some of the redundancy notices had to be delivered by taxi to reach their recipients within the legal time limit. In early October, Liverpool's famously left-wing Anglican and Roman Catholic bishops, David Sheppard and Derek Worlock, furious with the extremists, wrote an article in *The Times* headlined 'Stand Up to Liverpool's Militants'. Mrs Thatcher was winning what Letwin called the 'war of nerves'.

The hard left's rate-capping revolt deeply embarrassed the Labour leadership. In his speech to his annual party conference in October, Neil Kinnock aimed his fire at his own party's extremists. Taking the example of Liverpool, he railed against 'the grotesque chaos of a Labour council – a <u>Labour</u> council! – hiring taxis to scuttle round a city handing out redundancy notices to its own workers'. He was duly heckled by Militant and widely cheered in the country. By turning on his internal foes, however, Kinnock ensured that resistance to the Tories' local government reforms was seen as merely a left-wing cause. Not wishing to empower the militant left, Kinnock felt compelled to give Mrs Thatcher an almost free pass.

In mid-September, Redwood and Letwin advised Mrs Thatcher that Lawson's ideas for rate reform would be 'politically suicidal'. Capital valuations as the basis for rates would be seen by 'your supporters . . . as a wealth tax'. Yet the notion of a part-property tax remained popular because a poll tax alone would be a 'regressive' measure.* 'If I'm on *Question Time*,' Baker was heard to protest, 'and I'm asked, "Why do the Duke and the dustman have to pay the same?", there's no answer.' With the dustman in mind, Baker and Waldegrave had developed proposals that retained some property tax element. From the Policy Unit, Letwin and Redwood were now seriously worried about moving to a pure residence charge (or poll tax), which would, judged Letwin, produce 'too many big losers'. On the other hand, a mixed tax would be seen as two taxes. This could be unpopular and would undermine the beautiful simplicity of the 'residence charge'.† For a way out of this dilemma, the government looked to Scotland. As Letwin briefed Mrs Thatcher, George Younger 'is clearly extremely keen to use Scotland as a trail-blazer for the pure residence

---

* A tax is 'progressive' if the proportion of tax paid rises as the income rises, 'regressive' if the proportion decreases. These are not terms of praise or blame (necessarily), simply of fiscal description.

† The term 'residence charge' (or 'resident's charge' or 'residents' charge') was, at this stage, still competing with 'community charge'.

charge ... If the Scottish experiment worked, it could make a pure residence charge look sensible rather than extreme.'*

The eventual compromise between those who wanted the mixture of taxes, and the poll tax purists, was a transitional scheme, 'dual running'. Part of the rates would be replaced by a community charge. The remainder would never increase and would gradually wither away. It was vital, Letwin argued, with supportive double underlining from Mrs Thatcher, that the change be presented as 'a phased <u>replacement</u> of <u>rates</u> by the community charge'. There would be little point in the whole exercise if she could not say she was getting rid of the rates.

The difficulty at the heart of the new tax remained, however. On the same day as Letwin was crying 'Forward!', using Scotland as the battering ram, Brian Unwin, a senior Cabinet Office official, expressed it thus to Mrs Thatcher:

> There is a fundamental problem that if local accountability is to be effective the consequences of excessive spending must be painful for the electorate. Moreover, if the tax base is to be expanded, some people will have to pay who have not done so before. The local charge will therefore almost by definition have to be unpopular, at least in high-spending areas.

When confronted with this point in later years, Oliver Letwin said, 'That was the idea!' The strong argument of principle was hard to reconcile with the search for electoral popularity which drove the longing to abolish the rates.

None of this dampened support among senior ministers. Even the cautious Whitelaw was 'thoroughly supportive'. Norman Tebbit said, 'At last we're doing something for our own people.' Only Michael Heseltine and Nigel Lawson were full-throatedly opposed. The former, however, was too deeply embroiled in the Westland affair to dwell on the poll tax (see p. 505). The latter was rather sullen. 'I'm going to call these the Waldegrave reforms,' Lawson told the young minister with baleful humour.

At the turn of the year, Letwin urged Mrs Thatcher to push the Green Paper 'through Cabinet and out into the world as soon as possible – otherwise, the rats will start nibbling'. She now considered the decision of principle made. She was concerned that 'too extensive a discussion' at Cabinet 'would give an opportunity for sceptics to question the need for

---

* Thus began the idea that Scotland might be what critics later called the 'guinea pig' for the poll tax. It is worth bearing in mind, however, that a guinea pig has no say about experiments conducted on him. Scotland, on the other hand – as judged by public opinion at the time – was fiercely hostile to increased rates and eagerly demanding a different form of local taxation.

any reform at all'. She wanted the Green Paper as White as possible. She wanted to get on.

On 9 January 1986, the Cabinet approved the Green Paper which launched the community charge. By a strange stroke of fate, this was the meeting at which Michael Heseltine stormed out over Westland and resigned. The community charge was the first substantial item of business after he had left the room. The discussion by the shell-shocked gathering contained several passages where the 'rats', in Letwin's description, did manage a bit of nibbling. According to Robert Armstrong's scribbled record, the Energy Secretary, Peter Walker, was the most vehement.* 'I don't think this is going to be positively attractive – the opposite.' Noting that more than half of ratepayers would pay more than before, he warned: 'The disadvantaged will howl; the advantaged will keep quiet.' In the meeting, Nigel Lawson offered little opposition, confining himself to short, secondary points.

While arguing strongly in favour of the proposals, Kenneth Baker expressed doubts about the rush in Scotland. But George Younger insisted on legislation before the next election so that the community charge could begin there on 1 April 1989. Noting the 'full weight of Scottish feeling', Whitelaw backed Younger. If wise old Willie was for pressing forward, and Mrs Thatcher was firmly in favour, who could hold the line against them? The poll tax – as they were never allowed to call it – was agreed.

Given the weakness of Mrs Thatcher's political position after Westland, it is striking how little trouble from colleagues she encountered over the poll tax. The Green Paper, *Paying for Local Government*, was published the day after she had survived the last full-scale parliamentary assault over Westland. The fact that the new arrangements would not apply until 1989 in Scotland and 1990 in England and Wales, soothed anxieties. The parliamentary reception, on the Tory side, was mostly good. Baker did record, however, that Lawson reached over to him in the Chamber and whispered: 'It will be her King Charles's head.'†

Public attention now reverted to the GLC, which was abolished on 31 March 1986. This appeared to be a straightforward triumph for Mrs Thatcher. With the collapse of the miners' strike and the rate-capping revolts, Livingstone's extra-parliamentary campaign to bring down the

---

* Critics on at least some points included Howe, Joseph, Hurd, Brittan, Biffen, John MacGregor (by this time the Chief Secretary to the Treasury).

† Lawson, untypically, was muddling his reference. 'King Charles's head' is a phrase from Charles Dickens's *David Copperfield*. The amiable Mr Dick has a mental quirk which always returns his conversation to the subject of King Charles's head. Lawson seems to have used the phrase to suggest her fatal flaw. Perhaps he meant 'Achilles heel'.

Thatcher government had completely failed. Her victory, however, was perhaps too complete. Livingstone had been a bogeyman so long as he seemed on top, but sympathy turned his way at the idea that an elected body could be abolished by a government that happened to dislike its political complexion.

The problems of the poll tax remained. The essential difficulty was that the pure, beautiful idea of leaving local government alone to do the right thing when confronted by newly empowered electors was constantly being compromised. Even with enhanced accountability, Mrs Thatcher worried that left-wing councils would find ways of making trouble: 'indeed,' she wrote in her memoirs, 'before the end I would find myself pressing for much more extensive community charge capping than was ever envisaged for the rates'. As so often, she was right in her instinct about what was politically likely. She was less attentive to the illogic in her own policy.

Although the community charge was intended to be decentralizing, other, related measures were intended to centralize. The business rate was now to be made uniform and set centrally. This offered Whitehall the temptation to increase the burdens on business. Indeed, Nicholas Ridley, Environment Secretary from May 1986, was sufficiently concerned about the likely level of the community charge, that he looked to the business rate to bear as much of the strain as possible. The problems of which voters should have to pay the community charge and how they could be compelled were manifold. 'The virtue of the community charge', Ridley wrote, 'is its universality.' But that was its vice as well. It did not fit all cases and could not easily be collected from all its victims. With Scotland pressing ahead first, Michael Ancram, the Scottish Local Government Minister, argued for reductions for pensioners and exemptions for students and most non-working wives. It was the first time many of this last group had been directly taxed, and they would feel ill-used. The Treasury, however, was unsympathetic and such objections were overruled.

On 26 November, the Bill to abolish domestic rates in Scotland was introduced in Parliament. It advanced without difficulties. Such controversy as there was concerned the transitional period. So great were pressures to be rid of the rates that, in February 1987, Malcolm Rifkind, by now Scottish Secretary, decided to do away with dual running. The Scottish poll tax would come into full operation on 1 April 1989. This effectively decided matters. Once the poll tax had been introduced in Scotland, failure to proceed in England and Wales would have been a humiliating defeat. The government felt pleased that the ground for the general election was now prepared. It saw the new tax as a vote-winner.

*

The poll tax was not created on a whim of Margaret Thatcher, although it would never have happened without the force of her will. It was a serious, long-considered attempt to get to grips with several genuine problems – distorted property taxes and central grants, lack of local accountability, left-wing profligacy and extremism. Although it drew heavily on ideas from 'irregulars', it was fully worked through by the Civil Service machine: 'We did it so carefully, with *so* many papers,' recalled Terry Heiser. At least three problems, however, were observable in the early stages and never resolved.

The first was extreme complication. No one, however brilliant, fully understood what was being done. The second was a defect in the principle itself. What, exactly, was the justification for everyone paying the same? 'It is the same as a loaf of bread,' went the argument, '– you pay the same regardless of whether you are rich or poor.' This was related to the idea that councils should be accountable to all voters. But the loaf analogy did not really work. Customers can pay different prices for bread and buy more or fewer loaves. Besides, the poll tax cost much more than a loaf of bread and, in matters of tax, the amount is crucial. The third problem lay with Mrs Thatcher herself. As Sherbourne put it, 'It was the beginning of her losing touch with people, with a real electoral base.'

Perhaps she was too driven by anger that her 'promise' to abolish the rates had been so long unfulfilled. Ingham reported to her a sense from the lobby that the poll tax was fundamentally unfair. Quoting from the hymn 'All Things Bright and Beautiful', he emphasized the difference between 'the rich man in his castle' and the 'poor man at his gate'. Mrs Thatcher 'exploded'. 'The rich man in his castle is already paying through the nose in tax!' she exclaimed. Above all, 'she thought there *had* to be democratic control of local spending'. So strongly did she believe this that she did not think through the consequences.

From her first day in office, Mrs Thatcher had been arguing that Britain should get 'our money' back from the European Community. What had begun, in 1973, as a net contribution of £102 million had grown to £947 million by 1979. But for the temporary solutions negotiated during her first term, it would have increased further. She refused to allow the Community to embark on new endeavours until what she considered this gross imbalance had been rectified. More than five years later, on 26 June 1984, she finally succeeded. At the European Council in Fontainebleau, she secured a budgetary rebate of 66 per cent of the net British contribution. There would be no more *ad hoc* deals. It was settled.

At the previous Council, in Brussels that March, the stalemate had become almost unbearable. 'Everyone was furious with Margaret Thatcher,'

Kohl later wrote, 'François Mitterrand ... whispered to me at a meal, "I have had just about enough of these endless discussions ... I think we should agree between ourselves that we will offer her nothing, nothing, nothing."' Mitterrand and Kohl resolved to work for a final result at Fontainebleau. Meeting Kohl at Chequers on 2 May, Mrs Thatcher hinted that she, too, was ready to strike a deal. Britain did not lack loyalty to Europe: 'We were passionate Europeans,' she said. 'We joined the Community so that the conflicts that had occurred in the past could not recur in the future.' The 'big three' – Kohl, Mitterrand and Thatcher – were currently in strong electoral positions, she pointed out. Let them unite over a budget settlement and begin a new phase in the Community's development.

In her own, handwritten account of Fontainebleau, Mrs Thatcher recorded arriving unsure of what was likely to happen.* The choice for Mitterrand, she believed, lay between '1 – a solution & ∴ a triumph for France in the chair'† and '2 – a failure – all due to Britain!' She put forward her budget proposal, which was remitted to the foreign ministers for further study. She noticed that rather than getting down to work, the ministers, led by their French host Claude Cheysson, milled about outdoors drinking coffee and swapping funny stories. 'How dare they!' she exclaimed. 'We saved all their necks in the war.' Her own officials, Robin Renwick and David Williamson, chose this perilous moment to reveal to her that they had already been in secret negotiations with the French over the shape of a deal. Concerned more with 'Thatcher handling' than beating down the French, they left the actual percentage on which Britain would settle blank so that she could feel she had decided it: 'She glared, but gave us silent permission.' At 11.30 p.m., after dinner, Cheysson brought the heads of government the result of the foreign ministers' deliberations. It proposed a refund so low that Mrs Thatcher found it insulting: 'I was in despair and said we had never been treated fairly and if that was the best they had to offer Fontainebleau would be a disaster.'

Mrs Thatcher had arrived demanding a 70 per cent rebate, but the next day she told Kohl she would settle for two-thirds. Kohl countered with 65 per cent. As he recalled it, she 'became very vehement towards me. In essence, she said that the Federal Republic had to support Great Britain on the grounds that there were British soldiers stationed in our country.'

---

* The Fontainebleau European Council meeting was one of the few events in Mrs Thatcher's career as Prime Minister of which she wrote a personal account. Her desire to record her recollections probably reflected both her pleasure at ending the long quarrel and anxiety that Eurosceptic critics might think she had given too much away.
† The rotating six-month EEC presidency currently rested with France.

She then called a 'time out' to consult her officials. David Williamson said to Michael Butler, who was tasked with 'Thatcher handling', 'Tell her she's got to settle now,' but Butler wanted her to have the thought unprompted. 'I think we've almost got as much as we can,' she said, to his great relief, adding, 'If I've got it to 65 per cent, I can add one more per cent.' Returning to the full session, she asked for this, and Mitterrand conceded it with gallantry: 'Of course, Madame Prime Minister, you must have it.' The Germans did not dare gainsay the French presidency. Mrs Thatcher had secured what she called the 'essential points' – not only the percentage rebate, but acceptance that the deal would 'last as long as the problem'.

Fontainebleau was the sort of deal that delights diplomats. According to official Treasury figures, by 2015, it had saved Britain £78 billion. Robin Renwick claimed it as 'the most valuable financial agreement this country *ever* negotiated'. There were, however, other ways of looking at it. Hubert Védrine, Mitterrand's right-hand man, regarded it as the moment when the Kohl–Mitterrand axis forced Mrs Thatcher to accept compromise. Fontainebleau was *'le point de depart'* for their active alliance to shape the future of Europe. As part of the deal, Britain had agreed to a higher Community budget (the increase from 1 per cent to 1.4 per cent VAT receipts to fund the Community's 'own resources'). Now they could get on with European integration, whether she liked it or not. Mitterrand later told Jacques Attali that he had been surprised to see her 'almost in tears' when she made the deal.

Allowing for national exaggeration on both sides, it is fair to say that Fontainebleau was, indeed, a good financial deal for Britain. Mrs Thatcher had proved the superior of all her counterparts in knowledge, argumentative skill, force of personality and persistence, though not in diplomatic finesse. But French officials were not wrong to detect her anxieties about whether she had really got what she wanted. She had sought a higher percentage than she achieved.* Her Eurosceptic critics at home charged that Fontainebleau won a financial benefit at the cost of higher European expenditure, no reform of the CAP and further European integration. As the *Spectator* put it, she had 'passed up the only chance of real change by agreeing, before she had to, to more than she had to'. Detecting her

---

* Documents show that the 66 per cent which pleased officials so much when they reached it was only their minimum aim at Fontainebleau. 'The real crux', wrote David Williamson to Geoffrey Howe, just before the Council, '... is how far, if at all, we can get them above the refund of the two-thirds of the VAT share/expenditure gap.'

anxiety, Bernard Ingham told her she 'must present a successful outcome as a success and not grudgingly'. She obeyed, but her doubts lingered.

Sceptical though she was about closer European political links, Mrs Thatcher was interested in physical ones.* In 1981, through the ever-persuasive recommendation of Ian Gow, she was introduced to a scheme to link Britain and France dreamt up by Ian MacGregor, whom she had made Chairman of the British Steel the previous year. MacGregor was leading a group called EuroRoute, who rejected the traditional idea of a tunnel bored under the Channel in favour of a 'combined viaduct bridge and immersed tube for road and rail'. MacGregor's ambitions accorded with Mrs Thatcher's ideology, which feared exclusive reliance on rail because it was both nationalized and wholly unionized. The prevailing view of the relevant government departments was that a pure rail link was better. Others were sceptical of the project altogether. The Trade Secretary, John Biffen, reminded colleagues of the vast losses made on the Anglo-French Concorde aeroplane and the danger of being 'generally at the mercy of the French'.

Mrs Thatcher was cautious but, because of Mitterrand's helpful attitude during the Falklands War, she agreed with the Foreign Office that Britain should find 'a way of keeping the French in play and out of mischief'. So when she saw Mitterrand's Prime Minister, Pierre Mauroy, in May 1982, and he expounded his Channel vision, she agreed with him: 'She too harboured a dream of a fixed link.'† But she stressed that the private sector should take the initiative.

For quite some time, nothing happened. The situation had given rise to a private–public Catch-22. Several private promoters were now ready to push their case but could not do so without any government lead. The turning point came only during the Anglo–French summit in Paris in November 1984. Perhaps intoxicated by Mitterrand's Gallic charm, for which he was famed, Mrs Thatcher suddenly became animated about the fixed link. 'It would be nice to have something exciting getting under way,' she told her officials. 'I don't want the rail tunnel, I want EuroRoute.' Bernard Ingham recalled passing 'a note to Robin Butler which said: "When did this conversion on the road to Damascus take place?" "About 17 minutes ago,"

---

* Since the early 1800s, the idea of an underwater tunnel linking Britain with France had been promoted by enthusiasts on both sides of the English Channel. After the Second World War, the British and French governments began to take it more seriously. In 1964, a joint tunnel project was agreed in principle but proceeded very slowly because of concerns over financing.
† The phrase 'Channel tunnel' assumed there was no other possible built means of crossing the 22 miles between England and France. The wider term, adopted by the government, was 'fixed link'.

Robin replied. Mitterrand really did flirt with her.' The following day, the two leaders announced their amity on the fixed link (though without stating which scheme), promising to pursue the project with 'real urgency'.

Despite Mrs Thatcher's new-found zeal, her vision did not, in fact, prevail. As the Policy Unit complained, 'Ironically, the French team [the Socialist government] are embracing the positive spirit of the Thatcherite private enterprise formula ... with more inspiration and enthusiasm than the British.' Britain, not France, was the problem: there were 'too many hang-ups about rabies, plant health and terrorists'.* Moreover, the institutional forces in favour of a rail link were stronger than those favouring road. Sir Nicholas Henderson, hero of British diplomacy during the Falklands War and a former Ambassador in Paris, was Chairman of the Channel Tunnel Group which, with its French partner, Trans-Manche, was bidding for a rail tunnel. Lobbying Mrs Thatcher directly, the wily Henderson threw out an airy assurance that his company would offer a drive-through tunnel in addition to the rail one already planned. When, in November, the final bids were reviewed, Mrs Thatcher resisted pressure to weigh in on behalf of EuroRoute, and the bored-tunnel scheme of the Channel Tunnel Group/Trans-Manche emerged triumphant. As Henderson had calculated, the vague offer of adding a road tunnel made it much easier for everyone to accept. The decision was announced by Mrs Thatcher and Mitterrand at a ceremony in Lille on 20 January 1986. Charles Powell brought back a piece of paper on which he had written:

This – believe it or not – is a historic document ... please file:
THE UNITED KINGDOM AND FRANCE HAVE DECIDED TODAY, ON THE BASIS OF A REPORT BY EXPERTS, TO LINK THEIR TWO COUNTRIES BY A TWIN-BORE TUNNEL UNDER THE CHANNEL FOR RAIL TRAFFIC AND MOTOR VEHICLE SHUTTLE TRAINS.
LATER A DRIVE-THROUGH LINK SHOULD BE BUILT.

To this scrap of paper, François Mitterrand and Margaret Thatcher had appended their signatures.

The following month, on 12 February, Mitterrand visited Britain and

---

* Helmut Kohl, for one, believed that Mrs Thatcher shared these traditional British anxieties about Continental invasion. Richard Burt, the former US Ambassador to Germany, recalled the Chancellor's account of Mrs Thatcher's remarks on the subject: 'She started talking about her concerns that rats and animals with rabies would come through the Chunnel and spread rabies in Britain. Kohl saw this as a metaphor for her relationship with Europe. He said he'd never heard anything more stupid in his life.' The British press was full of such fears, including drug imports and damage to the ferry companies. Oddly, opportunities for illegal immigration, considered the great problem in the twenty-first century, were little mentioned.

Mrs Thatcher drove with him to Canterbury. 'He kept staring at her legs in the car,' recalled her detective, Barry Strevens. They signed a treaty to formalize the deal in the Chapter House of the Cathedral. Forty years on, the Channel Tunnel is extremely popular, although the high-speed rail link eventually installed had to be paid for by government, not the private sector. Of the drive-through link, there is no sign.

Through collaboration with a socialist French government, Mrs Thatcher had succeeded in bringing Britain and the Continent much closer, physically, than ever before. Yet she remained uneasy about the future direction of the European Community. At this stage, she did believe in the Community as embodying Western democracy and an aid to peace in Europe. And she had an agenda of bringing Thatcherite freedoms and disciplines to its economic affairs. In particular, she wanted the Single Market* to live up to its name. But she was scarred by the experience of European Councils over five years. 'These men!' she exclaimed after Fontainebleau. 'All they do is anecdote away ... So unbusinesslike!' Mrs Thatcher's Continental counterparts felt similarly annoyed. The fight had often been so fierce that it had permanently bruised them. 'These men' were fed up with 'that woman'.

Mrs Thatcher was already anxious about the ambitions her main European partners held for the Community's future. She never shared the deep emotion that underlay the drive for ever-closer union. On 22 September 1984, on the field of the terrible First World War Battle of Verdun, Kohl and Mitterrand stood hand in hand to symbolize the reconciliation of France and Germany. Mrs Thatcher watched it on television. Wasn't it moving, she was privately asked afterwards. 'No, it was *not*,' she answered. 'Two grown men holding hands!' She never shared the religion of Europeanism.

Like all religions, Europeanism needed its dogma. Mrs Thatcher often found herself accepting the expansive language favoured by her European partners. The 'Solemn Declaration' she had agreed to during the European Council at Stuttgart in June 1983 was a good example. The Declaration arose from the so-called Genscher–Colombo Plan of 1981, which had argued for greater European political integration, laying the ground for the creation of a European state. Both Lord Carrington, as Foreign Secretary, and his predecessor Francis Pym had argued that accepting this vague,

---

* The British still usually called this the 'Common Market'. It was also sometimes referred to as the 'internal market'. Mrs Thatcher did not like this phrase, though she did sometimes use it, because it implied that the EEC was an embryonic United States of Europe rather than a trading bloc.

aspirational rhetoric would do Britain little harm, while building goodwill with nations such as Germany (whose support Britain needed over the budget row). Mrs Thatcher resisted this for more than a year but the issue lingered. 'Do we have to sign it,' she wrote in February 1983. 'Can't we just adopt it. It is a <u>dreadful</u> document.' Pym insisted that failure to sign would leave Britain isolated, and all for something he believed 'has little real content'. Worn down, she agreed to sign. Officials assured her that a Declaration was much less than an Act. Nonetheless, by it, the Community was committed to 'progress towards Economic and Monetary Union' and to decide within five years 'whether the progress achieved should be incorporated in a Treaty on European Union'.

Mrs Thatcher was almost always advised that what officials characterized as the 'windy rhetoric' or 'theology' of European declarations was worth putting up with in return for concrete advantages. Sometimes this was good advice, but the windy rhetoric usually mattered to the men who uttered it. Theology always matters to a priesthood. The high priests of Europe would be sure to use it later. In this case, what was conceived by Genscher–Colombo in 1981 and solemnly declared at Stuttgart in 1983 would be framed as a treaty obligation at Luxembourg in 1985, included in the Single European Act of 1986, set in train at Hanover in 1988, confirmed at Madrid in 1989 and Rome in 1990, and implemented in the treaty which followed the Maastricht Intergovernmental Conference of 1991. Step by step, an increasingly integrated Europe was built. Mrs Thatcher was trapped: it was a condition of membership.

There was a strong contrast in underlying attitudes between her and her European colleagues. While Kohl was open about his desire for 'the political union of Europe', she was adamantly opposed. As she told *Die Welt* in October 1984, 'I do not believe that we shall have or can have a United States of Europe.' Her own thoughts about the EEC were limited, caustic and practical. Charles Powell helped her project, and sometimes harden, such views. He often sent her sarcastic notes about European affairs to stir her up. One, entitled '59 New Regulations in 1984', mockingly mentioned 'sewage sludge in agriculture' and laws on 'boat fittings'. 'They'll try to Harmonise Nursery Rhymes next!' he added.

Some of Mrs Thatcher's most consequential decisions concerned appointments to the European Commission. Given her vision of a largely economic Community, the choices she made were striking. In 1984, the Foreign Office favoured Jacques Delors, Mitterrand's Finance Minister, over the left-wing, anti-British Claude Cheysson to succeed Gaston Thorn as head of the Commission. Howe assured her that Delors would take a 'far more serious interest in the management of the community's finances', a point that naturally appealed to her.* There is, however, no record of Mrs Thatcher and British ministers discussing the candidates' attitudes to European integration. In terms of ability and experience, Delors was eminently qualified to run the Commission, but he was also trying to move Europe in a direction which was anathema to Mrs Thatcher. No one pointed this out to her. In the end, she supported his candidature.

A similar attempt to make the system work for her without questioning its overall direction lay behind Mrs Thatcher's 1984 appointment of Lord Cockfield as the new European Commissioner for the Internal Market. As a tax expert and believer in making markets operate efficiently, Cockfield had always impressed her. He was, she believed, 'one of us'. Once in harness, however, he proved a disappointment. Visiting her in May 1985, he said that creating the Single Market would naturally require 'the harmonisation of indirect taxes'. She blanched. There could be 'absolutely no question' of this, she told him: 'She was not going to be told by anyone outside the United Kingdom what rate of tax was to be charged here.' But that was exactly what she *was* going to be told, including by people she had thought shared her view. When Cockfield came up for reappointment in 1988, she was determined to replace him and settled on Leon Brittan – a strange choice as he was probably the most ardent Europhile in any of her Cabinets. She was surprisingly unaware that allies in other fields often adhered to a European creed almost completely at variance with her own.

When she met Delors after his appointment as President of the Commission, Mrs Thatcher urged him to avoid 'these constant references to European unity, something which could never come about'. Delors, who was to work unremittingly for just such unity, merely observed that there were two trends in the community – one of 'practical improvements' and the other 'those who aspired to a new treaty'. She declared that the idea of a new treaty was 'absurd'. Yet this was what Delors wanted. In such encounters, there was, no doubt, wishful thinking on both sides, but, broadly speaking, Mrs Thatcher was more deceived than deceiving. Europe was not, for the most part, going her way. This her officials and, with a very few exceptions, her ministerial colleagues did not tell her.

As well as being deceived, Mrs Thatcher must also have been self-deceiving. For the Single Market to function – which she wanted – individual states could not be allowed to impose their own regulations on imports from fellow EU members. To set European-wide standards,

---

* The following week, Mrs Thatcher met Howe's close ally Roland Dumas and discussed the appointment. The French Foreign Minister commended Delors to her on the grounds that 'M. Delors was very strict in budget matters.' These formulations are so similar, and occur so closely together, that might well conclude that Howe and Dumas colluded to persuade Mrs Thatcher.

she consciously supported the biggest ever extension of qualified majority voting (QMV) in the Community.* So when she complained later, she was in effect repudiating what she herself had driven forward.

It was true, however, that, post-Fontainebleau, Mrs Thatcher's public prestige in Europe stood high. Success in the Falklands, at the ballot box and in her domestic policies boosted her fortunes. She was the most arresting figure on the European, perhaps on the entire global stage. She had 'indisputable star quality'. European leaders still hoped to persuade her to go along with Community development rather than oppose it.

Britain was certainly seeking to mobilize the power of the EEC to bring about economic change, but not to increase that power more than was necessary for that change. It therefore urged Europe onwards towards some reforms while working hard to prevent others. As the debate continued through 1984 and 1985, it was not always easy to work out who was winning. Britain was successfully putting the Single Market at the top of the agenda. On the other hand, the country was at odds with the ultimately much more powerful Franco-German axis which sought greater European integration. The situation was further complicated by the fact that Helmut Kohl and Margaret Thatcher did not get on.

The new British Ambassador to Germany, Sir Julian Bullard, summed up his first impressions to Charles Powell in September 1984: 'the Anglo-German relationship at the highest level is not all that it should be'. Mrs Thatcher, he urged, should send Kohl a message 'saying something warm and special'. A letter was duly drafted. It would, Powell told her, be particularly effective, 'if you can bring yourself to put "Dear Helmut"'. Mrs Thatcher obliged by signing some words about Kohl's 'vision and statesmanship' but felt quite incapable of supplying the personal warmth pleaded for; 'My dear Chancellor,' she began.

The 'German Question' – the existence of an artificially divided Germany – was also a source of tension. Mrs Thatcher never doubted that the Berlin Wall was an abhorrent symbol of Soviet oppression, but equally was never happy with the idea of Germany united and strong. 'German reunification is an area where we have to say one thing and think another,' Powell wrote on an October 1984 despatch from Bullard on the subject. Mrs Thatcher underlined these words, but saying one thing and thinking

---

* Extending 'qualified' majority voting was usually favoured by those seeking greater European integration because removing the requirement for unanimity made progress towards this goal much easier. Such voting was 'qualified' because a straight majority was not good enough: it had to be additionally qualified by the right balance of voting 'weights' accorded in proportion to population, and a sufficient spread of different member states.

another was not her greatest skill. She tended to say what she thought: what she thought about German reunification was already uncomfortable. It was, to use an expression not then employed, the elephant in the room. Helmut Kohl's elephantine person reminded her unpleasingly of this fact. These difficulties, though real, usually stayed in the background. Both sides did make genuine efforts to foster a cooperative relationship. Rather surprisingly – for he usually tried harder than she did – it turned out to be Kohl, not Mrs Thatcher, who played a dirty trick.

It gradually became clear that the Milan European Council of June 1985 would decide whether a new treaty advancing European integration would come to pass. Under Community rules, a new treaty required an Intergovernmental Conference (IGC) of the member states to frame and agree it. Opposed to a new treaty, Britain naturally did not want an IGC.

Seeking to avoid the 'isolation' which, in the diplomatic mind, is always the worst result of any negotiation, the Foreign Office advised Mrs Thatcher to pre-empt France and Germany and develop her own ideas for Milan, sharing them with Kohl during his visit to Chequers in May. Her agenda, Powell proposed, should consist of the completion of the internal market, 'no more powers for the European Parliament', more qualified majority voting (subject to the Luxembourg Compromise being formalized),* and formalizing the existing arrangements for political cooperation ('PoCo'). Mrs Thatcher had always been in favour of PoCo (a closer approximation of a common foreign policy) because of her belief that Europe should speak up for Western ideas in the Cold War. Powell attached a draft on PoCo, which, he said, 'does not restrict our national independence of action. In short, it is dressing up mutton to look like lamb.' Although it would not convince the experts, Powell felt she could sell it 'as a British initiative, stake out a strong position, and make it impossible for others to put us in the dock as being a back marker on European union'. 'Yes,' wrote Mrs Thatcher, 'it seems fairly reasonable.' Despite Foreign Office pressure, she was determined that this remain an informal agreement, not a new treaty.

When the two leaders met, on 18 May, Kohl said he was 'basically positive' about the British document and agreed its ideas should be passed to the French. Apart from disagreement about increasing the powers of the European Parliament, the meeting was harmonious. Both publicly and

---

* The Luxembourg Compromise was the convention that each member state was free to veto any measure which it considered 'a very important national interest'. In theory, this could override qualified majority voting. The only time Britain invoked the Compromise was at the Agricultural Council of 16 May 1982. The Community ignored it – hence the British demand that it be formalized.

privately, however, Kohl reiterated his desire that PoCo should take the form of a treaty which should also, he wrote to Mrs Thatcher, 'stipulate the goal of establishing European Union'. Nonetheless, Geoffrey Howe assured her that, at Milan, both the British approach and the treaty option would be on the table. Howe boasted that Britain had 'taken the wind out of the sails' by making its own proposals: 'This has come as something of a shock to those who had expected us to place the emphasis on what we cannot accept – rather than on what we think can and should be done.'

But the shock was on the British side. The day before the summit, Horst Teltschik, Powell's counterpart in Kohl's office, rang to tell him, for the first time, that the French and Germans had prepared a draft treaty on European Union, which Kohl would table in Milan the following day. Outraged, Powell told Teltschik this was a 'black day for cooperation'. Kohl and Mitterrand had taken everything Mrs Thatcher had offered and 'then called it "Treaty on European Union"', creating the very thing that Britain had sought to avoid. By this stage, the Germans, French and Italians had agreed secretly to work to bring this about. By avoiding the need for any proposal requiring unanimity at the summit, they planned to outmanoeuvre Mrs Thatcher.

At the Milan Council, the Italian Prime Minister, Bettino Craxi, accordingly proposed an IGC and pushed it to the vote, the first ever taken in a European Council. Although a treaty required unanimity, a vote for an IGC required only majority support. This it received: an IGC was called for the end of the year, against Britain's wishes. After the summit, Howe told Mrs Thatcher that, having given way at Fontainebleau, Kohl and Mitterrand were 'determined to show themselves ready to go further than us'. But, in his view, 'Any reasonable German government should see that it is in their interests to go for things which we can agree. One's faith that the Germans may have a clear perception of their interests . . . cannot be great after Milan.'

Was that so? Howe did not contemplate the possibility that the German (and French and Italian) trick made perfectly good sense to its perpetrators. After years of being blocked, they had found a way of going forward which Mrs Thatcher could not stop. The Foreign Office policy of reining her in had failed. Howe felt rueful about it ever afterwards: 'Margaret worried about opening Pandora's box. I was more optimistic that we could play a trick on the Community and persuade them to develop conventions rather than have an IGC and a new treaty, but the wretched Craxi and Andreotti [at that time the Italian Foreign Minister] turned it upside down.' Howe himself, however, was a reason for the behaviour at Milan which he disliked. According to Teltschik, 'from summit to summit . . . there was a common strategy to isolate her'. The Germans felt emboldened in this because 'We knew the Foreign Office didn't agree with her. We knew this from Genscher [the German Foreign Minister], who knew it from Howe.'

Now Pandora's box was opened. Milan helped confirm Mrs Thatcher in her Eurosceptic instincts. In public, she was restrained, complaining only that an IGC delayed and complicated changes which could have been made at once. In private, she was furious: the actions of the French and Germans had been 'the sort of behaviour that would get you thrown out of any London club'. She felt that Kohl had shown his true colours. At his post-Milan press conference, he declared that he and Mitterrand were now the motors of change for Europe – 'the mission of the founding fathers had been to slowly dismantle national sovereignty ... At the end a European federal state could arise.' For Mrs Thatcher, the enemy was in plain view.

She did not, however, seize upon the humiliation at Milan and fight back. The ultimate direction of the European Community, and the problems this created for Britain, were not discussed in those terms within government. Instead, differences were suppressed. The British government coalesced still further round the project of the Single Market.

The now-agreed-upon IGC was set for December 1985, in Luxembourg. The British tactic was the opposite of that which had failed at Milan. Britain would wait to see who proposed what. When Mrs Thatcher met Kohl ahead of the summit, on 27 November, Powell advised her to 'let him out of the penalty box' for his behaviour at Milan, 'but to play on his guilty feelings (so far as anyone so thick-skinned has them) to induce him to pay particular attention to your points of view this time round'.* She should tell him she would not 'be bounced by another Franco-German ganging up ... You will in particular want to nail him down tight to opposing monetary amendments to the Treaty.'

With Delors already pushing for the abolition of national frontiers and the introduction of a single currency, the question of 'monetary amendments' was crucial. West Germany was torn – on the one hand wanting to keep the deutschmark, its proudest single creation of the post-Nazi era, on the other wanting never to compromise its devotion to European Union. When Mrs Thatcher and Kohl met, the Chancellor gave the impression that his dedication to sound money would prevail.

Yet at the European Council, Kohl changed his mind. What emerged was agreement to accept a symbolic reference to Economic and Monetary

---

* Powell went on in the same note to satirize Kohl: 'The first three or four hours – if you let him – will be devoted to gloating over the latest opinion polls in Germany, the state of the German economy, the fantastic sales of the latest biography of him (I am arranging to supply you with a copy. You might ask him to autograph it. He would never suspect a tease).'

Union (EMU) in the new treaty. In her memoirs, Mrs Thatcher claims that, by persuading Kohl to describe EMU in terms of 'co-operation in economic and monetary policy', she avoided any commitment to a single currency. No doubt these anodyne words gave her some comfort, but the fact that she accepted any reference to EMU showed the weakness of her position and the desire to ensure her Single Market agenda was not acrimoniously derailed. Not surprisingly, the belief gradually took root on the Continent that 'Mrs Thatcher always complains, but always comes along in the end.' This was an unflattering but essentially correct formulation.

Those on the British side who favoured greater European integration saw the concession on EMU as a chiefly symbolic gesture that produced more concrete Single Market gains. For Mrs Thatcher, though, symbols mattered. Although she had insisted publicly on the exact opposite, Delors emphasized that EMU was now to be considered 'a treaty objective'. From that point on, EMU would gather pace, making life extremely difficult for all succeeding British governments.

Advising Mrs Thatcher ahead of her post-Council press conference, Ingham urged her to highlight the completion of the internal market but take care over the extension of qualified majority voting ('which the press see as a weakening of our sovereignty'), animal and plant protections ('the rabies clause') and the monetary issue. She followed this advice. She also glossed over the fact that the treaty, against her wishes, increased the standing of the European Parliament.* And she emphasized that the 'reserves' (particular points to which an individual member state had not yet agreed) came from other countries as well as Britain. When one journalist incautiously remarked that these reserves made the agreement 'rather like a Cheshire cheese, full of holes', she retorted: 'A Cheshire cheese is not full of holes – that is Gruyere! A Cheshire cheese has got no holes in it – it is British!'

The one reserve Britain had entered involved extending qualified majority voting into matters concerned with health and safety at work. Mrs Thatcher worried that rules thus made would impose heavy burdens on small businesses. Colleagues and officials calmed her fears, and Britain belatedly signed up, but she was right: as one official admitted, QMV 'was abused to impose social legislation which Britain did not want'. This aggravated Britain's sense of being imposed upon by European legislation in future years.

Returning to Britain, Mrs Thatcher encountered no serious political opposition to what she had achieved at Luxembourg. The press, with the solitary exception of the *Spectator*, was in favour. Only seventeen

---

* It also insisted that, henceforth, it be known as the European Parliament rather than Assembly.

Conservative MPs rebelled against the Single European Act. Being a sceptic herself, she could marginalize the sceptics: if she said it was all right, who would listen to their objections? In that sense, Mrs Thatcher was the most effective promoter of European integration Britain has ever known.

The Single European Act (SEA), formally signed by the European member states in February 1986, became the first major revision to the 1957 Treaty of Rome. It established the goal of a single European market by the end of 1992 and provided for the extension of qualified majority voting to achieve this. There were undoubted British successes – the freeing up, for example, of the European airline market – but it gave much greater power to Delors and his team than it did to Mrs Thatcher and hers. He could use the extended QMV to get round whatever restrictions the SEA might appear to place on his ambitions for the Commission.

At the time, Mrs Thatcher saw the completion of the Single Market as a great prize. As David Williamson recalled, she '*positively*' wanted the Act'. In his view, these were 'the golden years' in which she redirected much of the Community's energies on to her agenda. He never countenanced the idea, later put about, that she did not understand the implications of the Act. 'I've read every single word of this treaty,' she told him at the time of ratification, 'and I am happy with it.' Charles Powell, though approaching the matter through a less Europhile lens, also believed she was genuinely in favour of the SEA: 'In relation to the EEC, she had different periods – like Picasso in his painting. The first period was the budget row; the second was that of the SEA; the third – the violent stage – came on with the rising power of Delors and the issue of EMU.' During the SEA stage, 'She was *not* a profound sceptic.' Her mistake, he considered, was failing to realize how hostile most Continental politicians secretly were to the Single Market because of their protectionist instincts, and how they would therefore try to frustrate its intentions.

Mrs Thatcher defended her decision to sign the SEA in her memoirs. But, by the time they were published, she was saying privately she regretted doing so, because of the push it gave towards the European Union which she feared. Before the Single European Act, she had never systematically developed her own vision of Europe. It was only later that she worked out – and publicly declared – what she thought. The result would cause delight and dismay in roughly equal measure.

20

The death-knell of monetarism

*'She's a moral coward when it comes to
dealing with people'*

As Mrs Thatcher was negotiating the Single European Act, her Chancellor of the Exchequer was changing the basis of British economic policy. Issues which at first appeared the preserve of experts gradually disclosed themselves as fundamental, altering Mrs Thatcher's relationship with Nigel Lawson and her ultimate political fate.

Of all her senior ministers, Lawson was the most technically accomplished advocate of 'monetarism'. It was he who had first articulated the Medium-Term Financial Strategy (MTFS). By 1984, he could point to its success. Inflation, above 20 per cent in 1980, was now steady at 5 per cent; markets had faith in the government's sense of direction; economic growth was recovering. Yet the explosion of economic activity which came from liberalization had led to dramatic changes in the money aggregates by which the policy was supposed to be judged. Policymakers found it hard to interpret these changes. Large increases in sterling M3, the chosen measure of money supply, had begun to weaken the value of sterling. The monetarist doctrine was that the government should control the quantity of money, not its traded price: it should, to use the favoured term, 'let the exchange rate go where it will'. Lawson began to think otherwise.

Mrs Thatcher greatly admired Lawson: 'She thought he was very clever and rather gutsy,' recalled Brian Griffiths, head of her Policy Unit from September 1985. She relied heavily on Lawson's intellectually self-confident advocacy of economic reform. But, as someone who saw economics more in terms of moral wisdom than prestidigitation, she felt she inhabited a different mental universe. 'Brian, he's a gambler,' she complained to Griffiths. Gradually, she came to believe that Lawson was gambling with the success of her entire economic project.

*

Equally gradually, though starting earlier, Lawson had come to believe Britain would be better off inside the Exchange Rate Mechanism (ERM) of the European Monetary System (EMS). The ERM was declaredly designed as the forerunner of a single European currency, but Lawson, who firmly opposed economic and monetary union, saw it differently. For him, the ERM could serve as a guiding star for managing sterling and hence controlling inflation. Since 1981, he later claimed, he had waited for 'the right opportunity'.* He meant not only the favourable economic conditions, but the right moment to persuade the person who, he knew, would be least persuadable – Margaret Thatcher. His first move, however, was more accident than act of persuasion.

In January 1985, prompted in part by the strength of the dollar and a perceived indifference on the part of the British government to the value of sterling, there was a run on the pound. On 11 January, it fell to $1.12, less than half its level in 1981. Whatever Mrs Thatcher might say about leaving the market alone, she saw a weak pound as an affront to British pride and self-confidence. So worried was she that she berated Lawson for not joining the ERM earlier. At this point, recalled his private secretary, Rachel Lomax, he 'was not yet stuck on the exchange rate: it was she that was pushing for change'. Invoking the existing policy that Britain should join the ERM 'when the time was right' (or, sometimes, 'ripe'), he proposed the government should revisit the matter. Mrs Thatcher duly called a meeting of senior ministers for 13 February. By the time they met, Lawson had raised interest rates from 9 per cent to 14 per cent.

In the meantime, on 15 January, Mrs Thatcher sought help with sterling from President Reagan. Reagan reassured her that the USA stood by its pledge at the 1983 Williamsburg summit to consider 'coordinated intervention where it was agreed such intervention would be helpful'. On 17 January, the G5 finance ministers, meeting in Washington, took the unprecedented step of pledging coordinated intervention 'as necessary', sending a clear signal to markets. This helped alleviate the pressure on sterling.

Those meeting on 13 February included Mrs Thatcher, Lawson, Geoffrey Howe, Robin Leigh-Pemberton, the Governor of the Bank of England, Eddie George, the Bank's expert on markets, and Peter Middleton and Terry Burns from the Treasury. This would be the main cast of characters in all subsequent discussions. Alan Walters, an inveterate opponent of the

---

* One of Lawson's motives, in 1981, for favouring ERM membership was political. He thought that if he could link financial discipline with the European project this would outflank Wet critics of Mrs Thatcher's economic policy, who felt bound to support almost anything they considered pro-European.

ERM, remained across the water in the United States, but retained a constant line to Mrs Thatcher. He was the ghost at every feast.

The official record shows no falling-out. Lawson put his case that Britain 'should not close the door' on the ERM but stressed it should not enter at such a turbulent moment. Geoffrey Howe spoke in similar terms. A contemporaneous note, kept by Terry Burns, shows that Mrs Thatcher doubted Lawson's case: 'Superficially membership attractive but . . . in detail it looks less attractive,' and she even protested against the existing policy: 'wonder if we should drop that line that we will go in when the time is ripe'. While the official record shows her summing up by stressing agreement that this was not the right moment to join, the key point went unrecorded. For the first time, she was confronted by support for ERM entry from the three most important people concerned – the Chancellor, the Foreign Secretary and the Governor.

This was part of the unhappy context for Lawson's 1985 Budget. 'High interest rates and the weakness of sterling have upset Budget plans,' John Redwood wrote to Mrs Thatcher. Nonetheless, he argued, it was vital that 'The Budget should be clear, purposeful, addressed to jobs, and pledged to lower interest rates and lower taxes'. On the night of Sunday 3 February, seeking to take advantage of Mrs Thatcher's habitual good mood after a weekend at Chequers, Lawson discussed his Budget plans with the Prime Minister. He told her the PSBR for 1984–5, an expected £10.75 billion, would represent an overrun of £3.5 billion.* The two agreed that for 1985–6 this had to come down to £7 billion, but not on how to achieve it. As in 1984, Lawson sought to extend VAT to newspapers. Mrs Thatcher again resisted. She also strongly disagreed with his proposal to confine mortgage interest tax relief to the basic rate of tax. She regarded such relief as one of the best ways of helping young people get on the housing ladder, however much economists urged her that it merely led to higher house prices. What Lawson wanted to reduce, she wanted made more generous. They agreed to leave the rate where it was.

Before the pre-Budget discussion in Cabinet the following week, Redwood was almost beside himself at the figures emerging: 'Taxes up, public spending up, interest rates up, unemployment up, even Income Tax and National Insurance up (as a percentage of earnings). That is the story since 1979 told in these dismal documents.' Mrs Thatcher thrice underlined '1979', as if in pain at what her governments were failing to achieve. 'You never give in,' Redwood urged her. 'Don't let others give in for the government at such a vital juncture.'

---

* £2.5 billion of this could be attributed to the coal strike.

At the Cabinet meeting, the consensus favoured caution. The Budget that Lawson presented to Parliament on 19 March reflected this. VAT was extended only to newspaper advertising, with a promise to go no further. Lawson did, however, alter the income tax burden to favour the low-paid by increasing the personal allowance by double the rate of inflation, and he hit the better off by removing the ceiling on employers' National Insurance contributions. He also committed large sums in this 'Budget for jobs' to the Youth Training Scheme and the Community Programme.

Reviews were mostly tepid. His Budget attracted criticism not only from Wets like Ted Heath and Jim Prior, but also from Thatcherites. In the *Spectator*, the paper Lawson had formerly edited, his old friend and former ministerial colleague Jock Bruce-Gardyne lamented that 'This was actually the last ideal year for radicalism' before the next general election. Although the Budget was no U-turn, the government was losing pace.

The mood was dour. Lawson felt it himself. After delivering his Budget, he gave a small party with a sense of 'anticlimax' and went to bed very early. Woken at 11 o'clock by the doorbell of his flat, he stumbled to the door and found the Prime Minister outside: 'Margaret was very chic in a black, frilly dress, and had obviously come on from somewhere to look in, as she thought, on our post-Budget party. She was naturally somewhat taken aback to find me barefoot and naked from the waist up . . .'

In September Lawson returned to the ERM charge. He was now clearer in his own mind. The pound, the reserves and interest rates were in better shape. On 22 September he and fellow G5 finance ministers signed the Plaza Agreement,* promoted by Reagan's new Treasury Secretary, James Baker. This was designed to lower the value of the US dollar and move away from 'free-floating' exchange rates by accepting that serious imbalances required coordinated intervention. As Baker recalled, 'Nigel was particularly enthusiastic.' Knowing Mrs Thatcher's much greater respect for American decisions than for EEC ones, Lawson believed this would soften her up: 'She remarked to me that the agreement created a favourable prelude to ERM membership.' She consented to a meeting on 30 September.

Ahead of this meeting, the Treasury paper did not mince words: 'It is the considered view of the Chancellor and the Governor that we should become full members of the EMS, joining the ERM at the earliest practicable opportunity.' 'The Treasury, Bank and City are uniting behind a new fashion,' Redwood warned Mrs Thatcher. He advocated a 'more pragmatic approach' which 'keeps our destinies in our own hands and not in those

---

* The name came from the Plaza Hotel in New York, where it was negotiated.

of the Germans; and still leaves us free to try and track the DM exchange rate if we wish'. She underlined the word 'fashion' three times. David Norgrove, her new Treasury private secretary, drew her attention to the high stakes: 'joining the ERM could turn out to be the most important economic decision of this Parliament and quite possibly of your Administration . . . Your discussions with the Chancellor have moved this question to the point where it may look to the Treasury that it is a foregone conclusion that we shall join.'

The 30 September meeting, billed as a 'seminar', was much fiercer than its February predecessor. Mrs Thatcher was by now fired up against joining. 'Need to prove the case for change' are her challenging words which begin Terry Burns's record. As each grandee – Chancellor, then Governor, then Foreign Secretary – said his emollient and stately piece in favour of entry, she would jump in with objections: 'Frightened about what proposing. Scared to death – don't think can do it . . . Up go interest rates months before election . . . Divide own side . . . Forfeit capacity to do our own thing . . . cannot fix exchange rate . . .'

At no point did she concede anything to the Lawson thesis. When Burns suggested her criticisms amounted to 'arguments for not joining ever', she baldly answered 'Yes.' To this Howe replied, in what amounted to a four-word summary of all his European attitudes, 'Can't be independent indefinitely.' 'Why limit manoeuvre? Argument of weakness,' said Mrs Thatcher, exemplifying all hers. Only Brian Griffiths supported her view. As Burns abbreviated it, she said, 'Know who to blame if went wrong,' which was her unnerving way of implying permission, but not support. With these tart, even menacing words she closed the meeting.

Mrs Thatcher now called for a full ministerial discussion in search of new allies. Lawson, meanwhile, made part of the argument public. In his annual Mansion House speech, he announced he was dropping the £M3 target. Though not billed as such, this was the death-knell of monetarism in British government policy. 'At the end of the day,' he declared, '. . . The inflation rate is judge and jury.' It was a rash thing to say without offering some mechanism, such as an independent central bank, to oversee inflation-rate targeting: the 'judge and jury' would try Lawson in front of its kangaroo court in the years to come.

Ahead of the broader ministerial meeting to discuss ERM membership, set for 13 November, Lawson delivered an ultimatum. Failure to join now, he wrote, would be 'a historic missed opportunity which we would before very long come bitterly to regret'. While he lobbied colleagues separately beforehand, Mrs Thatcher made no equivalent push. Even Willie Whitelaw had not been squared. John Wakeham, the Chief Whip, was also asked to the meeting to lend her support, but had not been briefed on what was at stake. Not for the first time, Mrs Thatcher was strangely innocent of Cabinet-level politics. By ill chance, her main advisers and officials – Nigel Wicks and David Norgrove in her private office and Brian Griffiths in her Policy Unit – were all new to their jobs. None had the relevant experience to fight the Whitehall battle effectively. Despite her astonishing personal dominance, hardly anyone was working the system to get her what she wanted.

The meeting of 13 November contained almost all the important ministers in the government – Mrs Thatcher, Lawson, Howe, Whitelaw, plus Biffen, Brittan, Tebbit and Wakeham. In substance, the argument added little to the debate of 30 September. Its significance was political and personal. As Wakeham recalled, Mrs Thatcher 'batted everything off in her best style'. But she found little support. Of those politicians present, only Biffen, a long-standing 'free floater' and Eurosceptic, opposed ERM entry. Even Tebbit, despite his Thatcherite reputation, supported Lawson.

After the arguments had been heard, Whitelaw spoke: 'We have said we will join when the time is right. Now we are told it is right. If CX [the Chancellor] and Governor say time is right then that is OK for my money.' Mrs Thatcher, however, refused to accept this. 'It was clear', recalled Norgrove, 'that she would resign rather than join.' In this impasse the only thing to do was, as the official record expressed Mrs Thatcher's summing up, 'to maintain rigidly the line which had been taken so far that the UK would join when the time was right'.

This outcome was a disaster because it flummoxed all those taking part. According to Terry Burns, the expectation had been that Mrs Thatcher would agree to look at ERM entry further, but 'she brought the trap door down sharply'. Neither side had prepared the ground with the other. 'I became aware of more personal animosity than I had realized,' Wakeham recalled. For Lawson it was 'the saddest event of my time as Chancellor'. After it his relations with Mrs Thatcher never fully recovered. 'How do I stand as Chancellor when I've had a big meeting like that, won the argument, but lost the battle?' Lawson asked himself. 'I did think of resignation.' For his part, recalled Norgrove, Nigel Wicks 'was determined that there shouldn't be another meeting like that, and therefore policy was never really discussed again between the two'. In this strange vacuum, Lawson decided to pursue his own approach.

There was no doubt the showdown had upset Mrs Thatcher, although she was buoyed up by the adrenalin of arguing so fiercely. In her memoirs she played down its importance. In particular, she failed to see the significance of her own remark that her arguments against ERM entry 'applied to the principle – not just the circumstances'. If the time could never be right for entry, she was effectively opposed to her own government's policy. History later showed that, as Terry Burns put it, 'she was fundamentally correct', but being right is not necessarily the same as governing well. The Thatcher–Lawson clash made it harder to run the British economy, and the British government, properly.

The fateful ERM meeting came towards the end of a year when politics, partly because of disappointing economic performance, had persistently gone badly for the government, especially for Mrs Thatcher personally. Although her defeat of Arthur Scargill was arguably the most important single achievement of her entire career, public opinion seemed to feel that the great argument for her – dire necessity in a crisis – no longer applied. Tired of conflict, voters cast about for something softer. Opinion polls gave strong backing to the SDP leader, David Owen. Even Labour, under Neil Kinnock, was starting to look less fractious and extreme. People spoke of Kinnock's 'decency', contrasting it with Mrs Thatcher's harshness.

As the Conservatives' position deteriorated, so internal discontent with Mrs Thatcher naturally grew. The terminology of Wets and Dries had given way to 'consolidators' and 'radicals'; but the fault lines were the same. Unemployment remained well above 3 million.* When Peter Walker, for example, spoke publicly in favour of full employment in May, it was readily understood that he was criticizing Mrs Thatcher. Later in May, Francis Pym and other senior Tories displaced by Thatcherism launched a grouping called Centre Forward to promote their ideas. Like many other critics, they praised Mrs Thatcher's courage and determination, but called for a more 'compassionate' style. If she was no longer necessary, they implied, she was unnecessary.

Perhaps more worrying for Mrs Thatcher was the lack of stirring support from the new generation of Conservative MPs. Her pool of reliable backers had not been well replenished, nor had enough able Thatcherites gained office. In part, this reflected her desire to avoid leaving her opponents on the back benches to make trouble. Oddly, though, for one who valued ideological affinity highly, she was not skilful at identifying and promoting those who showed it.†

Mrs Thatcher's ideological soulmates on the back benches had begun

---

* Total unemployment stood at 3,272,565 that April.
† One of the best examples of this came with the promotion of John Major, who first entered government in the 1985 reshuffle. For quite some time she considered Major a true believer, but events would later prove her wrong. 'We thought he had a better brain than he had' was how she (unfairly) put it later.

to organize shortly after the 1983 election. From this emerged, in 1985, the No Turning Back Group,* whose early members included Michael Forsyth, Michael Fallon, Francis Maude, Neil Hamilton, Peter Lilley and Richard Ryder. They were a counter to the Blue Chip group including Chris Patten and William Waldegrave, which had been a thorn in Mrs Thatcher's side in the previous Parliament. They wanted to keep up the pressure for Thatcherite market reform and were, according to Gerald Howarth, their convenor, 'very much designed to help her'. She treated them in a friendly manner, but nevertheless 'failed to secure the supply line' with her supporters. At a later dinner, Mrs Thatcher turned to Eric Forth, the group's leading eccentric, and said, 'Eric, you've been untypically silent. What do you have to say?' 'Well, Prime Minister,' said Forth, 'since you ask, when are you going to appoint some decent people to your government?' She seemed a little surprised by this thought.†

From May 1985, Mrs Thatcher's unideological counsellors began to plan her administration's recovery. Thoughts turned to the manifesto for the next election, but the lack of an obvious draftsman posed a problem, as did the unspoken thought that asking Geoffrey Howe to repeat the task which he had performed well in 1983 now seemed unimaginable. Plans for a Cabinet reshuffle had also begun. Over supper with Mrs Thatcher, Whitelaw and Wakeham pushed for reliability and better presentational skills, not radicalism – George Younger and Kenneth Baker moving up, Patrick Jenkin, Peter Rees and Tom King moving out. The most controversial thought was the return of Cecil Parkinson to his old job at the DTI. Tebbit, its incumbent, would then displace Gummer as Party Chairman to fight the presentational battle and prepare for the next election, whenever it might come.

As Mrs Thatcher continued to mull over possible changes, more controversy arose. Lord Plowden, the Chairman of the Top Salaries Review Body (TSRB), recommended extremely large increases for civil servants at the highest level. Believing that Plowden's recommendations 'would make an important contribution to better motivation and management of the Higher Civil Service', Mrs Thatcher dismissed Lawson's objection that the rises were simply too large for the public to swallow. When the report was published in July there was widespread political outcry. Yet she held fast. 'There was no doubt in my mind', she wrote in her memoirs, 'that we could not retain the right people in vitally important posts . . . unless their salaries

---

* The name came from the group's eponymous pamphlet, brought out in November 1985, which called for 'a revolution of choice, a revolution of opportunity'.
† At the end of the dinner, a perplexed Michael Alison, never at ease with political nuance, went round politely asking the guests who these decent people might be.

bore at least some comparison with their counterparts in the private sector.' Such views did little to sway the rebels. Before it rose at the end of July, the Commons rebuked the Prime Minister by cutting the government's huge majority to seventeen over the issue. This had come on top of a bad by-election. On 4 July, the Conservatives fell to third in the previously safe seat of Brecon and Radnor. Tory MPs had what Mrs Thatcher described as 'a bad case of the wobbles': there was 'an unmistakeable whiff of panic'.

The Prime Minister was inundated with end-of-term advice. Bernard Ingham warned her that the government was seen as 'arrogant' and 'insensitive'. More attention to presentation was needed, including making him 'privy to the sensitive issues before decisions are taken'. He applied his argument to the coming reshuffle: 'Your actions cannot be ruled by presentation; but they must, in my judgment, be seen to recognise its importance.' Although what Ingham wrote was self-serving, it was also true. Mrs Thatcher often gave little thought to how to introduce issues to the world. Ingham sought to bring more coherence to the government's actions in the public mind. In essence she accepted his suggestions, boosting his role and influence. She had made him, in effect, a forerunner of the modern 'spin-doctor'.* Naturally, this earned him the jealousy and suspicion of Cabinet members.

Before leaving the Policy Unit, John Redwood offered Mrs Thatcher a different perspective. Throwing at her the various unkind phrases widely used about the government – 'Uncaring Britain', 'class-ridden Britain' and the feeling of 'Time for a change' – he sought to link, rather than contrast, economic reform with concern for the social fabric. Before the next election, the charge that she did not care about public services like health and education should be countered by her commitment to patient and parent power. And the proceeds of privatization should go to provide a 'generous Family credit accompanied by a cut in income tax rates'. With his eye firmly on the election, he added: 'This really is the last chance.'

Because she believed her government was fundamentally on the right track, Mrs Thatcher was more disposed to follow Ingham's advice and reshuffle with presentation in mind than to review policy. She spent much of August pondering her September reshuffle, a process she hated. Politically ruthless though she was, she had a vivid sense of how shattering it could be for ministers to lose office.† She also realized she would be creating enemies.

---

* The term was not then current in Britain.
† Mrs Thatcher had resisted pressure from Whitelaw and Wakeham to make changes to her Cabinet in July. It was one of her pet theories that it was kinder to reshuffle colleagues in September, 'bearing in mind that they would leave my office without a ministerial salary, without a

On this occasion, one change she had hoped for was immediately frustrated after Lord Gowrie, the Arts Minister, told her he wished to leave government.* Wanting him for Education, she had finally plucked up the courage to retire her beloved but increasingly ineffective Keith Joseph. She was enamoured of Gowrie, whom she considered 'very lucid with an excellent mind'. She thought he would 'electrify' Education. But it was not to be. Gowrie insisted that people would not accept someone from the Lords in such a post.† She came to regard Gowrie's departure as 'the greatest loss'. Keith Joseph, unknowing of his near-dismissal, soldiered on.

Mrs Thatcher's actual appointments came about in a less eccentric manner, though not easily. Wakeham warned her against Parkinson's return, which would look like 'going backwards'. He also sought to quash the idea that the millionaire novelist Jeffrey Archer might be made 'Minister for Sport'. Because Archer was neither an MP nor a peer, this would require elevating him to the Lords, a controversial step given his chequered business career. Stephen Sherbourne also warned her against Parkinson because he was 'unpopular with many women in the Party'. Sherbourne feared 'further revelations from Sarah [sic] Keays and this time they would rebound on you and not just him'.‡ To improve presentation he recommended that Norman Tebbit replace Gummer as Party Chairman, that Jeffrey Archer come in as Deputy Chairman (for which membership of neither House was required), and that communicators – Kenneth Baker, John Moore, Kenneth Clarke – be chosen for key posts. Mrs Thatcher gave red ticks to every name except Clarke's.§

Norman Tebbit also submitted his thoughts. By this time, he knew he was Gummer's likely successor as Chairman. But his relationship with Mrs Thatcher was complicated. He was close to her ideologically and revelled

---

car and without the prestige'. Then they would earn the money for longer and have less media frenzy surrounding them than when Parliament was sitting.

* That summer, at Gowrie's request, Mrs Thatcher had visited the reclusive oil heir Paul Getty in the London Clinic where he was recovering from drug addiction. Gowrie knew that Getty was minded to donate a large sum to the National Gallery, but hoped for a knighthood in return. He felt a visit from Mrs Thatcher would indicate that the 'gong' would be his. Always eager to see private money going to Britain's greatest cultural institutions, she was happy to oblige. Getty received her in his dressing gown. She was flattering and briskly helpful: 'Oh, Mr Getty, we must get you out of here.' He happily received the implied promise of the knighthood and soon afterwards gave the National Gallery £50 million. 'It sort of cured Paul,' Gowrie recalled. 'He remade his marriage and became a pillar of society.'

† It was rarely a bar in Mrs Thatcher's mind that a minister was a peer, since this meant that, as Gowrie put it, he would be one of the 'eunuchs in the seraglio'.

‡ There were. Miss Keays's book *A Question of Judgement* was published to coincide with the Tory conference and attacked Parkinson once again.

§ Nonetheless, she commented that Clarke had 'outstanding ability' and 'deserves promotion'.

in the satirical television programme *Spitting Image*'s depiction of him as her loyal skinhead. He was also grateful for her personal kindness after the Brighton bomb.* According to Andrew Lansley, Tebbit's private secretary, she was 'utterly charming and supportive' to Tebbit, 'beyond what convention demanded'. But in Tebbit's view, his presence provoked 'a feeling that somehow she was responsible. She had been the target but others had paid the price. Every time I walked into the room, she remembered how narrowly she'd escaped death. Because she *was* a good woman, there was an element of feeling bad about this.' Thus did her very sympathy for her injured minister make his presence unwelcome.

At the same time as Mrs Thatcher felt sympathy and guilt, she also felt anger. The rumour spread that Tebbit was organizing his own leadership plans from his hospital bed. She seems to have believed this. 'He wanted the chairmanship', she recalled privately, 'as a springboard to take over from me.' Michael Dobbs, Tebbit's special adviser, however, insisted that after the bomb Tebbit had 'completely ruled himself out of any leadership bid'. Yet there may still have been some truth in Mrs Thatcher's perception of Tebbit's ambition. Senior politicians are rarely unequivocal in their refusal to contemplate becoming prime minister. In Lansley's view, the effect of the Brighton bomb on Tebbit was extremely painful psychologically. Just as he realized he had the ability and possibly the party backing to become leader, he understood that his own health, and even more that of his wife, made it impossible. This 'added a bitter edge. He had a sense of lost ambition afterwards, without having fully had that ambition before.' None of this made for a harmonious relationship between Chairman and Prime Minister. Dobbs came to believe that, uneasy about Tebbit, Mrs Thatcher was inclined to permit 'a parallel operation' to intervene in party matters without consulting him.

In his note about the reshuffle, Tebbit assumed no change in the top jobs, and said he took it 'for granted' that she would feel unable to sack Michael Heseltine or Peter Walker. He was unequivocal, however, in his view of the former. 'Defence is in a mess and we cannot afford things to get worse,' he wrote, continuing with characteristic acerbity, '. . . Michael is not really thinking things through and although I would like to see him carry the can for the errors he has made you may feel that he should be moved.' If so, Tebbit proposed his great rival be given Energy and Walker be sent to Health and Social Security. Parkinson ('If he doesn't come back now,

---

* Because Tebbit's wife Margaret had been lying paralysed by her Brighton injuries in Stoke Mandeville hospital near Chequers, Mrs Thatcher had invited him to stay in her country house for several weeks so that he could easily visit 'his Margaret'.

he never will') should go to Defence. In fact, Mrs Thatcher dared neither promote nor demote Heseltine. Attracted, perhaps, by Tebbit's suggestion that he might 'carry the can', she left him in place.

Mrs Thatcher's most striking decision was to move Leon Brittan to Trade and Industry. This reflected her desire for better presentation. 'I've got Geoffrey at the Foreign Office, Nigel at the Treasury and Leon at the Home Office,' she told Ingham. 'Between them, they can't sell anything.' She still considered Lawson vital to her government, and had no proper excuse for moving Howe, so Leon Brittan was the weakest link.*

Despite his undoubted ability and his importance in the miners' strike, Brittan had never won a parliamentary following. The victim of behind-the-hand backbench anti-Semitism, he also suffered from rumours that, though married, he was homosexual, and even that he had been a child abuser (too often in those days the two were conflated). No one produced any evidence for either accusation. Those involved in the reshuffle – Wakeham and Ingham – denied that the rumours affected Mrs Thatcher's decision. But they did reinforce prejudices against Brittan, weakening him politically.

In Brittan's view, he was the 'fall guy' for the government's unpopularity, set up chiefly by Mrs Thatcher's main window on the media world, Ingham. Mrs Thatcher sought to soften the blow for Brittan, assuring him that his seniority remained unchanged, but he felt insecure and ill-used. Although the DTI was undoubtedly a job more central to Mrs Thatcher's reforming mission than the Home Office, it was traditionally lower in the hierarchy.† Douglas Hurd – whom Mrs Thatcher thought 'a very calm person of great stature', though in no sense a Thatcherite – became Home Secretary in Brittan's stead. He was replaced as Northern Ireland secretary by Tom King.

As foreshadowed, Tebbit became Party Chairman. Jeffrey Archer was made his deputy, with a brief to revive the party's grass-roots enthusiasm. Tebbit, who had not been consulted, felt 'a bit miffed'. According to Dobbs, Mrs Thatcher also expected Archer 'to keep an eye on Norman for her', part of the parallel operation. Cecil Parkinson was not brought back. The justified fear of a further assault from Sara Keays prevented this. Concerned, in this exercise, more by presentation than by ideology, Mrs Thatcher promoted several from the left of the party whose strengths,

---

* Mrs Thatcher was also displeased with Brittan for what she considered a lacklustre performance in a battle with the BBC over a series called *Real Lives* in which the Corporation had outraged her by offering airtime to the IRA Chief of Staff, Martin McGuinness.

† In a moment that could have come from *Yes Minister*, one of Brittan's first acts as DTI Secretary was to write to oppose a levy on blank audio-cassettes which had recently been proposed in a letter from the then Home Secretary – himself.

she believed, lay in this realm. Sacking Patrick Jenkin, she made Kenneth Baker Environment Secretary to advance the 'community charge' and take on the left-wing Labour councils. She also made Kenneth Clarke Paymaster-General, with a seat in the Cabinet. He became the Department of Employment's main representative in the Commons because she had made a peer, Lord Young of Graffham, Secretary of State.

Young could now do by stronger means what he had already been doing, originally at the Manpower Services Commission, and then as a minister. Ministerial colleagues instinctively resented him since he was not a professional politician. Mrs Thatcher was alleged to have said, 'Other people bring me problems, but David brings me solutions.' This naturally enraged his fellow ministers, who thought of him as 'teacher's pet'. Much of this resentment was justified. He had, for example, maintained a channel to No. 10 while nominally working for Tom King: 'She was asking me to double-check on her Employment Secretary,' recalled Young. 'She's a moral coward when it comes to dealing with people'. Now she put Young in charge, telling him, 'I want you to deal with unemployment by the next election.' Young duly got to work on tackling everything that made getting a job difficult or undesirable – the benefit trap, poor technical and vocational training and the tax and regulatory difficulties which stopped small businesses thriving. He became one of the few important appointments which she did not partially regret.* As she later put it: 'I reckon he won the '87 election for us because of his employment policies.'

Perhaps because of these new faces, the Conservatives received more favourable media coverage during the conference season than they deserved. At Labour's gathering in Bournemouth Neil Kinnock scored a palpable hit with his attack on the behaviour of the Militant Tendency in Liverpool (see p. 471). The Tories had no comparable message of change. In her leader's speech, Mrs Thatcher tried to make a virtue of her government's lack of startling economic progress by speaking of 'the realities of power exercised responsibly' and 'idealism tempered by realism'. She was at pains to emphasize her commitment to dealing with unemployment. 'No problem ... occupies more of my thinking,' she said, almost truthfully. She was applauded loyally, not rapturously.

In political terms, it was perhaps a grim form of luck for Mrs Thatcher that riots had recently broken out in several black inner-city neighbourhoods.

---

* Alan Clark, who found himself one of Young's junior ministers and had previously been much opposed to him, recorded their first meeting after Young's appointment: 'He is pleasant, charming almost, and fresh ... He talks at twice the speed of Tom King, but listens too, cracks jokes, is full of bright ideas. I can quite see why the Lady fancies him. He is utterly different from the rest of the Cabinet – yet without being caddish.'

Although not nearly as extensive as their predecessors in 1981, the riots were fierce, one even bestial. In October, in Broadwater Farm, Tottenham, PC Keith Blakelock received forty injuries from cuts or stabs. He became the first policeman to die in a mainland British riot for more than 150 years. Bernie Grant, the black local Labour Leader of Haringey Council, said: 'The youths around here believe that the police were to blame for what happened on Sunday and what they got was a bloody good hiding.'

The ferocity of PC Blakelock's murder gave the Tories, gathering for their conference, a new solidarity. Mrs Thatcher turned the traditional Tory subject of law and order into the centrepiece of her speech. She attacked 'crime masquerading as social protest' and won her biggest applause for saying that most British people 'regard the police as friends'. Rather than merely asserting authority, she injected a note of compassion: 'We are all involved. We cannot pass by on the other side.' She was appalled by PC Blakelock's death and sent a handwritten sympathy letter to his widow. 'The agony will be almost unbearable, and words of little comfort,' she wrote. 'But I want you to know that without the bravery of your late husband and others like him Britain would not be the country we know and love. This new terrorism in our midst is like a cancer – and similarly it must be overcome.'

Mrs Thatcher had, in fact, been thinking about the inner cities for some time, which was partly why she had made David Young Employment Secretary. Instead of seeing the inhabitants of what were called Urban Priority Areas as passive victims of government neglect, she wanted them to be participants in shaping a better future. For this to happen, business opportunities had to be made easier.* The official papers on inner cities show her confronted with a piquant contrast. As bad news poured in about riots, so did good news about her largest urban regeneration project – Canary Wharf in London's Docklands. This huge development, which attracted £1.5 billion in private money, remains part of the financial success of London to this day. The London Docklands Development Corporation (LDDC), invented by her and Michael Heseltine in 1981, was achieving these results because it had the power to overcome local government objections and grant planning permission for commercial development and private housing. It was harder to extend such opportunities to other inner cities, most of which were less depopulated than the London Docks and therefore more difficult to transform.

* This was one of the reasons behind Mrs Thatcher's determination to reform local government finance. If, for example, left-wing councils could set their business rates prohibitively high without electoral retribution, they would, and jobs would leave their areas. This contributed to her thinking about the poll tax.

More broadly, there was a half-stated disagreement in the government between the more One Nation Conservatives, who thought that government money would transform the inner cities, and the Thatcherites, who were more interested in economic opportunity, non-state institutions and human failings. Hartley Booth and Oliver Letwin, idealistic young moralists at the Policy Unit, wrote to Mrs Thatcher noting the extensive wish lists of her ministers – black middle-class entrepreneurs for Lord Young, refurbished council blocks for Kenneth Baker, a reduction in youth alienation for Douglas Hurd. None of this, they argued, reached the root cause: 'Riots, criminality and social disintegration are caused solely by individual characters and attitudes. So long as bad moral attitudes remain, all efforts to improve the inner cities will founder. David Young's new entrepreneurs will set up in the disco and drug trade.'

Into this discussion broke the Church of England. That November, the Archbishop of Canterbury, Robert Runcie, sent Mrs Thatcher a copy of *Faith in the City*, the large-scale report of his Commission on Urban Priority Areas. It offered, by its own account, 'a disturbing picture' of those major cities 'where economic, physical and social conditions are at their most acute and depressing'. 'It is not, of course, a comfortable read for Archbishops or for Prime Ministers,' Runcie told her, but 'despite some reservations which I have about certain sections, I believe the contents have to be taken seriously.'

Chaired by Sir Richard O'Brien, the commission to which Runcie gave this somewhat tepid endorsement was made up almost exclusively of leading figures of the Anglican liberal-left.* Although Runcie had not intended a political onslaught,† his more ideological fellows had chosen to attack Mrs Thatcher (without naming her) and all her works. The report put forward an unreconstructed 1945-style programme of Keynesian government-sponsored works dressed in ecclesiastical vestments. It referred respectfully to Marx and disparaged the Protestant work ethic. It quoted with approval one submission: 'The exclusion of the poor is pervasive and not accidental.' When she read this Mrs Thatcher put heavy lines below 'not accidental', well aware that she stood accused. In the view of Richard Chartres, later Bishop of London, the report's recommendations and data about the life of the urban Church were valuable, but its theology was 'pathetic'.

Even the combative Ingham advised Mrs Thatcher against 'a pre-emptive

---

* They included David Sheppard, Bishop of Liverpool, Canon Eric James, the Director of Christian Action, and Professor A. H. Halsey, the leading socialist sociologist and former Reith lecturer.
† According to his chaplain at that time, John Witheridge, Runcie was 'a bit of a Tory Wet' who was 'quite confused politically'. He had a 'quiet respect for Mrs Thatcher'.

strike', since this would 'draw more attention to the report'. One unnamed minister, however, speaking to the *Sunday Times*, described it as 'pure Marxist theology', thus lighting the blue touchpaper. The resulting publicity served mainly to amplify the idea that the government, and the Prime Minister in particular, were 'uncaring'.

Mrs Thatcher had never wanted a fight with the Church. John Gummer, who discussed the report with her, noticed she felt 'hurt' by it. There was a strong moral and religious base to her politics and she 'saw the Church as an important part of the stability of society'. 'She didn't like its implication that she didn't care: she did.' She felt frustrated that the Church was trading on its spiritual and moral prestige to pronounce on economic matters which it failed to understand.

Seeking friendlier religious authorities, Mrs Thatcher was pleased by the writings of the Chief Rabbi, Immanuel Jakobovits. He wrote a commentary on *Faith in the City* entitled 'From Doom to Hope' in which he argued that Jews had broken out of the ghetto because 'we worked on ourselves, not on others' and 'hallowed our home life'. He thought it sad that *Faith in the City* 'falls short of hailing work as a virtue in itself'. Mrs Thatcher is supposed to have told Jakobovits she wished she could make him Archbishop of Canterbury.* Perhaps not coincidentally, she came to the view that his co-religionist, David Young, should be put in charge of inner-city initiatives, driving private-sector 'task forces' to 'develop a viable private sector base in the inner cities'.

In a scribbled note to Mrs Thatcher, Robert Armstrong suggested that the task force plan be announced soon to 'pre-empt ... the Member for Henley (Mr Heseltine) [who had resigned from the government over the Westland crisis three weeks earlier] who – Lord Young suspects – may before long turn his restless energies to the problems of inner cities and (especially) Liverpool'. Mrs Thatcher acted accordingly.

---

* Since she could not, Mrs Thatcher made Jakobovits a peer in 1988, the first chief rabbi to enter the House of Lords.

21

Helicopter crash

'Her hands were not entirely clean'

When she came to compose her memoirs in the early 1990s, Margaret Thatcher was heard to remark, 'I can't even remember what the actual Westland thing was about now.' She was not alone. To many, it seemed mysterious that an argument over the future of a £30 million West Country helicopter company should have convulsed a successful government with a parliamentary majority of 140. Yet that is what happened. For the first time, Mrs Thatcher would find her personal reputation assailed not only by her political opponents but by at least one 'enemy within'. Her methods of exercising power would be exposed and her integrity seriously questioned.

The immediate cause of the explosion was the character of the Defence Secretary, Michael Heseltine. Said to dislike working for a woman, Heseltine had never been close to Mrs Thatcher, personally or politically. She considered him lazy. 'At Defence he didn't take work home . . .' she recalled in retirement. 'He did actually give quite a lot of luncheon parties at his large house. It is usually a sign.'* Nonetheless, Heseltine had performed well for her politically at Defence, notably by his vigorous campaign for the installation of US cruise missiles in Britain. But he always maintained markedly different views from hers – more pro-European, more corporatist, more enthusiastic about regional policy. By 1985, seeing no prospect of further advancement under her, he was chafing at the bit.

In April 1985, Heseltine informed Mrs Thatcher that Westland, Britain's only helicopter manufacturer, was running out of work. He favoured a 'market solution' with new management and did not think Britain should

---

* Mrs Thatcher had in her head a charge list of minor incidents against Heseltine – how, for example, when she was at Education he had ordered her officials, without asking her, to brief him on which were the best schools for his own children; or how, at the fortieth anniversary of D-Day in 1984, he had failed to ensure, until she intervened, that war widows could be flown out for the ceremony.

place extra orders to rescue Westland.* Over the summer, as the company's plight worsened, the government sought to stave off receivership and the consequent loss of 1,700 jobs in Yeovil in Somerset.† No. 10 had good links with Sir John Cuckney, the Chairman of Westland, who came from an MI5 background. Cuckney hoped that Sikorsky, the helicopter division of the American company United Technologies, might buy a big minority stake. The Trade and Industry Secretary, Norman Tebbit,‡ openly discouraged the prospect of American involvement, but Mrs Thatcher made clear that an American offer 'would have to be judged on its merits'.

The Cabinet reshuffle that September had significant consequences for the Westland story. While Heseltine stayed at Defence, Leon Brittan replaced Norman Tebbit at the DTI. Brittan's demotion from the Home Office hit him hard. It was in this grumpy frame of mind that he now confronted the problem of Westland. Heseltine, who had always hankered after the job which Brittan had just reluctantly accepted, was not disposed to make matters easy for him. He had been hardened by a battle in 1984 about the building of two new Type 22 naval frigates. Tebbit had wanted them both built at Swan Hunter on Tyneside. Heseltine, who always pushed the cause of Liverpool, felt differently. When Tebbit insisted that Cammell Laird, based on Merseyside, be allowed to bid for only one frigate, Heseltine threatened resignation. Reluctantly Mrs Thatcher backed Heseltine but was left 'seething' at his tactics.

Norman Tebbit was also a significant figure in the drama, but a somewhat uncertain ally for Mrs Thatcher. He was close to Willie Whitelaw, the Deputy Prime Minister, who told him Heseltine had been a 'bloody shit' over Cammell Laird.§ Watching Heseltine's behaviour over Westland,

---

* Despite this, Mrs Thatcher jumped at an eccentric request from Kenneth Kaunda, the President of Zambia, who wrote asking for twelve Westland helicopters paid for out of the British overseas aid programme to check on poachers of elephants and 'the rhino, the eland, the leopard, cheetah and the black lechwe'. 'I hope this can be done very quickly,' Mrs Thatcher scribbled on the covering letter. 'It may help Westlands.' Concerned about the propriety of the aid programme, the Foreign Office quashed the idea.

† Yeovil was of particular concern to the Conservative government because a Liberal, Paddy Ashdown, had gained the seat from the Tories at the previous general election. They wanted to win it back. The seat remained in Liberal hands until 2015.

‡ The Department of Trade and Industry was the 'sponsor' department in the Westland affair because the Ministry of Defence, as an actual and potential customer, had an interest to declare. This involvement of two departments, though inevitable, was to prove incendiary.

§ Heseltine believed that Whitelaw 'never approved of me', for reasons that he never exactly understood. It may have been something to do with Whitelaw's view of business, which he once expressed to Heseltine thus: 'I hate businessmen. I hate businessmen. I hate businessmen.' 'Willie,' Heseltine replied, 'I am a businessman.'

they concluded quite early on, Tebbit recalled, that he was 'fishing for an issue on which to resign'.

In early October, when Leon Brittan first wrote to Mrs Thatcher about the future of Westland, the tone of discussion was rational. He considered Sikorsky the most likely buyer, but felt Westland 'should be encouraged to pursue the possibility of a European solution'. Heseltine, who would later make much of this suggestion, set to work. It was true that Heseltine instinctively preferred European projects and Mrs Thatcher instinctively favoured American ones. She thought in terms of free markets, he in terms of government intervention. But the Westland issue was not framed in pro- or anti-European terms, or even much in terms of market theory, at that time. Nevertheless, a difference of emphasis began to emerge. Tebbit, Charles Powell and – most important – Cuckney were suspicious of a European bid, which they considered an attempt to block Sikorsky. Heseltine, however, came to believe that Sikorsky wanted Westland as a vehicle to sell their own Black Hawk helicopters to the Ministry of Defence. He now sought to repeat his Cammell Laird victory over Westland. Powell encountered Heseltine sitting outside the Cabinet Office. 'She's not going to beat me on this one,' Heseltine told him. So Powell prepared Mrs Thatcher for battle.

In late November, Heseltine brilliantly, if precariously, cobbled together a European bid for Westland. Crucially, he combined this with an understanding among European National Armaments Directors (NADs) that European governments would buy helicopters only from European companies. If this stood, a European defence cartel would be established, annihilating any Sikorsky bid. Already worried by disagreement over Westland between the MOD and Brittan's DTI, Cuckney decided to exploit his connections: 'The monkeys are squabbling. I must go to the organ grinder.' He wanted Mrs Thatcher on his side.

Whitehall battle was joined. John MacGregor, the Chief Secretary to the Treasury, objected to the NADs' recommendations, which had 'placed Westland in an impossible position'. Brittan agreed and Mrs Thatcher supported him. As her Policy Unit put it, in a way guaranteed to rouse her ire: 'Michael Heseltine is proposing that a Conservative Government should intervene to kill a private sector rescue of Westlands – which amazingly costs the Government nothing – in order to promote a European deal which will reduce competition and result in the stripping of Westlands, such that it will only survive long term with state subsidy. This surely isn't on.' She strongly agreed.

As the government geared up to settle the matter collectively, Heseltine sought to strengthen his hand. On Thursday 5 December, he revealed that 'he has just (?) discovered that BAe would be ready to join a European consortium, thus making it less "foreign"' as Powell put it with sarcastic quotation marks. With colleagues the next day, Heseltine asked whether Westland should come under 'foreign control' (that is, Sikorsky) or be rescued by a European consortium? Mrs Thatcher, chairing, saw a 'clear majority' ready to reject the NADs' recommendation (and thus undermine the European bid), but noted that a minority 'strongly opposed' this view. The minority included Howe and Tebbit, who could see merit in a European solution. 'She thought Tebbit was a traitor,' recalled Heseltine, 'and was very rude to him.'* Rather than decide immediately, she now agreed, with an ill grace, to refer the issue to a full meeting of E Committee on Monday. She invited Cuckney and his colleagues to attend to explain their views, a highly unusual device which, she believed, would assist his cause.

Tension ran high over the weekend as Heseltine sought to sweeten the European bid. Powell believed that Brittan was not countering him robustly: 'In the face of all this figure skating, DTI look positively flat-footed,' he warned Mrs Thatcher. Westland now seemed willing to delay a decision. That would strengthen Heseltine by giving him more time to lobby for his rushed European option. Powell urged the DTI to refer the matter to full Cabinet, confident that Mrs Thatcher could prevail.

Seen from Heseltine's office, this ever-greater No. 10 engagement was a provocation. It was particularly noticeable that Powell had, in his own words, 'seized' the subject, squeezing out others, including his nominal senior, the principal private secretary, Nigel Wicks. Powell was an effective – perhaps too effective – projection of his principal's combative personality, bringing out the conflict between Prime Minister and Defence Secretary inherent not only in their views but in their characters. Mrs Thatcher had once remarked to Heseltine: 'You must realize, Michael, you and I are quite similar people.' Her crisp analysis helps explain the Westland debacle. A collision between these two was becoming almost inevitable. Powell believed that Heseltine had 'made up his mind early: it was win or leave'. The same 'win or leave' mentality well describes Mrs Thatcher – and she had absolutely no intention of leaving.

The E Committee meeting of 9 December did not go as smoothly as Mrs Thatcher had hoped. Although Cuckney performed well, ministers were irritated by his presence and felt that she was putting them under undue pressure. They therefore inclined to sympathize with Heseltine. This

---

* Tebbit later claimed he only wanted to 'give Michael enough rope to hang himself', but Mrs Thatcher was not aware of this.

meeting took place shortly after Mrs Thatcher had found herself isolated among colleagues over ERM entry (see p. 494): there was a lack of friendly feeling. There was no groundswell of support for the European bid, but rather than reject it outright, it was agreed to allow the Westland board until 4 p.m. that Friday (13 December) to decide whether to recommend it to shareholders. If it chose not to, ministers would reject the NADs' recommendation, leaving the way clear for Sikorsky. Heseltine did not dissent but, in a rather desperate gambit, asked for a special meeting after the Westland board decision on the Friday afternoon. Once the European bid was better developed, he believed he might yet sway colleagues.

Without realizing it, ministers departed with different views of what exactly had been agreed – an issue that would come to assume great significance. Heseltine 'believed (or affected to believe)' – as Robert Armstrong put it – that a further committee meeting had been promised. Mrs Thatcher believed that a meeting had merely been provided for should the circumstances surrounding the European bid change. Outraged that No. 10 had stopped an early Cabinet Office effort to ring round and line ministers up for a Friday meeting, Heseltine raised the matter at Cabinet on Thursday 12 December. Mrs Thatcher's view was that the ring-round was only to gauge availability, not set a definite meeting. She refused any further discussion. According to Heseltine, he protested, although this is not recorded in Armstrong's contemporaneous note. 'There was some force in Heseltine's claim that there wasn't a full Cabinet discussion,' Brittan recalled. 'I thought he had the right to refer it to the Cabinet.'

Heseltine had begun to attribute overwhelming importance to the Westland issue. He now worked furiously to get a European bid, higher than Sikorsky's, in time to impress colleagues on Friday.* He realized it was unlikely the Westland board would accept the European bid on the Friday. But he felt that if Cabinet colleagues were convinced, the European option would be kept alive and shareholders might be persuaded to reject the board's likely Sikorsky recommendation. In Heseltine's mind, 'If I had accepted the cancellation of the meeting, I would have been finished.' Brittan thought this correct: 'It was the only thing he had.'

After the Westland board meeting on Friday, Cuckney informed Powell that it had decided not to recommend the European bid to shareholders. He then sent Mrs Thatcher a letter complaining of undue interference from the MOD in Westland's future. He asked that 'no UK Government

---

* Heseltine's efforts included obtaining a letter offering GEC's financial support from his former Cabinet colleague and anti-Thatcherite Jim Prior, now the company's Chairman, for the European bid. GEC's involvement added to the notion that the European bid was 'British'.

statement is made to the effect that Her Majesty's Government will never purchase the Black Hawk', since to do so would be inconsistent with full and fair competition.

So ended the first full week of explicit hostilities. Heseltine was, on balance, losing. It was still not impossible, however, that the European bid might ultimately prevail with the Westland shareholders. Mrs Thatcher's private office – really Charles Powell – increasingly took control of the issue. Given the inadequacies of the DTI, this was understandable, but it was likely that Mrs Thatcher would be touched with pitch as the fight got nastier. She was as tough as anyone in politics, but not a good Machiavellian. Rather than seeking to avoid the meeting Heseltine coveted, she would surely have been wiser to let it happen, making sure that he did not prevail. In Heseltine's view her behaviour ensured that 'the disaster was cast in steel'.

By this time the press were excited, and the Westland disagreements between ministers were publicly exposed. Brittan made a statement to the Commons on Monday 16 December explaining that the government was not taking sides over Westland bids but leaving matters to the market. Sitting on the front bench with him, Heseltine was seen to shake his head in disagreement.

Mrs Thatcher believed that Heseltine was now consciously breaking collective Cabinet responsibility. Discussing the matter with the Chief Whip, John Wakeham, Whitelaw and Brittan on Wednesday, she accepted their suggestion that she send Heseltine a letter to force his hand. Robert Armstrong produced a draft that was short and blunt. 'You were on the front bench in the House yesterday when I made clear the Government's position concerning the future of Westlands,' he had Mrs Thatcher writing, 'namely that it is a matter for the company to decide.' An ultimatum followed: 'In this situation no Minister should use his position to promote one commercial option in preference to another – so long as he remains in government.'

Mrs Thatcher, however, could not decide whether the letter should be sent. She consulted Ingham, who said: 'I think it's weak.' 'Weak!' exclaimed Mrs Thatcher. 'What's strong?' 'Sacking him,' said Ingham. 'Are you saying that I should sack him?' 'No, I'm just saying what's strong.' The press secretary's view was that, if Heseltine received such a letter, 'he would just resign'. She later recalled Ingham saying, 'The public aren't ready for it, and wouldn't understand it.' She accepted this and the letter was not sent.

So nothing happened. To Ingham, here was an example of how Whitelaw, for all his prestige as a fixer, was 'a lightweight': 'He did nothing about

Westland. He should have said to Heseltine, "We're not having this."' In retrospect, Mrs Thatcher felt that the most justified criticism of her was not for provoking Heseltine but for not disciplining him. Her counter-self-justification took its cue from Ingham's argument about public reaction: 'I knew the politics of it.' Heseltine, in other words, was too popular with the party in the country. The ground for his departure had not been prepared.

At Cabinet the following day, Mrs Thatcher sought to bring the issue to a head. Westland's shareholders were due to decide the company's future on 13 January 1986. 'No Minister', she told the Cabinet, '... is authorised to lobby for one side or the other.' When Heseltine sought to quibble, she held firm. Lawson and then Whitelaw supported her. The Prime Minister had to answer questions in the House that day, Whitelaw said. He turned to her: 'Hope Cab. can agree you are speaking for whole Govt.' 'Is that confirmed?' Mrs Thatcher asked. '<u>Cab</u>: Confirmed,' noted Armstrong. Whatever Heseltine's private thoughts, he acquiesced in the unanimity. At Prime Minister's Questions that afternoon, when Neil Kinnock sought to exploit the issue, she could respond simply that the future of Westland was 'a matter for the company to decide ... That is the position ... reaffirmed by the Cabinet this morning.' In private, Heseltine complained to friends of his 'humiliation'.

Both sides now spent the Christmas season preparing for a showdown, with the struggle continuing through a series of letters. Heseltine's camp had been claiming that, were a non-European entity (i.e. Sikorsky) to hold even a minority stake in the company, Westland would be shut out of the European market. So Cuckney sought an assurance from Mrs Thatcher that this would not be the case. She wished to oblige, but soon after her draft reply to Cuckney reached Heseltine's office for comment, Downing Street received a letter giving the opinion of the Solicitor-General,* Sir Patrick Mayhew. It warned that the government would be 'at serious risk' if it did not convey 'the fact that there are indications from European governments and companies' that Westland might lose a number of European projects were the Sikorsky offer to be accepted.

This letter, which infuriated Mrs Thatcher, had clearly been inspired by Heseltine. Heseltine and Patrick Mayhew were old Oxford friends. The Defence Secretary, seeking to trump Mrs Thatcher's proposed response to Cuckney, had rushed the Solicitor-General into it. The use of the Law Officers in government was (and is still) a sensitive issue because of the distinction between law and politics. Under the British system the Law Officers are politicians but, when giving legal advice, they are not allowed to

---

* Mayhew's superior, the Attorney-General, Sir Michael Havers, was absent because of illness.

behave politically. By the same token, ministers are not supposed to abuse Law Officers' advice for political purposes or ever to disclose it – even its existence – without the officers' agreement. Paradoxically, therefore, the advice can be a potent political weapon because its apparent objectivity makes it difficult to challenge. Heseltine knew that Mrs Thatcher, faced with such advice, would have to go carefully.

In her reply to Cuckney on New Year's Day, Mrs Thatcher followed Mayhew's legal advice. But she also confirmed that while Westland remained in the UK, the government would continue to regard it as a British – and therefore as a European – company: 'The Government would wish to see Westland play a full part in existing and future European collaborative projects.' Two days later, Heseltine fought back by other means. In a letter to Lloyds Merchant Bank, acting for the European bid, he set out arguments to sway the shareholders against the Sikorsky bid. 'The Government ... has no intention of procuring the Black Hawk,' he wrote. Mrs Thatcher was not shown the letter before Heseltine sent it. The MOD subsequently leaked it to *The Times*.

Although the government remained formally neutral about who should buy Westland, both camps – Heseltine and 10 Downing Street – were now expending immense energy fighting for one side or the other. The next move came from Mrs Thatcher. Aware that Heseltine's letter to Lloyds contained a factual mistake, she instructed Powell to contact Mayhew. Revenge was about to be executed. As Powell put it, 'Heseltine tried to deploy the Law Officers and got it right back between the eyes.' On 4 January, Powell reported that, having reviewed Heseltine's letter, Mayhew had concluded that 'it contained a material inaccuracy'. Powell wanted Mayhew to write to Heseltine, pointing this out and suggesting the Defence Secretary 'issue a letter of correction'. Shortly afterwards, as he later recalled, he explained directly to Mayhew 'what was expected of him'. Mayhew made no objection.

The following day, a Sunday, Mrs Thatcher met Whitelaw and Wakeham at Chequers. They agreed that Heseltine should be brought to order at the next Cabinet meeting on Thursday 9 January. She still did not want to sack him. Nor were she and her colleagues trying to engineer his resignation – though they realized it was a strong possibility. They were trying to force Heseltine into line.

In the morning of Monday 6 January, the Solicitor-General sent his letter to Heseltine. Throughout the affair Mayhew was friendlier to Heseltine than to Mrs Thatcher: his rebuke did little more than go through the motions. But it did note 'material inaccuracies' in the letter to Lloyds and advised

Heseltine to correct them.* Passing this on to Mrs Thatcher, Powell wrote on it: 'Very satisfactory'. Like the first, this second Mayhew letter had been transparently inspired by ministers in their internecine war. The conflict now intensified. As Brittan recalled, 'She and her entourage were extremely keen it be in the public domain.' In a breach of accepted practice, the Law Officer's letter was leaked to the press. Colette Bowe, Brittan's press officer, read part of it over the telephone just after 2 p.m. to Chris Moncrieff of the Press Association.

Not only was the leak improper, it was also partial. Bowe had read Moncrieff only the passage damaging to Heseltine. 'It was', Moncrieff recalled, 'a major act of deception.' It also – not surprisingly – enraged Mayhew. 'I was furious,' he remembered, insisting he had a 'substantial interest in Law Officers not being perceived to be used for tendentious purposes'. Since he had, in fact, allowed himself to be used twice that week for tendentious purposes – first by Heseltine, then by Thatcher/Brittan – Mayhew must have been particularly irritated that his role had become visible. He now threatened resignation. Mayhew was supported by the Attorney-General, Michael Havers, who threatened privately to put the police into No. 10 to investigate. Havers also wrote to Robert Armstrong demanding a formal leak inquiry.† This was a dangerous development. If it could be proved that 10 Downing Street had been abusing a Law Officer's advice for political purposes, Mrs Thatcher's integrity would be in question.

Mrs Thatcher knew she had to find a way to rein Heseltine in at the Cabinet meeting that Thursday. Her draft speaking note reminded her that the affair had 'brought ridicule on the government at home and abroad'. One simple sentence read: 'We cannot go on like this.' This was no more than the truth.

When the Cabinet met on Thursday 9 January, Mrs Thatcher warned of 'great damage ... just as things were getting better'. She asked everyone to observe collective responsibility and the conclusions of the Cabinet meeting before Christmas. Given the sensitivity, she insisted, as Armstrong's scribbled notes recorded, that 'Answers to qu must be cleared through the Cabinet Office, so that they can be cleared with depts. concerned. That

---

* The nature of the 'material inaccuracies' was hardly earth-shattering. Heseltine had been mistaken in saying, said Mayhew, that *all* the companies in the European bid had stated that a Westland link with Sikorsky would rule out Westland participation in a European battlefield helicopter. Two had; one (the Italians) hadn't.

† Mayhew considered this 'very brave' of Havers, because he (Havers) wanted to be Lord Chancellor and was risking this ambition by displeasing Mrs Thatcher. In fact, she gave Havers the job he wanted in June the following year. It probably would have looked too vindictive for her to have done otherwise. Charles Powell was less impressed: 'The biggest leaker was Havers – every lunch-time to his chums at the bar of the Garrick Club.'

is what collective responsibility means.' Heseltine objected. He agreed he would not make any new statements, but he must be able to answer questions himself about the European bid since the answers depended on government defence policy.

Norman Tebbit acted the role of candid friend to Heseltine. He had 'a great deal of personal sympathy' for the European bid, he said, but 'with reasonable good will' all ministers could stick to the same line. Lawson, Howe and others also urged Heseltine to accept what Howe called the 'need for unity', but Heseltine would not let go. Mrs Thatcher stuck to her guns. At last she tried to end the debate, insisting all answers about Westland be cleared through the Cabinet Office. Heseltine said: 'There has been no coll. responsibility in the disc [discussion] of these matters. There has been a breakdown in the propriety of Cabinet discussions. I cannot accept the decision. I must therefore leave this Cabinet.' With these words, at 11.05 a.m. he swept up his papers, rose from the table and walked out.

Observed by Powell, Heseltine went straight from the Cabinet Room into the lavatory to 'comb his hair'.* When he emerged, he walked out of the front door of No. 10 and was approached by a solitary waiting cameraman. 'I've resigned from the Cabinet,' he declared, 'and I shall be making a full statement later on.'† Then he headed across the road to the Ministry of Defence. Heseltine later insisted he resigned on the spur of the moment, 'because of what the No. 10 machine would have done to me if I had accepted this humiliation'. Resignation was not in his best interests: 'It is very likely that I would have been Prime Minister if I hadn't resigned: but I'd never have faced myself.'

Mrs Thatcher adjourned the Cabinet meeting for half an hour. By her own account, she was one of the few not surprised. She knew that resignation was the logical outcome of Heseltine's dramatically uncompromising stance. She had not expected it at that moment but she had prepared, even hoped for it. After she asked George Younger to replace Heseltine at Defence, the Cabinet resumed its meeting.

That afternoon, Heseltine made a resignation statement that was very damaging to Mrs Thatcher. He accused her of organizing 'ad hoc' meetings to get round colleagues and 'close off the European option'. He protested at the leak of the Solicitor-General's letter, and about its content ('My answer needed no correction.'). He complained that Brittan, meeting the Managing Director of BAe, had tried to interfere with the bid by warning

---

* Heseltine denied this.
† Clive Whitmore, Heseltine's Permanent Secretary, dining with him the night before, formed no sense that he was about to resign. He wondered whether, if no cameraman had been in Downing Street, Heseltine would have resigned at all.

him to sever his company's link with the European consortium. He said he could not accept the silence demanded of him at that morning's meeting. Hence his action: 'if the basis of trust between the Prime Minister and her Defence Secretary no longer exists, there is no place for me with honour in such a Cabinet'. Heseltine successfully wrung the occasion for every drop of drama it possessed.*

Mrs Thatcher was not displeased with the resignation itself. She believed, probably rightly, that most Conservative opinion thought Heseltine had gone too far over such a minor issue. What she failed to see, however, was that, in the process he had damaged her, and she had damaged herself. Stephen Sherbourne, the head of her political office, sent her an acute analysis of the political effects. 'I am not worried about the attack on your so-called "style of Government",' he wrote. 'People want Prime Ministers to be in charge and they expect that of you.' The problem lay the other way: 'The most damaging effect of the Heseltine affair has been to show the Government in serious disarray and you looking, uncharacteristically, as though you are not in control.' Ingham suggested a coordinated press response, spreading the load among ministers. Instead, Mrs Thatcher chose to lay the unpleasant parliamentary duty of making a statement on the affair solely upon Brittan. His shoulders were not big enough to bear it.

On the following Monday, 13 January, Brittan addressed the House, only to be ambushed by Heseltine. Brittan denied Heseltine's accusation that he had put any pressure on BAe to withdraw from the European bid. But Heseltine knew that a letter had been received in Downing Street from the company complaining about Brittan's meeting with its Managing Director. When he asked whether the government had received any such letter, Brittan, who knew of its existence, said: 'I have not received any such letter.'† Late that night he was forced to return to Parliament to apologize and correct the record. There were numerous calls for his resignation. John Smith, the shadow DTI spokesman, pointed out that Mrs Thatcher could have lent over to correct him in the House that afternoon but had not chosen to do so.

The following day, Mrs Thatcher responded to growing pressure by

---

* The journalist Nicholas Coleridge was ill when Heseltine resigned, and so lay in bed watching the story continuously on television. He noted that he wore six different ties in one day – blue and yellow designed by Gianfranco Ferré, a white tie 'embossed like a pie frill', a plain black tie, then 'green geometric Pucci of Florence, followed by the Guards tie for the *Six O'Clock News* and a restrained red polka dot on a black background for the late headlines'.

† Brittan had been advised by Downing Street not to refer to the letter in Parliament because it was labelled 'private and confidential'. His denial was a lawyer's answer – literally true, since Downing Street, not he, had received it, but wholly misleading.

announcing a private inquiry into the leak of the Solicitor-General's letter, headed by Robert Armstrong. She had little choice, given the anger of the Law Officers, but her decision greatly increased the danger to her. Any discovery that the Prime Minister had a hand in the affair could, in the febrile circumstances, prove fatal.

By this time, friends of Mrs Thatcher were seriously worried about her political position. They knew that if, after all this, the European bid for Westland were to succeed, she would be badly wounded. So they began to take matters into their own hands. In early January, a mystery buyer bought nearly 15 per cent of Westland shares. This was quickly revealed to be Lord Hanson. According to John Nott, Hanson, Gianni Agnelli (the boss of Fiat) and Sir James Goldsmith had considered forming a 'concert party' to buy sufficient shares in Westland to take control of the company.* Rupert Murdoch, the media mogul, who was also a Director of United Technologies, the owner of Sikorsky, contemplated getting Sikorsky to 'do a deal' over Westland. It would go in with BAe and GEC, exclude the Europeans and thus save Mrs Thatcher's bacon. Meanwhile, Lord Weinstock, GEC's Managing Director, was trying to get Sikorsky-Fiat to join the European consortium 'and all would be a great united family'.

In fact, neither the Agnelli–Weinstock nor the Murdoch scheme came to fruition, but the combined efforts of Mrs Thatcher's supporters in business gave her welcome allies among Westland's shareholders. Murdoch himself bought just under 5 per cent of Westland's shares, the limit which required disclosure of the buyer. As well as believing that Mrs Thatcher was good for his business and for Britain, Murdoch had a particular reason to prevent her fall. He was about to make the dramatic move to produce all his papers on new technology at his plant in Wapping, taking on the might of print unions. He was counting on her support in the coming battle. Westland and Wapping were intertwined.

On Wednesday 15 January, Mrs Thatcher had to speak in the parliamentary debate which, after the Heseltine resignation, she had hoped to avoid. Although she made no catastrophic individual error, she was weak. This was no accident. She had to avoid attacking Heseltine, she explained to Woodrow Wyatt on the phone that morning,† because she feared giving

---

* A 'concert party' is the term used when individuals, secretly acting together, buy up a company's shares to acquire control. When taxed with the suggestion of a concert party to back the Sikorsky bid, John Cuckney preferred a different phrase: it was a 'fan club', he said.

† Wyatt, who wrote columns for the *News of the World* and *The Times*, liked to act as an informal intermediary between Mrs Thatcher and Rupert Murdoch, who owned both. He was close to Mrs Thatcher and interpreted her to his readers. He telephoned her most Sundays and

him 'an excuse to do even more harm'. Wyatt advised her to clear the air about the charge that Brittan had leaked the Solicitor-General's letter, but she knew she could not. Because of her own role, she was feeling vulnerable. Two days after the debate, Westland shareholders voted in favour of the Sikorsky bid, but not by the 75 per cent required to settle the matter. So the battle continued.

On Sunday, John Whittingdale, Brittan's special adviser, had an alarming conversation with Colette Bowe, who had leaked the key words from the Solicitor-General's letter. So far, she had not been publicly identified. She informed Whittingdale that she had told Armstrong the true circumstances of the leak and 'would tell Select Cttee if asked'. Until this point, those involved had assumed that the facts could be covered up; now this might be impossible. Bowe's account to Armstrong was bound to implicate some of her political masters. In his diary Whittingdale wrote, 'May finish us all.' Three days later, news spread that Armstrong's leak inquiry had identified the DTI as the source. The Labour MP Tam Dalyell named Colette Bowe in the House.

Rumours began to circulate that Brittan would have to resign. On 22 January, after he and Mrs Thatcher were briefed on the findings of Armstrong's inquiry, it was agreed she would make a statement in the Commons the next day. Geoffrey Howe, a friend of Brittan, argued for a form of words which made his position more publicly defensible, conveying the sense that Brittan had been acting with her authority. Although she resisted, Mrs Thatcher did concede some of what Howe and Brittan wanted. She felt close to being trapped.

On 23 January, Mrs Thatcher set out the findings of Armstrong's report before the House. She explained it had been 'a matter of duty' that Heseltine's 'material inaccuracies' be corrected and become public knowledge by 4 p.m. on 6 January before Cuckney's press conference announcing the board's recommendation of the Sikorsky bid. She explained that, at 1.30 that day, on becoming aware of what Mayhew had written, Brittan wanted it leaked (she stuck with the word 'disclosure'). He would have preferred this be done by No. 10, but gave authority for it to come from the DTI, subject to the agreement of her office.

Mrs Thatcher moved on to her own role. Her office, she said, had given 'cover' (a key word that Brittan had demanded): 'They did not seek my agreement: they considered – and they were right – that I should agree

---

she usually took his calls. His diaries, which begin in 1985 and were published posthumously, are a good source for the 'off duty' remarks and attitudes of many of the leading figures of the age, including Mrs Thatcher.

with [Brittan]' that the material should be disclosed quickly. Her office 'accepted' that the DTI would disclose the letter by ringing the Press Association. 'Had I been consulted,' she went on, 'I should have said that a different way must be found of making the relevant facts known.' The Attorney-General, she added, having read Armstrong's report, saw no need for prosecutions under the Official Secrets Act. She named none of the officials involved. She was in the awkward position of half-admitting that something bad had happened but not admitting that anyone (apart, of course, from Heseltine) had been at fault.

Her statement failed to clear the air. One Tory MP asked her pointedly if she was 'satisfied that the statement she has made this afternoon has enhanced the integrity of her Government'. On the other side, both Neil Kinnock and, more effectively, David Owen asked about what she herself had known and when. The mood within the parliamentary Conservative Party now became restive. Her statement had opened a gap between herself and Brittan, because it said that he definitely had ordered the leak and she definitely had not. This made Brittan vulnerable. At the 1922 Committee meeting that night, the current went strongly against him. The whips did not exert themselves to save Brittan. 'The mood was wholly supportive of her,' Alan Clark recorded, 'and the Scapegoat was duly tarred.'

This was unwelcome to Mrs Thatcher, partly because she felt that Brittan deserved to be backed, but chiefly because she feared for her own political life. Brittan, feeling ill-treated, might try to blame her and bring her down. She knew he knew things which could do this. Brittan himself seems to have toyed with this possibility. After the Solicitor-General's letter had been disclosed he told his PPS, Gerry Malone, that 'Mrs Thatcher personally authorised the leak.' Speaking to the present author, he put it a bit differently – the leak was '*in effect* authorized by her'. Although Brittan was naturally inhibited from turning against Mrs Thatcher by past loyalty, by hope of future advancement and by fear of being involved in the ensuing ruin, he was also angry. She now had to tread carefully.

The next morning, 24 January, Brittan contemplated the conflicting signals. The press was full of headlines suggesting he resign, so much so that he believed Ingham was briefing against him. Willie Whitelaw advised him to stay,* but John Wakeham told him he had lost the support of the party. In the afternoon, Brittan told Mrs Thatcher he must go. She begged him to stay, with a strong show of sincerity. He refused. In his resignation letter he said, 'Since your statement in the House yesterday it has become clear to me

---

* Characteristically, the next day, after Brittan had resigned, Whitelaw told Woodrow Wyatt that 'Of course Brittan had to go.'

that I no longer command the full confidence of colleagues . . .' There was an implied criticism here, perhaps a threat of revenge. In reply, Mrs Thatcher was much warmer. Expressing her regret at his departure, she added, 'I hope that it will not be long before you return to high office to continue your Ministerial career.' This was an unusual thing to say to a resigning minister. It had the force, in Brittan's mind, of 'an informal understanding'.

There was a sense in which Brittan's resignation was worse for Mrs Thatcher than Heseltine's. Unlike Heseltine, Brittan had tried to do what the Cabinet, and particularly she herself, had wanted. He had also conspired with her about how best to do Heseltine down. So the thought that she had been as weak in protecting an ally as she had in fighting an opponent was damaging. She now faced the Westland debate called by Labour for the coming Monday without a praetorian guard to protect her.

Mrs Thatcher's team made huge efforts to prepare her for the showdown. Sherbourne begged Nigel Wicks and Powell to go through the whole thing with her 'very precisely . . . "Brian Walden style"* . . . Because the PM has <u>got</u> to be pinned down to be as precise as possible.' 'I was worried', he recalled, 'that Kinnock would kill her with two or three questions.' For example: did her office know that the DTI intended to disclose the letter by partial leak? If so, why didn't they seek her agreement, or counsel against? If neither, wasn't it 'tacit approval of something which the Prime Minister has since said was wrong?'. Exhausted and perplexed, Mrs Thatcher allowed herself to become a passenger. As a lawyer, and one with a keen sense of the proprieties, she felt particularly awkward to be caught up in a scandal involving the Law Officers. She must also have had an uneasy conscience. Briefly at least, she seems to have felt like a rabbit in the headlights.

Mrs Thatcher was heartened, however, by a call from President Reagan, who told her 'he thought she might like to hear a friendly voice'.† 'He was furious that anyone had the gall to challenge her integrity. He wanted her to know that "out here in the colonies" she had a friend. He urged the Prime Minister to go out and do her darnedest.'

The biggest fear (or, for some, hope) was that Brittan would use his power to bring her down. Her vulnerability was emphasized on Sunday, when Douglas Hurd defended her on television but called for proper Cabinet government – a coded attack. He also said, 'The worst thing for the country now would be to lurch into discussion of the leadership,' thereby making such discussion more likely. Hurd's performance led to grumbles

---

* A reference to the heavyweight television political interviewer.
† Reagan was clearly fond of opening his calls in this disarming manner. He had used exactly the same words when calling Mrs Thatcher during the Falklands conflict in May 1982 (see p. 310).

from Howe's camp. According to Howe's PPS, Richard Ryder, 'Geoffrey believed he would become leader' if Mrs Thatcher fell: 'He'd got all his ducks in a row.'

On the morning of the debate, Monday 27 January, fear of Brittan's reaction had not receded. The problem was not just Brittan himself but the mutinous feelings of his officials, who resented being outmanoeuvred by Ingham and Powell. Sources among their ranks alleged to that morning's *Financial Times* that Mrs Thatcher had given an incomplete version of events to the Commons on Thursday.

Discussing her speech with a small group in Downing Street just before she headed to Parliament, Mrs Thatcher declared, 'I may not be Prime Minister by six o'clock tonight.' Those present inwardly acknowledged she might be right, and so did not protest. Howe found it piquant to be helping her in her hour of need because 'Even to my cautious eye it was not possible to discern any successor but myself.'

The House was packed, with Members overflowing the benches and perching in the gangways. Neil Kinnock opened the debate. Although he got in a few pertinent questions, he was quickly blown off course and soon fell back upon the rhetorical generalities for which he was well known. As Alan Clark put it, 'For a few seconds Kinnock had her cornered, and you could see fear in those blue eyes. But then he had an attack of wind, gave her time to recover.' The mood of the House changed. Tony Blair, then a young Labour MP in his first Parliament, learnt from Kinnock's failure as he watched in the Chamber that day: 'She was vulnerable to a forensic dissection. It needed a scalpel. All she got from Neil was a rather floppy baseball bat.'

When Mrs Thatcher answered, she got the worst bit out of the way quickly. She admitted how closely she had been involved in the decision to drum up an opinion from the Solicitor-General, repeating her previously expressed regret that the letter had been leaked without reference to him. This was one of 'a number of matters that could have been handled better, and that, too, I regret', she added. Attempting to account for the respective behaviour of her office and Brittan's, she took refuge in Armstrong's self-parodically careful mandarin phrase: there had been 'a genuine difference of understanding' between the two offices. This was a better formulation than 'misunderstanding' would have been, because it implied fault on neither side. Her speech was successful. 'A brilliant performance, shameless and brave,' Alan Clark wrote. 'We are out of the wood.'

Heseltine himself seemed to confirm this. Later in the debate, he declared that Mrs Thatcher's expression of regret had been 'a difficult and very brave thing for a Prime Minister to say in such circumstances' and admitted regrets about his own actions. She had, he said, now brought 'the politics of this matter to an end'. The Tory benches loudly cheered his apparent magnanimity. Speaking for the first time since his resignation, Brittan upheld the truthfulness of Mrs Thatcher's account and took responsibility for his role in the leak. The great traditional Tory combination of loyalty and humbug had reasserted itself. She had survived.

On 12 February, after much City jiggery-pokery, the Westland shareholders finally accepted the Sikorsky bid, sparing Mrs Thatcher further embarrassment. But by then the political caravan had moved on. The details of the scandal, which lacked the preferred ingredients of sex, spies and money, faded into boredom.

Oddly, though, Heseltine had been too merciful to Mrs Thatcher in declaring the politics of the crisis at an end. The questions about what had really happened and what she had known still lurked. These doubts were used against her officials and the way she governed. On the evening of her parliamentary triumph, Charles Powell wrote her a private letter of congratulation thanking her 'for fighting so hard for Bernard & for me'. He nonetheless stood ready to sacrifice himself: 'If you conclude that you would be better served by a less notorious Private Secretary, I would readily understand and offer to slip away . . .' Powell's letter was clearly couched as an offer she could not accept, but in describing himself as 'notorious' he drew attention to an important aspect of the Westland affair. Until then, although he had made a strong mark in Whitehall, Powell had been unknown to the public. The idea that a non-political official might be a known player was anathema to the Civil Service. It was also not what Powell wanted. The brilliant 'regular', the top-class professional civil servant, had begun to look like one of her 'irregulars', using dark arts. Ingham, although much better known to the public than Powell, was also, unlike twenty-first-century media operatives, a career civil servant with no party affiliation. The suggestion that Powell and Ingham were the two most powerful people below the Prime Minister was explosive, especially as it was not completely untrue.

It did not help that the two often had uneasy relations with each other. Part of the difficulty arose from what was, in more normal circumstances, a huge advantage. Both were outstandingly able. No one else had Ingham's power for a crisp summation of a story, nor his instinct for Mrs Thatcher's attitudes and idiom. Powell, for his part, was a man of astonishing industry and intelligence, and of speed and precision in writing. His memos to Mrs Thatcher, flowing almost constantly through day and night, expounded policy lucidly and gave masterly, often witty explanations of diplomacy. They also mirrored and prompted her thoughts, which enhanced their power. 'Please don't misunderstand this, but in a strange sense it was quite hard to tell what was me and what was her,' Powell reflected.* Mrs Thatcher was right to value both men extremely highly and to trust them. As the Westland trouble blew up, her principal private secretary, Nigel Wicks, though able and hard-working, was too cautious, anxious and reactive to give the necessary lead. Powell saw the vacuum and filled it with panache. Indeed, it is impossible to imagine Mrs Thatcher being able to find her way through the Westland crisis without his help.

Once Powell and Ingham were so widely reported, this became a problem in itself. Great efforts were made to avoid officials being called before the select committees investigating the Westland affair. In the end, Robert Amstrong appeared on behalf of the No. 10 officials as, for the DTI, did Brian Hayes, its Permanent Secretary. As a result, both Ingham and Powell survived and grew in their importance to Mrs Thatcher. If they had fallen, that would have been disastrous for her, but the fact that they stayed on, their power undiminished, was damaging too. The pattern of Westland, the idea of a kitchen Cabinet more powerful than the real one, was established. It would recur.

After months of hearings and deliberations, the Defence Select Committee reported in terms which, though scarcely pleasing to the government, did not cause Mrs Thatcher further personal damage. If the committee had known and published what had really happened, it is hard to see how she would have been able to remain in office. She was lucky that the official at the centre of the leak row, Colette Bowe, was a highly professional civil servant and, in her private views, a strong supporter of the Thatcher 'revolution'. If she had not been, she could probably have brought the Prime Minister down.†

As Bowe recalled, John Mogg, Brittan's private secretary, first made Brittan aware of the Solicitor-General's letter to Heseltine (concerning his 'material inaccuracies') at lunchtime on Monday 6 January. Mogg reminded Brittan that the Westland board would hold its press conference at 4 p.m. 'It's her [that is, Mrs Thatcher's] letter,' Brittan replied. 'If she wants it done, fine. Get it in the public domain, but clear it first with

---

* In Powell's case, the master–servant relationship occasionally teetered on the edge of inverting itself. Returning from their gruelling trip to sign the Hong Kong Declaration (and see Reagan at Camp David) just before Christmas in 1984, Robin Butler arranged an informal drinks gathering for Mrs Thatcher. During the party, the phone on Charles Powell's desk rang. Mrs Thatcher picked it up without hesitation, saying, 'I'm sorry, he's busy. Can I take a message?'
† Until speaking to the present author for this book, Bowe put all her personal records of the saga in a bank vault and said nothing to anyone, other than Armstrong's inquiry, about what had happened. This was despite numerous media provocations. One, from the *Sun*, was the headline 'DTI mole was nude model'. The paper felt able to write this because Colette Bowe, when a student, had taken part in a life-class for a friend at the Slade School of Art.

No. 10.' Mogg then called Powell, who told him the letter must be made public. In Mogg's view, both men spoke on the implicit assumption that if the private secretary says something is wanted, he does so on behalf of his principal. Besides, 'Charles was extremely good at interpreting what his boss wanted: he was speaking with her authority.' When Mogg asked how best to get the letter out, Powell said he had passed a copy to Ingham, while conveying 'that No. 10 did not want to do the business itself'. Mogg therefore asked Bowe to ring Ingham.

Bowe and Ingham were colleagues: he was not her boss but the most senior of her tribe. Because of the Mogg–Powell conversation, she did not believe that, in ringing Ingham, she was raising a question of whether the letter should be leaked. She thought she was having a conversation about 'ways and means' of leaking (she preferred the word 'disclosing'). In Ingham's recollection, Bowe asked him to leak the letter and he refused. According to Bowe, he acknowledged the need to get the letter out, but said, 'I've got to keep the PM above the fray.'* 'I took a deep breath,' Bowe recalled, 'and thought "OK, I'll have to do it."' 'I'll give it to Chris [Moncrieff of the Press Association],' she told Ingham, who agreed. All hell duly broke loose that afternoon.

The next morning, John Whittingdale came to see Bowe. He had just been to No. 10, he said, where it had been made clear to him that 'the PM is very relaxed about the Solicitor-General's letter'. The idea was that this should be conveyed to Brittan. The DTI thus believed they had been given cover from No. 10 both before and after the fact. No one at No. 10 had criticized them for the leak. They were stunned when Mrs Thatcher announced the inquiry. 'We gasped. We said, "What on earth is this inquiry for?"'

Powell gave a different account of his conversation with John Mogg. He believed that Mogg, 'a fairly devious fellow', had set him up for use 'posthumously' when people started to ask questions. Powell denied giving the DTI oblique permission to leak, maintaining that press relations were not his job.†

These 'who did what?' arguments might not have mattered much had it not been for Armstrong's inquiry. But once this began, the officials feared it might turn into *sauve qui peut*. To prevent a hunt for scapegoats, Brian Hayes insisted on accompanying Bowe to her meetings with Armstrong

---

* Ingham's recollection, which supports Bowe's, was that he said, 'I have to keep the PM above that sort of thing.'
† Powell recalled Mogg asking, 'Is this all going to reach the press?', to which Powell replied, 'I expect it will: everything else seems to.' Powell then pointed to the conversation between Ingham and Bowe 'which seems to have gone rather further than that'.

and threatened to resign if his officials were punished. Bowe told Armstrong the full story, including about the message from No. 10, relayed by Whittingdale, to the DTI. She warned that if she were charged under the Official Secrets Act, 'I'll see you in court.'

Bowe's story explains why Armstrong's inquiry found as it did, and why the officials concerned could not be permitted to appear before the select committee. In his own evidence, Armstrong had to give an accurate account of what had happened which nevertheless involved a good deal of *suppressio veri*. If Bowe had revealed what she knew about Mrs Thatcher's support for the leak, the storm would have broken upon the Prime Minister's head. As the select committee was accumulating its material, Mrs Thatcher more than once wrote to her officials warning against what she called 'spurious accuracy'. She meant that people asked for formal evidence sometimes answer with a precision that their memory does not justify. But what she really feared in this case was accuracy itself. As Powell himself put it, 'Her hands were not entirely clean.'

At the end of January, Mrs Thatcher received two contradictory signals. Ingham warned her that, among the lobby, the government was seen as 'tossing on a sea of trouble'. Cabinet ministers were extremely worried about the next election. But her postbag told a different story. During the week of 31 January she had received some 700 letters (five times the usual number). 'Virtually all these letters expressed their <u>unqualified support</u> for your leadership.'

As Mrs Thatcher tried to move on from the affair, it was what Westland exposed beyond the issue itself which proved so difficult. Not much worked well that December and January – not Cabinet government, nor the Cabinet Office; not the whips' management of party opinion, nor media presentation; not interdepartmental relations, nor her private office. Blame naturally attached to the woman in charge. This blame was not only *ex officio*: it also dwelt on her personal defects. Two of her strongest qualities – her leadership competence and her integrity – fell under question. This had not really happened before.

In the end, Mrs Thatcher learnt the wrong lesson from the Westland debacle. According to Ingham, 'Her arteries certainly hardened.' After Westland, 'She was always playing things very close to her chest.' Powell noticed 'no regret or revision' in her mind about how to govern.* Nor did

---

* Indeed, Mrs Thatcher became more arbitrary in her attitudes. She was angry, for example, that Clive Whitmore, her former principal private secretary, had not helped her deal with Heseltine. She ignored the fact that, as his Permanent Secretary, Whitmore owed his loyalty to him,

she see the need to start cultivating backbenchers in the tea room, as she had done in her early days. 'They've chosen someone to lead them, and that's what I do,' she told Powell. She was reinforced in her self-confidence by the view – surely correct in itself – that she had been right about the subject. She often was right when others were wrong, thanks to her courage and independence of mind; but, at this crucial juncture, she failed to pause and think self-critically about what had gone amiss.

The other big event in Britain in early 1986 was Rupert Murdoch's coup against the print unions. For years these unions had refused to agree to relocate to Wapping from the papers' separate, existing 'hot-metal' sites at the back of their respective newspapers. In the spring of 1985, Murdoch decided to move against his long-standing tormentors. Wapping would be made ready, in secret, with the new technology to prepare and print all his British newspapers.*

On 24 January 1986, the day, by coincidence, of Leon Brittan's resignation, 6,000 News International workers went on strike against the company's attempts to modernize. This confrontation suited Murdoch's plan. On the same day, he activated it. Instead of the print unions, he had arranged with the right-wing Electricians' Union (the EETPU) to replace the printers with their members overnight and get the papers out. He sacked all the strikers. To circumvent the attempted union boycott of newspaper distribution that followed he used his own freight company, TNT, to transport the papers by road rather than rail. Large crowds of often violent pickets assembled outside the Wapping plant to prevent workers going in. Some journalists refused to take part in the move to Wapping. The Labour Party announced it would not deal with representatives of the Murdoch papers.

Naturally, Mrs Thatcher was not part of this plan. Murdoch avoided all contact with her during the dispute, 'so that if anyone asked, she'd be in a stronger position'. But in the summer of 1985, Charles Douglas-Home, then Editor of *The Times*, had given her some warning of what was in the offing. Murdoch believed that, as a result, Mrs Thatcher informed the then Home Secretary, Brittan, about the potential need for large numbers of police, as had been required so often in the miners' strike. As Murdoch himself put it, 'We would probably not have done it if she hadn't reformed the unions.' News International's Wapping victory was extremely important to

---

not to her. 'It cost Clive Whitmore any possibility he might have had of being Cabinet Secretary,' she said when writing her memoirs, 'because I really felt at this time he should have warned us.'
* These were *The Times*, the *Sunday Times*, the *Sun* and the *News of the World*.

her. This was the first front-rank private-sector fight with the unions since her reforms. If it turned out that the newspaper industry could be beaten, then the issue which made so much of Fleet Street support her so strongly would have been lost.

Yet the astonishing fact is that, among the Prime Minister's official papers, there is no file about the Wapping dispute, and virtually no mention. The same is almost equally true of Mrs Thatcher's private papers. The truth is that there was nothing to record. She had brought about a reform of the law so successful that the battle needed no management by government. But there is a further reason. Because of the Westland effect, Mrs Thatcher was so weakened that she did not dare engage in the argument which raged about Wapping. Kenneth Clarke, her anti-Thatcherite Employment Minister, felt emboldened to criticize Murdoch for his bad 'public relations' in the dispute and she did not feel strong enough to slap him down. Luckily for her, Murdoch prevailed: after about a year, the picketing collapsed. A new era for British newspapers had begun.

The weekend the Wapping dispute began coincided with Mrs Thatcher's preparation for her final showdown over Westland in the Commons. Murdoch consulted Woodrow Wyatt: 'He says, "There's an unfortunate cartoon in the *News of the World* showing Mrs Thatcher choking on leek soup. Do you think she'll mind?"' Wyatt thought not. 'When I spoke to Rupert,' he recorded, 'I said I had two friends in difficulties, him and Margaret, and he said, "Yes, but I'm winning."'

22

That Bloody Woman

'We are in danger of a major disaster'

The immediate effect of the Westland affair was to cut Mrs Thatcher down to size politically. Douglas Hurd told the BBC that she 'must not run the Government as a one-woman band', earning the headline in the *Evening Standard*: 'Hurd warns Maggie'. All those Cabinet colleagues irritated by her approach and style now did their best to rein her in. She suspected that many senior Tories were trying to get her out. 'I am not going,' she told Woodrow Wyatt, 'I will fight them all the way.'

The spring of 1986 proved tough for Mrs Thatcher. She later wrote that 'the most damaging effect of the Westland affair was the fuel which had been poured on the flames of anti-Americanism'. The future of British Leyland (BL) provided an opportunity to stoke the fires higher. By 1986, BL had received some £2 billion from the British taxpayer over a ten-year period. Impatient with the company's failure to fulfil its promises of improvement, Mrs Thatcher wanted to split it into its constituent parts and, where possible, privatize. This had happened successfully with Jaguar, which demerged from BL and became a separate publicly quoted company in July 1984. As international interest grew, General Motors (GM) in the United States expressed a desire for Leyland Truck and Bus and, separately, for Land Rover. Norman Tebbit, DTI Secretary, sought to discourage American involvement, insisting that Land Rover was 'strongly identified with ... British excellence'. Mrs Thatcher had little patience with such objections. 'There weren't any British solutions,' she later recalled, and she harboured her own fear: 'I didn't want it to go German.'

Tebbit's move to Party Chairman in the September 1985 reshuffle avoided a showdown. His replacement at the DTI, Leon Brittan, pursued the GM discussions. In late November, as the Westland crisis loomed, Brittan was informed that Ford was interested in buying a different part of BL: Austin Rover, BL's volume car-maker. In one way, this was great news for Mrs Thatcher's revolution in industry. At last, the world wanted to own bits of the once-moribund company. In another, it was terrible timing.

'The downside', Peter Warry of the Policy Unit warned her, 'is the political difficulty of selling the whole of BL to foreign multinationals.' The GM project was codenamed Salton, the Ford bid Maverick. Both were likely to stir up potent opposition, including on the Tory back benches.

In early December, Mrs Thatcher, Brittan and Nigel Lawson agreed to pursue the Ford discussions. Wisely, no one informed Michael Heseltine. Mrs Thatcher was acutely aware of the tricky politics. If the American bids went forward without British or European companies having a chance to bid, it would be Westland all over again, magnified. On 27 January 1986, as Westland finally calmed down, she learnt that Tebbit felt that the combination of two American bids was too controversial. He preferred the idea of Austin Rover and Ford coming together to form a 'European holding company'. If her greatest maverick did not like Maverick, what hope did it have?

The next week, after both potential deals were leaked to the press, the matter was debated in Parliament. Edward Heath, relishing his moment, led the charge against the government. The public, he said, 'do not want to see our country and our industries handed over more and more to the American firms'. Like Tebbit, he called for 'a European arrangement'. This was the mood of the House, reflected in the media. Mrs Thatcher considered it 'a kind of pseudo-patriotic hysteria'. In Cabinet the next day, only Lawson supported her desire to push on with Maverick. She had no choice but to drop the Ford bid, a decision the press reported as a 'humiliation'.

Inevitably, opposition now moved to the GM bid. Mrs Thatcher was furious. But her ministers offered little encouragement. In Cabinet on 20 February, colleagues warned her that it could not go ahead – 'My postbag enormous, & universally hostile' (Tebbit), 'We are in danger of a major disaster' (Whitelaw). On 25 March, the government announced the bid would not proceed. The fact that the most pro-American of modern British prime ministers was compelled to abort both these deals showed how politically weak she had become.

Just two weeks later, in early April, Mrs Thatcher found her pro-American sympathies brought to the fore once again. For some time, Libyan-sponsored terrorism had been a growing problem. This culminated in attacks at Rome and Vienna airports on 27 December 1985, killing nineteen people. On 7 January 1986, President Reagan had announced sanctions against Libya. He wrote privately to European leaders, asking for their support.

Britain was in no doubt about the unpleasantness of Colonel Gaddafi's

Libyan regime. On 17 April 1984, WPC Yvonne Fletcher, policing an anti-Gaddafi protest outside the Libyan Embassy in London, had been killed by a shot fired from an Embassy window. Nonetheless, Mrs Thatcher had a long-standing dislike of economic sanctions. She believed, most notably in the case of South Africa, that they were ineffective and damaged the people who imposed them. She feared that Reagan, who had supported her over South Africa, was now undermining the general case.

Worse was the possibility that the Americans might resort to military action. If so, she told Wyatt in confidence, 'we can't support them'. At a press conference on 10 January she tried to head the President off: 'I do not believe in retaliatory strikes which are against international law.' She was, of course, against terrorism, but insisted 'one has to fight it by legal means'. With the Westland crisis in full flow, the last thing she needed was entanglement in a controversial military adventure. Replying to Reagan's letter, however, Mrs Thatcher concentrated on her case against sanctions, saying little about retaliation. 'The letter is perhaps more important for what it does not say . . .' commented an NSC staffer shrewdly. 'She does, however, subtly ask that "we remain in close touch as our thinking develops".' The Americans were not wrong in noticing this careful positioning. She sensed that Reagan meant business and did not want to rule herself out of the discussion.

Mrs Thatcher's mind was now churning about how she could help Reagan against Libya without sanctions and within the bounds of legality. Meeting President Mitterrand on 20 January, she pondered whether military action against terrorist training camps could be justified. He said he would support 'precise attacks', but also suggested the allies should create 'internal difficulties' for Gaddafi, in secret. A few days later, large quantities of Libyan rifles and ammunition – Gaddafi's supplies for the IRA – were discovered in the Republic of Ireland. This may well have strengthened Mrs Thatcher's desire to assist the United States. The British government looked into ways of impeding Gaddafi. 'The (reluctant) conclusion', Charles Powell wrote to her, 'is that there is not much we can do.'

On 5 April, three people, including one American serviceman, died following the bombing of La Belle discotheque in West Berlin. Intercepts of Libyan cable traffic (obtained, in part, through Britain's GCHQ) suggested that Gaddafi was responsible. With this 'smoking gun', the Americans decided to hit back. On 8 April, Reagan requested the use of British airfields where US F-111s were based to attack Libya. The Americans assumed that agreement would be pretty much automatic. But Mrs Thatcher played for time. Her reply, sent the following day, sought more information about the proposed targets.* She also raised wider concerns – the risk of 'getting us into a cycle of revenge and counter-revenge, in which many more innocent lives will be lost'. She wanted to know the exact justification: 'I have to live with the border between Northern Ireland and the Republic across which terrorists come daily. We have lost 2,500 of our people in the last ten years, but we have never crossed that border to exact revenge.' 'Indeed,' she added tartly, 'I wonder what the reaction would be in the United States if we did.'† Self-defence was a much better legal justification. 'I am deeply troubled by what you propose,' she concluded, but added that she wrote 'in the spirit of loyalty and friendship'.

In her memoirs, Mrs Thatcher wrote that 'this initial response was probably too negative'. Certainly, 'This was not the sort of cable we had expected to get back from Mrs Thatcher,' recalled Howard Teicher, an NSC staffer, but her questions did force the Americans to produce answers. Reagan's reply, which she received soon after midnight on 10 April, was firm. He said that, although her concerns were 'understandable', the cycle of revenge which she feared had started long ago. The lack of a firm Western response, the President wrote, 'builds up Qadhafi and his prestige': there was 'ample legal justification' for such an attack. His targets would be Gaddafi's 'primary headquarters and immediate security forces'. Then the President made her feel the iron fist in his velvet glove: 'You should not underestimate the profound effect on the American people if our actions to put a halt to these crimes continue to receive only lukewarm support or no support at all from our closest allies whom we have committed ourselves to defend . . .'

The next day, Charles Powell remembered Mrs Thatcher appearing in the private office unusually early: 'She sat in the armchair beside my desk and said, "Charles, I've been thinking about this all night. We have to support the Americans on this. That's what allies are for."' That morning she secured the acquiescence of George Younger, the new Defence Secretary, and, far less willingly, Geoffrey Howe‡ and wrote to Reagan to pledge

---

* One problem that the British did not reveal to the Americans was that they were far from sure whether the 1952 agreement on US use of British bases required British *permission* for such flights. Officials thought that the worst outcome would be for Britain to refuse the request, 'but for the United States Government to go ahead all the same'. To avoid this, was the implication, Britain had better agree.

† Mrs Thatcher later conceded that her parallel was unsound. 'The difference is that Libya was directly state-sponsored terrorism. The Republic of Ireland is not, they are trying to stop the terrorists.'

‡ Howe grumbled about 'whether the action proposed by the President would have the intended effects'. The Libya episode put further strain on Mrs Thatcher's relationship with her

'unqualified support for action directed against specific Libyan targets demonstrably involved in ... terrorist activities'.

Mrs Thatcher later put this down to her determination not to appease Gaddafi. While this was important to her, at the time she weighed all the arguments. As Powell recalled, what concerned her most was the fate of British citizens held hostage by Libyan proxies: 'She agonized over it beforehand, because the advice was that they would be bumped off ... It was a decision she took, knowing that she could be signing the death warrant of those guys.' She also wanted to be certain there was proper justification in international law for any attack and so leant heavily on the Article 51 right to self-defence in the UN Charter.

While Mrs Thatcher had to satisfy herself on these points, what really swayed her was her judgement of American attitudes. Once she realized the United States was determined to proceed, she had to decide whether Britain wanted to repeat the row over Grenada. But this time, Reagan had reasoned with her and invoked their overriding common interests. If she had refused to cooperate and he had gone ahead anyway, she would have exposed for all to see that she had been unable to sway him. So, while acutely conscious that neither British public opinion nor her colleagues would be supportive, she decided to back Reagan. As with so many decisions, she had been all hesitation, doubt and niggling until the moment of decision. Once she had decided, she was adamantine.

At noon on Monday 14 April, the issue was discussed and agreed at the Cabinet's OD Committee. Mrs Thatcher's speaking note summed up the problems of backing the USA, but concluded: 'We have got to stand by them as they stood by us over the Falklands.' At 5.20 p.m. Downing Street heard that the F-111s would shortly take off from their British bases, and immediately informed the Queen. As the bombers were taking off, Mrs Thatcher was also facing a political crisis of an almost absurdly different kind.

In the Commons that night, the House was debating the controversial Shops Bill, designed to liberalize Sunday opening. This reform had been brewing for several years. In deference to Christian principles, the law had always restricted Sunday trading, but social and technological change had eaten away at this. Despite her Sabbatarian background as a Methodist girl from Grantham, Mrs Thatcher was in favour of reform to help business and, possibly, create more jobs.

Among her advisers, counsels were divided. Free-market beliefs favoured

---

Foreign Secretary: 'It was the measure of Geoffrey Howe,' she later recalled. '... It was George Younger who was very strong.'

reform and business interests, represented by the likes of Tim Bell and David Young, were powerful. On the other hand, Brian Griffiths, in charge of the Policy Unit, and her PPS, Michael Alison, were strong evangelicals and opposed it. Many of her supporters, Griffiths told her, 'welcome your moral stance on economic and social matters'. Her support for this Bill, he warned, confused them.

Tory MPs noticed the strength of grass-roots opposition. By early March more than 32,000 letters against the Bill had arrived in Downing Street. 'The perceived inflexibility of the Government is now damaging your personal reputation,' hazarded Hartley Booth from the Policy Unit, adding that 'The Church in Scotland has come out strongly in favour of changing the law to restrict trading.' 'They would wouldn't they?' wrote Mrs Thatcher, in imitation of Mandy Rice-Davies.

There was a reputational danger for Mrs Thatcher here, partly because the Shops Bill coincided with her wider post-Westland unpopularity and the resistance to selling BL to Americans. Her personal support for the Bill, not matched by her doubting Cabinet,* added to the feeling that she was uncaring, that her god was money and even that she was somehow un-British. There was hypocrisy here, since the great majority of British people, including churchgoers, shopped on Sunday where and when they could; but hypocrisy is a permanent British quality which politicians ignore at their peril.

As the revolt grew, even the ultra-loyal Michael Alison sought Mrs Thatcher's permission to abstain. Because the contentious nine-hour debate stretched late into the night, Mrs Thatcher feared that the House would still be sitting when news of the Libyan bombing raid broke and she would be called to explain then and there what was going on. This did not come to pass. The government lost the Sunday Trading Bill by fourteen votes, with more than seventy Conservatives rebelling, the only occasion during her time in office when a government Bill was lost on the second reading. The House then adjourned before news of the raid broke.

It being much earlier in the evening in the United States, Reagan broadcast to the nation. This speech had been the subject of considerable lobbying on Mrs Thatcher's behalf. 'We were conscious of her insistence that we frame the attacks in terms of self-defence . . .' recalled Teicher.

---

* A list drawn up at the time of the Shops Bill suggests that most of the Cabinet were opposed to it, with ten 'For' and twelve 'Against'. At junior levels of government, opposition was even stronger. The totals were: minister of state four For/eighteen Against, parliamentary under-secretary nine For/thirty-eight Against, whips six For/seven Against, parliamentary private secretary nine For /thirty-four Against.

Reagan now provided the words she needed: 'Self-defense is not only our right, it is our duty. It is the purpose behind the mission undertaken tonight, a mission fully consistent with Article 51 of the United Nations Charter.'

At Cabinet that day, and again on Thursday, ministers were extremely unenthusiastic. Tebbit was particularly fierce. He said that Reagan's style was 'OK for Little Rock, Arkansas, but it grates on electors of Ryedale [the Yorkshire constituency, normally a safe Tory seat, where a by-election was imminent]'. Because she had already secured OD support, Mrs Thatcher was not in serious political danger. The episode, however, did little for her already strained relations with Tebbit, who was disgruntled by his exclusion from her inner counsels. At the time, he recalled, he was also worried that the permission for the raid would be politically damaging, but in retrospect formed the view that 'she was right: it was not'. Certainly, the immediate public reaction was overwhelmingly negative. Stephen Sherbourne informed her that Conservative Central Office had received an 'unusually large number of calls expressing concern... the biggest reaction since the Falklands'. 'Terrorism thrives on appeasement,' she wrote on the back of this note.

That afternoon, in the House she defended her ground firmly against an angry Opposition and faced no serious criticism from her own side. Afterwards, Reagan telephoned to thank her. He said that 'when, in the speech of the previous night, he had referred to the cooperation of European allies, he had only one country in mind: the United Kingdom. He was deeply grateful.' No doubt these words produced a warm glow in Mrs Thatcher, but she did not conceal her anxiety. She told Reagan she feared the raids had not been hugely effective or well targeted. It was, she added, 'a difficult task to secure wide public understanding and support for this in the United Kingdom'. She was effectively saying that he was in her debt.

What Mrs Thatcher called 'public understanding' did not improve much, from her point of view. BBC reporting of the bombing was clearly hostile, as was much comment in the British press. Mrs Thatcher was unrepentant. 'Terrorism has to be defeated; it cannot be tolerated or side-stepped,' she told the Commons the following day. And she tried to reassure doubters by saying – which Armstrong had agreed with the administration in advance – that no further US strikes would be launched from British bases without her express permission.*

---

* Mrs Thatcher had hoped to be able to bolster her case publicly with intelligence linking Libya to terrorism, but her officials insisted the sources were too sensitive. Always ultra-conscious of such concerns, she accepted this: 'She understood,' recalled Percy Cradock, 'she never compromised intelligence in any way.'

A MORI opinion poll recorded 71 per cent disapproval of US use of the bases, and a dissatisfaction rating with Mrs Thatcher personally of 68 per cent, up 7 per cent from March. On 18 April, the bodies of British hostages Leigh Douglas and Philip Padfield were found in Beirut. Naturally, Mrs Thatcher was upset. 'She says she's been feeling very lonely,' Wyatt recorded. Charlie Price, the US Ambassador in London, warned Reagan it looked likely she would 'pay the price for her decision. As a result, I think it unlikely that Mrs Thatcher would support another similar strike absent an extremely compelling case.' Price was right in thinking that she wanted no more of this, but she did not draw a red line. As Powell told the Foreign Office, the government gave the Americans 'no blank cheque', but nor did it rule out further action.

When Jacques Chirac, the French Prime Minister, visited Chequers that weekend he told Mrs Thatcher that French opinion polls showed support both for the US attacks *and* for the French government's position (France had denied the US aircraft overflight rights en route to Libya). She exploded with rage: 'that reflected a cynical attitude: let the United States do the job and let France keep out of it.' She stressed that Britain 'did not offer the United States blind devotion. Indeed, we frequently spoke very frankly to them. But there was a matter of loyalty.' She added acidly that 'France and the United Kingdom felt differently on this.'

Mrs Thatcher's political difficulties rumbled on. In early May, the government lost the Ryedale by-election, as Tebbit had predicted. Yet her stance on Libya, unpopular though it was, helped restore the respect for her leadership which had been weakened by Westland. Whatever else might be said, her actions were not indecisive or cowardly. As time went on, she could also point to a reduction in Libyan terrorism. With the glaring exception of the Lockerbie bombing in December 1988, Gaddafi was much subdued.*

More important, her loyalty was recognized in Washington and greatly increased her political capital. Reagan himself repeatedly expressed his gratitude. Howard Teicher believed that 'the UK could have asked for and received almost anything it wanted'. And so attention turned to long-standing British efforts to improve its ability to extradite terrorists from America. A loophole in the existing extradition treaty barred extradition if the acts concerned were 'political' in nature. In December 1984, the extradition of an IRA gunman, Joseph Doherty, had been denied on these grounds. The Reagan administration readily agreed to remove the

---

* According to Paul Bremer, then the State Department's Ambassador-at-Large for counter-terrorism, 'the Libyans had been planning 34 or 35 subsequent attacks on American targets in Europe. Those were stopped immediately.'

loophole, but the resulting 'supplementary extradition treaty' was held up in the Senate.*

At the prompting of Charlie Price, Reagan seized the issue. That May, he appealed to the American people in his weekly radio broadcast. Failure to close the loophole, he declared, 'would be an affront to British Prime Minister Margaret Thatcher, one European leader who, at great political risk, stood shoulder to shoulder with us during our operations against Qadhafi's terrorism'. On 17 July, the Senate ratified the treaty by eighty-seven votes to ten.

Mrs Thatcher believed that the Libyan affair vindicated her loyalty to the American alliance and proved the unreliability of European allies: 'they are a feeble, weak lot . . .' she said later. In late May, as Reagan's campaign on her behalf reached its climax, she was asked to contribute to a book about transatlantic relations.† Charles Powell redrafted what he called 'a late and poor draft from the Foreign Office'. 'I think you have done wonders,' she scribbled, deleting just one sentence. This came in answer to the question, 'Is there a special bond that exists between the United Kingdom and the United States that does not exist between the UK and any other country?' Powell had affirmed this, but added a qualification about close ties with Europe and the Commonwealth. Mrs Thatcher struck this out. Her answer ended with the unqualified words 'Special means unique, unique to Britain and the United States.'

As America made ready to attack Libya, Mrs Thatcher was at Chequers discussing, for the first time, how to approach the next general election. She was in an edgy mood, made edgier because she was not free to explain to colleagues why. The political high command were present – Howe, Lawson, Tebbit, Young and Whitelaw – assisted by Sherbourne, Brian Griffiths and Michael Dobbs, and also by John Sharkey, the Managing Director of Saatchi & Saatchi, who had retained the Conservative account ever since 1978. Their specific purpose, on Sunday 13 April, was to consider strategy for the election run-up, scrutinizing Saatchi opinion research commissioned by Tebbit.

The research was presented by Dobbs. It showed, as Sharkey recalled, that 'Perceptions of Mrs Thatcher had turned from largely positive to slightly negative.' She took this badly. At this time, the press were talking about the so-called 'TBW factor' counting against the Conservatives. TBW

---

* Leaders of the opposition to the change included John Kerry (who was to win the Democratic nomination for the presidential election of 2004 and later become President Obama's Secretary of State) and Joe Biden (who in 2021 would become President of the United States of America).
† This was *The Rich Tide* by David Frost and Michael Shea.

stood for 'That Bloody Woman'.* Although the offensive acronym naturally went unmentioned in the presentation, Mrs Thatcher sensed this lay behind it.† There was no shouting match, but when Dobbs was about to display the illustrative boards which summarized his talk she seized them, he recalled, and 'threw them into a corner'.

Dobbs soon found himself 'disinvited from every election planning meeting'. Since he was Tebbit's right-hand man this was, in effect, a rejection of Tebbit. She feared Tebbit's ambition and, post-Westland, with her leadership insecure, these concerns were magnified. In Young's view, 'Norman was just too popular: she suffered from ageing-lion syndrome in relation to him.' She particularly feared his close relationship with Saatchis, hence her suspicion of Dobbs.

Even before the Chequers meeting, some of those close to Mrs Thatcher had fed her anxieties. Tim Bell, the man who – with Gordon Reece – she liked most of all in the world of advertising, had fallen out with Saatchis and left them. But he continued to see her privately, offering advice. Tebbit, however, was against Bell. He was aware that Bell's drug-taking during the 1983 election campaign had made him almost impossible to deal with. Bell was now undergoing rehabilitation, and Mrs Thatcher herself chose not to hold the past against him,‡ but Tebbit remained uneasy. His decision that he did not want Bell involved set him on a collision course with her.

Bell's ally in all this – and Tebbit's challenger for Mrs Thatcher's ear – was David Young. Although unelected and thus no threat to her leadership, Young had strong political ambitions. He yearned to be Party Chairman. In Sherbourne's view, Mrs Thatcher 'loved David and adored Tim'. She had much more ambiguous feelings about Tebbit. Outside the stricter structures of policy and government, she was vulnerable to flattery and manipulation. There was too much of the atmosphere of a court. 'I began to understand Tudor history better,' Tebbit recalled.

The presence of Bell and Young created a parallel operation to prepare for the general election. They disparaged Tebbit's efforts and the work of Saatchis, persuading Mrs Thatcher to look secretly at research produced

---

* Mrs Thatcher had known about this moniker since the previous June, when David Frost had introduced her to the phrase on air.
† These findings were confirmed in ordinary opinion polls. In April 1986, Mrs Thatcher was viewed positively by only 28 per cent of those questioned. She had not had such low ratings since 1981.
‡ Mrs Thatcher, though extremely innocent about drugs, did know that all had not been well with Bell during the 1983 campaign. 'How is Tim now?' she used to ask while he was out of action. In 1985 he wrote to her to say he had overcome his drug problem. Her friendly response was 'If you've stopped, there's an end of it.'

by a rival firm, Young and Rubicam.* There was some truth in their criticisms. Saatchis was going through an uncreative phase. Tebbit, though a brilliant public performer, was not an organizer. As even Dobbs admitted, 'Norman couldn't reach out to the people at Central Office. They didn't like not seeing enough of him. He'd be thinking about his wife at home.'

Against this widespread ill feeling, the Tories suffered a series of by-election reverses. Just before the unhappy Chequers meeting Labour had gained Fulham from them. In early May, after trouncing the Conservatives in Ryedale, the Liberals came within 100 votes of taking West Derbyshire. Shortly after these results John Biffen, Leader of the House, articulated what many were thinking. 'Nobody seriously supposes that the Prime Minister would be Prime Minister throughout the entire period of the next parliament,' he told Brian Walden on television. He spoke of the need for a 'balanced ticket' at the next election, with the Prime Minister and her colleagues standing 'as a team'.

Speaking as usual through the anonymity of the lobby system, Bernard Ingham described Biffen as a 'semi-detached' member of the Cabinet. In his view, this was a pleasantly jokey (and accurate) way of defending Biffen's character against accusations of disloyalty, but Biffen interpreted it as meaning he might be sacked. While accepting that his comments had been 'ham-fisted', he resented this. 'I do feel she got out of kimber in the second half of her time,' he said later. 'She got to the point of "If I don't do it no one else will."' This was well put. Mrs Thatcher did resemble the Little Red Hen in the folk tale of that name. The hen seeks help from a pig, a cat and so on, to plant a grain of wheat. All refuse. '"Cluck, cluck, then I'll do it myself," said the Little Red Hen.' Because of her efforts the grain grows. Now the other animals want it, but she refuses them as a punishment for their laziness and eats it all alone.

Yet a 'balanced ticket' was, in effect, what those senior Tories who wished Mrs Thatcher to survive wanted too. They could appreciate the energy of the Little Blue Hen, though they found it exhausting. They sought a means of getting the government to work as one rather than she alone clucking around the political farmyard.

Within days of Biffen's remarks to Walden, Mrs Thatcher reshuffled her Cabinet. The faithful Keith Joseph had indicated his wish to depart and so, with some relief, given his underperformance as a minister, she replaced him with Kenneth Baker, whose communicative skills she admired. With research showing the Conservatives 'weak ... on the so-called "caring

---

* The 'Young' of 'Young and Rubicam' was no relation of David Young.

issues"', she meant to move Education fast up her list of priorities.* Her new Secretary of State for Transport was John Moore, whose youthful good looks and Thatcherite success in advancing privatization made him stand well in her eyes. She also promoted Nicholas Ridley from Transport to Environment. She knew this would do little for presentation, but wanted 'radical policies' for the manifesto and believed that Ridley's 'penetrating intellect' could help provide them. She kept Biffen in place, but he felt 'on the skids'.

Partly to improve government unity and partly to prepare better for the election, Sherbourne proposed an informal inner Cabinet. What emerged, with the support of John Wakeham, the Chief Whip, was a Strategy Group which the newspapers immediately christened 'the A-Team'. It consisted of Mrs Thatcher, Whitelaw, Howe, Lawson, Tebbit, Hurd, Wakeham, but neither Biffen nor Young.† The clear majority of the A-Team thought of themselves as 'consolidators', but the policy groups it spawned – Lawson on the economy, Moore on young people, Ridley on planning and the environment – were often led by 'go forwards', temperamentally and ideologically closer to Mrs Thatcher. These different schools of thought represented permanent tendencies in the Conservative collective mind. If the Conservatives were to succeed politically, they had to be held in balance. In fact, according to Robin Harris, secretary to the group, the A-Team's products were 'not very useful': its great virtue was that 'It proved we wanted to win the election and we wanted to win under *her*.'

Stephen Sherbourne now returned, more tactfully, to the territory tackled so unproductively by Dobbs and Tebbit. 'In the next election,' he wrote to Mrs Thatcher, 'the main issue will be you and your personality.' The question for voters, he suggested, was '"What is there to be done in this third Parliament that only Mrs Thatcher can do?": in other words, "why do we need this strong woman?"' By June, less under threat politically, she felt readier to consider such questions. Although the Conservatives had previously won three general elections in a row (1951, 1955 and 1959), no party in the twentieth century had ever done this under one leader. A Thatcher-led third victory would be unprecedented.

Despite the improving sense of direction, all was still not well between leader and Party Chairman. In late July, after the conflict appeared in the press, Tebbit demanded a meeting with Mrs Thatcher alone. Arriving in Downing Street, recalled Sherbourne, he 'had his dark face on'. He bore a

---

* She had made these 'caring issues' the theme of her speech to the Scottish party conference a few days earlier. A programme of public engagements was also drawn up which would show Mrs Thatcher in 'informal and human contexts'.

† Biffen considered that his exclusion proved he would not survive the next election.

sheaf of press cuttings which he dumped in front of her, accusing her people of inspiring the stories. She denied all knowledge. Tebbit threatened resignation if the stories did not stop. Mrs Thatcher asked him not to resign, but the meeting served only to produce a new flood of press coverage. On 5 August, she went into hospital for an operation on her right hand.* Denis and her children were absent. Barry Strevens, her detective, who accompanied her, was troubled by 'how lonely she looked in the hospital, clutching a teddy bear that the Garden Room girls had given her'.

She emerged after two days to a note from Sherbourne begging her to sort out the row and a curt handwritten letter from Tebbit (a '*cri de coeur*', warned Nigel Wicks). He wished her a speedy recovery, but then stated, as through clenched teeth: 'the press speculation about my position as Party Chairman has continued and seems likely to do so until something is done to end it'. This prompted Mrs Thatcher to act. 'Have phoned Norman,' she scribbled to Wicks, '& asked Jim Coe [a No. 10 press officer] to kill the story.' She did not banish Young and Rubicam (as Tebbit wished), but she did express her confidence in Tebbit and permit him to continue with Saatchis. At Sherbourne's suggestion, she set up regular meetings with Tebbit. It was a truce, at least. Tebbit and his wife went off on holiday to France. Mrs Thatcher and Denis stayed with the Wolfsons in Cornwall, where they agreed to be photographed – she with her bandaged hand – holding a rather unruly borrowed dog on the beach.†

Yet another antagonist with whom Mrs Thatcher was wrestling was the BBC. Egged on by Denis, who enjoyed railing against its 'pinkoes', she had always considered the Corporation politically and personally hostile. She disliked its 'extravagance', its broadcasting of material she considered indecent, its overmanned, unionized workforce, its journalistic methods‡ and its privilege of being funded by a flat licence fee imposed on every owner or renter of a television. She thought the BBC should be funded, in part at least, by advertising – which, in the BBC's strict theology, was a sin against the Holy Ghost. There was almost nothing she liked about the

---

* Mrs Thatcher suffered from Dupuytren's contracture, a condition which causes the fingers to bend into the palm of the hand.
† Mrs Thatcher, who was fond of animals, always wanted a dog or cat as a pet but Denis forbade it.
‡ These became a matter of passionate concern during the Falklands conflict, when she felt the BBC was making life difficult for the Task Force and preaching defeatism. In 1982, she was asked whether senior civil servants should take part in a BBC *Panorama* programme about information and propaganda during the Falklands War. 'Neither Ministers nor officials should appear on this programme,' she wrote. 'It is not being put on to reach the truth – but to try to justify the BBC.'

BBC, with the important exceptions of its original high-minded 'Reithian standards' (so named after its original Director-General, Sir John Reith), and its External Services, which helped bring accurate news to the Communist world.

Her criticisms notwithstanding, Mrs Thatcher had found reform difficult, because none of her successive Home Secretaries – the ministers responsible for the BBC – agreed with her. Of these the most important was Willie Whitelaw, who continued to champion the status quo even after leaving the Home Office in 1983. In 1986, he suggested he might resign if the BBC were to carry advertising. For Mrs Thatcher, this was not a price worth paying. As was quite often the case, her rhetoric was therefore more radical than her actions.

In her second term, Mrs Thatcher was determined to use the government's power to set the licence fee to exercise leverage over the BBC. In December 1984, she was secretly visited by Ian McIntyre, the Controller of Radio 3, a conservative-minded critic of his own organization. In a paper full of criticisms of the BBC's 'poor leadership', he warned her that the 'liberal consensus' had 'put its stamp on the BBC ... Contemptuous of politicians and patronising towards its audience, it appears increasingly to see itself as a state within a state.' Mrs Thatcher underlined the last phrase three times. She itched to overthrow that state. McIntyre recommended that she seize her chance and set up a committee of inquiry into the 'objectives, organisation, management and scope of the BBC'.*

Mrs Thatcher followed McIntyre's advice, though she reluctantly accepted the Home Secretary Leon Brittan's recommendation to narrow the inquiry to future financing of the BBC, because of the political dangers of inquiring into journalistic standards. She was unimpressed by Brittan's suggestion of Professor Alan Peacock, a leading free-market economist, to lead the inquiry. 'Not strong enough,' she scribbled. She told Brittan that Peacock would not be able to 'prevent the wool being pulled over his eyes', but eventually accepted his choice.

When Peacock reported in June 1986, he recommended, as the Home Office had hoped, that the BBC should not take advertising. He also pointed out that technological change, with its multiplicity of channels, would eventually create a genuinely competitive broadcasting market. The long-term consequences of Peacock were radical. The cosy system of the regional ITV franchises would be opened up to competitive tender. His

---

* A private office covering note to Robin Butler warned him that Mrs Thatcher had squirrelled away McIntyre's paper: 'If you agree this should go to the Home Secy we shall need to recover it from the handbag.'

recommendations provided the framework for reform of all television. Mrs Thatcher was to wrestle with this in her third term. But the short-term consequences were that her assault on the BBC was foiled, as she had suspected it would be. The licence fee was secure and was indexed to the Retail Price Index from 1 April 1988.*

At the end of August 1986, Stuart Young, the Chairman of the BBC, died of cancer aged only fifty-two. As she searched for a successor who might make a difference,† two particular programmes were making the BBC vulnerable to her attack.

The case of a *Panorama* programme, 'Maggie's Militant Tendency', had been running since it was broadcast in January 1984. It had alleged that three Conservative MPs – Neil Hamilton, Harvey Proctor and Gerald Howarth – had taken part in far-right activities, but provided little evidence. Hamilton and Howarth sued. The BBC executives, led by the Director-General, Alasdair Milne, assured the governors that the case was 'fire-proof'. It was not. When it became clear the action would come to court, the BBC capitulated. Their victims eventually received roughly £1 million in libel damages.

The other programme was the BBC's *Nine O'Clock News* on the night of the US raid on Libya. Mrs Thatcher and Tebbit were outraged by what they saw as its readiness to accept Libyan government propaganda about civilian casualties. Unlike his predecessors as Party Chairman, Tebbit wanted to harry the BBC for bias and inaccuracy. Armed with an independently reviewed dossier documenting the inadequacy of the Libyan coverage, Tebbit contacted Lord Barnett, the acting BBC Chairman: 'You may conclude', he wrote on 30 October, that such coverage was 'a mixture of news, views, speculation, error and uncritical carriage of Libyan propaganda which does serious damage to the reputation of the BBC.'

In trying to appoint Young's successor, Mrs Thatcher had almost no friends at the BBC to help her. A rare exception was Patricia Hodgson, whom she had met in the 1970s when Hodgson ran the Bow Group. She took what Hodgson considered a motherly/sisterly interest in her career

---

* A minor recommendation of Peacock was that the BBC should auction off the late-night hours of broadcasting which it owned but did not use to much effect. At a ministerial meeting, Mrs Thatcher asked what was broadcast at these times. No one knew. Her private secretary was sent out to get a copy of the *Evening Standard* and Mrs Thatcher and colleagues then pored over its TV listings. 'Oh, look,' exclaimed Mrs Thatcher, lighting on the schedule for 3 a.m. 'There's one of Ronnie Reagan's films! I wonder if Denis knows.'
† The rule was that the government appointed the Chairman of the BBC. The Chairman and governors then appointed the Director-General.

and invited her to tea or dinner every year. While Hodgson's politics were Conservative, her view of the BBC was old-fashioned, public-service Reithian rather than free-market. When appointed Secretary to the BBC in 1985 she was forced to promise to give up her friendly meetings with the Prime Minister, but through Brian Griffiths, who attended the same London church, she ensured that her views continued to reach Mrs Thatcher.

After Stuart Young died, Hodgson advised Mrs Thatcher against appointing Lord King of British Airways as his successor. 'I thought the chairman should understand the journalism,' she explained. Griffiths agreed and proposed Marmaduke 'Dukie' Hussey. Hussey had been Managing Director of Times Newspapers during the papers' trade union battles and was well connected.* Recognizing his business toughness, Mrs Thatcher appointed him. It was not considered important that he barely watched television. According to John Birt, whom Hussey would bring in to help transform the BBC, Hussey's 'own views and convictions chimed with Mrs Thatcher's. But he was an old soldier and he had strong views on public service.' If the BBC under Hussey was to be Thatcherized it would be in Reithian form, not according to the principles of market purity.

In January 1987, Hussey sacked Alasdair Milne and put in a sober accountant, Michael Checkland, as the new Director-General, with a brief to get the BBC's affairs in order. Mrs Thatcher felt well pleased. A few months after Hussey's appointment, Patricia Hodgson met her at a public function. 'Dukie is proving a great success,' said Hodgson. 'He's not frightened of BBC barons or journalists.' 'Of course he isn't,' said Mrs Thatcher, rather as if she alone had thought of the appointment. 'He lost his leg in the war.'†

For all of Mrs Thatcher's difficulties, 1986 saw the government's fortunes begin to improve. The first seeds of recovery had been sown in Lawson's March Budget. With growth up to 3.75 per cent, inflation down to 3.4 per cent and the PSBR a modest 1.5 per cent of GDP, Lawson eyed a broad tax cut. The politically extraordinary fact was that the 'tax-cutting' Tories had not cut the basic rate since Howe had reduced it to 30 per cent in 1979.‡ Lawson could afford only a 1 per cent cut, which would bring

---

* Hussey was married to Susan, a lady-in-waiting to the Queen, and brother-in-law to William Waldegrave, who also recommended him to Mrs Thatcher.

† Hussey was severely wounded in the spine at the Battle of Anzio, was captured by the Germans and eventually lost a leg. He was reputed to remove his tin one occasionally and bang it on the table to alarm people.

‡ Lawson's preferred, more targeted method of cutting income tax had been to raise the thresholds above inflation to take more of the lowest earners out of tax.

the rate to 29 per cent. But what might be seen as derisory, or plain silly when set against the round rate of 30 per cent, could be presented as a promise of more to come. Announcing the one penny cut in his Budget, Lawson revived the aim, first declared by Howe, of a basic rate of 25 per cent, but to achieve this voters would need to re-elect a Conservative government. Mrs Thatcher warmly supported the cut, but was so weakened by Westland that she was little more than an observer of the process. With the tax cut the Tories were starting once again to 'weaponize' tax issues politically. Kinnock's Labour Party found it hard to respond in a united way. By the autumn party conference season, tax and the state of the economy would take on electoral focus. Lawson's Budget set the right political framework.

That autumn, both the Labour and Liberal party conferences voted for unilateral nuclear disarmament. The Labour conference also voted to renationalize British Telecom and British Gas, which was about to be privatized, to remove the right to a secret ballot before a strike and to end the right to buy a council house. It promised punitive taxes on the rich. David Blunkett, the rising star of the left, proudly proclaimed that Labour's plans could not be paid for without increasing the standard rate of income tax as well.

There was nothing Mrs Thatcher liked better than a clear dividing line. In her speech to the Conservative Party's conference in Bournemouth on 6 October, she boasted of the lowest inflation rate for twenty years, the lowest basic rate of income tax for forty years and the lowest number of strikes for fifty. She put her strongest powder and shot into defence, emphasizing the 'utmost gravity' of the Labour decision the previous week: 'Exposed to the threat of nuclear blackmail, there would be no option but surrender.' A Labour Britain 'would be the greatest gain for the Soviet Union in forty years'. 'I believe the interests of Britain can now only be served by a third Conservative victory.' The opinion polls put the Conservatives ahead of Labour for the first time since well before the Westland crisis.

A fortnight after the conference, Jeffrey Archer was forced to resign as Deputy Party Chairman after being accused in the *News of the World* of arranging a cash pay-off for a prostitute. Norman Tebbit, who had never wanted the peripatetic novelist appointed, was relieved. He had, in fact, already taken on another Deputy Chairman, Peter Morrison, to help him prepare Central Office for the general election. Liked by Mrs Thatcher and respected by colleagues as a hard-working if unglittering junior minister, Morrison seemed a suitable choice – loyal, well connected in the party and no political threat.

There were two problems with Morrison. The first was that he drank too much. In a culture where being drunk was commonplace, his rather quiet drinking did not stand out but it did cause anxiety. The second concerned rumours about his sexual behaviour. There were no precise allegations, but suggestions that Morrison might have attended gay parties and engaged in casual pick-ups. Once Morrison became Deputy Chairman, however, Tebbit recalled allegations that Morrison was 'excessively interested in schoolboys. I faced him. He swore absolutely that there was no truth in it. I wasn't absolutely convinced.'

Mrs Thatcher was aware of rumours about Morrison, some coming from MI5, but never evidenced. With Morrison denying the claims, her attitude was to be careful but not punitive. Anything else would, in her mind, have been unfair. An informal ceiling was placed on Morrison's career, blocking his ambition to be Party Chairman after the 1987 election.

By late 1986, Tory spirits, particularly those of Mrs Thatcher herself, recovered. Almost all the economic indicators were favourable. Even unemployment, having hit its highest point ever in January, was now starting to fall.* Bernard Ingham recalled, that, one day towards the end of the year, as he sat with Mrs Thatcher in Downing Street, 'She seemed to experience a moment of pure joy. She believed that, at last, her policies really were working.'

---

* In November, after the third monthly drop (and the sharpest since May 1983), unemployment stood at 3,237,154.

23
Against Queen and Commonwealth
'Blacks and their families out of work? Moral? Poof!'

Over the summer of 1986, as Mrs Thatcher sought to recover her domestic standing, she was also engaged in an international struggle over her approach to South Africa. Her opposition to the imposition of economic sanctions and her decision to maintain contact with the State President P. W. Botha, leader of the white minority government, were extremely controversial. She was accused of sympathizing with apartheid. She was, in fact, more ambitious than her predecessors to influence change. But, while seeking a peaceful end to apartheid and white minority rule, she believed she must keep in mind the importance of British trade and kinship with South Africa and Soviet adventurism in the region. She opposed economic sanctions because they would damage British business, but also because she believed they would end up impoverishing the black population. As early as 1980, she chided South Africa's Foreign Minister, R. F. 'Pik' Botha, insisting that what was at stake was not 'only a question of economics and hunger: questions of dignity mattered'. This simple sentiment would fill out into a considered, if disputed, policy.

In the mid-1980s, the Cold War factor was uppermost in Mrs Thatcher's mind. To the frustration of most Commonwealth leaders, she shared President Reagan's determination to get Cuban forces – proxies of the Soviet Union – out of the former Portuguese colony of Angola and to make sure that independence for Namibia, illegally occupied by South African forces, should be linked with the Cuban withdrawal. She was suspicious of the largest black grouping in South Africa, the African National Congress (ANC), because of its links with the Communist Party and its intermittent use of violence. She feared its monopoly power: 'They don't represent all the Africans, all the interests must be protected.' Nonetheless, as F. W. de Klerk, the last of the white leaders of South Africa, recalled, he and his predecessors knew that she 'never supported apartheid'. Indeed, she regarded it with what she called 'total abhorrence and loathing'. From

1984, she believed that Nelson Mandela, the most prominent imprisoned black leader, should be released from prison. 'She *is* an enemy of apartheid,' he said after his release in 1990.

Mrs Thatcher sought the replacement of white power, but not its violent overthrow. In this sense, her attitude resembled her approach to the Soviet Union in the Gorbachev era. Unlike with the Soviet Union, however, she had personal sympathies with the 'white tribe' who dominated South Africa. Denis Thatcher had relations there, and often visited on business.* He always called it 'God's own country' and was caustic about the capacity of the Commonwealth either to understand or to improve the situation. This was what the Commonwealth Secretary-General, 'Sonny' Ramphal, called Mrs Thatcher's 'pillow-talk'. Denis's wife shared her husband's irritation with the Commonwealth but was much less cynical about the possibility of majority rule. She firmly believed, however, that British interests in South Africa must be looked after.† So her strategy was peaceful transition, and her tactic was one of engagement with the people central to such a change – the white government itself.

Mrs Thatcher was correct that Britain, because of its history and its economic and human presence, had greater salience in South Africa than any other Western country. But she knew that the ruling Afrikaner National Party saw itself as the proud anti-imperialist heir of the men who had fought the Boer War against Britain. Lectures from a British prime minister could easily backfire. P. W. Botha was the almost perfect representative of the Afrikaner mentality. Born into a 'bitter-ender' anti-British Boer family, he liked to boast that Afrikaners 'had nearly brought the British Empire to its knees'. In 1979, a year after becoming Prime Minister, he made a famous speech, telling Afrikaners they must 'adapt or die'. But his ensuing reforms fell short. In November 1983, at Botha's urging, white voters endorsed a new Constitution. It ended all-white voting, but gave votes only to Indians and so-called 'Cape Coloureds'.‡ Blacks remained voteless. A state president was invented to take charge of a multiracial but white-dominated President's Council. This role Botha designed for himself.

Although most international and internal black reaction to Botha's changes was hostile, the British government cautiously welcomed them.

---

* It was to South Africa that Denis went in 1964, when he suffered a nervous breakdown and thought that his marriage to Margaret was on the rocks (see p. 80).
† These included the interests of British passport-holders in the country – of whom there were about 800,000.
‡ 'Cape Coloureds' was the term used to describe mixed-race South Africans, so called because they were the predominant ethnic group in the Western Cape.

The following year, Mrs Thatcher received Botha at Chequers.* When they met, on 2 June 1984, she spoke of the 'natural reservoir of goodwill for South Africa in Britain'. Nonetheless: 'our political attitude was affected by one enormous problem: we felt strongly that people's rights should not be determined by the colour of their skin'. Her scribbled speaking notes reveal her priorities. They read:

> Good to break isolation
> Potential goodwill in West – but cannot be manifested because of internal situation
> Our foreign policy dependent on internal liberalisation.

Beside the last point she had written Botha's famous phrase: 'Adapt or Die'. Botha defended his constitutional changes and introduced a rag-bag of topics, trying, unsuccessfully, for example, to persuade Mrs Thatcher to close the ANC office in London. She, in turn, 'took the opportunity to raise the case of Nelson Mandela'. Botha replied that 'he was not able to interfere in the judicial process'.† This passage of arms – the seeking of an imprisoned dissident's release and the attempted fob-off – mirrored almost exactly what happened whenever she pressed Soviet leaders for the release of prisoners of conscience.‡ Nelson Mandela had been imprisoned since 1963, but Mrs Thatcher seems to have been the first British prime minister to request the South African government to release him.

The meeting was no breakthrough. Mrs Thatcher, as she later wrote, 'did not particularly warm' to the anti-British Botha, but the encounter did establish a basis of dialogue. In these early stages, she had some hopes of him. She felt that reform would only come from within South Africa, and that, when it did, the South African government would consider her a trustworthy external interlocutor. Her greatest fear was that the combination of white oppression and black violence would set the country aflame.

---

* Botha arrived in a helicopter, but Mrs Thatcher did not meet him as he landed because of the danger that the helicopter's blades would blow her hair all over the place. Whenever she travelled in a helicopter, Mrs Thatcher had to wear the headphone link hanging beneath her chin rather than sitting on top of her head, in order not to disturb her coiffure.
† The suggestion in Mrs Thatcher's speaking note was that she intended to raise Mandela's fate at the plenary session, but in the event raised it only in their *tête-à-tête*. She may well have hoped that Botha would be more receptive one on one than with a broader audience. Finding little give, she jotted down Botha's excuses on the back of her speaking notes: '"Nelson Mandela / ANC / Unpopular among electors / Under pressure from right / Never possible to satisfy internal opinion / Country of minorities."'
‡ By using the phrase 'raise the case' rather than 'demand the release', Britain could avoid provoking a direct refusal.

The following year, 1985, that fear threatened to become reality. In March, the anniversary of the 1960 Sharpeville massacre saw violent disturbances during which at least nineteen people died at the hands of the police. In June, South African forces raided suspected ANC bases in Botswana. Mrs Thatcher was furious. She warned Botha that, if it happened again, she would repudiate his actions. Botha, however, tried to draw a parallel with her struggle against the IRA. Incensed, she reminded him that some 2,000 people in Northern Ireland had lost their lives to the IRA: 'What would the international community think if Britain retaliated by launching attacks across the border into the Irish Republic, where many of the terrorists are?' His IRA comparison did not work: Irish republicans could vote in democratic elections, supporters of the ANC could not. Britain, she reminded him, 'stood almost alone in the international community . . . attempting to resist pressure for economic measures against South Africa'. Soon thereafter, Botha imposed a state of emergency, the first since Sharpeville.

France now imposed a unilateral freeze on new investment in South Africa, while the big American banks stopped rolling over loans to South African companies and froze all unused lines of credit. There was a run on the rand. In August alone, $400 million – about a tenth of the banks' loans – was withdrawn from South Africa.

With internal reform stalled, Desmond Tutu, the future Archbishop of Cape Town, accused Botha of wanting to 'bludgeon the blacks into submission. He knows he will be supported by Mrs Thatcher and President Reagan and Chancellor Kohl* . . . blacks in their view are expendable.' So far, Mrs Thatcher had reaped precious little benefit from her stand against sanctions, and plenty of obloquy. The Commonwealth now decided to make her feel her isolation.

Mrs Thatcher was always suspicious of the Commonwealth. She resented its unwillingness to look at the tyrannical practices of some members, and felt that its too-easy unity over South Africa was designed to put Britain in the dock. The Commonwealth Heads of Government Meetings (CHOGMs) were, she thought, inordinately long, pointless and ill organized. They often took place in hot holiday places, where pictures of leaders having fun at taxpayers' expense played badly at home.

The CHOGM at Nassau, in the Bahamas, in October 1985, toxically combined these pet hates with the determination of many Commonwealth

---

* Tutu was right that Kohl was an important figure in the sanctions controversy. West Germany needed South African coal and was opposed to sanctions. Kohl and Mrs Thatcher, despite their other differences, were to work together quite closely on this.

leaders to impose sanctions on South Africa. Planning her trip, as always Mrs Thatcher rejected anything that might be considered extravagant. This included turning down Lord King's offer to fly the British delegation on Concorde, fearing this would upstage the Queen, who, as usual, was attending as head of the Commonwealth.* As the conference approached, Charles Powell warned her that the outcome on South Africa 'appears to be of great concern to the Palace'. The Queen sought an audience with Mrs Thatcher the day before the conference began, 'in the hope that she may be able to use what you tell her with other Commonwealth leaders'.

At the conference itself, Mrs Thatcher dug in. The Canadian Prime Minister, Brian Mulroney, who later wrote that 'the Queen personally asked me to work with other leaders to prevent a major split', tried to win Mrs Thatcher over: a British initiative over South Africa, he said, would make Commonwealth members 'all stand in line and salute'. She was not tempted, believing that the Commonwealth liked to treat Britain as a target, not a guiding star. The Labor Prime Minister of Australia, Bob Hawke, pushed her to support a Commonwealth mission of eminent persons to South Africa but got nowhere. 'The South African regime would never negotiate with a pistol to its head,' she insisted. She also thought it 'unrealistic', in South Africa, to envisage 'one man, one vote in a unitary state': better to look to federal solutions to replace apartheid.

In discussions with Robert Mugabe of Zimbabwe, she rejected the idea that a revolution was the answer. She reminded him that his own Patriotic Front had been made to give up violence. Insisting she wanted to be 'a builder not a destroyer', she said she would not support economic sanctions, a view she repeated to the BBC. No one could accuse her of not being clear.

On the Saturday, Mrs Thatcher resisted efforts by the Commonwealth leaders to foist upon her a joint text she considered unacceptable. Instead, the British now sought to prepare their own. Sonny Ramphal was 'dejected ... and spoke of a damaging and perhaps irreparable split in the Commonwealth'. The next day's plenary session was worse still: 'The Prime Minister was lectured on morality, on preferring British jobs to black African lives, on being concerned for pennies rather than principles,' reported Powell. Characteristically, she 'reminded her critics of their own trade and other links with South Africa'† and attacked their records

---

* She also rejected a plan for daily hair appointments as too indulgent, but Caroline Ryder slipped them back into the programme without permission because she thought they would be needed in the Bahamian heat.

† Countries such as Canada and the 'Frontline States' (the informal grouping of those bordering South Africa – Angola, Botswana, Lesotho, Mozambique, Tanzania, Zambia and, from

on human rights. While perfectly genuine in her principled opposition to sanctions, Mrs Thatcher was also playing a game to minimize the demands made upon Britain. Contemptuous though she was of the Commonwealth's moral pretensions, she did not want a formal split. With her officials, she now agreed that if the conference called for 'a suspension of violence',* Britain might 'offer two very modest additional measures' – a ban on the import of South African Krugerrands (gold coins) to Britain and the ending of official support for trade promotions to South Africa.

Mrs Thatcher now changed her act from anger to injury. That afternoon, as she later wrote, 'I began by saying that I had never been so insulted as I had by the people in that room.' She said she felt 'deep hurt' at some of the morning's remarks. Feeling bad at this spectacle of a woman scorned, some of those present 'urged her not to take the remarks personally'. She exploited the moment to offer her two concessions. If her offer were not accepted, the United Kingdom would make a unilateral statement. After a brief discussion, the text she sought was approved and the final meeting ended, Powell recorded, 'with a round of applause for the Prime Minister'. 'I suddenly became a stateswoman for having accepted a "compromise",' she wrote mockingly in her memoirs. The compromise was that the Commonwealth would indeed send an Eminent Persons Group (EPG) to South Africa. If the eminences reported unfavourably on progress to ending apartheid, the issue of sanctions would be reopened.†

In Powell's loyal but, in this case, correct view, Mrs Thatcher had overcome the difficulties she had faced with 'consummate skill'. She had used her complete isolation to make her opponents feel guilty and won the two things she most wanted – no sanctions, for now at least, and no serious compromise of Britain's right to take an independent view.

She had no love for the EPG, but realized she could strongly influence its choice of members. In Nassau, Howe seemed open to her suggestion that he chair it, but asked how his job could be done in his absence. Mrs Thatcher airily replied, 'Oh, that's all right. I'll be my own Foreign Secretary!' Howe,

---

1980, Zimbabwe) carried on trade with South Africa while pretending not to. Privately, some Frontline States were quite open about their reliance on such trade. In 1986, a note passed to Mrs Thatcher from the British High Commission in Zimbabwe reported the Deputy Prime Minister saying, 'We will never commit suicide by imposing sanctions on South Africa.' Another local politician explained: 'I am surprised that the British, who taught us hypocrisy, should find our attitude surprising.'

* The call for 'suspension' rather than an 'end' to violence was itself a concession by Mrs Thatcher. She reluctantly accepted expert advice that the ANC would never forswear violence in principle, but might suspend it in practice.

† Instead of 'sanctions', the compromise included the Thatcher-driven phrase 'further measures', which was designed to water down the concept.

who shrank from conflict, made no direct protest, but this was, for him, 'the killer-blow'. She was soon dissuaded from putting him forward, but she had clearly, almost artlessly, expressed her true wishes.* For him, they were unforgettably humiliating.

At Nassau, Mrs Thatcher was proud not of what she had agreed, but of what she hadn't. When questioned on television, she put her forefinger and thumb close to each other to show she had moved only 'a tiny little bit'. 'With four little words', wrote Howe, she 'humiliated three dozen other heads of government, devalued the policy on which they had just agreed – and demeaned herself.' There is a vehemence here which perhaps tries to make up for his failure to protest at the time. He chewed the toad, as before, but with increasing distaste.†

As with the Cold War, for insights into South Africa Mrs Thatcher looked beyond official channels. Of all her 'irregulars', the writer Laurens van der Post was one of the most unusual. A brilliant, charming, beautiful old man of Afrikaner birth, he was a long-standing opponent of apartheid, and also of the ANC, whose Communist elements he mistrusted.‡ His romantic obsession with the un-Westernized glory of the black African led him to admire the Zulus, particularly the Inkatha movement led by the Zulu Chief Minister, Mangosuthu Buthelezi. Buthelezi was the only non-ANC leader with a large popular following. He opposed sanctions and, in Powell's view, van der Post 'fooled' Mrs Thatcher into thinking he was more influential than he was. Her determination to avoid the ANC ending up with a political monopoly inclined her to try to keep Buthelezi in play.

Van der Post had real influence with Mrs Thatcher and gave her the feeling, which she needed in all controversial policy areas, that there were genuine alternatives to official advice. Thanks to him, No. 10 also had an informant at the top level of the South African government: from 1979, the minister Piet Koornhof secretly provided information about the

---

* Privately she complained that her Foreign Secretary had been 'feeble' at Nassau: 'Howe has not got the calibre to be Prime Minister,' she told Woodrow Wyatt.

† It had at first been planned that Denis should accompany Mrs Thatcher to the CHOGM in Nassau. In the end, he did not. The meticulous government records noted who in the prime ministerial party bought what at the duty-free shop. Mrs Thatcher bought a multipack of Rothman's cigarettes for $6.50 and a bottle of gin for $4.97. Since she neither smoked nor drank gin, these must have been her present to her husband, who did both.

‡ Unknown to Mrs Thatcher, van der Post had also been something of a fantasist, claiming knowledge and experience he did not always possess, and using these to establish connections with important people. He said he had been brought up by a Bushman nanny, though this was not so. He also said he had been military-political adviser to Lord Mountbatten at the end of the Second World War, which was also untrue.

opportunities for change. Such intelligence helped Mrs Thatcher feel that her pressure might get somewhere.

Her other source of alternative views was Fritz Leutwiler, the former President of the Swiss National Bank and head of the Bank for International Settlements. She had come to know and like Leutwiler while staying with Lady Glover in Switzerland. She admired his success in orchestrating the rescue of South Africa from the bank crisis. Leutwiler shared her desire for an orderly end to apartheid. At this time, he became her 'main contact' with P. W. Botha.

Much as she preferred van der Post's gleaming-eyed accounts of warrior races and Zulu honour to being lectured at Commonwealth conferences, Mrs Thatcher retained a practical grasp of what was happening. In November 1985, she told Botha bluntly that he must end his refusal to cooperate with the EPG. He did so at once. At the same time, she was hearing from intelligence sources that the ANC would 'call a halt to all violence' if Mandela and fellow imprisoned ANC leaders were released and the organization unbanned. Despite her refusal personally to talk to the ANC so long as it espoused violence, she allowed MI6 to do so secretly. In December, Botha told her he wanted to 'get moving with the negotiations ... we are reconciled to the disappearance of white domination'. Cheered by all this, Howe told her that Botha 'obviously trusts you – you are perhaps the only Western leader in whom he feels he can confide'.

In early 1986, Julian Amery told Mrs Thatcher he was planning to visit Botha. Did she wish him to pass on a message? She did, scribbling:

> The one L van der Post put to me – namely – he must get a majority against the extreme blacks by forming an alliance of
> Whites
> Indians
> Coloureds
> Zulus
> S. African Swazis
> Which together with some of the blacks they would carry with them, would give him a majority.

This was a rough summation of how she wanted an internal settlement to come about.* In a speech in January 1986 promising further reform,

---

* Mrs Thatcher, however, recognized that any settlement involving Buthelezi would not succeed if it fell short of meaningful reform. She told the Conservative MP Robert Jackson that this meant a 'firm commitment to the abolition of apartheid ... The hope nurtured by some Afrikaners of a political deal which effectively maintains their power with the consent of the government does not seem to me a realistic one.'

Botha spoke of the possibility of releasing Mandela. Perhaps naively, Mrs Thatcher considered this 'very courageous', and was annoyed that the Foreign Office reaction was, as Powell minuted, 'rather wan'. Soon after, however, P. W. Botha rebuked his own Foreign Minister, Pik Botha, for saying South Africa would one day have a black president. The international community remained unconvinced that real change was coming.

Some things *were* shifting. In March, the EPG met Mandela, who had choice words for Lord Barber, its British member: 'I am told Mrs Thatcher says President Gorbachev is a man with whom she can do business,' Mandela told him. 'Will you please tell her that it would be far, far easier and very much safer to do business with Nelson Mandela.' Barber did as bidden. He also told her and Howe that the EPG's meeting with Botha had been a 'disaster': the South African government, he said, did not envisage the full dismantling of apartheid. In that case, said Mrs Thatcher, it must change its position. At Barber's request, she introduced the EPG's 'negotiating concept' to Botha. Under this, the white government would end the state of emergency, withdraw troops from the townships, release Mandela and other ANC leaders and unban the ANC. In return, the ANC would agree to suspend violence and enter talks. She told Botha that unless he moved, she would have no chance of persuading Commonwealth colleagues to stay their hand on sanctions. Botha responded positively, tacitly dropping his demand for the absolute forswearing of violence from the ANC. On 18 April, she defended the ANC to Botha: 'There is a readiness on their part to talk, but realistically they will need something they can show to their supporters to justify calling for a suspension of violence.' Irritated though she was by the Commonwealth, she genuinely wanted the breakthrough the EPG 'concept' sought.

On 19 May 1986, South African forces suddenly launched ground and air raids on ANC offices in Zambia, Zimbabwe and Botswana. These ended the EPG's mission. The raids evoked the same fury from Mrs Thatcher as the Botswana raids the previous June. She wrote to Botha asking 'what possible advantage to South Africa could outweigh the immense damage done to your international position and in particular to the Commonwealth initiative . . . I myself find them hard to reconcile with the relationship of trust and confidence which I had thought we had established.' It was, she declared, 'a watershed'. From then on, she seems to have decided that real change would not come from Botha. She began to look out for an Afrikaner Gorbachev.

Botha professed himself equally angry with Mrs Thatcher. Over eight pages, he complained of his 'deep disillusionment' with her letter. On 12 June, he reimposed the countrywide state of emergency. The EPG report was published the same day. It said South Africa was not making progress towards abolishing apartheid. Meeting the report's co-chairmen, also that day, Mrs Thatcher insisted that, ultimately, there would have to be 'negotiations in South Africa between the Government and blacks'. She believed 'Mandela held the key': his release should be the focus of discussions with Pretoria. The next day, Powell communicated her emphasis on the release of Mandela to the South African Ambassador. 'I am not passing this on to the Foreign Office,' he told her.* South Africa had become a subject, like certain aspects of the Cold War or relations with Saudi Arabia, for which Mrs Thatcher and Powell alone worked out the direction of policy, cutting out Geoffrey Howe and his officials.

Ahead of the European Council in The Hague at the end June, Hawke and Mulroney lobbied Mrs Thatcher for the EEC to introduce sanctions. Still seeking delay, she proposed instead that Howe should visit southern Africa as the European Council's special envoy. This was agreed: Howe's mission was given three months to bear fruit before a ban on the import of gold coins, iron, steel and coal, but not full-bodied sanctions, would take effect. This would make it more difficult, Mrs Thatcher hoped, for the Commonwealth London 'review conference', scheduled for early August, to throw its weight about. 'We must at all costs avoid bringing [his visit] to a premature conclusion,' she told Howe, perhaps subconsciously pleased that he would be away a lot. This ploy, according to Sonny Ramphal, left Commonwealth leaders 'enraged'.

Botha, little more impressed, haughtily refused to commit to receive Howe as EEC emissary. Once again, Mrs Thatcher weighed in forcefully – this 'perturbs me considerably', she wrote – and once again Botha backed down. As for poor Howe, he resented the poisoned chalice which Mrs Thatcher had passed him, but could scarcely reject such an important role.

The ensuing month, up to and including the London review conference, was the most difficult in diplomatic terms Mrs Thatcher had ever endured. She had to deal not only with discontent among her ministers, but the combined opposition of the Commonwealth leaders and the Commonwealth Secretariat (based in London), and the consequent anxieties of the

---

* On 6 June, Mrs Thatcher wrote to Lord Paget of Northampton, a Labour peer who supported her position on economic sanctions, outlining the case for Mandela's release: 'As you know, I loathe terrorism. But the status of Nelson Mandela as a black leader is accepted on all sides and I am convinced that his release is a necessary step on the way to creating the right conditions for dialogue ... I realise that Nelson Mandela has not been prepared to renounce violence as a condition for his release (that of course is not the same as declaring that he would engage in terrorist activities).'

Queen. Elizabeth II, as head of the Commonwealth, was worried about divisions between it and Britain. Against this, Mrs Thatcher had only the genuine but *sotto voce* support of Ronald Reagan and Helmut Kohl, and the backing of public opinion at home. South African sanctions provided a classic example Mrs Thatcher's leadership – reaching over policy elites and foreign leaders by reiterating what she saw as home truths, enduring isolation in the belief she would eventually be proved right.

In late June, the Queen had received an emotional letter from Desmond Tutu, warning of impending catastrophe in South Africa: why, he asked, were there no sanctions against the 'most vicious system since Nazism'? 'Your Majesty, this is a *cri de coeur*. Please help us bring about a new South Africa.' The letter immediately raised the ticklish problem of who should answer it. Was this a matter for the Palace on behalf of the Queen as head of the Commonwealth or even, since Tutu was a bishop, as supreme governor of the Church of England? On the other hand, since it dealt with foreign policy, should it not be a matter for the Queen's ministers? Howe favoured a reply from the Queen's private secretary, Sir William Heseltine. Heseltine's draft spoke of the Queen's 'great concern' at recent developments in South Africa: she sought 'an end to the suffering' and emphasized the 'special responsibility of those in positions of influence to speak out against violence'. Powell was chary, warning that the press might stir up trouble. He suggested Howe should reply, in uncontroversial terms. Mrs Thatcher agreed: 'I think the proposed draft <u>does</u> involve The Queen in politics ... The Press is bound to claim that there is a rift between The Queen and Her Government.' A week later, however, Heseltine reported that the Queen had decided that the balance of the argument rested with a letter from the private secretary. This was duly sent. Although the final draft differed little from the one that had so worried Powell and Mrs Thatcher, it did not lead to a press explosion. Nonetheless, the overall situation remained uneasy.

Mrs Thatcher was incensed by the suggestion that her stand against sanctions was immoral. One of her favourite points, formulated by van der Post, was 'the immorality of sanctions' themselves. On 9 July, the day after Howe began his mission, she publicly denounced her critics. 'I find nothing *moral*', she told the *Guardian*, 'about them sitting in comfortable circumstances, with good salaries, inflation-proof pensions, good jobs, saying that we, as a matter of *morality*, will put x hundred thousand black people out of work.' The proposed fruit and vegetable boycott alone, she claimed, would destroy 95,000 jobs: 'Blacks and their families out of work. *Moral*? Poof! *Moral*? No social security. *Moral*?'

Mrs Thatcher's critics on sanctions now increasingly combined against her. She was inundated with messages from EPG members and other Commonwealth leaders trying to change her mind. There was even talk of the Commonwealth breaking up. What made things worse was the increasing restiveness of Geoffrey Howe. On 24 June, he confided in Peter Marshall, Deputy Secretary-General of the Commonwealth, that 'the trouble is with the Prime Minister'. Trying, as with the British Leyland question after Westland, to rein in Mrs Thatcher through the power of ministers, Howe recruited senior colleagues, causing Peter Walker to write to her: 'Willie [Whitelaw], Norman [Tebbit], Quintin [Hogg, Lord Hailsham], the Chief Whip [Wakeham] and I all have expressed our political judgment that we must be seen as positive in our desire to negotiate.' The following day, in Cabinet, Howe won general support for further measures should his mission to South Africa fail.

The *Sunday Telegraph* built on this, reporting on 6 July that Howe was threatening to resign if Mrs Thatcher would not impose sanctions after his return.* Two days later, before setting off, Howe warned her that continued opposition to sanctions had produced the impression of Britain as 'the sole defender of apartheid'. He urged her to concede something at the review conference.

Stories grew of royal anxieties and dissatisfaction. At lunch in Clarence House, Queen Elizabeth the Queen Mother told Woodrow Wyatt 'without prompting ... "How disgraceful it is that the press and people are trying to involve the Queen in the row about sanctions."' She denied that her daughter was at odds with Mrs Thatcher. 'I suspect', Wyatt added, 'she wants me to let Mrs T know the Queen is not against her.' There is certainly no known evidence that the two women ever exchanged hard words over South Africa. But Buckingham Palace did have different interests from Downing Street and was working to promote them.

Reflecting the Queen's lifelong commitment to Commonwealth unity, the Palace did what it could to keep things together.† William Heseltine stayed in close touch with Ramphal, asking how best to outmanoeuvre Mrs Thatcher. On 23 June, shortly before The Hague summit, Ramphal met the Queen: 'It went very well,' he reported to Peter Marshall. '... She will do all she can to help.' On 10 July, Powell informed Mrs Thatcher that the Queen was now 'actively considering giving a dinner on the Sunday evening' (the

---

* Four days later, freed since January from the constraints of ministerial office, Leon Brittan became the first senior Conservative to break with Mrs Thatcher and call publicly for the imposition of sanctions.
† Such efforts were reinforced by the fact that Sir William Heseltine, only recently promoted to the top job, was himself an Australian, the first non-Briton in the role – and therefore had Commonwealth fellow feeling.

first day of the meeting). This royal bid to save Commonwealth unity made life considerably more difficult for Mrs Thatcher.

On 20 July, the campaign to change Mrs Thatcher's mind took a dramatic turn. Under the headline, 'Queen dismayed by "uncaring" Thatcher', the *Sunday Times* reported that the rift between monarch and Prime Minister over South Africa and the Commonwealth was real, and went wider: the Queen felt the government should be more 'caring' towards the less privileged in society and feared that as a result of the miners' strike 'long-term damage was being done to the country's social fabric'.

Buckingham Palace rushed out a statement: 'As with all previous prime ministers, The Queen enjoys a relationship of the closest confidentiality with Mrs Thatcher, and reports purporting to be The Queen's opinion of government policies are entirely without foundation.' This was not, in fact, a denial, although it was intended to give that impression. A complete denial was impossible because the story had been fed to the *Sunday Times* by Michael Shea, the Queen's press secretary. Shea had even privately boasted about what he done, before publication. An unrelated meeting of senior court officials from Continental monarchies, at Buckingham Palace, on 19 July, had included discussion of press handling. Shea, Heseltine recalled, had described his 'wonderful coup' with the *Sunday Times*, saying he had 'led them to publish a very sympathetic picture of the Queen: concerned about the coal miners and concerned for the Commonwealth'. Later in the day, Shea 'came in with his tail between his legs, looking thoroughly abashed, saying there's a sensational story appearing in the *Sunday Times* which says there's a rift between the Prime Minister and the Queen, and Bernard Ingham was in a state of frenzy'.*

After frantic discussions between the Palace and No. 10, Heseltine suggested to the Queen, at Windsor, that she might wish to call the Prime Minister, at Chequers. This the Queen immediately did. She told Mrs Thatcher that (in Heseltine's paraphrase) she 'could not imagine how the story came to be circulated, and anyway it bears no relation to the truth as I understand it ...' Queen and Prime Minister 'had a very amicable conversation'.

Many people were naturally disposed to believe the Palace statement. But because the *Sunday Times* stood by the story, Mrs Thatcher realized that it contained some truth. For a woman almost paralysingly correct in her relations with the monarch, this was difficult to handle. After her weekly audiences in Buckingham Palace – which, by tradition, never have

---

* Ingham had been informed because the *Sunday Times* had run the story past him.

officials in attendance – Mrs Thatcher would emerge, 'panting for a whisky and soda'. The audiences were rarely very productive, because she was nervous. She sat on the edge of her chair and launched into an anodyne recitation of current business. Heseltine once asked the Queen if it was like Queen Victoria's experience of Gladstone – 'He speaks to me as if I were a public meeting.' 'No,' said the Queen. 'It wasn't at all like that ... but I wasn't given much encouragement to comment on what was said.' Mrs Thatcher lacked the confidence to make a friend of the Queen so their relations were 'absolutely correct and perhaps not very cosy'. In Heseltine's view, 'There might have been fault on the Queen's side,' for not trying to turn the talk into more of a discussion. So, following Shea's damaging disclosure, Mrs Thatcher felt, Robin Butler thought, 'desperately hurt. She would freeze, as she did over the row about her honorary degree at Oxford [see p. 590]. She never said how upset she was.' Besides, she sensed political danger. 'Those little old ladies will say Mrs Thatcher is upsetting the Queen. I'll lose votes,'* she told Powell. There was also risk the other way round. Peter Marshall worried that the Queen's pro-Commonwealth stand might cause problems in the UK, where there was strong sentiment against sanctions.

Aware of Mrs Thatcher's political vulnerability, Howe pressed harder against his boss. She worsened her own position by giving a very frank interview to a friend, the journalist Graham Turner, on 19 July, for the following week's *Sunday Telegraph*. Reviewing the transcript, ahead of publication, Powell was alarmed. Through Ingham he tried to dissuade the paper from using its more incendiary passages. Mrs Thatcher had expressed trenchant views. It was not the *British* Commonwealth, she reminded Turner, 'it is their club. It is their Commonwealth. If they wish to break it up, I think it is absurd.' Numerous Commonwealth members were not democracies, she pointed out: 'some of them have had terrible internal massacres'. To the suggestion that her sanctions policy was divisive, she cried, 'Poppycock!' 'I am bound to say', Powell wrote to her, in the restrained language of the loyal adviser, 'that ... the article runs the risk of exposing you to sharp criticism for dealing too vigorously with South African problems', particularly with Howe, still 'engaged in delicate

---

* In the short term, at least, Mrs Thatcher's fears were probably justified. The monarchy, buoyed up by the popularity of Prince Andrew's marriage to Sarah Ferguson on 23 July, was a dangerous thing for an elected politician to fall foul of. An opinion poll in *The Times* on 1 August showed a sudden nine-point Labour lead; and the percentage thinking that the government was 'not tough enough on the South African government' had moved sharply up from 42 per cent to 56 per cent.

negotiations' there. She saw Powell's point. 'By all means try <u>very hard</u> to negotiate the deletions,' she told him.

Finding he could not stop the *Sunday Telegraph*, Powell thought he should warn Howe in South Africa. The reply, from Howe's private secretary, revealed half-suppressed anguish: 'although [the interview] contains some positive things, it also contains some material that could not be less helpful'. He pleaded that Mrs Thatcher should stop attacking 'the immorality of sanctions': people would think the British government were 'defenders of apartheid'.

Strangely, the *Sunday Telegraph* interview did not produce further outcry. But the Howe–Thatcher problem was now more serious than Commonwealth hostility. When a battered Howe returned home he told Mrs Thatcher the United States would soon adopt additional measures; so should Britain.* She agreed that Britain should contemplate further measures if the EEC would participate, but remained opposed to sanctions because she was 'absolutely convinced' they 'would not achieve internal change'. She said British public opinion supported her position. Ahead of the OD Cabinet committee on 31 July, Powell advised her to avoid an argument with Howe. He feared senior colleagues might support Howe, and saw danger in stories of disunity.

OD passed off without incident, but the trouble came afterwards. Although ministers had agreed to support further EEC measures, Howe learnt that Ingham was briefing that the government was 'not in the business of further sanctions'. Two weeks earlier, Howe had promised the Commons that further measures were likely. Calling this an 'albatross', Ingham had said he would not mind if the review conference were to 'break up'. Rumours now circulated that Howe would resign. Urged on by Elspeth, he sat down and wrote Mrs Thatcher a long, agonized letter, setting out how Ingham's behaviour risked the review conference. But his last point was, he said, 'more fundamental'. 'We have worked together closely, and I like to think successfully, for more than 11 years.' He wanted to continue but, for their partnership to survive, they must 'continue to have confidence in each other'. This was not possible if the No. 10 press secretary set 'Minister against Minister' – the issue must be tackled. Mrs Thatcher chose to see this as neither threat nor plea, but as a cowardly attempt to get her loyal press secretary sacked. When Howe raised it briefly

---

* That October, overriding President Reagan's veto, the US Congress passed the Comprehensive Anti-Apartheid Act imposing punitive sanctions on South Africa. According to Powell, rather than leading to a change of heart this only left Mrs Thatcher 'more embattled'.

in the margins of pre-conference meetings, she replied, 'Bernard isn't like that. But we can't talk about it now.'

Howe had got close to Michael Heseltine's situation over Westland. Because he was far more central to the Thatcher project, and more respected than Heseltine, the damage done to Mrs Thatcher would have been much greater if he had resigned. She was lucky that little of this became public and that her Foreign Secretary was both too loyal and too indecisive to press his point home.

On 3 August, the first night of the review conference, the seven leaders present, including Mrs Thatcher, plus Ramphal and Howe, dined at Buckingham Palace. In Ramphal's view, the Queen 'made clear that the Commonwealth must not break up over this. Margaret did not like it. The Queen indicated her disagreement with Mrs Thatcher without ever having to say so.'

The conference itself did not, in fact, end in disaster. Mrs Thatcher accepted Powell's analysis that 'for all the talk . . . [Commonwealth leaders] would relish avoiding a bust-up'. Since her position was so difficult, that was her attitude too. The review conference agreed that apartheid was not being dismantled. She said Britain would implement the EEC measures agreed at The Hague if the European partners would do the same.* These limited sanctions came into force in September. She did not repeat Nassau by belittling the deal afterwards.

Everything suddenly calmed down. The Howes went off on holiday. Mrs Thatcher went into hospital for the long-planned operation on her hand (see p. 539). Over time, the government's low opinion of Michael Shea's behaviour was borne in upon Buckingham Palace. He was quietly edged out.

What had this all been about? Certainly Mrs Thatcher had caused unnecessary antagonism and, at this stage, had little positive to show for her attempts to move the white government. But it was a strength as well as

---

* There was a piquant, *Yes Minister*-style postscript to the review conference. In November 1986, Mrs Thatcher received a letter from Nigel Lawson in his role as Master of the Mint. He said he wanted to strike a new one-ounce gold coin called the Britannia, 'following the virtual demise of the Krugerrand'. 'I assume we buy the gold from South Africa,' Mrs Thatcher inquired. Lawson replied that some of the gold probably would be South African. Geoffrey Howe wrote to Lawson to protest at this, given the Commonwealth ban. 'I trust that there will be no <u>Russian</u> [underlined three times] gold in it?' wrote Mrs Thatcher caustically. The Mint informed her that some of the gold probably would indeed be South African and some Russian. 'Go ahead,' instructed Mrs Thatcher, '– but I am at a loss for words! We can't import Krugerrands so we are going to strike a new coin which may . . . contain S. African & Russian gold. What a policy!!'

a fault that she did business in a unique way. Certain that economic sanctions would prove ineffective, she was not, unlike most politicians, cynical enough to agree to them for the sake of a quiet life. She believed South Africa could change peacefully to a multiracial government, negotiated after the release of Mandela, if the right interlocutors could be found. As in her attitude to Gorbachev and the Soviet Union, she believed a productive partner would emerge and hoped to help influence that process.

She paid a higher price with Geoffrey Howe. Their South African disagreements had been foreshadowed by Howe's frustration with her handling of the Anglo-Irish negotiations in 1984–5. There was 'a fiery Celtic element to Geoffrey', recalled Richard Ryder, 'a Welsh *hwyl*. On the rare occasions when he gets angry, he gets very, very angry.' In July 1986, he was angry about many things – about being made a fool of on his South African mission, about being disregarded by Mrs Thatcher, about her being, he thought, too kind to the white South African government and too rude to the Commonwealth.

He was also, perhaps, angry with himself for having failed to challenge her more forcefully over Westland. Had he already missed the chance to succeed her, only to be blackguarded by Ingham? He was uneasily aware that when Mrs Thatcher failed to answer his letter about Ingham, he had done nothing further about it. The issue festered.

On the review conference's last day, Peter Marshall had a long talk with Robert Armstrong: 'He says Mrs T doesn't trust Howe ... She is filled with a sense of mission and there is no one to support her (Tebbit is out of favour).' This was a fair summation.

24
To Moscow

'The light is coming from the West'

On 19 November 1985, Ronald Reagan and Mikhail Gorbachev held their long-awaited first summit in Geneva. Reagan came away with his confidence in Mrs Thatcher's judgement confirmed. 'Maggie was right,' he told his aides. 'We can do business with this man.' The actual business transacted had not been great, but the symbolic value was considerable. The leaders agreed to two more summits, in Washington and Moscow. Mrs Thatcher encouraged them both to get on with it. When they finally did so, however, she experienced a tremendous shock. In October 1986, Reagan and Gorbachev met alone in Reykjavik. Privately she described the result as an 'earthquake': 'It was the first time in her life that she had felt that there was no place on Earth on which she could put her feet and feel secure. It appeared that all Europe was to be sacrificed.' Her most powerful friend and greatest ideological soulmate had, she believed, come within a whisker of getting rid of the West's guarantee of freedom – the nuclear deterrent.

The strength of her relationship with Reagan caused Mrs Thatcher to be caught off-guard. Before Reykjavik, the two had been in close touch on the central question of reducing nuclear armaments. In early 1986, Gorbachev sought to exploit Reagan's aspiration for a nuclear-free world with a proposal, which the Russians immediately made public, for the complete abolition of nuclear weapons by the year 2000, providing the President gave up SDI. While he had no intention of dropping SDI, Reagan pledged that he and the NATO allies would give the suggestions 'careful study'.

Mrs Thatcher's 'careful study' made her no less sceptical. A world without nuclear weapons, she told Geoffrey Smith for *The Times*, was 'pie in the sky'. On 11 February she wrote to Reagan, offering the sort of warning about Gorbachev which, a year earlier, the Americans had been inclined to give her: 'He is clearly a more astute operator than his predecessors, far more aware of the scope for playing on public opinion in the West. But under the veneer he is the same brand of dedicated Soviet Communist that we have known in the past . . .' Praising Reagan's 'noble vision of a world without nuclear weapons', she warned that Gorbachev had 'latched on to this'. A nuclear-free world, she reminded Reagan, 'would be a very risky place indeed unless there were concurrent steps to reduce the massive imbalance in the Soviet Union's favour in conventional forces'. Such talk risked 'undermining public support for our agreed strategy of deterrence and flexible response'.*

To meet 'genuine Soviet anxieties', Mrs Thatcher proposed offering the Soviet Union more 'reassurance about the likely shape, scope and timescale of possible development of the SDI'.† She also stressed that Britain's nuclear deterrent should not be drawn into the arms control talks. She cautioned against seeking the removal of Intermediate-range Nuclear Forces (INF) from Europe (the 'zero option'), fearing for the credibility of NATO's nuclear deterrent.

Mrs Thatcher's broad concerns chimed with many within the President's administration. To temper Reagan's ambition, officials drafted wide-ranging conditions to be met before contemplating nuclear disarmament. These included not only complete conventional-force parity, but also the vague need for 'a demonstrated Soviet commitment to peaceful competition'.

The President's response to the Prime Minister, later in February, included all these conditions. According to Charles Powell, she was relieved: the conditions 'seemed so unachievable' that they were, *de facto*, 'an absolute guarantee' against abolishing nuclear weapons: 'So we could rest easy.' Reagan's letter emboldened her to write at once to Gorbachev: 'I know that both you and President Reagan have embraced the goal of freeing the world of nuclear weapons. But this is a long-term aspiration.' She expected nuclear weapons to continue to 'make an essential contribution to preserving peace and stability' for the foreseeable future. Reagan also told her he would keep the British and French independent deterrents out of any INF

---

* Under 'flexible response', NATO, if attacked, could draw on a range of options, beginning with conventional forces, but escalating to tactical nuclear weapons, intermediate missiles and ultimately strategic nuclear forces. NATO's nuclear deterrent was credible because it allowed the alliance to respond in kind to Soviet attacks of differing magnitudes.
† These included 'strengthening and refining the ABM Treaty, extending the period of notice required for unilateral withdrawal from it and a commitment not to enter particular phases of defensive programmes before certain specified dates'.

deal. But he said virtually nothing about SDI. Even with his closest ally, he wished to remain unencumbered on the subject.*

While Mrs Thatcher was trying to nudge Reagan in her direction on SDI, Geoffrey Howe was trying to push her in his. In April, he sent her a fifteen-page letter about the importance of not going beyond the research stage. 'The Foreign Office gets more verbose by the day,' she commented. Four days later, Lawson wrote in support of Howe's letter. 'The Foreign Secretary is finding some allies,' Powell warned her, 'I can't think what the Treasury is doing writing a letter like this,' she scribbled. It was indeed unusual and reflected her domestic weakness after Westland. To adapt a phrase from the SDI debate, one might say that a Howe–Lawson collaboration to keep her under control was now entering the research stage.

In July, Reagan wrote to Mrs Thatcher with a new proposal. The two superpowers, he said, should agree to keep all SDI research, development and testing within the bounds of the ABM Treaty for at least five years. He went on, however, to offer a striking new proposal: after five years, negotiations over how to share the benefits of strategic defence and to eliminate offensive ballistic weapons entirely would begin.†

Abolishing these missiles, the most potentially devastating nuclear weapons in existence, was an astonishing thought. It naturally appealed to Americans, however, because the Soviets had a large numerical advantage in them. It also undermined the Soviet argument that SDI was designed to give the USA an advantage in defending itself against ballistic missiles: if such missiles no longer existed, this could not be the case. The scheme looked less dazzlingly brilliant in London. Not only would it undermine 'flexible response', but it would put Britain's proposed new Trident in jeopardy, since Trident was itself a ballistic missile supplied by the USA. Reagan also expected 'other nuclear powers' to participate in the arms reduction talks. Was Britain's nuclear deterrent to be negotiated away?

It is surprising that Mrs Thatcher made no great protest at this letter. Although she persuaded Reagan to remove the reference to 'other nuclear powers', the idea of eliminating all offensive ballistic missiles – anathema to her – stayed. On 25 July, Reagan shared these proposals with Gorbachev. As Powell put it, 'Whether we *should* have taken his comments on

---

* An NSC analysis of Mrs Thatcher's suggestions cast doubt on whether a viable SDI research programme could be sustained under the limitations she was proposing, but grudgingly concluded that 'When all the smoke clears, we may ultimately have to make some move in the general direction suggested by the PM.'

† Reagan's proposal suggested that if no agreement were reached after two years, each side would be free to deploy SDI unilaterally after six months' notice.

abolishing ballistic missiles seriously is something you can argue about, but we *didn't*. I think the attitude was "Oh, the old boy's got ideas of his own about nuclear weapons, but NATO strategy is NATO strategy and therefore it will all be fine."'

Around this time, Gorbachev was anxious to set a date for his second summit with Reagan, in Washington, and sought Mrs Thatcher's help. She passed on his concerns to Reagan, who was receptive but non-committal. The President was 'very keen to have a second summit', she assured Gorbachev in August, although a date remained elusive. Gorbachev had more luck with Mrs Thatcher herself, who accepted his invitation to visit Moscow in the first half of 1987.

That September, Gorbachev suddenly proposed an informal meeting with Reagan in advance of the Washington summit. The two agreed to meet in Reykjavik.* Offering Reagan her thoughts on the key issues, Mrs Thatcher contemplated a likely reduction in INF. As to how many US and Soviet missiles should remain, she said she would accept 'any equal ceiling in Europe' so long as 'other Allied conditions, above all on SR [Short Range] INF, are met'. On SDI, she repeated the need to reassure the Russians there would be 'no sudden break-out from research to deployment'. Like the US administration, she saw Reykjavik as laying the ground for a major summit, nothing more. Indeed, she worried that her original draft to Reagan was too long: 'We have to remember', she scribbled, 'that this is <u>NOT</u> the <u>Summit</u>.'

Reagan saw his trip to Reykjavik in much the same way. 'I do not anticipate any formal agreements,' he told Mrs Thatcher. He stressed that his 'highest priority' was 'significant and stabilising reductions in strategic offensive weapons'. Powell told her the American approach was 'generally reassuring': with the administration concentrating on reduction, not abolition, Mrs Thatcher felt comfortable.

Gorbachev, however, had something very different in mind. Meeting the Politburo beforehand, he warned that, if Reykjavik failed, they would be pulled into an arms race: 'and we will lose this race' because 'we are presently at the limit of our capabilities'. His goal was to undermine NATO by driving a wedge between Reagan and his allies. 'In order to move Reagan we have to give him something ...' he said, namely, the 'liquidation of nuclear weapons'. As Anatoly Chernyaev, Gorbachev's foreign policy

---

* Gorbachev, in fact, offered two possible venues for the meeting: London or Reykjavik. According to George Shultz, 'The President was tempted by London because he would have loved it if Margaret had sat in on the meeting, but he knew that was not proper.' The Americans decided in favour of Reykjavik because of its much greater isolation.

adviser, understood it, Gorbachev meant to 'sweep Reagan off his feet'. In Mrs Thatcher's eyes, he very nearly succeeded.

When the two leaders met in Reykjavik on Saturday 11 October 1986, Gorbachev unveiled a bold package. It included a 50 per cent cut in strategic arms and the abolition of all INF in Europe (with French and British missiles ignored). Gorbachev also proposed that both sides agree to abide by the ABM Treaty for not less than ten years, during which research on SDI could proceed but 'not outside of laboratories'. These sweeping proposals caught the Americans completely by surprise but Reagan declared them 'very encouraging'. Officials on both sides got to work. By the Sunday morning, agreement had been reached on the 50 per cent cut in strategic forces and the removal of all INF from Europe. These were dramatic shifts in favour of long-standing US positions, the INF deal reflecting Reagan's 1981 'zero option' (see p. 243). They were far from what Mrs Thatcher had been expecting. While she had told Reagan she would accept a 'ceiling' on INF in Europe, this did not, obviously, mean zero. With a complete news blackout at Reykjavik, no one knew what was going on. It was not until midday on Sunday that the Americans began calling European capitals to relay what they considered the great triumph of the proposed INF deal. Around lunchtime, Mrs Thatcher rang Charles Powell from Chequers. 'Have you heard what is going on at Reykjavik?' she asked anxiously. 'We've got to do something, Charles.' Powell leapt into a car and drove to Chequers immediately.

Back in Reykjavik, the stumbling block was SDI. Reagan was determined not to confine it to the laboratory for ten years, while Gorbachev was unconvinced by the US offer to share it. To break the deadlock, the Americans introduced a new proposal based on their zero ballistic missile idea of 25 July: neither side would withdraw from the ABM Treaty for ten years. During the first five, both sides would halve their strategic nuclear forces; during the second five, they would abolish all remaining offensive ballistic missiles. Discussions now went to the brink. Gorbachev began by pressing for the elimination of not only ballistic missiles, but all strategic arms.* This would have left the USA with no nuclear weapon capable of reaching the Soviet Union from within the homeland. Advised against accepting this, Reagan raised the game still further: he said it would be fine with him 'if we eliminated all nuclear weapons'. Gorbachev replied, 'We can do that. We can eliminate them.' 'Let's do it,' echoed George Shultz.

---

* Gorbachev preferred this to the abolition of all offensive ballistic missiles because the Soviets had many more such missiles than the Americans.

But the problem of SDI remained. Gorbachev had insisted throughout that everything hinged on SDI being confined to the laboratory for ten years, and the Pentagon had equally insisted to the President that this would kill the programme. Reagan therefore refused Gorbachev's demand and the meeting broke up without agreement. Because Gorbachev's offer had been a 'package', no part of it now survived. All offers were off the table.

With this lack of agreement, the summit was immediately seen as a failure. For Mrs Thatcher, its failure was the only good thing about it. She did not immediately know exactly how far Reagan had gone. Few people did, even within the administration. Nonetheless, she picked up enough to be horrified. According to Jacques Attali, then Mitterrand's special adviser, the aftermath of Reykjavik was 'the first time I heard Margaret Thatcher say the Americans were crazy'.

When Reagan telephoned Mrs Thatcher the following day, her sixty-first birthday, he admitted candidly that, with Gorbachev, he had sought to eliminate all US and Soviet nuclear weapons. She was equally candid, telling Reagan that such a proposal 'caused her grave concern'. They found little common ground. He denied the conventional situation in Europe was as imbalanced as she suggested. She was careful to praise the President – he had 'performed marvellously', she said, though she certainly did not believe this at the time – but she clearly stated her anxieties. Reagan gave no ground: 'He showed no sign of backing down from his concept of eliminating nuclear weapons within ten years, indeed showed considerable pride in it.'

In fact, Reagan's 'concept' proved short-lived. Understanding just how incendiary it was, Reagan's top aides persuaded the President to focus instead on the elimination of offensive ballistic missiles. For Mrs Thatcher, this was a small mercy. As John Poindexter, the National Security Advisor, reminded Reagan, she questioned 'whether we can have effective deterrence without ballistic missiles. She does not believe it prudent to make major reductions without redressing conventional and chemical weapons imbalances. Mrs Thatcher also fears that elimination of ballistic missiles will undercut her domestic political position.'

This last point weighed heavily on her mind. Only a day before Reykjavik, she had been cheered at her annual party conference after excoriating Neil Kinnock's unilateralism. She considered this a key winner for her in the general election she planned for 1987, just as it had been in 1983. Now it looked as if Reagan had started dancing to Labour's tune.

'Giving up nuclear weapons is the sort of thing that Neil Kinnock advocates,' Mrs Thatcher chided the President over the phone. 'This would be tantamount to surrender, so we must be very, very careful.' Despite everything, she ended their call by thanking him for 'a job well-done in

Reykjavik. You lived up to the confidence we have in you.' She was able to praise him without total hypocrisy because he had, in the end, held the line against Gorbachev and refused to give in over SDI. In the years to follow she came to see SDI as the saviour of the West. Reagan's pet project had shot Gorbachev's fox.

Those observing Mrs Thatcher closely differed about her attitude to Reagan. Reykjavik was a prime example. As Poindexter put it, 'My instinct was that she didn't really respect the President. I don't think she thought the President was very smart.' Robin Butler held a similar view: 'Regularly after international meetings she would say, "But Robin, he didn't know anything about it!"' Others, however, thought that her regard was sincere. Colin Powell, Deputy National Security Advisor from late 1986, noted: 'A lot of foreign leaders might reflect the fact that they didn't think they were dealing with an intellectual equal. But Margaret never displayed that. She knew that she was dealing at the top level of abstraction and conceptualization with an intellectual equal.' Powell was right. She thought Reagan grasped the political and ideological challenges of the age in a way that other Western leaders did not. This is why she clung to him through thick and thin.

Reykjavik greatly strained her trust in Reagan's wisdom, but did not break it. She tried to maintain a sort of platonic idea of what Reagan really wanted. As she put it to Henry Kissinger, 'Her main concern remained to bring home to the President that the effect of what he had done at Reykjavik ran flatly contrary to his real objectives.' As it happened, she was due to visit Reagan at Camp David that November, a trip that now assumed pivotal importance. Because her trip had not been previously announced, it appeared to the world as a response to the summit. In preparing, Mrs Thatcher and Powell operated almost alone. 'You have a bilateral with the Foreign Secretary,' Powell reminded her nine days after Reykjavik, '– the plump chap with glasses who used to work across the road and whom we haven't seen for a long while! . . . He has been kept posted about your various discussions and the line you are taking.' There was no suggestion Geoffrey Howe should help craft the policy. Instead, Powell disparaged advice from the Foreign Office/MOD that Britain should 'try to get the Americans to negotiate agreed limits on SDI research'. 'One has to ask how far this is realistic,' he wrote. 'It is precisely the point on which the President stood firm at Reykjavik and reaped great credit for doing so.' Mrs Thatcher underlined and ticked approvingly. 'We want the President to pay attention to our political needs – deterrence, Trident –' Powell went on, 'so we must respect his political interests which are above all SDI.' Powell invented a private speech that Mrs Thatcher could make at Camp David. She underlined it carefully.

'Ron, you did wonderfully at Reykjavik in <u>reading Gorbachev's game-plan and refusing to let him bounce you into giving up the SDI</u>.' Reagan, Powell continued, should hold out against 'unreasonable constraints' on SDI, while pocketing the real concessions on INF already made and going for deep cuts in strategic nuclear weapons. He should 'break up the Reykjavik package into its constituent parts'. Then came the tough bit: 'The area where we have a real problem, Ron, is when you talk of the elimination of ballistic missiles within ten years. Now, <u>I know why you do that</u> ... But you do need to take account of the <u>impact in Europe</u>.' Without the US nuclear umbrella, Europe, exposed to superior conventional Soviet forces, would turn towards neutralism.'

The imagined oration ended with a personal plea: 'You will also cause me very real political difficulties if you pursue your proposal for eliminating ballistic missiles <u>too actively</u>. In our people's minds it will raise two questions: isn't Labour right after all in wanting to get rid of nuclear weapons ... ? And why on earth should we pay out all <u>that money for Trident, if it's going to be abolished in 10 years</u>?' The next British general election, she should warn him, could 'turn' on these points.

Rarely does a civil servant's draft so clearly set out policy thinking and political tactics and understand so well his principal's mind. Powell's skill in doing so shows why he had become so indispensable to Mrs Thatcher. At the heart of his advice lay a crucial concession. To stave off the elimination of ballistic missiles, she needed to welcome the proposed zero for INF missiles in Europe. 'She didn't like the plans to get rid of INF,' recalled Powell. 'To be perfectly honest she never liked any disarmament at all.' Now, however, 'she was sufficiently pragmatic to realize that there was no alternative to some sort of deal'.*

Just as Mrs Thatcher was preparing for Washington, revelations emerged that threatened the stability of Reagan's presidency: his administration had been secretly engaged in efforts to sell weapons to Iran in return for the release of American hostages held by Iranian proxies in Lebanon. What became known as 'Iran-Contra'† not only undermined US policy towards negotiating with terrorists but was also, very likely, contrary to US law. There was talk of impeachment if Reagan's knowledge of the

---

* Powell was also skilful in his methods. He had cultivated a close relationship with Charlie Price, the US Ambassador, and ensured that she privately passed Price her pre-Camp David thoughts so they would go '<u>directly</u> to the President, not put in telegrams which get [Mrs Thatcher underlined] <u>splattered all round the State Department</u>'.
† The word 'Contra' was added when it emerged that money from these sales was diverted to arm Contra troops against the left-wing Sandinista government in Nicaragua.

operation could be proved. What had happened, it eventually emerged, was that the NSC staff, under Poindexter, had been running the scheme without reference to the State Department. As the story grew, the day before Mrs Thatcher arrived in Washington Reagan declared publicly that it was 'utterly false'.

The White House probably did not realize it, but Mrs Thatcher knew Reagan was not telling the truth. Through what Charles Powell called 'the extraordinarily close intermeshing of GCHQ, Cheltenham and NSA [the US National Security Agency] operations', the British had worked out what was going on. She was unhappy but could not raise it with the Americans 'because we weren't supposed to know about it', Powell recalled. 'We didn't want to do anything frankly that would cut us off from the extraordinary flow of information which we got from the NSA.' The best line open to her, therefore, was 'Defend the man, not the policy.' This she did throughout the scandal, publicly and in private, earning Reagan's deep gratitude.

In Washington, there was considerable support for Mrs Thatcher's views on the abolition of nuclear weapons, and sympathy with her difficult political position. While eliminating offensive ballistic missiles within ten years remained US policy, Shultz told Reagan their task at Camp David was to agree a 'mutually acceptable formula' so that Mrs Thatcher 'returns to London stronger politically and reassured about the direction of our policies'. Bernard Ingham's briefing for Mrs Thatcher expressed matters differently, but with a similar aim: 'You want to show back home that the old magic works with the Americans and that in your hands the West's defence is secure.'

Arriving in Washington on Friday 14 November, Mrs Thatcher took out her frustration on Reagan's officials. Shultz recalled that she gave him 'unshirted hell'. She 'could not emphasise too much the degree to which the United States proposal on ballistic missiles, and the failure to consult in advance about it, had undermined confidence in Europe'. The proposal would 'undermine the security of Western Europe', she told Shultz, before delivering her *coup de grâce*: if pursued, it would 'cause you to lose me and the British nation'. All this only made the need for the 'mutually acceptable formula' which Shultz had advocated to Reagan more pressing. Powell and others worked on this into the night and the next morning, flying to Camp David, presented a draft joint statement to Shultz and Poindexter, who accepted it. Mrs Thatcher's tenacity impressed Poindexter: 'I remember thinking afterwards, that's why they refer to her as "the lady with the iron pants". Very tough.'

At Camp David, Powell recalled, Mrs Thatcher was 'very nervous about her meeting with Reagan and needed intensive hand-holding'. The visit began well. As Powell recounted, 'there is a rather romantic photograph of her coming off the helicopter with Reagan holding his hands out. It's real "Gone with the Wind" stuff.' But her mood shifted once she climbed aboard the President's golf cart: 'She was petrified being driven around by Reagan. She was absolutely convinced he was going to tip her into the woods ... She hated it.' Back on *terra firma*, in their *tête-à-tête* Reagan reported on his talks at Reykjavik. Mrs Thatcher repeated, in more measured terms, the arguments she had put to Shultz. At her prompting, he accepted the proposed joint statement 'without demur'.

Mrs Thatcher was delighted, with good reason. The statement released that day announced that the West's priority in arms control would be 'an INF agreement with restraints on shorter-range systems; a 50 per cent cut over five years in United States and Soviet strategic offensive weapons; and a ban on chemical weapons'. It stressed both leaders' support for 'the SDI research programme, which is permitted by the ABM Treaty'.* This was followed by a reassertion, crucial for Mrs Thatcher, of the importance of nuclear deterrence,† while 'reductions in nuclear weapons would increase the importance of eliminating conventional disparities'. Finally, the statement recorded Reagan's 'full support' for Britain's independent nuclear deterrent.

Ingham gleefully reported that the press was full of 'glowing praise' for Mrs Thatcher's performance. The only important omission from her prized statement was any language repudiating the idea of abolishing ballistic missiles. But what mattered was that the President had agreed to give priority to her proposals. This would push any discussion of eliminating ballistic missiles into the indefinite future.

There were several factors in the weakening of Reagan's Reykjavik agenda for nuclear disarmament. There was institutional opposition: the Chairman of the Joint Chiefs of Staff, Admiral William Crowe, for example, said abolishing ballistic missiles within ten years was 'completely unacceptable'. There was outside expert opposition, including from Henry Kissinger.

---

* Geoffrey Howe remained unhappy that Mrs Thatcher might be allowing Reagan too much leeway. A letter from his private office argued that what she had said about SDI research had been 'merely stating a common sense fact' and should be expanded. Mrs Thatcher scrawled on top: 'I do not accept that the common sense meaning of words should play no part in foreign policy.'

† The statement read: 'We confirmed that NATO's strategy of forward defence and flexible response would continue to require effective nuclear deterrents based upon a mix of systems.' Each party could take refuge in the ambiguity of this 'mix of systems'. There was neither an agreement, nor an agreement to disagree: it was more an agreement to pretend to agree.

Above all, there was the effect of the Iran-Contra scandal. On 25 November, Poindexter resigned after revelations that profits from arms sales to Iran were being diverted to the Contras in Nicaragua. He was replaced as National Security Advisor by Frank Carlucci, who 'disagreed with Reykjavik' and told Reagan so. He was also happy to pray Mrs Thatcher in aid: 'I finally said, "Mr President, if you move to get rid of nuclear weapons, Margaret will be on the phone in five minutes." "Oh, I don't want that," he said.' By the end of the year, the talk was of nuclear arms reduction, not of a nuclear-free world. As Shultz recalled, the proposal to abolish ballistic missiles 'just sort of faded. She was the exclamation point, after which there was nothing much.'

In her memoirs, Mrs Thatcher took a kinder view of Reagan's achievement at Reykjavik. She praised his refusal to give up SDI as 'crucial to the victory over communism. He called the Soviets' bluff.' In principle, she accepted the argument that Reagan had elicited concessions from Gorbachev which could never be taken back but, as Ingham put it, the lesson she took 'was that Reagan wasn't really reliable in international affairs. He had to be kept on a strict rein.' The aftermath of Reykjavik, however, confirmed her sense of her own ability to influence events favourably and make good use of their friendship. Her staunch personal support over Iran-Contra – the reassurance of a friend in need – helped keep the relationship strong.* Once the Reykjavik difficulty had been overcome, the rest of Reagan's term would, by comparison, be plain sailing for her.

Mrs Thatcher was understandably eager to communicate her success in moving Reagan away from the Reykjavik agenda to Mikhail Gorbachev. Rather than seeking an 'all-embracing arms control agreement in one leap', she wrote to him, 'Events convince me that a progressive approach based on smaller, more attainable steps has a better chance. I hope very much that you will revert to that.'

On 15 December 1986, Bryan Cartledge, the British Ambassador, presented Mrs Thatcher's letter to Gorbachev. Cartledge reported receiving 'strong and at times angry criticism from Gorbachev of British positions post-Reykjavik'. Gorbachev said he had a high regard for the Prime Minister, but wanted 'to find out whether she looked to the future with a rifle

---

* Mrs Thatcher's moral support for Reagan made a difference. In early December she sent him, by private means, a handwritten letter of solidarity: 'The press and media are always so ready to criticise and get people down. I know what it's like. But your achievements in restoring America's pride and confidence and in giving the West the leadership it needs are far too substantial to suffer any lasting damage. The message I give to everyone is that anything which weakens you, weakens America; and anything that weakens America weakens the whole free world.'

in her hand or, as he believed, ready to reach out with a handshake'. He complained of '"panic" in London and Paris' at the Reykjavik proposals. 'The world was changing. The British Conservatives, however, were not.' Their attitude had 'the damp stagnant smell of the prehistoric cave'.

Cartledge then read out Mrs Thatcher's letter, emphasizing the importance of the step-by-step approach. This provoked displeasure. Gorbachev said that 'Mrs Thatcher had given him and President Reagan an "oral whipping" for getting carried away, "like small boys", in Reykjavik.' What she had achieved at Camp David had produced only impasse: 'her great potential influence should be used to better effect than to read a sermon to the Soviet Union'. Despite all this, Cartledge found Gorbachev 'not unfriendly'. The dates for her visit to the Soviet Union (28 March–1 April 1987) were finally agreed. Gorbachev asked Cartledge to convey his 'warm personal greetings'.

Mrs Thatcher was pleased, as well she might be, by this flattering interpretation of her power, and by Gorbachev's correct, if critical, reading of her role.* She felt a great hostility to the Soviet Union but also a growing curiosity about how it might change for the better. In this she was not naive. The previous month, receiving the Russian dissident Yuri Orlov, she noted that people 'could easily be misled by the smooth, smart Gorbachevs' into thinking that 'the Soviet Union itself had changed'. She wanted to look beyond arms control: 'The genius of the Helsinki Accords was that they gave the West a locus for asking about human rights in the Soviet Union.' Orlov encapsulated a point important in her thinking: the great Soviet 'fallacy' was that 'disarmament and peace were the same thing'. She was interested both in highlighting Soviet oppression and in engagement which might improve matters. In December, Gorbachev allowed Andrei Sakharov, the dissident and eminent scientist, to return to Moscow from his KGB-supervised exile in Gorky. She, who had long supported Sakharov, insisted on being allowed to see him as part of her Moscow trip in the spring.

In preparing for her Moscow visit, Mrs Thatcher was anxious to learn more about what was happening inside the Soviet Union, and to understand Gorbachev's famous concepts of *glasnost* (openness) and *perestroika* (restructuring). 'You need to reach a judgment on how far Gorbachev really intends to change the Soviet Union and what the prospects of doing so successfully are,' Powell advised her. 'A great deal depends on that judgment . . .' Mrs Thatcher duly organized another seminar at Chequers. As in

---

* Charles Powell conveyed Mrs Thatcher's congratulations to Cartledge for the way he had conducted the meeting. The Prime Minister, he wrote, had read Cartledge's telegram 'with great interest (and some merriment)'.

1983, she brought in outside experts and excluded all but the most indispensable officials.* The result, however, was divided counsel. In his record, Powell split the attendees into two camps – 'enthusiasts' (who tended to be more expert on the USSR) and 'sceptics' ('principally non-specialists'). The enthusiasts sensed big change in the air in the Soviet Union, noting 'signs of greater pragmatism' about ideology and human rights cases. The sceptics, however, felt they 'had seen it all before' and saw Gorbachev as 'a transient figure'. The conclusions drawn, noted Powell's record, were that 'fundamental change was not on his agenda' and 'The Soviet Union might at best evolve in 20 years' time into something resembling Yugoslavia today.'† One person whose view was not sought was poor Geoffrey Howe. When he made as if to speak, Mrs Thatcher forestalled him: 'Don't worry, Geoffrey. We know exactly what you're going to say.' She herself formed no clear conclusion about Gorbachev's ultimate destination. By nature she was in the sceptic camp, but she also hoped the enthusiasts might be right.‡ The questions she was asking could be answered only by her visit.

Mrs Thatcher also consulted Oleg Gordievsky. When they first met at Chequers the previous May, he had been irritated by her loquacity – 'she talked and talked and talked' – but impressed by what she said: 'She had the same instinctive understanding of Communism as Reagan, but better than Reagan because more nuanced.' She had 'no historical understanding, but excellent moral understanding'. She said 'she did not expect to see any change in the nature of the Soviet Union in her time. But she was interested to know how that system could be influenced.'

Their second encounter, the following March, proved more productive. Mrs Thatcher wanted advice on what to say publicly during her upcoming visit. Gordievsky told her to be 'as clear and pungent as possible': she should 'spell out with statistics the reality of western prosperity'. He also told her that Gorbachev's likely reforms would not lead to democracy. As

---

* The experts attending included veterans of her 1983 seminar such as Ronald Amann, Archie Brown and Christopher Donnelly as well as Robert Conquest, Sir Michael Howard, Hugh Thomas and the American academic Seweryn Bialer. As for the officials, she excluded Robert Armstrong, the Cabinet Secretary, and his deputy Christopher Mallaby. Those permitted were Charles Powell and Percy Cradock, Bryan Cartledge and David Ratford (Foreign Office) and Martin Nicholson (Cabinet Office).

† Powell wrote that these conclusions 'seemed to command broad assent', but conceded that his record 'may err slightly on the side of conveying too negative a view of what is happening in the Soviet Union'.

‡ Archie Brown, whose comments on the next generation of Soviet leaders had attracted Mrs Thatcher's attention during the 1983 Chequers seminar, proved too much of an 'enthusiast' for her taste on this occasion. 'I'm not asking him again,' she told Robert Conquest afterwards.

for economic reforms, 'there was no one who would know how to take advantage of even a modest move towards a market economy'. The Soviet Union did want good relations with the West because it was desperate for money, but Gorbachev's 'long-term aim was to denuclearise and neutralise Western Europe'. The Prime Minister 'should not mince her words' in pointing out that the West 'must rely on nuclear weapons in the absence of conventional dominance'.

Mrs Thatcher wanted to know what Gorbachev would be expecting from her visit. On the one hand, Gordievsky told her, he sought 'a chance to build up his prestige'. On the other, 'he would fear that the Prime Minister's strong line on arms control might derail progress towards another US/Soviet Summit which he very much wanted'. The combined effect, especially when set against Reagan's weakness in the aftermath of the Iran-Contra scandal, was to put Mrs Thatcher in a pivotal position.

In planning the Moscow visit, electoral calculations bulked large. In Powell's view, election timing 'dictated' the date: she was looking for a *coup de théâtre*. Crawfie, Mrs Thatcher's personal assistant, who had noticed that Mrs Thatcher was much taken with Gorbachev's 'wonderful sparkly eyes', set about expanding her wardrobe. 'Mrs Gorbachev always wears Yves Saint Laurent,' she told her, 'so you'd better look nice.' Crawfie saw a black coat in the window of Aquascutum, which she got on approval. She also found a camel-hair coat with a sable collar and borrowed a sable hat from a friend. Mrs Thatcher intended to make a splash. Everyone was conscious of how much the visit mattered. Denis, who did not accompany her, said, 'Good luck, love' with untypical anxiety: 'We were all on edge.'

Mrs Thatcher was also careful to communicate with her allies. On 23 March 1987 she saw, separately, both François Mitterrand and Helmut Kohl. The French President fell into the 'enthusiast' camp: 'He believes Mr G prepared to go a very long way to changing the system,' her handwritten notes recorded, '– "when you change the form, you are on the way to changing the substance".' The German Chancellor, on the other hand, qualified as a 'sceptic': Gorbachev 'wants modern Communist system. Not a democratic system. More anti-religious than ever before.'*

Two days later, Mrs Thatcher wrote to Reagan. In Moscow she intended to assess Gorbachev's internal reforms and whether these might affect Soviet foreign policy: 'I am sceptical whether he is really able to take the

---

* While Mrs Thatcher was the first Western leader to forge a relationship with Gorbachev, Kohl was one of the last. In October 1986 the German leader had caused much offence in Moscow by drawing parallels between Gorbachev and the Nazi propagandist Joseph Goebbels. Kohl was not granted a meeting with the Soviet leader until the autumn of 1988.

necessary steps, or fully understands what is needed. People who have only lived under communism find it difficult to comprehend the workings of a free market.' As for arms control, she would aim to get Gorbachev to accept the Camp David agenda. At the forefront was a deal on INF, which Gorbachev had recently announced he would consider. She would accept the removal of intermediate missiles (the 'zero option'), so long as this was not a step, as Reagan was all too prone to see it, to denuclearizing Europe entirely. She also warned she would raise with Gorbachev the possibility of giving him 'some assurance' about 'the shape, scope and timescale' for SDI, something Reagan had so far refused to countenance.

Arriving in Moscow late on Saturday 28 March, she descended from the plane in her black coat and fur hat, carrying a black crocodile-skin handbag. Presented with a bunch of roses, as Crawfie recalled, 'she looked stunning'.

A unique aspect of the Moscow visit was that Mrs Thatcher was permitted to go where she had asked, to meet Christians, dissidents and ordinary Soviet citizens, and to speak at length on Soviet television. Gorbachev encouraged this to reinforce his claim to openness, and because he thought her endorsement of his reforms would help him at home.* In Powell's view, 'The most memorable aspect was the reaction of the Russian people ... There were huge crowds everywhere ... She symbolized the opposition to communism.' People began to gather on her first day, when, in smart beige boots and the camel coat with sable collar, she visited the Orthodox monastery at Zagorsk. She noticed that at least some of her priestly interlocutors were supporters of the regime:† 'Discarding my own prepared text, I answered [a speech by a patriarch against nuclear weapons] by stressing instead the need to release prisoners of conscience.'

That afternoon, Mrs Thatcher went to a supermarket and a show flat in Moscow.‡ Friendly crowds gathered outside and, as Amanda Ponsonby, accompanying her, put it: 'She started to be mobbed.' 'I was determined to see some real live people,' Mrs Thatcher recalled. '... The KGB would push them back and I would say "Stop it! Stop pushing them back!"' By the last day of the visit, which ended in Tbilisi, Georgia, people stood 'seven-deep'

---

* Scholars who were cynical about Gorbachev's reforms liked to point out that *glasnost* really meant not 'openness' but 'publicity'.
† The KGB had thoroughly penetrated what remained of the Orthodox hierarchy.
‡ Mrs Thatcher remembered that the supermarket was 'the most sparse for goods which I had ever seen in my life, there were one or two bits of bacon, very fat but not much, and there was some fish and some tinned fish and there was a little bit of chocolate. I had taken quite a lot of chocolate with me and I left some for the children.'

31 Denis listens attentively to one of his wife's election platform speeches. During her more informal 'stump' speeches, he was often to be found at the back of the crowd, shouting 'Hear, hear'.

32 General elections, 1983: Shouting down the hecklers in Salisbury, with the Conservative candidate Robert Key, who won.

33 On the morning of victory on 10 June 1983, Mrs Thatcher, Denis and Cecil Parkinson wave to supporters from the window of Conservative Central Office. She already knew that Sara Keays, Parkinson's former secretary, was pregnant with his child.

34 Lines of police confront the NUM pickets at the Orgreave coking works on 18 June 1984. The controversial defeat of the pickets' attempt to prevent supplies leaving the plant was a turning point against Arthur Scargill in the strike. The NUM were incensed by police tactics.

35 Mother and daughter. Mrs Thatcher takes six hours off over the Bank Holiday weekend, May 1984, to help Carol decorate her new house – a rare moment of shared domesticity.

36 Mother and son. Mrs Thatcher, suitably dressed for her holiday at Imlau, Austria, in August 1985 receives a slice of cake from Mark to celebrate his thirty-second birthday.

37 The very special relationship: President Ronald Reagan is welcomed by his greatest ally at the London Economic Summit, June 1984. Nancy Reagan stands between them.

38 Mrs Thatcher turns away from European partners at the Fontainebleau European Council, June 1984. It was here that she at last prevailed in the five-year row about the British contribution to the European Community. The other member states would get their own back on her later.

(*Above left*) 12 October 1984: Still dressed in her ballgown, Mrs Thatcher is driven with Denis (in pyjamas) from the Grand Hotel, Brighton, after the bomb went off at 2.54 a.m., accompanied by her assistant Cynthia Crawford ('Crawfie').

(*Above right*) The front of the Grand Hotel after the explosion. Only one vertical section of the building's construction, which did not include Mrs Thatcher's suite, was destroyed.

Within spitting distance (note the bowl), Mrs Thatcher and the Chinese leader, Deng Xiaoping, discuss the future of Hong Kong much more amicably in December 1984 than when they met two years earlier. Their interpreters, and William Ehrman (right) of the British Embassy, sit behind.

42 The US President steers his guest in a golf buggy round Camp David on 22 December 1984. She was terrified of his driving but successful in their talks.

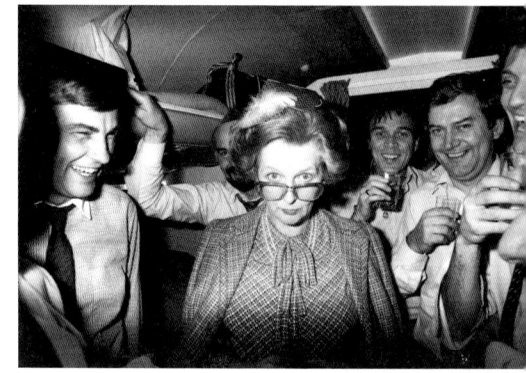

43 On the flight home, a rare moment of clowning with the press.

44 Mrs Thatcher and Garret Fitzgerald, the Irish Prime Minister, present one another with the Anglo-Irish Agreement in Hillsborough Castle, November 1985. She was uneasy about what she was doing. Behind them, left to right, are Dermot Nally, the Irish Cabinet Secretary, Tom King, the Northern Ireland Secretary, Geoffrey Howe and a painting of Windsor Castle.

45 Mrs Thatcher puts her feet on the sofa – her only concession to informality – and studies her red boxes. It is just after nine o'clock at night – very early for her.

46 (*Above left*) Michael Heseltine, ex-Defence Secretary, arrives with characteristic brio at the Westland heliport, Battersea, 12 January 1986. Three days earlier, he had resigned in Cabinet over the Westland crisis.

47 (*Above right*) With Prince Bandar and the Downing Street Christmas tree, December 1984. He and she persuaded King Fahd of Saudi Arabia to agree the Al-Yamamah deal – the biggest defence contract in British history.

48 Mrs Thatcher deploys her arts of flattery on King Fahd in London in 1987. He found her extremely attractive.

49 (*Above left*) 'Thy rod and thy staff comfort me': On holiday with Denis in Imlau, Austria, August 1984. Back home, the miners' strike raged.

50 (*Above right*) On holiday in Cornwall, August 1986, with a borrowed dog. Margaret always wanted a pet, but Denis would not allow it. Her bandaged hand is the result of a recent operation for Dupuytren's contracture.

51 Mrs Thatcher and President Mitterrand agree the Channel Tunnel project in the chapter house of Canterbury cathedral, February 1986. She was seduced by Mitterrand's idea for 'something exciting'.

52 Denis and Mrs Thatcher receive the Queen in Downing Street, October 1985, for a dinner to mark the 250th anniversary of No. 10 as the prime minister's residence. Always deferential to the monarch, Mrs Thatcher curtsies very low.

3 (*Above left*) Nigel Lawson, Chancellor of the Exchequer from the start of the second term, and economic mastermind of the period. She admired him greatly, but considered him 'a gambler'.

4 (*Above right*) Rupert Murdoch (right), with Kelvin Mackenzie, editor of his paper, the *Sun*, on the day it was first printed at Wapping in January 1986. Without Mrs Thatcher, Murdoch believed, he could not have beaten the print unions.

5 Mrs Thatcher visits workers' housing in Moscow, March 1987. She got a hero's reception from the crowds.

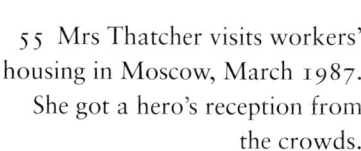

6 With Gorbachev in the Kremlin. Neither of them could stop talking.

57 Striding out in her constituency, Finchley, during the general election campaign of 1987 – but her steps were often uncertain.

58 The winners: on election night, at the window of Conservative Central Office, Mrs Thatcher at last gives Norman Tebbit his due.

59 Mrs Thatcher inspects wasteland at the former site of the Head Wrightson works in Thornaby, Middlesbrough, in September 1987. This is one of a series of pictures designed to show her commitment to inner-city regeneration; critics said they showed the problem she had created.

60 Flying visit: Mrs Thatcher and Mikhail Gorbachev greet each other at RAF Brize Norton, 7 December 1987. Their talk was fast but friendly. George Younger, the Defence Secretary, stands in the shadow between them.

on the pavements. 'There was a feeling that she was a tremendous breath of fresh air,' Ponsonby remembered. 'She adores attention. She played to that.'

On Monday, Mrs Thatcher began her full talks with Gorbachev at the Kremlin, with Geoffrey Howe conspicuously absent. Although she had failed to prevent him coming to Moscow, she ensured that whenever she was meeting Gorbachev he was engaged elsewhere. Her talks with Gorbachev went on for seven hours. As Powell recorded, they were 'frank with no quarter asked or given. The Duke of Wellington would have recognised it as hard pounding. The mood varied considerably throughout, with some thunderstorms and occasional squalls but also some bright periods.'

Gorbachev's aide, Anatoly Chernyaev, recorded the scene:

> She was, as always, extremely attractive,* earnest but determined, stubborn, sometimes didactic. He was ironic, sarcastic, at times even abrupt ... Thatcher, for all her practical intelligence and astonishing competence, always showed a feminine side as well. She 'tenderly' looked over the men sitting in front of her as if also making sure about the impression she made as a woman.

To Mrs Thatcher's surprise, Gorbachev began by raising her speech in Torquay nine days earlier, in which she had promised 'realism and strength' against oppressive Soviet behaviour: ' "Once again, communism and the Soviet Union were presented as 'evil forces'," he said ... We were very surprised by this. To tell you the truth, we even wondered if the prime minister would cancel her visit." "I can't believe this," she retorted. "You couldn't have thought that!" '

Mrs Thatcher tried to explain why the West feared the Soviet Union. There was 'no evidence', she said, that the Soviets had 'given up the Brezhnev Doctrine'.† They were subverting Southern Yemen, Ethiopia, Mozambique, Angola, Nicaragua, backing Vietnam to conquer Cambodia and occupying Afghanistan. She wanted to know whether his internal reforms would lead to changes in these external policies. Gorbachev's immediate answer was that Communist world domination was 'only an extrapolation of Soviet theory ... It was no more than a scientific concept,' but her mention of the Brezhnev Doctrine stuck in his mind. For the moment, he hit back with

---

* Chernyaev, who had a reputation as a ladies' man, encouraged Gorbachev to build a close relationship with Mrs Thatcher. He himself not only admired Mrs Thatcher but, according to his private diary, harboured sexual fantasies about her.

† In explicitly referring to the Brezhnev Doctrine she was taking up a suggestion of Robert Conquest's. This doctrine held that efforts to introduce capitalism into socialist countries were a problem for the entire socialist bloc, not merely for the country concerned. Such reforms would be resisted, if necessary through force.

an attack on Western meddling in the affairs of other countries, such as 'Britain's support for the racist regime in South Africa'. 'Apartheid cannot last. It must go,' Mrs Thatcher responded, while insisting that sanctions against South Africa 'only aid mass starvation'.

Gorbachev insisted that each must respect the other's system. He would not be able to make a Communist out of Mrs Thatcher and she should not expect to make a capitalist out of him. Communism, she countered, destroyed all choice. Bourgeois democracy, he retorted, was a mechanism 'for fooling people about who really controlled the levers of power'. Mrs Thatcher and the Conservative Party, he complained, were 'too closely linked to the interests of the haves'. She countered that 'the capitalist system had shown that it could distribute far greater benefits to ordinary every day people than socialism could'. As she later recalled, she told Gorbachev 'what I was trying to do was to create a society of "haves", not a class of them'.

The argument was fierce and, given the stubbornness of the participants, circular. Sometimes the tension was so great, Powell recalled, that 'I thought we'd be thrown out at once.' But it was Mrs Thatcher who, according to Gorbachev, 'struck a more conciliatory note'. The record shows that she professed herself 'appalled' by some of Gorbachev's remarks, but it had been 'helpful to clear the air'. Yes, said Gorbachev, it had stirred up 'the stagnant pond'. And so the talk turned readily to arms control.

Gorbachev focused his anger on her efforts to move Reagan away from eliminating nuclear weapons: 'You, Madam Thatcher, with your stance on nuclear weapons, hamper the negotiations and hinder efforts to start a process of genuine disarmament ... When you solemnly declare that nuclear weapons are beneficial, it's clear that you are an ardent supporter of them who is prepared to accept the risk of war.' This stung Mrs Thatcher. 'You had to see what those words did to her,' wrote Chernyaev:

> She got very tense, blushed, and her expression hardened. She reached out and, touching Gorbachev's sleeve, began to talk without letting him get in a word. She poured forth the reasons why she considered it impossible to give up nuclear weapons ... She became so excited that the conversation got completely out of hand. They started to interrupt each other, repeat themselves, assure each other of their best intentions. And compliments, compliments for Gorbachev and his new policies, which she hoped would be successful.

When matters calmed down, Mrs Thatcher stressed that she supported both a 50 per cent reduction in the strategic nuclear weapons of the two superpowers and an INF agreement. She urged Gorbachev to take advantage of the eighteen months before President Reagan left office to make a deal.

The meeting broke for lunch, which Mrs Thatcher (arriving late) had with Soviet dissidents led by Andrei Sakharov. When they told her that they supported Gorbachev's reforms, she insisted that was not enough. They needed to support Gorbachev 'when the going got rough'. She then returned to the Kremlin and a sixty-five-minute exposition of Gorbachev's internal reforms. *Perestroika*, he explained, had barely begun. He spoke with what Mrs Thatcher, writing later to Reagan, called 'almost messianic fervour'. Gorbachev wanted businesses to be free to earn foreign currency and sought 'democratization'. Individual enterprises would acquire their own rights. There would be much more scientific development. The West 'should forget any notion of putting the Soviet Union on the ash-heap of history and should abandon its evil-empire rhetoric'. This time, Mrs Thatcher did not pick an argument. Her goal was simply to find out more about what was happening.

They also discussed SDI. Despite Reagan's efforts to discourage her, Mrs Thatcher told Gorbachev 'she quite understood the Soviet Union's wish for predictability in this area'. Proposed activities on both sides could be set out, with an undertaking not to deploy SDI for a fixed period. Gorbachev commented carefully that this was 'an interesting, practical proposal'.

The discussion was less combative than in the morning. Mrs Thatcher made a series of strong points about human rights, including better treatment of Jews, but added she was 'far more optimistic about the Soviet Union than she had ever been'. The talks so overran that she had no time to return to the Embassy to change before the official banquet.* Her speech at dinner struck a constructive tone: 'you have certainly embarked upon a great endeavour,' she said of Gorbachev's reforms, 'and we most earnestly wish you and your people well'. Nonetheless, during the dinner, stirred up by Mrs Gorbachev, the two leaders clashed once more over arms control. Gorbachev concluded the evening by saying that 'he was beginning to think it would be easier to talk to the Americans than to the Prime Minister'. It was, noted Richard Pollock, Mrs Thatcher's interpreter, 'a somewhat sour tone on which to end the meal'. Gorbachev's complaint, however, reflected one side of his double-edged feelings about Mrs Thatcher – that she was his inveterate ideological opponent. The other side – which he felt, perhaps,

---

* This forced Mrs Thatcher to forsake her normal regard for formality and attend the dinner 'in the short wool dress I had been wearing all day'. Amanda Ponsonby recalled hurrying round with a change of shoes and a hairbrush to get her ready.

even more strongly – was that she was an honest, intelligent and powerful leader with whom agreement could be reached.

The highlight of the following day was Mrs Thatcher's interview on Soviet television. The Foreign Office had advised that 'an interview with a <u>visiting</u> Prime Minister will probably <u>not</u> be regarded as the occasion for cut and thrust'. Mrs Thatcher, who always thrived on cut and thrust, did not take this to heart. Readily challenging, interrupting and contradicting her three stolid male interrogators, she explained how well the Soviet Union was stocked with nuclear weapons and stressed the importance of the nuclear deterrent. She defended SDI and praised Gorbachev's reforms. The effect was sensational, principally because the Soviet authorities allowed it to be broadcast in its full, unedited form. Such a thing had never happened before. As Tony Bishop recalled, the Soviet public learnt much 'that had hitherto remained concealed. Her handling of the interviewers evoked widespread if sometimes rueful admiration . . . One Soviet trade unionist remarked, unattractively, to our Ambassador shortly afterwards: 'She squashed them like kittens.' 'Yes, I took a risk,' Gorbachev said later, '. . . I wanted her and everyone else to see that my policy of *Glasnost* was not a trick.'

In the evening, Mrs Thatcher attended a small, informal dinner given by the Gorbachevs, far more relaxed than that of the previous night. Ideas flowed freely as Gorbachev speculated on his plans for reform. 'Some of his ideas appear simplistic,' Mrs Thatcher later wrote to Reagan, but she was impressed by his direction of travel.* As Charles Powell reported, 'As we sat down to dinner Mr Gorbachev pointed to a landscape on the wall depicting a farming scene with a clear sky in the background and observed that it reminded him of his talks with the Prime Minister, tempestuous but with great clarity. The Prime Minister pointed out that the light was coming from the West.'

After Mrs Thatcher took leave of Gorbachev the following morning, there was no doubt on either side that her visit had been a great success. 'Remember how long we debated whether to invite her or not?' Gorbachev asked his Politburo colleagues. 'Now we can say we made the right choice.' In his report to Howe, Bryan Cartledge noted that 'The areas of disagreement dwarfed those of agreement: but the warmth of the atmospherics, both personal and political, was striking. Despite – or perhaps, because of – these contradictions, I have no hesitation in describing the visit as historic.'

---

* At one point, Gorbachev raised the suggestion of 'paying people more and then charging them something for services like health and education', a notion which even capitalist Britain tended to find heretical and dangerous. To hear such radical notions from the lips of a Soviet leader was indeed remarkable.

It established a new bench-mark for the quality of East–West dialogue.' Mrs Thatcher also won press plaudits across the political spectrum. In an April Fools' Day send-up, the *Daily Mirror*'s front page carried a mocked-up picture of Mrs Thatcher kissing her host marked 'Exclusive – Maggie Disarms Gorbachev'.

Mrs Thatcher had arrived in Moscow not quite sure what to make of *glasnost* and *perestroika*. She left believing that, while Gorbachev remained a committed Communist, his effort at delivering reform was genuine and deserved Western support. This was not lost on him: 'Probably unexpectedly to herself, she said too many positive things about us,' he told the Politburo. 'Something happened inside her.' Her support for *perestroika* was important, Gorbachev continued; 'The Americans are calling this her biggest mistake.' Her support for Gorbachev's reforms would grow, even though, as Gorbachev suggested, many in Washington questioned the wisdom of this course.

The visit boosted Mrs Thatcher's standing at home and abroad. Here Gorbachev was complicit: 'It is in our interest to raise the British role in international affairs,' he told his colleagues, stressing that her views could influence the Europeans and the Americans. Gorbachev had also accepted more of what Mrs Thatcher said than his combative style betrayed. 'She's sure that we have not given up the Brezhnev Doctrine,' he told the Politburo. 'This is really something to ponder, comrades. We can't just brush it aside . . .'

The Russians followed up fast. On 8 April, Powell reported a visit from an official at the Soviet Embassy who had told him that 'Mr Gorbachev wanted to maintain his "special relationship" with the Prime Minister.'* The British official reaction registered pleasure at this use of a phrase usually reserved for Britain and America. The Foreign Office judged that the idea was 'no doubt intended to be both flattering and wedge-driving. But we should not discount the possibility that it is also genuine.'

Mrs Thatcher did not forget, however, where her real special relationship was. Her account to Reagan was full. She told him she thought she had been able to move Gorbachev towards their Camp David priorities and saw a 'pretty reasonable prospect' of reaching an INF agreement by the end of the year. She had not fallen for Gorbachev's blandishments: 'If ever I had any doubts whether Gorbachev is a true "believer" in the Communist system, my talks with him dispelled them.' But she argued strongly

---

* The official was Nikolai Kosov, with whom Powell would develop an informal backchannel relationship.

that her visit had been 'very well worthwhile'. The West had an interest in supporting his reform policies.

There could be no better message for the election she secretly planned for June than that the Iron Lady was also the person to bring peace. But the Moscow visit had greater importance. As Powell put it, it was, 'in some ways, the beginning of the end of the Cold War'.

25
What they saw in her
'Mrs Thatcher is the point at which all snobberies meet'

The success of the Moscow visit reinforced Mrs Thatcher's standing as a bold and brave champion of the West. As she approached her ninth year as Prime Minister, her battles at home and abroad were well known. To many she had become a mythological figure: the archetype of the 'strong woman', the patron saint, some said, of taxi drivers and all who strove to improve their lot. Possibly for this very reason, she had become uniquely hated by many British writers and intellectuals.

Ahead of the 1987 general election, these critics spoke out. 'The chief function of this election', wrote the novelist Julian Barnes, 'is to turn out Mrs Thatcher and her spayed Cabinet, whose main achievement in the last eight years has been the legitimation of self-interest.' David Hare thought voters would eventually recognize her promotion of greed, and so her influence would disappear quickly after she left the political scene, 'leaving nothing but the memory of a funny accent and an obscure sense of shame'. His reference to her accent gives a clue to the visceral dislike harboured by her intellectual critics. She not only upheld ideas they found obnoxious; she almost physically embodied everything bad they conjured up in the word 'suburban'. As the novelist Hanif Kureishi later declared: 'England has become a squalid . . . intolerant, racist, homophobic, narrow-minded, authoritarian rat-hole run by vicious, suburban-minded materialistic philistines.'

Mrs Thatcher as philistine-in-chief was a popular theme with Britain's leading cultural figures, many of whom spoke to the journalist Graham Turner for the *Sunday Telegraph*. According to the novelist Jonathan Raban, 'she doesn't appreciate doubleness, contradictions, paradox, irony, ambiguity'. Alan Bennett, in words not printed, saw her as 'a kind of maiden aunt who knows all about marriage'. Mary Warnock, the philosopher and Mistress of Girton College, Cambridge, felt that Mrs Thatcher had 'a total lack of understanding of what universities were about'. Even were her views to change, she would still not be acceptable because 'Watching her choose clothes at Marks and Spencer there was something really quite obscene about it.' Dr Jonathan Miller, the theatre director and polymath, called her 'loathsome, repulsive in almost every way' with 'the diction of a perfumed fart'.

Any show of cultural interest by Mrs Thatcher met with derision. Visiting her in 1980, the poet Philip Larkin had been impressed when she had quoted from one his poems, 'Deceptions', which concerns the rape of a Victorian poor woman. She had referred to the line 'Her mind was full of knives', which was not quite what Larkin had written.* Alan Bennett wrote scornfully: 'Larkin liked to think that Madam knew the poem or she would not have been able to misquote it. Inadequate briefing seems a likelier explanation.'† Any other woman politician would have got some credit from the left for drawing attention to a poem about rape. But it was a special gift of Mrs Thatcher to goad her opponents into an extravagance of condemnation. As the novelist Ian McEwan perceptively put it after her death in 2013, 'It was never enough to dislike her. We *liked* disliking her.' This self-indulgence by her critics tended to work to her advantage. 'She reads best-sellers' was one of the attacks hurled at her by the novelist Anthony Burgess, as if that were a crime.

Across British fiction, film, drama and music from and about the Thatcher era, a similar extravagance of feeling dominated. The singer/songwriter Billy Bragg described Mrs Thatcher as his 'greatest inspiration . . . Like an angry line of kettling coppers, Thatcher's Tories pushed me around, forcing me to question the assumptions I had made about the British state and my place in it.' In his song called 'Thatcherites' (1997), Bragg complained, 'You privatize away and then you make us pay / We'll take it back some day, mark my words, mark my words.'

Other songs about – and against – Mrs Thatcher included 'Margaret on the Guillotine' by Morrissey and 'Tramp the Dirt Down', in which Elvis Costello sang, 'But when they finally put you in the ground / They'll stand

---

* The original words are 'All the unhurried day, / Your mind lay open like a drawer of knives.'
† Despite Bennett's doubts, Mrs Thatcher had a genuine taste for poetry – especially Tennyson and Kipling – and knew a good deal by heart. One reason why Denis Thatcher decided to propose to her was that, when he visited her once in her flat and quoted a line of verse, she capped the quotation and recited the whole poem. Mrs Thatcher was never attracted by the avant-garde in the arts and knew little about it. One day, at a meeting, she described something as being like 'Waiting for Godot', sounding the t in Godot. Lord Carrington whispered to her, 'It's pronounced Godo, Prime Minister.' 'How is it spelt?' she asked him sharply. He explained. 'Then it's Godot,' she insisted, sounding the t harder than ever.

there laughing and tramp the dirt down.'* In Britain, the best-known song about Mrs Thatcher comes from the wildly successful musical *Billy Elliot*, set against the backcloth of the miners' strike of 1984–5: 'Merry Christmas, Maggie Thatcher/,' sing the cast, 'We all celebrate today / 'cos it's one day closer to your death.'†

Newspaper cartoonists found Mrs Thatcher a challenging subject. Nicholas Garland, political cartoonist at the *Daily Telegraph* and then the *Independent*, found her 'very very difficult to draw', partly because of her sex: 'Women change more than men – hair, outfits, make-up. They are elusive.' Observing Mrs Thatcher in the flesh, however, he was surprised to find that 'This woman turned out to be rather attractive, with considerable presence.' He began to study her more carefully and noticed that 'She had slow eyes – the outside corners lower than the inside ones – strong, high cheekbones and a little, pursed mouth.' He tried to draw in her face 'the power and the activism, which gave her a slightly bad-tempered look', and 'the underlying possibility of panic' in her flashing eyes. Her handbag, often wielded as a weapon, was an essential accoutrement for the cartoonist, like a crown for the Queen. Garland's Thatcher followed several phases. Through the Falklands War, 'I drew her more strong, frowning and vigorous.' Then she became a 'fixture' on the national scene, and he made her Britannia or Queen Victoria. Finally, from around 1988, she became 'omnipotent; a bit mad'.‡

Other cartoonists treated her as mad – or bad – all along. Steve Bell at the *Guardian* emphasized the fact that her left eye was rounder than her right. He made both eyes huge and threatening, and the left one crazed. He turned Mrs Thatcher into a shark, a vampire, a zombie and a sculpture worked out of South Atlantic penguin guano. Bell's work could be powerful and inventive, but the relentless hostility of most cartoonists left little room for degrees of satire.

The subsidized theatre almost invariably attacked Mrs Thatcher. Indeed,

---

* Oddly, the most successful anti-Thatcher song was never released in Britain. By Renaud, 'the French Bob Dylan', it was called 'Miss Maggie' and reached number one in France in 1984. It celebrated women for not being hooligans, assassins and committers of genocide, but proclaimed Mrs Thatcher as the sole exception. Its conclusion, translated from the French, was 'If I can't stay on earth, I will change into a dog so that I can use Madame Thatcher daily as a lamp-post.'

† When Margaret Thatcher actually did die in 2013 the show went on, with the words unaltered.

‡ During the defence cuts of the early 1980s Garland drew Mrs Thatcher wearing a full suit of armour but with her knickers hanging round her ankles. His Editor, Bill Deedes, spiked the drawing on grounds of bad taste. Such qualms were rare in newspapers even then, however, and became rarer.

A Short, Sharp Shock (1980) provoked an apology in the Commons for the fact that public money had been spent on it. Written by Howard Brenton and Tony Howard, the play showed, among many lurid scenes, Mrs Thatcher forcing Jim Prior to drink the sperm of the free-market economist Milton Friedman from a Coca-Cola bottle. Brenton also, with David Hare, wrote a much more observant play called *Pravda* (1985) which satirized the power of Rupert Murdoch in the Thatcher era.

Such plays did reflect strong feelings amid elements of the theatre-going classes. Hare later recalled 'a tremendous blast of energy from the audience because they wanted an anti-Thatcher, anti-Murdoch blast'. 'It may seem exaggerated,' said Brenton of the Thatcher era, 'but it was as if some kind of evil was abroad in our society, a palpable degradation of the spirit.'

Only one play – *The Falklands Play* by Ian Curteis – went strongly against the trend. Commissioned for television by the BBC, the drama made Mrs Thatcher the unambiguous heroine of the Falklands story. After early enthusiasm, the BBC cancelled the drama, to avoid controversy ahead of the 1987 general election. Altogether, the BBC ran seven dramas which were anti the Falklands War and none which was pro.

In cinema, two films scripted by Hanif Kureishi sought to anatomize Thatcher's Britain unfavourably. *My Beautiful Laundrette* (1985), which was extremely successful, highlighted what Kureishi saw as her bad effects on race relations. *Sammy and Rosie Get Laid* (1987), about the breakdown of communities, was ambitiously intended, said its director, Stephen Frears, 'to bring the government down'. In this it failed, but the ardour of intent reveals the mood of the moment. *Top Girls* (1982), an explicitly anti-Thatcher play by Caryl Churchill, depicted Marlene, a ruthless businesswoman who does not help other women and models her behaviour on unscrupulous men. The idea that Mrs Thatcher was not 'really' a woman was a common motif among her critics.

On television, BBC2's *Boys from the Blackstuff* by Alan Bleasdale, a series about five Liverpool tarmac-layers, was later described by the British Film Institute as 'TV's most complete dramatic response to the Thatcher era', although the original play had been written in 1978, when Labour was still in power. Sometimes such responses were well satirized by her critics themselves. A BBC comedy called *The Young Ones* (1982–4) featured four students sharing a squalid house while studying at Scumbag College. It contained lines like 'The bathroom is free. Unlike the country under a Thatcher junta!' Its stars and authors included Ben Elton, Rik Mayall and Alexei Sayle.

Even *Doctor Who*, the long-running children's programme, began a surreptitious effort to attack Mrs Thatcher. According to Sylvester McCoy, who acted the Doctor from 1987 to 1989, 'We were a group of politically motivated people and it seemed the right thing to do ... Our feeling was that Margaret Thatcher was far more terrifying than any monster the Doctor had encountered.' In *The Happiness Patrol* (1988), the Doctor persuaded a colony of enslaved humans to rise up against a tyrant named Helen A. The trouble for the BBC children's TV subversives, however, was that any explicit declaration of their political intent might have been fatal to their jobs. It seems no one noticed what they were up to.

By far the most popular programme dealing with Mrs Thatcher was *Spitting Image*, the ITV puppet show which ran from 1984 to 1996. It depicted her as the authority figure bossing her Cabinet,* frequently dressed as a mannish dominatrix in a pinstripe suit and tie, sometimes with a Churchillian cigar. Although the programme treated her harshly, its message constantly reinforced the impression of her power, so it probably did her more good than harm.

The written word was generally slower to get to grips with the Thatcher era although, in *The Satanic Verses* (1988), Salman Rushdie did make a passing reference to 'Mrs Torture'. Most Thatcher-related novels appeared after her departure from office and tended to use her as a straw woman. Even novels with unpolitical subjects – Ian McEwan's *The Child in Time* (1987), for example – liked creating Thatcher-era settings that were dystopian, brutal, materialistic and decayed.

Sue Townsend's great comic creation, the disaffected teenager Adrian Mole, wrote a poem in his fictional diary entitled 'Mrs Thatcher':

> Do you weep, Mrs Thatcher, do you weep?
> Do you wake, Mrs Thatcher, in your sleep?
> Do you weep like a sad willow?
> On your Marks and Spencer's pillow?
> Are your tears molten steel?
> Do you weep?
> Do you wake with *'Three Million'* on your brain?
> Are you sorry that they'll never work again?
> When you're dressing in your blue, do you see the waiting queue?
> Do you weep, Mrs Thatcher, do you weep?

---

* *Spitting Image* embedded itself so deep in the public consciousness that the present author has often been approached by people who tell him a story about how Mrs Thatcher was asked by a waiter serving the Cabinet what meat she wanted. She answered, 'A raw steak, please.' Then the waiter asked, 'And the vegetables?' Mrs Thatcher replied, 'Oh, they'll have the same as me.' This is a *Spitting Image* skit, but people have turned it into a true story in their minds.

Few authors tried to imagine sympathetic Thatcher-era characters, such as 'upwardly mobile' members of the working class or women who felt empowered to pursue more ambitious careers. As the novelist and critic D. J. Taylor put it, 'Scarcely a single contemporary novelist bothered him- or herself to try and comprehend the nature of Thatcher's appeal.'

One exception was Philip Hensher, who drew on his experiences as a clerk of the Commons at the end of Mrs Thatcher's period in office for his second novel *Kitchen Venom* (1996). The book, which never names her, notes her parliamentary technique – how she used the hubbub of Prime Minister's Questions as 'the ritornello to an aria', for example. Although Hensher was, by his own account, 'a weak-willed lefty' at the time, he saw that the older generation of writers was inattentive to the way Britain had altered. So 'Paradoxically, she was fresh material': as a novelist, 'You always want a clear voice. The Gloriana mode. It is a wonderful voice to carry a novel.' A homosexual, Hensher was also conscious of her as a 'gay icon'. She had a 'magnificent, diva-like presence'.

A paperback edition of *Kitchen Venom* shows a picture of the prime ministerial feet in high-heeled shoes treading on a cigarette, drawn from Hensher's description: 'When she walked, she seemed to extinguish a cigarette beneath every pace; in her walk, it could be seen that she was in the right.' He was not the only novelist to observe her gait. Alan Hollinghurst, in *The Line of Beauty* (2004), writes of Mrs Thatcher's 'gracious scuttle, with its hint of a long-suppressed embarrassment, of clumsiness transmuted into power'.

Since the days of 'milksnatcher', Mrs Thatcher had learnt not to waste emotional energy on how others saw her, particularly if those others did not help win votes. She was, however, persuaded to attend a charity performance of *Anyone for Denis?*, the stage version of the *Private Eye* 'Dear Bill' letters. These, composed by John Wells and Richard Ingrams, purported to be written by Denis to an old chum, Bill, who was widely taken to be W. F. (Bill) Deedes, the Editor of the *Daily Telegraph*, describing the slings and arrows of life under 'the Boss' or 'the old girl'. She was, in Carol's words, 'acutely offended' by the play, though she dutifully declared it a 'marvellous farce'.* The spoof letters themselves, however, did much to humanize the Thatcher marriage. They also helped convince people that Denis could not possibly have any political influence over his wife, although this was not the case. As Bill Deedes put it, *Private Eye* 'put everyone off the scent'.

Meeting Mrs Thatcher in her old age, the novelist Sebastian Faulks

---

* In her dislike of it she took her cue from Denis, who was irritated to be portrayed as a drunken halfwit (though the adjective did not always lack foundation).

urged her to read *The Line of Beauty*, since she appeared in it. She had not heard of the book, but as they parted said to Faulks, '*The Line of Duty*: I shall remember that.' Her characteristic mishearing illustrated the gap between her way of thinking and that of British metropolitan literary culture.

There were, of course, members of the intelligentsia who did admire Mrs Thatcher. To Graham Turner, Kingsley Amis who, like many refugees from earlier leftism, was particularly attracted to her, praised her for something which most enraged her cultural critics: 'the less the Government was involved with the arts, the better it was for the arts'. He detected a certain jealousy of her on the left: 'The Labour Party were supposed to have the first woman prime minister – the Tories have nipped in and stolen that.' Noël Annan, the leading academic and historian of British intellectual life, insisted it 'was not true that there was no place for intellectuals in her scheme of things': it was merely that she had changed who those intellectuals were. Even the novelist John le Carré, remote from Mrs Thatcher politically, found himself thinking well of her after the Falklands War. He did not like the way left-wing writers 'cast her as the nanny, the tyrant'. To him she seemed 'a totally democratic person. Naturally adversarial. Entirely, in her own way, fair.' He also found her very attractive, sensing that she 'gave a cry for protection which made me feel like one of her courtiers'.*

Intellectuals with direct experience of real tyranny thought of Mrs Thatcher very differently from her left-wing critics in Britain. She was greatly admired, for example, by Andrei Sakharov, the Soviet nuclear physicist and dissident, and by Vladimir Bukovsky, the imprisoned writer who was granted asylum in the West. 'She was an intensely loyal person,' Bukovsky recalled, 'which always amazed me. We'd have a great quarrel [Bukovsky vehemently disapproved of her closeness to Gorbachev], and then she'd go round introducing me in most flattering terms.'

While Mrs Thatcher would certainly flatter intellectuals, her respect for what she called 'big minds' was genuine. This admiration for mental greatness was particularly apparent in her attitude to leading scientists. 'The only time I can remember seeing Mrs Thatcher in a flap, behaving just like a schoolgirl, meek and mild,' recalled Charles Powell, 'was when her

---

* There were a few occasions when even some of Mrs Thatcher's most dedicated foes did admire her. By chance, David Hare and Howard Brenton happened to be in Brighton, writing a play together, in the week of the 1984 bomb. When they watched her speech on the day that followed the bomb, Brenton said: 'I don't approve of her as prime minister, but by God she's a great tank commander.'

former Oxford tutor, the Nobel-Prize-winning chemist Dorothy Hodgkin, came to tea at No. 10.'

In Whitehall, Mrs Thatcher was notorious for hijacking interesting works from the government art collection for display in Downing Street. She formed a friendly relationship with the collection's director, Wendy Baron, asking her for examples which 'displayed the greatness of Britain'. Dr Baron supplied portraits of scientists like Sir Humphry Davy, Ada Lovelace, who invented the first algorithm intended to be carried out by machine, and a bust of Grantham's other most famous citizen, Sir Isaac Newton; also portraits of Wellington and Nelson. Under the influence of Lord Gowrie, she was persuaded to display more modern work as well, including a sculpture by Henry Moore. One August, thinking she would be away, Dr Baron visited No. 10 to check the collection. She was surprised to come upon the Prime Minister busily dusting her cabinet full of porcelain on loan from the V&A. 'You know, Dr Baron,' she said, 'one of the things I shall most miss when I leave here is having all these beautiful pictures.'

The *locus classicus* for the conflict between Mrs Thatcher and intellectuals was the 1985 row over her honorary degree at Oxford. In 1983, the Royal Society, the country's most eminent scientific academy, had elected her, as the first scientist Prime Minister, to its fellowship. She only narrowly secured the two-thirds majority needed, with opposition focused on her government's approach to the NHS and cuts in medical research funding. When Oxford's Hebdomadal Council proposed her for an honorary degree late in 1984, some of those who had failed to stop her at the Royal Society tried again.

Mrs Thatcher was not well informed about the state of Oxford opinion. The Conservative historian Robert Blake, Provost of the Queen's College, Oxford, insisted a challenge to the degree was 'very unlikely', but should it come to a vote in Congregation (that is, among all the university's academic staff) she would win. Spurred on by Lord Blake, she rejected advice from Robin Butler, who feared a left-wing campaign against her, to defer the invitation. 'Robin,' she said, 'if Oxford wants to confer an honorary degree on me, who am I to make terms about it?' In her letter of acceptance, she said that the proposal gave her 'the greatest pride and pleasure', which was true.

Her opponents, more diligent than her supporters, collected 275 protest signatures, including eleven Fellows of the Royal Society. Their campaign rejected a vision of the universities which was considered too utilitarian, but also harboured a particular animus against Mrs Thatcher heightened by the miners' strike, then still in progress. On 29 January 1985, Oxford's Congregation debated the issue. Denis Noble, a leading physiologist, argued against the degree. 'We are here to protect the intellectual heritage of hundreds of years', he said. History would probably judge this as 'the watershed in determining whether we are *philistine* [his emphasis] enough to let this particular national heritage crumble'.

That word 'philistine' tapped into intellectuals' widespread feeling against Mrs Thatcher. Peter Pulzer, a political scientist and co-leader of the Oxford anti-Thatcher camp, later reflected that there had been a strong 'aesthetic' objection. He considered this 'probably the biggest single common factor' among her opponents. According to Pulzer, who came from a modest grammar-school background, this was not because dons looked down on her socially: 'There was if anything this feeling that "She ought to be one of us, but isn't."' Ill prepared for this level of controversy, the Council's leaders did not know how to fight back. Congregation rejected an honorary degree for Mrs Thatcher by 738 votes to 319. No woman spoke in the debate.

In a general assessment of Mrs Thatcher's place in history, Professor John Vincent, one of the few prominent academics to sympathize with her subversive conservatism, identified why she was hated:

> It was because she offered 'earnest and practical dissent' to progressive orthodoxy. Mrs Thatcher is the point at which all snobberies meet: intellectual snobbery, social snobbery, the snobbery of Brooks's [the whiggish London club], the snobbery about scientists among those educated in the arts, the snobbery of the metropolis about the provincial, the snobbery of the South about the North, and the snobbery of men about career women.

What seems strangest is how little prominence was given to the point about Mrs Thatcher being Oxford's own, and the first of her sex to lead her country.* Although she offered little public complaint, Robin Butler felt 'The degree of hurt was huge.' Oxford had been the foundation of her public career, and she revered the place. To her friend Daphne Park, the Principal of her old college, Somerville, she wrote: 'I do assure you that the vote does not detract one jot from the affection I feel for the university which I knew, especially for Somerville ... Without that, I should never have been here [that is, in Downing Street].'†

---

* As Robin Butler, much later Master of University College, Oxford, recalled, Oxford's decision to deny Mrs Thatcher an honorary degree had 'a disastrous effect upon fund-raising for the university, especially in the United States'.
† By way of commiseration, the friendly Oxford don Michael Gearin-Tosh sent Mrs Thatcher a gift of a rare edition of *Gulliver's Travels* by Jonathan Swift. She told him that 'The book

Mrs Thatcher later recalled taking solace from her family. Mark had rung her at once from America: 'Don't worry, Mummy,' he said, and 'within about two hours there were some flowers here.' That she cited this example indicates how upset she felt. Denis, who was outraged, wrote a real-life 'Dear Bill' letter to Bill Deedes. 'Why anybody takes this terrible job and lives in this awful atmosphere only our God knows. I literally wept.' Denis later told the present author that this saga upset his wife more than anything else that happened to her in office, apart from her exit.

When informed, in 1991, that Mrs Thatcher had been genuinely hurt by the vote, her leading Oxford opponent, Peter Pulzer, said: 'I have no sympathy with that. I think that a politician like her, who loses no time lecturing absolutely everybody on absolutely everything, must be prepared to accept snubs.'

This snubbed woman, so suburban, harsh and philistine in many literary and academic minds, presented a very different persona to those who worked for her every day. Her staff – as opposed to her much-bullied Cabinet colleagues – found it a considerably more pleasurable experience than, given her rather terrifying reputation, they had expected.

John Coles, Mrs Thatcher's foreign affairs private secretary from 1981 to 1984, wrote about his experience. Physically, Coles found her 'Slightly dumpy, smaller than the popular imagination would have it.' Her physical features, he noted, were 'not particularly good, apart from her face which had great mobility; it was capable of an almost spitting fierceness, a beatific calm, flirtatiousness and the deepest concentration. You learned to watch the mood.' Despite her fondness for expressing the great simplicities, Coles felt that 'everything about [her character] was complex': 'The dominant characteristic was determination,' by which he meant that 'having rigorously examined the arguments' and reached a conclusion, she insisted on its application.

Much of Mrs Thatcher's behaviour, Coles thought, derived from her unique situation as the only woman in power. She feared she would be considered unfit to lead if she made public displays of human emotion or 'could be shown to be given to unreasonable feminine behaviour'. And so 'To assert her will this very feminine woman had to – or at least chose to – adopt a strident tone with nearly all of her colleagues. At times her style was abusive, rude and unpleasant.' She was perfectly happy to take

---

has long been a favourite of mine – but it had not previously struck me that Swift was such a perceptive economist, as well as such a devastating satirist. I agree with everything you say in your letter about the economic and industrial facts of life – if only there were more realists among the clouds of Laputa!'

advantage of the sexist belief in female irrationality: 'Not for her the logical chain of argument if she saw the chain leading in the wrong direction.' While she was capable of 'a quite unfeminine toughness and crudeness', Coles stressed her 'femininity. She was a loving mother, with a mother's emotions.'

Although no intellectual, she was 'passionately attracted by ideas'. Coles recalled that she 'seized on what to her was a new idea with all the avidity and enthusiasm of a parched traveller, emerging thirsty from the desert to be presented with a goblet of ice-cold water'. He considered her 'the least pompous of all British Prime Ministers', welcoming ideas whether they came from a Cabinet minister, an academic, an entrepreneur, 'or indeed the doorkeeper'.

Coles asked himself what motivated her. First, he concluded, it was her upbringing, especially her commitment to work, even when it entailed sacrifice: 'She always had a stricken conscience that if she had spent more time with her children, their lives would have been easier.' He added, rather tentatively, the idea that 'had the emotional side of her character been fully satisfied, she would never have developed the prodigious energy and determination that are two of her strongest qualities'. He was implying that never, in her marriage or any other relationship, had she known the full force of sexual passion or unguarded love.

David Goodall, another senior civil servant, whose strong sympathy with Irish Nationalism left him with less natural rapport with Mrs Thatcher, found that he 'liked, admired, and was repelled and exasperated by her in about equal measure. In retrospect, however, and on the whole, the admiration predominates.' He liked, for example, the fact that she could be teased. On one occasion, fed up with objections by officials, she exclaimed, '"Don't keep saying 'No, no, Prime Minister.'" We substituted "But, Prime Minister". "But, but, but; too many buts," she complained. "If we can't say no and we can't say but, how are we to disagree with you?" I asked. She had the grace to laugh.'

'What I liked', said Goodall,

> was her downrightness, her clarity of mind, her ability to cut to the heart of a problem ... and the courage and resolution with which she stuck to her guns. She was stimulating, capable of kindness and could be fun. What was less attractive was her narrowness of vision and above all what seemed to me a certain ungenerosity of spirit: she bridled at the word 'magnanimity' and the idea itself seemed alien to her.

Robin Butler, one of her closest aides, was in many ways an admirer, but as he recalled: 'My heart always fell when I had to sit next to her.' She had no small talk and he felt 'at risk'. Dealing with her face to face was 'like feeding a fierce animal'.

Although almost no women had formal power during Mrs Thatcher's premiership, several were important in her 'court'. They testified to aspects of her character which men tended to understand less well. Carla Powell, Charles's vivacious Italian wife, frequently helped her with clothes and home decoration: 'Everything about her was totally, totally feminine,' she recalled. 'She adored the details of clothes. I called her La Bionda [The Blonde] because she loved the boys [her private secretaries].' Carla recalled being lectured by Robin Butler: 'Remember that Mrs Thatcher is a woman, so don't overdress as you usually do.' It was important not to upstage the Prime Minister. Because of her own attention to dress, she used to fret about her daughter Carol's more casual attitude: 'She wanted Carol to be better dressed. She looked as if she wanted to put her in a washing machine.' This was connected in Mrs Thatcher's own mind, thought Carla, with her longing for her daughter to marry.* The subject of Carol, about whom Mrs Thatcher felt guilty, would bring tears to her eyes.† Her own marriage was undoubtedly strong and even, according to Carla Powell's testimony, flirtatious. She recalled a scrap of dialogue: 'Denis: "You know I don't like you dressed in black." Mrs Thatcher: "I have to. I'm the Prime Minister." Then Denis made a "Go on with you!" gesture.' According to Cynthia Crawford, however, the marriage was 'not a huge love affair though they were great soulmates', and Mrs Thatcher always felt uneasy about Denis's first marriage, whose break-up had hurt him greatly. 'Crawfie,' she once said, 'I shall always be only the second Mrs Thatcher.' For all her success, she always suffered from insecurity.

Mrs Thatcher, said Carla Powell, was ready to 'use her femininity' and could be 'totally, utterly ruthless'. 'Carla,' she once said, 'if a woman takes on a battle, she has to win.' She believed that men would close ranks against a woman: every inch had to be fought for. She also had a surprising cosiness about her. Caroline Ryder recalled that she liked to

---

* Some years after her mother's death, Carol married her long-term partner, Marco Grass.
† If she felt her own children had been wronged she was utterly unforgiving, although she tried also to appear to act professionally. In 1986, for example, Max Hastings, the new Editor of the *Daily Telegraph*, decided to sack Carol from his features staff 'with the other dead wood'. 'Naively, I thought the PM would regard this as a normal piece of newspaper business, but she went potty, told CB [Conrad Black, the paper's proprietor] that I had behaved disgracefully etc ... She never spoke to me again.' At the same time, however, Mrs Thatcher made sure to keep her relations with the Telegraph Group in good repair, courting Conrad Black and Andrew Knight, the then Chief Executive, who recalled her behaviour over the sacking of Carol as 'magnanimous'.

have her secretaries 'around early morning, late at night, late afternoon, to talk to. We were her daughters.'* Mrs Thatcher was always trying to find husbands for these younger women, often fastening on 'suitable' men who were, unbeknown to her, homosexual. She enjoyed gossip about such matters, especially about the absurdities of men in pursuit of women. Early in her leadership, for example, when Alison Ward told her how a young bachelor MP had made a 'massive lunge' at her in a taxi, scattering the contents of her handbag all over the floor, Mrs Thatcher 'cried with laughter'. Although she had traditional views about marriage, she was not personally censorious.

Mrs Thatcher was often criticized by prominent women and feminists for not doing enough for the cause of her sex. Certainly, she was in no hurry to surround herself with female talent in Parliament. But she did show some sisterly solidarity. Beginning in 1976, she kept up a friendship with Patricia Hodgson, then Chairman of the Bow Group, the influential party ginger group. Mrs Thatcher occasionally asked for help drafting speeches, but otherwise had no 'agenda'. She wrote Hodgson a couple of letters of support when she was experiencing a difficult pregnancy. Looking back at these various kindnesses, Hodgson said, 'I ask myself "Why?" and I conclude that she simply wanted to maintain links with other women.'†

Mrs Thatcher also kept in mind the pressures which women could experience in a man's world. On one occasion, her private office complained that too many ministers' wives were seeking to accompany their husbands on official trips abroad. Would she intervene? 'I think not,' wrote Mrs Thatcher. 'Some wives have a rotten time because husbands are away so much and late at the House so often that the odd visit is a kind of compensation.' Most ministers' wives, however, considered themselves ignored by her. She visibly preferred the conversation of the men and in questions of equality did not necessarily take the woman's side. She was, for example, instinctively against women priests, worrying that the issue would split the Church. One of her parliamentary private secretaries, Archie Hamilton, told her that, as a woman Prime Minister, she could not oppose the ordination of women. He urged her not to worry: 'Women are capable of greater spirituality than men and are less prone to sexual temptation'. 'Oh,

---

* Carol, her real daughter, was generous about this, and welcomed the fact that she was 'mightily fond of "her girls"'.
† Once Hodgson became Secretary to the BBC, she was forbidden from continuing these meetings (see pp. 541–2), so the two women had a 'farewell' lunch at Chequers at which they drank cheap Liebfraumilch. 'It's terribly good, you know,' Mrs Thatcher told her. 'It's a special offer from the *News of the World*.'

I don't know about that,' Mrs Thatcher replied. Eventually, however, she came out in favour of women priests.

As if to confirm the left-wing caricature of her habits and attitudes, Mrs Thatcher became, while Prime Minister, a suburban house owner. In 1984, the Thatchers decided not to renew the lease on their house in Flood Street, Chelsea. Over the Whitsun recess, she discovered a development of new executive houses in Dulwich. Although they were still under construction, she was smitten. This was to be their bolthole and their place of retirement. It was within 10 feet of the Dulwich and Sydenham golf course. She thought this would be nice for Denis, though in fact he had played on the course, which has heavy clay, and had 'absolutely loathed it'. For his part, Denis decided it would be nice for Margaret because she could 'walk out and watch the Dulwich boys playing rugby'. 'I wondered', recalled Robin Butler, 'how two people married to each other for so long could know so little about each other's tastes.' The Thatchers bought the mock-Georgian five-bedroom house, 11 Hambledon Place, for about £350,000 shortly before her sixtieth birthday. She relayed to the media Denis's view that it was important 'to get back into bricks and mortar' because prices were shooting up. 'For the first time in my life,' she enthused to *Woman's Own*, 'I've got the kitchen I've always wanted ... a country kitchen.' She probably spoke the truth when she said that 'planning the house and where everything will go will be the only relaxation I'll have'. Quite soon the house was habitable, neatly and brightly furnished in the chintzy Peter Jones style which Mrs Thatcher favoured.

In fact, 11 Hambledon Place was, in Denis's view, 'a great mistake'. Its purpose, he said privately, was 'not for me, you know. It's for the widow woman on her retirement. I shall be pushing up the daisies but she will be still on the go. She can toddle down to the village shops with her basket. And if they need her for anything in the Lords, they can send a car.'

But in fact, as Mrs Thatcher soon began to notice, it was too far from central London and with too little security. The Thatchers spent only a handful of nights there while in Downing Street, and the twins were not attracted to the place.* As well as sheltering their money, however, the house performed a valuable psychological function which they naturally did not want to disclose at the time. Denis well remembered Ted Heath

---

* Despite describing the golf course as 'lousy', Denis did play there, joining a group of like-minded retired members called the 'Wednesday Old Gentlemen', whose politically incorrect acronym amused them.

being homeless after his ejection from Downing Street: 'I said to Margaret we've got to have somewhere to go when we go.' If No. 10 failed, they now had No. 11.

Suburban housewife though, in some sense, she still was, the Margaret Thatcher of 1987 was a publicly much more majestic figure than when she had taken office eight years earlier. She had learnt to dress accordingly. Those who advised her on clothes felt she finally achieved her best style by 1987, both for her Moscow visit in March and for the general election in June. Mrs Thatcher had become a convert to the dictum of the famous *Vogue* Editor Anna Wintour that 'everything comes from the shoulders', lessening the bust and narrowing the waist. Crawfie enlisted the help of Margaret King at Aquascutum to find 'power suits' which would give Mrs Thatcher the greatest possible confidence. She had moved from the 'provincial woman looking smart' of the 1950s and 1960s, through the almost municipal styles of the 1970s, to a clearer, stronger look which worked better on television. This clothed her in block colours – sapphire, cerise, jade-green, canary-yellow – which stood out against grey men, as well as the staple black, which suited her well. In some respects she came to dress like the Queen, wearing, for example, thick-heeled patent-leather shoes and carrying the famous patent-leather handbag. For someone who was so busy and needed to change fast, dresses were vulnerable and complicated: suits were better. It was important to use materials which would not crease easily. As she told Angela Huth for the BBC, she preferred tweeds, brocades and British wool to frail silks or linen and was preoccupied with 'a very good line'. Blouses provided the required element of softness.* She understood signifiers, and secretly regretted the fact that hats were too out of fashion to wear except on special occasions. She also understood the importance of sentiment in jewellery, wearing a watch from Mark and a South African bracelet of semi-precious stones in a gold setting and an eternity ring, both presents from Denis.

Mrs Thatcher was thus well upholstered, well covered and always perfectly groomed and coiffed, although when travelling she never took a hairdresser but relied on local stylists. 'She had very nice hair [although] a little bit on the fine side,' recalled Eivind Bjerke, her US stylist of choice. 'She liked it – in today's parlance – a little bit old fashioned. She liked her hair soft. She liked it teased. She liked it rolled. She liked it sprayed. It also

---

* From her mother's expertise as a seamstress she had learnt about attention to detail and quality, and various tips, such as not pressing a hem so hard that it became 'a knife's edge' and could not be let down later.

had to be something that, when she was photographed from all angles, would look good.' She was never informal, because she instinctively recognized that this would invite a familiarity which would weaken her. Could she ever afford to be 'flamboyant, daring, sexy', Angela Huth asked her: 'Never! Nor would I wish to be.'* The BBC had insisted on asking Mrs Thatcher where she bought her underwear. The reassuringly unsexy answer was Marks & Spencer.

Although Mrs Thatcher's style was, in a sense, conventional, she rejected the cliché of the female executive which sought to imitate men – the pinstripe, the dull navy suit. In a way, her attitude to her clothes was like that of a medieval knight to his armour. What she wore had to be beautiful and well made but also combat-ready. Her clothes must attract all eyes and repulse all attacks. Thus armoured, she could feel ready for her third general election as Leader of the Conservative Party.

---

* Once, at a dinner in Washington, the liberal film director Mike Nichols had sat next to Mrs Thatcher and found her monologue about the evils of the Soviet Union punishing. After the dinner, she came and sat with him again, sticking with the subject. Desperate, Nichols said, 'My friend John le Carré says you are a very sexy woman.' 'Well,' replied Mrs Thatcher, 'I'm not,' and resumed her diatribe.

26

The last victory, 1987

'There's a woman who will never fight another election'

'No one with a conscience votes Conservative,' said Norman Tebbit. So *Guardian* readers were informed by Hugo Young at the beginning of 1987, which was expected to be election year. The article, benefiting from malicious but well-informed briefing, set out the differences between the Party Chairman and Mrs Thatcher: 'He is, she now thinks, the worst appointment she has made in her 12 years as party leader.' In fact, Tebbit had never uttered these words. He sued the *Guardian* for libel and won.

Young's error was a striking example of a trap into which the left repeatedly fell. Many of them – including the moderates – really hated Mrs Thatcher. They thought she was not merely mistaken, but evil. To such people Tebbit was even worse. They believed that to win an election, they need only proclaim this wickedness loudly enough. Never, in three general elections fighting Mrs Thatcher, did they coldly analyse why she was winning. The sense of moral superiority fired up the Opposition parties but made them ill-disciplined and unelectable.

One person who understood this was Peter Mandelson, who since 1985 had been working to 'rebrand' Labour. Although he disagreed with Mrs Thatcher he did not hate her, and he saw Tebbit as the man who 'embodied her appeal to the aspirant working class'. Mandelson wanted Labour to understand that some of what she was doing – controlling the deficit, reforming trade unions and nationalized industries, and maintaining the Bomb – was right. The young Labour MP Tony Blair agreed. Blair understood why she had 'broken through to some of our support': 'My dad was a huge supporter of hers: he had working-class Tory attitudes.' He felt that Labour had failed to recognize that Mrs Thatcher's philosophy 'posed certain hard questions for us, a philosophy around aspiration'. The task, Blair believed, was to sift out 'what was Tory in her and what was radical', opposing the first and harnessing the second.

In the run-up to the 1987 election, Labour was still not ready for this task. Although Neil Kinnock was trying to modernize his party, his time and energy were consumed fighting the hard left. As Kinnock put it, 'She was partly winning because we were so brilliantly losing.' A few days after Hugo Young's article, the Conservatives were projected to win a majority of 100 in the next Parliament. Despite Mrs Thatcher's habitual hesitation on this subject, early-summer election dates were beginning to pencil themselves into her diary.

At the end of February, the Alliance trounced Labour in a by-election in the previously marginal Labour seat of Greenwich. The fact that Labour's losing candidate was notably left-wing was encouraging for the Conservatives. It suggested the party had not really changed. There were other favourable auguries. In the same month, British Airways was privatized, with share applications eleven times oversubscribed. Days earlier, the print unions had surrendered in the Wapping dispute. Rupert Murdoch's success allowed other newspapers to follow suit, transforming their businesses. Given the difference this made to Fleet Street, Mrs Thatcher could now expect a good press in any election campaign.

These events confirmed Mrs Thatcher's power and ability to bring change. So, on a global scale, did her visit to Moscow. Her willingness to confront the Soviets had earlier been presented by the left as a threat to world peace. That she was now talking to the Soviet leader – toughly, but in a friendly spirit – took this card away. The prospect of her visit made it crucial for Kinnock to seek respectability on the world stage, which required getting on terms with the US administration.

In 1984, Kinnock had visited Washington and met Reagan for the first time. The President had been reluctant to receive him ('He thinks all the wrong things,' Reagan told an aide), but the meeting passed off amicably enough. The two men found common cause in the horror of nuclear weapons, though Reagan specifically stated his opposition to unilateral disarmament. In the ensuing years, the US Ambassador in London, Charlie Price, became increasingly worried by Kinnock's unilateralism and increasingly partisan in supporting Mrs Thatcher. Price's Deputy Chief of Mission, the career diplomat Raymond Seitz, worked to keep channels to Labour open, but understood how a potential Labour government was seen in Washington: 'The State Department, the Pentagon and the CIA were all concerned about the possibility that the security arrangements with Britain would unravel... Our entire defence posture in Europe rested on the British Isles. If Kinnock had won... the result would have been catastrophic.'

Against this uneasy backdrop, the White House agreed that Reagan would receive Kinnock in Washington on 27 March 1987, the day before Mrs Thatcher landed in Moscow. In preparation, Kinnock shifted his defence policy: a Labour government would now accept cruise missiles on British soil, assuming continued progress at the Geneva arms control talks. No one, however, expected a meeting of minds. 'While Kinnock will want to accentuate the positive,' Frank Carlucci, the National Security Advisor, told Reagan, 'our objectives are different: we want to make it clear that Labor's defense policies would adversely affect our common security interests and severely strain US–UK relations.' At the same time, he should bear in mind that Kinnock might be the next prime minister. 'Well,' said Reagan simply, 'I want Margaret to win.'

The Oval Office meeting seemed, to the Labour contingent, to pass off peacefully. Kinnock picked up on Reagan's un-Thatcherite dislike of nuclear weapons, and briefed the press accordingly: 'The President stated unequivocally that he wanted to see ... the elimination of all nuclear weapons ... Both I and Denis Healey [accompanying Kinnock] stated that we shared this desire.'

The White House did not like this. In its view, by ignoring fundamental disagreements, Kinnock was misrepresenting the meeting. Marlin Fitzwater, the White House press secretary, decided it could not stand: 'I knew it would be a big story and me slapping down Kinnock,' he recalled. 'But I could see no option.' At a press briefing he insisted that the President had told Kinnock that 'we disagree with Labor's defense policy'. It would have 'a strong effect on NATO, on East/West relations and would undercut our negotiating position at Geneva'. Fitzwater added that the meeting had lasted 'slightly less than 20 minutes', even shorter than the time originally allocated.*

The British press leapt at Fitzwater's briefing. 'Reagan takes his revenge on Kinnock', said the *Mail*. Even the *Guardian* used the word 'debacle'. While Mrs Thatcher, triumphant in Moscow, was cast as a global superstar, Kinnock was left looking like a pipsqueak.

Kinnock believed that 'The thing was set up' by Reagan's staff. He was correct. 'I'm afraid we rather sabotaged the meeting,' Charles Powell told

---

* A story (which was accurate) also began to seep out that Reagan had failed to recognize Healey and had greeted him with the words 'Nice to see you again, Mr Ambassador.' According to Antony Acland, the new and actual Ambassador, this was not necessarily a preposterous or deliberate mistake by the President. He (Acland) was not yet well known to Reagan, and his predecessor, Oliver Wright, 'was not wholly unlike Healey in appearance. He was dark and had bushy eyebrows.'

the present author. 'We wanted to diminish the impact of the visit. Charlie Price read our signals and arranged that . . . the whole thing would be really rather perfunctory. I'm ashamed to admit it now, but it is true.' Wisely, Powell kept Mrs Thatcher out of these machinations. But Kinnock was foolish to imagine he might break the Reagan–Thatcher bond.

On 17 March, Nigel Lawson had presented his fourth Budget, clearly designed for an election. The Chancellor gave himself a glowing report – good revenues, low inflation and the largest six-monthly fall in unemployment since 1973.* Britain was enjoying the longest period of steady growth since the war. What Lawson called 'genuine popular capitalism' was spreading so successfully that 8.5 million people now owned shares – almost three times more than in 1979. Lawson then translated this good news into eye-catching measures. There would be no rise in excise duties on alcohol and tobacco and, as previously foreshadowed, an additional two pence cut in income tax, to twenty-seven pence. He reaffirmed the aim of bringing it down to 25 per cent soon.

In Lawson's view, backbenchers considered this 'a good election Budget but not blatantly so'. But commentators spotted, in his managing down of the sterling exchange rate and his increasingly casual approach to monetary targets, the seeds of inflationary trouble to come. It was, however, politics that now took centre stage. Lawson's background and interests were as much political as economic: no one worked harder to calculate how to win the election.

Naturally, Mrs Thatcher raised no objection. When they discussed Budget plans in February, Lawson asked whether she wanted him to continue as Chancellor after the election. 'Yes, of course I do,' she replied. The only fly in the appointment came with a recommendation from Lawson's policy group that Britain should join the ERM. Objecting, Brian Griffiths suggested the idea be reconsidered after the election. Mrs Thatcher agreed: neither she nor Lawson pushed the argument further. But she had clocked what he and Geoffrey Howe – also involved in the scheme – were up to. The almost complete absence of Howe from any election plans showed just how far he and she had drifted apart.†

Despite the improvement in Tory fortunes, agreement had not been reached about how any election campaign should be run. Tebbit and Michael

---

* Inflation stood at 3.5 per cent. Unemployment, despite the drop, was still more than 3 million.
† In a later meeting about the contents of the manifesto, Howe complained that there was not enough foreign policy included and demanded an encouraging reference to Conservative Members of the European Parliament. 'This is a British election, Geoffrey,' said Mrs Thatcher. 'I don't need to be reminded of that, Prime Minister,' snapped Howe.

Dobbs at Conservative Central Office were not at one with Mrs Thatcher, nor with those close to her on these matters – David Young and (behind the curtain) Tim Bell. Early in 1987, the first of a series of 'war councils' was held at Alistair McAlpine's house. There was no row, nor real ideological difference, nor even deep division about campaign strategy. It was less a matter of what Mrs Thatcher wanted than of whom she wanted. Elections made her intensely anxious: she had to have people whom she liked and trusted.

Since the Chequers meeting of April 1986 (see pp. 535–6), Dobbs had remained out of favour. She considered him the agent of Tebbit's supposed leadership ambition, a view not discouraged by Tim Bell, who saw Dobbs as his opponent in his feud with Saatchis, or by Lord Young, who was seeking a bigger role.* Bell had a real gift for dealing with Mrs Thatcher. 'Tim amused her,' Cecil Parkinson recalled: 'He was also one of the very few people who could hint at the truth to her. He could say something like: "The public think you are very bossy," and he would know how to balance it by adding, "But they think you're a great leader." As a result, she did listen to him.' Bell saw it as his job to make her happy, to 'deliver the things she liked'. Mrs Thatcher ensured she had Bell with her, even as Saatchis continued to work for Central Office. Thus the 'parallel operation', begun early in 1986, never stopped.

By now Alistair McAlpine had become Mrs Thatcher's longest and closest associate in the party set-up. His value was immense, as a skilled treasurer and fundraiser and as a friend who, unlike many, was not seeking anything from her. Close to Bell and Gordon Reece, McAlpine felt some resentment against Tebbit, who wished to exclude them and him. In a wily, low-key way, McAlpine knew how to talk people up or down with Mrs Thatcher.† It was he who, once Tebbit became Chairman, had spread stories about his ambitions. He had also worked Bell back into Mrs Thatcher's company and now proposed David Young as an effective replacement for Tebbit during the election campaign.

On 17 March, Young visited Tebbit to explain that he was about to see Mrs Thatcher to discuss the ways in which he might 'help in the election'. Tebbit, Young recorded in his diary, 'seemed quite agreeable'. He told Young that he planned a campaign to expose the dangers of the Alliance by reminding people how the Lib-Lab Pact in the late 1970s had enabled

---

* Although not personally involved with any of the agencies, Young had found his much-trusted special adviser, Howell James, through Tim Bell. Young and James, though not umbilically linked in the manner of Tebbit and Dobbs, were effectively allies against them.
† It was McAlpine, indeed, who first suggested to the present author that Tebbit had been organizing his leadership campaign from his hospital bed after the Brighton bomb.

the Winter of Discontent. This idea did not find favour. 'It was too complicated for Margaret,' Tebbit recalled. Her preferred tactic was always to concentrate fire on Labour and marginalize the Alliance, treating it mainly as the subject for comedy.* Young then saw Mrs Thatcher and told her she should employ him to prepare for a general election. '"Yes," she replied. "You must. You must first help with the presentation of the manifesto – the way it looks."' Young advised her that the only really important thing was to get her on television all the time 'being met by adoring crowds'. Later that day she broke the news of Young's new job to Tebbit. According to Young, 'Norman looked only slightly surprised and said, "Well, of course that's no problem, I'd love that."' He did not love it at all.

Before his new role was announced, Young saw Peter Morrison, who warned him that 'Norman was not the same Norman that we both worked for three years back, for since the bomb he was a different person.' This refrain about Tebbit was frequently used against him.† For Young, as for Bell, it was a means of legitimizing efforts to marginalize him. A covert struggle was in progress to take credit for the expected victory. Tebbit considered the 'intensely ambitious' Young 'the prime briefer' against him to Mrs Thatcher.

All this was a recipe for conflict. On 5 April, Young was informed that 'Norman was spitting blood about my appointment'. When they met, Tebbit complained that Mrs Thatcher did not like the election tour plan he had devised for her. 'Norman ... you know what she's like,' Young replied, '... if you produce the tour it's no good, if I produce the same tour it'll be fine.' Young intended this as 'a laugh' at Mrs Thatcher's expense. It is doubtful if Tebbit found it amusing. A non-working relationship was established even before the election campaign began. This extended to Mrs Thatcher. As Dobbs put it, Tebbit 'felt, rightly, that he wasn't part of her inner circle'.

The same day as the Tebbit/Young confrontation, the *Sunday Times* reported the Conservatives 12 points ahead of the Alliance, with Labour in third place.

Despite the atmosphere of intrigue, the preparation of the manifesto had been relatively orderly. Mrs Thatcher felt that the 1983 manifesto had

---

* Mrs Thatcher did, however, hold a meeting about the Alliance threat at the end of April. One of those present was John Major, who afterwards wrote to her to set out the 'specific SDP/Liberal policies which would damage the self-interest of potential Tory defectors'. Towards the end of the campaign, Major was present at the daily press conferences as the minister with responsibility for Social Security. According to John Whittingdale, 'He did well in those briefings ... I always thought it was during that campaign that she noticed him for the first time.'
† More rarely it was deployed for Tebbit by those who argued he had become a deeper, wiser man.

missed a chance to set out a full agenda. She wanted the next one to 'keep the forward momentum ... on the lines of the fundamental principles'. This would mean more new ideas and more specific promises. The chief draftsman was John O'Sullivan of the Policy Unit, assisted by Ronnie Millar, who contributed the more purple passages. The argument, which Mrs Thatcher accepted, was that 'We needed to prove *why* again.' The Conservative case had to be shown as a historical development which would reveal its logic: it was 'rolling Thatcherism'. The first term had been about rescuing the economy from disaster. The second had been about creating the right conditions for economic opportunity. The third would turn to 'social Thatcherism' – responsibility and choice applied to public services. On health, however, there were no radical plans: the only tactic was to boast about how much had been spent.

With a June election looking ever more likely, Mrs Thatcher held an all-day meeting at Chequers on Easter Monday. As Young recorded, she started off 'at a tremendous rate of knots, saying that the manifesto wouldn't do and that it wasn't enough to talk about the past'. By late afternoon, she 'started to get fidgety about the timing of the election', while criticizing Young's proposed campaign. She kept saying, 'I must go to large factories, I must go to large factories.' Meetings such as this, with Mrs Thatcher sometimes fastening on tiny things, sometimes reaching for the big picture, sometimes confident, sometimes unbearably anxious, were a constant feature. Still no agreement was reached about several vital aspects. Tim Bell's role remained vague, and hidden from colleagues. Young's role remained unclear. Even as he made himself more central to the campaign, he kept asking Mrs Thatcher what she wanted him to do. She rarely gave a clear answer.*

In the local elections on 7 May, the Conservatives received 40 per cent of the vote, Labour 30 per cent and the Alliance 27 per cent. There was now no reason to delay the general election.† At Chequers on Sunday 10 May, Mrs Thatcher's closest ministers and advisers pushed hard for 11 June. With the polls encouraging and an extrapolation from the local election results suggesting a majority of ninety-four, she did not seriously demur. At a special Cabinet meeting the following morning, she announced that the election date would be 11 June. She then went to the Palace to

---

* To the informed exterior eye it was not obvious why the electoral 'virgin' Young should take over the campaign. 'His was a ludicrous appointment,' Nigel Lawson considered.

† Rupert Murdoch had already decided to come to Britain for the duration of the election, without waiting to know the exact date. He wanted to be there to help Margaret Thatcher and, according to Woodrow Wyatt, 'we [Wyatt and Margaret Thatcher] can also perhaps tell him what we would like his newspapers to be saying ... "He's marvellous," she replied.'

seek the formal agreement of the Queen. Parliament would be dissolved a week later.

The intervening seven days did not go very well for Mrs Thatcher. The Conservatives, she told the BBC on the very first evening, had such a big agenda that it would take her some time to accomplish. 'Yes,' she continued, 'I hope to go on [pause] and on.' Her eyes then dropped from the camera, as if she realized her mistake. The idea of 'going on and on' fed into public anxieties about her domineering personality. It was quickly used against her. Over the week, the Tory lead in the polls shortened and Labour pulled well ahead of the Alliance.

In retirement, Mrs Thatcher recalled Tebbit laying the blame on her. 'He'd say "People say 'TBW'." I'd say, "What do you mean 'TBW'?" He'd say: "That Bloody Woman!" . . . He came to the conclusion that I was stopping the party from winning, and I really wasn't going to admit that.' In this context, a Central Office election video became a new source of tension.* The film, with Tebbit as compere, showed six other ministers lauding the achievements of the past eight years. Mrs Thatcher was not interviewed, though the film ended with rousing film clips of her with foreign leaders. When Young showed it to her, at first she declared it 'Marvellous'. 'Then she added, "Well, on the other hand it only shows me overseas. The manifesto is mine, but it all appears to be Norman. It is *my* manifesto!" She worked herself up in a rather embarrassing way . . . Really for the first time ever I thought she appeared very much a woman . . .' Young left Downing Street promising to sort everything out: 'I really felt as if my whole world had come to an end . . .', he wrote in his diary, 'she somehow felt I'd let her down.'

To avoid a blow-up with Tebbit, Young and Wakeham told him they had seen the video without showing it to Mrs Thatcher. Concerned that it played to the Alliance attack line that she was 'happy to go to Moscow, but never goes to Middlesbrough', they suggested adding a new contribution from her. Tebbit swallowed this. That afternoon, Mrs Thatcher, always good in a tight corner, recorded a well-delivered encomium about the 'transformation' that Britain was undergoing.† When aired publicly, the video passed off without incident.

This farcical sequence of events was the result of too many cooks

---

* This video, originally espoused by Young and Bell, was designed to be shown to the candidates' conference after the launch of the manifesto.
† As he often did for party political broadcasts, Tim Bell sat between the legs of the cameras looking straight at Mrs Thatcher and smiling, to reassure her.

spoiling the broth, and of the fact that, over the question of who should be head chef, Mrs Thatcher's indecision was final.

The following morning, the Conservatives unveiled their manifesto. The efforts to show 'the team' meant that too many ministers were crammed into the small room at Central Office, sweating under television lights. The effect was to suggest tension rather than amity. The manifesto, though, was a thoughtful and coherent document. 'I knew exactly what I wanted,' Mrs Thatcher claimed later. Now that the Conservatives had established 'Pride of ownership of homes, shares and pensions', said the manifesto, it was time to offer 'greater choice and responsibility' in areas like housing and education. A core national curriculum would be introduced for state schools, which would also now be free to opt out of management by their local education authority (LEA) and receive money directly from central government.* 'The abuses of left-wing Labour councils' would be ended by replacing the rates with 'the fairer Community Charge'. The Youth Training Scheme would help young people find new jobs,† while the inner cities would be revived through private investment. As for the Bomb, the Conservatives alone promised to modernize the British deterrent, with Trident replacing Polaris.

The Labour manifesto, launched the same day, had no comparable depth. Its main policies – unilateral nuclear disarmament, increasing the basic rate of income tax, repealing all Tory trade union laws – lacked broad appeal. But journalists contrasted the slick modernity projected by Labour, who launched their manifesto in the suave and spacious surroundings of the Queen Elizabeth II Centre, with the stuffiness of the Conservatives. A contrast between the fresh young personality of Kinnock and the strident one of Mrs Thatcher gathered pace – 'Mr Nice Guy vs TBW' was the shorthand.

Two days after the manifesto launches, Labour produced its first party election broadcast.‡ Filmed by Hugh Hudson, director of the Oscar-winning film *Chariots of Fire*, it marked a revolution in the genre. This film, which never mentioned the word 'Labour', showed Neil and Glenys

---

* Strenuous and repeated efforts had been made to include a pledge in the manifesto to close down asylums and hand the mentally ill over to 'care in the community', but Mrs Thatcher resisted on the grounds that such care would, in reality, be cruel.

† The manifesto promised a place on the scheme for all sixteen- and seventeen-year-olds and all up to the age of twenty-five who had been out of work for six months or more.

‡ Party election broadcasts were prescribed in their maximum length and the number permitted to each party, by law. When each party's broadcast went out it was shown simultaneously on all television channels, so there was no escape for viewers. As a result, the broadcasts were unpopular in principle, but widely watched.

Kinnock strolling hand in hand on the Great Orme headland by Llandudno. It was interspersed with Kinnock explaining his compassionate attitudes and likeable working-class background. Although the broadcast did not move the polls much, it galvanized interest in the campaign and convinced the media that Kinnock was the man of the moment. Making much of Kinnock's youth (he was forty-five to Mrs Thatcher's sixty-one), the film also suggested the political mortality of the Thatcher era.* Although Mrs Thatcher did not see the broadcast she was naturally displeased by its success. In her recollection, 'The media were just determined that whatever Kinnock did was right.'

At the daily press conference after the Kinnock broadcast, Mrs Thatcher made her second gaffe. She suggested that schools opting out of local-authority control might be able to charge fees on top of what they received from the government and pursue selective admission policies. Under pressure from her advisers, she backed away from the idea, but the incident revealed a carelessness which, in past campaigns, she had rarely shown.

At midnight, Mrs Thatcher telephoned Young. Her daughter Carol, she said, had told her: 'We're about to lose the election the way things are going.' Two days earlier, John Wakeham, almost completely inexperienced on television, had performed very poorly on *Election Call*. The papers spoke of a 'lost week' for the Tories. That night, she had Bell and Young in for drinks with Denis, Carol and Stephen Sherbourne. Denis, Bell recalled, seemed 'a bit aloof', saying things like 'The woman's getting grumpy: watch it!' Mrs Thatcher raged against Wakeham's performance and seemed in despair: 'It's hardly worth bothering, let's give up, it's the end.' Denis kept telling her to listen to Bell and Young. They in turn urged her to 'release Norman the assassin' to destroy Kinnock.

She calmed down a bit, but the next day she was again full of anxieties. She twice telephoned Young, telling him she wanted to appear in more party election broadcasts herself and was appalled by the scruffy appearance of her ministers on television: 'Nigel's got to get a haircut.' 'Absolutely right.' 'Will you tell him?' 'No, Prime Minister . . . you've got to tell him.' 'All right.' In fact she did not; his own wife did. She also decided to strip Wakeham of his role coordinating television broadcasts for ministers. Young resented the fact that she forced him to pass on the bad news. This

---

* Age probably did play a small part, for the first time, in Mrs Thatcher's tetchiness during the campaign. Those close to her noticed that she tired more easily. 'She used to yawn a lot in meetings,' recalled David Young. 'She could have done with seven hours' sleep, but wouldn't admit it.' Shortly after the election, Young said in a private interview that 'you had to recognise she was ageing'.

atmosphere of unhappiness, anger, irresolution and intrigue dominated the whole campaign.* Everything came back to Mrs Thatcher's deep insecurity and lack of a united team she could trust.

The wider political realities were much better for her. The opinion polls held steady throughout May. On policy, the Conservatives made hay with Labour's spending promises, highlighting implicit hidden tax rises. Even more helpful was Labour's policy of unilateral disarmament. Saatchis produced an advertisement with the slogan 'LABOUR'S POLICY ON ARMS': it showed a British soldier with his hands held up in surrender. On television, Kinnock declared that, were Britain attacked, the choice would be between 'exterminating everything you stand for' (a nuclear response, which he opposed) or seeking to 'make any occupation totally untenable'. By using the word 'occupation' he seemed to concede the idea of defeat and surrender. 'Norman the assassin' struck: 'Britain has no ambition to live under the red flag of socialism or the white flag of surrender,' he declared. On the Tuesday night (26 May), Mrs Thatcher offered her own biting denunciation. She quoted Kinnock's words about occupation – 'So now we know that Labour's non-nuclear defence policy is a policy for defeat, surrender, occupation and finally, prolonged guerrilla fighting ... I do not understand how anyone who aspires to government can treat the defence of our country so lightly.'†

At the start of the last full week, the polls showed little change. The least favourable gave the Tories an 8.5 per cent lead over Labour. Travelling the country, Lawson recalled an even better atmosphere than in 1983, 'a huge, popular, positive response, a real feeling of a British economic miracle'. He was talking his own book, but there was a widespread sense that good times had arrived.

Mrs Thatcher, however, remained extremely uneasy. With reports in the Sunday papers that Labour would move to more personal attacks on her arrogance and dictatorial ways, Young told her that 'we must stay on the ATTACK ... [using] the fear issues ... "They will destroy our industrial

---

* Part of the trouble was that, by this stage, Mrs Thatcher had very few associates senior enough to stand up to her. Once, when she was firing so many angry questions at David Willetts that he could not get her to read the brief, David Wolfson intervened: 'Just shut up and read the bloody brief,' but such courage was memorable by its rarity.
† Two people who were not supposed to help her campaign, but did, were Ronald Reagan and Charles Powell. Reagan spoke publicly of Labour's 'grievous errors' on the nuclear issue. Powell admitted that he took the Civil Service practice of scanning the manifesto for consistency with government policy to unusual lengths and suggested amendments to the defence aspect. He also proposed wording on foreign affairs and defence in Mrs Thatcher's speeches because policy was 'too important to leave in the hands of Central Office hacks'.

peace, they will destroy our safety on the streets and they will destroy the money in your pocket."' Mrs Thatcher always liked attacking and was pleased to concentrate on the simple case against Labour, the Alliance's fortunes having faded. On Tuesday 2 June, in Edinburgh, she denounced Labour's resort to 'personal abuse' and warned of what lay behind the 'mask of moderation'. To much applause, she reminded her audience of the abolition of domestic rates and the imminent introduction of the community charge.

That night, a new poll put the Conservative lead at just under 4 per cent, the smallest of the campaign so far. Still away in Scotland, Mrs Thatcher was beside herself, her mood exacerbated by the onset of 'extremely painful toothache' (later diagnosed as an abscess). When she returned to London the next day (3 June), matters only deteriorated. Rumours in the City that afternoon had started share prices falling. A Gallup poll the following day put the Tories only four points ahead of Labour. At Downing Street, Sherbourne recalled, 'Panic gripped us all. "Is this a horrible turning point?" we asked ourselves.'

Mrs Thatcher passed a sleepless night, racked by tooth pain, until given pills by Crawfie in the small hours, so the next morning she was groggy. Arriving at Central Office, she lashed out at Tebbit and Young: 'You and David, you've been on too much and you're too old. We must have younger people on television.' Although older than both of them, she wanted to be seen more herself. At the press conference, she allowed herself to be trapped by a question about private health care. She said she had been treated privately in the past 'to enable me to go into hospital on the day I want, at the time I want and with the doctor I want'. Afterwards, David Willetts, at Central Office, recalled, she did not seem to understand why it was so problematic to suggest that the NHS, for which she was responsible, was inadequate for her needs but sufficient for everyone else. She would be pursued for her remark until the end of the campaign.

By now Mrs Thatcher was 'almost hysterical, with her arms sweeping everywhere'. 'Her eyes flashed: hatred shot out of them, like a dog about to bite you.' She demanded to see Saatchis' proposed advertising. When Dobbs brought it in, 'She flayed me,' he recalled. 'She was screaming, foaming at the mouth. Norman was trying to talk sense into her. David Young was saying "Leave it to me, Margaret." Willie Whitelaw was rolling his oyster eyes.' Her only coherent demand was that the material dwell more on Conservative achievements. Young now hurried off with Tim Bell to try to fix matters. Mrs Thatcher meanwhile went to visit Alton Towers, the Staffordshire theme park, in heavy rain, an ill-fated attempt to lighten the atmosphere. After she had set off, Whitelaw turned to Dobbs and said, 'There's a woman who will never fight another election.'*

Rumours were sweeping Westminster of another poll about to appear showing the Tory lead at just 2 per cent. Young and Bell, scared by Mrs Thatcher's mood, now came up with a new advertising slogan: 'BRITAIN'S A SUCCESS AGAIN – DON'T LET LABOUR RUIN IT'.† At the same time, Saatchis and Tebbit were frantically working to replace their own offering that had been rejected that morning.

After Mrs Thatcher returned from her dismal outing, both teams arrived in Downing Street unaware of the other's presence. Young took Tebbit aside and showed him Bell's work, about which, until then, he had known nothing. '"Who did this?" he asked . . . I said "Tim Bell." He said, "Well, that's it then, that's it."' Young then 'got him by the shoulders and said, "Norman listen to me, we're about to lose this fucking election, you're going to go, I'm going to go, the whole thing is going to go. The whole election depends upon her being right for the next five days doing fine performances on television – she has to be happy, we have got to do this."' Rather cool-headedly, Tebbit inspected the competing offerings and decided that the one produced by his rivals was the better and more likely to please Mrs Thatcher.

Maurice Saatchi was 'enraged' at this but, encouraged by Tebbit, agreed to accept Bell's proposal with the face-saving modification of 'BRITAIN'S GREAT AGAIN: DON'T LET LABOUR WRECK IT'. Mrs Thatcher was then presented, at last, with a single, agreed suggestion. 'She looked very relieved,' and accepted it. Early that evening the dreaded poll arrived. Contrary to the panicky rumours, it showed the Conservatives a comfortable ten points ahead of Labour. Suddenly, the appalling past twenty-four hours looked ridiculous. That night Mrs Thatcher, exhausted, fell asleep at her desk.

Many seasoned campaigners considered the whole business of Wobbly Thursday, as it came to be known, absurd. Some blamed it on Lord Young. 'David panicked,' Nigel Lawson believed. 'It was infectious.' The ultimate problem, however, lay with Mrs Thatcher herself, who spent much of the campaign sure of nothing except that everything was going wrong. So Young and Bell were right to think that the key issue was to humour her, thus coaxing the best performances out of her. In Charles Powell's view,

---

* It was this highly charged occasion which inspired Dobbs to write his novel *House of Cards*.
† This had been inspired by the Conservatives' victorious campaign for a third term in 1959: 'LIFE'S BETTER UNDER THE CONSERVATIVES. DON'T LET LABOUR RUIN IT'.

Wobbly Thursday 'made some of us feel that she had to be saved from herself'.

It is strange that tensions with Tebbit ran so high, given that he had told Mrs Thatcher in April that he would not accept office after the election. Possibly she found this impossible to believe. Certainly she tried, including on election night itself, to get him to stay. Perhaps she just never felt at ease with the stern Tebbit as she did with louder, easier, more self-consciously charming men. For his part, Tebbit was deeply hurt by what had happened. At the 1987 party conference, he treated one colleague to 'a 10-minute fusillade of RAF expletives about his election treatment by the ghastly——, an overrated PM'. There was something tragic in this falling-out. Mrs Thatcher admired Tebbit greatly and yet, despite everything they had done together, their sense of common purpose had declined. In this sense, Wobbly Thursday was not so much a one-day wonder as a watershed.

In the final days, Mrs Thatcher recovered form. With a clear battle to fight under a clear slogan, she performed strongly in interviews. On the eve of poll, however, she stumbled again when pressed by David Dimbleby about why she did not seem to care about the unemployed. 'If people just drool and drivel that they care,' she said, 'I turn round and say "Right, I also look to see what you actually do."' Very untypically, she immediately retracted the phrase on air. If it had come earlier in the campaign, it would probably have created as much trouble as her remarks on health. Yet the words were of the essence of Margaret Thatcher. First, they expressed fierce antagonism to the left's pretension to any moral high ground. Second, they encapsulated her tendency to judge by results and by action rather than by words. In all her social teaching she kept asking the question, 'What is to be *done*?' and so got angry at critics who cared, as she saw it, only about what should be said.

On the day before polling day, Young told Mrs Thatcher he did not think she would get near a majority of eighty. 'I must have an 80 majority, I must have it,' she replied. 'It won't look right if I don't.' Once the votes were counted, the Conservatives received a majority of 102. In Finchley, Mrs Thatcher saw her majority slightly reduced to 8,913. The results were:

Mrs M. Thatcher (Conservative)	21,603
J. R. M. Davies (Labour)	12,690
D. Howarth (Liberal)	5,580
Lord Buckethead (Independent)	131
M. J. St Vincent (Independent)	59

The Conservative vote nationwide was 13,763,066 (42.2 per cent of the total) – a higher numerical, though not proportional, haul than in 1979 or 1983. Labour's vote share had risen from 27.6 per cent in 1983 to 30.8 per cent. The Alliance, with 22.5 per cent, was three points down. The only serious blot on the Tory success was Scotland, where voters had suffered from rate revaluation: Tory seats fell from twenty-one to ten.

On polling day, Bernard Ingham prepared Mrs Thatcher to comment on 'your historic winning of a third term': 'While savouring your triumph you <u>must</u> give no impression of resting on your laurels . . .' She should signal that she intended 'to get on with the major "caring" tasks which were interrupted by the General Election'. Mrs Thatcher's own handwritten notes suggest she followed this advice. She wanted 'more choice in housing and education. Especially for those in inner cities.' What she actually said to the cameras was 'We must do something about those inner cities.' Those were the words that were remembered.

But the facts spoke louder than anything she herself could say. No prime minister in the era of universal suffrage had ever won a third consecutive term. Despite her own misjudgements in the campaign, she had triumphantly done so. Thatcherism was now the dominant creed of the age.

The day after the Conservatives' victory was declared, Charles Powell wrote a letter of congratulation to his boss. 'If ever a party and a country were carried to success on the shoulders of one person,' he told her, 'it has been over the last eight years.' But then he gave some brave advice: 'All the same, I hope you will not put yourself through it again . . . In two or three years' time, you will have completed the most sweeping change this country has seen in decades and your place in history will be rivalled in this century only by Churchill. That's the time to contribute in some other area!'

In her moment of greatest triumph, Mrs Thatcher was being reminded by her closest associate that she was mortal.

27
Bourgeois triumphalism
'What's to stop us?'

On Friday 12 June 1987, David English, the Editor of the *Daily Mail*, sent Mrs Thatcher congratulations on her third general election victory: 'Well, we certainly agreed the right headline on Wednesday night!' he declared, '... you not only wrote it, you worked for it, you earned it and you deserved it.' On the eve of polling day, English had most improperly let her compose his paper's headline. She had suggested 'THATCHER SET FOR A WINNING TREBLE', which the paper published. Although British electoral contests are based on parties, not individual leaders, there was something in what English said. The British people had voted on a record overwhelmingly associated with one woman. This was Mrs Thatcher's victory.

After the fractiousness of the campaign, the change of mood inside 10 Downing Street was complete. Tessa Gaisman, Mrs Thatcher's diary secretary, noticed how happy were the civil servants as well as the political appointees: 'It was lovely how pleased the Garden Room girls were. It was because she was always kind to them. They queued up to shake her hand.' Archie Hamilton, appointed her PPS in succession to Michael Alison, recalled 'a general feeling of happiness, but no sitting around drinking champagne'. Norman Blackwell, in the Policy Unit, felt 'elation – the sense that we could tackle things that had been hard before'. The Unit now hoped to extend Thatcherism to social policy – reforming the National Health Service and schools, regenerating the inner cities and introducing democratic accountability into local government through the community charge.

Mrs Thatcher's third win reverberated across the world just as the Cold War was moving in the West's favour. President Reagan called her from Berlin after issuing his rousing appeal there: 'Mr Gorbachev, tear down this wall.' He congratulated her on her 'magnificent victory'. It had, she said, 'been beyond her wildest expectations . . . It looked like she was set to remain in office for another 3-4 years,' a period which would see Reagan leave office. Mrs Thatcher's personal success, reported the US Embassy in London, was 'good news for the US': 'As her ministers and bureaucrats look increasingly toward Europe and European institutions like the EC . . . she remains a firm Atlanticist.'

There were also strong political reverberations at home. Opposition parties realized they would soon have spent a decade failing to defeat Mrs Thatcher. Tony Blair, a young Labour frontbencher, felt in awe of her achievement as 'a modernizer against outdated collectivism'. He added: 'I liked the simplicity of her intellect. It's the biggest thing I learnt from her.' Peter Mandelson believed that her third victory forced further modernization upon the Labour Party. Until then, reformers such as he had concentrated on fighting Labour's internal problems. Now 'We had to concentrate on *her*.' For the Alliance, the result showed it had failed to 'break the mould' of British politics. As its two component parts sought a merger, most were not disposed to learn lessons from Mrs Thatcher. The important exception was the SDP leader, David Owen, the most radical of the Social Democrat 'Gang of Four'. Early in July, when Ted Heath, 'mortified' by Mrs Thatcher's success in the election, attacked her 'reactionary, regressive policies', Owen came to her defence. As Bernard Ingham's daily press digest recorded, 'Owen tells MPs your majority of 101 was a far greater triumph than the 144 won in 1983.' From then on there were frequent overtures to Owen to join the Tory Party, but he always refused.*

The media accepted that Mrs Thatcher had changed the terms of public argument. As Hugo Young, her hostile but perceptive biographer, conceded, the 1987 election 'locked the Thatcher era into place'. *The Times* ran a leading article declaring 'We are all Thatcherites now'. Oddly, perhaps, this was less accepted in the Conservative parliamentary party itself. The old antagonisms between Wet and Dry had diminished, but enthusiasm for Thatcherism did not reach right across the party. Lord Hesketh, a government whip, complained to Woodrow Wyatt that colleagues were 'already talking about her not going the whole of her third term. "It's all these ghastly middle and lower middle class people we have at the top of

---

* There was even the occasional suggestion that Owen could become a minister in the government without becoming a Conservative. In May 1988, following a poor showing for the SDP in local elections, Mrs Thatcher herself in effect invited David Owen to join her party, publicly extolling his political 'feel' and his dislike of socialism, but he still rejected the idea.

the party. They can't understand how wonderful she is. There'll be a lot of intrigue against her."'*

Before the election campaign began Mrs Thatcher's astute Chief Whip, John Wakeham, had warned her that, even in victory, 'The management of Parliament and the colleagues will continue to be difficult.' He considered Willie Whitelaw's role essential. After the election Wakeham emphasized the need for balance and consolidation. Hoping for promotion, he urged her to give his job to either John Major or Peter Brooke – the first a young rising star, the second a trusted member of the party establishment. The Chief Whip's post should not go, he insisted, to a candidate she favoured, her close supporter Peter Morrison, who 'is I fear a non-runner'. Wakeham said this not so much because of the unproved allegations against Morrison of sexual activities with young men (see p. 544), but because he knew, though he did not say this directly to Mrs Thatcher, that Morrison had developed a severe drink problem. Wakeham felt she should replace no more than two Cabinet ministers, proposing mostly non-Thatcherites for advancement.† Wakeham also reminded Mrs Thatcher that 'you wanted to give all the possible contenders for the leadership, when you retire, some chance to show themselves'. While she realized she would have to leave eventually, she considered the prospect both distant and unpleasing. Besides, her political nose told her that to discuss the succession was to risk advancing it. Wakeham judged that, on current showing, 'leaving aside Geoffrey Howe, the only serious contender ... is Ken Baker'. He urged her to keep Peter Walker, her only surviving Wet, in the Cabinet to avoid him joining forces with Michael Heseltine and producing 'the first serious opposition' from the back benches.

Wakeham advised that party organization needed renewed attention. The legendary Central Office machine of the early 1980s and the voluntary party's grass-roots were beginning to decay. Mrs Thatcher wished to tackle this problem, but organization was something for which she had no gift. She preferred to leave it to the right people. The trouble was

---

* When editing the *Spectator* during the 1987 election campaign, the present author, assuming that the Conservatives would win, drafted a cover piece arguing that this would be the moment for Mrs Thatcher to plan her early departure. He dropped his own piece after Ferdinand Mount, the magazine's political columnist, argued it would be interpreted as incomprehensibly hostile. The fact that such a piece was under consideration shows that thoughts of Mrs Thatcher's political mortality were widespread.

† Wakeham's list included Tony Newton, Tim Renton, David Mellor, John Gummer, John Patten and William Waldegrave. No one on his list, with the semi-exception of the flamboyant Alan Clark, was what Mrs Thatcher called 'one of us'.

that, after so many years in office, she no longer knew who the right people might be.

Weighing these conflicting factors, Mrs Thatcher chose her new Cabinet on Saturday 13 June, accompanied by Whitelaw, Norman Tebbit and her new Chief Whip, David Waddington. Waddington, suggested by Nigel Lawson, was a well-liked and competent man, and wholly loyal to her. She later described him as 'the best Chief Whip I had', but he lacked the worldly guile and intelligence-gathering skills of his predecessor. As Waddington remembered it, the meeting was overshadowed by Tebbit's decision to leave government, a 'bombshell' even though he had made his plans clear to Mrs Thatcher well in advance (see p. 611). She now insisted that Tebbit stay on as Chairman until the October party conference to receive the acclaim of the party's supporters.

Mrs Thatcher followed Wakeham's counsel against too much change. Howe stayed at the Foreign Office, Lawson – whose economic success made him, in many people's eyes, the architect of victory – at the Treasury and Hurd at the Home Office. With the first two her relations were by now strained, and with the third not close. She removed John Biffen from the Cabinet because of his persistent criticism of her style of government. John Wakeham became Leader of the House. According to Waddington, Mrs Thatcher and he cast around for 'true Thatcherites' but 'There weren't so many able men: you can't say she overlooked a bright star.'*

Lord Hailsham was forced into retirement, allowing the Attorney-General, Sir Michael Havers, to become Lord Chancellor.† Following Wakeham's advice, Mrs Thatcher made Peter Walker the almost insultingly junior offer of the Welsh Office. He accepted, and was replaced at Energy by Cecil Parkinson. Parkinson's return fuelled hopes among her loyalists that they might now gain advancement, but the Sara Keays scandal and the lapse of four years had sapped a good deal of his political

---

* There were not many able women either. Following the 1987 election there were just seventeen female Conservative MPs (including Mrs Thatcher) in Parliament. In Mrs Thatcher's eyes, none of these women constituted a star.

† Havers had been half-promised the job to soothe him over the Westland embarrassments. In late October, however, he fell ill and had to resign after only four months. Mrs Thatcher seems seriously to have considered the idea of forcing Geoffrey Howe, who, as a former Solicitor-General, was well qualified, to take this eminent but politically impotent position. Howe got wind of this plan, which would have ended his front-line political career, and protested. In the end, Mrs Thatcher did not make the appointment because she feared losing the by-election consequent on Howe's departure from the Commons. Much future trouble might have been spared if she had bitten this bullet.

strength. He was still Mrs Thatcher's friend but no longer central to her counsels.

She also promoted her close associate Lord Young from Employment to Trade and Industry. Under him at the DTI, but in the Cabinet for the first time, was Kenneth Clarke, who was no Thatcherite, but whose taste for a scrap made him a strong partner in public service reform. The other two representatives of the rising generation were Thatcher favourites. The first was John Major, who became Chief Secretary to the Treasury. The second was John Moore, who filled the place at Health and Social Security vacated by Norman Fowler, now moved to Employment. Both these youngish Johns came from modest backgrounds and exemplified the upward mobility that she preached. Both were seen as advocates of Thatcherism. Mrs Thatcher liked both but knew neither well.

The greatest personal anguish of the reshuffle followed her decision to offer Michael Alison, her outgoing PPS, no government position. 'It was a shattering blow,' the saintly Alison wrote to Mrs Thatcher, deeply hurt. He reminded her that 'the office of your PPS should be seen as a coveted and enviable prize', not a dead end. He hoped she would, after all, find space for him: 'The Leader of the Long March is to be applauded for favouring her foot-men, the more so if they appear a bit old and battle-scarred.'* Alison's complaint reflected her failure to value the role of PPS highly enough. Archie Hamilton, the new incumbent, thought she 'didn't understand what a PPS did. She saw him as passive, a messenger boy.' This was a serious mistake. Alison was right about her general failure to reinforce loyalty. Many Long Marchers felt increasingly disgruntled.

Mrs Thatcher may have been lulled into a false sense of security not only by her third consecutive victory, but also by her trust in her non-party Downing Street team. As Stephen Sherbourne recalled, 'Bernard Ingham and Charles Powell were the two most powerful people in No. 10 and were disconnected from the party. Yet the party was her base.' Therefore 'My role was one which, oddly, no one else in No. 10 had – to make sure that she remained PM.'

The only part of the United Kingdom where the Conservatives lost ground in the 1987 election was Scotland, where their seat tally fell from twenty-one to ten.† Labour were the main beneficiaries, winning fifty seats in all.

---

* Despite his protest, Michael Alison was never again made a minister, but Mrs Thatcher did appoint him Second Church Estates Commissioner, a task well suited to his ecclesiastical interests. On all Christian and Church matters, he continued to influence her.
† The Conservative percentage share of the vote had fallen by a less dramatic 4.4 per cent to 24.0 per cent.

Scotland seemed the most extreme example of the so-called 'North–South divide' – political and economic – with the added national factor making it still more intractable for Mrs Thatcher. Beyond rage against rate revaluation in Scotland, the deeper cause of the Tory losses was disputed. Was it, as more upper-class and rural Scottish Tories tended to believe, because the Conservatives had set their face against devolution and because free-market economics were too strong meat for a deindustrializing Scotland? Or was it, as their lower-middle-class, pugnacious, reformist counterparts liked to argue, that Scotland had not yet been offered vigorous revived Unionism and a proper dose of Thatcherism? Malcolm Rifkind, Scottish Secretary since January 1986, was in the first camp. Michael Forsyth, whom Mrs Thatcher brought into government after the election, was in the second.

Not surprisingly, Mrs Thatcher tended to prefer the views of Forsyth (perhaps the most ideologically Thatcherite of all her ministers) to those of Rifkind. When she appointed Forsyth as a junior minister to the Scottish Office, she told him that Rifkind's department 'needs strengthening'. She felt some frustration that Scotland had so far 'opted out of Thatcherism'. She was not likely to warm to Rifkind's view that 'The problem, as seen by the Scots, was that she was a woman, an English woman and a bossy English woman,' even though this contained an element of truth.

Although a strong Unionist, Mrs Thatcher had some difficulty in understanding the nature of loyalty in the non-English parts of the United Kingdom. On one occasion, she stayed with the Scottish industrialist Lord Weir shortly before a football match between England and Germany. When he told her that every one of his workers would 'support Germany, she simply could not believe what I was saying'. As a patriotic political campaigner without rival, Mrs Thatcher found it disturbing that in Scotland she could not play that card without being trumped by parties from the left. Conscious that, without dominant patriotic appeal north of the border, the Tories risked becoming a small middle-class party of business, she sought ways in which the party might be more successfully 'wrapped in tartan'. Instinctively, however, she was uncomfortable with this. She told colleagues privately that she 'Had [the] impression that when we stopped being Unionist and started trying to be Scottish, our supporters began to lose identity.' That the Tory Party could be at once Unionist and Scottish seemed to be beyond her ken.

Following the 1987 election, Scottish Labour began to define its own patriotism in terms of a devolved, collectivist Scotland standing as a proud bulwark against the selfish individualism of Tory England. As the appeal of this grew, Mrs Thatcher struggled with the idea that the Conservatives, having won a UK general election, could lack legitimacy in Scotland. In Edinburgh that September, she tried to scotticize Thatcherism by claiming it as a version of 'Adam Smithism' and thus a product of Scotland's most famous economist, but this did not resonate.

As Mrs Thatcher sketched out her mission for the third term, Robert Armstrong recalled her as 'more driven' than ever before: 'she knew that this would be her last innings and there was so much more still to do'. Norman Blackwell remembered working with her on a speech when she pulled out a copy of *On Liberty* by J. S. Mill and turned quickly to the passage she sought: 'A state that dwarfs its men,' she read aloud, 'in order that they may be more docile instruments in its hands even for beneficial purposes – will find that with small men no great thing can be accomplished.' 'She was trying', Blackwell believed, 'to liberate people to do things.'

But what did this mean, in her political context? For all her enthusiasm for bold change, she never found the formulation of a programme easy. Particularly on social policy, she was uncertain about how to proceed. A telling sentence in Mrs Thatcher's memoirs exemplifies this. Early on, in her account of her third-term reforms in schools, housing and health, she writes: 'So the Government soon found itself embarked on even more far-reaching social reforms than we had originally intended.' It is surprising but true that she embarked on such reforms with little resembling a grand plan. One reason for her hesitation was that the subject matter came less readily to her than that of economics. She was seriously interested in social questions, but instinctively happier with quantifiable matters. She also believed more unambiguously in freedom of choice in economic questions than she did in social ones, where her instincts were more conservative. Once, when David Willetts spoke approvingly to her of *laissez-faire*, she brought him up sharply: 'Not *laissez-faire*, David – ordered liberty.' She did not think, for example, that pornography was justified by freedom of speech, or that a couple living together unmarried were making as legitimate a 'lifestyle choice' as a married one. Although she might, in theory, have preferred health or school systems which were market-based, she considered these politically unattainable. Her plans to improve choice in these fields, therefore, tried to replicate market freedoms within state systems. This made them easier for bureaucracies to frustrate.

Mrs Thatcher relied heavily on her Policy Unit to drive reform. From 1985, its Director was Brian Griffiths, an academic economist, but also an active Christian keen to deepen the moral dimension of policy. She too wished to apply her beliefs to political action, but was hesitant about doing this too explicitly. Willetts felt that Griffiths tended to exaggerate the Christian element in her thinking.* He shied away from basing modern Conservatism on explicitly Christian terms: 'We had to find the right moral basis for a *secular* society.' In Griffiths's view, however, Mrs Thatcher well understood that Christianity should not be pushed too hard politically. What she sought was to express the altruism of Conservatives: 'She felt the Conservatism which centred on economic success was viewed as heartless. She wasn't heartless; she was Victorian. She thought what she was doing in helping put families on their feet *was* moral.' The Policy Unit's Hartley Booth, a Methodist barrister, felt that her Methodist Christianity underpinned many of her attitudes. Although personally she 'was a quiet Christian, with a Bible by her bed', her Christianity helped direct her reflections on social policy.

During the election campaign, writing in the strongly Tory *Sunday Telegraph*, its Editor, Peregrine Worsthorne, complained of Mrs Thatcher's 'bourgeois triumphalism'. Her utopia, he insisted, was 'riddled with worms'. These worms were 'more social than political, eating into the moral base and values of a ruling class'. The jibe of 'bourgeois triumphalism' stuck, and she longed to refute it.

Before Parliament rose for the summer, Mrs Thatcher delivered her annual speech to the backbench 1922 Committee. She linked her economic policies, particularly those of ownership, which she believed had won the general election, to the coming programme. The independence created by ownership could also be accomplished through social policy. The 'Great Education Reform Bill' would give parents 'a deciding voice' in schools. Housing reforms and the revival of inner cities would build on the same theme. As for the community charge, it would mean that 'councils really will be accountable'. She was reported to have added that the community charge was 'the flagship' of her programme.

Over the summer, Mrs Thatcher became aware of strong opposition to appointing Lord Young as Party Chairman. She had always liked Young and believed his business connections would help raise money for the party. As a peer, he would not use the chairmanship to challenge her leadership. Colleagues, however, were envious of his advancement. They argued that a man with no party background could not understand the Conservative Party well enough to run it. Others asked how Young could raise money from businesses while also, as Secretary of State for Trade and Industry,

---

* In 1987, for example, Griffiths told Willetts that he had persuaded Mrs Thatcher to read all the prefaces from *Crockford's Clerical Directory*, the annual reference book for the Church of England, for the past ten years. Willetts did not regard this as a good use of her time.

adjudicating fairly between those businesses? At Lawson's urging, Mrs Thatcher therefore decided to appoint Peter Brooke, a Tory grandee whose family had a distinguished party history.* Brooke becoming Chairman guaranteed respectability, but he was not terribly effective as an organizer or public presenter. The chance to rebuild Conservative Central Office as an election-winning machine was missed.

At the party conference in Blackpool Mrs Thatcher was hailed as the conquering hero. Her own speech did nothing to discourage this, seizing on the nineteenth-century precedent of Lord Liverpool as the last leader to win three consecutive elections: 'And he was Prime Minister for 15 years. It's rather encouraging.' In the third term, she explicitly rejected the post-Westland notion of reining back: 'Is this where we pitch our tents? . . . Absolutely not . . . Would "consolidate" be the word that we stitch on our banners?' The next stage was 'to extend opportunity – and choice – to those who have so far been denied them'.

In education, she accused left-wing councils of low standards and propaganda. Her remedies were 'a national curriculum for basic subjects', while empowering parents and governors to create 'independent state schools', free of local-authority control. To this she added plans for the reform of council tenancies, a bonfire of building controls and the new community charge. Summing it all up, Mrs Thatcher declared: 'To coin a phrase it is "an irreversible shift . . . of power . . . in favour of working people and their families".' At this her audience laughed and cheered: she was appropriating the famous words of Labour's leading left-winger Tony Benn.† The cheeky idea, present in council house sales and trade union reforms, that the Conservatives were the true workers' party continued to be politically transformative. If it were true, what was left for Labour?

Concluding, she quoted her beloved Rudyard Kipling's famous poem 'Recessional', about the need for 'a humble and a contrite heart'. This was, perhaps, her nod towards the danger of 'bourgeois triumphalism'. But she went on to declare that 'we have both a right and a duty to remind the whole free world that, once more, Britain is confident, strong, trusted. Confident, because attitudes have changed. "Can't be done" has given way to "What's to stop us?"' Her words accurately reflected the state of politics. Her opponents – outside and within her party – had

---

* This decision was, in part, a nod to the High Tory side of Mrs Thatcher's character. Brooke's mother, Lady Brooke of Ystradfellte, whom she admired, had been a Vice-Chairman of the party, and his father, Henry, had been Home Secretary.
† In 1976 Benn had called for an 'irreversible shift in the balance of power and wealth in favour of working people and their families'.

spectacularly failed to stop her. This did not mean, of course, that they would not try again.

Three weeks later *Woman's Own*, then the biggest-selling women's magazine in Britain, published an interview with Mrs Thatcher. Buried deep within it was one potentially explosive sentence. She had said: 'There is no such thing as society.' To critics this summed up her creed of selfish individualism. It would be forever used against her. Her words, however, had a distinct context. As she had told the magazine:

> Too many people have been given to understand that if they have a problem, it's the Government's job to cope with it. 'I have a problem, I'll get a grant.' 'I'm homeless, the Government must house me.' They're casting their problem on society. And you know there is no such thing as society. There are individual men and women, and there are families. And no government can do anything except through people, and people must look to themselves first. It's our duty to look after ourselves and then, also, to look after our neighbour.*

If Mrs Thatcher had used a late-twentieth-century gesture, she would, when uttering the word 'society', have flipped her fingers in the air to indicate quotation marks. She was trying to identify the drivers of social improvement: she concluded they were the people who composed society and were aware of their responsibilities. Far from advocating selfishness, she was arguing against it, on the grounds of duty to neighbour. It was not 'the dole' that paid people not to work: 'It is your neighbour who is supplying it and if you can earn your own living then really you have a duty to do it.' She was reflecting on the balance between dependence and independence, arguing that the former could be sustained only by plenty of the latter.

Her *Woman's Own* interview only gradually became common currency among her opponents. It was not until the following July that Downing Street, unusually, put out a statement clarifying her views, views which she then repeated on *The Jimmy Young Show*: 'Well, who is society? You say society is to blame. It is you and me and our next-door neighbour and everyone we know in our town, in our school, in our business.' She was denounced two days later by Paddy Ashdown, just elected leader of the

---

* The complete, unpublished transcript shows that Mrs Thatcher repeated her point. It was not good if people thought that 'If children have a problem, it is society that is at fault. There is no such thing as society. There is living tapestry of men and women and people and the beauty of that tapestry and the quality of our lives will depend upon how much each of us is prepared to take responsibility for ourselves and . . . prepared to turn round and help by our own efforts those who are unfortunate.'

newly merged Liberal Democrats. From then on her alleged rejection of the reality of society was repeatedly thrown at her. Taken alone, the sentence would prove a constant embarrassment. But she herself did not take it alone: the *Woman's Own* interview, as a whole, is a key to her approach to social reform, indeed to society itself.

Given the importance she attached to the community charge, Mrs Thatcher was keen to get on with it. The Scottish legislation had been passed before the election: now the flagship, as the manifesto had promised, could be launched in England and Wales. In Scotland, where a full rate revaluation had already taken place, the tax would be introduced immediately to mitigate the shock of much higher bills. But in England and Wales, where revaluation was still pending, the poll tax would run alongside the existing system for four years, with the former gradually rising as the latter fell away. This 'dual running' was meant to soothe transitional pain.

As Environment Secretary, Nicholas Ridley had to introduce the community charge. The problem, according to his private secretary, Robin Young, was that Ridley was 'not *that* in favour of the poll tax', though this was well concealed by his intense loyalty to Mrs Thatcher. In her mind, Ridley, who had entered the Commons with her in 1959, was her equal rather than her subordinate, and her intellectual soulmate. In turn, Ridley had 'a fantastic fondness' for her and greatly admired her courage and convictions. Accepting the community charge as government policy, he did not try to go back on it.

Ridley's dismissive upper-class manner often came across as arrogant, so he was not a good frontman for the poll tax, but he was admired as a minister. His civil servants and colleagues respected his courtesy, grasp of issues and courage in leading from the front. His practical sense cast doubt on important aspects of the poll tax. Mrs Thatcher liked to say in private, 'My father always said that everybody should pay something, even if it's only sixpence,' but Ridley worried whether getting the sixpences would be worth the trouble.* He took a similar view of dual running; 'Those who were gaining would not gain fast enough, and those who were losing would angrily contemplate their growing losses year by year.'

The solution, in Ridley's mind, was to abandon dual running and introduce the tax quickly and fully. Colleagues, however, were sceptical. So, with Mrs Thatcher's support, he sought to harness the enthusiasm of activists at the

---

* Students, for example, were eligible for rebates of 80 per cent. Ridley thought it would be pointless to try and wrest the remaining 20 per cent from them: 'You couldn't find the blighters and they would spend their time protesting, not paying.'

annual party conference, most of whom hated the rates. At his behest Gerald Malone, a defeated Scottish MP seeking a new seat, delivered a punchy and loudly applauded speech on the subject from the conference floor: 'We've had the courage to take on this challenge,' he declared. 'Let's do it properly. Let's do it as soon as we can.' On cue, and on camera, Mrs Thatcher turned to Ridley and said something approving. In his speech, Ridley responded, 'All I'm saying is that we have listened to this conference ... We'll have to have another think about it.' Dual running could be dispensed with.

By the end of 1987, several men important to Mrs Thatcher had left their jobs. The Cabinet Secretary, Robert Armstrong, retired and was replaced by Robin Butler, who had been her principal private secretary from 1982 to 1985. She liked his type – tall, athletic, active and enthusiastic. Butler had been the head boy at Harrow, the school to which she had sent her son, Mark. When she appointed Butler he asked her: 'How long will you continue?' 'Not more than a couple of years,' she replied. 'Denis is getting older, you know.' This hint of *fin de régime* conflicted with other things she had said about 'going on and on' and brewed confusion.

Armstrong was almost the last Whitehall mandarin whose eminence predated hers. He and Mrs Thatcher were, in Butler's words, 'never buddies, though there was great respect'. Thirteen years her junior, Butler had been raised up by her, and was therefore less well placed than Armstrong to stand out against her. Armstrong recalled that, not long after he became Cabinet Secretary, she had objected to a memorandum he had sent her:

> After five minutes or so I heard myself say: 'No, Prime Minister, you're wrong.' As I said it, I wondered whether it was something I ought not to have said to the Prime Minister, remembering the rebuke of Queen Elizabeth I to Robert Cecil when he told her in her last illness that she must go to bed: 'Must! Is must a word to be addressed to princes? Little man, little man, thy father, if he had been alive, durst not have used that word.' But Margaret stopped at once, and said: 'Why do you say I am wrong, Robert?' Having gone so far, I told her ... she said: 'You're right, Robert; I was wrong.' I think that this episode was very good for our relationship and went far to establish mutual trust.

Returning to the heart of Mrs Thatcher's government after three years in the Treasury, Butler noticed a definite difference: 'She was no longer prepared to argue. If someone disagreed, she didn't want to know ... There was much less listening.' Richard Wilson, who joined the Cabinet Office in the summer of 1987, thought that 'She had become a performance by the time I met her.' She remained absorbed in the issues but had become harder to reach, more dependent on a very few: 'Charles Powell was absolutely crucial, and he knew it,' Wilson recalled. 'He was always there to greet her when she came back late at night.'

It was usual for private secretaries to move on after three years, which for Powell would be the summer of 1987. But by the time Butler became Cabinet Secretary, Mrs Thatcher was showing no sign of wanting Powell to leave her side. In the Foreign Office, stories circulated of Geoffrey Howe visiting No. 10, only to be told that the Prime Minister was too busy to receive him and he would be seeing Charles Powell instead. He would come 'limping back', recalled one official, 'rather like Piggy in *Lord of the Flies*, having had his spectacles smashed'. In the press, Powell was satirically entitled 'the deputy Prime Minister'. Butler believed that he was 'trying to exclude anyone else who might have an influence on her, including Geoffrey Howe and Nigel Lawson'. He himself felt 'slightly estranged' from her. This came as a particular shock, as the Butlers and the Powells were friends in private life. When Butler was in the running for Cabinet Secretary, Powell had put in a word for him with Mrs Thatcher. In 1984, Butler had argued for Powell to become her foreign affairs private secretary. Accepting this suggestion, she had predicted, with an acuteness which, about appointments, she often lacked: 'If we appoint Charles Powell, he will be controlling us all within six months.' In Butler's opinion, she was proved all too right. As he recalled, 'We had got to a point where Charles was quite a serious barrier between Mrs Thatcher and the Foreign Office.' Soon after his appointment, Butler embarked on a lengthy struggle to ease Powell out of No. 10. In time, this would strain his relationship with Mrs Thatcher almost to breaking point.

On 14 December 1987, Willie Whitelaw suffered a minor stroke in front of the carol service congregation in St Margaret's, Westminster. The doctors advised Whitelaw, sixty-nine, to retire. Mrs Thatcher scolded him – 'But Willie, you have never been ill' – as she visited him in hospital. She was most upset that he would not return to government. As an instance of her famous failure to understand *double entendre*, she was often quoted as having said: 'Every prime minister needs a Willie.'* Now she had not got one.

Whitelaw was irreplaceable, because of his party history and his unique character. As a loyal Heathite, and her main opponent in the second ballot of the 1975 leadership contest, he could have made endless trouble for

---

* Although colleagues always asserted that she did make this remark, and it has been sourced by some to a session with her speech-writers at a party conference, the present author has not found anyone, dead or alive, who actually heard her say it.

her in the early years. That he did not was remarkable, not least because he was not personally close to Mrs Thatcher or her politics. In private, he was said to refer to her as 'that awful woman', but he saw it as both his duty and his best future in politics to be her faithful deputy. Whitelaw felt a regimental loyalty to the Tory Party and its unity. His longing for consensus helped make peace in an administration run by a woman who scorned the very idea. His main contribution lay in averting disasters behind the scenes. Mrs Thatcher loved people with can-do attitudes, but she badly needed someone with can't-do ones to warn her of danger. 'Willie was the buffer,' said Charles Powell. 'Others came to cry on his shoulder. He took for her the strain of their woes. Because of this, and because of his seniority, she respected him.'* Bernard Ingham doubted how effective a protector Whitelaw was when the situation became highly unpleasant, as during the Westland affair, but he considered him invaluable to her because 'she knew that if she couldn't get something past Willie, she had better hold her hand'.

After Whitelaw's departure,† the only person entitled by his seniority to become Deputy Prime Minister was Geoffrey Howe, but by now Mrs Thatcher increasingly mistrusted him. Having failed to move him from the Foreign Office, she did not want to promote him. With Whitelaw gone, there was no one left in the highest positions of government whom she trusted. Although no change was visible to the public, the effect, both on her and on the government, was marked. Nigel Lawson's judgement was sweeping: 'The Thatcher Government, which for more than eight years had been such a great and glorious adventure, was never the same again.' Shortly before he left the government, Whitelaw shocked Butler by saying: 'The trouble is that, when Margaret leaves, she will leave the Conservative Party divided for a generation.'

At the turn of 1987/8, Mrs Thatcher also saw her political secretary, Stephen Sherbourne, depart. His replacement by John Whittingdale marked

---

* Mrs Thatcher's respect for Whitelaw was such that she would often, in a rather formal manner, seek his opinion in Cabinet. He did not always have one ready. On one occasion he had recently returned from Brazil, having represented Britain at a state funeral. 'I'm sure the Lord President would like to tell us about Brazil,' said Mrs Thatcher. Whitelaw, who had been half asleep, looked slightly bewildered and said, 'Well, Prime Minister, all I can tell colleagues is that Brazil is a very big place.'

† Once he had left the government, Whitelaw felt rather hurt that Mrs Thatcher so seldom took up his offer – which she had gratefully accepted when he made it – of giving her occasional advice. She may have been right not to do so, however. The great value of Whitelaw did not lie in any power of abstract analysis but in understanding exactly what was going on. So, when out of office, he was no great use to her. The only Tory grandee outside the government whose advice she quite often sought was Lord Carrington, who had resigned as Foreign Secretary during the Falklands crisis in 1982. According to Charles Powell, 'she adored Carrington. This amused him because, as he said, "I couldn't be further away from her in the party."'

another generational shift. Sherbourne had worked in the party organization since 1970 and knew it intimately. He was effective at tactfully conveying to Mrs Thatcher the perceptions of supporters outside No. 10. Whittingdale, by contrast, lacked this independent standing. Archie Hamilton, Mrs Thatcher's PPS, considered Sherbourne 'exceptional' and Whittingdale 'lightweight'. Others were kinder to Whittingdale, admiring his intelligence and devotion to Mrs Thatcher, but his appointment was another symptom of No. 10 becoming more cut off from party, Parliament and public opinion.*

Although she commanded a majority of over 100, Mrs Thatcher did not find the parliamentary passage of the community charge easy. Few MPs wanted to keep the rates, but it was becoming obvious that the poll tax would involve unwelcome new bills for millions and bear much more heavily on the ordinary voter than on the rich. In December 1987, Tory rebels introduced an amendment that would band the tax to take account of differences in income among those paying it. This ploy was defeated, but the government's majority was cut to 72. The unfavourable publicity for the poll tax emboldened Michael Heseltine to speak, but not vote, against it.† Following agonizingly long sessions in committee,‡ the Bill returned to the House for the 'report stage' in April 1988. Michael Mates, a close ally of Heseltine, then introduced an amendment again seeking to band the tax, mirroring income tax rates. Lawson, otherwise (privately) hostile to the poll tax, disliked this idea even more. With his radical income tax cuts earning widespread acclaim, he did not want his fiscal revolution undermined. As Mrs Thatcher put it privately, it 'would just be a local income tax by another name'.

On 18 April, the Mates amendment was lost, but the government's majority fell to just 25. Before the vote, Commons business managers had warned Mrs Thatcher of the scale of the rebellion. 'This is such a mess,' she responded. 'Our reputation is based on being good on taxes and fairness.' Thirty-eight Conservative MPs – this time including Heseltine§ – defied

---

* Mrs Thatcher conducted her interview with Whittingdale for the Downing Street job most characteristically: 'I received a half-hour diatribe about Helmut Kohl. I was not interviewed at all.'

† Seventeen Conservative MPs, including Ted Heath, voted against the government and thirteen others, including Heseltine, abstained.

‡ To avoid the Bill getting bogged down completely, the government decided to 'guillotine' its passage after seventy hours, only seventeen of the Bill's 129 clauses having been debated.

§ In the debate, Heseltine had been the first to make the bold suggestion that the rates should not, after all, be abolished. He saw his vote as political. To his friend Mates, he said words to the effect of 'I'll support you, so long as you understand that your amendment is rubbish.'

the whips to vote for the amendment, while thirteen abstained. Three days later, a Gallup poll showed that the Tory lead – 11 per cent in March – had given way to a Labour lead of 1 per cent. Only 26 per cent supported the community charge.

The controversy now moved to the Lords, where opponents redoubled their efforts. Mrs Thatcher brought forward her annual address to Conservative peers to rally the troops: 'May I ask your Lordships to recall that the fundamental <u>structure</u> and <u>detail</u> of the Bill <u>was</u> <u>before</u> the <u>electorate</u> and it was <u>that</u> which was endorsed by them.'* Willie Whitelaw spoke persuasively in the debate, his last great service to Mrs Thatcher over a piece of legislation, though many considered he would have done better to have warned her against the poll tax in the first place. On 13 July, with support from the Tories' 'backwoods' hereditary peers, the Lords approved the Bill by 317 votes to 183. Already scheduled to begin in Scotland in April 1989, it would start in England and Wales a year later.

Mrs Thatcher was concerned by the nature of the revolt. 'What is worrying is that they are now a gang,' she told Woodrow Wyatt, '. . . they are all the embittered, the discontented and disappointed people.' She was right to sense danger. 'The vote turned out to be the first brick to come out of the wall,' Mates recalled. 'A tide of resentment was slowly coming in.' He 'began to collect intelligence'.

Mrs Thatcher's zeal for reform, however, was undimmed. Her aim was to reach those who, to date, had felt few of the benefits of Thatcherism. When she had said, immediately after her election victory, 'Now we must do something about those inner cities,' she did not have exact policies in mind but she did have a strong sense of mission. The loose phrase 'inner cities' covered most areas in which her government was criticized for having failed – schools, crime, unemployment, racial tension, public housing, family breakdown and the creation of what was becoming known as 'the underclass'. To Mrs Thatcher, the inner cities were political battlegrounds in which the enemy were the left-wing Labour councils who wasted huge amounts of taxpayers' money† and denied the inhabitants

---

* This was, in part, a response to serious suggestions, fiercely attacked by Thatcher loyalists, that the Upper House should defy the constitutional convention ('the Salisbury Convention') that it should not vote down Bills promised in the governing party's election manifesto.
† The spending profligacy of some Labour local authorities was indeed astonishing. In December 1986, David Norgrove sent Mrs Thatcher a copy of the debt charges of Inner London boroughs. In Labour Islington, where he lived, they amounted to 44 per cent of income, as opposed to 5 per cent in Tory Westminster. 'I think I had better move house!' he exclaimed to Mrs Thatcher. 'Not to <u>Southwark</u>!' she replied, where the percentage was 37 per cent.

the opportunity to improve their lot. The party had lost seats in the northern cities in the 1987 election and she believed that this presented a political opportunity. According to Kenneth Clarke, her Cabinet minister most closely linked with the subject, 'She thought we could win all these Labour strongholds.' She believed that the community charge would empower voters in decayed urban areas to throw off their chains by voting for prudent local government. Above all, she wished to break the cycle of dependence. To her, the 'inner cities' represented the unfinished business of Thatcherism.

Some work had begun well before the election. Lord Young's employment and training programmes had already helped turn the tide of unemployment. Kenneth Baker's reforms of schools were being developed (see p. 636). Social security reforms to break the 'poverty trap' had been scoped out. But so many different subjects and departments were involved that there was duplication and rivalry. Nicholas Ridley's Department of the Environment (DoE), which expected to take the lead, found its role contested by the DTI, run by Young and Clarke.

The conflict was not only about ministerial turf; it was also ideological. Early in her premiership, Mrs Thatcher had delegated inner-city problems to her then Environment Secretary, Michael Heseltine. He had annoyed her, both by rather successfully using the job to advance his own ambitions and by seeing central government intervention as the solution. She was suspicious that a report was being prepared, at Young's suggestion, by Eric Sorensen, a DoE official who had drafted Heseltine's report after the Toxteth disturbances in 1981, entitled 'It Took a Riot'. Sure enough, when Sorensen's final report was submitted in late September, her Treasury Secretary, David Norgrove, told her that it 'lacks vigour and bite . . . What output are we achieving?' The underlining was Mrs Thatcher's.

Mrs Thatcher wanted to show her active interest so, in September 1987, she took off on a northern tour. At the Teesside Development Corporation in Stockton-on-Tees, she was photographed, alone except for her handbag, standing in the grounds of the derelict Head Wrightson ironworks. Pictures of what was branded 'the Walk in the Wilderness' became both instantly famous and a liability, seeming to present her as the cause of northern industrial decay, not the cure.*

From the summer onwards, a power struggled ensued between Clarke

---

* Mrs Thatcher's televisual error had been to stand among the ruins, in smart office clothes, without displaying any visible means by which things could be put right. It was notable, nearly thirty years later, that when the Conservative Chancellor, George Osborne, developed his concept of the Northern Powerhouse he was always careful to be photographed in a hard hat and on a site where something was being built or made.

and Ridley over inner-city policy. Increasingly concerned about presentation, Ingham favoured Clarke, but others, such as Robert Armstrong, felt the matter rested properly with Ridley. Mrs Thatcher proved reluctant to bring the matter to a head. Ridley was, in this matter, more troublesome for her than Clarke. His free-market beliefs made him mistrust interventions skewed to favour a particular area. 'Mr Ridley believes', wrote Norgrove to Mrs Thatcher, 'there is no such thing as inner city policy. There is only policy towards housing, transport, social services, blacks and so on . . .' She was sympathetic to Ridley's insistence that the subject was his department's business but knew he had no presentational skills. Besides, how could he sell a coordinated policy which he instinctively opposed? Often indecisive over disputes between colleagues, she dithered for six months. Only in December did she finally settle on Clarke.

She had resisted Clarke partly out of affection for Ridley, but also because she well knew he was not 'one of us'. What would be the point, she asked herself, of trying to Thatcherize social policy, only to find it hijacked by the same old state intervention against which she had set her face? Clarke, however, could see his way through this problem. In his broad-brush manner, he felt he shared Mrs Thatcher's main aim for the inner cities, which was 'not just bulldozers' (as he saw the DoE's approach) but 'economic regeneration creating employment for the population'. He also understood the need to show that 'our transformation of the British economy could benefit everybody' and reach the poorest parts of cities. Pugilistic by nature, he was as anxious as she to take on the 'very extreme left-wing councils and trade unions'. As Richard Wilson observed, Clarke, 'unlike most ministers, but like Mrs Thatcher, really, really liked arguing'. In the end, Clarke recalled, 'She left me alone. She was quite happy. She didn't think I was trying to undermine her.'

Mrs Thatcher was beginning to feel her way towards a general theory of urban life and what made it thrive – a theory of how 'society', the concept she allegedly rejected, develops or decays. In notes she scribbled for her party conference speech that autumn, she wrote of 'Cities as a focus, as a <u>whole</u> . . . Won't come back by sitting around waiting for handouts . . . Must have rules – to enable people to know where they stand and to help them do better than their best. Like architecture – have to observe rules.'*

---

* These words did not survive into the speech as delivered, but in Blackpool Mrs Thatcher did lament the modern planning system and physical environment of the inner cities, explaining how the right rules of architecture had been flouted. 'They [planners] replaced them [familiar city centres] with a wedge of tower-blocks and linking expressways, interspersed with token patches of grass and a few windswept piazzas, where pedestrians fear to tread.'

Eager for partners in the recovery of inner cities other than Labour councils, she pounced upon the work of Business in the Community (BiC), an organization set up by the Prince of Wales and chaired by her friend the leading businessman Sir Hector Laing. She liked Prince Charles's pioneering concept of 'community entrepreneurs' and enthusiastically met some of them privately in Liverpool.

By November, the Policy Unit warned against 'losing sight of our basic philosophy – that local leadership is the key source of initiative'. In Clarke's view, however, the most important thing was to hurry up and do something. He now chose several areas 'rather too rapidly because they were largely based on places we'd heard of' to receive 'Task Forces' of bright young officials. 'I ask for a policy,' Mrs Thatcher told him. 'All you give me is dry ice and lasers,' but she was not displeased to have the burden of this complicated subject lifted off her shoulders by the straight-shooting Clarke.

Bernard Ingham also understood that the inner-cities programme was more a symbol of government commitment than a set of exact policies. In the published report (based on Sorensen's document), he wanted 'before and after pictures' of successes. As always, he sought to place Mrs Thatcher at the heart of the presentation: 'I think it is very important for you to indicate you will be a "hands on" Prime Minister so far as inner cities go – for that is what will give confidence to all those you want to get involved with a development.' She underlined the words 'hands on' and 'confidence'.

Mrs Thatcher launched the report, *Action for Cities*, on 7 March 1988, with the restored Salford Quays on the cover. The bundle of announcements enabled her to declare that £3 billion would be spent on the inner cities over the next year, although only a small proportion was 'new money'.*

Her attitude to all of this was strongly affected by something far bigger in scale – the progress of Canary Wharf and the associated regeneration of the London Docklands, a project she and Heseltine had launched in 1981 (see p. 502). In July 1987, the secretive Canadian property developer Paul Reichmann stepped in after the withdrawal of other interests. Believing in Canary Wharf's future, Reichmann persuaded Mrs Thatcher to attend the project's launch to convince major banks that it would happen.† This illustrated in her mind Ingham's point in relation to the inner cities launch. She, personally, was the key to investor confidence. This in turn

---

* They included more Urban Development Corporations, more derelict-land reclamation, training programmes, funding for housing associations, roads, home improvements, City Technology Colleges and City Action Teams.

† In the early 1990s, Reichmann's property company, Olympia and York, went bust but, by the end of the decade, Reichmann returned, leading a new consortium which bought it back and achieved the long-term success he had foreseen.

helped give her confidence to throw herself into the politically unpromising arena of the inner cities.

She also saw the whole issue as necessary combat. Preparing her for her press conference, Ingham drafted her reply to an imaginary question: 'Is not your entire inner city policy designed to marginalise local government?' As so often, his draft answer (not used) almost uncannily captured her true thoughts: 'No. But equally we cannot allow anti-enterprise, spendthrift, irrelevant local government to condemn urban areas to deprivation for which the Government is then blamed. The attachment of some local authorities to high rates, gay rights, Nicaragua* and nuclear free zones does not offer much hope to their residents.'

As Ingham's fantasy press conference answer mentioned, one of the contentious activities of left-wing Labour councils was the promotion of gay rights. At the time, this was widely considered a fringe activity: an abuse of the councils' powers and money and, to many, objectionable in itself. There was a particularly strong feeling about the issue in relation to schools. A Harris poll from January 1988 found 83 per cent support for a ban on the promotion of homosexuality by schools and councils. In 1986, a stir had been caused by a book called *Jenny Lives with Eric and Martin*, about a young girl who lives with her father and his male lover. It contained photographs of her, clothed, in bed with them, apparently naked. It was reported to be available in the library of a Haringey school run by the Inner London Education Authority (ILEA).†

In March 1987, the issue came to Mrs Thatcher's attention after the leading backbench MP Dame Jill Knight sought to attach an amendment to the Local Government Bill to 'prevent local councils from promoting "positive images"‡ for homosexuals'. At Prime Minister's Questions, Knight begged for her support to stop 'very young children in our schools from being encouraged to grow up as homosexuals'. Mrs Thatcher praised her 'great concern for protecting family life' and encouraged her to 'bring the bill back' after the election. When Knight did just that, Mrs Thatcher arranged for her Private Member's Bill to become an amendment to the Local Government Bill – later notorious as 'Section 28' (of the resulting

---

* At this time Nicaragua was run by the Marxist Sandinista regime and was a fashionable cause on the left, particularly because the Sandinistas were actively opposed by the Reagan administration.
† In fact, the one and only copy of the book was not in a school library but available for loan to teachers from a central facility run by the ILEA.
‡ The phrase 'positive images' was used by the local authorities who themselves had such programmes for homosexuals.

Act). It sought to prevent any local authority from promoting homosexuality and 'the teaching in any maintained school of the acceptability of homosexuality as a pretended family relationship'.

Although the legislation was popular with the wider public, it caused outrage among gay activists, who saw it as vindictive and bigoted, and among many in the arts who saw it as an attack on free speech. Many in the gay rights movement – notably the actor Ian McKellen, who came out as gay in protest – saw the Bill as a watershed, both because they had failed to organize to stop it and because it radicalized many gay people. Section 28 also demonized Mrs Thatcher in the eyes of the movement. The Bill became law in May 1988.

Mrs Thatcher's own view was unambiguously, though not militantly, in favour of the legislation. Like many in her generation, she was almost completely ignorant of homosexuality. She disapproved of homosexual behaviour as part of her acceptance of traditional Christian teaching, but the subject did not preoccupy her. She worried more that children might be corrupted and the traditional family threatened. Her bigger motivation, however – almost an obsession – was the misuse of public money for ideological ends by left-wing councils. Thus it was that Section 28, though it concerned education, was included in a local government Bill. If it was vindictive in spirit, it was against the councils, not against gay people.

A couple called Dennison wrote to Mrs Thatcher to express their support for Section 28. She replied, in her own hand, on Easter Day: 'People are free to live their own lives in private,' she wrote, 'but should not expect to flaunt their lifestyle on the local authority rates to the offence of their fellow citizens.' To someone of her generation these would have seemed almost uncontroversial thoughts, but they were not. It was repealed in Scotland in 2000 and in the rest of the United Kingdom in 2003. Nowadays, schoolchildren are taught about the shameful past persecution of gay people. Section 28 is held up as a prize exhibit.

28
Schools, AIDS and health
'Do we have to do the section on Risky Sex?'

Writing, as so often, without punctuation, Mrs Thatcher scribbled:

> If you are not taught some facts
> you wont have much to think
> If you are not taught memory at school
> You will miss a lot in life and restrict your future abilities
> If you are not taught methods of thought
> You won't know where to start.

These jottings, for her 1987 party conference speech, summarized her attitude to what should be taught and why. She was interested in what she described as 'the basic deposits in the bank of the mind to draw on for ever more'. She believed that British education had done far too little to secure and build up those deposits.*

It was surprising for a British prime minister to be seriously interested in education, a subject traditionally viewed as too 'female' to command the interest of top-rank men. Mrs Thatcher's long-standing interest regained urgency after the Conservatives were badly beaten in the Brecon and Radnor by-election in July 1985. Told that low education standards had become a major issue, she concluded there were votes to be won. In the following May's reshuffle she replaced Keith Joseph as Education Secretary with the much bouncier figure of Kenneth Baker. Although Baker was originally a Heath man, his energy and presentational skills had captured her attention.

The legislation being prepared became known as GERBIL (the Great Education Reform Bill). It was not as herbivorous as it sounded, but highly

---

* Another symptom of Mrs Thatcher's concern for 'the bank of the mind' was her constant refusal, going against her other instincts about public expenditure, to make people pay for library books: 'People must always have access to pull themselves up – that is why I will *never* have charges for libraries.'

ambitious. By inventing 'grant-maintained' schools, which could vote to opt out of local-authority control and manage their own affairs with central government money, it broke the council monopoly which, as in so many other areas of social policy, Mrs Thatcher detested. A new class of schools called City Technology Colleges (CTCs), partially funded from private sources (though not by fees), would come into being.* A National Curriculum for schools would be introduced for the first time. Higher and further education would also be removed from local-authority control. Academic tenure would be abolished at universities.

Although Mrs Thatcher and Baker agreed on the broad aims, she was obsessed, largely justifiably, with the fear that DES officials would try to thwart the government's plans, and considered Baker liable to cave in. Brian Griffiths maintained vigilance on her behalf. She told him, 'If I retire, I should really like to run a school.' This, obviously, was fantasy, but her attitude to Baker was a bit like that of a head teacher to a bright new head of department – friendly encouragement, tempered by anxiety and a tendency to interfere.

As Baker's proposed solutions gathered pace, Griffiths was quite prepared to denounce them to the headmistress where necessary. On the National Curriculum and on grant-maintained (GM) schools, for example, there were serious disagreements over the extent of centralization required. No. 10 sought to keep intervention to a minimum, while many at the DES saw a chance to augment their power and money. The GM schools, Griffiths told Mrs Thatcher in July 1987, were 'the jewel in the crown of the forthcoming Education Bill' but would come to nothing if the department strangled them with excessive restrictions. She underlined Griffiths's argument that Baker's approach would be 'far too dirigiste'.

At the same time, Griffiths reported that the planned National Curriculum had become appallingly over-elaborated. Instead of concentrating on raising minimum standards and improving the 3Rs (reading, writing and arithmetic), Baker was now proposing ten prescribed curriculum subjects, no pass or fail, a single authority over public examinations and an intrusive inspectorate. Supporters of the reforms would be 'desperately unhappy',

---

* Mrs Thatcher was keen that these colleges should be genuinely technological, and was therefore suspicious of Baker's suggestion of a City Arts College for the performing arts. 'Emphasis on the performing arts does not seem right for special grants ... We are NOT short of such people,' she wrote. Such students would almost certainly be left-wing. Baker recalled that 'I could only persuade her by making it seem like a technical school for sound recordists.' The result, funded as a CTC, was the BRIT School for Performing Arts and Technology in Croydon, whose students eventually included Amy Winehouse and Adele.

Griffiths warned, while 'progressive educationalists will judge them as a Thatcherite takeover. We risk pleasing no one.'

Mrs Thatcher raised these concerns with Baker, but his revised document offered No. 10 little comfort. Although he made much of his newly invented distinction between 'core' subjects – maths, science, English – and the lesser, more numerous 'foundation' subjects, David Norgrove, Mrs Thatcher's private secretary, dismissed this as 'cosmetic'. As Norgrove explained, there would still be 'no such thing as passing and failing' – a point which she underlined. Overall, he wrote, 'this is a long way from your own conception of minimum requirements to be set in three or four subjects with "driving test" assessments'.

Hostilities resumed after the summer break, with Baker demanding 800 extra inspectors to monitor the implementation of the National Curriculum. 'It is utterly ridiculous,' Mrs Thatcher wrote. 'The result will come through in tests and exams ... It is also a very autocratic approach – a "takeover" of edn by DES through the inspectorate.' 'Try to knock it out immediately,' she ordered Griffiths. By the end of October, the struggle had become sufficiently heated for Baker to protest over the minutes of the education Cabinet committee, E(EP), which he felt recorded conclusions over the National Curriculum to which he had not agreed.

By questioning the minutes, Baker was implying dishonesty. Such a grave charge risked producing a breakdown of process, as had happened during the Westland crisis (see pp. 507–14). 'But the minutes are *accurate*,' declared Mrs Thatcher, having reviewed the original notes. 'The record must not be changed.' Informal negotiations followed and Baker, not wishing to imitate Heseltine, swiftly backed away from his complaint.

Mrs Thatcher's disagreements with Baker, particularly those over the National Curriculum, revealed a contradiction at the heart of her education reforms. Like the poll tax, they were both decentralizing and centralizing. She genuinely sought to return power to parents, head teachers and schools; but the agent enabling this was the central government. As Griffiths admitted, 'The state became more powerful than she or I would have wanted.'

By the same token, the establishment of a National Curriculum was an invitation to everyone who wished to control the minds of children to pitch in.* As the lead department, the DES selected the National Curriculum

---

* Something similar happened in the discussions in E(EP) committee, in which Cabinet ministers would air random views based on their memories of their own schooldays and try to influence the curriculum accordingly. 'I loved art,' Nicholas Ridley liked to recall, 'hated PE.'

working parties for each subject. The results often dismayed Griffiths, who passed on his anxieties to Mrs Thatcher. History, perhaps predictably, proved incredibly fraught. Even after Baker selected an aristocratic former naval commander, L. M. M. Saunders Watson, as the working party's chairman, Griffiths found the group's proposals 'extremely disturbing'. This is 'the New History!' he protested to Mrs Thatcher, referring to a fashionable school of thought which exalted 'skills' and 'concepts' above narrative and facts. 'This won't do at all,' she responded. 'Better not have a core curriculum than one based on this.' To her private secretary, Paul Gray, she expressed irritation that the working group had such a free hand: 'I thought our purpose was to <u>tell</u> them some of things that must be taught.' The working party, meanwhile, resented what they saw as 'very strident rubbishing' of their work by Mrs Thatcher's supporters in the press.

Mrs Thatcher was equally disappointed over proposals for the study of English, which had little to say about grammar and rejected English tests. It was, complained Griffiths, much too 'child-centred': 'The alternative view that there is a body of knowledge which exists outside of the child and his/her experience which the child needs to be taught in order to develop into a mature adult is absent.' Mrs Thatcher ticked this point. She was viscerally opposed to views of education which looked inwards to the child rather than outwards to the world.* On this, Kenneth Baker held similar views. He changed the draft National Curriculum to require that pupils should be able to write formal Standard English by the end of their compulsory education (the age of sixteen). 'Very good,' wrote Mrs Thatcher.

The introduction of the National Curriculum opened up an unexpected front in one of the trickiest areas in British education – religion. Since the Butler Education Act of 1944, a collective act of worship and the teaching of religion had been the only educational elements compulsory in all state schools. Could this be the moment to remove these provisions or, conversely, should religious education become part of the core curriculum? Was it time to institutionalize a more multi-faith form of religious education?

In the Lords, Caroline Cox, a conservative Christian sociologist, set about tabling amendments to ensure that the new Act provided for explicitly Christian religious instruction in schools. Both Michael Alison and

---

* Mrs Thatcher also had a strong belief, inculcated in her childhood, in the importance of being taught great poetry and learning it by heart. One day, at a meeting in which she made this point, she launched into a recitation of a poem by Robert Browning and then dried up halfway through. 'Well, Mr Wilson,' she demanded of the nearest civil servant, 'what comes next?' and seemed quite surprised when he didn't know.

Brian Griffiths supported her efforts. Mrs Thatcher herself wanted the law to ensure that schools could teach 'the essentials of the Christian faith'. This should include 'good teaching about the Bible', she told Baker. 'Otherwise, children could not appreciate the culture, history and way of life of their own country.' The trouble was that the Christian Church leaders, fearing demands for compensatory rights to teach in schools from other faiths, or even atheists, did not really agree with her. Although she did not like this, Mrs Thatcher quickly understood it and concluded that the government could not support Lady Cox's amendments. A compromise was reached whereby teaching and worship in schools would 'in the main reflect the broad traditions of Christian belief'.

More annoying to Mrs Thatcher was the opposition of the Church leaders to allowing schools to 'opt out' of existing management structures. A large minority of publicly funded schools were Church ('voluntary-aided') schools. While she sought greater independence for each school and greater parental choice, the Church, wishing to maintain influence, clung to the status quo.*

Mrs Thatcher found these episcopal difficulties tiresome. In May 1988, ahead of a lunch in Downing Street for the Swedish Prime Minister, she cast her eye over the seating plan. 'Why are you sitting so far off?' she asked the British Ambassador to Sweden, Sir John Ure. 'You're an ambassador. You should be higher up.' Ure explained that ambassadors have higher precedence in the country where they serve, 'but they don't count for much in their own country. It's the exact opposite with bishops.' 'Well,' said Mrs Thatcher, 'as far as I'm concerned, bishops don't count for much here.'

Amid the immense problems of schools reform, Mrs Thatcher took solace from her belief that her approach would ultimately prove popular. A highly visible example of this phenomenon arose in Scotland, where good political opportunities for the Conservatives were few and far between. In the autumn of 1987, it emerged that the Labour-controlled Strathclyde Council wanted to close the ancient and popular Paisley Grammar School. The fight to save this school could 'easily mark the turning point of Thatcherism in Scotland', Griffiths advised Mrs Thatcher; failure to do so would 'be another nail in our coffin north of the border'. With her support, fast-tracked legislation empowered the Secretary of State for Scotland to

---

* An extreme example was the Archbishop of Westminster, Cardinal Hume, who saw the opportunity for individual schools to opt out as an assault on his authority and hence on the Church itself. The very successful Cardinal Vaughan School in his archdiocese elected to opt out, with the parents strongly supportive, but he threatened to prevent it by illegally replacing the governors and imposing compliant ones. Hume was eventually forced to back down.

prevent the closure of any school with enough pupils to survive. 'For once,' Griffiths enthused, 'the Tories in Scotland are seen to be backing a popular issue!' Paisley was saved. Griffiths urged her to pursue the campaign further, legislating to allow schools to opt out of local-authority control across Scotland. This was achieved in 1989, but it never really took off. The parents of Paisley Grammar voted heavily against opting out in 1993.

Seen nationally, however, the effects of the reforms were huge and, in many cases, successful. GERBIL became law on 29 July 1988. Three months later, Griffiths sent Mrs Thatcher a note listing the main changes. For schools, these included financial delegation, the National Curriculum, grant-maintained schools, City Technology Colleges. There would also be new funding arrangements for universities and polytechnics, with the latter made independent of local authorities.*

Almost all these reforms persisted into the twenty-first century. The model of higher standards nationally imposed and greater freedom for individual schools to achieve, though threatened by the government of Sir Keir Starmer, remains dominant today. Mrs Thatcher is loudly praised for her achievement in council house sales, but more often criticized for her educational reforms. Yet both effected an emancipation. Her invention of the National Curriculum, on the other hand, has, as she herself feared, led to creeping nationalization.

In only one area of school policy did Mrs Thatcher refuse to consider innovation. In May 1989, the Health Secretary, Kenneth Clarke, informed her he wished to end free milk for children in day care, which would save £4 million a year. This awakened evil memories of her 'milksnatcher' furore in 1970. 'No,' she replied, 'this will cause a terrible row . . . I know – I went through it 19 years ago . . . Any scheme for saving £400 million or more I will look at. But not £4 million.'

By the mid-1980s, AIDS (Acquired Immune Deficiency Syndrome)† had become a problem recognized across the Western world. Mrs Thatcher was informed that, by the end of August 1985, 206 cases of the disease had been confirmed in the United Kingdom and 114 patients had died. In the view of the Chief Medical Officer, Sir Donald Acheson, it was likely that the virus that caused AIDS could be transmitted heterosexually as well as

---

* The replacement of block grants with per capita funding made it easier, in time, to introduce a system of student loans and to permit expansion of numbers.
† This disease later became known as 'HIV/AIDS', reflecting the classification of the transmittable virus (HIV) that leads to the onset of AIDS. In these early years, however, the condition was referred to simply as 'AIDS'.

homosexually. More public information was needed. 'We have to walk a difficult tightrope between being accused of bureaucratic inertia,' David Willetts of the Policy Unit wrote to Mrs Thatcher, 'and being so active as to whip up public hysteria.' Willetts recommended she show her concern by visiting the Blood Products Laboratory in Elstree: 'It combines attractive themes – high-quality British science, action to protect innocent victims of AIDS, and spending on health infrastructure.'

This 'tightrope' made the subject of AIDS a difficult one. If Mrs Thatcher were thought to be ignoring it she could be depicted as complacent or prudish. It might be taken to imply prejudice against homosexuals, the main bearers and victims of the disease. If, on the other hand, she intervened, she would raise the political temperature. She also had to consider public attitudes. A clue to this lay in Willetts's use of the word 'innocent'. A widespread view at this time was that, if the disease was spread by homosexual promiscuity and/or drug abuse, blame should attach to those involved. Therefore the 'innocent' victims of AIDS were, for example, the children of drug-addicted prostitutes, or haemophiliacs who had received transfusions of contaminated blood. The implication was that victims who were not 'innocent' were guilty.

Although Mrs Thatcher was later accused of 'homophobia' (a coinage little used at the time), there is no recorded incident of her expressing a view about the strictly moral question described above. Her main concern, as so often, was to establish the facts. 'She did believe in evidence: she was a scientist,' recalled one official, but the problem with AIDS was that 'Nobody knew what would happen.'

As public anxiety mounted, pressure grew for a big publicity campaign. In February 1986, Willetts informed Mrs Thatcher that 'Norman Fowler is proposing to place explicit and distasteful advertisements about AIDS in all the Sunday papers.' If this sounded like advice against doing so, it was not: 'The AIDS problem is now so serious that we must do as he proposes.' Mrs Thatcher duly reviewed the proposed advertisement. 'Do we <u>have</u> to do the section on Risky Sex?' she wrote. 'I should have thought it would do immense harm if young teenagers were to read it.' She feared putting into the minds of young people sexual practices, notably anal intercourse, which might not otherwise, in that pre-internet age, have occurred to them. Her views drew no support from the Home Affairs Committee, but she persisted: 'It would be better in my view to follow the [wartime] "VD" precedent of putting notices in surgeries, public lavatories etc.' Fowler pleaded with her: 'Given that there is no vaccine and no cure the <u>only</u> option open is public education.' He begged that mention of anal intercourse, 'which has been linked with 85 per cent of AIDS cases so far', should remain. After carefully marking an article in the *Lancet* which set out all the risky practices in detail, Mrs Thatcher reluctantly agreed.*

As the number of AIDS cases grew, her caution persisted. 'AIDS is probably the most important public health issue this century,' Willetts warned her private office in October, yet 'There is a perception that the Government in general, and the Prime Minister in particular, is reluctant to treat the issue with the seriousness it deserves.' Robert Armstrong now proposed a new Cabinet subcommittee devoted to AIDS public education, chaired not by the Prime Minister but by Willie Whitelaw. This she accepted. The desire to keep her away, Armstrong recalled, stemmed in part from a concern that she 'might be too ready to regard AIDS as being in the nature of a divine judgment on homosexuals'. But the 1980s was also a time when men were embarrassed to talk in front of women about the details of sexual behaviour, especially when the woman in question was someone as serious as Mrs Thatcher. There was always a certain amount of giggling sympathy among ministers and officials for anyone who had to talk to her about sexual matters. It was much easier with dear old Willie in the chair.

At the end of 1986, it was expected that deaths from AIDS in Britain would reach 4,000 by 1990. Mrs Thatcher nonetheless opposed Fowler's plan for a television ministerial public-health broadcast in early 1987, fearing it would create 'an atmosphere of panic and crisis'. Discussing it in Downing Street on New Year's Eve, Fowler noted in his diary, she was 'at her best – relaxed, intelligent, sympathetic. She has difficulties in her attitudes to AIDS. She recognises it as a profoundly serious health threat but another part of her would like to see us putting all our efforts into reducing waiting lists or giving further help in other disease areas.' No doubt Mrs Thatcher's stated reasons for opposing the broadcast were genuine, but she may also, with her eternal job insecurity, have disliked the idea of a minister attracting so much publicity.

In her approach to AIDS, Mrs Thatcher needed to have regard to the views of her natural supporters.† They were expressed to her by Hartley

* The only remaining objection to the advertisement came from Lord Hailsham, the Lord Chancellor. 'I am convinced that there must be some limit to vulgarity,' he wrote, adding in his precise hand: '... and illiteracy. "Sex" means that you are either male or female. It does not mean the same thing as sexual practices. Nor does "having sex" mean anything at all.'

† Such anxieties affected even matters such as honours. In 1988, privately discussing a possible knighthood for a Conservative MP whom she knew to be homosexual, she had to confront the rumour that he might have AIDS: 'Does it make any difference if he has AIDS?' she asked a private meeting. 'Perhaps it does. Better wait.' Her own views were not strong either way: she was more worried about the reaction of others.

Booth in her Policy Unit, who complained that by advocating the use of condoms the government was 'not stressing the importance of abstinence and faithfulness sufficiently'. Her favourite religious leader, the Chief Rabbi, Immanuel Jakobovits, argued similarly. She listened carefully to such complaints, but did remarkably little about them.*

Although she treated the subject of AIDS gingerly, Mrs Thatcher was always moved by dramatic examples of human suffering. In August 1989, she visited London's Mildmay Mission Hospital, the first AIDS hospice in Europe. Unlike most politicians on errands of compassion, she ensured her visit had no publicity and thus no potential political benefit. According to her private secretary, Caroline Slocock, she was anxious to avoid comparison with the Princess of Wales, who had recently been filmed visiting AIDS victims: 'To many, Diana was the beautiful young princess; Mrs T the ugly old witch.' In Slocock's view, she may also have feared being seen to condone homosexuality.

At the Mildmay, Mrs Thatcher met two men who were dying. One, an American, was suffering from delusions, and at first thought that he was not meeting the real Margaret Thatcher. When he realized that he was, Slocock recorded, he begged her to ring President Bush so that 'action is taken now to help people like him ... He is overexcited ... and it is very, very sad.' Mrs Thatcher behaved 'as if she has all the time in the world. She places her hand on his arm ... and listens, in a way that demonstrates that she is real, not a phantom, and is there because she cares and wishes him well. He calms down in response. It is simple, human stuff, but I am in awe of it.'

A few days later Mrs Thatcher learnt that both patients had died 'peacefully'. She had handwritten a note of thanks to the Mildmay matron ('I

---

* It was also as a scientist that Mrs Thatcher took a particular interest in AIDS. According to Professor Raymond Dwek, who was a friend and colleague of the Nobel Prize-winning molecular biologist Max Perutz, Perutz met Mrs Thatcher in the summer of 1987 and warned her that 'she'd be remembered as the Prime Minister who failed to tackle AIDS'. In part because of this conversation, she allocated urgent government money to set up the Medical Research Council's AIDS Directed Programme and established what Dwek called 'a constant dialogue' with members of its steering committee, including himself. Dwek and Perutz worked on the development of antiviral drugs. Mrs Thatcher was aware that Dwek had secured a large industrial grant to work on sugar molecules attached to proteins. Her own scientific knowledge told her that this might be relevant to AIDS research because 'The HIV virus is covered with sugars.' Dwek believed that it was for this reason he was recruited for the AIDS work and considered that 'We wouldn't have got to the drug without her.' The relevant drug, a modification of the DNJ molecule, isolated from the leaves of mulberry trees, had too severe effects to be deployed against HIV/AIDS in the required doses, but was eventually used to treat Gaucher's disease. Dwek's summation was that 'The result of her intervention was that virology was stronger in the UK.'

learned so much and am very grateful'). With the letter she enclosed 'a small cheque to help with fund-raising' for £1,000 from her own resources.

One reason why Mrs Thatcher worried about too much government attention to AIDS was that she was even more concerned by the wider problems of the National Health Service. Aware that the NHS had the potential to destroy her electorally, her approach to reform was circumspect. She felt that the system delivered poor outcomes and was so constructed that, whatever extra money the government provided, 'you never see anything for it'. She longed for health reform to be part of her third-term drive to improve public services. But she reserved the right to move her foot from the accelerator to the brake. When Richard Wilson, working on health reform in the Cabinet Office, suggested the NHS should be broken up into its component parts, she disagreed. 'Oh no, Mr Wilson,' she replied. 'The Health Service is safe in our hands.' She stuck to this mantra, both in public and in private, and probably believed it.*

As early as 1984, David Willetts had written the first government paper on the 'internal market' – the idea that there should be a 'purchaser/provider split' in health care by which those commissioning services were separated from those who supplied them, thus directing money more efficiently towards patients who needed it and exposing true costs. Discreet discussions of these ideas took place ahead of the 1987 election, but Mrs Thatcher did not dare offer explicit reform to the voters.

The subject had gone awry in the 1987 campaign after Mrs Thatcher's clumsy answers about the right to private treatment had fuelled the suspicion that she wished to privatize the service. Willetts advised her to reposition herself: 'I argued that we were in the worst of both worlds to be attacked for having a secret agenda on the NHS when we did not have one.' The Policy Unit agreed. Norman Blackwell and John O'Sullivan took the lead in developing 'a gradualist approach that would capture the benefits of markets while leaving open the long-term structure of health funding. We would compare them [health policies] to our present education policy.' 'Everyone knew you couldn't privatize the NHS,' recalled O'Sullivan. 'It was never an aim.' The aim was 'to deal with demand' – the way extra injections of money disappeared with little tangible benefit – 'and with

---

* At one point in the discussion of reform, the Treasury began to oppose reference in documents to 'the National Health Service' as the name for the future shape of health care, preferring quietly to jettison it in favour of the looser phrase 'a health care system that is once again the envy of the world'. This change of nomenclature would have made it easier to introduce radical reform of the system. Mrs Thatcher never countenanced it.

blame' – the way problems were always seen as the fault of politicians, never the producer-dominated service itself.

In her post-election reshuffle, Mrs Thatcher replaced Norman Fowler at the Department of Health and Social Security (DHSS) with John Moore. Moore, aged forty-nine, was one of the rising generation of Conservative politicians – others included John Major, Chris Patten, Norman Lamont, William Waldegrave, Michael Portillo and Peter Lilley – whom Richard Wilson remembered as 'young men who caught each other's eye ... They performed for her, but marked each other's performance. She was beginning to be a figure of another generation.' Many believed she had singled out Moore as her preferred successor. She certainly had a high regard for Moore, who was ideologically sound and a gifted performer on television. Yet in appointing him to the DHSS she did him few favours. 'She didn't charge me with bringing about change at all,' he recalled. 'She saw it in terms of presenting things better.' It is not easy to present something well if you have little to present and neither Moore nor his boss had clear ideas about how to proceed. At the party conference that October, Moore's speech was poorly received.

Matters did not improve after John Major, the new Chief Secretary to the Treasury and leading rival for the role of Mrs Thatcher's blue-eyed boy, persuaded Moore to seek too little money for the DHSS in the upcoming spending round. According to Richard Wilson, Major said to Moore: '"You know the PM will expect you not to be too demanding on the NHS." He played him quite cunningly. Moore took the bait.' Although Moore himself denied this hotly, the Major version of events prevailed in people's minds. The Health Service unions noticed Moore's defeat and fought back. Unrest within the NHS followed, projecting a sense of crisis that went beyond the customary seasonal routine.* This called for decisive leadership, but the government appeared unwilling or unable to oblige.

The strain proved too much for Moore. In late November 1987, he collapsed during a meeting with Mrs Thatcher and had to be taken, unconscious, to a hospital which, by no choice of his own, was private. The strain was also visible on Mrs Thatcher herself. A few days after Moore's collapse she felt giddy and almost fainted at a reception at Buckingham Palace.† Pressure continued to build for action. Although she had an instinctive dislike for reviews and inquiries, by December, noted David Norgrove, Mrs

---

* Unrest in the NHS usually became most apparent in the run-up to Christmas when ministers were most sensitive to media attacks about being Scrooge-like. This time, however, it began earlier and with greater intensity.
† Mrs Thatcher tended to faint when tired because she suffered from low blood pressure.

Thatcher was 'prepared to think seriously about holding an inquiry (not a Royal Commission) into the future of the NHS'.*

Blackwell and O'Sullivan now warned her of 'a Tory version of the Winter of Discontent' of 1978–9. But they also sensed opportunity: 'We believe it is time to throw caution to the winds.' They advocated establishing 'a competitive market' within the NHS – words which Mrs Thatcher replaced with the more human phrase 'patients' choice'. These ideas were designed to counteract her latest, panicky view that NHS reform should be delayed until the next election. Such was the pressure for emergency cash that, on 16 December, the government produced another £100 million (with promises of a further £700 million the following year) to stave off political revolt. This came the day before the Commons vote on the poll tax, for which Michael Heseltine was fomenting trouble.

In this fraught period, Mrs Thatcher veered all over the place. Sometimes she rejected more spending; sometimes she called for it. She went back and forth on the inquiry into the future of the NHS. 'You slam door on desperate parents of children waiting for heart operations' (*Daily Mirror*) was one of many disturbing headlines Ingham passed on during these months. It was a bloody time and coincided with her maximum anxiety about Nigel Lawson's policy of shadowing the deutschmark (see pp. 656–7). She was on edge.

Moore returned to work in mid-January 1988, but he was far from recovered and unable to give a lead. The broader situation so alarmed Mrs Thatcher's former chief of staff, David Wolfson, that this normally reticent man intervened. 'I believe you are now more at risk than with the Falklands or Westland . . .' he wrote to her on 23 January. 'You are now unable to formulate a strategy to deal with a crisis which you maintain does not exist.' Knowing how best to make her feel insecure, he added, 'I read Geoffrey Howe's speech today as putting himself in a good position to authorise an "inquiry into the NHS".'† Wolfson was warning her, in effect, of her growing vulnerability to a leadership challenge. She knew that he always helped protect her position, so she took his warning seriously.

On 25 January, on BBC *Panorama*, Mrs Thatcher declared that the government would set up its own inquiry. She gained strong headlines proclaiming 'Maggie takes charge', while giving the impression that radical

---

* Mrs Thatcher disliked and avoided Royal Commissions because their complicated rules and procedures made them, in her view, an excuse for delay. She liked inquiries to be narrow and practical in their remit, and short.

† Howe's speech, to students in Liverpool, was ostensibly friendly to Mrs Thatcher, advocating an honest debate about the need for a mix of public and private provision, but Wolfson was probably reading its subtext correctly.

reform, including the 'internal market', would emerge. Her own policy entourage at last felt they had permission to press ahead. 'She'd burnt her boats,' judged Kenneth Clarke, probably deliberately. Reform now had to happen.

An 'NHS Working Group' came into being. Chaired by Mrs Thatcher, it included Moore, but also Lawson and Major. John O'Sullivan had warned her against a partnership between the Treasury, which 'sees reform of the NHS as a synonym for charging', and the DHSS, which was in thrall to medical pressure groups. Neither had 'a deep interest in money following the patient'. After O'Sullivan begged her to keep all options for reform open, she ensured he became part of the Working Group.

The progress of the group was complicated by the physical and political weakness of John Moore. He sought to separate 'the buying and provision of health care', but came up against a Chancellor who wanted to kill most of his ideas, a Policy Unit which, though sympathetic, doubted his capacities and a Prime Minister having great difficulty making up her mind.

Although, in March, O'Sullivan had told Mrs Thatcher that the Working Group had 'accepted such ideas' as money following the patient, the hospital self-management and possibly GPs as budget-holders, much of the summer was consumed by arguments with Lawson, who feared that such reforms would undermine the Treasury's control of public-service finances.* The Chancellor was also against tax relief for those who took out private medical insurance because of the 'deadweight cost' of funding those previously paying their own way, and because, given the controversy over the poll tax, he fought shy of defending help to the better off.

A combination of Moore's department and the Treasury was trying to maintain the status quo. In May, O'Sullivan warned Mrs Thatcher that Moore's proposal for self-governing hospitals was rife with 'unnecessary' controls: 'The old bureaucratic Adam is reasserting itself.' Lawson piled on: 'What happens if the money runs out before the end of the year – is it realistic to think that we can tell a profligate buyer that he has made his bed and must lie in it?' As the Working Group began dithering again, O'Sullivan told her, 'A "mouse" of reform . . . would dispirit your own supporters . . . it would be presented in the media as a defeat for you. It would postpone any further health reform for a decade.'

While the real object of these warnings was Mrs Thatcher, the natural scapegoat was John Moore. At the end of July, she removed him from his

---

* As with the poll tax and with grant-maintained schools, the Treasury opposed financial freedoms for individual institutions, such as hospitals or GP practices, which would weaken its control over, for example, the wages of nurses and doctors.

post, splitting the gigantic DHSS into its component parts. Moore stayed at Social Security but lost Health. His time at Health, he reflected later, 'ultimately destroyed me'. Mrs Thatcher, he complained, was not committed to reform: 'What she wanted was peace.' He had endured an utterly miserable time under a boss who, though she liked him, had not properly supported him.

John Moore was replaced by Kenneth Clarke. In some important ways, Clarke had 'flatly different' ideas from Mrs Thatcher about health policy. She firmly believed that a person who could afford private care was right to do so, partly because this freed up NHS space for those who could not. Clarke, however, believed in the essential, original concept of the NHS – the best vehicle for 'the delivery of health care regardless of wealth on the basis of need'. Unlike Mrs Thatcher, he had always used its services. Nonetheless, Clarke was the right man for the task in hand. While never 'right-wing', he came to think that Mrs Thatcher had proved him and his fellow Wets wrong in accepting the post-war economic consensus. He shared her readiness to take on the producer interest in the public services and, like her, enjoyed an argument. 'I could stand the heat of the kitchen,' he boasted, the kitchen in which poor John Moore had melted.

In September 1988, Clarke presented Mrs Thatcher with his preliminary thoughts. His chief proposal was that the money should 'flow to those GPs who were most responsive to the needs of their patients, and to those hospitals that were most efficient and cost-effective in providing treatment'. Unlike the Working Group, Clarke stated that 'The adoption of GP budgets would be fundamental.' Breezily egotistical, Clarke erroneously believed that she – and indeed everyone else – 'had not contemplated this' before. Sensing she 'flatly disagreed', he sought to persuade her. 'Boy, did she oblige me to do some work,' he recalled. 'Very disappointing & sketchy,' she wrote, in headmistress mode, on one of his early papers. According to Clarke, 'She loved a bloody great row about policy. I tried to bury her under paper. You'd find she'd read every word . . . She'd take you apart and leave you bruised and you'd revise things. Rows with Margaret did you a lot of good.' One paper over which she had scribbled heavily was praised by the Policy Unit as 'very much better than anything we have had to date'. It could discern a welcome pattern into which Clarke's ideas could fit: 'The Government is loosening its control over education and housing. Kenneth Clarke's paper needs to reflect a faster pace of change in health.'

Formidable obstacles remained – chiefly the Treasury. 'Yet again,' the Policy Unit complained to Mrs Thatcher, 'the Treasury is attempting to destroy the concept of GP budgets.' Part of the purpose of the reforms was, as she put it privately, 'to distance decision making to the point of delivery of health service care'. She wanted to move from 'political to medical management of the NHS'. Lawson feared that this could go wrong. A self-governing hospital or GP practice could never be allowed to go bankrupt, so the government would end up footing the bill for local financial mismanagement. In the end, however, he conceded a real-terms increase in health spending of 4.5 per cent – the largest ever – in his Autumn Statement of November 1988. In his memoirs, Lawson glossed over most of the sharp disagreements. He considered the reforms a success with which he wished to be associated.

Towards the end of 1988, Mrs Thatcher used the drafting of the Health Service White Paper to enforce her will. She was very particular about the choice of language, excising anything which sounded too 'impersonal'. Patients, for example, should not be described as 'customers', nor self-governing hospitals as 'businesses'. Clarke unveiled the White Paper, entitled 'Working for Patients',* to Parliament on 31 January 1989. He was ever afterwards pleased with the support he received: 'She never wavered. Once you did a deal with Margaret your back didn't feel uncomfortable.'

For Mrs Thatcher's video message for the launch of the White Paper, Ingham suggested 'At its best, Britain's National Health Service is without equal. Time and again, we have all seen just how much we owe to those who work in it.' Against this she wrote: 'The nation has – I haven't been treated in it myself.' This was literally the case. In her childhood and youth, the NHS had not existed. In her adult life, she had invariably gone private, supported by Denis. She therefore had no share in – and so less understanding of – the joys and sorrows of the Health Service known to most people. To her credit, she was both too cautious and too honest to imply that she had.

In his memoirs, Kenneth Clarke sought to contrast his own unwavering support for 'the founding principles of the NHS' with Mrs Thatcher's preferred approach. 'Margaret was privately convinced', he wrote, 'that the US insurance-based model was the ideal system to follow.' But Mrs Thatcher, the conservative ideologue sounding off behind the scenes, was often quite unlike Mrs Thatcher the pragmatic Prime Minister. Throughout

---

* Much agony was expended over the title. 'Caring for the 1990s', suggested Clarke, but Mrs Thatcher objected crossly: 'what does "Caring for the 1990s" mean??!! Don't we care now? And it's not the years but the patients we care for.'

her time in office she never made a serious attempt to dismantle the NHS, let alone privatize it.

What was remarkable about Mrs Thatcher and Kenneth Clarke was not how much they disagreed but – in practice – how little. He had learnt to be more Thatcherite, while she understood that public support for reform rested on a belief that the NHS was safe in Tory hands. Today, the basic principle of the 'purchaser–provider split', which Clarke introduced, endures. Hospital trusts and GP fundholding (nowadays called 'clinical commissioning') remain the basic units of the split system, yet the ills of the NHS increase.

29

The shadow of Lawson

'You can't buck the markets'

At Mrs Thatcher's insistence, the 1987 Conservative manifesto had made no mention of British entry into the Exchange Rate Mechanism (ERM). The official line, that Britain would join 'when the time is right', masked a growing and dangerous disagreement at the heart of government. During the second term, Nigel Lawson had tried – and failed – repeatedly to persuade Mrs Thatcher to accept ERM membership. Rumours of divisions appeared in the press, but the extent of her opposition remained hidden from all but a select few.

Lawson cared so much about the subject because he had, some time before (see Chapter 20), lost faith in the monetarist doctrine he had formerly so eloquently expounded. As inflation began to rise, he sought salvation in exchange rate management – if he could not join the ERM, he would replicate it. Mrs Thatcher, however, retained her monetarist faith and was alarmed that Lawson might be throwing away the key to the control of inflation.* Under the tutelage of Alan Walters, she vehemently opposed any effort to fix exchange rates. She was even more uneasy about a European scheme to do so because she understood that the project was political as well as financial.

On 10 June 1987, the day before polling, David Norgrove, Mrs Thatcher's Treasury private secretary, warned her of a 'widespread expectation that we shall become full members of the EMS† after the election. It will

---

* Having reached a twenty-year low of 2.4 per cent over the summer of 1986, inflation rose to 4.5 per cent by the autumn. By the time of Mrs Thatcher's 1987 election victory, it was causing real concern.

† Strictly speaking, Britain was in the European Monetary System (EMS) throughout Mrs Thatcher's time in office, but not in the ERM. The EMS was a project launched by the EEC in 1979 to stabilize exchange rates with the eventual aim of monetary union. The debate, as Norgrove wrote, was about becoming a 'full member', which meant joining the ERM of the EMS, thus tying the national currency to particular parities (within bands). Officials and ministers sometimes elided the difference between the two things.

be a priority for the Chancellor.' Norgrove wanted to avoid a repeat of the disastrous meeting of senior ministers in November 1985 (see p. 494) at which Mrs Thatcher had stood alone against ERM membership. Views had not shifted, Norgrove warned, so further discussion of the issue 'could well prove exceptionally difficult ... You could again find yourself isolated.' One option could be to tell Lawson she remained opposed and refuse any further discussion, but: 'You will want to consider whether that would be a sustainable position, in view of the support the Chancellor would receive from the Foreign Secretary and possibly others also.' Such thinking reveals what a strange position she was in. Despite her third consecutive election victory making her seem mistress of all she surveyed, Mrs Thatcher was being advised – almost certainly correctly – that she would not prevail over a central matter of economic policy.

Following the November 1985 meeting, Mrs Thatcher had, as Charles Powell put it, become 'convinced Nigel and Geoffrey were scheming against her on the ERM'. Both Howe and Lawson denied this, but they kept in close touch. John Kerr, who had been principal private secretary to both men and was intimate with Howe, believed they had decided that 'Geoffrey should stay out of the ERM argument, so that it could be made on economic grounds alone.' Howe's leadership ambitions were well known. Lawson's one remaining ambition, after Chancellor, was to be Foreign Secretary.* The only mutually satisfactory way a vacancy could be created was if Howe were to become prime minister. It would be an exaggeration to say there was a plot against Mrs Thatcher at this stage, but she had reason to feel uneasy.

At the beginning of July, Alan Walters furnished Mrs Thatcher with his thoughts for the coming battle. ERM entry, he insisted, would be 'a gift to speculators', increase uncertainty for investors and make interest rates more volatile. To Willie Whitelaw, Mrs Thatcher stressed her implacable opposition to ERM entry, hoping he might prepare the ground with Lawson. As so often, however, Whitelaw was trying to play both sides in what he saw as the interests of Cabinet unity. His efforts left Mrs Thatcher feeling comforted but Lawson emboldened.

On 27 July, at his regular bilateral with the Prime Minister, Lawson argued that now, post-election and with the reserves much stronger, was a good time to enter the ERM. He reminded her of her earlier view that 'the first year of a new Parliament would be the right time'. He was not, he stressed, 'a great believer in UK membership of the European Community,

---

* In retirement, Lawson explained that he felt that 'the party at that time wouldn't want someone of Jewish descent as leader. So I didn't bother to make friends.'

but this was one of the few areas where membership had benefits to offer'. Mrs Thatcher disagreed. She emphasized how, since 1979, Britain had built up its own reputation for prudence. Joining the ERM would imply that we needed 'the restraint provided by Germany and the Deutchmark [*sic*]'. She threw in most of Walters's arguments, adding some of her own. By reducing exchange rate flexibility, ERM entry would 'lead to higher unemployment'.

Lawson countered with an argument unlikely to appeal to her, stressing that the government was, in any case, 'bound by the reactions of business and the markets. Membership had clearly helped France during its difficulties.' Mrs Thatcher retorted that imprudent France was quite different from steady Britain. 'The two', Norgrove felt, 'were completely missing one another's arguments.' Mrs Thatcher also suffered because, while vehemently opposed to the ERM, she had no ready alternative. When Lawson suggested they revisit the issue in the autumn, she insisted she wanted no further ERM discussion until the new year.

Greatly dismayed, Lawson felt that Mrs Thatcher had gone back on her promise: 'I could never trust her completely again.' But, according to his then private secretary, Alex Allan, there was no sense at the time that trust had broken down. Nor did Mrs Thatcher see the meeting as a climacteric. For now, Lawson realized there was little more he could do. As he put it, 'my political position was stronger than it had ever been before: I had been widely credited, much to her annoyance, with being the true author of the 1987 election victory. But by the same token Margaret, as the leader who had just won a third election victory in succession – an unprecedented achievement – was at the peak of her authority.' The two were locked in conflict, each made impotent by the other's eminence. Their mutual unease at clashing directly meant that communication began to break down.

Lawson had for some time been pursuing by other means the policy which Mrs Thatcher continued to forbid. In February 1987, the G7 (minus Italy) had agreed the Louvre Accord, which aimed to stabilize the dollar and, by extension, international exchange rates. Lawson used its slipstream to pursue a new policy to reduce the pressure on sterling. He indicated to journalists that the current rate of DM2.80 would now be the floor for sterling and that there would be a ceiling too (taken to be DM3). Lawson was pursuing an exchange rate target without quite saying so. He intended to replace this with ERM membership after the election. The policy which came to be known as 'shadowing the deutschmark' had begun.

It was not publicly so described by its Treasury authors. Peter Lilley, who became Economic Secretary to the Treasury after the election, concluded that 'Nigel was pursuing a highly contentious policy without having got clearance.' But others, such as Allan, argued that because it was never formally discussed with Mrs Thatcher, Lawson 'didn't need her agreement to pursue it'. The Treasury certainly never explained in explicit terms what it was up to. David Willetts, who came to the Policy Unit from the Treasury, considered that the Treasury 'tried to keep its papers away from her', relying instead on the Chancellor's weekly meeting with the Prime Minister. Lawson was determined to run his own show. He detected in Mrs Thatcher 'the desire to do it herself' and wanted to frustrate her.

The lack of Treasury paper was also, paradoxically, the result of the long-standing good relationship between Lawson and Mrs Thatcher. She had an almost maternal attitude to her Chancellor: 'I remember her telling him to get his hair cut,' recalled Norgrove. This relationship led Lawson to believe he could handle her more deftly than was the case. With the economy responding so well under Thatcherism, it was natural to skirt round their differences.

In the admittedly hostile view of Alan Walters, Lawson feared losing the argument: 'She'd anticipate what he was going to say. Nothing annoyed Nigel more than a woman anticipating him.' Mrs Thatcher was also gradually losing her trust in him. At bilaterals which Lawson remembered as productive, others recalled her as 'quite wary'. The record of such meetings never mentions the phrase 'shadowing the deutschmark'. It does, however, refer frequently to foreign exchange market interventions and the pursuit of exchange rate stability, so she was not completely in the dark. In Lawson's view, 'she knew perfectly well what I was doing'. Both were pursuing an unacknowledged policy of 'Don't ask; don't tell.'

With the election won, observers began to notice the failure of monetary discipline and the enormous growth in credit. In late June 1987, for example, the *Spectator* carried a cover cartoon of Lawson as Monty Python's Mr Creosote growing fatter and fatter* just before he explodes. The headline was 'Inflation returns'. The accompanying piece, by the leading monetarist Tim Congdon, pointed out that 'broad money' was out of control and bank lending was 25 per cent higher, in real terms, than during the worst excesses of the 1972 'Barber boom'.† Students of monetary policy began to sense that the Lawson magic might be too much of a good thing.

Lawson, well aware of the problem, often complained – with justice – that

---

* At this time, Lawson was noted for being increasingly tubby. After he left office he went on a famously successful diet.

† With the ERM being 'widely canvassed' as the solution to these economic problems, Congdon saw the real anchor as the independence of West Germany's central bank: Britain should

Mrs Thatcher was 'completely schizoid' about rises in interest rates needed to dampen down demand. Her love of prudence clashed with her support for 'our people' getting their feet on the housing ladder. In early August, she resisted his wish to raise rates by a further 1 per cent. Such a rise 'would look as if the Chancellor was defending a particular exchange rate prior to entry into the EMS'. Her suspicions had been aroused.

Lawson did his best to disregard Mrs Thatcher's views. In September 1987, in a speech not shown to her in advance, he told the IMF in Washington that he sought 'to build a more permanent regime of managed floating'. His move away from standard monetarism was pretty much complete. He still had a monetary account of inflation but had, in effect, contracted out the work to the Bundesbank. Even now, no change in government policy had been agreed. This was his way back towards ERM entry. Though she did not directly tell him so, Mrs Thatcher was angry. On 14 October, Norgrove told her that Eddie George, her favourite expert within the Bank of England, was concerned about the scale of intervention in the money markets ('in the last 24 hours . . . some $660 million') ordered by Lawson. The Chancellor's fixed-rate quest was becoming dangerously expensive.

Events, however, temporarily blew these anxieties away, replacing them with new ones. Over the night of 15–16 October, Southern England experienced the worst storm in living memory, with huge destruction and the loss of eighteen lives. On the following Monday – 19 October – a comparable storm hit shares. 'Stock prices across the world plunge up to 20 per cent,' declared Bernard Ingham's press digest. A year after the Big Bang in the City of London, some feared – and some hoped – that the great Reagan–Thatcher recovery of capitalism was collapsing. Following what became known as 'Black Monday', the tycoon Sir James Goldsmith telephoned Downing Street from New York and told Charles Powell that politicians were 'losing their heads completely' and 'the only person who can give a lead' was Mrs Thatcher. Shortly afterwards, she wrote a letter of tactful anxiety to President Reagan, welcoming his willingness to consider tax rises to tackle the budget deficit: 'The priority now has to be for sound money and sound finance.' In reply, Reagan gave her guarded comfort, agreeing that prompt action to control the 1988 budget was needed.

The crash, however, was good, at least temporarily, for Thatcher–Lawson relations. To keep the show on the road, she accepted his two proposed interest rate cuts, each of 0.5 per cent. She also supported his

---

make the Bank of England independent, he contended, then policy would not be debauched by electoral politics.

decision to proceed with the planned sale of the government's remaining BP shares, despite market turmoil.* This proved a success. Both Lawson and Mrs Thatcher emerged from the crash with their reputation for steady nerve enhanced. She felt, however, that the informal system of exchange rate management created after the Louvre Accord had helped cause it in the first place. Such intervention, she told Terry Burns, 'throws all the noise on to other markets'. She added she would 'never' join the ERM.

The simmering, half-acknowledged disagreements came to a head a few weeks later. On 23 November, under the headline 'Thatcher stands firm against full EMS role', the *Financial Times* carried an interview with the Prime Minister in which she questioned the efficacy of a managed international exchange rate system and opposed British entry to the ERM. In his press digest, Ingham added, 'You also deny that there is any exchange rate target for sterling or that the pound is unofficially tied to just under or about DM3.' The news story was strong because it challenged Lawson, though not by name. The most striking thing about the encounter, however, was how amazed Mrs Thatcher seemed when the *FT* interviewers showed her a chart suggesting that sterling was pursuing a DM3 exchange rate target. Peter Riddell, present, felt she seemed genuinely not to have understood before what had been happening. The scales now fell from her eyes, but they could surely have fallen earlier if she had wanted them to. Lawson believed she was shocked only at the possibility of his policy going public: 'To her it was slightly sinful, and she could sin only in private.'

The *FT* article prompted Brian Griffiths into a full denunciation of Lawson's approach, which Mrs Thatcher underlined excitedly. It has now become clear, he argued, that the Treasury, 'having been frustrated in their intention to join the EMS . . . have pursued a *de facto* policy regarding the £/DM rate as if we were full members'. He pointed to 'the inflationary potential of buying in foreign currency to protect the rate'. Mrs Thatcher now prepared to fight her Chancellor's policy.

The opportunity quickly presented itself. In early December, Mrs Thatcher was informed about Lawson's plan to switch interventions from buying dollars to buying deutschmarks, which, as a breach of EMS rules, had angered the German Bundesbank. She fastened on a broader point: 'Why intervene at all,' she scribbled to Charles Powell. 'We cannot go on day after day without having high inflation following.' Lawson continued to think differently. As he told the Commons Treasury Select Committee on 9 December, 'keeping [the pound] in line with the mark was likely over

---

* This course ran contrary to advice from the Bank of England, a great deal of City opinion, the Canadian government and James Baker, the US Treasury Secretary.

a period to be a strong anti-inflationary discipline'. He was still trying to force her to accept the policy she had denied. In the very short term, to avoid loss of market confidence, Mrs Thatcher felt she had to let Lawson do what he wanted.

At the end of 1987, Paul Gray succeeded David Norgrove as Mrs Thatcher's Treasury private secretary. He noted that she and Lawson never talked directly about shadowing the deutschmark and was 'conscious of a bad feeling' between them: 'She would fulminate. She was deeply uneasy.' In early March 1988, as the cost of intervention mounted, Gray sent her a recommendation by Brian Griffiths that sterling should be allowed to go through DM3. Appalled by the scale of intervention, which reached $1.8 billion in two days, on Friday 4 March Mrs Thatcher informed the Treasury that intervention should cease. Lawson resisted. So at Griffiths's suggestion, and somewhat improperly for a prime minister, she telephoned Eddie George and asked him, 'Are you in favour of getting out of shadowing?' George's answer was 'Yes.' He stressed how worried he was by the scale of intervention. She then saw Lawson twice that afternoon in 'fraught' meetings. Eventually he conceded that, on Monday morning, 'the rate should be allowed to go above DM3'. Lawson continued to argue, however, for more limited interventions as required. Mrs Thatcher told him sternly that on Monday they would need 'regular contacts at least every half hour between this office and your office'. The Chancellor's liberty was at an end. At 9.20 on the morning of Monday 7 March, the DM3 cap was removed from sterling.

On the ensuing Thursday, at Prime Minister's Questions, Mrs Thatcher was assailed. Neil Kinnock threw at her a CBI statement that the pound needed to stay below DM3, and then quoted Lawson's remark of 9 December about keeping the pound in line with the deutschmark as an anti-inflationary discipline. Did she agree with Lawson? She replied that she and Lawson were 'absolutely agreed' on the importance of getting inflation down, but 'The Chancellor never said that aiming for greater exchange rate stability meant total immobility. Adjustments are needed ... There is no way in which one can buck the market.'*

In the context of the controversy, this last sentence was subversive. For while Lawson was still attempting managed floating (with a new sterling

---

* Paul Gray, who was learning to spot how Mrs Thatcher would sometimes go 'off script' in her public pronouncements, wondered where she had got the phrase about bucking the markets. Then he met Denis Thatcher at a No. 10 reception. 'Suddenly Denis raised the subject of Lawson's policy and told me how awful it was. "I was talking to Margaret the other day," he recalled, "and I said to her 'You can't buck the markets.'"' She often used her husband's economic views to fortify herself in difficulty. She saw them as those of 'a commonsense businessman'.

target of DM 3.10), Mrs Thatcher had just declared it could not be done. The press seized upon this, making it appear that Lawson was being pushed into a corner by Mrs Thatcher – which indeed he was. He, however, had tried to push her into a corner; now she had her revenge. It was a wretched background against which to launch his Budget the following Tuesday.

On Friday 11 March, the atmosphere became still more unpleasant after Mrs Thatcher demanded changes to Lawson's Budget speech. She felt he was still trying 'to play God with the exchange rate', Griffiths told Terry Burns. This led to a 'stop press' drama in which the official Budget 'Red Book' had to be changed just before printing. Mrs Thatcher wanted monetary policy described without any reference to the exchange rate, but accepted Lawson's compromise, which acknowledged a continuing role for 'the objective of exchange rate stability'. This episode left a sour taste. In Lawson's mind, the Budget and shadowing the deutschmark 'came together in one issue: whether she trusted me'. It was now clear to him – though not, interestingly, to her – that she did not.

On that Monday, 14 March, Lawson saw the Queen for the Budget audience. He told her that this might be his last Budget, since Mrs Thatcher was 'making the conduct of policy impossible'. The Queen, he considered, was 'clearly sympathetic but appropriately non-committal'. Already Lawson was contemplating a way out. He consciously prepared the 1988 Budget as the culmination of his Chancellorship, so if necessary 'it could have been my grand finale'.

Annoyed as she was, Mrs Thatcher did not want Lawson out. Almost as much as he, she wanted his Budget to represent the culmination of economic success. As usual, she had been involved in its preparation but, also as usual, without being fully informed. Through Gray, she learnt that Lawson was planning to cut the basic rate of income tax to either 27 or 25 per cent and the top rate from 60 per cent to 40 per cent or perhaps 45 per cent. On inheritance tax, Lawson sought to raise the threshold and establish a single rate of 40 per cent.* Against this last idea, Mrs Thatcher wrote a typical plea for the home-owning classes: 'Matrimonial home to <u>children</u> – 40% much too high.' The total cost of all the changes was estimated at £4–5 billion.†

---

* The existing arrangement consisted of staged rates, with the highest at 60 per cent.
† Paul Gray also informed her that Lawson wanted to impose VAT on newspapers, a long-standing Treasury objective. She had been lobbied, however, at a meeting with the newspaper proprietors, led by Rupert Murdoch and Conrad Black (the owner of the Telegraph Group), a couple of months earlier. She had refused to give any commitment about VAT on their papers. But she had warmed them up by holding forth against VAT harmonization in the EEC: she did not 'want to see our tax system determined by the European Community' or the right to

With Lawson and others in January, Mrs Thatcher professed herself 'deeply worried about inflation' and fretted that tax cuts might be 'too big'. She complained, 'We are running an inflationary/growth economy with a balance of payments deficit.' But her desires pulled in both directions. As Terry Burns observed to Lawson, she 'liked the idea of fiscal toughness but also wanted to reduce taxes'.

What most annoyed Mrs Thatcher was that taxes and National Insurance contributions (NICs) formed a higher percentage of (non-North Sea)* GDP (37.4 per cent) in 1987 than when she came into office in 1979 (34.1 per cent). After the necessary pain of the early 1980s, she and Lawson were determined to produce substantial gain for the individual against the state. Thatcherism, they agreed, had to pay a dividend.

Lawson's Budget statement on 15 March could fairly claim to do just that. He delivered it with great confidence, boasting that 'the British economy is stronger than at any time since the war'. The mood on the Opposition benches was febrile: so great were the interruptions that proceedings had to be suspended twice. Alex Salmond, the Scottish Nationalist MP (and eventual First Minister of Scotland), shouted, 'This Budget is an obscenity' with sufficient persistence that he was expelled from the House. Such behaviour, unknown in a Budget in modern times, helped to emphasize Lawson's claim to be the bringer of dramatic change. He ended thus:

> I have radically reformed the structure of personal taxation, so that there is no rate anywhere in the system in excess of 40 per cent.†
>
> After an Autumn Statement which substantially increased public spending in priority areas, I have once again cut the basic rate of income tax, fulfilling our manifesto pledge of a basic rate of 25 pence in the pound and setting a new target of 20 pence in the pound.
>
> And I have balanced the Budget.

Although these words would come to seem hubristic, they resounded at the time. The occasion represented an important moment in British history – the first in the era of universal suffrage – when lowering income tax rates and removing all punitive rates of tax became politically advantageous. It 'Thatcherized' the future too. More than thirty-five years later, successive governments, even that of Sir Keir Starmer, had not dared move

---

apply zero rating restricted. As before, Mrs Thatcher told Lawson to drop the idea of VAT on newspapers.

* North Sea oil, being priced in dollars and therefore vulnerable to exchange rate movements, was treated separately by the Treasury. It was also seen as a windfall, and therefore not permanently reliable.

† This was the figure Lawson settled upon for the higher rate.

very far from the new rules laid down by Lawson's 1988 Budget. Mrs Thatcher was genuinely delighted. 'Only Nigel could be such a revolutionary, brilliant Chancellor,' she said to Paul Gray. Talk of a dysfunctional relationship between Prime Minister and Chancellor gave way to a sense of shared accomplishment: the *Express* declared her revolution now 'unstoppable'.

Nos. 10 and 11 Downing Street reached a 'concordat' shortly afterwards, acknowledging a role for exchange rate intervention, albeit on a highly restricted scale. The fundamental, bitter disagreement, however, remained and could not be long concealed. A day before the 'concordat' had been agreed, Geoffrey Howe said, in Zurich, that exchange rate stability was 'necessarily coming to play a more significant role in both domestic monetary discussions and international policy cooperation'. In repeating, almost exactly, a phrase from Lawson's Budget, Howe nailed his colours to the mast. His aim was to turn the collapse of 'shadowing' into a reason for joining the ERM. On 12 May, at Prime Minister's Questions, Neil Kinnock asked Mrs Thatcher if she agreed with her Chancellor that a further rise of the pound against the deutschmark would be 'unsustainable'. Although she lavished praise on Lawson, she avoided stating she agreed with him. The next day, at the Scottish Conservative Party conference in Perth, Howe departed from his text to attack the formula about joining the ERM 'when the time is right': 'We cannot forever go on adding that qualification.'

The media naturally picked up Howe's words, linked them to the previous day's exchange in Parliament and made mischief. This angered Mrs Thatcher. In New York, the pound hit DM 3.18 despite heavy intervention. Gray warned her that Lawson might now have to cut interest rates but, with Griffiths, counselled against: 'The whole "feel" at the moment is that the monetary position is too loose.' 'I agree,' she wrote, 'I fear ½% off interest rates would not stop the rise.'

Three days later, with Cabinet splits still in the headlines, Howe called Mrs Thatcher asking to meet her later that day, accompanied by the Chancellor. She demurred. As Powell recorded, if all three of them met, she said, 'it would increase speculation about difficulties. The best thing which the Foreign Secretary could do would be to keep quiet . . . he had succeeded [by his Perth speech] in making life very difficult.' Howe persisted and began to advocate for ERM membership. She cut him off: 'We were not going in at present. The Foreign Secretary had caused havoc over the weekend by his remarks.' Once again, she demanded he 'keep quiet'. There would be no meeting. Mrs Thatcher was coldly furious, Howe simultaneously nervous and unrepentant. Their exchanges were tense and untrusting. As Powell put it, she did not want to see Howe and Lawson together because 'she rightly assessed that they were going to form up to her and threaten to resign'. Being, for now, 'in a strong enough position to fend them off', she did so.

Howe was, said his close friend Richard Ryder, 'obsessed by the ERM'. He genuinely believed it was the right way forward. But, at least since his angry letter to Mrs Thatcher about Ingham's behaviour over South African sanctions in July 1986 (see pp. 559–60), he had found his relationship with her almost impossible and expected a denouement. Whether on policy – the ERM, South Africa, the poll tax – or because of the personal humiliations he endured from Mrs Thatcher, Howe felt growing cause to rebel. His ambition to succeed her remained intact.

In his memoirs, Howe shows how he and Lawson kept in touch over issues where they disagreed with her. He even states that he tried to create 'a wider three-handed team' with Lawson and the Home Secretary, Douglas Hurd. But this effort stumbled: they should 'have pre-emptively agreed that an attack on any one of us would be treated as an attack on us all . . . [but] we never did'. What this amounted to was a conspiracy not to conspire: inevitably ineffective, but enough to arouse Mrs Thatcher's suspicions.

Mrs Thatcher still faced a challenge following her refusal to support Lawson's claim that a further rise of sterling against the deutschmark would be 'unsustainable'. To find a way out, she suggested to Lawson that the half per cent cut in interest rates he had earlier advocated should be announced just before Prime Minister's Questions on 17 May. This action, she hoped, would speak louder than the words she refused to utter, lowering the value of the pound. Lawson – 'to his eternal regret' – accepted this. Mrs Thatcher, equally uneasy with her own idea, later called it 'the price of tolerable relations with my Chancellor'. The rate came down (for only a fortnight) to the lowest level ever reached during her time as Prime Minister, 7.5 per cent.

At Prime Minister's Questions, Kinnock warmly welcomed 'today's cut in interest rates and the Chancellor's victory over the Prime Minister'. Did she now agree with Lawson that further rises in the pound would be unsustainable? Reading out what she had prepared, Mrs Thatcher said recent interest rate cuts were 'clearly intended to affect the exchange rate. We use the available levers, both interest rates and intervention, as seems right in the circumstances, and it would be a great mistake for any speculator to think at any time that sterling was a one-way bet.' Was there now 'complete and utter unanimity' between Chancellor and Prime Minister, asked another MP: 'Yes,' she said.

Too late, Lawson saw he had accepted a 'poisoned chalice', though he did not accuse Mrs Thatcher of having poisoned it deliberately. Reducing interest rates at the height of a boom would damage his reputation. Besides, Kinnock's idea that Chancellor had defeated Prime Minister was not something, Lawson realized, that she could let stand.

With the row over entry into the ERM played out in almost purely economic terms, it is striking how little the political dimension was discussed by Mrs Thatcher and her senior colleagues. The ERM was part of the aim, declared in EEC treaties from the Treaty of Rome onwards, of bringing about European Economic and Monetary Union (EMU). The political dimension in the European grand political design was even more important than the economic one. It followed that most British pro-Europeans were in favour of ERM entry and most Eurosceptics were against, regardless of the economic questions involved. Early in 1984, for example, a Foreign Office document warned that: 'Our line that we shall join when the time is right is less and less convincing to our partners.' As the ERM developed, therefore, 'we would not want to find ourselves anywhere but in the central group'. This was the prevailing official doctrine.

What confused the picture, however, was that Lawson was never a pro-European true believer and was always opposed to a European single currency: 'I saw ERM entry as entirely an economic issue, part of the battle against inflation. I was with Margaret on Europe.' Since the Treasury rather than the Foreign Office took the lead on the policy, the deeper questions of Britain's relationship with Europe were almost completely suppressed.

Mrs Thatcher's opposition to ERM entry on economic grounds was genuine; but she – and Alan Walters – were also instinctively against Europe, and especially Britain, moving towards one currency. She consistently opposed extensions of political power to the EEC at the expense of nation states. But the European tide was now going so clearly the other way that it threatened to beach her. In Walters's view, 'She lost most power when she signed the Single European Act.' By this he meant not her personal political power (though that, too, was damaged), but British sovereignty itself. The political project of European integration lay behind everything. With the passing of time, it gradually came to the fore.

After the Single European Act, the tensions within the EEC temporarily abated. Discussion returned to the thorny but less existential issues of agriculture and budgets. Mrs Thatcher's approach was intentionally provocative.* She thought of herself as speaking truth to people who did not

---

* Occasionally, her remarks were aided by refreshments. Charles Powell recalled that when, at European summits, she began to tire, he would bring her a surreptitious whisky and soda:

like it. Drawing on her unique ability to combine occupation of the moral high ground with calculations of her best political interest, she deliberately cultivated her Euroscepticism for the domestic audience. In the new year of 1986, Charles Powell had sent her a boldly cynical memo. Britain was to assume the EEC presidency later that year: 'Bearing in mind the political calendar,'* Powell wrote, '... there seem to me good reasons for continuing the tactic of "Community-bashing" both because it is necessary in its own right to get some sense into the institution and because you will be a much more convincing exponent of it than the Opposition and will therefore cut the ground from under their feet'. Focusing on reform of the Common Agricultural Policy, Mrs Thatcher resolved to refuse the next increase in the Community's 'own resources' (that is, the percentage of member-state taxation the EEC was free to spend) without agricultural reform and much better budget discipline.† It would be a 'nightmare', said her speaking notes for a quarrelsome Council in Brussels in July 1987, if an increase in 'own resources' 'were simply swallowed up in the storage and disposal of agricultural surpluses'. Another nightmare was the vast proposed expansion of 'structural funds' – the subsidies from the richer northern countries to the poorer southern ones. A third bad dream was that the increase in 'own resources' would threaten the British rebate, won at Fontainebleau in 1984.

Matters came to a head at the specially convened Brussels Council of February 1988. As ever at European summits, Mrs Thatcher faced a presentational problem with her domestic audience. As Bernard Ingham warned, if agreement were reached it would give rise to 'the inevitable suspicion that you have sold out ... have you been taken to the cleaners?'. If, on the other hand, the Council 'failed', 'you will be ... able to present yourself as the champion of the taxpayer and the housewife while not forgetting the farmer'. EEC 'success' was therefore 'failure' in Ingham terms, and vice versa.

In fact, the Council result was not amenable to either type of media treatment. Mrs Thatcher did not lose outright, but was more knocked

---

'sure enough, it revived her spirits wonderfully'. When Helmut Kohl got wind of this he said to Powell: 'I wish you would stop doing that, you're just making her more difficult.' 'To be honest, Mr Chancellor,' Powell replied, 'that's the whole point.'

* This was a reference to the provisional date for the next general election, which in Mrs Thatcher's mind was the summer of 1987.

† This approach notwithstanding, Mrs Thatcher remained sensitive to the electoral needs of her Conservative colleagues abroad. When, in October 1986, Howe suggested agriculture take centre stage at the London Council in December, Mrs Thatcher scribbled in the margin, 'We have to remember that Kohl has an election in January and he may therefore not want much discussion on agriculture.' She returned to agriculture only after the German elections.

about by the power of Helmut Kohl than she liked to admit.* David Hannay, who passed the fraught evening with her, noticed that she 'shed a tear or two ... tears of rage and not submission'. Britain had won on some things (for example, continuing the budget rebate, by now saving £1,750 million a year), but lost on others (such as structural funds). Such messy inconclusiveness did not fit either of Ingham's pigeonholes.

The broader trajectory of Europe was going gradually against Mrs Thatcher. For Europhiles it was clear why. From Germany, Julian Bullard, the British Ambassador, writing to the Foreign Office in October 1987, believed the problem lay with Britain, by which he meant Mrs Thatcher, failing to give a lead: 'We don't seem interested in any particular objective except the Internal Market in which Smarties can be sold in the same packet everywhere from Copenhagen to Constancia ... What I think is missing: Vision.'

To the Foreign Office, however, 'vision' meant further European integration, to which Mrs Thatcher was adamantly opposed and about which British public opinion was unenthusiastic. As Charles Powell put it, 'by far and away the dominant feature of Europe in her mind', at least in private conversation, 'was its intrusion upon our national sovereignty'. On this matter she did have a vision, but one that sat uneasily with the diplomatic establishment. When, the following year, she tried frankly to set out a new direction for Europe they would complain even more.

Mrs Thatcher's belief in the central importance of national independence was sharpened, as fitted her surprisingly emotional temperament, by the personal. Her resentment against Jacques Delors was mounting. She disagreed with his centralizing, socialist vision of Europe and was jealous of his growing power. This problem first became acute during the London European Council of 1986, when, without warning, Delors revealed that 'the Community would not get through 1987 without a major financial crisis'. He wanted either savage cuts or an increase in 'own resources', overthrowing the 1984 Fontainebleau settlement. 'In plain terms, the Community was broke,' Mrs Thatcher said tartly to her fellow leaders. 'Heads of government should have been told this before ... ' She resented an unelected official seeking, as she saw it, to bounce his elected superiors. It was a moment of awakening. In Ingham's view: 'She identified him as a force to be reckoned with.'

---

* Mrs Thatcher later wrote about Kohl's well-calculated aggression, 'He was never above banging the table.' She much disliked and often referred disparagingly to Kohl's way of saying 'Germany pays, so Germany must have its way.'

At the Council press conference she exacted revenge, inviting 'Monsieur Delors'* to answer a question about the imminent lack of Community resources. When he grumpily declined, she said, 'I had no idea you were such a strong silent man.' As Delors recalled, 'She humiliated me.' Two days later, reporting, alongside Mrs Thatcher, on the London Council to the European Parliament, he attacked Britain over unemployment, demanding 'other than lip service' to 'social dialogue'. Not one to pass over such a challenge, Mrs Thatcher immediately demanded the chance to reply. She regretted Delors had said none of this at the London press conference: 'some people do not like me to reply quite as vigorously as they attack me'. This set-to disturbed Geoffrey Howe. He was increasingly upset by what he considered her 'excessive rhetoric'.

With Delors coming up for reappointment during 1988, it became clear that no one, including Mrs Thatcher's favoured choice, the Dutch Prime Minister Ruud Lubbers, would be able to oust him. To contain the Delors–Thatcher antagonism, the Foreign Office concocted the idea that she should support his reappointment but that, as a *quid pro quo*, David Williamson, an official whom, despite his Europhilia, she both liked and respected, should take over as Secretary-General of the Commission (the chief civil servant, in other words, of Delors). John Kerr recalled that Helmut Kohl and Delors both supported the Williamson candidacy as 'the best way of civilizing her'. But Mrs Thatcher had no desire to be 'civilized', or rather she rejected the EEC definition of what being civilized meant.

European development under Delors increasingly acquired what Mrs Thatcher considered a socialist tinge. She resisted his talk of the 'social dimension' of the Single Market on the grounds that state authorities should not interfere with markets and contracts and because she saw that it would arrogate more power to Brussels. It was also an area in which the Commission sought to exploit its new powers conferred in the Single European Act by qualified majority voting (QMV). Mrs Thatcher had supported QMV because she had been assured it would allow the Community to run more expeditiously. The idea that it might now reimpose socialism by stealth was incendiary.

At the Hanover Council in June 1988, the question of how to advance EMU came to a head. Beforehand, Mrs Thatcher had fought off an attempt by the former French President Valéry Giscard d'Estaing – joint Chairman, with Helmut Schmidt, of the committee on EMU – to see her to discuss 'European monetary construction'. 'No point in talking to me about this,'

---

* Mrs Thatcher never used the title of 'President', though Delors preferred it, because she did not want to confer on him anything which implied the status of a head of state.

she wrote crossly. Informed that Giscard's diary was filling up fast, she wrote, 'Let it fill right up.' She disliked both the haughty Frenchman and his message.

Mrs Thatcher was assured by Helmut Kohl, always frightened of losing the deutschmark, that a European Central Bank was 'premature'. He privately backed her in opposing the suggestion of his Foreign Minister, Hans-Dietrich Genscher, that a committee of 'five wise men', not necessarily financial experts, should investigate how to bring EMU about. Mrs Thatcher preferred to trust in central bankers, particularly Karl Otto Pöhl, the Bundesbank President, who had written against the need for a European Central Bank.

President Mitterrand, who had just won a second seven-year term, told Mrs Thatcher in June that he did not want to leave the work to central bank governors. 'In particular,' he added, 'Herr Pöhl would be an obstacle to progress.' This was exactly what Mrs Thatcher did not want to hear. A European Central Bank, she replied, 'presupposed a common currency, common economic policies and a readiness to surrender national control over monetary policy. None of these conditions was remotely likely to be met, so a study was pointless.' 'It was nice', Mitterrand commented drily, 'to be reminded that the Prime Minister knew how to say no.'

At Hanover, however, things seemed to go well for her. The compromise, negotiated by Kohl, was that a study of 'further concrete steps' towards EMU would be carried out by central bankers, chaired by Delors. Having already agreed to support Delors's second term as Commission President, Mrs Thatcher could hardly oppose this. Hanover thus ended harmoniously. The trouble, from her point of view, was that Delors's chairmanship gave him control of the process.* He was determined to clear the path to create a European Central Bank. She had won nothing significant.

At the same time as she was fighting over the future of the European Community, Mrs Thatcher was involved in very different European negotiations. In February 1988 her friend Sir Peter Smithers, a former Conservative MP now living in Switzerland, had informed her that his neighbour, Baron 'Heini' Thyssen, was interested in Britain as a permanent home for his extraordinary art collection (the 'most important private collection . . . in

---

* Bernard Ingham, in fact, foresaw this. 'Your press conference should be a tame affair,' he told Mrs Thatcher at Hanover, 'given the remarkable degree of harmony in the council and the fact that you will be seen to have won over an European Central Bank.' 'As a consequence,' he continued in jocular tone, 'I would expect journalists to argue that there is nothing to stop the inquiry team from investigating the idea of a European Central Bank and that, therefore, your victory is hollow.' That is exactly what happened.

the world'), but had not found the government receptive. Smithers urged Mrs Thatcher to intervene.

Mrs Thatcher was excited. The recovery of the British economy and her dominance of the political scene had made her feel more secure about involving herself in the arts. One small-scale example came with her decision, in 1988, to renovate parts of 10 Downing Street. Quinlan Terry, a famous architect in the classicist tradition, was charged with an extensive remodelling of the three State Drawing Rooms. 'She thought the rooms were boring,' he recalled, '. . . she felt that after the Falklands War, the time had come to do something mildly triumphalist and confident.' His designs incorporated intricate new mouldings, many with gold leaf.*

Olga Polizzi, the head of design for the Forte Hotel group, oversaw the renovation. She considered Mrs Thatcher's taste 'quite conventional. The place had become rather shabby and she ... was a stickler for it looking proper.' Her approach was practical: she wanted no pelmets on the curtains because they were so difficult to clean.† Partly because 'her sight wasn't that brilliant', she preferred bright lighting and bright colours. 'All the paintings had to be British, with portraits of national dignitaries preferred.' Mrs Thatcher enjoyed the process. Once she bumped into Polizzi and the delivery men bringing up a new sofa. 'Ooh, let's have a look,' she said, and chatted to the workmen while happily bouncing on the sofa. The changes increased the grandeur of the place, adding to the perception that Mrs Thatcher was becoming a Gloriana figure, though she had, as usual, insisted on keeping the cost to taxpayers impossibly modest.

Mrs Thatcher had earned much odium from the world of the subsidized arts for challenging the notion that it was the automatic duty of the state to underwrite artistic endeavour; but she did not agree that government had no place in enhancing the nation's cultural assets. She successfully sought much more private and commercial patronage to magnify what the state provided. In her view, 'the public manifestation of a nation's culture is as much a demonstration of a nation's qualities as the size of its GDP is of its energies'. She enjoyed seducing the rich into helping the arts. The Thyssen collection contained first-rank paintings in the Western tradition from the thirteenth to the twentieth century. Here was a unique opportunity, requiring first-rank flattery.

At Smithers's suggestion, Mrs Thatcher agreed to see his friend, the deal-maker Claude Hankes-Drielsma, who then got moving with a speed which

---

* In tribute to his patron, Terry included a small portrait of a male thatcher in the corner of one of his friezes.

† When Olga Polizzi insisted on pelmets Mrs Thatcher agreed, on condition that brown paper was stuck on top of them so it could collect the dust and be replaced annually.

alarmed the bureaucracy. On the day of Lawson's Budget, 15 March, Mrs Thatcher saw Thyssen in 10 Downing Street. She was at her most charming. 'She chatted to Heini about art in a way which left all of us standing,' Hankes-Drielsma recalled, but then, as he put it, 'the waffle started'. He blamed Ridley, the Environment Secretary, and others for scuppering his plans for a firm proposal by the end of April.

Hankes-Drielsma was alarmed that the Baroness had not accompanied her husband to the Downing Street luncheon. He knew that 'Tita', Thyssen's fifth wife and a former Miss Spain, badly wanted the collection to go to her native country. Charles Powell reported to Mrs Thatcher the following day that Hankes-Drielsma had telephoned him 'in some agitation'. The family trustees would meet in June to decide matters: 'Baroness von Thyssen – fifth edition – was of course pressing very strongly for Madrid,' Powell wrote.*

In British government circles, there was resistance. The Treasury thought the £200 million earmarked to cover housing the collection and related costs was too high. Neil MacGregor, Director of the National Gallery, was among those complaining about plans to spend public money on a 'foreign' collection when existing British ones felt starved. Mrs Thatcher pushed forward regardless. On 2 May, however, it all seemed for naught, after Thyssen informed Ridley that he was 'most attracted by the proposal of the Spanish government'. Thyssen did not make clear – and Mrs Thatcher did not know – that on 7 April his trustees had told the Spanish government that they wished to accept its offer.

Mrs Thatcher appeared to accept Thyssen's disappointing news: 'at least it is a <u>clear</u> decision and NOT of <u>our</u> making'. Two days later, however, Smithers told her that the Thyssen trustees were '<u>not</u> in favour of the pictures going to Spain'. That day, Hankes-Drielsma extracted a letter from the Baron himself, promising to give the British proposal 'my utmost consideration'.

Amid this chaos, Bernard Ingham questioned the entire project. 'I have the gravest misgivings about the "saleability" of the Thyssen collection,' he told Mrs Thatcher. The arts lobby would 'grumble loud and long', as would others, 'especially the poverty lobby; in this respect the timing [shortly after Lawson's tax-cutting Budget] could not be worse'. She usually found wisdom in her press secretary's growls of warning, but on this occasion pressed ahead regardless. On 14 May, at the suggestion of Hankes-Drielsma, the Prince of Wales met Thyssen in Lugano. He reported to Mrs Thatcher that the Baron

---

* As the saga dragged on, Mrs Thatcher considered desperate measures to counter the Baroness. 'I'm very worried, dear, about this Spanish girl,' she confided in Lord Gowrie, the former Arts Minister, Chairman of Sotheby's. 'Can't you find the Baron a nice English girl?' Gowrie failed to produce the 'honeytrap', or possibly sixth Baroness Thyssen, she sought.

remained open to proposals but had been unaware of the Cabinet's intention to discuss a British offer. It was 'all a terrible muddle', she lamented.

The Cabinet now agreed to proceed with the British offer and Hankes-Drielsma flew out to see Thyssen, accompanied by Robin Butler bearing a letter from Mrs Thatcher supporting the British bid. As Butler recalled, 'Everything went wrong. There was an industrial dispute at the airport and we were late for lunch. At the lunch, the Baroness declined to be present because her dog was ill. The dog *was* ill, but this seemed to me a pretext.' Although Thyssen professed himself delighted with Mrs Thatcher's letter and the proposal, little had changed, because of Thyssen's wife. When he returned home Butler received a note from Charles Powell: 'The Baroness's views were still an unknown quantity: her dog had died yesterday (not so far as I can establish as a direct result of your visit) and she was in consequence distraught and had not studied the proposals.'

Once the Baroness *had* studied the proposals, she scotched them. On 30 May, Baron Thyssen informed Mrs Thatcher that he, his wife and his son felt they must honour the agreement already reached with Spain. In the end, Butler judged that Thyssen had 'only been playing with Mrs Thatcher all along'. Hankes-Drielsma, however, believed that he and she, if unimpeded by the bureaucracy, would have secured the collection. She later wrote that her failure to do so was her 'greatest disappointment' in the field.

The Thyssen story is characteristic of 'late-period' Thatcher. It was ambitious, daring and romantic, and relied too heavily on her personal intervention and on her 'irregulars'. As Powell put it, 'It reflected well on her boldness.' Yet it failed. Even at her zenith, her writ did not automatically run. Although the arts were far better endowed than when she arrived in office, she left behind no one great symbol of her artistic legacy.

Back at home, Mrs Thatcher was becoming ever more worried about inflation, now running at 4 per cent, and Nigel Lawson was nearer to his wits' end about how to respond. In May 1988, alarmed by the balance of payments current account figures,* she argued for interest rate rises. Lawson, convinced the current account deficit would be transitory, wanted only half a per cent rise, and not yet. Through the politeness of the official record one can hear Mrs Thatcher upbraiding Lawson: the Prime Minister 'wondered whether such an approach would convince the markets that the authorities were taking the situation sufficiently seriously'. Rates, which had risen by

---

* The deficit was £1.2 billion for May 1988, making the cumulative deficit for the year so far £4.7 billion, compared with £1.7 billion for the whole of 1987.

half a per cent two days earlier, went up again by another half per cent to 9.5 per cent – 2 per cent above May's low – on 28 June.

New economic figures gave greater ammunition to Mrs Thatcher against Lawson. On 1 July, she received a memo from Brian Griffiths warning starkly of 'increasing excess demand' in the economy. The result would be an inflation rate of 7 per cent. At the time of the Budget, output and expenditure had been 'growing much more rapidly than we thought'.* The 'Lawson Boom' was now apparent. Monetary growth had been way out of control since 1985–6, driven, Griffiths wrote, by 'intervention in the foreign exchange markets'. Mrs Thatcher underlined this sentence vigorously. Here was the consequence of Lawson's exchange rate targeting. Griffiths recommended the government acknowledge mistakes in the conduct of monetary policy, 'however unpalatable this may be'. At a meeting on 18 July, Mrs Thatcher again pushed for higher interest rates. Pointedly, she declared that 'nothing had been done since 1983 to get inflation down': 1983 was the year in which Lawson had become Chancellor. The press began to speculate about his future.

Tensions were made worse by increasingly frequent public pronouncements from Alan Walters. On 14 July, in the *Independent*, he criticized Lawson's 'misguided shadowing of the mark' and warned of the inevitable inflationary consequences. In a phrase that would later become famous, he described the ERM as 'half-baked'.† With Walters rumoured (accurately) to be returning to No. 10 as Mrs Thatcher's economic adviser, his words were taken as hers.

Lawson protested to Mrs Thatcher about Walters's return (planned for the following year), but accepted it nonetheless.‡ On 19 July, however, Walters popped up again, suggesting in the *Evening Standard* that Lawson might well be 'thinking of moving on' from his job as Chancellor. Contrary to what many assumed, Walters had not been prompted by No. 10. Wicks wrote to Walters to press Mrs Thatcher's view that he must stop talking in public 'if you are to return here'. But Tory MPs resented what they saw as No. 10 undermining ministers: sympathy for the Chancellor grew.

On 21 July, Lawson again resisted Mrs Thatcher's call to increase

---

* One factor in the overheating was the enormous temporary growth in mortgages caused by Lawson's desire to rein them back. His four-month window, announced in the Budget, before the interest tax relief on the double mortgage for one house came to an end caused a rush of new applications. House prices to the end of July 1988 rose 28 per cent on the previous year.
† By this Walters meant it lacked both the flexibility of fully floating currencies and the certainty of fixed rates.
‡ In later years, Lawson wondered whether he himself should have communicated with Walters, whom he had, in the past, liked. 'I didn't try to talk to him. Maybe I should have done. I am very lazy.'

interest rates: 'We really do need to have an interest rate increase very early next week,' she scribbled to Paul Gray. 'His reputation is at stake.'*
At the 1922 Committee 'end of term' meeting that night, she hailed Lawson for his 'brilliant' Budget. She 'particularly disliked' being forced to say this, Powell recalled, but felt it necessary for political peace and market stability. This truce ended the political summer. Neither Mrs Thatcher nor Lawson quite knew which of them was winning. Both increasingly turned to the European stage to argue out their case.

Despite the superficial harmony at the Hanover Council, Mrs Thatcher's public hostilities with Delors resumed in the summer of 1988. Addressing the European Parliament on 6 July, he predicted that 'ten years hence 80 per cent of our economic legislation, and perhaps even our fiscal and social legislation as well, will be of Community origin'. He spoke of an embryonic European government. This provocation was, in Powell's view, a 'turning point' for Mrs Thatcher: 'In her mind a Rubicon had been crossed.'

On *The Jimmy Young Show* later that month she hit back. 'I think he [Delors] was wrong,' she said baldly. The Commission wanted more power, she went on. She would not 'surrender many fundamental economic decisions' through the creation of a central bank. 'Europe', she said, 'has only been single under tyranny, not under liberty.'

That September, Mrs Thatcher had been invited to address the College of Europe in Bruges. Over the summer, Powell drafted the speech himself, effectively cutting out the Foreign Office.† As he put it, 'She felt the time had come to spell out an alternative vision' for the future of Europe. At the end of August, Powell's draft reached the Foreign Office, where it caused unease, though not panic. John Kerr, who ruefully admitted that 'Charles had a golden pen', tried to soften its asperities. He crossed out disparaging references to 'a European super-state' and criticism, by name, of the views of Delors. But he did not question the central drift. There were also some noises of protest from Geoffrey Howe, but one passage earned his praise: 'Let me say bluntly on behalf of Britain: we have not embarked on the business of throwing back the frontiers of the state at home only to see a European super-state getting ready to exercise a new dominance

---

* Mrs Thatcher had to wait until 8 August, when rates rose by half a per cent to 11 per cent.
† The unlikely catalyst for this was a terrorist attack over the summer. On 20 August an attack on British soldiers near Ballygawley in County Tyrone by the Provisional IRA left eight dead and twenty-eight injured. Condemning the attack, Mrs Thatcher broke her holiday and returned to Downing Street. Charles Powell accompanied her: 'She didn't want to go on holiday again. So we got to work on the Bruges Speech.'

from Brussels.' 'The Secretary of State strongly agrees,' wrote Stephen Wall, Howe's private secretary. The final version of these words was to cause more controversy than any other part of the speech.

Kerr orchestrated an extensive rewrite, excising whatever seemed 'off-beam, and in some cases unnecessarily provocative'.* Shortly afterwards he wrote to the Permanent Under-Secretary, Patrick Wright, permitting himself some self-congratulation. Powell's revised version had accepted 80 per cent of their suggestions, he said. They were now seeking 'to secure another 10%. The remaining 10% don't really matter (and concern areas where No 10 are probably incorrigible). It thus looks as if our damage limitation exercise is heading for success.'

It was odd that the Foreign Office felt calm before the coming storm, because Delors himself had leapt into combat so fiercely that Mrs Thatcher was bound to respond in kind. On 8 September, he addressed the annual conference of the Trades Union Congress in Bournemouth. Emphasizing the 'social dimension' of Europe, he called for 'a platform of guaranteed social rights', including every worker's right to be covered by a collective agreement. Mrs Thatcher passionately rejected such talk. For the unelected official of an organization she considered little better than an illegitimate foreign power to address her sworn enemy was, in her mind, an insult. The delighted trade unionists sang 'Frère Jacques', while she seethed.† The British trade union movement has remained broadly pro-European ever since.

Wishing to supply Mrs Thatcher with more ammunition against Delors, Alan Walters passed on a powerful private letter from Bernard Connolly, a British economist who worked at the European Commission but did not share its political agenda. Connolly warned that Delors had 'publicly exulted in having pulled the wool over the eyes of legislatures and electorates across Europe' and got the Single European Act through. Mrs Thatcher must kill the idea of the European Central Bank 'if Thatcherism is to survive Thatcher'. For the composition of her speech, Connolly's warning was timely.

---

* Kerr circulated Powell's draft and his own redraftings and collected departments' unfavourable opinions of the former, but thought it would be more effective if Downing Street did not know about this collusion: 'The other departments will I think tell No 10 that they regard our version as greatly preferable to its predecessor: it might be best that such advice appears to be sua sponte!'
† In the 1970s and 1980s, the British trade union movement had tended to look unfavourably on the EEC as a capitalist ramp. After Delors's TUC speech it changed overnight, and decided that Europe was an anti-Thatcherite bulwark.

When she rose to speak to the College of Europe on 20 September, Mrs Thatcher joked that inviting her to speak on Britain and Europe was rather like inviting 'Genghis Khan to speak on the virtues of peaceful coexistence'.* It was a position she relished. Europe, she reminded her audience, had often been threatened by tyranny and Britain had often fought 'to prevent Europe from falling under the dominance of a single power': 120,000 British troops lay buried 'only miles from here'. 'Had it not been for their willingness to fight and die, Europe would have been united long before now – but not in liberty, not in justice . . . It was from our island fortress that the liberation of Europe itself [in 1944] was mounted.' Pointing east of the Iron Curtain, she declared that liberation incomplete: 'We shall always look on Warsaw, Prague and Budapest as great European cities.' Europe was also a gift to the wider world, a culture which nurtured the values which built the United States of America. On these terms, Britain wanted no 'cosy, isolated existence' on the fringes: 'Our destiny is in Europe, as part of the Community.'

So she was worried, she continued, that the Community wasted so much time on 'arcane institutional debates' instead of cultivating 'willing and active cooperation between independent sovereign states'. Just as the Soviet Union was beginning to recognize the problems of centralized power, the European Commission seemed to be going the other way. Here she unleashed the sentence which Geoffrey Howe had enthusiastically endorsed, made more pointed by Delors's remarks in Bournemouth: 'We have not successfully rolled back the frontiers of the state in Britain only to see them re-imposed at a European level, with a European super-state exercising a new dominance from Brussels.'

This dislike of centralized bureaucracy also impelled her to warn against a European single currency. The Community should consider what was happening as Communism weakened: 'freedom is on the offensive . . . for the first time in my life-time'. She called for a Europe which 'looks outward not inward, and which preserves that Atlantic Community – that Europe on both sides of the Atlantic – which is our noblest inheritance and our greatest strength'.

The Bruges Speech was immediately reported as a sensational attack upon Delors. The Foreign Office blamed this spin on Ingham. Powell agreed: 'Bernard mis-sold it to the British press as "Smash Brussels".' In

---

* The original draft made a similar joke about the speech being 'rather like inviting King Herod to speak on the subject of nursery education', but Mrs Thatcher rejected this because the simile implied the murder of children.

fact, the speech provided, in good faith, Mrs Thatcher's suggestions for a better Europe. Here was the 'vision' for which Julian Bullard and his like called, though not the one they wanted. Much more fervently than most of her Continental colleagues, she believed in the triumph of pan-European freedom, unrealized since the Second World War, and was working to bring it about. 'It was', said Kerr, 'a great moment in British foreign policy – and we all missed it.'

It is not hard, however, to understand why. The speech 'caused absolute horror' in Brussels. Delors himself felt it was 'well written' with 'beautiful phrases', but he was in no doubt about its purpose: 'I think she thought she could put a stop to the European project.'* He was determined to prevent her. To European integrationists, Bruges was a declaration of war. It was also both what its admirers praised and what its critics attacked – a visionary declaration of a way forward for Europe *and* a fierce piece of score-settling with people whose power threatened Mrs Thatcher's own. In the light of posterity, the former looks more important than the latter, but posterity is never around when you need her.

In both the bravely prophetic and the angrily combative, the speech was pure Margaret Thatcher. No doubt, Patrick Wright noted in his diary, the Prime Minister 'is delighted by the storm she has caused, and by comparisons drawn with de Gaulle'. As Powell put it, this 'was the single occasion on which she fully articulated her view of Europe: the suspicion, the desire to work together but not to be glued together: and the importance of Eastern Europe and the US. It's all there. She was Luther: here she stood, she could do no other.'

There was also a sense in which she could do no more. Howe noted this was the first time a British prime minister had called into question the legitimacy of EEC institutions, rather than specific policies. After Bruges, therefore, the EEC and she – not to mention Howe and she – were on a collision course. Because of their disagreement, Mrs Thatcher's vision would not be translated into actual, coherent policy change. As Powell put it, 'Not a single member of our own government, let alone the Foreign Office, was prepared to go out and argue for its [the Bruges Speech's] ideas: instead they went around apologising for it.'

The other consequence of Bruges was to provide her own party's establishment with an issue on which it might break her. In July 1988, Alan Clark dined with Tristan Garel-Jones, a government whip and ardent Europhile.

---

* Delors also detected in the speech the hand of Charles Powell, whom, rather than Mrs Thatcher herself, he chose to blame for the worsening of his relations with her: 'It was easier for me to talk directly with the PM than with her secretary. I had the impression he had it in for me.'

The subject turned to Europe: 'Tristan said that "confrontation" in Cabinet (what did this mean?) was inevitable "one way or another" . . . he said, the Prime Minister will find herself isolated by her three "heavies" – Howe, Hurd and Lawson – and in a crisis Brittan [shortly to become a European Commissioner] would go native and add to her troubles'.

His prediction was well informed.

30

Bush turns away

'I respect her. I like her. But I'm the President of the United States!'

Even as her domestic troubles mounted, Mrs Thatcher retained a seemingly unassailable position in world affairs, particularly in relation to the Cold War. In Opposition she had been the first British leader to challenge the Soviet Union's renewed aggression, but first too, in office, to engage with Mikhail Gorbachev, and encourage Reagan to do likewise. She had won the right to act, though she shunned the phrase, as a bridge between the United States and the Soviet Union.

Reagan, her greatest friend and ally, was in a weaker political position. In the first half of 1987, his administration faced protracted investigations into the Iran-Contra scandal. Throughout, Mrs Thatcher had maintained strong personal support for Reagan but kept her distance from the matter itself. In May 1986, she resisted an effort to ensnare Britain directly in the affair, refusing an American request to approve the covert transfer of British-made weapons from Chile to the Contras in Nicaragua. 'As you know,' Charles Powell wrote to John Poindexter, Reagan's National Security Advisor, 'the Prime Minister always tries to respond helpfully to requests from the President. After careful reflection she would prefer not to be pressed on this one.'

Her decision was prudent. If she had authorized the proposed transaction, the woman known for upholding the rule of law might have been ruined by supporting a friend who had chosen to evade it. Because she was not tainted, Mrs Thatcher felt comfortable defending Reagan vigorously in public and comforting him in private.* In February 1987, the Tower Commission, appointed to investigate the scandal, concluded that the administration had indeed traded arms for hostages in Iran, although

---

* After the President had undergone prostate surgery in early 1987, Mrs Thatcher told him of her pleasure at his impressive recovery. 'As for any residual problems with Congress and the press on Iran,' she wrote, 'I recall some words of Harry Truman: "I never gave them hell. I just tell the truth and they think it's hell!"'

Reagan had been unaware of the diversion of funds to the Contras. The picture was of a president who had lost his grip. In a televised address, Reagan took responsibility and apologized to the American people. Over the phone, Mrs Thatcher told him she was 'thrilled by the speech . . . things were well "back on track"'. In fact, Congressional hearings were only just beginning, but Reagan's address pulled him up from his low point. Her call was 'instrumental in the follow-up to that speech', said Ken Duberstein, Deputy White House Chief of Staff. 'She said, "Ronnie, you did what you had to do. You put this to bed."'

In June 1987, Mrs Thatcher told Charlie Price, the US Ambassador, how pleased she was that her first foreign trip after the election was to the USA, 'since support for President Reagan was her highest foreign policy priority'. One of those who sensed her global opportunity was the former US President Richard Nixon. In a paper, passed on to her, he wrote that she could fill the 'vacuum of leadership' because she 'will be the only qualified Soviet expert among Western leaders for the next five years . . . She <u>knows</u> Gorbachev. The doves like the fact that she says she can do business with him. But . . . the hawks have confidence that she is not going to allow Gorbachev to give us the business [that is, to take advantage of us].' Mrs Thatcher, Nixon wrote, had 'demonstrated that she can get in the ring with [Gorbachev] and take him on toe-to-toe'.

Preparing Mrs Thatcher for her July visit, Powell focused Nixon's themes on Reagan's weak position: 'There is a real risk of a vacuum in the leadership of the West at the very moment when the Soviet system has thrown up an articulate and appealing leader . . . Your role is to rally the West. It is not a question of supplanting American leadership . . . Rather you need to propel the United States forward with the force of your own ideas and personality.'

There was, nonetheless, a danger that if Mrs Thatcher stood too tall she would make Reagan look small. As the *Washington Post* journalist and Reagan biographer Lou Cannon put it in June: 'Thatcher reinforces Reagan while also patronizing him. When the two leaders share a world stage, their constituents instantly recognize that Thatcher is both the superior intellect and the more elemental force.' While Mrs Thatcher did have a keener intellect than Reagan, she maintained a genuine admiration for his strong convictions and communicative gifts. Besides, she was, by temperament, someone who, once committed, strengthened that commitment in adversity. She had long ago put her eggs in Reagan's basket, and found it sound, so there her eggs would stay, no matter what anyone said.

*

Mrs Thatcher flew into Washington on 16 July, as the Iran-Contra Congressional hearings reached a climax. She found Reagan 'hurt and bemused'. Far from avoiding the controversy, she toured the television studios to support him. On CBS's flagship programme *Face the Nation* she told the interviewer, Lesley Stahl: 'Cheer up! America is a strong country with a great President, a great people and a great future! ... Why are you doing your level best to put the worst foot forward?' As Stahl recalled, Mrs Thatcher 'chewed me up, stomped on me, and left me in tatters'.

After Mrs Thatcher had returned to London, Reagan rang 'to thank her from the bottom of his heart' for her 'stalwart performance'. He then orchestrated a round of applause from his assembled Cabinet. Mrs Thatcher said she was 'very touched'. According to Duberstein, 'Her encouragement ... helped President Reagan not only to get back on his feet, but to get back on his feet with some bounce left in him.'

Her staunch support increased her power within the US administration. The East–West arms control agenda now centred on the future of Intermediate Nuclear Forces (INF). Mrs Thatcher had already conceded, reluctantly, that negotiations should proceed to remove all INF missiles from Europe (see pp. 569–71). When George Shultz visited Moscow in April 1987, Gorbachev went further. He wanted to add the abolition of shorter-range INF systems to the deal. At Camp David the previous November, Mrs Thatcher and Reagan had agreed to give priority to an INF agreement 'with restraints on shorter range systems'. Abolishing these systems (known as the 'second zero') went further still: other than the British and French independent deterrents, the only nuclear weapons remaining on European soil would be very short-range forces (SNF) with a range of under 500 kilometres. Shultz brought these sweeping proposals home for consultations.

Opposition gathered in Republican circles. Nixon and Henry Kissinger came together for the first time since Nixon's resignation in 1974 to write a joint article in the *Washington Post*, expressing their anxiety. At the end of the month, Kissinger called on Mrs Thatcher. 'The doctor', Powell recorded, 'was in sombre and apocalyptic humour ... The President seemed hell bent on pursuing disarmament proposals that even CND would applaud. The effect would be to ... undermine the few strong West European leaders and to drive the Germans into neutralism and nationalism ... some blunt speaking was needed and only the Prime Minister could provide it, rather like Churchill in the 1930s.' As Kissinger later recalled, 'I thought she was the only one who could have an impact, because I knew how much Reagan revered her.'

As Powell recorded, 'The Prime Minister took this [Kissinger's] catalogue of woe with equanimity (that, I suppose, being the only alternative to suicide) ... She agreed that European concerns needed to be voiced more bluntly.' Mrs Thatcher was never keen on doing away with central parts of NATO's nuclear deterrent. Nonetheless, she would now make a sacrifice for the greater good. On 28 April, she wrote to Reagan accepting that the West 'should agree to consider' the second zero, but if and only if it refused to contemplate negotiations over the remaining SNF. Shultz urged support for Mrs Thatcher's formulation. He warned Reagan, however, that compromise 'might be necessary to meet the very real problem facing Kohl – a staunch friend and ally'.

For all their differences, Mrs Thatcher had always considered Kohl steadfast in his devotion to the Western alliance. But once the two accepted the second zero, their views on further reductions began to diverge. For her, it became crucial to preserve the shortest-range weapons. Without them there would be nothing to deter Soviet troops from overwhelming the small number of British forces serving in Germany. NATO's doctrine of 'flexible response' would be obsolete. For Kohl, retaining only the shortest-range nuclear weapons seemed to make Germany the theatre of any nuclear exchange – a politically toxic thought.

This argument came to a head, against Mrs Thatcher's will, at the Venice G7 summit in June. With polling day approaching in Britain, she feared that any hint of weakening resolve would prove an electoral liability. Over dinner, however, as she later relayed to Powell, Kohl had wanted to hold out the prospect of follow-on negotiations, aimed at removing the remaining SNF missiles from Europe (the so-called 'third zero'). She had strongly argued against. The Canadian Prime Minister, Brian Mulroney, remembered the set-to thus: 'There will be no denuclearization of Europe because you will destroy NATO,' Margaret thundered. 'It's my skin,' Kohl replied before she cut him off. 'No, our soldiers are there.'

By her own account, Mrs Thatcher stressed the importance of eliminating chemical weapons and achieving conventional parity before any 'third zero'. She noted that 'Reagan had intervened helpfully' in favour of this stance. Rather characteristically, she blocked out of her mind Reagan's less welcome remarks. In his diary, the President recorded: 'Margaret & Helmut did battle over whether to go to zero on the very short range and tactical nuclear weapons. She says no & I had to differ with her although I explained it shouldn't happen until after we had negotiated an end to chemical & reduced conventionals.'

Mrs Thatcher told Powell that 'President Mitterrand had been little help.

He had claimed not to believe in the doctrine of flexible response, and to attach importance only to strategic nuclear weapons.'* To Mitterrand's senior foreign policy aide, Hubert Védrine, this dinner was a key moment when the leaders all expressed their versions of the truth about the nuclear deterrent. It was typical of Mrs Thatcher that she was so committed to fighting her corner that she did not notice that Reagan, her closest ally, was in fact disagreeing with her underlying argument.

While the Venice Statement on East–West Relations pledged 'the continuing importance of nuclear deterrence in preserving peace', the whole truth was less comforting. The Americans were increasingly ready to shape policy around Germany. The day after Mrs Thatcher's third general election victory, Ronald Reagan issued his famous challenge to Mikhail Gorbachev at the Brandenburg Gate in Berlin. It was the high point of the conservative revolution. Yet by this stage, Mrs Thatcher was the only front-rank Western leader who still fully believed in NATO's nuclear doctrine.

Mrs Thatcher and Reagan met again, in Washington, just over a month later. By this stage in his presidency he was more easily satisfied in conversation than she was.† As Frank Carlucci, the National Security Advisor, recalled, once Reagan had gone through his talking points he 'wanted to tell jokes and have a light conversation. But Margaret was constantly business. She with her steel-trap mind . . .' None of this diminished the importance of their relationship. She now persuaded Reagan to re-pledge allegiance to their 1986 'Camp David agreement'. Following an INF agreement, he would seek a 50 per cent cut in strategic nuclear weapons but would concede nothing on shorter-range missiles 'until chemical weapons and the conventional imbalance were dealt with'.

Back in Britain, Mrs Thatcher immediately reported her Washington trip to Gorbachev. She emphasized how she had told Reagan that Gorbachev's reforms were 'historic and courageous and that you had my support for what you were trying to achieve. I mention this only to underline that <u>what</u> I say is not governed by <u>where</u> I say it.' She insisted that Reagan sought an INF agreement, but that the narrow Camp David agenda, not the cosmic talk of Reykjavik, would be his guide. She closed by inviting Gorbachev

---

* Mitterrand disliked flexible response because he feared that by allowing a nuclear exchange to be confined to the European theatre, the doctrine did not force the United States to give a total guarantee: it was America's way of 'playing for time and leaving it too late: if the Russians are in Bonn, it's too late'.

† This was due, in part, to their difference in temperament, but also reflected the slight wane in Reagan's mental acuity evident later in his second term.

to visit Britain again. Gorbachev replied that he appreciated her readiness to convey her thoughts, but his bottom line was clear: 'You shouldn't have a shadow of doubt as to our determination to translate into life the entire complex of Reykjavik.'

Mrs Thatcher's message hinted at a clear difference between her and the Reagan administration. In an unpublished draft of his memoirs, George Shultz put the matter succinctly: 'Gradually, she came to believe that it was important not only to engage with Gorbachev but to help Gorbachev. She was more the advocate of this view than Ronald Reagan ever was.' As Charles Powell put it, although Mrs Thatcher considered Gorbachev 'misguided . . . she still trusted him'. She therefore became almost his advocate in the West – or in Powell's teasing phrase, 'something of an agent of influence for Gorbachev'. Reagan was more cautious, repeating almost *ad nauseam* the Russian expression '*Doveryai, no proveryai* – trust but verify'. In his speech at the Brandenburg Gate, Reagan challenged Gorbachev to prove his intentions: 'if you seek liberalization: Come to this gate! Mr Gorbachev, open this gate! Mr Gorbachev, tear down this wall!' Mrs Thatcher had no misgivings about Reagan's rhetoric, but she put things differently. 'There are historic and courageous things happening in the Soviet Union,' she said three weeks later. She hoped Gorbachev's 'courageous plan' would succeed.

Before Mrs Thatcher's meeting with Reagan that July, Carlucci addressed the divergence. While 'no cause for quarrel', her positive approach to Gorbachev, he warned, was helping him become 'the media darling, especially in Europe, that she herself finds dangerous'. Gorbachev might be a true reformer, but so far he had not 'really earned the label fully'. Carlucci also felt that her desire to encourage Gorbachev's reforms could encourage the West to give him 'dangerous, gratuitous, or at best premature concessions'. The USA should push the Soviet Union in the right direction without falling into Gorbachev's traps: 'I doubt Prime Minister Thatcher would differ with any of this.'

Carlucci was probably right. The difference in assessing Gorbachev arose from the two Western leaders' respective situations and characters. At home, Mrs Thatcher could take bolder risks. Reagan, out of luck because of Iran-Contra, and out of time because of being in his final term, had to be conscious of strains among Republicans on this issue. Perhaps because he was, by temperament, less inquiring than Mrs Thatcher, he was slower to be interested in Gorbachev's internal reforms. On the whole, Reagan's trajectory on this issue followed hers, not the other way round.

In November, eager to improve her understanding of Gorbachev's reforms, Mrs Thatcher received several of his top officials.* Shortly afterwards, Powell told Charlie Price she 'had the impression that Gorbachev's domestic difficulties were even more formidable than she had imagined'. Attentive to intelligence sources, she balanced her support for his reforms with alertness to Soviet behaviour abroad. In this she was reinforced by Percy Cradock, who was always highly suspicious of Soviet intentions. As Chairman of the Joint Intelligence Committee (JIC), Cradock presented Mrs Thatcher with the 'Red Book' of JIC reports every Friday morning, together with his own covering notes. In a typical example from August 1987, Cradock warned there was 'no diminution in the long-term politico/military threat posed to Western Europe. In fact the new flexibility, coupled with western credulity, makes the Soviet Union in some ways a more formidable adversary.' These sentences excited Mrs Thatcher to a series of heavy underlinings.

Cradock was keen, too, to point out splits within the Soviet hierarchy. In late October, increasingly frustrated by the pace of reform, Boris Yeltsin, the reformist Mayor of Moscow, accused Gorbachev publicly of indulging in a 'cult of personality'. On 11 November, Gorbachev denounced Yeltsin, confirming his removal from his Moscow job. Summing up the JIC reaction, Cradock described the affair as 'a distinct setback'. If Gorbachev proceeded faster with reform, 'it could risk unseating him'. The problem, replied Mrs Thatcher, was that Gorbachev 'wants to improve the system without realising the system is hopeless'.† Already anxious that Gorbachev's reforms might founder on hardline opposition, Western leaders now saw that he might also be outflanked by those wanting more radical change. His personal prestige was diminishing. That November Mrs Thatcher told the French Prime Minister, Jacques Chirac, that 'for the first time, she was worried whether Mr Gorbachev was going to survive'.

Also in November, Gorbachev agreed to visit Britain en route to his summit with Reagan in Washington. This welcome news made it less likely she could be excluded from American counsels, as at Reykjavik. Seizing the opportunity, she wrote to Reagan to remind him of their agreed agenda for arms control. Although slightly taken aback by the news of Gorbachev's

---

* They included Gorbachev's Deputy Prime Minister, Valentin Tolstykh, his chief economic adviser, Abel Aganbegyan, and Gury Marchuk, the President of the Soviet Academy of Sciences.
† On 22 November, the *Observer* splashed with a story unfavourable to Mrs Gorbachev, about Yeltsin's attack on her and the cult of the 'First Lady'. Mrs Thatcher was irritated – 'Yes,' she replied to Charles Powell's suggestion that she convey to the Gorbachevs how sorry she was about the piece, 'I too suffer from the *Observer*.' (The paper had exposed her son Mark's involvement in a controversial building contract in Oman (see p. 440).)

British stopover, the Americans saw value in demonstrating Western unity. Reagan sent Mrs Thatcher a reassuring reply.

Before Gorbachev and Mrs Thatcher met, on 7 December, at RAF Brize Norton in Oxfordshire, Bernard Ingham warned her that the US media wanted to paint the meeting as engineered 'to upstage Reagan' and '"to ensure that Gorbachev knows what the West's real position is" – i.e. before Reagan blurts out his objective of a nuclear-free world'. They would seek confirmation that the meeting was designed '"to put on a show to convince American conservatives INF really is OK"'. This was a pretty good summary. That night, Mrs Thatcher spoke to Woodrow Wyatt on the telephone: 'It's quite exciting,' she said of the impending visit. Wyatt noted that 'she spoke with that schoolgirl eagerness I love ... She said, "The others" (meaning the European leaders) "are as jealous as hell".'

The principals could hardly wait. As one witness recalled: 'the evident mutual chemistry ... was such that, on catching their first glimpse of each other and before [Gorbachev] was clear of his aircraft or the engines had gone quiet, the two of them began smiling, greeting and speaking to each other, fully 10 paces apart!'

At the meeting, Gorbachev flattered Mrs Thatcher. He 'wanted to say to the Prime Minister, personally, since there was a rather special relationship based on mutual sympathy between them, that he was ready to go a very long way indeed with the policy of perestroika', which would include 'a policy of democratisation'. As Mrs Thatcher returned to the comparison between their two situations that she enjoyed making, Gorbachev 'interjected that the Prime Minister's understanding was remarkable. The Prime Minister added that her own first two years in office had been her most trying, but she had pressed on. The most difficult undertaking of all was to change people's attitudes.'

She said 'she found it irritating that the exponents of the old psychology in the Soviet Union were described as conservatives. She wanted nothing to do with Mr Gorbachev's conservatives. (Mr Gorbachev thought this a tremendous joke.)' He said that his next step would be to build a democracy with 'a proper legal foundation to make it irreversible'. When the talk turned to arms control, the two soon became enmeshed in their habitual arguments over the morality of nuclear deterrence. She also told him the atmosphere of disarmament discussions and INF ratification would improve if the Soviets agreed to move on human rights and Afghanistan. Powell noted: 'Mr Gorbachev, who by now was getting very restless, said that a solution in Afghanistan would be made easier if the United Kingdom would stop supplying the rebels with missiles which they used to shoot down civilian aircraft.'

At the press conference, Mrs Thatcher declared that Gorbachev's account of *perestroika* had been 'absolutely fascinating. He is a bold, determined and courageous leader and I hope that he succeeds in his colossal task.'* Soon afterwards she called Reagan: Gorbachev, she said, both wanted and needed further arms control agreements: '. . . She thought he was a man with a sense of history and was genuinely prepared to work for improved East/West relations in a new spirit of co-operation.'† Reagan replied that she had 'clearly softened him up'. Indeed, 'He wondered whether she would like to come over and sit in on the meetings.' Mrs Thatcher had the sense to see this was a joke: in truth, nothing would have given her more pleasure.

The Reagan–Gorbachev Washington summit, at which the INF Agreement was signed, was a success. Telephoning Mrs Thatcher afterwards, Reagan thanked her. He 'thought our consulting so closely had made it clear to Gorbachev that he could not split the Alliance'. It also helped Reagan secure his right flank. As Peter Robinson, Reagan's speechwriter, recalled, conservatives 'were afraid Reagan was going soft. But if Margaret Thatcher was also dealing with Gorbachev, it made it much harder to conclude that he had simply gone soft . . . she gave him cover.'

With a deftness she rarely displayed in her dealings with European politicians, Mrs Thatcher retained her uniquely high standing with the Republican right while probably doing more, in practical terms, to assist the more centrist elements in the administration. As her influence grew, her support was highly coveted. As Ken Duberstein recalled with some chagrin, 'There were people in the US government who would call her . . . and say it would be great if she could weigh in with President Reagan. So, at times, we discounted her advice because she was being put up to it.' Mrs Thatcher's method of intervening with the President was considered 'astute' by his staff. As one recalled, 'She would grab him by the arm and say, "Ronnie, I want to talk to you about this or that after the meeting" . . . I think she

---

* It is notable that in Washington, the next day, Reagan neither encouraged nor showed an interest in Gorbachev's reforms. When the Soviet leader attempted to open a discussion of the issue Reagan cut him off with an unflattering joke about the failings of Communism, much to the embarrassment of the Americans present. 'Gorbachev colored,' Shultz recorded, and said nothing more about the issue.

† There were, however, limits to that spirit of cooperation. Richard Pollock, Mrs Thatcher's interpreter, recorded that when Mrs Thatcher privately mentioned to Gorbachev her 'request that whatever could be done for a certain family should be done if possible . . . MSG [Gorbachev] strides purposefully on, without reaction . . . MSG clearly registered the point, with palpable if unexpressed emotion.' The 'certain family' was that of the prominent Soviet defector to Britain, Oleg Gordievsky.

manipulated him much more cleverly than the official record will show.'*
Mrs Thatcher, recalled Powell, was also 'not unaware that [Reagan] was ageing and was less in command of some of the day-to-day issues than he once was'. Her own attitude to Reagan in decline was loyal, but sad. One day in 1988, Chris Donnelly, an expert on the Soviet armed forces, suggested involving Reagan in the matter under discussion. Mrs Thatcher pulled a face and replied: 'Unfortunately, his mind is such now that we'll see no more initiatives from him.'†

The strongest specific example of the power of the Thatcher–Reagan relationship was over arms sales to Argentina. In the years following the 1982 Falklands War, Buenos Aires tried repeatedly to buy US Skyhawk A-4 fighter aircraft from Israel. This deal required US approval. Repeatedly America moved to approve it, and repeatedly Mrs Thatcher stamped it down. Ahead of her visit to Camp David in November 1986, US officials persuaded the President to take up the issue himself: 'You will want to tell Mrs Thatcher that we cannot continually put off how best to nurture Argentina's democracy,' wrote Poindexter. 'And that sooner rather than later, we will want to return to the question of military aircraft for Argentina. You should expect a typical Thatcher barrage.'

John Kerr, at the Washington Embassy, had got wind of this effort and warned Mrs Thatcher. She said:

> Just not possible ... 'He can't do that.' And she put it on her shopping list. Like going to Sainsbury's ... and she put it in her handbag. [At the end of her meeting with Reagan she] got out the handbag ... found the shopping list and said: 'there is something we have forgotten ... Ah yes ... Arms to Argentina.' And she looked at him and said, simply but sternly, 'You won't, will you?' And Reagan said, 'No, of course I won't, Margaret.' And that was the end of three months of the US interagency process.

---

* One area in which Margaret Thatcher's influence in Washington was less pronounced was the Middle East. During her second term she had played a modest role in bringing the parties together (see pp. 434–7), but she was less influential, particularly after Peres was succeeded by Yitzhak Shamir, a Likud hardliner. 'Shamir is, as Begin was, "a biblical times man",' she told George Shultz in March 1988. 'He cannot give the territories [land occupied by Israel since the war of 1967] back ... Something is needed to move Shamir.' Reagan had his own frustrations with Shamir, but Mrs Thatcher's pleas to put greater pressure on the Israeli leader fell largely on deaf ears.

† Speculation notwithstanding, it was not until 1994 that Reagan's regular exhaustive medical examinations found any evidence of mental loss beyond that due to age. Later that year, he was diagnosed with Alzheimer's disease.

In March 1988, the State Department sought to back an Argentine resolution at the UN Security Council calling for negotiations to resolve the future of the Falkland Islands. This, Charlie Price reported to Washington after seeing Charles Powell, had left Mrs Thatcher 'absolutely livid': '[Powell] said Thatcher found the very idea that we would even consider such an action after all they have done for us "insulting". The Prime Minister was "gravely affronted" ... he had not seen [her] so "hopping mad" ... it was "breathtaking", "outrageous", and "inconceivable" that we would support Argentina on a matter like this ...'

The Americans duly backed off. Taking stock, Price advised Washington that there was 'no point in going down that road if we are not prepared to withstand the British storm at the end of it. That means the President and, at this late stage, his willingness to impair his close personal relationship with the Prime Minister.' Reagan was not willing. So long as he was in the White House and she was in 10 Downing Street, the United States was not going to side with Argentina over Britain.

By 1988, Mrs Thatcher sensed that Western unity against the Soviets was weakening because of the very changes under Gorbachev's leadership which, for wider reasons, she welcomed. She wanted NATO to reassert its shared purpose. Visiting Brussels in mid-February, ahead of a special NATO summit in March, she found 'disturbing signs of weakness', especially among the Germans, and 'an air of torpor', wrote Powell: 'The real problem is that they are not frightened any more: the new-look Soviet diplomacy is having its effect.' On 8 February, Gorbachev had revealed that the Soviet Union would withdraw from Afghanistan – an announcement timed, perhaps, to make NATO waver.

Mrs Thatcher was alarmed. The JIC saw 'no evidence' of a diminished threat from the Warsaw Pact. The INF Treaty would only drive the Soviets to compensate for their loss of nuclear strength by improving their conventional forces. This was not, Percy Cradock, stressed, 'a prediction of a Soviet invasion' but a warning that the Soviet aim was to 'intimidate and overawe'.

Reports of Mrs Thatcher's increasingly tough stance displeased the Kremlin. Nikolai Kosov, a contact of Charles Powell's at the Soviet Embassy with direct personal access to Gorbachev, warned Powell 'in some agitation' that Zamyatin, the Soviet Ambassador, had just returned from Moscow 'with a considerable flea in his ear from Mr Gorbachev'. Why this 'sudden change' from her tone at Brize Norton? Was it any longer 'worth his while' for Gorbachev to visit the United Kingdom at the end of the year, as planned? 'I am not at all surprised by this approach,' Powell commented: the Russians hoped to 'frighten us off'.

In Downing Street the following day, Mrs Thatcher told Zamyatin there had been no change in her views. Indeed, she expressed her admiration for the 'boldness' of Gorbachev's policies, especially his decision to leave Afghanistan. Kosov later told Powell that these comments had helped Gorbachev keep Soviet reaction to the NATO summit 'fairly low-key'. Slightly mollified, Mrs Thatcher wrote: 'I think we should perhaps recognise that they really are making an effort.'

In the end, the NATO summit went off almost spookily well. Kohl rejected both the third zero and denuclearization. Mrs Thatcher urged vigilance against Gorbachev trying to detach allies from one another. In striking remarks delivered extemporaneously, Reagan reiterated the importance of NATO and its nuclear deterrent. When he concluded, Mrs Thatcher turned to him with some relief: 'Brilliant, Ron,' she said softly. 'Brilliant!' The resulting summit declaration avoided a promise to 'modernize' nuclear systems, but used the phrase 'kept up to date where necessary'.*
In her press conference, Mrs Thatcher referred to the withdrawal from Afghanistan: 'We have perhaps begun to see some signs of change in the Soviet Union's external policies.'

As Reagan's summit with Gorbachev in Moscow approached, his administration began to move. In May, Reagan publicly endorsed Mrs Thatcher's support for Gorbachev's domestic reform. A day later, offering her advice for his summit, Mrs Thatcher emphasized there was 'absolutely no need to be disappointed that a START [STRATEGIC ARMS REDUCTION TREATY] agreement is not ready for signature'. She then wrote to Gorbachev in strikingly similar terms. As ever, she wanted no rush for an agreement and to avoid any effort to resurrect the Reykjavik agenda. Her second point drew on her own experience of visiting Moscow. She urged Reagan to 'let the Russian people experience at first hand the deep sincerity of your commitment to peace and freedom . . .' She hoped he would have the chance to move among them: 'the impact of such direct contact will be enormous'.

So it proved. In his speech at Moscow University on 31 May, Reagan spoke about freedom and human rights. As Jack Matlock, the US Ambassador in Moscow, described it, 'his speech rang out as a paean to Gorbachev's *perestroika*'. Mrs Thatcher was right about the President's

---

* The debate over 'modernization' was a crucial one. Defenders of 'flexible response' insisted that short-range systems must be modernized to ensure their effectiveness. But those who sought a third zero had no interest in modernization. Here was an effort to find a form of words both sides could live with.

personal encounter with the Russian people. He and Gorbachev walked together in Red Square, greeting Muscovites and kissing babies. When a journalist asked Reagan if he still considered the Soviet Union an evil empire, the President said he did not: 'I was talking about another time, another era.'

It had been arranged that Reagan would visit London on his way back from Moscow. Mrs Thatcher was doubly happy because Reagan had, in turn, invited her to Washington that November. Her visit would be central to the plan to round off Reagan's eight-year reign and, as Nancy Reagan put it, 'tie it up with a bow'.

Reagan and Mrs Thatcher met in London on 3 June 1988, almost exactly four years since they had last come together in the same city and discussed the then chilly state of the Cold War. Now all was transformed. In his speech in Guildhall, Reagan declared that the 'forward strategy of freedom' he had spoken of in his previous set-piece speech in London in June 1982 was bearing fruit: 'quite possibly, we are entering a new era in history, a time of lasting change in the Soviet Union'. Reagan crowned this review with a high compliment:

> I want to say that through all the troubles of the last decade, one such firm, eloquent voice, a voice that proclaimed proudly the cause of the Western alliance and human freedom, has been heard. A voice that never sacrificed its anti-Communist credentials or its realistic appraisal of change in the Soviet Union ... Prime Minister, the achievements of the Moscow summit as well as the Geneva and Washington summits say much about your valor and strength, and, by virtue of the office you hold, that of the British people.

In response, a flattered Mrs Thatcher said she believed there was 'now more hope between East and West than ever before in the lifetime of most of us here'. She saw Reagan's visit as a celebration of their shared triumph. It was both natural and politic that, when the President of the United States himself gave her generous credit, she should bask in it. She had become more important in the world than any British prime minister since Churchill. Given how often she had struggled to contain Reagan's propensity for nuclear disarmament, she also felt sheer relief at having prevented him.

Between June and November 1988, Anglo-American political traffic slowed for the US presidential election. Mrs Thatcher was delighted when George Bush, Reagan's Vice-President, defeated the Democratic candidate, Michael Dukakis. In her mind, this signalled continuity in foreign policy. Before the handover, however, she would visit Reagan one last time. 'It was largely a theatrical visit. *Fin de siècle* stuff,' judged Charles Powell. No detail was too small for the Reagans and little expense was spared.* Via Powell, the White House inquired as to whether the Thatchers might wish to stay after dinner to dance with the President and First Lady. 'This would be an exceptional gesture,' commented Powell. 'Yes,' wrote Mrs Thatcher, who had an ill-suppressed passion for dancing, 'love to.' Fred Ryan, Reagan's director of appointments and scheduling, recalled, 'There's always jockeying to come to State dinners, but this one ... because it was Margaret Thatcher, <u>everyone</u> wanted to go.'†

At the arrival ceremony at the White House on 16 November, Reagan welcomed Mrs Thatcher with a nineteen-gun salute. 'The atmosphere', recalled George Shultz, 'was that the Cold War was basically over. We had worked hard together and it had worked.' As was surprisingly often the case for a woman who enjoyed good health, Mrs Thatcher had a nasty cold and, in the Oval Office, her voice began to fail. Duberstein remembered: 'I had never seen Ronald Reagan dote over somebody before. He himself got her a pot of tea. He himself found her tissues ... I remember him scurrying around the Oval Office trying to make her comfortable ... It said everything about their relationship.'

Some substantive discussion took place through the sniffs and sneezes, most notably a warning from Mrs Thatcher against ready acceptance of Gorbachev's suggestion of a human rights conference in Moscow. Without proper preconditions, she feared, it could become a propaganda triumph for the Soviets.‡ However, even she saw that this was not the moment to press the retiring President. Their meeting ended thus: 'As the Prime Minister was set to depart, the President told her that, in his discussions with the

---

* Reviewing the guest list for the President's dinner, Mrs Thatcher crossed out the veteran BBC correspondent Alistair Cooke and replaced him with Charlton Heston. She ticked Weinberger, Kissinger, Paul Volcker, Alan Greenspan and several others. She pointedly did not tick General Al Haig, who had so annoyed her during the Falklands War. Other guests included Alexander Solzhenitsyn, Michael Caine, Tom Selleck, Andrew Lloyd Webber and David Hockney.
† To make the dinner feel special, both Carol and Mark were invited, but, as Antony Acland recalled, 'Mark was extremely difficult. He was upset that he hadn't been placed at the main table and he made all sorts of objections.' 'He was a spoilt brat who behaved very badly,' said one senior US official involved in arranging the visit. 'He exploited his mother's position.'
‡ The idea for a human rights conference in Moscow had been proposed by Gorbachev as early as 1986. Mrs Thatcher had always been opposed unless the Soviets agreed to stiff preconditions. Reagan had warmed to the notion, both because he wanted to recognize Gorbachev's reforms and because it was essential to completing the Vienna talks (on the implementation of the Helsinki Final Act) before he left office. In November 1988, Mrs Thatcher met Andrei Sakharov, the Soviet dissident scientist, who told her that such a conference could be 'useful' under 'certain conditions', thereby hewing closer to the American position than to hers. In early January 1989, Mrs Thatcher reluctantly gave in. The conference took place in October 1991.

Soviets, he would not do anything that would jeopardize Britain's nuclear program. Prime Minister Thatcher responded, "I never doubted you."' This was a factual untruth. Yet there was perhaps a broader, poetic truth. She had never doubted that Ronald Reagan was a friend to her and to Britain, that their joint endeavour for what they both believed in would prevail.

Toasting Mrs Thatcher over lunch at the State Department, George Shultz was so bold as to present her with what he called 'the first and perhaps only Grand Order of the Handbag'. Handing her a handsome bag, he offered a dictionary definition: '*Handbag*, verb transitive, bag, bagging; 1. to inspire through leadership, energy and special powers of persuasion, agreement on alliance programs and priorities that advance the achievement of the Western cause; 2. to employ a unique diplomatic satchel; 3. to bag is generally considered more desirable than to be bagged.' Inside Shultz had placed choice quotations from her speeches, which he read out to the assembled company. Thus did the verb 'to handbag', already in use in reference to Mrs Thatcher, gain formal authorization.

The climax of the visit came that evening with dinner at the White House. Reagan expressed 'considerable satisfaction' that Mrs Thatcher would remain in her post as President Bush succeeded him: 'Nancy and I are proud to claim the Thatchers as our friends, just as America is proud to claim the United Kingdom as a friend and ally.'

Mrs Thatcher replied in kind. She revealed 'the feeling of sheer joy at your election eight years ago, knowing that we thought so much alike ... and convinced that together we could get our countries back on their feet, restore their values and create a safer and, yes, a better world'. She ended by quoting the famous lines of Arthur Hugh Clough's 'Say not the Struggle naught Availeth':

> And not by eastern windows only,
>   When daylight comes, comes in the light;
> In front, the sun climbs slow, how slowly,
>   But westward, look! The land is bright.*

After dinner the Reagans and the Thatchers enjoyed 'Shall We Dance',

---

* The poem was a favourite of Mrs Thatcher. She later told Peggy Noonan, Reagan's speechwriter, that she remembered hearing Churchill use the words on the radio to rally the nation. She was correct. Churchill cited Clough in a broadcast on 27 April 1941, when Britain's situation against Hitler was almost desperate and the United States had not yet entered the war. By speaking of the bright land to the west, Churchill was in effect imploring the Americans to help. When she heard this, Margaret Roberts was fifteen.

and changed partners for 'Hello, Dolly'. Afterwards, back at their official lodging, an elated Mrs Thatcher characteristically tried to convene a post-dinner meeting of her officials. 'Calm down, dear,' Denis exclaimed, perhaps thinking of his wife's cold. 'You must go to bed.'

After she returned home, Mrs Thatcher wrote to thank the Reagans. She confessed to feeling a 'little sadness' during the visit, knowing that your historic Presidency was drawing to a close ... But I am sure George will be no less true to those fundamental beliefs and he can look to our complete loyalty and support.'

Rarely can a US presidential transition have seemed as smooth, from the British point of view, as that from Ronald Reagan to George H. W. Bush. During Bush's eight years as Vice-President, Mrs Thatcher had taken care to cultivate him, always calling on him when she visited Washington* and welcoming him when he visited Britain.† The relationship was professional, trusting and pleasant. 'Margaret and I became good friends,' Bush recalled. Mrs Thatcher also liked Bush's intelligent, no-nonsense (and somewhat left-wing) wife Barbara, probably preferring her company to the pricklier Nancy Reagan. 'Prime Minister Thatcher's delight at your victory is almost palpable,' Charlie Price told Bush after the 1988 presidential election. 'No doubt you sensed it when she called election night.'‡ Mrs Thatcher was 'gratified' that she knew not only Bush and his incoming Secretary of State, James Baker, but others he might pick for his new team.

The smoothness of the transition, however, concealed one problem and perhaps exacerbated another. Bush and Mrs Thatcher were not complementary characters. At their first encounter, in 1977, Bush had described her as 'frighteningly bright' (see p. 158). This unease would always be present. Bush felt he had to be on his best behaviour with her and found this irritating. She, according to Charles Powell, also felt difficulties: 'Bush was a man's man, liking off-duty to wear jeans and cowboy boots and drink beer out of a can. She was always in her high heels.' She was also inclined to think that Bush lacked Reagan's clear conviction, even that he was wet. She tended to hector men whom she thought of in this way.

Her hectoring particularly irritated Bush because, unlike Reagan, he

---

* The Vice-President's official residence is next door to the British Embassy. Mrs Thatcher often exploited this to have a working breakfast with Bush.
† Mrs Thatcher even had Bush to stay at Chequers (in February 1984), an unusual honour for a vice-president.
‡ It shows Mrs Thatcher's sense of international isolation that she confided in Rodric Braithwaite, the incoming British Ambassador to the Soviet Union: 'If Dukakis wins this election, Gorbachev will be my only friend left.'

came to the White House with a wealth of foreign policy experience (including CIA Director and UN Ambassador). According to Brent Scowcroft, Bush's National Security Advisor, she would 'try and speak without letting Bush get a word in . . . He would feel patronized.' Political commitment as well as character was at issue. Baker thought the two were '*philosophically* birds of a feather'. But there was quite a difference between Bush, the child of American wealth and privilege, and Mrs Thatcher, the grocer's daughter, who saw herself as having fought a lonely battle for the truth against feeble and complacent men. In her mind Reagan, resisting Communism in the political wilderness of the 1970s, was her analogue in a way that Bush, the Yale-educated insider, could never be.

Under Reagan, both Bush and Baker had witnessed the disproportionate influence Mrs Thatcher had enjoyed. According to Robert Zoellick, Baker's closest aide, Baker admired her but complained 'how he'd watched Margaret Thatcher wrap Ronald Reagan around her little finger'. When asked in later years if Reagan had allowed Mrs Thatcher too much influence, Bush agreed: 'I think he was just smitten by her. She really spoke for Reagan. In all international meetings: "Ronnie and I think this. Ron and I want to do that."' 'I just can't continue the way President Reagan did with her,' Bush told Scowcroft shortly before taking office. 'I respect her. I like her. But I'm the President of the United States!'

Few of these undercurrents registered with Mrs Thatcher. And in the early days, all went well. Her farewell visit to Reagan in November also included time with the President-elect. On the main East–West issues, Bush spoke reassuringly. He promised 'no hairpin bends' in arms control negotiations. His views on nuclear weapons were indeed robustly traditional; he never shared Reagan's iconoclastic approach.

Agreement was such that, on the official record of his conversation with Mrs Thatcher, Bush scribbled, 'No real hot news here'. But he had not chosen to raise any controversial matters, above all her increasing difficulties with Helmut Kohl. The NSC staff warned that among the Europeans she was 'perceived as imperious and preachy'. The task ahead was 'to balance our special relationship with Britain with our bedrock requirement to work with other key European allies, in particular the Germans'. For the time being, however, all was sweetness and light. Shortly after inauguration day, Mrs Thatcher called the new President: 'The United States could always rely on Britain,' she told him. Flatteringly, Bush told her he hoped he could 'feel free to call on the Prime Minister for her advice'.

As the US presidential election played out, Mrs Thatcher had been an active mover elsewhere in East–West relations. On 2 November 1988, she flew to Poland at the invitation of the Communist government, led by General Wojciech Jaruzelski. Taking his cue from Mikhail Gorbachev in opening up to the West, Jaruzelski sought to harness Mrs Thatcher's popularity in his country.* She, in turn, saw a visit to Poland as a natural extension of her efforts to reach out to Eastern Europe. Nervous of her capacity to boost opposition forces, above all the trade union Solidarity, led by Lech Wałęsa, Jaruzelski sought to prevent her from visiting Gdańsk, Solidarity's birthplace. But when Mrs Thatcher insisted, he allowed the visit to go ahead.

Just before Mrs Thatcher set off, however, the Polish government set a trap. It announced that the loss-making Lenin shipyard in Gdańsk would be closed, under reforms aimed at bringing some market freedoms without political liberty. It was an attempt, the British Ambassador in Poland told her, 'to cut off Solidarity from its birthplace'. Would she, who had fought the NUM so fiercely over pit closures, support Solidarity,† or would she side with the economic rationale of the Communist government? Grappling with this dilemma, Mrs Thatcher scribbled down her thoughts. Parliamentary democracy in Britain, she wrote, allowed the expression of political freedom: 'It is where there is no political freedom that the task of pol. opp. [sic] falls to the Trade Unions. Moreover because there is no forum for open debate, their only method of political expression is through strikes. So the economic condition of any enterprise is really not economic but political. And everyone knows it.' She hewed to this line throughout her time in Poland.

When she met Jaruzelski on 3 November, he praised her reforms, seeking to persuade her that his government understood the 'broader current' of reform sweeping Eastern Europe. But such change, he said, must be adapted to Poland's 'specific conditions'. Mrs Thatcher told him that earlier that day she had visited the church of Fr Jerzy Popiełuszko, the priest who had been kidnapped, tortured and murdered by the Polish security service in 1984. There 'she had felt the power of the Solidarity movement. As a politician, her instinct told her that power could not be denied.' At Jaruzelski's request, she agreed to help persuade Solidarity to take part in 'Round Table' talks with the government. When she praised the Polish people, many of whom were 'very good Conservatives ... General Jaruzelski permitted himself a wintry smile'. Afterwards she told Powell that

---

* Even before her visit, Mrs Thatcher had acquired mythical status among Poles. The journalist and historian Timothy Garton Ash recalled seeing in a market in Warsaw earlier that year a handwritten poster exclaiming (in English), 'Mrs Thatcher – Buy Poland!'
† The origins of Solidarity did cause a little difficulty for Mrs Thatcher's world view. She once said to Malcolm Rifkind, when the junior minister for Eastern Europe, 'Solidarity is a marvellous anti-Communist organization, but why does it have to be a trade union?'

Jaruzelski was 'a patriot trying to do the right thing'. Early the following morning, Mrs Thatcher flew to Gdańsk. She wore a green suit, advised by a Polish assistant at Aquascutum as being the colour of hope. A dramatic brimless hat completed her ensemble. She was amazed by the scene as her boat moored at the shipyard: 'Every inch of it seemed taken up with shipyard workers waving and cheering.' Once her official programme ended she was taken to a hotel, at which point all Polish television and media coverage was cut off. She wondered what would happen next. After about ten minutes, Powell recalled, there was a 'timid knock' and 'a rather nervous Wałęsa was shoved into the room by his supporters'.*

Wałęsa led her on foot to the presbytery of his priest, where they talked. Wałęsa told her that 'The Communist system was finished. The only question was how to get out of it.' His union was open to the idea of Round Table talks, but not under threats like that of closing the shipyard. Mrs Thatcher urged that Solidarity make its willingness to talk clear. She asked how Solidarity could best get its points over to the government. 'Mr Walesa pointed to the ceiling and said that all its meetings were bugged so there was no problem.'

After lunch with a wider group, Mrs Thatcher visited the Church of St Brigit, the spiritual heart of Solidarity. It was packed with supporters making the V for victory salute. As Powell recalled, her eyes 'did moisten', especially at the singing of the Solidarity anthem ('That Poland Be Poland'). She gave what she described as 'a short emotional speech'. Back at the shipyard gates, she laid a wreath at a monument for workers killed by the security forces. Vast, cheering crowds, forcibly kept at a distance, climbed on buildings to wave and shout, in English, 'Thank you. Thank you.'

Mrs Thatcher saw Jaruzelski again in Warsaw later that day (4 November). Her visit to Gdańsk, she said, had been 'moving'. Solidarity's strongest resentment was that it was illegal. If it got assurances of good faith, she thought it would probably say yes to talks. Jaruzelski appeared to give no ground. He complained that Solidarity wanted to be 'the only ruler' of Poland: it must demonstrate responsibility before it could be legalized. At the same time, he told Mrs Thatcher how much he respected her. He wanted Britain and Poland to 'play a role bridging a gap between the two parts of Europe'. Although she loved the idea of working with a free Poland, she was highly suspicious of its Communist incarnation. Speaking

---

* This nervousness in the presence of Mrs Thatcher was a rather touching aspect of the attitude of Solidarity and the Polish dissidents towards her. The left-wing poet Adam Michnik, who attended the lunch in the Gdańsk presbytery, wore a tie, the only occasion he had ever been seen in one.

at dinner with Jaruzelski the night before, she urged him, quoting Shakespeare's *Julius Caesar*, to acknowledge the 'tide in the affairs of men' and take it at the flood.

In accordance with protocol, the Polish Prime Minister accompanied Mrs Thatcher to the airport to say farewell. As she was about to board the plane, however, there was 'a screech of brakes on the tarmac'. Out jumped General Jaruzelski, who presented her with a large bunch of flowers. As she later wrote: 'not even Marxism could suppress Polish gallantry'.

In later years, Lech Wałęsa said that without his meeting with Mrs Thatcher 'there would have been no victory'. According to Timothy Garton Ash, the prominent journalist and later Professor of European Studies at Oxford, claims that Poland was 'bound' to liberalize suffer from 'the illusion of retrospective determinism'. With her notable theatrical abilities, Mrs Thatcher had dramatized Poland's situation at the crucial moment. In the ensuing weeks, Solidarity did take part in Round Table talks. Legalization followed in January 1989 and in semi-free legislative assembly elections that June, Solidarity won a huge victory. Through her government's policy of getting close to the 'soft under-belly of the Soviet Union' Mrs Thatcher was well prepared to help. She was the main Western leader who had been in the right place, with the right ideas, at the right time.

In February 1989, Mrs Thatcher faced an unexpected challenge from the Middle East. On St Valentine's Day the Ayatollah Khomeini pronounced a fatwa on the British novelist Salman Rushdie, whose novel *The Satanic Verses* he declared blasphemous. It invited the faithful to kill Rushdie. This was Khomeini's way of celebrating the tenth anniversary of his Islamic revolution and part of widespread Iranian support for terrorism overseas and the taking of Western hostages.* For some time, the Foreign Office had been edging towards reforging diplomatic ties, partly to help get the hostages released. Mrs Thatcher disapproved of any rapprochement. The Rushdie affair made it easier for her to freeze the process.

When Powell presented her with evidence of 'the Iranians officially trying to carry out the Ayatollah's threat to execute Salman Rushdie', Mrs Thatcher requested all British Embassy staff withdrawn from Teheran at once. In the Commons, Howe stressed that the fatwa was an attack 'on the fundamental freedoms for which our society stands'. Mrs Thatcher wholeheartedly agreed, though she did not warm to Rushdie himself. He

---

* Several of these were British – the businessman Roger Cooper, for example, in Iran; and Terry Waite, the Archbishop of Canterbury's special representative, and the journalist John McCarthy in Lebanon.

was a classic salon leftist and a member of the 20 June Group of writers who met in the Holland Park house of Harold Pinter and Lady Antonia Fraser to try to concert an intellectual fight-back against Thatcherism.* When Alan Clark later complained to Mrs Thatcher that Rushdie was 'a tiresome piece of work', she wrote: 'Whether or no we have any sympathy with Rushdie's views is not the point. We must react strongly to any <u>state murder</u> hunt made against one of our citizens.' 'Rather to the astonishment of everybody, we didn't hesitate to protect him,' recalled William Waldegrave, then a Foreign Office minister, 'against the advice of people like John le Carré and others, who felt he should be left to look after himself.'

The Rushdie affair also raised, in vivid terms, the problematic relationship between Islamist extremism in the Middle East and the attitudes of Muslim citizens on British streets. After the fatwa, Mrs Thatcher's freelance adviser David Hart warned her that 'Islam may now present a greater threat to Western security than the Soviet Union.' Powell told her this was 'a lot of bombast', but Hart was on to something which Powell – and Mrs Thatcher herself – did not quite take in. Neither properly grasped that the issue was inextricably both global and local and was likely to stay that way.

In early March, Iran broke off diplomatic ties with Britain.† Three months later Khomeini died. His death did not end the fatwa, but it created greater possibilities. Offers came from all sorts of potential intermediaries, but the basic problem, as Powell put it, was that 'You can't mediate a threatened assassination.' Rushdie remained under constant protection. It was only in September 1990, following the Iraqi invasion of Kuwait, that Iran agreed to restore diplomatic ties, with a statement promising no interference in the internal affairs of the United Kingdom.

At the time, there was frustration within government that, as Waldegrave put it, 'Rushdie and Pinter were so antipathetic to Mrs Thatcher that they could not admit to anything done right by her.' After her death, Rushdie softened somewhat, conceding that she 'offered me protection when I needed it'. When they met he found her 'very considerate, and, surprisingly, touchy-feely . . . She would tap you on the arm and say, "Everything OK?" I hadn't expected that touch of tenderness.' Mrs Thatcher was certainly sympathetic to Rushdie's personal plight, but it was principle, not

---

* Early in the crisis, Charles Powell reported to Mrs Thatcher that Rushdie had been telephoning the Liberal leader, Paddy Ashdown, to complain, falsely, that she was doing nothing for him. 'What a creep!' he wrote, words which Mrs Thatcher underlined.

† Towards the end of the month, Mrs Thatcher was informed that four named individuals chosen by Hezbollah (the Iranian-backed Shia Islamist militant group) would soon be sent to Britain to kill Rushdie. '<u>Home Office</u> Assume they will be <u>refused</u> admission,' she wrote, perhaps superfluously.

tenderness, which actuated her – the rule of law and the basic freedoms of British citizens, whatever their beliefs.

Following President Bush's inauguration in January 1989, the first action of the new administration in relation to East–West affairs had been deliberate inaction. 'The pause', as it was known, reflected the Bush team's fear that Reagan had become 'too enamoured' of Gorbachev and pushed ahead too fast on arms control. Washington's decision to pull back naturally left Mrs Thatcher with more space on the world stage. With Gorbachev due to visit Britain for the third time in April,* Rodric Braithwaite, the British Ambassador in Moscow, offered this assessment: 'The PM is perhaps the only foreign leader with whom [Gorbachev] can discuss domestic and foreign relations on equal terms ... If he cannot secure her understanding of Soviet positions, his chances of influence [sic] Western policy are diminished. And he may hope for some clues in interpreting the continuing silence from Washington.'

Mrs Thatcher's standing in the Soviet Union was high. She was much admired by two of Gorbachev's most senior and reformist advisers, Anatoly Chernyaev and Alexander Yakovlev, and favourably reported in the Soviet media. 'Prime Minister, you are top of the pops in the Soviet Union!' Powell scribbled on a report detailing her highly positive Soviet press profile. Gorbachev's difficulties, meanwhile, only grew. As Gorbachev's visit approached, Percy Cradock told her that the JIC considered the Soviet economy worse than when Gorbachev took over in 1985. Cradock noted almost uncontrollable demands for political autonomy in the nationalities† and 'the paradox of a man in considerable difficulties at home but performing with a great deal of skill abroad'. None of this discouraged Mrs Thatcher. Her entire strategy towards Gorbachev was a balance between endorsement and criticism. The more he was at risk, she felt, the more the West had an interest in helping him. A memo from Powell, ahead of Gorbachev's visit, declared that while Britain would disclaim any suggestion to be mediating between Moscow and Washington, 'there is no harm in letting it be known that you will be passing on your impressions to President Bush'. On this Mrs Thatcher simply wrote: 'Plenty of <u>flowers</u> in all <u>rooms</u>'.

Gorbachev arrived in London on 5 April 1989, direct from balmy Cuba. 'It is a cold, sleet-driven scene,' Braithwaite noted in his diary. 'The arrival ceremony is chaotic, with the RAF band playing the Soviet national

---

* The visit had been originally scheduled for December 1988, but Gorbachev had been forced to postpone after a terrible earthquake struck Soviet Armenia.
† The Soviet Union consisted of fifteen Soviet Socialist Republics harbouring varying degrees of nationalistic feeling.

anthem at half the usual speed. Mrs Thatcher looks grim.' Indeed, she was furious. The talks between the two leaders, however, were almost merry. Gorbachev, recorded Powell, was 'in lively and good-humoured form and . . . remarkably frank'. Mrs Thatcher took her briefing cards from her bag. 'Mr Gorbachev observed with much jollity that this must be the famous handbag. The Prime Minister retorted that it was the most secure place in 10 Downing Street.'

Gorbachev was worried that the Bush administration seemed distinctly less friendly than its predecessor. 'People were asking whether it was worth tying the whole destiny of the West to Mr Gorbachev . . . he sensed that the Prime Minister shared this more cautious approach.' Mrs Thatcher denied this vigorously. She wanted *perestroika* to succeed, but a 'secure defence' was the 'soundest basis' from which to welcome it. She praised Gorbachev's political reform,* but pointed out that real economic reform could be harder. On this Gorbachev agreed. As for Bush, she said, he would 'continue most of President Reagan's policies even if his personal style was rather different'.

As always, they clashed over nuclear deterrence.† On this occasion they also sparred about Gorbachev's announcement, at the UN that past December, of sweeping unilateral cuts in Soviet conventional forces.‡ When Mrs Thatcher pointed out that, even with these reductions, he would still have a 2:1 conventional superiority over the West, Gorbachev interjected sarcastically, 'Poor little West.' When she threatened to get out her maps to explain the conventional imbalance, 'Mr Gorbachev said that he knew the Prime Minister's maps all too well: they were specially prepared by Mr Powell to support her arguments.'

As in previous encounters, clear differences, clearly expressed, reinforced the sense of sincere goodwill. In Anatoly Chernyaev's view, Mrs Thatcher persuaded Gorbachev that Bush 'was not about to depart from the policy of US–Soviet cooperation'. At her press conference she pledged her 'full support' for his 'historic mission' of domestic reform.

Some of the Soviet party noticed that Mrs Thatcher's ardour – what one described as her 'look of sheer rapture and adoration' – did not seem fully reciprocated. On the plane home, Chernyaev rebuked Gorbachev for

---

* In recent free elections to the Congress of People's Deputies, Boris Yeltsin, the anti-establishment candidate in Moscow, had won nearly 90 per cent of the vote.

† Gorbachev apologized for having not yet congratulated Mrs Thatcher on the birth of her first grandchild, Michael, the previous month: 'he had rather hoped this would soften her views on nuclear weapons'. Mrs Thatcher did not rise to this bait.

‡ Gorbachev had declared his intention to reduce Soviet forces by 500,000.

not being sufficiently appreciative: 'She raised the prestige of perestroika, and of you personally, so much that Kohl, Mitterrand, and even Bush will have to try and keep pace ... Why pretend this isn't significant? Besides, she's a woman, not a man in a skirt ... And she's English ... If she's done this and doesn't get an appropriate response, the pride will take over. And we'll lose a lot.' Perhaps taking this to heart, Gorbachev spoke warmly of Mrs Thatcher to the Politburo on his return.* She was the most important person in persuading the West, he believed, that *perestroika* needed help. But he added an important point: 'In Europe and America people consider that she's overdoing her attempt to become the leader of the West. Both Bush and Kohl saw these ambitions of hers and regard her with some scepticism.' He was well informed.

Mrs Thatcher now hastened to brief Bush. Gorbachev, she told him, had been 'frank' about his enormous problems. He had said he was 'absolutely determined to go ahead with perestroika and I believe him'. At the same time, she commented on the 'rather menacing tone' of his Guildhall speech (which had followed their talks) in relation to nuclear modernization,† and urged Bush to use this at the upcoming summit to strengthen NATO.

On Gorbachev's problem with Bush himself, she was tactful but clear: 'He professed concern about delay in the United States coming forward with new policies ... He is clearly looking for reassurance about continuity.' Gorbachev believed that Mrs Thatcher's views were 'taken into account', because when Jim Baker came to Moscow some six weeks later he did so 'in a constructive spirit'. Brent Scowcroft confirmed that her advice was taken seriously: 'It told me we'd better be getting along and getting our act together.'

Following Gorbachev's visit, Mrs Thatcher decided to proceed with long-standing plans to expel a number of Soviet spies masquerading as diplomats at the Soviet Embassy. She had resisted pressure from Howe and others to take this action earlier in the year, fearing it would mar Gorbachev's visit. But now she wanted to move ahead with the expulsions (eleven Soviet spies, plus four Czechs) 'before the NATO Summit, to show that our resolve had not weakened'. At Powell's suggestion, she warned Gorbachev of what was coming. This was, she wrote on 18 May,

---

* A non-political explanation for Gorbachev's comparative reserve towards Mrs Thatcher is that his wife was not pleased by any suggestion of his closeness to her.
† Gorbachev, Percy Cradock warned Mrs Thatcher, had urged NATO not to modernize its nuclear weapons, based on the 'direct lie' that he was not modernizing his own. NATO must agree to modernize at the coming NATO summit, advised Cradock, 'or the rot will set in'.

'a decision I had hoped not to take'. Seeking to keep the affair low-key, she said she would not make it public. Howe, again more hawkish than she, thought this 'over-protective of Soviet sensibilities', but she stuck to her chosen course.* Some considered that Mrs Thatcher had been untypically pusillanimous: 'She was terrified of damaging her relationship with Gorbachev,' judged Rodric Braithwaite. After the expulsions on 19 May, the Russians retaliated in kind. While, privately, Gorbachev was furious, in public he declared the Anglo–Soviet relationship unaffected: 'Everyone has trouble from time to time about spies.'

Throughout the Bush 'pause' – from January to May 1989 – Mrs Thatcher continued to balance firm support for Gorbachev's reform with equally firm backing for maintaining strong defence. On the latter, she saw West Germany as NATO's weak link. The arguments about SNF negotiations now focused on plans to replace the ageing LANCE nuclear missile with the Follow-on-to-Lance (FOTL). While Mrs Thatcher considered this modernization essential, in Germany desire to get rid of SNF altogether (the third zero) was growing. The changes being introduced by Gorbachev were welcomed with what Christopher Mallaby, the new British Ambassador in Bonn, called 'uncritical enthusiasm . . . and a willingness to believe that the Soviet threat has gone'. Helmut Kohl, though passionately opposed to German neutrality, felt he must bend to this anti-nuclear wind. He had to contend with his governing coalition partner the Foreign Minister, Hans-Dietrich Genscher, of the FDP liberal party, whose policy towards the Soviet Union was much softer. In February, Kohl bowed to Genscher and formally requested that NATO members put off SNF modernization until 1991 or 1992.†

With NATO's landmark fortieth anniversary summit to be held in Brussels that May, Mrs Thatcher and Bush seemed at one in wanting Kohl to remain tough. In March, she suggested to Bush they 'help Helmut' overcome his 'loss of political nerve'. The President should stress the importance of SNF modernization: 'If Helmut gets the feeling that we are not united on this, Genscher's arguments will more easily prevail.'

At first, Bush backed Mrs Thatcher wholeheartedly. Later in March, however, she suggested that 'the United States should stand down and let her work the problem out with [Kohl]'. This did not find favour: 'We

---

* According to Rodric Braithwaite's diary, she unfairly suspected Howe and Hurd of 'deliberately timing the expulsions to foul up her relationship with Gorbachev because they were jealous of it'.

† Kohl did not want rows over nuclear modernization to overshadow the fortieth anniversary celebrations for the Federal Republic of Germany in May.

didn't think that she was, shall we say, diplomatic enough to deal with the Germans,' recalled Brent Scowcroft. This marked the first specific US rejection of her Reagan-era role of speaking for the President. As Bush put it, it 'was very clear to the leaders in these meetings, Kohl and so forth, that that had changed'.

On 21 April, Kohl's ruling coalition voted to support immediate SNF negotiations and refused to rule out a third zero. Bush rang Mrs Thatcher: 'To put it diplomatically, he, the President, was annoyed.' Such negotiations 'at this time would be a grave mistake'. She, of course, agreed. 'In the last resort,' she said, 'if the US and the UK could stand firm for NATO on its 40th anniversary, Kohl would not depart from his American and British allies. The consequences would be too horrific. It was up to Washington and London to rescue NATO.' Bush said 'he was not surprised by the Prime Minister's reaction and was delighted by it'. Disturbed though he was by German tactics, this was not wholly true. Bush was already unhappy with Mrs Thatcher's aggressive attitude towards Kohl. For now, however, he offered her encouragement.

Fortified by her conversation with Bush, Mrs Thatcher flew to Germany on 30 April for a special meeting with Kohl. The Chancellor had persuaded her to visit his home town of Deidesheim, in the Rhineland-Palatinate, so that she could 'get a better understanding of Germany' and indeed of Kohl personally. The two held short talks, followed by lunch in an old inn. Afterwards she reported to Bush that Kohl was opposed to a third zero but wanted the prospect of SNF negotiations preserved. She advocated keeping the fight going right up to the summit. Kohl, she said, had lost the argument domestically to Genscher: 'I doubt he will be too unhappy if we can win it for him in the wider NATO framework.'

Whether or not Mrs Thatcher was right about Kohl's attitudes, the day had not made each more persuasive to the other. She had greatly disliked the local delicacy – pig's belly – which Kohl had produced with great pride at lunch: 'She kept chasing it round her plate. She ended up trying to hide it under her fork.'* After the lunch the pair did some tourism, ending up in Speyer Cathedral. 'Now she sees me in my home environment,' Kohl said to Powell, 'she should understand that I'm not really German. I'm European.† You must convince her.' 'I'll do my best, Chancellor,' replied Powell.

With the visit concluded, Mrs Thatcher sank wearily into her seat on

---

* Kohl was a statesman noted for marching on his stomach, whereas Mrs Thatcher was usually indifferent to what she ate.
† Kohl's hope that Mrs Thatcher might see him as 'European' was misconceived because Mrs Thatcher found this concept, in the sense that people like Kohl meant, difficult to understand or admire.

the plane. 'Oh, Charles,' she exclaimed, 'that man is *so* German.' Powell aborted his mission to persuade her otherwise.

Mrs Thatcher's exhortations to keep the pressure on Kohl reached Washington as a major US rethink of East–West relations was coming to fruition. At its heart was the very nature of the Cold War. In November 1988, Mrs Thatcher had declared publicly 'we're not in a Cold War now', an idea the incoming Bush administration considered premature. For them, an end to the Cold War required an end to the division of Europe, and therefore the reunification of Germany. The implication was spelt out in a NSC memo for Bush dated 20 March. 'Today,' it began, 'the top priority for American foreign policy in Europe should be the fate of the Federal Republic of Germany.' Mrs Thatcher's warnings about Kohl's attitude thus fell on ever more stony ground. The denouement came later in May, just days before the all-important NATO summit.

The full extent of the change broke in an almost insulting manner. On 19 May, Powell had succeeded in extracting from Scowcroft an agreed position for the summit: SNF negotiations were 'at present premature' and would, in any case, not take place without a commitment to deploy the FOTL missile. Just hours later, however, the American approach shifted. James Baker, concerned for Kohl's position, succeeded in moving Bush away from Scowcroft's assurances. Baker's surviving notes from his conversation with Bush, headed 'Thatcher', make the points succinctly:

TAIL WAG DOG
SHE WON'T PAY COST – YOU WILL
YOU'VE GOT TO LEAD.

Baker insisted that Mrs Thatcher's approach would lead to the fall of Kohl's government and the failure of the summit. Bush therefore agreed that his administration would concede SNF negotiations in principle, without making modernization a precondition. 'We knew what Mrs Thatcher's reaction would be . . .', Scowcroft later wrote, 'had we consulted the British, it would have been very awkward to proceed over their strong objections.'

Reflecting nearly thirty years later, Powell was clear: 'Once Bush turned to Germany, that was the end of it all.' By this he meant the end of the Anglo-American dominance in international affairs which Mrs Thatcher and Ronald Reagan had achieved and which, she believed, had brought victory in the Cold War. From that moment, Powell thought, the world began to pass her by.

*

While the Americans had now agreed to negotiations over SNF, the Germans continued to want more. Genscher, for example, sought the complete removal of SNF.* To find a way through, Baker introduced another new and – for Mrs Thatcher – difficult element. He wanted radical cuts in US conventional forces in Europe (CFE). This would be popular in Germany and might nudge Bonn towards the US position on SNF. Bush resolved to propose cutting US forces by 20 per cent and Soviet forces by even more, leaving 275,000 troops on both sides.

This left Mrs Thatcher bewildered. After Bush's initial wariness in dealing with Gorbachev, she now seemed to be dealing with an American president less cautious on the subject than she. Realizing she had to give him something before the summit, she decided to pledge support for the CFE proposal but not the emerging language on SNF. This left Bush apprehensive: 'How *are* we going to manage Margaret?' he asked Scowcroft.

Powell helped Mrs Thatcher order her mind. She faced, he wrote, 'a difficult task': 'You are being cast in the role of the one who says no to everything ... an antediluvian adherent to outdated Cold War concepts.' So she must 'keep President Bush with you'. This would require her to give in on everything except SNF. But there could be political consequences: move 'too far towards the German position, and people will perceive it as NATO support for Labour's new defence policy and a major defeat for you. We therefore have a lot to fight for and only one, slightly unsure ally.'

As the Brussels summit began, Mrs Thatcher was agitated. Over dinner, Bush confided to his diary, she 'was lecturing all the other participants'. 'My first impression: Margaret is principled, very difficult, and most people are far more down on her than I would have thought possible. Indeed, they talk about her a lot and laugh about her, and say that she always stands alone in EC meetings.' In the SNF discussions, Baker made a point of working closely with Howe to accommodate the British position. As the end approached, Robert Zoellick recalled, 'Baker says to Genscher, "I think we need to help Geoffrey, I think he's in a difficult spot." And Genscher's eyes light up. He realizes ... that he's not really negotiating with Baker. That he's got a shrewd counterpart, who's trying to say "How do we get everybody along with this?" And Genscher responds, "Ach ja. That terrible woman!"'

Around midnight, Baker rang Bush with the foreign ministers' formulation: the allies would enter SNF negotiations, but only for a 'partial' reduction of SNF and after conventional force reductions had been agreed. Bush was sceptical that Mrs Thatcher would accept this, but she put on a brave face and, he recalled, 'waxed enthusiastic'. At least she could say

---

* The US proposal insisted that some SNF would remain, even after negotiations.

that the third zero had been ruled out.* The truth, however, in Powell's view, was 'she knew she was beat'.

The wider world agreed. Commentators were now linking Mrs Thatcher's loss of standing with the Americans to her hostility to European integration. 'Mrs Thatcher is a reluctant European,' wrote R. W. 'Johnny' Apple in the *New York Times*. 'That undercuts her country's standing in NATO as well as the European Community, and that makes it hard for Washington to visualize London as the avenue into the new Europe.'

In Mainz, Bush gave a set-piece speech calling for the creation of 'a Europe whole and free'. He also referred to the United States and West Germany as 'partners in leadership', a snub to Britain. In private discussion, Kohl gave Bush a soliloquy about 'the problem with Prime Minister Thatcher'. Bush's response made his recalibration clear: 'The President said he wanted to be sure that the US did not appear to have exclusive friends in Europe.'

The final leg of Bush's European journey was London. The intention of both parties was conciliatory. 'Prime Minister Thatcher has been a rock of support . . .' briefed Scowcroft. Bush should 'project a shared world-view and an undiminished U.S.–U.K. "special relationship"'. In a long, friendly meeting, Bush told his host that 'there was no one else he could talk to in this totally uninhibited way'. Mrs Thatcher put on a good, flattering performance, congratulating him on the 'triumph' of his European tour.

The President asked her whether she feared German unification 'as a threat to the stability of Western Europe'. She confessed that 'she did indeed, although she could not say so openly. More generally, she was concerned by signs of resurgent German nationalism . . . We had to find ways to keep Germany anchored in the West.' He then praised her for being the alliance's 'anchor to windward', a phrase which became public. 'This was kindly meant,' commented Percy Cradock, 'but was not exactly reassuring: the anchor to windward is a lonely position and not the one we had imagined we occupied.'

But the visit was a success. In his diary, Bush reflected on their relationship: 'Ronald Reagan worshiped her, and she knew it, and their personal respect for each other was enormous. I don't feel that Margaret feels that way about me; but I do feel that she thinks I'm conversant with the issues, and I think she was pleased with the agreement we reached at NATO.' In

---

* On the issue of modernization, the declaration promised that SNF would 'continue to be kept up to date where necessary'. It was a fudge, but allowed Mrs Thatcher to maintain her position.

fact, she was not pleased, but Bush's words are evidence that their relationship remained amicable.

Patrick Wright's diary that day suggests that the mind of the British establishment was elsewhere. By this stage, Mrs Thatcher's preference to do without her Foreign Secretary was increasingly obvious. 'At the Queen's lunch for the Bushes, Virginia [Wright's wife] and I had a talk with Elspeth Howe about the possible sacking of Geoffrey, about which she seems pretty fatalistic, saying that they only need to get their domestic arrangements in place. "It's bound to happen sooner or later."'

31
Secrets and lies
'They're as bad as Nazis'

The Cold War inclined Mrs Thatcher to set great store by secret intelligence. As Colin McColl, her last 'C' (head of the Secret Intelligence Service, or MI6), put it, 'The Cold War was to a large extent an intelligence war ... Mrs Thatcher gave us wonderful support.' While this secret world brought clear benefits, there were problems too. Well into her third term, Mrs Thatcher was still wrestling with the legacy of treachery bequeathed by the Cambridge spy ring, which included Guy Burgess, Donald Maclean, Kim Philby and Anthony Blunt.* She also faced modern demands for greater openness. In a curious way, the first gave her an opportunity to deal with the second.

On 25 June 1985, Robert Armstrong wrote to Mrs Thatcher to confirm that Peter Wright, a senior member of MI5 until 1976, was proposing to publish a book revealing all about his time in the service. Wright, who nursed a justified grievance about his government pension, was living in Australia. Armstrong reported that Sir Antony Duff, the Director-General of MI5, proposed that the government seek injunctions in both Britain and Australia to prevent the publication of Wright's book. Did she agree? 'Yes,' wrote Mrs Thatcher.

That one-word assent set in train a process of immense labour, complication and expense over nearly four years. To understand the manifold problems that arose, one must first consider the trouble Mrs Thatcher's administration had faced with an earlier book. After she had exposed Anthony Blunt in 1979 (see p. 207), rumours began to recirculate that the late Sir Roger Hollis, head of MI5 from 1956 to 1965, had himself been a traitor. Although exhaustive investigations had found nothing against him, a disaffected faction of former MI5 officers, including Wright, still believed in Hollis's guilt.

---

* Burgess, Maclean and Philby had been exposed in the 1950s and 1960s.

In the early 1980s, the government learnt that the well-known investigative journalists Barrie Penrose and Roger Courtiour were preparing a book about Hollis that would stir the pot. No. 10 then got wind that Chapman Pincher, a long-time espionage journalist on the *Daily Express*, had approached the Conservative peer Lord Rawlinson, seeking help with his own book about Hollis. This gave Robert Armstrong an idea. He wanted it leaked to Pincher, considered more sympathetic than Penrose and Courtiour, that Hollis had been cleared of suspicion, most recently in a secret review by the former Cabinet Secretary Lord Trend. When he discussed this with Mrs Thatcher, he recalled, 'Her first instinct was not to say anything to Pincher, but Howard Smith [the Director of MI5] and I persuaded her.' In surprisingly explicit terms, Clive Whitmore, her principal private secretary, set out her endorsement: 'The Prime Minister thinks there would be advantage if you saw Lord Rawlinson . . . and put him in the picture', knowing 'that he would pass on what he was told to Chapman Pincher'. Armstrong duly obliged.*

Some time before Pincher's book, *Their Trade is Treachery*, was published in March 1981, Armstrong had been slipped the galley proofs. These demonstrated that the Rawlinson gambit had failed. Pincher's book accused Hollis of treason. Worse, officials concluded that Pincher must have been briefed by someone from the Hollis investigating team who did not agree with Hollis's exoneration. There was 'some reason to think', Armstrong told Mrs Thatcher, that this was Peter Wright, now in Australia, 'out of reach of the Official Secrets Act'.

Armstrong forwarded her an MI5 document listing all Pincher's dangerous revelations. This also noted that 'Pincher is known to be acquainted with Lord Rothschild.' This reference concealed a far more complicated relationship which would later loom large. Victor Rothschild, the senior British member of the famous banking family, had served with distinction in MI5 during the Second World War and remained close to its senior officers. As the head of Ted Heath's 'Think Tank' from 1971 to 1974, he had taken a close and controversial interest in security, which had brought

---

* To the modern mind, it seems extraordinary that governments – and a prime minister – so preoccupied with propriety and secrecy were nevertheless happy to slip information to favoured writers. This hypocrisy arose from the fact that the secret services were not what was called 'avowed', that is, publicly acknowledged. Since nothing could legally and formally be said about them, reasons of state sometimes required that information about them reach the public domain by surreptitious means. There were no other.

him into regular contact with Wright. Rothschild loved the secret world.* Shortly after Mrs Thatcher took office, he urged her to appoint him to a new role in which, with full access to MI5's personal files, he would seek to root out subversives. This proposal alarmed both officials and her. It was seen off.

Rothschild stayed in the picture, however. He had been a Cambridge friend of Blunt and Burgess before the war. During it, they had lived with him in London. Some hinted that Rothschild might himself have been a traitor, though MI5 never found any evidence. When Mrs Thatcher unmasked Blunt, Rothschild wanted her also to include a statement exonerating himself. Her decision not to do so left Rothschild bearing a grudge. Pincher's book contained no suggestion that Rothschild was involved. But MI5's mention of his acquaintance with Pincher may have been a coded warning that the situation was more complicated than it seemed.

There was no serious thought of trying to stop Pincher's book being published, because the government was compromised by its secret acceptance of the galley proofs. A court battle which might reveal Pincher's links with the services, and perhaps the Thatcher-approved conversation with Rawlinson, was unthinkable. But the general accuracy of Pincher's account, combined with its untruth about Hollis, was incendiary. Something had to be done. So, in the Commons on 26 March 1981, Mrs Thatcher declared Pincher mistaken: Lord Trend had found no case against Hollis.

In the summer of 1984, the issue of Peter Wright returned. For Granada Television's *World in Action*, Wright alleged that Hollis had been the Soviet 'mole' in MI5. The government got hold of an early Wright manuscript, and by the summer of 1985 his plan for a book was clear. Mrs Thatcher now endorsed Armstrong's suggestion that it should be injuncted wherever it might be published. Surprisingly, the difficulties of a court case in a foreign jurisdiction were not raised.

News of Wright's book stirred Lord Rothschild, already in touch with Downing Street over the community charge (see p. 466). In September 1985, he told Armstrong that if his MI5 connection were mentioned, he wanted an official statement put out. Armstrong batted this away, but said the government would endorse an agreed form of words that Rothschild himself could issue. Rothschild's purpose here was to warn

---

* Rothschild delighted in being a man of mystery, sometimes pretending, for security purposes, to be called Simpson. He was equipped with a briefcase engraved with the single letter 'S' to complement this disguise.

obliquely that, if the government tangled with Wright, it risked tangling with him too. Christopher Mallaby, at the Cabinet Office, warned Mrs Thatcher's private office: 'we are evidently committed to confirm that we are content with a statement by Lord Rothschild if he is mentioned in the Wright book and it is published. It could be taken as evidence of collusion.'

As Armstrong later explained, his conversations with Rothschild had gone further. Rothschild had told him that, in 1980, he had seen an early draft of Wright's manuscript. Recognizing that Wright was determined to publish, he had bought him a plane ticket to Britain and introduced him to Pincher, with 'a view to his turning the material into something publishable. He assumed . . . that Pincher or his publisher had made some payment to Wright.' It would later emerge that Rothschild's account was neither the whole truth nor nothing but the truth. Although Rothschild did not say so, his support had been 'conditional on there being no mention of himself or of Lady Rothschild in Pincher's book'.* It is nonetheless surprising that Armstrong's new knowledge of Rothschild's history did not make him more anxious about any court case.

In September 1985, the government won a temporary injunction against the publication of Wright's book, *Spycatcher*, in Australia. To make this permanent, someone from the government would have to appear in Sydney to speak for it. Normally the British government would have been represented by the Attorney-General, but Sir Michael Havers was considered a leaky vessel. So it fell to Armstrong, as principal adviser to the Prime Minister on intelligence and security, to go to Sydney.

A year later, with proceedings about to start, Armstrong updated Mrs Thatcher on the book. Wright's subsequently most famous line was that, for five years, he and a colleague had 'bugged and burgled our way across London at the State's behest, while pompous bowler-hatted civil servants in Whitehall pretended to look the other way'. Although many of the revelations had appeared already in Pincher and elsewhere, Armstrong advised that it was 'much worse for a former member of the Security Service to make revelations' himself. The case for enforcing the lifelong duty of confidentiality was strong, and indeed had recently been upheld by the English Court of Appeal. For this principle, the government now prepared

---

* Rothschild was worried about the possible exposure of wife, Tess, who was alleged to have been a member of the Communist Party in the 1930s and a lover of Blunt in her youth (although Blunt was homosexual).

to do battle.* Oddly, the problem of earlier, officially approved cooperation with Pincher was not raised.

Armstrong reported that Wright's side was seeking settlement out of court, which would involve negotiating various cuts to the book. This, however, would effectively concede the key point of the case – the author's freedom to break his duty of confidentiality and profit from it. With legal advice showing that the government had a better than 50 per cent chance of winning, Armstrong argued the government should press forward. It must try to deter. 'We must,' wrote Mrs Thatcher. 'I am utterly shattered by the revelations in the book. The consequences of publication would be enormous.' What had shocked her was Wright's breach of confidence. 'She had a simple conviction', recalled Armstrong, 'that a man who had behaved like a traitor should be pursued.' She felt that imitators must be frightened off. The case before the New South Wales court was set down for 17 November 1986.

Things went badly for the British government. The 'optics' of the former colonial power trying to protect its secrets against a poor old man in Tasmania were well played up by Wright's ambitious young Australian barrister, Malcolm Turnbull (later Prime Minister of Australia). This made for a disagreeable experience for Armstrong in the witness box. Turnbull seized upon the failure to object to Pincher's earlier book. The British government had acquiesced, he challenged Armstrong, 'so that this affair would come out in the open through the pen of a safely conservative writer rather than some ugly journalist on the left'. Armstrong declared this 'Totally untrue.' Splitting hairs, he could perhaps say that he and Mrs Thatcher had not 'agreed to let Pincher write his book' but merely permitted a briefing relevant to it, though this would not have impressed the court. At a different point in his testimony, Armstrong conceded he had been 'economical with the truth'. The phrase, originally Edmund Burke's, was taken to epitomize the cast of mind of the British mandarin. It became proverbial.

On 24 November, *The Times* ran a story, inspired by Wright's side in Sydney, which made public Lord Rothchild's role in the affair. This revealed that Rothschild had arranged for Pincher to meet Wright, saying that he wanted him 'to meet someone who wanted to expose MI5 traitors'. It also

---

* In order not to have to 'discover' (that is, disclose) secret documents to the court, the British government decided to take its stand solely on the lifelong duty of confidentiality owed by servants of the Crown. It therefore agreed, for the purposes of the court case alone, to admit the truth of Wright's allegation and information, disputing only the author's right to publish them. Although this was a legal technicality, the press treated this as a 'Hollis was guilty' story. It was one of many clashes between the needs of secrecy, the requirements of the law and the arts of public presentation with which the government had to struggle.

claimed that Armstrong had 'got his hands on' a copy of *Their Trade is Treachery* six weeks before publication, but still asked the publisher for copies just before it came out. (It was about this that he had been 'economical with the truth'.) It also noted that Pincher had paid Wright 'substantial sums'. Although this made Wright look mercenary, it increased the danger to the government. If such a powerful person as Lord Rothschild had been orchestrating Pincher and Wright to disclose things illegally, why were he and Pincher not being chased by the authorities? Had there been collusion with the government?

In London, Rothschild now sought advice from No. 10 on what he could tell his legal advisers without breaking the Official Secrets Act. This barely veiled request for prime ministerial protection threatened to compromise Mrs Thatcher. Rothschild had orchestrated and helped pay for what was probably, at that time, the biggest leak of British state secrets ever made.* Yet he wanted the Prime Minister to protect him from the consequences.

In the *Sunday Express*, Pincher wrote a piece praising Rothschild's discretion – he was 'so tight-lipped I used to call him the Great Clam of Chowder' – and said his aim in facilitating Wright's collaboration with Pincher was simply 'to prevent Wright himself producing a book which would be far more damaging to MI5 than a book by me'. Rothschild, who had prompted Pincher's article, commended it to the Cabinet Office as 'very accurate'. On 4 December, Rothschild's anxiety reached such a pitch that he unilaterally sent a letter for publication in the *Daily Telegraph*, demanding MI5 state publicly that they held 'unequivocal, repeat unequivocal, evidence that I am not, and have never been a Soviet agent'. While 'not pleased' by this extra pressure, Mrs Thatcher agreed to put out a statement declaring: 'I am advised that we have no evidence that he [Rothschild] was ever a Soviet agent.'

Rothschild told Mrs Thatcher he was 'deeply touched and grateful'. In fact, he was displeased, because he had not got the 'unequivocal' wording he had demanded. The supposedly tight-lipped Great Clam of Chowder went on talking at a great rate, frequently telephoning Armstrong. He worried that the police would ask him about his dealings with Wright and Pincher, which might have put him on the wrong side of the Official Secrets Act.

Mrs Thatcher's views on Rothschild were ambivalent. Armstrong recalled her 'respect for his talent. She liked a Rothschild.' Nigel Wicks thought 'He charmed her, like François Mitterrand.' Powell, on the other

---

* Rothschild had even arranged for Wright's share of Pincher's royalties to be funnelled through his own family bank. This was known, in correspondence from Pincher to Wright, as 'the V channel'.

hand, said, 'She thought he was a bloody nuisance and a troublemaker. Too much magic attached to him.' Rothschild's attempt to manipulate Wright and Pincher for his own ends had not only put the government in a farcical position but dragged Mrs Thatcher directly into the mire. Although Rothschild had insisted to Wicks that she and he had never discussed Wright, the situation was not clear-cut. In court evidence, Wright recalled that, when visiting Rothschild in Cambridge in 1980, he had asked how he could make his concerns known to Mrs Thatcher. Rothschild had replied that they had been discussing intelligence matters 'sitting on that couch only a few days ago'. In Downing Street, a frantic check of Mrs Thatcher's engagements diary showed she had indeed had tea with Rothschild at his Cambridge house on 27 August 1980. Had intelligence been discussed on the sofa? How could anything be proved either way?* In the Commons, the eccentric but persistent Labour MP Tam Dalyell called for Rothschild to be prosecuted for suggesting an unlawful enterprise to Wright.

Rothschild now made a new claim to Armstrong. The real reason he had put Wright in touch with Pincher, he said, was that he had been urged to by a friend (now deceased) who felt that Pincher could assure Wright that his manuscript 'contained nothing new or worth publishing'. Rothschild refused to divulge his friend's identity to the police because this would be used 'to support the theory that the Government sought, promoted or connived at the publication' of Pincher's book. He would, however, tell the Attorney-General in confidence. The friend was Sir Maurice Oldfield, the former head of MI6. Armstrong immediately told Rothschild that he should disclose this to the police. As he recalled, he 'was not inclined to believe' Rothschild's story, but could not prove its untruth, Oldfield being dead.† Rothschild was, in effect, issuing a threat. The suggestion that Oldfield had been involved would lead the entire Wright–Pincher deal to be seen as an establishment plot. Rothschild was hinting that to prosecute him would be immensely unwise. After the 1987 general election, the new Attorney-General, Sir Patrick Mayhew, decided to take no action against either Rothschild or Pincher.

On 12 March 1987, the government lost its case in Sydney. The judge held that the government had removed most of Wright's confidentiality duty

---

* So anxious did 10 Downing Street become about the Rothschild connection that it even prepared a 'contingency note' detailing his works of art on loan to the official residence, in case they might seem compromising. These consisted of 'Four silver cups, bowls and salts [salt-cellars] which are the property of Lord Rothschild.'

† Armstrong carefully recorded that this was the only occasion that he had heard Oldfield's name being mentioned in relation to the Wright–Pincher relationship. He also forewarned the Attorney-General.

by its earlier acquiescence in the Pincher book. Mrs Thatcher immediately authorized an appeal. Among Wright's many claims, press attention had shifted to his assertion that in 1975 a right-wing faction within MI5 had harboured suspicions that the Labour Prime Minister, Harold Wilson, had links to the KGB.* This was soon exaggerated, in the press, into a full-scale MI5 plot against Wilson.

Although, in Armstrong's view, Mrs Thatcher herself 'did not take [the plot story] very seriously', Jim Callaghan, Wilson's successor, called for a full independent inquiry into the secret services. Suspecting that Mrs Thatcher sought a general election that summer, Labour wanted to cause embarrassment.

By now, some were beginning to see the blanket secrecy surrounding the services as more curse than blessing. Douglas Hurd, then Home Secretary, advised her that 'We are increasingly recognising that our position on the Official Secrets Act is under strain.' The notorious 'catch-all' Section 2 of the 1911 Act, which made disclosure of any official information whatsoever unlawful, should go, he argued. Not for the first time, Armstrong urged Mrs Thatcher to consider legislating for formal 'oversight' of the Security Service. Tony Duff, on behalf of MI5, wanted her to rebut Wright's claims publicly: 'The allegations of plotting against a Prime Minister are so uniquely awful that, in my view, they call for open and categorical denial.'

Only Bernard Ingham, hardened by the media, felt robust. Any inquiry, he advised, 'is doomed before it begins to eventual dismissal as a whitewash'; 'I consider that a far more effective remedy would be for the secret services (who have, after all, largely got themselves into this mess) publicly to shut up and secretly to grit their teeth, pull themselves together and get on with it.' That same day Mrs Thatcher told colleagues she 'did not believe an inquiry was warranted'. She fought and, on 11 June, won the general election without any announcement about the future of the security services.

The move towards oversight was harder to resist, particularly when attitudes began to shift within the security services themselves. Following the election, Armstrong reminded Mrs Thatcher that she had been 'impressed' by Duff's concerns that 'the Security Service's ability to undertake operations and the readiness of the Security Service to carry them out was being inhibited by the lack of legislative cover'. By November, she was telling Jim Callaghan that the service 'might have to be put on a statutory basis'.

---

* At the time, Wright did not reveal that he had been one of the thirty people with suspicions. He later admitted that, in fact, only he and one other official had taken these suspicions seriously.

In June 1988, the government lost its final appeal over *Spycatcher* in the Australian courts. Thanks to Mrs Thatcher's battle against him, Wright would eventually sell nearly 2 million copies of his book and die, in 1995, a millionaire. In October 1988, with the book's contents widely known in Britain, the Law Lords refused to make permanent the interim injunction against the *Sunday Times* (which had serialized Wright's book). They did, however, affirm that Wright owed a lifelong duty of confidence to the Crown. 'Those who breach it, such as Mr Wright,' said Lord Keith, 'are guilty of treachery.' Mrs Thatcher took comfort from having sustained the principle on which she had been fighting.*

By this time, much of the heat had dissipated. The Security Service Bill, designed to put MI5 on a statutory footing without making it subject to parliamentary oversight, was accepted by Mrs Thatcher, although she fought many of its details.† The Security Service Act came into force in December 1989. In March 1990, a reformed Official Secrets Act also became law. It removed the unpopular 'catch-all' Section 2, but tightened control on more closely defined areas, such as intelligence. To demonstrate her commitment, on the day the Act came into force Mrs Thatcher signed her own Acknowledgment of Notification Notice, accepting that she was herself subject to Section 1(1) of the Official Secrets Act.

The Peter Wright saga revealed much about Mrs Thatcher – for good and ill. On the one hand stood her determination to punish disloyalty and her fierce devotion to keeping secrets secret. On the other, she and her government were consistently outmanoeuvred by the legal complications of pursuing Wright, with her the most pig-headed of all in the chosen methods of fighting.

There was a sense, however, in which Mrs Thatcher exercised remarkable patience. Bernard Ingham was right to say that the secret services had 'largely got themselves into this mess'. After the terrible treachery of Philby, Blunt and others a generation earlier, the legacy of ill feeling lingered. Hence Wright's behaviour. From the ill-fated off-the-record briefing to Chapman Pincher, via the failure to elucidate the real risks in fighting the case in Australia, to the shocking behaviour of Lord Rothschild, Mrs Thatcher could with reason have complained that she had been condescended to

---

* In November 1991, a year after Mrs Thatcher had left office, the government lost in the European Court of Human Rights, which held that the attempt to ban *Spycatcher* had been contrary to free speech: the *Sunday Times* serialization had been justified, the court ruled.
† She was particularly exercised by its proposal for a tribunal: 'This is impossible,' she wrote, '– the trumped up complaints will be endless because of the people and organisations whose purpose is to abuse freedom.'

and, in Rothschild's case, cheated by an out-of-date security establishment. Yet – apart from her dismay at Rothschild's behaviour – there is no record of her criticizing, even privately, the leading figures of the secret world. On the contrary, she backed them. By appointing Tony Duff, whom she greatly admired, to head MI5 she helped the service move to better times.

Paul Greengrass, Wright's ghostwriter and Mrs Thatcher's opponent throughout the *Spycatcher* story, came to believe that the 'arc' of Mrs Thatcher's relations with intelligence looked much more successful than had seemed possible at the height of the Sydney court fiasco. 'Through the farce and nonsense and theatre of it all, Britain ended up – thanks to her reforms – with what we certainly needed.' This led, after her time, to a statutory basis for MI6 as well. Before her, the secret services had suffered serious embarrassments in the Cold War. By the end of her time in office, they were more secure and more admired.

But Mrs Thatcher's prejudice in favour of maximum secrecy for the intelligence and security services never left her. Robin Butler remembered the moment he discussed MI6's planned move to its new custom-built headquarters at Vauxhall Cross with her in her Downing Street study. She looked out of the window at the ivy-covered wartime Admiralty building across Horse Guards. 'Why can't they go in there?' she asked. 'There are no windows,' Butler replied. 'That's what's so good about it,' said Mrs Thatcher.

As the *Spycatcher* case approached its crisis, Mrs Thatcher faced another security embarrassment. It had hung over her since 1979. That summer, she had summoned Sir Maurice Oldfield back from retirement to serve as the newly created security coordinator in Northern Ireland.* She admired Oldfield greatly for, in her view, restoring MI6's morale in the Cold War. She had got to know this son of a Derbyshire farmer slightly in Opposition and she liked his droll, owlish, bachelor manner.† Oldfield reciprocated Mrs Thatcher's admiration, feeling that she was the only prime minister he had known who properly appreciated his service's work. Because of Mrs Thatcher's personal entreaties, Oldfield accepted the Northern Ireland job. He took up the post in October 1979.

Just a month later, however, Willie Whitelaw, the Home Secretary, briefed

---

* This came after the IRA assassination of Lord Mountbatten and the murder, on the same day in August 1979, of eighteen British soldiers at Warrenpoint, Co. Down. Oldfield's appointment was designed to improve intelligence and security in the province.
† In his performance as the legendary spy chief George Smiley in the television adaptation of John le Carré's novels, Alec Guinness, who knew Oldfield, drew on his character for the portrayal.

Mrs Thatcher on a disturbing development. Oldfield's close-protection officers* had come across pictures – described as 'fairly horrific stuff' – suggesting that Oldfield was homosexual and was using rent boys. Mrs Thatcher now agreed that Oldfield's appointment must be brought to an end as soon as possible. The reasons for this included not only the belief, orthodox at that time, that Oldfield's homosexuality left him vulnerable to blackmail, but also that he had lied about the matter during positive vetting over many years.

In early March 1980, John Junor, the Editor of the *Sunday Express* and a strong supporter of Mrs Thatcher, warned her that Oldfield's homosexuality was no longer a secret. Junor said he would like to run the story but felt that 'wider loyalties should have precedence and that he owed it to the Prime Minister to warn her'. He would find it difficult to sit on the story, however, if rivals got wind of it. This hint of Fleet Street menace spurred the authorities. Days later, in a meeting which Armstrong remembered as 'inexpressibly horrible', he confronted Oldfield with evidence of his homosexual conduct. Oldfield confessed. He 'broke down, really: he felt his whole career was ruined'. Oldfield also insisted he had never been blackmailed or compromised, or even approached by a hostile intelligence service. This was accepted. Crushed, he agreed to retire from his job on health grounds in June.

For Mrs Thatcher the whole business was painful. Although she had the mild distaste for homosexuality common in her generation, she felt 'strong personal loyalty, and was not sniffy about colleagues' sexual peccadilloes'. She felt guilty about Oldfield because, by dragging him out of retirement, she had unintentionally caused him to get caught. Oldfield soon became seriously ill. Early in 1981, Mrs Thatcher visited him in hospital. In the view of Armstrong, 'It was a generous instinct.' Part of her motive, he speculated, was that 'she wanted to apologize to him'. On 11 March, two days later, Sir Maurice Oldfield died.

His death increased the danger of exposure. Freed from the laws of libel (which apply only to the living), the press might be emboldened. The post-Blunt atmosphere also made stories much harder to suppress. Armstrong warned Mrs Thatcher that if the Oldfield story broke at the same time as Chapman Pincher's *Their Trade is Treachery* was published, 'we shall have the makings of a major security scandal'. 'None of this is made any easier', he added, 'by the fact that the . . . existence of the SIS is not avowed.' Any

---

* It has been suggested that the RUC Special Branch and MI5, irritated by Oldfield being parachuted into the province over their heads, deliberately dug up the story to use against him. No evidence for this has been produced.

statement about Oldfield's lies could not acknowledge the organization which his lies might have compromised.

For several years, the dam held. In April 1987, however, news reached No. 10 of an imminent new book by the ever-productive Chapman Pincher called *Traitors*, which discussed Oldfield's sexual activities and his consequent resignation. There was particular anxiety because the book was said to contain the untrue allegation that Mrs Thatcher had known about Oldfield's conduct before appointing him to Northern Ireland.* The possibility of an injunction was considered, but before any action was taken the book was serialized in the *Mail on Sunday*.

Mrs Thatcher agreed to make a statement. Nigel Wicks expressed concern about a draft passage praising Oldfield's past achievements because it implied 'his contribution to the success of his old service in some way excuses his conduct'. She, however, was adamant: 'I think we owe him some counterbalancing statement to the one which I regret having to make.' She was, noted Patrick Wright in his diary, 'particularly (and characteristically) concerned about the effect on Maurice Oldfield's family'.

On 23 April 1987, in a Written Answer, Mrs Thatcher recounted Oldfield's admission to engaging in 'homosexual activities', noting that this had not resulted in security being compromised. Oldfield had 'contributed notably to a number of security and intelligence successes which could not have been achieved had there been a breach of security'. The main practical effect was to increase pressure within government to put the intelligence services on a statutory footing.

For Mrs Thatcher personally, it was a sad business, with a melancholy postscript. During the general election campaign the following month a Conservative branch chairman, James Greig, wrote to her to say that he had met Maurice Oldfield's sister, Mrs Sadie Pearce, while campaigning. She had told him that she could no longer vote Conservative because Mrs Thatcher's statement about her brother 'made no reference to his patriotism and service to his country [though this was not really the case]'. Greig suggested she write to Mrs Pearce.

Officials strongly advised against this, recommending instead that they send (and sign) any reply to Greig themselves. They also warned against sending it before polling day, lest it be used against her electorally. Mrs Thatcher accepted that the letter should be addressed to Greig, but instinctively took responsibility: 'my visit to him in hospital 2 days before his death was in a way to pay my quiet tribute to him. I think it would be

---

* In fact, Pincher's book described how Oldfield's sexual proclivities had come to light only after he had assumed this post.

better if I signed the letter to Mr Greig.' Her letter, sent before polling day, said all this and expressed her 'great regard for Sir Maurice as a loyal and devoted public servant'. She asked Greig to feel free to show the letter to Mrs Pearce and her family.

Although she never found the subject congenial, Northern Ireland was seldom far from Mrs Thatcher's mind. In February 1987, Garret FitzGerald, the Irish Prime Minister, was defeated by Charles Haughey's Fianna Fáil party. Leaving office, FitzGerald wrote her a note of striking warmth. Celebrating their relationship as 'extraordinarily fruitful for both our countries', he confided that he wanted her re-elected 'for Ireland's sake'. Mrs Thatcher's reply was guardedly friendly. She described the Anglo-Irish Agreement (AIA) as 'uniquely valuable and lasting', but then her more distinctive tone of voice cut in – 'though goodness knows it has brought us difficulties enough'.

In speaking of 'difficulties enough' Mrs Thatcher was referring to several things. One was Haughey. Chiefly because of his unfriendly attitude during the Falklands War (see p. 265), he aroused what Charles Powell called her 'irreparable' feeling about successive Irish governments, going back to their neutrality in the Second World War.* She considered them ambivalent towards violence against the British, a subject – perhaps *the* subject – about which she felt most passionately. As leader of the more aggressively Nationalist of the Republic's two main political parties, Haughey had little political incentive to make life easy for her.†

His unhelpful position affected her overriding difficulty – how to defeat terrorism from both sides, chiefly the Republican terrorism of Sinn Fein/IRA.‡ In Mrs Thatcher's eyes, the great virtue of the AIA was its promised security cooperation between North and South. While she had conceded to the Republic a role in the affairs of the province, she felt 'the Irish' had not reciprocated. By 'the Irish' she meant not only the Dublin government, but also the Nationalist Social Democratic and Labour Party (SDLP) in Northern Ireland itself. Its leader, John Hume, had not engaged in the political development he and FitzGerald had led her to expect. She therefore 'lost confidence' in Hume. While most people involved saw political

---

* 'The Irish were worse than neutral,' she said privately, suggesting their formal neutrality had given comfort to the Germans.
† Haughey had been forced to resign from the Irish government in 1970 because of his alleged involvement in a plot to import arms for the IRA. Despite his being rehabilitated politically, Unionists (and Mrs Thatcher) never really trusted him.
‡ 'Loyalist' terrorism, though equally extreme, was on a smaller scale and less well organized than that of the IRA. It was essentially reactive.

development as the key issue and security as secondary, Mrs Thatcher considered them inextricably linked: how could any political development succeed if each side still feared the other might kill them?

All this caused Mrs Thatcher to feel guilt, as well as impatience. She was a Unionist yet had signed the AIA without consulting either the Ulster Unionist Party (UUP) led by James Molyneaux or Ian Paisley's Democratic Unionist Party (DUP). In the view of Robin Eames, the Church of Ireland Primate, who was close to the Ulster Unionists, Molyneaux saw the Agreement as a 'personal betrayal'. Mrs Thatcher was troubled. 'It was strangely similar to the agreement she made over Hong Kong,' Charles Powell believed. 'She privately felt she had betrayed people.' Because security had not improved, the British soldiers, policemen and ordinary citizens, for whom she cared so much, continued to be murdered.* At her final meeting with FitzGerald as Taoiseach, she mused on 'whether she could continue, in all seriousness, to send young men to their death in Northern Ireland'.

Her final difficulty was the Unionists themselves. Since the AIA, Unionist MPs had refused all contact with ministers. Some had encouraged a campaign of civil disobedience. Mrs Thatcher resented their behaviour, feeling they should improve matters instead of sulking. Only after the 1987 election did Molyneaux and Paisley agree to meet Tom King, who had stayed on as Northern Ireland Secretary. King told Mrs Thatcher of their interest in 'replacing' the Agreement and he proposed 'a form of internal government' which might edge matters along outside its framework. Mrs Thatcher stamped on his idea. King's plan was 'tantamount to suspending' the Agreement, she wrote that September, and 'WE HAVE NO AUTHORITY to do so . . . the consequences of giving in to Paisley/Molyneaux positions would be <u>disastrous</u>. The sooner this proposal is consigned to oblivion, the better.' So, when it came to Northern Ireland, Mrs Thatcher began her third term friendless and frustrated.

On 8 May 1987, the security forces in Northern Ireland had won a famous, if controversial victory. British intelligence had learnt of IRA plans to attack the RUC barracks in Loughgall. The barracks were evacuated and a trap was set. After the IRA drove a digger carrying a bomb into the (now empty) barracks, the SAS shot dead all eight members of the IRA attack unit. It was the Republicans' largest single loss during the Troubles. Seeing

---

* She was particularly upset by the rise in so-called Loyalist attacks on the security forces in the AIA aftermath. 'They say they are British. If they are British, why are they attacking British soldiers?' she would ask.

the IRA hit so hard encouraged Unionists to enter so-called 'talks about talks' with the British government.

Despite Loughgall, in July the Defence Secretary, George Younger, told Mrs Thatcher that 'the army feared that the battle against the IRA was being lost'. This grave warning reflected, in part, a complaint that the army were not receiving full intelligence from the RUC (part of a long internal struggle for primacy over security in Northern Ireland). But it also reflected the help the IRA had been receiving from abroad. That November, the French Navy intercepted a ship named the MV *Eksund*, carrying 100 tonnes of weapons (including missiles that could bring down helicopters, rocket-propelled grenades and heavy machine guns) originating in Colonel Gaddafi's Libya and destined for the IRA. Presenting Mrs Thatcher with intelligence that Libya had accomplished 'four previous successful shipments of arms since 1985', Percy Cradock noted the 'chilling implications'. The capture of the *Eksund* was, she recalled, 'a real plus for us'. The Libyan link put her in a stronger position to press Dublin to stop dragging its feet in ratifying the European Convention on the Suppression of Terrorism (ECST), which would facilitate the extradition of terrorist suspects from the Republic.

On 8 November, an IRA bomb at the annual Remembrance Day ceremony in Enniskillen killed eleven people, including a woman aged twenty, Marie Wilson. This was the worst attack on non-military targets since the Troubles had resumed in 1969. Mrs Thatcher shared the 'deep loathing that British people felt' for the perpetrators: 'They're as bad as Nazis.'* A fortnight after the attack the Remembrance ceremony in Enniskillen was rerun, this time in the cathedral, and she flew in – unannounced, for security reasons – to take part. Archbishop Eames had encouraged her to come because feelings in the Unionist community were running so high. The reaction to her visit, he recalled, was 'extremely positive, and I think she benefited greatly in stature'.

Mrs Thatcher rejected demands for new special powers for the province, however. She wanted to do nothing that would give Haughey an excuse to avoid ratifying the ECST, a step he suggested he might now be ready to take. A week later Powell warned her that 'The Taoiseach is wriggling disgracefully.' He was now insisting on qualifications to the ECST, such as

---

* In the Commons, a small group of the Labour hard left sounded a very different note. An Early Day Motion signed by Ken Livingstone, Tony Benn, Diane Abbott and the future Leader of the Labour Party, Jeremy Corbyn, stated that the violence and bloodshed in Northern Ireland 'stems primarily from the long-standing British occupation of that country and the partition imposed by force in 1921'.

giving the Irish Attorney-General the power to refuse to certify any British extradition request. This was worse than nothing, protested Mrs Thatcher.

Just before Christmas, Tom King and George Younger sought to answer her persistent worries about border security by proposing the army take over certain anti-terrorist operations from the police.* Powell, backing, for once, a suggestion from Geoffrey Howe, recommended that she explain this plan to Haughey. 'I see no reason to make <u>any</u> statement about it <u>whatsoever</u>,' wrote Mrs Thatcher crossly. '<u>Nor</u> to tell the Taoiseach. No <u>General</u> warns his opponents of his next moves.' Presumably the 'opponents' in her mind were the IRA, not the Dublin government, but her words implied a low level of trust with the Republic.

Relations continued poor. Dublin resented the British government's announcement, in January 1988, that the results of inquiries by senior British police officers John Stalker and, later, Colin Sampson into the security forces' alleged policy of 'shoot to kill' would not be published; there would be no prosecutions.† The Irish government was also angered after the English Court of Appeal dismissed efforts to overturn the convictions of the 'Birmingham Six'.‡ As the temperature rose, on 10 February Powell advised Mrs Thatcher to meet Haughey at the Brussels European Council that began the next day: 'If you don't it will be taken as a complete breakdown in our relations ... It does not cost us anything to allow them to let off steam.' She duly turned on her charm in Brussels. Her meeting with Haughey had little concrete result, but both sides calmed down.

The respite was brief. For some time, MI5 had been tracking IRA terrorists preparing to attack British soldiers in the British colony of Gibraltar. Mrs Thatcher now granted permission to deploy the SAS to catch the terrorists red-handed. On 6 March, the IRA operatives entered Gibraltar. They parked a car close to their target, the daily guard ceremony outside the Governor's residence, before dispersing on foot. Suspecting a car bomb, the SAS followed them. When they attempted to reach for what the SAS soldiers feared was a weapon or remote bomb trigger, all three were shot dead. In the immediate aftermath, the Provisional IRA confirmed that the three 'on active service' had been supplied with a large amount of Semtex.

---

* Robin Butler recalled 'an absurd discussion about moving the border'. Mrs Thatcher tended to regard the border purely in terms of what would be best for security and forget that any reshaping of Northern Ireland's boundaries would be impossibly controversial.
† The phrase implied that terrorists suspected of being on missions to murder could be killed by the security forces without any attempt being made to arrest them. While Stalker had found there had been no 'shoot to kill' policy, the government feared that publishing the reports would compromise security.
‡ The Birmingham Six were six Irishmen who had been found guilty of the Birmingham pub bombings in 1974. Their convictions were finally overturned in 1991.

In fact, all three had been unarmed and no bomb had been found in the car. It was only the next day, much to the government's relief, that a vehicle carrying sixty-four kilos of Semtex was found across the border in Marbella. The SAS had been following the dummy run.

Although the Gibraltar shootings were highly controversial, Mrs Thatcher retained strong support for them on the British mainland. 'The moral for the IRA is a simple one,' said the *Sun*. 'If they don't want to be killed, they should not try to kill others.' Elsewhere it was a different story. The bodies of the IRA dead were flown to Dublin, where some 2,000 people welcomed them. As they were driven north for the funeral in Milltown cemetery, Belfast, crowds came out to watch. Mrs Thatcher found this 'very revealing . . . It really just shows you the nature of the people we were up against.'

The funeral itself brought forth another atrocity. Michael Stone, a freelance 'Loyalist' terrorist, threw hand grenades into the crowd and fired on mourners. Three people died. Three days later, on 19 March, two British Army corporals in civilian clothes became caught up by accident in the funeral cortège of one of the Milltown dead. A hostile crowd, suspicious of an ambush, gathered round their car and the corporals were pulled out and badly beaten up. They were then driven to waste ground nearby and shot dead. The IRA put out a statement confirming it had killed them and that they had been – which was untrue – soldiers of the SAS.* Pictures and films of these atrocities went around the world.

To Mrs Thatcher, the corporals' murder was 'the single most horrifying event in Northern Ireland during my term of office'. When she went to RAF Northolt to receive the bodies she found the families in a terrible state, 'screaming, shouting and crying'. 'Come on,' she said, 'we must do this properly. We must greet the coffins.' As Powell recalled, 'everyone pulled themselves together'.

The Irish government found plenty to complain about in this shocking sequence of events. Nicholas Fenn, the British Ambassador, sent a despatch to Geoffrey Howe listing the Irish grievances, without adverse comment. Mrs Thatcher annotated them: Stalker-Sampson, the Birmingham Six ('not a crisis'), extradition ('they made this one'), the shootings at Gibraltar and many more. 'This is appalling,' she wrote, '– the crisis in some of these is

---

* It was said that what sealed their fate was a document on one of the men which mentioned the German town of Herford (which housed a British garrison). The mob misread it as Hereford, the headquarters of the SAS.

for us not them,' and added, 'Cowardly PIRA'. When Fenn reported that 'we have lost Irish confidence', she riposted, 'They never had ours.'

Charles Powell now sent a letter of rebuke to the Foreign Office on Mrs Thatcher's behalf.* 'The Prime Minister is shaken by the gap in comprehension which the despatch reveals,' it began cuttingly, 'not so much between the British and Irish Governments as between the British Government and its Ambassador in Dublin.' The complaints from the Irish authorities were 'secondary' compared with 'the inadequacy of their commitment to deal effectively with PIRA terrorism'.

Poor Fenn was the semi-accidental victim of Mrs Thatcher's exasperation. 'The Irish seem to have no understanding of the enormity of what happened,' she wrote in mid-April. In her eyes, Haughey confirmed this later that month by airing his grievances in speeches in the United States. 'It is outrageous,' wrote Powell against Haughey's text. 'No mention of PIRA violence, no acknowledgment of the need for cross-border cooperation, no commitment to the Anglo-Irish Agreement.' In a blunt letter to Haughey, Mrs Thatcher said his speeches had 'deeply upset' her: he had blamed terrorism on the existence of Northern Ireland outside the Irish Republic. 'To me,' she said, 'such an admission would be tantamount to a surrender to terrorism.'

The next day, a documentary called *Death on the Rock* ran on Thames Television, despite the government's best efforts to prevent it.† It sought to show that the IRA operatives had not been challenged before being killed and had been shot, variously, in the back, on the ground or with their hands up. It also speculated that MI6 had known that there would not be a bomb in the car that day. The programme pushed for a judicial inquiry. There was outcry against the programme in several newspapers.‡ Mrs Thatcher reacted angrily. She was incapable of seeing that journalists must uncover stories which governments want concealed. She was also appalled by the refusal of the BBC and ITN to hand over their footage of the lynching of the two corporals to help with police inquiries. Wishing to uphold their independence, the television executives invoked the legal rights of journalists. With ministers, Mrs Thatcher, normally so attentive to

---

* The letter was Powell's idea, but Mrs Thatcher felt she, not he, should sign it: 'Such a note coming from you may harm you.' Powell, however, persuaded her it should go under his name.
† The MOD had refused to cooperate with the programme-makers. Protesting that the timing of the programme might prejudice the coroner's inquest, Geoffrey Howe had tried twice, without success, to prevent it being broadcast.
‡ Eventually, an inquiry by the Independent Broadcasting Authority (IBA) found, with minor qualifications, in favour of the programme. Seen today, *Death on the Rock* looks fairly low-key, and certainly not biased in favour of the IRA, though it strains too much to prove its case against the government and makes some mistakes about the evidence.

legality, protested that 'it was not just a question of law, it was a question of duty. As she had said in the House earlier, if one was not on the side of justice, one was on the side of terrorism.'

She felt something similar about the Gibraltar shootings. But she may also have wished to conceal that the operation had not gone perfectly. Robin Butler probably represented the view at the heart of government when he recalled that the programme had revealed the SAS might have been 'a bit quick on the trigger'. He had 'no feeling of guilt', he said, because three 'very bad people' had been prevented from killing the innocent, but he felt some embarrassment.

On 15 June, some seven weeks after her anguished letter to Charles Haughey, Mrs Thatcher received a reply. The Taoiseach pronounced himself 'deeply perturbed by some of the things you have written ... and reject many of them'. He suggested they talk at the forthcoming European Council in Hanover. The resulting conversation was frank. Haughey protested how much the Republic was doing to fight terrorism, but warned of a backlash if he conceded too many British demands: the Republic must not be 'constantly bully-ragged'. Mrs Thatcher hit back. She complained vociferously of 'bombs, guns, explosions, people being beaten to death and naked hatred'. The killers, she insisted, had 'a safe haven in the Republic and a great deal of sympathy from people there'. The Republic had to furnish 'more pre-emptive intelligence'. Did the Taoiseach not realize that the island of Ireland contained more terrorists than anywhere in the world, apart from Lebanon? He seemed to want a united Ireland, she said. Did he not understand that this would produce 'the worst civil war ever'? According to the Irish record, Mrs Thatcher said she would '<u>never</u> be prepared to walk out and let the terrorists win'. She added, 'I have one objective: to beat the IRA.'

Haughey appeared somewhat abashed. He accepted 'they could do more', but begged her to stop the 'constant belittling' of the Republic. Now it was Mrs Thatcher's turn to be slightly apologetic. She did not mean to belittle, she said. Both needed to do more: 'We were not winning the battle.' This 'outspoken exchange', Powell recorded, was 'conducted without anger or personal rancour on either side. The mood was perceptibly better at the end.' Shortly afterwards, Haughey was taken to hospital with kidney stones. Mrs Thatcher sent him flowers.

Towards the end of the year, however, relations again deteriorated. Haughey's government refused to back British extradition requests for Patrick Ryan, a former Catholic priest suspected of being the IRA's main conduit for procuring arms from Libya.* Just before Christmas Mrs Thatcher told Haughey she found his refusal 'astonishing and dismaying'. She complained to Archbishop Eames that it was difficult to make political progress or even 'to keep the Anglo-Irish agreement in existence' when confronted by such phenomena.

Throughout her third term, Mrs Thatcher was bitterly disappointed by the Republic's attitude towards terrorism and increasingly disillusioned with the AIA. She was also dissatisfied with her own government's approach. In May 1988, for example, Charles Powell sent her the latest policy options from the Northern Ireland Office (NIO). 'I am afraid we can only conclude', he wrote, 'that there are many good intentions, <u>but nothing very much is happening</u>,' the underlining being hers.

On 20 August 1988, a bus carrying thirty-six soldiers was blown up by an IRA roadside bomb at Ballygawley. Eight died, the second-greatest military loss of life in Northern Ireland (after Warrenpoint in 1979). Mrs Thatcher cut short her holiday in Cornwall immediately and returned to work. Although Northern Ireland was not his specialist subject, Charles Powell took this moment to send her his own paper. His approach was tough: it included identity cards within Northern Ireland and leaning harder on the Republic about security. Someone like Christopher Curwen (due to step down as the head of MI6) should be sent in to sort out the province's security coordination, he urged: 'At the moment the terrorists are disrupting us: we have got to disrupt them.' Powell advocated more 'direct action e.g. Loughgall and Gibraltar . . . surely we must consider giving the SAS a much more direct and active role in the province'. He advised Mrs Thatcher that, by Christmas, she would need to consider replacing Tom King as Northern Ireland Secretary: 'there must be some doubts whether he can raise his game to deal with the new level of threat'.

Powell's bold note was in the same spirit as the Bruges Speech which he was also busy composing (see p. 671), circumventing the NIO just as Bruges circumvented the Foreign Office. With political development notably absent, it showed the same mindset as Mrs Thatcher's. She marked

---

* Ryan had been arrested in Belgium in July 1988, but that November the Belgian government overruled its country's own legal processes and put him on a plane to Ireland without informing the British government. At the European Council in Rhodes at the beginning of December, Mrs Thatcher confronted the Belgian Prime Minister, Wilfried Martens. 'The tone was robust,' Charles Powell recorded. Mrs Thatcher told Martens that the Belgian attitude 'contrasted vividly' with all the cooperation given to Belgium over those charged in relation to the horrors at the Heysel Stadium: 'We were mystified and deeply wounded.'

Powell's note closely, doubly underlining the bit about the SAS. To address his suggestion of improving security coordination she charged Sir Colin Figures (Curwen's predecessor as head of MI6) with producing an urgent report. A week after Powell's note, the SAS, aware of an IRA plan to murder a member of the Ulster Defence Regiment in Drumnakilly, lay in wait and killed the three terrorists. Two days later, however, the army warned Mrs Thatcher that 'PIRA have the capability and intention of further escalating their campaign of violence and can sustain the present level for up to two years.' Ministers now focused heavily on military and anti-terrorist solutions. Unable to agree on proscribing Sinn Fein as an organization, they suggested instead prohibiting its broadcasts (and those of the Ulster Defence Association) on the airwaves. There was considerable support for this ban, which came in on 19 October 1988, because it would deny terrorists the moral legitimacy associated with public debate. As early as 1985, Mrs Thatcher had enthusiastically adopted a phrase given her by the Chief Rabbi, Immanuel Jakobovits, that violent extremists craved 'the oxygen of publicity' and should be denied it. Naturally, the idea was greeted with outrage and ridicule by the broadcast media. Television programmes quickly worked out it was legal to have the words of, say, Gerry Adams or Martin McGuinness voiced by an actor and dub them over film of them. So the ban became little more than a consolation prize for Mrs Thatcher, far short of the prohibition on Sinn Fein itself that she wanted.*

Mrs Thatcher's attitude to security at this time also needed careful management by ministers and officials. She had sent Figures to Northern Ireland because her sympathies for soldiers had been strongly aroused. His findings did not answer this problem. 'I have NEVER read a more inadequate report,' she wrote. 'It is pathetic and seems very biased in favour of the RUC.' Figures had highlighted RUC suspicions that 'what the army are really after is an anti terrorist campaign on the lines of what was done in Malaya, Borneo, and other places where insurgency created serious problems'. Instead Figures recommended 'further evolutionary change'. 'We shall never defeat the terrorists if this attitude prevails,' lamented Mrs Thatcher. 'Is there no urgency?'

Percy Cradock, however, supported Figures's defence of the existing arrangements and rejected the army's claim that it was being denied effective intelligence by the RUC. He stressed that police primacy must be preserved. What was needed was better coordination. Back-pedalling rather, Powell supported Cradock. Before the end of October, Mrs Thatcher

---

* Four years after Mrs Thatcher left office, the ban was lifted.

fell in behind Cradock's suggestions for a new coordinator of intelligence with enhanced powers.

In September 1988, the inquest on the Gibraltar shootings took place. To secure a friendlier reaction from Dublin, the British government privately briefed Haughey's government about the background. The suggestion that the briefing include the SAS rules of engagement provoked Mrs Thatcher's ire. 'We do NOT hand over the rules of engagement,' she scribbled. 'It would be RECKLESS and DAMAGING to do so, and TOTALLY UNFAIR to OUR ARMED FORCES.' The inquest jury found that the terrorists had been lawfully killed. The successful Gibraltar operation and the inquest result were two of the few things in the saga of Northern Ireland which gave Mrs Thatcher deep satisfaction.

Behind the apparent political stasis, some things were going forward. In January 1988, Gerry Adams and John Hume had begun a series of meetings.* After the first, Mrs Thatcher was informed that Adams might accept that change in the status of Northern Ireland could come only by consent and constitutional means. She was 'unimpressed', Powell commented to Robin Butler, 'and has no doubt that Mr Hume is being led up the garden path. She does not intend to modify the line in dealings with Sinn Fein.'

This was Mrs Thatcher's undeviating position throughout her premiership. She never believed that Sinn Fein had any potential for good. She would never talk to terrorists, she always said, and she personally never did. She was, however, aware of the backchannel link between the British state and the IRA, informally sustained by the SIS officer Michael Oatley and the Londonderry fish and chip shop owner Brendan Duddy, and reactivated with her knowledge in 1980 to exchange messages during the Republican hunger strikes (see p. 255). 'She did know about it,' confirmed Charles Powell, 'but she pretended she didn't.' She had a comparable approach to political initiatives, particularly those involving the Republic. She steered clear of them, but did not seek to stop others pursuing them.

In this cautious manner, some change started to take place. Tom King was sympathetic to John Hume's view, post the AIA, that 'Now is the time for Irishmen to persuade Irishmen.' In a speech in Belfast in September 1988, King encouraged that process. He was careful to emphasize that the Unionist majority were British 'and intend to remain so', but stressed

---

* Several of these meetings were acknowledged in public, but Hume and Adams later continued to meet in private. The Irish government had also maintained its own backchannel with Adams since 1986.

that the interests of the British state were not involved: 'there is no secret economic or strategic reason [for the British presence in Northern Ireland], but simply ... the self-determination of the people of Northern Ireland'.

This was significant. Sinn Fein had always held that Britain would never give up Northern Ireland because of its strategic importance. King's speech was not a declaration of neutrality, but he did later accept that the phrase about 'no secret economic or strategic reason' had probably come, through intermediaries, from Adams. The true significance of this concession would become apparent before Mrs Thatcher left office.

When Mrs Thatcher was shown this speech in advance, she marked the early pages. King's vital phrase, however, went unmarked. She either did not reach it, or failed to see what it meant. It was a rare example of her attention wandering. Stealthily, British policy towards Northern Ireland was beginning to move in a manner she opposed.

32
Ten years, then an ambush

'No resignations yet, I see!'

On Thursday 4 May 1989, Mrs Thatcher officially celebrated the tenth anniversary of her premiership. Months earlier, Denis Thatcher had offered typically level-headed counsel: 'I think this <u>10th</u> is going to be badly over played ... Pl. let us be <u>v.</u> careful.' His wife was similarly minded, but the occasion had to be marked. No prime minister, since Lord Liverpool, had lasted so long in office.*

At Bernard Ingham's suggestion, Mrs Thatcher gave just one anniversary interview – to the Press Association's Chris Moncrieff. Ingham advised her to 'avoid altogether discussing your successor', but stress her 'determination to go on doing for Britain what you have so successfully done so far'. She duly looked forward, telling Moncrieff about the importance of combating global warming.† Inevitably she looked back too. Her achievements had come through refusing to take the 'easy way': 'The easy way is the difficult way in the end.' Implicitly acknowledging criticism of her combative style, she said: 'one tends ... to defend oneself. Of course, most women defend themselves – it is the female of the species, the tigress ...'

The 'tigress' image excited the media, and she was asked about it again: 'you remember that poem of Kipling's,' she replied, '... the female of the species is rather better than the male at many many things, and I was pointing out therefore that it is ... the tigress who defends her cubs because she is always interested in the future'. As Mrs Thatcher well knew, Kipling had not said that the female of the species was 'rather better' than the male, but 'more deadly'. Her message about her unique and necessary impact as the one and only woman in power was unaltered after a decade.

On the day itself, the tigress went on display with her cubs. Mrs Thatcher emerged from No. 10, flanked by Mark and his Texan wife Diane Burgdorf

---

* Lord Liverpool held the office from 1812 to 1827, an era when the electorate numbered fewer than 500,000.
† In the previous year, Mrs Thatcher had been the first to make the subject of global warming her own (see p. 781).

(but not, despite Ingham's urging, by Denis). In her arms was their first-born, Michael. This was a bit of a gamble. After news of Michael's birth had first broken on 3 March, she had been much mocked for her awkward declaration that 'We have become a grandmother.' Cited as an example of her pseudo-royal grandiosity, this had in fact been a clumsy effort to include Denis (who was absent).*

At sixty-three, Mrs Thatcher could not avoid talk of retirement. Ingham's suggestion that she embrace the fact of ageing was probably the right one. She looked happy and Michael slept throughout. The almost dynastic pictures dominated the news.

By now, the fortunes of Mrs Thatcher's government were beginning to decline. Ingham dated the start of the trouble to December 1988, with the strange story of Edwina Currie and the eggs. 'After that', he recalled, 'nothing went right for the Government.' Other than Mrs Thatcher, Mrs Currie, a junior minister at the Department of Health, was the government's only well-known woman minister. On 3 December she made the soon-infamous claim that 'most of the egg production of this country, sadly, is now infected with salmonella'.† Sales of eggs slumped, to the fury of producers.

At first, Mrs Thatcher avoided the row. By 13 December, however, with producers reporting a 50 per cent drop in forward orders of eggs, she convened a meeting of relevant ministers. As one who tended to believe that farmers were feather-bedded at public expense, she leant against the producer interest.‡ Besides, she looked favourably on Mrs Currie, one of the rising generation of Thatcherite meritocrats. She was usually pleased to advance able women, unless, perhaps, they posed a direct threat to her. On the other hand, she did not want egg farmers going bust, particularly at the taxpayers' expense.

Mrs Thatcher summed up the meeting, saying there was 'a genuine and growing problem of infection of eggs by salmonella enteritidis PT4'. This, however, was a long way from saying all eggs were unfit to eat. Downing Street had let it be known that Mrs Thatcher had eaten scrambled eggs for

---

* The phrase quickly mutated, in popular memory, to 'We are a grandmother.' It reflected Mrs Thatcher's perpetual embarrassment at use of the word 'I', which she avoided wherever possible.
† As Currie later pointed out, saying that most of the *production* was infected with salmonella was not the same as saying that the infection was present in most, or even many, eggs, but this distinction was obliterated in the excitement.
‡ Mrs Thatcher's direct acquaintance with agriculture came almost entirely through the big Essex farm of her sister Muriel and her husband Willie (who had probably wanted to marry Margaret – see p. 44).

lunch. When Mrs Currie heard this, she recalled, she knew 'I was sunk.' As the parliamentary party turned against Mrs Currie, Mrs Thatcher summoned her to 10 Downing Street and, rather apologetically, accepted her resignation. Afterwards, Mrs Currie recorded, she 'gave me a cuddle and it creased me for a minute ... she said, "That is because we are friends", and that was that'. While the Currie crisis was a storm in an eggcup, it was telling that Mrs Thatcher had failed to protect a ministerial colleague from backbench hostility.

As 3 May 1989 drew nigh, the media was filled with what Ingham called 'an orgy of criticism and unflattering poll'. *Spitting Image* depicted Mrs Thatcher, in a man's suit, bursting into 'My Way' during a television interview. Harriet Harman, the rising feminist Labour politician, wrote that 'Having climbed the spiked ladder to leadership, Mrs Thatcher has pulled it up after her ... It seems there is only room at the top for one woman.' In a television programme called *The Thatcher Factor*, the fashion journalist Brenda Polan traced how, over the decade, Mrs Thatcher had moved from 'middle-class mimsy' to 'what Englishmen find very frightening, which is a sort of hard-edged chic'. She had been accused of looking more royal than the Queen, Polan continued, 'but in fact she's expressing what the Queen doesn't have, which is power'.

In an interview, Willie Whitelaw delivered several 'Willieisms' in which praise and criticism were inextricably intertwined. 'I don't pretend that I liked her [when she beat him for the party leadership in 1975], because I didn't ... But I decided to force myself to try to get on with her ... the fact is that she has got things through.' If he were still in government, he revealed, 'I would be urging caution as far as the parliamentary programme is concerned. I really must say that the dangers of going too fast are there.'

Whitelaw, still Deputy Leader of the Conservative Party, had always been one to urge going slower, but now his warning matched the general mood. Although opinion polls continued, unusually for the mid-term, to put the Tories ahead of Labour,[*] they also reflected a certain weariness. A Mori poll showed 55 per cent finding the country 'heading in the wrong direction'. At a small 'family' dinner in Downing Street on 3 May, Tim Bell made the congratulatory speech. But as he informed Mark Lennox-Boyd, Mrs Thatcher's PPS from 1988, he 'made it quite clear that the perception in the country was that the Govt was doing too much on too many fronts'.

Mrs Thatcher celebrated the anniversary herself with an informal

---

[*] The Gallup poll published on 5 May had the Conservatives at 40.5 per cent and Labour on 37.5 per cent.

luncheon at Chequers on Sunday 7 May. Mark and Diane (but not Carol) were joined by a range of powerful supporters and friends.* From politics, the guests were mainly those safely in the Lords – Whitelaw, Carrington, Gowrie, Thorneycroft and Bruce-Gardyne; plus Norman Tebbit and Cranley Onslow, the Chairman of the 1922 Committee, from the Commons. Her only serving Cabinet minister present was John Major. This seemed to single him out as her favoured successor.

By her tenth anniversary, Mrs Thatcher had no serious health problems, but those closest to her noticed some loss of energy, concentration and self-restraint. Ever since Westland, Charles Powell felt that 'The stress had seemed to build. She started to drink a bit more† and said slightly wild things. There was increasing excoriation of some colleagues.' His inward assumption was that she would not contest the next election. Sensing that his wife was 'getting terribly, terribly tired', Denis now broached the possibility of her stepping down. 'I think you're probably right,' she told him, and began to contemplate when to tell the Queen: 'I have to choose the time to play it right with Her Majesty.' The plan fell apart, however, after she consulted Whitelaw, who insisted that, with no obvious heir, her departure would split the party. Then, as Denis recalled, 'we had rows over the whole damn thing, and that really upset her. And that's the first time her nerve began to go a bit.' In the end, she reverted to her natural inclination and decided to continue until the next election. 'Well, maybe we'll scrape by,' Denis told her, unconvinced.‡

On 4 May, the Cabinet attended a tenth-anniversary dinner in the Carlton Club. Geoffrey Howe, as Mrs Thatcher's most senior surviving minister, delivered a lavish eulogy. He ended with words from her long-standing

---

* They included Rupert Murdoch, Bill Deedes, John Junor, Alastair Burnet and Woodrow Wyatt from the world of journalism; Lords Sieff, Forte and King, plus Sir Hector Laing, Sir Phil Harris, Garfield Weston and Michael Richardson from the world of business; close counsellors like Alistair McAlpine, Ronnie Millar, Tim Bell, David Wolfson, Mark Lennox-Boyd and Cynthia Crawford (Crawfie); and, in tribute to her murdered colleague, Airey Neave's widow, Lady (Diana) Airey.
† According to her detective, Barry Strevens, her favourite was 'the low flyers' – that is, Famous Grouse whisky.
‡ Denis himself, eleven years older than Mrs Thatcher, was a source of some anxiety to her coterie. At a dinner towards the end of the previous year Charles Powell had suggested to Mark Lennox-Boyd that 'the only thing that would stop the PM going on and on would be if something happened to Denis'. Powell added that 'some time ago' Denis 'had a car accident ... just the wing scratched. He drove on & when he got home said it had been s.o. else's fault – but Charles and the PM I guess suspected he had been drinking. Charles said to me that if anything did happen he only hoped Denis would be killed outright rather than injured. Then she would carry on. Charles is a brutal man.'

critic, Peter Jenkins, in that morning's *Independent*: 'History will surely recognise her achievements as Britain's first woman Prime Minister, a leader with the courage of her convictions who assailed the conventional wisdom of her day, challenged and overthrew the existing order, changed the political map, and put the country on its feet again.' Howe's decision to quote Jenkins was, in fact, artfully mischievous. For immediately after Howe's chosen quote, his column continued thus: 'She did all this with ruthlessness and much injustice and at a high cost in human misery, but she did it. Yet note how, ten years on, we begin to slip into the past tense.'

As if to ram home Jenkins's point, in a by-election in the Vale of Glamorgan that day, Labour took the seat from the Conservatives on a swing of 12.5 per cent, the biggest from Tory to Labour for half a century.

For all his praise at dinner, earlier that day Howe had been plotting a serious challenge to Mrs Thatcher's authority. His accomplice was Nigel Lawson. As economic Thatcherites, but also victims of the Thatcher style of government, they were natural allies. They did not, in fact, agree about Europe – Howe being wholly pro-European and Lawson sceptical – but they had maintained, indeed deepened, their faith in British membership of the ERM, to which Mrs Thatcher remained adamantly opposed. On that anniversary morning, increasingly frustrated by her attitude, they resolved to make her an offer she could not refuse.

Preparations for this showdown had begun more than six weeks earlier. If it was hurt feelings towards the domineering Mrs Thatcher which gave Howe and Lawson the motive, it was changing events in Europe which presented them with the cue. The Delors Committee (see p. 666) formally reported on 17 April 1989, recommending a three-stage process of Economic and Monetary Union (EMU). The first stage required the entry of all member states into the Exchange Rate Mechanism (ERM). The second created a European Central Bank. The third completed the single currency. The key difficulty, from the British point of view, was paragraph 39, which insisted that entry into Stage 1 compelled eventual entry into all stages.

It was in opposition to this linkage that the entire British government could agree. With the June European Council in Madrid planning to approve the Delors agenda and move forward to an Intergovernmental Conference (IGC) later in the year to accomplish EMU, ministers considered their response. Mrs Thatcher was naturally opposed to the entire thing. Howe and Lawson, however, believing it would be disastrous for a single currency to go ahead with Britain standing aside, argued the government must make a concession favourable to the ERM. This would gain Britain a purchase on the process: it might postpone the IGC and perhaps even frustrate Stages 2 and 3 altogether. They now sought to persuade Mrs Thatcher of this course.*

In forming their plans, Howe and Lawson were not cut off from their Continental counterparts. Delors had what he called 'a quiet friendship' with Howe and discreet conversations took place. Leon Brittan, Howe's close ally and the senior British European Commissioner, understood what was afoot. In mid-March, after discussion with Howe, he recorded in his diary: 'As he is contemplating leaving the Government this yr or next in any event, he is thinking of getting together with Nigel and making this a resignation issue. I did not discourage him.' Meanwhile, in the *Financial Times* Leon Brittan's brother Sam, a close friend of Lawson, whose work Mrs Thatcher had long admired, assiduously promoted ERM entry on economic grounds.

Scouring the European scene for help, Howe sought to recruit the Dutch Prime Minister, Ruud Lubbers. Mrs Thatcher thought highly of Lubbers, whose free-market views she shared and whose good looks she was thought to admire. Howe persuaded a doubting Lawson to use Lubbers's summit meeting with Mrs Thatcher at Chequers that April to push her towards the ERM. The occasion was a disaster. Mrs Thatcher listened impatiently as Lawson's counterpart, Onno Ruding, put forward the Lawson case for the ERM. An ill-tempered exchange followed: 'She was very harsh to these colleagues,' Ruding recalled. 'You don't say that sort of thing in front of foreigners.' When Lawson next met Mrs Thatcher, on 3 May, she complained of the nonsense that Ruding had talked. Lawson disagreed, putting forward his case for ERM entry in order to prevent Delors Stages 2 and 3. Mrs Thatcher drew herself up imperiously and replied with finality that she 'did not want the issue of UK membership of the ERM to be raised at this stage'. Lawson vividly recalled her last words: 'I must prevail.'

Thus enraged and frustrated, Lawson met Howe the following day, that of Mrs Thatcher's tenth-anniversary celebrations. With the Prime Minister evidently unconvinced of the economic case for ERM membership, Lawson felt they should focus on the tactical argument ahead of Madrid. But Howe, always putting faith in what he saw as reason, wanted both the political and economic arguments made. It was agreed that a joint paper, incorporating both, should be worked up.

As they exchanged drafts, Howe and Lawson continued to agonize. Both men felt uneasy about their political careers. Both realized they had

---

* Given the determination of the European leaders to press forward, it seems strange that Howe and Lawson could have believed so strongly that ERM entry would derail EMU, but it was only after the fall of the Berlin Wall in November 1989 that EMU was to become an unbreakable Franco-German deal. At this earlier stage Germany was more equivocal.

little chance of being prime minister – though Howe did contemplate it. As Howe suspected, he was being considered for a reshuffle. On 4 June, while planning her ministerial changes for July, Mrs Thatcher raised the possibility of sending him to the Lords (as Lord Chancellor) but feared he would refuse. For his part, 'Nigel was on the skids' because of the growing problems of the British economy. He told Robin Leigh-Pemberton, the Governor of the Bank of England, that he was thinking of going, noting how 'difficult' things had become with Mrs Thatcher. Rumours circulated in the press.

As the date of Madrid approached, both Howe and Lawson fretted. Lawson in particular 'got cold feet' about the planned *démarche* and went along with it chiefly 'because of being loyal to Geoffrey'. Although Mrs Thatcher still liked Lawson, she already mistrusted Howe. So, in her eyes, by ganging up with Howe Lawson weakened his case.

On 13 June, Lawson saw Whitelaw and cried on his shoulder. Ever friendly, but ever canny, the oracle told Lawson he hoped he would not step down but would 'fully understand' if he did. This decided nothing. If Whitelaw had sided with Lawson the whole thing would have amounted to a coup against Mrs Thatcher, which is probably why he was not tempted. Hours later, Lawson and Howe finally agreed to send their joint minute to Mrs Thatcher.

On the same day – 13 June – as her two most senior ministers settled upon this ploy, Mrs Thatcher came under attack from two of her most senior bureaucrats, Robin Butler, the Cabinet Secretary, and Patrick Wright, the head of the Foreign Office. At issue was the fate of Charles Powell, whom Butler had been seeking to dislodge from Downing Street ever since he became Cabinet Secretary in early 1988 (see pp. 625–6). Mountains had been moved to persuade Mrs Thatcher and the Foreign Office to allow Powell to become Ambassador to Spain. She, however, had now gone back on it all and said Powell must stay.*

Butler was at his wits' end. He believed that Mrs Thatcher's reliance on Powell – and, to a lesser extent, on Bernard Ingham – worked against the proper processes of government: 'I was chief executive of a government that was falling apart.' Her senior ministers felt it strongly, he knew. He considered her perceived dependence on Powell akin to a 'cancer' at the heart of government. 'Miss this chance, and it would be too late to cut

---

* A snapshot of Mrs Thatcher's engagement diary indicates the omnipresence of Powell in her life. In May 1989, he attended twenty-seven official meetings with her, compared with sixteen attended by Paul Gray and eleven by Andrew Turnbull. So Powell's rate was exactly that of the two, neither of whom was idle, combined.

it out,' he thought. On the morning of 13 June he threatened to resign if Powell stayed at Downing Street.*

That afternoon, Mrs Thatcher met Butler and Wright, with Andrew Turnbull in attendance, for 'a full hour of very tough talking'. Butler told her frankly that Powell 'excluded other sources of advice'. His influence on policy was too great. Butler laid his own position on the line: 'He did not believe that, having given that advice [that Powell must go to Madrid], he could continue if it were rejected.'

But Powell, Mrs Thatcher insisted, was so 'exceptionally competent'. He was brilliant both at writing speeches and at advice – '(She indicated that on many issues she was dissatisfied with the advice from the FCO)'. She 'lashed out savagely', Wright noted in his diary, 'accusing Robin Butler of twisting the constitutional position – saying that she was not bound to accept either his advice or mine'. Then she raised the stakes: 'She several times implied that she could not go on without Charles, and that she might resign herself. At another point, she said that it would be either Charles or Geoffrey Howe' – implicitly accepting the widespread view that Powell was, in effect, her Foreign Secretary.† She begged Butler to go away and reflect. He told Wright that he thought he really must resign.

Andrew Turnbull set out the issues on paper for her. Keeping Powell, he said, was 'a decision you are entitled to make'. Yet he registered his own concern 'at the way Charles' role has developed ... it does weaken the authority of the Foreign Secretary'. On the other hand, Turnbull thought Butler was wrong to threaten resignation and inwardly puzzled: 'Robin was not a guy who throws wobblies. It was uncharacteristic, and constitutionally odd.'

In a minute for Mrs Thatcher, Butler stressed that 'We have all found [Powell] increasingly brusque and difficult to work with.' These were the 'symptoms of someone who has been in No. 10 too long'. He also professed

---

* A subsidiary anxiety for Butler was the glamorous and fiery Carla Powell. She was often in the office and was close to Mrs Thatcher, to the annoyance of those who worked there and who thought that she 'traded on her relationship with Margaret'. Her Latin flamboyance, which perhaps overexcited British civil servants, was also considered a problem.

† A vignette of Charles Powell in his pomp is provided by Mark Lennox-Boyd. After dining with the Powells just before the tenth anniversary, he noted: 'The Prime Minister is, more than previous PMs, running her foreign policy and Charles is designing it ... When I am present when foreign policy is discussed, she rarely fails to take his advice. On Tuesday morning ... the PM in exasperation with Chancellor Kohl over his desire to have negotiations by NATO over SNF said "If I am asked at questions about the Germans I will say they were good allies once." Charles frowned & said sternly "I think you might try & win the argument rather than indulge in abuse" and added sarcastically "if you are going to argue it at all that is". She took it like a lamb.'

concern for 'the welfare of the Powells themselves. I have worried about the intensity – almost the obsessiveness – with which Charles Powell works and the effects on his marriage . . . If there is some sort of breakdown, that will reflect badly on No. 10.'

When Prime Minister and Cabinet Secretary met again, on 17 June, to Butler she seemed 'like a mad woman'. She considered parts of Butler's minute 'libellous', so 'She might want to consult the Solicitor-General. Sir Robin was acting as if she was not free to reject his advice.' It was 'cruel' and 'selfish'. 'She had to fight the FCO all the way (i.e. needed Mr Powell's help to do it).' If she let Powell leave, 'The only reason would be that Sir Robin had threatened to resign.'

Mrs Thatcher's rage was real enough – more vividly expressed here, perhaps, than in any other official record. She was deeply affronted at being told, as she saw it, whom she could have in her own office, and genuinely terrified of losing Powell. But context is crucial. Even as she dealt with the Butler-Powell problem, she was also dealing with the Howe-Lawson one. The latter is often referred to as the 'Madrid ambush'. Butler's resignation threat must have seemed like an ambush too – also, coincidentally, involving Madrid. She was bound to link the two and feel under unprecedented assault. 'You could see why she didn't want to lose the one person she could absolutely count on,' Turnbull recalled. Noting he did not make this connection at the time, he felt he and Butler 'were guilty of failing to spot her sense of isolation'.

The next day, Charles Powell sent Mrs Thatcher his pre-emptive rebuttal. He answered Butler's criticism about access: 'I have tried to extend the number of people whom you see outside the government machine – Soviet dissidents, refusniks [sic], the Bob Conquests, the David Harts* and many others. Of course the FCO don't like that . . .' In the end, 'the only point in staying is to help you . . . You are wonderfully loyal to the people who work for you – but you must think of yourself, and I would understand and accept [a request to leave] without question: and that is meant very sincerely.' These words, appealing simultaneously to Mrs Thatcher's protective, motherly instincts and to her personal desires, could not have been better calculated to ensure Powell's continuance in Downing Street.

Mrs Thatcher now faced a crisis with the potential to bring the whole edifice crashing down. The next day, however, Butler took a step back. In a memo, he noted Mrs Thatcher had said that if he threatened resignation,

---

* Powell had passed to Mrs Thatcher, before writing his note to her, an impassioned memo from David Hart urging her to fight back against the 'sustained, unrestrained attack on you personally' with 'a thorough shake-up' of her Cabinet and new 'radical action', so his was a good name to deploy at that moment.

she would have to concede: 'I have no wish to win the argument by holding a pistol to your head,' he went on. 'So I remove the pistol: I will not resign whatever you decide.' She had got her way.*

Throughout, Wright had kept Howe abreast of these machinations. The day after Butler withdrew his resignation threat, Wright noted in his diary: 'The next crunch will come with Geoffrey Howe, who told me this afternoon that he was not prepared to let Charles stay on.' There was a shared assumption among senior ministers and officials that Mrs Thatcher was the problem, and they must remedy it.

Mrs Thatcher had received the Howe–Lawson minute, typed, at Lawson's insistence, on Foreign Office paper, on 14 June.† This warned of a 'dangerous confrontation' with the French EEC presidency. If Britain did not shift its position the IGC would happen, and British opposition would be seen 'to reflect a new insularity': Britain would lose investment and have less influence with the Bush administration. Better to produce a 'non-legally binding timetable' for ERM entry by the end of 1992 and postpone discussion of EMU until 1993. Could they meet her to discuss the matter?

Powell immediately sensed, to use the word Mrs Thatcher employed in her memoirs, an 'ambush'. He questioned whether this was 'genuinely a tactical move to help us over Madrid? Or is it a ploy to increase the pressure on you to agree to early membership of the ERM?' Mrs Thatcher double-underlined and ticked the word 'ploy'. Powell concluded: 'The joint minute's offer of peace in our time is superficially attractive. But is it realistic and deliverable? And when all is said and done, you are being asked to bind us to joining the ERM by a fixed date.'

This note illustrated perfectly why Mrs Thatcher depended upon Powell so heavily. It displayed his clarity of thought and expression, his exact alertness to any risk to his chief and his cunning way of influencing her reaction. Referring to the 'offer of peace in our time', he was consciously echoing the language used by Neville Chamberlain when he returned from meeting

---

* Mrs Thatcher did not want the notes of these exchanges kept, telling Turnbull to ask Butler to agree to destroy the records. 'This was the only time she ever asked me to do this, and the only time I ever did,' Butler recalled. 'I feel ashamed I did so.' Andrew Turnbull saved them, however, by keeping his own copies.

† Lawson's uncertainty about how best to handle the impact of his own joint minute was such that, only two days after sending it, he and his wife Thérèse, at the prompting of Ian Gow and Mark Lennox-Boyd (neither of whom knew about the minute), invited the Thatchers to supper with them that Sunday. He was being both confrontational and diplomatic at the same time. Mrs Thatcher 'felt too tired to accept'.

Hitler in Munich in 1938. As he well knew, this would prejudice Mrs Thatcher against what Chancellor and Foreign Secretary were proposing.*

Not that she needed much encouragement. With her unusual combination of high principle and base suspicion, Mrs Thatcher took violently against what she saw as both a cowardly piece of Foreign Office-style compromise and a plot against herself. She at once requested a meeting with Alan Walters (Lawson's bugbear, who had returned to Downing Street as her economic adviser the previous month). She postponed the meeting that Howe and Lawson sought to 20 June, but she dared not prevent it. Despite the impending confrontation, she was not certain they were flat wrong. She was painfully aware that her position in the coming negotiations was insecure. Her instinct against ERM entry never changed but, guided by Walters, she began to edge towards a more positive approach: Britain would be willing to join the ERM, but only after certain rigorous conditions were met. These were the complete abolition of exchange controls, and the deregulation and mutual recognition of all financial and capital markets and businesses across the EEC. Such concessions, Walters told her, would make ERM membership a price worth paying.

In between the receipt of the Howe-Lawson letter and the meeting of 20 June came the European Parliament elections in which the Conservatives ceded thirteen seats to Labour. These were the first nationwide elections Mrs Thatcher could be said to have lost since becoming party leader. 'Tories put blame on Thatcher for campaign "flop"', splashed the *Daily Telegraph*. Electoral failure greatly strengthened her critics within the party and weakened her political position. The following day, when Mrs Thatcher met officials and advisers ahead of seeing Howe and Lawson, Mark Lennox-Boyd noted that she seemed 'curiously pragmatic' in her approach to what they were proposing. In the end, the Walters line, treated as a serious offer over ERM entry, prevailed.†

Seeing Lawson and Howe on 20 June, Mrs Thatcher advanced the Walters view. Invoking the tactical spirit of the Howe-Lawson proposals, she said she wanted to keep all options open for Madrid. She 'remained very wary of setting a date for sterling's membership of the ERM because of the extent to which this would constrain the Government in future'.

The next day, Patrick Wright and Howe discussed the Powell situation. Even as Howe tried to convince Mrs Thatcher over Madrid, he was also

---

* When confronted by the present author with his use of this phrase, Charles Powell had the good grace to blush slightly.
† Only Bernard Ingham was utterly unconciliatory. He, 'passionately and mischievously, believes her position should not change', Lennox-Boyd recorded in his journal. '"Does this mean that we will never join?" he asked enthusiastically.'

trying to get rid of her closest counsellor. This was now the same contest, conducted on two fronts. Mrs Thatcher's attitude on the ERM the day before, Howe told Wright, had left him gloomy. Even if she did shift her position, she would 'do it with such bad grace, and setting such impossible conditions, that all negotiating advantage would be lost': 'He was about to see Nigel Lawson, and told me (very privately) that both of them were getting very near to resignation. He was seriously worried about the PM's state of mind, and the damage it was doing to the nation.' Offstage, Howe was being pushed forward by Elspeth. At lunch on 22 June, she told Wright's wife, Virginia, that 'Margaret Thatcher was totally impossible, and that it was a pity to go back on one's word as Robin Butler had done. "We should all stick together, and to our guns." She said that it was a pity that all this could not be leaked.' It was notable that Lady Howe included the Wrights and Robin Butler as part of the 'we' who should 'stick together' against Mrs Thatcher. The Prime Minister was not paranoid to discern a conspiracy.

At Cabinet, Mrs Thatcher maintained the line that, at Madrid, she would try to 'shunt away' Stages 2 and 3 of Delors without 'binding commitments' about ERM entry. She might, however, be willing to spell out the conditions for deciding that 'the time was right'. She asked for 'tactical flexibility' at the summit. This was not good enough for Howe and Lawson. In an unprecedented act of rebellion they demanded to see her once again, at almost the last minute. On Friday 23 June, two days before her departure for Madrid, in another minute they insisted she offer a target date for ERM entry at Madrid, which was crucial to 'killing Delors para 39 and kicking Stages II and III into the long grass'.

Mrs Thatcher was furious. Once para 39 suffered this fate, she wrote, 'it will be found very quickly thrown back into the ring again'. She now felt certain that Howe and Lawson were seeking to trap her. As Powell recalled it, 'This was an ultimatum, the sort of thing that starts World War I or World War II.' After failing to put them off, Powell advised Mrs Thatcher to receive Lawson and Howe in Downing Street at 8.15 on Sunday morning.

Also that Friday, Patrick Wright learnt that Powell was to stay in post. He passed this on to Howe, 'who became more and more determined to oppose the decision'. Meanwhile Mrs Thatcher discovered that, in Paris, the idea of the EEC agreeing not to push for the automatic Stage 2 of Delors in return for British ERM entry was being described as 'the Lawson compromise'. Suspecting collusion between Howe-Lawson and foreigners, she was lost for words: '!?' she wrote on the note.

Ahead of Sunday's meeting, Powell spoke to Lawson. As he told Mrs

Thatcher, 'Geoffrey* has been making the running in pressing for the meeting. Nigel has allowed himself to be persuaded.' While both men wanted Britain to join the ERM by the end of Delors Stage 1, 'In Geoffrey's case it goes wider than that. He is worked up about the elections, about our general tone on Europe and about divisions within the Party.' There was a risk of resignation: 'Geoffrey is getting quite emotional about it and those close to him are not certain quite what he will do . . .' Powell then rehearsed all the arguments against setting a date for ERM entry. She might deploy these at the meeting, he advised, or 'simply listen'. Mrs Thatcher underlined this second option.

When Howe and Lawson arrived in Downing Street they were met by Andrew Turnbull: 'I greeted these two portly gentlemen at the door and showed them up to the study. I felt like a mahout with a couple of small Indian elephants.' With the meeting considered political, no one was present except for the three principals, and no record was taken. Led by Howe, the two produced their formulation for Madrid, insisting on a date for ERM entry. If she did not agree, said Howe, he would resign. Lawson followed suit: 'You should know, Prime Minister, that if Geoffrey goes, I must go too.'† Robin Butler's resignation threat of ten days earlier must have seemed to her like a rehearsal for this. Confronted with so sudden an ultimatum, Mrs Thatcher experienced three reactions: 'First, I was not prepared to be blackmailed into a policy which I felt was wrong. Second, I must keep them on board if I could, at least for the moment. Third, I would never, never allow this to happen again.' She said she would spell out the conditions in which Britain would enter the ERM, but she would not set a date. 'They left,' she later wrote, 'Geoffrey looking insufferably smug. And so the nasty little meeting ended.'

If Howe looked smug, this did not reflect his inner feelings. Mrs Thatcher not having disclosed her hand, he did not know what she would do. He had not, despite his fighting words to Wright, raised the question of Charles Powell.

That Sunday afternoon, Mrs Thatcher flew to Madrid in the same plane as Howe. She did not, however, speak to him. She was so furious that she stayed with Ingham and Powell behind the curtain screening off the Prime Minister's part of the plane. When her speaking note for the Council was

---

* It was highly unusual at that time for an official to refer to a minister by his first name in a document. It indicates the way that Powell saw himself as an equal of the other players.
† Howe's threat to resign had not been settled with Lawson in advance. When it came, Lawson recalled, he was 'taken by surprise. My statement of support was spur of the moment to stop her driving a wedge between us.'

drawn up, Powell was 'forbidden to show a copy to anyone from the Foreign Office. It was petty, but I was loyal to my instructions.' As Ingham recalled, 'The atmosphere was *appalling*.'

At the Council meeting, Mrs Thatcher did not do what Howe and Lawson had asked. She avoided setting any date for ERM entry. She did, however, greatly soften her tone. She set out what became known as the Madrid Conditions – the completion of the internal market, the abolition of exchange controls and a free market in financial services. If the above applied, she went on, and 'provided inflation in Britain has indeed been brought down significantly as we intend* – the conditions would clearly exist for sterling to join the ERM'. She was indicating a change, a genuine readiness to join.

Also in calm tones, but firmly, Mrs Thatcher then explained Britain's objections to Stages 2 and 3 of the Delors Report. She questioned the binding fiscal rules and the massive subsidies to the periphery which would be required by a European single currency. She emphasized the implications for sovereignty: 'I question the acceptability, to Community public opinion, of arrangements as lacking in democratic accountability as the Report describes.' She did not want any date for an IGC.

For the post-Council press conference in Madrid, Ingham advised Mrs Thatcher to 'demonstrate, contrary to all the petty propaganda of people who should know better, that you remain a positive, constructive force in Europe'. 'The simple story', he said, 'is whether you won or lost.' Put in those simple terms, she won. The Council, telegraphed David Hannay, was 'unexpectedly successful' and agreed conclusions on everything except the Social Chapter (which Britain, alone, opposed): 'The Gospel according to paragraph 39 does not appear.' Contrary to French wishes, no date was set for an IGC. Seen in the rather less simple overall picture, however, she lost. Britain won some delay and avoided obloquy, but British ERM entry became much more likely, as did the European federalist project. Besides, Madrid was damaging to Mrs Thatcher because it was clear that the Iron Lady had been forced to bend. Her aura of invincibility never fully recovered.

In immediate British political terms, however, there was relief. Mrs Thatcher had, it appeared, managed to bring the party together. Privately, she told staff that 'there may have to be a 2 tier Europe'. She began to see a parting of the ways. But she did feel some satisfaction that she had got out of a tight corner in Madrid without following the Howe-Lawson recipe for success. Howe and Lawson realized that, in the circumstances, they

---

* This was a reference to the need for inflation to 'converge' with Continental rates.

could not possibly resign over Mrs Thatcher's failure to set a date. Andrew Turnbull summed it up: 'Seen from London, it seemed that the judgment of the Chancellor and the Foreign Secretary was faulty.' The business of setting a date had been a bluff, which Mrs Thatcher had called.

Still seething at the ambush, Mrs Thatcher exulted in its failure. When the Cabinet assembled after the Madrid Council she stood by the door and, as Howe and Lawson entered the Cabinet Room, hissed, 'No resignations yet, I see!' Like Robin Butler, they had chickened out. Howe later claimed he failed to notice 'this piece of retrospective theatre'. He described her behaviour as 'private gloating' and asked, 'Don't you find it baffling?' After so many years working with Mrs Thatcher, he should not have been baffled. She thought him unmanly for not understanding that a threat to resign, solemnly made but not carried out, disqualified the person making it from her respect. How could he continue as her Foreign Secretary, she asked herself? In Cabinet she found a way of putting down Lawson too: 'when she reported on the Summit, the Chancellor raised the desirability of joining the ERM. She dealt with his intervention by changing the subject, rather to his consternation.'

The 14th of July 1989, shortly after Madrid, marked the bicentenary of the French Revolution. Before attending that month's G7 in Paris (timed to coincide with the celebrations), Mrs Thatcher gave a remarkably frank interview to *Le Monde*. 'Human rights', she declared, 'did not begin with the French Revolution' but stemmed from 'a mixture of Judaism and Christianity . . .' In 1689, she continued, England had its 'silent quiet revolution [the Glorious Revolution], where Parliament exerted its will over The King . . . it was done quietly without the bloodshed'. She compared the French Revolution unfavourably with the home-grown variety: 'Liberty, egality, fraternity; they forgot obligations and duties I think. And then of course it was the fraternity that went missing . . . It heralded an age of terror.'

As with the Bruges Speech (see p. 673), the inspiration for these remarks was a combination of Mrs Thatcher's own thoughts and suggestions from Charles Powell.* Her purpose was threefold: to state that the British way of doing things was best; to support the peaceful type of revolution ('velvet' revolutions) now taking place in Eastern Europe; and to speak out because, in Powell's view, 'the chance to stick it to the French was too good to miss'. This was Margaret Thatcher, the Burkeian conservative, the guardian, as she saw it, of the particular anti-revolutionary English form of liberty. Her

---

* As Powell described his own role: 'Since [the Glorious Revolution] was at the heart of my history degree, it may well have been me.'

desire to preach what she believed to be the truth was integral to her leadership. Frequently this was uncomfortable and occasionally it was reckless, but it enabled her to help set the agenda both at home and abroad. In this, indeed, she resembled a great Frenchman, General de Gaulle. Her problem, by the middle of 1989, was that a dissonance was gradually emerging between her controversial but respected presence on the international stage and her growing troubles at home.

Back in March, Powell had offered Mrs Thatcher ideas for a reshuffle.* He told her that she would wish to avoid a repetition of Harold Macmillan's 1962 'Night of the Long Knives', but 'There is a case for quite extensive changes ... You don't want to go into the election with the risk that people will vote for a change of government when all they want is a change of faces. The time for a reshuffle is probably the end of July.' Powell then addressed what he called 'The Big Three' – Lawson, Howe and Hurd: 'I imagine you will want the Chancellor to go through to the election ... Your comments suggest that you may consider moving or even dropping the Foreign Secretary and the Home Secretary.' Without such changes, Powell warned, 'it will not be a radical reshuffle'. This remarkably frank memo formed the basis for most of what was to follow.

At dinner with close colleagues on 19 July, Mrs Thatcher made the final decisions. Howe would be offered Leader of the House. If he refused, he would be offered the Home Office. 'The ostensible reason', wrote Mark Lennox-Boyd, 'is that a powerful figure is needed in the House for TV but the real reason is his disloyalty at Madrid ... I think she hopes he will resign altogether.' John Major, the Chief Secretary, would leap up to the foreign secretaryship. Nick Ridley would move to Trade and Industry, making room for Chris Patten at Environment. Kenneth Baker was made Party Chairman, becoming the bookmakers' favourite to succeed Mrs Thatcher. The one person she wished would depart, but dared not move, was Nigel Lawson.

The first reaction to the reshuffle on 24 July was favourable, with excitement at the first arrivals of the younger generation – Major and Patten. Major's promotion suggested a moderate, modernized Thatcherism with a human face.† Patten was more obviously from the left of the party, but Mrs Thatcher felt he had 'moved a long way towards us'. On the key

---

* It was notable that the Prime Minister's foreign affairs private secretary, traditionally a post which had nothing to do with ministerial appointments, was giving her advice on how to reconstruct her entire administration.
† In June, Major had given a speech to the Adam Smith Institute which was described as 'one of the toughest speeches ever by a Treasury Minister at this stage of the public spending round'. This burnished his Thatcherite credentials.

pending economic decision, however – entry into the ERM – Patten and Major agreed with Howe, not with her. Patten's arrival was also thought to presage a more emollient approach over the poll tax.

Howe was the problem. Until Mrs Thatcher summoned him in the morning on Monday 24 July, he had had no premonition of disaster. So when she told him what she wanted he was surprised and confused. She offered him the leadership of the House and the office of Lord President of the Council and then, when that appeared not to find favour, the Home Office. Howe would have to give up the Foreign Secretary's grace-and-favour house, Chevening, of which he was very fond, but she softened the blow by offering him Dorneywood, the Chancellor's residence, instead. As Howe recorded, she said she wanted 'a younger face' at the Foreign Office but admitted that 'our pre-Madrid exchanges' had been 'a factor in her mind'. By Mrs Thatcher's account, Howe 'just looked sullen and said that he would have to talk to Elspeth first'. As usual, she was irritated by his slowness and the role of his wife. The meeting ended with nothing decided.

Discussing all this with Elspeth and Richard Ryder, Howe seemed 'very shocked and very sad'. According to his close friend Tim Renton, 'He did consider leaving and throwing in his dice behind Michael Heseltine.' Howe also consulted Leon Brittan, who suggested he would be 'better off, even in political terms, if he . . . went to the back benches'. Howe drafted a letter of resignation, citing their differences over Europe and the Madrid Council.

By Ryder's account, Elspeth Howe was 'hawkish', but did not consistently advise her husband to leave the government. Ryder's own view was that Howe's relationship with Mrs Thatcher was 'beyond repair and would likely end in continuing unhappiness and frictions unless he tendered his resignation'. Howe now telephoned Nigel Lawson. As Ryder recalled, 'He sort of said to Nigel, "Where do you stand if I resign?" Nigel was very cautious and quite abrupt. It was clear that he didn't want to have anything to do with it . . . the conversation lasted only about thirty seconds.' Ryder was sure Howe was sounding out Lawson to see if he, too, would resign. Such a step would have plunged her into a possibly terminal crisis. But Lawson fought shy of another Howe-led drama. His caution made it easier for Howe to decide that he might as well accept Mrs Thatcher's offer.

Later that morning, Howe went to the Foreign Office, where his private secretary, Stephen Wall, found him 'sitting at his desk in tears, very, very shaken. He had the underlying feeling that he'd been on the Long March.* He thought it counted for more than it did.' Sensing that Howe

---

* The phrase was Denis Thatcher's comic borrowing from Chairman Mao's Communist struggle, which he used to describe those who had started the Thatcher revolution in the 1970s.

was really seeking a reason to accept some version of Mrs Thatcher's offer, his allies suggested he ask also to be made Deputy Prime Minister, an informal title vacant since Willie Whitelaw's retirement, and chair certain Cabinet committees. In this cross-government role, he could rein in Mrs Thatcher's wilder instincts. Through David Waddington, the Chief Whip, Howe ascertained that the title of Deputy Prime Minister was on the table.* Elspeth and his advisers now told him to accept, once he had heard from Mrs Thatcher's own lips the terms of the job.

The two met at No. 10 that afternoon. When Mrs Thatcher offered the deputy prime ministership, Howe accepted. She clearly thought the worse of him for that. Howe may even, in retrospect, have agreed with her: 'It might have been better if I had gone ... if it had then been followed by Nigel's departure, it would have created a completely different structure in the party, wouldn't it?' But, at the time, he was in a muddle and getting no help from Lawson. In the short term, Mrs Thatcher was successfully practising divide and rule.

Mrs Thatcher's decision to appoint Major as Howe's successor grievously injured Howe's vanity: 'To promote someone of that total inexperience to that job at that time was itself crazy.' She, however, liked the fact that Major was 'untainted' by the Foreign Office and could offer a fresh perspective.† More important was the chance to build up Major as her eventual successor. 'She did not think he would be a master diplomat,' said Powell. 'In her eyes, this was going to be a crash course in introducing him to the world as a future senior figure.' Major himself had real concerns over his lack of experience. He agreed to take the role, but 'I wasn't happy about it: it would absolutely label me as someone there to do her bidding. I remembered Icarus.'

When Howe appeared in the Commons for his first performance as Leader of the House, he was greeted by a sustained roar of approval from the Conservative benches, signifying affection for him and criticism of his treatment at Mrs Thatcher's hands. As the week ended, Mark Lennox-Boyd noted in his journal, 'I suppose if we lose the next election ... this last week will be portrayed by commentators as a significant one.' The Conservatives

---

* Mrs Thatcher had been hoping to hold this back, regarding it as an honour peculiar to Willie Whitelaw and not something to be conferred on people she did not trust ('I don't want him in charge while I'm abroad'); but Waddington had – by his own account 'wrongly' – advised her to offer it, and now did so on her behalf.

† Major told Patrick Wright that 'he was worried by the implications in the Press that he had been sent to the FCO to change Community Policy in an anti-European direction. He said that this was quite false.'

were now well behind in the polls.* Interest rates stood at 14 per cent. On top of this were strikes – rail, dock, local government workers – and, far worse, continued Lennox-Boyd, 'the Tory Party suddenly woke up to the pain of the community charge'.

The community charge had become law in October 1988. Now it was about to be implemented. One of its central goals was to widen the local tax base, forcing more of those who benefited from local government services to contribute. This was supposed to improve local accountability. But a recipe for popularity it was not. By the summer of 1989, many Conservatives felt deeply apprehensive.

Two problems took centre stage. The first was the so-called 'safety net'. For a transitional period of four years, councils predicted to be better off under the poll tax (owing to the redistribution of central government grants and non-domestic rates) would be required to provide relief for councils that lost out. The beneficiaries of the new tax (prudent, usually Tory, councils) would thus be forced to levy a higher poll tax to subsidize the losers (spendthrift, usually Labour, councils). This enraged many Conservative backbenchers. Some feared this might lose the party the next election. The second problem was the sometimes huge losses which the poll tax was likely to throw up. Original talk of an average poll tax of £50 was now being replaced by figures like £350 – many households were going to pay much more than that.

On 19 July, Nicholas Ridley announced limits on the contribution prudent councils would make to the safety net, and additional local authority grants of over £2 billion. But these failed to appease many Tory MPs, who resented the safety net in principle and considered the extra grants some £1 billion short of what was needed. Ridley's statement was thus badly received in Parliament. In her 'end of term' speech to the 1922 Committee the following day, Mrs Thatcher defended the community charge. Her notes† show her reminding MPs that reform was much better than the catastrophic increases associated with rate revaluation. She hailed the day when the principle would prevail: 'WHAT YOU VOTE FOR, YOU PAY FOR'. She stressed that the safety net was being modified to the benefit of Conservative councils. The government, she said, had 'NOT tied [its] hands' for future years: it proposed to 'learn from first year's experience'. These remarks tacitly admitted all was not well.

Four days later came the reshuffle. Over-zealous, as most new ministers

---

* Labour was 14 per cent ahead in the *Observer*'s Harris poll on 25 June.
† There is never any formal record of the proceedings of the '22.

are, the new Environment Secretary, Chris Patten, quickly told the Commons that 'The community charge puts the community in charge.' He quickly came to regard this as a 'terrible mistake'.

As the summer recess began, Cranley Onslow, the Chairman of the 1922 Committee, warned Mark Lennox-Boyd that he should 'at least consider the remote possibility that someone might seek to challenge the leader at the next leadership election'. As Lennox-Boyd recorded, 'I certainly think this is wrong, but it is clearly a good thing that the House has risen.' Three weeks later, he told Mrs Thatcher that while a leadership challenge was 'theoretically possible', neither he nor Onslow had heard that any individual was considering making one. Yet he urged her to pay more attention to the parliamentary party, such as by including backbenchers in her Monday lunches with ministerial colleagues. Mrs Thatcher objected: 'We are not going to have luncheons every Monday. They are too repetitive.'

Over the summer, Patten sought a way forward for the poll tax. Early in September, he cut out Nigel Lawson and went straight to Mrs Thatcher. He wanted an extra £650 million to fund the safety net fully, vigorous charge-capping of some high-spending authorities and targeted interim relief for vulnerable households. His aim was to soften the blow for those 18 million who would 'for the first time receive a bill for local authority services', while also addressing backbench concerns about the safety net.* Mrs Thatcher was well aware of the likely political damage if nothing was done. In early September, she saw a secret survey of Conservative marginal seats which showed that, assuming a 7 per cent increase in council spending, 73 per cent of households and 82 per cent of individuals would pay more under the poll tax.

Lawson was naturally furious at Patten's attempt to get past him. He refused, point blank, to consider full funding; instead he wanted the safety net, planned to last four years, withdrawn after the first. This would allow all the planned benefits of the tax to accrue to prudent councils in the second year of operation. He proposed no additional transitional relief for those losing out during the remaining three years.

Mrs Thatcher was impatient, out of sheer political anxiety: 'I can't tell you the row there is ... I have never seen the 1922 Executive in such a state.' So she accepted Lawson's offer to end the safety net after one year,

---

* Patten also took to Mrs Thatcher a secret report for Westminster Council by the expert on London politics Tony Travers, revealing the devastating potential effect of the poll tax on Tory marginals in Greater London, especially the poorer ones. 'I think she was really surprised,' he recalled.

but also approved Patten's request for additional transitional relief.* Patten regarded the settlement as inadequate in scale. Among his officials there was a sense that 'The thing was being horribly obfuscated . . . the original ideal of equity and clarity was collapsing.'

In the run-up to the party conference, the media increasingly linked poll tax problems with the leadership question. BBC Television's *Panorama*, broadcast on the eve, presented that moment as Michael Heseltine's best chance, after nearly four years in the wilderness, to replace Mrs Thatcher. The programme ran interviews with MPs complaining about the community charge and how Mrs Thatcher was not listening to them. Viewers were given intimations of her political mortality by being reminded that she would be sixty-four that week. In Chris Patten's view, Heseltine supporters now saw their chance in relation more to the poll tax than to Europe: 'She'd said it was the flagship. So now they could say to doubters that the ship would sink them in their constituencies unless they could get rid of the admiral of the fleet.'

Nevertheless, the party conference itself, at Blackpool, went fairly well for Mrs Thatcher. To the irritation of some ministers, cheering party members chanted 'Ten More Years!' when she appeared.† While the poll tax did not blow up a storm, the economic situation remained a major political anxiety. Just before the conference, she had reluctantly conceded Lawson's demand to raise interest rates by 1 per cent to 15 per cent, despite a drop in inflation the previous month, to curtail overheating.‡ As public confidence in Lawson continued to fall, the presence of Alan Walters as her adviser in No. 10 became ever more irksome to him. Walters had an undue influence

---

* Around this time, officials had to get to grips with the politically delicate and surprisingly complex question of what community charge Mrs Thatcher herself should pay. In May 1989, Paul Gray explained that she and Denis would pay the charge in 10 Downing Street and the standard second-home charge ('Mr Thatcher has already returned the standard declaration form') for their house in Dulwich. The Thatchers were duly registered by Westminster Council as 'tenants' on 'Rooms First Floor, 10 Downing Street'. In June, however, it emerged that the correct description of their chargeable accommodation was 'Living Accommodation, 2nd floor, 10 Downing Street'. Mrs Thatcher filled in the form for Denis and herself and signed, registering as charge number C7455211000017. In October, it emerged that the community charges registration officer had lost Mrs Thatcher's form. Later that month, Gray finally handed over the completed form in person to the relevant official, to make sure it did not go astray. Any perceived delay would have been quickly used against her by hostile media.

† As usual, Michael Heseltine addressed a packed fringe meeting of the conference. Mrs Thatcher watched a television newsclip of it with Kenneth Baker. 'Look how he uses his hair!' she snorted.

‡ In August, annual inflation had fallen to 7.3 per cent, down from 8.2 per cent in July. But September's data reversed this trajectory. A rise in the RPI of 0.7 per cent pushed annual inflation to 7.6 per cent. This probably influenced Lawson's decision to raise rates.

over Mrs Thatcher, Lawson believed, because of his complete political loyalty to her. Understandably, Lawson deeply resented it when Walters's careless talk reached the public domain: 'Why did the markets think that the PM had a different policy from her Chancellor?' he asked rhetorically. 'Because Alan Walters couldn't keep his trap shut.' As Powell put it, 'she brought Alan back solely in order to poke a finger in Nigel's eye after their falling out'. Less reasonably, Lawson resented the very idea that the Prime Minister should have economic thoughts unless they coincided with his own. She in turn resented how his seniority and prestige inhibited her ability to intervene. The strange stand-off between the Treasury and everyone else over the poll tax was a by-product of this situation.

At the same time, Lawson must have realized that the Madrid démarche and subsequent reshuffle had left him more exposed. Although Mrs Thatcher had undoubtedly been weakened by the events of the summer, so had he. The state of the economy prevented him appealing over her head to the court of public opinion. It therefore made sense to fight for the moral high ground and, if he did not win, to leave, honour vindicated. The Walters problem appeared to give him his best chance.

The *casus belli* with Walters was an odd one. In October, Walters was quoted in the *Financial Times* as describing the ERM as 'half-baked':* the arguments for British entry had 'never attained even a minimum level of plausibility'. He had, in fact, written these words eighteen months earlier for an academic journal only now being published. But Lawson chose to take them as a provocation.

On the day of publication, Mrs Thatcher had left for the CHOGM in Kuala Lumpur. Lawson made no formal protest, but telephoned Mark Lennox-Boyd to say that Mrs Thatcher should get rid of Walters. As Lennox-Boyd noted in his journal: 'I sympathised but said I didn't think that would happen.' Lawson did not mention resignation, so Lennox-Boyd felt he was letting off steam. Lawson, however, felt that Lennox-Boyd missed the point: 'It was clear (or should have been) that I was sending a message to Mrs Thatcher.'

While Lawson's anger with Walters was a major concern in Downing Street, it was not seen as a crisis about to explode. On the evening of Monday 23 October, however, Lawson had a private word with Howe. Howe's special adviser Anthony Teasdale was witness: Lawson said, 'I'm really reaching the end of my tether. She just doesn't listen any more.' Howe

---

* In using this phrase Walters had a particular, rather than merely an insulting, meaning. The ERM was half-baked, he thought, because it neither abolished exchange rate fluctuations nor let them work freely.

replied: 'Nigel, you've just got to keep going. It's very difficult, but you've just got to.' Teasdale felt Lawson's resignation was imminent.

At 8.45 a.m. on Thursday 26 October, Lawson came to see Mrs Thatcher, who had returned from Kuala Lumpur the previous day. As Lennox-Boyd recorded, Lawson insisted she 'get rid of Walters by Xmas'. When she told him this was 'unreasonable', Lawson said 'he would have to consider his position'. Mrs Thatcher 'was astonished and I guess did not believe him'. Yet a little after 1 p.m., as she prepared for Prime Minister's Questions, Lawson demanded to see her again. As Lennox-Boyd recorded, 'Alarm bells begin to ring very seriously.' She then 'has a brief meeting with him in the study (& puts his letter [of resignation] in her desk drawer because she did not dare bring it to the House)'.

With less than an hour before the beginning of Prime Minister's Questions, 'Nigel insists that it is all announced at 3.15 pm! When she starts questions! And before a major & most difficult statement [on Kuala Lumpur]! And before there has been time to tell the Palace! And before a successor has been announced! What about the markets!!!' Luckily for Lennox-Boyd's store of exclamation marks, Lawson was dissuaded from this course, agreeing they would speak again immediately after the statement. As Mrs Thatcher set off for the Commons, Lennox-Boyd felt in awe of her 'Devotion to the task in hand. Stuffing the briefing coolly & professionally into her brain even though I can scarcely focus my eyes on a piece of paper. I know by now there is no political alternative to a giant political crisis.'

In a contemporary account Mrs Thatcher wrote of Lawson's resignation, she branded his ultimatum over Walters, from their first meeting that morning, 'an absurd, indeed reprehensible proposition': 'Alan was a trusted consultant & Nigel was a Chancellor ... no Chancellor allowed himself to be offput by an adviser and in my view no-one could possibly resign on the basis of such a flimsy and unworthy proposal.'

In Lawson's account of the meeting, he recorded 'something more revealing than everything else taken together' – she said: 'If Alan were to go, that would destroy my authority.' This, Lawson considered, was 'absurd: her authority owed nothing to Walters'. Lawson failed – or chose not to understand – that for the Prime Minister to sack her adviser because of the Chancellor's threat of resignation would indeed undermine her authority. Her anxiety was rational. He also recorded that in his second meeting à deux with her that day, she reminded him of his earlier ambition to succeed Robin Leigh-Pemberton as Governor of the Bank of England: did he want to throw that away too? 'In fact, she said everything except the one thing which would have persuaded me to stay.' She refused to sack Walters.

Mrs Thatcher's performance in the Commons, noted Lennox-Boyd, was 'Brave, beautiful, well briefed and confident.' Afterwards, she informed John Major that she might very shortly want him to become Chancellor of the Exchequer. Shocked, Major provisionally accepted. Returning to Downing Street, she saw Lawson for a third meeting and accepted his resignation. Before it was announced,* she had to reshuffle her Cabinet. In the circumstances Major, so recently Chief Secretary, was the only realistic choice for Chancellor. Mrs Thatcher privately lamented not offering the post to Nicholas Ridley, by now her only Cabinet co-resister against the ERM, but she felt she could not because he was 'so bad at presentation'. At no point did she raise the question of the ERM with Major.

In the middle of her reshuffle discussions, Mrs Thatcher suddenly exclaimed, 'My God what about the Deputy Prime Minister?' With Howe busy in the Chamber, she had forgotten about him entirely. She now sought his view, too late to influence the appointment of Major. To Howe (and Elspeth), Mrs Thatcher's inadvertent omission was as insulting as a deliberate one.

In a rush, Douglas Hurd was made Foreign Secretary, though Mrs Thatcher's original preference had been for Tom King. She respected Hurd but considered him too much a product of the Foreign Office. 'If I appoint Douglas,' she asked John Major, 'will he be on my side?' 'You can rely on him to be absolutely loyal,' Major replied, which was not quite the assurance she was seeking. David Waddington replaced Hurd at the Home Office. Into his place as Chief Whip came Howe's ally Tim Renton. Waddington told her this was a 'crazy' choice. 'That's the end for Margaret,' he said to himself. This was a widespread view. Despite his ardent Europhilia, the Deputy Chief Whip, Tristan Garel-Jones, considered the Whips Office 'the Prime Minister's Praetorian Guard. Was there not the risk that Tim Renton would on occasions be loyal to Geoffrey Howe?' John Major was so concerned that he rang – too late – to see if Renton's appointment could be stopped.

It remained only for Alan Walters to resign. While Mrs Thatcher felt she could not accede to Lawson's threat, now that it had been carried out she could not let Walters stay. Walters was prevailed upon by Brian Griffiths and reluctantly she accepted his resignation. With a loyalty close to

---

* Lawson and Mrs Thatcher agreed not to release the news until 6 p.m., but this embargo failed to hold. Chris Moncrieff of the Press Association got a call from the Treasury ahead of time. One reason for Lawson's haste throughout the day is that he did not want No. 10 to get control of the story.

madness, she now proposed making Walters a life peer immediately. 'She will be dissuaded,' wrote Lennox-Boyd, 'but my God what secrets we have to keep.'

Once it was all over, Lawson was overwhelmed: 'I can't tell you how sad I felt.' As for Mrs Thatcher, she took comfort, as in stressful situations, in the motherly side of her nature. That evening, she sat down with Paul Gray: 'She kicked off her shoes and I poured her the obligatory "small" whisky, and we chatted about the events in which the world had seemed compressed into a day.' Suddenly she turned to the clock on the mantelpiece and remembered that Gray commuted to work from out of town more than an hour away. 'Paul, it's half past nine! You must be going home.'

On Lawson's part, the fuss about Walters had been chiefly a ruse to get out while appearing morally in the right. The manner of his going inclined Mrs Thatcher to draw the wrong lessons. Rather than reflecting on the way she was running the government, she moralized it all into a situation in which Lawson had not been brave enough to face the difficult economic situation which he had himself created. 'Her private view', noted Lennox-Boyd, 'is that Nigel is a coward.' In a handwritten letter to Walters she complained that Lawson had 'left us with very high inflation, an own goal, and a very high trade deficit ... Not to mention the very high interest rate.' Walters had been 'such a <u>wonderful adviser and friend</u>', she wrote. She wanted the friendship to continue, with 'perhaps a little advice too'.

For Mrs Thatcher's critics, Lawson's resignation seemed to prove she was impossible for senior ministers to work with. With her two greatest companions in the Thatcher revolution, she had covered the political waterfront – Howe the centrist pro-European, Lawson the bold libertarian, she the almost Powellite voice of the Tory right.* Now this triumvirate, one of the most successful in the history of British government, had been broken up. The only people with whom she could work, the critics complained, were her gang of over-mighty courtiers or ideologues – Walters, Powell, Ingham, Griffiths.

Then there was the issue itself. It is hard to understand how lonely (and brave) was Mrs Thatcher's stand against British membership of the ERM. Control of exchange rates had once again become the dominant orthodoxy: most Conservative MPs and Cabinet minsters, the Foreign Office,

---

* Enoch Powell, though no longer an MP, continued to command Mrs Thatcher's respect, and he in turn was increasingly supportive of the Prime Minister's position. Around this time, Lennox-Boyd began sending her copies of Powell's speeches on Europe, which she would read, underlining the most Eurosceptic passages with approval.

the Treasury, the Bank of England,* the main political parties, the CBI, the grander newspapers, the BBC, the Europeans and the US administration were all in favour. To them the ERM offered a stability which Britain had failed to achieve alone. Still more important, the rise of Delors's plan for EMU and the thawing of the Cold War led people to believe that European integration was the future. Two weeks after Lawson's resignation, the Berlin Wall fell. She had prayed for this: now she feared it.

The turmoil caused by Lawson's resignation did not quickly abate. On the Sunday (29 October), Mrs Thatcher faced Brian Walden. Although Walden was close to her,† their interview proved anything but friendly. She maintained that Lawson had been 'unassailable' as Chancellor, so Walden pressed her repeatedly to say why, after so many conversations with her Chancellor, she thought he had resigned. She naturally did not want to answer. Walden asked her if Lawson would have stayed if she had sacked Walters. She said, 'I do not know. I do not know.' Walden told her this was a 'terrible admission'. He added that backbenchers were saying she was 'slightly off her trolley'. Mrs Thatcher was extremely angry with Walden, until now her secret friend on the silver screen: 'She never really spoke to me again.'

On Tuesday 31 October, Lawson delivered a resignation statement to the House that did Mrs Thatcher no favours. Directly afterwards she gathered John Major, Ian Gow and Lennox-Boyd in her Commons room. She was 'in a very bad state', noted Lennox-Boyd. She complained about Howe, Walden and 'the difficulties of being a woman'. Those present worked to 'calm the situation and help the PM overcome her blackest feelings'. What she had no wish to calm, however, were her own views on the European question. At the diary meeting the day before, she had suddenly come out with the suggestion that, if necessary, Britain could hold a referendum on ERM membership. As she became more beleaguered among colleagues, her idea of appealing over their heads to the wider British public grew.

Mrs Thatcher was in the psychologically difficult position of having achieved great success over many years, believing she was right on this issue and yet making all sorts of mistakes which weakened her own position. In

---

* It says something about the disposition of power at the time that, when Lawson resigned and was briefly homeless in London, Robin Leigh-Pemberton, the Governor of the Bank of England, invited him to live temporarily in his official flat in the City.

† Walden had, in fact, telephoned Woodrow Wyatt in advance to ask him (improperly) to pass on to Mrs Thatcher what his questions would be. As Wyatt put it, Walden wanted to 'phrase them in the most helpful way'.

an interview, she now failed to rule out the possibility that she might fight even a *fifth* election as Conservative leader. In private she was thinking about an earlier succession: 'we have to win the election first,' she told Ken Baker, 'and we still have "beloved Geoffrey" to cope with. Then after that, there will be several of you . . . who can take it on next time.'

On 1 November, Leon Brittan saw the Prime Minister: 'I was shocked at her state of exhaustion, both physical and mental . . . She is still in a violently anti-German frame of mind . . . it was an encounter the like of which I had never previously had.'

In Parliament, everyone was taking soundings of everyone else for a possible challenge to Mrs Thatcher's leadership. Cranley Onslow warned Lennox-Boyd that a 'stalking horse' candidate, an unimportant figure put up to conceal the intentions of the real challenger, might emerge to test the strength of feeling against her: 'we both agreed . . . that Anthony Meyer would be the sort of fool who might do it'. Meyer was an eccentric, elderly, friendly baronet on the extreme-left, Europhile wing of the party. If Mrs Thatcher were wounded in the first ballot, Michael Heseltine might then challenge her on the second. 'Meyer *was* the stalking horse,' recalled Michael Mates, Heseltine's informal campaign manager. 'Our plan was always to wait, so this was helpful.'

Despite these reports, Lennox-Boyd advised Mrs Thatcher that a challenge was unlikely. Tristan Garel-Jones, closer to Commons opinion, thought the opposite. On 2 November, he wrote offering his advice for the Prime Minister: 'None of those who would regard themselves as successors (Howe, Baker, Heseltine) will stand. They don't have the guts she had when she stood against Heath and, more important, they know they would lose!! . . . If a lunatic stands he will be defeated – and substantially . . . All the wets who matter – Hurd, Patten, Major (is Major a wet? – discuss) and second rankers like myself would not only vote for her with enthusiasm but would use every means at our disposal to bring others with us.'

On 22 November, Anthony Meyer declared he would challenge Mrs Thatcher. Denis, she told Lennox-Boyd, 'says to me that if any more than a handful vote against or abstain I should resign immediately. To which I said that would not be fair to my supporters. It might be one day but not at this stage.' Writing in *The Times*, Meyer laid out his reasons for contesting the leadership. His most passionate argument concerned Europe: 'Never has Mrs Thatcher's insistence on the retention of every scrap of national sovereignty seemed so dangerously unwise.' With the ending of the Cold War (discussed in Chapter 35), Meyer wrote, Germany would be reunited. Handling this required 'a closely integrated Europe': 'This concept is utterly alien to Mrs Thatcher,' Meyer added. '... And it is vital to the survival of us all.' These words were an eloquent, unguarded expression of the semi-concealed views of many Cabinet ministers, including Howe, Hurd, Patten, Clarke and – more cautious though he was – Major. At the top of the party, they provided a more powerful anti-Thatcher motivation than did the poll tax (unmentioned in Meyer's article), which no surviving senior Cabinet minister had opposed.

Given that Meyer was not a serious candidate, Mrs Thatcher's supporters focused on organization rather than policy. With George Younger as its titular head, her campaign team included Ian Gow, Garel-Jones, Richard Ryder and, *ex officio*, Lennox-Boyd. To ascertain truthful answers, they determined that MPs should not know they were being canvassed. The team chose eight MPs from different wings of the party to act as what they called 'Apostles', each tasked with canvassing among people who trusted them. They calculated that there were thirty-three 'Untouchables', considered beyond persuasion, and a larger number of doubtfuls ('Dodgies') on whom they set to work.

Warning signs soon emerged. As Lennox-Boyd drove Garel-Jones to Chequers on Saturday 25 November, they agreed that 'this was not the end but was probably the beginning of the end'. At Chequers, Mrs Thatcher's team told her that abstentions could be high – 'certainly over 50' – and that 100 was a possibility. All agreed there should be no stated minimum target of votes needed for political security, but privately Lennox-Boyd and Garel-Jones 'agreed ... at least 300 out of 375'.

The ballot, on 5 December, produced 314 votes for Mrs Thatcher, 33 for Meyer and 27 spoilt ballot papers and abstentions.* The result was slightly better than the Thatcher team had privately predicted, but worrying nevertheless. As John Whittingdale, her loyal political secretary, put it, 'the writing was on the wall'. Mrs Thatcher, however, was not inclined to listen to voices of gloom. All the same, George Younger wrote her a frank report. 'Result not as good as the figures,' it began. 'At least 40 who voted for the PM did so very reluctantly. They cannot be counted on another time.' To right the ship, Young recommended 'an early and visible change in Downing Street top advisers' and a change of tone about Europe. When Lennox-Boyd put these points to Mrs Thatcher, however, she batted away the first. On the second, Younger told her: 'It is the hearts of the pro-Europeans that need to be reached, not their heads ... They can

---

* Anthony Meyer amused and dismayed the Chief Whip by saying, 'That was great fun. I think I'll do it again next year.' In January 1990, however, Meyer was deselected as a candidate by his constituency association, a reminder to any would-be challengers that Mrs Thatcher remained popular in the party.

be persuaded to be hard-headed on bad policy proposals, provided they believe our leadership passionately believes in Europe too.' Mrs Thatcher could not supply such a belief. Her heart was elsewhere.

The result further emboldened MPs who feared the poll tax. Just before Christmas her new Chief Whip, Renton, reported that the whips' canvass was 'ominous': the government would not win the Commons vote required to levy the first community charge. She and John Major agreed to consider further concessions with Chris Patten.

Visiting her in Downing Street, Garel-Jones offered some blunt advice: 'The community charge has to go out of the window,' he said, 'because MPs are scared.' As for her post-Madrid policy of moving towards ERM entry, 'you've got to pretend to like it . . .' He recalled that 'My parting words were "You've won easily this time, but remember, there are 100 assassins lurking in the bushes."'

Tough as this may have sounded, Garel-Jones pulled his punches. As he put it in a private note for his chief, Renton:

> I believe that this is the beginning of the end for Mrs Thatcher. The job of the [Whips'] Office . . . is to try to manage that end in a way that does not split the Party. This means avoiding the daylight assassination of the Prime Minister by her enemies. I . . . would rather lose the next election with the Prime Minister we have than risk the bitter factionalism that would follow her forced removal. But that may not be an option. Heseltine will, I suspect, run next year. The Prime Minister . . . might well say that she has not come this far to simply walk away. We have no power to stop Heseltine. So all the ingredients exist for a fight. Unless . . .

Unless what? Garel-Jones did not say, but he had shifted markedly from his assurances to Lennox-Boyd just a month earlier. Now he wanted the whips and other party managers to find a decorous way of easing Mrs Thatcher out. He deplored 'daylight assassination' but not, by implication, her night-time replacement by her Cabinet 'friends'. Those same managers could help put in the right leader, who was not, he considered, Michael Heseltine. When the time came, they would be ready.

33
Unfinished business

'The proposals are bold ... Please go ahead indicating my full support'

Mrs Thatcher's political difficulties mounted, but her radical ambitions remained undimmed. In her third term, she took on British institutions that had so far proved resistant to Thatcherite remedies. These included public-service broadcasting, the legal profession and remaining pockets of trade union obduracy. She also advanced more controversial ideas for privatization. Five days after Nigel Lawson resigned, she held a meeting of ministers to consider privatizing British Rail. She chose not to pursue the railways but pressed ahead with electricity and water privatization. Water, indeed, passed into private ownership just days after she defeated Anthony Meyer's leadership challenge. For Mrs Thatcher, political turbulence was rarely a reason for retreat. She still wanted to get things done.

On 21 November 1989, the daily proceedings of the Commons were televised for the first time. Mrs Thatcher had opposed this change.* Staunchly traditional, she feared for 'the dignity and authority of Parliament'. She also mistrusted the people who ran television. Challenged by Neil Kinnock, in February 1988, to let the British people 'have the chance to see her on television in this House', Mrs Thatcher gave a romantic, almost metaphysical reply. Amid Labour cries of 'Frit!'† she declared, 'I do not think television will ever televise this House.' Her emphasis was on the word 'this'. She meant that Members would act up to the camera; the peculiar magic of the place would be lost. Many MPs shared Mrs Thatcher's view but, after skilful lobbying by the broadcasters, the Commons voted by

---

* In 1985, with Mrs Thatcher's support, the Commons had narrowly rejected the cameras, even though the House of Lords had recently introduced them. It seemed comical that the unelected House was the one televised.

† This was the Lincolnshire dialect word for 'frightened' which she had herself used against Denis Healey in Parliament before the 1983 election.

318 votes to 264 to admit television cameras. Mrs Thatcher now relied on Ingham to steer any change. 'My instructions', he recalled, 'were to get tight rules that prevented TV from making theatre – e.g. no panning.' His job was to prevent parliamentary television from turning into 'Barnum and Bailey's circus'.

Mrs Thatcher's advisers argued that the change would work to her personal advantage. 'I don't think you can lose,' Ingham told her. Because 'television thrives on personalities', he believed, 'women Ministers are likely to have a head start over mere males unless the males are particularly photogenic.' Mrs Thatcher wrote, simply, 'No.' Perhaps because, as a woman who knew how hard it was for her sex to succeed in the male-dominated media and Parliament of the day, she did not share this view. Although she had her share of personal vanity, she was never easy with television and did not enjoy watching her own performances. As always, however, she saw the point of detailed preparation. Following the Commonwealth Conference in Kuala Lumpur, there was a live but unbroadcast 'pilot' of the exchanges between her and Kinnock. Her voice, which she had been advised to lower, worked well. Careful consideration was also given to her outfits. The result, under the advice of Crawfie, her long-standing personal assistant, was 'less tweed; more power-blue'.

The Canadian Prime Minister, Brian Mulroney, whose country had been the first in the Western world to televise parliamentary proceedings, warned her that British Labour Party operatives were studying the Canadian experience in order to 'destroy you in Question Time': 'They would be advising the Leader of the Opposition to bring out your stridency and imperiousness.' Mulroney's tips included: 'Show your human side to viewers ... the occasional acknowledgment of error, some good humour, and an engaging smile [are] all very helpful.' Mrs Thatcher underlined these messages. Although acknowledgement of error was never her strongest suit, she took them to heart.*

Channel 4 asked for an interview to coincide with the arrival of the cameras. Ingham advised her to accept. He wanted Mrs Thatcher to explain how, as a woman, she dealt with the barrage of insult and noise in the House: 'Part of the test', he urged her to say, 'is the tumult and the shouting which you have not allowed to get you down these last ten years ... you

---

* In his last meeting with Mrs Thatcher before he fell from grace over his interview with her about Lawson's resignation, Brian Walden advised her to 'speak more softly' and thus give 'more chance for vague, pleasant propaganda with a smile on your face'. She should alter her stance towards the despatch box: 'I would do it at more of an angle, almost face the Speaker ...'

won't allow it to do so now.' By echoing the words of Kipling ('The tumult and the shouting dies; / The Captains and the Kings depart') and appealing to Mrs Thatcher's pride in her own sex, Ingham perfectly calculated how to persuade her to take part.

In those days, Prime Minister's Questions were a twice-weekly event. Despite the questions not being known to her in advance, it was Mrs Thatcher's proud boast that she had never, in ten years, been forced to pass on a question because she did not know the answer. She told her interviewer about her methods. At one o'clock every Tuesday and Thursday, she met her Question Time team over sandwiches and soup ('You do not really want a very full stomach before you are going in to bat in the House') to consider possible answers. In the Chamber, the sound system was not very good, so it could be difficult to hear a question above the noise. Television would make things worse, she predicted, because at the 'tall Despatch box', as she leant forward to the microphone, she feared the cameras would see only the top of her head.* Was it true she was 'shrill'? 'No, no,' she replied: MPs 'quite deliberately raise the volume of sound to make one raise one's voice . . .' but 'The great advantage of a woman's voice is that it can be heard through the hubbub' because of its 'different pitch'.

Mrs Thatcher claimed to find the ordeal worthwhile. Whenever she was negotiating abroad, she said, it was 'invaluable' to ask herself, 'Could I get this through the House of Commons?' The interviewer asked her to predict the result of televising. 'I only know that when you televise anything, it changes,' she replied. She worried about 'that ghastly phrase called a soundbite',† something, in fact, she successfully deployed. Whatever happens, 'I have to take what comes and . . . just get on with it. But then that is what most women do anyway.'

On the first day of the real thing, 21 November 1989, Mrs Thatcher followed Crawfie's suggestions and wore 'cobalt blue with a dagger brooch'. Kinnock and Mrs Thatcher were, unnaturally for both, on their best behaviour. 'Commons TV voted big yawn', said the *Sun* the next morning, though 10 million people watched. Ingham rounded up the reviews for Mrs Thatcher: 'One says you were masterful and another says Tories won fashion stakes, with you a knock-out.' Her distinctive style, personality and sex made her much more watchable than the average suited male politician. More important still was her mastery of the House, attained over many years. It was hard to find a chink in her armour. Now the world could

---

* These were the remarks of quite a small woman (5 feet 5 inches): most men in Parliament did not regard the despatch box as tall.
† The term had only recently washed up on British shores from the United States.

watch her, her authority was enhanced. The steadfast opponent of cameras in the Commons was probably their biggest twentieth-century beneficiary.

Within the British Conservative mind there existed two contrasting approaches to the BBC. One – the more libertarian, market-driven and disrespectful – saw the BBC, and the duopoly it formed with the private-sector ITV, as the enemy of freedom, innovation and choice. The other – more traditionalist and consensual – saw it as a civilized, uniquely British institution which contributed to national unity.* Broadly speaking, the market-based reformers were to be found at the Treasury and DTI, led by Nigel Lawson and Lord Young, whereas the traditionalists, led by the Home Secretary Douglas Hurd (and his predecessor, Willie Whitelaw, who retained influence), were to be found at the Home Office, which had charge of broadcasting.

Although Mrs Thatcher was identified with the market-oriented approach, she held conflicting views. She was a fierce critic of the BBC. She hated its embedded soft leftism, considered its funding by compulsory licence fee iniquitous and deplored its gross inefficiencies. In this she was strongly reinforced by Denis.† She also disliked the BBC's claim to be essential to national life. Reacting to the argument that paying the BBC licence fee should be no different from standing charges for water or other utilities, she wrote crossly, 'Nonsense You <u>must</u> have water or some kind of drainage – you don't need a BBC.'

On the other hand, Mrs Thatcher greatly admired the seriousness of the BBC's first (pre-war) Director-General, Lord Reith. She told Marmaduke ('Duke') Hussey, whom she had appointed as Chairman in 1986 (see p. 542), that 'The BBC had a duty to uphold the institutions and liberties of the country from which we all benefited . . . the only reason for having a BBC was to maintain public service standards.'‡ She had no desire to abolish or privatize it. Instead, she wanted to return the BBC to what she

---

* The only thing on which Conservative politicians of all stripes agreed was that the BBC was biased against them.
† One of the features both Thatchers disliked was the grotesque overmanning by technicians and cameramen which arose from trade union restrictive practices. On one occasion, according to John Birt, who later became Director-General of the BBC, a television crew booked for 10 Downing Street to interview Mrs Thatcher sought security accreditation for 'more than 100 technicians and assistants'. This enraged Denis, who told Birt about it shortly afterwards. Although Denis thought the offending group had come from the BBC, they were from London Weekend Television (LWT), for which Birt was then working. Birt did not pluck up the courage to correct Mr Thatcher.
‡ This was her first conversation with Hussey. The fact that it took place two years after he had assumed the post gave the lie to the claim that Mrs Thatcher was forever interfering in the BBC.

saw as its essential national purpose and leave the rest to competition – contradictory aims. Her view went against the BBC doctrine of 'wider still and wider' in response to new technologies.

The advice Mrs Thatcher received reflected these mixed views. While Ingham was quite favourable to the status quo, Brian Griffiths, at her Policy Unit, was more of a free-market radical. Like Mrs Thatcher, he was interested in allowing advertising on the BBC so that the licence fee could be abolished, or at least cut. A serious evangelical Christian, Griffiths also reinforced her view that Reithian broadcasting standards had to be more strictly upheld. His aim was not to dismantle the BBC but nudge it in the right direction.

Mrs Thatcher's most influential nudge proved to be Hussey's appointment as Chairman. Through bringing in the low-key accountant Michael Checkland as Director-General and John Birt as his deputy, Hussey sought not to Thatcherize the BBC politically but to bring greater rigour and objectivity to news and current affairs. These changes altered the BBC fast. Shortly before the 1987 election, through the private channel established between Griffiths and the Secretary to the BBC, Patricia Hodgson, (see p. 542) Mrs Thatcher was told that 'The authority of the Board has now been re-established.' Hussey's message to his troops was that 'fact must be separated from comment, comment sourced and adjectives expunged'. The implication was that the BBC could now be safely left alone.

The strength of Mrs Thatcher's approach was that she saw new technology as her ally against duopoly. In their 1987 election manifesto, the Conservatives had promised a new Broadcasting Bill.* At a seminar hosting TV executives from both the BBC and the independent sector on 21 September 1987, Mrs Thatcher explained her vision of choice and innovation. She was determined to harness technological change – including satellite broadcasting and the coming fibre-optic network – to make many more channels available. On each subject, except in relation to standards – which 'have an effect on society as a whole, and therefore was [sic] a matter of proper public interest for the Government' – Mrs Thatcher favoured a more open market. According to John Birt, the effect of the meeting was profound. She insisted the moguls recognize and welcome the coming technologies – about which she displayed surprising knowledge – and the

---

* One of its aims was to force the BBC and ITV to accept that 25 per cent of their programmes would be made by independent producers. As late as Christmas 1989, frustrated by delay in implementing these quotas, Mrs Thatcher exploded: 'the T.V. companies want to continue their monopoly powers and hate the independent producers,' she scribbled. 'They try every way to cut them out. But there are young people with initiative . . . We must support them MORE VIGOROUSLY.' Today, independent producers are an essential part of broadcasting.

choice they would bring. One of the recommendations from Alan Peacock's 1986 report (see p. 540) had been that rather than having the Independent Broadcasting Authority (IBA) award ITV regional franchises on untestable criteria of suitability, they should be auctioned off to the highest bidder. Embracing this, Mrs Thatcher warned the franchise companies they would face open competition.

'ITV was an inward-looking dinosaur,' Birt recalled. Its chiefs arrived 'untutored in what Mrs Thatcher was like'. They had thought they could see Peacock off: 'Now they realized they had the fight of their lives.' Birt came away thinking to himself, '"My God she's formidable." I was a radical, but I wasn't that radical.'

Despite Mrs Thatcher's force of will, her direction of travel was not entirely clear. Shortly before the seminar, Griffiths had written to her to confess a 'nagging feeling that our policy, post-Peacock, is not quite right'. Fretting about how to 'deal with standards in a competitive market', he sought 'a fundamental rethink of broadcasting policy'. The subject of standards bothered Mrs Thatcher greatly, but she always found it difficult to resolve. Rhetorically, she used standards as a stick with which to beat those who attacked her over quality: 'The real difficulty is in defining quality. We don't see much of it on our television but the T.V. companies constantly give the impression we do. The ordinary person considers bad language ... violence, bad and discourteous behaviour and undermining what used to be acceptable standards as bad and that it should be cut out of all programmes.' She later insisted on setting up a new Broadcasting Standards Council (BSC) but, as a purely advisory body, it was largely ignored. She never quite confronted the fact that her enthusiasm for a proliferation of channels made it much harder to impose any general set of standards.

Almost a year after the Downing Street seminar, the expected broadcasting White Paper was still some way off. Griffiths wanted it to specify how and when the licence fee would be abolished. Mrs Thatcher agreed, but then the BBC began to soften her up. In September 1988, Hussey told her he was pushing his views down through the BBC 'so that the decline in attitudes and standards, discernable [sic] since the time of Sir Hugh Carleton Greene, was reversed'. It was well judged of Hussey to disparage Greene, the notoriously progressive Director-General of the BBC in the 1960s and bugbear of the morality campaigner Mary Whitehouse. Everything he said was calculated to help her feel that a problem was being solved. Ingham encouraged this view. He believed the government would get better control of television by making the right friends within the existing system rather than root-and-branch reform.

Argument also swirled about the second independent channel, Channel 4, established in Mrs Thatcher's first term. It interpreted its official commitment to programming for minority groups as a way of advancing a left-wing agenda hostile to Mrs Thatcher. She responded by seeking to privatize it. This was strongly opposed by Douglas Hurd and others, who wished to preserve Channel 4 (together with a proposed Channel 5) as 'a third force' in television. As arguments over 'quality' became prominent, Mrs Thatcher challenged the notion that competition would necessarily reduce quality. 'CNN, Wall St Journal is marvellous,' she told Brian Walden, 'and some of BBC is terrible.'

While Griffiths reinforced this view, Ingham argued the opposite: 'Politically you are most vulnerable in the area of quality. You, of all people, must not go down in history as the person who ruined British television.' The 'quality' issue played on the idea, beloved in the arts world, that she was a philistine; and it had wider traction because of genuine public affection for the existing British broadcasting order. Eventually she gave in. Plans for the privatization of Channel 4 were sidelined.

The 'quality' argument also applied to the future of ITV franchises. Willie Whitelaw, now out of office, was sufficiently stirred to write to Mrs Thatcher privately, warning that he 'would be horrified and deeply antagonistic if [ITV] franchises were automatically to go to the highest bidder without clear safeguards' on quality. Although efforts had been made to include such protections,* the results of the first franchise auction (which took place in 1991 after Mrs Thatcher had left office) were considered disappointing. When GMTV won against a bid by TV-am, Mrs Thatcher wrote to Bruce Gyngell, the Chairman of TV-am, to say she was 'mystified' and 'heartbroken': 'I am only too painfully aware that I was responsible for the legislation.' She was much more successful in reducing the duopolistic privileges of ITV than in creating the right successor environment.

Satellite broadcasting was perhaps the biggest change-bringer for television in the late Thatcher era. By 1988, a battle royal over this emerging technology had broken out between British Satellite Broadcasting (BSB) and Sky Television. The former, part-owned by Pearson (owner of the *Financial Times*) and by Granada Television, was the establishment candidate. The latter was owned by Rupert Murdoch. By February 1989, Sky was working, beamed to the UK from the Luxembourg-owned Astra satellite, while BSB had yet to launch its satellite.

---

* There would be an initial 'quality threshold' to be cleared before any would-be franchise-holder could compete, and an 'exceptional override' if quality were to deteriorate.

In the Labour Party, the media establishment and even among many Conservative MPs, the idea that Murdoch might become a power in television was alarming. It was argued he could have a controlling interest in television or newspapers, but not both. Mrs Thatcher vehemently disagreed. 'She loved the whole idea of competition with the BBC,' Murdoch recalled. She duly sought ways to help him. In February 1989, she told ministers that 'an enterprising initiative should not be obstructed by excess bureaucracy, or worse, by favouritism of other operators'. That July, Woodrow Wyatt warned her that the Office of Fair Trading was seeking to 'dispossess' Murdoch of Sky, actuated by the political motive that Murdoch had moved *The Times* to the right. 'She cried out: "But this is censorship."' By September she was able to indicate to Wyatt that any threat to refer Murdoch's ownership of Sky to the Monopolies Commission would probably not succeed. In May 1990, a Lords amendment to the Broadcasting Bill, threatening to restrict Murdoch's cross-media ownership, was defeated.

By this time, the losses involved made it logical for BSB and Sky to merge. It was probably the closest Murdoch ever came to going under: 'Was I pretty desperate?' he recalled. 'You bet.' Having negotiated a favourable Sky-BSB merger, Murdoch wanted the support of his most powerful ally. On 29 October 1990, he called on Mrs Thatcher in Downing Street. According to Murdoch, 'I went and said, "I may have to close Sky News." She just said, "If that's how it is, that's how it is." I never asked her for anything.' Nonetheless, Mrs Thatcher understood that Murdoch wanted her support against any possible official objections. By seeing him at this key moment she was, without clear impropriety, giving it. The merger was announced four days later. Brian Griffiths informed her it was 'effectively a takeover of BSB by Sky'. For her this was a victory. BSkyB, as Murdoch's new company was called, ushered in the new era of television which, with mixed success, she had sought. For Sky to take flight was almost as important, both for her political interests and for her world view, as had been Murdoch's victory over the Wapping pickets in 1986.*

In her third term, Mrs Thatcher also decided to settle unfinished business with the trade unions. Previously, even after the defeat of the NUM, she had fought shy of taking on the most extreme remaining example of

---

* Mrs Thatcher did not make the mistake of some of her successors in cultivating a personal friendship with Rupert Murdoch, although he did sometimes attend her Chequers dinners. Indeed, she was always shy about her connection with him while privately understanding how much it mattered. Given his importance to her, the fact that she does not mention his name in her memoirs is quite a feat of omission. The memoirs were published by HarperCollins, a firm owned by Murdoch.

outdated, uncompetitive trade union practices – the Dock Labour Scheme (DLS). Under the DLS, all member ports had to guarantee dockers a well-paid, partly government-subsidized, permanent job and pay them whether or not there was work. While smaller ports, such as Dover and Felixstowe, that were outside the scheme prospered, the DLS ports decayed. Accounting, as they did, for 70 per cent of the country's port trade, they damaged economic opportunity.

Mrs Thatcher's victory over the NUM had depended on slow, painstaking preparation, so she did not want to rush. She knew that a dock strike could paralyse the country. In 1985, she rejected ministerial pressure to act, saying it would be better to 'let the Scheme wither on the vine'. But, as the Chairman of Associated British Ports, Keith Stuart, put it, 'The ports would wither away: the Scheme couldn't.' It was backed by law: it had to be abolished by law.

Following the 1987 election, Mrs Thatcher finally accepted there was 'no realistic alternative to out-right abolition'. Although she allowed detailed preparations to begin, Norman Fowler, the Employment Secretary, recalled her 'caution to a very late stage'. Not until April 1989, with the media distracted by Mikhail Gorbachev's visit to London (see p. 697), was she content for Fowler to announce the proposed abolition to Parliament. It was received by deafening Tory cheers. The dockers voted heavily to strike, but the Labour Party mounted only nominal opposition. Labour realized the scheme was indefensible and did nothing to support the unions. The strike, which began on 10 July, lasted only three weeks. The last union restrictive practice with the power to close down the country had been defeated.

Richard Wilson, handling the issue at the Cabinet Office, considered that the saga displayed her skill, not her indecisiveness: 'She sniffed the air, decided what the public were thinking, quite independently of everyone else, and acted accordingly . . . I don't recall anyone regarding it as timorous.' In the end, the almost peaceful passing of the Scheme showed how complete was Mrs Thatcher's victory in the area which, when she came into office in 1979, had seemed most difficult of all – the defeat of trade union political power.

If dockers were to be forced to end restrictive practices, why not lawyers? It had been a criticism of early Thatcherism that it did not apply its market rigours to the Conservative-voting middle classes. It became a criticism of late Thatcherism that it did.

In October 1987, Mrs Thatcher surprised the legal profession by appointing James Mackay Lord Chancellor. Mackay, the first Lord Chancellor plucked from the separate Scottish legal system, began to develop what were, by the extraordinarily slow-moving standards of the profession, startling ideas for reform. The most controversial was to alter 'rights of audience' so that solicitors as well as barristers could appear in court and, by extension, hold the highest judicial appointments. The goal, in reducing these restrictive practices, was to make legal services cheaper and more accessible to the public.*

'The proposals are bold,' Mrs Thatcher wrote, having reviewed Mackay's submissions over Christmas, 'but <u>very</u> well and persuasively argued. Please go ahead indicating my full support.' Published, to Lord Mackay's pleasure, on Burns Night (25 January), the reforms were initially well supported in the broadsheet press. But the legal profession soon hit back. 'This is all developing into quite a dirty fight,' Paul Gray warned Mrs Thatcher. Numerous judges spoke out against the plans, including the Lord Chief Justice, Lord Lane, who called the Green Paper 'one of the most sinister documents ever to emanate from government'. As opposition grew, the Policy Unit urged the Prime Minister to hold firm, advice which Mrs Thatcher underlined: '<u>If the Government were to cave in now . . . it would be pilloried mercilessly as too feeble to take on the middle class equivalent of the National Union of Mineworkers.</u>' Lord Mackay warned her that almost all the lawyers in the Lords would oppose the government. He and Mrs Thatcher agreed that 'details could be modified', but they would not 'retreat on the broad lines of the Lord Chancellor's reform package'.

While much of the opposition was self-serving, the debate raised a deeper question. Did Thatcherism leave room for the professions and their culture of institutional independence, or did its vision of society recognize only two entities, the government and the individual? In the *Spectator*, John Casey wrote a High Tory denunciation bemoaning the government's failure to '"understand and love" . . . historic institutions and the traditions on which they depend'. There was some truth in such criticisms, but it was hard to take too seriously the Bar's claim that its monopoly of rights of audience was a pillar of the Constitution. Some allege that Mrs Thatcher had it in for the Bar because of the difficulty she experienced there, as a woman, in getting a place in chambers in the 1950s, but there is no evidence of this. In Mackay's recollection, while 'completely supportive' of his position, she never aired her personal views. Her support for the removal

---

* Another reform aimed at the liberalization of conveyancing, further reducing the monopoly of solicitors in that area. Another would allow the introduction of contingency fees, using the Scottish 'speculative action' practice rather than the American model.

of the Bar's monopoly mirrored her support for an end to the privileges of the Stock Exchange in Big Bang (see pp. 409–13). It was based on the belief, more practical than ideological, that freer competition was a good thing.

In the end, the greatest danger to reform was the specific threat that the Attorney-General, Patrick Mayhew, who would be charged with taking the Bill through the Commons, would resign. Mayhew was a traditionalist in these matters, and Mrs Thatcher knew well from the Westland crisis (see Chapter 21) that his disaffection must be avoided. A deal was struck, at Mackay's suggestion, whereby solicitors recommended for rights of audience should be approved by a committee of senior judges. This was enough for Mayhew and the Bill became law in 1990. In the twenty-first century, wider rights of conveyancing, contingency fees and the gradual spread of rights of audience to solicitors have not brought the legal profession to its knees.

Privatization had been one of the greatest themes and – with significant exceptions – greatest successes of Mrs Thatcher's second term (see Chapter 16). By the time of her third, the big remaining subjects were the utilities – water and electricity. With the problem of natural monopolies, the question of whether free markets could work to the public good in such industries was more contested than in sales of more competitive businesses. The politics accordingly became harder.

While the sale of water was unpopular,* unlike electricity, the problems it presented were quite simple in concept. The government accepted that water was a natural monopoly. The question, therefore, was not about creating competition but about how best to finance the industry to improve the service. As Michael Howard, the junior Environment Minister in charge of the privatization from 1988, put it, in the public sector investment in water 'could never compete for money with much more popular demands like schools and hospitals. Once privatized, it would no longer need to.' Such investment would now be financed by separate, regulated charges.

The need for investment was environmental too. The decaying system was not delivering good-quality drinking water, clean rivers or clean beaches. Despite his reputation for free-market ruthlessness, the Environment Secretary, Nicholas Ridley, insisted that regulation must be a matter for government. Regulation and supply should be separated and a National Rivers Authority created, even though this would reduce the flotation price.

---

* For some, selling off water companies was wrong because water was God-given. Bernard Ingham gave crisp advice on how to counter this argument: 'Water may be a gift from heaven but it does need trapping, collecting and storing and then purifying and delivering to the customer – which makes it an industry.' It was strange that people did not acknowledge this since, even before privatization, about a quarter of Britain's water companies were privately owned.

61 With Lech Wałęsa, the leader of the Solidarity trade union, being fêted by crowds in Gdańsk, 4 November 1988. Polish state television blacked out the Gdańsk part of her visit, but this only added to its prestige. The Communist government fell the following September.

62 A house-proud Mrs Thatcher straightens the tablecloth on the Downing Street mahogany in 1990. More than any other post-war prime minister, she saw the place as home. Winston Churchill watches from the wall.

63 As his boss greets Gorbachev outside 10 Downing Street, 6 April 1989, Charles Powell is the power behind the scene.

64 'We have become a grandmother': the first known photograph of Michael Thatcher with Mrs Thatcher and his parents, Mark and Diane Thatcher, in Downing Street, May 1989.

65 A rare informal shot of the Prime Minister during her annual stay with the Queen at Balmoral. The corgi looks away.

66 This picture was taken at the July 1989 G7 summit in Paris a couple of weeks after the unsuccessful 'Madrid ambush' of Mrs Thatcher by Geoffrey Howe and Nigel Lawson. Her expression shows her feelings about Howe. Ten days later, she demoted him from the Foreign Office.

67 Behind the hand: John Major, the new Foreign Secretary, and the new party Chairman, Kenneth Baker, exchange private remarks on the platform of the Conservative Party conference at Blackpool, 12 October 1989.

68 At the same conference, Mrs Thatcher looks coldly at Nigel Lawson, the Chancellor. By the end of the month, he had resigned, protesting at her refusal to sack Alan Walters as her economic adviser. She replaced him with John Major.

69 Uneasy triangle: President George Bush and Chancellor Helmut Kohl have eyes for each other and not for Mrs Thatcher at the Paris G7, 14 July 1989. She found her new isolation galling.

70 Mrs Thatcher arrives in snow for her first Camp David meeting with President Bush, 24 November 1989. There was a clash of styles, and a clash of views about Europe and German reunification.

71 Mrs Thatcher's new Cabinet in July 1990. Except for Geoffrey Howe (on her immediate right), who removed himself on 1 November, these were the men who would later tell her she could not win a second ballot in the leadership contest. Standing (left to right) are Tim Renton, David Hunt, Norman Lamont, Peter Brooke, Tony Newton, John Wakeham, Cecil Parkinson, Lord Belstead, Chris Patten, John Gummer, Michael Howard, Peter Lilley and the Cabinet Secretary, Sir Robin Butler; seated (left to right) are John MacGregor, Kenneth Baker, David Waddington, Douglas Hurd, Sir Geoffrey Howe, MT, Lord Mackay of Clashfern, John Major, Tom King, Kenneth Clarke and Malcolm Rifkind.

72 (*Above left*) 'She is an enemy of apartheid': Nelson Mandela pays his first visit to No. 10, 4 July 1990. Mrs Thatcher thought him 'most dignified', but worried about his socialist economics.

73 (*Above right*) The Foreign Secretary, Douglas Hurd, walks uncomfortably behind Mrs Thatcher as she arrives at the ballet and dinner at Versailles during the CSCE conference in Paris. She tries to put a brave face on her first-ballot disappointment.

74 'I'm enjoying this': Mrs Thatcher lays about her in the House of Commons no-confidence debate on Thursday 22 November 1990. Earlier in the day, she had announced her resignation. John Major permits himself a smile.

75 (*Above left*) 'Eleven-and-a-half wonderful years': Mrs Thatcher speaks on the steps of Downing Street for the last time as prime minister. Crawfie, inside the door, holds her hands to her eyes.

76 (*Above right*) Denis and Margaret leave for Buckingham Palace. She sheds a tear.

77 Emerging from her temporary offices at 17 Great College Street on 28 June 1991, Mrs Thatcher announces that she will leave the House of Commons at the next general election. It had taken her months to accept that she could not hope to return to power.

78 Camp Pendleton, California, on 14 March 1991: among the US Marine Corps after they had helped win the Gulf War.

79 (*Above left*) Visiting the Reagans at their simple Californian ranch in February 1993. Despite being told that they would be casually attired, she dressed up as usual.

80 (*Above right*) Dressed with an oriental touch, Lady Thatcher signs copies of her memoirs in Hong Kong, April 1995. She was readier as the book's promoter than as its author.

81 Michael and Amanda Thatcher with the woman they called 'Grammy', and Denis, 1994.

82 The Rt Hon. Baroness Thatcher of Kesteven KG, OM, FRS in her place in the House of Lords for the state opening of Parliament, 21 June 2001.

83 (*Right*) The bereft widow at Denis's memorial service, Guards Chapel, 30 October 2003.

84 (*Far right*) Lady Thatcher welcomes the Queen to her 80th birthday party at the Mandarin Oriental Hotel, Knightsbridge, 13 October 2005. She was the only one of her prime ministers to be thus honoured.

85 Lady Thatcher grieves beside the casket of President Reagan on Air Force One, with Crawfie and Mark Worthington, June 2004. They flew with the Reagan family from the service in Washington to the interment in California.

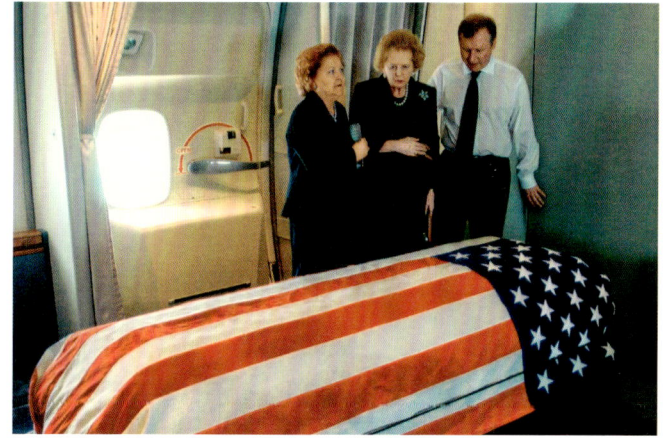

86 Frailty: Sir John Major helps Lady Thatcher at the Garter service, St George's Chapel, Windsor, June 2007.

87 (*Above left*) Return to Downing Street: at the door of No. 10 after being received there by the new Labour Prime Minister Gordon Brown, September 2007. New Labour treated her more kindly than many Conservatives.

88 (*Above right*) With Crawfie in the garden of Count Giovanni Volpi, Venice.

89 At the ceremony to inaugurate the Margaret Thatcher Infirmary at the Royal Hospital, Chelsea, 14 February 2008. She loved the Pensioners. The ashes of both Denis and Margaret are interred in the hospital grounds.

90 The pallbearers carry the coffin to the hearse after Lady Thatcher's funeral at St Paul's Cathedral on 17 April 2013, watched by her family. Standing above them is the Queen, with Prince Philip. Behind the Queen, on her right, is Richard Chartres, Bishop of London, who had given the address.

In this he was strongly supported by Mrs Thatcher, who was becoming increasingly green. Water privatization is 'going to do a great deal for the environment, improving the quality of it', she told Woodrow Wyatt. To facilitate this, on privatization the industry's £4.4 billion debts were written off and an extra £1.5 billion, described by the government as the 'green dowry', bestowed upon it.

As well as environmental regulation, strong statutory economic regulation was necessary to impose standards on the privatized companies and prevent overcharging. A regulatory body, known as OFWAT, was invented. The sale, in November 1989, was deliberately pitched on the low side and slightly oversubscribed. It brought in more than £5 billion for the Treasury. Coinciding with the fall of the Berlin Wall, Lawson's resignation and Meyer's leadership challenge, the successful sale was a relief to Mrs Thatcher and was supported within the party. Many years later, it would become clear that the regulatory structure frequently failed to protect water quality.* The problem of 'producer capture' within the industry was never properly addressed.

Electricity was more momentous, complicated and, for Mrs Thatcher herself, sometimes awkward. Here the monopoly question was different. The wires themselves came close to being natural monopolies, but what went down them did not. It was not always easy to see the opportunity presented. After all, as one adviser put it, 'Nowhere in the world was there a competitive electricity system.' Britain had to create a new, untested model.

In doing so, Mrs Thatcher had to contend with one of her favourites, Lord Marshall, the Chairman of the Central Electricity Generating Board (CEGB). In January 1987, John Redwood, who remained Mrs Thatcher's privatization guru, advised her that nuclear power (because of its unique costs and safety issues) should be kept in the public sector but five new companies be created, and then floated, to own the remaining power stations. Marshall, Redwood warned, would fiercely resist this and demand to privatize the industry entire. Marshall was 'an extremely powerful character', but 'It would be a pity to let individual personalities ruin a major privatisation opportunity.'

Mrs Thatcher liked Marshall's strong personality.† She was deeply grateful to 'dear Walter', as she called him, for helping her defeat the NUM by keeping power stations running during the miners' strike. They also shared

---

* The most notorious example was the plight of Thames Water, which became a public scandal in the mid-2020s.
† Marshall himself once boasted that he was 'on kissing terms with Margaret', after she pecked him on the cheek while preparing for a party at his house.

a firm belief in nuclear power as the alternative to the coal dependence. Yet she believed privatization must break down monopoly wherever possible. She did not wish to repeat her failure to achieve this for British Gas.

After the 1987 election victory, Lord Marshall pledged his support for CEGB privatization, but said that 'to sell it otherwise than exactly as it stood was to cause the lights to go off'. Mrs Thatcher's principal ally against this view was Cecil Parkinson, who had succeeded Peter Walker as Energy Secretary in 1987. In the view of William Rickett, the senior departmental civil servant handling electricity privatization, 'Parkinson had come with a brief from the PM to introduce competition' and was supported by Nigel Lawson. Back in office after four years in the wilderness, Parkinson strove not to displease Mrs Thatcher, but how to give her what she wanted was a puzzle, torn as she was between her desire for competition and her tenderness towards Marshall.

Mrs Thatcher had an equal tenderness for nuclear power, both as a secure source of electricity against strikes and because of her growing concern for the environment. The idea that nuclear electricity could come at low cost was more an article of faith – based on assurances from Marshall's CEGB – than a statement of fact. The stage was now set for faith and fact to clash.

At Parkinson's behest, the electricity industry was discussed at Chequers on 14 September without Marshall. The idea was floated that the National Grid be separated from the CEGB, thus opening up the generation market, and that the CEGB be split. While Parkinson left the meeting convinced that electricity would not be privatized as a monolith and that the nuclear industry should be part of the sale, others were less convinced. Mrs Thatcher continued to worry about Marshall: 'He's a great friend of mine – mustn't let him down.'

After months of intense argument, in early December Parkinson proposed the creation of two generating companies. The first, known as Big GENCO, would include nuclear power and would own 70–80 per cent of capacity. Little GENCO would own the rest.* Marshall was 'almost certain' to oppose the plan. Wicks reminded Mrs Thatcher that Lawson preferred splitting the CEGB into four or five companies, but Parkinson feared that this would delay privatization and reduce proceeds '(which implies some monopoly pricing under Mr Parkinson's preferred model)'. Big GENCO (known as 'Big G') was Parkinson's compromise, a successor

---

* Parkinson's plan also specified that all private generators must have equal access to the grid. The twelve area boards would become twelve separate distributing companies, which would own the grid.

to the CEGB which might permit some real competition and yet persuade Marshall to stay on. Mrs Thatcher accepted Parkinson's plans but suggested keeping Lawson's more radical idea in play to alarm Marshall into accepting Parkinson's more modest proposal. In all this, the urgent was being preferred to the important, but in politics the urgent is often unavoidably important. If electricity privatization could not happen soon, it might not, given the electoral cycle and the complex legislation involved, happen at all.

In February 1988, Mrs Thatcher, with Parkinson at her side, met Lord Marshall.* Marshall was unequivocal. Parkinson's plans would lead to 'the end of nuclear power in this country', he said. 'Divorcing transmission from generation would separate the industry's brain from its body.' It was the CEGB's 'fundamental obligation' to maintain supply. If it failed, there would be 'catastrophic national consequences'. Marshall declared solemnly that he had 'spoken as a scientist', a credential he knew weighed with Mrs Thatcher. Her response, however, was firm. She took everything Marshall said very seriously, she assured him, but there had to be competition: 'The Government could not put itself in a position where it could be said that they had created a private monopoly from a public monopoly.'

Nevertheless, Marshall's dire warnings were difficult to brush off. As Rickett summed it up, Mrs Thatcher was 'being asked to overrule the Chairman and Board of the CEGB on a technical issue which concerned the safe management of the country's electricity supplies'. Three days later, she fretted over the possibility of a serious interruption of electricity supply soon after privatization. Parkinson, Lawson and Lord Young worked to convince her that the present planned economy of generation ran a much greater risk of supply failure than did a competitive system. Her wobble passed.

Parkinson's way through the problem was working. As the deadline approached, Marshall decided he would prefer chairing the new Big G to trying to pull the plug on the whole enterprise. It was to Mrs Thatcher's credit that she was, in the end, willing to stand up to Marshall and make the hardest decision of the whole privatization saga. The pull of personal loyalty was always strong with her. Luckily, in this case her loyalty to the consumer proved stronger.

Lord Marshall's acquiescence cleared the way, but rested on his belief that Britain's nuclear power would remain in his hands. It was one of the effects

---

* Considerable efforts had been made to evade Mrs Thatcher's wish to agree a one-on-one meeting with Marshall. Officials feared that such a meeting would lead her to back down. Parkinson's presence at the key meeting with Mrs Thatcher was mortifying to Marshall.

of privatization in general, however, that gathering information to establish a market price often brought awkward facts to light. In the case of nuclear power, these facts soon became very awkward indeed.

By October, Nigel Wicks was pointing out to Mrs Thatcher that the 'nuclear obligation' of Big G would have to be quantified. The government, he warned, would have to cover the 'back-end' costs (waste, reprocessing and eventual decommissioning) to achieve privatization. With the extent of this obligation unclear, she demanded more rigorous investigation.

The following summer, Mrs Thatcher received signals of distress from another part of the battlefield. These came from Roy Lynk, Leader of the Union of Democratic Mineworkers (UDM), representing the Nottinghamshire miners who had continued working during the strike. With the privatization of electricity, orders for coal would inevitably fall away. Lynk now warned Mrs Thatcher that 'a smaller Industry virtually kills off the U.D.M. pits and puts the coal production back in the hands of Arthur [Scargill]'. 'I have always comforted myself with the knowledge that the U.D.M. has a friend in the Prime Minister,' he went on. He now sought her help.

With Parkinson already devoting considerable effort to the UDM, his office discouraged a meeting between Mrs Thatcher and Lynk as premature. As well as the UDM, there was considerable discontent from both the National Coal Board and Scargill's NUM. Recognizing the danger of united opposition from the coal industry, Mrs Thatcher ensured the privatization settlement included three-year contacts between the industry and the generators to give coal producers time to adjust. On the whole, however, the government was much less anxious about coal than in the mid-1980s. The decline of coal was an inevitable part of electricity privatization, and the future of electricity mattered more. It struck some of those observing Mrs Thatcher that 'She just didn't want to get involved.' She had defeated Scargill. In the wider scheme of things, that was what mattered.

During the Bill's passage through Parliament, damning evidence against the cost of nuclear power began to accumulate. It fell to John Wakeham, who replaced Parkinson as Energy Secretary in July 1989, to bring the issue to a head. Through Alan Walters, Wakeham had made sure that the seed of a nuclear retreat was planted in Mrs Thatcher's mind. That November, he wrote to warn her that 'so long as nuclear remains substantially more costly than fossil power,* the banks will see investing in a nuclear con-

---

* In late June 1989 Mrs Thatcher had been informed that the cost of nuclear power, nine months earlier pegged at 4.2 pence per kilowatt hour, was now estimated at 7p. This contrasted with 2.6/2.7p for fossil fuels.

struction programme as a high-risk venture'. He urged the establishment of a separate state-owned company to take over all the CEGB's nuclear assets and liabilities.

Wakeham's view was strongly backed by Mrs Thatcher's Policy Unit. 'Nuclear power is quite simply uneconomic,' it told her. The CEGB had hidden its true costs for years. The Unit complained that the entire structure of privatized generation had been built around 'the perceived necessity of finding "private" solutions for nuclear'. As a consequence, 'National Power [when privatized] will be completely fossil-fuelled and private sector generation will therefore begin as a cosy duopoly,' words which Mrs Thatcher heavily underlined.

The next day Mrs Thatcher and ministers accepted Wakeham's suggestion. Walter Marshall's dream had finally fallen apart. As Wakeham told her, Marshall was now 'prepared to resign quietly once a package of financial compensation satisfactory to him had been agreed'. He resigned just before Christmas. Although she lamented his loss, Mrs Thatcher no longer feared the consequences. She understood the new situation perfectly well. She was not forced publicly to admit that her own vision of a new generation of nuclear power was crumbling away.

Despite manifold imperfections and improvisations, Mrs Thatcher was not unduly alarmed. Wakeham's final proposals, presented just before Christmas 1989, sought to increase the value of the electricity industry and reduce possible political problems by imposing short-term restrictions. There was a four-year monopoly on the supply of electricity to commercial customers and an eight-year one for domestic. 'Once the contract period was over,' Wakeham recalled, 'new generators would have much more freedom. After that, in came gas.' 'The package involves various administrative constraints on the immediate operation of free competitive forces,' Mrs Thatcher's private secretary, Paul Gray, wrote. 'But this seems inevitable if the timetable and other constraints are to be met.' 'Yes,' she scribbled, 'I think he [Wakeham] has done a superb job.'

The actual asset sales began in December 1990, after Mrs Thatcher had left office. The twelve distributing companies saw their shares 10.7 per cent oversubscribed, with total net proceeds a little over £7.7 billion. The later sale of the generators raised £2.8 billion net and the Scottish privatizations £3.5 billion.

The process had been elaborate and sometimes uneasy. The breaking of the CEGB into only two parts rather than five could probably have been avoided if the nuclear problem had been recognized earlier. Gradually, this structure allowed vertical integration and therefore monopoly power to creep back in. It was nevertheless a considerable achievement to create a structure which made Britain far less dependent on coal without incurring a strike; which forced government to look realistically at the problems of nuclear power; which opened up opportunities for new, greener sources of energy; and which, over time, introduced real competition. During the 1990s, the British energy market opened up and prices fell.

Privatization was not an untarnished legacy, but it was a remarkable one. It was a tribute to the partnership between Mrs Thatcher and Nigel Lawson which, until it fell apart in 1989, had been such an important engine of reform.

34
God; climate; South Africa
'No generation has a freehold on this earth'

On 20 May 1988, Brian Griffiths was summoned to see the Prime Minister. He had just reviewed a speech she was to give in two days' time: 'It was appalling,' Griffiths recalled, 'wishy-washy in the extreme.' Now, entering her study, he found her 'kneeling beside the coffee table ... fishing crumpled pieces of paper out of her wastepaper basket. "Brian," she said, "you're right: it's no good. Please help me say what I need to say."'

The speech was Mrs Thatcher's address to the General Assembly of the Church of Scotland. She had accepted this unusual invitation because of continued ecclesiastical criticism of her government for hard-hearted materialism. Disturbed by the Anglican *Faith in the City* report of 1985 (see p. 503), she wished to reassert the Christian basis of her economic and social beliefs. The invitation promised her a wider audience, not least in Scotland, which had proved largely resistant to Thatcherism. She believed that without a solid Christian – or, as she preferred to say, Judaeo-Christian* – underpinning, Britain's social order might not survive. Privately, she lamented that the 'common acceptance that Christianity is the accepted religion and is good – [is] now being chipped away like the ozone layer'. She felt emboldened to preach to the preachers.

Mrs Thatcher's approach was strongly personal. It fell to Griffiths, an evangelical Protestant theologian as well as an economist, to check the soundness of the theology and supply the right biblical quotations. Mrs Thatcher told him that, in matters of faith, you could not get the 'fruits' without the 'roots'. Those roots were her Methodist upbringing in Grantham. Her speech would be 'first and foremost a declaration of her real and meaningful personal faith in Christ'. From this faith she derived her idea of the importance of individual responsibility and choice: the Methodist idea of turning to Christ required God's grace,

---

* Mrs Thatcher was fond of pointing out that 'You cannot have the New Testament without the Old.'

but also a real personal decision. Her dislike of collectivism arose from a fervent belief that society could thrive only if each person recognized his or her duty to it.

The General Assembly Hall of the Church of Scotland is situated on The Mound in Edinburgh, so Mrs Thatcher's speech was christened 'The Sermon on the Mound'. Dressed in a hyacinth-blue suit with a matching shallow toque, she cut a striking, solitary figure among the male, Presbyterian black. At the heart of her speech was an effort to identify Christian values as the bedrock for her political beliefs. Mrs Thatcher explained how the Old Testament laid down social rules and the basis of law through the Ten Commandments and the injunction to love our neighbour; whereas the New was a record of the Incarnation, the teachings of Christ (which confirmed that love of neighbour) and 'the establishment of the Kingdom of God'. Taken together, they provided 'a proper attitude to work, and principles to shape economic and social life'. The love of money was wrong; the creation of wealth was not: 'How could we respond to the many calls for help, or invest for the future ... unless we had first worked hard and used our talents to create the necessary wealth?'

Christians could legitimately disagree, Mrs Thatcher said, about political and social institutions, but must uphold individual responsibility. She ended by both separating and linking state and Church. It was for politicians to legislate for the rule of law, while the Church 'can teach the life of faith'. Picking what was perhaps her favourite hymn, she explained the complementary role for each set out in Cecil Spring Rice's 'I Vow to Thee, My Country'. The first verse was 'a triumphant assertion of ... secular patriotism'. The second spoke of 'another country I heard of long ago', the heavenly country which advances 'soul by soul and silently'. 'Not', Mrs Thatcher very characteristically added, 'group by group, or party by party, or even church by church – but soul by soul – and each one counts.'

Most Church reaction to the speech was unfriendly. Its senior figures treated her slightly churlishly, like members of a trade union resenting an outsider crossing their demarcation lines. The Episcopalian Bishop of St Andrews complained of her 'laywoman's use of the Bible with a vengeance'. Robert Runcie, Archbishop of Canterbury, felt the speech 'lacked ideological sophistication': she had 'a high doctrine of moral standards but a lower doctrine of caring for the outcast and the sinner and the muddled seeker'. This was a rerun of earlier contretemps.

Mrs Thatcher was piqued. Privately that September she complained it was she, more than the Church, who was advocating the continuing importance of Christian values in a society which was becoming more plural – 'With Moslems and Hindus. People want children to be taught all that is good.' She felt that the Church was neglecting its own social duty: 'It has been the transfer of responsibility from everyone to the Government which is the great mistake of the 20th century. People not always ready to go out and help others.'

Among those close to Mrs Thatcher, opinion was divided about the wisdom of venturing into religious territory. Charles Powell thought the context and place of delivery 'disastrous': she was not going to make converts in Scotland 'by calling on religion in aid of her policies'. Bernard Ingham, however, reported that no speech of Mrs Thatcher's had ever attracted so many requests for copies: 'you have clearly launched a thousand sermons'. Her seriousness impressed many. Mary Whitehouse told Mrs Thatcher that her words were 'echoed in the hearts of many people up and down the land, many of whom never go to Church'. As a political manoeuvre, the Sermon on the Mound may have been an error; but as a mark of moral courage and intellectual energy it deserved credit, and showed she was more than a workaday politician. It was part of her desire, which her father had taught her, to 'dare to be a Daniel'. It was part of Thatcherism.

As for the Established Church of England, Mrs Thatcher did make one considerable difference to its leadership through her power of appointment.* Under the prevailing conventions, the Prime Minister was privately presented by the Crown Appointments Commission with two names for each diocesan vacancy, in order of preference. She was permitted to reverse the order, or to reject both appointments, but not to add a new name. In addition, she could express privately her general preferences. As Runcie recalled: 'She'd say to me, "Why can't we have any Christian bishops?"'

In July 1990, she chose George Carey, the relatively junior Bishop of Bath and Wells, to succeed Runcie at Canterbury. Carey accepted and they met for the first time. 'She talked non-stop,' Carey recalled, 'until, when she mentioned John Wesley, I said, "Yes, a great socialist," which must have displeased her.' He was favourably impressed: 'I really admired her. She made me think of the Book of Esther: "And who knows whether you have not come to the kingdom for such a time as this?"'

Carey was very different in background from his predecessor. A boy from Dagenham who went to neither Oxford nor Cambridge, he was

---

* More formally, this was the power to recommend appointments to the Queen.

outside the normal circles of power and influence. His appointment marked a shift in the leadership of the Church to its fast-growing evangelical wing. The other name on the list had been John Habgood, Archbishop of York. An Etonian of some academic distinction, with the usual liberal-left views of the episcopal bench at that time, he was much senior to Carey and would have been the obvious choice. It was widely alleged that Mrs Thatcher had picked Carey even though he was second on the list to Habgood, though this was never proved.

In the Established Church, Carey was the anti-establishment candidate. Mrs Thatcher liked that. Under his archiepiscopate, the Church moved away from its twentieth-century role of being the spiritual conscience of the moderate left to a greater concentration on preaching the Word, which is what she had sought. Carey maintained his admiration for her because she 'enjoyed wrestling with ideas and indeed relished arguing'. In this, her faith meant that she 'wasn't drawing from an empty well'.

In November 1987, Mrs Thatcher received an invitation to speak at the 1988 annual dinner of the Royal Society. 'The Royal Society', she wrote, 'is rather special, because I am a member [fellow, to be precise] Provisional acceptance.' Mrs Thatcher was proud of her fellowship of the most eminent scientific body in Britain. She liked to say it was more important that she was the first prime minister with a science degree than the first woman. Her interest in science was a subject on which she could be flattered, and her connection with the Royal Society flattered her greatly. She wanted to say something important, although, accepting the invitation to speak on 27 September 1988, she had no idea what.

The answer emerged in late August. In a meeting with Dominic Morris, from her private office, Mrs Thatcher drew from her handbag an article from the *New Scientist*: 'This is exciting!' she declared. The report, headed 'The Challenge Of Global Change', gave a synoptic account of man-made climate change and the potential threat to the planet. For any world leader at that time, a speech addressing climate change would be a momentous departure.* Most of Mrs Thatcher's officials had scarcely heard of it.

The Royal Society dinner did not necessarily require a serious speech,

---

* The only national leader already to have made a long-term international mark about climate change was the Norwegian Prime Minister, Gro Harlem Brundtland, whose *Our Common Future* report of the previous year was the first to give common currency to the phrase 'sustainable development'. G7 leaders, including Mrs Thatcher, had endorsed the concept in Toronto in June. The Canadian Prime Minister, Brian Mulroney, had also raised the issue in international forums.

but that is what Mrs Thatcher delivered. She declared that because of rising population, the greater use of fossil fuels and changing agricultural practices there had been 'a vast increase in carbon dioxide' in the atmosphere. Perhaps, she said, 'we have unwittingly begun a massive experiment with the system of this planet itself'. She warned of dramatic temperature rises and the danger of melting polar ice. She also noted concerns over the hole in the ozone layer which the British Antarctic Survey* had discovered in 1985 and about acid rain. Although she announced no policy initiative, she staked a great deal on getting the issues right: 'Stable prosperity can be achieved throughout the world provided the environment is nurtured and safeguarded. Protecting this balance of nature is therefore one of the great challenges of the late 20th century.'

Mrs Thatcher's embrace of the radical idea of climate change received little coverage.† In part, this was because Bernard Ingham, unversed in the subject, was not sure how to present it. The scientists, however, noticed their chance. 'Her timing was so important,' recalled John Houghton, the Director-General of the Meteorological Office: her speech came just two months before the first conference of the Intergovernmental Panel on Climate Change (IPCC), the UN body set up to assess the state of public knowledge. She intended the speech to have consequences, and it did.

Mrs Thatcher's speech showed her acting in character – as the science graduate handling matters closed to most politicians, as the eager seeker after truth who loved to preach a new crusade and as a political operator. Despite her victory in the miners' strike, the fear of another strike never completely left her. As Nigel Lawson noted, the suggestion that coal was damaging to life on earth, and that other sources of energy would be required, was 'quite convenient'.

Two weeks later, Mrs Thatcher returned to the theme in her annual speech to the Conservative Party conference seeking clear political advantage. 'It's we Conservatives who are not merely friends of the Earth,' she insisted, teasing the well-known pressure group. 'We are its guardians and

---

* Mrs Thatcher was considerably influenced by the British Antarctic Survey in her attitude to climate change. She had been very grateful when its knowledge of terrain proved so useful in the Falklands War, and ever afterwards ensured that it was generously funded. David Drewry, the Survey's director, recalled that she was interested in retaining British Antarctic Territory ('It's our land'), in the exploitation of marine and mineral resources there and in the ozone-layer discovery, which he told her was 'a harbinger for global change'. The 'harbinger' phrase stuck in Mrs Thatcher's mind.

† Mrs Thatcher notes in her memoirs that, because the subject of the speech was scientific, the media could not be bothered with it, and the expected television lights were not present at the dinner. As a result she had to read her speech by the light of the flickering candles of the Fishmongers' Hall.

trustees for generations to come ... No generation has a freehold on this earth. All we have is a life tenancy – with a full repairing lease. This Government intends to meet the terms of that lease in full.' The phrase about the 'full repairing lease' has been quoted ever since.

Although the Royal Society speech was a genuine expression of Mrs Thatcher's views, its content was not purely her own. The man who most influenced her over climate change was not a scientist but a diplomat. Crispin Tickell, a handsome, charismatic official with the ex-Guards bearing which Mrs Thatcher always admired, had become her guru. Drawing on his personal interest in the subject, he persuaded her to include a climate discussion in the 1984 G7 London summit. Tickell was taken with the 'Gaia' theory of the scientist James Lovelock, which posits that living organisms interact with their inorganic surroundings to form a self-regulating planetary system which ensures life on earth. This theory, controversial among scientists, was deployed by environmentalists to demonstrate the dangers of drastic human interventions in the biosphere. Tickell shared all this with Mrs Thatcher. When he arranged for her to meet Lovelock, she was impressed.

'She didn't know much about climate change,' Tickell recalled, 'but she found it interesting as a scientific hypothesis ... As the only woman and the only scientist, she wasn't going to be pushed around by people who knew about Thucydides.' Tickell always denied authorship of the Royal Society speech, but her text drew on a memo he had written advocating a British environment initiative at the UN (where, from 1987, he served as Britain's Permanent Representative). With Mrs Thatcher's blessing, Charles Powell redrafted Tickell's thoughts, including a call for an international commission on climate change and 'a world levy on fuel prices to support improved energy efficiency'. The Foreign Office objected to the international commission idea, while her proposal of universal fuel levies, and debt relief for developing countries in return for preserving their rainforests, outraged the Chancellor: 'These bizarre ideas are contrary to Government policy, and are political dynamite': they 'must be deleted', Lawson insisted. They were. The groundwork, however, was laid. As Tickell recalled: 'I persuaded her that international bodies were the right thing.' Mrs Thatcher had now bought into a global method of tackling the problem.

After the Royal Society speech, Tickell wrote to Powell, 'I agree that the next thing is to make sure that something happens.' Mrs Thatcher ticked this and added, 'I think we need to take some international initiative quickly or the French will try to take the lead.' She arranged for Britain to host an international ministerial conference, that same year, about CFCs (chlorofluorocarbons), the chemicals which were thought to damage the ozone layer.

The issue of global warming was moving quickly from something in which world leaders were uninterested to a competition to be the greenest. Rapid, man-made climate change was now widely considered a hypothesis sufficiently strong to shape policy. 'There is as yet no firm evidence of climatic change resulting from the greenhouse effect,' noted a Cabinet Office paper from December 1988. 'But there is no serious disagreement within the scientific community that man's activities will lead to global warming.'* Mrs Thatcher underlined these words approvingly.

Mrs Thatcher's 'Saving the Ozone Layer Conference' took place in London in March 1989, under UN auspices. She told the BBC she hoped for 'agreement to cut [ozone-depleting CFC gases] by 85 per cent within the next decade'.† According to Bernard Ingham, what the press really wanted to know was 'How green is Mrs Thatcher?' The answer, it soon emerged, was green enough to put real conviction into the conference. At its formal dinner, the then Prince of Wales (now King Charles III), one of the gloomiest of the environmental prophets, praised her for giving 'a firm lead'. He called for an 'obligation to intervene' on behalf of the environment to be imposed on government. William Reilly, the new US Environmental Protection Agency Administrator, had come bearing a letter of support for Mrs Thatcher from President Bush: 'I agree on CFCs!' the President had added in his own hand. Reilly, who was finding his environmentalism outgunned by scepticism from Bush's Chief of Staff, John Sununu, and others, was thrilled to find Mrs Thatcher on his side. 'Her conference', he reported to the President, 'was a *tour de force*' which 'set the stage for a genuinely global response to the problem of ozone depletion'.‡

During the London conference twenty nations agreed to sign the Montreal Protocol, with fourteen more seriously considering it.§ Politically, as

---

* This paper was drafted by Richard Wilson, who had been put in charge of an officials' committee to sort out the issues involved. He christened it 'The Committee on the End of Mankind as We Know It'.
† Mrs Thatcher's conference received a significant boost when, on 2 March, the EEC agreed to phase out CFCs completely by 2000. This was echoed shortly afterwards by the Americans.
‡ Mrs Thatcher was asked whether the issue was rather more urgent for her 'since the arrival in this polluted world of a new little Thatcher?' (Michael had been born just over a week earlier). 'Shall we say that it has a perhaps even greater and deeper personal meaning?' she replied. From then on, young Michael's inheritance would become a sub-theme in her speeches on the future of the planet.
§ Known, more formally, as the Montreal Protocol on Substances that Deplete the Ozone Layer, this committed its signatories to action to reduce emissions damaging to the ozone layer.

Reilly observed to Bush, Mrs Thatcher had 'managed to reposition herself and her Government. The Germans and the Dutch looked on incredulous as Mrs Thatcher received huge and very positive publicity throughout Europe.'*

Tickell quickly capitalized on the success of the ozone conference to apply it to global warming. Using the Montreal Protocol as a model, he argued that Britain should start working on an International Convention on Climate, including a code of 'good climatic behaviour'. Although this was almost as extreme as Prince Charles's suggestion, Mrs Thatcher seemed to accept Tickell's proposal of 'the obligation of states to protect and preserve the atmosphere'. In April, her support for an international convention found its way into *The Economist*. Nudged by Tickell, Mrs Thatcher had moved in a few months from virtual silence on the subject to something close to global leadership.

On 26 April 1989, she hosted leading scientists for a seminar on climate change in Downing Street. James Lovelock noted the amazement of his scientific colleagues: 'They'd never thought they'd be at a meeting where the head of government presided as if she'd presided over science meetings all her life.' 'She was dying to do some science,' recalled John Houghton. 'Her poor ministers ... kept looking at their watches.' The mood of the seminar was all but unanimously in favour of the theory of global warming. Tickell expounded his concept of a 'loose framework' for curbing climate change overseen by the UN Security Council.

Mrs Thatcher's new-found environmental interest notwithstanding, in the June European Parliament elections the Greens received almost 2.3 million votes – more than in any previous British election. The Conservatives came second to Labour. Dominic Morris felt that she rather lost heart at this point: 'She was global cooling quite rapidly. The subject was helping a party that was hurting her party.' But she did not give up. In her reshuffle that July she replaced Nick Ridley at Environment with the explicitly and eloquently green Chris Patten. This was, in part, an effort to reorient the party on the environment. Patten, felt Richard Wilson in the Cabinet Office, 'altered the whole flavour of government thinking'.

Another aspect of the environment, much less intellectually challenging but also dear to Mrs Thatcher's heart, was the problem of litter. In this, as in several areas of social policy, she was, felt Dominic Morris, 'a little unmoored':

---

* One consequence of the CFC ban she supported did, however, dismay Mrs Thatcher. Some years after she left office, at a dinner at the British Embassy in Washington, Mrs Thatcher turned to Bill Reilly's wife and said: 'Do you find that, ever since we banned those ozone depleters, it's been impossible to find hair lacquer that works?'

'she had her instincts, but no road-map'. With her encouragement, her Environment Secretary, Nicholas Ridley, devised a series of pilot schemes, often involving private initiatives, to try out litter solutions. At Ridley's request, Mrs Thatcher attended the launch of one of these, on 22 March 1988, in St James's Park. To illustrate the extent of the problem, all the litter found in one day in the park (three cubic metres) was to be laid in front of her. Her programme, headed 'you should wear a stout pair of shoes', explained that Ridley would provide her with a stick 'to collect litter that has been dumped'. 'I would expect you', warned Ingham, 'to be up against a very cynical audience.'

The press were indeed cynical, but delighted by Mrs Thatcher's bravura comic performance. Despite being beautifully dressed as always, she started scurrying across the grass, stabbing fiercely at the litter, while Ridley loped behind her, grinning sheepishly. In a short speech, she identified the first cause of litter – people. If people 'knowingly or thoughtlessly' made a mess they should clear it up, she said. What she called an attempt at the restoration of 'civic and national pride' provided rich material for satire, for which Mrs Thatcher happily fulfilled her caricature as the bossy headmistress. For her it achieved at least one of the desired effects, linking her in everyone's mind with a longing to make Britain tidy.

In the summer of 1989, at Tickell's urging, Mrs Thatcher agreed to make climate change the subject of her address to the UN General Assembly that November. With her agreement, Tickell took charge of preparing the speech (cutting out the Foreign Office) with help from Chris Patten and Patten's special adviser, the green economist Professor David Pearce. While open to their ideas, Mrs Thatcher also listened carefully when Nigel Lawson warned her against Pearce's economic calculations, criticizing his idea that sustainable development was 'an operational concept'. For all her belief in climate change, she was careful never to lose sight of economic realities.

Two weeks before her UN speech, Mrs Thatcher received a fax which struck her very much. It came from an ocean physicist, Dr Peter Wadhams, on board 'FS "Polarstern"'. At sea, Antarctic Ocean.' He told her that his measurements revealed that ozone depletion was worse than ever. Over eleven years, there had been a 15 per cent loss of the average thickness of the ice over an area twice the size of Britain. The lesson, said Dr Wadhams, was that man-produced climate change might 'take on a self-sustaining or "runaway" quality'. All this was fed into the speech composition process.*

---

* Peter Wadhams had some reputation as a maverick, and some experts doubted whether he could have seen what he said he saw from where he was travelling in the ship at that time. This objection was not known to Mrs Thatcher.

On 8 November, Mrs Thatcher stood before the UN General Assembly and warned of 'the prospect of irretrievable damage . . . to earth itself' with 'Mankind and his activities' to blame. Having deployed Dr Wadhams's Antarctic fax to dramatize the urgency of the task, she conveyed the full Tickell remedy – a 'framework convention on climate change', taking the Montreal Protocol as its model and developing binding agreements for the control of CO_2 emissions.

Mrs Thatcher found it harder to apply her green ideas to the nitty-gritty of policy than to air them in major speeches. In early December, she chaired the first meeting of the new Cabinet committee, MISC 141, set up to address environmental policy. Here she was warned by the Chancellor, John Major, against pronouncements which might increase tax, and about the 'enormous liability in the electricity industry' if international agreement forced Britain to cut CO_2 from coal-fired power stations. If restraints on emissions were in place before electricity privatization, they would badly damage the price at which the industry could be sold. Principles which sounded good in the abstract were unattractive in real life. As Patten prepared his Environment White Paper, Mrs Thatcher warned him against 'comfortable phrases, the meaning of which were [*sic*] far from clear'. She singled out 'sustainable development', forgetting that she had signed Britain up for it in Toronto a year earlier. In policy terms, she felt happier dealing with the more exact problem of CFCs and the ozone layer than with the more inchoate one of CO_2.

Her approach was to be cautious and flexible – not to say political – about the detail while keeping up a high rhetorical volume. In the view of Richard Wilson, who ran MISC 141, 'It was all uphill work, and the skies had started darkening for other reasons, such as the poll tax and the cuts in public spending.' Climate change 'seemed a funny little creature, which could be pushed aside by the above. Her views on climate change did not alter, but I think she knew she wasn't winning.'

In private, Mrs Thatcher had already decided to follow the implication of John Houghton's striking IPCC report, which she had discussed with him before publication. It predicted a rise in global temperature of between 1.3 degrees Centigrade and 2.5 degrees from pre-industrial levels by 2020.*
On 25 May, publication day, she announced Britain's willingness to set

---

* In 2018 an IPCC report found that man-made climate change had, it estimated, led to a rise of approximately 1.0 degree Centigrade above pre-industrial levels, with a rise of 1.5 degrees expected between 2030 and 2052.

its own targets to help stabilize global emissions by 2005.* In embracing targets, Mrs Thatcher was placing herself on the side of the Europeans and against the Bush administration. She also banged home Houghton's confirmation that man's activities were responsible for climate change. Taking up her own phrase about the 'full repairing lease', Mrs Thatcher declared, 'we have the Surveyor's Report and it shows that there are faults and that the repair work needs to start without delay'.

The next conference on the ozone layer was due that June. To encourage the wider participation of countries such as China and India in the Montreal Protocol, Mrs Thatcher ignored her usual principles and supported the establishment of a $260 million fund to help finance the measures required. The US administration, led by John Sununu, opposed this. Passing on to the British what he called 'the disappointing but unannounced' US position, William Reilly urged that Mrs Thatcher intervene personally with Bush. Writing to the President, she praised the US role in getting the Montreal process going, but said it was now necessary to provide money 'additional to existing aid flows' to get other countries to participate. Bush's advisers recommended doing as she asked. Bush agreed. Mrs Thatcher was therefore able to launch the world's first global environmental fund to be overseen by the UN. Her behaviour was highly un-Thatcherite. There is no evidence, however, that she did not mean it.

Despite this accord, Mrs Thatcher and the Bush administration continued to disagree about the extent of global warming and how to address it. In Aspen, in August 1990, just after Saddam Hussein's invasion of Kuwait (see p. 856), she warned that if the world delayed, 'the damage will be counted not only in dollars, but in human misery as well. Spending on the environment is like spending on defence – if you do not do it in time, it may be too late.' Administration critics, such as Sununu, feared that the efforts made to solve the CFC problem would now be applied to environmental issues more widely. But to green advocates such as Chris Patten, this was precisely the point. 'The [London] meeting marks a new phase in international cooperation on major environmental issues,' he told Mrs Thatcher that summer. 'We can build on this to try to solve the other – more difficult – environmental problems that we face, such as biodiversity and global warming.'

Margaret Thatcher, of all people, had done more than any other non-American to encourage the United States towards a global, well-funded approach to climate change, advantaging believers in anthropogenic global

---

* This was designed to dovetail with Houghton's assertion that 'the scientific position will not be clear until 2005', and indeed Mrs Thatcher's speech was written with his assistance. He later recalled her, 'pencil and eraser in hand', as she carefully drafted and redrafted the text: '"I'm a scientist," she said a few times, "I've got to get it absolutely right."'

warming. The process itself, and subsequent US resistance to it, continue to cause unresolved controversy to this day.

In her last book, *Statecraft*, published in 2002, Mrs Thatcher appeared to recant on climate change. She asserted that the science had now shifted against warming theories and that the plan to deal with climate problems globally 'provides a marvellous excuse for worldwide, supranational socialism'. Referring to her Royal Society speech, she stressed she had always emphasized the importance of economic growth in dealing with environmental problems.

This was the truth, but by no means the whole truth. Mrs Thatcher did not admit that, when in office, she had been the most prominent advocate of global remedies, helping to put the UN on the course of a global framework to tackle climate change. In her sense of herself, Margaret Thatcher loved to claim absolute consistency. Part of the fascination of her character lies in the fact that this claim was sometimes false.

More consistent with her broader world view was Mrs Thatcher's longstanding approach to South Africa. In June 1987, despite all the effort of her second term, few signs of change were visible. Less than a month earlier, the State President P. W. Botha had convincingly won his election, his National Party receiving more than 50 per cent of the all-white vote. He now wrote to Mrs Thatcher declaring his readiness to enter discussions with black leaders, but offered few specifics. His message 'says disappointingly little', Charles Powell told her '– at considerable length'.

The received Western wisdom was that Mrs Thatcher had gained nothing from her readiness to engage with the white government and her resistance to economic sanctions. Nonetheless, her approach received reasonable support in British opinion polls and strong backing from party grass-roots. She was disappointed by the lack of progress. Nelson Mandela, for whose release she had been campaigning since 1984, remained in prison, while her relationship with Botha was, in the words of Powell, 'virtually nonexistent'. But she still believed an 'Afrikaner Gorbachev' would emerge.

Mrs Thatcher knew that F. W. de Klerk – considered a centrist on the National Party's spectrum – was already pushing for the extension of black political rights. George Guise in her Policy Unit, well connected to South Africa, advised her that the National Party would now move faster with reforms: 'people who say that South Africa now is in a right wing laager ... are hopelessly wrong'. This chimed with Mrs Thatcher's instincts.

By this stage, she had effectively removed South African policy from the Foreign Office's purview, putting Charles Powell in charge. As he later admitted, Powell now 'shamelessly promoted a friend of mine', Robin Renwick, who became Ambassador to South Africa shortly after her election victory.* Because of the isolation of white South Africa, and because of Mrs Thatcher's patronage, Renwick was able to act like a nineteenth-century ambassador, making important decisions himself on the spot and engaging with all major elements of opinion.

In September, Renwick met de Klerk, who, he reported, was 'tough-minded, but committed to reform according to his lights . . . He is universally regarded here as the most likely successor to P. W. Botha.' For the time being, however, there was little movement. Ahead of the Commonwealth Heads of Government Meeting (CHOGM) in Vancouver that October, Powell felt compelled to warn Mrs Thatcher that 'The reform process in South Africa is dead in the water,' and therefore the conference would be difficult.

In her opening speech, on her sixty-second birthday, Mrs Thatcher told the Commonwealth leaders there was 'nothing to be gained by parading our differences . . . what we do all agree is that apartheid is an utterly repulsive and detestable system and that it must go'. This won her a round of applause, but the harmony did not last. She felt particularly annoyed by the hypocrisy on display. For all the solemn words of support for sanctions from Canadian Prime Minister Brian Mulroney, his country's exports to South Africa were rising. When Ingham allowed these figures to reach the press there was outrage. Mulroney, who denied the figures, saw this as an attempt by Ingham to 'sabotage the conference'. This led the other leaders to call a press conference to attack Mrs Thatcher, he recalled, because 'they were so Goddam mad at her'. She, however, was unrepentant. As was becoming the norm, the final communiqué included calls for sanctions 'with the exception of Britain'.

There was more controversy at the press conference. Angered by a statement from an African National Congress (ANC) spokesman that British businesses in South Africa might become the target for violent attacks because of British opposition to sanctions, Mrs Thatcher hit back. 'This shows what a typical terrorist organisation it [the ANC] is,' she declared. 'I fought terrorism all my life and if more people fought it . . . we should not have it.'

Her outburst was characteristic, but unnecessary. The ANC's 'armed struggle', which had such emotional resonance, was not, in reality, very effective, yet it felt it could never resile, in principle, from this position until apartheid was fully ended. It was partly because Mrs Thatcher understood

---

* Renwick had earlier won Mrs Thatcher's confidence in Rhodesian and then in European negotiations.

this that she was so keen on political reform. Her words would now be used against her, and distorted over time to the damaging claim that she had called Nelson Mandela himself a terrorist, though she never did.

Besides, Mrs Thatcher was open to the charge of hypocrisy. As was quickly pointed out, there were already British official and even ministerial contacts with the ANC which she had approved. In April 1985, she had allowed consideration of 'a relationship with the ANC through intelligence channels'. That October, Geoffrey Howe had urged links with the exiled ANC leader Oliver Tambo via Zambia. Mrs Thatcher's first reaction was 'hostile', but Powell urged her to accept. There were risks, he admitted – 'We shade our position on contact with terrorists' – but there were greater advantages. Contact would lead to more influence with both the ANC and the white South African government.* Mrs Thatcher agreed.

After the first meeting between the ANC and British officials, in February 1986, Geoffrey Howe argued for ministerial contacts, believing British influence could restrain the ANC from violence. 'Not much hope of that,' wrote Mrs Thatcher tartly. Nonetheless, she agreed to grant Howe some discretion. He duly met Tambo at Chevening, his official country residence, in September. These closer links reflected a change of heart by the ANC. During 1986, they – particularly Mandela – had come to believe that apartheid must end through negotiations. This did not exclude the 'armed struggle' but marginalized it.

So the immediate task facing Downing Street following Vancouver was to maintain contacts despite its mistress's own public words. After a predictably angry reaction from the ANC, Powell sought Mrs Thatcher's permission to continue 'intermittent contact' at a ministerial level, so long as 'the main purpose of such contact is to urge the ANC to abandon violence'. Salving her conscience by multiple underlinings of 'main purpose' and 'abandon violence', Mrs Thatcher gave her consent.†

As Robin Renwick worked within South Africa to bring about change, he exploited Mrs Thatcher's high standing among the whites. In October, the leading article in the main Afrikaans newspaper, *Beeld*, declared: 'She is trying

---

* There was a Machiavellian justification in that the Botha government had encouraged Britain to build up ties to the ANC 'no doubt hoping that we will pass them some information'. In fact, Mrs Thatcher later decided not to allow such information to be passed to the South Africans, but the point stood that contacts with the ANC might strengthen Britain's influence over the white government.

† Part of that intermittent contact would soon be Charles Powell himself. Through the good offices of Anthony Sampson, the journalist, writer and friend of Mandela, Powell twice met Oliver Tambo in Sampson's house in Ladbroke Grove, London, finding him 'very indignant' at Mrs Thatcher's description of the ANC as a 'terrorist organisation'. Powell's visits were freelance: he told Mrs Thatcher about them afterwards.

to create an opportunity for us to make progress ourselves. Let us not waste the opportunity.' Botha, however, seemed unconvinced. In February 1988, he sent Mrs Thatcher a message that she complained contained nothing which enabled her to say that progress without sanctions was being made. She was particularly disappointed that Mandela remained in prison; if he were to die there, 'he would become a legend which could never be erased'. As if to confirm her fears, Botha imposed a new clampdown on anti-apartheid political activity. She protested. Botha told her she was 'simply ill-informed'.

Renwick reported to London a striking follow-up conversation with Botha, who, he felt, for the first time did not seem very well. Botha argued that 'Mandela was keeping himself in jail. If he renounced violence, he could be released at any time. We would not be prepared to consider releasing convicted IRA prisoners. Why should he be expected to release Mandela with no assurances as to what might happen thereafter?' On this telegram Mrs Thatcher wrote: '<u>Very interesting</u>. He seems to be trapped and does not have the vigour to get out of it.'

Beyond South Africa's borders, the Gorbachev era was changing the political climate. For geopolitical, ideological and financial reasons, the Soviets lost interest in the post-colonial countries of southern Africa. Their previous assistance to the ANC – in money, weaponry and training – fell away, forcing the ANC to turn towards a settlement within South Africa. Mrs Thatcher backed Gorbachev in his policy of disengagement.

She argued similarly against US intervention on an ideological basis. Mozambique provided a telling example. Here President Reagan faced pressure from his right-wing supporters to back the anti-Communist RENAMO forces in their struggle against the pro-Soviet government. Mrs Thatcher persuaded Reagan instead to support her efforts to cultivate Mozambique's President Samora Machel and his successor. As Chester Crocker, the US Assistant Secretary of State for African Affairs, put it, 'she believed in something that we in the State Department believed in: you can wean Marxists. But you've got to know what you're doing.' She understood that, if the region were no longer a theatre for East–West tensions, violence would become less likely. The fear factor which bolstered white rule would diminish.

Mrs Thatcher's most reliable ally over South Africa was Helmut Kohl.* German business interests made him almost as hostile as she to economic

---

* Mrs Thatcher's naturally closest ally on this was President Reagan, but the Comprehensive Anti-Apartheid Act, passed against his wishes by Congress in 1986, kept him on the sidelines of any engagement with South Africa.

sanctions, and he shared her instinctive Cold War anxieties about Communist (and Soviet) influence in the region. In July 1988, however, during a visit to Chequers, Kohl confessed to feeling domestic pressure to support sanctions: 'the churches in Germany', he said, '... were very steamed up'. Fearing even greater isolation, she persuaded Kohl instead to agree to send a joint emissary to Botha to advance reform and the release of Mandela. The envoy would be Fritz Leutwiler, the former President of the Swiss National Bank and Mrs Thatcher's informal adviser on South Africa. His visit was arranged for December.

In the intervening period, Mrs Thatcher learnt privately of significant changes of view from both sides of the struggle. In October, South African officials told the British that Mandela would be released but, because many white voters considered foreign intervention in domestic affairs anathema, there should be no public link between his release and any possible visit to South Africa by Mrs Thatcher. The South Africans reported that their Cabinet 'as a whole' had decided that 'blacks could no longer remain outside the constitutional system'. New constitutional change would be announced early in 1989. One South African official declared boldly that Botha was 'old fashioned and out of touch'. His reign was drawing to a close.

The ANC was also adjusting. In November, Mrs Thatcher received word of private discussions with Thabo Mbeki, a rising star of the ANC. Mbeki considered efforts to establish a direct relationship between her and the ANC paramount. He understood her difficulties in engaging with an organization that had not renounced violence, but believed that were she to meet Oliver Tambo it would demonstrate to the South African government that they too would eventually have to engage with the ANC.

Mbeki's comments were striking in their recognition of Mrs Thatcher's salience, but also a possible trap. If she agreed to meet Tambo, she might seem to legitimize the ANC and sacrifice her hard-won influence over the white government. Charles Powell wrote, 'A meeting with Tambo is surely unthinkable.' Mrs Thatcher ticked the word 'unthinkable' and underlined it three times. But she clearly *did* think about it. A more accurate word would have been 'premature'.

In December, Leutwiler met Botha, telling him that support from Britain and Germany would cease unless he stepped down to allow the changes required, including the release of Mandela. This hit Botha hard. Six weeks passed before Leutwiler reported to Mrs Thatcher in person on his visit. By this stage Botha had suffered a stroke, which she knew was much more serious than publicly reported. 'President Botha was the slave of his fears and vanities,' she told Leutwiler, '... we could expect nothing much more from him.' On 2 February 1989, P. W. Botha resigned as National Party leader while staying on as State President. His successor was F. W. de Klerk.

Less than a month after de Klerk's rise, Mrs Thatcher heard the disturbing news that South Africa was planning to assassinate ANC personnel in London. Powell advised her this would be 'a devastating setback' to British policy in South Africa: Britain should issue a 'veiled warning'. She replied, 'Yes – a pretty firm warning. This is totally reprehensible and must not happen.' Pretoria got the message; no assassinations occurred.

Although Botha remained in ultimate charge, de Klerk presided over an immediate change in atmosphere. Telling Renwick of his enthusiasm for Mrs Thatcher, he explained his great difficulty was to get his own party to accept that white rule was 'morally unjustifiable'. In winning this change of heart, sanctions and international disapproval were not effective because they were so blankly hostile: 'Mrs Thatcher had a much bigger influence.' Three weeks later, Renwick was told by one of Mandela's lawyers that Mandela had asked him to convey 'his appreciation of your Prime Minister's role in opposing apartheid, notwithstanding his difference of opinion on the sanctions issue'.

In April, as de Klerk prepared for a European tour, events in Namibia provided a test of his country's intentions. Ruled by South Africa, Namibia (known previously as South-West Africa) had seen a long-standing violent struggle for independence led by the South West African People's Organization (SWAPO), backed by Cuban troops based in neighbouring Angola. To resolve this, Chester Crocker had persuaded the South Africans to accept independence for Namibia so long as Cuban forces were withdrawn from Angola. The resulting plan, under UN auspices, happened to be coming into force when Mrs Thatcher arrived in the Namibian capital, Windhoek, on 1 April 1989* during her second African tour as Prime Minister.† That day it emerged that SWAPO troops had mounted an incursion into Namibia, killing several police officers. SWAPO seemed to be trying to

---

* Before Namibia, Mrs Thatcher had visited Blantyre, Malawi. En route to Blantyre from Zimbabwe, she later discovered, her plane had been attacked by seven Sam 7 missiles fired from Mozambique. The attackers missed. In her memoirs Mrs Thatcher attributes the shooting to the RENAMO fighters to whom she was hostile, but the best information at the time suggested that 'excited Mozambican [that is, FRELIMO] troops' were responsible. The attack was later pinned on 'a drunk Frelimo air battery commander'. The British government decided to take no action in response to this probably freelance attack.
† She had paid a successful visit to Kenya and Nigeria the previous year. Otherwise, her only visit to sub-Saharan Africa as Prime Minister had been to the Commonwealth Conference in Lusaka in 1979.

pre-empt the implementation of the agreement and take over. It was a major provocation to the South Africans.

Mrs Thatcher was well positioned to tackle this crisis. As Crocker put it, 'Unique among our allies, the British had significant credibility in both Luanda [the Angolan capital] and Pretoria.' Her policy of cultivating influence with the South African government was about to be put to the test. At Windhoek airport, against the advice of her officials, she met the South African Foreign Minister, Pik Botha. To pre-empt unilateral action by Pretoria she undertook to persuade the UN Special Representative, Martti Ahtisaari, to authorize the South African forces to block the SWAPO invasion without reoccupying the country. If South Africa did not do as she said, she told Botha, 'The whole world will be against you – led by me!' After some bluster, Botha agreed. Mrs Thatcher promptly met Ahtisaari and the crisis passed.

By her chance presence and her own presence of mind, Mrs Thatcher had helped foil a potential *coup d'état*. An unusual combination of sources praised her. Pik Botha said he 'warmly appreciated' her efforts, while, in Moscow, Mikhail Gorbachev reported to the Politburo his 'high appreciation of the important role' she had played. Following elections in November, Namibia became an independent state on 21 March 1990.

Mrs Thatcher relished this episode of derring-do. Robin Renwick recalled: 'She was really rather enjoying this – taking over Namibia for a bit. Denis was keen to get her back on the plane. But for his efforts she would have stayed on for another day or two.'

On 23 June 1989, Mrs Thatcher received F. W. de Klerk at Chequers. This unusual mark of favour was designed to boost his standing when world leaders still shunned South Africa's white leadership. Despite de Klerk's outward deference to Botha, Mrs Thatcher knew the way he was heading. At secret discussions between the South African government and the ANC at Mells Park in Somerset, the South Africans had raised the possibility of instituting talks about talks with the ANC, who responded positively. The suggestion was mooted that she herself could play some role as an 'honest broker', but she demurred. She wished to 'encourage' what was happening, Powell told the Mells Park chairman, but not 'intervene directly'.

At Chequers, Mrs Thatcher knew de Klerk would be cautious ahead of his country's September elections. All the same, she insisted he was not going far enough. When de Klerk replied that Mandela 'could not be released into a void', she said there was 'no prospect of negotiations before Mandela was released. She could not emphasise . . . this too strongly.'

Charles Powell recorded that 'Mr de Klerk was rather taken aback by this opening salvo,' but explained that although he was determined to release Mandela 'He had a bottom line . . . Whites had to have unity and a guaranteed future.' He later recalled that he found her 'very well informed, very friendly, but she listened more than she talked'. 'I think we got on well,' he added, 'because we were both completely frank. Also, both of us admired – and accepted the need for – political courage.' Although Mrs Thatcher immediately liked de Klerk much better than Botha, she found him reserved. After bidding him farewell, she turned to Renwick and said, 'I'm not sure how far he will go.' 'I think you will find he will go further than you imagine,' Renwick replied.*

On 8 July, Mrs Thatcher was privately informed that P. W. Botha had recently met Nelson Mandela. With *de facto* recognition of Mandela's leadership, the ANC knew that, sooner or later, white rule would end. Increasingly marginalized, Botha resigned as State President in August. The National Party won the ensuing general election. The combined votes of the reformist Democratic Party and the National Party showed that 70 per cent of votes had gone to parties advocating the end of white rule. De Klerk was fully in charge.

In her message of congratulation to de Klerk on 15 September, Mrs Thatcher mentioned her own most pressing concern – that at the looming CHOGM in Kuala Lumpur, 'international pressure for more negative action against South Africa' would grow. With de Klerk at the helm, she felt more justified than ever in not only opposing sanctions but trying to roll back measures already imposed. For her, the situation was maddening. She believed that her approach to South Africa was beginning to bear fruit and yet she had to listen to Commonwealth colleagues indulging in what is nowadays called 'virtue signalling'. She was therefore even more argumentative than usual, frank to the point of rudeness.†

---

* Mrs Thatcher reported her de Klerk meeting to George Bush, urging the President to meet him during his visit to the United States next month. Bush replied encouragingly. Under pressure from Congress, however, Bush later refused to see de Klerk while Mandela remained in prison, and so the two did not meet until the following autumn. One unintended consequence of the domestic pressure Bush faced, not least from the Congressional Black Caucus, was that the United States played a surprisingly marginal part in the ending of apartheid.
† As usual at CHOGMs, Mrs Thatcher was probably a little bit on edge because of the presence of the Queen, the head of the Commonwealth, which sharpened her perennial anxieties about correct behaviour. When she received an invitation from the King of Malaysia to reply to his speech at the royal banquet with which the conference would open, Mrs Thatcher wrote, 'I don't think it would be right to do so in the presence of the Queen. I should have thought the occasion required a Head of State.' Denis was more relaxed about the trip. 'I NEVER join in with "official" jaunts for spouses,' he wrote to Charles Powell, but he would happily

As the gathering in Malaysia got under way, the Australian Prime Minister, Bob Hawke, suggested the Commonwealth could be 'very significant' in helping change. Mrs Thatcher told him 'she disagreed profoundly . . . When someone was doing the right thing, it did not help to beat them about the ears.' During the conference debate she accused those present of aiming to 'multiply the number of those who were hungry'. She later provoked a row by releasing, via Powell, a statement opposing sanctions shortly after the official communiqué had been published.

This infuriated the Commonwealth leaders. Hawke and Brian Mulroney jointly protested. Hawke 'did not understand this way of doing business. First you accepted a document, then you repudiated it.' Mulroney demanded an explanation. Mrs Thatcher gave one, sort of: 'She was astounded that anyone should object to a nation putting its own viewpoint' and was 'frankly appalled that anyone should try to stop her'. She was unrepentantly uncollegial. When asked how she felt about being isolated from every other Commonwealth country, Mrs Thatcher replied: 'If it is one against forty-eight, I am very sorry for the forty-eight.'

The British press saw Mrs Thatcher's unilateral statement as a snub to John Major, whose agreement had not been sought and who was attending his first (and last) CHOGM as Foreign Secretary. 'I was pretty shocked,' Major recalled, '. . . I swallowed hard.' These arguments were quickly swept away because when Mrs Thatcher arrived back in London she was immediately confronted with the resignation of Nigel Lawson (see p. 751). Her tactlessness had been extreme, even by her own standards in Commonwealth meetings; but those shaping British policy saw merit in her approach. As Robin Renwick put it, the situation was 'just ludicrous. Here is this great reforming leader [de Klerk], who appears, and what do they want to do? Intensify sanctions against him . . . Three months later, he released Mandela. She was absolutely right in Kuala Lumpur.'

The fact that the CHOGM took place in Malaysia had much to do with Mrs Thatcher. She had persuaded Mahathir bin Mohamad, the country's powerful, volatile and intermittently anti-British Prime Minister, that Malaysia would improve its standing in the Commonwealth by playing host. This was part of her long campaign to restore Anglo–Malaysian relations after a difficult period in the early 1980s. At the heart of this was the trade relationship, especially British defence sales. Mahathir was open to such sales, but wished to make purchases of British defence equipment

---

agree to two rounds of golf. For this he would 'have to BORROW a set of light wieght [sic] LEFT-HANDED clubs'.

contingent on receiving British overseas aid for civil infrastructure projects. Mrs Thatcher did not explicitly accept this idea, but nor did she repudiate it. In Kuala Lumpur in March 1988, the Defence Secretary, George Younger, allowed himself to sign a defence protocol explicitly establishing this link. British aid for 'non-military aspects' should 'amount to no less than 20 per cent of the value of defence equipment'. The protocol was designed to bring Britain defence business worth £1 billion (thus requiring British aid contribution of £200 million).

Such a link, though not illegal, was against the international rules governing overseas aid and provoked sharp protests from the Overseas Development Administration (ODA), the Foreign Office sub-department responsible for aid, and the Treasury. On behalf of Mrs Thatcher, however, Powell told Younger's office that, since the protocol had been signed, 'the commitment would have to be met some way or other'.* For her, what really mattered was furthering British business – particularly British defence business – abroad. 'She thought it was quite right to link aid and trade,' Powell recalled. 'The Japs did; the French did. We were aware that we couldn't do it in relation to defence. We sailed close to the wind.' A link, of sorts, between arms and aid thus endured.

This was quite subtle. While the official minutes consistently show Mrs Thatcher stating to Mahathir that any defence package would be 'quite distinct' from any aid package, she always followed any mention of the defence deal with discussion of British aid. 'A nod and a wink' were not her style, but in effect that is what she was giving Mahathir. On 27 September, the two leaders signed a Memorandum of Understanding (MOU) on defence equipment procurement. Mrs Thatcher led the conversation straight from defence sales to aid, repeating the promise of funding to follow. The main upcoming project for which the Malaysians sought aid was the construction of a hydroelectric power station known as the Pergau Dam.

In January 1989, Mahathir suffered what the Malaysian public were told were chest pains but was actually a major heart attack. 'We must send flowers,' Mrs Thatcher scribbled. Early in March, his private visit to London for medical treatment provided an opportunity. 'The Prime Minister', the Foreign Office advised, 'might mention our close interest in the

---

* Younger wrote to his Malaysian counterpart to explain that 'the linking of aid to projects is governed by international rules which would preclude the sort of arrangement which you seemed to envisage at our meeting. However, I assure you, on behalf of my government, that we will continue to explore new avenues of cooperation.' He was saying, in effect, that the link would persist but could not be acknowledged. The official line was that arms and aid had thus been 'disentangled'.

important Pergau hydroelectric scheme (about £200 million UK content)' and praise the 'track record' of the relevant British contractors Balfour Beatty, GEC and Cementation. Through an informal backchannel, Charles Powell knew that agreeing these civil contracts was much on the Malaysian leader's mind. Mahathir would be 'surprised if you do not mention them', Powell had warned her. More than mentioning them, she made an offer of up to £68.25 million in grants alone for the Pergau project.

Less than a month later, the cost of building the dam had risen so high that, in theory, it could now be disqualified from ODA funding for failing to offer 'value for money'.* It was hard, however, to pull out now, said the Foreign Office, presumably thinking of the knock-on political consequences. For the remainder of Mrs Thatcher's time in office, plans stalled. Mahathir began to get cold feet over the cost of British Tornado aircraft, while the ODA, by now with Tim Lankester as Permanent Secretary, was deliberately moving slowly. Lankester was 'hoping that the Malaysians would see sense' and abandon the project. The arms link was 'unmentionable' by that stage, but 'I was personally very conscious that Pergau was part of it in the minds of Mrs Thatcher, the DTI, the FCO, the Malaysians and, of course, the MOD.' The aid offer made by Mrs Thatcher to Mahathir was twice renewed but expired on 17 October 1990.

It was only after Mrs Thatcher left office in November that a deal was reached. On 10 December, Malaysia signed a contract for twenty-eight Hawk aircraft. Over the deep reservations of ODA and the Treasury, the new Prime Minister, John Major, decided that Britain's contribution to Pergau should go ahead. 'If Mrs Thatcher gave her word we must keep it,' he wrote in February 1991. Three years later, and after the overall price had spiralled, rows and scandals about the Pergau Dam became public. Judicial review followed, at which the High Court determined the Pergau Dam grant unlawful.† This heralded a new era of judicial activism, with greater protections against ODA money being used for wider political purposes.

While critics assailed Mrs Thatcher for using unsuitable policy instruments to pursue her ends, she was unmoved. She believed in getting good defence and other commercial deals for Britain. She positively disliked the doctrine that development aid should be separated from the wider national interest. In her view, the controversy over Pergau was a small price to pay for defence contracts worth £1.3 billion between 1989 and 1993.

---

* This was a test the ODA was entitled to apply, a covert way of identifying corruption.
† The High Court judges decided that the project had failed to meet the relevant statute's stipulation that each aid grant should have a sound economic purpose.

For the historical observer, the Pergau Dam affair is a microcosm of the late-Thatcher style. She used her global power and prestige with considerable dash to win direct benefits for her country. On the other hand, she let Mahathir grab too much British taxpayers' money. She also disdained the conventions of government, producing bad effects later. She made bigger omelettes than anyone else, but therefore broke more eggs.

At midnight on 1 February 1990, President de Klerk telephoned Robin Renwick to say he would announce the release of Nelson Mandela the following morning. Only the precise timing was a surprise. The previous November, Mrs Thatcher had learnt from a secret report that de Klerk had decided on the release and to unban the ANC. So, that January, she had ordered preparations. She wanted an end to all British measures against South Africa and asked Renwick to tell de Klerk she would welcome him to Chequers. Her preconditions, expressed obliquely, were the release of Mandela and a partial lifting of the state of emergency. She accepted 'it would be right for her to offer to see Mandela once he was released', but 'would not want to rush in, appearing to claim credit'. Douglas Hurd's office warned her that 'Quite a lot of Mr Mandela's ANC advisers would urge him to turn down an invitation to visit Britain.'

The analogy with the end of the Cold War bulked large. Mandela himself told Renwick that Mrs Thatcher's ability to persuade Gorbachev and Reagan to do business together had been 'breathtaking developments'. He accordingly sought her help in bridging the divide with the South African government. While Mrs Thatcher had always been much more hostile to Soviet Communism than she was to white South Africa, the similarity was strong. She had helped confront leaders of impossible systems with the need to change and had stuck by them – despite much criticism from allies – along the path of reform. For her, the release of Mandela was a triumphant but also a delicate moment. After de Klerk announced the release, Mrs Thatcher put out a statement of congratulation, inviting him to Chequers: 'She will similarly invite Mr Mandela to make a visit to the United Kingdom when he is free.'

Nelson Mandela walked out of Victor Verster prison at 3 p.m. on 11 February 1990, greeted by huge crowds. The impact of his presence among the people was overwhelming. Mrs Thatcher watched him speak on television. As she told Bernie Grant, one of Britain's first black MPs, Mandela 'was clearly a most dignified and distinguished man, but the speech had been rather a disappointment in its references to armed struggle and nationalisation': it would give 'little comfort' to de Klerk. Renwick reassured her, however, after meeting Mandela privately, that he 'is a man of much higher calibre than any of his colleagues and he clearly does want to try to play a statesman-like role'.

Mandela's attitude to Mrs Thatcher was to show respect but advance with care. He told Renwick that he 'had high personal regard for the Prime Minister and wanted "to get her on my side"'. He expressed a desire to meet her when he visited London in mid-April, but said he would be guided by the ANC.* 'Very disappointing,' Charles Powell wrote on Renwick's telegram. Mrs Thatcher had never courted Mandela, but she had worked for his release longer than any other Western leader. It would be a heavy blow if he were now seen to snub her. In the event, Mandela did not see her during his April visit. Instead, addressing an Anti-Apartheid Movement pop concert in his honour at Wembley Stadium, he criticized those 'who wish to support the South African government by giving it rewards and carrots', a barb seemingly in her direction. But face was saved when, three days later, Charles Powell learnt that Mandela would like to see her in London that July.

For her part, Mrs Thatcher continued somewhat disheartened by Mandela, saying privately that 'he ought to lead from the front'. She was irritated that he publicly maintained the need for sanctions while privately indicating they should soon end. With President Bush in Bermuda, just before Mandela's Wembley concert, she worried that 'Mandela was evidently much more constrained than we had hoped by ANC dogma.'

In May, F. W. de Klerk embarked on a grand tour of Europe, ending at Chequers. Powell set the scene for her: 'You had to be pretty tough on de Klerk at your first meeting and it worked. He has done virtually everything you asked of him then. This time you can afford to be much nicer to him.' She was. In her speech at lunch she recalled the shared sacrifice of Britain and South Africa in two world wars: 'We have not forgotten the days when we were allies. We would like those days to come again, and I believe they will.'

De Klerk told her that he had a 'good rapport' with Mandela. What mattered now was to start negotiations. He hinted he would probably lift parts of the state of emergency in June and thought he could do a deal with the ANC: 'Without Soviet backing, it was a political movement and manageable.' He was impressed that she 'accepted axiomatically that cooperation

---

* The question of Mandela's relationship with the ANC was a complicated one. His greatest gift was to be the public voice of reconciliation, whereas the ANC had to work out how to gain power. There was an element of 'good cop; bad cop'. In a later conversation, Mandela told Robin Renwick that he had always to bear in mind that 'No political leader was of any value unless he could take his constituency with him.'

with the ANC was essential for the success of the negotiation process'.*
Mrs Thatcher felt that de Klerk had 'grown considerably in stature since
their last meeting a year ago'. This meeting, wrote Powell, proved 'a very
happy occasion'. The tensions and uncertainties about Mandela and the
ANC remained, yet the unfreezing of the Cold War made the overall context much more favourable. That April, the Soviet Foreign Minister, Eduard
Shevardnadze, told Douglas Hurd that the Soviet Union and Britain should
'cooperate to encourage progress' in ending apartheid. †

Behind the scenes, the secret contacts with the ANC which Mrs Thatcher
had authorized now came into their own. One factor was that the ANC,
losing Soviet intelligence back-up, were pleased to have help from the
British. In May 1990, Mrs Thatcher was informed that the ANC sought a
'private holiday' for Mandela. Exhausted, he wanted to spend a weekend
in England before flying to North America. She raised no objection,‡ and
so an elegant country house in Kent was provided. As well as seeking rest,
Mandela wished to meet Oliver Tambo, the other grand old man of the
ANC, whom he had not seen since his imprisonment in 1963.

The Mandelas were duly reunited with the Tambos. During the visit,
Mrs Thatcher was told, Mandela showed 'charm, warmth and friendliness
... to everyone irrespective of their position' and 'a slight quality of otherworldliness and vulnerability', but when the talk turned to politics he was
less gentle, saying that Britain should do more to stop township violence.

Acting impulsively, after drinking 'a tumbler and a half of hot port' at
dinner, Mandela decided to try to reach his ultimate host.§ As Powell at
once reported to Mrs Thatcher, 'Nelson Mandela telephoned me out of the

---

* At Chequers, de Klerk was accompanied by his wife Marike. Mrs de Klerk wrote to thank Mrs Thatcher, mentioning the flowers in their room which had used the colours of the South African flag, her speech at the lunch, and her 'insight ... and courage'. 'Forgive me if I say it needed a woman to do just that!' Perhaps because English was not Mrs de Klerk's first language, it was not perfectly clear which of these good things was distinctively female: perhaps she meant it was the combination of all of them.

† Shevardnadze felt that the British should concentrate on the South African government and the Russians on the ANC. Thus a problem which had until recently been seen as a bitter power struggle was now treated more as a division of labour.

‡ Presuming too much on her goodwill, the Foreign Office sent a further message saying that Mandela wanted money to help returning ANC exiles. Even though Charles Powell informed her that the South African government supported this request, Mrs Thatcher exploded: 'No ... We don't finance VIOLENCE ... Only a few days ago I was told the F.O. had no money and would have to go to the Treasury to finance NATO. They speak with forked tongue ... The ANC have been generously financed for violence by the [European] Community ... They are still committed to armed struggle. We DO NOT FINANCE VIOLENCE.'

§ Mandela did not like cold alcohol because, he said, it 'gave him a cough'. Powell scribbled to Mrs Thatcher that he would arrange for this unusual drink to be provided when Mandela came to see her in Downing Street: 'GHF [the Government Hospitality Fund] will be appalled!'

blue at about a quarter to midnight tonight . . . He said that he was very anxious to see you before leaving . . .' With Mandela's imminent departure, meeting in person was impractical, so she rang him at 7.30 the following morning. This was the first time the two had spoken.

Typically, she began by worrying about his health. She 'said that we were very concerned that Mr Mandela was taking on too much . . . He had a great and historic task ahead in South Africa, and he must be fresh and ready for it.' Mandela replied by thanking her for his 'lovely day' in Kent: he 'felt much refreshed'. However, he wished to dissuade her from pushing for an end to sanctions at the forthcoming European Council in Dublin: 'The Prime Minister had played a great part in securing his release' he said. '. . . He was very anxious that her influence should be preserved.'

Mrs Thatcher responded by trying to make Mandela see her concerns. He should 'suspend' the armed struggle.* Just as she had avoided his sanctions point, he avoided hers about violence. He assured her of the ANC's good faith in the negotiations: this 'was "my baby"', he said, 'and he was keen that it should succeed'. Mrs Thatcher said she 'would be blunt with Mr Mandela: sooner or later one had to say publicly what one was prepared to say privately'.

Powell recorded that the conversation ended amicably, but that Mrs Thatcher had commented afterwards that she was 'a bit disappointed with Mandela, who seemed to have rather a closed mind'. Mandela, however, told his hosts that he was very pleased with her call. He had been particularly touched by her concern for his health.

Before the two met at Downing Street on 4 July, Renwick and Powell both tried to coach Mrs Thatcher. To let the conversation be as frank as possible she and Mandela should meet alone, save for Thabo Mbeki and, to keep the record, Powell. Renwick, supported by Mbeki, told her that Mandela wanted to 'establish some kind of personal rapport (which should not be difficult, given the character of the man)'. Mandela, Renwick explained, considered himself, rather than de Klerk, to be the South African equivalent of Gorbachev. He wanted to be seen as 'the kind of person we can do business with'. In an oblique rebuke, Renwick suggested she give her guest a chance to talk. Mandela 'had waited 27 years to tell his side of the story'. She said: 'You mean I mustn't interrupt him?'

When Margaret Thatcher met Nelson Mandela in 10 Downing Street on 4 July 1990, she let him speak at length. Mandela thanked her for her role in his release and for her opposition to apartheid. She told him that

---

* Saying 'suspend' rather than 'abandon' was a notable concession on her part.

apartheid was 'wrong, immoral and contrary to the dignity of man'. She tried to move him on his support for nationalization, giving him a lesson on the nature of an open economy. Both accepted, though, that, as Mandela put it, their disagreements were not important 'so long as they agreed on the main goal of getting rid of apartheid'. They talked for so long that the press waiting outside began to chant 'Free Nelson Mandela!'

Mrs Thatcher afterwards recalled Mandela's 'genuine nobility of bearing', which was high praise since 'bearing' was something which she particularly admired. At their press conference Mandela endorsed Mrs Thatcher's integrity. 'She *is* an enemy of apartheid,' he said. 'Our differences are in regard to the methods of inducing the [South African] government to dismantle apartheid.' He declared Mrs Thatcher 'a woman I can do business with'.*

Were Mrs Thatcher to look back on her policy over South Africa, she could feel pleased. Her main aims had been engagement with the white government to end apartheid, the release of Mandela and holding the line against sanctions. This approach had isolated her from much world opinion, enraged the Commonwealth, worried her Sovereign and hastened Geoffrey Howe's estrangement. Yet she had carried her commitment to peaceful change through real gifts of leadership which Mandela himself recognized.

F. W. de Klerk, who, with Nelson Mandela, won the Nobel Peace Prize in 1993, was asked by the present author who, of all the world leaders he had known, stood highest in his esteem. 'Margaret Thatcher straddled the world stage. She was principled,' he said, 'I rank her number one.'

---

* An index of the level of trust between the British government and the ANC came in September, after Mandela had finally announced the suspension of the armed struggle. Thabo Mbeki privately asked Britain to help train and advise bodyguards for Mandela. His personal protection, said Mbeki, was 'wholly inadequate' and had received poor training from Romania and Cuba. Niël Barnard, head of the South African National Intelligence Service, informed the British government that he agreed with the idea and that de Klerk supported it too: 'He [de Klerk] would much prefer us to do it than anyone else to whom Mr Mandela might turn.' Charles Powell replied that Mrs Thatcher was 'content' so long as de Klerk had personally agreed.

35
The Wall falls; Germany rises
'Toad is at the wheel'

The fate of South Africa mattered to Mrs Thatcher intensely, but the central focus of her foreign policy was always the Cold War. By 1989, she saw the momentous changes under way in the Soviet Union and in Eastern Europe vindicating her approach. But she sensed danger too. While, to her, the fall of Communism was thrilling, the rise of Germany was not. As a rational strategic thinker, she had a strong, traditionally British sense of the need for a balance of power in Europe. As a child of the 'home front' in the Second World War, she had a visceral dislike of German power. Her enforced acquaintance with Helmut Kohl unfortunately strengthened her feelings. She could be moved to tears by the plight of the Poles under Communism, less so by that of the East Germans, despite her detestation of the Berlin Wall. According to Charles Powell, she suffered from 'a fundamental ignorance of Germany and Germans' to which she added a certain 'envy of Germany', not least for its economic performance. In her eyes, Germany had twice made terrible trouble in the world and might do so again.

By 1989, two related issues sharpened her anxieties about Germany. The first – moving quickly from distant dream to real possibility – was the idea that the two parts of the country divided by the Cold War might reunify.* The second was the suggestion that the only solution to the problems thus created was ever-closer European integration, particularly Economic and Monetary Union (EMU). She saw 'more Europe' not as controlling German power, but as cloaking it. Privately, she put it thus: 'The Germans need to have Europe to prove Germany is

---

* There was disagreement about how to describe the union of the two Germanies. Kohl, and most diplomats, usually preferred the term 'unification', since they wished to avoid seeming to recreate the greater Germany of Adolf Hitler. Mrs Thatcher preferred the more controversial but fundamentally more accurate term 'reunification'.

all right, and they only need to prove that Germany is all right because it isn't.'

Mikhail Gorbachev's opening up of the Soviet Union inevitably weakened his power. By the early summer of 1989, Percy Cradock was warning Mrs Thatcher of plots against the Soviet leader's life, which, if successful, would lead to bloodshed on a grand scale. As pro-democracy protests developed inside the Soviet Union, it became clear that if its citizens were given a voice, most of the 'nationalities' – the subsidiary, non-Russian republics of the Soviet Union – would seek freedom from it.

To help shore up his boss, Anatoly Chernyaev, Gorbachev's equivalent of Charles Powell, sought a 'public gesture from Mrs Thatcher to dramatise her continued support for the man and his policy'.* Rodric Braithwaite, the British Ambassador, suggested she might stop over in Moscow after attending a conference in Tokyo that September, an idea she accepted with alacrity. 'The poor man's in trouble,' she told Braithwaite. She felt a moral duty and a political imperative to help him. If he failed, she thought the liberation of Eastern Europe, which she had always strongly supported, would be at risk. She feared 'the hardliners would come back'.

By the time of Mrs Thatcher's meeting with Gorbachev, the pace of change in the Eastern bloc was quickening. In Washington, incoming Bush appointees encouraged this trend.† As one, Philip Zelikow, recalled: 'we were trying to promote as rapid change as we felt the market could bear'. The transformation in Poland, which in August saw its first non-Communist government in over forty years, and growing political liberalization in Hungary, electrified East and West. Since the early 1980s, Mrs Thatcher had sought to nurture the green shoots of democracy across Eastern Europe. These early signs of peaceful change gave her great heart.

In East Germany, where the ailing leadership of Erich Honecker refused to acknowledge the change, the populus became increasingly restive. Over the summer of 1989, growing numbers, taking advantage of Hungary's decision to open its borders to Austria, fled to the West. By the end of

---

* Chernyaev's motivation may also have been to reconcile Gorbachev to Mrs Thatcher after the affair of the spy expulsions that May (see p. 699). Despite the official line that all was well, Charles Powell's confidant Nikolai Kosov reported that Gorbachev had 'gone through the roof' over the issue. She had not mentioned it in London in April, and so 'He had been made to look a fool in the eyes of his critics for trusting the British.'
† James Baker and his close aide Bob Zoellick were especially active in this regard. Brent Scowcroft, the National Security Advisor, was more cautious.

September, some 40,000 East Germans had escaped. 'Suddenly the myth that East Germany is a real country has been totally dispelled . . .' Rodric Braithwaite wrote in his diary; 'it is an artificial country . . . created and sustained by the Russians.' 'Suddenly it has become respectable', he continued, '. . . to talk about reunification as a real prospect.' If Braithwaite was right, the natural question now was: 'Would the GDR still be sustained by the Russians?' Mrs Thatcher sought Gorbachev's answer.

As one of the Four Powers (the others being the United States, the Soviet Union and France) guaranteeing the post-war order of divided Berlin, and with 60,000 troops in West Germany, Britain was entitled to a substantial say. Since, to Mrs Thatcher, Germany remained a country on probation for its past sins, she was thoroughly alarmed that it might now add more than a quarter to its population and claim its full place among the comity of nations. On 1 September, President Mitterrand visited her at Chequers. He was, recalled Powell, extremely anxious about 'the German problem'. This was the first time Mrs Thatcher had heard a fellow Western leader speak thus. Four days later, she discussed the issue with Oleg Gordievsky. She had always assumed, she told him, that the Soviets would never permit German reunification; 'now she was less sure'. Gordievsky confirmed that attitudes might be altering: 'He thought that there was actually less fear of reunification in the Soviet Union than in the West.'

Briefing Mrs Thatcher for her Moscow visit, Powell put first the need to help Gorbachev, who was 'up against it in a big way', with *perestroika*. But he also suggested she 'test his reaction to renewed talk of German reunification'. Gorbachev had not yet spoken about this publicly, added Braithwaite: he might be 'more forthcoming in the intimacy of his exchanges with the Prime Minister'.

When Mrs Thatcher arrived at the Kremlin on 23 September, Gorbachev began by humorously alluding to the London spy expulsions: their dialogue had been 'a continuous one stretching over five years now, although the Prime Minister had sometimes tried to interrupt it (this said with much laughter)'.* He wanted them to 'keep their dialogue going'. This broke the ice and set the tone.

On *perestroika*, Gorbachev expressed concerns about implementation. It would take time, Mrs Thatcher stressed, noting she had to wait two years for the results of her own reforms: 'All that time I was criticised, and when the success came it was received as something natural, and nobody

---

* Given his original anger at the expulsions, Gorbachev's light touch on this subject was a sort of concession to Mrs Thatcher.

thanked me.' Gorbachev noted the danger that the extremes of reaction and revolution could yet coalesce against him. The USSR was inhabited by 120 different nations and peoples: if the problem of the nationalities blew up, 'it would be curtains for *perestroika*'.

Mrs Thatcher emphasized that the West did not intend 'to undermine Soviet security interests in Eastern Europe' and praised Gorbachev for his conduct towards Poland. Gorbachev confirmed that the internal developments of Eastern European countries were 'a matter for the countries themselves, but the structure of the Warsaw Pact must hold'. When she stressed that Bush would welcome a US–Soviet summit the following year, 'Mr Gorbachev said rather grumpily that President Bush had taken his time about it.'

On Moscow TV she praised Gorbachev's 'great historic mission ... we look forward to the Soviet Union becoming as well as a great military power, a great international power, a great and strong economic power'. So warm were these words that, according to Braithwaite, even Charles Powell considered then 'a bit overboard'. Braithwaite, meanwhile, noted with pleasure that 'The magic of their relationship is undimmed.'

So confident was Mrs Thatcher with Gorbachev that she chose to share her candid concerns about the German question. As Powell's highly restricted note* recorded, she said that 'Although NATO traditionally made statements supporting Germany's aspiration to be reunited, in practice we would not welcome it at all . . . She had discussed the matter with at least one other western leader.'† Gorbachev confirmed, as Powell recorded, that the Soviets 'did not want German reunification any more than Britain did. It was useful that the matter had been raised and that he and the Prime Minister knew each other's mind on this delicate subject.'

The Russians welcomed Mrs Thatcher's opinions, but with a characteristic reservation. As Chernyaev recorded, 'They want to prevent this with our hands.' This was probably unfair on Mrs Thatcher. She certainly did seek Soviet assistance in stopping or slowing reunification, but only as part of the broadest coalition she could assemble. Arguably, her behaviour was duplicitous. She ordered that the discussion of reunification not be shared with President Bush. She was, according to the historian of Germany and Eastern Europe, Timothy Garton Ash, being 'spectacularly disloyal to a very long-term, faithful, close ally [West Germany]'. This was not Mrs Thatcher's view. She saw real danger to the international order (including Gorbachev's continuation in power) in early reunification.

---

* At Mrs Thatcher's suggestion, no notes were taken of the German discussion but, relying on memory, Powell produced a separate, very tightly held record.
† This was Mitterrand.

Less than a fortnight after meeting Mrs Thatcher, Gorbachev visited East Germany, where he refused Honecker's pleas for military intervention to preserve the GDR. Ten days later, Honecker fell from power, to be replaced by the more 'moderate' Communist Egon Krenz. Later in October, 300,000 protesters took to the streets of Leipzig, demanding not just the right to travel to the West but fundamental democratic reform at home.

Mrs Thatcher's attitude caused consternation in the Foreign Office. In late September its head, Patrick Wright, complained in his diary of her 'Germanophobia ... any talk of German Reunification is anathema to her'. Rather than trying to discourage reunification, officials urged that Britain seek 'to exert influence over the speed and timing of any moves in that direction'. This view was swiftly taken up by Douglas Hurd after he replaced John Major as Foreign Secretary in October.

There was also tension with the Bush administration. In mid-September, Bush declared publicly that he saw nothing to fear in reunification. At the same time, his anxieties about Mrs Thatcher's attitude were conveyed. Robert Blackwill, a senior NSC staffer, confided in a British diplomat that 'President Bush is accustomed to, but uncomfortable with, the Prime Minister's dismissive references to the Germans ... Was there ... any way that the President could say to the Prime Minister "please don't cut yourself out of the game" without causing offense?'* This was the starkest US warning to date about Mrs Thatcher's attitude to Germany. On 24 October, at Kohl's request, Bush again weighed in publicly. 'I don't share the concern that some European countries have about a reunified Germany,' he told the *New York Times*, 'because I think Germany's commitment to and recognition of the importance of the alliance is unshakeable.' These words made it all but impossible for any NATO ally to oppose reunification in public.

Mrs Thatcher's attention, however, was elsewhere. Two days after Bush's comments she was forced to contend with the resignation of Nigel Lawson (see p. 751). At the same time, she confronted striking news elsewhere. On 27 October, a Soviet biochemist, Vladimir Pasechnik, sought refuge in the British Embassy in Paris. Percy Cradock briefed that he was 'the most serious senior scientist to defect to the West for at least 20 years' and claimed to be involved in a highly secret programme producing biological warfare agents 'which he suspected was in breach of the 1972 Biological

---

* The British diplomat Michael Alexander told Blackwill that the President should 'speak to her frankly and personally about his concern': to manage the German problem he should tell Mrs Thatcher to support stronger European cooperation.

Warfare Convention'. The suggestion that the Soviets might have illicitly acquired an extensive arsenal of biological weapons was deeply troubling. It also raised awkward questions for Mrs Thatcher's relationship with Gorbachev. 'Gorbachev can't know about this!' she exclaimed. When Cradock produced intelligence to the contrary she was 'furious', recalled Powell. 'She felt she had been deceived.' An intense study of Pasechnik's claims was put in train.

As the Thatcher/Bush gulf over reunification became ever clearer, her officials scrambled to obfuscate her position. At the Commonwealth conference in Kuala Lumpur in October, Patrick Wright covertly arranged for her blunt remarks on the German question to be removed from the record. It was axiomatic among Foreign Office ministers and officials that Mrs Thatcher was wrong and her views should not become known, much less acted upon. On 3 November, Wright recorded a call from Cradock 'confirming Christopher Mallaby's account of the PM's obsessions about the European Community and Germany. Percy commented that there are signs of her obsessions becoming policy.' There is unintentional Sir Humphreyish comedy in the outrage that the head of the British government should be able to affect its foreign policy.*

Mrs Thatcher felt supported, however, by word from Moscow. In a private message, Gorbachev referred explicitly to their conversation that September. He 'would like to emphasise, that new leadership of GDR adheres to the interests of stability of two German states'. He wished to encourage her to maintain the line against German reunification.

In the evening of 9 November 1989, Mrs Thatcher watched on television in Downing Street as huge crowds breached the Berlin Wall. As the extraordinary scenes unfolded, her first reaction, as Powell paraphrased it, was ' "This is wonderful, everything we ever dreamed of, and the people are doing it, not the government." Her second thought, only micro-seconds afterwards, was "My goodness! This is dangerous! We'd better be sure this doesn't get out of hand." '† As Wright recorded, 'She was apparently

---

* Mrs Thatcher was extremely conscious of this. One of the subjects she had raised with John Major at their first meeting after she had made him Foreign Secretary in July was the need for 'regular bilaterals with him and the closest possible working together, so that the FCO is an instrument for carrying out Government policy not FCO policy'. In his short time in the job, Major did not really oblige.
† One who watched the unfolding events in Germany with disgust was the young Vladimir Putin, a KGB officer in Dresden. This display of Soviet weakness appears to have convinced him that his country had been humiliated by the West. Mrs Thatcher feared such reactions, believing they might lead to the fall of Gorbachev.

appalled to see pictures of the Bundestag singing *Deutschland über Alles*, which she described as "a dagger in my heart".'

The next morning, at Hurd's urging, Mrs Thatcher stood outside Downing Street and proclaimed 'a great day for freedom'. But, when asked if she could live with a united Germany, she answered, 'I think you are going much too fast. The first thing is to get a proper, genuine democracy, a multi-party democracy, in East Germany.' That evening, when Kohl rang her from Berlin, she congratulated him and repeated this message. Kohl promised that his government 'would do everything possible to avoid anything provocative which could lead to conflicts or upheavals'. He would 'contact her immediately if there was anything dramatic'. According to Powell, she was 'enormously relieved and pleased'. Hard upon Kohl's call came a 10 p.m. visit from the Soviet Ambassador bearing a message from Gorbachev. This worried that 'emotions might run high, leading to demonstrations and calls for reunification. There seemed to be some in West Germany who were keen to whip up such feelings.' Mrs Thatcher felt able to squash this: 'The Prime Minister said there had not been the slightest evidence of this in her talk with Chancellor Kohl.'

In the ensuing days, Mrs Thatcher continued to stress the need 'to see genuine democracy' in East Germany. At Cabinet on 15 November, she declared that 'German reunification should not be treated as an immediate issue. Governments should take due account of the implications of the present turn of events for President Gorbachev's position.' Increasingly, the destabilization of Gorbachev became what Powell called 'her number one worry': it would be 'very selfish' of the Germans to put his goals for the freedom of Eastern Europe at risk. Some, like William Waldegrave, a Foreign Office minister, considered this a pretext: 'If it had been the Poles reunifying she would have seen off such timidity in no time. The truth is, she really didn't like the Germans, and nor did Denis.'* Waldegrave was surely right that, even without Gorbachev, Mrs Thatcher would have opposed reunification, but her anxiety for him was genuine.

Mrs Thatcher was reluctant to accept that Gorbachev might have an interest in the reunification of Germany. As her trusted informal adviser, Robert Conquest, put it to her, Gorbachev's 'new thinking' entailed withdrawal from the Soviet 'empire' in Eastern Europe. The Soviet leader 'sees no real possibility' of preventing reunification, he argued, so the fight now would be about whether such a Germany would be in NATO. Although she underlined Conquest's words repeatedly, she clung to the more convenient idea that the whole process would destabilize Gorbachev.

---

* Denis Thatcher did indeed express robust views about the Germans in private.

Mrs Thatcher's reply to Gorbachev's recent message agreed about the risks of instability and reiterated the allies' determination not to damage Soviet interests. This impressed Gorbachev, who declared: 'Our views are at one.' She copied her letter to Kohl. His right-hand foreign policy adviser, Horst Teltschik, noted that she ticked every West German wish for East German reform: 'The agreement with the Federal Chancellor on this point is impressive.'

At the time, agreement with the Americans seemed equally impressive. President Bush's public reaction to events in Berlin had been notably restrained.* On 13 November, Powell had advised Mrs Thatcher that 'The tide of opinion has begun to swing towards a more prudent assessment . . . The United States and Germany have come to share your prompt recognition of the danger . . . for Gorbachev.' Four days later, she and Bush discussed the German question on the phone. As Bush recalled in his memoirs, 'Margaret seemed to feel that it was time to pull in the reins on the subject. "After the East Germans started coming out, there was too much euphoria, too many efforts to try to see into a crystal ball," she said.' What went unmentioned in Bush's account is that he offered what seemed like unequivocal backing: 'The President said they were indeed very, very close: really eye to eye . . . he wholeheartedly agreed with the Prime Minister's approach.'

In reality, Bush agreed only about the need for a cautious line in public. According to the NSC's Condoleezza Rice, Bush's 'support for unification was unequivocal . . . Germany should unify as quickly as the Germans themselves desired, he told us.' Mrs Thatcher's failure to accept this left him exasperated. 'It's very emotional with her,' Bush said privately. 'It's hard to even focus because it's just so emotional.' As he told the present author, 'she had the history of Germany . . . more tenaciously in mind. I . . . felt that the time had come to move on.' This difference was masked from Mrs Thatcher, though she could probably have noticed it if she had wanted to.

Buoyed up by her illusory sense of agreement with Bush, Mrs Thatcher flew to Paris the following day, 18 November, for a special meeting of EC leaders. Kohl now hit back at her efforts to stymie thoughts of reunification out of concern for Gorbachev, reminding her that NATO had

---

* Like Mrs Thatcher, Bush was worried by the threat to Gorbachev, and mindful of the events in Tiananmen Square, Beijing, that summer, where student-led protests calling for greater freedom and accountability had been dispersed by the Chinese military with shocking brutality. Thousands had lost their lives. Bush did not wish to do anything that might encourage similar scenes in the streets of Berlin.

endorsed German reunification in 1970. As the historian Mary Elise Sarotte recorded: 'Thatcher, according to Kohl, snapped that this endorsement happened because nobody believed it would ever take place; Kohl responded that ... the NATO decision still stood. His reply angered Thatcher so much, he remembered, that she started stamping her feet in fury.'

Five days later, on 23 November, Mrs Thatcher visited Bush at Camp David. As the visit coincided with Anthony Meyer's leadership challenge, Powell advised that she needed a 'visible success'. She must make sure the President shared her underlying strategic assumptions – that 'Gorbachev needs to be supported' and that 'we want to avoid/postpone German reunification for as long as possible'. She should persuade Bush to avoid implying that the US supports 'European integration, as opposed to cooperation' (the former being damaging to America's own interests), but the most important thing was to get Bush to agree 'not to allow a tide of opinion to build up that defence is no longer necessary' because of the likely end of the Cold War.

Mrs Thatcher arrived in Washington with new cause to be irritated with Kohl. The German Chancellor had just told the European Parliament that he considered 'German and European unity as two sides to the same coin'. Worse, Jacques Delors had suggested that the coming European Council in Strasbourg should call an Intergovernmental Conference (IGC) to push forward EMU.

Bush arrived at Camp David well prepared. Brent Scowcroft's briefing offered a blunt expression of Mrs Thatcher's hostility to German reunification: she might seek Bush's support for reunification 'remaining a distant and hardly attainable goal'. Though she felt genuine concern for Gorbachev, she might 'use arguments about Moscow's fears to cloak her own'. The purpose of the meeting was not, however, to set Bush against her. Scowcroft urged he tap into her 'generally shrewd perspective on East–West relations' ahead of his imminent summit with Gorbachev in Malta. He also counselled Bush to question her attitudes to her European Community colleagues: 'We share her distaste for central control by bureaucrats in Brussels, but doubt she will achieve her goals by distancing herself from almost every potential ally on the continent.'

When Mrs Thatcher reached Washington she dined with the Ambassador, Antony Acland, Powell and Ingham. With Bush the next day, she told them, 'I'm going to say there's a real danger in a unified Germany.' Acland and Powell bridled: 'We said, "This won't go down at all well here. They think that the coming down of the Berlin Wall and the unification of Germany is the best thing that's happened in years. She said, "I don't care."' 'And then old Bernard Ingham, with his jowls wobbling, said, "All right, Prime Minister, if that's what you're going to say I'm going to go out and commit suicide," and he walked out of the room ... But then, when we took her up to bed, she said to me "Don't worry, Antony, I won't be as bad as that in the morning."'

At Camp David the next day, Bush started their talks by seeking her advice about his Malta meeting with Gorbachev. This allowed Mrs Thatcher to launch into her view of the West's approach to the Soviet Union and Eastern Europe. The 'first and overriding objective', she said, was 'genuine democracy', but this could not be established without 'a background of stability in which no country felt threatened'. She wanted to preserve both NATO and the Warsaw Pact. A united Germany would not only undermine Gorbachev but 'raise fears in Western Europe ... To have a country of 80 million people at the heart of the European Community would fundamentally change its nature.'

For Mrs Thatcher, the problem of borders applied also to the Baltic states: 'better to say nothing about it' at present, she told Bush. If the Baltics sought to secede, 'it would be cruel to raise false hopes' of Western help. Bush agreed, but felt they could not simply 'give Gorbachev *carte blanche*'. He would be 'troubled' if the West were to support the continuation of the Warsaw Pact: it could not keep countries in it against their will.

Asked about the European Community, Mrs Thatcher expressed her familiar concerns about a centralized, protectionist EC. She was 'a passionate European, but she wanted a free Europe and would fight for it'. Their only stated disagreement came over defence spending. As Bush confided in his diary, 'I couldn't find any change that would convince her that we've got to do less in the way of defense spending, a position I disagree with ... she is as rigid as can be.'

At the press conference afterwards, no difference between Bush and Mrs Thatcher about Germany emerged. She felt able to report to Gorbachev that the two had agreed about the priority of genuine democracy in Eastern Europe against a background of stability 'for all parties', preserving existing alliances and borders. She seemed unwilling to comprehend that 'genuine democracy' in the GDR would surely consign the country to oblivion and, with it, the Warsaw Pact.*

In reality, the Camp David visit had not been a great success. There

---

* Mrs Thatcher did not spot the difference between the German question and similar debates in Poland, Hungary and (with qualifications) Czechoslovakia. Those last three countries equated greater freedom with the recovered identity of their nation states from Soviet control. For the East Germans, however, their very country was an artificial creation of Soviet control. Their

was no repeat of her Reagan-era triumphs there. In her memoirs she noted that Bush 'seemed distracted and uneasy'. Bush, meanwhile, found Mrs Thatcher 'uptight. I think she's worried about what's happening at home,' he wrote in his diary. By this stage 'a sourness crept into their conversations', recalled the State Department's Raymond Seitz. What Bush considered her 'hectoring was really not very appreciated'. Bush liked to use humour to get on terms, but as Scowcroft recalled, he 'found Mrs Thatcher relatively humourless'. Years later, when asked about her sense of humour, Bush adopted a wry expression: 'I don't recall it being profound.' Bush felt constrained, unable to tell his sometimes risqué jokes in front of Mrs Thatcher – a woman, and an apparently starchy woman at that.

One might imagine Mrs Thatcher as a girl on a new date after many happy years with her previous boyfriend. Bush was an eligible man whom she respected, but she sensed they would never really click. He was not Ronnie, and he knew she knew it.

On 28 November, Helmut Kohl unveiled a 'Ten Point Plan' with the ultimate aim of German reunification. He gave no timescale, but the destination was clear. The following day the mass-circulation *Bild* newspaper printed the word 'Reunification' on its front page, in the colours of both the East and West German flags. Mrs Thatcher was now deeply worried. Kohl's public words seemed to conflict with private assurances received, not least his telephone call of 10 November. Unlike other leaders, she had been given no advance warning of the speech. The Germans felt emboldened to isolate her, explained Teltschik, because 'We knew the Foreign Office didn't agree with her. Geoffrey Howe had told Genscher this early in 1989.' She did not now publicly denounce Kohl, but neither did she support him. This was noticed. In Teltschik's view, 'She should have told Kohl, "It's difficult for Gorbachev. Be careful. But I will support you. Stay in close touch." But no gesture was given.'

Bush, on the other hand, called Kohl and welcomed the Ten Points. In return, Kohl outlined his complementary vision of a more united Europe: 'A week from now in Strasbourg [at the coming European Council], I will see to it that we make progress with respect to the Economic and Monetary Union. I think it is a great mistake on Maggie's part to think that this is a time for caution.'

On 2–3 December, Bush met Gorbachev in Malta. There the Soviet leader agreed not to block reunification, while Bush pledged not to speed

---

idea of national freedom naturally had a bigger expression – becoming part of a much greater historic Germany once again.

it up. Bush then headed to Brussels to report to NATO leaders. Dining with Kohl, he threw his weight behind the Chancellor's vision for a united Germany. Kohl tactfully described Britain as 'rather reticent' on the subject. 'That is the understatement of the year,' replied Bush. Thus encouraged, Kohl expanded: 'Thatcher says the European Parliament can have no power because Whitehall cannot yield a bit of sovereignty. Her ideas are simply pre-Churchill . . . She thinks history is not just. Germany is so rich and Great Britain is struggling. They won a war but lost an empire and their economy. She does the wrong thing. She should try to bind the Germans into the EC.'

At the summit, Bush not only backed reunification but followed Kohl's line on the European debate, calling for 'a continued, perhaps even intensified, effort of the [EC] 12 to integrate'. Kohl proposed that the meeting should signal support for Bush's approach and adjourn. The Italian Prime Minister, Giulio Andreotti, objected and Mrs Thatcher supported him, saying she 'wanted to study Bush's proposal more carefully'. But she was heavily outnumbered. 'I'm feeling a little strained with Margaret Thatcher,' Bush confided in his diary. She gave what Hurd described as 'an adequate press conference, but fails to stem stories yet again of isolation'. Flying home, she went to bed with a cold.*

Mrs Thatcher was indeed greatly strained by Bush's summit remarks. According to Wright, she left 'muttering that this was the thanks one gets for being a loyal ally'. What really upset her was his call for EC integration, so obviously at odds with her own position, which dominated the British press.

Bush's comments had come the day before Tory MPs were due to vote on Meyer's leadership challenge, thus aggravating their impact. After Powell made Mrs Thatcher's dismay known to the Americans, Bush quickly reassured her on the telephone that he had been referring only to EC economic, not political, integration: 'she was very relieved', he wrote in his diary. But she doubted whether his remarks meant what he told her: 'I hoped they did – or that at least from now on they would.'

In the White House there was a post-mortem. The episode, Scowcroft told Bush, was a warning of how 'the bitter debate between Thatcher's and Delors' visions of Europe can affect our own policy objectives'. 'It would

---

* At this time, Mrs Thatcher's state of health was attracting attention from some inside the government machine. On 20 December, Patrick Wright recorded: 'Percy Cradock spoke to me very privately today about Margaret Thatcher's health and mood; he suspects that she is taking pills or vitamins for her perpetual colds . . . and combining this with occasional drinks. He is finding her much less lucid than usual.'

be best all round,' said Scowcroft's memo, 'if Mrs Thatcher took a more constructive attitude toward the EC': she would ultimately achieve more if 'she changes her tone and tactics, so that Helmut Kohl will not continue to refer to her as "that woman"'.

This was the orthodoxy of the policy elites but, as was often the case with orthodoxies, Mrs Thatcher could not accept it. The idea that European 'integration', with its requisite loss of national sovereignty, would be accomplished with American help because the West was winning the Cold War was her nightmare. On the world stage, she now confronted an unpleasant choice: would she stick to her beliefs and face isolation or abandon them and join the consensus?

On 8 December, Powell informed Hurd's office that Mrs Thatcher wanted 'to try to assert a greater degree of Allied influence over the actions of the West German government and to reassure the Russians that we are doing so'. Bush had recently scotched the idea, which Mrs Thatcher favoured, of a meeting of the Four Powers to discuss German issues. But she was not willing to give up her search for leverage. As Powell wrote, 'We do not want to wake up one morning and find that events have moved entirely beyond our control and that German reunification is to all intents and purposes on us.'*

Mrs Thatcher was not alone. As Scowcroft recalled, 'nobody supported German reunification except Kohl and Bush. The French were opposed. Mrs Thatcher was opposed. Gorbachev was opposed.' The United States worried 'they would all get together and prevent it happening and that would be a catastrophe'.

On the day of Powell's message, Mrs Thatcher flew to Strasbourg for the latest European Council. Over dinner, she later recalled, Kohl 'was just a bulldozer'. He protested that Germany had paid for the last war by losing a third of its territory: 'A German must be able to speak of reunification.' Kohl feared not a united Germany but a neutral one. He wanted a Germany 'anchored in the EC and NATO'. According to Kohl, Mrs Thatcher exclaimed, 'Twice we've beaten the Germans! And now they're here again!' 'I will never forget her remarks,' he said.† Kohl now lost interest in bringing Mrs Thatcher with him. 'Forget about her,' he told Teltschik.

Despite her private objections, Mrs Thatcher understood the weakness

---

* In a probably vain attempt to reassure Mrs Thatcher about Foreign Office tactics towards the Germans, Stephen Wall, Hurd's private secretary, replied to Powell that the idea was to surround them with 'activity which we would present as assiduous "help and support . . ." We should, so to speak, smother them with diplomacy.' 'How very unpleasant!' wrote Powell.

† Her scribble on her Council briefing about EC 'Social Issues' expressed some of her irritation: 'More Communists in Western Europe than in Eastern Europe at the moment.'

of her position. In this spirit, she agreed a communiqué which spoke about self-determination within existing treaties and international agreements and the 'perspective of European integration'. Kohl's plan to bind a united Germany into an integrated Europe was gathering steam.

At the summit, Wright had noted Mrs Thatcher's 'remarkably good humour'. One reason – in addition to prudence – for Mrs Thatcher's public equanimity may have been her private meeting in Strasbourg with Mitterrand. The French President had poured out what she took for his heart: 'He was very worried about Germany. Gorbachev had spoken to him very harshly on the subject and the time had come for action.' Mrs Thatcher responded enthusiastically: 'If we were not careful, reunification would just come about ...' The two agreed they must use the Four Powers 'to stop this happening'.*

'Mitterrand was even more alarmist than she was,' Powell recalled. 'They got together like two old ladies.' Mitterrand said he was 'fearful that he and the Prime Minister would find themselves in the situation of their predecessors in the 1930s who had failed to react in the face of constant pressure by the Germans ... At moments of great danger ... France had always established special relations with Britain. He felt that such a time had come again. We must draw together and stay in touch.'†

Mrs Thatcher chose to take Mitterrand's fears about Germany at face value, although aware that Mitterrand was saying something different to Kohl. But Powell felt she was right to do so. Mitterrand, he recalled, 'was shit-scared ... He wanted her support and thought that perhaps they could prevail.' Certainly, Mitterrand's comments encouraged her resistance to reunification. When, on 19 December, she met the Soviet Foreign Minister, Eduard Shevardnadze, she assured him she knew of Gorbachev's worries about it. Yes, said Shevardnadze eagerly. The Soviet Union had 'grave anxieties'. Nonetheless, he told her that if the GDR 'suddenly voted for reunification' it was 'unthinkable' that Soviet forces 'would shoot'. The logical next question, which Mrs Thatcher seems not to have asked herself, was that if the Soviets were not willing to use force, what power could prevent reunification if the people willed it?

By this stage, relations between Mrs Thatcher and senior Foreign Office officials were uneasy. In early January 1990, for example, Christopher

---

* Her hopes that the Four Power framework might help block reunification came to naught. Although the Soviets called for such a meeting, the Bush administration insisting on downgrading it to ambassadorial level with a strictly curtailed agenda.
† In one remark, unrecorded by Powell, which Mrs Thatcher vividly recalled, 'Mitterrand told me that ... Kohl will achieve what neither Bismarck nor Hitler could achieve.'

Mallaby aroused her ire by reporting from Bonn the candid impression that 'the UK is perceived here as perhaps the least positive of the three Western Allies and the least important'. The telegram so annoyed her that Powell told the Foreign Office: 'She thought it showed a lack of understanding of our policy which she finds alarming.' With a seminar at Chequers on the German question arranged for the end of the month, the Foreign Office debated how to 'manage' the Prime Minister. William Waldegrave wanted to present 'the stark truth about what is likely to happen . . . I thought we could have gone into bat and said, look, you're getting this really, really wrong.' His boss, Hurd, however, favoured caution. 'I don't think I needed to be dramatic,' he recalled. '. . . The tide was running against her and she knew that.'

From his pro-Thatcher point of view, Powell was as irritated as Waldegrave by the timorous negativity. 'I have been impressed (or rather depressed) again this year by how slow off the mark the FCO often are in following up good ideas, let alone having any,' he wrote to Mrs Thatcher. While she was often very difficult for the Foreign Office to deal with, Powell was right that boldness in foreign policy had much more often come from Downing Street than from King Charles Street.

The day after the memo rebuking Mallaby, Mrs Thatcher met Hurd. 'Works up into a rage', Hurd wrote in his diary, '. . . against German selfishness in interesting themselves solely in unity. Will be 1913 again, she said.' Her suggestion now was that policy should spell out certain conditions to be met before Britain could support German unity.* Hurd accepted this, but plucked up the courage to say that 'What we could not produce was a blue print for stopping German reunification.' Mrs Thatcher assented but told him not to approach the question 'in the spirit that reunification was inevitable'.

In fact, reunification now looked not only likely but imminent. Worse, perhaps, for her was the ever-growing sense that reunification must be secured by deeper European integration. In early January, she learnt that James Baker had warned Antony Acland that to retain its central role in East–West relations, Britain must 'find some way of working more effectively than at present with the Germans . . . especially in the EC context'. The Americans wished 'where practicable to regard the Community rather than any individual member of it as their principal partner in Europe'. 'This is a very worrying telegram,' Powell told Mrs Thatcher. She considered it

---

* These familiar stipulations included the establishment of freedom, the rule of law and democracy 'throughout Eastern Europe' and support for reunification only after understanding the implications for NATO, the GDR's relationship with the European Community, 'the wider application of the principle of self-determination' and the consequences for Gorbachev.

'very muddled thinking on the part of the Americans', he informed Hurd's office. The government must show Washington how this approach would damage its own interests: 'We clearly face a major task.'

On 20 January, Mrs Thatcher flew to Paris for another meeting with Mitterrand with almost amorous allure. As Powell put it to Mitterrand's aide, Jacques Attali, just before Christmas, 'I said the Prime Minister would be ready to slip across to Paris for a few hours . . .' Before she did so, however, he warned her against seduction. Although, 'face to face with the German Frankenstein', the British and French 'ought to jump into each other's arms', the chances of a successful partnership were slim. Whatever Mitterrand might say, the French were publicly encouraging reunification. Far more important than 'sidling up to the French' was building 'closer cooperation with the Americans'.

Mrs Thatcher was still inclined to sidle. When they met, Mitterrand excited her with dark thoughts: the 'sudden prospect of reunification', he suggested, had turned the Germans 'once again into the "bad" Germans they used to be. They were behaving with a certain brutality and concentrating on reunification to the exclusion of everything else . . .' This, however, proved to be the prelude to a volte-face. 'In reality there was no force in Europe that could stop' reunification, Mitterrand declared, so 'it would be stupid to say no'. In Powell's view, 'He had egged her on only, in characteristic French fashion, to abandon her.' Mitterrand was much closer to Kohl than to Mrs Thatcher, and Germany, for obvious reasons, mattered more to France than Britain. As his foreign policy adviser, Hubert Védrine, recalled, while Mitterrand agreed about the dangers of reunification he saw no 'point in stopping it. He thus went along with it and exacted certain conditions from Kohl.' One was EMU, to which Mrs Thatcher was even more opposed than German reunification.

Six days after Mrs Thatcher saw Mitterrand, her frustration burst forth in print. In the *Wall Street Journal* she protested against reunification at speed, which 'could destabilise everything' and prove 'bitterly unfair' to Gorbachev. She urged Germany's leaders to 'put this longer view of Europe's needs before their more narrow, nationalistic goals'. These words, the Germans told the Foreign Office, 'caused "unheimlich viel Weh" (enormously great pain) in the Chancellor's Office'. Mrs Thatcher probably did not realize that in Germany, 'nationalism' usually refers specifically to the Nazi era.

By this time, her isolation on German reunification was almost complete. Powell analysed it thus: 'First, like most others she was caught out by the sheer speed of events . . . Second, others adjusted to the situation more rapidly . . . by a conscious decision to accept the inevitability and desirability of unification.' The third reason was more specific to Mrs Thatcher: her isolation was 'the downside of being an Iron Lady. It made retreat difficult.'

Powell might have added that her arguments, ably reinforced by him, had much to commend them. On 21 January, in preparation for the Chequers seminar, he sent her his own views. In a passage she underlined heavily in approval, Powell wrote that, having won the Cold War, 'we shall find the next decade altogether more complex, with a multiplicity of dangers and threats'. Powell was arguing explicitly against Francis Fukuyama's 'End of History' thesis, which had hailed liberal democracy as a final form of government of all nations. Powell wrote presciently that the next decade would 'mark the return of history'. In the 1990s, the West would once again be 'confronting nationalism', made stronger by having been suppressed for so long by Communism. It would also, he predicted, be 'fuelled by Islam'. He argued that the Soviets should withdraw from Eastern Europe, but US and British forces should stay. Better than trying to prevent German reunification, Powell suggested, would be the 'containment' of a united Germany. Britain should engage the newly liberated Eastern European countries to 'pull the Eastern European blanket to our side of the bed' and thus dilute German influence.

This view of the dangers was far-sighted. It both reflected – and influenced – Mrs Thatcher's thinking. It showed an understanding of the realities of power when an empire dies.

The Chequers seminar on 27 January, which brought together ministers and officials to debate the German question, represented a success for the Foreign Office. Despite the urgings of Waldegrave, the Foreign Office 'didn't go in to bat' with great vigour. By his own, possibly unreliable account, the only person who stood up to Mrs Thatcher was the maverick junior defence minister, Alan Clark:

> I argued cogently for accepting, and exploiting, German reunification while they still needed our support.
> No good. She is determined not to . . .
> During the coffee-break I cornered her.
> 'These are just a re-run of the old Appeasement arguments of 1938.'
> 'Yes,' she said, eyes flashing (she's in incredible form at the moment), 'and I'm not an appeaser.'

The conclusions of the seminar were that Britain should aim to slow down reunification, but only for a 'transition' period, not as a covert attempt to prevent the process. With the word 'transition' the Foreign Office won Mrs Thatcher's acquiescence in reunification.

Early that Saturday afternoon, with the seminar in progress, Bush telephoned to say he wanted to reduce US troops in Europe from the existing 275,000 to 195,000. His argument that they should pre-empt the changes under way in Eastern Europe left her unconvinced: 'It looks like we're being hustled.' Hurd watched as she took the call 'looking out over grey rainy rose gardens ... bracelet occasionally striking against the desk as she scribbles, receiving, questioning and not welcoming the news ... Feel sorry for her, a "rout" she says.'

On 29 January, Hurd visited Washington. At this stage, recalled Philip Zelikow, the Foreign Office 'increasingly makes it clear to us that we are not the problem. The Prime Minister is the problem.' Hurd drew closer to James Baker. 'He was clear about the fact that his boss wasn't on the same page,' Baker remembered. Meeting Bush, Hurd explained that Mrs Thatcher was 'reluctant to endorse unification, a reluctant unifier. Not against, but reluctant. She sees things that need to be sorted out. Will Germany be part of NATO or not? Will East Germany be in the EC? What about Russian sensitivities? We need a framework in which these issues can be discussed.'

The next day, Powell reported to Mrs Thatcher that the Americans also sought a framework and agreed 'on the need for a period of transition before unification', words she underlined approvingly. In these two ideas the British government now had a policy around which they could publicly unite.

That same day, Gorbachev announced that the Soviet Union now recognized that the reunification of Germany would take place. In retirement Mrs Thatcher recalled, 'This is one thing I really think Gorbachev got very wrong. If he was going to sell the reunification of Germany ... He sold it much too cheap.' She now had little choice but to accept Hurd's sobriquet– the 'reluctant unifier'.

Back home, Hurd sought to press his advantage. On 2 February, ahead of a speech in Bonn, he told Mrs Thatcher he wanted to talk about reunification in a friendly way in order not to 'weaken our influence in the transition'. 'If you agree,' he continued, 'I would like to have a short tête à tête with Kohl, giving him a message from you – to the effect that you think it crucially important ... that the CDU should win in the autumn, [and] will do whatever you can to help ...' 'Yes,' she wrote, '– we must get things agreed between the 5 US/USSR/UK/France and FRG – to present to the wider NATO–Helsinki nations.'

The chief, unstated purpose of Hurd's visit was to right the Anglo–German relationship. In Hurd's view, 'we were quite near danger' that she might 'upset the applecart between us and Germany'. He also wanted to hint to the Germans not to equate British policy with Mrs Thatcher's views. In Bonn, after expressing his indignation at Mrs Thatcher's *Wall Street Journal* article, Kohl asked if Hurd could be his future political contact. Reporting to Mrs Thatcher, Powell called this 'far from satisfactory'. Kohl 'appears to want to deal with someone other than you. We can't allow that: he must take his medicine like a man. Only you will tell him what we really think.' She agreed. Powell told Hurd that she was 'in principle ready to meet' Kohl herself but, given his recent comments, 'doubted whether he would relish a meeting'.

On 5 February, Mallaby relayed that, fearing the imminent collapse of East Germany, the FRG was seeking the immediate economic and monetary union of the two Germanies. 'This is it,' Powell warned Mrs Thatcher, 'the Germans are going full tilt for reunification, without waiting for anyone.' 'I think we should have another Berlin 4 meeting,' she wrote, desperately seeking a framework to restrain the rush for German unity. 'Cabinet now consists of three items,' Hurd told Patrick Wright, 'parliamentary affairs; home affairs; and xenophobia.'

On 9 February, Powell flew to Bonn to assess the situation for himself. He told Mrs Thatcher he encountered a 'heady atmosphere': 'For the Germans, this is the breakthrough. After decades of sober and cautious diplomacy . . . they are in the driving seat and Toad is at the wheel . . . The Germans' moment has come: they are going to settle their destiny.'

In retrospect, Powell conceded, his talk of Toad 'might seem a little insulting', but its purpose was to convey the atmosphere 'in a way which someone like Mrs Thatcher would have understood'.* He was right. Below the mention of Toad she wrote: 'Nationalism, n'est-ce pas?' Powell told her he had warned Teltschik of Britain's fears that the 'economic might' of a united Germany 'could come to dominate Europe'. Teltschik had responded that the FRG was 'simply reacting to an ever-worsening crisis in East Germany'. The truth was that no one knew what would happen after the GDR elections on 18 March and 'No-one could control what might happen.' In the margin Mrs Thatcher wrote crossly, 'No study of its implications or its possible effect on others.'

Much depended on Kohl's forthcoming meeting with Gorbachev in

---

* In referring to Toad, Powell was likening Helmut Kohl to Kenneth Grahame's fat, brash anti-hero Mr Toad of Toad Hall, in his novel *The Wind in the Willows*. Toad is, among other things, a noisy and domineering motorist.

Moscow. Although he emphasized Kohl's total commitment to NATO, Teltschik told Powell that 'If the Russians were to make a nuclear-free Germany a major issue, he doubted whether any German government could resist.' 'This', Powell told Mrs Thatcher, 'is a most worrying signal ... unification is the only subject which matters.'*

Despite all the jitters, the allies – and even the Soviet Union – were moving towards agreement. The idea was that reunification would be overseen by a framework of the Four Powers plus the two Germanies. Its American progenitors called this the '2+4', which implied that the two Germanies were in the driving seat. For Mrs Thatcher, however, it was the '4+2', with the Four Powers taking the lead.†

In London on 9 February, she received Hurd's proposal that British policy should seek to keep a united Germany in NATO. She accepted this, but worried about Soviet sensitivities over Germany's eastern border: 'who defends?' she wrote. 'Or do Germans pour over that and have the Berlin argument over again[?]' Powell told Hurd that taking account of Gorbachev's position might require Soviet forces to remain in the GDR for 'a substantial transition period': 'To put it bluntly, we have to bear in mind – although not say – that we might one day need the Soviet Union as a counter-balance to a united Germany.'

This message was in part superseded by events in Moscow. Hosting Kohl, Gorbachev agreed that the Germans alone would decide whether to unify and accepted the American conception of the '2+4'. Two days later (12 February), Braithwaite found Mrs Thatcher 'appalled by the speed of events'. She railed against 'the "wetness" of James Baker, whom she deeply distrusts. Bush, she thinks, is showing more backbone. Even Gorbachev, she fears, is wavering ... We need a settlement which makes it clear that the Germans are still not fully trusted.' Toad, to use Charles Powell's formulation, was driving the car too fast. At the Open Skies conference‡ in

---

* Horst Teltschik took exception to Powell's version of their meeting: 'His record gave an account of how tough he had been. Actually, he said to me, "Don't forget Margaret Thatcher belongs to another generation."' His impression was that Powell had tried to distance himself from her views when they met and had then given Mrs Thatcher a different version of their encounter.

† Gorbachev, like all others who feared reunification, shared this view. On 8 February, he accepted Baker's suggestion of a six-power framework but put the 4 first. It was, Chernyaev later told Braithwaite, 'an arithmetic which he and Gorbachev preferred'.

‡ The formal purpose of this conference was to discuss a long-standing US initiative, resurrected by President Bush, that would allow the USA and its allies to conduct surveillance flights over Soviet and Warsaw Pact territory and vice versa.

Ottawa from 11 to 13 February, the plans for the '2+4'/'4+2' were settled. The fact of reunification was now broadly accepted.

Like all successful agreements, the one made at Ottawa was open to different interpretations. For the Germans, it calmed their critics. For the Soviets, it was burden-sharing of the dangers ahead. For the United States, it was almost exactly the opposite of what Mrs Thatcher envisaged. As Condoleezza Rice recalled, it 'made certain that our allies could not slow down unification'. The trick was 'Give the US, Soviet Union, France, Britain nothing to do but sign away their Four Power rights and responsibilities, determine the status of Berlin and determine the Polish border. Nothing more.'

For some time, Powell had felt that Mrs Thatcher (who always disliked the telephone) had been too reluctant to initiate conversations with President Bush. 'I think we have to be careful not to appear stand-offish,' he warned her. With her agreement, he set up a call to Camp David for 24 February, hours before the President would meet Kohl there. Before she and Bush spoke, Powell pointedly reminded her that Kohl had been 'admirably robust' over Germany's membership of NATO. 'You continue to attach the highest priority to helping Chancellor Kohl's re-election,' Powell added, lest she forget.

When they spoke, Bush and Mrs Thatcher soon disagreed over the '4+2', which she told him 'must deal with the big issues'. These were the Polish border, the relationship between Germany and NATO and the balance of power in Europe. When she reported Polish anxieties that a united Germany might seek to reclaim territory yielded to Poland after the Second World War (thus breaching the agreed post-war border known as the Oder–Neisse line), Bush was unreceptive. 'Surely everyone was agreed that the Polish borders were permanent and inviolable,' he said. 'This was guaranteed by the Helsinki Accord.' Pointing out that 'Helsinki was not a treaty', Mrs Thatcher urged him to raise the need for something legally binding with Kohl.*

On Germany and NATO, they started much closer together. Bush sought a statement from Kohl supporting 'full membership of NATO for a united Germany. This is very, very important.' She agreed, but added a

---

* This point about Helsinki reflected a recent anxiety of Mrs Thatcher's. The Foreign Office, attempting to squash the view, which Gorbachev had urged upon her, that under Helsinki the consent of the thirty-five-nation CSCE was required for German reunification, had warned her that Helsinki was not a treaty and its Final Act was 'not legally binding'. 'Does the Foreign Office therefore say that it is not morally binding,' she had asked angrily, 'and that any frontier can be changed easily and without reference to any other state? If so we need a PEACE TREATY SOON.'

plea to consider Gorbachev who, she feared, 'will feel isolated if all the reunification process goes the West's way'. She argued that NATO should not deploy non-German forces in the former GDR and Soviet troops should remain even after unification for a transitional period.

Bush was having none of it. 'I'm not comfortable with Soviet troops staying there,' he told her. Their disagreement boiled down to their clashing views on Germany. Bush recalled that Mrs Thatcher's fears 'came ringing through … Germany is in the heart of a continent of countries, most of which she has attacked and occupied. Germany has colossal wealth and trade surpluses. So we must include a bigger country, the Soviet Union [or] you, in the political area.' Bush was troubled. As he wrote in his diary: 'There is a certain insult to the Germans suggesting that they will give up democracy and give way to some new Hitler once they're unified.'

By the time he wrote the words above, Bush had also spoken to Kohl. 'I can't understand her,' Kohl said of Mrs Thatcher. 'The Empire declined fighting Germany – she thinks the UK paid this enormous price, and here comes Germany again.' Bush told Kohl he did not share this view: 'We don't fear the ghosts of the past; Margaret does.' Nonetheless, they 'must bend over backwards to consult'. Bush stressed that Mrs Thatcher was worried about the uncertainties of reunification. 'When you say Germany will be staying in NATO with full membership that helps.' The two men agreed that US forces would remain in Germany, but all Soviet troops would leave after a limited transition period. Only on the Polish border did Bush feel disappointed. For electoral reasons, Kohl did not wish to make public his private assurance that the border would not be altered.*

There was an aftermath to all this which caused anxiety in London. On 26 February, Andrew Wood, Minister in the British Embassy, reported an approach from the ever-loquacious Bob Blackwill of the NSC staff. Bush, Blackwill told him, had been 'puzzled and concerned' by what he had taken as Mrs Thatcher's wish for a demilitarized GDR and a European system 'containing' Germany, which would include the Russians. The Americans seemed to be getting the idea, Wood continued, that 'we [the British] may be beginning seriously to dust off memories of the war-time coalition [of the US, the Soviet Union and Britain]'. Blackwill added that 'the Americans had been struck once again by how very bad the Anglo-German relationship now was'. He, Blackwill, 'found it painful to see us dealing ourselves out of the game'.

---

* Kohl's CDU was leading a coalition called the Alliance for Germany, contesting the first free elections in the GDR, to be held on 18 March. With the SPD expected to come out on top, Kohl was reluctant to do anything which might hurt the feelings of East German voters.

Powell told Mrs Thatcher the 'alarming' reporting in Wood's telegram reflected 'the President's own lack of understanding'. He urged that when she next speak to Bush, she explain her points 'in very simple language and repeat them'. Powell also asked the Foreign Office to tell Blackwill that Downing Street was 'flabbergasted'* by his impression that Mrs Thatcher was proposing a new alliance with Russia. She remained a staunch supporter of NATO. Her broader point was that, in the long term, the Soviet Union was the only European country which could balance the power of Germany.

As for the Germans, Powell admitted that 'We do have a problem and need to sort it out before and at the Anglo-German Summit [at the end of March].' He ended with a flourish: 'If Wood cares to add that Blackwill's innuendo . . . that No. 10 is inhabited by a combination of Dr Strangelove and General Curtis B. LeMay,† in contrast to the cool, rational thinkers of the FCO and the NSC, has been greeted with some surprise in view of the Prime Minister's consistent and successful record of managing East/West relations over the last eleven years, that would be fine with me.'

While Blackwill may have been exceptionally blunt, British officials understood he represented a genuine concern: Bush was more alarmed by Mrs Thatcher's attitude than he was letting on. She and her advisers felt a tinge of fear that she might be putting herself beyond the Washington pale.

Mrs Thatcher's balance-of-power approach confused the Americans. As Robert Zoellick explained, it would have been 'a very foreign argument to us. The idea that we would have to rely on *the Soviets* to balance our ally Germany? Our strategy was to embrace Germany!' Mrs Thatcher, however, was trying to turn the Soviet Union into a co-worker for European peace. Bush did not realize how much her approach to the Soviet Union had altered because of her support for Gorbachev's reforms.‡ There was misunderstanding on both sides. His thought process was not speculative and he found her deliberately challenging manner off-putting.

In her memoirs, Mrs Thatcher wrote that Bush had 'failed to understand that I was discussing a long-term balance of power in Europe rather than proposing an alternative alliance to NATO'. But the truth may not have

---

* Andrew Wood recalled that Powell's word 'flabbergasted' was reported to him. 'I decided not to pass it on to Blackwill.'

† Curtis E. LeMay, former Commander of the US Strategic Air Command (1948–57) and Chief of Staff of the US Air Force (1961–5), was famous for saying, during the Vietnam War, that 'We should bomb them [the North Vietnamese] back into the Stone Age,' though he denied it, asserting that he had said only that the United States had the capacity to do this.

‡ Nor was Bush as concerned as Mrs Thatcher with the link between threats to Gorbachev and the end of the division of Germany. This would prove a factor in Gorbachev's eventual loss of power.

been quite so simple. When Powell noted that Bush 'could not conceive how you could think of the Russians as possible allies against Germany', Mrs Thatcher scribbled the words '1941–45' – the period of the Soviet alliance with Britain and the United States against Hitler. Perhaps she really did dream that something comparable should again be constructed to hold down German power.

On 6 March, Helmut Kohl at last announced his agreement to a fixed Polish–German border, guaranteed by treaty.* Delighted, Mrs Thatcher congratulated him on these 'most statesmanlike steps'. In the GDR elections of 18 March, Kohl's alliance won 48 per cent of the vote, held the SPD to a mere 22 per cent and pushed the Communists lower still. Although this was a mandate for swift reunification, Mrs Thatcher was, in Powell's words, 'rather chuffed . . . it showed that people without a voice in Europe had moved to the Right'. The result also made it likelier that a united Germany would be a member of NATO. At Powell's prompting, she wrote at once to Kohl, hailing a 'great day for the people of Germany and for Europe', a message that Teltschik reported 'had been brilliantly effective in improving relations'.

At Mrs Thatcher's request, another seminar on Germany had been arranged for 24 March at Chequers. Powell, whose idea it was, sought to remedy the fact that 'she'd got herself hopelessly out on a limb on Germany . . . We needed to try to get her more back into line.' She would not accept this from the Foreign Office, so the seminar must draw on outside experts. In a memo, Powell suggested they might address historical lessons about the 'character and behaviour of the German-speaking people', and whether the Germans had changed in the last forty years ('or 80, or 150', added Mrs Thatcher). 'Or are we really dealing with the same old Huns?'

On Powell's paper, Mrs Thatcher set out at unusual length what was in her head:

> I want to use our experience of the past to help us shape the future. But not to be dominated by the past . . . We have to build a new framework for the future – for defence, for co-operation beyond Europe and try to see how we can bring the Soviet Union to a real western democracy with economic as

---

* Some disagreement quickly emerged over whether, now that the makeshift division of Germany agreed in 1945 was coming to an end, a broader 'peace treaty' was necessary. Britain did not want a full peace treaty – not least because that would have to involve all the fifty-seven belligerents – but, as Hurd put it, 'an overall settlement of some sort is needed'.

well as political freedom. We <u>must</u> consider Central Europe and its minorities, and how our security could be upset from the Middle East.

At the bottom she added:

> We must <u>widen</u> the discussion to include the future of the USSR – (and of Russia) and whether we pursue spheres of influence, or <u>alliance</u> <u>of</u> <u>democracy</u> or geographical alliances . . . We must . . . consider some of the old <u>balance</u> <u>of power</u>. But it seems to me that while in the past, history was determined largely by the personalities and ambitions of the <u>rulers</u> of the people, in future it will be decided much more by the <u>character</u> of the people. However, the lesson of the past two years is that neither character nor pride has been suffocated by oppression.

She was searching for the full context for the changes happening right across Central and Eastern Europe.

Of the six experts who arrived at Chequers on Saturday 24 March, only Professor Norman Stone could be described as Thatcherite. The others were Professor Gordon Craig; Professor Fritz Stern, a notable liberal; the historian Hugh Trevor-Roper; George Urban and Timothy Garton Ash, the journalist whose criticisms of Mrs Thatcher's attitude towards the EC were well known. Mrs Thatcher did not harangue them. 'She appeared', George Urban wrote, 'to be genuinely anxious to find out what all these "distinguished" observers and historians had to tell her.'

As Powell recorded, the seminar began with a discussion of German character:

> Like other nations, they had certain characteristics . . . It was easier – and more pertinent to the present discussion – to think of the less happy ones: their insensitivity to the feelings of others (most noticeable in their behaviour over the Polish border), their obsession with themselves, a strong inclination to self-pity, and a longing to be liked. Some even less flattering attributes were also mentioned as an abiding part of the German character: in alphabetical order, <u>angst</u>, aggressiveness, assertiveness, bullying, egotism, inferiority complex, sentimentality.

But had the Germans changed? Powell noted 'a strong school of thought . . . that today's Germans were very different from their predecessors . . . We should have no real worries about them.' This summary approach hid the fact that Mrs Thatcher was heavily outnumbered. Douglas Hurd noted in his diary, 'They, none of them, share her extravagant suspicions of Germany, but this just makes her flail about more.'

Garton Ash recalled 'a crucial moment when Hugh Trevor-Roper (exactly the kind of man ... that she would respect and listen to) said words to the effect that "I was in Germany in 1945, and if you had told us then that we could have a united Germany as part of the West, we would not have believed our luck." I believe that really struck home.' Powell's record echoed this, in part, noting that the West had now won the democratic united Germany it had sought in 1945: 'Far from being agitated, we ought to be pleased ... The overall message was unmistakable: we should be nice to the Germans.'*

While there is every reason to think that Mrs Thatcher accepted this, the positive intentions of the Chequers seminar were dashed almost immediately. Two days before the seminar, Mrs Thatcher had given an interview to *Der Spiegel*, which appeared in print shortly after it. She cast doubt on Kohl's promise to guarantee the Polish border, which she had earlier welcomed. 'You know what happened to the previous assurances,' she told *Der Spiegel*; '... I heard Helmut say: "No! I will not guarantee the present borders ...". I heard him say that at Strasbourg after dinner.'

This, naturally, infuriated the Germans. The interview overshadowed Kohl's visit to Britain days later for a joint appearance with Mrs Thatcher at the Königswinter conference in Cambridge. During dinner at St Catharine's College, the two 'barely exchanged a word', but when it came to the speeches she was generous in her praise of 'Helmut'. She went so far as to 'underline that Britain, at least as much as other countries, has been instrumental in creating the conditions in which German unity could be achieved in freedom'. Kohl was pleased. The following day, at a joint press conference, he declared: 'Margaret is a wonderful woman,' recorded a rather stunned Horst Teltschik. Asked about the Polish–German border, Mrs Thatcher recalled that she had congratulated Kohl for his promise of a treaty 'before he came here and I congratulate him upon it now'. Then she asked Kohl if he had anything to add. 'No,' he replied, 'that was a perfect answer.'

On 13 April, Mrs Thatcher travelled to Bermuda to see President Bush. Baker warned the President that she would arrive 'with greater political

---

* While Mrs Thatcher now received almost unanimous advice against stigmatizing Germany, one exception was President Mitterrand. When she entertained him in May, he warned that the Germans were 'very vulnerable to demagoguery' and might turn against NATO membership as they united. Mrs Thatcher opined that the Germans 'were displaying increasing arrogance', leading Mitterrand to share his worry that Kohl had 'hesitated' over the Oder–Neisse line: 'In *Mein Kampf*, Hitler had regarded war with Britain and France as undesirable: it was to the East that the Germans had traditionally sought lebensraum.' Mitterrand admitted that 'The Germans were democratic these days ... but there seemed to be something in the genetic structure of the Germans which made them a danger.' Such Mitterrand–Thatcher conversations produced nothing of substance and are perhaps best seen as mutual therapy.

liabilities than at any other time during her 11 years in office'. The British, advised Henry Catto, the US Ambassador, wanted the meeting 'to counteract incessant press stories here that the Americans no longer care very much about Britain or Maggie Thatcher'. Having no wish for a Labour government, the administration was anxious to oblige. As Brent Scowcroft briefed the President: 'Under Mrs Thatcher's leadership Britain is the only major European power that is unequivocally and reliably pledged to the achievement of the security objectives we consider to be so essential.' On Air Force One, en route to Bermuda, Bush turned to an aide and said: 'I don't know why I'm going through the briefing book, because Margaret will do all of the talking.'

Preparing Mrs Thatcher, Powell warned that the State Department had been briefing against the UK: 'It is a mixture of spite: a feeling that the Brits had it too good under President Reagan: that your experience and prestige threatened to put Bush in the shade: and an almost hysterical obsession with getting Germany "right".' The Americans, Powell added, would 'react badly to anything which they regard as anti-German'. Powell then offered astute advice about Bush-handling: 'The mood and style of the meeting will be important,' he wrote. 'The President likes informality. He does not have your grasp of substance . . . nor is he a good debater. You need to be careful not to dominate him or get too much into the detail . . .' 'Even if we have to swallow hard sometimes,' he wrote, 'nothing is more important to us than the US.'

In Bermuda, the talks began well. Bush, with James Baker in attendance, insisted he wanted the USA and the UK to stay 'on the same wavelength', united at the heart of the alliance. Mrs Thatcher agreed. Having in effect abandoned her struggle against German reunification, she was at one with Bush about the importance of NATO membership for a united Germany. They consequently agreed on a NATO summit soon to help Kohl stand firm. Bush was flatteringly keen that it should be held in Britain.

At the press conference afterwards Mrs Thatcher said, 'We have discussed just about everything and I think we agree on just about everything.' Bush called her 'a tough, courageous leader'. The new tactics with the President had worked: 'we handled him really with kid gloves,' she commented years later. Bermuda, she felt, marked the 'turning point' in their relationship. Mrs Thatcher 'isn't always easy to deal with', Bush told Kohl a month later, 'but I am happy she is there now – and not Kinnock'.

Throughout these anxious months, Mrs Thatcher also faced the ever-greater difficulties of the Soviet Union. By early March, Gorbachev had announced the end of the Communist Party's political monopoly. British experts considered these changes a boost for Gorbachev's prestige, but also 'a momentous breach in the party dyke'. Percy Cradock warned that 'instability in the country can only grow as the Party's authority withers'.

Nor could the Soviet Union itself survive. On 11 March, Lithuania became the first Soviet republic to declare its independence.* Gorbachev immediately denounced this as 'illegitimate and invalid' and signs emerged that Moscow was preparing to intervene militarily. On 28 March, Mrs Thatcher and Gorbachev discussed Lithuania by telephone.† She found the conversation 'alarming', Powell reported to US officials: Gorbachev had sounded 'like a man whose father had just died'. She begged him not to use force, but he replied that this was entirely an internal matter for the Soviet Union. He complained that some in the West were now asking whether it was worth supporting him or his policies. 'As far as we were concerned,' replied Mrs Thatcher, 'we expected Mr Gorbachev to be there for 10 years and hoped it would be 20.'‡

Although Mrs Thatcher supported independence and democracy for all Baltic states, she worried continually about Gorbachev's position. After he threatened economic sanctions against Lithuania, she asked Hurd not to protest. She placed her faith in Gorbachev not going over the top. 'I know that you have done everything you can to avoid the situation becoming a public trial of strength,' she wrote to the Soviet leader. 'Western public opinion, however, is bound to take a highly critical view of any escalation of economic pressure.' The Soviet Union edged up to extreme measures

---

* Similar moves were mooted in the other Baltic states and even in Georgia, Moldavia and Ukraine.

† The Soviets had suggested this call take place over the 'hotline'. In fact no such line existed, and the call was embarrassingly interrupted by bad reception and a Russian operator shouting 'Mrs Thatcher? Mrs Thatcher?' Charles Powell, trying to get a proper line installed, drew on Ian Fleming as he fantasized about what it would be like: 'Yes, Moneypenny, that telephone is connected directly to Gorbachev's study; that's why it's red. And there's a direct tap to the KGB. Saves so much trouble.' The complication and expense were frightful, and Powell decided that 'security is less of a concern than audibility'. In July, an unencrypted direct line was finally installed.

‡ A severe complication in Anglo–Soviet relations arose at this time because of the Gordievsky case. Oleg Gordievsky's wife, still stranded in Moscow with their young children, sought relief from her mistreatment by the KGB. 'I hear that our "samovar lady" is shortly to visit Moscow,' she wrote to her husband. 'Perhaps something can be done . . .' The 'samovar lady' was, of course, Mrs Thatcher – a private joke because of her personally administering tea to Gordievsky in Chequers. Sadly, the 'samovar lady' did not succeed in persuading Gorbachev to release Gordievsky's family while she was Prime Minister, but in 1991 they were eventually allowed to move to Britain. It is evidence of the underlying strength of Soviet–British relations in the Thatcher-Gorbachev era that a row of this sort could be pursued without other dealings being compromised.

but did not quite use them. The West edged up to support for Lithuanian independence, but urged restraint. Both sides played for time.

In May, Mrs Thatcher saw Mrs Kazimira Prunskienė, the *de facto* Prime Minister of the as yet not formally recognized independent state of Lithuania.* Stressing her support for the aspiration of Lithuanian independence, she nonetheless urged Mrs Prunskienė to work with Gorbachev. Encouraged by her response, Mrs Thatcher wrote to Gorbachev: 'My judgment is that Mrs Prunskienė is ready to make a significant move towards your position.' This did not prevent Kremlin denunciations of Lithuanian leaders, but nor did Gorbachev order any irreversible clampdown. His bark was worse than his bite.

Mrs Thatcher also had to decide how to tackle the Soviets over biological weapons. By February, the Soviet defector Vladimir Pasechnik had confirmed the existence of a massive, secret biological warfare programme. William Waldegrave recommended Mrs Thatcher be advised of this urgently 'with a view to tackling Mr Gorbachev directly'. The Americans were also briefed about Pasechnik's revelations. Despite their magnitude, Washington's inclination was to let sleeping dogs lie. 'We were trying to get [a unified] Germany into NATO,' recalled a senior aide to Baker. '. . . And you're going to introduce this?'

Mrs Thatcher considered the American position too cautious and raised the issue herself with Bush in Bermuda. Given Gorbachev's uneasy balance on the political tightrope, they agreed, recalled a US official, to handle the problem 'behind the scenes . . . drawing his attention to it and insisting he do something about it'. The two Ambassadors in Moscow, Rodric Braithwaite and Jack Matlock, delivered a joint démarche in May. A few days later the Defence Secretary, Tom King, visiting Moscow, was told that Pasechnik was an 'insane scientist', a 'liar with personal problems'. Mrs Thatcher now realized she would have to address this matter with Gorbachev herself.

Although she disliked the thought, Mrs Thatcher knew that Gorbachev might not survive and that she must keep her eye open for his potential rivals. On 27 April 1990 she received Boris Yeltsin, recently elected to Russia's Congress of People's Deputies, at No. 10.†

Tony Bishop, who interpreted, recalled that they 'met with mutual and

---

* The meeting, Powell noted subversively, 'was rather longer than originally planned, but women Prime Ministers – of all nationalities – do like to have their say'.
† Yeltsin, in London for a book tour, had requested the meeting. The Foreign Office sought to discourage this, but Mrs Thatcher kept the door slightly ajar. Braithwaite consulted Chernyaev

lively interest, but ... rather like two creatures from quite alien species and different parts of the zoo, sniffing around each other'. Mrs Thatcher was always impressed by well-dressed men and Yeltsin ticked this box. She began by stating squarely her 'special affinity' for Gorbachev and his policies. Yeltsin, however, argued that Gorbachev had missed his big chance. *Perestroika* was supposed 'to make Communism more efficient ... But that was impossible.' The key thing, in Yeltsin's view, was to introduce a real market economy. He now saw a rising risk of revolution from below which 'could be much more like Rumania'* than like Hungary [that is, 1989, not 1956] or Czechoslovakia. He told her of his ambition to become President of the Russian Republic. Mrs Thatcher learnt much from this encounter. As Powell recorded, 'Her conclusions were that there is rather more to him than she had been led to expect. She was quite impressed.'

Later in May, Yeltsin was elected Chairman of the new Russian parliament. Although Cradock advised that this was 'a clear defeat for Gorbachev', Mrs Thatcher felt no qualms about sending Yeltsin a letter of congratulation. Soon thereafter, the Foreign Office sent her a note under the capitalized headline 'SUPPORTING SOVIET REFORM DOES NOT NECESSARILY MEAN SUPPORTING GORBACHEV'. She did not welcome this thought, but she certainly did not dismiss it.

After Bermuda, Bush and Mrs Thatcher tried to persuade Gorbachev to accept NATO membership for a united Germany. This would require far-reaching reform of NATO itself. 'Margaret Thatcher, one of freedom's greatest champions of the last decade,' Bush declared in a speech on 4 May, 'told me that while NATO has been fantastically successful, we should be ready now to face new challenges.' It should reduce conventional and nuclear forces, but only with the assurance of a continuing American presence in Europe. At Mrs Thatcher's urging, Bush also advanced the idea, which Gorbachev favoured, of developing the Conference on Security and Cooperation in Europe (CSCE) as a forum for European political dialogue and the development of free societies.

On 30 May, Powell's contact in the Soviet Embassy, Nikolai Kosov, told him that 'we were probably all better off with Germany subjected to the discipline of an alliance'. But if Gorbachev were to say this, his

---

and reported that, though such a visit would be unwelcome to Gorbachev, it would not be opposed.

* Shortly before Christmas 1989, in what was at that stage the only seriously bloody conflict of the end of the Cold War, the Romanian tyrant Nicolae Ceaușescu had been overthrown and quickly executed, along with his hated wife Elena, without a proper trial. These scenes had shocked Mrs Thatcher.

enemies would accuse him of 'giving away the shop', so a way of enabling Gorbachev 'to present agreement to Germany's membership of NATO as a bargain' had to be found. Mrs Thatcher underlined the word 'bargain' four times.

The next day, Gorbachev and Bush met in Washington. To consternation from his advisers, Gorbachev accepted Bush's formulation that Germany had the right to choose its alliances. With the press afterwards, Bush suggested he and Gorbachev had agreed that whether a united Germany joined NATO was, 'in accordance with the Helsinki Final Act, a matter for the Germans to decide'. This potential breakthrough gave a heightened importance to Mrs Thatcher's next visit to Moscow on 7 June. Bush told her that Gorbachev had 'left the impression he was still feeling his way and that his position may not yet be fixed'. The Americans wanted her impression of what was really going on.

When Mrs Thatcher and Gorbachev met in the Kremlin for four hours of talks and lunch she found him 'a bit less ebullient than usual, but ... seemingly well in control of events'. Seeking to press the case for a united Germany in NATO, she argued that the presence of American troops inside the country would offer security for both the Soviets and Western Europe. If that were agreed, then each side could allay the other's concerns. The CSCE could then become 'a forum for regular political consultation between East and West'.

Gorbachev repudiated none of this. If he and Mrs Thatcher 'could join hands in seeking a solution', he declared, 'they would succeed'. He spoke of a possible joint declaration by NATO and the Warsaw Pact. What would be unacceptable was unilateral reunification: 'The Soviet Union would feel its security in jeopardy.' All this left Mrs Thatcher encouraged. She told Bush she felt confident the Soviets 'will accept a united Germany in NATO and that we need not ... pay a high price for that'. Back in London, Kosov reported that Gorbachev had found their talks 'very frank and direct ... His relations with the Prime Minister were more important to him than those with any other Western leader.'

From Moscow Mrs Thatcher flew to Kiev, where she was enthusiastically received by the Supreme Soviet of the Ukraine, some of whose members unsuccessfully urged her to back them in schism from Moscow. The next day she visited the city of Leninakan in Armenia, which had been devastated in the 1988 earthquake. Huge crowds, probably more than 200,000, turned out to greet her. Partly they wished to thank her for Britain's prompt aid after the earthquake. Partly, too, they cheered her as the most vivid champion of the freedom and independence they sought. 'People hung out of windows, climbed lamp-posts and cheered and screamed,' reported the *Daily Telegraph*. This would be Mrs Thatcher's last public lap of honour, while in office, as a victor in the Cold War.

With Gorbachev Mrs Thatcher had raised the secret Soviet biological weapons programme. It was 'a very serious matter', she told him: were the reports she had received correct? Gorbachev 'said emphatically that they were not'. Nonetheless he promised to summon those concerned 'and quiz them thoroughly'. 'Because Mrs Thatcher had a belief in Gorbachev's truthfulness,' said Powell, '. . . she was prepared to give him the benefit of the doubt.'

According to Powell, Gorbachev and Mrs Thatcher returned to the subject in the margins of the CSCE conference in Paris in November. As Powell recalled, Gorbachev said something like, 'Well, it looks as if you might be right.' His inquiries, he suggested, had produced 'things which he was unaware of'. In Powell's view, this was 'astonishing: what other Soviet leader would have said that?' It seems likely, however, that Gorbachev's startling admission was in fact a form of evasive action. By that stage, agreement to mutual inspections (to confirm that neither side was pursing biological weapons) had been reached and the West's inspectors were due in the Soviet Union soon. So Gorbachev needed some plausible deniability, some suggestion of a rogue element. Sure enough, in January 1991 the inspectors found evidence of what Cradock called a 'massive' biological weapons programme, containing 'some of the most dangerous toxins known to man'. In September 1992, Russia signed an agreement with Britain and the United States which formally ended its biological weapons programme.*

Through this story, some believed that Mrs Thatcher was being too credulous about Gorbachev. William Waldegrave felt that Pasechnik's information proved that Gorbachev was 'lying through his teeth . . . She didn't want to hear that at all . . .' The Soviet documentary record indeed demonstrates, beyond doubt, Gorbachev's awareness of the programme.† So Gorbachev had misled her, offering a tactical admission only when he knew the game was up. Her behaviour was probably less the result of naivety – though she did trust Gorbachev too much – than of high policy. Since she was doing everything she could to try to bring the Cold War to a peaceful end – and here she rightly trusted Gorbachev's determination

---

* The implementation of this agreement, however, has never to this day been properly verified.
† The records show, for instance, that in February 1986 Gorbachev signed off on a five-year plan for the development of biological weapons.

not to use force – she did not want his other evasions to distract her from maintaining her aim.

Home after seeing Gorbachev, Mrs Thatcher developed her thoughts about the coming NATO summit. On 17 June, she wrote to Bush: 'Our main task is to provide Gorbachev with convincing evidence, which he can use with public opinion and the military, that NATO will not represent a threat to the Soviet Union.' She backed Gorbachev's call for a joint NATO–Warsaw Pact declaration 'to make clear NATO's defensive intentions, our commitment to arms control and to strengthening CSCE'.

The Americans, however, had already settled on a different approach, even producing their own draft of the final summit declaration. When, on 21 June, Bush sent Mrs Thatcher a copy, she was dismayed. Although his plan deferred to her proposals for the role of the CSCE, Bush rejected a joint NATO–Warsaw Pact declaration, fearing that this would portray the two groupings as 'equivalent'. A more central disagreement – the heart of Bush's message – was about nuclear weapons. NATO's strategy of flexible response, he declared, was 'becoming out of date'. While rejecting a policy of 'no first use' of nuclear weapons, Bush wanted them described as 'weapons of last resort'. Below this an angry Mrs Thatcher scribbled, '– then they have no deterrent effect in the shortest ranges'.

The Americans believed this gloss was necessary to prove to the Soviets that NATO had changed. Mrs Thatcher disagreed. She worried that such changes might lead some 'to question the very need for NATO'. Bush's proposals were exactly the unnecessarily 'high price' she had warned against after seeing Gorbachev. She now sought to bring together officials to negotiate an agreed text, but the Americans resisted. Instead they sent Bush's proposals to the other allies: 'This should build support for our text,' minuted Bob Blackwill, 'and further isolate Thatcher.' Replying to her letter, Bush stood his ground. As he prepared for the summit, Douglas Hurd, as so often, saw the issue in terms of managing Mrs Thatcher. 'PM in full rampage against Bush . . . on the nuclear,' he told his diary on 3 July. 'Quite absurdly, she puts on the mantle of Churchill in the 1930s. I hope that having blown herself out, she will not make a similar exhibition at the summit itself.'

The meeting unfolded at Lancaster House on 5 July. The mood was mostly cooperative, although there was 'ongoing sniping' between Kohl and Mrs Thatcher. The day before, the Germans had defeated England in the semi-final of the World Cup. In Sarotte's account: 'Kohl gloated that the Germans had beaten the English at their national game; Thatcher shot back that the English had beaten the Germans at theirs twice in the twentieth century.'

In discussion, Bush stressed that, even as 'weapons of last resort', nuclear weapons could still be used 'early' in conflict to deter large conventional attacks. Mrs Thatcher was extremely tart in response: 'To me... last means last and nothing else and yet I am told that is not so, that their expression is ambiguous... to be told that clear words are confusing is, to me, a new dimension of diplomacy. Of course, as colleagues... round this table will know, I never had much use for diplomacy anyway, and I've got on very well without it.' After further negotiations,* the alliance confirmed that there would be 'no circumstances in which nuclear retaliation in response to military action might be discounted'. The final sentence, however, reflected Bush's victory over Mrs Thatcher: 'in the transformed Europe, they [the allies] will be able to adopt a new NATO strategy making nuclear forces truly weapons of last resort'.

At her press conference Mrs Thatcher hailed the success of the declaration, but in her memoirs she wrote, 'I cannot say that I was satisfied with this unwieldy compromise.' Nonetheless, at breakfast on the last morning Bush found her 'in a good frame of mind'. He sensed that their relationship had changed – and for the better. Famously, Mrs Thatcher respected men who stood up to her and bullied those who did not. Now that Bush had faced her down and, without gloating, defeated her, she probably felt an increased respect for him.

Despite her fondness for the Soviet leader, Mrs Thatcher made a firm alliance with Bush against Gorbachev's request for money from the West. At the Dublin European Council in June, Kohl and Mitterrand had argued for the West to hand over large sums. 'I just sat back horrified,' she later recalled. 'You don't just come, put a proposition for 3 billion dollars on the table. No papers, no reasoning.' When the issue re-emerged at the G7 in Houston, Texas a couple of weeks later,† she again knocked it down. With Bush's support, she prevailed.‡

On the morning of Mrs Thatcher's return from Houston, 12 July, Nicholas Ridley broke cover, possibly unintentionally, in an interview with

---

* Douglas Hurd succeeded in removing a draft reference to 'further far-reaching reductions' in conventional weapons and, Bush's earlier opposition notwithstanding, Mrs Thatcher's proposal for a NATO–Warsaw Pact declaration was accepted.

† Mrs Thatcher was much oppressed by the extreme heat in Houston. On the university lawn for the group photo, air conditioning was blown in from the side to try to cool everyone down. According to local legend, Mrs Thatcher's staff sewed weights into the hem of her skirt to prevent it from billowing up like Marilyn Monroe's in *The Seven Year Itch*.

‡ Hurd, whose diary over these months gradually becomes more open in its disdain for Mrs Thatcher, recorded a meeting with her at the summit during the Wimbledon Finals, which she was watching on television: 'Sensible on the agenda, she is demonic against the Germans, wanting Becker to lose (which he does).'

the *Spectator*. European Monetary Union, he told the magazine, was 'all a German racket designed to take over the whole of Europe'.* Attacking the European Commission as 'seventeen unelected reject politicians', he said: 'The idea that one says, "OK, we'll give this lot our sovereignty," is unacceptable to me ... You might just as well give it to Adolf Hitler.' The cover of the magazine carried a cartoon of Ridley running away having painted a Hitler forelock and moustache on a poster of Helmut Kohl.

There was an immediate outcry. Although Ridley, while angry at what he considered a *Spectator* set-up, offered a complete retraction, the Chief Whip, Tim Renton, warned Mrs Thatcher that unless Ridley resigned his views would be taken to be hers (which, to a large extent, they were). The writing was on the wall. She could not bring herself personally to ask such a close ally to go, so, on 14 July, Powell did her work for her. He found Ridley 'very bitter'. Ridley went. In the *Independent on Sunday* the next morning, Powell's incendiary minute of the Chequers seminar in March about the Germans was leaked, almost certainly by Ridley's aides. Naturally, the Germans were upset.† But the reaction was less dramatic than it would have been a few months earlier. Mrs Thatcher's repeated infractions of diplomacy were now taken more as symptoms of her declining importance than as cause for new affront.

On the day that Ridley resigned, Kohl was with Gorbachev in Moscow, where Gorbachev formally dropped his opposition to NATO membership for a united Germany. This had been made possible, a Soviet official told Braithwaite, because of 'the NATO London declaration that NATO no longer considers the Soviet Union an enemy'. On 3 October 1990, East and West Germany unified. Mrs Thatcher, Wright noted, 'watered down a draft statement produced by the FCO, omitting any reference to "rejoicing"'. But she nonetheless offered her 'warmest congratulations' to Kohl: 'Together with Allies, we withstood the difficult period of the Cold War. Now Germany is to be united in peace and freedom.'

'We wanted the Cold War to end with a whimper, not a bang,' recalled James Baker. 'It did.' This was an achievement for which Mrs Thatcher deserved significant credit. Of all the Western leaders, she had shown the

---

* Ridley later claimed that the incendiary passages of the interview had not been intended for publication.

† There was anger too among some participants at the seminar, who were embarrassed by what they saw as Powell's over-dramatization and skewing of their views. Powell privately defended himself, admitting only to one mistake: 'all the pejorative words were used, but to arrange them in alphabetical order was perhaps a step too far'.

clearest sense of the architecture of victory. First, face down the Communist threat by building up Western defences, military and moral. Second, once in a position to bargain from strength, be open to the possibilities of change in the USSR. Gorbachev exemplified that possibility, and Mrs Thatcher grabbed it with both hands. She backed his reforms early on, when others dismissed them, realizing they would have far-reaching and lasting effects. Throughout all this she gave help, hope and voice to the peoples of Eastern Europe who were struggling to be free.

When victory came, however, her joy was highly qualified. She worried that, in its euphoria, the West would let down its defences. She was deeply uneasy about the economic and political power which would inevitably accrue to a reunited Germany (a concern many came to share in the early twenty-first century); and she was horrified by the emerging orthodoxy that the only way to deal with this problem was to bind Germany – and most of the rest of Western Europe – into a single currency. In articulating her doubts in public she was, perhaps, at her most characteristic – part rude, unreasonable and backward-looking; part brave, truth-seeking and prophetic. She set out to speak what she saw as truth to power. The trouble was that, in the process, she lost enough of her own power for allied counterparts to stop listening to her.

36

Trouble at home

'I'd never seen her flailing before'

On 9 March 1990, Mrs Thatcher was forced to deny rumours she had resigned as Prime Minister. That she had to squash this story indicated she had a problem. Sterling slid quite steeply.

Little had gone right in the year so far. Although she had easily beaten off the challenge from Anthony Meyer the previous December, it had weakened her air of invulnerability. To Bernard Ingham it 'suggested a level of discontent which I don't think [we] took as seriously as we should have done'. In January, Norman Fowler resigned as Employment Secretary, as he put it, 'to devote more time' to his family.* This voluntary departure, coming after both David Young and George Younger had left the Cabinet of their own volition six months earlier, added to a *fin de régime* feeling. Following March's groundless resignation story, the papers carried surveys suggesting that a quarter of Conservative backbenchers wanted Mrs Thatcher to step down. ICM posted the Labour lead at a massive 21 per cent, while more than half of those polled wanted her to leave office at once. 'It's me they don't like . . .' she told Woodrow Wyatt, 'I don't expect any gratitude in politics.'

That January, the Conservative Party Press Office warned her that 'the critical "C2" [upper working-class] group which supported us in 1979, 1983 and 1987 has now gone to Labour . . . winning this group back is the key to the election'. The cherished C2s were suffering from returning inflation and, with interest rates at 15 per cent, huge monthly mortgage repayments. From 1 April, many would receive poll tax bills much larger than the previous domestic rates.† Besides, something had gone wrong in the political

---

* Following Fowler's departure, the phrase 'to spend more time with my family' became a euphemism to conceal the real reason for a resignation.
† Infuriated by these economic woes, Mrs Thatcher deeply regretted her earlier decision, under pressure from Nigel Lawson, to hold down mortgage interest tax relief. 'Could have avoided most of this had we dynamised mortgage relief . . .' she burst out, in private. 'If I had had my way, would have increased mortgage relief at least twice by now.'

atmosphere. As the true-blue Tory backbencher Sir John Stokes complained at a 1922 Committee meeting in February, 'People talk politics in pubs – a bad sign for Tories. People should not talk politics if they are happy (laughter).' People were not happy. Naturally, many blamed the Prime Minister.

Mrs Thatcher was not happy herself. She told Kenneth Baker she was 'fed up with the party': they 'do nothing but complain'. The threat of immigration from Hong Kong was one bone of contention, although the economy was a greater problem. Economic recovery had been the Conservatives' best selling-point at three successive general elections, yet now, with the return of inflation and high interest rates, the recovery was withering. For all this, as her MPs thought ahead to the next general election and the local contests that May,* the poll tax was where the shoe pinched.

In early January 1990, the normally chirpy Kenneth Baker warned Mrs Thatcher of 'considerable unease' among backbenchers over the poll tax. Its unpopularity was projected to cause heavy losses in the upcoming local elections. This would lead many Conservative MPs to 'consider their seats at risk. I think they will start to campaign for a fundamental change in the Community Charge.' Baker advocated the basic line that the charge would be lower under the Tories but urged extra funds to reduce its impact.

On 18 January, the government cleared the final parliamentary hurdle to implement the poll tax. Its majority of nearly 100 was cut to 36, but the whips had expected an even bigger rebellion. The projected level of the tax was less reassuring. In late February, the government conceded that the average charge would be £370, nearly £100 over Chris Patten's earlier estimate. As Ferdinand Mount pointed out in print, 'The ultimate reality about a universal flat-rate tax is that it remains tolerable only when levied on a smallish scale.' It was already feeling intolerable, even to loyalists. On 4 March, the outspoken backbencher Rhodes Boyson, a Thatcherite turned poll tax rebel, publicly reminded Mrs Thatcher that the Conservative leadership was 'a leasehold not a freehold'. The same words had been used to threaten Ted Heath before he fell in February 1975 to a challenge from one Margaret Thatcher.

In his first Budget on 20 March, John Major tried to take the sting out of the poll tax by making more pensioners eligible for rebates. These concessions, however, would not be made retrospective for Scotland, which had started paying the tax a year earlier. After the Scottish Secretary, Malcolm Rifkind, threatened resignation, it was left to Major to agree a compromise whereby Scottish pensioners would receive an *ex gratia* payment. Patrick Wright

---

* This was widely expected to take place in the course of 1991, although the last possible date was 9 July 1992.

noted in his diary that Rifkind's resignation became a 'damn close thing' which Charles Powell told him, rightly, would have been 'disastrous for the Government'. From then on, Rifkind became Mrs Thatcher's opponent.

Major increasingly made himself the indispensable problem-solver between Mrs Thatcher and colleagues, usually tilting in favour of the latter. Following the U-turn, Alan Clark recorded that 'practically every member of the Cabinet is quietly and unattributably briefing ... about how awful she is ... Malcolm Rifkind is actually quoted today as saying, "I'll be here after she's gone."' The Rifkind fracas was followed immediately by the mid-Staffordshire by-election on 22 March. Dubbed 'the poll-tax by-election', it saw a Conservative majority of 14,654 become a Labour majority of 9,449. The implications for the imminent local elections were alarming.*

The government's crushing loss in mid-Staffordshire came just two days after Major's underwhelming first Budget. With little to tackle the high inflation, high interest rates and excessive public spending, it left many natural Conservative supporters disillusioned. Nor did it impress the markets, seeking a clear signal about ERM entry. Sterling fell accordingly.

From his first day in No. 11, Major made clear privately that he planned to join the ERM. Mrs Thatcher understood that membership had become likelier after she had set out the Madrid conditions in June, but not, she felt, inescapable. After all, the conditions, including the convergence of Britain's inflation rate with Continental ones, would not be satisfied in the foreseeable future.

After Madrid, and Howe's removal from the Foreign Office, ERM entry had become unmentionable within government. Mrs Thatcher wanted to move on, yet was conscious she lacked a clear alternative. She was as flummoxed as her colleagues about the best way to stop fast-growing inflation.† She feared a bust.

Major approached the matter differently. Although he shared (less passionately) Mrs Thatcher's dislike of a single European currency, he had no such reservations about the ERM. Privately, he concluded that entry was necessary as the 'belt and braces' for defeating inflation and, as John Kerr put it, was 'preparing to have a go at her about it'. Besides, he was at his wits' end: 'Interest rates were 15 per cent; inflation was up, unemployment

---

* A small problem Mrs Thatcher's officials had to handle was whether Margaret's and Denis's poll tax bills from Westminster Council would receive the transitional relief now available to old-age pensioners, both being over retiring age. Mrs Thatcher had asked that she and Denis not receive this relief, but there was a danger that the computer would pay it automatically, causing great political embarrassment. This was averted.

† In June 1989, inflation had reached 8.3 per cent, a dramatic rise from a recent low of 3.3 per cent just sixteen months earlier. After a brief dip in October, underlying inflation rose sharply.

was up; the trade gap was awful; we were heading for recession ... what option was I left with?' he later recalled. 'How about the external discipline of the ERM?'

Major also had a personal political motive. His meteoric rise to Foreign Secretary and now Chancellor had painted him as Mrs Thatcher's compliant heir. She herself accidentally bolstered this impression, regarding him, as Powell put it, as 'a bit of a junior boy'. This riled him. According to John Gieve, his private secretary, support for ERM entry 'showed that he was a player, an independent political force'. So he set out to overcome Mrs Thatcher's objections.*

To this end, Major moved with astute caution. The last thing he wanted was a repeat of the Lawson-Howe/Thatcher battles. But he quickly formed what Powell called 'a bond of steel' about the ERM with Douglas Hurd, who had succeeded him at the Foreign Office. As a mainstream, pro-European Tory centrist, Hurd wanted to contain rather than empower Mrs Thatcher. As Major himself put it, 'We wished to persuade.' So their method was gentle: 'We approached it crabwise.'

Hurd–Major cooperation was a necessary, but not a sufficient, condition for success. Major knew he must reach Mrs Thatcher through people she trusted, which Howe and Lawson had failed to do. In December 1989, he approached Bernard Ingham. '[Major] does not believe that the ERM matters one way or the other economically, but the politics of it are important and conceivably crucial,' Ingham recorded. To avoid Kinnock making hay with the issue, 'might it not make sense to announce entry in six months' time in a surprise coup ... That, he says, would take a lot of tricks and would convince everybody that we were going to be at the heart of Europe.'

Major also worked his methods of political seduction on Mrs Thatcher directly: 'I felt from the outset that she could be persuaded,' he recalled, 'if the decision to enter did not humiliate her.' She was susceptible. In the view of Richard Wilson, 'She did have an eye for younger men. Not in a bad way: she was marvellously innocent.' Nigel Wicks, who had attended the ill-fated ERM meeting in November 1985, told Major she would never agree to join. Major smiled: 'Leave it to me, Nigel. Leave it to me.'

In the early months, Major reiterated in a newspaper article – as in Parliament – the government's existing, pro-ERM line that it was 'not a

---

* The strongly pro-European Leon Brittan had noticed Major's sentiments even before he was made Chancellor. After lunching with him at the Foreign Secretary's residence in Carlton Gardens in early September, he wrote in his diary: 'He was reasonable & cautious. Clearly aware of the need not to be Mrs Thatcher's poodle. Quite sympathetic on European issues' and on 'gradual moves to EMU'.

question of whether, but when'. Mrs Thatcher pronounced Major's draft 'Excellent – straightforward and direct', but scribbled, 'It is ironic that at a time when Eastern Europe is moving towards greater democracy the Community proposes to take the heart of monetary and economic policy away from our national Parliament to a non-elected non-accountable body. To our Parliament this is totally unacceptable.'*

Attention turned to the Strasbourg European Council in December, which would decide whether Delors's proposals for EMU should be taken forward by an Intergovernmental Conference (IGC). This could only add pressure for Britain to join the ERM. The one minister now actively urging Mrs Thatcher to stick to her anti-ERM line was Nicholas Ridley. Having been disappointed in his ambition to become Chancellor, he was even less disposed than usual to run with the pack. On 1 December, he sent her a minute setting out the ERM's flaws and stressing its inevitable link with EMU, which would produce an 'unthinkable' transfer of sovereignty. He urged her not to accept that ERM entry would be just 'a token of our good European intentions'.†

At Strasbourg, despite Mrs Thatcher's efforts to prevent it, an IGC was called for a year's time. A British plan for competing currencies within the European system, an 'evolutionary' counter to Delors's mandatory move to EMU, gained little traction. After the fall of the Berlin Wall, most people felt that the more 'Europe' there was, the better. Mrs Thatcher was out of step. In early March 1990, Leon Brittan told Douglas Hurd it was 'absolutely essential that he, John Major and Geoffrey Howe should get together to press for ERM entry between July and December'.

Major's more pressing task, however, had been to prepare his first Budget. Mrs Thatcher was frustrated because there was so little to play with. The January forecast showed growth at only three-quarters of 1 per cent in 1990, and government expenditure growing as a proportion of GDP. 'One is left with an uncomfortable feeling that everyone else knows how to keep down inflation, and we don't,' she scribbled in February. In these circumstances, ERM entry seemed to offer stability, yet it was tricky to join at a time of weakness. In January, Mrs Thatcher and Major had agreed that the state of inflation was a 'key issue' for entry (the higher, the worse) and so it seemed unlikely entry could be contemplated until much later in the year. Introducing his Budget on 20 March, Major therefore

---

* These comments came a week after the Commons had rejected the Delors version of EMU (in the adjournment debate on 2 November).
† Mrs Thatcher liked Ridley's paper and wanted it published as a pamphlet, but eventually allowed the idea to be squashed by officials, lest it reopen controversy.

confined his mention of the ERM to repeating the Madrid Conditions. In contrast to the Howe–Lawson dramatics, he proceeded cautiously, building alliances and allowing the pressure to grow.

As Mrs Thatcher's political difficulties mounted, she faced a domestic challenge from an international event. In the latter half of 1989, controversy arose over whether large numbers of Hong Kong people should receive British passports. Ever since her warning in 1978 that people were worried about being 'rather swamped' (see p. 163) Mrs Thatcher had been identified with strict immigration controls, but now she was siding with those who might want to flee Communism and come to Britain. She had good reason to do so, but little room for political manoeuvre.

The crisis in Hong Kong came from China. On 4 June 1989, the Tiananmen Square crackdown shocked the West. Western diplomats estimated that, across China, roughly 10,000 people were killed. This was a special agony for Mrs Thatcher, who feared that the carefully constructed guarantees of the Anglo-Chinese Joint Declaration she had signed in 1984 (see p. 363) might not survive. Would confidence in Hong Kong collapse? On 11 June, she rang President Bush and asked him to help 'steady nerves'. There was 'renewed clamour' in Britain to give full citizenship to all the 3.25 million Hong Kong people who were 'British nationals'.* She told Bush she would not do this, but wanted to enlarge the categories of those eligible for full British passports. She sought further guarantees from the Chinese, notably on democratic rights for the people of Hong Kong, without provoking an extreme reaction. In its current mood, China might want to punish the colony.

In Hong Kong itself, the feeling after Tiananmen was desperate. Lydia Dunn, the Senior Member of Hong Kong's Executive Council (EXCO), flew to London to express the collective anguish to Mrs Thatcher: 'I found her shattered. Her instinct was very like that of the people of Hong Kong. She waved the famous picture of the man confronting the tank at me,† saying "This is just terrible."' But while her heart was with Hong Kong people, Mrs Thatcher's head was much influenced by Percy Cradock, who always put agreement with Peking first. After Tiananmen, Cradock recalled, 'She was appalled, but I told her we already knew what China was like; and I pointed out that it showed no sign of wanting to tear up

---

* Most Hong Kong people at this time were British Dependent Territories Citizens (BDTC), a status which gave them passports but no automatic right to live in Britain.
† A reference to the iconic photograph of a man blocking the path of a line of tanks in Tiananmen Square on 5 June 1989.

the Hong Kong agreement.'* On British citizenship, Cradock was wary of inflaming China. Reluctantly, Mrs Thatcher felt compelled to follow his approach. She told Dunn that Hong Kong's demand for British citizenship for all 3.25 million British nationals was unrealistic, explaining the more limited plan she had outlined to Bush. Mrs Thatcher should act now, pressed Dunn, or Hong Kong would 'wither away'.

Acting on the issue, however, was far from simple. Tim Renton, the Chief Whip, watched Mrs Thatcher 'arguing more passionately than anyone else in Cabinet about our duty to Hong Kong, even if the issue would cause us to lose a lot of blood in the Commons and would anger her friends on the right'. In November, she pressed a plan to offer passports for 50,000 heads of household (implying up to 200,000 people) upon her new and decidedly sceptical Home Secretary, David Waddington. There were two aims, she told him – to safeguard Crown servants and 'to sustain the prosperity of Hong Kong' by securing the base of the business and professional elite. Before this was announced, the Prince and Princess of Wales visited Hong Kong to help boost morale. Writing afterwards to Mrs Thatcher, the Prince reported his impression that Hong Kong people wanted a British passport as an insurance policy rather than as a ticket to leave. He feared the strength of feeling aroused if Britain failed to recognize the issue's importance to many in Hong Kong. This struck a chord with Mrs Thatcher. 'Very good letter,' she scribbled.

When, later in December, Hurd, now Foreign Secretary, announced the passport proposals to the Commons, Norman Tebbit accused him of breaking the party's long-standing pledge 'that there will be no further large-scale immigration'. Hurd implicitly rebuked him, saying that the 'last chapter' of Britain's colonial story 'should not end in a shabby way'. In the wider debate, Tebbit's attack may have actually helped Mrs Thatcher, since it showed Hong Kong people what she was up against and made her very modest proposals look less stingy. At the time, however, she did not feel comforted. She doubted Tebbit's loyalty. There was a certain irony in the fact that the most right-wing of all modern Conservative prime ministers was facing trouble from such quarters. As Prime Minister Mrs Thatcher had not lost a Commons vote on a second reading except over Sunday shopping (see p. 531), but now she feared defeats on both the poll tax and Hong Kong.

In late February 1990, Tebbit announced that eighty-one Conservative

---

* Cradock always disdained what he considered the naivety of those who complained about China's repressive behaviour. 'When we entered into the Joint Declaration,' he would say, 'we did not do so believing they were Asquithian Liberals.'

MPs had lent their names, privately, to a letter protesting against the measures. They feared the effect on 'critical seats, particularly in London, the Midlands and the North West'.* But when Mrs Thatcher saw Tebbit and his fellow rebels, she was having none of it. The offer of citizenship was 'a matter of straight moral duty', she said. She was 'not prepared to see Britain rat on its duty'.

Difficulties over Hong Kong and Europe were worrying enough for Mrs Thatcher, but it was the problems over the poll tax that truly alarmed her. The punishing defeat in mid-Staffordshire and the possibility of deep losses in the local elections to be held on 3 May hung uncomfortably in the air. On 25 March, she rang John Major, thoroughly disenchanted. The community charge was 'not bringing about increased accountability', she said. She wanted to reimpose methods of control which it was supposed to supersede. There must be immediate capping of the charge in the worst cases that year and a review which would consider 'direct control over levels of local authority expenditure' for the next. She was reverting to her longstanding instinct towards local government – trying to contain its power.

It fell to Andrew Turnbull, Mrs Thatcher's principal private secretary, to hold the line. He stressed that accountability required transparency and, at present, those paying the charge 'do not know who to blame'. Transparency would improve over time: 'It would be a tragedy if, having got this far, you were publicly to concede in the first month of the charge operating in England that accountability was a dead duck.' Astutely mentioning her former Environment Secretary as bogeyman, Turnbull insisted it would be a disaster to go back to 'the Heseltine regime of targets and holdback'. In Turnbull's view, she was 'flailing around'. Chris Patten agreed, and he worried, because 'I'd never seen her flailing before': 'I was aware of her not being able to concentrate long enough or hard enough. Too many other things were pressing on her, especially Europe.'

Mrs Thatcher did not reject Turnbull's advice, but her immediate priority was to shore up her leadership. By the time she rose to address the annual Conservative Central Council at Cheltenham, Norman Tebbit had declared he would stand if Michael Heseltine were to challenge for the leadership and she were to step down. Although technically a gesture of support for Thatcherism, this was a reminder of her political mortality. At Cheltenham, a town famous for its large population of former army

---

* They rubbed in the electorally significant point that Labour – for the first time since 1970 – had found a way to oppose an immigration increase. The Opposition had contrived this by deciding that the Hong Kong plan was 'elitist' because it excluded passports for poorer people.

officers, she joked, 'at the risk of disappointing a few gallant colonels, let me make one thing absolutely clear. I haven't come to Cheltenham to retire.' At the insistence of her advisers, she sought to offer reassurance on the poll tax: those looking to the government for protection from excessive bills 'will not look in vain'.

Mrs Thatcher did not know, as she spoke, that a full-scale riot against the poll tax was developing in central London. Reports she received from Downing Street spoke of 'Lots of fighting', 'People are being attacked in their cars', a 'hard core of 3–3½,000' out of a crowd of 40,000–50,000. The next day she learnt of 340 arrests, with fifty-eight police officers and roughly 100 civilians injured. The eventual figures were higher still. 'Police Commissioner's view was that it was sheer wanton violence.'

Wantonness was certainly an element in the poll tax riots, and so was hard-left political motivation. In this sense, the riots were grist to the mill of her assertions that an extremist underclass was trying to sabotage a tax which gave citizens more power and responsibility over local affairs. But although the violence disgusted most, the majority wanted to see the poll tax go. The riots added to the uneasy question: 'What on earth is the point of all this?' In his diary, Alan Clark recorded that MPs were 'now talking openly of ditching the Lady to save their skins. This is the first time I've heard it *en clair* since a bad patch (1977?) when we were in opposition.' That month her approval rating dropped to the lowest since she came to office.* With hindsight, Major believed the riots marked 'the turning point' for her premiership.

Across the grander parts of London, similar expressions of fear, disillusionment and dislike were heard among important people.† Even Queen Elizabeth the Queen Mother, probably the only member of the royal family to be an ardent fan of Mrs Thatcher, asked Woodrow Wyatt in March, 'Can't you get her to be a bit more flexible?' Her friends felt almost powerless to help. Two of them, Tim Bell and Gordon Reece, did raise her dire political situation over dinner in Chequers. They reported to Whittingdale that she 'shouted at them that they did not understand the pressures'. Over dinner at Bledlow, his country house near Chequers, Lord Carrington confronted her boldly. 'Margaret,' he said, 'you're going to lose the next

---

* In March, according to Gallup, it fell to 24 per cent. In April it dropped further.

† Woodrow Wyatt supported Mrs Thatcher even more fervently than Clark, but his diaries for the first half of 1990 record almost daily denunciations of her from others – Willie Whitelaw, Andrew Neil, George Soros, Lord Home, Lord (Leonard) Wolfson, Lord Carrington and many more.

election to Kinnock. Shouldn't you consider resigning?' He did not receive a response.*

On 3 April 1990, Chris Patten announced plans to cap the community charge in twenty councils in England, all of them Labour. He emphasized the difference between the proposed community charge of £573 in Labour Haringey and of £148 in Tory Wandsworth. Labour's frontbench spokesman, Bryan Gould, pertinently objected: 'If accountability is the key, why could he not wait for voters to pass judgment on 3 May?'

Increasingly concerned at what that judgment was likely to be, Mrs Thatcher scratched around to limit future damage. Quite uncharacteristically, she suggested a surcharge on the poll tax payable by everyone earning more than £50,000 a year. 'I know there are lots of snags,' she concluded, 'but we must try to remove the unfairness feeling.' This angst notwithstanding, the argument that the charge could still produce political benefits remained strong. In February, Ingham had informed Mrs Thatcher that Westminster Council would soon announce a community charge of only £200. He advised her to discuss with Kenneth Baker spreading a loud Westminster Council-style message across the country: 'DON'T BETRAY THE WESTMINSTER SUCCESS WITH THE COMMUNITY CHARGE'. As local election day neared, Conservative Central Office focused on the simple slogan: 'Conservative Councils Cost You Less'. But the polls showed little respite. Heavy Conservative losses were widely predicted.

Amid this political turmoil, John Major sought to wear down Mrs Thatcher's resistance over Europe. His goal was to entwine three strands – ERM entry, preventing a European single currency *à la* Delors and improving Britain's competing currencies idea. Finding Mrs Thatcher as opposed as ever to the first, he turned in desperation to Charles Powell. Aware of Powell's hostility to Howe and Lawson before Madrid, Major knew that if he were to succeed where they had failed he needed Powell on his side. Powell reluctantly agreed: 'I thought entry was wrong, but politically necessary,' he recalled. 'I thought it was essential to preserve her.'

On 8 April, Powell reported his conversation with Major to Mrs Thatcher: 'The Chancellor is in quite a state – unusual for a normally calm man – about both ERM membership and EMU.' She should heed Major's

---

* The only known example of a backbencher brave enough to make a similar suggestion was the irascible right-winger Tony Marlow. At a small meeting in May 1990, Marlow told her, 'There is a great deal of animosity to you personally. How do you assess whether it is best for the party for you to lead us into the next election?' When Mrs Thatcher tried to brush this off, Marlow persisted: 'But level of animosity is greater than ever before.' Mrs Thatcher: 'I do not want to see all that has been achieved thrown away. It needs a firm hand.' Marlow: 'Are there no other firm hands?'

suggestions. On the ERM, he wrote, the Chancellor felt that 'he has very few options left for managing the economy if we are to avoid further interest rate rises this year'. Were Britain to join the ERM in September, the Madrid Conditions would not have been met, Powell noted, but Major felt this could be outweighed by the 'political effects for you'. Adding his own well-tailored arguments, Powell stressed that the decision to enter should not be seen as 'something you are being reluctantly dragged into'. She might consider 'some warming-up' of her public references to the ERM.

The other half of Major's plan, as served up by Powell, was that ERM entry would gain Britain goodwill for the IGC. Major wanted Britain to propose a 'hard ecu',* which might eventually emerge as a common currency used by consent rather than a single currency imposed by fiat. Even with this plan, Major warned, the other eleven member states would still insist on a treaty specifying the goal of fixed exchange rates and/or a single currency.† To maintain influence, he would have to go along but negotiate a national 'opt-in' permitting Britain to enter later. The single currency would be conceded in principle, though possibly avoided for Britain in practice.

Powell gave Mrs Thatcher his own views. He doubted the 'hard ecu' would make any difference. He also recognized the dangers of signing up in any form for the single currency. On ERM entry, Powell spoke very frankly:

> I am very conscious that much of this thinking . . . stems from the present political 'low' . . . you clearly <u>are</u> going to face a concerted effort from your closest colleagues this year to get us in. The questions to be answered are whether it is politically feasible to resist this once again: and, if you did decide that we should go in, how to extract the maximum advantage from it politically.‡

Major's own minute, sent to Mrs Thatcher the following day, applied more pressure. Declaring himself 'very startled at the attitude of our European partners', all of whom 'were determined to agree a Treaty for full EMU', Major insisted that 'we need to confront this issue now'. He worried too about 'the electoral timetable', given that the subject was 'a hugely

---

* Ecu stood for 'European Currency Unit', which already existed in European monetary arrangements but had historical resonances, because the *écu* had been a coin in pre-Revolutionary France.
† In law, no treaty could be signed without the unanimous agreement of the member states; but in practice, if the other eleven member states wanted to go ahead without Britain, they would do so, British officials warned Mrs Thatcher, by creating parallel institutions. This was sometimes referred as 'putting everything in the wife's name', like a tax ruse.
‡ Mrs Thatcher also received, three days later, a valedictory memo from her able Treasury private secretary, Paul Gray. He told her he shared 'your instinctive worries about fixed exchange rate systems', but that if the market believed that ERM membership would give government policies greater credibility 'then it will, at any rate for a period'. Bernard Ingham told her that, in relation to the ERM, 'she was running out of political options'.

divisive party issue for us'. His aim was to convey a sort of controlled panic. He did not use the phrase, of course, but he was saying to Mrs Thatcher, 'There Is No Alternative.'

Mrs Thatcher reacted less fiercely than expected. She understood her political weakness. As she said to Paul Gray: 'I lost one Chancellor: I can't really lose the next one. Besides, I think he's the person who ought to succeed me.' If she could somehow stick to her wider economic beliefs while Major helped her find her way out of her present hole, she would be delighted. Powell's conciliatory attitude also made a huge difference. She always listened to Charles.

To Charles, and probably to Charles alone, she confided her inner thoughts. 'She said explicitly that she couldn't get away with not going in this time. It was a question of politics. She realized she was beaten.' When Mrs Thatcher and Major met she did not endorse ERM entry, but she raised no objections. As Major remembered it, 'It was what she was *not* saying that made me think she'd give in.'

Mrs Thatcher's political position began to show some signs of improvement. On 19 April, the Commons voted twice on the much-anticipated Hong Kong Bill. The government won the first by 97 votes and the second by 115. Many of the Tebbit faction had abstained rather than voted against. Labour too had split. As a domestic political problem, Hong Kong suddenly went away. Although her passports offer was not very impressive, she had done just enough to reassure Hong Kong. There was no mass exodus. Business confidence recovered.

On 3 May came the local elections. To the surprise of most observers, including Mrs Thatcher, the Conservatives did all right on the night. Against a predicted loss of 600 seats, a net total of 172 losses looked by no means catastrophic. Given that, as Mrs Thatcher was informed, 90 per cent of households had 'seen their local tax bills rise by around 50 per cent', it was remarkable that the results were not much worse. Shrewdly managing expectations, Baker had done little to discourage talk of extravagant losses. 'You've certainly saved Margaret,' Willie Whitelaw told him. 'I don't think there will be a leadership election this year.'

Despite this respite, Mrs Thatcher remained deeply concerned by the unpopularity of the poll tax. Still unconvinced the tax had delivered accountability, she sought to impose 'income limits' (in effect, cash limits) on local-authority spending. Most ministers disliked this approach. Malcolm Rifkind pointed out that in Scotland accountability was already improving. If income limits were to prevail, 'the Government will be defining almost all local-authority spending, and consequently the level of local taxation. But if so, what is the point of a system of local taxation? We're setting the level of our own unpopular tax!'

By June, Mrs Thatcher's new Treasury private secretary, Barry Potter, warned her that Major and Patten 'seem to have agreed, privately, on an enhanced capping solution' rather than the income limits that Mrs Thatcher sought. Just as Major had used his close relationship with Hurd to pursue ERM entry, so his axis with Patten helped force her hand over the poll tax. Richard Wilson, an informal poll tax adviser to Mrs Thatcher, felt that Major and Patten viewed her efforts to strengthen controls over local-authority spending as 'a very bad idea, mainly, I suspect, because it would have put them more in the firing line': 'They were a canny couple ... thick as thieves on the poll tax.' In Wilson's view, they realized the tax 'was a disaster ... they preferred Mrs Thatcher to carry the can on her own'. As Wilson put it: 'Looking back, this was the beginning of the end. Mrs Thatcher was increasingly isolated ... and she was surrounded by ambitious young Ministers who caught each other's eye at meetings around the Cabinet table and who sensed that big political movement was afoot under the surface.'

Naturally, these relative youngsters looked ahead to the next general election and how the poll tax might affect the party's fortunes. Also in their minds was the idea that Mrs Thatcher might not be leader by then. As Patten put it: 'There was a need to get her to take rational decisions, one of which was about how long she could go on for.' This was an echo of the strategy set out by Garel-Jones the previous December (see p. 757).

By early July, ministers, led by Patten and Major, combined to prevail over the capping issue. On 19 July, Patten announced yet another cash injection – £3.26 billion – to keep the next year's average community charge increase to £22, with threats to make 'vigorous use' of his capping powers. Things went quiet for the time being. Nothing was solved, however. A policy which had begun as a harmonious product of Cabinet government was now being hung firmly round the neck of one woman.

On the question of ERM membership, Major now suggested entry as early as 18 May. Sensing a change in their mistress's mood, opponents of ERM entry began to change too. Alan Walters told her he and the Chairman of the Fed, Alan Greenspan, whom Mrs Thatcher much admired, thought that 'Entry to the ERM is a political necessity; and properly timed and managed, it can give economic benefits.'*

By mid-May the timing was still not settled, but opposition to entry fell silent

---

* Walters did warn, however, that the short-term economic bonus would 'tend to unwind', so the timing of entry would be 'important in the context of the next election'.

within government. Major now pushed ahead with his argument about EMU, sending Mrs Thatcher a paper that Powell warned she would find 'unpalatable'. She did. Powell asked whether Major's pessimism about the other eleven countries going ahead alone was justified. 'NO,' said Mrs Thatcher. The 'crucial point', said Powell, was whether, if Britain conceded Major's argument about the 'opt in', 'we are throwing in the towel on the substance of EMU and arguing only about tactics'. 'That', she concluded, 'is the correct assessment.' She thought the best tactic was to table the hard ecu proposals. She ended her comments thus: 'I will have a long talk with the Chancellor.'

At the ensuing meeting, Major raised every terror, including German domination and the danger of British isolation, 'particularly with the approach of the general election'. Mrs Thatcher was unmoved. She rejected the inevitability of EMU: it was 'psychologically wrong' to accept it. She felt the Germans would ultimately agree with Britain that EMU would dilute the commitment to anti-inflation policies. As for the poorer countries, without massive transfers EMU 'could be unsustainable for their economies'. Britain should tell them so, 'playing also on their fears of German domination'. Besides, EMU was wrong for non-economic reasons – 'a way of getting to a federal Europe by the back door'. She insisted Britain do everything it could to 'undermine' Delors Stage 3 (which provided for EMU).* 'We should be more crusading,' she declared.

No crusader himself, Major changed the subject. He sensed, correctly, that Mrs Thatcher's adamantine stance was in part her inner compensation for getting ready to concede. At a meeting on 14 June, 'The Prime Minister said that she no longer had reservations about the UK joining the Exchange Rate Mechanism (ERM). The issue was when was the right time to join.' Which, in theory at least, had always been the policy anyway.

At the Dublin European summit at the end of June, Mrs Thatcher introduced Major's 'hard ecu' proposal, but not his 'opt in' initiative for EMU. Predictably, the hard ecu alternative was considered a diversionary tactic and went nowhere.† Returning from Dublin, Major urged she accept ERM entry the very next month. Inflation was too high (9.7 per cent), he

---

* She also urged that Britain try to build a wider trade dimension by bringing together the European members of NATO and the free trade area established between the United States and Canada.

† Towards the end of the Dublin Council, when Mrs Thatcher was tired and irritable, she had still to sign off a Declaration on Anti-Semitism, Racism and Xenophobia. 'What's xenophobia, anyway?' she asked crossly, knowing perfectly well. 'It means an inveterate hatred of foreigners, Prime Minister,' Douglas Hurd replied, 'and I have to tell you that the declaration is against it.' This made Mrs Thatcher laugh. It illustrated Hurd's sangfroid as her Foreign Secretary, a quality which, in her presence, Geoffrey Howe always lacked.

admitted, but she need not worry because 'attention would focus on the favourable reaction to entry, not on whether the strict Madrid conditions had been met'. Like an over-keen salesman, he was discouraging her from reading the small print. If she did not hurry, inflation might be even higher, so it would 'look like the UK was clutching at entry as a support'. The problem with this argument was that inflation was already far too high, so Major wanted to clutch at entry then and there.

Don't do it, Brian Griffiths advised her in early July, describing Major's inflation forecast as 'quite shocking'. 'You are known to stick to your word. As a result, the Madrid conditions really matter.' Griffiths was raising a point which Major had ignored: where would it leave Mrs Thatcher herself? Major was in danger of ignoring his own rule that she must not be humiliated.

Having made little progress, Major shifted his target date for ERM entry again, now advocating early autumn. Mrs Thatcher agreed that 14 September and 5 October were 'two candidates' but committed only to reconsider dates at the end of August.

On 14 July, Nicholas Ridley was forced to resign after his *Spectator* interview describing EMU as a 'German racket designed to take over the whole of Europe' (see p. 836). Mrs Thatcher thus lost her last senior Cabinet ally on the ERM.* Ridley had entered Parliament, with Mrs Thatcher, in 1959. Like Keith Joseph, he was an intellectual, of grander social background than she, who had supported her against the grain of establishment thinking. Also like Joseph, he lacked political skills; but many was the late night when he had fortified Mrs Thatcher's views over whisky in Downing Street. With Ridley's departure, she reverted to the essential loneliness with which her political career had begun.

Nine days after Ridley's resignation, there followed a reshuffle of junior posts. Two of these mattered for Mrs Thatcher's future. The first was the appointment of Peter Morrison as her PPS in succession to Mark Lennox-Boyd. She was attached to his loyalty and by her belief that he knew the parliamentary party extremely well. She remembered his help in her election as leader fifteen years before. Morrison was delighted to be offered the position, but he was already out of touch with younger MPs and his drink problem was worsening. In Richard Ryder's view, 'it looked as though he was slowly committing suicide'. This damaged man would be her main protector in the leadership challenge expected that autumn.

The other significant move was that of Tristan Garel-Jones, who left the Whips Office for the job he craved: Europe Minister in the Foreign

---

* Ridley's replacement, Peter Lilley, was equally Eurosceptic, but lacked Ridley's standing.

Office.* The consequence, as Tim Renton, the Chief Whip, later admitted, was that Garel-Jones would no longer act 'as the unofficial contact between the whips' office and the Prime Minister and her team' as he had done during the Meyer contest: 'Now he followed his natural loyalties and acted as the firelighter of the opposition [to Mrs Thatcher].' For Mrs Thatcher, this boded very ill indeed.

On the morning of 30 July, leaving his house in Sussex, Ian Gow was blown up by a car bomb planted by the IRA. Charles Powell conveyed the news to Mrs Thatcher. It was the only time he ever saw her completely break down, weeping uncontrollably. She drove straight to Sussex to comfort Gow's widow, Jane. As Mrs Thatcher later recalled, after the explosion Jane had found her husband 'moaning. She said, "Margaret, I ran back into the kitchen and just prayed to God that he had died: it was so terrible. I don't think he had any legs." ... Six months later, she said to me, "They say time heals, but it doesn't, it gets worse."'

Gow had always been Mrs Thatcher's true friend and supporter. He had given his career and, in a sense, his life for her. In murdering him the IRA were seeking to punish him not only for his Ulster Unionism, but also for his closeness to her. There was a sort of chivalry about his death, with an untold cost to his family.

Two weeks before the murder, and the day after Ridley's resignation, the Gows had invited the Thatchers to dinner. Jane recalled that Mrs Thatcher had insisted on defying security and drinking Gow's favourite cocktail – white ladies – in the garden. Indoors, as they ate, Denis raged, 'They're all trying to kill her.' He was referring not to the IRA but to his wife's parliamentary colleagues.

Amid the extraordinary pressures of 1989–90, Mrs Thatcher had devoted less time than before to the affairs of Northern Ireland. When she appointed Peter Brooke to replace Tom King as Northern Ireland Secretary in July 1989, Brooke recalled: 'She made it clear she didn't want anything happening, except keeping the place on an even keel.'† Brooke, however, detected

---

* Despite Renton's urging, Mrs Thatcher had been reluctant to put Garel-Jones in the Foreign Office. He was not, she complained to Renton, 'in line with the general direction policy has taken over the last 10 years' – 'meaning', Renton interpreted, 'he's an awful wet!' In July, however, after Garel-Jones declared himself ready to return to the back benches, Mrs Thatcher gave in.
† Brooke's appointment was more significant than Mrs Thatcher had anticipated. In the words of Sir John Chilcot, Permanent Secretary of the Northern Ireland Office: 'I doubt she ever realized how profoundly Irish Peter Brooke was. His capacity to build relationships not only with Unionism but across to the constitutional Nationalists ... she might not have sympathized with it.'

an opportunity for political re-engagement. If Republicans renounced their terrorism, he said publicly, 'I think that Government would need to be imaginative in those circumstances as to how that process should be managed.' These words caused displeasure in Downing Street. But Brooke was trying to interest Mrs Thatcher in the discussion within the IRA 'about the circumstances when violence might come to an end', a phrase under which she wrote a wiggly line of scepticism.

Drawing on 'sensitive sources', the Northern Ireland Office reported that Gerry Adams and Martin McGuinness had started to indicate interest in ending the armed struggle without 'complete loss of face'. McGuinness, in particular, had given interviews echoing Brooke's use of the word 'imaginative' and speaking of Sinn Fein's readiness 'to take part in a peace process'. The Provisionals were looking ahead: '"Outlasting Mrs Thatcher"', continued the Northern Ireland Office brief, 'is becoming a significant part of the leadership thinking.'

These words were not well calculated to please the Prime Minister. Through Powell she sent a severe reply, commenting that 'it is best to be guided by the facts, which are continued murder and mayhem perpetrated by the PIRA. We must not give them any reason to think there is weakening in our resolve to defeat them.' She had little appetite for a political deal.

Perhaps because of this, Brooke maintained a bare minimum of discussion with Mrs Thatcher about his developing political ideas. On 10 November 1990, echoing Tom King over two years earlier (see p. 727), he delivered a speech declaring that Britain had no 'selfish strategic or economic interest' in Northern Ireland. This speech, cleared by Mrs Thatcher, was likely also shown to the Republican leadership in advance. After she left office it was to have important consequences, helping lead the IRA to rethink its attitudes to peace.

In 1990, however, peace was a long way off. The IRA's immediate preoccupation was to hit mainland British targets once again. That summer, the Carlton Club and the Stock Exchange in London were bombed and high-profile individuals targeted. These included Alistair McAlpine, who escaped unscathed, and Sir Peter Terry, Governor of Gibraltar at the time of the SAS shootings in 1988, who was wounded. Gerry Adams seemed to be trying to fulfil his earlier pledge that 'Mrs Thatcher and rich and powerful people' would be made to suffer for the successful SAS assault at Loughgall (see p. 719).

Always punctilious about bereavement, Mrs Thatcher attended Gow's funeral on 8 August, where she read the lesson, and his memorial service in October. In a handwritten letter to Jane she wrote: 'I shall miss him so very much. True friends who believe the same things . . . and who are loyal whatever the weather – are rare indeed.' These were genuine sentiments, but in fact Mrs Thatcher and Gow had drifted somewhat apart. This had been another symptom of her growing isolation. By 1990, recalled Jane, even Gow 'believed she ought to go'.

Beyond the broader sufferings of Northern Ireland, the Troubles punctuated Mrs Thatcher's life personally. In March 1979, her Northern Ireland spokesman and campaign manager for the 1975 leadership contest, Airey Neave, had been murdered (see p. 174). In October 1984, at Brighton, she had endured the Grand Hotel bombing (see p. 448). And now she had lost Gow. His death added to her isolation. The IRA must have intended this. Although Mrs Thatcher did not dwell on it, she felt it.

On 18 October, at the Eastbourne by-election following Gow's death, the Conservatives lost to the Liberal Democrats. As Jane Gow recalled, 'I think it affected her very badly.' Four days later, Geoffrey Howe delivered the eulogy at Gow's memorial service. The two had been great friends. His speech was eloquent and touching, but even on such an occasion Mrs Thatcher could not restrain herself. 'Why don't you speak up, Geoffrey?' she said afterwards. 'You mumble.'

As the autumn political season resumed, Mrs Thatcher, surveying the scene, could see only repeated losses instead of the successes that had accumulated ever since the Falklands triumph in 1982. Abroad, the Cold War victory to which she had contributed so much had sidelined her in relations with the United States and been converted, as she saw it, into a ramp for European integration. At home, the public's sense that she, though often unpopular, was necessary had faded. It had become possible, even enticing, to imagine politics without her. Her poll tax 'flagship' was hit below the waterline. She could find no guiding star to bring down inflation. And then, perhaps hardest to bear, she had experienced the parting of friends and the distancing of colleagues. In some cases, most notably with Geoffrey Howe and Nigel Lawson, she had fallen out with boon companions of the Long March. In others, most notably Nicholas Ridley and Alan Walters, she had been unable to save trusted allies or, as in the case of Charles Powell, had been forced to fight for them almost to the death of her political career. In the case of Ian Gow, real, violent death at the hands of her fanatical enemies had removed her most loyal and once-closest political lieutenant.

Mrs Thatcher was, perhaps, too busy to indulge such melancholy musings for long, but the burden weighed heavily and her essential loneliness now increased. Opponents within her own party had thought about all this much more clearly than she had. They had been working for a long time to achieve her isolation. Soon they would at last feel ready to exploit it.

37
'No. No. No.'

'She was determined to have the fight'

On 1 August 1990, two days after Ian Gow's murder, Mrs Thatcher flew to Aspen, Colorado. While she was in the air, Iraqi troops, under the orders of Saddam Hussein, began to invade Kuwait.

Aspen had been intended as a semi-holiday. To overcome Mrs Thatcher's aversion to taking time off, Charles Powell had arranged for her to give a major speech to the Aspen Institute and visit the SDI National Test Facility. This could be combined with healthy mountain walks, accompanied by Denis and joined by Mark and family.* President Bush, it emerged, would also be addressing the Aspen conference. Powell begged her to keep her first evening free: 'you will probably be fairly tired'. Mrs Thatcher wrote a wiggly line under these words to indicate her irritation at the very idea.

Shortly after she arrived in Aspen, Powell informed Mrs Thatcher of the Iraqi invasion.† However shocking the news, her spirits rose. With a crisis on her hands, the dreaded prospect of a holiday receded. As she put it years later: 'I identified right from the word "Go" two things. You never appease an aggressor and ... British foreign policy is at its worst when it is giving away other people's territory, as in the Sudetenland and Czechoslovakia.' This approach, she said, drew on her family's view that 'we should have stopped Hitler when he went into the Rhineland' and her 'experience of dealing with Galtieri' in the Falklands War. Her immediate priorities were to ensure that Bush would still come to Aspen and to urge the UN Security Council to pass an emergency resolution calling for Iraqi withdrawal. The first was swiftly achieved: cancelling Bush's trip 'would have sent the wrong signal', said Brent Scowcroft. The second was

---

* As it turned out, Saddam Hussein got in the way, and Mark and his family did not come to Aspen.
† Powell had learnt of the attack in a phone call from Brent Scowcroft.

drafted in Washington and London overnight and passed in New York in the small hours.

There had been warnings. Iraq's military build-up on the Kuwaiti border had been reported, yet as late as 20 July top-secret intelligence assured Mrs Thatcher that 'the risk of armed confrontation in the immediate future is low'. After the end of the Iran–Iraq War in 1988, Britain, like the United States, had sought to improve relations with both sides. Mrs Thatcher had never met Saddam, whom, said Powell, she 'saw as a monster', but she preferred dialogue, better oil deals and growing exports to confrontation. Ministers began to interpret guidelines forbidding 'lethal' exports to Iraq with a new elasticity.

By early 1990, it became clear that Saddam, resentful of the West's unsupportive attitude to his war debts, was seeking leadership of the Arab world against it. In March, the summary execution of Farzad Bazoft, a British-based, Iranian-born journalist, for alleged spying highlighted the regime's brutal self-assertion.* Later that month, customs officials at Heathrow intercepted eight large steel tubes bound for Iraq as parts of a so-called supergun.

Britain and America were uneasy, but not yet inclined to get tough with Saddam. At their Bermuda summit in April, Mrs Thatcher told Bush that King Fahd of Saudi Arabia had begged her: 'Don't cut off ties; keep the channel open.' Over the summer, Saddam began to build up forces against Kuwait, from whom he demanded huge sums in compensation for Iraqi efforts in the Iran–Iraq War. The British government, however, continued to rely on assurances from friendly Gulf leaders that there was no cause for alarm.

The Americans had a similarly false sense of security.† Shocked by the invasion, the Bush administration initially struggled to respond. In Washington, on 2 August, before an NSC meeting to address the crisis, Bush told the press he was 'not contemplating' sending troops. This left a distinctly weak impression which the NSC meeting did nothing to correct. Brent Scowcroft was 'frankly appalled at the undertone of the discussion which suggested resignation to the invasion and even adaptation to a *fait*

---

* Documents captured by American forces after the US invasion of 2003 record Saddam discussing the case privately: 'We will execute him quickly during Ramadan . . . as punishment for Margaret Thatcher.' He wanted to punish her for trying to get her friend King Hussein of Jordan to mediate in the case and for thinking that 'Iraq is a piece of cake'.
† This was exacerbated by a meeting between Saddam and the US Ambassador to Iraq, April Glaspie, on 25 July, in which she accidentally gave Saddam the impression that the USA would not take sides in Iraq's long-standing border disputes with Kuwait.

accompli'. As they flew together to Aspen, Scowcroft found that Bush agreed: the President felt 'We've got to do something about this. He didn't know exactly what . . . but we cannot accept this kind of naked aggression.'

In Aspen, on 2 August, Mrs Thatcher awoke to a briefing from Charles Powell: the Arab response had been 'most unsatisfactory', he wrote. Her dear friend King Hussein was 'actually trying to excuse the Iraqi action' and 'The Gulf Arabs are plainly petrified.' Powell was emphatic about the significance of the attack: 'A major issue of principle is at stake: the need for the international community to prevent large, bullying countries from simply marching in and taking over small ones. We cannot just let this go by.' Mrs Thatcher underlined 'cannot' four times.

At lunchtime, the two leaders sat down to talk. Mrs Thatcher, Henry Catto, the Ambassador to Britain, recalled, 'sat, as always, bolt upright, spine straight as a queen's, an expression of concern on her face'. Bush 'as usual, sprawled in his chair'. As Powell recorded, Bush and Mrs Thatcher 'were in very close agreement in their assessment of the situation and what should be done . . . The President seemed reassured.'

Bush explained that he had already told Hosni Mubarak of Egypt and King Hussein of Jordan that the 'Arab solution' they sought 'must include Iraq's withdrawal and restoration of the lawful government of Kuwait'. Mrs Thatcher stressed two points. First, if Iraq could get away with this, 'no small state would ever be safe again'. Second, it was 'unacceptable' that more Middle East oil should be 'falling under the control of Iraq'. Measures should now include a full trade embargo, backed by a naval blockade. She shared Bush's apprehensions about an 'Arab solution', fearing that Saudi Arabia 'might even urge acceptance of the [new] status quo'. The two agreed that the only bright spot was that the Soviet Union, under Gorbachev, was thoroughly cooperative. This had never happened before in the Middle East.

The only shade of difference was that Mrs Thatcher felt more urgency than Bush about deploying forces. At this stage, military planning was defensive: the sole aim was to prevent Saddam invading Saudi Arabia.

After lunch, the two leaders faced the press. While they declared their unity of purpose, there was a contrast. Bush confirmed he was not contemplating military action, saying only that no options would be ruled out. Mrs Thatcher was much more forceful. The Iraqi invasion, she said, was '*totally* unacceptable'. 'You cannot have a situation', she asserted, 'where one country marches in and takes over another.'

This comparison, unfavourable to Bush, was reinforced by demeanour.

Bush, in a lightweight suit, stood with his hands in his pockets, looking awkward and speaking in a low, passionless key. Mrs Thatcher, dressed, as ever, with great care, stood erect with her hands clasped in front of her, and spoke with much more passion and command. She, Bernard Ingham recalled, 'was all resolve, flashing eyes, assertive language and purpose' whereas Bush was much more restrained.

After the press conference ended, Bush addressed the Aspen Institute. On the Iraqi invasion he said little, except to pay tribute to Mrs Thatcher: 'I felt very comforted by the fact that as I spoke Prime Minister Thatcher was there with me answering the tougher questions and standing shoulder to shoulder with the United States.' Bush's words were generous, but they contributed to the impression that she was the dominant character.

Bush then returned to Washington. Still, in theory, on holiday, Mrs Thatcher remained in Aspen for the next three days,* but in touch with officials and world leaders. On 3 August, she asked Royal Navy ships to start moving towards Oman. Bush also rang her that day: having spoken to the Saudi Ambassador, Prince Bandar, he remained 'rather depressed about the likely Saudi attitude'. She took the opportunity to thank him 'for all the kind things you said at Aspen'. 'It's easy when you believe them,' he replied.

The next day, she spoke on the phone to Bandar, who sounded more robust than Bush had described. Antony Acland informed her that the Saudis were now 'seriously considering' accommodating US troops. If this happened it would be a breakthrough. The presence of Western troops in Arab countries was a highly charged political and religious issue. The House of Saud had, until now, fought shy of it.

Back in the White House, Bush became clearer. 'The enormity of Iraq is upon me now,' he wrote in his diary on 3 August. 'The status quo [created by Saddam in Kuwait] is intolerable.' At a second NSC meeting, he declared it 'fortunate [that] Mrs Thatcher is at Aspen. I am glad we are seeing eye-to-eye.' A more robust US approach now emerged. As Richard Haass of the NSC staff later summarized, 'US and other forces would be dispatched to the region to deter further Iraqi aggression against Saudi Arabia – Desert Shield – and to provide a backdrop to economic sanctions so that Iraq would either have to capitulate and leave Kuwait or get pounded. A blockade of Iraq would add to the sanctions. This would require a new UN resolution ... to get the others on board.' On Sunday

---

* Mrs Thatcher sought the distraction of a nearby hiking trail and amused her local guide by setting off in a buttoned-down red dress, her only concession to the mountain terrain being a pair of tennis shoes.

5 August, Bush announced his position: 'This will not stand,' he told the press. 'This will not stand, this aggression against Kuwait.' The phrase had, as Colin Powell later wrote, 'a Thatcheresque ring' but was all the President's own. His public stance had moved a long way in three days.

That same afternoon, Mrs Thatcher delivered her Aspen speech. Designed, in Powell's words, as 'Bruges II', it sketched out a post-Cold War role for Europe with 'the closest possible partnership with the United States'. She wanted the Soviet Union brought closer to the G7; all European countries with democracy and adequate economies should be accepted by the EC. Declaring the Cold War 'over', she wanted the UN to step up as a global institution: 'Iraq's invasion of Kuwait defies every principle for which the United Nations stands. If we let it succeed, no small country can ever feel safe again. The law of the jungle would take over from the rule of law ...' Mrs Thatcher was, once again, amplifying and fortifying Bush's message.

Out of these dramatic days grew the idea that Mrs Thatcher had 'stiffened George Bush's spine'. When the crisis broke, James Baker was abroad. His perspective, as Bush became more hawkish, was that 'Thatcher had moved him,' recalled an aide. This displeased Baker: 'He said: "We're headed towards war."'* The idea of her 'stiffening' effect was fed by briefing on both sides of the Atlantic. It was even claimed that at Aspen she had turned to Bush and said, 'Remember, George, this is no time to go wobbly.' Although these words became famous they were not, in fact, uttered at Aspen. They came much later, in a different context.

Once the 'wobbly' line is stripped out, what is left of the stiffening thesis? Charles Powell dismissed 'the patronizing view that Bush only bucked up because she told him to'. Bush himself rejected the idea that 'she strengthened my resolve ... We just saw eye to eye.' Nor did Mrs Thatcher ever suggest that Bush was at sea over Kuwait. On 9 August, they spoke on the telephone: 'The President finished by thanking the Prime Minister for her leadership. The Prime Minister said that leadership came from the President. She was just a chum.'

She was a powerful chum, though. Without her supportive presence in Aspen, the almost instantaneous unity between the main allies would not have been visible. It was a given of US policy that only America could solve the Kuwait problem, but not America alone. If Mrs Thatcher had, to use

---

* Another American who ascribed to Mrs Thatcher a decisive role was Henry Kissinger. On 12 August, he rang Charles Powell, asking him to pass on the message that 'you [Mrs Thatcher] had clearly done a marvellous job in Aspen in stiffening the President. The White House party had gone out to Aspen convinced there was nothing much to be done, but had returned braced and determined. You were the new element in their thinking. You should keep it up.'

her own word, 'wobbled', who would have stood steady with the United States? This understanding of her role quickly spread. As King Fahd put it: 'Your Prime Minister was terrific – she strengthened me, she strengthened President Bush and she helped unite the whole coalition against Saddam.' In a word, she had been more confident than Bush, and that confidence had proved contagious.

On 6 August, Mrs Thatcher broke her homeward journey in Washington and spent two hours with Bush at the White House. What impressed Powell, he recorded at the time, was 'the total frankness and confidence which the President showed to the Prime Minister. She was drawn directly into the US Administration's decision-making . . . I have had a worm's eye view of Anglo-American relations at the highest level for quite a long time now. I have never seen it operate with this degree of closeness and trust.'

During the Oval Office meeting, news arrived that the Saudis had agreed to accept American forces on their soil: indeed, King Fahd had said that he would welcome a force which was not just American but multinational. This naturally led to the question of British participation. 'If the Americans needed our support,' Powell recorded her saying, 'we would give it.' Some of the Americans, however, were sceptical about how much this would mean in practice. As Jim Baker drily recalled, 'Margaret had an uncanny ability to flex our muscles.' In fact, that same day she reminded Bush of the secret Nixon–Heath understanding, recently renewed, that the United States could use the British Indian Ocean atoll of Diego Garcia for military purposes. Two days later, she informed Bush that Britain would contribute to a multinational force in Saudi Arabia.*

Mrs Thatcher's role in the Oval Office meeting was to offer her distinctive mixture of strong support and close interrogation of the facts. One important disagreement concerned the UN. Drawing on the Falklands, she was enthusiastic for the condemnatory Security Council Resolution 660 invoking Article 51 (asserting the right of self-defence), which had already been passed, believing it provided sufficient legal grounding for an allied armed response. She was worried about going further down the UN route, fearing it would be strewn with obstacles. As she and Bush met, the Security Council passed Resolution 661, which imposed sanctions on Iraq, albeit without providing the means to enforce them. 'Oh, this is just unacceptable,' she declared. 'It's not strong enough!' As Richard Haass

---

* The initial British deployment consisted of one squadron of twelve Tornado F3 fighters, one squadron of twelve Jaguar ground attack/fighter aircraft, a detachment of Rapier surface-to-air missiles, three minehunters and the necessary support forces.

analysed it, she worried that 'we would now be required to go back and get another resolution authorising us to enforce sanctions'. These concerns aside, Mrs Thatcher left the White House elated and, perhaps for the first time, deeply impressed by George Bush. She wrote in her memoirs: 'He was firm, cool, showing the decisive qualities which the Commander-in-Chief of the greatest world power must possess. Any hesitation fell away. I had always liked George Bush. Now my respect for him soared.'

Mrs Thatcher also felt an inward satisfaction. All through the period when Germany seemed to eclipse Britain in American eyes, she had comforted herself that 'When there's a crisis, they always find out who their real friends are.'* So it was now proving.

'Today's press is good,' Charles Powell informed Mrs Thatcher on 8 August, 'particularly the pops who are very strongly for you (the *Mail* above all).' The sense that she, after so many troubles, was in command, working harmoniously with allies, was powerful. After months of her lagging behind Neil Kinnock, the Gallup poll put her six points ahead on 'Who would make the best Prime Minister?'

Mrs Thatcher now largely refrained from public comment on the Iraq situation as she prepared behind the scenes. The Cabinet Secretary, Robin Butler, envisaged 'a proper War Cabinet, properly minuted and organized by the Cabinet Office', but she preferred a more intimate body, with Charles Powell taking the minutes. The membership was Mrs Thatcher, Hurd, King, the Defence Secretary, Patrick Mayhew, the Attorney-General, and the Energy Secretary, John Wakeham.

On 12 August, leaving to finish what was left of her holiday in Cornwall, Mrs Thatcher scribbled her priorities. These included: 'We must get the blockade going'; 'We must constantly put the case against Saddam and his appalling record'; 'I do not think we should provoke a clash. One will almost certainly occur in the way events happen';† 'We must keep the Soviets on side.' In pursuit of this last aim, she wrote to Gorbachev to thank him for Soviet cooperation on the Security Council. While on holiday, she told Hurd that 'our aim must be to resist the aggression against Kuwait, not to overthrow Saddam Hussein'. The deployment of a third

---

* A report Mrs Thatcher received of US reactions to her Washington visit relayed a question Bush had received at his press briefing. The ABC White House correspondent 'could not resist asking if the President had recently consulted "the man who was described by some of our colleagues only a few weeks ago as the colossus of the West, Helmut Kohl".' He got no clear answer.'

† Mrs Thatcher was disagreeing with Henry Kissinger's recent suggestion that the allies should 'draw the Iraq air force into a clash which would force us to eliminate it'.

squadron of British aircraft (Tornado GR 1s) was announced by Tom King on 23 August.

When she returned to London, Mrs Thatcher encountered serious problems, as she had feared, about the enforcement of sanctions. On 18 August, five Iraqi tankers, heading for Yemen, refused to yield. Most of Bush's advisers, and the President himself, were inclined to stop the ships by force. Jim Baker, anxious to keep the Soviet Union on side, disagreed. He wanted to give the UN the chance to pass a new Security Council resolution explicitly authorizing the enforcement of sanctions. On the telephone on 20 August, Mrs Thatcher and Bush agreed that, under Article 51, they had authority to stop ships by force. But they also accepted that, as she put it, the use of force 'would be better with a UN approach'. She said the same in public.*

The Iraqi tankers, however, continued to run the blockade and the Security Council failed to agree a new resolution. On 23 August, as Bush waited for the Soviets to come round, Powell warned that 'the Americans risk being diddled by the Russians'. Events proved otherwise. After Saddam rejected Gorbachev's entreaties, the Soviets came on board. On 25 August, UNSCR 665 passed, with no votes opposing. It banned all trade with Iraq and was interpreted as authorizing military means of enforcement. Despite Mrs Thatcher's misgivings, Baker's suggestion had clearly worked. The degree of international amity as the Cold War ended was remarkable.

Mrs Thatcher now wanted the resolution quickly acted upon. Bush called her that evening from his home in Kennebunkport. 'If Iraqi shipping tried to break the embargo,' he said, 'we must not vacillate.' She agreed: 'The key was not to go wobbly now.' Mrs Thatcher emphasized the need for momentum while waiting for sanctions to work. 'We must not', she urged in her most characteristic style, 'let the faint-hearts grow in strength.' As the call closed, Bush said Mrs Thatcher had been 'superb'. She praised his 'outstanding lead'.

This was the wholly genial context in which the famous 'wobbly' word

---

* Mrs Thatcher was already using her influence covertly to prevent sanctions-busting. Learning that the South African government's Strategic Fuels Office planned to evade the Iraq oil embargo through a swap deal with the controversial businessman Marc Rich, Britain had protested to Niël Barnard, the head of South Africa's National Intelligence Service. She was told that President de Klerk would prevent the circumvention. He wanted Mrs Thatcher to know that South Africa was the UK's firm ally in this situation. However, he also wished to point out that he 'hoped the world would realise that it was the oil embargo [against South Africa] that was directly responsible for the growth of the South African arms industry'. He also hoped that his 'positive response should one day be rewarded by the lifting of these sanctions'.

appeared.* One official remembered Bush laughing as he hung up the phone. Bush's entourage shared his amusement. Vice-President Dan Quayle recalled, 'Whenever something else came up, we'd say, "Now, don't go wobbly, Mr President! Don't go wobbly, or you'll hear it from Thatcher!"' She had not been upbraiding the President but, in her rather nanny-like way, urging him on. It was only later, once mythology had mislocated her remark to the Aspen meeting, that the 'wobbly' quotation played to the picture of Bush as weak. 'The common wisdom' that 'she stiffened my spine pisses me off', Bush said years later. By this time even he had become confused about when and why the word 'wobbly' was originally uttered.†

When interviewed for this book about how he would characterize her comment, George Bush called it 'gratuitous'. Was she being patronizing? Bush paused: 'I think it was Margaret Thatcher.'

From the first, Mrs Thatcher had believed war the likely, but not inevitable, outcome of the invasion of Kuwait. She knew that, for the sake of public opinion, sanctions would need to be given time to work, but was sceptical of their ultimate efficacy. If they failed to dislodge Saddam speedily she would turn to force. Because this strategy depended on the United States, she positioned herself to nudge Bush in her favoured direction.

Following the invasion, Mrs Thatcher had feared that the Americans might act unilaterally. She thus took comfort from the close relationship between Charles Powell and Brent Scowcroft – a personal channel set apart from her government. On 21 August, Powell reported an assurance from Scowcroft that 'the President would want to share even their most secret plans with you'. There was 'a growing feeling' within the administration that 'the United States might have to acquire a military option,' but not quite yet. 'No need to say anything to others,' she wrote on Powell's memo. As Scowcroft recalled, 'In my mind and I think the President's mind, there was no doubt after the first week that, unless the Iraqis changed their views, force was going to be used.'

That same day, Mrs Thatcher had the uncongenial task of seeing King Hussein, who had all but sided with Saddam. Powell advised firm words, but from a friendly standpoint: 'We must encourage him to behave like

---

* The word was much on Mrs Thatcher's mind and lips at that time. In a meeting with Prince Saud of Saudi Arabia the following day, she told him she was worried that 'some other countries might get wobbly' and that 'No one must get wobbly and start talking about negotiations.'
† Bush's published account added to this confusion by implying, erroneously, that Mrs Thatcher's wobbly comment came on 22 August, after he had decided to hold off intercepting ships at Moscow's request. Exhorting the President not to 'go wobbly' at this juncture would have constituted a clear criticism of his chosen course.

a white man over Iraq <u>and</u> ensure that he can survive doing so.' During the meeting, neither side pulled their punches. Mrs Thatcher said she was 'frankly amazed by the King's account': the Iraqi invasion was 'one of the most blatant cases of aggression which she had ever seen'. But after a calmer lunch, the King said 'he hoped he and the Prime Minister were still friends. The Prime Minister agreed that they were.' Jordan was much beholden to Saddam for oil, and Palestinian pro-Iraq opinion piled pressure on the beleaguered King. But it was also much beholden to Britain's support and to Mrs Thatcher personally.

Parliament was recalled to debate the Iraq crisis in early September, with polls showing over 80 per cent support for military action, and Labour saw little benefit in opposition. The only political danger seemed to be attempts, pushed by the Liberal Democrat leader Paddy Ashdown, to bind Mrs Thatcher to the 'UN route' of further Security Council resolutions. On 6 September, the Commons endorsed the government's policy by 437 votes to 35. Her line to the Cabinet, as summarized by Powell, was that force might be required 'if sanctions are patently not working. We have sufficient legal cover for it ... We do <u>not</u> accept that we have to go back to the UN for authority.'*

Although she was against rushing, Mrs Thatcher now told Hurd she was 'increasingly certain' that force would be needed. On 14 September, she told Bush Britain would send the 7th Armoured Brigade – with 120 tanks, helicopters, 7,500 ground troops and more Tornados – to the Gulf. 'Why that is just marvelous,' Bush responded: '... the icing on the cake.' The President's pleasure was unfeigned. British support 'was terrifically important', recalled Jim Baker, 'both politically and militarily ... The brutal truth of the matter is that the only forces that counted were UK forces and US forces.'

Mrs Thatcher was determined that such a significant deployment should have the right commander. Over the opposition of Tom King and the Ministry of Defence† she insisted upon General Peter de la Billière, whom she had admired ever since he commanded the daring SAS operation which ended the Princes Gate siege in 1980 (see p. 221). His appointment was widely celebrated in the press. It raised questions, however, about Mrs

---

* The legal advice Mrs Thatcher received suggested that, so long as the Amir of Kuwait made a formal request for help, military action would be permitted under international law.
† As de la Billière himself recalled, 'The very understandable wisdom of the day was, look, here's this guy who's never commanded anything, he's never been in the MOD, didn't even go to Sandhurst, never been in Germany, never been in Northern Ireland, never even served in a division. He's not the man to run a conventional war ...'

Thatcher's style of leadership. As Chief of the Defence Staff, Sir David Craig, saw it, 'Margaret had done the Falklands. All of the things that were done militarily there, rules of engagement etc., she was very up to speed with, or thought she was. So one was inclined to find she was in the lead here rather than waiting for military advice; which . . . did get a bit out of hand.'* In Patrick Wright's view, 'There was a danger that she and Charles Powell would try to run the war alone.'

On 30 September, Mrs Thatcher saw Bush in New York. 'As is usual when the chips are down, the British have been there when it counts . . .' Scowcroft briefed the President. 'The Prime Minister should know how deeply you appreciate, and rely on, this partnership.' When the two leaders met, alone except for Scowcroft and Powell, Mrs Thatcher was impatient to plan for early military action. Recalling the 'very brief window' for military action in the Falklands, she stressed that in this case they had to 'move during the cool months – November to March. If we waited for sanctions to work it would take us to the following November.' She believed that 'The whole reputation of the US and the UK was on the line.' As Hurd noted in his diary, 'The secret record of her private talk shows that she egged Bush on and on and up and up in the nicest way.'

Bush, though sympathetic, worried about American public opinion. He wondered whether Iraqi provocation would free him to act faster. This could take the form of terrorism, the abuse of foreign nationals in Kuwait or the 'ruination of Kuwait'. Indeed, Bush thought the USA had 'initially defined its objectives too narrowly . . . He was now convinced "this guy is going to have to go" . . . The status quo ante was not good enough. The Prime Minister agreed with this.'

Talk of a 'provocation', however, displeased her. She thought an attack should be made only when the coalition was best prepared. But without a provocation, the idea of seeking cover from the UN Security Council was gaining ground in Washington. Earlier in September, Bush, like Mrs Thatcher, had opposed this course: 'She does not want to go back to the UN on use of force,' he wrote in his diary, 'nor do I.' Since then Baker, in particular, had sought to shift his position. Joining the meeting in New York, Baker stressed that without UN backing they risked losing public support. There followed what Baker called 'a very spirited debate . . . Her point, . . . well taken, was that we've got authority to do this under Article

---

* Craig thought, for example, that she tended to use the War Cabinet to focus on secondary issues, such as clothing, rather than the necessary strategic planning.

51. "Oh, George!" she said, "Let's just go do it!"' With Baker at one end and Mrs Thatcher at the other, Bush was undecided.

The following day, unbeknown to Mrs Thatcher, Hurd and Baker tasked the British and American UN Ambassadors, David Hannay and Tom Pickering, with constructing the next steps that might be taken at the UN. When Hannay reported this to London Mrs Thatcher was furious.* 'I am <u>appalled</u>,' she wrote, 'I have NOT consented to any such instructions being given to David Hannay . . . My confidence in the Administration is <u>diminished</u>. I do <u>NOT intend that our forces will be answerable to anyone other than the U.K. govt</u>.'

Mrs Thatcher's reaction was understandable, given that her Foreign Secretary seemed set on a policy which she vigorously opposed. But the problem arose partly because she had kept the Foreign Office out of her innermost counsels.† On 4 October, Hurd felt Mrs Thatcher's anger: 'PM, increasingly Boadicean, is now definitely of the war party.'

Once back from New York, Mrs Thatcher had to make up her mind about the ERM. By this stage, in John Major's view, she was coming to look at British entry 'like ageing – you don't like it, but you can't avoid it'. As he encouraged her, he was growing in confidence. In the late summer both Francis Maude and Peter Morrison had approached him, separately and in secret, to urge he consider himself the next Prime Minister. Morrison gave Ian Twinn, Major's PPS, the sense that he was acting on behalf of the Tory establishment. 'I think Major would have thought he had it in the bag after this,' recalled Twinn, 'and that "the men in suits", such as Wakeham, would support him.'

On 3 October, matters came to a head. An anxious Major warned Mrs Thatcher that September's RPI figure would be even higher than August's. By the logic of the Madrid Conditions, this was a strong argument for not joining – Britain's inflation rate was not converging with the European average – but Major was desperate to reverse the argument. 'The monetary squeeze', he said, 'was clearly biting hard' and so a reduction in interest rates would soon be justified. The government had three options – to cut

---

* Hannay recalled an 'enormous row' which led to his telegram being formally withdrawn. This was an extremely unusual step, signifying deep displeasure. As Hannay recalled: 'I just thought, "How silly! She obviously thinks she can tell the Americans how to do this."'

† Mrs Thatcher also had an issue with David Hannay, whose talents she admired but whose manner she found irritating. When it had been suggested that he become head of the Foreign Office in succession to Patrick Wright, she had commented: 'David is very good, but it would be rather like having a pneumatic drill in the next room. He should go to the UN in New York – they like that sort of thing.' That is what happened.

interest rates without ERM entry, to cut them on entering, or to enter and then delay action on rates 'for a few days' to study immediate reactions. He preferred the last.

Mrs Thatcher, however, preferred the second. But, as she told the key, final meeting the next day, she wanted 'to avoid the impression that the cut in interest rates was a bonus flowing from ERM entry – it was better to present it as fully justified by domestic conditions, with ERM providing an essential underpinning of counter-inflationary policy'. Even now she remained unconvinced by the economic benefits of entry, but she could see clear political gain in an interest rate cut. In the view of Terry Burns, it was her way of 'checkmating' everyone else. Those present had no choice but to grant her wish.

The meeting decided that the Chancellor would announce Britain's entry on Friday 5 October, the very next day, just after the markets had closed, revealing the 1 per cent cut in interest rates at the same time. Sterling seemed stable at the rate of 2.93 deutschmarks, so the entry rate chosen was 2.95 DM to the pound.*

Mrs Thatcher spent part of the Friday preparing her speech for next week's party conference. With the Liberal Democrats threatening to win the upcoming Eastbourne by-election, she needed to attack them. To do this, John O'Sullivan, the speech's joke-master,† had proposed she compare their new logo, an unidentifiable bird taking wing, to the dead parrot in John Cleese's famous *Monty Python* sketch. Mrs Thatcher, however, had not heard of *Monty Python* and was confused when O'Sullivan explained the sketch, surreal humour not being her thing. With her customary conscientiousness, she insisted on studying a video, which she did carefully, without smiling. 'She did not seem terribly impressed,' John Whittingdale noted in his diary, 'and did not think that he [Cleese] delivered it very well.'‡ At 4 p.m. she put all this to one side to tell those present that Britain would shortly be joining the ERM. 'She brushed over that we were joining,' Whittingdale noted, 'saying "But we've got the cut in interest rates."'

At 5.30 p.m. on 5 October, Mrs Thatcher gave a press conference, her Chancellor silently in attendance, outside 10 Downing Street. She put the

---

* Sterling entered the ERM in the wider bands, which permitted up to a 6 per cent variation up or down. Wider bands in the mechanism were normally seen as temporary, with the eventual aim being to confine the currency to tighter bands of 2.5 per cent.

† This was an onerous position. Three days earlier, O'Sullivan had had to explain to Mrs Thatcher the phrase 'Beam me up, Scotty.'

‡ Aware that Cleese was an active Lib Dem supporter, Mrs Thatcher was probably even less receptive to the sketch than she would otherwise have been.

interest rate cut first and ERM entry second. She and Major, she said, were 'both very pleased'. For Major this was indeed a happy moment. He had achieved what most of the great and the good had long advocated; he was Mrs Thatcher's persuader and, by implication, her successor.*

Although Mrs Thatcher had got her interest rate cut, she had given in without being converted. As John Kerr put it, 'We didn't think she'd signed up. We'd just dragged her over the line.' As events would prove, however, her instincts had been correct. The timing of ERM entry was wrong, partly because British inflation was not under control and partly because of tying sterling to a deutschmark relationship when, because of reunification, German monetary needs were changing. She had raised this point earlier but allowed herself to be overruled. 'Our big mistake', said Terry Burns, 'was not foreseeing the scale of what subsequently happened to German interest rates.' New strain on sterling was inevitable.

Above all, Mrs Thatcher had lost politically. Major, now clearly the 'heir apparent', had stepped out of her shadow. 'On the night we went in,' Powell remembered, 'I felt it was a necessary compromise': the truth was 'She no longer really had the power.'†

The timing of entry was interpreted more politically than economically, with the press predicting a 'boomlet' ahead of a likely general election. Ingham told Mrs Thatcher she might now expect 'a more cohesive government as necessity exercises its own discipline over the self-indulgent . . . You should be spared a leadership contest this year.'

On 9 October, the Conservative party conference, in Bournemouth, began in more confident mood. In a fringe speech, Geoffrey Howe welcomed ERM entry as the start of Britain's new engagement in Economic and Monetary Union (EMU). Teasing Thatcherites, he added: 'There can and should, if I may coin a phrase, be "no turning back".' In a second speech, he incited Britain to be in the 'driver's seat', not the 'rear carriage' of the 'European train'. His close friend Leon Brittan spoke in the same vein. 'PM was v. upset,' noted Whittingdale. In her platform speech she thanked all prominent members of her Cabinet except Howe.

---

* For Geoffrey Howe the event was less happy, although he fervently supported entry. By chance he was with the Queen when the story broke, but when she mentioned the news, 'I didn't know what she was talking about because I hadn't been informed about our entry. This showed how I was now kept out of all important decisions,' he recalled. 'It was wounding.'
† There can be little doubt that Mrs Thatcher was not really reconciled to ERM entry. On 23 October, preparing for an ERM debate in Parliament, she was informed that John Biffen, a lifelong Eurosceptic, planned to vote against her government. Her private reaction was 'Good old John.'

When she made her sixteenth speech as party leader, Mrs Thatcher was less nervous than usual. Ingham had laid down a challenge to her mettle, telling her to offer 'the firm slap of leadership' against Kinnock. She willingly obliged. She justified ERM entry as the fruit of 'our own financial discipline' and emphasized that it did not imply agreement to a single currency and what she called 'a federal Europe through the back-Delors'.* Her bravura passage concerned the Liberal Democrat bird. Just before going on stage she had asked Whittingdale, with doubt in her voice, 'This Monty Python, John, is he one of us?' 'Oh yes, Prime Minister,' said Whittingdale, with some presence of mind, 'he's a great supporter.' Reassured, she delivered the lines with superb, though uncomprehending aplomb: 'I will say only this of the Liberal Democrat symbol and the party it symbolises. It is an ex-parrot. It is not merely stunned. It has ceased to be, expired and gone to meet its maker' etc. Her speech earned a standing ovation of nine minutes, with repeated chants, to the mortification of Cabinet colleagues, of 'TEN MORE YEARS!' It was the eve of her sixty-fifth birthday.

On 18 October, the Conservatives lost the Eastbourne by-election to the Liberal Democrats on a 20 per cent swing. Shortly afterwards Ingham sent Mrs Thatcher a note demonstrating a candour few would have dared emulate. He warned of a broadly held impression that 'You have lost your touch and drive.' 'The plain truth is that the Government and your party need to be made to snap out of it; to recover their purpose; and to jump to it.' This advice fell on deaf ears. Peter Morrison told Ingham that Mrs Thatcher was 'deeply hurt "after all these years"' by what he had written. The matter was not pursued.

The Monday after the Tory conference, Mrs Thatcher met the US Defense Secretary, Dick Cheney, in London. Cheney set out the latest plan for liberating Kuwait, should sanctions and diplomacy fail. If an extensive air campaign proved unable to dislodge Iraqi forces, ground troops would be used. Were Saddam to deploy weapons of mass destruction (WMD), the US would probably 'rely on massive conventional response' rather than use such weapons itself. Could Britain envisage the use of nuclear weapons in such circumstances? She said she would be 'most reluctant to consider this, indeed she would rule it out'.

Mrs Thatcher summarized her own views. Saddam would not withdraw from Kuwait, so 'We would have to eject him.' If he did withdraw, though, 'we must demand reparations, the dismantling of his CW and BW

---

* The fact that she used this semi-pun indicated a hardening of her line: she had rejected it for an advertisement in the European elections the year before.

capability and an end to his military nuclear programme'. Otherwise, 'we should all be sitting here in President Bush's second term discussing how to achieve what we ought to do now'. She wanted to agree on dates for military action. Brent Scowcroft felt such pressure helped avoid 'foot-dragging ... There was Margaret, behind the scenes, constantly pushing, "Let's get going, let's get going. We know that this is what we have to do."'

President Bush, however, now returned to his fixation with an Iraqi provocation. He wanted a new Security Council resolution to include the 'right to reprovision nationals (or extract them if needed)'. If Saddam refused, or attacked helicopters sent in to rescue US personnel, this could provide the trigger for military action. When Mrs Thatcher and Bush spoke on 18 October, she objected: 'we need no more triggers for military action, and if you send helos in they could be shot down – they are sitting ducks'. What she understood, perhaps better than Bush, was that the United States would have an interest in its helicopters being shot down. Though she did not put it in such terms, this would be morally wrong. Bush agreed to drop the idea.

On 23 October, Mrs Thatcher presented Britain's strategic objectives to David Craig, the Chief of the Defence Staff. As well as Iraqi withdrawal and the restoration of Kuwait's legitimate government, she wanted those responsible for atrocities to be brought to justice and for Iraq's WMD capability to be eliminated. She stressed that 'military action would in all likelihood have to be initiated before the end of the year' and efforts should continue to 'wean' the USA from seeking a further UN resolution. The overthrow of Saddam was not a specific goal of British policy: as Powell put it, she 'just assumed' he would be 'toppled in the process'.

Although Mrs Thatcher continued to be influential with the Bush administration, she had obviously mattered more in the uncertain days of August than in the more organized ones of October. David Hannay, no friend to her,* was caustic: 'She thought she was running the show but she wasn't. The illusion that we were driving it faded in September, October, November for everyone, except her.' On 30 October, against all her advice, President Bush resolved that the USA would seek a UN Security Council resolution before using force.† An ultimatum would be issued to Saddam that he should leave Kuwait by a certain date, or be forced out. This decision was communicated personally to Mrs Thatcher by James Baker, in London,

---

* By this time Hannay was annoyed with her because of her attitude to Europe, her failure to make him head of the Foreign Office and his exclusion from the Iraq policy loop.

† This UN strategy was, in fact, a conditional one. Without UN backing, or even Congressional approval, recalled Bob Gates, Deputy National Security Advisor, 'The President was still willing to go. In fact, he told us in the Oval Office that he was prepared to be impeached.'

on 7 November. Baker stressed the importance of a further resolution in overcoming domestic opposition. 'You don't need it politically,' Mrs Thatcher replied. 'With all due respect, ma'am,' said Baker, 'I think you need to let us be the judge of what we need politically in the United States.' Grudgingly, she conceded that work should begin on a draft resolution. On 30 October, Bush had also resolved to raise the US troop commitment to 450,000, almost doubling current levels. While not inevitable, military action seemed ever more likely.

As she grappled with these developments, Mrs Thatcher also had to prepare for the Rome European Council in late October, which threatened to bring the Delors EMU plan to a head. In the run-up, Helmut Kohl had called for the Council to agree 1994 as the start date for Stage 2 of EMU, although what Stage 2 would consist of remained unclear.* On 20 October, at Chequers, Mrs Thatcher received the Italian Prime Minister, Giulio Andreotti, who would chair the Rome meeting. The two, recalled Powell, 'cordially disliked each other and disagreed profoundly on progress towards greater European integration'. Powell told her that the Italians, 'hopelessly advanced' on EMU, might press for a Stage 2 starting date. Warning of a likely 'ambush on this from the French, Germans and Commission', he advised her to speak to Andreotti 'in resolute but not volcanic mode'. She put an exclamation mark beside the word 'volcanic' but, with Andreotti, she was certainly smouldering. Attacking EMU and political union, she insisted that only 'the traditional nation states of Europe' could prevent the Community being 'under the thumb of the dominant nation [Germany]'. After the meeting, Andreotti said that they had agreed on 'absolutely nothing'.

John Kerr warned Mrs Thatcher that, at the summit, Andreotti would not accept her request to discuss the GATT talks† which were being held up, she believed, by EC refusal to reform its protectionist Common Agricultural Policy (CAP). The push was on for EMU Stage 2 and steps towards political union. 'None of these are ripe for decisions . . .' Kerr went on, 'The risk is that the Italian presidency nevertheless rush their fences.' Powell continued to warn of the likely ambush. On 24 October, he asked whether she would prefer 'to come out with a clear 11:1 split', or to build tactical alliances on the practicalities involved? While Powell favoured the latter, her mind tended towards a clear split.

In later years, Kerr dismissed talk of an 'ambush' at the Rome summit.

---

* Stage 3 would be the start of the single currency.
† The General Agreement on Tariffs and Trade (GATT) was the forerunner of what is now the World Trade Organization (WTO).

While it is true that Mrs Thatcher had some sense of what would happen,* in Powell's view, 'the Foreign Office did not draw out the risk'. More broadly, her officials did not expose her to the full extent and momentum of EC integrationist ideology. Under the pressures of Delors and the end of the Cold War, the centralizers were gaining ground. By 1990, as Kerr admitted, 'The EMU dossier had picked up a momentum of its own.' British officials believed the EMU 'juggernaut' was bound to roll on, but neither they nor their political masters told Mrs Thatcher this. 'She thought she could stop it,' recalled Kerr. 'We thought she couldn't.' Besides, they did not share her extreme anxiety. As Kerr put it, 'She thought the pound was part of nationhood. The rest of us didn't think that. It was *not* one of the stripes in the Union Jack.'†

On arriving in Rome, Mrs Thatcher gave lunch to President Mitterrand. As was often the case, he was inclined to minimize differences. When she declared that Britain 'would never give up our sovereign right to issue our own currency', he affected to agree: 'That was where France stood too: a common currency, not a single currency.'‡ She complained about a recent interview given by Delors in which he had 'talked of the Commission as the Executive of Europe, the European Parliament as the Legislature, and the Council of Ministers as the Senate'. She saw this as 'proof positive of his ambitions'. Mitterrand, who had always looked down on Delors, murmured sympathetically that his remarks were 'not at all wise'. The Delors interview would soon bulk even larger in Mrs Thatcher's mind.

Seeking, perhaps, to tap into Mitterrand's earlier concerns about Germany (see pp. 815–7), Mrs Thatcher told him that 'the idea you could bind Germany into the Community and tie it down that way was wrong'. If all countries were forced to surrender their national sovereignty, 'you would soon find that Germany was dominant'. The problem went wider still: 'A move towards a federal Europe would be going up a blind alley in history, just . . . as the formation of the Soviet Union had been.' Mitterrand suggested that the Soviet Union had been 'broken by economic failure and bureaucratic centralisation'. Mrs Thatcher 'hazarded that Europe was going in the same direction'.

---

* The Italian plan had been carefully concocted: ahead of the summit, an informal delegation had been visiting all member-state capitals, except London, to concert immediate agreement against Britain and for a Stage 2 date.
† Kerr's personal opposition to Mrs Thatcher's attitudes towards the EC was notable. Leon Brittan, meeting him at the end of September, wrote, 'his heart is very much in the right place, and he is quite candid and critical of the Government as and when he feels like it'.
‡ Mitterrand's line was by no means French policy, so Powell added: '(Ed. That's what he said.)'

As they talked over lunch, almost all the virtually irreconcilable differences between Mrs Thatcher's world view and the EC leadership were set out – free trade versus protection,* national monetary and political sovereignty versus integration, opposing views about how to handle a reunited Germany. But the atmosphere remained civilized. According to Sophie-Caroline de Margerie, Mitterrand's note-taker, 'Each was at ease in one another's company. It was friendly, bordering on flirty.' Mrs Thatcher enjoyed the occasion.† She did not, however, gain anything useful for the forthcoming Council meeting.

That meeting proved unpleasant. As Kerr had warned, Mrs Thatcher failed to substitute a discussion of GATT for EMU. Instead, her partners insisted that the communiqué include warm references to political union and set a start date (1 January 1994) for Stage 2 of monetary union. 'My objections were heard in stony silence,' Mrs Thatcher later recalled. 'I now had no support. I just had to say no.' The 'clear 11:1 split' of which Powell had written was becoming a reality.

On the morning of 28 October, as Hurd continued to negotiate the text, Mrs Thatcher called a press conference. As Kim Darroch, a diplomat at the Rome Embassy, recalled, the room was 'heaving' and very hot: 'And she comes in and sits down, and you sense, they [the journalists] smell the blood.' She denounced the Council and implied she would veto efforts to bring EMU into being through a treaty amendment. On GATT and the CAP, she condemned obstructionism by France and Germany motivated by 'plain straightforward nationalist interests'.

The assembled leaders made no effort to arrive, as was customary, at an agreed text. For the first time ever, the conclusions of the meeting included one member state – the United Kingdom – dissenting in a separate paragraph. 'We were pretty shocked,' said Michael Jay of the British delegation. 'This was not the way you do things.' In his view, the Foreign Office had 'underestimated the real drive toward EMU and political union ... We were too much in the weeds.'

---

* Mrs Thatcher had warned that she would insist that the Community table proposals to advance the GATT talks (about which was France being particularly obstructive): 'Failure would be a signal to the world that Europe was protectionist.' Mitterrand was unmoved: 'Of course the Community was protectionist,' he interjected: 'that was the point of it.'

† Sophie-Caroline de Margerie, whose first European Council this was, also enjoyed the encounter. 'Mrs Thatcher said to me "Good luck, my dear." It was kind and sweet of her to notice a very junior woman. I would have jumped into the Tiber for her.' She recalled that Mrs Thatcher had 'energy, charm and vision – especially energy – to an extent I had never seen before and never saw since in anyone else'.

Geoffrey Howe, briefed by the Foreign Office,* now appeared on Brian Walden's Sunday television programme and suggested that the government did not oppose the principle of a single currency. For all Howe's mildness of manner, this was a provocation, intended as such.

With characteristic speed, Mrs Thatcher wrote a thank-you letter that very day to her host in Rome, the British Ambassador: 'It was frustrating not to be able to see rather more of Rome, which was looking lovely in the sunshine today – perhaps next time.' Her assumption that there would be a next time was looking shaky.

Mrs Thatcher returned to London in fighting form. The leader in *The Times*, whose Editor she had briefed, declared she had been 'absolutely right. This summit was a disgrace.' On the following evening, 29 October, the present author encountered her at a Downing Street reception: 'She seemed absolutely confident ... She was happy to fight the next election on Europe. "I wd say to the voters, 'Ask the candidates "Do you want to go to Parlt to decide things for me, or do you want just to hand over those decisions to foreign powers?"'" I said what cd she do about G. Howe & she said with a sly look, "Ah well, Geoffrey must speak for himself."' He soon would.

The next day, Mrs Thatcher reported on the summit to Parliament. Despite the decision on EMU, she reiterated that Britain would retain its own currency unless Parliament and the people decided otherwise. Neil Kinnock, attacking her handling of the summit, quoted Leon Brittan as saying, 'You don't have to lose the pound sterling under the single currency plan.'† This was a good way of annoying Mrs Thatcher, since Brittan irritated her by working for, as she increasingly saw it, 'the other side'. She answered:

> Leon Brittan is a loyal member of the Commission ... it is a non-elected body and I do not want the Commission to increase its powers at the expense of the House, so of course we differ. The President of the Commission, Mr Delors, said in a press conference ... that he wanted the European Parliament to be the democratic body of the Community, he wanted the Commission to be the Executive and he wanted the Council of Ministers to be the Senate. No. No. No.

---

* Geoffrey Howe's exceptional closeness to several British officials with their own strong pro-European views was an important factor in his way of thinking. 'He was surrounded by Michael Butler, David Hannay, John Kerr,' recalled Richard Ryder. 'They were absolutely vehement.'
† Brittan was suggesting that a single currency could have notes and coins with values in both pounds sterling and the European currency unit (known then as the ecu).

These three words were endlessly – and rightly – quoted afterwards. They were part of a classic, combative statement of her views, but were almost always wrenched from their context. Mrs Thatcher was not attacking the EC and all its works. She was attacking the Commission and its ambitions for more European integration, which the government and the great majority of Conservative MPs opposed. Her words were part of a long-held position which she was now 'weaponizing' for political struggle. As Powell put it, 'She was determined to have the fight.'

Mrs Thatcher also predicted that the hard ecu for which Britain had been advocating (see p. 851) could evolve into a single currency, but 'would not become widely used throughout the Community'. As John Major recalled in his memoirs, 'I nearly fell off the bench. With this single sentence she wrecked months of work and preparation.' Should he have been so surprised? He knew Mrs Thatcher's views and was aware that the hard ecu was unlikely to get anywhere. Her expression of her opinion was an almost predictable response to Howe's comments on Walden's show. What happened at Rome, and how Mrs Thatcher and Howe reacted to it, had now brought matters to a head. For those long waiting to make their move, 'No. No. No.' was not so much a shock as a cue.

38
Downfall
'But it's a coup'

Shortly after Mrs Thatcher's statement on the Rome summit, Geoffrey Howe decided he must resign. This had been long meditated, but the moment itself was unexpected, even to him.

Since losing the Foreign Office in July 1989, Howe had been all but terminally disaffected. His hope for a greater influence over policy had come to nothing. By the end of June 1990, he was in a 'dreadful mood', Ian Gow warned Mark Lennox-Boyd – 'his voice broken, a look of mournful sadness, and of course feelings of rejection'. Mrs Thatcher spurned Lennox-Boyd's suggestion that she appoint him Leader of the Lords as a viscount: 'Never, never, never a Viscount,' she replied. 'He is a loyal dog,' Lennox-Boyd recorded, 'loves her, but is boring and indecisive and gets kicked.' She casually told Howe he could stay until the general election, 'whilst', Howe told one associate, 'pointedly saying nothing about what might happen after that'. Howe realized he was running out of time to influence events. He was spoiling for a fight to stop Mrs Thatcher derailing his beloved European train. For him, ERM entry was just the first stop, whereas Mrs Thatcher hoped it would prevent the full journey. 'Geoffrey was in favour of a single currency,' recalled Charles Powell. 'It went back a long way.'

Howe's opportunity was sudden. Dismayed by Mrs Thatcher's performance in Rome and her subsequent statement to the House, that same day he told his special adviser, Anthony Teasdale: 'She is using her political capital to shift the centre of gravity of the Conservative Party in an anti-European direction. Unless she is resisted, she will succeed.' Howe knew the rules: any formal challenge to her leadership before November 1991 had to come in November 1990 – in other words, within weeks.

The following day, Howe addressed a university gathering. One student asked how, given Mrs Thatcher's language the day before, he could possibly stay in the government. 'That's a very good question,' replied Howe, 'it is one I think about a lot.' That night, he decided to resign.

Mrs Thatcher's advisers, though unaware of Howe's plans, sensed danger as the leadership deadline approached. The country at large resented divisions over Europe, the return of double-digit inflation and the poll tax, while Mrs Thatcher was seen as increasingly imperious. Her approach to Iraq's invasion of Kuwait commanded broad support but had not restored her political fortunes.* MPs increasingly believed that their leader was dragging them down.

At Cabinet, on 1 November, Mrs Thatcher rebuked Howe rudely over delays in parliamentary business. 'It was embarrassing,' recalled John Major, 'lots in Cabinet did not like it.' Although she did not know it, by then Howe had already decided to resign and had told Leon Brittan as much on the phone that morning.

Despite his determination to go, Howe struggled with his resignation letter. Arabella Warburton, his political assistant, was puzzled that his draft did not readily set out the reasons for his departure: 'No one will understand what's actually forced you to go. It could be so much more punchy.' To which Howe replied: 'I just don't want to do that to her – nor do I want to bring down the government.'† At 5.50 p.m., in Downing Street, Howe informed Mrs Thatcher of his decision. She asked if anything could persuade him to stay. When he said no, she made no further effort.

The immediate reaction in Downing Street was of private pleasure. As Mrs Thatcher later wrote, 'In a sense it was a relief he had gone.' It was 'marvellous news', Brian Griffiths told John Whittingdale. With Tim Renton, the Chief Whip, away at home in Sussex, those now gathered in the Policy Unit saw a chance to re-Thatcherize the Cabinet. Perhaps Norman Tebbit could return? As Whittingdale noted in his diary: 'It may be we have turned disaster into triumph.'

That evening, the exchange of letters customary on resignations was published. Howe's characteristically long, careful and earnest text stuck almost wholly to European policy. Only in the thirteenth paragraph did he summon the courage to declare, 'I am deeply anxious that the mood you have struck – most notably in Rome this weekend and in the House of Commons this Tuesday – will make it more difficult for Britain to ... retain a position of influence in this vital debate.' On European policy, he added, 'I now find myself unable to share your view of the right approach.'

---

* In 1987, her Gallup approval rating as Prime Minister had climbed to 52 per cent. Over the summer of 1990, its peak was 33 per cent.

† Elspeth Howe was constantly irritated by her husband's reluctance to hit back at Mrs Thatcher: 'I've never heard him make any of the comments he could have made about her behaviour. If it had been me, it would have been different. But that's him.'

Mrs Thatcher replied, with Powell's assistance. She regretted his decision and thanked Howe for his 'courage and fortitude' as her Chancellor. More backhandedly, she praised him as Foreign Secretary because he had won 'the highest respect and admiration of your Foreign Minister colleagues'. She had long complained that he craved the approval of foreigners more than he fought for British interests. Even now, she could not quite repress her scorn.

Howe's resignation was a big story. The last survivor of Mrs Thatcher's first Cabinet, he had, with the arguable exception of Nigel Lawson, been the most important minister of the Thatcher 'revolution'. His resignation not only reflected poorly on Mrs Thatcher's management of people, but also, as she recognized, drew 'disparaging attention to my longevity'. Speculation grew that a challenger – Michael Heseltine – would now come forward. But Heseltine was not prepared. He and Howe were friendly allies over Europe and so he was 'very surprised' not to have been given advance warning of the resignation. He was off to Jordan for four days and had no plan ready. Nor did Howe.*

On the night of Howe's resignation, with Renton out of touch, Alastair Goodlad, the Deputy Chief Whip, went to 10 Downing Street, where he found Mrs Thatcher and Denis 'enjoying some drinks', and 'surprised' but not 'dismayed' by the resignation. Goodlad feared that the Policy Unit's idea of bringing Norman Tebbit back would 'solidify support' against her and so sought to scotch it. Denis was noisy in support of Tebbit, particularly because Tebbit was so strong against immigration. When Mrs Thatcher rang Renton, in Sussex, he argued against Tebbit's return. 'You're always on the wrong side,' she said crossly. 'Look at the people you've been suggesting to me.' The next morning, returning early and unwillingly to London to see Mrs Thatcher, Renton continued to resist Tebbit's return. The issue, however, became moot after Tebbit himself arrived at No. 10 and said he would not join the Cabinet.† Thus passed Mrs Thatcher's last chance to fortify her Cabinet with a strong, front-rank supporter.

It was eventually agreed, against Mrs Thatcher's preferences, that

---

* In deciding what to do next, Howe was also influenced by Nigel Lawson's advice that 'probably the best thing to do was to wait until there was an opportunity [to speak] in the Commons and turn down media requests'.
† Tebbit kept the promise he had made to his wife, Margaret, paralysed by the IRA bomb at Brighton, not to return to front-line politics. He may also have felt the Education job on offer to be a little junior.

Kenneth Clarke should move to Education, replacing John MacGregor (who replaced Howe as Leader of the House), and that William Waldegrave should replace Clarke at Health. Both were firm Euro-enthusiasts. Whittingdale conveyed this news to Robin Harris and Andrew Dunlop in the Policy Unit: 'Both of them said: "Right. That's it. She's lost."' Whittingdale blamed Renton for the changes. He regretted that Peter Morrison (away shooting) had not been around 'to talk her out of it'. From then onwards, Renton felt excluded from her counsels. Taking advantage of the brief parliamentary recess, he spent the following Monday shooting in Lincolnshire rather than helping to secure Mrs Thatcher.

On Sunday 4 November, while Heseltine was in Jordan, a letter he had written to his constituency chairman was published. Noting Howe's departure, Heseltine warned that the Tories had 'lurched violently away from the mainstream'. 'The issue, of course, is Europe,' he continued: in his view, the wide range of views in the party could easily be held together, were it not for Mrs Thatcher. In using Europe to isolate her, Heseltine's letter made no mention of any leadership challenge or of the poll tax.

On the Monday, when asked if his letter had been a direct challenge to Mrs Thatcher, Heseltine joked, 'No. No. No.' Mrs Thatcher flew to Geneva to deliver a speech on global warming. Peter Morrison returned from his shoot just as she left, bearing a brace of pheasants for John Whittingdale.

At the shooting tea in Lincolnshire that afternoon, Tim Renton was telephoned by Cranley Onslow, the Chairman of the 1922 Committee, to discuss the rules for a leadership challenge. It was decided that nominations should be in by 15 November and the first ballot, if there were a contest, should take place on 20 November. No one seems to have objected that, at the time of any first ballot, Mrs Thatcher would be at the Conference on Security and Cooperation in Europe (CSCE), a summit in Paris to mark the formal end of the Cold War.

The rules required a proposer and seconder. Onslow informed Renton that, in the event of a contest, Hurd would propose Mrs Thatcher and Major would second her. Renton immediately objected, noting that last year: 'I had proposed and Tristan Garel-Jones [as Deputy Chief Whip] had seconded.' Renton sought to maintain this precedent, for reasons of both propriety* and politics. He worried that should Douglas Hurd,

---

* There was no justification for this. Richard Ryder, himself a former Chief Whip, regarded Renton's view as 'codswallop'. It also contradicted his other doctrine – for which there was genuine precedent – that the whips should remain 'neutral' in a leadership contest. Obviously they were not neutral if their two chiefs had nominated the Prime Minister. Mrs Thatcher had

for example, wish to become a candidate in any second round, having proposed Mrs Thatcher in the first round 'could be acutely embarrassing'. Sure enough, the following evening, Hurd told Renton that 'he had not been overwhelmed by the thought of proposing the Prime Minister, nor had John Major with whom he had had words ... but it was obviously impossible for him to refuse'. Foreign Secretary and Chancellor were closely in touch.

Under the rules, to win outright on the first ballot a leadership candidate needed both an overall majority and '15 per cent more of the votes of those entitled to vote than any other candidate'. With 372 Conservative MPs eligible, the winner must receive at least 56 more votes than her or his nearest rival. But the exact number of votes required to win depended on the number of abstentions. If the threshold were not reached on the first ballot, there would be a second, in which new candidates could join.

On 7 November, during the debate on the Queen's Speech, Geoffrey Howe 'sat deep in thought', reported the *Daily Telegraph*, as Mrs Thatcher said how much she regretted his resignation and that there was not 'any significant policy difference on Europe' between them. This attempt to placate Howe annoyed him. He had explained their policy differences in his resignation letter.

On Thursday 8 November, by-elections in the safe Labour seats of Bradford North and Bootle saw dramatic swings to Labour from the Conservatives. The next day came more awkward news. Richard Needham, a minister at the Northern Ireland Office, had been illegally recorded saying privately: 'I wish that cow would resign.'* Mrs Thatcher rang Renton. 'You mustn't take it too seriously, Tim,' she said, 'I've been called much worse things before. After all this is only a three-letter word.' Even Renton noted that 'her resilience was astonishing'.

Over the weekend of 10–11 November, facing immense pressure to stand, Heseltine hesitated. Saturday's *Guardian* reported that his camp was seeking a stalking horse so he might enter on the second round. That same day, Heseltine sought backing from the Editor of the *Sunday Times*, Andrew Neil, who, unlike his boss, Rupert Murdoch, was a Heseltine supporter. Neil told Heseltine: 'We're likely to be very sympathetic' but refused to pledge his paper's endorsement: 'You have to declare first!' Shortly

---

benefited from this muddle over how the whips should behave when she challenged Heath in 1975. Now she suffered from it.

* This recording had been delivered to the Northern Ireland Office by the *Sunday Times*.

afterwards, Murdoch rang Neil and told him that 'Heseltine would be a disastrous Prime Minister.'

Balancing these two egos, Neil deferred for now to the one who paid his wages. That weekend, the *Sunday Times* did not endorse Heseltine. Ingham informed Mrs Thatcher that, while several papers said that the country needed another leader, he did not think this would spur Heseltine to action. 'Sir Geoffrey Howe is the key,' he wrote. 'While he is to speak about the "substantive" reasons for his resignation, there is no sign he will provide . . . "the dream ticket" in which Howe forces a second ballot and then Heseltine moves effortlessly to win the leadership. This begs the question as to whether Sir Geoffrey is content always to be the bridesmaid.' Mrs Thatcher herself was much less sanguine. Ingham sensed she felt Heseltine would stand: 'She vouchsafes that if it runs to a second ballot, all is lost.'

Conservative Central Office, led by Kenneth Baker, insisted Heseltine should 'put up or shut up'. Baker also suggested that Howe had resigned in a fit of pique. In Arabella Warburton's view, this 'tipped Geoffrey over the edge . . . He was hurt and he was angry, which is always a powerful cocktail.'

Seeing Mrs Thatcher on the Monday, Renton detected 'a great tenseness in her'. She seemed 'really uncertain about what to do'. For all this, at the Lord Mayor's Banquet that evening, wearing a particularly elegant, close-cut black-velvet evening gown, she projected an almost regal confidence. Her opening sally led the news: 'I am still at the crease, though the bowling has been pretty hostile of late. And in case anyone doubted it, can I assure you there will be no ducking the bouncers . . . The bowling's going to get hit all round the ground.'

Her metaphor inspired Howe as he put the finishing touches to the resignation statement he would make the next day.

Earlier on the Monday, Mrs Thatcher's leadership campaign, still covert, began canvassing MPs. Using less research and more subjective judgements than the year before, they divided Members into 'Sound', 'Dodgy' and 'Untouchable'. Howe's entry of 12 November said 'Deemed sound'. Even before his resignation statement, this was incomprehensibly mistaken.

That day, Alan Clark noted that the whips had 'gone into "neutral" mode. Secret policemen burning the old files, ready to serve.' The pace of the contest now quickened, shifting hour by hour.

TUESDAY 13 NOVEMBER

Before Howe's resignation statement that afternoon, Mrs Thatcher offered a weaker than usual performance against Kinnock at Prime Minister's Questions.* In the Howe camp, meanwhile, the mood had changed. Richard Ryder recalled that 'Heseltine was known to be on manoeuvres, and Geoffrey knew this. Maybe they'd spoken and Heseltine had said, "I'm in your hands, Geoffrey."' Teasdale denied Howe's impending speech was 'a call to arms to Heseltine', but shared Ryder's view that Howe was now 'more relaxed about whether Mrs Thatcher survived or not'. Ryder was aware that Howe was fired up – 'the dead sheep on steroids'.

The packed House was in expectant mood, like a theatre audience before a new show. Howe, sitting next to Lawson, spoke with great care, dry wit and contained passion. His words drew gasps as they hit home. The spine of his narrative of estrangement was European policy, particularly the attempts to join the ERM. He revealed that he and Lawson had threatened to resign before Madrid and suggested that Britain should have joined five years earlier (monetarism alone having proved insufficient to contain inflation). Attacking Mrs Thatcher's attitude to Europe and EMU, Howe used against her Harold Macmillan's words about living in 'a ghetto of sentimentality about our past'. He compared favourably Winston Churchill's vision of a wider, shared sovereignty with the 'nightmare image sometimes conjured up by my right honourable friend', who seemed to 'look out upon a continent that is positively teeming with ill-intentioned people . . . scheming . . . to lead us through the back-door into a federal Europe'.

It was 'disturbing', Howe said, and 'tragic' that Mrs Thatcher had recently dismissed the idea that the hard ecu might come into common use, thus undermining the Chancellor and the Governor of the Bank of England. Both were 'cricketing enthusiasts', he added: 'It is rather like sending your opening batsmen to the crease only for them to find, the moment the first balls are bowled, that their bats have been broken before the game by the team captain.' This provoked loud guffaws from the Labour benches; Mrs Thatcher forced a thin smile.

Citing her 'No. No. No.', Howe said much damage had been done because the world assumed the country shared her views. Her attitude to Europe was 'running increasingly serious risks for the future of our nation'.

---

* Mrs Thatcher had been worried that Kinnock might make play with her cricketing metaphor from the night before and so had spent too much of her preparation time brainstorming obscure cricketing analogies. As Whittingdale recorded, 'she hadn't properly briefed herself . . . because she was so nervous'.

He had tried but failed to make Cabinet government work, he said, so 'The time has come for others to consider their own response to the tragic conflict of loyalties with which I have myself wrestled for perhaps too long.'

At the time, it not immediately clear what Howe intended by these words. Was he inviting challenges from inside the Cabinet or from Heseltine? Might he himself challenge? Hearing what he called 'Geoffrey's chilling words', however, Heseltine had no doubt: 'I knew Geoffrey would not stand,' he recalled. Therefore he must.*

Mrs Thatcher walked to her parliamentary office with John Major: 'She was hurt. She was wounded. She was shaken,' he recalled. 'I think she realized it was self-inflicted. I'm a tactile person and reached across, taking both her hands in mine . . . she kept them there for a good deal of the conversation.' To Dominic Morris, she said Howe's speech 'was far worse than expected'. It was indeed, despite Howe's quiet voice and sub-fusc manner, an oratorical masterpiece. 'I believe we are now in for a real battle,' Whittingdale confided to his diary, 'and I am not sure we are going to win.' It was not until 16 November, three days later, that Mrs Thatcher's campaign changed Howe's canvass return from 'Sound' to 'Untouchable'.

The whips' notes on MPs' reactions started to flow into Renton's office. 'G. HOWE – TEAROOM CONSENSUS' began one: 'Generally felt . . . as having been extremely crafty and damaging.' Two Cabinet ministers were also recorded expressing their excitement. Chris Patten was 'worried that the P.M. is finished: "Is it all over now?"' Malcolm Rifkind was reported to be briefing the press: 'In any ballot the P.M. is going to be seriously damaged.' A populist backbencher, Terry Dicks, epitomized a good many colleagues when he told his whip, 'She's a lame duck. I'll vote for <u>anyone</u> as long as it's not her. I want to hold on to <u>my</u> seat. That's what I care about.'

Whittingdale now learnt that 'Carol was in the flat and needed reassurance and Mark had twice rung from Dallas in tears.'

WEDNESDAY 14 NOVEMBER

At 10.30, Michael Heseltine announced his candidacy, claiming the support of more than 100 MPs. Declaring that Mrs Thatcher's 'views on Europe'

---

* As he left the Chamber, Heseltine met Michael Jopling, the experienced former Chief Whip, and sought his advice. 'Do nothing,' said Jopling, 'and you'll be leader in eighteen months.' He meant that it would be better to let the leadership fall into Heseltine's lap after a general election defeat rather than risk the odium of challenging Mrs Thatcher directly. 'But I don't want to be leader of the Opposition,' Heseltine replied, 'I want to be prime minister.'

had divided the Cabinet, he insisted he would restore unity. He cited the opinion polls. (That morning's NOP poll showed a Heseltine leadership cutting the Labour lead from 15 per cent to 4 per cent.) Very importantly for Conservative MPs beleaguered by angry constituents, he promised an 'immediate and fundamental review' of the poll tax, relating it to people's ability to pay. The press led strongly with Heseltine's successful launch.

That morning, Mrs Thatcher's campaign belatedly took formal shape. Its front men were supposed to be George Younger, Norman Tebbit, Michael Jopling and John Moore. But their roles were more apparent than real.* Only Tebbit campaigned actively on her behalf. Although a brilliant media performer, particularly when attacking Heseltine, he was not well placed to win over middle-ground Conservative MPs. So the campaign was in practice led by Peter Morrison, with Michael Neubert and Gerry Neale in support. Neubert and Neale were competent lieutenants, but Morrison was complacent. 'He just didn't know how to do it,' recalled Shana Hole, who ran the secretarial side of the campaign. 'He was so busy being important. He was so busy drinking. He'd send me out for vodka in the middle of meetings.' Morrison had rejected much earlier offers of help from Garel-Jones and Ryder. This made it easier for Garel-Jones to execute his plan of the previous year with a clear conscience.

Mrs Thatcher's team made no serious attempt to persuade her to mix with her MPs.† In Charles Powell's view, she felt 'it was not for her, as a three-term prime minister ... to skulk around the Commons tea-room cadging votes'. Although the CSCE conference in Paris would make her miss the first ballot, she was determined to attend. This approach infected her ministers: if she was going abroad rather than campaigning, why should they pitch in for her?

Tebbit had told Alan Clark that they must fight 'to the death'. But Tristan Garel-Jones told Clark 'he was *very* against NT's [Tebbit's] idea of a "last stand". He thinks he can fudge up a solution which will keep H [Heseltine] out. "Of course," I said. "If it works." "It's got to fucking work," he answered.' Keeping Heseltine out, however, was not the same thing as keeping Mrs Thatcher in office.

---

* Younger explained that, since he had just become Chairman of the Royal Bank of Scotland, he was very busy in Edinburgh. Jopling declined to take a formal role in her campaign but promised to do what he could to help. As an old and close friend of Geoffrey Howe, he did not prove an enthusiastic campaigner. John Moore, meanwhile, was yet to return from business in the United States.

† Against the wishes of his chief, Greg Knight, one of the whips, sought to pass Morrison a piece of paper with the names of four potential supporters whom he felt could be won over if only Mrs Thatcher would speak to them. 'He batted the piece of paper out of my hand and said, "We don't need this," and off he went. It potentially cost her four votes.'

THURSDAY 15 NOVEMBER

In her first interviews since the challenge, Mrs Thatcher spoke to the *Sunday Times* and the *Sunday Telegraph*. Combative in tone, she raised the possibility of holding a referendum before joining a European single currency.* By proposing something never formally discussed with colleagues, she reinforced Howe's complaint that she governed as a one-woman band. She seemed full of fire, but unfocused. Both interviews contained long passages about the sweep of European history.† Her mind was racing. Her blood was up. Preoccupied with the great European questions, she and her supporters had no tactics for her immediate struggle.

Privately, people were now preparing for her political demise. Garel-Jones rang Major to warn him that 'Norman Lamont has canvassed me on your behalf.' 'If he's doing that it's not my wish . . .' said Major, 'I intend to vote for the Prime Minister.' 'Good,' said Garel-Jones. But, as Major added, 'We both knew . . . that this might not be the end of the matter.'

That evening 1,000 red roses were delivered to 10 Downing Street anonymously in support of Mrs Thatcher. They filled the entrance hall.

FRIDAY 16 NOVEMBER

Early in the morning, Mrs Thatcher flew to Northern Ireland for one of her customary, pre-Christmas visits to boost morale. Owing to tight security and poor communication, Whittingdale learnt of the trip only when he arrived in Downing Street that morning. She was out of action politically for an entire day – her leadership campaign was not integrated into official thinking. Woodrow Wyatt rang her at Chequers that evening, to warn that the *Sunday Times* might come out for Heseltine. Wyatt was distressed: 'The dear darling doesn't deserve this treachery from the cowardly mob of Tory MPs who can't see what she has done for them.'

Mrs Thatcher's two most senior Cabinet colleagues now dropped hints on their own behalf. When Hurd was asked whether there were no circumstances in which he would stand, reported the *Daily Telegraph*, he 'replied

---

* When asked what the question would be, Mrs Thatcher answered: 'Quite simple: Do you give up the power to issue your own currency? Do you give up the pound sterling?'

† Writing in the *Spectator*, the present author, who had conducted her *Sunday Telegraph* interview, put it thus: 'Her unusable answer went on for more than five minutes and encompassed (I am not exaggerating) the Old and New Testaments, the Emperor Justinian, the Renaissance, the scientific and industrial revolutions, the Ottoman Empire, the Mogul Empire and China.'

forcefully, but carefully, "Against her"'. The media joked that Heseltine had become 'the stalking stallion' for Hurd and others who might enter a second ballot if Mrs Thatcher stood down. Major, too, declined to rule out entering a second ballot. He told his political adviser, Judith Chaplin, that Mrs Thatcher was 'finished'. Major, Chaplin noted later, had 'discussed his chances' of succeeding Mrs Thatcher with Norman Lamont 'before the weekend before the first ballot'.

SATURDAY 17 NOVEMBER

At home at Saltwood, his castle in Kent, Alan Clark was becoming 'more and more dejected' about Mrs Thatcher's prospects. From Tristan Garel-Jones, he learnt that Hurd and Major were planning to confer over the phone 'in that first critical hour' following the first ballot, to 'settle what should happen next'. 'I don't like the sound of this,' Clark continued. 'It will be Halifax, Churchill and George VI [in May 1940], and they may decide who runs.' In which case, Clark thought, Hurd would take the Halifax role and stand aside: 'We're then left with John Major who, being calm and sensible, is infinitely preferable to that dreadful charlatan, H [Heseltine].' Garel-Jones told Clark that if, following the first ballot, there was any 'uncertainty . . . a group of us are to meet at Catherine Place after the 10 p.m. vote that evening'. Plans were being laid to fulfil his hopes of 'managing the end' of Mrs Thatcher.

At Chequers that afternoon, Mrs Thatcher used an interview with Simon Jenkins, Editor of *The Times*, to attack Heseltine directly for the first time. He would, she said, 'jeopardise all I have struggled to achieve', by making the state a partner in business enterprises just when 'you've seen the crumbling of the more extreme forms of that philosophy in the Soviet Union'. She accepted that the rise of inflation under the influence of Lawson had been her error, but insisted her line on Europe was right. She defended her resistance to consensus: 'When a woman is strong, she is strident. If a man is strong, gosh he's a good guy.'

Mrs Thatcher then told Jenkins to turn off his tape recorder. 'Can you imagine', she said, 'my being at the CSCE conference next Tuesday night and someone handing me a note saying, "You've lost on the ballot?" What will the rest of the world think of us?' 'Tuesday', she added, 'will be the worst day of my life.'

That evening, Morrison brought her his 'worst-case' rough predictions of the first ballot. They were 220 for Mrs Thatcher, 110 for Heseltine and 40 abstentions. Charles Powell noted Morrison's habit of 'tapping his breast pocket knowingly to imply he had the necessary votes to see her through'. As of the night before, however, figures collected by the pro-Thatcher MP Michael Brown gave Mrs Thatcher just 177 votes.

The Thatchers now hosted a cheerful dinner at Chequers for close friends.* As Whittingdale recorded, 'Everybody was absolutely confident of victory.' That 'everybody' did not include Mrs Thatcher. She recalled that Ted Heath had been shown similarly encouraging figures before she defeated him in 1975. But without a rigorous campaign to support her, she could not intervene. She was like the grandest passenger on the *Titanic* – offered every comfort and deference, but still headed for the iceberg.

SUNDAY 18 NOVEMBER

Ingham's Sunday-morning press digest recorded that the *Mail on Sunday*, the *Observer* and the *Sunday Times* had all come out for Heseltine. Nonetheless, at teatime, Morrison reported that his figures were now 'if anything ... slightly better than last night'. Mrs Thatcher left for Paris, with Douglas Hurd and Crawfie, but without Denis. Before she departed, Denis confided to Crawfie: 'Beloved Crawf [his invariable way of addressing her], she's done for now.'

Before lunch that day, calling Renton in Suffolk, Morrison disclosed that he, Baker, Wakeham and Tebbit had agreed that Mrs Thatcher should hold a press conference in Paris immediately after the result. They would telex her to advise on what her reaction should be. 'My suspicions were aroused,' wrote Renton, who insisted he and Cranley Onslow would also need to weigh in. 'I could see a cabal forming of those friendly ... to the Prime Minister.' He was concerned that this cabal might seek to retain Mrs Thatcher for self-interested reasons. At the same time, Renton accepted that his own position was 'not wholly unbiassed'. As he later wrote, he strongly disapproved of her 'position on European issues and I felt she would lose the next Election if still our leader. For those reasons I did not vote for her.' Renton's hostility was crucial. He never bestirred the whips' office to help save her.

By the Sunday night, Mrs Thatcher was out of the country. Almost no one in Westminster, outside her immediate entourage, was actively working to secure her re-election. Ewen Fergusson, the British Ambassador in Paris, gave her tea at the Embassy, where she was staying. He knew Mrs

---

* The guests included Mark and Carol, the Bakers, the Wakehams, Tim Bell and his wife, Alistair McAlpine, Gordon Reece and the active campaign managers Morrison, Neubert and Neale.

Thatcher well and greatly admired her: 'For the first time ever, I felt her laser-like focus was not on me, or on anyone.'

MONDAY 19 NOVEMBER

The world leaders with whom Mrs Thatcher was gathering in Paris tended to believe that she remained unassailable. 'She is very skilful,' President Mitterrand told President Bush, 'and I can't believe she is threatened within her own party.' At the summit, East and West pledged themselves to 'respect and cooperation', while signing the Conventional Forces in Europe (CFE) Agreement, the largest single act of disarmament since 1945. Yet victory in the Cold War already seemed so complete that Mrs Thatcher gained little domestic benefit.

When Mrs Thatcher met Bush for breakfast on 19 November, she began with her domestic political situation: 'This is a historic day which has been completely overshadowed.' Bush empathized, but 'All he could say was, good luck.' They discussed the Gulf and Mrs Thatcher promised Britain would send a further brigade and minesweepers. Her main concern remained delay.

During the first formal signing ceremony at the Élysée Palace that morning, Mrs Thatcher, reported the White House press pool, 'appeared to be in a determinedly jaunty mood'. She told the press, 'I most earnestly believe that I shall be in No. 10 Downing Street at the end of this week and a little bit longer than that.' That evening, over dinner, Helmut Kohl assured her it was 'unimaginable' she should fall. Despite their poor relations, Mrs Thatcher was 'very moved by his words, and by the real warmth of his feeling'. 'There is much personal sympathy with Mrs Thatcher here,' Hurd noted, 'even amongst those – Mitterrand, Kohl – whom she has most exasperated. Impossible not to share this.'

Back in London, 'The battle hots up,' Renton noted in his diary. At 11.30 a.m. he attended a meeting with Mrs Thatcher's campaign advisers, including Wakeham,* Tebbit, Morrison and the campaign's titular (and previously absent) leader, George Younger. Talking through the possibilities, they agreed to advise Mrs Thatcher that should she win a majority in the following day's ballot, but not the lead of 56 votes required for outright victory, she should immediately declare her candidacy in the second ballot. Otherwise, as Younger put it, 'rats would start nibbling away at her

---

* Wakeham's virtual absence from Mrs Thatcher's campaign until this point had been another problem for her. He had been too busy with electricity privatization to play a full part.

position'. Morrison's prediction was now 236 for Mrs Thatcher, 78 for Heseltine and 58 undecided.

In the Commons, Alan Clark bumped into Tristan Garel-Jones:

> I don't think he wants 'Hezzy', as he (spastically) calls him, to win. It would be disruptive of the Blue Chip* long-term plan. But he's high on the whole thing.
>
> Tristan said, 'Of course every member of the Cabinet will vote for the Prime Minister in the first round.' Like hell they will.
>
> I said to him, hoping he'd deny it, 'One cannot actually exclude the possibility that Heseltine will score more votes than her on the first ballot.'
>
> 'No, I'm afraid one can't.'
>
> ... This was really chilling. Apocalypse. Because time is horrendously tight if we have to organise an alternative candidate.

Garel-Jones, however, had given more forethought to an 'alternative candidate' than Clark: the 'Blue Chip long-term plan' had indeed been laid (see p. 757).

That afternoon, Clark visited Morrison's office: 'He was asleep, snoring lightly, in the leather armchair, with his feet resting on the desk. Drake playing bowls before the Armada and all that ... This was ten minutes past three in the afternoon of the most critical day of the whole election.' When Morrison awoke, he told Clark that Heseltine's vote was '115. It could be 124, at worst.' 'Peter is useless,' wrote Clark, 'far worse than I'd thought ... sozzled. There isn't a single person working for her who cuts any ice at all ... And she's in Paris. "*Où est la masse de manoeuvre? – Aucune.*"'†

Allies of John Major, such as Graham Bright (his PPS) and Norman Lamont, were already manoeuvring for a second ballot in which he would stand.‡ Major later insisted they were working 'categorically not with my approval or knowledge'. Lamont recalled being impressed by Major's 'brilliant ambivalence' in his loyalty to Thatcher and Thatcherism. 'John Major', he judged, 'is much cleverer than people imagine, and not quite as nice.'

---

* For a discussion of the Blue Chips see p. 496.
† Clark was quoting Churchill's famous question to the French Commander-in-Chief, Gamelin, in the face of the German attack on 15 May 1940, and Gamelin's equally famous one-word reply.
‡ On 19 November, for example, the Conservative MP Robert Hayward was approached by his fellow MP David Davis and invited to join John Major's team for the second ballot. Since there was, in theory, no John Major team, because all ministers were supposed to be supporting Mrs Thatcher, this was striking. Hayward observed that Davis was working closely with Graham Bright, who was close to John Major, but 'wanted clean hands'.

On the Monday, Major was convalescing from a wisdom teeth operation at home – Finings, Great Stukeley, near Huntingdon – in the company of Jeffrey Archer. According to Major's biographer, Bruce Anderson, Major told Archer that if Mrs Thatcher withdrew before the second ballot, the whips should 'take a sounding' as to whether he or Hurd would 'have the better chance of stopping Heseltine'. As Major noted, 'We were friends more than we were rivals.' They agreed to 'compare notes as soon as the results were known'. Thus did the two most senior ministers in the government plot not to plot.

TUESDAY 20 NOVEMBER

On the morning of the first ballot, the *Daily Telegraph* led with a Gallup poll showing that more than 20 per cent of voters would consider switching to the Conservatives under a new leader. John Major, the paper noted, was 'being pressed' to stand if there were a second ballot.

Arriving in Paris, Peter Morrison told Ewen Fergusson that 'Even allowing for a 15 per cent lie factor, I think she's got the votes.' But Morrison's own figures belied this. Pegging Mrs Thatcher's support at 236, if the lie factor operated in full, she could fall well short of the 56-vote margin required. Fergusson sent up champagne to Mrs Thatcher's rooms nonetheless to await the result.

Mrs Thatcher now conducted a rush of meetings with world leaders, during which Mikhail Gorbachev told her he saw 'absolutely no difficulty' with a further UN resolution on the Kuwait crisis. Indeed, he sought this 'without delay'.* In the late afternoon, she returned to the British Embassy to await the ballot result. On the phone to London, Powell told Whittingdale they were taking bets. Powell predicted that Mrs Thatcher would get 230 votes, Bernard Ingham had chosen 220 and John Sununu, Bush's Chief of Staff, was down for 228. By then, the whips' office believed she had 226 votes, with Heseltine on 107 and 39 abstentions. Any of these results would have avoided a second ballot.

Ian Twinn, one of the tellers, was a young MP who had been Peter Morrison's PPS.† His role was to convey the result to the Thatcher team before it was announced. And so, at 6.35 p.m., he handed a piece of paper to John

---

* Ten days later, UNSCR 678 was passed with Soviet support and China abstaining, allowing 'all necessary means' to expel Iraqi forces from Kuwait.
† The count was not well conducted. Twinn noticed that two ballot papers had fallen through the cracks between desks on the raised dais where the count was taking place. He retrieved them in time: both were for Mrs Thatcher.

Wakeham: 'She's won,' he said, 'but it's not good enough.' The figures were 204 for Mrs Thatcher, 152 for Michael Heseltine and 16 abstentions. With just two more votes from Heseltine's tally, Mrs Thatcher would have won outright. In his diary, Alan Clark quoted the old proverb 'For want of a nail a kingdom was lost.'

Whittingdale now tipped off Powell in the British Embassy before Renton informed Morrison. Powell, Morrison, Ingham, Ewen Fergusson and Crawfie were with Mrs Thatcher, who was sitting at the dressing table in Morrison's bedroom. Powell made a thumbs-down sign to Crawfie, but then he realized that Mrs Thatcher could see him in her mirror. 'She could see my grimace. I'm sure she knew it was over.' After hearing the news from Renton, Morrison turned to Mrs Thatcher and said, 'Not quite as good as we had hoped and not quite good enough.' After a brief silence, Mrs Thatcher took the telephone, '"Does this mean a second ballot, Tim?" in a voice with a perceptible catch in it. "Yes, I'm afraid so Prime Minister."'

Mrs Thatcher descended at once to the courtyard of the Embassy, where she commandeered a microphone from the BBC's John Sergeant, already live on the *Six O'Clock News*: 'I am naturally very pleased that I got more than half the Parliamentary Party and disappointed that it is not quite enough to win on the first ballot, so I confirm it is my intention to let my name go forward for the second ballot.' Whatever she felt, she looked strong and confident. Returning indoors, she rang Denis, who offered his usual support. Shortly afterwards, however, Denis gave a drink to Wakeham. 'I hope she packs up,' he said.

While Mrs Thatcher was outside, Douglas Hurd had been on the phone to John Major, convalescent at Finings. Hurd now promised his and Major's continued support. Under pressure from Ingham and Morrison, Hurd came down to the courtyard and pledged his 'full support' for Mrs Thatcher, adding 'I am sorry that this destructive, unnecessary contest should be prolonged in this way.' There was the faintest hint that it was she who was prolonging it.

Realizing she would be late for that evening's ballet at Versailles, Mrs Thatcher had asked the other guests not to wait, but they did, at Mitterrand's insistence, out of respect. During the car journey, Morrison recalled that 'Her right arm leapt out and grabbed just above my left knee and she dug her nails in – quite painfully – and all she kept saying was "We must fight on, we must fight on, there's so much more to do."' She arrived almost an hour late, but, according to Brian Mulroney, 'with all her dignity and all her splendour and all her jewellery'. The leaders there, Fergusson recalled, 'found it inconceivable that she would not have the votes . . . She had great difficulty in framing answers to all their questions.'

That evening, Charles Powell drafted speeches for Mrs Thatcher's two forthcoming performances in Parliament: her statement on the Paris summit on Wednesday and the no-confidence debate Labour had tabled for Thursday. He and Ingham had privately agreed that she was doomed. As Powell recalled, 'all we could do now was protect her'.

In the Commons, however, Thatcher supporters endeavoured to stem the tide. Ian Twinn sensed that the grandees leading her campaign thought 'she was finished'. He felt, 'Sod the generals – let the majors get on with it' and went round the tea room declaring 'She's won.' The trouble was that the No Turning Back group (NTB), the main Thatcherite backbench grouping, was not united. That night there were acrimonious words between those who now doubted she could survive, such as Francis Maude and Peter Lilley, and loyalists such as Michael Forsyth, Michael Fallon, Neil Hamilton and Michael Brown, the NTB's convenor. 'Maude and Lilley had clearly been talking to Major,' Fallon recalled. 'It was such a shock.' The loyalists were fired up to defend their heroine, but coordination with her campaign was absent. When the NTB gathered that night, Brown recalled, 'Maude came in and said, "There's nothing more we can do." When we accused him of treachery, he burst into tears.'

By this time, the whips had 'anecdotal evidence' of twelve defections from Mrs Thatcher to Heseltine. But, if that was the extent of the losses, she would still win since, in round two, only a majority of one was required. As Alastair Goodlad recorded, '11 of the office, including myself, thought that she could probably win on the second round. 3, including Tim Renton, thought she could not.' Shortly after this meeting, Michael Heseltine told Renton he could stay on as Chief Whip under his premiership. 'I found myself being swept up in some of the euphoric enthusiasm that emanated from Michael,' Renton recorded.

As MPs gathered for the division that evening, Tristan Garel-Jones started to round up selected colleagues. 'We're meeting at my house, straight after this,' he told Alan Clark. 'Who's "we"?' Clark asked. 'Oh just a few mates; *Chris* [Patten] and people. We need to talk through the next steps.' 'How do you mean?' 'Ways of supporting the Prime Minister.' This was, in the circumstances, an amusing phrase. Although Garel-Jones would always insist the gathering, later legendary as the 'Catherine Place conspiracy', was an impromptu get-together, he had, in fact, mentioned the idea to Clark the previous Saturday. It is also significant that Major, according to Bruce Anderson, ordered Graham Bright not to attend, because 'he didn't want to be involved in anything that looked like a plot'. Major could not have known about Bright's possible attendance unless there had been some prearrangement.

The Catherine Place gathering included five Cabinet ministers,* all from the generation below Mrs Thatcher – Lamont, Rifkind, Waldegrave, Chris Patten and Tony Newton. The meeting had no formal agenda and no chairmanship. Waldegrave remembered 'the sense of excitement with Chris and co that she might go'. He was the only person present who spoke words sympathetic to Mrs Thatcher. There was little time left, because nominations for the second ballot had to be in by noon on Thursday 22 November. If nothing was done, it would be Thatcher versus Heseltine.

The majority at the meeting tended to favour Hurd, but part of the purpose was to mingle Hurd and Major supporters in amity. Lamont's advocacy for Major was important because it showed that the Chancellor's campaign was under way with significant Thatcherite support. Both Lamont and Patten spoke positively about Heseltine. In a dig at Mrs Thatcher, who, he told Lamont, was 'off her trolley', Patten said of Heseltine, 'Well, he's not mad, is he?', but this was not a pro-Heseltine meeting. The prevailing mood was that, if Mrs Thatcher withdrew, two candidates from the Cabinet could enter, one of whom could ultimately beat Heseltine. As Patten recalled, 'All of us would have been comfortable with either Hurd or Major.' This was what Garel-Jones, backing Hurd, but also very close to Major, had desired. It was the answer to the 'Unless . . .' which had ended his note to Renton nearly a year earlier (see p. 757).

Following the meeting, the five Cabinet ministers, led by Rifkind, went to see the Chief Whip to report its conclusions. Their message, recorded Alastair Goodlad, was that 'the Prime Minister probably would not win and even if she did that she should not carry on'.† When asked whether they would be willing to share this opinion directly with the Prime Minister, 'they demurred amongst some foot shuffling'. Renton now agreed with Goodlad that he would have breakfast with Willie Whitelaw. Part of Whitelaw's informal constitutional role was to advise the Prime Minister when it was time to go. He could lend valuable respectability to any attempt to get rid of the leader.

As Mrs Thatcher was preparing to leave the banquet in Versailles alone, she was swept up by George and Barbara Bush: 'We went on either side of her,' Mrs Bush recalled '. . . She had her head held high – a really brave woman . . . She said to George, "Now, don't worry, George. I'll go home and get this straight."' Mrs Thatcher was touched: this was 'one of those

---

* Garel-Jones had also wanted a sixth, Kenneth Clarke, to attend, but had been unable to find him.
† All those present at Catherine Place, with the possible exception of Alan Clark, had agreed that Mrs Thatcher should go.

little acts of kindness which remind us that even power politics is not just about power'.

Returned to the British Embassy, Mrs Thatcher retired to her room with Crawfie. 'This was the first time', Crawfie recalled, 'that I had ever seen her slumped. She complained of turncoats and being stabbed in the back.' Eventually, however, she became more peaceful, talking about 'her mother and father and Denis and the twins and her ambitions'. She did not go to bed. Early in the morning, Crawfie did Mrs Thatcher's hair herself, and helped apply extra make-up to her face 'because everyone thinks you're going to be a sad little person'.

WEDNESDAY 21 NOVEMBER

Over breakfast, Renton asked Whitelaw what message he might convey to Mrs Thatcher. Whitelaw said that there was 'a danger of her being humiliated in the second ballot'.* Even if she won by a low margin, 'she will not be able to unite the party'. They agreed 'for the sake of the press' to say that Whitelaw had asked to see Renton, although in fact it had been the other way round. The 'optic' of the Chief Whip consulting the great tribal elder would make it obvious enough that Mrs Thatcher was in deep trouble.

Later, Leon Brittan rang the young William Hague, now Norman Lamont's PPS: 'He says that there is a massive withdrawal of support for the Prime Minister, and that she will have to back down before the day is out . . . as a result of pressure from people like Willie Whitelaw. He [Hague] is getting geared up to help organise the John Major campaign.'†

The night before, Morrison had called Wakeham from Paris. Mrs Thatcher 'did not trust Tim Renton', he said, and so wanted Wakeham to produce an honest appraisal of her support on her return. Wakeham agreed and deputed John MacGregor to take the temperature among ministers. That same evening, Wakeham had been chatting to John Gummer when Ken Clarke entered the room and said, 'She hasn't a chance. She's got to go.' Gummer did not demur. So Wakeham was under no illusions. At Wednesday lunchtime he was due to give Mrs Thatcher the true state of opinion.

Meeting at 10.30 a.m., the whips concluded, 'the situation seemed to be moving against the Prime Minister': the count of net defections had moved

---

* This phrase was becoming the euphemism among those not formally opposed to Mrs Thatcher who nevertheless wanted her to go.
† Brittan's contemporary account is at variance with Hague's memory nearly thirty years later. Hague insisted that there was no organization for Major until after Mrs Thatcher had resigned.

from a dozen the previous night to twenty-five. The whips felt the result would be 'a close-run thing'.

At 12.30, Renton saw John MacGregor. By now, he knew of six Cabinet ministers who would not support her. MacGregor reported that 15 per cent of junior ministers also took this view, but the rest were firm. At 12.45, Renton and Cranley Onslow agreed that the available evidence did not permit them to tell her 'that she certainly should not go forward'. By implication, only the Cabinet could stop her.

That morning, Alan Clark was trying to reach Mrs Thatcher in Paris to warn her about what had happened at Catherine Place. He was blocked by Peter Morrison (Morrison: 'There's a Working Breakfast'; Clark: 'With a lot of fucking foreigners, I suppose'). Garel-Jones, however, reached his old schoolfriend Charles Powell with his version of the Catherine Place events. 'Probably everyone in the room, except for Alan Clark, didn't vote for her in the first round.'* 'Tristan wanted me to get the message to her that her position was now ... almost irretrievable,' Powell recalled. 'I passed it on.' Garel-Jones, Powell wrote to Morrison, also told him that 'both Peter Lilley & Michael Howard had been in touch to say that the game was up. The only hope was to unite quickly on a "stop Heseltine" candidate – with John Major preferred.' Garel-Jones knew that the defections of Lilley and Howard – two Thatcherites – would hit her hard. Accompanying her to Orly airport, Fergusson recalled: 'She seemed limp; sub-fusc. The oomph wasn't there.' Mrs Thatcher returned to Downing Street at 11.50, and went straight up to the flat, where Denis told her, 'Don't go on, love.' This had been, roughly speaking, his view for the previous eighteen months. Mrs Thatcher appreciated his frankness, but 'I felt in my bones that I should fight on.'

Around this time, John Wakeham was publicly announced as her new campaign manager. This came as a surprise to Wakeham, who was unaware that he had been offered the post. He took it on with great reluctance. Bumping into him in the House, Cecil Parkinson formed the impression that he 'didn't want the job, and he didn't intend to do it'. Mrs Thatcher now saw Norman Tebbit, soon joined by Wakeham and Morrison. Encouraging her to fight, Tebbit suggested she see Cabinet ministers collectively: if she arranged for her strongest supporters to speak first, the doubtfuls

---

* If this was accurate, it was a startling fact, since all had pledged their allegiance to Mrs Thatcher. Indeed Garel-Jones had assured Clark, just two days earlier, that every member of the Cabinet would vote for Mrs Thatcher.

might yet fall in line.* Mrs Thatcher said that 'if she could see the Gulf crisis resolved and inflation brought down she could choose the time of her own departure'. Her talk of departure was a concession, but Tebbit regarded it as 'a nonsense' and suspected she did too. She also wanted to know whether, 'if she withdrew, Mr Major could win'. She did not want Hurd, because his beliefs were not hers. Morrison, understanding the purpose of the Catherine Place meeting, explained that Hurd and Major had a 'pact': they would, 'if allowed, stand against each other in an effort to take the election to a third ballot, with the weaker candidate's votes being transferred'. Mrs Thatcher maintained it was better for her to fight on.

Wakeham advised that, were it suggested that she should stand down for the sake of party unity, she should 'test the proposition thoroughly': 'Could someone else other than Mr Heseltine win?' The aim of saving Mrs Thatcher was being nudged into stopping Heseltine.

All four present then moved down to the Cabinet Room to meet Baker, Renton, MacGregor, John Moore and Cranley Onslow, a combination of her campaign team and the 'men in suits'. In Tebbit's opinion, Wakeham was now acting more as Chief Whip than campaign manager, collecting opinions, not trying to win. Renton reported his somewhat gloomy but by no means conclusive opinion about the likely result. He claimed, falsely, that Whitelaw had approached him to give his negative advice. Although MacGregor had told Wakeham that two-thirds of the Cabinet were against Mrs Thatcher continuing to fight, he chose not to share this at the meeting. Baker, however, told her that 'those who feared the Prime Minister could not win were her strongest supporters', including Lamont, Gummer, Howard and Lilley. Wakeham advised her to see Cabinet ministers individually to get their views.

'My clear impression', Renton recorded, 'is that she intends to stand as none of the seven of us have clearly and firmly told her that we do not think she has a chance of winning herself, nor have we stressed that any other candidate, Major or Hurd, would do better than her against Heseltine.' The 'men in suits' had quailed before the woman with the handbag, as most had done for the past eleven and a half years. At Wakeham's insistence, Cabinet ministers were now lined up to see her in Parliament individually that evening.†

---

* It was sometimes alleged that Tebbit had other fish to fry. The previous night, he had, by Kenneth Clarke's account, seen Clarke and subtly suggested to him a pact by which, if he supported him in a leadership bid, he (Tebbit) could become his deputy in the ensuing government. Tebbit firmly denied, however, that any such meeting ever took place.
† Wakeham was anxious that the encounters should take place in Parliament rather than Downing Street. This would make their comings and goings much less conspicuous to the

Mrs Thatcher then left Downing Street to make her Commons statement on the Paris summit. She called out to the press the words Ingham had prepared for her: 'I shall fight on, I shall fight to win.'

After her statement, Clarke, Patten and Lamont met in the corridor behind the Speaker's Chair and found themselves 'in complete agreement' that she should go. Clarke now maintained 'constant conversation' with fellow Cabinet members, doing everything he could to make sure she stood down.

That afternoon, Tebbit persuaded Mrs Thatcher to visit the tea room to rally support. This was the right gesture, but far too late. Those she met complained that Heseltine had already approached them two or three times for their vote: 'Then I realized that many of these were supporters complaining that my campaign did not seem to be really fighting.'

Returning to her room, she saw Hurd, who agreed at once to renominate her. There was now an urgency about the nominations, because of the deadline of noon the following day. She telephoned John Major in Great Stukeley to ask that he second her nomination: 'The hesitation was palpable,' she later wrote. 'No doubt the operation on John's wisdom teeth was giving him trouble. Then he said that if that was what I wanted, yes.'

Major had been irritated by Mrs Thatcher's call, which he recalled as 'rather breathless and abrupt ... I did think she had an obligation to have a discussion about tactics.' He said none of this to her: 'Hand on heart, there was no hesitation from me because of manoeuvring.' It was not, perhaps, quite as simple as that. By lunchtime, Major knew that he had eighty supporters signed up as part of the campaign that supposedly did not exist. He knew what had happened at Catherine Place and how fast opinion was running against Mrs Thatcher. With many urging him to stand, he felt 'It would be rather cowardly to shrink away from it.' If he renominated Mrs Thatcher and she went forward to the second ballot, he would put himself out of the running. He had to solve this problem urgently.

Back in Parliament, Alastair Goodlad found Wakeham in his room with colleagues, 'sitting surrounded by cigar smoke' holding a list of Cabinet ministers who felt that the Prime Minister should not go on. 'She is living in cloud-cuckoo land,' Wakeham declared. This was an extraordinary line for her campaign manager to be taking, just as she was about to begin, at his suggestion, her individual meetings with Cabinet ministers. Goodlad

---

media, but had the disadvantage for her that ministers could easily concert tactics in their nearby rooms.

moved on to see Clarke and Patten. He asked whether they were 'resolved to take a robust line with the Prime Minister and they said that they were'.

As Mrs Thatcher's individual sessions with Cabinet ministers began, Andrew Turnbull took notes. The first to see her was Francis Maude. Although only a junior minister, Maude mattered because of his leading role in the NTB. If Maude were despairing, it would suggest that even Mrs Thatcher's closest allies had lost hope. He was: 'I think you're going to lose this election,' he told her, 'and Michael Heseltine is going to win and that will be a disaster.' Maude was already conscious of why Wakeham had proposed such meetings: 'It was to get them individually to tell her it was over.' Her response was, Maude thought, 'magnificent: she was at her most fiery' – 'But it's a coup,' she said. According to Turnbull's record, Maude left 'visibly distressed'.

Next in was Kenneth Clarke, speaking with characteristically genial brutality: 'Personally happy to support you for 5–10 more years,' he said. 'Most of the Cabinet think you should stand down as you are not only going to lose but to lose big.' Clarke urged that Hurd and Major be allowed to stand against Heseltine: 'Either has a better chance than you.' Clarke told Leon Brittan that he passed on what he had said to other Cabinet ministers awaiting their turn and 'thereby stiffened [their] resolve'.

Peter Lilley, the purest Thatcherite in the Cabinet, followed Clarke: 'Will support you if you stand but inconceivable that you will win.' He urged her to 'make way for John Major'. Then came Rifkind, who warned her that she was 'holed below the waterline'. She asked if Rifkind would vote for her if she did stand. 'I'll have to think about it but I will never campaign against you,' he replied.* This answer, which she considered evasive, enraged her.

Peter Brooke came next: 'You can win if you go in with all guns blazing,' he told her. She replied that 'she could not win unless all guns did blaze'. Michael Howard followed. Turnbull recorded his contribution laconically: '"Will support you and will campaign vigorously for you but you cannot win." In tears.' At about 6.45, while William Waldegrave was telling her that it would be dishonourable for him, a Cabinet minister for only three weeks, not to support her, a note was brought in for Mrs Thatcher. Wakeham needed an urgent word: 'The position had got very much worse than he had thought.'

She quickly saw John Gummer and Chris Patten, who both pledged their support but warned she could not win. Then she made room for Alan Clark, who, though not a Cabinet minister, had managed to insert himself

---

* Rifkind, in his memoirs and subsequently, disputes what Turnbull recorded. He denies telling Mrs Thatcher that she could not win and recalls that he promised he would not vote against her.

and urged her to fight on: 'I do not believe you can win but it is better to go out this way than any other.'*

Ejecting Clark, Wakeham and Kenneth Baker told Mrs Thatcher most of the Cabinet now wanted her to stand down. This she already knew. But Wakeham now added that Tristan Garel-Jones and Richard Ryder had refused to help with her campaign 'as they did not believe she could succeed'. This was a substantial blow. It was also untrue. Garel-Jones and Ryder insisted they had, in fact, agreed to Wakeham's request, earlier that afternoon, to join the campaign, while pressing for a new political strategy and the replacement of Peter Morrison. There is, however, no evidence that Wakeham passed this on to Mrs Thatcher at the time. Instead, by 7 p.m., needing to show her that her campaign would fail, he staged a dramatic interruption giving the misleading impression that Garel-Jones and Ryder had refused to help. Wakeham wanted her to resign, so that her succession could be secured in the manner he favoured.

Mrs Thatcher continued the sad encounters with her Cabinet. None held out hope of victory. By 7.45, Turnbull recorded, it was clear that twelve Cabinet ministers thought she could not win. Although Hurd and Major had promised to sign Mrs Thatcher's nomination papers, both were now recognized as opponents of her standing. Neither said this to her. Many Cabinet ministers told her they did not want to see her humiliated. In Turnbull's view, what they meant was, 'If you don't stand aside, we can't come in and stand against Heseltine.'

Outside Mrs Thatcher's room, like schoolboys outside the Head's study, Cabinet ministers compared accounts. 'How many did you get?' someone asked Gummer, meaning how many strokes of the cane. Patten made play of the same thought. 'There he was,' recalled David Waddington, 'rubbing his bottom and saying, "She gave me a good whacking." I could've killed the bloody man.'

Mrs Thatcher now saw Wakeham again. He explained away his more upbeat advice at lunchtime by saying 'he had discovered the true depth of the problem only when he had sought, and failed, to recruit the campaign team'. 'It was the end,' Mrs Thatcher later wrote, 'I was sick at heart ... what grieved me was the desertion of those I had always considered friends and allies and the weasel words whereby they had transmuted their betrayal into frank advice and concern for my fate.' She privately recalled that 'the atmosphere that night was like witchery, it was like the

---

* Clark's diary offers a fuller version of their exchange, in which Mrs Thatcher questions his suggestion of fighting to a third ballot, because others have entered the race, and then losing. Clark says, 'what a way to go! Unbeaten in three elections, never rejected by the people. Brought down by nonentities!'

three witches in *Macbeth*'. The witchery, she mistakenly thought, was Heseltine's.

Mrs Thatcher dictated a statement declaring her intention to withdraw, which would be read at Cabinet the next morning. But before making a final decision, she wanted to return to No. 10 to talk to Denis.

Before she left, Mrs Thatcher received a visit from the 92 Group, a parliamentary club of the Tory right, staunch Thatcher supporters. 'We rushed to her room,' recalled Michael Portillo. 'We may have pushed Peter Morrison aside.' They found her with Tebbit, and in tears. She listened politely to their appeal, thanked them and then asked Portillo, as a minister, to stay behind. 'Almost every member of the Cabinet has told me to resign,' she told him, so what could she do? 'You know all the electors,' Portillo told her. Had she forced each to tell her personally they were going to vote against her, 'half of them would be carried out in tears'. He was implying that, with greater personal involvement, she could have stemmed the tide. He saw from her face that she realized, too late, that things could have been different.

Returning to Downing Street at 8.10, Mrs Thatcher talked to Denis in the flat. 'There was not much to say,' she recorded, 'but he comforted me. He had given his own verdict earlier and it had turned out to be right.' This was probably the moment she really decided to resign. Even so, she kept to her usual rule and said that she would sleep on it.

For those trying to make absolutely sure that Mrs Thatcher would go, the situation remained unsettled. Hurd and Major now both agreed to stand ('on a wholly friendly basis to give colleagues a choice') so long as Mrs Thatcher left the race. Major, however, was fretting about Mrs Thatcher's nomination papers, which he was due to return, signed, to Downing Street. Jeffrey Archer's driver was standing by to ferry them back to London.* There remained the possibility that, having received Major's signed paper (and already holding Hurd's), the Thatcher team might decide to use it. Could she still pull off a coup against the coup?

In Downing Street, Peter Morrison was worried: 'Between you and me,' he scribbled to Turnbull, 'John Major is now jibbing at seconding the nomination, if she went on & then there is a row in Cabinet tomorrow morning then he may not do so.' On this, Turnbull wrote: 'Because he has

---

* The need for Archer's driver arose because Major had said he was not well enough to get to London to sign the papers. Andrew Turnbull decreed that, because the leadership was a party matter, no government driver could be used to ferry the papers. The ever-eager Archer, who had not obtained from Mrs Thatcher the peerage for which he had been pushing for some time, therefore stepped in.

been offered a glimpse of his own candidacy.' Effectively, Major was saying he would nominate Mrs Thatcher for the second ballot only if she would not stand in it. There would be an explosive story if it were known that the Chancellor would not renominate the Prime Minister, but an even worse disaster, from his point of view, if his nomination took effect. That would rule him out of the contest.

A Cabinet meeting had been arranged for 9 a.m. the next day. Renton and Goodlad now recommended Major send the signed nomination papers back with a covering letter requesting they not be submitted until after Cabinet, in case circumstances arose 'which might lead him to stand himself'. At Goodlad's behest, Morrison had given 'his word of honour that he would ... not release the nomination papers without John Major's consent'.

At about 10.30 p.m., Morrison confirmed to Major on the telephone that Mrs Thatcher would not stand. Reassured, Major sent Archer's driver off to London, bearing Mrs Thatcher's nomination signed by him. He also took Major's papers for his own entry into the contest for delivery to Graham Bright. With Mrs Thatcher's nomination, he enclosed two handwritten letters, both to Morrison. The first – 'Strictly Private' – said:

> The following is <u>for your eyes only</u> as a former Whip.*
>
> I gather that there is a possibility of resignations from the Cabinet <u>if</u> the PM proceeds against the wishes of colleagues. This would obviously be awful – for the PM <u>and</u> the Party. Could <u>you</u> please hold the nomination until after Cabinet – refer to me if such a problem arises (<u>before</u> the nomination goes in).
>
> I am anxious to protect the PM from any further unpleasantness wherever possible – and also protect the Party.

Thus did Major artfully set out to Morrison what they had earlier agreed, without committing anything to paper which could prove any agreement had been made.

Major's second letter to Morrison concerned his own application to contest the leadership: 'I haven't enclosed a Consent Form for me for the moment but will reflect later this evening. I <u>may</u> then send one up to Graham Bright – but it merits some thought first, I think. Keep in touch!' In fact, he was sending his consent form to Bright so that it could be ready, without any interference from Morrison, for delivery to Cranley Onslow the following morning.

---

* Major mentioned Morrison's status as a former whip to invoke the *omertà* of the whips' office. It was the ultimate sin to pass on to others any information shared on whips' terms.

In these two envelopes, Mrs Thatcher's fate was, almost literally, sealed, and John Major's entry into the contest – on highly favourable terms – was sealed too.

Although Mrs Thatcher seemed resolved, John Whittingdale had not given up. At 11.30 that night, as she worked on her speech for the next day's no-confidence debate, he summoned Michael Portillo. Michael Forsyth, Michael Fallon and Neil Hamilton appeared too. They all met her, 'urging her to fight on', but without any useful result. Denis kept saying, 'We've got to get you to bed, old dear.' She went up with him at 12.45.

When Jeffrey Archer received from his driver the envelope containing Major's nomination of Mrs Thatcher, he took it round to Downing Street and handed it to Morrison. He detected, from Morrison's absolute lack of interest, that the nomination was not going to be used.*

THURSDAY 22 NOVEMBER

At 6.30 a.m., Michael Brown and his fellow Thatcherite Edward Leigh ran to Downing Street, determined to convince Mrs Thatcher she could still win. It was a forlorn hope. Denied an audience, they waited, and at 8 saw Peter Morrison pass by. Brown grabbed him by the lapels. 'You stupid, stupid idiot,' he shouted, as Morrison went puce. 'Go and tell her she can win.' He did not. Indeed, by then, he could not, since, just after 7.30, Mrs Thatcher had told Turnbull and Morrison that she would resign. At 7.40, Morrison informed Hurd and Major. At 7.45, Turnbull informed the Treasury and the Bank of England before the markets opened and, at 7.50, confirmed with the Palace.† At 9, the Cabinet gathered.

Normally, Turnbull recorded, ministers would be 'milling around in the ante-room and there is a hubbub of conversation', but:

> As she came down the stairs no one could be seen and there was no noise ... Then, as she passed the Macmillan portrait, one could see the Cabinet standing silently, pushed back against the walls of the ante-room, trying to look as

---

* Morrison told Whittingdale that the envelope was 'damp and looked as if it has been steamed open' by the famous writer of fiction.
† At 10 p.m. the night before, Turnbull had rung Robert Fellowes at the Palace 'to confirm that Mrs Thatcher had decided to stand down, but would sleep on it ...' 'I cleared with the Queen', wrote Fellowes, 'that there could be an announcement of intent (as arranged) at about 9.45 a.m.'

invisible as possible. By then they had realised the full significance of what was about to happen.

As the meeting began, Mrs Thatcher started her statement,* but then almost broke down.† Trying to help, Cecil Parkinson put his hand on her arm and said, 'The Lord Chancellor [the minister most senior in terms of protocol] will read it for her.' 'No, the Lord Chancellor won't,' replied the Lord Chancellor, Lord Mackay. 'She'll deal with it herself.' 'I felt she'd regret it all her life if she didn't do it herself,' he recalled. 'She got immediate strength.' Thus fortified, Mrs Thatcher read out:

> Having consulted widely among colleagues, I have concluded that the unity of the party and the prospect of victory in a General Election would be better served if I stood down to enable Cabinet colleagues to enter the ballot for the leadership. I should like to thank all those colleagues in Cabinet and outside who have given me such dedicated support.

Mackay then delivered a short tribute on behalf of the Cabinet: 'Your place in our country's history is already assured.' Then Mrs Thatcher spoke more ad-lib: 'She could not bear it if all they believed in were not to continue ... The Cabinet should stand together to back the person most likely to beat Mr Heseltine.'‡ Short tributes from Baker and Hurd followed.

As she had broken down, so had others. Renton noticed David Waddington 'sitting opposite her openly in tears'. Caroline Slocock, the only woman private secretary Mrs Thatcher ever had, had little sympathy with Mrs Thatcher's politics, but recalled, 'It was like watching Mary, Queen of Scots, being beheaded. I had tears streaming.' 'Crocodiles mostly,' recalled Chris Patten of his colleagues' tears. 'The majority of us just stared at the table.' Renton, though no friend to Mrs Thatcher, was impressed by her 'fighting spirit. It is like shaking a very firm apple off a tree ... she

---

* While rehearsing her statement with Powell and Morrison, Mrs Thatcher had at first suggested that she should read it out at the end of the meeting, but they had counselled that it would be too emotionally difficult for her to wait till the end. It occurred to Morrison in retrospect that her motive 'might have been one last roll of the dice ... to see whether any of them upped and off' because she was not announcing her departure.

† In Robin Butler's manuscript Cabinet Notebook, on which he drew when writing up the minutes formally, this scene is recorded by only one word: 'Pause'.

‡ Her reference to Heseltine by name on such an occasion verged on the improper. Robin Butler admitted he had 'consciously misrepresented what happened when I wrote up the minutes': he replaced any reference to Heseltine by name with a phrase along the lines of 'continuing the spirit of what the Government has done'.

comments that with three more supporters she would have won ... That is an extraordinary thought.' He was one of those who had withheld his backing.*

After formal proceedings concluded, around 10.15, Mrs Thatcher invited ministers to stay for coffee. But some were extremely anxious to leave and run the campaigns for Hurd or for Major. When the latter returned to London, from Great Stukeley, at noon, a crowd had gathered.† 'I was astounded,' wrote Major, 'I had no idea I was likely to find such strong backing so quickly.' He cannot, in reality, have been quite so surprised.

Beyond the Westminster village, there was virtually global pandemonium. People shouted out 'She's gone', and everyone knew whom they meant. A friend told the present author that his ten-year-old daughter asked him, 'Daddy, in England, can a man be prime minister?'

At 12.45, Mrs Thatcher gave the Queen formal notice of her intention to resign.‡ 'When she emerged from her audience,' Sir Robert Fellowes, the Queen's private secretary, recorded, 'she was in a very distressed state and unable to speak.' As soon as she returned to No. 10, Crawfie recalled, 'She went straight upstairs to the flat and ran to the bathroom and she absolutely wept. She said: "It's when people are kind to you that you feel it most. The Queen has been so kind to me."'

In the Commons that afternoon, Mrs Thatcher wore one of her favourite suits, a royal blue with a blue-satin trim, catalogued by Crawfie as 'Blue Bouclé'. At Prime Minister's Questions, Tory critics fulfilled the uniquely long and strong Conservative tradition of hypocrisy by larding her with praise. Tony Marlow, one of the most vocal in trying to get rid of her, now spoke of the 'great well of affection' which was felt for her in the House. Shortly after Questions, Mrs Thatcher repaired to her room before Labour's motion of no confidence. As she and Morrison walked back, alone, 'She turned round and burst into floods of tears and she said, "I can't go through with this."' Morrison said: 'Prime Minister ... no human

---

* The press the next day reported that Mrs Thatcher had said it was 'a funny old world', when a person gets pushed out after winning three general elections in succession. These were not, in fact, her words. They were Andrew Turnbull's paraphrase of what she had meant by what she said to the Cabinet. Bernard Ingham repeated them in his briefing and the press took them as her own expression.
† Major was nominated by Norman Lamont and John Gummer. Hurd, nominated by Tom King and Chris Patten, also declared his candidacy that afternoon.
‡ Her resignation, though announced, could not take effect until a new prime minister had been chosen.

being could go through what you're being asked to do. However you have always proved you are the exception to every rule . . .' Mrs Thatcher rallied – 'we mopped ourselves down', as Morrison put it – and she entered the Chamber.

Just before 5 p.m., she rose to rebut the Opposition no-confidence motion. Neil Kinnock's speech had badly misjudged the mood of the House because he failed to acknowledge the change wrought by her imminent departure. His denunciation of all Tory wickednesses made no acknowledgement of Mrs Thatcher's achievements. She, by contrast, felt liberated. Her own benches now wished to assuage their guilt by loudly backing her. Their backing – and the adrenalin flowing through her – drove her forward.

The best moments, as so often in her speeches, came in her impromptu responses to interruptions. To accusations that she had widened the gap between rich and poor, she declared: 'they [socialists] would rather the poor were poorer': 'Once they start to talk about the gap, they would rather that the gap were that – [indicating] – down here, not this – [indicating] – but that – [indicating]. So long as the gap is smaller, they would rather have the poor poorer. One does not create wealth and opportunity that way.'

During this, Mrs Thatcher's index fingers sank low and close together to indicate socialism's idea of wealth and rose high, but further apart, to indicate hers. This mixture of gospel-preaching with high-spirited theatricality was all her own. Surveying the House, pointing, sweeping her arm, even resting her elbow on the despatch box, she was full of vigour and yet at ease.

As her speech turned to Europe, she was asked whether she would continue her fight against the single currency and an independent central bank after leaving office. Dennis Skinner, the hardest-left Labour backbencher and full-time heckler, shouted out, 'No. She is going to be the governor.' Mrs Thatcher beamed at him. 'What a good idea,' she replied. And then, after a short passage on the iniquity of the single currency, she exclaimed: 'Now where were we? I am enjoying this.'* Michael Carttiss, a Tory backbencher, shouted out, 'Cancel it [meaning her resignation]. You can wipe the floor with these people.' Even the Labour benches cheered.

Paddy Ashdown, the Liberal Democrat leader, who spoke next, was prophetic, and more generous than Neil Kinnock. He warned 'whoever is successful in the leadership election to watch out': 'she will be a powerful

---

* When Mrs Thatcher's Treasury private secretary, Barry Potter, afterwards congratulated her on this particular riposte she told him, with a twinkle in her eye, 'And I nearly added, "so I think I'll stay on".'

voice in months to come. We shall be interested to see how much that voice will be used to unite her party or, on the issue of Europe, to divide it.'

Returning to Downing Street a little after 6 p.m., Mrs Thatcher received a call from President Bush. The news of her resignation had been 'quite emotional' for Bush, recalled his press secretary, Marlin Fitzwater: 'it was right at the beginning of the war. He and she had put this together. And now she was going to be gone.' In his diary, Bush recorded, she seemed 'resigned and tired, but determined; she will be with us . . . End of a long marvellous chapter. What a courageous woman.'

'She came back from the House on a complete high,' Amanda Ponsonby, now her diary secretary, recalled. Part of Mrs Thatcher's temporary happiness derived from having accepted the Major–Hurd candidacies as a 'stop Heseltine' move. Conservative MPs wanted to give her something to assuage their 'Oh my God, what have we done?' feeling. All they could offer was the right, in effect, to choose her successor. That evening, Major cunningly played to this on television by emphasizing how he had signed Mrs Thatcher's nomination papers and would have supported her if she had gone forward. Heseltine's whole campaign, meanwhile, had been constructed against her. He had nothing left to say.*

Before the second ballot on Tuesday 27 November, Whittingdale considered Mrs Thatcher 'desperate for Major to win'. At this stage, she was not disposed to blame him for her fall. It was the Cabinet, she told Woodrow Wyatt, who had 'sold me down the river', and he had been absent throughout. At the request of the Majorites, she agreed to use her farewell lunch on Monday 26 November to work on those who might still favour Heseltine.†

The intervening days were spent packing and clearing up.‡ Having had no expectation of leaving office, Mrs Thatcher was unprepared emotionally,

---

* In after years, he said, 'There was an alternative that no one considered at the time. After the first ballot I could have said that I did not wish to exploit a technicality and withdrawn. I could have been prime minister within a year. But no one thought of that.'
† Major's camp knew she could deliver many of her supporters to his cause; equally, they realized that too much Thatcher backing, too publicly given, would make it harder for him to be his own man. In later years, Major tended to say that Mrs Thatcher's backing had not been necessary for his victory: 'It was not true that I won because Margaret supported me. I think I was sufficiently ahead: my team told me.' This was said, however, after the two had fallen out.
‡ There was also the enormous – if pleasurable – burden of 30,000 letters, almost all of them complimentary, which arrived in the six days between Mrs Thatcher's announcement of her resignation and her departure. It was important to answer as many of these as possible then and there, while she still had the full resources of the Civil Service at her disposal.

domestically, financially and practically. All her energies, including her strong instincts as a home-maker, had for more than a decade been concentrated on 10 Downing Street and Chequers. 'Her whole life was in No. 10,' Caroline Slocock felt, 'and we were her family.' Retirement loomed like enforced exile.

Along with many of Mrs Thatcher's personal staff, both Charles and Carla Powell helped her pack – he getting papers into boxes, she stowing Mrs Thatcher's collection of Crown Derby. Crawfie procured empty boxes and asked Mrs Thatcher to sort out what she wanted. But this proved futile. 'You'll have to do it, dear,' she said. In Crawfie's view, 'She couldn't face it: she was bewildered.'* For all her famous practicality, Mrs Thatcher was at sea. In the middle of packing, she received another call from George Bush, his last to her in office. Almost as if nothing had happened, she spoke yet again about the Gulf, stressing that Saddam Hussein should not be given more time. At the end of the call, Bush mentioned her departure. He said 'she had courage and guts', noted the US record: 'we feel you have served magnificently. Thatcher said to remember that one still has influence and she is watching everything. I shan't stop.'

On Sunday 25 November, she and Denis went to church from Chequers. Then, in the failing light of the winter afternoon, they walked through its rooms and the great hall, past the piano she used to play in her more private moments, for the last time.

The next morning, Monday 26 November, Mrs Thatcher visited Conservative Central Office to thank the staff. Referring to the impending Gulf War, she said of Bush: 'He won't falter, and I won't falter. It's just that I won't be pulling the levers there. But I shall be a very good back-seat driver.' The BBC took these words out of context and suggested she was applying them to John Major, should he win. But Major was right to be worried. As Charles Powell put it, 'Her *real* attitude to him *was* that of a back-seat driver.'

Back at No. 10, at her farewell lunch,† Mrs Thatcher worked to shore up support for Major. Morrison briefed her beforehand on the waverers.

---

* The one exception was her father's Bible, which Mrs Thatcher herself secured.
† Those attending included one or two elderly grandees, such as her much-loved patron, Keith Joseph, and her first Party Chairman, Lord Thorneycroft. The senior ministers or ex-ministers present included Nick Ridley, Tebbit and Parkinson. Among the others were the 'four Michaels', Forsyth, Fallon, Portillo and Brown; Edward Leigh, Gerald Howarth and the campaign men Neale, Neubert, Twinn and Morrison. A few ministers less trusted by Thatcherites because of their role in the downfall – Wakeham, Lilley, Gummer and MacGregor – were also there.

Edward Leigh, for example, needed: 'a firm talking to as well as reassurance that Major had no part in the conspiracy'.* All the best silver was on show and the room was heavy with the scent of her well-wishers' flowers.

Twinn observed that Mrs Thatcher was 'bullish as ever'. As Michael Forsyth came in, 'She said, "You must vote for John Major." I said, "Why? He is not the Thatcherite you think he is. He took a very long time to sign and return your nomination papers." She replied, "That's not true. We must stop Heseltine." ... She was insistent and lobbying hard so I voted for Major.' Over lunch, Keith Joseph toasted what he called 'the most beautiful giant in history'. She was cheerful, now and again exclaiming, 'No tears! No tears!' But as the guests lined up to shake her hand before leaving, 'Everyone', Portillo recalled, 'was getting tearful.' Denis was outside the dining room when they emerged sad-faced. 'We're not bloody dead, you know,' he shouted.

On Tuesday 27 November, Mrs Thatcher faced her 698th – and last – Prime Minister's Questions. Throughout the day, Conservative MPs voted in the second round. The results were 56 votes for Hurd, 131 for Heseltine and 185 for John Major. Major's tally, like Mrs Thatcher's in the first round, was two votes short of preventing a further ballot. This time, however, both Hurd and Heseltine immediately fell in behind Major. With nineteen fewer votes than Mrs Thatcher received when forced to resign, John Major became the new Conservative leader, and therefore would shortly become Prime Minister.

Mrs Thatcher went through from No. 10 to No. 11, where celebrations were already under way. Clearly excited, she congratulated Major warmly, and told his wife Norma that it was 'what I have always wanted'. When Major made to meet the press in the street outside, Mrs Thatcher suggested she accompany him. As Major recalled, 'I should have agreed ... But my team were over-sensitive to the Labour line that I was the political "son of Thatcher" ... Norman Lamont peeled her away.'

Mrs Thatcher went instead to the upstairs window, where Renton observed her 'cooing with evident delight at the success of her favourite candidate'. The photographers noticed her too and grabbed the picture, which was exactly what the Major team did not want. The dynamics at the party itself were notable. 'Within two minutes,' said Dominic Morris, 'everyone clustered round Major, leaving her alone.' Picking up on this,

---

* It is notable that Morrison wrote as much while knowing full well what Major's part in her downfall had been.

Mrs Thatcher soon returned to No. 10. Supper that night was with Denis, Mark and Carol.

One other matter needed to be settled. It had been indicated that the Queen wished to confer some sort of honour. Since Mrs Thatcher had no immediate plan to leave the Commons, talk of a peerage was premature. Nonetheless, she toyed with the idea that any peerage, when it came, should be hereditary. This gave rise to two problems. First, there was no regular provision for an English hereditary peerage to be held by or pass through a woman. The second was that, as Powell put it, she 'was determined that Mark should inherit something'. This was controversial.* The solution was to make Denis a baronet, the order of hereditary knighthood. Mark would then eventually become Sir Mark, but since a baronetcy does not create a legislator, it was felt that not much harm could be done. Denis became Sir Denis, and so Mrs Thatcher became Lady Thatcher.† As to honouring Mrs Thatcher herself, attention focused on the Order of Merit (OM). This (along with the Order of the Garter) is the most distinguished honour in the personal gift of the Sovereign. It seemed a natural choice for a Prime Minister who had been the greatest champion of meritocracy.‡

At 9 a.m. on Wednesday 28 November, elegantly coiffed and looking immaculate in a burgundy suit, Mrs Thatcher descended to the Downing Street entrance hall with Denis. She found it crowded with all the staff waiting to say goodbye. 'That's what brought her to tears,' recalled Amanda Ponsonby. Everyone clapped her. When she emerged into the street, with Denis beside her, she was composed, except for the slightest quaver in her voice as she began:

> Ladies and Gentlemen,
>
> We're leaving Downing Street for the last time after eleven-and-a-half wonderful years, and we're very happy that we leave the United Kingdom in a very, very much better state than when we came here eleven-and-a-half years ago.
>
> It's been a tremendous privilege to serve this country as prime minister – wonderfully happy years – and I'm immensely grateful to the staff who

---

* Mrs Thatcher would have liked something for Carol also, but felt defeated by the system's bias against women.

† There may have been a private reason for Mrs Thatcher's enthusiasm for the baronetcy. Denis's first wife had left him for a baronet. She may have seen it as a small victory if the Queen could make him one half a century later.

‡ Only five women had joined the order in its ninety-year history. These included Florence Nightingale, and Mrs Thatcher's former tutor at Oxford, Dorothy Hodgkin.

supported me so well, and may I also say a word of thanks to all the people who sent so many letters, still arriving, and for all the flowers.

Now it's time for a new chapter to open and I wish John Major all the luck in the world. He'll be splendidly served and he has the makings of a great prime minister, which I'm sure he'll be in very short time.

Thank you very much. Goodbye.

After she had got into the car, the camera caught the tear in Mrs Thatcher's eye. Instead of the poise of the Prime Minister, it captured a glimpse of the distress of Margaret Roberts from Grantham, who had risen so high and was now cast down. The car proceeded to Buckingham Palace. Denis, untypically, was holding her hand. As they approached, he muttered, 'Steady the Buffs.'*

As always, the Prime Minister saw the Queen alone. When Fellowes told her she was about to be offered the OM, she was 'surprised and delighted'. It was the Queen's personal suggestion. She may also have hinted at the baronetcy. The audience finished after twenty minutes and then the Queen said goodbye to Denis as well. 'The couple', so downcast before, 'looked better as they emerged,' Fellowes recalled. Shortly after they left, John Major arrived to 'kiss hands'. Mrs Thatcher was no longer prime minister.

She was driven to Alistair McAlpine's house in Great College Street, where her closest aides were gathered. 'Can I get you a cup of coffee, Prime – Mrs Thatcher?' said Shana Hole, struggling to escape the force of habit. Later that day, Amanda Ponsonby accompanied the Thatchers to their house in Dulwich. 'There was no food. She and I sat in the kitchen. She was completely broken.'

---

* As Denis was a man of Kent, the phrase 'Steady the Buffs', an exhortation to stay calm in the face of adversity, was a favourite of his. That it originated with the Royal East Kent Regiment ('the Buffs') of the British Army appealed to him.

39
The lioness in winter

'The Almighty had shaped her to be prime minister, but not to do anything else'

The young Margaret Roberts kept a schoolgirl 'autograph book' of improving thoughts and poetical quotations (see p. 19). As Prime Minister, and after leaving office, Margaret Thatcher returned to the genre. One of her selections, by the Scottish Chartist poet Charles Mackay, was called 'No Enemies':

> You have no enemies, you say?
> Alas! My friend, the boast is poor;
> He who has mingled in the fray
> Of duty, that the brave endure,
> *Must* have made foes! If you have none,
> Small is the work that you have done.

Mrs Thatcher thought of herself in this way. She was proud of enemies made 'in the fray of duty'. In her sudden fall, however, she had learnt she had far more enemies than she had realized, including among her closest colleagues. The effect was shattering: she had had little idea of their resentments and even less that some might be justified. As Prime Minister she had been too busy, too innocent and, latterly, too haughty to consider such matters. Now, with an empty diary and a broken heart, she could not understand what had happened.

Her bewilderment was not unique. Across the world, people were amazed that such a successful figure could have been ejected with such sudden discourtesy. King Fahd of Saudi Arabia said, privately, that she must have been the victim of an actual *coup d'état*. She had won handsomely all three general elections into which she had led her party. She had good claims to have restored the British economy, reversed national decline and helped win the Cold War. Yet she was out, denied the chance to put her record to the electorate again.

Her critics insisted that, as leader, she would have lost the next general election. They pointed, with justice, to serious problems such as the poll tax, renewed inflation and high interest rates, the clash about Britain's European destiny and her growing personal unpopularity. It is striking, however, that Tony Blair, then emerging as a bright new Labour star, felt that 'She could still have won the 1992 election. She was able to govern with a strength and party unity her successors were lacking.' Perhaps some of Mrs Thatcher's Cabinet colleagues worried less that she might lose the next election and more that she might win it. Her dominance would then have become intolerable: the generation beneath her – that of John Major and Chris Patten – might never have found their place in the sun.

Mrs Thatcher's removal was the result of a conspiracy in the tradition of the Tory establishment – a loose, virtually all-male club whose habits of mind were profoundly different from her own. In 1981, over economic difficulties, and in 1986, over Westland, they had toyed with getting rid of her but she had outwitted them. From late 1989, her failure to learn the lessons of the Meyer challenge, combined with the unpopularity of the poll tax and the split over Europe, had given them their chance.

So when Tristan Garel-Jones wrote his secret note to Tim Renton in December 1989, identifying the coming 'end of the Thatcher era', he was merely 'weaponizing' the sentiments of the Tory club to, as he put it, 'manage that end in a way that does not split the Party'. In the ensuing months, most of the men involved did not need to plot much. The hand not stretched out to save Mrs Thatcher was usually a more effective weapon than the hand raised to strike her down. The tribe acted largely by instinct against the leader whom it had never fully accepted. Only in the last weeks did the conspiracy become active. Only after the first ballot did men such as Garel-Jones, Major, Hurd, Goodlad, Renton, Clarke, Lamont, Patten – and, more ambiguously, Wakeham and Whitelaw – cooperate to remove the woman whom they were publicly committed to support. It was this behaviour that Mrs Thatcher would later describe on television as 'treachery – with a smile on its face'.

They were not necessarily wrong to conspire. To senior colleagues, her manner was often insufferable. There was an extreme contrast between Mrs Thatcher's ability to inspire the love and loyalty of her immediate staff who worked *for* her and her ability to insult and antagonize those, chiefly Cabinet ministers, who worked *with* her. There was something attractive in her inversion of normal hierarchies, but it was bad man-management. Once Geoffrey Howe, her patient and longest-serving Cabinet minister, could stand it no more, the dam broke. Most colleagues, understandably sick of her, were ready to push her out. Embodying their wish with immense subtlety, John Major came out on top.

In the British system, the Cabinet is the ultimate decision-making body. Mrs Thatcher would never have denied the theory of collective decision-making but often ignored the practice. By her third term she felt she had been proved right against doubting colleagues so often that she tended to make up her own mind, aided by officials and advisers, and then tried to ram her decision through or avoid Cabinet altogether. This left Britain worse governed.

The saga surrounding ERM entry is a case in point. Mrs Thatcher had powerful economic and political arguments about the risks of entry; but, after the painful meeting in November 1985, she never really sought a way of persuading the Cabinet. Instead she sniped at her own government's policy until, just before the end, she ungraciously succumbed. As often with great leaders, her vices were inseparable from her virtues. Her intelligence, courage and commitment set her way above the common run, but these involved a pig-headedness which was more than frail Tory flesh and blood could bear. So when she slipped, too few were left to break her fall. As she had begun, so she ended, a woman isolated in a man's world – herself alone.

The manner of her fall engendered bitterness within the Conservative Party that lingers still. 'We were mistaken,' admitted Chris Patten in hindsight. 'The Conservative Party would have been better served if she had been despatched by the electorate.' On the deeper level of human drama, they were also mistaken. They created an unforgettable, tragic spectacle of a woman's greatness overborne by the littleness of men.

On 29 November 1990, having led her country for 4,227 consecutive days, Mrs Thatcher began her first full day as a former Prime Minister. The sudden loss of office was impossible to process: it was, she said, like 'having a mosaic smashed into little pieces'. Her lack of a suitable place to live or work added greatly to her disorientation.

Soon after leaving Downing Street, she and Denis went to stay at Easton Neston, the great Northamptonshire house and seat of Lord (Alexander) Hesketh.* Charles and Carla Powell were fellow guests, as was Sabrina Guinness. Ignoring the women, Mrs Thatcher 'flirted' with

---

* Hesketh had been one of her whips and a junior minister in the House of Lords. She liked him very much, not least because he was one of the handful of men who could make her laugh.

the men and stayed at the dinner table when the women left, just as she had done forty years earlier in the farmhouse of the man who wanted to marry her (see p. 45). She was, felt Sabrina Guinness, in 'a very wobbly state'. Having been cut off from the Downing Street switchboard, she was also out of touch. No one, including Mark and Carol, rang for her that weekend. After dinner, Denis sat at her feet in the drawing room, patting her knee as her eyes filled with tears. Snow fell so heavily that the planned guests could not come to lunch the next day, so the small party walked outside as the snowflakes fell about them: 'Everyone was kind, embarrassed, sympathetic,' recalled Sabrina Guinness. 'It was like being with someone who had just lost a relation.' She also noticed that Mrs Thatcher had 'nothing to do'. She could see the experience was as unwelcome as it was new.

Mrs Thatcher's plight was sharpened by the fierceness of the British system, which leaves no time for transition. Once she had resigned she received only her MP's salary (£21,000 a year) plus an annual £25,000 prime ministerial pension.* There was something admirably democratic about this penny-pinching, but for her it created real difficulties. Mrs Thatcher left office with virtually no money in her bank account.† The decisions about what to do with her life would determine her financial future, but she was too distraught to make them. Even the small things of life were a puzzle for her. She had probably not dialled anyone direct on the telephone since 1979 and consequently had no idea what anyone's number was. For Christmas, Carol gave her a book containing the contact details of her closest friends.

The same official attitude which kept the purse-strings tight was peremptory in enforcing other rules. A fortnight after leaving office, Mrs Thatcher received a letter from Robin Butler revoking her 'notification' under the Official Secrets Act which governed her access to classified information. This bald letter deeply upset her. Drafting the reply herself, she called Butler's letter 'hardly a model of clarity or consideration'. If Cabinet Secretaries, she said, 'had to go through the experience of leaving office but still remaining a public figure, with such little consideration and help for the realities of public life as we Prime Ministers receive, I

---

* She was also provided with close protection officers and a bullet-proof car (plus driver) as she was at risk from terrorist attack.
† Although Denis was comfortably off, he had never paid for her life in Downing Street and, according to Julian Seymour, who would soon take charge of her affairs, he 'never voluntarily put his hand in his pocket from 1979 till the day he died'.

think such Cabinet Secretaries would take a more reasonable, not to say sympathetic, view'.*

As she began her life in exile, Mrs Thatcher felt genuine, if not unqualified, goodwill towards her successor. Because she believed his victory 'locked in' her legacy, she felt she had a right to be consulted about important matters. While Major hoped to draw privately on her experience, he also had to contend with the accusation that he was her creature: 'Once she had said she was going to be a good back-seat driver, it made it much more difficult for me to consult her.' He contemplated offering her the Embassy in Washington, but this risked a rerun of her offer of the same thing to Edward Heath in 1979, a suggestion he had deeply resented (see p. 184).† Besides, Mrs Thatcher was simply too big a figure to be thus contained.

Major knew he was vulnerable, both politically and personally, to any backlash from her. As she sought culprits in her downfall, he was not high on her list, but nor was he in the clear. She remembered his hesitation before nominating her for the second ballot. Peter Morrison also conveyed Major's reluctance to help. All this left her slightly suspicious of Major, a suspicion which would fester.

Major's statement in Downing Street immediately after becoming Prime Minister – 'I want to see us build a country at ease with itself' – was judged a reproach to his predecessor. His first Cabinet brought Michael Heseltine back as Environment Secretary. This left Heseltine in charge of the poll tax, which he promptly jettisoned.‡ All this was wormwood and gall to Mrs Thatcher. Major also chose to include no women. There was a sense that, after eleven and half years, the men felt they deserved a break. There emerged a jolly, all-male affair, soon branded 'the Cabinet of chums'. Major disliked the description, but added: 'there's no point in having a Cabinet unless you listen to them,' as too often Mrs Thatcher had not. This was a fair point, but a Cabinet from which the tension was

---

* Butler showed more consideration when he oversaw the creation of the 'public duty cost allowance' in March 1991. In direct response to Mrs Thatcher's difficult financial situation, this entitled former prime ministers to extra funds for expenses incurred as they fulfilled duties associated with their previous position in public life. Mrs Thatcher wrote to Butler to offer her 'grateful thanks . . . It will be an enormous help.'

† According to Major, the Bush administration was, in any case, unenthusiastic about the idea.

‡ The community charge was replaced by a new council tax, based on the value of the property and the number of occupants. Mrs Thatcher chose not to make a public fuss, realizing how little support she would receive. She never fully recanted about the poll tax, but she did lament her handling of it. One day, during a discussion for her memoirs, she mentioned the decision to get rid of 'dual running' and exclaimed, 'I wish to God we'd kept it!', before sweeping out of the room.

released tended to produce less decisive government. She watched all this with increasing dismay.

The most urgent problem facing the government after her fall was the easiest for Mrs Thatcher to support. Before she left office, war to expel Iraq from Kuwait had been mapped out. Major immediately established good relations with George Bush – much better, on a personal level, than hers had been. The plan to drive Iraq out of Kuwait was meticulously enacted. At Major's request, Charles Powell (who had stayed in 10 Downing Street for the war) kept Mrs Thatcher well briefed. On 16 January 1991, the day hostilities began with an intense air campaign, she stayed up late into the night 'with her ear glued to the wireless, listening to what was happening'. Although frustrated by not taking part, she was appreciative of Major's consideration, and on 28 February, after Iraqi forces had been routed, promptly congratulated him on victory. These were her first words spoken in Parliament since her fall.

Even on Iraq, however, two points of difference emerged. One, voiced only privately, was her belief that the surrender should have been absolute, and exacted from Saddam in person. She was disturbed that the Iraqi leader had escaped punishment. Major complained to Bush about her attitude: 'These conversations get out and create problems for us.' Speaking just before Easter, she also called for action to help the Kurdish refugees from Saddam. This annoyed Major because he was already trying to persuade the Americans, privately, to do just that: 'She really impeded the policy,' he recalled. Nonetheless, within hours of her comments Major authorized extra funds for the Kurds, soon afterwards making public his plan to establish 'safe havens' in Iraq. The Americans, somewhat reluctantly, agreed.

One of Mrs Thatcher's most pressing problems after leaving Downing Street was her lack of a proper home. Her Dulwich house was simply too far – nearly six miles – from Parliament and, as Andrew Turnbull put it, 'from the nearest armed response'. Shortly before Christmas, she accepted the loan of a flat, 93 Eaton Square, Belgravia.* In these and other temporary provisions, like using Alistair McAlpine's house in Great College Street as her office, she was reliant on the kindness of friends and admirers, some of whom transferred money directly to a bank account she

---

* This came from Kathy Ford, the widow of Henry Ford II of the Ford Motor Company, and was found for Mrs Thatcher by Charlie Price, the former US Ambassador to Britain. Mrs Ford herself had never met her.

could draw on.* As to staff, Crawfie continued as Mrs Thatcher's informal, uniquely close personal assistant, now in greater demand than ever. Peter Morrison was replaced as PPS in 1991 by Gerald Howarth. Robin Harris and John Whittingdale stayed much longer.

To run Mrs Thatcher's office Amanda Ponsonby recruited Andy Bearpark, who had served Mrs Thatcher earlier as a private secretary and had a reputation for good logistics. Informally, however, Charles Powell remained of immense importance. When she left office, he stayed in frequent touch on the phone and would see her regularly. At first, she turned to Powell for virtually anything. Once she rang him on a Saturday morning to complain she had no hot water. Powell encouraged her to find a plumber, but the idea overwhelmed her: 'The episode only ended after I went round there and helped her to get the water running again.'

Powell's own idea of his role was expressed in a letter he wrote to Mrs Thatcher when he left Downing Street in March 1991. 'Dear Prime Minister,' he wrote, never dropping the now out-of-date usage, 'My last letter from No. 10 could only be to you.' He thanked her for 'The incomparable years spent here with you . . . although I shall miss it, in a way I am also glad to go. You can't transfer loyalty.' He was ready to be her lifelong counsellor.

Bearpark's role was much less cosmic, but urgently needed. He realized Mrs Thatcher was 'disorientated': 'As prime minister, her entire day had been rigidly determined . . . She had suddenly lost that.' So he set about creating a mini-Downing Street. Just as in No. 10, Monday mornings began with a diary meeting; Fridays remained a constituency day. Mrs Thatcher received three boxes of papers each night to work on, just as if she were in office. Within a few months, her staff cut this back to just one. There was some difficulty about how to address her after so many years of 'Prime Minister'. Luckily, Denis's baronetcy, announced, with his wife's OM, on 7 December 1990, offered escape. She was Lady Thatcher. Quite quickly, most of her staff began to call her 'Lady T' – a mixture of deference and intimacy which suited her.

Thanks to Bearpark and Ponsonby, daily life could go on, but there was still no one able to take the key decisions about the future. Denis, who decades earlier had decided to preserve his own independence by offering 'just two things – love and loyalty', stuck to this rule. Carol, too, kept her

---

* Sir Hector Laing and Sir Geoffrey Leigh helped pay for secretaries. At a later stage Sir James Goldsmith made large contributions, and Peter Palumbo also contributed. Under a rule instigated to help look after Winston Churchill in retirement, the tax authorities permitted what they called 'gifts of esteem' free of tax. Palumbo had been ennobled in the resignation honours list always permitted to outgoing prime ministers and Leigh had been knighted, as had Peter Morrison.

distance. This seemed to provide an opening for Mark. When Crawfie saw him just after his mother left office, she said, 'Oh dear. It's over.' 'No, Crawfie,' Mark replied, 'it's only just beginning.' Parachuting in from the United States for brief periods, he was keen to capitalize on the Thatcher 'brand'. For a while, recalled Ponsonby, 'he was rather enjoying being a slight doorkeeper to her,' but he could not sustain a coherent operation. Besides, he was not, as Bearpark put it, 'a team player' and so 'he was not reporting to us on his conversations/activities'.

About two months after her fall, Richard Wilson, who had worked closely with Mrs Thatcher in the Cabinet Office, was invited to call on her. His description of the visit, which lasted two hours, can stand for many such encounters:

> We drank whisky throughout and, to be honest, got fairly tipsy. We talked, in a rambling way, mainly about three things: her sense of betrayal, her grief at losing office and what she should do now ('what does one do with so much energy? I've got so much energy').
>
> She said she couldn't bear seeing the things she stood for being distorted and attacked ... At the beginning she was her usual brisk self but ... I said something about her chosen profession, politics ... its brutality, and her mood changed quite suddenly and she looked as though she was going to weep. She said the worst thing was waking up feeling depressed and realising that she was no longer Prime Minister. She couldn't get used to not taking decisions.

Wilson recalled her bitterness against 'the younger men who owed everything to her and had deserted her'.

> She cheered up enormously when she heard Denis come in. He proceeded to pour out further huge whiskies and the conversation became quite jolly and domestic. I suggested she should take up golf. She looked at me with mock horror and said: 'Oh, no, Mr Wilson. I don't like little balls (gesture with finger and thumb), I like playing with the globe (huge expansive gesture).'

Wilson's visit captured her predicament – her sense of bereavement, her anger, her eagerness to be up and doing on behalf of her country without much sense of how. It also showed the consistent notes of her character – her egotism, directness, oddly cosy moments of domesticity and flashes of humour.

Around this time, Geoffrey Howe, who had an uneasy conscience, decided to write Mrs Thatcher a personal letter of apology. He was unrepentant about his resignation, but as Arabella Warburton recalled, until the day he died he was 'deeply saddened that, after everything they had achieved together, her own leadership had had to end that way'. He often described his relationship with Mrs Thatcher as 'a marriage' which eventually went wrong. He wanted to be back on good terms. Amanda Ponsonby passed the letter to Mrs Thatcher and saw her 'grimace' as she read. She never answered it.

By early 1991, Mrs Thatcher's dejection and her office's unease about Mark's interventions were becoming increasingly difficult to handle. Mark's participation in the proposed philanthropic Thatcher Foundation was considered impossible by potential backers. In April the *Sunday Times* ran a story headlined '"Mark is wrecking your life", friends tell Thatcher'. Weary of such conflicts, which Mark's mother never confronted, Bearpark left. His replacement, Lois Stuart-Black, had her troubles with Mark too. His way of muscling in upset people. In May 1991, for example, Mark insisted on accompanying his mother to dinner at the Kremlin during her first post-office visit to Russia. This displeased Mikhail Gorbachev, who joked teasingly about one of Mark's previous fiascos (see p. 280): 'Why don't you come more often, Mark? We've got plenty of deserts for you to get lost in.' To Mrs Thatcher, joking in a different spirit, Gorbachev said, 'it wouldn't be a bad thing if you were to become Prime Minister here . . . we would probably work well together'.

Some offers of public service came Mrs Thatcher's way. She rejected both a private suggestion that she might become Secretary-General of the United Nations and the idea of heading an international institute to spread awareness of global warming. She did not want to leave the political game.* Her fundamental problem was encapsulated by Mark Worthington, later her political secretary: 'The Almighty had shaped her to be prime minister, but not to do anything else. She was made to sit there and take decisions. If there were no decisions to take, she did not know what to do.' In Powell's view, 'she never had a happy day after being ousted from office'.

After a few months, at the prompting of Tim Bell and Alistair McAlpine, Bell's friend and former colleague Julian Seymour became overall head of the Thatcher operation. He was tasked with bringing order, getting her memoirs written, 'how she might earn her living in a dignified fashion' and how she could make her foundation work. As he saw it, Mrs Thatcher quickly needed the security of a permanent home and workplace and, above all, money. With the help of David and Frederick Barclay, twin brothers who had made their fortunes chiefly in the property business, in May

---

* In the case of the UN job, Mrs Thatcher had insisted at once that she was unsuited to all the patient committee work involved.

1991 the Thatchers took up residence at 73 Chester Square, Belgravia.* They quickly became fond of the five-storeyed, white-stuccoed townhouse. Its many flights of stairs provided Mrs Thatcher with nearly her only form of exercise. She and Denis were to live there almost to the end of their lives.

In terms of gainful employment, it was Ronald Reagan who pointed the way. Just a week after her fall, the Reagans had tea with Mrs Thatcher in London. According to Fred Ryan, the former President's Chief of Staff, 'Reagan felt very badly. He felt that she was a giant of that period and that she should not have been removed in that way.' Reagan suggested she follow the long-standing American tradition of the paid lecture tour at which famous Britons such as Oscar Wilde and Winston Churchill had excelled. She was a natural at this form, being a born preacher and a uniquely forceful public performer. At Reagan's suggestion, she signed on with the Washington Speakers Bureau (WSB), which retained her to make thirty to forty speeches a year. For each speech she was paid upwards of $50,000.†

According to Amanda Ponsonby, Mrs Thatcher did 'love being courted – she loved to smile and wave at someone if they were cheering her'. In the United States, the Far East, the Gulf and Eastern Europe, smiles and waves were guaranteed. Besides, she wanted to spread her gospel. She was invariably fluent on 'the strenuous defence of liberty – and not just liberty, but law-based liberty'. Speaking became her main source of continuous income, bringing in more than $1.5 million per annum.

On Seymour's advice, Mrs Thatcher resolved not to join any company board (with the associated legal responsibilities) nor to advertise anything. For about half a million dollars a year, she took an advisory role with the American tobacco company Philip Morris. This caused controversy, 'but she didn't mind,' recalled Seymour, 'because Denis was a convinced smoker'. She also promoted British industry abroad without payment. She retained an extraordinary ability to open doors. From the Chinese Politburo to the King of Thailand, a visit from Mrs Thatcher brought British diplomats access that their counterparts could rarely match.

---

* The Barclays were great admirers of Mrs Thatcher. David Barclay, who owned the lease on 73 Chester Square, arranged with Mark Thatcher for this to be sold to a trust established for his children. Denis and Margaret then moved in as tenants of the trust.

† Separately, and outside the United States, Seymour negotiated with Citibank Asia that Mrs Thatcher be paid for speaking tours mainly in the Far East, including Japan, which would earn her roughly $300,000 for each country visited. Anxious always to behave with propriety, she decided not to accept payment for speeches made in Britain. She also refused payment for Hong Kong or China speeches, so that she could not be compromised in the dealings which she, as a signatory of the Hong Kong Agreement, continued to have with the Chinese government about the future of the territory after 1997.

She spent a good deal of time raising money for the Margaret Thatcher Foundation, which sought to assist, through education, the development of entrepreneurial skills, particularly in former Warsaw Pact countries. It financed numerous scholarships for education in the West.* Unfortunately, although Mrs Thatcher genuinely favoured such causes, in Seymour's view the Foundation 'bored her absolutely sideways'. She was skilled at winning millions of pounds for it, but to her action-oriented mind, academic study seemed remote. While she loved ideas, she was temperamentally unsuited to the detachment of academic life. She was never detached about anything.

The single most important decision, both for Mrs Thatcher's pocket and for her reputation, concerned her memoirs. On leaving office she told Bearpark that she thought 'Rupert would be able to help me.'† A deal was duly struck with HarperCollins, which Murdoch owned, worth in the region of £6 million. The book, combined with the speeches, made Mrs Thatcher, for the first time, rich.

Although she recognized the need to write the book, Mrs Thatcher was not at first much interested in it. Still a player in politics, and constitutionally averse to retrospection, she was reluctant to create the mental space required. Her formal writing style was wooden, almost lawyerly, removing all the colour which, in real life, she gave to words. As to the book's purpose, part of her saw it as an urgent contribution to current political battles. Part hoped it could be a work of lasting, almost philosophical merit: 'a historical version of Hayek's *Constitution of Liberty*', she told the present author. What became clear very early on was that she was incapable of writing a single successful paragraph unaided. The one thing she did decide for herself was the book's title – '*Undefeated!*'.‡

Robin Harris, who understood Mrs Thatcher's mind and had long

---

* It later contributed £2 million to setting up the Chair of Enterprise Studies at the Judge Institute in Cambridge. A separate Margaret Thatcher Foundation in the United States supported other projects, including founding the Margaret Thatcher Center at the Heritage Foundation, the conservative think tank in Washington.

† For her 'resignation honours' Mrs Thatcher had recommended Rupert Murdoch for a knighthood (in honorary form because he was an American citizen). Her citation had noted that his 'entrepreneurial and journalistic flair, though often controversial', had brought about 'a great technological leap forward', including satellite television (Sky) and 'new zest and quality to British journalism'. Her suggestion was opposed, however, by the Public Honours Scrutiny Committee and prudently she did not push the point. The committee also opposed her suggestion of a peerage for Jeffrey Archer. John Major wanted a peerage for Archer too, but each was slightly embarrassed by their desire to reward the energetic and exceedingly colourful supporter of the party. Major tried to get Mrs Thatcher to press Archer's case but she batted this away. He was left to ennoble Archer, his friend and country neighbour, himself.

‡ This title, a reference to the fact that she had never lost an election as leader, did not survive the editing process. The first volume became *The Downing Street Years*.

experience of drafting for her, was the most obvious 'ghost'. But things nearly went off the rails after Alan Clark sought to interpose himself. At first Mrs Thatcher was enthusiastic: 'I want *you* to do it, Alan, because you are a believer,' she told him in January 1991. But the two had different conceptions of the project. Clark wanted to write her biography, but 'what she wants, I fear, is *Margaret Thatcher. My Story*'. Eventually, the need for professional work and quick progress won the day. Harris stayed in the saddle.

The work began in November 1991, with the book timed for the Christmas market and party conference in October 1993. Such a tight deadline required immense discipline. Harris was, as he put it, the 'clerk' and the main drafter. John O'Sullivan was brought in to charm stories out of her and add stylistic touches. An Oxford historian, Christopher Collins, handled the necessary research. Mrs Thatcher was engaged but reactive, submitting to frequent interviews and going through the drafts carefully.

Problems arose, however, because of her extreme dislike of public disclosure. According to Harris, by far her most common response was, 'Oh, we can't say that.' This applied absolutely to stories about the Queen, and almost absolutely to any mention of intelligence or special forces. If she had got her way, the book would have been shorn of almost anything interesting. Until quite late in the day, she also eschewed all mention of Neil Kinnock. Eventually her editor, Stuart Proffitt, tackled her on this surprising omission. 'I refuse to have his name in my book!' she replied, although she later relented. Nor did she like to admit disagreement with those whom she most respected. It was difficult, for instance, to extract any admission of her fundamental difference with Reagan about nuclear weapons. As for her family, Denis, Mark and Carol were assumed to be off-limits. Almost everything private was kept at bay.

Robin Harris, loyal but sometimes of explosive temper, quite often 'resigned' from the project in frustration. After these contretemps, Mrs Thatcher, who was a bit frightened of him, would knock on his door very politely. 'He would say "Enter" and she would put her head round expressing concern in pantomime-style. "Are you *free*, Robin? I'm not *disturbing* you, am I?"'

Despite these trying circumstances, progress was made. Harris's own prose style managed to capture Mrs Thatcher's gift for tart expression. Sometimes, perhaps, there was a sense that he was writing what he thought she ought to have thought. But everything was scrupulously submitted to Mrs Thatcher and she rarely objected.

*

Out of office, Mrs Thatcher did not shy away from current controversies, both national and international. Her interventions were often stimulating, and sometimes original and brave. But there was a tension between her public-spirited desire to advance important policy questions and her wish to fight passionate battles with those who, she believed, had wronged her and were harming Britain. In her mind, the two things were all but synonymous. This tension could never be resolved.

Indeed, for the first six months after her fall Mrs Thatcher was suffering from the well-known ex-prime ministers' affliction of believing that she might return to power. In Finchley, in March 1991, she said what a 'jolly good thing' it could be for the Conservative Party 'to have a senior elder statesman, especially a matriarch, to stand behind our present Prime Minister and see him carried forward to victory at the next election'. Such remarks, innocently made, were bound to irritate Major. At the same time Mrs Thatcher was, because of her continuing hurt, easily upset. For example, she felt wounded when Major gave a farewell dinner for Charles Powell without inviting her. Such snubs – merely perceived or otherwise – took a toll on their relationship.*

For Mrs Thatcher, Europe remained the burning issue. It was the repository of her most passionate feelings of frustration, in part because it had been an instrument of her downfall. Denis reinforced her concerns: 'Europe', he was forever telling her, was 'a racket', run by 'crooks'. With the Delors plan for EMU approaching fruition, she was keen to fight on. At the beginning of 1991, she had accepted the presidency of the Bruges Group, the all-party body named after her famous speech. For the Major government, sidling towards a more pro-European policy, this was an unwelcome signal. In March, Major declared in Bonn that he wanted to see Britain 'at the very heart of Europe. Working with our partners in building the future.' Major, who considered his speech 'anti-federalist', was 'astonished' by the hostility this generated among his Eurosceptic critics.† He was also wounded by Mrs Thatcher's failure to communicate: 'If she had bothered to speak to me personally about this, she would have understood.' But their rare

---

* On another occasion, watching the news, Mrs Thatcher noticed Norma Major wearing a brooch which had been given to her as Prime Minister, most likely by some Arab potentate. Mrs Thatcher had surrendered such gifts on leaving office, as the rules required, but in her mind they were for prime ministers, not for prime ministers' wives. She despatched Denis to his old rugby friend Robin Butler to ensure that henceforth only women prime ministers would wear such jewels.

† Seen in terms of European diplomacy, the Bonn speech was a success. It built on the easy personal relations which Major had quickly established with Helmut Kohl to make up for the years of high tension with Mrs Thatcher.

bilaterals were unproductive. Neither was frank with the other and so they failed to clear the air. Major's Bonn speech seemed to confirm he was not the true heir to Thatcher. Her mostly tacit but intermittently noisy backing now emboldened his critics.

Mrs Thatcher wanted to influence the debate before the EC incorporated the Delors plan into its treaties at Maastricht in December. That June, in speeches in America, she attacked the EC on protectionism, on anti-Americanism and on its selfishness in not encouraging the former Communist countries to join more quickly. In New York, she hinted she had been mistaken to take Britain into the ERM.

Tensions between the Prime Minister and his predecessor were now coming to the surface. '"I'm disappointed in Major", says bitter Thatcher', headlined the *Sunday Telegraph* on 2 June. The paper quoted her, unsourced, as saying of Major, 'He stands for nothing. He is grey. He has no ideas. I have been totally deceived.'*

Later in June, Parliament debated the upcoming Maastricht Intergovernmental Conference (IGC). When Mrs Thatcher rose from the back benches she was assiduously polite to the government and the Prime Minister, even claiming, contrary to her private view, that Major was right in 'his wish to see Britain at the heart of Europe'. Her concern lay with the Delors proposals, the results of which, she said, would be 'a kind of federal Europe achieved by stealth' and a single currency, leading to 'the greatest abdication of national and parliamentary sovereignty in our history'. She offered the government 'my full support' in the Maastricht negotiations, but clearly raised the standard of revolt.

Two days later, Mrs Thatcher announced that she would leave the Commons at the next election. Reluctantly she had heeded the advice of those she trusted: staying in the Commons could only foster vain hopes. She needed a calmer, quieter place – the House of Lords – to come to rest. In her diary Judith Chaplin, in Major's Policy Unit, contrasted her boss's 'gracious [public] tribute' following Mrs Thatcher's announcement with his private comments: 'PM often makes foul remarks about her – "mad", "loopy", "emotional" – very unattractive considering what he owes her. One night he says, "I want her destroyed."'

By November 1991, Mrs Thatcher finally had a properly functioning office. The large premises at 34 and 35 Chesham Place, Belgravia were more

---

* At a private dinner in New York that summer, which did not leak, one questioner asked bluntly about her recent comments: 'Are you trying to show your contempt for your successor?' 'On the contrary,' Mrs Thatcher replied, 'I was trying to conceal it.'

suited to a statesman than a belligerent and accorded with her sense of status. She became happier and more settled. She now felt able to consider world affairs more systematically. She maintained her consistent interest in reform of the Soviet Union and support for Gorbachev, even though the skies were darkening for him. In late August, while Gorbachev was on holiday in the Crimea, the Soviet army and security force commanders mounted a coup in Moscow. They confined Gorbachev to his dacha and cut off the telephones. Standing on a tank outside the Russian parliament building in Moscow, Boris Yeltsin, by now President of Russia,* immediately denounced the coup and barricaded the building.

While Western leaders weighed their words, Mrs Thatcher moved fast to encourage resistance, even placing a call to Yeltsin in the besieged Parliament. Yeltsin said he thought the 'eight conspirators sitting in the Kremlin' had underestimated the popular resistance: 'I've asked for a general strike. The eight will soon be standing trial.' Yeltsin was thrilled by her call: 'I'll tell the press we've spoken.' On the steps of Great College Street, Mrs Thatcher declared: 'We should not necessarily assume that the coup will succeed.' She called on the Soviet people to stand by Yeltsin. The next day she tried but failed to reach Gorbachev.† Calling Bush, John Major reported on her statement: 'She said people won't give up democracy lightly. Then she was starting to say there should be no cuts in defense spending. Unhelpful. <u>The President</u>: You handled it well. We don't need to increase defense spending because of this.'

Three days later, the coup crumbled. Gorbachev stayed President, but Yeltsin now took charge. As the Baltic states and other Soviet republics declared themselves independent, he removed all formal aspects of Communism from government. The world's first Communist state had not long to live.

Mrs Thatcher's behaviour greatly irritated Major and Hurd. 'I think she was wrong to encourage the public to take to the streets in protest,' said Major. 'Wrong to ask people to put their lives at risk.' In his diary, Bush noted her attempt to reach Gorbachev: 'This obviously annoys John Major tremendously. Some people simply can't let go.' This was more pique than good sense. Her intervention to champion democracy and good order rather than bowing to force had been statesmanlike. When Rodric Braithwaite delivered Major's belated support to Yeltsin's office, his interlocutor

---

* Gorbachev, at this time, was President of the Soviet Union.
† In doing so, she first called Ronald Reagan in California and secured his support for her efforts.

thanked him, but added that 'it was Mrs Thatcher's telephone call which gave [Yeltsin] the greatest pleasure'.

Mrs Thatcher understood that *éclat* in one place made her more sought after in another. A couple of weeks after her call to Yeltsin, she was on a plane to Beijing.* Travelling privately, but in contact with the Foreign Office, she was to see, among others, Li Peng, the Prime Minister, the hardliner widely blamed for the violent suppression of the 1989 Tiananmen Square protests. According to John Gerson, her favourite sinologist, who accompanied her, she regarded the 1984 Anglo-Chinese Joint Declaration with 'an extraordinary mixture of guilt and pride'. She felt that the killings in Tiananmen Square had undermined trust and thus weakened confidence in Hong Kong. Now, because the coup in Russia had failed, she arrived in China 'fizzing like potassium in water'.

Her interview with Li Peng took place with some 200 Chinese high officials bearing witness. Gerson advised that these officials were there to judge Li Peng's performance, but they offered an opportunity to spread her message throughout the Chinese hierarchy. Mrs Thatcher went on the attack immediately, though subtly. She asked warmly after Zhao Ziyang, her co-signatory of the Joint Declaration, who had been arrested on Li Peng's orders for being too soft on the Tiananmen students. When he explained it would not be possible for her to see Zhao, she opened her handbag, produced a tie and asked Li to give it to Zhao on her behalf. Conscious of his colleagues sitting in judgement, Li 'held the tie as if it were a cobra', Gerson recalled.†

Mrs Thatcher then explained how the Tiananmen events had weakened confidence in Hong Kong. When Li spoke to her about the shortcomings of capitalism, she said that it was Communism and its 'archpriest' Mao Zedong that had brought about the murderous Cultural Revolution of the 1960s. Li, 'growing red in the face', almost lost his self-control. Mrs Thatcher then raised human rights problems in China, speaking up for 'brave intellectuals' who were being denied their freedom.

As the meeting ended, Li Peng asked if she would be willing to tell the press that 'we had a frank and amicable conversation'. Mrs Thatcher 'drew herself up, "Mr Premier, I have no intention of talking to the press"'. Most Western leaders were ingratiating with the Chinese in private but then told the press

---

* By this time, most Westerners were using this version of the name rather than 'Peking'.

† Mrs Thatcher thenceforward made it a habit to produce a tie and handkerchief for Zhao during most such meetings with Chinese dignitaries. As she put it to Chris Patten, 'If I'm known to have handed over the present, they won't be able to kill him.'

how tough they had been. She behaved in the opposite way. To Gerson 'It was the most impressive leader-to-leader conversation I've ever heard.'

Until the handover to China in 1997, Mrs Thatcher felt responsibility for Hong Kong. When Chris Patten became Governor of Hong Kong in 1992, she did her best to support him. Although Patten was no Thatcherite, she shared his belief that the principles of the Joint Declaration – the rule of law, China and Hong Kong as 'one country: two systems' and the commitment to democratic development – should be upheld, especially after Tiananmen. His efforts to boost the territory's democratic structures fell foul of Beijing (whose views found support from Percy Cradock and Ted Heath). In the Lords, Mrs Thatcher defended Patten as 'new, imaginative and competent'. The people of Hong Kong, she said, were 'our charge and our responsibility'. Until the handover, she visited Hong Kong more than once a year, on average, often going to Beijing as well to maintain the British position. Given her popularity in Hong Kong, her visits to the colony boosted morale. As Patten wrote to Lady Thatcher in 1995, 'You were, are, and always will be Hong Kong's greatest friend and staunchest champion.' She and Julian Seymour were the last official guests to stay in Government House before Hong Kong ceased to be a colony. In her heart, she would have liked Britain to hang on to Hong Kong. With that impossible, she did her best to keep the rule of law and therefore the existing society in place.

The British political season resumed in the autumn of 1991 with the Conservatives' conference at Blackpool. Although not invited to speak, Mrs Thatcher was asked to appear on the platform. This led to deafening cheers, stamping and shouts of 'We want Maggie!' The ovation lasted six minutes. She had proved her popularity without any act of disloyalty, indeed without having to deliver a single word.

This experience may have helped embolden Mrs Thatcher in the run-up to the IGC at Maastricht in December. For the Commons debate on 20 November she wore a black suit with wide white lapels which some called the 'black widow' look. When she rose, purportedly in support of Major's motion, she urged him to take out what he himself had branded 'quite unacceptable' proposals from the draft treaty: 'In my day, that would have required the occasional use of the handbag. Now it will doubtless be the cricket bat, but that is a good thing because it will be harder.' The transfer of powers on EMU, she warned, was 'the most dangerous of all'. Pressed by the Eurosceptic Labour left-winger Tony Benn on the possibility of a referendum before any transfer of sovereignty, Mrs Thatcher was clear. Without an explicit electoral mandate to abolish the pound, she said, 'the only thing to do was to hold a referendum'. This was extremely awkward for Major, who had been contemplating offering a referendum of his own. But, as he recalled, 'the fact that *she* had called for the policy killed the policy. I couldn't get it through the Cabinet.'

As a result, in part, of Mrs Thatcher's performance, Major led his country's delegation to the IGC in Maastricht amid a febrile political atmosphere. Rather than stopping the single currency in its tracks, he won important opt-outs for Britain, both from the Social Chapter on workers' rights and from the single currency. The negotiation was widely proclaimed as 'Game, set and match' to Major. Privately Mrs Thatcher did not believe this, but publicly she was very civil. On 12 December, the Thatchers celebrated their Ruby Wedding at Claridge's. Major was invited and was photographed in amity with Mrs Thatcher. 'I'm absolutely thrilled,' she said, referring to his Maastricht deal, 'I congratulated him.' She was now in election mode. This was a ceasefire, not peace.

On 11 March 1992, Major called a general election for 9 April. Five days later, Mrs Thatcher spent her last day as a Member of Parliament. Following the prorogation ceremony, MPs returned to the Commons Chamber, where Mr Speaker Weatherill gallantly kissed her hand to a great cheer. As she left the Chamber for the last time, Yusef Azad, a young clerk, watched her look back into the Chamber in which she had met with triumph and disaster for thirty-three years. After half a minute she turned again and walked on. 'Packing it all away,' she said: 'that's the most awful part.'

The Conservative leadership envisaged little role for Mrs Thatcher in the election campaign. The manifesto, composed under the social-market, strongly European direction of the Party Chairman, Chris Patten, mentioned her only once. But as Labour's poll lead grew, Tory high command felt compelled to recall her to the front line. For the Westminster rally of all Conservative candidates, Mrs Thatcher was suddenly given a starring role. 'The Governments that you led, Margaret,' Patten gamely declared, 'have transformed Britain, and no one should ever forget that.' Labour, Mrs Thatcher responded, wanted 'more power for them over our own money, less power for the citizen'. She also attacked Labour's pro-Europeanism: 'When will they learn? You cannot build Jerusalem in Brussels.' Campaigning in twenty-nine constituencies where the Tory candidates were Thatcherites, she was enthusiastically received. Didn't the Tory campaign need more 'oomph', asked a well-wisher in Maldon? 'That's what I'm providing, dear,' she replied.

For his part, an energized John Major took to the streets, standing on a soapbox to make well-judged extempore speeches which combined his natural amiability with a new readiness to fight. On election night the Conservatives won 14,093,007 votes, the largest total ever and 2.5 million more than Labour. With 336 seats, they had achieved an overall majority of 21, guaranteeing the longest period of government by one party since the nineteenth century.

For the first time since 1955, Mrs Thatcher had no constituency of her own, so watched the results come through at 17 Great College Street, crowded with friends, family and colleagues.* When the Heseltines appeared on the screen the Thatchers all groaned. Chris Patten lost his seat at Bath, at which several Thatcherites shouted out 'Tory gain!' Mrs Thatcher rebuked them sharply. Then she was driven to the *Telegraph* party at the Savoy where she moved happily among the guests, like a victor.

'With the Conservative victory,' Mrs Thatcher later wrote,'... a result achieved in equal measure as a result of my record, John Major's admirable grit and the Labour Party's egregious errors, I felt newly liberated to continue the argument about Europe's future.' Days after the election, she collaborated with the American magazine *Newsweek* to produce an article. It proved incendiary: 'I don't accept the idea that all of a sudden Major is his own man.' It was she who had revived the 'fundamental principles' which understood the British character and the nature of liberty: 'Thatcherism will live. It will live long after Thatcher has died.' There was, Chris Collins recalled, 'a huge row', with most of her circle, from whom she had withheld the final draft, complaining loudly and Major justifiably furious.

Mrs Thatcher was not seriously repentant. By now, as she brooded, she began to harbour resentments about Major's role in her fall. She also did not believe her legacy was safe in his hands, agreeing with Denis that he was 'a nice, useless man, who cannot lead'. And on Maastricht and Europe she had a clear, defensible position which she felt it her patriotic duty to articulate. So as her political secretary, Mark Worthington, put it, 'She did undermine Major's position,' not out of spite towards him but because 'she was opposed to it'. She was also driven by guilt at having signed away too much sovereignty in the Single European Act. She saw Maastricht as an opportunity to warn against repeating the mistake.

On 30 June 1992, Mrs Thatcher entered the House of Lords as a life peer† – Baroness Thatcher of Kesteven. Her coat of arms depicted, to some mockery by heraldic experts, an admiral of the fleet holding binoculars (a

---

* Mrs Thatcher had been scrutinizing Glenys Kinnock arriving with Neil at the polling station: 'She was very smartly dressed and I thought, "Silly girl. Silly girl to wear Yves St Laurent before you know the result."'

† She was introduced by Keith Joseph, her key political patron, and John Boyd-Carpenter, her departmental Cabinet minister when she had first become a junior minister (for pensions) in 1961.

nod to her Falklands victory) and her fellow child of Grantham, Sir Isaac Newton. Her chosen motto was 'Cherish freedom'. She was now Lady Thatcher in her own right. Woodrow Wyatt sat in the Lords when she was introduced. He thought she looked 'like a lioness entering into what she must realise is something of a cage'.

There was now little to stop Lady Thatcher advancing whatever she considered important. By 1992, second only to Europe in her mind was the fate of the former Yugoslavia. Her attention focused on the increasingly aggressive actions of Slobodan Milošević, the Communist elected President of Serbia in 1989. Under the cloak of holding Yugoslavia together, Milošević sought an ultra-nationalist Greater Serbia,* trying to suppress secessions by Croatia and Slovenia through ever more violent means. From October 1991, his forces laid siege to the historic Croatian city of Dubrovnik. In November they pulverized Vukovar in eastern Croatia, where his proxies murdered Croatian prisoners of war.

Amid these atrocities, Mrs Thatcher identified Milošević, as she had identified Saddam Hussein, as an aggressor who would take everything unless he was stopped. Rejecting an EC or NATO 'peace-keeping' mission, she wanted military support to deter Milošević's aggression, combined with help for refugees. Conscious of her relative ignorance of the area, she was guided by Robin Harris, who knew it well, with advice from the historian and Balkan expert Noel Malcolm. As she had demonstrated so often in relation to Eastern Europe, she wished to give a voice to the voiceless in the part of Europe long dominated by Communism.

Initially, Mrs Thatcher's sense of political propriety, encouraged by Charles Powell, had held her back. This annoyed Harris: 'I certainly did keep him [Powell] (and others) at a distance, because they would have tried to stop her intervening.' But in November 1991, after Dubrovnik and then the Vukovar barbarities, she called publicly for Britain to recognize and arm Croatia.

By the summer of 1992 the scene had moved to Bosnia, where the fledgling multi-ethnic state was fighting for its life against Milošević and Radovan Karadžić, the Bosnian Serb leader. Lady Thatcher supported Bosnia's plea for arms to defend itself, which the West resisted. On 30 July she wrote to both Major and Douglas Hurd, calling for the West to step in. 'I am appalled that the countries of the west have taken no <u>effective</u> action to deal with the massacres taking place in the midst of Europe', read her letter to Hurd. 'It isn't that we <u>can't</u>, it's that we <u>won't</u> ...'

---

* It was because of Milošević that the phrase 'ethnic cleansing' first came into international parlance.

Hurd's response suggested she had been 'misinformed' about the West's position, but the disagreement was real. The government considered the Balkan crisis a matter of 'ancient ethnic hatreds' and 'violence' with no specific direction. Therefore the only solution was containment. Lady Thatcher, however, insisted that Serbia had war aims, aims of conquest. Britain's support for an arms embargo was one-sided because Serbia was already well armed, whereas the Bosnian government had scarcely anything. She believed Milošević could be beaten by ending the embargo and providing Western air cover to his opponents.

That August, during a book-writing retreat in Gstaad, the Swiss mountain resort, Lady Thatcher received Ejup Ganić, the Bosnian Vice-President, who had been smuggled out of a besieged Sarajevo. What she called his 'horrific story' prompted her to write a piece for the *New York Times*. Headlined 'Stop the Excuses. Help Bosnia Now', this was a watershed moment because it was her first direct appeal to the US administration and American public opinion. Although Republican support for her position was growing, the balance of opinion inside the Bush administration remained unfavourable.

In the spring of 1993, at the time of the first killings in Srebrenica, she told the BBC there should be a Western ultimatum to the Serbs with the threat of force. At present, the West was being 'a little like an accomplice to massacre'. This time her views attracted considerable sympathy in Washington. The new administration of Bill Clinton embraced a more forward policy against Milošević, at odds with the European status quo.* 'On Bosnia, the John Major government was abysmal,' recalled Jenonne Walker of Clinton's NSC staff, '. . . some of us on the staff muttered to each other, "If only Thatcher were still in power . . ."' In September 1995, NATO launched its first airstrikes on the Serb forces and the tide began to turn. The Dayton Accords followed in December, but a full and lasting peace took much longer. In March 1999, with support from Tony Blair, the new Labour Prime Minister, NATO airstrikes finally forced the Serbs to withdraw from Kosovo. Mrs Thatcher felt vindicated. How much the issue mattered to her is evident in her private letter to Blair when he left office in 2007: 'Because of you,' she wrote, 'we saw an end to the horrors of genocide in the Balkans.'

As Lady Thatcher became more vocal over the former Yugoslavia, she became increasingly willing to take on Major's government over Europe. On 15 May 1992, she gave a speech in The Hague developing her critique

---

* Writing to congratulate Clinton on his victory in November 1992, Lady Thatcher offered her encouragement: 'I am so pleased to see your deep concern for the terrible things that are being done in Bosnia.'

of EMU. She attacked the European Commission's vision as 'yesterday's tomorrow', which combined 'all the most striking failures of our age'. She prophesied that large-scale immigration caused by free movement would cause 'ethnic conflict' and bring about the rise of extremist parties. There would be 'national resentment' because of one-size-fits-all financial and economic policies under a single currency. The following week, the government won a vote in the Commons approving Maastricht with a majority of 244.* This was to prove its high-water mark.

Mrs Thatcher's attitude to Major was hardening. Two days after her speech in The Hague, over dinner with the Wyatts, 'she started saying that John Major and the government had let the whole thing slide and it was inevitable that we were going to have a federal state, a single currency and a Central European Bank'. She later complained to Wyatt that Major was 'too weak': 'He always wants to be popular.' Major, she now realized, did not fulfil her ideal of manhood: what she called a 'fine mind', or a dashing man of the world, or a person of unimpeachable, soldierly loyalty. On the future of Europe, she wanted the nation to wake up, whereas Major hoped it would keep calm.

On 2 July, in her maiden speech in the Lords, Lady Thatcher proposed to depart from the convention that such a speech should not be argumentative: 'I have never knowingly made an uncontroversial speech in my life.' She complained that since all three parties at the general election had supported Maastricht Treaty ratification, the voters had been denied a democratic choice.

September 1992 brought a turning point both for Major's premiership and Britain's relationship with Europe. With Britain still suffering from the recession that had begun in 1991, sterling came under growing pressure. On 16 September, despite spending billions of pounds and aggressive interest rate rises,† the government proved unable to stave off the speculators. That evening sterling's membership of the ERM was 'suspended'. Thus collapsed the economic strategy of the Major government, and the *raison d'être* of its 'heart of Europe' political strategy too. The day became known as 'Black Wednesday'. The British economy, no longer fettered by an artificial exchange rate, recovered quickly. But the economic reputation and political standing of the Major government did not. It was the biggest smash-up of a British government policy since Suez.

Britain's ERM exit seemed to vindicate Lady Thatcher's long-standing

---

* Although twenty-two Conservatives voted against, Labour abstained.
† Interest rates were raised by two full percentage points that day with a promise to raise them another three points the next day.

opposition to entry. As she was indecently happy to say in a speech shortly after the debacle, the markets could not be bucked.* The facts began to look much more Thatcherite than when Major had won his 'game, set and match' in Maastricht.

Just before the Conservative Party conference that October, Lady Thatcher attacked Maastricht head on in the *European*. Opt-outs, she wrote, were not nearly good enough because they would, over time, be whittled down by the ineluctable central machine. Building on her speech in The Hague, she said, 'The Government must recognise that Maastricht, like the ERM, is part of the vision of yesterday. It is time to set out the vision of tomorrow.' She was claiming, in effect, the right to oppose the main direction of government policy.

What Lady Thatcher considered a principled stand Major viewed as self-aggrandizement and disloyalty. With the government's majority having fallen to 21 at the recent election, Lady Thatcher's stance was now likely to have practical consequences. In early November, the Maastricht Bill returned to the Commons, requiring two 'paving' votes to proceed. Lady Thatcher held what Major described as 'a whole series of personal salons in which she advised acolytes to vote against the government'.† Although no master parliamentary tactician, she assisted revolt by encouraging people with opinions on Europe similar to hers. These included her many admirers among the new Tory intake of MPs, such as the future Conservative leader Iain Duncan Smith. According to John Whittingdale, 'They saw her as their *de facto* leader.' In the paving votes the government scraped through, with majorities of 6 and 3. Lady Thatcher wrote to the stoutly rebellious Duncan Smith praising the 'clarity, persistence and excellence of your arguments'. She raised the prospect of a lunch or supper soon at Chesham Place for 'our most devoted people'.

By the time Maastricht reached the Lords in June 1993, Lady Thatcher's opposition remained undimmed. Speaking in the debate on ratification, she half admitted she had been mistaken in signing the Single European Act because it had led Britain down the road to Maastricht, and she quoted Kipling on how 'the burnt Fool's bandaged finger goes wabbling back to the Fire'. It was wrong, she insisted, to 'hand over the people's parliamentary rights' without a referendum. Despite her efforts, the Bill was carried by a huge majority – 445 in favour to 176 against, one of whom was Margaret

---

* This was a deliberate repeat of the formula she had used about Lawson's shadowing of the deutschmark.

† Major even began to feel that 'it would have been better if she had stayed and lost the election', which he believed she would have done. Then what he called the 'compelling narrative' which dominated after Britain's exit from the ERM would never have got going.

Thatcher.* When urged for reasons of party loyalty to abstain, she replied, 'I can't. I may want to take action later consistent with having voted against.'

Lady Thatcher's renewed insistence on a referendum, first made public in the final weeks of her premiership, was starting to make political headway. In private, she was now telling Eurosceptic ministers to resign. Charles Powell feared she would damage her legacy: 'I made the point that she had expected loyalty over the Single European Act and her successor was entitled to expect the same over Maastricht.'

On 22 July, after the government lost a vote in the Commons seeking approval of its efforts to secure an opt-out from the Social Chapter of the Maastricht Treaty, Major was forced to turn the issue into a vote of confidence. This he won quite easily, since Tory rebels were not prepared to provoke a general election. But, with the Cabinet at odds, he no longer seemed in control. In a 'hot mic' moment, Major branded his Eurosceptic colleagues – including Peter Lilley, Michael Howard and Michael Portillo – 'bastards'.

As contracted for, Lady Thatcher's memoirs were ready for the autumn party conference season. *The Downing Street Years* covered solely her eleven and a half years in office. Thanks to the intense efforts of the ghosts and the researcher, her account was full, forceful, clear and factually accurate. It set out what she saw as the purposes and achievements of her premiership. The ideas of Thatcherism were present, expressed not so much in theoretical argument as through the story of one remarkable woman. This was fitting, because Thatcherism is not a philosophy so much as a disposition. It has many intellectual antecedents but came out of one person, who was not herself an intellectual. This the memoirs captured. In a thoughtful review for the *Independent*, Andrew Marr wrote of 'a damaging book, a partial book, an unreflective book, a book which is sometimes dull and is often exhausting', but ultimately judged it 'a clear and indispensable insider's history of the most extraordinary period in post-war British history. She was a unique and courageous politician cut off in her prime, and her wounds still bleed.'

The book was, at times, bad-tempered. This reflected its author. Lady Thatcher was not usually a vindictive person, but she could be an angry and acid one. The book contained too many sharp criticisms of colleagues and foreign leaders, made worse by her boasts about how she had defeated such people in argument. Except for her description of Major's 'hesitation'

---

* This was only the second time in her career that she had voted against the policy of a Conservative government. The first was when she voted against the banning of corporal punishment in 1961 (see p. 71).

before seconding her nomination for the second ballot, her book included few personal digs at her successor. She did, however, speak frankly about their policy differences in office.

The memoirs had faced the customary Cabinet Office pre-publication review process. On Major's behalf, Robin Butler had sought to excise certain passages addressing these differences, particularly over the ERM and EMU when Major had been Chancellor. Such references, Butler asserted, broke the Radcliffe Rules on 'confidential relations' between ministers. Lady Thatcher resisted. Refusing to remove one passage, she wrote, 'It is crucial to showing how the difference between the present Prime Minister and me over what was to become Maastricht was evident in our discussions well before I left office.' This was precisely what Major did not want revealed.

The stories the book disgorged were mostly not, in terms of hard news, sensational. More powerful in this respect was the four-part television series based on the book and bearing the same name. Lady Thatcher had been attracted by an independent company, Fine Art Productions, whose impartiality she trusted. Despite her many disagreements with the Corporation, she insisted that the series be shown on the BBC.* During the thirty hours of interviews that she gave for the programmes, Denys Blakeway, the Director, found her 'totally unmanipulative and open'. She did not demand to see the tapes before screening or block interviews with any former colleagues: 'She had no fear of what others might say.' Blakeway considered her performance extremely professional, noting her 'tremendous theatricality'.

On camera she did not hold back. Blakeway thought she saw the series as her 'platform for revenge', which he reflected by using her famous quotation about 'treachery with a smile on its face' in the opening minutes of the first programme. Her comments could be almost too eloquent. Speaking of Howe's resignation speech, for example, she remarked on how 'cleverly' he was 'wielding the knife ... too cleverly': instead of assassinating her politically, she insisted, he had 'assassinated his own character'. The sheer force of her words made great television but, as so often, injected too much drama for her own good.

During the filming, the press were investigating rumours that Denis was suffering from cancer. One day, Lady Thatcher came into the room and told the assembled film crew, 'Denis does *not* have cancer. He has *no* cancer.'

---

* Julian Seymour secured roughly £800,000 for Lady Thatcher from the programmes. The deal stipulated that, after one repeat, copyright reverted to the Thatcher Foundation and much of the money she received came from the sale of foreign rights.

Then she went to the window and looked out at the photographers below and exclaimed, 'Vultures!' In fact (though she probably did not know this), he did have cancer – of the prostate – but after radiotherapy it went into remission. Although he suffered remarkably little from many years of heavy smoking (forty a day) and drinking, Denis was eleven years older than his wife and edging towards old age. This made Lady Thatcher anxious on his behalf, and sometimes cross with him.

The television series served to confirm strong feelings about Lady Thatcher on both sides. To her critics she was a self-righteous, egocentric, right-wing ranter. Watching her overly dramatic, at times wild-eyed performance, some even said she was mad. To her admirers she was a brave, forthright and patriotic woman – the victim of devious pygmies. Enduring interest in her, at home and abroad, was reflected in the great excitement at her numerous book signings and the large sales of *The Downing Street Years*.* Blakeway was probably right that writing, publishing and speaking were therapeutic. Julian Seymour noticed that, once book and programme were done, she became 'far more rational', readier to get on with the rest of her life.

In June 1995, the second volume of Lady Thatcher's memoirs, *The Path to Power*, appeared. It covered her life up to her victory in the 1979 general election. Her ghostwriters found that she had few early memories: only when describing her time as a young Tory candidate in Dartford did she come alive. This was the period when she fell in love (with Robert Henderson,† before Denis), just as she realized she was a born political campaigner. To make up for the deficiency of anecdote, the book also discussed public events after she had left office. Developing arguments about the future of Europe, she became directly critical of her successor: 'I knew that John Major was likely to seek some kind of compromise with the majority of heads of government who wanted political and economic union ... But I was not prepared for the speed with which the position I adopted would be entirely reversed.' She echoed Geoffrey Howe's famous resignation statement: 'I offer some thoughts about putting these things right. It is now, however, for others to take the action required.'

On 22 June, a few days after the book's publication, Major announced an unusual step. Fearing a leadership challenge in the autumn, he decided to pre-empt his critics by calling an immediate contest himself, daring them, as he put it, 'to put up or shut up'. He told the *Financial Times* that Lady

---

* Sales reached 300,000 hardbacks in the United Kingdom alone; the book was even, to general surprise, top of the bestseller list in France.
† One of several earlier boyfriends whose existence Lady Thatcher refused to acknowledge until the present author raised the evidence directly with her (see pp. 46–52).

Thatcher's criticisms had 'played a part' in persuading him to fight. The cumulative effect of her opposition to his European policy on top of the collapse of Britain's ERM membership was crushing. As Richard Ryder, his Chief Whip, put it, the parliamentary party's 'untrusting attitude' to the leadership's European policy was a price the Tories had to pay for the way Mrs Thatcher had been overthrown.

As in 1990, one possible contender for the succession was Michael Heseltine but, after Westland, he could scarcely resign from the Cabinet once again. Another likely runner was Michael Portillo, whose career Lady Thatcher had privately encouraged, but he hesitated. The only Cabinet minister prepared to challenge Major was the Welsh Secretary, John Redwood. A former head of Mrs Thatcher's Policy Unit, he was *plus royaliste que la reine* in his commitment to competition and free markets, and equally hostile to Maastricht and EMU.

Publicly, Lady Thatcher declared both candidates 'sound Conservatives'. This non-committal phrase reflected a tussle behind the scenes. She looked favourably on Redwood and 'admired his courage in challenging'. Robin Harris was active in Redwood's campaign. Julian Seymour, however, was close to Major's campaign manager, Lord Cranborne, and exercised a restraining influence. He strongly advised Lady Thatcher that for a former Conservative leader publicly to back a challenge to a sitting one would cross a Rubicon. As Seymour summarized her attitude: 'heart will have said Redwood, head will have said no'.

Support for Redwood would also have laid Lady Thatcher open to the same charges of disloyalty which she had thrown at her former colleagues. Endorsing Major, she declared: 'I fully support the prime minister and would vote for him if I were still a member of the House of Commons.' Perhaps because her backing was more formal than full-hearted, it seemed to pass Major by: 'I don't think I ever knew that she supported me against Redwood,' he said later.

In the contest on 4 July, Redwood won 89 votes to Major's 218. Major survived, but without the convincing mandate he had hoped for.* His administration limped on, with him a prisoner of the leading Europhiles, including Heseltine.

On 13 October 1995, Lady Thatcher was seventy. She had reached the time of life when old friends begin to die. When they did so, she always and at

---

* Major's well-organized campaign immediately claimed the result as a strong victory; but in fact, as he later revealed in his memoirs, he had planned, if he had got three votes fewer, to resign.

once wrote condolence letters in her own hand. Her loyalty and sense of duty to those who had been close to her was strong: no one was a more faithful attender of funerals and memorial services than she.*

Nick Ridley – like Denis, a heavy smoker – died in March 1993, aged sixty-four. Lady Thatcher, who had been very fond of him, and perhaps felt guilty that she had never made him Chancellor, spoke at his memorial service. He had been, she said, quoting Tennyson, 'A man who never sold the truth to serve the hour'. Less than a year later, Keith Joseph died. Again there was an element of guilt in Lady Thatcher's mind because, though she truly loved him, she had found his honourable ineligibility for practical politics maddening. She was eternally grateful to 'dear Keith' for having made way, in late 1974, so that she could stand for the party leadership. In July 1995 Peter Morrison died, aged only fifty-one, of the drinking that had been a serious problem in the 1990 leadership campaign and subsequently became worse because he felt he had let Lady Thatcher down.

Mark Worthington, Lady Thatcher's political secretary, recalled that when informed of the death of each of these three men she retired to her office, shut the door and sat alone for a long time, something she hardly ever did.†

At seventy, Lady Thatcher showed no signs of slowing down, although she had, perhaps, mellowed. She maintained her punishing lecture schedule around the world but enjoyed visiting the Lords, despite being temperamentally ill suited to its uncombative style of debate. On its red benches, she found it possible to speak civilly to Geoffrey Howe, who had also become a peer after the 1992 general election. In April 1995, she became a Lady of the Garter. In 1987, the Queen had changed the rules to allow non-royal women to join this medieval Order. Queen Elizabeth the Queen Mother had at first resisted this change but, learning of her daughter's wish to give the Garter to Lady Thatcher, became a warm supporter. Of all the royal family, she was the most admiring of the first woman Prime Minister. Lady Thatcher herself was thrilled. The honour touched the romantic spirit in her. 'There is something very special about an "Order of Chivalry",'

---

* After leaving office she attended at least 116 of them, always immaculately dressed in elegant hats.
† Lady Thatcher did not confine her respect in death to her own side. Immediately after she had resigned in 1990, she received a letter from the hard-left Labour MP Eric Heffer which touched her. 'Politically, I cannot be sorry that you are no longer PM,' he wrote. 'Yet in a personal sense I am terribly sorry as although I disagreed with you, no one could say you were not honest, courageous and with great integrity.' Heffer died the following year and she attended his memorial service.

she wrote to a schoolfriend. 'The very word conveys all that is best in this country.' The Queen also honoured Lady Thatcher by attending her seventieth-birthday dinner at Claridge's. She had not done this for any of her previous prime ministers.

For someone of her age, Lady Thatcher was in good health.* Her only enduring trouble came from her teeth. In 1995, she completed a series of operations to put in dental implants. These caused her prolonged discomfort, making eating more difficult so she got too thin, and slightly impeded the clarity of her speech.†

Ronald Reagan, now suffering from Alzheimer's disease, had been unable to attend Lady Thatcher's seventieth-birthday dinner. His wife Nancy came alone. 'Ron is always in our minds,' Lady Thatcher wrote to her afterwards. 'Fate has dealt him and you a cruel blow . . . The best medicine in life is the kindness of real friends and you have many more than you know.'

The friendship between the Thatchers and the Reagans had become increasingly personal in the post-office years. In June 1989, five months after Reagan left office, Mrs Thatcher had honoured him with a small but splendid dinner in 10 Downing Street.‡ When she was pushed out of Downing Street, the Reagans responded in kind. The watchword, as expressed by Reagan's Chief of Staff, Fred Ryan, was 'When the question involves Margaret Thatcher, the answer is "yes!".'

In 1993, to celebrate Reagan's eighty-second birthday, Lady Thatcher flew to California to help raise money for the former President's Library.§ For the first time, she saw that something was not right. When Reagan toasted her at dinner he repeated his toast, using the very same words. The following year, in Washington for Reagan's eighty-third birthday, she delivered a tribute to him at another fundraiser. Beforehand, however, she found the President disorientated. 'Ronnie, we're in Washington,' she

---

* During her time in office she had had minor operations for varicose veins, a detached retina and the procedure to correct Dupuytren's contracture in her right hand. She also continued to suffer slightly from low blood pressure, which occasionally caused her to faint.

† As speculation grew in the later 1990s about whether Lady Thatcher was beginning to suffer from dementia, the lengthy general anaesthetics required for these operations were cited as a possible cause.

‡ Knowing of Reagan's interest in wine, Mrs Thatcher had arranged for 1970 Château Pétrus, a rare and valuable wine, to be served. The dinner also included a Chardonnay from Matanzas Creek in California, alongside 1982 Bollinger vintage champagne, 1945 Warre port and a Grands Fins Bois cognac from 1878. According to Fred Ryan, such exquisite choices were considered a real mark of respect by Reagan and his staff.

§ Presidential libraries in the United States are what in Britain would be called their archives. They are always sited in the relevant president's home state.

assured him. She also realized that he at first did not recognize her, and felt momentarily hurt. After this 'bad night', Reagan wrote her an emotional letter: 'I feel that the Lord brought us together for a profound purpose . . . I am proud to call you one of my dearest friends, Margaret; proud to have shared many of life's significant moments with you; and thankful that God brought you into my life.' Already Reagan had slipped into the past tense.

Later that year, Reagan published his famous letter to the American people, announcing his Alzheimer's: 'I now begin the journey that will lead me into the sunset of my life . . .' Reagan had asked that, in due time, Lady Thatcher deliver a eulogy at his funeral. She made sure she was always ready. In August 2000, for example, she went to stay in Vail, Colorado, with Gay Gaines, a leading Republican fundraiser. Mrs Gaines recalled helping her unpack her 'enormous case':

> I've never seen a more beautifully packed bag. She showed me how she laid clothes over the edge, in each direction, and then put tissue. And then more clothes and then more tissue. So that when you folded the pants or dress back there were no creases or wrinkles . . . at the very bottom of her suitcase were black pantyhose, black slip, black dress, black purse, black shoes. I said, 'What's that?' . . . She said, 'Gay dear, I never know when Ronnie might pass.'*

The next general election could be held no later than June 1997. Major would face Tony Blair, the archetypal modernizer. Blair's election as Labour leader in 1994, following the death of John Smith, had changed the political landscape and caught Lady Thatcher's attention. Blair and his team shared few of her opinions, especially on Europe, but they admired her political style and her thirst for change. They saw that the 'New Labour' which they wished to create must accept much of the Thatcher legacy in order to move beyond it. They agreed that, as Peter Mandelson put it, 'there *was* a sense that in the 1970s the trade unions had brought the country to its knees'. They hated what they saw as the self-indulgence of the left in preferring to denounce Mrs Thatcher than to defeat her party at elections. They envied and copied her way of creating 'dividing lines' between the two main parties from which she could gain electoral advantage.

On the other hand, Blair and his allies believed that the Thatcher years had exalted greed over the interests of the wider society and considered her 'oblivious to the social consequences of her economics'. They saw votes to be won by saying so. By adopting the vigour of Thatcherism without its

---

* In American English, 'pass' means 'die'; it is unlikely Lady Thatcher followed that usage.

divisiveness, while also denouncing the weakness of John Major's government, they hoped to create 'the perfect storm'. As Blair put it, 'I was ready to say that if we'd been in government we should have been doing some of what she was doing, albeit in a different way.' He sought the support of 'a generation of 35–45-year-olds, who were economically in Margaret's place, but socially liberal'. Blair also learnt something from the manner of her fall: 'our first evidence that the Tory Party might just destroy itself'. As New Labour sought to foment Tory divisions, friendly feelers were extended to Lady Thatcher herself through Blair's close adviser Jonathan Powell, brother of Charles. She was too deep-dyed a Conservative Party woman to take the bait, but was certainly susceptible to flattery.

In public, however, Lady Thatcher gave Blairism little comfort. In January 1996, for the first Keith Joseph Memorial Lecture, she insisted that Blair was 'by instinct a man of the Left'. She gave no cover to disillusioned Conservative voters hoping it might be safe to defect.* Her underlying message, however, was much less pleasing to the Major government, because she saw Blairism as a symptom of a wider move to the centre which she regarded as a mistake. Taking up an old theme of Joseph's, she said that what mattered was the 'common ground', not the 'centre ground', and linked the good aspects of the government with named Eurosceptic members of the Cabinet – Peter Lilley, Michael Howard and Michael Portillo. She was making the 'bastards' legitimate. According to Mark Worthington, after the Joseph Lecture relations between Lady Thatcher and Major 'pretty well broke down'.

Lady Thatcher was more impressed by New Labour – or at least by Blair – than she stated publicly. Paul Johnson, the former Labour supporter turned ultra-conservative writer, quoted her as saying privately that voters had 'nothing to fear' from Blair because he 'would not let the country down'. Imitation being the sincerest form of flattery, she was beguiled by the fact that Labour was becoming more Thatcherite, especially as her own party's leadership was showing her less respect. She found Blair fresh, energetic and capable of talking her language.

On Europe, Lady Thatcher now concentrated increasingly on the referendum question. She was friendly with Sir James Goldsmith who, in November 1994, had founded the Referendum Party, wholly devoted to

---

* Lady Thatcher also became more careful than she had been shortly after leaving office about what might be said in private but nevertheless get reported. At a large Carlton Club dinner early in 1996, for example, Woodrow Wyatt watched an 'exceedingly drunk' Denis Thatcher 'shouting out "He [Major]'s awful, he's weak, he's hopeless, he should be got rid of" ... At which point, Margaret said quite sharply, "You must be quiet, Denis ... This is not the place to say it."'

achieving a referendum on Britain's membership of the European Union. Lady Thatcher was also close – as was Goldsmith, who helped pay for it – to the European Foundation of Bill Cash, one of the strongly Eurosceptic MPs whose career she had not advanced when in office. She regarded Cash, said Seymour, as 'the ultimate torch-bearer' on European questions.

One of the last votes Mrs Thatcher cast before leaving the Commons in 1992 had been in favour of a Private Member's Bill put forward by Richard Shepherd and Cash which sought to impose referendums before any change in the European treaties. During 1996, pressure on the issue had forced first the Tories, and consequently Labour, into committing themselves to a referendum on whether Britain should join the European single currency. Alongside Cash and Goldsmith, she could take considerable credit for getting this method of popular approval into the mainstream. Eventually the referendum idea would be applied to the broader question of EU membership, with Britain voting to leave in 2016.

Going right up to the wire, John Major called the general election of 1997 for 1 May. In April, he briefed Lady Thatcher privately about his election plans. All she would say to staff afterwards was, 'Well, it's not very promising.' Some time earlier, she had decided to play only a modest part, focusing on the constituencies of her friends. But she agreed to one joint appearance with John Major, in Stockton-on-Tees – the scene of a new enterprise zone which had arisen out of the Conservatives' inner-city initiative (see pp. 629–33).

Lady Thatcher flew to Teesside in the early morning of 16 April, only to be told that the Prime Minister would be at least an hour and a half late.* According to Mark Worthington, she saw this as a snub and 'an insult to the people of the North'. When Major did show up the pair went to plant a tree. Lady Thatcher dug with her normal vigour, whereas Major made a few token jabs at the earth. 'Come on,' she said, 'nothing will get planted at this rate.' As they travelled in the battle-bus to a supporters' lunch, the pair barely spoke. Lady Thatcher kept noticing crowds watching them pass. 'There are voters out there,' she declared. 'All wave to the left. More voters over there: all wave to the right.' Poor Major waved.

The 1997 general election returned a result for the Conservatives even worse than that of 1945, the campaign in which the young Margaret Roberts had made her first public speech. Labour won 418 seats, the

---

* Faced with widespread rebellion from Tory candidates who wanted the party to rule out a single currency under any circumstances, Major had taken the emergency decision to film a new election broadcast in which he was seen begging voters, 'Do not bind my hands' in any future European negotiations. Hence his lateness.

Conservatives 165, giving Blair an overall majority of 179.* Thus ended the eighteen years of Conservative government which had begun when Margaret Thatcher entered Downing Street on 4 May 1979.

On 2 May, Tony Blair's first day as Prime Minister, Lady Thatcher wrote in her own hand to offer her 'warm personal congratulations on a famous victory'.

That same day she also wrote to John Major:

> You fought a valiant and energetic campaign across the whole country. Few could have foreseen the devastating result – you deserved <u>much</u> <u>better</u> . . .
>
> Opposition does not come naturally to Conservatives. Nevertheless we shall have to analyse and vigorously criticize everything that we consider wrong or unwise for Britain . . .
>
> Please tell Norma that she was <u>absolutely marvellous</u> throughout.

Jonathan Powell had maintained a friendly conduit to Lady Thatcher through Julian Seymour. Before the election, Seymour had refused all suggestions that Blair and Mrs Thatcher should meet, knowing the cries of treachery such a meeting would have provoked. Once Blair became Prime Minister, however, such difficulty vanished. His reply to her letter, also in his own hand, read:

> Dear Margaret,
> Thank you so much for writing to me. It meant a lot to me . . . I would like to meet soon. There is much I would like to talk about, with you. Thank you, again.
>
> > Yours ever,
> > Tony

---

* There was a nearly 4-million-vote gap in Labour's favour, with the Conservatives falling below 10 million votes for the first time since 1945.

40
The light fades
'Good night, Margaret. Sleep well'

At the handover of Hong Kong to China on 1 July 1997, Julian Seymour noticed all was not well with Lady Thatcher. She seemed 'a little bit wandery' and not quite herself. Seymour put it down to the tiredness of a woman in her seventies after strenuous long-distance air travel. Looking back, however, he came to think this had been an early symptom of mental decline.

In 1997, there was no general perception of trouble, nor any slowing in Lady Thatcher's pace. On 22 May, just three weeks after his landslide victory, Tony Blair received her privately in Downing Street. Their discussion concentrated on foreign policy: they agreed on the fundamental importance of the American alliance, while on the former Yugoslavia Lady Thatcher reinforced Blair's nascent liberal internationalist impulses. She also held forth about Europe, but to no avail. According to Mark Worthington, a basis of trust was established, paving the way for future meetings.* While she was flattered by Blair's attention, she still wanted the Conservatives to recover. Because of the divided state of the party she had some direct influence over its future.

John Major having stepped down abruptly, there was an immediate contest. Michael Portillo, the best-known Thatcherite candidate, had lost his seat and so was out of the running. Lady Thatcher favoured Michael Howard, the most senior candidate on the right, to oppose Kenneth Clarke, the obvious favourite of the left, but Howard was outmanoeuvred by William Hague and withdrew after the first ballot. Clarke came first, very narrowly in front of Hague in the second ballot, with John Redwood lagging third. Many of the strongest Thatcherite Eurosceptics favoured

---

* On the few occasions she returned to No. 10, Lady Thatcher took a keen interest in the decor. In April 2002, when Tony Blair hosted a dinner for the Queen attended by all living former prime ministers, she commented on 'how worn the carpets were and how the colours in the green room did not coordinate. She almost fainted when she went into her old office and found out that it had been turned into a spartan meeting room.'

Redwood, until he and Clarke formed an unlikely alliance seeking to unite the opposites on Europe. This left Lady Thatcher 'deeply shocked'. Calling the pact 'incredible',* she threw her weight behind Hague. When she appeared with the thirty-six-year-old candidate, she waved her finger at the camera: 'I am supporting William Hague. Have you got the name? Vote for William Hague to follow the same kind of government I led.' This awoke the 'back-seat driver' image that had haunted Major. It was also effective, however, especially after she went with Hague into the Commons tea room to buttonhole startled Tory MPs. Several Thatcherites, including John Whittingdale, defected from the Redwood camp. With such a depleted electorate – just 164 MPs – this proved decisive. In the third ballot, Hague won, with 90 votes to Clarke's 72.

Hague's victory mattered. Had Clarke become leader, the European position Lady Thatcher represented would have been pushed to the margin. The episode would prove a milestone in the gradual move away from the Europhilia which still dominated the Tory elites. Throughout Hague's time as leader, Lady Thatcher was, in his own words, '90 per cent helpful' but '10 per cent disruptive'. Her advice was 'very sweeping' and her presence 'overpowering'.

At the party conference that October, Lady Thatcher caused one memorable incident. In the spirit of the 'Cool Britannia' image invented by Tony Blair, British Airways had introduced 'ethnic' tail fins, with semi-abstract designs of an African appearance. These proved unpopular: customers could not see why the nation's flag-carrier had abandoned the traditional Union flag livery. Touring the conference, Lady Thatcher stopped at the BA stand which displayed scale models. 'Absolutely terrible!' she exclaimed to the cameras. 'We fly the British flag, not these awful things.' To laughter, she covered the offending fin with her handkerchief. The publicity that ensued led BA's rival, Virgin, to steal the Union flag livery. BA eventually admitted defeat, dropped the tail fins and restored the flag.

The year 1997 saw the settlement of Lady Thatcher's political legacy in physical form. She decided that the best home for the vast number of personal papers she was allowed to take with her on leaving office would be at Churchill College, Cambridge.† Given that her own university had denied her an honorary degree (see p. 590), the thought that Oxford's main rival would benefit pleased her. She and Denis were

---

* Lady Thatcher was using the word in its exact meaning of 'not to be believed'.
† In making this choice, Lady Thatcher turned down an offer of £7–8 million from an American university.

also impressed by Churchill College, where the papers would be looked after in purpose-built archives which already housed the papers of Winston Churchill.* Complementing the work of the Churchill archive, in 2001 the Margaret Thatcher Foundation established a website, margaretthatcher.org, edited by Christopher Collins, which in time made millions of pages of documents relating to Mrs Thatcher's life freely available to the public.

Those advising Lady Thatcher suggested that, rather than leaving her history completely to chance, she should authorize a biographer who could have full and immediate access to the papers and to her. This was agreed in 1997, giving rise to this book. Although punctilious as ever about these matters, Lady Thatcher did not obsess over them. Her attitude to history was 'I did it: somebody else can write it.' Egotistical though she was, she did not try to edit her past. She liked to say, 'My father told me, "It's always the next thing that counts."'

Although Lady Thatcher now had more time for family, this part of her life was not entirely satisfactory. Her motherly instincts were more successfully fulfilled with her close staff than with her own children. Mark was living in Dallas, so she saw little of her grandchildren, Michael (instantly famous by being born when she was in office) and Amanda, whose middle name was Margaret and was four years younger. Whenever Mark visited, Lady Thatcher's staff always noticed a sharp rise in her level of anxiety. He would sometimes shout at his mother: one of her team remembered her 'going like jelly' when he told her angrily that she was travelling with the wrong briefcase instead of one he had given her. He was often generous to her too, but his presence was not a calming one.

Lady Thatcher delighted in her grandchildren but saw them only on special occasions like Christmas. Michael Thatcher had taken his first steps on Christmas Day 1989 at Chequers – the last Christmas Margaret and Denis spent there. According to Mark's then wife, Diane, only the presence of the grandchildren could make Lady Thatcher, whom they called 'Grammy', kick off her shoes: she would sit on the floor to get on their level. She deluged them with presents. On one occasion in London, Grammy arranged a private, after-hours visit to Hamleys, the famous toy

---

* In 1997, a deal was struck and the papers were consigned to Churchill on permanent loan. Lady Thatcher retained personal ownership of a few of the most valuable papers, such as her manuscript account of the Falklands War, but placed them in the archives. The only financial comfort was the likelihood that the state would consider accepting these special papers in lieu of inheritance tax.

shop. As Michael recalled, 'we got, as kids, to run through Hamleys and grab whatever we wanted'.

Both Michael and Amanda remembered their grandmother as 'very loving and doting', but with 'an air of formality'. As Amanda put it, 'Grammy ... was very stately, and she was always the driver of the conversation. However, I never feared her – she managed to retain this regal presence all the while being open towards us.' Her greatest interest was in what the children were learning at school. She was thrilled when Michael decided to study chemistry at university, as she had done.

Amanda remembered a typical example of Lady Thatcher's grandmotherly conversation. When she was five or six, Grammy broke off from reading her a bedtime story to tell Amanda about the Falklands War: 'Did I understand why it was important for the UK to reclaim its territory? Did I understand why troops had to stay behind even after the war was finished? I was extremely perplexed at the time but it's one of my most delightful memories of her now.'

In 2005, Mark and Diane's marriage ended. Lady Thatcher grieved. She was fond of Diane and feared it would become harder to see Michael and Amanda. There were difficulties with Carol too. Although fiercely loyal to her daughter in her career as a journalist,* she wished Carol could somehow be different: more elegant, less casual, someone who would settle down to marry and have children. Carol naturally resented this futile desire to change her. There were occasions when she would even say, like a teenager, 'I hate my mother.'

Whereas Mark was attracted to fame and power, Carol tended to shun them. She preferred to travel, and to see her father rather than her mother. Indeed, Carol rarely visited her mother in old age – much more rarely, in fact, than Mark. Sometimes she said she would come and Lady Thatcher would wait for her, looking out of the window, and she would not appear. The only relation of Lady Thatcher who could be relied on for caring was her niece, Jane Mayes (née Cullen), Muriel's daughter. She visited Chester Square roughly every three months. 'I felt her sense of loneliness,' Jane recalled, 'and I wanted to support her because the children weren't around much.'

There was an element of absenteeism even in the relationship with Denis. His loyalty to his wife was absolute but, as Crawfie put it, he had 'had enough' of relentless activity and high drama. He enjoyed coming home to his wife in the evening, having a large drink and complaining

---

* Lady Thatcher never forgave Max Hastings for having sacked Carol from her job on the *Daily Telegraph*.

about what was wrong with the country, but he made himself scarce during the day, at first with his business interests and golf and then, as he got too old for either, still having lunch with what he called his 'chummoes'. Lady Thatcher was instinctively 'jealous' of his lunch companions. She fussed if he was at home and she fussed if he wasn't. One of her most common remarks was 'Where's DT?', an expression both of irritation and of love.

Her jealousy was not completely unreasonable, although there are no grounds for thinking that Denis was unfaithful. From the mid-1980s, through a business connection he got to know Ken Foreman, the Chairman of an American company called Attwoods, and his wife Mandy. Mandy felt that Denis, though he 'adored' his wife, was 'rather lonely'. She befriended him: 'He liked strong women, quite bossy women, which is why he liked me.' She liked his modesty and sense of humour. On one occasion, she complimented him on his trim figure. 'Yes,' he replied, 'I owe it to alcohol and nicotine.'* In younger days, Mrs Foreman had been well known by her maiden name, Mandy Rice-Davies. With Christine Keeler she had been one of the two leading women in the Profumo scandal of the early 1960s.

In London, Denis would quite often call at the Foremans' flat, sometimes without warning. He also wrote Mandy affectionate letters ('Mandy dear'). Mandy concluded that Denis's marriage was strong, but he felt the need to put some distance between his wife and himself. She was herself a great admirer of Mrs Thatcher. The two women met only fleetingly, at one or two parties. Mandy noticed her gaze: 'She had a kind of forensic stare . . . She was working me out.'

Given the family difficulties, Lady Thatcher depended more for company – which, despite her fundamentally solitary character, she always craved – on friends. In the USA, she particularly enjoyed staying with Carroll Petrie, a rich philanthropist and socialite, at her house in the Hamptons, Long Island.† Mixing with America's elite, for whom the Hamptons was a favoured holiday destination, she found 'huge intellectual stimulation'. There was also light entertainment. At one of Mrs Petrie's parties, put on for Nancy Reagan, the Mulroneys and the Thatchers, the pianist struck up 'There'll Be Bluebirds Over The White Cliffs Of Dover'. As Brian Mulroney recalled, 'Margaret stood up and started singing. Everybody was both startled and

---

* These reduced his consumption of food. Denis enjoyed the companionship of meals but was not much interested in eating. He would push food around his plate, incurring 'cosmic obloquy from Her'.
† In addition to the Reagans, her other American friends included Charles Price, the former US Ambassador in London, and his wife Carol, the Annenbergs, Gay Gaines, Steve Forbes and Henry Kissinger.

delighted. And when she kept singing, I got up and joined her. She brought the house down.' In England, the equivalent figures, with equivalently hospitable houses, tended to be people closely linked with her Downing Street life – Archie Hamilton and his wife Anne, the Heskeths, the Wolfsons, the Lennox-Boyds and, until his premature death, Peter Morrison. Some of her personal employees, existing or former, would also invite her to see them in the country.* Crawfie used to take her off to a quiet hotel at Great Malvern, near her home in Worcester. Charles and Carla Powell entertained her at their villa outside Rome, and the McAlpines looked after her in Venice. Her only family retreat was Mark's house in Constantia, near Cape Town.

As a guest, Lady Thatcher was simultaneously appreciative and exhausting. She loved seeing beautiful houses, works of art and gardens and the tamer sort of country walks. But this intensely active woman was, in a rural environment, rather passive. She always dressed with intimidating formality, which went against the English country-house spirit of relaxation. 'It was a bit like having royalty to stay,' recalled Archie Hamilton. 'You always had to think of things for her to do.' Whenever Denis came too that made everything easier.

People longed to meet or see Lady Thatcher. Not since Winston Churchill had a British prime minister held such allure. People would applaud her in the street and wanted, sometimes literally, to touch the hem of her garment. She almost never passed unnoticed, anywhere in the world.

In 1998, Denis decided that he and his wife should make their church attendance more regular. From then on, most Sundays, the Thatchers could be found in Christopher Wren's large and distinguished chapel at the Royal Hospital, Chelsea. Both liked the 'comfortable words' of the 1662 Prayer Book liturgy, the hymns and the military good order. Denis was quite a high Anglican, Margaret a Methodist by background. He took Communion in the chapel but she never did.

Through her post-office years, Lady Thatcher remained top of the death list of the Provisional IRA.† The need for heavy protection reinforced her isolation. As Tony Blair pursued the peace process, she watched with some scepticism, but in silence. This self-imposed rule came under considerable strain over aspects of the 1998 Belfast Agreement. On 21 June 1999, for

---

* These included Amanda Ponsonby, Alison Wakeham, Tessa Gaisman and their families and Julian and Diana Seymour.
† The IRA made active attempts to kill her after she left office, although none got far. One such was plotted when the Greek shipping magnate John Latsis lent her his house in Gstaad to get on with her memoirs. She had to be confined indoors at all times, which spoilt the trip's small element of holiday.

example, the Northern Ireland Secretary, Mo Mowlam, informed her that Patrick Magee, in prison for having planted the Brighton bomb, would be released the following day under the terms of the Agreement: 'I know that this will cause you particular distress given the loss of so many close friends and colleagues, and the infliction of horrific injuries on many others.' Lady Thatcher replied with cold anger: 'You rightly conclude that this will cause great distress – and a sense of injustice – to many of my friends including Margaret Tebbit. I don't think that any of the IRA terrorists should be released until all their weapons have been decommissioned.' She did not explicitly reject the *Realpolitik* behind the process, but she was forever opposed to what she saw as the false moral equivalence between terrorism and legitimate state force.

The fate of General Augusto Pinochet, the former President of Chile, was the final major issue on which Lady Thatcher provoked controversy. In October 1998, Pinochet was held in London under an international arrest warrant issued by a judge in Spain, who sought his extradition there. This action was popular with the left, who focused on the human rights abuses after Pinochet had seized power in 1973. It was extremely controversial, however, because Pinochet was being denied the normal immunity granted to a former head of state. He remained under house arrest in England for nearly eighteen months until the British judicial system eventually found that he could be put on trial.

The case aroused Lady Thatcher's passions because she felt strongly that Britain owed Pinochet a great debt for his secret actions during the Falklands War in 1982. Just days before he was arrested, he had been to tea with the Thatchers in Chester Square.* Julian Seymour advised her to intervene: 'Quite aside from the issues of principle as regards Chile, there is a much wider principle which is of direct relevance to you.' He was aware of efforts to bring legal action against her in Spain for Argentine deaths during the Falklands War: 'What will be this Government's attitude if an arrest warrant for you is issued at the hands of a Left-wing Spanish judge?' On 22 October 1998, in a letter to *The Times*, she stressed that Chile had reached its own internal agreement over its recent past, including the status of General Pinochet: 'It is not for Spain, Britain or any other country to interfere.' She noted the imminent visit of Argentina's President, Carlos Menem, to build bridges over the Falklands War, even as the British authorities were holding 'under arrest someone who, during that same

---

* Lady Thatcher had never met Pinochet until she visited Chile in 1994; since then they had kept in friendly touch.

conflict, did so much to save so many British lives'. In Robin Harris's view, her emotions were heightened because she knew just how far Chile had gone in Britain's aid but could not, for security reasons, make this public.*

In the spring of 1999, Lady Thatcher made a point of visiting Pinochet publicly in his gilded cage in Virginia Water. In July, in a rare speech in the Lords, she decried Pinochet's treatment. That October, almost a year after the arrest, she took her cause to the Conservative conference in Blackpool. Her address, to a fringe meeting, overshadowed William Hague's speech as leader the next day. It also left many puzzled. Why, having not spoken at the conference for nine years, had she chosen to break her silence on an issue outside the Conservative mainstream? Her reason was almost certainly the one stated in her speech – her outrage that Pinochet had been the victim of what she called 'judicial kidnap'. Might he yet die in Britain, she asked, 'as this country's only political prisoner'? After extensive medical examinations, in March 2000 Pinochet was allowed to return to Chile because of declining mental health.

In taking up Pinochet's cause, Lady Thatcher had shown her courage and sense of honour. Yet, with the media convinced that Pinochet was a monster, she was marginalized as one of a gallery of right-wing grotesques. There was an additional problem. When he had first briefed her about the Pinochet case in 1998, Robin Harris had found her still pretty good at absorbing new information. A year later, when she was about to address the conference fringe, this was markedly less true. The vehemence of Lady Thatcher's demeanour may have been a symptom of her mental struggle to hold on as she felt her powers fade.

A similar problem arose during the composition of Lady Thatcher's last book, *Statecraft*. Its themes of grand strategy included the state of great-power relations post-Cold War, the rise of 'rogue states' and terrorist actors, the Balkan controversies and the European Union. At the time, its European chapters, which called the EU 'a classic utopian project ... whose inevitable destiny is failure', were disregarded for being out of touch, but they accurately reflected Lady Thatcher's direction of travel. In private, she had come to think that Britain should find a way to leave the EU. Christopher Collins recalled Harris 'expressing frustration that she would not go that far in *Statecraft* – almost, but not quite'. Instead,

---

* At Britain's request, Pinochet had installed military radar at Punta Arenas, near enough to pick up what was going on at the Argentine air base of Comodoro Rivadavia. An RAF officer there was given real-time information on Argentine aircraft movements. It was only when the radar station was briefly shut for repairs that Argentine aircraft got through and hit British landing ships at Bluff Cove. Fifty-six British servicemen died. Pinochet had also helped shelter British special operatives who had tried and failed to attack Argentine planes on the ground at Comodoro Rivadavia.

the book argued that Britain should renegotiate with the EU to recover national sovereignty. In the view of Nile Gardiner, its researcher, *Statecraft* was a 'revolutionary work' because of the role these ideas played in 'shaping the momentum towards Brexit'.

The trouble was that Lady Thatcher's attention began to break down. As Harris remembered, 'By the time we finished, in 2001, she had really gone.' Lady Thatcher would read every page of the draft put before her, but when she had approved it at the bottom he found she could not remember what she had just read at the top.* The book ends with a quotation from one of Lady Thatcher's favourite Kipling poems, 'The Reeds at Runnymede',† a paean to English liberty:

> And still when Mob or Monarch lays
> Too rude a hand on English ways,
> The whisper wakes, the shudder plays,
> Across the reeds at Runnymede.

Margaret Thatcher was a great champion of English ways, but perhaps the whisper in the reeds was also that it was time for her to rest.

Tony Blair called a general election for 7 June 2001, rightly confident that he would win it easily. Despite Lady Thatcher's increasing frailty, demand for her in the campaign endured: 'she was brilliant at motivating our people to bother to vote,' recalled William Hague. She duly agreed to address the party's spring conference in Plymouth. However, after she spoke out against multiculturalism in an interview for the *Daily Mail*,‡ a row broke out. Michael Portillo, who had returned to Parliament and rebranded himself as a Tory modernizer, was now Shadow Chancellor. Seeking to distance himself from Thatcherite social and cultural attitudes, he wanted Hague to withdraw her invitation or at least denounce her. This Hague chose not to do, not least because of the potential damage to party morale. Lady Thatcher thus took the stage in Plymouth on 22 May. From her point of view, this was probably a mistake. Despite small signs of frailty, she put in a stirring performance for the faithful, which included a self-mocking joke about having just seen a local cinema hoarding which

---

* Since the book arose so closely from Lady Thatcher's speeches, and from views she had long held, it retained its authenticity. But there were occasions – her recantation of her earlier support for tackling global warming, for example – when the book fell too easily into an identikit right-wing mode which was not her own.

† It was on the banks of the Thames at Runnymede that King John signed Magna Carta in 1215.

‡ She told the paper: 'I want a society of opportunity for all, irrespective of colour or ethnic background. But I don't wish to have what they call a multicultural society ... There's something greater than a culture: it's a fundamental belief in liberty. A multicultural society will never be a united society.'

announced 'The Mummy Returns'. The audience loved it, but the media gleefully suggested Lady Thatcher was indeed something out of a horror film haunting poor Hague. Labour quickly concocted a poster sequence in which Hague's features morphed into those of Lady Thatcher. In her speech she attacked New Labour for being 'embarrassed by our history', but her difficulty was that leading Tories were embarrassed by theirs.

Labour went on to win the election by 413 seats to the Conservatives' 166, a margin only fractionally smaller than in 1997. Hague immediately resigned and a leadership contest ensued, long drawn out because the party had now changed its voting system to include party members. By the third ballot of MPs, there remained Kenneth Clarke, Michael Portillo and a Member from the 1992 intake with no ministerial experience, Iain Duncan Smith. To take on Clarke, Eurosceptics had to decide between Portillo and Duncan Smith.

Two days before the third ballot on 17 July, the *Sunday Telegraph* proclaimed that Lady Thatcher was supporting Portillo. But when the present author, then Editor of the *Daily Telegraph*, rang her she explained that while she had inclined towards Portillo at first, his campaign had worried her: 'If you start with legalising a soft drug [one of Portillo's ideas], where do you end?' She was now backing Duncan Smith, a preference duly reported in Monday's paper. In the third ballot Portillo was eliminated, one vote behind Duncan Smith. On 11 September 2001, Duncan Smith convincingly beat Kenneth Clarke among party members and became the new Conservative leader.*

As with the choice of Hague four years earlier, a late Thatcher endorsement had probably been decisive. Also as in 1997, the candidate of the Europhiles had been defeated, and so the cause of Euroscepticism had survived. The 2001 leadership election would prove Lady Thatcher's last significant intervention in British politics.

In December 2001, the Thatchers celebrated their Golden Wedding. While visiting Madeira over Christmas, scene of their 1951 honeymoon, Lady Thatcher temporarily lost the power of speech. Denis, who hated illness, could not cope

---

* Since the ballot was counted on the same day as the devastating Al-Qaeda attacks in the United States, the news disappeared from view. The *Daily Telegraph* got a scoop of the result (which was to be declared the following day), but could find no room for it on the front page. The events of 9/11 prompted a strong reaction in Lady Thatcher. On a copy of a collection of speeches by George W. Bush made in the wake of the atrocities she wrote, 'God gave us choice – some choose evil: their purpose is defeated by the overwhelming number who choose goodness, being always ready to help when things go devastatingly wrong. Those of us who still have life must comfort friends & neighbours who mourn their loss and we must show the undefeated spirit of a free and honourable people.'

and pretended nothing had happened. His wife, inclined always to equate illness with weakness, also brushed aside concern. When, back in England, a neurologist found ischaemic changes on her MRI scan, Lady Thatcher continued to downplay what had occurred. In early March, however, after a further episode, the risk of a major stroke was considered high. Her doctors recommended she withdraw from public life. This was announced on 19 March 2002, the day after the publication of *Statecraft*. The statement noted her 'small strokes', adding she would now 'cancel all her speaking engagements'. This was a hard decision, because Lady Thatcher's greatest fear was of 'a life without work', and she objected strenuously. 'There's nothing wrong with me,' she said. But her withdrawal from public life was overdue. Noticing her general decline, Denis remarked, 'It's not how many miles there are on the clock. It's how hard you drive the car.'

Policing the new regimen was challenging. Mark Worthington recalled that 'She was *constant* trouble about making speeches and it was all but impossible to contain her.' All formal speaking invitations were now declined, with the one exception of the eulogy after the death, whenever it should come, of Ronald Reagan.

When the decline in Lady Thatcher's mental powers had really set in was disputed. Opinion tended to reflect the attitude of the person speaking. In 2018, for example, John Major went public with the view that she had shown some symptoms even in office. He noted that in 1990 'she didn't understand' certain details of his hard ecu proposals, and sometimes showed 'irrationality'. He also felt that some of her anger with him after leaving office had been related to her mental health: 'It became more and more clear that she was simply unwell.'

However, those who worked with Mrs Thatcher daily when she was Prime Minister, as well as her doctors, had detected no loss whatsoever of mental powers while she was in office. To an extent, remarks by male colleagues about Mrs Thatcher's mental condition had been a trope from the start of her leadership. Men of that generation often talked about the 'irrationality' of women. In later years such talk sometimes amounted to a retrospective 'gaslighting'. Obviously, forcing her out would seem more forgivable if she had been, in Chris Patten's phrase, 'off her trolley'.

After Major made his remarks, Julian Seymour and Mark Worthington wrote to the *Daily Telegraph* to disagree. At the time of leaving office, they said, Lady Thatcher had not been 'ill', but distraught. Only later did she suffer memory loss.* By the late 1990s, she had become quite deaf and

---

* Among those close to her, Robin Harris was probably the first to identify the problem, when working on *The Path to Power* in 1994. Seymour noticed touches of it in 1997. One day in

refused to wear a hearing aid. Her strange responses because she had not quite heard led some to diagnose mental decline prematurely.

Not long after her official withdrawal from public life, the couple's health troubles got worse. After a rather unhappy Christmas in Tenerife, Denis, who had kept the news from her, had an aortic valve replacement in January 2003. In February, Lady Thatcher developed polymyalgia rheumatica. This was remedied by steroids, but the drugs also induced anxiety. Because Denis needed to rest after his operation, Mark had him out to South Africa, which reawakened anxious memories in his wife of his 1964 midlife crisis when he had fled to South Africa and she had thought he might not return. In her more troubled moments, she now thought he might be leaving her. That May, fretting over his absence, she decided to fly to South Africa to join him. There they had a successful holiday together.

The following month, after Denis became ill again, he was found to have cancer of the pancreas. On 26 June 2003, in the Lister Hospital, with his wife and children by his bed and her holding his hand, he died, aged eighty-eight. Lady Thatcher recalled the moment: 'Suddenly I saw the colour drain from his face. He had gone.' After a funeral in the chapel of the Royal Hospital, Denis's ashes were buried in the hospital's grounds.

As Mark's ex-wife Diane put it, 'Denis was always the quintessential English gentleman – old-school and chivalrous . . . She was effectively his leader as prime minister, but she . . . willingly deferred to him in private, because she knew he would not ever give her reason to distrust him.' She valued his common sense and knew his honest advice always had her best interests at heart. Denis Thatcher was an able man with his own ambitions and traditional views, and yet, in an age when it was almost unheard of, he had sacrificed himself for his wife's career. When asked how he felt after her first-round victory in the leadership contest in 1975, he said, 'Delighted. Terribly proud. Naturally. Wouldn't you?' He remained terribly proud to the end.

Now Denis's widow became, as her doctor, Christopher Powell-Brett, put it, 'depressed and lonely'. 'She didn't put on her usual, practical face,' recalled Worthington. 'She was grief-stricken.' She lived in a mixture of loss and confusion. Before the service in the Royal Hospital chapel, she seemed to think she was attending the funeral of her father rather than her husband. It was a strange trick of her failing memory both that she sometimes thought he was still alive and that she missed him so much. 'Where's DT?' came her old question, sometimes adding, 'I must go home now and get his

---

2000 she was sitting in Worthington's office, talking, when she suddenly could not get words out. She was shaking. This was probably an early transient ischaemic attack.

supper.' 'It's so lonely at night,' she also said, 'with no one to come back to. Without my faith, I don't know how I'd keep going.'

In 2004, full-time, live-in carers arrived at Chester Square and her life became chiefly private at last. Stories of the outside world would still reach her, which sometimes prompted a simple, clear thought. When Carol was the victor in the television programme *I'm a Celebrity ... Get Me Out of Here!* in 2005, Lady Thatcher neither watched it nor knew what it was about, but she understood the point. 'She's WON, you know,' she would repeat excitedly. As late as the formation of the coalition between the Conservatives and the Liberal Democrats in 2010, she was still capable of sharpness. When someone asked her, 'If you hadn't won the election, what would you have done?' she answered at once, 'I didn't have that problem, dear.'

On 5 June 2004, President Reagan died, aged ninety-three. It had become clear from 2002 that Lady Thatcher would not be well enough to deliver her eulogy in person. The decision was taken to film her speech so that it could be played at the funeral. Now, on 11 June 2004, in Washington's National Cathedral, Lady Thatcher, dressed in a broad-brimmed black hat, had the unusual experience of sitting in the congregation to watch herself projected on plasma screens. Brian Mulroney, sitting next to her, had been forewarned that when her speech was introduced she might, by instinct, get up to deliver it. Sure enough, she turned to him and said, 'Brian, should I say anything?' 'No, Margaret,' he said, '... it's going to be on TV.' The eulogy, drafted chiefly by John O'Sullivan, began: 'We have lost a great president, a great American, and a great man, and I have lost a dear friend.' She celebrated her friend's work in 'the great cause of cheering us all up', which he had turned to a 'purpose beyond humour' by leading the successful effort to 'free the slaves of communism ... With the lever of American patriotism, he lifted up the world.' After the tape had finished, Lady Thatcher turned to Mulroney: 'Brian,' she said, 'I went on too long.'

The speech marked the importance of a real alliance and a real friendship and provided an epitaph for the English-speaking dominance of the twentieth century. Alone of all the cathedral congregation, Lady Thatcher then joined the Reagan family party as it left for California on Air Force One. That evening at sunset, the interment service was performed against the backdrop of the Santa Susana Mountains. After the family had said farewell to the casket, Lady Thatcher was the first to come forward, walking up to it unassisted and bowing her head. By this stage, 'she was absolutely exhausted,' recalled Anne Wold, who accompanied her. 'We got back to the hotel and I said, "Lady Thatcher, let's take off your shoes." And she said, "Can we?" She looked almost childlike.' The whole thing had been almost too much for her, but her quality as a trouper saw her through.

In early 2005, thanks to better medication and proper care, Lady Thatcher emerged from the darkness caused by the loss of Denis. There was never any chance of her reverting to her former vigour, but her condition allowed her to 'plateau'. On 13 October, a party for more than 300 people was held at the Mandarin Oriental Hotel to celebrate her eightieth birthday. As she had for her seventieth, the Queen came. She circulated with Lady Thatcher at her side. The two old ladies looked cosy together – two grandmothers enjoying themselves. It also pleased the company that Geoffrey Howe was present – a mark of the reconciliation she had refused fifteen years earlier. Lord Carrington made a short speech, praising her kindness and her courage. Then Lady Thatcher stood forward. She began, 'I'd like to thank' – then a pause – 'the speaker' – then another pause – 'Peter' and everyone laughed and clapped with relief. No one could tell whether she had almost forgotten his name or had paused for effect. Then she spoke fluently about the trouble and strife of politics and all the adventures she had enjoyed. After the speeches the Queen said to Lady Thatcher, 'I'm afraid I must go now.' 'What a good idea,' she replied, 'I think I'll go too.' 'You'd better not!' said the Queen. 'It's your party.'

The secret of the success of the years that followed was that Lady Thatcher had such good care. Her chief carers, Kate Sawyer and Janice McCallum, understood what she needed. Kate, who was with her for ten years, described Lady Thatcher as 'one of the most compassionate and easy people I ever looked after'. She loved meeting people and so Kate and Janice would take her on small outings. She particularly enjoyed picnics, shared with 'her boys' her personal protection officers and drivers – in Richmond Park. Because she gradually ceased to be able to participate in substantive conversation, rather than staying with friends she would make use of their houses when they were away. When staying at the comfortable Clock House of Wafic Saïd's Tusmore estate in Oxfordshire, she would sit for hours in front of a Victorian painting – *The Leamington Hunt – Mr Harry Bradley's Hounds* by John Frederick Herring – finding it therapeutic to count the hounds depicted.* When visiting parks, Lady Thatcher particularly liked talking to dog owners. One said to her, 'You look like Margaret Thatcher, don't you?' 'Do I?' she replied with a secret smile.

The carers realized that dignity and a good appearance were, if anything, even more important for Lady Thatcher as she lost her memory. They spent

---

* The answer is twenty-two and a half couple.

much time on her hair and make-up, and choosing the right jewellery. She still made no concession to convenience in clothes. Crawfie once bought her sensible stretch skirts and easy jumpers. 'These are not mine,' she said coldly. What she wore was part of the 'bearing' that she so admired in others.

Because of the confidence her care gave her, Lady Thatcher could still take part in major public occasions with grace and success. She was determined to attend commemorations of the twenty-fifth anniversary of the Falklands War in June 2007,* and made appearances to support causes she believed in, such as Women2Win, the organization encouraging more women to become Conservative parliamentary candidates.

She even made a few foreign visits. In May 2009, as part of her annual Italian stay with the Powells, she attended a general audience of the Pope, Benedict XVI. Having first laid a wreath on the tomb of Pope John Paul II, the Pope she most admired, she was received by Pope Benedict, who offered a few shy, courteous and unchallenging words. After this, she spotted the pen of newly married couples awaiting papal blessings. She hurried up to them and said, 'We did that once [meaning getting married], and it is wonderful,' at which they smiled and cheered. Then she went down through the crowd. Before she got into her car, someone said, 'Lady Thatcher, they want to photograph you.' 'I must get this thing off first,' she said, referring to her mantilla. She removed it, adjusted her hair and gave a regal, all-embracing wave to loud applause. She had performed brilliantly. An hour later she remembered nothing about it.

The carers also noticed Lady Thatcher's strong aesthetic sense, notably her love of language. Kate learnt from her how, as a girl, she had read and recited poetry. So she and Lady Thatcher began to read poems to each other – Kipling, Tennyson, Ella Wheeler Wilcox, Longfellow, Thomas Hardy. 'She was the better reader,' Kate judged. She liked to watch *Songs of Praise* on Sunday nights. Charles Powell had to time his visits before or after the programme or else sit and sing along with her.

Although Lady Thatcher was not one to look back, Kate realized that there were times she did want to remember – childhood, and also Denis. It upset the carers that Lady Thatcher's children did not do more to comfort her. Kate once had words with Mark: 'I said, "I can't cope with you any more. I'll resign." He said, "You can't do that. You know too much."'

Rather to her carers' surprise, Lady Thatcher never talked about politics. Her long agony about being thrown out of office had disappeared. She

---

* At a celebration for Falklands veterans at the Painted Hall in Greenwich, Gerald Howarth, who attended, remembered 'the most astonishing roar from men who had been maimed' as she got up to leave them.

lived for the day and liked simple things. They also detected her dry sense of humour. One evening, a clip of Lady Thatcher speaking appeared on the television. 'Could you turn that woman off, please?' she said to Kate, deadpanning, 'I've had enough of her.'

At all times, the staff would address her as 'Lady Thatcher' or 'Lady T' (and she, having increasing trouble with names, would always call them 'dear'). There was one exception to this, however. When Anne Lawther, one of her carers, put her to bed when she was very old, 'I would say, for the sense of security, "Good night, Margaret. Sleep well."' It was many years since anyone had said that to her. 'Thank you, dear,' Lady Thatcher would reply. 'Good night.'

Even in old age, Lady Thatcher had to face troubles with her children. In August 2004, Mark was arrested for alleged financial involvement in a mercenary coup plot in Equatorial Guinea. Because, under South African law, a third party has to stand bail, he needed someone to raise the requisite 2 million rand (about £175,000). Lady Thatcher was desperate to help him, but knew she must not be dragged in and risk making the affair political. So she agreed to produce the money, on condition that he paid her back. Mark denied the coup-related accusations, but in January 2005, to avoid extradition to Equatorial Guinea, he made a plea bargain. He received a four-year suspended prison sentence and a fine of about £300,000 and was then allowed to leave the country. In his view, the whole thing was 'politically driven'. Lady Thatcher naturally found the episode distressing. In this one respect, at least, her loss of memory was a blessing.

In 2008, in a memoir called *A Swim-on Part in the Goldfish Bowl*, Carol gave the first public account of her mother's dementia and memory loss. Carol's decision to disclose this unilaterally shocked Lady Thatcher's staff and friends. 'On bad days,' Carol had written of her mother, 'she could hardly remember the beginning of a sentence by the time she got to the end.' When Lady Thatcher got wind of what Carol had done she was 'incredibly angry'. According to Michael Forsyth, 'It set her back months because she was frightened she would be caught out in public.' In her rage she began steps to disinherit Carol, until dissuaded by Julian Seymour.

Carol's disclosure started open season on her mother's dementia. In 2012, a full-length feature film, *The Iron Lady*, was released. Directed by Phyllida Lloyd and starring Meryl Streep as Lady Thatcher, the film centred on her mental decline. Among friends, family and supporters it provoked outrage. They considered it cruel to show the dementia of a living person, especially for commercial gain. There was also complaint about the film's inaccuracies, which included the suggestion that whereas Mark rarely visited his mother, Carol was always there to comfort her.

Streep's portrayal of Lady Thatcher, however, which won an Oscar, was almost eerily good.* One consequence was an increase in sympathy for her subject. Since the Thatcher caricature had always been of hardness and invincibility, new audiences were touched to think that she had been vulnerable. Women, in particular, noticed this.

Lady Thatcher, of course, never saw the film, but knew of its existence. Mark Worthington showed her a photograph of Meryl Streep in the part. 'Hmm,' she said, with some satisfaction. 'She's attractive, isn't she?'

As Lady Thatcher's general health declined, her office prepared for the inevitable. In 2009, Julian Seymour and Mark Worthington produced an aide-memoire laying out her funeral plans, codenamed by No. 10, under Tony Blair, 'Project True Blue'. Based on her wishes, she was to have a funeral and no memorial service, her ashes interred alongside those of Denis at the Royal Hospital, Chelsea. As to the venue, she felt Westminster Abbey might suggest monarchical airs, so preferred St Paul's, which was not royal and could hold more people.

The Seymour-Worthington aide-memoire also reported an 'interesting message' from Buckingham Palace that 'HM the Queen would wish to attend if she was able'. The only other prime minister to whom she had extended this privilege had been Winston Churchill. The expected presence of the Queen shifted attitudes. While the possibility of a state funeral was mooted, Seymour and Worthington argued that a ceremonial funeral (one notch down from a state funeral) would 'attract less public controversy' and thus be a more prudent choice.† This was agreed.

Lady Thatcher herself chose the hymns and the readings, and much of the music, including Brahms's *German Requiem*.‡ She also hoped that at least one of her grandchildren should play a part in the service. Michael

---

* Some of the small details aroused suspicion that the film-makers had been given inside information about life at Chester Square, though no culprit was ever discovered.

† A state funeral is accorded to all monarchs, and had previously been given to Nelson, Wellington, Gladstone and Churchill. But because state funerals can be the subject of parliamentary motions, there was the potential for mischief. A state funeral also involved the body lying in state in Westminster Hall, something Lady Thatcher herself refused. 'That was for Winston,' she insisted, and therefore too exalted for her.

‡ The readings and prayers she drew from the Authorized (King James) Version of the Bible and the Book of Common Prayer. For the hymns she selected John Bunyan's 'He Who Would Valiant Be', 'Love Divine, All Loves Excelling', by Charles Wesley, brother of John and the most famous Methodist hymnologist, and Cecil Spring-Rice's 'I Vow to Thee, My Country', whose meaning she had expounded in her 1988 'Sermon on the Mound'.

having read at Denis's memorial service, it was natural for Amanda to read one of the lessons. Lady Thatcher's other notable wish had been for the armed forces to participate, 'perhaps to remember in particular those units involved in the Falklands conflict'. This too was arranged. The coffin would be borne on a gun carriage and escorted by the military.

Pondering long and hard about who might give the funeral oration, Lady Thatcher and her advisers found themselves drawn to Richard Chartres, the long-standing Bishop of London. He was known for his stately bearing, impressive conduct of services of national importance – and his high-quality jokes. He was also, in cultural terms, a conservative.

Over 2010–11, Lady Thatcher had several more small strokes and, in 2012, a recurrence of polymyalgia. Her life now became very quiet, and although she did not seem unhappy, she retreated further into silence.

Amanda Thatcher last visited her grandmother in 2012, aged nineteen:

> Throughout the visit, I did not tell Grammy that I was her granddaughter. It would've been too confusing, because the young adult I had grown into was too unlike the little girl she could remember ... Although Grammy's memory had waned, her personality was still very strong. She was still able to remark on everything she saw and she still seemed to be enjoying herself. And sometimes, if I asked her too elementary a question, she'd respond with a tone that sent the message 'I'm not a dimwit, so stop treating me like one.' Her dignity was still very much intact.
>
> We were watching a gospel choir together on the TV and I would prod with simple questions and remarks. She responded amicably with nods and small affirmations, but when I asked if 'Denis had a good singing voice' she immediately lit up and said with the utmost inflection 'Oh yes.'

In December 2012, Lady Thatcher fell ill. Tests revealed a high-grade bladder cancer. Five days before Christmas the tumour was removed, after which she remained in hospital for a week. She then repaired to the comfort of a suite at the Ritz Hotel, offered to her by its owners, Sir David and Sir Frederick Barclay. Radiotherapy followed. Three or four weeks later she felt much better. 'She loved the Ritz,' Worthington recalled. 'She was looked after by beautifully dressed young men: the world wasn't bothering her any more.' Towards the end of March 2013, however, she had several more small strokes. It became clear that she would not live much longer. Carol came to visit her and left in tears at her condition, afterwards ringing Mark in Barbados to update him.

*

Saturday 6 April was a bad day. Sunday was worse. Until then Lady Thatcher had spent most of each day up and dressed, but now she kept to her bed. That evening she was visited by Charles Powell, who watched part of *Songs of Praise* with her. Powell spoke to her quietly and showed her photographs of Carla's puppies, which evoked a smile. 'Before leaving I leant over the bed, took her hand and lightly kissed her forehead.' He went home, 'and told Carla that I thought the end was very near'.

In the morning of Monday 8 April, Lady Thatcher experienced a powerful stroke, and at 11.28 a.m. she died. The life which had begun in a bedroom above her father's shop in Grantham had ended, eighty-seven years later, in a suite at the Ritz.*

---

* A bronze head and shoulders of Lady Thatcher was placed just inside the inner doors of the Ritz by the Barclays to commemorate her time at the hotel.

Epilogue

Mark and Carol announced Lady Thatcher's death shortly before 1 p.m. on 8 April. Her death certificate described her as 'Stateswoman (retired)'. Hearing the news in Madrid, the Prime Minister, David Cameron, came straight home. Lady Thatcher 'didn't just lead our country; she saved our country . . .' he declared. 'I believe she'll go down as the greatest British peacetime Prime Minister.' President Barack Obama, whose politics were very far from Lady Thatcher's, said, 'The world has lost one of the great champions of freedom and liberty, and America has lost a true friend.' She had shown women that 'there is no glass ceiling that can't be shattered'. With striking generosity, Helmut Kohl described her as 'a great woman [for whom] there was no substitute'.

The funeral was set for 17 April and the Queen's decision to attend announced immediately. Parliament was recalled for a day of tributes, led by Cameron. While generous, he put a little distance between himself and Lady Thatcher: her confrontational style, he said, had led 'yes, even to division'. The Labour leader, Ed Miliband, said she had left communities 'angry and abandoned', but his tone was respectful: she was a Prime Minister 'who defined her age'. Several Labour MPs were more hostile, the most extreme the actress Glenda Jackson. 'To pay tribute to the first Prime Minister denoted by female gender, okay,' she declared; 'but a woman? Not on my terms.' Jackson was updating the old sexist trope that a strong female leader must be 'really' a man.

To avoid controversy, Miliband discouraged leading Labour figures from speaking about Lady Thatcher between death and funeral. This produced a vacuum into which stepped her more extreme critics, whose voices dominated the BBC. The song 'Ding Dong! The Witch is Dead' from *The Wizard of Oz* reached no. 2 in the official UK singles charts, and some held anti-Thatcher street parties. Such events were reported out of all proportion (most drew no more than 200–300 people) and attracted global attention. It was a backhanded compliment to Lady Thatcher that she was capable of stirring such passions. The only real danger was that concerns about possible disorder would deter the public from paying their respects during the funeral procession in London. This could become a story that she had died unmourned.

At 4 p.m. on Tuesday 16 April, Lady Thatcher's coffin, draped in the Union flag, was received in the Chapel of Parliament. The following morning, at 10 a.m., it was carried from Parliament up Whitehall and along the Strand in a hearse before being switched to a gun carriage. On it lay white roses with a card which said 'Beloved Mother – always in our hearts. Mark and Carol', a rare joint initiative by the twins. The carriage was preceded by the band of the Royal Marines.* A tri-service bearer party 'found by Arms and Services represented in the Falklands' followed. As the cortège neared St Paul's Cathedral, the crowds, so large that movement was difficult, clapped – a departure from tradition prompted by the desire to counter the recent anti-Thatcher sentiment in the media. The threatened protests turned out to be small and unremarkable.†

Inside, a congregation of 2,000 was seated, led by the Queen and the Duke of Edinburgh. It included almost all surviving members of the Thatcher Cabinets, notably Geoffrey Howe and Michael Heseltine. Because this was not a state funeral, heads of state were not invited, but senior world leaders, such as F. W. de Klerk, Dick Cheney and Henry Kissinger, attended in a personal capacity. The only controversy concerned the US representation. The Obama administration chose to assemble a delegation headed by the former Secretaries of State George Shultz and James Baker. There was a logic to this, but the failure to send a high-ranking serving official was resented,‡ especially because Lady Thatcher, America's most important foreign friend since Winston Churchill, had herself made such efforts for President Reagan's funeral.§

The cortège arrived at the cathedral at 11 a.m. A single half-muffled bell

---

* Normally in such processions the band is kept apart from the gun carriage, which moves in silence, but Mark Worthington had worried that this silence might be disturbed by a protester shouting insults, and so it had been agreed that gun carriage and band should proceed together, the latter playing as it went.

† Nothing, however, had been left to chance. A spare Union flag was ready in the cathedral in case the one on the coffin had been splashed with protesters' paint. It was not needed.

‡ Donald Trump, who at the time held no public office, weighed in by tweet: 'It is terrible that neither Obama, Biden nor Kerry attended Lady Thatcher's funeral. They would all run to Muslim Brotherhood Morsi's.'

§ George H. W. Bush, himself too old to manage the trip, had been worried that the United States looked ungrateful. As compensation, he contributed an article to the *Daily Telegraph* in praise of Margaret Thatcher.

tolled as the bearer party lifted the coffin up the steps, lined by Chelsea Pensioners. The men bore it down the aisle and placed it under the dome just forward of the family, and of the Queen. Amanda read the first lesson, from Ephesians 6: 'Stand therefore, having your loins girt about with truth, and having on the breastplate of righteousness.' Her confidence and clarity of diction were widely admired. David Cameron read the second lesson, the famous passage from John 14: 'Let not your heart be troubled . . . I go to prepare a place for you.'

In his address Bishop Chartres began, 'After the storm of a life lived in the heat of political controversy, there is a great calm.' He played on one of her most famous phrases, 'Lying here, she is one of us, subject to the common destiny of all human beings.' Chartres expounded how her views had been formed by her provincial Methodist upbringing – which had inspired her perseverance in facing 'the immense hurdles she had to climb' and her courage in saying what she thought was true. She believed in independence because society's interdependence required each person to fulfil his or her own responsibilities. When she said there is 'no such thing as society', she was trying to show not that society did not exist but that each person was responsible for it. His intention, he later explained, was 'to rescue her humanity'. His address implied a rebuke to those who did not give Margaret Thatcher her due as a principled leader and a woman who tried to practise virtue.

After a blessing from the Archbishop of Canterbury, the coffin was carried back to the West Door. As it emerged into the light someone in the crowd shouted, 'Three cheers for Mrs Thatcher!' These were given. Everyone began to clap, and the sound of clapping swept into the cathedral. Then there was silence as the coffin was borne back down the steps and loaded into the hearse. At the top of the steps stood the Queen. Bishop Chartres was impressed by her 'hieratic stillness' as she watched the dignified farewell to her eighth prime minister.* The coffin proceeded to the Royal Hospital, thence to Mortlake cemetery, where Lady Thatcher's body was cremated in a private ceremony.

Shirley Ellis (née Walsh) used to walk to school with the young Margaret Roberts during the Second World War. In the intervening sixty and more years, the two had exchanged the odd friendly card or letter. She was Margaret's only childhood friend to attend the service. After it she said,

---

* Afterwards the Queen's former private secretary, Robert Fellowes, remarked to her how well it had gone, but ventured a slight question about whether Lady Thatcher should have had a gun carriage. Fellowes came away with the clear impression that the Queen thought the gun carriage decision had been absolutely right.

'As the coffin passed me, I suddenly burst into tears. I thought to myself, "So much has happened."'

On 28 September, Lady Thatcher's ashes were buried close to those of Denis, after a service in the chapel of the Infirmary named after her at the Royal Hospital. A separate memorial stone with nothing but her name and dates marks the spot. No casual passer-by would know it was there.*

At a small party he gave for Mrs Thatcher on the day she left office, Robin Butler told the assembled company, 'The thing that will be most interesting about us in our later years is that we worked with Margaret Thatcher.' Partly, seen through the eyes of civil servants, this was because of the sheer size of the task she had set herself and them. The volume of her work for well over a decade was stupefying. Somehow she managed to combine minute attention to detail with a cracking pace of change.†

As well as the quantity of the work, there was its sense of purpose. In her commonplace book, Lady Thatcher included a quotation of Emerson about power: 'Concentration is the secret of strength. To the inquiry of how he had been able to achieve his discoveries, Newton answered, "By always intending my mind."' Isaac Newton had come from Grantham. Like Newton, Margaret Thatcher intended her mind. She was a near-revolutionary reformer – in economic matters, though not in constitutional ones. Her 'housewife economics' directly challenged the post-war orthodoxy that the state could run the economy. Countries could not become richer, freer or even fairer, she asserted, if government and trade union leaders controlled labour, forever increased public debt and nationalized the means of production. Individual liberty was both an economic and a moral imperative. Before her, no modern leader had successfully acted on these assertions. She did. There were many errors – those privatizations

---

* The last formal matter occasioned by Lady Thatcher's death was the granting of probate on 26 November 2013. In her will, she left her estate equally – a third to Mark, a third to Carol and a third shared between Mark's two children. In a codicil of June 2003 – only eight days, as it turned out, before Denis died – she left £50,000 and a flower brooch with emerald and ruby diamonds to Crawfie, and 'my tiger brooch with sapphire' (a piece of very high quality which Lady Thatcher used to wear in the evening) to her granddaughter Amanda. The gross value of her estate at probate was £4,768,795 and the net value before inheritance tax was £4,694,605. The eventual inheritance tax paid was substantially reduced by the tax authorities' 'acceptance in lieu' of her personal retained papers in Churchill College, which produced a tax credit of just over £1 million.

† Political colleagues recognized this too. When one of her junior ministers, Michael Forsyth, was hurrying through the Central Lobby of the House of Commons one afternoon, a colleague called out, 'Slow down, slow down! Rome wasn't built in a day.' 'Well,' Forsyth replied, 'Margaret Thatcher wasn't the foreman on the job.'

which failed to break monopolies; the rise, in her later years, in inflation; ERM entry – but her successes were copied across the world and endured. Before the miners' strike, Britain had been unable to answer the question which Ted Heath, in February 1974, had put to the electorate, 'Who governs Britain?' With her defeat of Arthur Scargill, Mrs Thatcher answered it in favour of the elected government. She won at a high cost, both human and financial, but it was as nothing to the cost of defeat.

Although much criticized for her 'divisiveness', Mrs Thatcher won office in 1979 precisely because the nation was deeply divided. In that year, over 29.4 million working days were lost to strikes. In 1990, the year she left office, the figure had fallen to fewer than 2 million working days. However warlike her rhetoric, her victories brought industrial peace.

Something similar happened with her foreign policy. From 1976, Mrs Thatcher's attacks on *détente* led to accusations of warmongering. Yet by 1984, recognizing the importance of Mikhail Gorbachev before any other major leader did, she was the first to see that the West could bargain from the position of strength which Reagan, she and Helmut Kohl had achieved. Her readiness to confront Soviet Communism was not reckless: it was both a careful calculation about power and the result of her optimism that freedom would prevail.

In all Cold War matters, Mrs Thatcher was the sole British leader, apart from Winston Churchill, who thought not only in balance-of-power terms but also felt deeply about the suffering of the millions oppressed by Communism. When she said in her 1988 Bruges Speech that 'We shall always look on Warsaw, Prague and Budapest as great European cities,' she was, to some degree, stating the obvious. Yet the European Community had fought shy of this, seeing the matter mostly in terms of great-power stability. She was a missionary for the cause of democracy in Eastern Europe. Her persistence helped the whole of Europe become free.

This does not mean that her critics were flat wrong. She did polarize opinion, sometimes unnecessarily. Her sense of righteousness, though inspiring to some, was distasteful to others. Her angry rhetorical tone could be disproportionate and off-putting. So could her inability to recognize the validity of the other person's point of view. Archbishop Runcie's complaint that she offered little to the 'muddled seeker' after truth (see p. 776) had force: in her mind, muddle and truth were opposites.

Related to this was her intellectual and perhaps emotional failure to understand some ways of thinking. She found it hard, for example, to see why a Scot might regard the governance of the United Kingdom differently from an Englishwoman (or man), or why a substantial minority in Northern Ireland might feel allegiance to a foreign country rather than its own.

She liked binary choices: Conservative or Labour, freedom or socialism, good or bad.

This difficulty could affect foreign relations too. Mrs Thatcher had an innate sympathy for the United States, as for all the English-speaking peoples, and for Poles, and all victims of Communism. But towards Western European nations which she believed had not distinguished themselves in the Second World War, including the then-neutral Republic of Ireland, she felt some disdain. For Germany, she felt actual dislike. In her mind, Britain had rescued the Continent from its own follies twice in the twentieth century, with great sacrifice of blood and treasure. This sacrifice obsessed her, not only as a political leader but as a mother. In her commonplace book, she included lines from A. E. Housman about 'The lads that will die in their glory and never be old'. To her, the sins that had caused these tragedies had not been fully expiated. This meant that her thoughts about the future of Europe – in some ways more prophetic than those of her opponents – were often discounted because they were seen merely as unfriendly. On the one hand, she framed better than any other leader the problems of sovereignty, democracy and identity in modern Europe. On the other, her words seemed to impugn the motives of many people of goodwill. It would be wrong to say that Margaret Thatcher was unimaginative – she was capable of great leaps of bold thought – but her imagination was inspired only if her sympathies were engaged. Otherwise, she tended to become more hectoring and dogmatic.

Mrs Thatcher's behaviour, for good or ill, must be understood in the light of her character. Its contradictions were striking. She was high-minded and highly educated, yet had a common touch. She was fierce, but kind; rude, and courteous; calculating, yet principled; matter-of-fact, yet romantic; frank, yet secretive; astute, yet innocent; rational, yet capricious; puritanical, yet flirtatious. She had an icy stare and a warm heart. Mrs Thatcher combined an immense assurance about following her own way with a permanent uneasiness in life. In Crawfie's view, she had 'not been allowed the time to be happy' in her childhood. So she sought the laurels of fame and power but could never rest on them. Applying her high standards to herself, she found herself wanting. So she pressed ever onwards.

In this, her sex was the key factor. Combined with her lower-middle-class background, it gave her a lifelong sense that she was living dangerously. To succeed, she would have to do everything twice as well as the men who surrounded her. It was the privilege of the ruling class and sex of her time to be almost careless about their own careers. They knew they would be all right in the end. None of them felt Mrs Thatcher's anguish – about what to wear, how to speak, how to look after her family, how to survive. She never ceased to be alone.

As the years passed, however, her sense of mastery grew. By 1987, when she fought her final general election, she had tamed the union leaders and was widely believed to have pulled off an economic miracle. She had also gained a pivotal position in the relationship between the two superpowers, becoming a political pilgrimage site for world leaders and an icon, without rival, of female leadership.

Since Mrs Thatcher had achieved so much against the grain of most senior ministers, she came to believe in her own invincibility. This was bad for her character. She lost some of her ability to catch the political wind and some of the caution which had earlier balanced her crusading zeal. Combat became her default mode. She drove a lot of powerful men to distraction and turned voters against her. By remaining so long in office she outstayed her welcome, but she also attained a continuity of governmental purpose not known in Britain since before the age of Queen Victoria. The pronoun 'she' became synonymous with power.

In her famous handbag, Mrs Thatcher hid many secrets – not just literally in the papers she carried within, but metaphorically too. Near allied to her unique vulnerability was the secret of her unique power. 'Never look in a lady's handbag' was the traditional, gallant rule. But anyone trying to understand Margaret Thatcher needs to do just that. This was implicitly recognized by the extraordinary interest in the Christie's sale of her clothes and effects in December 2015. Many items sold for ten or more times their estimate, including her red despatch box for over £240,000 and the bag she used on her last visit to Downing Street, which went for £47,500.* The excitement showed how deep and universal was her mythological status as the archetype of a strong woman.

Mrs Thatcher's character and situation make her politics hard to classify. Was she a traditionalist or a radical? An unqualified monarchist, she showed reverence for the Established Church (her irritation with Anglican bishops notwithstanding). She was thoroughly respectful of parliamentary tradition and tried to stop the place being televised. She even revived the creation of hereditary peers. She admired ancient institutions such as Oxford and Cambridge, even though Oxford slighted her. She fought and won a war 8,000 miles

---

* Bids came from forty-four countries all over the world, including the United States, China, Russia, Korea, Singapore and Switzerland. The total reached was £4,516,038, with 100 per cent sold. A sale of lesser items in May 2019 raised more than £1 million. It included the pebble bracelet Mrs Thatcher had worn when she first met Nelson Mandela in 1990, which was estimated at £2,500 but sold for £40,000. Taken together, the two auctions raised a substantial six-figure sum for Great Ormond Street Hospital from the sale of items set aside for this purpose by the beneficiaries after Lady Thatcher's death.

away to recapture a small colony. To her, the habits of ancient institutions represented something deep and proud in the history of her country. Behind her actions as Prime Minister there was a task of restoration. Obviously she did not seek to bring back the British Empire, but she did consider British civilization the country's greatest global export; and she had an instinctive understanding – one of the reasons she liked Kipling so much – of how that civilization depended more on its engineers, warrant officers and small traders ('the Sons of Martha') than it did on its proconsuls in plumed hats.

Yet she was a radical too. She had the radical's total lack of embarrassment about arguing from first principles and a permanent angry impatience for change. While huge issues like trade union reform had to be tackled, she did not have to seize upon climate change, or fight South African sanctions, or try to break the lawyers' monopolies or allow Sunday trading, yet her energy and zeal demanded such things. John Bunyan's character says, on the point of death, 'I do not repent me of all the trouble I have been at to arrive where I am.' Nor did she: she saw herself as Mrs Valiant-for-Truth.

Reflecting on her legacy, Tony Blair considered Mrs Thatcher 'a great reformer, but a bad nostalgic'. This nostalgia, he felt, 'collides with her record as a modernizing reformer'. A clue as to how she reconciled this apparent contradiction between tradition and change lies in words pasted into her commonplace book, attributed to Confucius: 'How may we recognise a good craftsman? First by the reputation of his ancestors for honesty and sincerity: then by his ability to create something new with an experience that is old.' Her passionate love of freedom should be seen in this context: not a global assertion of abstract rights, but a belief about the value of the long British experience, and that of its offshoots, particularly in the United States. She thought Britain had a legacy of liberty under the law which it should cherish and bestow on others.

If there was one uniting force in everything Mrs Thatcher did, it was her love for her country. What she loved – its liberty, its lawfulness, its enterprise, its readiness to fight, its civilizing, English-speaking mission – was not always visible, nor was her love always requited. But great loves such as hers go beyond reason, which is why they stir others to achieve extraordinary things.

In her 'Sermon on the Mound', Mrs Thatcher offered her vision through the words of Cecil Spring-Rice's hymn 'I Vow to Thee, My Country', both in its first verse about patriotism and in its second about 'another country', the heavenly one. She asked that it be sung at her funeral. It summed up what she thought and felt. The woman so often criticized for being 'uncaring' cared more than any prime minister before or since about what she thought was her task. She gave everything she could.

Acknowledgements

The acknowledgements in my three volumes amounted to twenty-eight pages. My thanks to the many hundreds of people involved (most of whom were interviewees) remain heartfelt; it would be otiose to particularize them again here.

An exception must be made for the late Lady Thatcher herself. She invited me, in 1997, to embark on this project and gave me the opportunity to meet the necessary family, friends and colleagues and consult the necessary papers. The liberal conditions she set ensured that proper history could be written.

I must also thank Lord Wilson of Dinton, the then Cabinet Secretary, who gave me the freedom to consult and quote from the government archives, a permission which continued under his successors. Without this access, the biography could not have been authoritative.

The man most closely involved in the project on Lady Thatcher's behalf was Sir Julian Seymour. He was its greatest 'friend at court' and generously helped me solve numerous problems along the way. It was a tremendous shock when he died unexpectedly after a hospital operation in March this year. So many people miss his kindness and practical wisdom. This centenary volume is dedicated to his memory.

As in the past, Chris Collins, the master of www.margaretthatcher.org, and Andrew Riley, the Thatcher archivist at the Churchill Archive Centre, Churchill College, Cambridge, have been the oracles I have consulted. They are the two people who know the most about Margaret Thatcher.

Penguin Books have been my publishers from start to finish. The editor of all three volumes and of this centenary edition, which was his idea, has been the great Stuart Proffitt. His devotion and judgement have been outstanding.

I also want to thank the following at Penguin: Rebecca Lee, my superb editorial manager; Vartika Rastogi, Stuart Proffitt's able assistant, Linden Lawson, who copy-edited the text, and Pen Vogler, for her creative and sympathetic approach to publicity. Thanks also to Daniele Roa for the jacket design, Sandra Fuller for production work, and Stephen Ryan and Joe Barnes for proof-reading. The Index was compiled by Mark Wells.

*

Clare Alexander, head of Aitken Alexander, has continued as my doughty literary agent, accompanied by Lesley Thorne, who has dealt with all television and filmic aspects.

David Shiels, who did such important research for the three volumes, has contributed further expert knowledge on Northern Ireland. Virginia Utley, guardian of my manuscripts, has answered all my queries about the earlier ones, which helped in composing this book.

In previous volumes, Daniel Collings contributed the great bulk of primary research in the United States, as well as taking meticulous care over all drafts of the whole work to make sure that mistakes were corrected and clarity was maintained.

With this book, Daniel's role has been arguably even more important. He has given me the first and fullest advice on what could be cut or re-arranged, and helped ensure that a volume which contains only 40 per cent of the original does not short-change the reader and makes a proper book in its own right. His professionalism, patience and mastery of the subject are beyond praise.

As the book's editor, Daniel would like to acknowledge Laurence Norman, whose counsel is more important than he knows. He would also like to thank his two brilliant daughters, Clara and Lucy, for their patience as their father disappeared to edit (yet) another chapter. His ultimate debt, however, is to his wife Sonja, whose support and encouragement have exceeded all reasonable expectation. She has made this, and so much more, possible.

Our twins, William and Katharine, were seven when my Thatcher work began. Now our grandchildren are much the same age. The third volume was dedicated to our granddaughter, Elizabeth Persis Moore. This book is dedicated to her brother, Patrick Gillachrist Moore, who was born a few months after Volume Three appeared.

As with all the previous books, I owe my greatest gratitude to my wife Caroline, who was there before it all began and is with me still. Like the Abbé Sieyès, she can say, 'I have survived.'

Index

Entries with a symbol denote a footnote.

abortion issue, 84
Abrahamson, Lieutenant
  General James (1933–;
  educated Massachusetts
  Institute of Technology
  and University of
  Oklahoma; Lieutenant
  General (retired) US
  Air Force; astronaut;
  Associate Administrator
  at NASA, responsible
  for the US space
  shuttle program,
  1981–4; Director,
  Strategic Defense
  Initiative 1984–9), 425,
  429–30
Acheson, Dean, 303
Acheson, Sir Donald,
  640–41
Achille Lauro cruise ship,
  436
Acland, Sir Antony
  (1930–2021; educated
  Eton and Christ
  Church, Oxford;
  joined FCO, 1953;
  Ambassador to Spain,
  1977–9; Permanent
  Under-Secretary
  and head of
  Diplomatic Service,
  1982–6; Ambassador
  to the United States,
  1986–91; Provost of
  Eton, 1991–2000;
  Knight of the Garter,
  2001), 289, 304, 329,
  601*, 689†, 810–11,
  816, 859
Adams, Gerard (Gerry)
  (1948–; educated
  St Mary's Christian
  Brothers' School,
  Belfast; Vice-President,
  Sinn Fein, 1978–83,
  and President from
  1983; Sinn Fein MP for
  Belfast West, 1983–92
  and 1997–2011), 255,
  260, 261–2, 262*;
  elected MP for
  West Belfast, 445*;
  backchannel with Irish
  government, 727*;
  meetings with Hume,
  727*, 727; interest
  in ending the armed
  struggle, 854
Adams, John, 425*
Adams, Tom, 370–71, 373
Adele, 636*
Adelman, Kenneth (1946–;
  US Ambassador and
  Deputy Permanent
  Representative to UN,
  1981–3; Director,
  Arms Control and
  Disarmament Agency,
  1983–8), 243, 371, 426
Advisory Council for
  Applied Research
  and Development
  (ACARD), 186
Afghanistan: Soviet invasion
  of (1979), 239–41,
  240†, 419, 577, 683;
  West arms mujahidin
  resistance, 240†; Soviet
  withdrawal from, 686,
  687
African National Congress
  (ANC), 545, 547†,
  547, 550*, 551, 552,
  553; MT's terrorism
  comments, 787–8,
  788†; British contacts
  with, 788*, 788,
  790, 799; Gorbachev
  disengages from, 789,
  799; South Africa plans
  London assassinations,
  791; Mells Park
  discussions with
  South Africans, 792;
  Mandela's relationship
  with, 797–8, 798*, 800;
  De Klerk's negotiations
  with, 798–9
Aganbegyan, Abel, 682*
Agnelli, Gianni, 516
Ahtisaari, Martti
  (1937–2023; Special
  Representative
  of the Secretary-
  General for Namibia,
  1978–88; President of
  the Republic of Finland,
  1994–2000), 792
AIDS (Acquired Immune
  Deficiency Syndrome),
  640–41, 642†, 642–4,
  643*; public education
  on, 641–2, 642*, 643;
  Medical Research
  Council's AIDS
  Directed Programme,
  643*
aircraft industry,
  143–4, 144*, 144†,
  173*, 337
airline market, European,
  488
Aitken, Jonathan (1942–;
  educated Eton and
  Christ Church,
  Oxford; Conservative
  MP for Thanet East,
  1974–83; for Thanet
  South, 1983–97;
  Chief Secretary to the
  Treasury, 1994–5;
  journalist and author;
  jailed in 1999 for
  perverting the course of
  justice), 148
Alexander, Andrew, 88
Alexander, Sir Michael
  (1936–2002; educated
  St Paul's and King's
  College, Cambridge;
  diplomatic private
  secretary to the Prime
  Minister, 1979–82;

Alexander – *cont'd*
  Ambassador to Austria,
  1982–6; Permanent
  Representative to
  NATO, 1986–90;
  knighted, 1988), 214*,
  214, 237, 264, 806*,
  806
Alison, Michael
  (1926–2004; educated
  Eton and Wadham
  College, Oxford;
  Conservative MP
  for Barkston Ash,
  1964–83; for Selby,
  1983–97; Minister
  of State, Northern
  Ireland Office,
  1979–81; Department
  of Employment,
  1981–3; PPS to the
  Prime Minister, 1983–7),
  260, 261, 496†, 639; as
  MT's PPS, 352†, 352–3,
  353*, 358, 532, 618;
  not offered government
  position (1987), 618*,
  618
Alison, Rosie, 352
All Souls College, Oxford,
  468‡, 468
Allan, Sir Alexander 'Alex',
  653, 654
Allen, Jim, 18
Allen, Richard V.
  (1931–2024; advised
  Ronald Reagan
  on foreign policy
  and worked on his
  presidential campaigns,
  1976, 1980; US
  National Security
  Advisor, 1981–2), 189,
  232, 233, 259*
Alton Towers (theme park),
  610
Amann, Ronald, 366*, 574*
Amersham International,
  337‡, 337
Amery, Julian (1919–96;
  educated Eton and
  Balliol College, Oxford;
  Conservative MP
  for Preston North,
  1950–66; for Brighton
  Pavilion, 1969–92;
  Minister for Housing
  and Construction,
  DOE, 1970–72;

Minister of State, FCO,
  1972–4; created Lord
  Amery, 1992), 552
Ames, Aldrich, 430†
Amis, Kingsley (1922–95;
  educated City of
  London School and St
  John's College, Oxford;
  his novel *The Old
  Devils* (1986) received
  the Booker Prize;
  knighted, 1990), 97†,
  187*, 589
Ancram, Michael
  (1945–2024;
  13th Marquess of
  Lothian, educated
  Ampleforth, Christ
  Church, Oxford and
  Edinburgh University;
  Conservative MP for
  Berwick and East
  Lothian, February–
  September 1974;
  for Edinburgh
  South, 1979–87; for
  Devizes, 1992–2010;
  Parliamentary Under-
  Secretary,
  Scottish Office,
  1983–7; Chairman,
  Conservative
  Party in Scotland,
  1980–83; Chairman,
  Conservative Party,
  1998–2001; created life
  peer, 2010), 474
Anderson, Bruce, 891, 893
Anderson, Jack, 296
Andreotti, Giulio
  (1919–2013; Prime
  Minister of Italy,
  1972–3, 1976–9 and
  1989–92), 485, 813,
  872
Andrew, Prince, Duke of
  York, 290, 558*
Andropov, Yuri, 367, 369†,
  414, 415
Anglo-Irish Agreement
  (1985), 456, 457,
  718–19; early
  movement towards,
  257–8; negotiations/
  diplomacy (1983–5),
  446–8, 451–7; Unionist
  responses to, 457–8,
  459†, 459–60, 460†,
  719*, 719; signing of/

press conference, 458*,
  458–9, 459*; MT's
  retrospective view of,
  460†, 460–62, 725
Anglo-Irish
  Intergovernmental
  Council, 263–4, 445‡,
  445–6, 452
Anglo-Irish Treaty (1921),
  447*
Angola, 545, 577, 791–2
Annan, Noël (1916–2000;
  educated Stowe
  and King's College,
  Cambridge; Provost
  of King's College,
  1956–66; Vice-
  Chancellor, University
  of London, 1978–81;
  created Lord Annan,
  1965), 589
Annenberg, Leonore, 949†
Annenberg, Walter
  (1908–2002;
  businessman and
  philanthropist; US
  Ambassador to Britain,
  1969–74), 104, 949†
Anson, Charles (1944–;
  educated Lancing
  and Jesus College,
  Cambridge; seconded
  from FCO to No. 10
  Press Office, 1979–81;
  press secretary to the
  Queen, 1990–97), 188
Antrim, HMS, 301, 371
Anyone for Denis? (Ingrams
  and Wells stage play),
  321*, 588
APEX trade union, 152*
appeasement policy (1930s),
  15, 738–9
Apple, R. W. 'Johnny', 704
Aquascutum (fashion label/
  store), 575, 597, 694
Arafat, Yasser, 433*, 433,
  434–5
Archer, Jeffrey (1940–;
  educated Wellington
  School and Brasenose
  College, Oxford;
  best-selling novelist;
  Conservative MP
  for Louth, 1969–74;
  Deputy Chairman,
  Conservative Party,
  1985–6; created
  Lord Archer of

Weston-super-Mare,
1992; imprisoned
(2001–3) for perjury
and perverting the
course of justice),
891, 901*, 901, 902,
903; Deputy Party
Chairman, 498, 500;
scandal involving
prostitute, 543; Major
ennobles, 922†
Ardent, HMS, 313
Argentina: Falkland Islands
invasion (2 April 1982),
246, 247, 265, 281,
286–8, 288†; military
junta ruling, 281–2,
283; historic claim to
Falklands, 281, 283;
Reagan's relations with,
283–4, 284*, 285, 286,
294–6, 303, 314‡,
685–6; Israel's attempts
to sell fighter aircraft
to, 685; Menem's visit
to London (1998),
951–2; air base of
Comodoro Rivadavia,
952*; *see also* Falkland
Islands; Falklands War
Argonaut, HMS, 313
Armenian earthquake
(1988), 697*, 832–3
Armstrong, Robert
(1927–2020; educated
Eton and Christ
Church, Oxford; joined
Treasury, 1950; private
secretary to R. A.
Butler (Chancellor
of the Exchequer),
1954–5; joint principal
private secretary to Roy
Jenkins (Chancellor),
1968; principal private
secretary to the Prime
Minister, 1970–75;
Permanent Under-
Secretary, Home Office,
1977–9; Cabinet
Secretary, 1979–87;
created Lord Armstrong
of Ilminster, 1988):
Cabinet Secretary,
216–17, 224, 228,
271–2, 625; on
economic policy
making, 216–17;
and British Leyland

recovery plan, 220–21;
MT's dinner for the
permanent secretaries,
222; on MT's
Englishness, 250; and
Anglo-Irish relations,
257, 265, 445†, 445‡,
445–6, 451–2, 453,
455, 456, 457, 460;
Heath's principal
private secretary, 257;
and Northern Ireland,
257, 259, 260, 264–5;
and Falkland Islands,
282–3; and Falklands
War, 291–2, 317, 318†,
318‡; and MT's visit to
Falkland Islands, 341†;
on MT's reaction to
SDI, 366; and Grenada
crisis, 375; and GCHQ
dispute, 377, 378; and
miners' strike, 380,
393; on inner-city task
force plan, 504; and
Westland affair, 509,
510, 511, 513, 516,
517–18, 522, 523–4;
and US bombing of
Libya, 533; on MT
and Howe, 561; not
at Chequers seminar
(1986), 574*; and
MT's third term, 620,
625, 631; retirement
of (1987), 625; willing
to contradict MT,
625; and AIDS public
education, 642; and
Spycatcher controversy,
706, 707, 708–11,
712, 713; 'economical
with the truth' phrase,
710; and Oldfield
revelations, 716–17
Arnold, Matthew, 11
Ascension Island, 293, 298,
341†
Ashdown, Arnold, Baron,
156
Ashdown, (Jeremy) Paddy
(1941–2018; educated
Bedford School; served
in the Royal Marines,
1959–72; MP for
Yeovil, 1983–2001
(Liberal 1983–8, Liberal
Democrat 1988–2001);
Leader of the Liberal

Democrats, 1988–99;
knighted, 2000; created
Lord Ashdown of
Norton-sub-Hamdon,
2001), 506†, 624,
696*, 865, 906–7
Ashworth, John
(1938–2025; educated
West Buckland School
and Exeter College,
Oxford; Chief Scientist,
Central Policy Review
Staff, 1976–81; Vice-
Chancellor, University
of Salford,
1981–90; Director,
London School of
Economics, 1990–96;
knighted, 2008), 182,
186*, 186, 198
Assad, Hafez, 434
Associated British Ports,
766
Association of Chief Police
Officers (ACPO), 382
Astra satellite, 764
Atkins, Humphrey
(1922–96; educated
Wellington;
Conservative MP
for Merton and
Morden, 1955–70; for
Spelthorne, 1970–87;
Chief Whip, 1973–9;
Secretary of State for
Northern Ireland,
1979–81; Lord Privy
Seal, 1981–2; created
Lord Colnbrook,
1987): Chief Whip,
114, 123, 159;
Northern Ireland
Secretary, 182, 250,
253, 256, 259–60;
Lord Privy Seal, 289‡;
resigns over Falklands,
289; as MT's hope for
Speaker, 354
Atlantic Conveyor, SS, 314,
317*
Atlas Preservative Company,
41, 79
Attali, Jacques (1943–;
economist and senior
civil servant; special
adviser to President
of French Republic,
1981–91; founding
President, European

Attali, Jacques – *cont'd*
Bank for Reconstruction and Development, 1991–3), 290, 291*, 477, 567, 817
Attlee, Clement, 1st Earl, 29, 389‡
Attwoods, 949
Austin, Hudson, 370
Austin Rover, 527–8
Australia, 549, 554, 794; and *Spycatcher* controversy, 706, 707, 709, 710, 714
Aylward, Sean, 265
Azad, Yusef, 929

Babcock International, 404†
Bach Choir, Oxford, 32
Bahrain, 434, 437*
Baker III, James A. (1930–; White House Chief of Staff, 1981–5; US Secretary of the Treasury, 1985–8; US Secretary of State, 1989–92; White House Chief of Staff and senior counsellor, 1992–3) and MT's economic policy, 231, 656*; and Grenada crisis, 373; and Plaza Agreement, 492; MT and, 691, 692, 821, 827–8, 860, 861, 866–7, 871–2; on Reagan–MT relations, 692; visits Moscow (1989), 699; and Anglo-German relations, 702, 703, 816; NATO summit (1989), 702, 703–4; and SNF negotiations, 702, 703; and Howe, 703; and end of Cold War, 803†, 836–7; and Hurd, 819; and German reunification issue, 821†, 821, 830; at Bermuda meeting, 827–8; and Gulf crisis, 860, 861, 863, 865, 866–7, 871–2; at MT's funeral, 965
Baker, Kenneth (1934–; educated St Paul's and Magdalen College, Oxford; Conservative MP for Acton, 1968–70; for St Marylebone, 1970–83; for Mole Valley, 1983–97; Secretary of State for the Environment,1985–6;for Education and Science, 1986–9; Chancellor of the Duchy of Lancaster, 1989–90; Chairman, Conservative Party, 1989–90; Home Secretary, 1990–92; created Lord Baker of Dorking, 1997), 126, 496, 498; and local government, 467, 471, 473; and poll tax, 471, 473, 839, 847; Environment Secretary, 501; and policy on inner cities, 503; Education Secretary, 537–8, 630, 635, 636–9; as possible leadership candidate, 616; and GERBIL, 635–6*, 636–9; Party Chairman, 745; and local elections (3 May 1990), 849; on Howe's resignation, 882; and leadership contest (November 1990), 888, 897, 900; and MT's resignation, 904
Balfour, Harold, 1st Baron Balfour of Inchrye, 39
Balfour Beatty, 796
Balfour Club, 30
Balkan conflict, 931–2, 945
Baltic states, 811, 829*, 829, 926
Bancroft, Ian (1922–96; educated Coatham School and Balliol College, Oxford; head of the Home Civil Service and Permanent Secretary to the Civil Service Department, 1978–81; knighted, 1975; created Lord Bancroft, 1982), 173
Bandar bin Sultan, Prince (1949–; fighter pilot, trained RAF Cranwell; Saudi Arabia's Ambassador to the United States, 1983–2005; Secretary-General, Saudi National Security Council, 2005–15; Director-General, Saudi Intelligence Agency, 2012–14), 437–9, 438†, 439*, 440*, 440, 859
Bank for International Settlements, 552
Bank of England, 147, 198, 223†, 226, 228, 338*, 490, 492, 656*, 751, 754*, 883, 906
Banks, John, 97
Barbados, 370–71, 373
Barbara (nanny), 57
Barber, Anthony (1920–2005; educated Retford Grammar School and Oriel College, Oxford; Conservative MP for Doncaster, 1951–64; for Altrincham and Sale, 1965–74; Chancellor of the Exchequer, 1970–74; created Lord Barber, 1974. Barber had taken up the Chancellorship after Iain Macleod died suddenly little more than a month after the election): Chancellor of the Exchequer, 98, 100, 103, 106, 274, 654; expansionary policies, 106, 274, 654; EPG member, 553
Barclay, David (1934–2021; joint proprietor with Frederick Barclay of the *Daily Telegraph*, *Sunday Telegraph*, 2004–21; knighted, 2000), 920–21, 921*, 962, 963*
Barclay, Frederick (1934–; joint proprietor with David Barclay of the *Daily Telegraph*, *Sunday Telegraph*, 2004–23; knighted,

2000), 920–21, 921*, 962, 963*
Barnard, Niël, 801*, 863*
Barnes, Julian (1946–; educated City of London School and Magdalen College, Oxford, novelist, winner of the 2011 Man Booker Prize for *The Sense of an Ending* (2011)), 583
Barnett, Joel, 541
Baron, Wendy, 590
Barrington, Liz, 28
Bastiat, Frédéric, 110, 147*
Bauer, P. T. (*later* Baron Bauer), 147*
Bazoft, Farzad, 857*, 857
BBC (British Broadcasting Corporation): *Panorama* (television programme), 99, 127*, 301, 539‡, 541, 646†, 749; *Midweek* (television programme), 123, 128; coverage of Falklands War, 303–4, 316*, 316, 539‡, 586; *Real Lives* series, 500*; and US bombing of Libya, 533, 541; MT's views on, 539–42, 761†, 761–2; licence fee, 539, 540, 541, 761, 762, 763; Peacock Report, 540–41, 763; and appointment of Marmaduke Hussey, 542 and Patricia Hodgson, 541–2, 595‡, 762; coverage of US raid on Libya, 541 'Maggie's Militant Tendency' (*Panorama* programme), 541; portrayal of Thatcherism in drama and comedy, 586–7; and Northern Ireland, 723–4; Conservative views on, 761–2; and Reithian ethos, 761, 762; and Bosnian crisis, 932; series based on *The Downing Street Years*, 936–7
Bearpark, Andy (1953–; educated Balderstone Senior High School and University of London; private secretary to the Prime Minister, 1986–9; chief of staff to Margaret Thatcher, 1990–91), 918, 919, 920
Becker, Boris, 835†
Beeld (Afrikaans newspaper), 788–9
Begin, Menachem (1913–92; born Poland; commander, Irgun Zvai Leumi, 1943–8; Leader of the Likud Party 1973–83; Prime Minister of Israel, 1977–83; joint winner, Nobel Peace Prize (with Anwar al-Sadat), 1978), 433†, 433
Belaúnde, Fernando, 305
Belfast (Good Friday) Agreement, 449*, 454*, 460, 950–51
Belgium, 725*
Belgrano (Argentine cruiser), 304–5, 305*, 307, 309, 345*
Bell, Steve (1951–; educated Slough Grammar School; cartoonist, notably for the *Guardian*), 585
Bell, Tim (1941–2019; educated Queen Elizabeth's Grammar School, Barnet; Managing Director, Saatchi & Saatchi, 1970–75; Chairman and Managing Director, Saatchi & Saatchi Compton, 1975–85; Chairman, Bell Pottinger, from 1987; created Lord Bell, 1998), 164–5, 170†, 170, 171‡, 344*, 846; and Sunday trading debate, 532; closeness to MT, 536‡, 536, 603, 606†; drug taking of, 536‡, 536; and preparations for 1987 election, 536–7, 603, 605; 1987 election campaign, 606*, 606†, 608, 610–11; and party political broadcasts, 606†; and MT's tenth anniversary, 731, 732*; and leadership contest (November 1990), 888*; and MT after her departure from office, 920
Bell, Virginia, 888*
Beloff, Max, 93*, 93
Belton Estate (near Grantham), 13
Belvoir Hunt, 13
Benedict XVI, Pope (Joseph Ratzinger) (1927–2022; Pope 2005–13), 959
Benn, Tony (Anthony Wedgwood Benn) (1925–2014; educated Westminster and New College, Oxford; Labour MP for Bristol SE, 1950–60; 1963–83; for Chesterfield, 1984–2001; Secretary of State for Industry, 1974–5; Secretary of State for Energy, 1975–9. Benn became 2nd Viscount Stansgate on the death of his father. Determined to return to the Commons, he renounced this title after the passage of the 1963 Peerage Act and retook his former seat in a by-election), 103, 113, 279, 622†, 622, 928
Bennett, Alan, 583, 584
Berlin, Sir Isaiah, 147†
Berlin Wall, 333, 483, 754, 802, 807‡, 807–8, 842
Bermondsey by-election, 342
Berry, Sir Antony, 450†
Berwick and East Lothian by-election, 169
Bevan, Aneurin, 403
Beveridge, William (*later* 1st Baron Beveridge), 75–6
Bialer, Seweryn, 574*
Bible, 365†, 621, 639, 776, 908*, 961‡; Testaments, 19, 175, 775*, 776, 886†; idea of the righteous remnant, 54†

INDEX

Biden, Joe, 535*, 965‡
Biffen, John (1930–2007; educated Dr Morgan's School, Bridgwater and Jesus College, Cambridge; Conservative MP for Oswestry, 1961–83; for Shropshire North, 1983–97; Chief Secretary to the Treasury, 1979–81; Secretary of State for Trade, 1981–2; Lord President of the Council, 1982–3; Leader of the House of Commons, 1982–7; Lord Privy Seal, 1983–7; created Lord Biffen, 1997): in opposition, 146, 162; on Lady Howe, 150; Euroscepticism of, 162, 869†; as Powellite, 162, 183; Chief Secretary to the Treasury, 183, 203–4; and public spending control, 183, 273, 278; 'Inner Group' on economic policy, 216; Trade Secretary, 229, 478, 538; opposes despatch of Task Force, 287; and 1984 budget, 399; opposes Channel Tunnel project, 478; and ERM question, 494; Ingham's 'semi-detached' comment, 537; Leader of the House, 537; exclusion from Strategy Group, 538*; leaves Cabinet, 617
Bild newspaper, 812
Billy Elliot (musical), 585*, 585
Biological Warfare Convention (1972), 806–7
Birkin, Jane, 18*
Birmingham, 95–6
'Birmingham Six', 721‡, 721
Birt, John (1944–; educated St Mary's College, Liverpool and St Catherine's College, Oxford; Deputy Director-General,

BBC, 1987–92; Director-General, BBC, 1992–2000; created Lord Birt, 2000), 542, 761†, 762, 763
Bishop, Maurice, 370
Bishop, Tony, 415, 417, 419*, 420, 427–8, 580, 830–31
Bismarck, Otto von, 142, 815†
Bjerke, Eivind, 597
Black, Conrad (*later* Lord Black of Crossharbour), 594†, 658†
Black Hawk helicopters, 507, 510, 512
'Black Monday' (19 October 1987), 655
'Black Wednesday' (16 September 1992), 933–4, 938
Blackstone, William, 327
Blackwell, Norman (1952–; educated Latymer Upper, Royal Academy of Music and Trinity College, Cambridge; special adviser to the Prime Minister, No. 10 Policy Unit, 1986–7; head, No. 10 Policy Unit, 1995–7; created Lord Blackwell, 1997), 615, 620, 644–5, 646
Blackwill, Robert (1939–; Senior Director for European and Soviet Affairs, NSC, 1989–90; US Ambassador to India, 2001–3; NSC deputy for Iraq, 2003–4), 214, 806*, 806, 823–4, 824*, 834
Blair, Anthony 'Tony' (1953–; educated Fettes and St John's College, Oxford; Labour MP for Sedgefield, 1983–2007; Leader of the Opposition, 1994–7; Prime Minister, 1997–2007; Leader of the Labour Party, 1994–2007, Knight of the Garter, 2022): MT's influence on, 4, 615, 941–2; Paul Johnson on, 148; on

Kinnock in Westland debate, 520; understands MT's appeal, 599, 941; on MT's prospects at 1992 election, 913; and Balkan conflict, 932; as archetypal modernizer, 941; MT's views on, 942; wins 1997 election, 943–4; meetings with MT, 945; Northern Ireland peace process, 950–71; wins 2001 general election, 953–4; and MT's funeral plans, 961; on MT's legacy, 971
Blair, Colonel David, 207
Blake, Robert, 590
Blakelock, Keith, 502
Blakeway, Denys, 936, 937
Blatch, Bertie, 63–4, 84
Bleasdale, Alan, 586
Bledlow (Lord Carrington's country house), 846–7
Blood Products Laboratory, Elstree, 641
Blunkett, David (*later* Baron Blunkett), 543
Blunt, Anthony (1907–83; educated Marlborough College and Trinity College, Cambridge; Professor of the History of Art, University of London, and Director of the Courtauld Institute of Art, 1947–74; Surveyor of the Queen's Pictures, 1952–72; knighted, 1956, but the honour was cancelled and annulled, October 1979), 207–8, 706, 708, 709*, 714
Blyth, James (*later* Lord Blyth of Rowington), 440
Boetcker, William, 139†
Booth, Hartley (1946–; educated Queen's College, Taunton, Bristol University and Downing College, Cambridge; practising barrister, 1970–84;

special adviser and member No. 10 Policy Unit, 1984–8; Conservative MP for Finchley, 1992–7), 503, 621, 642–3
Bootle North by-election, 881
Bosnian crisis, 931–2
Bossom, Alfred (1881–1965; educated Charterhouse and Royal Academy of Arts; Conservative MP for Maidstone, 1931–59; created Baron Bossom, 1960), 55, 76†
Bossom, Sir Clive, 76†, 76
Botha, Peter Willem (P. W.) (1916–2006; Prime Minister of South Africa, 1978–84; State President, 1984–9), 545, 546–8, 552, 553–4, 786, 788*, 789; illness and resignation as leader, 790–91; resigns as State President, 793
Botha, Roelof Frederik ('Pik') (1932–2018; Minister of Foreign Affairs, South Africa, 1977–94; of Information, 1978–86), 545, 553, 792
Botswana, 548, 553
Bourdeaux, Rev. Michael, 366*
Bowe, Colette (1946–; educated Notre Dame High School, Liverpool, Queen Mary College, University of London and LSE; Director of Information, DTI, 1984–7; Chairman of Ofcom, 2009–14; created dame, 2014), 513, 517, 522†, 522–4, 523*, 523†
Bowyer, Sir Eric, 74
Boyd, Alan Lennox-Boyd, 1st Viscount Boyd of Merton, 192, 193
Boyd-Carpenter, John (1908–98; educated Stowe and Balliol College, Oxford; Conservative MP for Kingston-upon-Thames, 1945–72; Minister of Pensions and National Insurance, 1955–62; Chief Secretary to the Treasury, 1962–4; created Lord Boyd-Carpenter, 1972), 74, 75, 930†
Boyle, Andrew, *The Climate of Treason* (1979), 207, 706
Boyle, Edward (1923–81; 3rd Baronet, educated Eton and Christ Church, Oxford; President of the Oxford Union, 1948; Conservative MP for Handsworth, 1950–70; resigned as junior minister over Suez, 1956; Minister of Education, 1962–4; Vice-Chancellor, Leeds University, 1970–81; created Lord Boyle of Handsworth, 1970), 30*, 30, 31
Boys from the Blackstuff (television series), 586
Boyson, Rhodes (1925–2012; educated Haslingden Grammar School, Manchester University and Corpus Christi College, Cambridge; headmaster, various comprehensive schools, 1955–74; Conservative MP for Brent North, 1974–97; Parliamentary Under-Secretary of State, DES, 1979–83; Minister of State, DHSS, 1983–4; NIO, 1984–6; DoE, 1986–7; knighted, 1987), 839
Brace, Susan, 40
Bradford North by-election, 881
Bragg, Billy, 584
Brahms, Johannes, *German Requiem*, 961
Braithwaite, Rodric (1932–; educated Bedales and Christ's College, Cambridge; Ambassador to the Soviet Union, 1988–92; knighted, 1988), 237, 367*, 369, 691‡, 697, 700*, 700, 803, 804, 805, 821, 830†, 830
Bramall, Edwin (1923–2019; educated Eton; Commander-in-Chief, UK Land Forces, 1976–8, 1978–9; Chief of the General Staff, 1979–82; field marshal, 1982; created Lord Bramall, 1987; Knight of the Garter, 1990), 285, 312*
Brass, Laurence, 108, 114
Bray, Tony, 31–4, 37–8, 38*, 46, 52
Brazil, 310, 627*
Brecon and Radnor by-election, 497, 635
Bremer, Paul, 534
Brenton, Howard (1942–; educated Chichester High School for Boys and St Catharine's College, Cambridge; playwright), 585–6, 589*
Brexit, 6, 943, 953
Brezhnev, Leonid (1906–82; General Secretary of the Communist Party of the Soviet Union, 1964–82), 236, 239, 241, 249, 364–5
Bright, Graham, 890‡, 890, 893, 902
Brightman, John (1911–2006; educated Marlborough and St John's College, Cambridge; tax lawyer; judge of Chancery Division, 1970; judge of Industrial Relations Court, 1971; Lord of Appeal, 1982), 60
Brightman, Roxane, (Lady), 60
Brilliant, HMS, 313
BRIT School for Performing Arts and Technology, Croydon, 636*
British Aerospace (BAe), 337†, 439, 508, 514–15, 516

British Airways (BA), 343,
  400, 404†, 404–5;
  privatization (February
  1987), 404–8, 600;
  lawsuits against, 405–7;
  and treble-damages
  remedy, 407; 'ethnic'
  tail fins, 946
British Antarctic Survey,
  323*, 779*, 779
British Army: Royal
  Inniskilling Dragoon
  Guards, 33; Denis
  Thatcher's service in,
  54, 292, 314; Ulster
  Defence Regiment
  (UDR), 207, 454†,
  454, 460, 726;
  Falklands land war,
  313–15, 316*, 316–18,
  319–20; 2nd Battalion,
  Parachute Regiment,
  316*; and RUC, 720,
  721, 726–7; murder
  of corporals (March
  1988), 722*, 722,
  723–4; 7th Armoured
  Brigade, 865; Royal
  East Kent Regiment,
  911*
British Caledonian (BCal),
  405*, 405
British Empire, 11, 28, 39;
  MT's views on, 11,
  28, 39, 327; Imperial
  Preference, 41*, 41, 48;
  the Dominions (Old
  Commonwealth), 48–9,
  297, 315, 318
British Film Institute, 586
British Gas Corporation,
  402, 543; privatization,
  408–9, 770
British Leyland, 219†,
  219–21, 234, 343‡,
  400*, 402, 527–8
British National Oil
  Corporation (BNOC),
  337–8
British Nationality Act
  (1981), 328‡
British Olympic Committee,
  240*, 240
British Petroleum (BP): sale
  of government-owned
  shares, 204, 337†, 337,
  656*, 656; and Mark
  Thatcher, 441
British Rail, 758

British Satellite Broadcasting
  (BSB), 764, 765
British Steel Corporation
  (BSC), 217–19, 269,
  343‡, 385–6, 400*
British Telecom (BT),
  338*, 338, 343, 400,
  543; privatization of,
  338–9, 400, 402–4,
  403*, 404*, 464
Britoil, 338, 408
Brittan, Leon (1939–2015;
  educated Haberdashers'
  Aske's School, Trinity
  College, Cambridge;
  Conservative MP
  for Cleveland and
  Whitby, 1974–83; for
  Richmond, Yorkshire,
  1983–8; Chief Secretary
  to the Treasury,
  1981–3; Home
  Secretary, 1983–5;
  Secretary of State for
  Trade and Industry,
  1985–6; European
  Commissioner,
  1989–99; knighted,
  1989; created Lord
  Brittan of Spennithorne,
  2000): Chief Secretary
  to the Treasury, 229;
  as 'Cambridge mafia'
  member, 351†; Home
  Secretary, 351†, 351,
  382–3; and miners'
  strike, 382–3, 385, 500;
  as ardent Europhile,
  482, 869, 873†;
  and ERM question,
  494, 842; and 1985
  reshuffle, 500*,
  500, 506; Trade and
  Industry Secretary,
  500†, 500, 506, 527–8;
  anti-Semitism against,
  500; and Westland
  affair, 506, 507, 508,
  509, 510, 513, 514–15,
  515†, 517–19, 520,
  522–3; resigns over
  Westland, 518–19;
  on leak of Solicitor-
  General's letter, 518;
  and Wapping dispute,
  525; Peacock Report
  into BBC, 540;
  and South Africa,
  556*; as European

Commissioner, 675,
  734, 875; advises Howe
  to resign, 745; on MT's
  exhaustion (late 1989),
  755; on Major, 841*;
  on single currency,
  875†, 875; and Howe's
  resignation, 878; and
  Major campaign for
  leadership, 895†, 895
Brittan, Samuel
  (1933–2020; brother of
  Leon; educated Kilburn
  Grammar School
  and Jesus College,
  Cambridge; columnist
  at the *Financial Times*
  from 1966; knighted,
  1993), 147*, 148, 734
Brixton riots (April 1981),
  259, 271
Broadcasting Standards
  Council (BSC), 763
Brooke, Sir Alan (*later* 1st
  Viscount Alanbrooke),
  200
Brooke, Henry (*later* Baron
  Brooke of Cumnor),
  69, 70, 622*
Brooke, Peter (1934–2023;
  educated Marlborough,
  Balliol College,
  Oxford and Harvard
  Business School;
  Conservative MP for
  the City of London
  and Westminster
  South, 1977–97; for
  Cities of London
  and Westminster,
  1997–2001; Paymaster-
  General, Treasury,
  1987–9; Chairman,
  Conservative Party,
  1987–9; Secretary of
  State for Northern
  Ireland, 1989–92; for
  National Heritage,
  1992–4; created Lord
  Brooke of Sutton
  Mandeville, 2001), 616,
  622, 853†, 853–4, 899
Brooke of Ystradfellte, Lady,
  622*
Brown, Archie, (1938–;
  educated London School
  of Economics; Oxford
  University Lecturer
  in Soviet Institutions,

1971–89; Professor of Politics, 1989–2005; Emeritus, 2005–; his books include *The Gorbachev Factor* (1996) and *The Rise and Fall of Communism* (2009)); 366*, 367*, 367, 574*, 574‡
Brown, Michael (1951–; educated Andrew Cairns Secondary Modern School, Littlehampton, Sussex and University of York; Conservative MP for Brigg and Scunthorpe, 1979–83; for Brigg and Cleethorpes, 1983–97), 888, 893, 903, 908†
Brownlow, Lord, 13
Bruce-Gardyne, Jock (1930–90; educated Winchester and Magdalen College, Oxford; Conservative MP for South Angus, 1964–74; for Knutsford, 1979–83; Minister of State, Treasury, 1981; Economic Secretary to the Treasury, 1981–3; created Lord Bruce-Gardyne, 1983), 146, 492, 732
Bruges Group, 924
Brunner, Karl, 226
Brzezinski, Zbigniew, 157, 192, 238, 240
BSkyB, 765
Buchanan-Smith, Alick, 160–61
Buckethead, Lord, 612
Budgen, Nicholas (1937–98; educated St Edward's, Oxford and Corpus Christi College, Cambridge; MP for Wolverhampton South, 1974– 97; leading Eurosceptic backbencher, temporarily lost the Conservative whip over Maastricht Treaty), 284
Bukovsky, Vladimir (1942–2019; Russian dissident, author and human rights activist;

spent a total of twelve years in Soviet prisons, labour camps and so-called 'psychiatric hospitals' before his release and move to the UK in 1976), 589
Bullard, Julian (1928–2006; educated Rugby and Magdalen College, Oxford; Fellow of All Souls College, Oxford, 1950–57; joined FCO, 1953; Deputy Under-Secretary, 1979–84 (also Political Director, 1982–4); Ambassador to West Germany, 1984–8; knighted, 1982), 483, 664, 673
Bundesbank, 654†, 655, 656, 666
Bunyan, John, 971
Burgess, Anthony (1917–93: educated Xaverian College, Manchester and Manchester University; novels include *A Clockwork Orange* (1962) and *Earthly Powers* (1980)), 584
Burgess, Guy, 207, 706, 708
Burke, Edmund, 147*, 710
Burmah Oil, 79†, 141
Burnet, Alastair, 732*
Burns, Terence (1944–; educated Houghton-le-Spring Grammar School and University of Manchester; Chief Economic Adviser to the Treasury and head of Government Economic Service, 1980–91; Permanent Secretary, Treasury, 1991–8; created Lord Burns, 1998), 267, 269, 490, 491, 493, 494, 495, 656, 658, 659, 868; presentation on financial situation (1980), 224–5; on timing of UK's ERM entry, 869
Burt, Richard, 424
Bush, Barbara, 691, 894–5
Bush, George H. W. (1924–2018;

Vice-President of the United States of America, 1981–9; President, 1989–93): on MT, 158, 703, 704–5, 812, 828, 831, 864; attends Chernenko's funeral, 428; wins 1988 election, 688, 690, 691‡, 691; MT cultivates while Vice-President, 691*, 691†, 691, 692; foreign policy experience, 691–2; relations with MT, 691–2, 699, 700–705, 785–6, 809–12, 822–5, 834–5, 856–61, 862, 863–4, 894–5; MT's views on, 691, 698, 821, 824–5, 862, 863–4, 917; initial inaction on East–West affairs, 697, 698, 700; and NATO nuclear 'modernization', 700–701, 704*; and MT–Kohl relations, 701, 702; and SNF negotiations, 702, 703–4; supports reunification of Germany, 702, 806, 807, 809, 812–13, 814, 821–3; proposes cutting US forces in Europe, 703; Mainz speech, 704; and green issues, 781, 782, 785–6; and southern Africa, 793*; and end of Cold War, 803†, 803, 836; and Gorbachev, 805; and MT's attitude to Germans, 806; and fall of Berlin Wall, 809*, 809; MT at Camp David with, 810–13; Malta meeting with Gorbachev, 810, 811, 812–13; and MT's view of EC, 810, 813–14, 816; views on European integration, 813, 814, 816; reduces US troop numbers in Europe, 818; MT's telephone call (February 1990), 822–3; meets

Bush, George H. W. – *cont'd*
Kohl at Camp David, 822, 823; concern at MT's views on Russia, 823–5; MT meets in Bermuda, 827–8, 830, 857; on NATO, 831; meets Gorbachev in Washington, 832; at NATO summit (July 1990), 834–5; nuclear weapons policy, 834–5; at Aspen conference (August 1990), 856–9, 860; and Gulf crisis, 856–67, 862*, 862†, 870–72, 908, 917; military plans for liberating Kuwait, 861, 866, 870–72, 917; and MT's use of word 'wobbly', 863–4, 864*, 864†; MT meets in New York, 866–7; UN strategy over Iraq in Kuwait, 871†, 871–2; CSCE summit in Paris (November 1990), 889, 894–5; and MT's resignation as Prime Minister, 907; relations with Major, 917, 926; and Balkan conflict, 932; and MT's funeral, 965§
Bush, George W., 4, 954*
Business in the Community (BiC), 632
Buthelezi, Mangosuthu (1928–2023; Chief of the Buthelezi tribe, South Africa; founder of Inkatha Freedom Party, 1975; Leader, 1975–2019; Chief Minister, KwaZulu Legislative Assembly, 1976–94; Minister for Home Affairs, 1994–2004), 551, 552*
Butler, Adam (1931–2007; educated Eton and Pembroke College, Cambridge; Conservative MP for Bosworth, 1970–92; Minister of State, Department of Industry, 1979–81; Northern Ireland Office, 1981–4; Defence Procurement, 1984–5; knighted, 1986), 142, 147, 166†
Butler, David (1924–2022; educated St Paul's and New College, Oxford; Fellow of Nuffield College, Oxford, 1954–2022; author/editor of many publications, including, since 1951, the Nuffield Election Studies, a reference series for each UK election since 1945; knighted, 2011), 167, 344, 347
Butler, Michael (1927–2013; educated Winchester and Trinity College, Oxford; Ambassador and UK Permanent Representative to EEC, 1979–85; knighted, 1980), 209, 211, 477, 875*
Butler, R. A., 75, 77, 118, 167*, 290
Butler, Robin (1938–; educated Harrow and University College, Oxford; principal private secretary to the Prime Minister, 1982–5; Cabinet Secretary, 1988–98; knighted, 1988 created Lord Butler of Brockwell, 1998): at Treasury, 200; on MT and Reagan, 234, 568; on MT–Deng meeting, 329–30; and Franks Inquiry, 341; and MT's visit to Falkland Islands, 341; and MT's health, 357; and Parkinson's affair with Keays, 358; and Grenada, 372–3; on dispute with NUM, 379–80; and GCHQ dispute, 379; and miners' strike, 384, 387, 391, 393; with MT for Camp David trip, 421, 522*; and Brighton bombing, 448, 449; and local government, 469; and Channel Tunnel project, 478–9; and McIntyre's paper on BBC, 540*; and Oxford honorary degree issue, 590, 591*; on working for MT, 593–4; Cabinet Secretary, 625, 626, 735; seeks to dislodge Powell, 626, 735–8, 740; and Thyssen collection project, 669; and intelligence services, 715; and Northern Ireland, 721*; on Gibraltar shootings, 724; and Iraq 'War Cabinet' (1990), 862; and MT's resignation statement to Cabinet, 904†, 904‡, 904; revokes MT's access to classified information, 915–16; creates 'public duty cost allowance', 916*; and Denis Thatcher, 924*; and MT's memoirs, 936; and MT's departure from office, 967
Butskellites, 167*, 167
BX Plastics, Manningtree, Essex, 35–6

Cable and Wireless, 337‡, 337
Cadbury chocolate factory, Birmingham, 175
Caine, Michael, 689*
Callaghan, James (1912–2005; educated Portsmouth Northern Secondary School; Labour MP for Cardiff South (1945–83), Chancellor of the Exchequer, 1964–7; Home Secretary, 1967–70; Foreign Secretary, 1974–6; Prime Minister, 1976–9; created Lord Callaghan of Cardiff, 1987): halts South African cricket tour, 88; Home Secretary,

88; Foreign Secretary, 137; Prime Minister, 143–5, 144*, 144†, 161–2; background and character, 143; condescension towards MT, 143; MT's views on, 143; replaces Wilson, 143; IMF crisis, 144–5, 216; devolution proposals, 161*, 161–2, 162*; party divisions over Europe, 162; rejects British ERM entry, 163; decides against autumn 1978 election, 168; incomes policy, 168, 169–70; 'Winter of Discontent', 169–71; 'Crisis? What Crisis?' headlines, 169; on MT when provoked, 169; and 1979 election campaign, 171–2, 175, 176–7; invites MT to televised debate, 171–2; fall of government (March 1979), 171; departure from Downing Street, 180; as Prime Minister, 197–8; resigns as Labour leader, 227; and Falklands War, 285*; calls for inquiry into secret services, 713
Cambodia, 577
Cambridge by-election, 156
Cambridge spy ring, 207–8, 706, 708, 714
Camden School for Girls, 21
Cameron, David, 964, 966
Cammell Laird, Merseyside, 506, 507
Campaign for Nuclear Disarmament (CND), 333, 423
Campbell, John, 89
Campbell, Judy, 17–18, 18*
Canada, 346, 549†, 549, 554, 656*, 759, 787, 794
Canary Wharf, London, 502, 632*
Cannon, Lou, 577
capital punishment, 177, 355
Carbaugh, John, 215
Cardinal Vaughan School, Westminster, 639*

Carey, George (1935–; educated Bifrons Secondary Modern School; Bishop of Bath and Wells, 1982–91; Archbishop of Canterbury, 1991–2002; created Lord Carey of Clifton, 2002), 777–8
CARICOM, 371
Carlton Club, 732–3, 854, 942*
Carlucci, Frank (1930–2018; [Deputy Director, Central Intelligence Agency, 1978–81; US National Security Advisor, 1986–7; US Secretary of Defense, 1987–9), 572, 601, 680, 681
Carr, Robert (1916–2012; educated Westminster and Gonville and Caius College, Cambridge; MP for Mitcham, 1950–74; for Sutton, Carshalton, 1974–6; Secretary of State for Employment, 1970–72; Home Secretary, 1972–4; created Lord Carr of Hadley, 1976), 109, 114, 117, 129
Carrington, Iona, Lady, 130
Carrington, Peter (6th Baron Carrington) (1919–2018; educated Eton and Sandhurst; First Lord of the Admiralty, 1959–63; Leader of House of Lords, 1963–4; Secretary of State for Defence, 1970–74; for Energy, 1974; for Foreign and Commonwealth Affairs, 1979–82; Chairman, Conservative Party, 1972–4): Heath government, 106, 109; and party leadership, 114; Shadow Leader of the Lords, 129, 130, 160, 167; and Rhodesia, 160, 192–3, 204; and immigration, 164*; Military Cross

in Second World War, 183*, 289§; Foreign Secretary, 183, 184, 213, 215, 236, 237, 238, 242, 480–81; MT's relations with, 194*, 194, 213; at CHOGM in Lusaka (1979), 194–5; and ERM question, 209; and monetary policy, 209; and fight over EEC budget contribution, 211–12; and Dublin Council of Ministers (1979), 211; Lancaster House Agreement, 214, 215; in Washington with MT (1981), 234*, 234; and Soviet Union, 236, 237, 238, 241, 242; on MT and Reagan, 241; Trident missile system, 244; and unrest in Poland, 245; and Northern Ireland, 252–3, 262; and 1981 budget, 270; and public spending control, 272, 278; Falklands 'leaseback' proposal, 282–3; sends submarine to South Atlantic, 284–5; and Argentina's occupation of South Georgia, 284; and Falklands War, 286, 287, 288; resigns over Falklands, 289†, 289; and Arabism of Foreign Office, 433; on 'Waiting for Godot', 584†; and MT's tenth anniversary, 732; advises MT to resign (1990), 846–7; attends MT's 80th-birthday dinner, 958
Carron, Owen, 262†
Carter, Jimmy (1924–2024; Governor of Georgia, 1971–5; President of the United States of America, 1977–81): MT meets (1977), 153, 157, 159; MT's relations with, 157, 159, 189, 192, 212–14, 215; and Rhodesia, 158–9, 192–3, 213,

Carter, Jimmy – *cont'd*
214–15; congratulates MT on election as Prime Minister, 189; at G7 Tokyo summit (1979), 192; US Embassy siege in Teheran, 213; and Cold War, 237, 238, 239, 240, 242, 245; and Moscow Olympics boycott, 240; and Trident missile system, 244; and Northern Ireland, 251‡

Cartledge, Bryan (1931–; educated Hurstpierpoint and St John's College, Cambridge; diplomatic private secretary to the Prime Minister, 1977–9; Ambassador to Hungary, 1980–83; to the Soviet Union, 1985–8; knighted, 1985), 572–3, 573*; foreign affairs private secretary to MT, 180, 190, 191, 208, 237; visit to France (1979), 190, 191; and G7 Tokyo summit (1979), 191†, 191, 192; at CHOGM in Lusaka (1979), 194‡, 194; and Gordievsky, 430, 431; Chequers seminar on Soviet Union (1986), 574*; on MT's Moscow visit (1987), 580–81

cartoonists, newspaper, 585‡, 585

Carttiss, Michael (1938–; educated Great Yarmouth Technical High School and Goldsmiths' College, London University; Conservative MP for Great Yarmouth, 1983–97), 906

Casey, John (1939–; educated St Brendan's College, Bristol and King's College, Cambridge; lecturer, Cambridge University, and Fellow of Gonville and Caius College; founder (with Roger Scruton), Conservative Philosophy Group, 1975), 767

Cash, Bill, 943

Castrol (oil company), 79

'Catherine Place conspiracy', 893–4, 894*, 894†, 896, 897, 898

Catholic Church, 11, 51†, 51, 309, 315*, 315

Catto Jr, Henry (1930–2011; US Ambassador to the UK, 1989–91; Director, US Information Agency, 1991–3), 828, 858

Cazenove & Co., 411*

Ceaușescu, Elena, 831*

Ceaușescu, Nicolae, 831*

Cecil, Robert (*later* 7th Marquess of Salisbury), *see* Gascoyne-Cecil, Robert

Cementation International, 440–41, 442, 796

Central Electricity Generating Board (CEGB), 380, 769, 770–71, 773

Central Policy Review Staff (CPRS), 181–2, 466†, 466, 707–8; abolished (1983), 335, 353; public spending paper (1982), 335, 336, 356

Centre for Policy Studies (CPS), 109–10, 129, 131, 146, 221

CFCs (chlorofluorocarbons), 780–81, 781†, 782*

Chamberlain, Neville, 15, 738–9

Changing Gear (pamphlet by Blue Chips, 1981), 277

Channel 4 television, 386‡, 759–60, 764

Channel Tunnel Group, 479

Channel Tunnel project, 478*, 478†, 478–80, 479*

Chaplin, Judith (1939–93; educated Wycombe Abbey and Girton College, Cambridge; special adviser to Chancellor of the Exchequer, 1988–90; head of Prime Minister's Political Office, 1990–92; Conservative MP for Newbury, 1992–3), 887, 925

Charles, Eugenia, 373

Charles, Prince of Wales (*later* King Charles III), 231, 274, 632; and Thyssen collection project, 668–9; and the environment, 781, 782; visits Hong Kong, 844

Charteris, Sir Martin (*later* Baron Charteris of Amisfield), 130

Chartres, Richard (1947–; educated Hertford Grammar School, Trinity College, Cambridge, Cuddesdon Theological College, Oxford and Lincoln Theological College; Archbishop of Canterbury's chaplain, 1980–84; Bishop of London, 1995–2017; preached the address at Lady Thatcher's funeral at St Paul's Cathedral, 17 April 2013; created Lord Chartres, 2017), 503, 962, 966

Chase Smith, Margaret, 88

Checkland, Michael (1936–; educated King Edward's Grammar School, Five Ways, Birmingham and Wadham College, Oxford; Director-General, BBC, 1987–92; knighted, 1992), 542, 762

chemical weapons, 571, 679

Cheney, Dick, 870, 965

Chequers, Buckinghamshire, 185–6, 947; Anglo-Irish summit (November 1984), 451†, 451–3, 452*; meeting on local government finances (March 1985), 468–9; meeting to plan 1987 election, 535–7, 603; seminars on Germany (1990), 816, 818–19,

825–7, 836†, 836;
MT's last visit as Prime
Minister, 908
Chernenko, Konstantin
(1911–85; General
Secretary of the
Communist Party
of the Soviet Union,
1984–5), 415, 426–7
Chernyaev, Anatoly
(1921–2017; Russian
historian and author;
principal foreign policy
adviser to Mikhail
Gorbachev, 1986–91),
428, 577, 578, 697,
698–9, 803*, 803, 805,
821†, 830†
Chevening (grace-and-
favour house), 745
Cheysson, Claude
(1920–2012; French
socialist politician;
European Commissioner,
1973–81; Foreign
Minister, 1981–4), 476,
481
Chicago, 139
Chilcot, John (1939–;
educated Brighton
College and Pembroke
College, Cambridge;
principal private
secretary to the Home
Secretary, 1978–80;
Deputy Under-Secretary,
Home Office, 1987–90;
Permanent Under-
Secretary, 1990–97;
Chairman, Iraq War
Inquiry, 2009–13;
knighted, 1994), 222,
853†
Child Poverty Action
Group, 98
Chile, 297*, 297, 676,
951*, 951–2
China, 156*, 891*, 921;
and Hong Kong,
328–32, 361–4;
MT's visit to (1982),
329–30, 330*, 332;
MT's sense of regime
as evil, 331–2; MT's
secret letter to Zhao
Ziyang (1983), 331;
economic growth,
363*, 363; Joint
Declaration (December
1984), 363–4, 407,
416, 421, 843–4, 844*,
921†, 927, 928; 'One
Country, Two Systems'
concept, 363, 364, 928;
Tiananmen Square
(June 1989), 364, 809*,
843†, 843–4, 927, 928;
and green issues, 785;
MT's private trip to
(1991), 927–8; Cultural
Revolution, 927; human
rights abuses, 927;
handover of Hong
Kong to (July 1997),
945
Chirac, Jacques, 534, 682
Christian Action, 503*
Christian Democrats,
German, 332
Christianity: Methodism
of Alfred Roberts,
9, 10–11, 33, 149;
in MT's childhood,
10–11; sacramental
aspect of, 11*, 51*;
MT seeks justifications
for capitalism,
148–9, 158; and
MT's political beliefs,
148–9, 158, 620–21,
634, 775–7; and 'There
is no such thing as
society' comment, 149,
966; and MT's refusal
of consensus, 175;
and Falklands War,
323–4; and Michael
Alison, 352†, 352–3,
353*, 618*, 639; of
Gummer, 357†, 504; of
Reagan, 365†; MT's
reaction to *Faith in the
City*, 504, 775; and
Sunday trading debate,
531–2, 844; and Brian
Griffiths, 532, 542,
620–21, 621*, 639,
762, 775; Russian
Orthodox Church,
576†, 576; MT's view
on women priests, 596;
traditional teaching
on homosexuality,
634; and national
curriculum, 639; MT's
speech to General
Assembly of the
Church of Scotland
('Sermon on the
Mound'), 775–7, 961‡,
971; church attendance
at Royal Hospital,
Chelsea, 950
Chung, Sze-yuen
(1917–2018;
Member, Hong Kong
Executive Council,
1972–80; Senior
Member, 1980–88;
adviser to Government
of People's Republic
of China on Hong
Kong affairs, 1992–6;
knighted, 1978), 362
Church of England, 6, 11,
357†, 621*, 719, 777–8,
970; *Faith in the City*
(report), 503–4, 775;
evangelical wing, 778
Church of Scotland, 775–7
Churchill, Caryl (1938–;
educated Trafalgar
School, Montreal and
Lady Margaret Hall,
Oxford; playwright;
her plays include *Cloud
Nine* (1979) and *Top
Girls* (1982)), 586
Churchill, Lord Randolph,
160
Churchill, Sir Winston:
MT's admiration for,
28*, 28, 29; election
defeat (1945), 28–9;
wartime Prime Minister,
28, 75, 127, 200, 201,
291, 315, 322, 418,
690*, 890†; at October
1946 party conference,
29–30; MT's only
meeting with (1950),
50; wins 1951 election,
55; funeral of, 80; MT
invokes for political
purposes, 127, 425; use
of 'irregulars', 237*;
'Iron Curtain' speech
(1946), 247; views
on Communism, 247,
418, 968; on doctrine
of nuclear deterrence,
425; views on Europe,
883; tax free 'gifts of
esteem', 918*; lecture
tours in USA, 921;
archives at Churchill
College, 947

Churchill – *cont'd*
Churchill College, Cambridge, 1, 946–7, 947*, 967*
Citibank Asia, 921†
City of London, 204–5; Big Bang (October 1986), 409–10, 412, 655, 768; and stock exchange reform, 410–12
Civil Aviation Authority (CAA), 405*
Civil Contingencies Unit, 229*, 229
Civil Service: rules of confidentiality, 1; traditional impartiality of, 6; and MT's Private Members' Bills, 70; and MT's early career, 76; in Education Department, 94–5, 96–7, 100, 109, 180; MT's relations with, 173, 180–81, 221, 237; MT's need for pithy/concise briefs, 180†; arrival of MT in Downing Street, 180; pay settlements, 202, 496–7; 'Rayner Scrutiny', 221*, 221; MT's dinner for the permanent secretaries, 221, 222; strike action (1981), 271, 377; and MT's 1983 election victory, 359; GCHQ dispute, 377, 378–9; and the poll tax, 475; role of Ingham and Powell, 521–2, 523; and MT's 1987 victory, 614; *see also* entries for senior officials
Clark, Alan (1928–99; educated Eton and Christ Church, Oxford; MP for Plymouth, Sutton, 1974–92, and for Kensington and Chelsea 1997–99; junior minister at Employment, at Trade and Industry and at Defence, 1983–92), 187*, 284, 288, 320, 323, 674–5; as a junior minister, 352*, 352, 818; on Lord Young, 501*; and Westland affair, 518, 520; on Wakeham's list after 1987 victory, 616*; on Rushdie, 696; on MT's unpopularity, 840, 846; and leadership contest (November 1990), 882, 885, 887, 890†, 890, 893, 899–900, 900*; on first ballot result (November 1990), 892; and 'Catherine Place conspiracy', 893, 894†, 896; individual session with MT (21 November 1990), 899–900, 900*; offers himself as MT's 'ghost', 923
Clark, George, 124
Clark, Senator Joseph, 88
Clark, Judge William (1931–2013; Chief of Staff to Governor Reagan, Sacramento, 1966–9; Justice, Supreme Court of California, 1973–81; US Deputy Secretary of State, 1981; National Security Advisor, 1982–3; US Secretary of Interior, 1983–5), 246, 247*, 248, 308, 319*, 334, 448
Clarke, Colin, 395–6
Clarke, Kenneth (1940–; educated Nottingham High School and Gonville and Caius College, Cambridge; Conservative MP for Rushcliffe, 1970–2019; Paymaster-General and Minister for Employment, 1985–7; Chancellor of the Duchy of Lancaster and Minister for Trade and Industry, 1987–8; Secretary of State for Health, 1988–90; for Education and Science, 1990–92; for Home Department, 1992–3; Chancellor of the Exchequer, 1993–7; Lord Chancellor and Secretary of State for Justice, 2010–12; created Lord Clarke of Nottingham, 2020): and Falklands War, 289*; as 'Cambridge mafia' member, 351†; and 1985 reshuffle, 498§, 498, 501; Paymaster-General, 501; and Wapping dispute, 526; first Cabinet post at DTI, 618, 630; and MT's inner-city policy, 630–31, 632; as not 'one of us', 631; as pugilistic by nature, 631, 648, 899; Health Secretary, 640, 648–50; and NHS crisis, 647; 'Working for Patients' White Paper, 649*, 649; Education Secretary, 879–80; and leadership contest (November 1990), 895, 898, 899; alleged meeting with Tebbit (20 November 1990), 896*; individual session with MT (21 November 1990), 899; and conspiracy to remove MT, 913; leadership contest (1997), 945–6; leadership contest (2001), 954
Clarridge, Duane (1932–2016; served in a number of positions in the CIA, 1955–87; Chief, Latin America Division, 1981–4), 371
Cleese, John, 868†, 868
Clegg, Hugh, Pay Comparability Commission, 175, 195, 196
climate change, 182*, 182, 729†, 729, 778–81, 779†; 'Saving the Ozone Layer Conference' (London 1989), 781†, 781; MT presses USA on, 781–2,

785–6; Downing Street seminar on (April 1989), 782; MT's address to UN General Assembly, 783–4; loss of Antarctic ice, 783, 784; global temperature rise predictions, 784*, 784–5; MT's views on in later life, 786, 953*
Clinton, Bill (1946–; Governor of Arkansas, 1979–81 and 1983–92; President of the United States of America, 1993–2001), 4, 932*, 932
Clive of India, 326
Clough, Arthur Hugh, 690*, 690
CNN (Cable News Network), 764
coal industry: and oil price shock (1973), 106; and February 1974 election, 107–8; MT accumulates coal stocks, 191*, 229–30, 380; MT prepares for confrontation with miners, 191*, 229–30, 377, 380–81, 383; and oil shock (1979), 191*; pit closures, 229*, 230; MT concedes to NUM (February 1981), 230–31, 234, 379–80; Strategy for Coal, 230; secret 'hit list' allegations, 381*, 392; after 1984–5 strike, 396; and electricity privatization, 772; and climate change, 779; and green issues, 784; *see also* miners' strike (1984–5); National Coal Board (NCB)
Coalition government (2010–15), 957
Cockerell, Michael, 123
Cockfield, Arthur (1916–2007; educated Dover Grammar School and LSE; Director of Statistics and Intelligence, Board of Inland Revenue, 1945–52; Managing Director, Boots, 1961–7; Chairman, Price Commission, 1973–7; Secretary of State for Trade, 1982–3; Chancellor of the Duchy of Lancaster, 1983–4; Vice-President, European Commission, 1985–8; created Lord Cockfield, 1978), 150, 176*, 402, 405, 482
Coe, Jim, 539
Coke, Sir Edward, 327
Colchester, Essex, 35–7, 38, 42, 44
Cold War: ending of, 5, 754, 755–6, 799, 802, 803†, 803–4, 807–11, 836; and Reagan, 5, 238†, 241–9, 364–5, 368, 414–32, 562–9, 614–15, 676, 680–90; MT's relations with/ views on Soviet Union, 26*, 90, 134–5, 142–3, 191, 236–49, 333, 364–9, 414–32, 572–82, 697–700, 968 (*see also under* Gorbachev, Mikhail); détente, 134–5, 142, 236–42, 968; MT's speeches as Leader of Opposition, 134–5, 142–3; INF deployment in Europe, 238–9, 240, 242, 294, 332, 333, 346, 364, 372, 373, 414, 505; MT's desire to win, 238; Soviet invasion of Afghanistan (1979), 239–41, 240†, 419, 577, 683; Reagan/MT's language/tone over Soviet Union, 241–2; Reagan's 'zero option' stance, 243*, 243, 563, 566, 576; West's use of 'economic warfare', 245–6, 246*, 346; Reagan's Royal Gallery speech (1982), 247†, 247–8, 319†, 319; Churchill's 'Iron Curtain' speech (1946), 247; US Latin America policy, 294; and US response to Falklands, 294, 319; and MT's Falklands rhetoric, 317, 323; MT's 'peace with freedom and justice' mantra, 317, 968; Geneva summit (November 1985), 429, 431–2, 562; and 'PoCo' in Europe, 484; Cuban forces in Angola, 545, 791; Reykjavik summit (1986), 562, 565*, 565–9, 566*, 571, 572, 680–81; MT's ascendancy in late-Reagan era, 614–15, 676, 688, 689; and Bruges Speech, 673, 968; Bush's policy on, 702, 703–5; and British intelligence services, 706–15; fall of Berlin Wall, 754, 807†, 807–8, 842; anxieties over southern Africa, 789–90, 799; South African analogy, 797; fall of Communism in Eastern bloc, 803–4
Coleridge, Nicholas, 515*
Coles, John (1937–; educated Magdalen College School, Brackley and Magdalen College, Oxford; private secretary to the Prime Minister, 1981–4; Ambassador to Jordan, 1984–8; High Commissioner to Australia, 1988–91; Permanent Under-Secretary and head of Diplomatic Service, 1994–7; knighted, 1989): and Falklands War, 285, 287, 292, 318†, 322, 323; and Hong Kong, 329; and Kohl's visit, 332; and MT's insecurity, 356; on Grenada, 372, 373; on King Hussein, 434; Ambassador to Jordan, 436; on working for MT, 592–3
College of Europe, Bruges, 671, 673

Collingwood, Evelyn, 173–4
Collins, Christopher (1960–; educated Glyn Grammar School, Epsom and Exeter College, Oxford, 1978–81; Nuffield College, Oxford, 1981–8; lecturer in PPE, Lincoln College, Oxford, 1988–96; assisted Lady Thatcher in writing her memoirs, 1992–5; edited Mrs Thatcher's *Complete Public Statements* (1995–8); editor, www.margaretthatcher.org, 2000–), 389‡, 923, 930, 947, 952–3
Collins, Michael (Irish Republican leader), 458
Colville, Sir John, 237*
Comer, Tony, 378
Common Agricultural Policy (CAP), 211, 477, 663†, 663, 872, 874
Commonwealth, 48–9, 49*, 163, 193–5; and Falklands War, 297, 315; and apartheid South Africa, 546, 548–51, 553, 554–9; MT as suspicious of, 548–50; length of meetings, 548; Eminent Persons Group (EPG) to South Africa, 550–51, 552, 553–4; London 'review conference' on South Africa (August 1986), 554–5, 559, 560, 561
Commonwealth Heads of Government Meetings (CHOGMs): Lusaka (1979), 193, 194–5; Nassau (1985), 548–51, 551†; Kuala Lumpur (1989), 750, 751, 759, 793†, 793–4, 807; Vancouver (1987), 787–8
Community Programme, 492
Confederation of British Industry (CBI), 196, 204, 228
Conference on Security and Cooperation in Europe (CSCE), 822*, 831, 832, 833, 834, 880, 885, 887, 888–9, 891–2, 894–5, 896
Confucius, 971
Congdon, Tim (1951–; educated Colchester Royal Grammar School and St John's and Nuffield Colleges, Oxford; economist. On economics staff, *The Times*, 1973–6; economist, L. Messel and Co., 1976–86; founder, Managing Director, Lombard Street Research, 1989–2001, Chief Economist, 2001–5), 198†, 654†, 654
Connolly, Bernard (1949–; educated Xaverian College, Manchester and Worcester College, Oxford; head of the unit responsible for the EMS and monetary policies at the European Commission, from which he was sacked following publication of his book *The Rotten Heart of Europe: The Dirty War for Europe's Money* (1995)), 672
Connolly, James, 256†, 256
Conqueror, HMS (British submarine), 304–5
Conquest, Robert (1917–2015; educated Winchester and Magdalen College, Oxford; author of *The Great Terror*, *The Harvest of Sorrow*, poet. Though British, Conquest lived for many years in California as a Fellow of the Hoover Institution.), 134, 236–7, 239, 240, 574*, 574‡, 577†, 737*, 808
Conservative Central Office, 61, 62, 616–17, 622; MT's references (1949), 39–40; MT's 'Let Our Children Grow Tall' speech, 137*, 137; Reece, Bell and McAlpine team, 165; MT thanks staff at, 908
Conservative Party: and 1935 general election, 14; conference (1946, Blackpool), 29–30; 39–45 Group of Essex Tories, 36, 40; conference (1948, Llandudno), 38–9; leadership contest (1975), 54, 121–2, 123–7, 956; MT's growing stature in, 54; MT seeks a constituency (1956–8), 62–4; manifesto (1959), 69; conference (1961, Brighton), 73–4; conference (1963, Blackpool), 77; leader 'emerges' by consultation, 77; leadership contest (1965), 81; conference (1969, Brighton), 84; conference (1967, Brighton), 85–6; Selsdon Park Hotel conference, 92–3, 111; manifesto (1970), 93, 95, 102, 132; 1922 Committee, 103†, 109, 114–15, 121, 128, 288–9, 289*, 388–9, 518, 621, 671, 732, 747, 748, 880–81; manifesto (1974, October), 112–14; Home's review of leadership contest rules, 115, 120*, 120, 121; 'knights of the shires', 122, 128; conference (1975, Blackpool), 140–41; *The Right Approach*, 145–6, 160; conference (1976, Brighton), 145; decline in Scotland, 160*, 161, 612, 618–19, 619†; conference (1978, Brighton), 160, 169; divisions in Scottish party, 161; manifesto

(1979), 162, 172, 251, 253, 337*, 337; manifesto (1978, draft for assumed autumn election), 167–8; conference (1979, Blackpool), 209, 239; conference (1980, Brighton), 227, 241; 'Blue Chips' group, 277†, 277, 890; conference (1981, Blackpool), 277; conference (1982, Brighton), 325, 336, 339; business donors, 341–2, 404†; manifesto (1983), 342, 343, 344, 400, 463–4, 606, 607; triumphalism after 1983 victory, 348; 'Cambridge mafia' MPs, 351†; element of anti-Semitism in, 351, 500; conference (1983, Blackpool), 358–9, 360, 368; conference (1984, Brighton), 391–2, 448–50, 466, 589*, 604†, 604, 855, 951; conference (1985, Blackpool), 432, 501, 502; Centre Forward grouping, 495; No Turning Back group (NTB), 496*, 496, 893, 899; conference (1986, Bournemouth), 543, 567; Bow Group, 595; manifesto (1987), 604–5, 651; conference (1987, Blackpool), 622, 624–5, 631*, 631, 635; conference (1989, Blackpool), 749; leadership contest (1989), 755–7, 810, 813, 838, 880, 913; conference (1988, Brighton), 779–80; conference (1990, Bournemouth), 868*, 868†, 868, 869–70; leadership contest (1990), 880–81, 884–92, 891†, 893–903, 909; leadership contest rules (1990), 881;

'stop Heseltine' moves (November 1990), 885, 891, 894, 896, 897, 899, 900, 904, 907*, 907; 'Catherine Place conspiracy', 893–4, 894*, 894†, 896, 897, 898; the 92 Group, 901; second ballot result (27 November 1990), 909; conference (1991, Blackpool), 928; 1992 victory, 929–30; manifesto (1992), 929; leadership contest (1997), 945–6; conference (1999, Blackpool), 952; leadership contest (2001), 954; leadership contest rules (2001), 954
Conservative Philosophy Group, 148
Conservative Political Centre Lecture, 86, 87–8
Conservative Research Department, 110, 118, Con. Research Depto, 130, 146, 150, 156, 164*, 181, 348
Conventional Forces in Europe (CFE) Agreement (1990), 889
Cook, Beryl, 39, 54, 61
Cooke, Alistair, 689*
Cooper, Lady Diana, 13*
Cooper, Frank (1922–2002; educated Manchester Grammar School and Pembroke College, Oxford; Permanent Under-Secretary, Northern Ireland Office, 1973–6; MOD, 1976–82; knighted, 1974), 222, 291
Cooper, Jilly, 147
Cooper, Roger, 695*
Corbett, Robert, 252*
Coronation Street (TV programme), 133
corporal punishment, 71–2, 935*
Cosgrave, Patrick, 140*
Costa Méndez, Nicanor, 284*, 296, 297

Costello, Elvis, 584–5
Counter-Inflation (Temporary Measures) Bill (1972), 105
Courtiour, Roger, 707
Coventry, HMS, 314
Covid-19 pandemic, 6
Cox, Caroline (1937–; educated Channing School and London University; staff nurse, Edgware General Hospital, 1960; Director, Nursing Education Research Unit, Chelsea College, London University, 1977–84; created Baroness Cox, 1982), 639
Cradock, Percy (1923–2010; educated Alderman Wraith Grammar School, Spennymoor and St John's College, Cambridge; Ambassador to People's Republic of China, 1978–83; leader of UK team in negotiations over Hong Kong, 1982–3; Deputy Under-Secretary of State, FCO, supervising Hong Kong negotiations, 1984; Prime Minister's foreign policy adviser, 1984–92; knighted, 1980): and China, 328, 329, 330, 331–2, 361–4, 843–4, 844*, 928; as MT's foreign policy adviser, 416; as Chairman of JIC, 533*, 682, 686, 697, 699†, 720; and Soviet Union, 574*, 682, 686, 697, 699†, 803, 806–7, 829, 831, 833; and Bush–MT relations, 704; intelligence arrangements in Northern Ireland, 726–7; and Soviet biological weapons, 806–7, 833; and MT's health, 813*
Craig, Sir David, 866*, 866

Craig, Gordon (1913–2005 Professor of History, Princeton University, 1950–61; J. E. Wallace Sterling Professor of Humanities, Stanford University, 1961–79 (Emeritus), Chair), 826
Cranwell (RAF base in Lincolnshire), 438*, 438
Crawford, Cynthia ('Crawfie'), 184, 610, 732*, 969; and MT's clothing, 179, 186†, 575, 597, 759, 760, 905, 959; and Brighton bombing, 449–50; and MT's visit to Moscow, 575, 576; on nature of MT's marriage, 594; in Paris with MT, 888, 892, 895; helps MT pack, 908; serves MT after her departure from office, 918, 919, 948, 950, 959; and MT's will, 967*
Craxi, Benedetto 'Bettino' (1934–2000; head of the Italian Socialist Party, 1976–93; Prime Minister of Italy 1983–7; ended his days in judicial exile in Tunisia, under suspicion of handling bribes worth more than £100 million), 485
Critchley, Sir Julian, 289*
Croatia, 931
Crocker, Chester, 789, 791, 792
Crockford's Clerical Directory, 621*
Cromwell, Oliver, 447
Cromwell, Thomas, 2
Cropper, Peter (1927–2020; educated Hitchin Grammar School and Gonville and Caius College, Cambridge; special adviser to Chief Secretary to the Treasury, 1979–82; to Chancellor of the Exchequer, 1984–8; Conservative Research Department, 1951–3, 1975–9, Director, 1982–4), 348
Crosby by-election, 279
Crossmaglen, Northern Ireland, 207
Crossman, Richard (1907–74), 75
Crowder, Sir John, 64
Crowe, William, 571
Cuba: and Falklands War, 296; and Grenada, 370; forces in Angola, 545, 791
Cubbon, Brian (1928–2015; educated Bury Grammar School and Trinity College, Cambridge; Permanent Under-Secretary, NIO, 1976–9; Home Office, 1979–88; knighted, 1977), 382
Cuckney, John (1925–2008; educated Shrewsbury and St Andrews University; Chairman of Westland, 1985–9; knighted, 1978; created Lord Cuckney of Millbank, 1995), 506, 507, 508, 509–10, 511–12, 516
Cullen, Andrew (MT's nephew), 47
Cullen, Morton (MT's nephew), 51
Cullen, Muriel (née Roberts; MT's sister): and birth of MT, 9; on her upbringing, 11, 12; visit of penfriend, 15–16; education at KGGS, 16; visits MT at Oxford, 31; boyfriends, 38; Cullen courts, 45–7; engagement to Willie, 46–7; marries Willie (1950), 47; birth of children, 51, 57, 58; on sacrifices of her parents, 51; relations with MT, 58, 92†, 92‡, 92; on father's removal as alderman, 62; death of father, 92†, 92‡, 92; Essex farm of, 730‡
Cullen, William: courts MT, 40–41, 42, 44–6; courts Muriel, 45–7; Essex farm of, 45, 51, 730‡; engagement to Muriel, 46–7; marries Muriel (1950), 47
Cunningham, Sir Knox, 77
Currie, Edwina (1946–; educated Liverpool Institute High School for Girls and St Anne's College, Oxford; Conservative MP for Derbyshire South, 1983–97; Parliamentary Under-Secretary of State (Health), DHSS, later Department of Health, 1986–8), 730†, 730–31
Curteis, Ian, *The Falklands Play*, 586
Curwen, Christopher (1929–2013; educated Sherborne and Sidney Sussex College, Cambridge; Chief, MI6, 1985–8; knighted, 1986), 725, 726
Cust family, 13*, 13
Cyprus, 436
Czechoslovakia, 811*

Daily Express, 71, 119–20, 660
Daily Mail, 118, 133, 148, 166, 601, 615, 862, 953‡, 953
Daily Mirror, 133, 166*, 173–4, 581, 646
Daily Telegraph, 47, 93, 130, 148, 175, 279, 310, 711, 833, 881, 930, 954*, 955, 965§; Charles Moore edits, 1, 2, 954; and MT's leadership challenge, 123*, 123–4; ownership of, 138†, 658†; as main line to MT's natural supporters, 188; on Foot Cenotaph incident, 279†; political cartoons in, 585‡, 585; Carol Thatcher sacked by, 594†, 948*; and leadership contest (November 1990), 886–7, 891

Dalyell of the Binns, Sir
Thomas ('Tam')
(1932–2017; educated
Eton and King's
College, Cambridge;
Labour MP for West
Lothian, 1962–83; for
Linlithgow, 1983–2005;
Member, European
Parliament, 1975–9.
He never called himself
Thomas nor used his
title), 517, 712
Dam, Kenneth, 375–6
Darlington by-election
(March 1983), 342
Darroch, Kim, 874
Dartford: MT as
candidate for, 14,
41, 42–4, 46, 48–50,
53–5, 937; Conservative
Association, 39–40,
41–3, 49–50; Rotary
Ladies Day, 44*;
election result (1950),
49; the Woollcotts
(MT's landlords), 50*;
Free Church Federal
Council, 54†; election
result (1951), 55
Dartford Chronicle, 54
Davies, J. R. M., 612
Davies, John (1916–79;
educated St Edward's
School, Oxford;
Conservative MP
for Knutsford,
1970–78; Director-
General, CBI, 1965–9;
Secretary of State for
Trade and Industry,
1970–72; Chancellor of
the Duchy of Lancaster,
1972–4; Shadow
Foreign Secretary,
1976–8), 155
Davis, David, 890‡
Davis, F., 85
Davy, Sir Humphry, 327,
590
Dayton Accords (1995), 932
De Gaulle, Charles, 85*,
744
De Klerk, F. W. (Frederik
Willem) (1936–2021;
State President of South
Africa, 1989–94; Deputy
President, 1994–6;
winner, Nobel Peace
Prize (with Nelson
Mandela), 1993): on
MT's view of apartheid,
546; as National Party
centrist, 786, 787, 791;
becomes National
Party leader, 791; first
Chequers visit, 792–3;
takes full control in
South Africa, 793;
release of Mandela,
797–8; grand tour of
Europe (summer 1990),
798–9; negotiations
with ANC, 798–9;
second Chequers visit,
798–9, 799*;
appreciation of MT,
801; wins Nobel Peace
Prize, 801; and Iraqi
invasion of Kuwait,
863*; at MT's funeral,
965
De Klerk, Marike, 799*
De la Billière, Peter (1934–;
educated Harrow and
Staff College; Director,
SAS, and Commander,
SAS Group, 1978–82;
Commander, British
Forces Middle East,
1990–91; knighted,
1991), 222, 865†,
865–6
Deakins, Eric, 66
Death on the Rock
(Thames Television
documentary), 723†,
723‡, 723
Deaver, Michael
(1938–2007; educated
San José State College;
aide to Ronald Reagan,
1967–85 (known for
arranging memorable
photographic
backdrops for his
public appearances)),
345, 373
Deedes, William (W. F.)
(1913–2007; educated
Harrow; Conservative
MP for Ashford,
1950–74; Minister
without Portfolio,
1962–4; Editor, *Daily
Telegraph*, 1974–86;
created Lord Deedes,
1986), 54, 70, 116†,
169, 228, 592, 732*;
editor of *Daily
Telegraph*, 123*, 585‡,
588
defence policies: Labour
Party, 78, 142, 345,
543, 600–601, 609*,
609, 703; Heath
rescues Rolls-Royce,
102; 'Iron Lady' label,
142–3; Kensington
town hall speech
(1976), 142; 1979 Tory
manifesto, 173; cuts in
MT's first term, 229,
244†, 283, 286, 585‡;
Trident missile system,
244*, 244, 564, 568,
569; and end of Cold
War, 802–6, 807–35,
836–7, 926; *see also*
nuclear weapons;
Strategic Defense
Initiative (SDI, Star
Wars)
defence procurement:
arms sales to
Middle East, 437*,
437–8, 439–40, 440*;
European National
Armaments Directors
(NADs), 507, 508,
509; and Malaysia,
794–7; *see also*
Westland affair
Deidesheim (Rhineland
Palatinate), 701
Delors, Jacques
(1925–2023; Minister
of the Economy and
Finance, France,
1981–3; Minister of
Economy, Finance
and Budget, 1983–4;
President, European
Commission, 1985–95):
becomes European
Commission President,
481–2, 482*; support
for single currency,
486, 733; and extended
QMV, 488, 665;
centralizing, socialist
vision of, 664–5, 671;
MT's resentment
against, 664–5, 671,
672, 673–4, 870*,
870; and EMU,
666*, 666, 733–5,

Delors, Jacques – *cont'd*
740, 754, 810, 851, 870, 872–3, 924–5, 928–9; addresses TUC conference (1988), 672†, 672, 673; and Bruges Speech, 672–3, 674*; three-stage process for EMU, 733–4, 740, 741, 742, 754, 851, 870, 872*, 872–3, 924–5, 928–9; and Howe, 734; interview on European institutions, 873, 875
Democratic Unionist Party, 251–2, 719
Deng Xiaoping (1904–97; Leader of People's Republic of China, 1978–92. He never held formal offices that reflected his power, but was in complete control), 329–30, 332, 362, 363–4
Derx, Donald, 181
Desert Shield, Operation, 859–60
Desert Storm, Operation, 917
deutschmark, 486, 666; 'shadowing' of, 646, 653–4, 655, 656–8, 660, 670, 934*; DM3 rate, 653, 656, 657–8, 660, 661; and timing of UK's ERM entry, 869
devolution issue, 160–62, 171
Diamond, Jack, 82–3
Diana, Princess, 231, 274, 643, 844
Dickens, Charles: *Great Expectations*, 68; *David Copperfield*, 361, 363, 473*
Dicks, Terence 'Terry' (1937–2020; educated LSE and Oxford; Conservative MP for Hayes and Harlington, 1983–97), 884
Diego Garcia atoll, 861
Dilks, David (1938–; educated Royal Grammar School, Worcester, Hertford College and St Antony's College, Oxford; Vice-Chancellor of Hull University, 1991–9; biographer of Neville Chamberlain), 149
Dimbleby, David, 612
'Ding Dong! The Witch is Dead' (song), 964
Dobbs, Michael (1948–; educated Christ Church, Oxford and Fletcher School of Law and Diplomacy, Tufts University; government special adviser, 1981–7; chief of staff, Conservative Party, 1986–7; Deputy Chairman, Saatchi & Saatchi, 1983–6, 1988–91; Joint Deputy Chairman, Conservative Party, 1994–5; author of *House of Cards* and other political novels; created Lord Dobbs, 2010), 176, 179–80, 499, 500, 535–6, 537, 538, 602–3, 610; *House of Cards* (novel), 610*
Dock Labour Scheme (DLS), 766
Docklands, London, 411†, 411, 502, 632
Doctor Who (television programme), 586–7
Dodds, Norman, 43, 49, 55
Doherty, Joseph, 534–5
Dominica, 373
Donnelly, Christopher (1946–; educated Cardinal Langley, Lancashire and University of Manchester; Director, Soviet Studies Research Centre, Sandhurst, 1979–89; special adviser for Central and Eastern European Affairs to the Secretary-General of NATO, 1989–2003), 366*, 574*, 685
Donoughue, Bernard (1934–; [educated Northampton Grammar School, Lincoln College and Nuffield College, Oxford; senior policy adviser to Prime Minister, 1974–9; created Lord Donoughue, 1985), 107, 169, 170, 173, 177*; on MT in 1964 election, 78–9; on MT in October 1974 election, 113; on sense of collapse in Britain, 115*; on Conservative Party leadership contest, 124*; on MT facing Wilson in Commons, 142
Dorchester Hotel, London, 33
Dorneywood (Chancellor's residence), 745
Dorr, Noel, 451
Dostoevsky, Fyodor, *The Possessed*, 147
Douglas, Leigh, 534
Douglas-Home, Charles, 429, 525
Douglas-Home, Alec (1903–1995; educated Eton and Christ Church College, Oxford; became 14th Earl of Home, 1951; Secretary of State for Commonwealth Relations, 1955–60; Leader of the House of Lords, 1957-60; Lord President of the Council, 1957–60; Foreign Secretary, 1960-63; disclaimed his peerage, 1963; Prime Minister, 1963–64; Foreign Secretary, 1970–74; created Lord Home of the Hirsel, 1974): 77–8, 78*; steps down as leader, 81; reviews leadership election system, 115, 120*, 120, 121; and MT's leadership challenge, 125; dislike of Soviet Communism, 135*, 135; popular caricature of, 156;

INDEX

advice to Carrington
over resignation, 289†
Dover, port of, 766
drugs/narcotics, 131*, 536‡,
536
Du Cann, Edward
(1924–2017; educated
Woodbridge School
and St John's College,
Oxford; Conservative
MP for Taunton,
1956–87; Chairman,
Conservative Party,
1965–7; Chairman,
1922 Committee,
1972–84. A leading
figure in the City,
he was ultimately
discredited by his
controversial financial
record): Chairman of
1922 Committee, 103,
114, 115; in opposition,
109, 114, 115; and
party leadership, 109,
114, 115, 119*, 119,
120–21; business
career, 119*, 120
Duberstein, Ken, 677, 678,
684, 689
Dublin Castle, 256
Dubrovnik, 931
Duddy, Brendan, 255†,
261†, 261, 727
Duff, Antony (Arthur)
(1920–2000; educated
Royal Naval College,
Dartmouth; High
Commissioner, Nairobi,
1972–5; Deputy
Governor, Southern
Rhodesia,
1979–80; Deputy
Secretary, Cabinet
Office, 1980–84;
Director-General, MI5,
1985–7; knighted,
1973), 706, 713, 715
Duguid, Andrew, 235
Dukakis, Michael
(1933–; Governor,
Commonwealth
of Massachusetts,
1975–9 and 1983–90;
Democratic nominee
for the presidency of the
USA, 1988), 688, 691‡
Dulwich, 596–7, 911, 917
Dumas, Roland, 482*

Duncan Smith, Iain
(1954–; educated
HMS *Conway* (Cadet
School), Sandhurst and
Dunchurch College
of Management;
Conservative MP
for Chingford,
1992–7; for Chingford
and Woodford Green,
1997–; Leader of the
Conservative Party
and Leader of the
Opposition, 2001–3;
Secretary of State for
Work and Pensions,
2010–16), 934, 954
Dunlop, Andrew (1959–;
educated Trinity
College, Glenalmond
and Edinburgh
University; No. 10
Policy Unit, 1988–90;
created Lord Dunlop,
2015), 880
Dunn, Lydia (1940–;
Member, Legislative
Council of Hong
Kong, 1976–88; Senior
Member, 1985–8;
Member, Executive
Council, 1982–95;
Senior Member,
1988–95; created
Baroness Dunn, 1990),
364, 843–4
Dwek, Raymond, 643*

Eagleburger, Lawrence
(1930–2011; diplomat;
Under-Secretary of
State for Political
Affairs, 1982–4;
Deputy Secretary of
State, 1989–92;
Secretary of State,
1992–3; received
honorary knighthood
1990), 370
Eames, Robert 'Robin'
(1937–; educated
Methodist College,
Belfast, Queen's
University, Belfast and
Trinity College, Dublin;
Archbishop of Armagh
and Primate of All
Ireland, 1986–2006;
created Lord Eames,

1995; OM, 2007), 719,
720, 725
East Germany, 802, 803–4,
806, 808, 809, 815,
820–21; post-Cold War
national identity, 811*,
811; free elections
(March 1990), 820,
823*, 825
Eastbourne by-election, 855,
868, 870
Easter Rising (1916), 256†,
256
Easton Neston,
Northamptonshire
house, 914–15
Economic and Monetary
Union (EMU),
486–7, 662, 665–6,
734*; Delors' three-
stage process, 733–4,
740, 741, 742, 754,
851, 870, 872*, 872–3,
924–5, 928–9; Delors
Committee report
(1989), 733–5, 754;
Strasbourg Council
(1989), 810, 812,
842; Mitterrand–Kohl
agreement on, 817;
Ridley's *Spectator*
interview, 835–6, 836*,
852, 855; Commons
rejects Delors version
of, 841*; Britain's
competing currencies
plan, 842, 847; IGC
called for at Strasbourg,
842, 848; 'hard ecu'
proposal, 848*, 848,
851, 876, 883, 955;
Major's national 'opt-
in' idea, 848, 851; MT
rejects, 851, 932–3; and
UK's entry to ERM,
869; Rome Council
(1990), 872–6, 873*;
and Howe's resignation
statement, 883; *see
also* Exchange Rate
Mechanism (ERM)
economic policy: loss of
faith in ruling elites,
5–6; free market
philosophy, 5, 82, 102,
110*, 110–11, 138,
329, 531–2, 620, 844;
free-trade doctrine,
5, 41, 874*, 874;

economic policy – *cont'd*
Keynesian, 27–8, 75*, 89, 110, 198, 503; White Paper on Employment Policy (1944), 27–8, 75*, 75; Ministry for Reconstruction and Development, 28; Imperial Preference, 41*, 41, 48; MT's housewife analogies, 41, 43, 83, 224; devaluation of the pound (1949), 43; expansionary under Macmillan, 65, 76; incomes policies, 76, 86, 102, 104, 105, 106, 144, 145, 151, 167, 168, 169–71; MT favours financial stringency in early 1960s, 77; Resale Price Maintenance, 78†, 78; post-war consensus, 78; Wilson government (1964–70), 82–3, 102; devaluation of the pound (1967), 85; 'growth' becomes key, 86; Good Samaritan image, 87, 149; sterling floats freely (1972), 103; Heath's three-day week, 107; Labour government (1974–9), 117, 122–3, 144–5, 165, 167, 168–70, 197–8, 216, 337†; public spending control, 173, 183, 195, 196*, 197, 200, 202, 203*, 203, 227–9, 235, 271–2, 334, 355–6; in MT's first term, 195–206, 215–21, 224–5, 234–5, 267–8, 334–5; independent central bank concept, 198†, 493, 654†, 906; 'Wets' and 'Dries', 205–6, 222–3, 223*, 228, 270–74, 276–8; MT's 'Inner Group' on, 216–17, 222–3; Chequers seminar (January 1981), 235, 267; Dry narrative of

economic recovery, 280; in MT's second term, 355–6, 360; total public spending never cut under MT, 356; Big Bang (October 1986), 409–10, 412, 655, 768; Lawson boom of late-1980s, 413; run on the pound (1985), 490; in MT's third term, 646, 651, 653–62, 668–71, 734–5, 738–43, 749–54, 768–74, 839–43, 847–52, 867–70, 934*; balance of payments figures (May 1988), 669*, 669–70
Economist, 118, 126*, 335, 782
Eden, Anthony, 1st Earl of Avon, 59, 65, 286, 291, 348
Eden, Clarissa, Countess of Avon, 59†, 59
Edinburgh, Duke of, 965
education: private, 71*, 71; Butler Education Act (1944), 75*, 91, 638; comprehensivization of secondary schools, 90–92, 95–6; Labour Circulars 10/66 and 10/67, 91, 95; local authority control over, 91, 95, 96; Beloff's proposal for independent university, 93; MT's attitude to, 94; 'Black Papers' opposing progressive education, 97†; school milk controversy, 98†, 98–100, 640; Assisted Places Scheme, 197, 336*; education vouchers idea, 335, 336–7; student loans, 335; national curriculum introduced, 607, 622, 636–9, 640; school opt-outs from LEAs, 607, 608, 636, 635–9*, 639, 640; GERBIL (the Great Education Reform Bill), 621, 635–6*, 636–9, 640; MT's third term reform programme,

621, 622; 'independent state schools', 622; Baker reforms, 630; City Technology Colleges (CTCs), 632*, 636*, 636, 640; issue of 'promotion' of homosexuality in schools, 633–4; 'Section 28' of Local Government Act, 633–4; MT's concern for 'the bank of the mind', 635*, 635; 'grant-maintained' (GM) schools, 636, 640; contradiction at heart of MT's reforms, 637–8; national curriculum and religion, 638–9; in Scotland, 639–40
Edwardes, Michael (1930–2019; educated St Andrew's College, Grahamstown, South Africa and Rhodes University, Grahamstown; Chairman, BL (formerly British Leyland), 1977–82, 1984–5; knighted, 1979, 219–20, 220*
Edwards, Madeline, 20, 21, 23
Edwards, Nicholas (1934–2018; educated Westminster and Trinity College, Cambridge; Conservative MP for Pembrokeshire, 1970–87; Opposition spokesman on Welsh affairs, 1975–9; Secretary of State for Wales, 1979–87; created Lord Crickhowell, 1987), 225
eggs, salmonella scare over, 730†, 730–31
Egypt, 433, 435, 437*, 858
Eksund, MV, 720
Electricians' Union (EETPU), 525
electricity industry, 402, 409, 768, 769–74, 770*, 771*, 784, 889*

INDEX 997

Eliot, George, *Silas Marner*, 10*
Elizabeth, Queen (Queen Mother), 556, 846, 939
Elizabeth I, Queen, 625
Elizabeth II, Queen, 44, 73, 130*, 130, 531, 658, 705, 923, 945*; accession of, 56; MT 'kisses hands' (May 1979), 178, 179; MT's anxieties about correct behaviour, 194†, 194, 793†; at CHOGM in Lusaka (1979), 194; Reagan's visit to Britain (June 1982), 247; and Falklands War, 290, 301, 320, 324; as head of state in Grenada, 370, 371, 372, 373; visit to Jordan (1984), 378‡; at Nassau CHOGM (1985), 549; anxieties over Commonwealth–UK divisions, 554–5, 556–7, 558, 560, 801; Desmond Tutu's letter to, 555; MT's relations with, 557–8, 560; MT's weekly audiences with, 557–8; *Sunday Times* report of rift with MT, 557; at CHOGM in Kuala Lumpur (1989), 793†; and MT's resignation, 903†, 903, 905; awards MT Order of Merit, 910‡, 910, 911, 918; awards MT Order of the Garter, 939–40; attends MT's 70th-birthday dinner, 940; attends MT's 80th-birthday dinner, 958; expresses wish to attend MT's funeral, 961, 964; attends MT's funeral, 965, 966*, 966
Elton, Ben, 586
Emerson, Ralph Waldo, 967
Enders, Thomas, 283–4, 284*
Endurance, HMS, 283, 284
energy prices, 6, 191, 202
English, David (1931–98; Editor, *Daily Mail*, 1971–92; Editor, *Mail on Sunday*, 1982; Editor in Chief, Associated Newspapers, 1989–98, knighted, 1982), 166, 615
English-Speaking Union (ESU), 89†, 158
environmental/green issues: MT's speech to Royal Society, 778–9, 779†, 786; conferences on the ozone layer, 781–2, 785; and economic realities, 783, 784; 'sustainable development', 783, 784; global emissions targets, 784–5, 785*; MISC 141 Cabinet committee, 784; *see also* climate change; global warming
Equal Opportunities Commission, 150*
Equatorial Guinea, 960
Erith Observer, 41
Ethiopia, 577
European, 934
European Central Bank, proposals for, 666*, 666, 671, 672, 733
European Commission, 130, 191, 836*; Jenkins as President, 163*, 209; and European integration, 209, 481–2, 872–3, 933; Delors appointed to head, 481–2, 482*; appointment of Lord Cockfield, 482; Delors on role of, 873, 875
European Convention on the Suppression of Terrorism (ECST, 1977), 455, 457, 460*, 460, 720–21
European Council, Delors on role of, 873, 875
European Council meetings: Strasbourg (1979), 190–91; Dublin (1979), 191, 210–11; Maastricht (1981), 257; Stuttgart (1983), 353–4; Dublin (1984), 453; Milan (1985), 455–6, 484–6; Brussels (1984), 475–6; Fontainebleau (1984), 475, 476–7, 480, 485, 663, 664; Hanover (1988), 481, 665–6, 666*, 671, 724; Madrid (1989), 481, 733, 735, 740–43, 840; Rome (1990), 481, 872–6, 873*, 877; The Hague (1986), 554, 560; London (1986), 663†, 664–5; Brussels (1987), 663; Dublin (1990), 800, 835, 851†, 851; Strasbourg (1989), 810, 812, 814†, 814–15, 842
European Court of Human Rights, 714*
European Economic Community (EEC, European Union from 1993): Britain votes to leave (2016), 6, 943, 953; MT supports leaving in post-office years, 6, 952–3; France vetoes Britain's bids to join (1963), 76, (1967) 85*; MT's position on in 1960s, 85, 89; referendum on (1975), 132–3, 135†; MT and sovereignty issue, 133, 208, 486, 662, 664, 742, 755–6, 813, 814, 836, 842, 874, 925, 930, 952–3, 969; MT's position on in 1970s, 133; Franco-German axis, 162, 163, 477, 480, 483, 485–6, 817, 835; Britain's contribution to budget, 173, 190–91, 208, 209–12, 353–4; in Tory manifesto (1979), 173; MT's position on as Prime Minister, 190–91, 208–12, 481–8, 662*, 662–6, 671†, 671–5, 672*, 725, 743, 872–6, 968; agricultural policies, 190, 211, 477, 663†, 663, 872; and Foreign Office officials, 209–10; United States

EEC – *cont'd*
of Europe concept, 209–10; Brussels deal with UK (May 1980), 211–12; principle versus advantage/influence in dealings with, 212; and Maze hunger strikes, 259; and Falklands War, 297, 303, 312; Kohl's views on unification, 332–3, 481, 484–5, 486, 810, 812, 813, 814–15; moves towards greater integration, 354*, 354, 477, 480–83, 484–8, 662, 802–3, 807, 813, 814–15, 816, 872–6; Treaty of Rome (1957), 354*, 488, 662; Solemn Declaration on European Union (1983), 354, 480–81; MT secures UK budgetary rebate, 475–8, 476*; rotating six-month presidency, 476†; Kohl–Mitterrand axis, 477, 480, 485–6, 817, 835; Single Market, 480*, 480, 482–3, 486, 487, 488, 664, 665; Genscher–Colombo Plan (1981), 480–81; MT supports Delors Commission candidature, 481–2; Single European Act (SEA, 1986), 481, 487–8, 489, 662, 665, 672, 930, 934, 935; extension of qualified majority voting (QMV), 482–3, 483*, 487, 488, 665; MT's prestige/star quality, 483; Luxembourg Compromise, 484*, 484; 'PoCo' (arrangements for political cooperation), 484–5; Luxembourg IGC (December 1985), 486–8; Howe as emissary to South Africa, 554, 555, 556; and sanctions on South Africa, 554,
560; MT's post-SEA approach to, 662*, 662–6; special Brussels Council (February 1988), 663–5, 721; centralizing, socialist vision of Delors, 664–5, 671; Bruges Speech (September 1988), 671†, 671–5, 672*, 725, 743, 968; and Meyer's leadership challenge, 755–7; phases out CFCs, 781†; and German reunification issue, 809–10; and former Communist countries, 925; Major wins opt-outs for Britain, 929, 935
European Foundation, 943
European Monetary System (EMS), 162–3, 208–9, 277, 489, 490*, 490–91, 651†, 651–2, 656; *see also* Exchange Rate Mechanism (ERM)
European Parliament, 168, 484, 487*; elections (1979), 190; Luxembourg treaty (December 1985), 487; elections (1989), 739, 782; Delors on role of, 873, 875
EuroRoute, 478, 479
Evans, Abbey (nanny), 58*, 72†, 72
Evans, John, 328*
Evening News, 71
Evening Standard, 116, 125*, 230, 527, 670
exchange controls, lifting of (1979), 147, 199, 204–5, 410
Exchange Rate Mechanism (ERM), 162–3, 208–9, 277, 489, 490*, 602, 651†, 651; meetings over possible UK membership (1985), 490–91, 492–5, 509, 652, 841, 914; MT's refusal to join, 494–5, 509, 651, 652, 653, 656, 660–61, 662, 733–5, 753–4, 847–9, 933–4; Walters'
'half-baked' comment, 570, 670†, 750*, 750; Howe–Lawson collaboration over, 602, 652, 660–61, 733–5, 734*, 737, 738–43; political dimension, 662; Delors Committee report (1989), 733–5, 740, 754; MT's strategy for Madrid summit, 740, 742; MT's Madrid Conditions, 742, 840, 842–3, 848, 852, 867–8; MT considers referendum on, 754; Major's plan to join, 840–43, 847–9, 850–52, 867–8; Hurd–Major cooperation on, 841, 842, 850; Ridley's paper on, 842†, 842; Britain enters, 868*, 868–9, 869†, 870, 968; and Howe's resignation statement, 883; MT's views after leaving office, 925; 'Black Wednesday', 933–4, 938; British exit from, 933–4, 934†, 938

F-15 Strike fighter aircraft, 439
Fahd of Saudi Arabia (1921–2005; Crown Prince of Saudi Arabia, 1975–82; King, 1982–2005), 434, 438, 439*, 439‡, 439, 857, 861, 912
Falkland Islands: British rule, 281–3; Argentina's sovereignty claims, 281, 283; population, 281, 282, 283, 287, 288, 299, 308, 310–11, 341; Foreign Office view of, 282–3, 287; 'leaseback' of sovereignty proposal, 282–3; Shackleton report (1977), 282, 321; elected representatives, 283; Hong Kong comparison, 328; MT visits (1983), 341†, 341; after the 1982

War, 344†; future of
(after 1982 war), 686
Falklands War: Argentine
invasion (2 April
1982), 246, 247, 265,
281, 286–8, 288†;
and United States,
247, 284*, 285, 286,
293–300, 302†, 302–3,
305, 306–9, 310–11,
315–16, 318*, 318†,
318–19; consequences
for MT, 248, 321–3,
324, 325–6, 340,
970–71; MT's prestige
after victory, 249;
Irish government
during, 265, 305, 309,
312, 323, 444, 718;
historical origins of,
281*, 281–3; JIC's
warning prior to, 283;
and MT's defence
cuts, 283, 286; British
contingency plans
before, 284; British
doubts about chance
of recapture, 284,
285, 287; *Endurance*
despatched for South
Georgia, 284; Leach
suggests Task Force,
285–6; intelligence
indicates invasion
imminent (31 March
1982), 285–7; British
request to Reagan,
285, 286; Task Force
assembled, 286, 287,
288; initial Tory
backbench view, 288–9,
289*; international
opinion, 290–91, 297,
305, 311, 314–15, 318;
UN Security Council
Resolution 502 on,
290–91, 302†, 861;
and United Nations,
290–91, 301–2, 309–10,
311‡, 311–12, 313,
318–19, 319*; Task
Force sets sail, 290;
War Cabinet, 291,
293, 297, 298–301,
304–5, 311–12, 317;
MT's private account
of, 293*, 293, 302,
947*; need for active
American support,
293–6; Maritime
Exclusion Zone
(MEZ), 293; Haig's
diplomacy, 294–300,
302, 689*; MT's need
for diplomatic effort,
295–6; and Pinochet,
297*, 297, 951–2,
952*; US intelligence
support for UK,
298*; UK Rules of
Engagement (ROE),
299*, 299, 304–5;
Haig–Pym plan (24
April), 299–300, 300*,
302; repossession of
South Georgia, 299,
300–301, 302; British
public opinion during,
301; Total Exclusion
Zone (TEZ), 301,
304–5; BBC coverage
of, 303–4, 316*, 316,
539‡; military action
during, 303–6, 313–15,
316–18, 319–20; MT's
Mid Bedfordshire
speech, 303; US arms
and materiel supplied
to UK, 303, 314†,
314; sinking of the
Belgrano, 304–5, 305*,
307, 309, 345*; sinking
of HMS *Sheffield*,
305–6, 306*, 307, 317;
US-Peruvian 'peace
process', 305, 306–9,
308*, 309*; British
landings, 313–14; land
war, 313–15, 316–18,
319–20; Argentine air
attacks, 314; Darwin/
Goose Green operation,
316*, 317–18;
Argentine surrender,
320–21; total deaths
during, 320; service
of thanksgiving for
victory, 323–4; secular
celebrations of victory,
324; Franks Inquiry,
341; and 1983 election
campaign, 345*, 345;
MT rejects Grenada
comparisons, 374–5;
cultural depictions of,
586; MT tells
her granddaughter
about, 947;
twenty-fifth anniversary
commemorations,
959*, 959; armed
forces at MT's funeral,
962, 965
Fallon, Michael (1952–;
educated St
Andrews University;
Conservative MP
for Darlington,
1983–92; for
Sevenoaks, 1997–2019;
Secretary of State for
Defence, 2014–17;
knighted, 2016], 496,
893, 903, 908†
Farmer, Jean, 11, 13, 17,
20, 21
Farnborough, Kent, 59,
72–3, 80
Farr, John (1922–97;
educated Harrow;
Conservative MP for
Harborough, 1959–92;
knighted, 1984), 123
Faul, Father (Maze prison
chaplain), 262
Faulds, Andrew, 164
Faulkner, Brian, 251*
Faulks, Sebastian, 588–9
Fearless, HMS, 290†
Federation of Conservative
Students, 131
Felixstowe, port of, 766
Fellowes, Robert
(1941–2024; educated
Eton; assistant private
secretary to the
Queen; 1986–90;
deputy private secretary,
private secretary,
1990–99; Chairman,
Barclays Private Bank,
2000–2009; knighted,
1991; created Lord
Fellowes, 1999), 903†,
905, 910‡, 966*
Fenn, Nicholas
(1936–2016; educated
Kingswood School,
Bath and Peterhouse,
Cambridge; British
Ambassador to Ireland,
1986–91; High
Commissioner to India,
1991–6; knighted,
1989), 722–3
Fergusson, Ewen
(1932–2017; educated

INDEX

Fergusson, Ewen – *cont'd*
Rugby and Oriel
College, Oxford;
Ambassador to South
Africa, 1982–4; to
France, 1987–92;
knighted, 1987), 888–9,
891, 892, 896
Fermanagh and South
Tyrone by-elections,
259, 262†
Fermor-Hesketh, (Thomas)
Alexander (1950–;
succeeded his father
as 3rd Baron Hesketh,
1955; educated
Ampleforth; Minister of
State, DTI, 1990–91;
Government Chief Whip
in House of Lords,
1991–3; Treasurer,
Conservative Party,
2003–5, 615–16, 914*,
914–15, 950
Fieldhouse, John (1928–92;
educated Royal Naval
College, Dartmouth;
Royal Navy, 1945;
Commander-in-
Chief Fleet, 1981–2;
knighted, 1980; created
Lord Fieldhouse,
1990, 285, 292, 304*,
304, 313–14, 317, 318,
319–20
Fiennes, John, 69
Figueiredo, João, 310
Figures, Colin (1925–2006;
educated King
Edward's School,
Birmingham and
Pembroke College,
Cambridge; Chief,
MI6, 1981–5;
knighted, 1983), 726
film/cinema, 12, 17–18, 25
financial crisis (2008– 9),
5–6; and repeal of
Glass–Steagall Act,
412*; and universal
banking, 413
Financial Times, 148, 520,
656, 734, 764, 937–8
Finchley, London: MT's
adoption as candidate,
63–4; Jewish vote,
64–5, 69†, 69, 77, 79*,
88, 432–3, 434; MT
becomes MP for, 65–6;

election result (1959),
66; election result
(1964), 79; election
result (1966), 85;
election result (1970),
93; election result
(1974, February), 108;
election result (1974,
October), 114; election
result (1979), 178;
election result (1983),
348; election result
(1987), 612
Finchley Press, 64
Findlay, Neil, 30†, 30–31, 34
Fine Art Productions, 936
Finings, Great Stukeley, 891,
892, 898
First World War, 480
Fisher, Nigel
(1913–96; educated
Eton and Trinity
College, Cambridge;
MC, 1945; Conservative
MP for Hitchin,
1950–55; for Surbiton,
1955–83. His book *The
Tory Leaders* (1977)
includes a good account
of the 1974–5 leadership
contest), 114
Fitt, Gerry, 251*
FitzGerald, Garret
(1926–2011; educated
Belvedere College,
University College,
Dublin; PhD; Minister
for Foreign Affairs,
1973–7; Leader of
Fine Gael, 1977–87;
Taoiseach, 1981–2,
1982–7), 260–61, 261*,
262, 263–4, 444†,
444–5, 718, 719;
fear of the rise of
Sinn Fein, 445, 452,
456; November 1983
summit with MT, 446†,
446–7; November 1984
summit with MT, 451†,
451–3, 452*; meets
MT at Milan European
Council, 455–6; Anglo-
Irish Agreement (1985),
457, 458–9, 459*, 461,
718
Fitzwater, Marlin (1942–;
press secretary
to Vice-President

Bush, 1985–7; to
President Reagan,
1987–9; to President
Bush, 1989–93), 601,
907
Fjaelberg, Mrs, 395*
Fleming, Kate, 165–6
Fletcher, Yvonne, 529
Foot, Michael (1913–2010;
educated Leighton
Park School, Reading
and Wadham
College, Oxford;
Labour MP for
Plymouth Devonport,
1945–55; for Ebbw
Vale, 1960–83; for
Blaenau Gwent,
1983–92; Secretary of
State for Employment,
1974–6; Leader of the
House of Commons,
1976–9; Leader
of the Opposition,
1980–83), 113, 143,
171*; becomes Labour
leader, 227; leadership
of, 235, 272, 279, 340;
and nuclear weapons,
243; and Maze hunger
strikes, 260; Cenotaph
incident, 279†; and
Falklands War, 288,
301–2, 323†; Reagan
helps MT against,
333–4; MT refrains
from personal attacks
on, 344*; and 1983
election campaign, 345
football World Cup (1990),
834
Forbes, Steve, 949†
Ford, Gerald (1913-2006;
President of the United
States of America,
1974–77), 135‡, 136*,
136, 137–8, 157
Ford, Kathy, 917*
Ford Motor Company,
527–8
foreign exchange markets/
exchange rates, 200,
223†, 224, 267–8,
268*, 489, 490, 492;
lifting of exchange
controls, 147, 199,
204–5, 410; and
monetarism, 223†,
267–8, 268*, 489,

602, 651; Reagan aids sterling (January 1985), 490; Plaza Agreement (1985), 492; Lawson and deutschmark, 646, 653–4, 655, 656–8, 660, 661–2, 934*; Lawson's management of, 646, 651, 653–4, 655, 656–8, 660, 670, 934*; Louvre Accord (1987), 653, 656; DM3 cap removed from sterling (March 1988), 657; timing of ERM entry as wrong, 869
Foreman, Ken, 949
Foreman, Mandy (born Marilyn Davies, formerly Mandy Rice-Davies) (1944–2014; educated Sharmans Cross secondary modern school, Solihull; model, novelist, showgirl and entrepreneur), 949
Forsyth, Michael (1954–; educated Arbroath High School and St Andrews University; Conservative MP for Stirling, 1983–97; Chairman, Scottish Conservative Party, 1989–90; Minister of State, Scottish Office, 1990–92; Secretary of State for Scotland, 1995–7; knighted, 1997; created Lord Forsyth of Drumlean, 1999), 496, 619, 893, 903, 908†, 909, 960, 967†
Forte, Sir Charles (*later* Lord Forte), 732*
Forth, Eric (1944–2006; educated Jordanhill College School, Glasgow and Glasgow University; Conservative MP for Mid Worcestershire, 1983–97; for Bromley and Chislehurst, 1997–2006), 496
Foulton Hall, Essex, 45†, 45
Fowler, Norman (1938–; educated King Edward VI School, Chelmsford and Trinity Hall, Cambridge; Conservative MP for Nottingham South, 1970–74; for Sutton Coldfield, 1974–2001; Minister of Transport, 1979–81; Secretary of State for Social Services, 1981–7; for Employment, 1987–90; Chairman, Conservative Party, 1992–4; created Baron Fowler, 2001): as 'Cambridge mafia' member, 351†; Health and Social Security Secretary, 356, 641–2; and public spending control, 356; Employment Secretary, 618, 766; and AIDS, 641–2; resigns from Cabinet, 838*, 838
Fox, Sir Marcus, 358
Fox, Roy, 158
France, 190, 240, 720, 795; Common Agricultural Policy (CAP), 211; and Cold War, 242; nuclear capability, 244; and Falklands War, 290–91, 305, 318, 323, 478; and NATO, 346*; arms sales to Middle East, 437–8, 439; and US bombing of Libya, 534; and apartheid South Africa, 548; ERM membership, 653; bicentenary of French Revolution (1989), 743–4; German reunification issue, 804, 805†, 814, 815, 817; as one of 'Four Powers' after war, 804, 815*, 815, 821, 822; and Rome Council (1990), 872, 873‡, 873–4; *The Downing Street Years* as bestseller, 937*
Francis of Assisi, St, 179*, 179
Franks Inquiry, 341
Fraser, Antonia (1932–; daughter of the 7th Earl of Longford; first married to Hugh Fraser MP, who contested the leadership in the first ballot, which Mrs Thatcher won, in 1975; married Harold Pinter (1980); educated St Mary's Convent, Ascot and Lady Margaret Hall, Oxford; author of histories, biographies and detective fiction), 126†, 696
Fraser, Hugh (1918–84); younger son of Lord Lovat; educated Ampleforth and Balliol College, Oxford; Conservative MP for Stafford, previously Stafford and Stone, previously Stone, 1945–84; Secretary of State for Air, 1962–4; at this time married to Lady Antonia Fraser (née Pakenham)), 121, 125, 126†, 148
Frears, Stephen (1941–; educated Gresham's School, Holt and Trinity College, Cambridge; film director; his films include *My Beautiful Laundrette* (1985), *Dangerous Liaisons* (1988) and *High Fidelity* (2000)), 586
Freedman, Sir Lawrence, *The Official History of the Falklands Campaign*, 283
Freeman, Michael, 93
Friedman, Milton (1912–2006; economist and writer; Professor of Economics, University of Chicago, 1946–77; economic columnist, *Newsweek*, 1966–84; Nobel Prize in Economic Sciences, 1976), 110, 147*, 223†, 226, 268*; MT meets, 146, 149–50, 223
Frost, Sir David, 536*; *The Rich Tide* (with

Frost, Sir David – *cont'd*
  Michael Shea, 1986), 535
Fry, Christopher, *The Lady's Not for Burning*, 227*
Fukuyama, Francis, 'End of History' thesis, 818
Fulham by-election, 537

G5 finance ministers: meeting in Washington (1985), 490; Plaza Agreement, 492
G7 summits: Guadeloupe (1979), 169; Tokyo (1979), 191†, 191–2, 239; Versailles (1982), 247, 248, 318†, 318, 319; Ottawa (1981), 273*, 273; Williamsburg (May 1983), 341*, 345†, 345–6, 347, 490; Venice (1987), 679–80; Paris (July 1989), 743; London (1984), 780; Houston (1990), 835†, 835‡, 835
Gaddafi, Muammar (1942–2011; politician, soldier and revolutionary; seized power in 1969 and ruled Libya until the 'Arab Spring' uprisings of 2010–12), 393, 456, 528–31, 532–4, 533*, 535, 541, 720
'Gaia' theory, 780
Gaines, Gay (1938–; Republican Party fundraiser; Chairman, GOPAC (a leading organization supporting Republican candidates for office), 1993–7), 941, 949†
Gainsbourg, Charlotte, 18*
Gaisman, Tessa (née Jardine Paterson) (1954–2022; secretary to the Prime Minister's PPS, 1978–86; diary secretary to the Prime Minister, 1986–9), 185 449†, 615, 950*
Gaitskell, Hugh, 167*
Galtieri, Leopoldo, 283, 286, 287–8, 288†, 296–7, 303*, 309, 321

Gamelin, Maurice, 890†
Gandhi, Indira, assassination of, 451*, 451, 452
Gandhi, Rajiv, 263
Ganić, Ejup (1946–; Vice-President of the Federation of Bosnia and Herzegovina, 1994–7, 1999–2000 and 2001; President, 1997–9 and 2000–2001), 932
Gardiner, George, 142*
Gardiner, Nile, 953
Garel-Jones, Tristan (1941–2020; educated King's School, Canterbury; Principal, language school, Madrid, 1960–70; Conservative MP for Watford, 1979–97; government whip, 1982–9; Deputy Chief Whip, 1989–90; Minister of State, FCO, 1990–93; created Lord Garel-Jones, 1997), 674–5, 752, 755, 850; and Blue Chips group, 277†, 890; and Meyer's leadership challenge, 756, 757, 880; Europe Minister in Foreign Office, 852–3, 853*; and leadership contest (November 1990), 885, 886, 887, 896*, 896, 900; and 'Catherine Place conspiracy', 893, 894*, 894, 896; and conspiracy to remove MT, 913
Garland, Frances (née Roberts, MT's aunt), 67
Garland, Nicholas (1935–; educated Slade School of Fine Art; political cartoonist, *Daily Telegraph*, 1966–86 and 1991–2011;*Independent*, 1986–91; also drew regularly for the *Spectator*, 1979–95), 585‡, 585
Garrick Club, London, 513†

Garton Ash, Timothy (1955–; educated Sherborne and Exeter College, Oxford; commentator on Central Europe throughout the 1980s in the *New York Review of Books*, the *Independent*, *The Times* and the *Spectator*, of which he was Foreign Editor, 1984–90; Professor of European Studies, University of Oxford, 2004–; author of *In Europe's Name: Germany and the Divided Continent* (1993), 693*, 695, 805, 826–7
Gascoyne-Cecil, Robert (1946–; 7th Marquess of Salisbury, previously Viscount Cranborne, educated Eton and Christ Church, Oxford; Conservative MP for Dorset South, 1979–87; Leader of the House of Lords, 1994–7), 277†, 625, 938
Gates, Bob, 871†
Gaucher's disease, 643*
Gearin-Tosh, Michael, 591*
GEC (General Electric Company), 509*, 516, 796
General Agreement on Tariffs and Trade (GATT), 872†, 872, 874*
general election (1935), 14
general election (1945), 28–9
general election (1950), 47, 48–9
general election (1951), 53–5
general election (1959), 65–6, 349*, 611*
general election (1964), 78–9
general election (1966), 81, 83, 84–5
general election (1970), 93, 102
general election (1974, February), 6, 107–8

general election (1974, October), 113–14
general election (1979), 161†, 162, 171–8
general election (1983), 340–41, 343–8, 349
general election (1987), 535–6, 605–13, 618–19, 619†, 630
general election (1992), 929–30
general election (1997), 943*, 943–4
general election (2001), 953–4
General Motors (GM), 527–8
Genscher, Hans-Dietrich (1927–2016; Chairman, West German Free Democratic Party, 1974–85; Foreign Minister, 1974–92 in both Social Democratic Party and the Christian Democratic Union-Christian Social Union Ministries before and after German unification in 1990), 486, 666, 700, 701, 703
Genscher–Colombo Plan (1981), 480–81
George, Edward ('Eddie') (1938–2009; educated Dulwich College and Emmanuel College, Cambridge; Deputy Governor, Bank of England, 1990–93; Governor, 1993–2003; knighted, 2000; created Lord George, 2004), 490, 655, 657
George VI, King, death of, 56
Georgia, 829*
Gerda (nurse), 57
German reunification issue: MT's anxieties about, 483–4, 802*, 802–3, 804, 805, 806, 807–11, 814–18, 819, 822–3; and Bush administration, 702, 806, 807, 809, 812–13, 814, 821–3; Meyer on, 755–6; terminology, 802*; and greater European integration, 802–3, 807, 813, 814–15, 816; fall of Communism in Eastern bloc, 804; and 'Four Power' framework, 804, 814, 815*, 815, 821, 822; French anxieties, 804, 814, 815†, 815, 817; and Soviet Union, 804, 805, 807, 808–9, 812–13, 814, 815, 821†, 821, 822–3; and NATO, 809–10, 813, 821, 822–3, 827*, 828, 830, 831–2, 834; Kohl's 'Ten Point Plan', 812; Chequers seminars on (1990), 816, 818–19, 825–7, 836†, 836; sheer speed of events, 817–18, 821–2; and imminent collapse of GDR, 820–21; Ottawa agreement (February 1990), 821‡, 821–2; and Helsinki Final Act, 822*, 822, 832; Polish border issue, 822, 823*, 823, 825*, 825, 827*, 827; proposal for joint NATO–Warsaw Pact declaration, 832, 834, 835*; East and West Germany unify (3 October 1990), 836; and timing of UK's ERM entry, 869
Gerson, John (1945–; educated Bradfield and King's College, Cambridge; diplomat; First Secretary and Consul, Peking, 1974–7; First Secretary, later Counsellor, FCO, 1979–87; Counsellor, Hong Kong, 1987–92; Counsellor, FCO, 1992–9), 156*, 331–2, 927–8
Getty, John Paul, 384†
Getty, Paul, 498*
Gibraltar shootings (March 1988), 721–2, 723, 727, 854
Gieve, John, 841
Gillies, Miss Dorothy, 20, 22, 23
Gilmour, Ian (1926–2007; 3rd baronet; educated Eton and Balliol College, Oxford; Conservative MP for Norfolk Central, 1962–74; for Chesham and Amersham, 1974–92; owner (1954–67) and Editor (1954–9) of the *Spectator*; Secretary of State for Defence, 1974; Lord Privy Seal, 1979–81; created Lord Gilmour of Craigmillar 1992): Heath government, 106; and party leadership, 114, 115; Shadow Home Secretary, 129, 132, 154, 160–61; supports devolution, 160–61; Foreign Office spokesman in Commons, 183; Lord Privy Seal, 183; supports EEC, 210; and fight over EEC budget contribution, 211–12; and monetarism, 222–3; speech criticizing MT's economic approach, 222–3, 223*; and 1981 budget, 270; leaves Cabinet, 276; visits Washington (October 1981), 277*; and Falklands War, 289*
Giscard d'Estaing, Valéry (1926–2020; President of France, 1974–81; Member, European Parliament, 1984–9; President of the Convention on the Future of Europe, 2001–4), 190–91, 211, 240, 242, 665–6
Gladstone, William Ewart, 149
Glamorgan, HMS, 320
Glaspie, April, 857†
Gleysteen, Dirk, 104
global warming, 729†, 729, 781*, 781, 782, 785–6, 880, 920, 953*

Glorious Revolution (1689), 743*, 743
Glover, Eleanor, Lady, 14*, 226†, 226, 357, 390, 552
Glover, Sir Douglas, 226†, 226
GMTV, 764
Godfrey, Janet, 114
Goldsmith, James (1933–97; educated Eton; businessman, publisher and founder of the Referendum Party; Member for France, European Parliament, 1994–7; knighted, 1976), 516, 655, 918*, 942–3
Goodall, David (1931–2016; educated Ampleforth and Trinity College, Oxford; diplomat; Cabinet Office, 1982–4; Deputy Under-Secretary, FCO, 1984–7; High Commissioner to India (1987–91); knighted, 1987), 265–6, 324, 325–6, 445, 447, 453, 455, 458*, 460; on working for MT, 593–4
Goodhart, Sir Philip, 293
Goodison, Nicholas (1934–2021; educated Marlborough and King's College, Cambridge; Chairman, Stock Exchange, 1976–88; TSB Group, 1989–95; knighted, 1992), 410
Goodlad, Alastair (1943–; Conservative MP for Northwich, 1974–83; for Eddisbury, 1983–99; Deputy Government Chief Whip, 1990–92; High Commissioner to Australia, 2000–2005; created Lord Goodlad, 2005), 879, 893, 894, 898–9, 902, 913
Goodrich, Canon, 11–12
Goodrich, Margaret, 21, 23, 32

Gorbachev, Mikhail (1931–2021; General Secretary of the Communist Party of the Soviet Union, 1985–91; President of the Soviet Union, 1990–91): MT hears of for first time, 367*, 367; MT's first meeting with (Chequers, 1984), 407, 416, 417–21, 422–3; invited to Britain (February 1984), 415†, 415–16; in Gordievsky's reports, 417; character and vitality of, 418–19; MT's rapport with, 420–1, 424, 427–8, 432, 572–82, 677, 680–81, 698–700, 804–5, 807, 829‡, 832–4, 920; views on MT, 420–21, 579–80, 581, 683, 699, 792, 920; MT on, 420, 421, 422, 424, 427, 431–2, 562–3, 819; MT's 'a man to do business with' phrase, 420, 421; and SDI, 420, 427–8; desire to see No. 10 Downing Street, 421*; and MT–Reagan relations, 422–3, 424, 428, 429, 431–2, 562–5, 567; becomes president of Soviet Union, 426–7; MT meets in Moscow (1985), 427–8; Reagan invites to talks, 428; Geneva summit with Reagan (November 1985), 429, 431–2, 562; and Gordievsky row, 431*, 431; and Gordievsky's family, 431*, 684†, 829‡; nuclear-free world proposal, 562–3; Reykjavik summit (1986), 562, 565*, 565–9, 566*, 571, 572, 680–81; strategy for Reykjavik summit, 565–6; and British post-Reykjavik position, 572–3; criticizes MT's role at Camp David, 572–3; *glasnost* (openness), 573, 576*, 576, 580, 581–2; *perestroika* (restructuring), 573, 579, 580*, 581–2, 683, 684, 687, 698, 699, 804–5, 831; Gordievsky on, 574–5; and Brezhnev Doctrine, 577†, 577–8, 581; MT's talks with in Moscow (1987), 577–80; Nixon on MT's influence on, 577; 'second zero' proposals (April 1987), 678–9; MT's support/advocacy for, 681–8, 697–700, 789, 792, 803, 804–5, 808–12, 816*, 817, 822–5, 831–2, 837, 968; conflict with Yeltsin, 682†, 682, 698*; Washington summit with Reagan (December 1987), 682–3, 684*, 684; British stopover (December 1987), 682–4, 684†; domestic difficulties/destabilization, 682, 697, 803, 808–12, 828–34, 926–7; MT toughens stance with (1988), 686–7; withdrawal from Afghanistan, 686, 687; Moscow summit with Reagan (1988), 687–8; human rights conference in Moscow (October 1991), 689‡; suggests human rights conference in Moscow, 689‡; visits UK (April 1989), 697–9, 766; announces cuts to Soviet conventional forces, 698‡, 698; Guildhall speech (1989), 699†, 699; and southern Africa, 789, 792, 799†, 799; MT meets in Moscow (1989), 803, 804–5;

weakening of power of, 803; and German reunification issue, 805, 807, 808–9, 812–13, 814, 815, 819, 821†, 822–3, 824‡; refuses to intervene in GDR, 806; MT's anxiety over position of, 807†, 808–12, 816*, 817, 821–5, 824‡, 828–34, 926–7; and biological weapons, 807, 830, 833†, 833; Malta meeting with Bush (December 1989), 810, 811, 812–13; meets Kohl in Moscow (July 1990), 820–21, 836; ends Communist Party's political monopoly, 828–9; and Lithuania, 829–30; and Germany in NATO issue, 831–2, 834; Yeltsin on, 831; meets Bush in Washington (May 1990), 832; meets MT in Moscow (June 1990), 832, 833; request for money from the West, 835; drops opposition to German NATO membership, 836; MT's views on/ relations with, 837; Iraqi invasion of Kuwait, 858, 862, 863, 891*, 891; CSCE summit in Paris (November 1990), 891; meeting with MT in Paris, 891; and MT's first post-office visit to Russia, 920; Moscow coup (August 1991), 926–7; MT's continued support for, 926
Gorbachev, Raisa, 417, 418, 420*, 422, 424, 575, 579, 682†, 699*
Gordievsky, Oleg (1938–2025; joined KGB, 1963; posted to London, 1982; secret agent for SIS, 1974–85). 368, 369, 416–17, 574–5, 804; cover of blown, 430†; defects to UK, 430–31, 431*, 432, 684†; family of in Moscow, 431*, 431, 684†, 829‡
Gormley, Joe, 230
Gould, Bryan (1939–; born in New Zealand, educated Tauranga College and Balliol College, Oxford; Labour MP for Southampton Test, 1974–9; for Dagenham, 1983–94; Opposition spokesman on the environment, 1989–92), 847
Gould, Diana, 345*
Government Communications Headquarters (GCHQ): SIGINT activities, 377–8; union ban, 377–9, 378†, 387, 396; judicial review of union ban, 387; and 'Iran-Contra' affair, 570
Gow, Ian (1937–90; educated Winchester; Conservative MP for Eastbourne, 1974–90; PPS to the Prime Minister, 1979–83; Minister for Housing and Construction, 1983–5; Minister of State, Treasury, 1985; assassinated by the IRA, 1990): in opposition, 146; as MT's PPS, 186–7, 227, 235, 352; and Northern Ireland, 252, 253, 254, 258, 264, 265, 445, 458; and September 1981 reshuffle, 276; and Falklands War, 292*, 292, 323; and 1983 election date, 342–3, 343*; Minister of Housing, 352, 445; resigns over Anglo-Irish Agreement, 458; EuroRoute plan for Channel crossing, 478; and Lawson, 738†; and Meyer's leadership challenge, 756; murdered by IRA, 853, 854–5; on Howe's mood (June 1990), 877
Gow, Jane, 853, 854–5
Grachev, Andrei, 421
Graham, Kay, 138†, 138
Grahame, Kenneth, *The Wind in the Willows*, 820*
Granada 500 (television programme), 177
Granada Television, 764
Grant, Bernard 'Bernie' (1944–2000; Council Leader, London Borough of Haringey, 1985–7; Labour MP for Tottenham, 1987–2000), 502, 797
Grant, John, 39
Grantham: grocery shops of Alfred Roberts, 9–10; poverty in, 10; RAF bases near, 13–14; during Second World War, 13–14, 15, 17, 21, 31; Belvoir Hunt on Boxing Day, 13; growth in pre-war years, 13; local council politics, 14, 15, 61–2; Picture House, 17–18; eisteddfod, 19; 1945 general election in, 28–9; Roberts family house in, 36*; Central School for Boys, 94
Grass, Marco, 594*
Gray, Cardinal Gordon, 309
Gray, Paul (1948–; educated Wyggeston Boys' School, Leicester and LSE; assistant secretary, 1984–7; economic affairs private secretary to Prime Minister, 1988–90), 638, 657*, 657, 658†, 658, 660, 735*, 749*, 753, 767, 773, 848‡, 849
Gray, Roger, 30†, 30, 31
Great Ormond Street Hospital, 970*
Greater London Council (GLC), 339–40, 463*, 465†; 1983 manifesto

GLC – *cont'd*
commitment to
abolish, 343, 463–4;
legislation to abolish,
388; campaign against
abolition, 465, 473–4;
sets legal rate (1985),
469; abolition of
(March 1986), 473–4
Green, Maurice, 123*
Green Party (UK), 782
Greene, Sir Hugh Carleton,
763
Greengrass, Paul, 715
Greenspan, Alan (1926–;
chairman, US Council
of Economic Advisors,
1974–7; chairman, US
Federal Reserve Board,
1987–2006): 138,
689*, 850
Greenwich by-election, 600
Gregson, Peter
(1936–2015; educated
Nottingham High
School and Balliol
College, Oxford;
Deputy Secretary,
Cabinet Office,
1981–5; Permanent
Under-Secretary,
Department of Energy,
1985–9; Permanent
Secretary, DTI,
1989–96; knighted,
1988), 338, 380, 381,
390, 408
Greig, James, 717–18
Grenada, US invasion of,
369–76
Griffiths, Brian (1941–;
educated Dynevor
Grammar School
and LSE; Professor
of Banking and
International Finance,
City University,
1977–85; head of
No. 10 Policy Unit,
1985–90; created Lord
Griffiths of Fforestfach,
1991), 110*, 228, 535,
752–3; on risks of Big
Bang, 411–12; heads
MT's Policy Unit, 411,
489, 494, 532, 620–21;
and ERM question,
493, 494, 602, 852;
and Christianity, 532,

542, 620–21, 621*,
639, 762, 775; and
broadcasting, 542, 762,
763, 764, 765; and
GERBIL, 636–8, 639,
640; opposes Lawson's
exchange rate targeting,
656, 657, 658, 660,
670; on Howe's
resignation, 878
Grimstone, Gerald (1949–;
educated Whitgift
School and Merton
College, Oxford;
Assistant Secretary,
Treasury, 1984–6;
knighted, 2014; created
Lord Grimstone of
Boscobel, 2020), 402
Gromyko, Andrei, 415, 416,
419, 427–8
Grunwick industrial dispute,
152*, 152–3
Gstaad (Swiss resort), 932
Guardian, 99, 139, 228,
270*, 384, 400, 585,
601; Tebbit sues for
libel, 599
Guinness, Sir Alec, 715†
Guinness, Sabrina (1955–;
member of the
Guinness brewing
family; former
girlfriend of Prince
Charles; married
the playwright Tom
Stoppard, 2014),
914–15
Guise, George, 786
Gulf States, 433, 437*, 858
Gummer, John Selwyn
(1939–; educated
King's School,
Rochester and Selwyn
College, Cambridge;
Conservative MP
for Lewisham
West, 1970–74; for
Eye, 1979–83; for
Suffolk Coastal,
1983–2010; Chairman,
Conservative Party,
1983–5; Minister of
Agriculture, 1989–93;
created Lord Deben,
2010), 119*, 145,
278; as 'Cambridge
mafia' member, 351†;
Christianity, 357†,

504; Party Chairman,
357–8; and Brighton
bombing, 448–9; and
1985 reshuffle, 496,
498; on Wakeham's
list after 1987 victory,
616*; and leadership
contest (November
1990), 895, 897,
899, 900; individual
session with MT (21
November 1990), 899,
900; nominates Major
for leadership, 905†; at
MT's farewell lunch,
908†
Gyngell, Bruce (1929–2000;
Australian television
executive who invented
British breakfast
television; Managing
Director, TV-am,
1984–92), 764

Haass, Richard (1951–;
special assistant to
George H. W. Bush and
NSC Senior Director
for Near East and
South Asian Affairs,
1989–93), 859, 861–2
Habgood, John
(1927–2019; educated
Eton and King's
College, Cambridge;
Bishop of Durham,
1973–83; Archbishop
of York, 1983–95;
created Lord Habgood,
1995), 778
Hackett, Mrs, 397
Hackett, Terry, 397
Hadfields (private
steelworks), 217, 219
Hague, Sir Douglas, 110*; *A
Textbook of Economic
Theory*, 147
Hague, William (1961–;
educated Wath-upon-
Dearne Comprehensive
School and Magdalen
College, Oxford;
Conservative MP for
Richmond, Yorks,
1989–2015; Secretary
of State for Wales,
1995–7; Leader of the
Conservative Party
and Leader of the

Opposition, 1997–2001; Foreign Secretary, 2010–14; Chancellor, University of Oxford, 2025–; created Lord Hague of Richmond, 2015), 895†, 895, 945–6, 952, 953–4
Haig, Alexander (1924–2010; Assistant to the President and White House Chief of Staff, 1973–4; Supreme Allied Commander Europe, NATO, 1974–9; US Secretary of State, 1981–2): and MT's 1981 visit to US, 231; favours 'dual track' strategy, 242–3; and Soviet Union, 242–3, 246; replaced as Secretary of State, 249; and Falklands War, 286, 293, 294–300, 302–3, 305, 306–7, 308, 309, 312†, 315, 318, 319*, 319, 689*; political ambitions, 294; US-Peruvian 'peace process', 305, 306–7
Haines, Joe, 124*
Hall, Joan (1935–; educated Queen Margaret's School, Escrick and Ashridge House of Citizenship; Conservative MP for Keighley, 1970–74), 125
Halsey, A. H., 503*
Hamilton, Anne, 950
Hamilton, Archibald 'Archie' (1941–; educated Eton; Conservative MP for Epsom and Ewell, 1978–2001; PPS to Prime Minister, 1987–8; Minister of State, MOD, 1988–93; knighted, 1994; created Lord Hamilton of Epsom, 2005), 596, 615, 618, 628*, 950
Hamilton, Neil (1949–; educated Amman Valley Grammar School, University College of Wales, Aberystwyth and Corpus Christi College, Cambridge; Conservative MP for Tatton, 1983–97. In the 1990s, while still an MP, Hamilton became involved in the 'cash for questions' affair. He lost his seat in 1997, to the independent candidate, Martin Bell), 496, 541, 893, 903
Hamilton, Willie, 74
Hamleys toy shop, 947–8
Hammersmith, 44, 49–50
Hankes-Drielsma, Claude (1949–; Chairman, Management Committee, Price Waterhouse and Partners, 1983–9; assisted Dr Fritz Leutwiler in his role as independent mediator between South African government and foreign banks, 1985–6; Deputy Chairman, Leutwiler and Partners Ltd, 1992–6; trustee and adviser, St George's House, Windsor Castle, 2000–, knighted, 2006. In 2006, he dropped the 'Drielsma' from his name by deed poll], 667–8, 669
Hannay, David (1935–; educated Winchester and New College, Oxford; chef de cabinet to Sir Christopher Soames, European Commissioner, 1973–7; Ambassador and UK Permanent Representative to EEC, 1985–90; UK Permanent Representative to UN, 1990–95; knighted, 1986; created Lord Hannay, 2001), 209–10, 664, 742, 867*, 867†, 867, 871*, 871, 875*
Hanrahan, Brian, 303–4
Hanson, James (1922–2004; educated Elland Grammar School, Halifax; Chairman, Hanson plc, 1965–97; created Lord Hanson, 1983), 404†; as Westland 'mystery buyer', 516
Hardy, Thomas, 959
Hare, David (1947–; educated Lancing and Jesus College, Cambridge; playwright; his plays include *Plenty* (1978) and *Racing Demon* (1990); knighted, 1998), 583, 586, 589*
Hare, John, 61, 62
Haringey Council, 847
Harlech, David Ormsby-Gore, 5th Baron, 193
Harman, Harriet (1950–; educated St Paul's Girls' School and University of York; QC, 2001; Labour MP for Peckham, 1982–97, for Camberwell and Peckham 1997–2024; Deputy Leader of the Labour Party, 2007–15; acting Leader of the Opposition, May–September 2010 and May–September 2015), 731
HarperCollins, 765*, 922
Harris, Sir Phil, 732*
Harris, Ralph (1924–2006; educated Tottenham Grammar School and Queens' College, Cambridge; founder President, Institute of Economic Affairs, 1990–2006 (General Director, 1957–87; Chairman, 1987–9); Chairman, Bruges Group, 1989–91; created Lord Harris of High Cross, 1979), 110, 146, 149–50
Harris, Robin (1952–; educated Canford and Exeter College,

Harris, Robin – *cont'd*
Oxford; Director,
Conservative Research
Department, 1985–9;
member, No. 10 Policy
Unit, 1989–90; adviser
to Lady Thatcher,
1990–2003; author
of *Not for Turning:
The Life of Margaret
Thatcher* (2013)),
538*, 880, 918, 931,
938, 952–3, 955*;
'ghost' for MT's
memoirs, 922–3
Harrison, Brian, 36, 40
Harrods, 447
Harrow school, 71*, 434,
625
Hart, David (1944–2011;
educated Eton; political
adviser, novelist and
property developer),
384‡, 384–5, 391, 392,
394–5, 696, 737*, 737;
and legal actions against
NUM, 384†, 384
Hartwell, Michael Berry,
Baron, 123*
Hartwell, Pamela, Lady,
123*, 138†
Hastings, Max, 594†, 948*
Hatton, Derek (1948–;
educated Liverpool
Institute for Boys;
Deputy Leader,
Liverpool City Council,
1983; expelled from
the Labour Party in
1986 for belonging to
Militant), 388
Haughey, Charles
(1925–2006; educated
St Joseph's Christian
Brothers' School,
Fairview, Dublin and
University College,
Dublin; Fianna
Fáil TD, 1957–92;
Leader of Fianna Fáil,
1979–92; Taoiseach,
1979–81, March–
December 1982 and
1987–92), 254, 255,
256–7, 260, 718†; and
Falklands War, 265,
444, 718; and ECST
ratification, 720–21;
MT meets at Brussels

Council (February
1988), 721; speeches
in USA (April 1988),
723; and Patrick Ryan
extradition request,
724–5; MT meets at
Hanover Council (June
1988), 724
Havers, Michael (1923–92;
educated Westminster
and Corpus Christi
College, Cambridge;
lieutenant RNVR,
1941–6; called to Bar,
1948; Conservative
MP for Wimbledon,
1970–87; Attorney-
General, 1979–87;
created Lord Havers,
1987; Lord Chancellor
for three months in
1987 before retiring on
health grounds), 208,
219*, 304, 511*, 709;
and Falklands War,
291–2, 292†, 314;
Lord Chancellor,
513†, 617†, 617; and
Westland affair, 513†,
513, 518
Hawk aircraft, 796
Hawke, Robert 'Bob'
(1929–2019;
educated University
of Western Australia
and University College,
Oxford; Prime Minister
of Australia, 1983–91),
549, 554, 794
Hayek, Friedrich von
(1899–1992; educated
University of Vienna;
Tooke Professor of
Economic Science and
Statistics, University
of London, 1931–50;
Professor of Moral
and Social Science,
University of Chicago,
1950–62; Nobel
Prize in Economic
Sciences (jointly),
1974; Companion
of Honour, 1984),
146, 147*, 198†, 222,
268*; *The Road to
Serfdom* (1944), 27‡;
Constitution of Liberty,
146, 922

Hayes, Sir Brian, 522,
523–4
Hayward, Robert, 890‡
Healey, Denis (1917–2015;
educated Bradford
Grammar School
and Balliol College,
Oxford; Labour MP
for Leeds South East,
1952–5; for Leeds East,
1955–92; Secretary
of State for Defence,
1964–70; Chancellor
of the Exchequer,
1974–9; Shadow
Foreign Secretary,
1980–87; Deputy
Leader of the Labour
Party, 1980–83; created
Lord Healey, 1992):
Chancellor of the
Exchequer, 117, 120,
122–3, 144, 165, 216;
IMF loan, 144, 216;
'first law of holes', 224;
and Falklands War,
293, 301, 323; 'cut and
run' comments, 342;
MT's 'frit' accusation,
342, 758†; and US
invasion of Grenada,
372; with Kinnock in
Washington (1987),
601*, 601
health and safety matters,
487
Heath, Edward (1916–2005;
educated Chatham
House School,
Ramsgate and Balliol
College, Oxford;
served war of
1939–45 (mentioned
in despatches);
Conservative MP
for Bexley, 1950–74;
for Bexley, Sidcup,
1974–83; for
Old Bexley and
Sidcup, 1983–2001;
Government Chief Whip,
1955–9; Lord Privy Seal,
1960–63; Leader of
the Conservative Party,
1965–75; Prime Minister,
1970–74; captain,
Britain's Admiral's
Cup team, 1971,
1979; Knight of the

Garter, 1992): asks 'Who governs Britain?', 6, 106, 107, 153, 395, 968; February 1974 election, 6, 107–8; treatment of Young Conservatives, 43; in Douglas-Home government, 78; MT's views on, 81†, 81; becomes party leader (1965), 81; leader of the Opposition (1965–70), 81, 82, 86, 87; uneasiness with women, 81, 123; attitude to MT, 83; technocratic leadership, 87; Selsdon Park Hotel conference, 92–3, 111; appoints MT to Cabinet, 93–4; Prime Minister, 93, 95, 97–8, 99, 100–101; wins 1970 election, 93; economic policies, 97–8, 102–5, 106, 107; review of all public spending, 97–8; industrial relations, 100, 101, 102–3, 105, 106–8, 151, 382*, 382; and Cabinet government, 105*, 105; imposes direct rule in Northern Ireland, 105–6; and Northern Ireland, 105, 106–7, 250–51, 257; prices and incomes policy, 105, 106, 167, 168–9; Sunningdale Agreement, 106–7, 250–51, 252, 257; three-day week, 107; courts the Liberals after February 1974 election, 108; leader of the Opposition (1974–5), 109–10, 111–21; potential challenges to leadership, 109, 112, 114–21; Keith Joseph undermines, 111–12; notion of 'national unity' (October 1974), 113–14; as possibly homosexual, 116†; meeting with

MT (November 1974), 118–19; MT's leadership challenge, 121–6, 123*; first leadership ballot, 125*, 125†, 125–6; reaction to MT's election as leader, 126*, 126†, 126, 129; resigns as leader, 126*, 126†, 126; 'incredible sulk' with MT, 129, 133, 151, 168–9, 183–4, 277, 615; refuses post under MT, 129; and EEC referendum, 132*, 132–3; anti-Americanism, 135‡, 135; Kissinger on, 135‡; resignation of Wilson, 143; and *The Right Approach*, 145, 160; popular caricature of, 156; failed attempts to improve relations with MT, 168, 176; offered ambassadorship in Washington, 184, 916; attacks MT's economic policies, 277; Steinway piano at Chequers, 360*; and 1985 budget, 492; on foreign multinationals and BL, 528; as 'homeless' after 1974 defeat, 597; votes against poll tax, 628†; and Hong Kong, 928
Hedger, John, 97
Heffer, Eric, 939†
Heffer, Simon, 460†
Heiser, Terence 'Terry' (1932–; educated Windsor County Boys' School and Birkbeck College, University of London; joined Civil Service, 1949; Permanent Secretary of the Department of the Environment, 1985–92; knighted, 1992. He was the most senior civil servant dealing with the poll tax), 464, 466, 475
Helms, Jesse, 159, 215, 302†
Helsinki Accords (1975), 134–5, 142, 238, 432*,

432, 573, 822*, 822, 832; Vienna talks on implementation of Final Act, 689‡
Henderson, Josie, 52
Henderson, Nicholas (1919–2009; educated Stowe and Hertford College, Oxford; Ambassador to Poland, 1969–72; to West Germany, 1972–5; to France, 1975–9; to the United States, 1979–82; knighted, 1991): Ambassador to USA, 213†, 213, 233, 277*, 286, 296, 299, 305, 311, 315, 316, 318; and Falklands War, 299, 305, 311, 315, 316, 318, 322; chairs Channel Tunnel Group, 479
Henderson, Robert, 46, 47†, 47–8, 50*, 50, 51–2, 52†, 53, 937†, 937
Hensher, Philip (1965–; educated Tapton School, Sheffield, Lady Margaret Hall, Oxford and Jesus College, Cambridge; clerk to the House of Commons, 1990–96; his novels include *The Northern Clemency* (2008) and *Scenes from Early Life* (2013)), 588
Heritage Foundation, 922*
Hermes, HMS, 290, 304
Hermon, Jack, 260
Herring, John Frederick, *The Leamington Hunt – Mr Harry Bradley's Hounds*, 958
Heseltine, Michael (1933–; educated Shrewsbury and Pembroke College, Oxford; Conservative MP for Tavistock, 1966–74; for Henley, 1974–2001; Secretary of State for the Environment, 1979–83; for Defence, 1983–6; for the Environment, 1990–92; President of the Board of

Heseltine, Michael – *cont'd*
Trade, 1992–5; First
Secretary of State
and Deputy Prime
Minister, 1995–7;
Chairman, Haymarket
Publishing Group, from
1999; created Baron
Heseltine, 2001):
MT on, 104, 183;
and 1975 leadership
vote, 125†; on Joseph
paper, 132; seizes
Mace in Commons,
144; Shadow
Industry spokesman,
144; Environment
Secretary, 183, 201,
203; relations with
MT, 183, 505*, 505,
508; opposes lifting
of exchange controls,
204; as 'Minister for
Merseyside', 272*,
272–3, 630; attacks
Howe's spending cuts
(1981), 273, 278; on
unemployment, 334;
and local government,
340, 467†; Defence
Secretary, 351, 359,
499–500, 505; and
public spending
control, 355, 356;
rivalry with Tebbit,
359; and Soviet Union,
366*; and London
Docklands, 411†,
502, 632; with MT in
Washington (1985),
426; opposes poll
tax, 472, 628§, 628†,
628, 646; Westland
affair, 472, 473, 504,
505–14; resigns over
Westland, 473, 504,
514*, 514–15, 515*;
and 1985 reshuffle,
499–500; and Tebbit,
499, 506–7, 508*, 508,
514, 845; and policy
on inner cities, 504,
630; and US cruise
missiles in Britain, 505;
and Whitelaw, 506§,
506–7; and Westland
Commons debate,
520–21; as backbencher,
616, 628; 'It Took
a Riot' (report on
Toxteth riots), 630;
at 1989 conference,
749†; and MT's poll
tax problems, 749;
and Meyer as stalking-
horse, 755; and Howe's
resignation, 879,
880; hesitates over
leadership bid, 881–2;
and Howe's resignation
statement, 883, 884*,
884; announces
leadership candidacy
(14 November 1990),
884–5; faces 'stop
Heseltine' moves
(November 1990),
885, 891, 894, 896,
897, 899, 900, 904,
907*, 907; first ballot
result (20 November
1990), 891–2, 893;
and 'Catherine Place
conspiracy', 894; and
MT's resignation,
904‡, 904; second
ballot result (27
November 1990), 909;
as Major's Environment
Secretary, 916, 938;
poll tax jettisoned by,
916; at MT's funeral,
965
Heseltine, William (1930–;
educated University of
Western Australia; press
secretary to the Queen,
1968–72; private
secretary, 1986–90;
knighted, 1982), 555,
556†, 556, 557
Hesketh, Lady (Claire), 950
Heston, Charlton, 689*
Hezbollah, 696†
Hickman, Lady (Denis
Thatcher's first wife),
52*, 52, 54
Hickman, Sir Howard, 54
higher and further
education, 636, 640*,
640
Hillsborough Castle,
Northern Ireland, 457,
458–9
Hind, Rita, 21, 22
Hitler, Adolf, 18, 492*,
690*, 802*, 815†, 825,
836, 856; appeasement
policy towards, 15,
738–9; *Mein Kampf*,
245, 827*
Hockney, David, 689*
Hodgkin, Dorothy
(1910–94; educated
Sir John Leman School
and Somerville College,
Oxford; distinguished
chemist, famous for
her crystallographic
analysis of the
structure of molecules;
winner, Nobel Prize
in Chemistry, 1964;
OM, 1965), 26*, 26,
589–90, 910‡
Hodgson, Patricia (1947–;
educated Brentwood
High School and
Newnham College,
Cambridge; Deputy
Secretary, BBC,
1983–5; Secretary,
1985–7; Chair, Ofcom,
2014–17; created dame,
2004), 541–2, 595‡,
595, 762
Hogg, Quintin (1907–2001;
succeeded his father as
2nd Viscount Hailsham,
but disclaimed his
peerage for life in 1963;
educated Eton and
Christ Church, Oxford;
Conservative MP for
Oxford City, 1938–50;
for St Marylebone,
1963–70; First Lord
of the Admiralty,
1956–7; Chairman,
Conservative Party,
1957–9; Leader of
the House of Lords,
1960–63; Secretary of
State for Education and
Science, April–October
1964; Lord Chancellor,
1970–74 and 1979–87;
created Lord Hailsham
of St Marylebone,
1970; Knight of the
Garter, 1988), 77;
Shadow Minister
without Portfolio, 129,
132; Lord Chancellor,
183, 218; as special
minister for the
depressed North-East,

272; on Herbert
Hoover, 273–4; and
Argentina's occupation
of South Georgia, 284;
and South Africa, 556;
retirement of, 617; and
AIDS, 642*
Hole, Shana, 885, 911
Hollinghurst, Alan, *The Line
of Beauty*, 588, 589
Hollis, Roger (1905–73;
educated Clifton
College, Bristol and
Worcester College,
Oxford; Director-
General, MI5, 1956–65;
knighted, 1960), 706–7,
708, 710*
homosexuality, 84, 116†,
129*, 353*, 588, 595,
634, 715–16, 717;
and left-wing Labour
councils, 633‡, 633;
'Section 28' of Local
Government Act, 633–4;
and AIDS, 641, 642
Honecker, Erich
(1912–94; General
Secretary of the
Socialist Unity Party,
1971–89; Chairman of
the Council of State of
the GDR, 1976–89),
803, 806
Hong Kong, 328‡, 328–9,
361–4; people of, 328‡,
328, 329, 330, 331,
361, 362–4; sovereignty
question, 328, 329–32,
361; 'Unofficials' (or
EXCO), 362, 363,
364, 843–4; Joint
Declaration (December
1984), 363–4, 407,
416, 421, 843–4,
844*, 921†, 927, 928;
Basic Law, 363;
'One Country, Two
Systems' concept, 363,
364, 928; China's
National Security Law
(2020), 364; issue of
immigration from, 839,
843, 844–5, 849; MT's
visits after leaving
office, 928; Patten as
Governor of, 928;
handover of to China
(July 1997), 945

Hooley, Jim, 247†
Hoover, Herbert, 273–4
Hopkins, Stanley, 60†, 60
Hore-Ruthven, Alexander
Greysteil, 2nd Earl of
Gowrie (1939–2021;
educated Eton and
Balliol College, Oxford;
Minister of State,
Department of
Employment, 1979–81;
Northern Ireland Office,
1981–3; Minister
for the Arts, 1983–5;
Chancellor of the Duchy
of Lancaster, 1984–5),
378, 379, 498*, 498†,
498, 590, 668*, 732
Hoskyns, John
(1927–2014; educated
Winchester; head
of Prime Minister's
Policy Unit,
1979–82; Director-
General, Institute of
Directors, 1984–9;
knighted, 1982): on
MT, 131, 153–4, 182,
200, 201, 224, 227,
267; and monetary
policy, 154, 155, 200,
202, 217, 224–5,
227, 268; 'Stepping
Stones' process, 154,
155; and trade unions,
154, 200, 217; heads
No. 10 Policy Unit,
181, 182, 335; and
MT's lack of strategy,
181, 182, 200, 201,
221, 224; 'Government
Strategy' (paper),
200–201; Stabilization
process, 200, 202;
and British Leyland
recovery plan, 220; on
need for fundamental
reform, 234, 235, 267;
and 1981 budget, 268,
269; 'blockbuster'
memo from, 274–6;
and September 1981
reshuffle, 275; and
1981 conference
speech, 278
Houghton, Douglas, 75
Houghton, John
(1931–2020; educated
Rhyl Grammar School

and Jesus College,
Oxford; Professor
of Atmospheric
Physics, Oxford
University, 1976–83;
Chief Executive and
Director-General,
Meteorological Office,
1983–91; knighted,
1991), 779, 782,
784–5, 785*
House of Commons, 3;
effect on home life,
61; MT's early career
in, 67–75, 82–3;
Private Members' Bills,
68–71; 'Lady Members'
Room', 68; MT's
combativeness in
industry, 74–5, 82–3,
117, 120, 122–3; not
broadcast live or on
radio (until 1978),
133†; MT against
Wilson in, 142; MT
against Callaghan
in, 143, 144; Tory
rebellion over Rhodesia
(1978), 160; MT in
vote of confidence
debate (December
1978), 169; MT in
vote of confidence
debate (March 1979),
171; Prime Minister's
Questions, 180–81,
760, 883*, 883, 905,
909; and Falklands
War, 287, 288, 293,
301–2, 305, 310,
312–13, 320, 321;
MT's attempts to
influence Speakership
choice (1983), 350,
354; MPs' pay,
allowances and
expenses, 354†, 354;
and Grenada crisis,
372, 373, 374; and
miners' strike, 390,
392; and Westland
affair, 510, 511,
515†, 515, 516–21;
Westland debate (27
January 1986), 518–19,
520–21; passage of
poll tax, 628–9,
646, 839; Lawson's
resignation statement,

House of Commons – *cont'd*
754; televised for first time (1989), 758–61; rejects Delors version of EMU, 841*; debate on Iraq crisis (1990), 865; MT's 'No. No. No.' words in, 875–6, 877, 883; Howe's resignation statement to (13 November 1990), 882–4, 936; and MT's resignation, 905–7; MT in after her fall, 917, 925, 928–9; MT leaves (1992), 925, 929; approves Maastricht Treaty, 933; Maastricht Bill, 934; tributes after MT's death, 964
House of Lords, 77*, 464, 925; Judicial Committee of, 379*; passage of poll tax, 629*, 629; salisbury Convention, 629*; televising of, 758*; MT enters as life peer, 930†, 930–31; MT's maiden speech, 933; Maastricht Bill, 934–5; MT's visits to, 939
Housing Act (1980), 337
housing policy: MT at 1950 election, 48; Heath's policy (1974), 112–14; bourgeois aspiration of ownership, 112, 113, 197, 201–2; 'right to buy' in October 1974 manifesto, 113; MT's letter to Evelyn Collingwood, 173–4; right to buy, 197, 201–2, 337, 543; council house rents, 279; mortgage interest tax relief, 491, 670*, 838†; MT's third term reform programme, 621; reform of council tenancies, 622; Lawson's overheating of mortgage market, 670*
Housman, A. E., 969
Houston, Texas, 158, 159
Houston Post, 89
Howard, Michael (1941–; educated Llanelli Grammar School and Peterhouse, Cambridge; Conservative MP for Folkestone and Hythe, 1983–2010; Home Secretary, 1993–7; Leader of the Conservative Party and Leader of the Opposition, 2003–5; created Lord Howard of Lympne, 2010): as 'Cambridge mafia' member, 351†; privatization of water industry, 768; and leadership contest (November 1990), 896, 897; individual session with MT (21 November 1990), 899; and Major's 'bastards' label, 935, 942; leadership contest (1997), 945–6
Howard, Sir Michael (historian), 147†, 237, 574*
Howard, Tony, 585–6
Howarth, D., 612
Howarth, Gerald (1947–; educated Bloxham School and Southampton University; Conservative MP for Cannock and Burntwood, 1983–92; for Aldershot, 1997–2017; PPS to Margaret Thatcher, 1991–2; knighted, 2012), 496, 541, 908†, 918, 959*
Howe, Elspeth (née Morton Shand) (1932–2022; educated Bath High School, Wycombe Abbey and LSE; Deputy Chairman, Equal Opportunities Commission, 1975–9; Chairman, Broadcasting Standards Commission, 1997–9; created Baroness Howe of Idlicote, 2001), 150*, 150, 277*, 559, 705, 740, 745, 746, 752, 878†
Howe, Geoffrey (1926–2015; educated Winchester and Trinity Hall, Cambridge; Conservative MP for Bebington, 1964–6; for Reigate, 1970–74; for Surrey East, 1974–92; Solicitor-General, 1970–72; Chancellor of the Exchequer, 1979–83; Foreign Secretary, 1983–9; Lord President of the Council and Deputy Prime Minister, 1989–90; knighted, 1970, created Lord Howe of Aberavon, 1992): legal background of, 61; MT's views on in Opposition, 104, 150–51, 153; in opposition, 109, 111–12, 150–51, 152, 162; supports Joseph's rethink, 111–12; leadership bid (1975), 126, 127, 186; on MT's leadership victory, 128; Shadow Chancellor, 129, 132, 150–51, 153, 162; lifting of exchange controls, 147, 199, 204–5; character of, 150–51, 152, 560, 561, 877, 878†, 878; MT's attitude towards, 150–1, 182, 203–4, 228, 274, 279, 352, 429, 530‡, 551*, 554, 561, 571*, 705; and policy-making, 150, 152; Economic Reconstruction Group, 152; MT's behaviour towards, 153, 196, 203–4, 279, 291, 367, 426*, 550–51, 574, 577, 626, 745–7, 752, 855, 878; and ERM question, 162, 163, 490, 491, 493, 494, 652, 660, 661, 677, 733–5, 734*, 738–43, 842, 883; and monetary

policy, 163, 197–200, 216–17, 223, 224, 225; and VAT increases, 176*; Adam Ridley as special adviser, 181†; Chancellor of the Exchequer, 182–3, 196, 197–200, 203–5, 216–17, 227–9, 235; Gow's friendship with, 186–7; 1979 budget, 196*, 196, 197–200, 542; and monetarism, 198–200, 216–17, 223, 224; on MT, 199, 361, 379, 461, 551, 556; and public spending control, 200, 202, 227–9, 235, 271–2, 334; 'there is no alternative' phrase, 205; and fight over EEC budget contribution, 210; 'Inner Group' on economic policy, 216–17; MTFS, 216, 217, 224, 267, 268*; trade union reform, 217–18; and British Leyland recovery plan, 220*; Autumn Statement (1980), 227–8, 228*; 1981 budget, 259, 268–71; introduces cash limits, 269‡; 1981 public expenditure review, 273–4; MT considers removal of (1981), 274; visits Washington (October 1981), 277*; on Blue Chips group, 277; Autumn Statement (1981), 279; and Falklands War, 287; excluded from Falklands War Cabinet, 291‡, 291; and 1983 election date, 342; and 1983 manifesto, 342, 344; Foreign Secretary, 350, 352, 500, 617; and Hong Kong, 361–3, 364; and Soviet Union, 366*, 367, 369; and US invasion of Grenada, 370, 371, 372; and GCHQ dispute, 378*,

378, 379; on MT's failings, 379; and Gorbachev, 419; with MT in Washington (1985), 426*, 426; views on SDI, 428–9, 564, 568, 571; and Charles Powell, 429†, 568, 626, 677, 736, 738, 739–40, 879; and Northern Ireland, 454–5, 456, 457, 458, 461, 721, 723†; and Delors, 481–2, 482*; and Milan European Council (1985), 485, 486; excluded from 1987 manifesto, 496; and Westland affair, 508, 514, 517, 520; and US attack on Libya, 530‡; preparations for 1987 election, 535; in Strategy Group ('A-Team'), 538; basic rate of 25 per cent aim, 543; deteriorating relations with MT, 550–51, 554, 556, 558–60, 561, 568, 602†, 602, 627; MT humiliates over EPG, 550–1, 561; at Nassau CHOGM (1985), 550–1, 551*; rift/conflict with MT, 550–51, 554, 556, 558, 559–60, 561, 661, 705; and South Africa, 550–1, 552, 553, 554, 555, 556, 558–9, 560, 561, 661, 788, 801; as EEC emissary to South Africa, 554, 555, 556, 558–9; letter to MT (August 1986), 559–60; collaboration with Lawson, 564, 602, 652, 660–61, 675, 733–5, 734*, 737, 738–43; excluded from Gorbachev talks (1987), 577; excluded from 1987 election planning, 602; considered for Lord Chancellorship, 617†, 735; and NHS crisis, 646†, 646; leadership ambitions, 652, 661;

estrangement with MT, 660–61, 665, 674–5, 739–43, 745–7, 801, 855, 869*, 878, 882–4, 914, 919–20, 936; at London EU Council (1986), 663†; and MT's EU rhetoric, 665; and Bruges Speech, 671–2, 673; and Rushdie affair, 695; and expulsion of Soviet spies (1989), 699–700, 700*; and Bush administration, 703; and *Death on the Rock*, 723†; and MT's tenth anniversary, 732–3; and Delors Committee report, 733–5; joint minute with Lawson ('Madrid ambush'), 735, 737, 738†, 738–43; and Madrid summit (June 1989), 740–43, 741†; and July 1989 reshuffle, 744, 745–6, 840; Deputy Prime Minister, 746, 752; as Leader of the House, 746; advises Lawson not to resign, 750–51; and German reunification issue, 812; gives eulogy at Gow's memorial service, 855; and UK's entry to ERM, 869*, 869; supports single currency, 875, 877; Walden interview during Rome Council, 875, 876; decision to resign from government, 877–8; resigns from Cabinet (1 November 1990), 878–80, 879*; resignation statement to Commons (13 November 1990), 882–4, 937; Ingham on, 882; personal letter of apology to MT, 919–20; as life peer, 939; MT as civil to in later life, 939; attends MT's 80th-birthday

Howe, Geoffrey – *cont'd*
dinner, 958; at MT's funeral, 965
Howell, David (1936–; educated Eton and King's College, Cambridge; Conservative MP for Guildford, 1966–97; Secretary of State for Energy, 1979–81; for Transport, 1981–3; created Lord Howell of Guildford, 1997), 146, 183, 216, 230, 276, 380
Hudson, Hugh, 607
Hughes, Francis, 260
Hugo, Victor, 177†
Hume, Cardinal Basil, 309, 639*
Hume, John (1937–2020; educated St Columb's College, Derry and St Patrick's College, Maynooth; Leader of the SDLP, 1979–2001; MEP, Northern Ireland, 1979–2004; SDLP MP for Foyle, 1983–2005; joint winner of Nobel Peace Prize, 1998), 260, 445, 455, 718; meetings with Adams, 727*, 727
Hungary, 365, 414–15, 811*, 831*; fall of Communism in, 803, 804
Hunt, John (1919–2008; educated Downside and Magdalen College, Oxford; served RNVR, 1940–46; joined Home Civil Service, 1946; Cabinet Secretary, 1973–9; created Lord Hunt of Tanworth, 1980): Cabinet Secretary, 108, 180, 186, 190, 208–9; and economic policy, 195, 196, 202, 208–9; and Northern Ireland, 251
Hunt, Sir Rex, Governor of the Falklands, 281, 284, 323
Hurd, Douglas (1930–; educated Eton and Trinity College, Cambridge; joined FCO, 1952; political secretary to the Prime Minister, 1970–74; Conservative MP for Mid Oxon, 1974–83; for Witney, 1983–97; Secretary of State for Northern Ireland, 1984–5; Home Secretary, 1985–9; Foreign Secretary, 1989–95; created Lord Hurd of Westwell, 1997): in China with MT, 156*; on Saltley Cokeworks picket, 382*; Northern Ireland Secretary, 454–5, 456; Home Secretary, 500, 617, 713; and policy on inner cities, 503; criticizes MT's leadership style, 519–20, 527; on Westland affair, 519–20; in Strategy Group ('A-Team'), 538; and Howe–Lawson collaboration, 661, 675; and expulsion of Soviet spies (1989), 700*; Foreign Secretary, 752, 806, 808, 818, 829, 851†; and broadcasting, 761, 764; and South Africa, 797; and German reunification issue, 806, 816, 819–20, 821, 826; visits Washington (January 1990), 818; visits Kohl in Bonn (February 1990), 819–20; at NATO summit (July 1990), 834, 835; at G7 in Houston (1990), 835‡; 'bond of steel' with Major, 841, 842, 850; and ERM question, 841; and Hong Kong immigration issue, 844; and Iraq 'War Cabinet' (1990), 862; and Iraqi invasion of Kuwait, 862, 865, 867; and Rome Council (1990), 874; and leadership contest (November 1990), 880–81, 886–7, 888, 891, 892, 898, 900, 901–2; pact with Major over leadership, 887, 891, 894, 897, 901, 913; with MT in Paris (18–21 November 1990), 888, 892; and 'Catherine Place conspiracy', 894; agrees to renominate MT, 898, 900, 901; and MT's resignation, 904; leadership campaign (November 1990), 905†; second ballot result (27 November 1990), 909; and MT's behaviour over Moscow coup, 926; and Bosnian crisis, 931–2
Hussein, King (1935–99; educated Harrow and Sandhurst; King of Jordan, 1952–99), 291, 323, 433, 434–6, 439, 857*, 858, 864–5
Hussey, Marmaduke 'Dukie' (1923–2006; educated Rugby and Trinity College, Oxford; served in Grenadier Guards in the Second World War; Chairman, Board of Governors, BBC, 1986–96; created Lord Hussey of North Bradley, 1996), 542*, 542†, 542, 761†, 761, 762, 763
Huth, Angela, 597, 598
Hutton, Graham, 110*

Ilford North by-election, 164
Illustrated London News, 101
immigration: from the Muslim world, 5; Powell's 'Rivers of Blood' speech, 87, 163; MT's 'British character' coding, 93, 163–4; Jenkins relaxes controls, 163*, 163; MT's 'swamped'

comment, 163–4, 843;
  from Pakistan and
  New Commonwealth,
  163–4; in Tory
  manifesto (1979), 173;
  and 1979 election
  campaign, 177; and
  Channel Tunnel project,
  479*; and Hong
  Kong issue, 839, 843,
  844–5, 849; and EC
  free movement, 933
Independent, 585, 670,
  732–3, 935
Independent Broadcasting
  Authority (IBA), 723‡,
  763
Independent on Sunday, 836
Independent Television
  News (ITN), 123,
  723–4
India: Methodist
  missionaries in, 10;
  MT's childhood
  fascination with, 10,
  39, 327; Indira Gandhi
  assassinated, 451*,
  451, 452; and green
  issues, 785
industrial relations:
  Heath government,
  102–8, 151; dock
  strike (1970), 102; and
  The Right Approach,
  145–6; Grunwick
  dispute, 152*, 152–3;
  and 1978–9 manifesto,
  167–8; unrest in steel
  industry, 217–19; dock
  strike (1984), 387*,
  387, 388, 390; MT's
  achievements/successes
  in, 396, 968, 970;
  strikes (1989), 747; *see
  also* trade unions and
  entries for the three
  miners' strikes
Industrial Relations Act
  (1971), 102, 105, 146,
  151
Industry Bill (1972), 103
inflation: in 1950s/early
  1960s, 65, 76; and
  MT's housewife
  analogies, 83; under
  Labour (1964–70), 85;
  Heath government,
  102, 104, 106, 107;
  monetarist theory of,

111, 131, 151, 200,
  205, 651, 883; under
  Labour (1974–9), 132,
  168; MT describes
  as evil, 139; during
  MT's first term, 195,
  200*, 200, 205, 272,
  273; causes of, 200;
  Reagan's view of,
  232; in MT's first
  term, 271*; in MT's
  second term, 399,
  489, 542, 602*, 602,
  651*, 651; in MT's
  third term, 654, 659,
  669–71, 749‡, 749,
  838, 839, 840†, 840,
  842–3, 851–2, 867–8,
  878, 887; Lawson's
  overheating of
  mortgage market, 670*
Ingham, Bernard
  (1932–2023; educated
  Hebden Bridge
  Grammar School;
  reporter, *Yorkshire Post*,
  1952–61; *Guardian*,
  1961–5; Director
  of Information,
  Department of
  Employment, 1973;
  Department of Energy,
  1973–7; chief press
  secretary to the Prime
  Minister, 1979–90;
  knighted, 1990): press
  secretary to MT,
  188–9, 230–31, 272,
  497; background
  and character, 188;
  on MT's attitude to
  media, 189; attitude
  to EEC, 209; *Old
  Moore's Almanack*,
  229; and NUM, 230;
  on Reagan, 231–2; and
  1981 budget, 270*,
  270; on letter of 364
  economists, 270; on
  Royal Wedding (1981),
  274; and Autumn
  Statement (1981), 279;
  and Mark Thatcher's
  disappearance during
  motor rally, 280; and
  Falklands War, 310;
  and 1983 election date,
  342; on 1983 election,
  349; and public

spending control,
  355–6; and Parkinson's
  affair with Keays, 358;
  and Tebbit, 359; and
  miners' strike, 384,
  394; and 1984 budget,
  399; and Gorbachev,
  420; and Anglo-Irish
  Agreement, 458; and
  GLC abolition, 465;
  and poll tax, 475, 847;
  and EU budget rebate,
  478; and Channel
  Tunnel project, 478–9;
  and 1985 reshuffle,
  497, 500; on *Faith
  in the City*, 503–4;
  and Westland affair,
  510–11, 515, 520,
  521, 523*, 523†,
  523, 524; as career
  civil servant, 521–2;
  prominence of in MT's
  government, 521–2,
  618, 735, 753; 'semi-
  detached' comment on
  Biffen, 537; on MT's
  1986 revival, 544; and
  Howe, 559–60; and
  South Africa, 559, 661,
  787; and MT's visit to
  Reagan (1986), 570,
  571; and MT's views
  on Reagan, 572; and
  1987 election, 613,
  615; on Whitelaw,
  627; and MT's inner-
  city policy, 631, 632,
  633; and NHS crisis,
  646; and 'Working
  for Patients' White
  Paper, 649; and
  'Black Monday', 655;
  and 'shadowing the
  deutschmark', 656;
  and MT's EU strategy,
  663, 664, 666*; and
  Thyssen collection
  project, 668; and
  Bruges Speech, 672–3;
  and Gorbachev's British
  stopover (December
  1987), 683; on secret
  services, 713, 714;
  and MT's tenth
  anniversary, 729, 730,
  731; sees egg crisis as
  turning point, 730; and
  ERM question, 739†,

Ingham, Bernard – *cont'd* 841, 848‡, 869; at Madrid summit (June 1989), 741–2; and televising of Parliament, 759–60; and broadcasting policy, 762, 763, 764; and privatization policy, 768*; and MT's use of religion, 777; and climate change, 779, 781; and anti-litter schemes, 783; Camp David meeting with Bush (1989), 810–11; and Meyer's leadership challenge, 838; Iraqi invasion of Kuwait, 859; and 1990 conference speech, 870; sends warning to MT after Eastbourne by-election, 870; on possible leadership challenge, 882; and leadership contest (November 1990), 888, 891, 892, 893, 898; first ballot result (20 November 1990), 892, 893; and MT's resignation as Prime Minister, 905*
Ingrams, Richard (1937–; educated Shrewsbury and University College, Oxford; Editor, *Private Eye*, 1963–86; *Oldie*, 1992–2014), 588
Inkatha movement, 551
Inman, Bobby Ray, 294–5
Inner London Education Authority (ILEA), 633†, 633
Inns of Court Conservative and Unionist Association, 61
Institute of Directors, 136
Institute of Economic Affairs (IEA), 110, 146
intelligence and security services: Blunt scandal, 207–8, 706; monitoring of striking miners (1984–5), 388, 393, 417‡, 417, 418‡, 418; and Neave, 417*; MT's respect for, 417, 533*, 715, 923; and Cold War, 706–15; and Victor Rothschild, 707–9, 710–11, 714–15; Callaghan calls for inquiry into, 713; Ingham on, 713, 714; and Northern Ireland, 720, 726–7; *see also* Government Communications Headquarters (GCHQ); Secret Intelligence Service (SIS or MI6); Security Service (MI5)
interest rates: and globalism, 6; Barber's raising of, 106; Minimum Lending Rate (MLR), 106, 198, 205; monetarist approach to, 198†, 216, 223; in MT's first term, 198–9, 205, 216, 224, 225, 227–8, 267, 268–9, 276–7, 280; MT's initial objection to rises, 198–9, 205, 654–5; impact of high US rates on UK, 273; in MT's second term, 490, 491, 492; and ERM battle, 652, 840–41, 848, 867–9; in MT's third term, 654–5, 660, 661–2, 669–71, 747, 749‡, 749, 753, 838, 839, 840–41, 867–9, 913; Lawson–MT conflict over (1988), 661–2, 669–71, 671*; 'Black Wednesday', 933†, 933
Intergovernmental Panel on Climate Change (IPCC), 779, 784*, 784
International Committee of the Red Cross, 262
International Monetary Fund (IMF), loan to Britain (1976), 144, 216
Invincible, HMS, 290, 314
IRA (Irish Republican Army): murder of Ross McWhirter, 141†; murder of Mountbatten, 207, 252, 715*; Chelsea Barracks bombing (1981), 252*; 'special-category status' for prisoners demand, 254*, 254–5; Maze hunger strikes, 254–6, 259–63, 262*, 265, 727; Provisional–Official split, 255‡; bombing of the Grand Hotel, Brighton (1984), 391–2, 448–51, 452, 466, 499, 589*, 604†, 604, 855, 951; bombing of Harrods (1983), 447; Libyan aid to, 529, 720, 724–5; extradition from US to UK, 534–5; Botha on, 548, 789; Ballygawley attack (1988), 671†, 725; MT's desire to defeat, 718‡, 718, 724; Loughgall barracks trap, 719–20, 854; Gibraltar shootings (March 1988), 721–2, 723, 724, 727, 854; murder of British Army corporals (March 1988), 722*, 722, 723–4; backchannel with British state, 727; murder of Ian Gow, 853, 854–5; debate within over ending violence, 854; mainland attacks (1990), 854; MT as top of PIRA death list, 950†, 950
Iran: Islamist revolution in, 191; US Embassy siege in Teheran, 213; embassy siege, Princes Gate, 221–2, 865; war with Iraq, 437*, 857; taking of Western hostages, 570, 695*, 695; fatwa on Salman Rushdie, 695–7
'Iran-Contra' affair, 569†, 569–70, 572, 575, 676*, 676; Tower Commission, 676–7; Congressional hearings, 677, 678
Iran–Iraq War, 437*, 857
Iraq: and King Hussein, 434; Iran–Iraq War,

437*, 857; invasion of Kuwait (1990), 696, 785, 856–67, 862*, 862†, 870–72, 878, 891*, 891, 908; execution of Farzad Bazoft, 857*, 857; sanctions against over Kuwait, 859–60, 861–2, 863*, 863, 864; Desert Storm removes forces from Kuwait, 917; Kurdish 'safe havens' in, 917
Ireland, Republic of: MT's views on, 250, 252–3, 444–5, 447, 721, 722–3, 724–5, 969; and Neave's regional councils proposal, 251; and security situation in Northern Ireland, 252–3, 444–5, 447–8, 718, 720–21, 723–5; UK's direct dealings with over Northern Ireland, 254, 256–9, 258‡, 452–61; MT's Dublin summit with Haughey, 256–7; 'joint studies' concept, 256, 257–9, 258‡, 264; claim to the 'whole island' in Constitution, 258*, 258, 262, 446*, 446, 447, 448; and Maze hunger strikes, 259, 260–61, 262, 265; Anglo-Irish summit, London (November 1981), 263–4, 264*; principle of consent in relation to the North, 264*, 264; and Falklands War, 265, 305, 309, 312, 323, 444, 718; FitzGerald's New Ireland Forum, 445, 446–8, 452–4; partition of Ireland recognized by treaty (1925), 446*; 'basic equation', 447, 454–5; Reagan visits (1984), 448; terrorist extradition issue, 455*, 455–6, 457, 460*, 460, 720–21, 724–5; Garda Síochána, 460;

neutrality in Second World War, 718*, 718, 969; Haughey returns to office (1987), 718; poor relations with UK (1987–88), 718; poor relations with UK during MT's third term, 720–25; government backchannel with Adams, 727*
Irish American Voice, 442
Irish Commission for Justice and Peace (ICJP), 260*, 260–61
Irish National Liberation Army, 174
'Iron Hand' (Dire Straits song, 1991), 386‡
Iron Lady, The (Phyllida Lloyd film, 2012), 960–61, 961*
ISAs, 413
Islam, 818
Islamist terrorism, 5
Isle of Ely by-election (1973), 106
Islington Council, 629†
Israel, 88, 188, 284–5, 432–3, 434, 435*, 435, 436, 439†; MT visits (May 1986), 436–7; attempts to sell fighter aircraft to Argentina, 685
ISTC (steelworkers' union), 217–19
Italy, 485, 653, 813, 872, 873*
ITV (Independent Television), 540–41, 761, 762*, 763, 764*, 764

J. Lyons and Co., 44
Jackson, Glenda (1936–2023; educated West Kirby County Grammar School for Girls; RADA; actress, 1957–92; Labour MP for Hampstead and Highgate, 1992–2010; for Hampstead and Kilburn, 2010–15), 964
Jackson, Robert, 552*
Jaguar, 219, 220
Jaguar ground attack/fighter aircraft, 861*

Jakobovits, Immanuel (1921–99; educated University of London and Jews' College and Yeshivah Etz Chaim, London; Chief Rabbi of the United Hebrew Congregations of the British Commonwealth of Nations, 1967–91; knighted, 1981; created Lord Jakobovits, 1988), 504*, 504, 643, 726
James, Eric, 503*
James, Henry (press secretary), 188
James, Howell, 603*
Japan, 191, 795
Jardine-Paterson, Tessa, *see* Gaisman, Tessa
Jaruzelski, Wojciech (1923–2014; First Secretary, Polish United Workers' Party, 1981–9; Prime Minister, 1981–5; Chairman of the Council of State, 1985–9; President, 1989–90), 245, 692–5
Jay, Douglas, 83*, 83, 204
Jay, Michael, 874
Jay, Peter, 157*, 157, 159
Jefferson, Sir George, 338*, 403*
Jenkin, Patrick (1926–2016; educated Clifton College and Jesus College, Cambridge; Conservative MP for Wanstead and Woodford, 1964–87; Minister for Energy, 1974; Secretary of State for Social Services, 1979–81; for Industry, 1981–3; for the Environment, 1983–5; created Lord Jenkin of Roding, 1987): legal background of, 61; 'Inner Group' on economic policy, 216; Industry Secretary, 278; and public spending control, 278; and Falklands War, 307; and BT privatization, 338–9; and local

Jenkin, Patrick – *cont'd*
government, 465†,
465–6, 467†, 467; and
1985 reshuffle, 496,
501; leaves government
(1985), 501
Jenkins, David (1925–2016;
educated St Dunstan's
College, Catford and the
Queen's College, Oxford;
Professor of Theology,
University of Leeds,
1979–84; Bishop of
Durham, 1984–94), 391
Jenkins, Michael, 209
Jenkins, Peter, 228, 234,
732–3
Jenkins, Roy (1920–2003;
educated Abersychan
County Grammar
School, University
College, Cardiff, Balliol
College, Oxford;
Labour MP for
Southwark Central,
1948–50; for
Birmingham Stechford,
1950–77; Home
Secretary, 1965–67;
1974–76; Chancellor
of the Exchequer,
1967–70; President of
European Commission,
1977–81; Member of
'Gang of Four' that
founded the SDP, 1981;
SDP MP for Glasgow
Hillhead, 1982–87;
Chancellor, University
of Oxford, 1987–2003;
created Lord Jenkins
of Hillhead, 1987) and
immigration, 163*, 163;
President of European
Commission, 163*, 209,
210; and Labour split,
227†; Limehouse
Declaration, 234–5;
visits Washington
(October 1981), 277*
Jenkins, Simon (1943–;
educated Mill Hill
and St John's College,
Oxford; journalist
and prolific author;
Editor, *Evening
Standard*, 1976–8, and
The Times, 1990–92;
knighted, 2004), 887

*Jenny Lives with Eric and
Martin* (book), 633
Jews: persecution of in Nazi
era, 15, 16; in Finchley,
64–5, 69†, 69, 77, 79*,
88, 432–3, 434; MT's
views on, 64–5, 88,
110, 111, 351, 504*,
504; element of anti-
Semitism in Tory Party,
351, 500; in Soviet
Union, 418, 579;
Jakobovits on, 504;
Lawson as of Jewish
descent, 652*
Joachim, M., 348
John, King, 953†
John Brown Engineering,
246, 248
John Paul II, Pope (Karol
Wojtyła) (1920–2005;
Archbishop of Kraków,
1964–78; elected Pope,
1978), 244–5, 309,
315*, 315, 959
Johnson, Frank, 124*, 148,
175, 344
Johnson, Paul
(1928–2023; Editor,
New Statesman,
1965–70; author of
many works of history),
147*, 148*, 148
Joint Intelligence Committee
(JIC), 283*, 283, 682,
686, 697
Jones, Colonel 'H', 317–18
Jones, Nicholas, 381*
Jopling, Michael (1930–;
educated Cheltenham
and King's College,
Newcastle-upon-Tyne;
Conservative MP for
Westmorland, 1964–83;
for Westmorland and
Lonsdale, 1983–97;
Government Chief
Whip, 1979–83;
Minister of Agriculture,
Fisheries and Food,
1983–7; created Lord
Jopling, 1997), 182, 184,
274, 288, 307, 884*;
and 1983 election
date, 342–3; and MT's
leadership campaign
team (1990), 885*, 885
Jordan, 291, 323, 434–6,
437*, 864–5

Joseph, Helen, Lady, 117*,
117
Joseph, Keith (1918–94;
2nd baronet; educated
Harrow and Magdalen
College, Oxford;
Conservative MP for
Leeds North East,
1956–87; Secretary
of State for Social
Services, 1970–74; for
Industry, 1979–81; for
Education and Science,
1981–6; founder and
Chairman, Centre
for Policy Studies,
1974–9 (Director,
1991–4); created
Lord Joseph, 1987):
MT's admiration for/
closeness to, 81, 104,
110, 115, 116–18, 434;
in Heath government,
98, 104; opposes
deal with Liberals
(February 1974), 108;
and CPS, 109–10,
131; in opposition,
109–10, 111–12, 129,
146, 150, 152, 153;
influence on MT, 110,
111, 131–2, 360, 942;
Preston speech, 111*,
111; and monetarism,
111, 131, 217; and
party leadership, 114,
115, 116–18, 121;
Edgbaston speech,
116–17; withdraws as
potential leader, 117;
liberal view on drugs,
131*; *Notes Towards
the Definition of Policy*
(paper), 131–2; on
Communist subversion,
131; Secretary of
State for Industry,
182–3, 197; and public
spending control,
183, 197, 278; 'Inner
Group' on economic
policy, 216; and British
Leyland recovery plan,
220, 221; and 1981
budget, 270; Education
Secretary, 276, 635, 636*;
report on education
vouchers, 336–7;
character of, 337, 852;

and BT privatization, 338; and Brighton bombing, 449; and 1985 reshuffle, 498; leaves government (1986), 537; at MT's farewell lunch, 908†, 909; introduces MT in Lords, 930†; death of (1994), 939
Judge Institute, Cambridge, 922*
Junor, John (1919–97; educated North Kelvinside Secondary School and Glasgow University; Editor, *Sunday Express*, 1954–86; knighted, 1980), 716, 732*

Kaberry, Donald, 62, 63
Kádár, János, 414–15
Karadžić, Radovan (1945–; first President of Republika Srpska, 1992–6; convicted in 2016 by the International Criminal Tribunal for the former Yugoslavia of crimes including genocide. Sentenced to forty years' imprisonment, later increased to life), 931
Kaser, Michael, 366*
Kaufman, Gerald (1930–2017; educated Leeds Grammar School and the Queen's College, Oxford; Labour MP for Manchester, Ardwick, 1970–83; for Manchester, Gorton, 1983–2017; Shadow Environment Secretary, 1980–83; Shadow Home Secretary, 1983–7; Shadow Foreign Secretary, 1987–92; knighted, 2004), 344
Kaunda, Kenneth, 194‡, 194, 195, 506*
Kavanagh, Dennis, 167
Keays, Sara, 347–8, 357, 358–9, 498, 500, 617–18; *A Question of Judgement* (1985), 498‡
Keble College, Oxford, 141

Kedourie, Elie (1926–92; educated Baghdad, LSE and St Antony's College, Oxford; lecturer, then Professor of Politics, LSE, 1953–90; author of *The Chatham House Version* (1970)), 237
Keeble, Chris, 318
Keeler, Christine, 76‡, 949
Keith, Lord, 714
Kendall, Denis, 29
Kenya, 791†
Kerr, John (1942–; educated Glasgow Academy and Pembroke College, Oxford; principal private secretary to the Chancellor of the Exchequer, 1981–4; Head of Chancery, British Embassy, Washington, 1984–7; Assistant Under-Secretary, FCO, 1987–90; Ambassador and UK Permanent Representative to EU, 1990–95; Ambassador to the United States, 1995–7; Permanent Under-Secretary, FCO, 1997–2002; created Lord Kerr of Kinlochard, 2004), 279, 291‡, 652, 665, 671, 672*, 672, 673, 685, 869; and Rome Council (1990), 872–3; views on EC, 873†, 875*
Kerry, John, 535*, 965‡
Kershaw, Sir Anthony, 371
Kesteven and Grantham Girls' School (KGGS), 16–17, 19, 20–23
Keynes, John Maynard, 27–8, 75*, 89, 147*, 158; *Economic Consequences of the Peace*, 110
Keyser Ullmann (bank), 120
Khomeini, Ayatollah (1902–89; founder of the Islamic Republic of Iran and leader of the 1979 Iranian Revolution that overthrew the last Shah of Iran. Khomeini became Iran's supreme leader, a position he held until his death), 695
Kim Il Sung, 330*
Kinchin-Smith, Michael, 29
King, John (1917–2005; Chairman, British Airways plc, 1981–93; Chairman, Babcock International Group plc, 1970–94; master, Belvoir Hunt, 1958–72; knighted, 1979; created Lord King of Wartnaby, 1983), 404†, 404‡, 404–5, 405*, 542, 549, 732*
King, Margaret, 597
King, Tom (1933–; educated Rugby and Emmanuel College, Cambridge; Conservative MP for Bridgwater, March 1970–2001; Secretary of State for the Environment, January–June 1983; for Transport, June–October 1983; for Employment, 1983–5; for Northern Ireland, 1985–9; for Defence, 1989–92; created Lord King of Bridgwater, 2001): Employment Secretary, 359, 501; Northern Ireland Secretary, 456–7, 459, 500, 719, 721, 725, 727–8, 854; and 1985 reshuffle, 496; speech in Belfast (November 1988), 727–8; considered for Foreign Secretary, 752; Defence Secretary, 830; and Iraq 'War Cabinet' (1990), 862, 863; nominates Hurd for leadership, 905†
Kingston, Bob, 141–2, 449
Kinnock, Glenys (*later* Baroness Kinnock of Holyhead), 607–8, 930*
Kinnock, Neil (1942–; educated Lewis School, Pengam and University College,

Kinnock, Neil – *cont'd*
Cardiff; Labour MP
for Bedwellty, 1970–83;
for Islwyn, 1983–95;
Leader of the Labour
Party and Leader
of the Opposition,
1983–92; Vice-
President, European
Commission,
1999–2004; created
Lord Kinnock of
Bedwellty, 2005), 357,
359–60; Goose Green
comment (1983), 345;
and Grenada crisis,
374; and miners' strike,
390, 392, 394*; Leader
of the Opposition, 423,
600; attack on Militant
Tendency in Liverpool,
471, 501; battle with
hard left, 471, 501,
600; reform of Labour
Party, 495, 600; and
Westland affair, 511,
518, 520; and Westland
debate, 518, 520;
unilateralism of, 567,
600–601, 609; meetings
with Reagan, 600–602;
defence policy, 601,
609; 1987 election
campaign, 607–8,
609; on deutschmark,
657, 660, 661–2; and
televising of Parliament,
758, 759, 760; on
single currency, 875; at
PMQs (13 November
1990), 883*, 883, and
MT's resignation as
Prime Minister, 906; in
MT's memoirs, 923
Kipling, Rudyard, 19,
147*, 147, 303, 584,
729, 934, 959; 'Sons
of Martha', 12, 971;
'Recessional', 622,
759–60; 'The Reeds at
Runnymede', 953†, 953
Kirkpatrick, Jeane
(1926–2006; served
as Ronald Reagan's
foreign policy
adviser in his 1980
campaign and later
in his Cabinet; first
female US Permanent
Representative to the
UN), 294–5, 310, 311*,
313, 315, 319, 323
Kissinger, Henry
(1923–2023; born in
Germany; educated
George Washington
High School, New
York City and Harvard
University; National
Security Advisor,
1969–75; US Secretary
of State, 1973–), 135†,
136*, 137, 270, 414,
429, 568, 689*, 949†;
on MT, 135–6, 159,
678, 860*; on China,
330; and Reagan's
nuclear policy, 571,
678–9; and Iraqi
invasion of Kuwait,
860*, 862†; at MT's
funeral, 965
Kitson, Timothy
(1931–2019; educated
Charterhouse and
Royal Agricultural
College, Cirencester;
Conservative MP for
Richmond, Yorkshire,
1959–83; PPS to
Edward Heath,
1970–74; knighted,
1974), 129
Knight, Andrew, 126*, 594†
Knight, Greg, 885†
Knight, Jill (1923–2022;
educated King Edward's
School, Birmingham;
Conservative MP
for Birmingham,
Edgbaston, 1966–97;
created Baroness Knight
of Collingtree, 1997),
633–4
Koestler, Arthur, 110;
Darkness at Noon, 147
Kohl, Helmut (1930–2017;
Leader of the CDU/
CSU, 1976–98;
Chancellor of Federal
Republic of Germany,
1982–90; of reunified
Germany, 1990–98):
MT's immediate dislike
of, 135†, 333; views on
European unification,
332–3, 481, 484–5,
486, 810, 812, 813,
814–15; and INF
deployment, 332, 333,
346; and EU budget
settlement with MT,
475–6; relations with
Mitterrand, 477, 480,
815, 817, 835; on MT's
Channel Tunnel
anxieties, 479*; at
Verdun with Mitterrand,
480; MT's poor
relationship with, 483–7,
663–4, 664*, 679,
701–2, 704, 802,
809–10, 814, 827,
889; Luxembourg
IGC (December 1985),
486–7; and apartheid
South Africa, 548*,
555, 789–90; insults
Gorbachev, 575*;
and MT's Moscow
visit (1987), 575; and
MT's alcohol intake,
662*; MT sensitive
to the electoral needs
of, 663†, 822; and
Williamson candidacy,
665; and EMU,
666; and SR nuclear
weapons, 679–80,
687; at special NATO
summit (1988), 687;
increasingly difficult
relationship with MT,
692, 809–10, 814, 820;
and NATO nuclear
'modernization', 700†,
700–701; and SNF
negotiations, 700, 701,
702, 703–4, 736‡; and
Bush, 701, 702, 704;
German reunification
issue, 802*, 806,
808, 809–10, 812,
820–21; and fall of
Berlin Wall, 808, 809;
'Ten Point Plan', 812;
at Strasbourg Council
(1989), 814†, 814–15;
Hurd visits (February
1990), 819–20;
meets Gorbachev in
Moscow (July 1990),
820–21, 836; meets
Bush at Camp David
(February 1990), 822,
823; Polish border
issue, 822, 823*, 823,

825*, 825, 827*, 827;
MT congratulates over
Polish border, 825,
827; wins elections in
GDR (March 1990),
825; at NATO summit
(July 1990), 834–5;
MT congratulates on
unification, 836;
and Iraqi invasion
of Kuwait, 862*;
CSCE summit in Paris
(November 1990), 889;
Major's relations with,
924†; tribute to MT on
her death, 964
Königswinter conference,
Cambridge, 827
Koornhof, Pieter 'Piet'
(1925–2007; educated
Stellenbosch and
Oxford Universities;
National Party Cabinet
Minister in various
portfolios in 1970s
and 1980s; South
African Ambassador
to the United States,
1987–91), 551–2
Korean War (1950–53), 54
Kosov, Nikolai (1955–;
assistant, senior
assistant, attaché,
Third, Second and
then First Secretary,
Counsellor of the
USSR Embassy,
1977–92), 581*, 686,
687, 803*, 831–2
Kosovo, 932
Kosygin, Alexei, 191, 239
Krenz, Egon (1937–;
General Secretary,
Socialist Unity Party of
Germany, 18 October–3
December 1989), 806
Kurds, 917
Kureishi, Hanif (1954–;
educated King's College
London; his novel *The
Buddha of Suburbia*
won the Whitbread
Prize for best first novel
in 1990; his film scripts
include *My Beautiful
Laundrette* (1985)),
583, 586
Kuwait, 434, 437*; Iraqi
invasion of (1990),
696, 785, 856–67,
862*, 862†, 870–72,
878, 891*, 891, 908;
Desert Storm removes
Iraqi forces from, 917

Labour Party: use of
Thatcher-inspired
statecraft, 4–5; under
Blair, 4, 941–2;
Starmer government,
4, 5; and pre-war local
politics, 14; removes
Alfred Roberts as
alderman (1953), 61–2;
attitude to press, 69;
reactions to MT as
new young minister,
74; MT's 'other
people's money' phrase,
82; commitment to
comprehensive schools,
91–2; nationalizes
shipbuilding and
aircraft industry,
143–4, 144*, 144†,
173*, 337*; loses
overall Commons
majority (1976), 143;
devolution proposals,
161–2, 162*; attitude to
EEC, 209; splits, 227†,
227, 234–5; political
levy, 341–2; manifesto
(1983), 343–4; and
unilateralism, 345, 543,
567, 600–601, 609*,
609; and miners' strike,
389–90, 394*; and
Anglo-Irish Agreement,
459; and hard left's
rate-capping revolt,
471; Kinnock's reform
of, 495; and Murdoch,
525, 765; conference
(1986), 543; failure
to understand MT's
appeal, 599–600;
hostility of Reagan
administration to,
600–602; 1987 election
campaign, 607–8, 609;
1987 election vote,
612; Scottish Labour,
619–20; poll lead
in summer of 1989,
746–7, 747*; tables
no-confidence debate
(November 1990), 893,
905–7; 'New Labour',
941–2
Laing, Hector (1923–2010;
educated Loretto
and Jesus College,
Cambridge; Chairman,
United Biscuits,
1972–90; created Lord
Laing of Dunphail,
1991), 182, 187*, 218*,
218, 632, 732*, 918*
Laker, Sir Freddie, 405–6,
406*
Laker Airways, 405–6,
406*, 407
Lamb, Sir Larry, 137, 166
Lamberhurst, Kent, 80, 93,
96, 106*, 107, 112,
141, 169
Lamont, Norman (1942–;
educated Loretto
and Fitzwilliam
College, Cambridge;
Conservative MP
for Kingston-upon-
Thames, 1972–97;
Financial Secretary
to the Treasury,
1986–9; Chief Secretary
to the Treasury,
1989–90; Chancellor
of the Exchequer,
1990–93; created
Lord Lamont of
Lerwick, 1998), 909;
in opposition, 146;
as 'Cambridge mafia'
member, 351†; in
rising generation of
Conservative politicians,
645; and leadership
contest (November
1990), 886, 887, 890,
897, 898; and 'Catherine
Place conspiracy', 894;
nominates Major for
leadership, 905†; and
conspiracy to remove
MT, 913
Lancaster House conference
(1979), 195, 213, 214,
215
Lancet, 642
Land Rover, 219, 220, 527
Landon, Timothy, 441
Lane, Geoffrey, Lord, 767
Langton, Thomas, 63–4
Lankester, Tim (1942–;
educated Monkton

Lankester, Tim – *cont'd*
Combe School,
St John's College,
Cambridge and Yale
University; private
secretary to the Prime
Minister, 1979–81;
Permanent Secretary,
Overseas Development
Administration,
1989–94; knighted,
1994), 181, 441, 796
Lansley, Andrew (1956–;
educated Exeter
University; private
secretary to Secretary
of State for Trade and
Industry, 1984–5;
Conservative MP for
South Cambridgeshire,
1997–2015; Secretary
of State for Health,
2010–12; created Lord
Lansley, 2015), 499
Larkin, Philip (1922–85;
poet and novelist;
Companion of Honour,
1985), 237, 584*, 584
Lawson, Nigel
(1932–2023; educated
Westminster and Christ
Church, Oxford;
Conservative MP
for Blaby, 1974–92;
Financial Secretary
to the Treasury,
1979–81; Secretary
of State for Energy,
1981–3; Chancellor of
the Exchequer, 1983–9;
created Lord Lawson
of Blaby, 1992): in
opposition, 142*, 146,
150, 162–3; and ERM
question, 162–3, 490*,
490–91, 492–5, 602,
651–3, 733–5, 734*,
738–43, 750; and
monetary policy, 162–3,
216, 654–5, 887; and
VAT increases, 176*;
on MT, 177; Financial
Secretary to the
Treasury, 203–4; and
monetarism, 216,
223†, 223, 268*,
489, 651, 654, 655;
MTFS, 216, 489;
Energy Secretary, 276,
380, 408; and public
spending control, 278,
355, 356; Dry narrative
of economic recovery,
280; and Falklands
War, 287; and
privatization policy,
337–8, 355†, 355, 400,
401, 402*, 402, 408,
409, 770, 771, 774;
appointed Chancellor
(June 1983), 349–50,
381; and Walters, 353,
654, 670‡, 670,
749–52, 753, 754;
Chancellor of the
Exchequer, 355, 413,
500, 617, 887; public-
spending Cabinet
(21 July 1983), 356;
and tax policy, 360,
398–400, 465–6, 468†,
470, 472, 491–2, 542‡,
542–3, 602, 658–60;
and miners' strike, 380;
1984 budget, 398–400;
relations with MT, 399,
400, 470, 489–90, 494;
on Sir Denis Rooke,
408; and stock
exchange reform, 410;
and local government,
465–6, 468†, 468,
470, 471, 472; and
poll tax, 470*, 470,
472, 473, 628, 748–9,
750; opposes European
single currency, 490,
662; 1985 budget,
491–2; Mansion House
speech (1985), 493,
clash with MT over
ERM, 494–5, 651,
652, 653, 656–8, 661,
662; and Westland
affair, 511, 514; and
Ford interest in BL,
528; preparations for
1987 election, 535; in
Strategy Group
('A-Team'), 538; 1986
budget, 542–3; as
Master of the Mint,
560*; collaboration
with Howe, 564, 602,
652, 660–61, 675,
733–5, 734*, 737,
738–43; 1987 budget,
602; and Lord Young,
605*, 611, 622; 1987
election campaign,
608, 609, 611; and
Charles Powell, 626; on
Whitelaw's retirement,
627; exchange rate
management, 646, 651,
653–4, 655, 656–8,
660, 670, 934*; MT's
anxieties over, 646,
652, 654–5, 656–8,
660–62,669–71,738–43,
749–52; 'shadowing the
deutschmark' policy,
646, 653–4, 655,
656–8, 660, 670, 934*;
and health reform,
647, 649; Autumn
Statement (1988), 649;
as of Jewish descent,
652*; ambition to be
Foreign Secretary, 652;
and DM3 rate, 653,
656, 657–8, 660, 661;
MT's deteriorating
relationship with, 653,
654–5, 656–8, 660–62,
735, 738–43, 749–52;
and growth in credit
(summer 1987), 654–5;
1988 budget, 658–60,
659†, 668, 671; conflict
with MT over interest
rates (summer 1988),
661–2, 669–71, 671*;
balance of payments
figures (May 1988),
669–70; overheating
of mortgage market,
670*; and Delors
Committee report,
733–5; joint minute
with Howe ('Madrid
ambush'), 735, 737,
738†, 738–43; and
Madrid summit (June
1989), 740–43, 741†,
750; and July 1989
reshuffle, 744, 745,
746, 750; falling
public confidence in,
749–50; ultimatum
over Walters, 751–2;
resigns as Chancellor,
752*, 752, 753,
754, 794, 806, 855;
resignation statement
to House, 754; views
on BBC, 761; and

climate change, 779, 780, 783; holds down mortgage tax relief, 838†; and Howe's resignation, 879*; and Howe's resignation statement, 883
Lawson, General Sir Richard, 260
Lawson, Thérèse, 738†
Lawther, Anne, 960
Lawton, Frederick (1911–2001; educated Battersea Grammar School and Corpus Christi College, Cambridge; criminal advocate; QC, 1957; High Court judge, 1961; Lord Justice of Appeal, 1972; knighted, 1961), 59–60
Le Carré, John (pseudonym of David Cornwell) (1931–2020; educated Sherborne, Berne University and Lincoln College, Oxford; author of spy novels, including *The Spy Who Came in from the Cold* (1963), *Tinker, Tailor, Soldier, Spy* (1974) and *Smiley's People* (1980)), 589, 598*, 696, 715†
Leach, Henry (1923–2011; educated Royal Naval College, Dartmouth; Commander-in-Chief Fleet and Allied Commander-in-Chief, Channel and Eastern Atlantic, 1977–9; Chief of Naval Staff and First Sea Lord, 1979–82; Admiral of the Fleet, 1982; knighted, 1977), 285–6, 287, 291, 302*
Lebanon: US Marine barracks bombing, Beirut, 371–2; Israeli invasion of (1982), 437*; Western hostages held in, 570, 695*
legal profession, 766–8, 767*
legal system, 6; rarity of women at Bar, 60–61; Continental view, 60; principles of English law, 60; rule of law, 60, 105–6, 131, 167, 171, 172, 329, 374, 406, 696–7, 723–4, 921, 971; Bill of Rights proposals, 131*; trade union immunities, 172–3, 217–18, 276, 278; MT's view of history, 327; Judicial Committee of House of Lords, 379*; actions against NUM by working miners, 384, 388, 392–3, 395; judicial review of union ban at GCHQ, 387; miners' strike declared unlawful, 392–3; 'Diplock' courts in Northern Ireland, 454‡, 454; use of Law Officers in government, 511–13, 513*, 515–16, 517–19, 520–21, 522–4, 768; Scottish, 766–7; liberalization of conveyancing, 767*, 768; and Pergau Dam project, 796†, 796
Lehman, John, 294
Leicestershire County Council, 91
Leigh, Edward, 903, 908†, 909
Leigh, Sir Geoffrey, 918*
Leigh-Pemberton, (Robert) Robin (1927–2013; educated Eton and Trinity College, Oxford; Governor, Bank of England, 1983–93; created Lord Kingsdown, 1993), 490, 491, 492, 493, 735, 751, 754*
LeMay, Curtis B., 824†, 824
Lenihan, Brian, 257
Lenin, 418§, 418
Leninakan (Armenia), 832–3
Lennox-Boyd, Arabella, 950
Lennox-Boyd, Mark (1943–2025; educated Eton and Christ Church, Oxford; Conservative MP for Morecambe and Lonsdale, 1979–83, Morecambe and Lunesdale, 1983–97; PPS to Chancellor of the Exchequer, 1983–4; government whip, 1984–88; PPS to Prime Minister, 1988–90; Parliamentary Under-Secretary, Foreign Office, 1990–94; knighted, 1994), 732*, 732‡, 738†, 746–7, 748, 753*, 754, 950; as MT's PPS, 731, 852; on Charles Powell, 736†; and ERM question, 739†, 739; and Howe's demotion, 744; and Lawson–Walters issue, 750, 751, 752, 753; and Meyer's leadership challenge, 755, 756; on Howe, 877
Letwin, Oliver (1956–; educated Eton and Trinity College, Cambridge; member, No. 10 Policy Unit, 1983–6; Conservative MP for West Dorset, 1997–2019; Minister for Government Policy, Cabinet Office, 2010–15; Chancellor of the Duchy of Lancaster, 2014–16; Cabinet minister in overall charge of government policy, 2015): twins of, 11*; on MT and privatization, 338; in Policy Unit, 353†, 464, 466–7, 503; at Rothschilds, 412†; and local government, 466–7, 468, 469, 471–2; and poll tax, 468, 469, 471–2, 473
Letwin, Shirley, 147*
Leutwiler, Fritz (1924–97; President of Swiss National Bank, 1974–84; Chairman and President, Bank for International Settlements, 1982–4), 226, 552, 790–91
Lewin, Terence (1920–99; educated the Judd

Lewin, Terence – *cont'd*
School, Tonbridge;
Royal Navy, 1939;
served in Second World
War (DSC 1942); Chief
of Naval Staff and
First Sea Lord, 1977–9;
Chief of Defence Staff,
1979–82; created Lord
Lewin of Greenwich,
1982; Knight of the
Garter, 1983), 292–3,
300, 304, 306
Lewis, C. S., 147*; *Christian Behaviour*, 23; *The Screwtape Letters*, 352†
Lewis, Kenneth, 115
Li Peng (1928–2019; Acting Prime Minister of the People's Republic of China, November 1987–March 1988; Prime Minister, 1988–98), 927–8
Liberal Democrats, 624, 855, 865, 868†, 868, 870, 957
Liberal Party: in 1930s, 14; in Finchley, 69; 1966 election, 85; by-election wins (1973), 106; February 1974 vote share, 108; and Callaghan government, 143, 603–4; Lib-Lab Pact (late 1970s), 143, 603–4; SDP-Liberal Alliance, 341, 342, 346, 348, 600, 603–4, 604*, 606, 612, 615; Bermondsey by-election victory, 342; and 1983 election, 346, 348; and 1987 election, 515, 603–4, 604*, 606, 612; and unilateral nuclear disarmament, 543
library books, 635*
Libya, 393, 442, 456, 528–31, 530†, 532–4, 533*, 535, 541, 720, 724–5
Lilley, Peter (1943–; educated Dulwich College and Clare College, Cambridge; Conservative MP for St Albans, 1983–97; for Hitchin and Harpenden, 1997–2017; Economic Secretary to the Treasury, 1987–9; Financial Secretary to the Treasury, 1989–90; Secretary of State for Trade and Industry, 1990–92; for Social Security, 1992–7; created Lord Lilley, 2018), 496, 645, 653–4, 852*, 893, 896, 897; individual session with MT (21 November 1990), 899; at MT's farewell lunch, 908†; and Major's 'bastards' label, 935, 942
Lillis, Michael (1946–; educated University College Dublin; head of Anglo-Irish Relations, Department of Foreign Affairs, 1982–5; Irish head of the Anglo-Irish Secretariat, Maryfield, Belfast, 1985–6), 446, 453, 458, 459*, 460
Limehouse Declaration, 234–5
Lincoln's Inn, 50
Lithuania, 829†, 829–30
litter, problem of, 782–3
Liverpool, 170, 272*, 272, 632; local government in, 69*, 388, 464, 465, 470–71, 501; and Heseltine, 272–3, 506, 630
Liverpool, Robert Banks Jenkinson, 2nd Earl, 622, 729*, 729
Liverpool Daily Post, 72, 100
Livingstone, Kenneth 'Ken' (1945–; educated Tulse Hill Comprehensive School; Leader, Greater London Council, 1981–6; Labour MP for Brent East, 1987–2001; Mayor of London, 2000–2008), 388, 464, 465*, 466; campaign against GLC abolition, 465, 473–4
Lloyd, Elizabeth, 178
Lloyd, Phyllida, 960–61
Lloyd George, David, 447*
Lloyd Webber, Andrew, 689*

Lloyds Merchant Bank, 512–13
local government: Alfred Roberts' career in, 14, 15, 61–2; admission of press to meetings of, 69–70; MT's attitude to, 69–70, 463–71; and education, 91, 95, 96; council rates, 112, 113, 203, 339–40, 463; spending/finances, 112, 113, 203, 339–40, 463, 464, 465, 466–9, 629†, 629–30; and right to buy, 201; Rate Support Grant (RSG), 203; Metropolitan Counties, 339–40, 343, 388, 463*, 463; local elections (5 May 1983), 342; left-wing activism in, 388, 464, 465, 466, 470–71; and miners' strike, 388; rate-capping policy, 463, 464, 465, 467, 470–71; and Militant Tendency, 465*, 465, 470–71, 501; Jenkin review of, 465–6; Rothschild's review of finances, 466–7, 468–9; rating revaluation in Scotland, 467–8, 468*, 469, 470, 619, 624; rate-capping revolt, 467, 470–71; Chequers meeting on finances (March 1985), 468–9; *Paying for Local Government* (green paper), 473; business rates, 474, 502*; domestic rates abolished in Scotland, 474; local elections (7 May 1987), 605; and gay rights, 633‡, 633–4; 'Section 28' of Local Government Act, 633–4; local elections (3 May 1990), 839, 840, 845, 847, 849
Lockerbie bombing (December 1988), 534
Lomax, Rachel, 490
London Docklands Development Corporation (LDDC), 502, 632

INDEX

London Weekend Television (LWT), 761†
Longfellow, Henry Wadsworth, 959
Louis, John, 369–70
Louvre Accord (1987), 653, 656
Lovelace, Ada, 590
Lovelock, James (1919–2022; educated Strand School, London; independent scientist who originated Gaia theory in the late 1960s. He developed the theory in a series of books including *Gaia: A New Look at Life on Earth* (1979) and *The Ages of Gaia* (1989); Companion of Honour, 2003), 780, 782
Lowell, James Russell, 427
Lowry, Robert, Lord Lowry, 455
Lubbers, Rudolphus 'Ruud' (1939–2018; Senior Deputy Leader, then Leader of the Christian Democratic Alliance, 1977–82; Prime Minister of the Netherlands, 1982–94), 665, 734
Lucas, Ivor, 441*, 441
Luce, Richard (1936–; educated Wellington and Christ's College, Cambridge; Conservative MP for Arundel and Shoreham, 1971–4; for Shoreham, 1974–92; Minister of State, FCO, 1981–2, 1983–5; Minister for the Arts, 1985–90; Governor of Gibraltar, 1997–2000; Lord Chamberlain, 2000–2006; created Lord Luce, 2000): Minister of State at Foreign Office, 283, 284, 285*, 285; resigns over Falklands, 289; and US invasion of Grenada, 371
Luker, Pat, 43
Luxembourg Compromise, 484*, 484

Luxembourg IGC (December 1985), 486–8
Lynch, Jack, 190*, 251, 252–3
Lynk, Roy (1932–; educated Station Road Higher School and Healdswood School, Sutton-in-Ashfield and Nottingham University; National General Secretary, Union of Democratic Mineworkers, 1985–6; President, 1987–93), 772

Maastricht Intergovernmental Conference (1991), 481, 925, 928–9, 930, 933, 934–5
Maastricht Treaty (1992), 481, 925, 929, 930; Social Chapter, 742, 929, 935; MT proposes referendum on, 886, 928–9; Major secures opt-outs for Britain, 929, 935; in Parliament, 933, 934–5; and MT's memoirs, 936
Macaulay, David, 45
Macaulay, Enid, 35
MacGregor, Ian (1912–98; educated George Watson's College, Edinburgh, Hillhead High School, Glasgow and Glasgow University; Chairman and Chief Executive, British Steel Corporation, 1980–83; Chairman, National Coal Board, 1983–6; knighted, 1986), 219, 380; pit closure plans, 381*, 381; and secret 'hit list' allegations, 381*; and miners' strike, 382, 383–4, 386, 390, 391, 395*; NACODS strike ballot, 391, 392; EuroRoute plan for Channel crossing, 478
MacGregor, John (1937–; educated Merchiston Castle School and St Andrews University; Conservative MP for South Norfolk, 1974–2001; Chief Secretary to the Treasury, 1985–7; Minister of Agriculture, Fisheries and Food, 1987–9; Secretary of State for Education and Science, 1989–90; Lord President of the Council and Leader of the House of Commons, 1990–92; created Lord MacGregor of Pulham Market, 2001), 507, 880, 895, 896, 897, 908†
MacGregor, Neil, 668
Machel, Samora, 789
Mackay, Charles, 'No Enemies', 912
Mackay, James (1927–; educated George Heriot's School, Edinburgh and Edinburgh University; QC (Scotland), 1965; Lord Advocate of Scotland, 1979–84; Lord High Chancellor of Great Britain, 1987–97; created Lord Mackay of Clashfern, 1979; Knight of the Thistle, 1997), 766–8, 904
Maclean, Donald, 207, 706
Maclean, Muriel, Lady, 450†
Macleod, Iain (1913–70; educated Fettes and Gonville and Caius College, Cambridge; Conservative MP for Enfield West, 1950–70; Minister of Health, 1952–5; of Labour and National Service, 1955–9; Secretary of State for the Colonies, 1959–61; Chancellor of the Duchy of Lancaster and Leader of the House of Commons, 1961–3; Chairman, Conservative Party, 1961–3; Chancellor of the Exchequer, June–July 1970), 82, 103

Macmillan, Harold
(1894–1986; educated
Eton and Balliol College,
Oxford; Minister of
Defence, 1954–5;
Foreign Secretary,
1955; Chancellor of the
Exchequer, 1955–57;
Prime Minister
1957–63; created Earl
of Stockton, 1984): on
'events', 4; as Prime
Minister, 65–6, 272,
349*; on MT, 73*, 73;
and idea of national
government (1976),
144§; popular caricature
of, 156; criticizes MT's
monetary policy, 225–6,
226*; on consensus,
277; and Falklands War,
291; and Suez crisis
(1956), 291; on miners'
strike, 394; 'family
silver' speech criticizing
privatization, 412; 'Night
of the Long Knives'
(1962), 744; 'a ghetto of
sentimentality about our
past' phrase, 883
Macmillan, Maurice (later
Viscount Macmillan of
Ovenden), 98; and idea
of national government
(1976), 144§
Magee, Patrick, 449*, 449,
951
Magna Carta, 953†
Maguire, Frank, 259
Mahathir bin Mohamad
(1925–; Prime
Minister of Malaysia,
1981–2003 and
2018–20), 794–7, 795*
Maidstone, Kent, 62–3
Mail on Sunday, 717, 888
Major, John (1943–;
educated Rutlish;
Conservative MP for
Huntingdonshire,
1979–83; for
Huntingdon,1983–2001;
Chief Secretary to
the Treasury, 1987–9;
Foreign Secretary,
1989; Chancellor
of the Exchequer,
1989–90; Prime
Minister and Leader of
the Conservative Party,
1990–97; Knight of
the Garter, 2005), 209;
and Blue Chips group,
277†; MT's promotion
of, 495†; and 1987
election campaign,
604*; on Wakeham's
list after 1987 victory,
616; Chief Secretary
to the Treasury, 618,
645; first Cabinet
appointment, 618;
in rising generation
of Conservative
politicians, 645; rivalry
with John Moore, 645;
and NHS 'Working
Group', 647; and MT's
tenth anniversary,
722; speech to Adam
Smith Institute (June
1989), 745†; and
ERM question, 745,
752, 840–43, 841*,
847–9, 850–52, 867–8;
Foreign Secretary, 745,
746†, 746, 794, 807*;
Chancellor of the
Exchequer, 752, 784,
839–43, 867–8; and
Renton's appointment,
752; and poll tax,
757, 839–40, 850; and
Pergau Dam project,
796; 1990 budget,
839–40, 842; Brittan
on, 841*; 'bond of
steel' with Hurd, 841,
842, 850; as MT's 'heir
apparent', 841, 867,
869, 908–9; sees poll
tax riots as turning
point for MT, 846;
'hard ecu' proposal,
848*, 848, 851, 876,
883, 955; national
'opt-in' idea for EMU,
848, 851; and entry to
ERM, 868*, 868–9;
and leadership contest
(November 1990),
880–81, 886, 887, 890‡,
890, 892, 898, 900,
901–3; comforts MT
after Howe statement,
884; and conspiracy
to remove MT, 886–7,
890–91, 893–4, 897–8,
900, 901–4, 908–9,
909*, 913–14, 916,
930; pact with Hurd
over leadership, 887,
891, 894, 897, 901,
907, 913; Lamont on,
890; and 'Catherine
Place conspiracy', 893,
894, 898; leadership
campaign (November
1990), 895†, 895,
902–3, 905†, 905,
907†, 907; agrees
to renominate MT,
898, 900, 901*,
901–3, 907, 909, 916,
935–6; behaviour over
nomination papers
before second ballot,
898, 901*, 901–3,
907, 909, 916, 935–6;
MT's phone call to
(21 November 1990),
898; and MT's 'back-
seat driver' comment,
908, 916, 924, 946;
second ballot result
(27 November 1990),
909; becomes Prime
Minister, 909–10, 911;
as Prime Minister,
916–17, 924, 928–30,
931–3; no women in
first Cabinet of, 916;
and Desert Storm, 917;
relations with Bush,
917; ennobles Archer,
922†; relations with
MT deteriorate, 924*,
924–5, 925*, 930, 933,
942, 943; Bonn speech,
924†, 924, 925; MT
takes on government
over Europe, 925,
928–9, 930, 932–3,
934–5, 937–8, 942–3;
and MT's behaviour
over Moscow coup,
926–7; and MT's
interventions on EMU,
928–9; wins 1992
election, 929–30; at
MT's Ruby Wedding
party, 929; soapbox
of, 929; wins EC opt-
outs for Britain, 929,
935; and Bosnian
crisis, 931, 932;
'Black Wednesday',

933–4, 938; and MT's memoirs, 935–6; 'bastards' comment on Eurosceptics, 935, 942; calls leadership contest (June 1995), 937–8, 938*; 1997 election campaign, 943*, 943, 944; on MT's mental decline, 955

Major, Norma, 909, 924*, 944

Malawi, 791*

Malaysia, 793†, 793–7, 795*

Malcolm, Noel (1956–; educated Eton and Peterhouse, Cambridge and Trinity College, Cambridge; Fellow of Gonville and Caius College, Cambridge, 1981–8; journalist; political columnist, *Spectator*, 1987–91, *Daily Telegraph*, 1992–5; author of histories of Bosnia and Kosovo; Fellow of All Souls, Oxford, 2002–; knighted, 2014), 931

Mallaby, Christopher (1936–2022; educated Eton and King's College, Cambridge; head of Arms Control, Soviet and Eastern European Planning Departments, FCO, 1977–82; Deputy Secretary to the Cabinet, 1985–8; Ambassador to West Germany, 1988–92; to France, 1993–6; knighted, 1988), 237, 238*, 241, 574*, 700, 807, 815–16, 820

Malone, Gerald (1950–; educated St Aloysius' College, Glasgow and Glasgow University; Conservative MP for Aberdeen South, 1983–7; for Winchester, 1992–7; PPS to Secretary of State, DTI, 1985–6; Minister of State, Department of Health, 1994–7), 625

Mandela, Nelson (1918–2013; President, African National Congress, 1991–7; President of South Africa, 1994–9; sentenced to five years' imprisonment, 1962; tried for further charges, 1963–4, and sentenced to life imprisonment; released, 1990; winner, Nobel Peace Prize (with F. W. de Klerk), 1993), 546, 547†, 547, 552, 553, 554*, 554, 786, 789, 790; marginalizes 'armed struggle', 788*; appreciation of MT, 791, 797, 798, 800, 801; and De Klerk, 792–3, 793*; Botha meets, 793; relationship with the ANC, 797–8, 798*, 800; release of, 797–8; uses Cold War analogy, 797; speech at Wembley Stadium, 798; visits London (April 1990), 798; liking for hot port drink, 799§, 799; 'private holiday' in Kent, 799‡, 799–800; meets MT at Downing Street, 800 801, 970*; MT's first telephone call with, 800; announces suspension of armed struggle, 801*; bodyguards trained by British, 801*; wins Nobel Peace Prize, 801

Mandelson, Peter (1953–; educated Hendon County Grammar School and St Catherine's College, Oxford; Director of Campaigns and Communications, Labour Party, 1985–90; Labour MP for Hartlepool, 1992–2004; Minister without Portfolio, Cabinet Office, 1997–8; Secretary of State for Trade and Industry, 1998; for Northern Ireland, 1999–2001; for Business, Enterprise and Regulatory Reform (later Business, Innovation and Skills), 2008–10; created Lord Mandelson, 2008), 941; and Trump, 5; understands MT's appeal, 599; and 1987 election defeat, 615

Manpower Services Commission, 501

Mansfield, Lord, 327

Mantel, Hilary, 2

Mao Zedong, 927

Marchuk, Gury, 682*

Margadale, John Morrison, 1st Baron, 115†, 115

Margaret Thatcher Foundation, 389‡, 920, 922*, 922, 936*, 947

margaretthatcher.org website, 947

Margerie, Sophie-Caroline de, 874†, 874

Marjai, József, 365

Marks, Harold, 22, 23

Marks & Spencer, 139*, 184, 221, 449, 584, 598

Marlborough, Duchess of, 32–3

Marlow, Tony, 847*, 905

Marr, Andrew (1959–; educated Dundee High School, Loretto and Trinity Hall, Cambridge; journalist and television presenter whose positions have included Editor, *Independent*, 1996–8; Political Editor, BBC, 2000–2005; presenter, *The Andrew Marr Show*, BBC TV, 2005–21), 935

Marsh, Richard, 86*

Marshall, Alfred, 147*

Marshall, Peter (1924–2023; educated Tonbridge and Corpus Christi College, Cambridge; UK Permanent Representative to UN,

Marshall, Peter – *cont'd* 1979–83; Deputy Secretary-General of the Commonwealth, 1983–8; knighted, 1983), 556, 561
Marshall, Walter (1932–96; educated Birmingham University; Chief Scientist, Department of Energy, 1974–7; Chairman, United Kingdom Atomic Energy Authority, 1981–2; Chairman, CEGB, 1982–9; knighted, 1982; created Lord Marshall of Goring, 1985), 380, 388, 769†, 769–70, 771*, 771–2, 773
Martens, Wilfried, 725*
Mary I, Queen, 461
Marychurch, Peter, 378‡
Mastriforte, Sue, 141
Mates, Michael (1934–; educated Blundell's School and King's College, Cambridge; Conservative MP for Petersfield, 1974–83; for East Hampshire, 1983–2010; Minister of State, NIO, 1992–3), 628‡, 628, 629
Matlock, Jack (1929–; American academic and diplomat; US Ambassador to the Soviet Union, 1987–91), 416, 687, 830
Matthews, Victor, Lord, 440†
Maude, Angus (1912–93; educated Rugby and Oriel College, Oxford; Conservative MP for Ealing South, 1950–58; for Stratford-upon-Avon, 1963–83; Deputy Chairman, Conservative Party, 1975–9; Paymaster-General, 1979–81; knighted, 1981; created Lord Maude of Stratford-upon-Avon, 1983), 124, 129

Maude, Francis (1953–; educated Abingdon School and Corpus Christi College, Cambridge; Conservative MP for Warwickshire North, 1983–92; for Horsham, 1997–2015; Minister of State, FCO, 1989–90; Financial Secretary to the Treasury, 1990–92; Chairman, Conservative Party, 2005–7; Minister for the Cabinet Office and Paymaster-General, 2010–15; created Lord Maude of Horsham, 2015), 496, 867, 893, 899
Maudling, Reginald (1917–79; educated Merchant Taylors' and Merton College, Oxford; Conservative MP for Barnet, 1950–79; Chancellor of the Exchequer, 1962–4; Home Secretary, 1970–72; Shadow Foreign Secretary, 1975–6), 81, 126, 129, 132, 135
Mauroy, Pierre, 478
Maxse, Marjorie, 39
May, Richard, 178
Mayal, Rik, 586
Mayes, Jane (née Cullen, MT's niece), 47, 58, 948
Mayhew, Patrick (1929–2016; educated Tonbridge and Balliol College, Oxford; Conservative MP for Royal Tunbridge Wells, 1974–83; for Tunbridge Wells, 1983–97; Solicitor-General, 1983–7; Attorney-General, 1987–92; Secretary of State for Northern Ireland, 1992–7; knighted, 1983; created Lord Mayhew of Twysden, 1997), 511–13, 513*, 513†, 516, 517–19, 522, 712, 768, 862

Maze Prison, Northern Ireland, 254–6, 259–63, 262*, 265
Mbeki, Thabo (1942–; member, ANC NEC, 1975–2007; Director, Information and Publicity, ANC, 1984–9; head, Department of International Affairs, 1989–94; President, ANC, 1997–2007; President of South Africa, 1999–2008), 790, 800, 801*
McAlpine, Alistair (1942–2014; educated Stowe; Director, Sir Robert McAlpine & Sons Ltd, 1963–95; Deputy Chairman, Conservative Party, 1979–83; created Lord McAlpine of West Green, 1984), 139, 140, 165, 174, 178, 270, 449, 603, 732*, 950; animosity to Tebbit, 603†, 603; IRA target, 854; and leadership contest (November 1990), 888*; house in Great College Street, 911, 917, 930; and MT after her departure from office, 911, 917, 920
McAlpine, Romilly, 950
McCallum, Janice, 958–60
McCarthy, John, 695*
McColl, Sir Colin, 417, 430–31, 706
McCoy, Sylvester, 587
McDonnell, Joe, 261
McEwan, Ian, 584, 587
McFadzean, Sir Frank (*later* Baron McFadzean of Kelvinside), 139*
McFarlane, Brendan 'Bik', 260, 262*
McFarlane, Robert 'Bud' (1937–2022; counsellor, US Department of State, 1981–2; Deputy National Security Advisor, 1982–3; National Security

Advisor, 1983–5), 294, 370, 374–5, 422, 423, 426
McGahey, Mick (1925–99; miner and trade unionist; Vice-President, NUM, 1974–87), 106, 418
McGuinness, Martin (1950–2017; educated Christian Brothers' Technical College, Londonderry; Vice-President, Sinn Fein, from 1983; Sinn Fein MP for Mid-Ulster 1997–2013; Member, Northern Ireland Assembly, from 1998; Minister of Education, 1999–2002; Deputy First Minister from 2007), 255, 500*, 854
McIntyre, Ian (1931–2014; educated Prescot Grammar School and St John's College, Cambridge; Controller, BBC Radio 4, 1976–8; Controller, BBC Radio 3, 1978–87), 540*, 540
McKellen, Sir Ian, 634
McWhirter, Ross, 141†
media: Saatchi–Reece strategy, 165–7, 175; MT's relations with, 166–7; 'Crisis? What Crisis?' headline, 169; and 1979 election campaign, 173–4, 175–6, 177; MT's skills, 175–6; global interest in MT as Prime Minister, 188†, 188; Ingham's daily press digest for MT, 188–9; and 1983 election campaign, 344; coverage of MT's Grenada humiliation, 373; Shah's union-busting newspapers, 382†; MT vetoes VAT on newspapers, 399, 491, 658†; and Westland affair, 510, 513, 515*, 519–20; Murdoch at Wapping, 516, 525–6, 600, 765;

and US bombing of Libya, 533; and Tebbit–MT conflict, 538–9; newspaper cartoonists, 585‡, 585; and 1987 election, 601, 604; party election broadcasts, 607‡, 607; broadcast ban on Sinn Fein, 726; *see also* BBC (British Broadcasting Corporation); radio; television; and entries for individual newspapers/journals
Medical Research Council's AIDS Directed Programme, 643*
Meir, Golda, 188
Mellor, David, 616*
Mendelson, John, 75
Menem, Carlos (1930–2021; President of Argentina, 1989–99), 951–2
mental health, policy on, 607*
Meteorological Office, 779
Methodist church, 9, 10–11, 15, 33, 147, 149, 389‡, 621, 775–6, 950, 966
Mexico, 309†
Meyer, Anthony (1920–2004; 3rd baronet; educated Eton and New College, Oxford; Conservative MP for Eton and Slough, 1964–6; for West Flint, 1970–83; for Clwyd North West, 1983–92; challenged party for the leadership, November 1989), 755–7, 756*, 810, 813, 838, 880, 913
Michnik, Adam, 694*
Middle East, 685*; MT's views/policy, 432–9, 685*; arms sales to, 437*, 437–8, 439–40, 440*; MT's friendship with Bandar, 438†, 438–9, 439*
Middleton, Peter (1934–; Permanent Secretary to the Treasury, 1983–91; Chairman, Barclays Bank, 1999–2004;

knighted, 1984), 226‡, 490
mid-Staffordshire by-election, 840, 845
Mildmay Mission Hospital, London, 643–4
Milhem, Mohammed, 436
Miliband, Edward 'Ed' (1969–; educated Haverstock Comprehensive School, Corpus Christi College, Oxford and LSE; Labour MP for Doncaster North, 2005–; Leader of the Labour Party, 2010–15, Secretary of State for Energy Security (2024–)), 964
Militant Tendency, 388, 465*, 465, 470–1, 501
Mill, J. S., *On Liberty*, 620
Mill Hill public school, 41, 71*
Millar, Ronald (1919–98; educated Charterhouse and King's College, Cambridge; playwright and screenwriter; knighted, 1980), 139†, 139–40, 170, 179, 227*, 270, 278, 732*; Hoskyns' 'blockbuster' memo, 274–5; on 1983 election result, 359–60; and miners' strike, 387; and 1987 manifesto, 605
Miller, John, 39
Miller, Jonathan (1934–2019; educated St Paul's and St John's College, Cambridge; writer, academic, broadcaster and director of numerous plays, operas, films and TV programmes; knighted, 2002), 584
Milne, Alasdair (1930–2013; educated Winchester and New College, Oxford; Managing Director, BBC TV, 1977–82; Director-General, BBC, 1982–7), 541, 542
Milošević, Slobodan (1941–2006; President

Milošević, Slobodan – *cont'd*
of Serbia, 1989–97;
President of Yugoslavia,
1997–2000; died in The
Hague as a prisoner
of the International
Criminal Tribunal for
the former Yugoslavia,
charged with war
crimes), 931*, 931, 932
miners' strike (1972), 100,
102–3, 382*, 382
miners' strike (1973–4),
101, 106–8
miners' strike (1984–5):
MT prepares for,
380–81, 383;
government's build
up of coal stocks,
380, 381, 383, 385;
MT's non-intervention
fiction, 381–2; NUM's
refusal to call national
strike ballot, 381,
383, 384–5, 389–90;
policing during, 382†,
382‡, 382–3, 386–7,
395; flying pickets, 382;
Nottinghamshire
miners, 382, 383,
384–5, 395–6, 772;
working miners during,
382, 383, 384–5,
386–7, 392–4, 395–6,
397, 772; 'Daily Coal
Report', 383*, 383,
392, 395; MISC
101 Cabinet sub-
committee, 383;
violence during, 383,
385–6, 393–4; Policy
Unit during, 384*,
384; Orgreave, South
Yorkshire, 385–6,
388*; MT's 'reckless
ideas' during, 386*;
'Battle of Orgreave'
(18 June 1984), 386†,
386‡, 386–7; miners
returning to work
during, 386, 390, 394;
NCB–NUM talks
during, 386, 388, 389,
390; and Reagan, 387†,
387–8; Security Service
monitoring of strikers,
388, 393, 417‡, 417,
418‡, 418; MT's 'the
enemy within' phrase,
389‡, 389, 390; peace
plans during conference
season, 390; MT's
conference speech
(1984), 391–2, 466;
NACODS strike
ballot, 391, 392, 394,
450†; High Court
declares unlawful,
392–3; NUM receives
support from Gaddafi
and Eastern bloc,
393, 417‡, 417, 418‡,
418; end of (March
1985), 394–5, 395*,
968; murder of David
Wilkie, 394, 417†,
418; government's
internal post-mortem,
395; MT's conduct
during, 396–7; and BG
privatization, 408–9
Ministry of Pensions and
National Insurance
(MPNI), 73–6, 76*
Mirage aircraft, 438, 439
Mitchell, G., 93
Mitterrand, François
(1916–96; President
of France, 1981–95),
280, 290–91, 318,
323, 439, 480; MT's
personal bond with,
291*, 291, 318‡, 354,
478–9, 815, 817, 874;
at G7 Williamsburg
summit (1983), 346*,
346; and EU budget
settlement with MT,
476, 477; relations
with Kohl, 477, 480,
815, 817, 835; Anglo-
French summit (Paris,
1984), 478–9; and
Channel Tunnel project,
478–80; and action
against Libya, 529; and
MT's Moscow visit
(1987), 575; and EMU,
666; nuclear policy,
680*, 680; at G7
Venice summit (1987),
679–80; German
reunification issue, 804,
805†, 815†, 815, 817,
827*; at Strasbourg
Council (1989), 815;
views on Germany,
815, 817, 827*, 873;
and Rome Council
(1990), 873‡, 873–4;
on EC protectionism,
874*; CSCE summit in
Paris (November 1990),
889, 892
Mogg, John (1943–;
educated Bishop Vesey's
Grammar School,
Sutton Coldfield and
Birmingham University;
private secretary to
Secretary of State for
Trade and Industry,
1985–6; knighted,
2003; created Lord
Mogg, 2008), 522–3,
523†
Moldavia, 829*
Molyneaux, James
(1920–2015; educated
Aldergrove School, Co.
Antrim; Ulster Unionist
MP for Antrim South,
1970–83; for Lagan
Valley, 1983–97;
Leader of the Ulster
Unionist Party in House
of Commons, 1974–9,
and Leader of the Party,
1979–95; created Lord
Molyneaux of Killead,
1997), 252, 253, 445,
719
monarchy/royal family, 6,
194, 303, 324, 558*,
961†, 970; Blunt affair,
207–8, 706; Charles–
Diana engagement,
231; Royal Wedding
(1981), 274; Queen
Mother as MT fan,
556, 846, 939; *see also*
Elizabeth II, Queen
Moncreiffe, Sir Iain, 187*
Moncrieff, Chris
(1931–2019;
Political Editor, Press
Association, 1980–94),
513, 523, 729, 752*
Mondale, Walter, 159
Monde, Le, 743–4
monetarism: MT's first
references to, 86–7;
and Enoch Powell, 87;
Keith Joseph on, 111,
131, 217; theory on
inflation, 111, 131,
151, 200, 205, 651,

883; and Heathites/
Wets, 151, 200, 205–6,
222–3, 223*, 225–6,
226*, 228, 270–74; M3
(chosen measure of
money supply), 197–8,
217*, 217, 223, 224,
226, 232, 268*, 489;
Howe's first budget,
197–200, 216–17;
and control of interest
rates, 198†; money
supply targets, 198,
205, 217, 268*; and
Denis Healey, 216; and
Lawson, 216, 223†,
223, 268*, 489, 651;
as matter of principle
for MT, 216; Medium-
Term Financial Strategy
(MTFS), 216, 217,
224, 267, 268*,
489; and exchange
rates, 223†, 267–8,
268*, 489, 602, 651;
technical arguments
over, 223–4; Friedman's
view of money supply
control, 223, 226, 268*;
idea of no alternative
to, 224–5; Macmillan's
speedometer analogy,
226*; question of
narrower monetary
base control, 226‡,
226–7; and Walters,
226–7, 670; letter
of 364 economists
opposing, 270–71;
Lawson loses faith in,
493, 651, 654, 655; MT
retains faith in, 651
monetary policy: Barber
boom (1972), 106, 274,
654; M2 (monetary
aggregate), 138; M3
measure, 197–8,
217*, 217, 223, 224,
226, 232, 268*, 489;
Howe's first budget,
197–200, 216–17; crisis
of 1980/81 period,
205–6, 223–9, 234–5,
267–72; Medium-Term
Financial Strategy
(MTFS), 216, 217,
224, 267, 268*,
489; 'shadowing the
deutschmark', 646,
653–4, 655, 656–8,
660, 670, 934*; DM3
rate, 653, 656, 657–8,
660, 661; growth in
credit (summer 1987),
654–5; 'Lawson Boom',
670*, 670, 887; 'Black
Wednesday', 933–4,
938; *see also* Exchange
Rate Mechanism
(ERM); foreign
exchange markets/
exchange rates; interest
rates
Monopolies and Mergers
Commission, 339, 765
Montgomery, Fergus
(1927–2013; educated
Jarrow Grammar
School and Bede
College, Durham;
Conservative MP for
Newcastle-upon-Tyne
East, 1959–64; for
Brierley Hill, 1967–74;
for Altrincham
and Sale, 1974–97; PPS
to the Leader of the
Opposition, 1975–6;
knighted, 1985), 117,
121, 127, 129*, 129,
142
Montreal Protocol, 781§,
781, 782, 784, 785
Monty Python, 654, 868, 870
Moore, Henry, 590
Moore, John (1937–2019;
educated LSE;
Conservative MP for
Croydon Central,
1974–92; Economic
Secretary to the
Treasury, June–October
1983; Financial
Secretary to the
Treasury, 1983–6;
Secretary of State for
Transport, 1986–7;
for Health and Social
Services, 1987–8; for
Social Security, 1988–9;
created Lord Moore of
Lower Marsh, 1992),
498; and privatization
policy, 401, 402, 409;
and Strategy Group
('A-Team'), 538;
Transport Secretary,
538; Health and Social
Security Secretary,
618, 645, 646–8; ill
health of, 645, 646,
647–8; rivalry with
John Major, 645; and
split of DHSS, 647–8;
and NHS 'Working
Group', 647; and
leadership contest
(November 1990),
885*, 885, 897
Moore, Sir Jeremy, 320
Morris, Dominic, 778, 782,
884, 909
Morrison, Danny, 263*
Morrison, Peter (1944–95;
youngest son of Lord
Margadale; educated
Eton and Keble College,
Oxford; Conservative
MP for Chester,
1974–92; Minister
of State, Department
of Employment,
1983–5; of Energy,
1987–90; PPS to the
Prime Minister, 1990;
knighted, 1990), 115,
118, 122, 543–4, 902*,
909*; and Brighton
bombing, 604; drink
problem, 616, 852,
885, 890, 939; as MT's
PPS, 852, 870, 880;
sees Major as next
Prime Minister, 867;
and MT's leadership
campaign team (1990),
885†, 885, 887–8,
888*, 889–90, 891,
892, 895, 896–7, 900,
901–2, 939; first ballot
result (20 November
1990), 892; and
Major's behaviour
before second ballot,
901–3, 909*, 916;
and MT's resignation
as Prime Minister,
903, 904*, 905–6; at
MT's farewell lunch,
908†, 908–9; MT's
resignation honours
list, 918*; death of
(1995), 939, 950
Morrison, Sara, 114, 123
Morrissey, 584
Mortlake cemetery, 966
Mosley, Sir Oswald, 77

Moss, Stanley, 29
Moss Side riots, 272
motor industry, 219†, 219–21, 527–8
Mount, Ferdinand (1939–; educated Eton and Christ Church, Oxford; journalist and author; political columnist, *Spectator*, 1977–82, 1985–7; head of No. 10 Policy Unit, 1982–3; Editor, *Times Literary Supplement*, 1991–2002): heads No.10 Policy Unit, 335, 353; and education vouchers, 336–7; on Pym, 336; and local government, 340; on trade union reform, 342; and 1983 election date, 343; 'get well' postcard to MT, 357; on Civil Service, 359; on unemployment, 360; leaves Policy Unit, 361; at *Spectator*, 616*; on poll tax, 839
Mountbatten, Lord, murder of, 207, 252, 715*
Mowlam, Marjorie 'Mo' (1949–2005; educated Coundon Court Comprehensive School, Coventry and Durham University; Labour MP for Redcar, 1987–2001; Secretary of State for Northern Ireland, 1997–9), 951
Mozambique, 577, 789, 791*
Mubarak, Hosni (1928–2020; Vice-President of Egypt, 1975–81; Prime Minister 1981–2; President, 1981–2011), 433, 858
Mugabe, Robert (1924–2019; educated co-founded Zimbabwe African National Union (ZANU), 1963; detained in Rhodesia, 1964–74; led insurgency from Mozambique, 1975–9; Prime Minister of Zimbabwe, 1980–87; President 1988–2017), 160, 192, 214, 215, 549
Mühlbauer, Edith, 15–16
Muldoon, Robert, 323
Mulroney, Brian, 549, 554, 679, 759, 787, 794, 892, 949–50, 957
Mulroney, Mila, 949
Murdoch, Rupert (1931–; Chief Executive, News International plc, UK, 1969–81, Chairman, 1969–87 and 1994–5; Chairman, Times Newspapers Holdings Ltd, 1982–90 and 1994–2012; Chairman, British Sky Broadcasting, 1999–2007), 166*, 189*, 436, 658†, 732*; and unions at Wapping, 516, 600, 765; and Westland affair, 516; coup against print unions, 525–6; power of, 586; and satellite broadcasting, 764–5; not mentioned in MT's memoirs, 765*; publishes MT's memoirs, 765*, 922; views on Heseltine, 881–2; knighthood for rejected, 922†
Murphy, Jean, 36
Murphy, Richard, 435, 436
Muzorewa, Bishop Abel, 159–60, 192–3
My Beautiful Laundrette (Frears film, 1985), 586

Naipaul, Vidia (V. S.) (1932–2018; novelist; knighted, 1990; Nobel Prize in Literature, 2001), 237
Nally, Dermot (1927–2009; head of Northern Ireland Affairs, 1973–80; Secretary-General to the Department of the Taoiseach (and Cabinet Secretary), 1980–93), 253, 257, 259*, 445‡, 445–6, 452, 453
Namibia, 545, 791–2
NASA (US space agency), 89
Nasser, Gamal Abdel, 61, 64
National Archives, Kew, 2
National Association for Freedom, 141†
National Association of Colliery Overseers, Deputies and Shotfirers (NACODS), 390–91, 392, 394, 450†
National Coal Board (NCB), 230, 269, 380, 381, 383–4, 385, 386, 388, 389, 390; NACODS strike ballot, 390–91, 392; transfer of working miners after strike, 395*, 395–6; privatization of, 402; and electricity privatization, 772
National Council for Women, 186†
National Economic Development Council, 78
National Education Association, 92
National Freight Corporation, 173*, 337*
National Front, 114, 163*, 164†, 178
National Gallery, 498*, 668
National Government (1931–39), 14
National Health Service (NHS), 50, 75, 88, 202; prescription charges, 279; fears that MT might abolish/dismantle, 335, 336, 644; Tory manifesto (1983), 343†, 343; and Bevan, 403; and 1987 election, 610, 644; reform in MT's third term, 644*, 644–50; 'purchaser-provider split' principle, 644, 646–7, 649, 650; unrest/sense of crisis (winter 1987), 645–7; concept of GP budgets, 647, 648–9, 650; MT's 'Working Group', 647,

648; self-governing hospitals, 647, 649, 650; 'Working for Patients' White Paper, 649*, 649
National Industrial Relations Court (NIRC), 105
National Insurance, 75–6, 228*, 228, 279, 280, 398, 492, 659
National Power, 773
National Press Club, Washington, 138–9
National Rivers Authority, 768–9
National Theatre, 166
National Union of Mineworkers (NUM), 101, 103, 106–8, 153, 171; government's build up of coal stocks, 191*, 380, 381, 383, 385; MT prepares for confrontation with, 191*, 229*, 229–30, 377, 380–81, 383; MT concedes to (February 1981), 230–31, 234, 379–80; Gormley-Scargill relations within, 230; Scargill elected leader, 279; overtime ban (October 1983), 381*; refusal to call national strike ballot, 381, 383, 384–5, 389–90; legal actions against by working miners, 384, 388, 392–3, 395; talks with NCB during 1984–5 strike, 387, 388, 389, 390; receives support from Gaddafi and Eastern bloc, 393, 417‡, 417, 418‡, 418; and electricity privatization, 772
National Union of Teachers (NUT), 96, 98
nationalized industries, 202, 217–21, 227–8, 229, 234, 269; and privatization policies, 337–9, 400–401, 402–3, 408–9; case of natural monopolies, 338, 400, 402, 768–9

NATO, 90, 142, 209, 238–9, 243, 283, 294, 346*, 374, 679; ABLE ARCHER ('command post' exercise), 369*, 369, 417; 'flexible response' strategy, 563*, 563, 564, 679, 680, 687*; and Gorbachev's reforms, 686; special summit (March 1988), 686, 687; debate over nuclear 'modernization', 687*, 687, 699†, 699, 700†, 700, 702, 704*; Gorbachev's Guildhall speech (1989), 699†, 699; and West Germany, 700–701, 736†; fortieth anniversary summit (Brussels, 1989), 700, 701, 702, 703–4; and German reunification issue, 809–10, 813, 821, 822–3, 827*, 828, 830, 831–2, 834; Lancaster House summit (July 1990), 834–5, 836; air strikes on Serb forces, 932
Nazism, MT sees socialist aspect of, 164†
Neale, Gerrard 'Gerry' (1941–; educated Bedford School; Conservative MP for North Cornwall, 1979–92; knighted, 1990), 885, 888*, 908†
Neave, Airey (1916–79; educated Eton and Merton College, Oxford; prisoner of war, 1940–42; first British officer to escape from Colditz and make a successful 'home run'; Conservative MP for Abingdon, 1953–79; head of Mrs Thatcher's private office and Shadow Secretary of State for Northern Ireland; assassinated by Irish National Liberation Army, March 1979): and 1975 leadership battle, 54, 121–2, 123, 124, 125*, 125–6, 127; and challenges to Heath's leadership, 54, 109, 114–15, 119*, 119, 120–21; asks 'Who governs Britain?', 106; February 1974 election, 107; on sense of collapse in Britain, 115; views on MT, 117, 120; and Northern Ireland, 129, 141*, 174, 250, 251†, 251, 252, 253; in opposition, 129, 155; Shadow Secretary for Northern Ireland, 129, 141*, 174; heads MT's private office, 130; murder of (March 1979), 174*, 174, 186, 250, 855; at Katyn massacre commemoration, 244‡; purported deal with UUP, 251, 253; ties to intelligence world, 417*
Neave, Diana, Baroness Airey of Abingdon, 732*
Needham, (Sir) Richard, 6th Earl of Kilmorey, 881; and Blue Chips group, 277†
Neil, Andrew, 881–2
Nelson, Horatio, Lord, 327, 590
Neubert, Michael (1933–2014; educated Bromley Grammar School and Downing College, Cambridge; Conservative MP for Havering, Romford, 1974–83; for Romford, 1983–97; knighted, 1990), 885, 888*, 908†
New Scientist, 778
New York City, 137, 157–8, 159; stock exchange reform in, 410; Plaza Hotel, 492*
New York Times, 137, 157, 206, 213, 424, 704, 806*, 932
New Zealand, 323

News of the World, 133, 525*, 526
Newsweek, 930
Newton, Anthony 'Tony' (1937–2012; educated Friends' School, Saffron Walden and Trinity College, Cambridge; Conservative MP for Braintree, 1974–97; Chancellor of Duchy of Lancaster and Minister of Trade and Industry, 1988–9; Secretary of State for Social Security, 1989–92; Lord President of the Council and Leader of the House of Commons, 1992–7; created Lord Newton of Braintree, 1997), 616*, 894
Newton, Sir Isaac, 327, 590, 931, 967
Nicaragua, 569†, 572, 577, 633*, 633, 676
Nichols, Mike, 598*
Nicholson, Martin, 574*
Niehans, Jürg, 267–8, 268*
Nigeria, 791†
Nightingale, Florence, 910‡
Niles, Thomas, 247
Nixon, Richard (1913–94; Vice-President, United States of America, 1953–61; President, 1969–74), 134, 364, 677, 678
Nkomo, Joshua, 160, 214
Noble, Denis, 591
Noonan, Peggy, 690*
Norgrove, David (1948–; educated Christ's Hospital, Exeter College, Oxford, Emmanuel College, Cambridge and LSE; Treasury, 1972–8 and 1980–85; private secretary to the Prime Minister, 1985–8; knighted 2016), 494, 629†, 630, 631, 637, 645–6, 651–2, 653, 654, 655
Norman, Edward (1938–; educated Chatham House School, Ramsgate and Selwyn College, Cambridge; priest in the Church of England, 1971; lecturer in history, University of Cambridge, 1965–88; Dean of Peterhouse, Cambridge, 1971–88; historian of Church and society in Victorian England, and of modern Ireland; Reith Lecturer (published as *Christianity and the World Order*, 1979), 1978; Chancellor, York Minster, 1999–2004), 148†, 148, 149
North Sea Oil, 117, 136*
Northern Ireland: sectarian disorder in, 105–6, 207, 252; 'power-sharing' concept, 106–7, 174*, 250–51, 252; Sunningdale Agreement, 106–7, 250–51, 252, 257; and Airey Neave, 129, 141*, 174, 250, 251†, 251, 252; integrationist views, 174*, 251†; MT's views on, 174*, 174, 250, 252–4, 264†, 264, 444–5, 447, 968–9; MT visits (August 1979), 207; Warrenpoint attack, 207, 252, 715*; direct rule imposed (1972), 250–51; Loyalist Ulster Workers' Council general strike, 251*; power-sharing Executive, 251*; Irish-American lobby, 251‡, 448, 453–4, 459; devolutionist agenda, 251–2, 253*, 253, 264–5, 452, 455; Neave's regional councils proposal, 251, 253; Irish Republic and security situation, 252–3, 444–5, 447–8, 718, 720–21, 723–5; Atkins plan (1979–80), 253–4; growth of Paisleyism, 253–4; Maze hunger strikes, 254–6, 259–63, 262*, 265, 727; UK's direct dealings with Dublin, 254, 256–9, 258‡, 263–4, 445‡, 445–8, 452–61; Bloody Sunday (1972), 260; Prior's proposals, 264–5; FitzGerald's New Ireland Forum, 445, 446–8, 452–4; Lloyd George's Boundary Commission, 447*; 'basic equation', 447, 454–5; 'Diplock' courts in, 454‡, 454; Enniskillen Remembrance Day bombing, 460*, 720; Ballygawley attack (1988), 671†, 725; Oldfield's security role, 715–18, 717*; Loyalist terrorism in, 718‡, 718, 719*, 722; MT sees through security lens, 718–19, 721*, 726–8; Loughgall barracks attack, 719–20, 854; SAS action in, 719–20, 726; Hong Kong comparison, 719; MT visits Enniskillen (November 1987), 720; RUC and British Army, 720, 721; alleged policy of 'shoot to kill', 721†, 721; Hume–Adams talks, 727*, 727; King's 'no secret economic or strategic reason' speech, 727–8, 854; MT's pre-Christmas visits, 886; peace process, 950–51
Nott, John (1932–2024; educated Bradfield and Trinity College, Cambridge; Conservative MP for Cornwall St Ives, 1966–83; Secretary of State for Trade, 1979–81; for Defence, 1981–3; knighted, 1983): in opposition, 146; and public spending control, 183, 197, 273; Trade Secretary, 183, 197,

212; 'Inner Group' on economic policy, 216; Defence Secretary, 229, 244*, 244†, 244, 283; defence cuts, 244*, 283; and Falklands War, 285, 288, 291, 293, 297, 300, 301, 305, 313; offers resignation over Falklands, 289; in Falklands War Cabinet, 291, 299, 304; and Westland affair, 516
Nove, Alec, 366*
Now, Voyager (Irving Rapper film, 1942), 12
nuclear energy/power, 192*, 192, 769, 770, 771–3, 774
nuclear weapons: and Soviet Union, 26*; US use of (1945), 29; British development of, 54*, 54; MT's views on, 54, 243, 325, 365, 366, 420, 423, 425–6, 562–5, 569, 570, 578; Schlesinger doctrine, 138*, 138; Edward Norman on, 148†, 148; CND campaigns of early 1980s, 148; struggle over INF deployment in Europe, 238–9, 240, 242, 294, 332, 333, 346, 364, 372, 373, 414, 505; MT and British capacity, 238; Strategic Arms Limitation Treaty, 238, 240; 'dual track' strategy in Cold War, 242–3; Reagan's 'zero option' stance, 243*, 243, 563, 566, 576; Polaris submarine-based, 243–4; Reagan's views on, 243, 365†, 365, 366, 420, 422, 423, 425–6, 562–7, 600, 601, 923; Trident missile system, 244*, 244†, 244, 564, 568, 569; Truman–Churchill agreement (1952), 334*, 334; and 1983 election campaign, 345; unilateralism, 345, 543, 567, 600–601, 609*, 609; Anti-Ballistic Missile (ABM) Treaty, 365‡, 365, 422, 563†, 564, 566, 571; 'Intermediate Nuclear Forces' (INF) category, 365‡; Mutually Assured Destruction (MAD), 365; Soviet fears of pre-emptive strike, 369; and MT's first meeting with Gorbachev, 419–20, 421, 422–3; 'Four Points' agreement (Camp David, 1984), 423–4, 427–8, 429†, 429, 432; Gorbachev's nuclear-free world proposal, 562–5; Reykjavik summit (1986), 562, 565*, 565–9, 566*, 571, 572, 680–81; credibility of NATO's deterrent, 563*, 563, 564, 679, 680, 687*; INF 'zero option', 563, 566, 569, 576, 578, 678; offensive ballistic weapons, 564–5, 566–9, 570, 571–3; shorter-range (SR) systems, 565, 571, 678, 679 80, 687*, 687; INF and Camp David Agreement, 571; Gorbachev's 'second zero' proposals (April 1987), 678–9; short-range forces (SNF), 678, 679, 700–701, 702, 703–4, 736†, 834; 'third zero' option, 679, 687*, 687, 700, 701, 703–4; INF Agreement (December 1987), 683, 684, 686; debate over NATO 'modernization', 687*, 687, 699†, 699, 700†, 700, 702, 704*; Bush policy on, 834–5; military plans for liberating Kuwait, 870

Oatley, Michael, 255, 261†, 727

Obama, Barack (1961–; US Senator (Democrat) from Illinois, 2005–8; President of the United States of America, 2009–17), 964, 965‡
O'Brien, Richard (1920–2009; educated Oundle and Clare College, Cambridge; Chairman, Manpower Services Commission, 1976–82; Chairman, Archbishop of Canterbury's Commission on Urban Priority Areas that published the *Faith in the City* report in 1985; knighted, 1980), 503
Observer, 440–41, 682†, 888
O'Connor, Martin, 108, 114
Office of Fair Trading (OFT), 410, 765
Office of Telecommunications (OFTEL), 403
Official Secrets Act, 518, 524, 707, 711, 714, 915; Section 2 of, 713, 714
O'Fiaich, Cardinal Tomás, 262
OFWAT, 769
oil: oil price shock (1973), 106; North Sea Oil, 117, 136*, 659*, 659; oil shock (1979), 191*, 191, 192; and privatization, 338, 408; collapse in price (1986), 396
Old Moore's Almanack, 229
Oldfield, Maurice (1915–81; educated Lady Manners School, Bakewell and Manchester University; Chief, MI6, 1973–8; Co-ordinator of Security and Intelligence in Northern Ireland, 1979–80; knighted, 1975), 712†, 712, 715*, 715†, 715–18, 716*, 717*
Olivier, Laurence (1907–89; actor and director; co-founder of the

Olivier, Laurence – *cont'd*
National Theatre, and
its Director, 1973–4;
knighted, 1947; created
Lord Olivier, 1970),
165–6
Olympic Games, Moscow
(1980), 240
Oman, 433, 437*, 440–41,
441*, 859
O'Neill, Tip, 251‡, 453–4,
459
Onslow, Cranley
(1926–2001;
educated Harrow
and Oriel College,
Oxford; Conservative
MP for Woking,
1964–97; Chairman,
1922 Committee,
1984–92; knighted,
1993; created Lord
Onslow of Woking,
1997), 732, 748, 755,
880, 888, 896, 897,
902
Open Skies conference,
Ottawa (1990), 821‡,
821–2
Open University, 98
Oppenheim, Sally, 129
O'Rawe, Richard, 262*
Organization of Eastern
Caribbean States
(OECS), 369, 371
Orgreave coking works,
South Yorkshire,
385–6, 388*
Orlov, Yuri, 573
Orme, Stan, 394*
Orpington, Kent, 62
Orwell, George, *1984*,
414
Osborne, George, 630*
O'Sullivan, Colonel Sir John
William, 266
O'Sullivan, John (1942–;
educated St Mary's
College, Crosby and
London University;
special adviser to
the Prime Minister,
1986–8. His
journalistic positions
have included:
parliamentary sketch-
writer, *Daily Telegraph*;
Associate Editor, *The
Times*; Editor, *National

Review), 123*, 148,
605, 644–5, 646, 647,
868†, 868, 923, 957
overseas aid: international
rules governing, 506*,
795*, 795–6; MT
supports links with
trade, 795–7; Overseas
Development
Administration (ODA),
795, 796*, 796;
Pergau Dam project
ruled unlawful, 796†,
796; after Armenian
earthquake, 832
Overseas Scientific and
Technical Register, 39
Owen, David (1938–;
educated Bradfield and
Sidney Sussex College,
Cambridge; Labour
MP for Plymouth
Sutton, 1966–74; for
Plymouth Devonport,
1974–81; SDP
MP for Plymouth
Devonport, 1981–92;
Foreign Secretary,
1977–9; Leader of the
SDP, 1983–7; created
Lord Owen, 1992),
187*, 357, 495; and
Labour split, 227†,
234–5; Limehouse
Declaration, 234–5;
and Falklands War,
323; and Westland
affair, 518; attitude to
MT, 615*, 615
Oxford Conservative
Graduates' Association,
38–9
Oxford Union, 27*, 27, 30
Oxford University: refuses
to grant honorary
degree to MT, 1,
590–51, 946–7, 970;
MT coached for
entrance exam, 11–12;
MT applies to, 22–3;
MT at Somerville
College, 23–6, 27–8,
29–34, 451*, 591–2;
political life at, 24, 25,
27*, 27–8, 29–31; and
social opportunities,
27, 30, 31, 32–3, 34;
veterans at postwar,
29, 30; MT teaches

in Grantham during
vacation, 94*, 94†, 94
Oxford University
Conservative
Association (OUCA),
24, 27, 30, 32; policy
subcommittee report
(1945), 29; and social
advancement, 30, 31,
32–3, 34; at Randolph
Hotel, 32–3, 38*

Padfield, Philip, 534
Paget, Reginald, Lord Paget
of Northampton, 554*
Paisley, Ian (1926–2014;
educated Ballymena
Technical High
School, South Wales
Bible College and
Reformed Presbyterian
Theological College,
Belfast; ordained,
1946; moderator, Free
Presbyterian Church
of Ulster, 1951–2008;
Protestant Unionist
MP for Antrim
North, 1970–74;
Democratic Unionist
MP for Antrim North,
1974–2010; Leader of
Democratic Unionist
Party, 1972–2008;
Member of Northern
Ireland Assembly,
1998–2011; First
Minister of Northern
Ireland, 2007–8;
created Lord Bannside,
2010), 251–2, 253*,
253–4, 445, 459†, 459,
719
Paisley Grammar School,
639–40
Pakistan, 240†
Palestine: Arab–Israeli
conflict, 432–7, 439;
MT's views on, 432–7;
British Mandate in,
433; and terrorism,
433, 436; King
Hussein's initiative,
434–6, 439
Palestine Liberation Front
(PLF), 436
Palestine Liberation
Organization (PLO),
433, 434–6, 437

Palgrave, Francis Turner, *Golden Treasury*, 19, 32
Palliser, Michael (1922–2012; educated Wellington and Merton College, Oxford; joined FCO, 1947; private secretary to the Prime Minister, 1966–9; Ambassador and head of UK Delegation to European Communities, 1973–5; Permanent Under-Secretary and head of Diplomatic Service, 1975–82; knighted, 1973. Married to the daughter of the EEC founding father Paul-Henri Spaak), 210, 283, 312*
Palmerston, Henry John Temple, 1st Viscount, 420
Palumbo, Peter (*later* Lord Palumbo), 918*
Pannell, Charlie, 70†, 70‡, 70
Papillon, David, 38, 40
Pardoe, John, 79
Park, Daphne (1921–2010; educated Rosa Bassett School and Somerville College, Oxford; leading figure in the Secret Intelligence Service; Principal of Somerville College, Oxford, 1980–89; created Baroness Park of Monmouth, 1990), 25, 26*, 591–2
Parkinson, Cecil (1931–2016; Royal Lancaster Grammar School and Emmanuel College, Cambridge; Conservative MP for Enfield West, 1970–74; for Hertfordshire South, 1974–83; for Hertsmere, 1983–92; Secretary of State for Trade and Industry, June–October 1983; for Energy, 1987–9; for Transport, 1989–90; Chairman, Conservative Party, 1981–3 and 1997–8; created Lord Parkinson, 1992), 104, 117; and party leadership, 119*; in opposition, 146; Party Chairman, 276; and public spending control, 278; in Falklands War Cabinet, 291, 292, 303, 304, 306, 317; and 1983 election date, 342–3; and Sara Keays, 347–8, 357, 358–9, 498, 500, 617–18; 1983 election campaign, 347, 348; Trade and Industry Secretary, 348, 350, 402†, 410, 411; friendship/rivalry with Tebbit, 350*, 350; resigns from Cabinet, 358–9, 368; and 1985 reshuffle, 496, 498, 499–500; on Tim Bell, 603; Energy Secretary, 617–18, 770; returns to Cabinet (1987), 617–18; electricity privatization, 770*, 770–71, 771*; and leadership contest (November 1990), 896; and MT's resignation, 904; at MT's farewell lunch, 908†
Parris, Matthew (1949–; educated Waterford School, Swaziland and Clare College, Cambridge; Conservative MP for West Derbyshire, 1979–86; author, columnist for *The Times* from 1987), 173–4, 353*
Parsons, Anthony (1922–96; educated King's School, Canterbury and Balliol College, Oxford; Ambassador to Iran, 1974–9; UK Permanent Representative to UN, 1979–82; special adviser to the Prime Minister on foreign affairs, 1982–3; knighted, 1975), 195, 292; and Falklands War, 290, 291, 309–10, 311†, 311–12, 314–15, 319, 322; heads MT's foreign affairs and security policy unit, 335–6, 353
Parsons, Jane, 185
Partridge, Michael, 74
Pascall, David (1949–; educated Queen Mary's Grammar School, Basingstoke and the University of Birmingham; held various positions in British Petroleum, 1967–93; seconded by BP to the Central Policy Review Staff, Cabinet Office, 1982–3 and then to the No. 10 Policy Unit), 384*, 400, 401
Pasechnik, Vladimir, 806–7, 830
Paterson, Anthony, 178
Patten, Christopher 'Chris' (1944–; educated St Benedict's School, Ealing and Balliol College, Oxford; Director, Conservative Research Department, 1974–9; Conservative MP for Bath, 1979–92; Secretary of State for the Environment, 1989–90; Chairman, Conservative Party, 1990–92; Governor, Hong Kong, 1992–7; European Commissioner, 1999–2004; Chancellor of Oxford University, 2003–24; Chairman of the BBC Trust from 2011; created Lord Patten of Barnes, 2005): director of Conservative Research Department, 118, 130, 146, 150; *The Right Approach*, 145; on battle of ideas, 150;

1038 INDEX

Patten, Christopher – *cont'd*
  rejects Stepping Stones, 154; on immigration, 164; and 'Winter of Discontent', 170; and 1979 election campaign, 174; and Blue Chips group, 277; and Falklands War, 289*; as critic of MT, 341‡; in rising generation of Conservative politicians, 645; Environment Secretary, 745, 782; and ERM question, 745; and poll tax, 745, 748*, 748–9, 757, 839, 845, 847, 850; and green issues, 782, 783, 784, 785; and leadership contest (November 1990), 884, 898, 899, 900; and 'Catherine Place conspiracy', 893, 894; individual session with MT (21 November 1990), 899, 900; and MT's resignation, 904; nominates Hurd for leadership, 905†; and conspiracy to remove MT, 913; hindsight view on removal of MT, 914; Governor of Hong Kong, 928; and 1992 manifesto, 929; Party Chairman, 929; loses seat (1992), 930; on MT's mental health, 955
Patten, John (*later* Baron Patten): and Blue Chips group, 277†; on Wakeham's list after 1987 victory, 616*
Pattie, Geoffrey, 142*
Pattison, Michael, 185–6
Pay Comparability Commission, 175
Peacock, Alan (1922–2014; educated Grove Academy, Dundee High School and St Andrews University; Professor of Economics, University College at Buckingham, 1978–80; Principal, 1980–83; Vice-Chancellor, University of Buckingham, 1983–4; knighted, 1987), 540–41, 541*, 763
Pearce, David, 783
Pearce, Sadie, 717–18
Pearl Harbor, 422
Pearson, 764
Penrith and the Border by-election, 356
Penrose, Barrie, 707
pensions, 74, 75, 607; link with earnings broken, 176, 199; portable, 360, 411, 413
Pepper, Gordon (1934–; educated Repton and Trinity College, Cambridge; partner, Greenwell's, 1962; Chairman, Lombard Street Research from 2000), 147
Peres, Shimon (1923–2016; born Poland; Chairman of Israel's Labour Party, 1977–92 and 1995–7; Prime Minister of Israel, 1984–6 and 1995–6; Vice Premier, 1986–90; Minister of Foreign Affairs, 1986–8 and 1992–5; Minister of Finance, 1988–90; President of Israel, 2007–14; joint winner Nobel Peace Prize (with Yasser Arafat and Yitzhak Rabin), 1994), 433, 436–7, 685*
Pérez de Cuéllar, Javier, 301–2, 309, 312†, 312, 313, 323
Pergau Dam, Malaysia, 795–7, 796†
Perle, Richard, 243*, 244†
Personal Equity Plans (PEPs), 413
Peru, 305, 306–8
Perutz, Max, 643*
Peterhouse, Cambridge, 148
Petrie, Carroll, 949
Peyton, John (1919–2006; educated Eton and Trinity College, Oxford; Conservative MP for Yeovil, 1951–83; Minister of Transport, 1970; Minister for Transport Industries, DOE, 1970–74; created Lord Peyton of Yeovil, 1983), 126, 127
Philby, Kim, 207, 706, 714
Philip Morris (tobacco company), 921
Pickering, Tom, 867
Pile, Sir William, 94–5, 96, 100
Pimlico, London, 50–52
Pimlico Comprehensive School, London, 97
Pincher, (Henry) Chapman (1914–2014; educated Darlington Grammar School and King's College London; freelance journalist, novelist and business consultant; Assistant Editor, *Daily Express*, 1972–9; author of *Their Trade is Treachery* (1981)), 707, 712, 714; *Their Trade is Treachery*, 707, 708, 709, 710–11, 711*, 713, 716; *Sunday Express* article on Rothschild, 711; *Traitors*, 717*, 717
Pinochet, Augusto (1915–2006; Commander-in-Chief, Chilean armed forces, 1973; led coup against President Salvador Allende, September 1973; President of Chile, 1974–90), 297*, 951*, 951–2, 952*
Pinter, Harold (1930–2008; educated Hackney Downs Grammar School; actor, playwright and director. His best-known plays include *The Birthday Party* (1957), *The Homecoming* (1964) and *Betrayal* (1978); awarded the Nobel Prize in Literature, 2005), 696
Pitt, William, the Younger, 327

Plowden, Edwin, Lord
    Plowden, 496–7
Pöhl, Karl Otto
    (1929–2014; President
    of the Bundesbank,
    1980–91), 666
Poindexter, John (1936–;
    US Deputy National
    Security Advisor,
    1983–5; National
    Security Advisor,
    1985–6), 371, 567,
    568, 569†, 570, 572,
    676, 685
Polan, Brenda, 731
Poland, 802; Katyn massacre,
    244‡; Pope John Paul
    II, 244–5; Gdańsk
    shipyards, 245, 693, 694;
    martial law in, 245, 279,
    333; Solidarity in, 245,
    693†, 693, 694*, 694;
    MT visits (November
    1988), 692–5; MT's
    mythical status among
    Poles, 693*, 694; fall of
    Communism in, 803,
    805; post-Cold War
    national identity, 811*;
    Oder–Neisse line, 822,
    827*
Polaris submarine-based
    nuclear missiles, 243–4
Police Service of Northern
    Ireland (PSNI), 454*
policing/police forces: at
    Saltley coke depot
    dispute, 103, 152;
    MT's police protection,
    141–2; pay, 173, 202;
    inner-city riots (1981),
    271, 272; miners' strike
    (1984–5), 382†, 382‡,
    382–3, 385, 386†,
    386–7, 388, 395; and
    Brighton bombing, 449;
    inner-city riots (1985),
    502; and Wapping
    dispute, 525; murder
    of Yvonne Fletcher
    (1984), 529; and
    Spycatcher affair, 711,
    712; and poll tax riots,
    846, *see also* Royal
    Ulster Constabulary
    (RUC)
Policy Unit, Major's, 925
Policy Unit, MT's, 181,
    182, 335, 353†, 353,
    361, 384*, 384, 400,
    494; and privatization
    policy, 400–402, 773;
    and local government,
    464, 466–7; and
    Channel Tunnel project,
    479; and inner cities,
    503; and Westland
    affair, 507; and Sunday-
    trading debate, 532;
    and 1987 manifesto,
    605; and 1987 victory,
    615; and social reform,
    620–21, 644–5; and
    policy on inner cities,
    632; and AIDS, 641,
    642–3; and NHS
    reform, 644–5, 647,
    648–9; and reform of
    legal profession, 767;
    and South Africa, 786;
    and Howe's resignation,
    878, 879, 880
Policy Unit, Wilson's, 107
Polizzi, Olga (1946–;
    educated St Mary's,
    Ascot; Director, Forte
    plc, 1983–96. Polizzi
    was the daughter of
    Mrs Thatcher's strong
    supporter, Lord Forte),
    667†
poll tax (community
    charge): MISC 79
    Cabinet subcommittee
    (1982), 339; origins
    of, 463, 465, 468–9;
    naming of, 468†, 471†;
    Waldegrave–Rothschild
    team proposes,
    468–9; lack of data
    to aid planning for,
    469†, 469–70; Lawson
    opposes, 470*, 470,
    472, 473, 628; political
    impetus towards,
    470; in Scotland, 470,
    471–2, 472*, 473, 474,
    624, 839–40, 849–50;
    regressive nature of,
    471, 475; Cabinet
    agrees, 472–3; 'dual
    running' (discarded
    transitional scheme),
    472, 474, 624, 625,
    916‡; principle versus
    popularity issue, 472,
    474, 475; becomes
    law for Scotland, 474;
    as attempt to solve
    genuine problems,
    475, 502*; Baker's
    appointment at
    Environment, 501;
    in 1987 manifesto/
    campaign, 607,
    609–10; as third-
    term flagship
    policy, 621, 622,
    624–5; bill 'guillotined'
    in Commons, 628‡;
    parliamentary passage
    of, 628–9, 646, 757,
    839; and Chris Patten,
    745, 748*, 748–9, 757,
    839, 845, 847, 850;
    becomes law (October
    1988), 747; projected
    level of, 747, 839;
    'safety net'/transitional
    period, 747, 748–9;
    MT's own payment of,
    749*, 840*; rebates in
    1990 budget, 839–40;
    Rifkind threatens to
    resign over, 839–40;
    backbench discontent
    over, 839; MT as
    'flailing' over, 845,
    847, 849–50; riots
    against, 846; capped in
    Labour councils, 847;
    MT proposes 'income
    limits', 849–50; Major
    and Patten's enhanced
    capping solution, 850;
    and leadership contest
    (November 1990),
    885; replaced by a
    new council tax, 916‡;
    Heseltine jettisons, 916
Pollock, Richard, 579, 684†
Ponsonby, Amanda (née
    Colvin), 449†, 449,
    576–7, 579*, 907, 910,
    950*; serves MT after
    her departure from
    office, 911, 918, 920,
    921
Popiełuszko, Fr Jerzy, 693†
Popper, Karl, 147*
'populism', political, 5
pornography, 84, 620
Portillo, Michael (1953–;
    educated Harrow
    County Boys' School
    and Peterhouse,
    Cambridge;

Portillo, Michael – *cont'd*
Conservative MP for Enfield, Southgate, 1984–97; for Kensington and Chelsea, 1999–2005; Secretary of State for Employment, 1994–5; for Defence, 1995–7), 156, 164*, 164, 176*, 645, 901, 903, 938; at MT's farewell lunch, 908†, 909; and Major's 'bastards' label, 935, 942; loses seat (1997), 945; rebrands himself as Tory modernizer, 953; leadership contest (2001), 954
Potter, Barry, 850, 906*
Powell, Anthony (1905–2000; novelist, author of the *Dance to the Music of Time* sequence; Companion of Honour, 1988), 237
Powell, Carla, 594, 736*, 737, 908, 914–15, 950, 959, 963
Powell, Charles (1941– ; educated King's School, Canterbury and New College, Oxford; private secretary to the Prime Minister, 1983–91; created Lord Powell of Bayswater, 2000): MT's foreign affairs private secretary, 292, 361–2; and Hong Kong, 361–2, 363, 364, 719; on MT, 407, 430; and MT's Chequers meeting with Gorbachev, 419, 420, 421; at Camp David with MT, 423, 424; with MT in Washington (1985), 425*, 426; and MT–Gorbachev meeting in Moscow, 427; on MT's investment in Gorbachev, 428; and Howe, 429†, 568, 626, 677, 736, 738, 739–40, 879; and Middle East politics, 435, 436, 437, 438; on Robert Armstrong, 445–6; and Northern Ireland, 451, 455, 456, 457, 461–2, 720–21, 723*, 723, 725–6, 727; and Channel Tunnel project, 479; and MT's views on Europe, 481, 488, 664, 671; German reunification issue, 483–4, 804, 805*, 805, 807–8, 814*, 814, 817–18, 819, 821; and MT's relations with Kohl, 483, 486*, 486, 820; and Milan European Council (1985), 484, 485; and Westland affair, 507, 508, 510, 512, 513†, 514, 519, 520, 521, 522, 523, 524; as projection of MT's combative personality, 508; as career civil servant, 521–2, 522*, 601–2, 609*, 663; prominence of in MT government, 521–2, 523, 569, 601–2, 609*, 618, 625–6, 735*, 735–8, 736†, 744*, 753; and action against Libya, 529, 530–31, 534; and 'special relationship' with US, 535; and South Africa, 549–51, 553, 554, 555, 558, 560, 786–8, 788†, 790, 792–3, 794, 798, 799–800, 801*; on Nassau CHOGM (1985), 549, 550; and nuclear weapon negotiations, 564–5, 568–9; and Howe–Lawson collaboration, 564, 660, 738–41, 739*; and Charlie Price, 569*; at Camp David (November 1986), 570–71; and 'Iran-Contra' affair, 570, 676; Chequers seminar on Soviet Union (1986), 573–4, 574*, 574†; and MT's Moscow visit (1987), 575, 576, 577*, 577, 578, 580, 582; and MT's 1987 visit to USA, 577; and Kosov, 581*, 686, 687, 803*, 831–2; Hodgkin's visit to No. 10, 589–90; sabotages Kinnock's meeting with Reagan, 601–2; on Wobbly Thursday, 611; on 1987 election victory, 613; Butler seeks to dislodge, 626, 735–8, 740; on Whitelaw, 627; and ERM question, 652, 847–8, 849, 869; and MT's alcohol intake, 662*; and MT's 'EEC bashing', 662*, 663; and Thyssen collection project, 668, 669; Bruges Speech (September 1988), 671†, 671, 672*, 672–3, 674*, 725, 743; and MT–Lawson relations, 671; and Kissinger, 678–9; on MT–Gorbachev relations, 681, 805, 807; on Gorbachev's domestic problems, 682; and MT–Reagan relations, 685; MT's tougher stance with Gorbachev (1988), 686–7; and future of Falkland Islands, 686; on NATO, 686; MT's 'farewell' visit to Reagan, 689–91; and Bush–MT relations, 691, 822, 825; with MT in Poland, 694; and Rushdie affair, 695, 696*, 696; and Gorbachev's visit (1989), 697, 698; in Deidesheim with MT, 701–2; and Bush's turn to Germany, 702, 703, 704; on Victor Rothschild, 711–12; on Haughey, 720–21, 723; rebukes Foreign Office, 723*, 723; note on Northern Ireland policy, 725–6; on Denis Thatcher, 732‡; on

MT's stress levels, 732;
and Foreign Office,
736, 737, 738, 816;
and 'Madrid ambush',
738–41, 739*; at
Madrid summit (June
1989), 741–2; and
Le Monde interview,
743–4; and July
1989 reshuffle, 744;
on recall of Walters,
750; and MT's use
of religion, 777; and
Royal Society speech,
780; and Malaysia,
795, 796; on MT's
ignorance of Germany/
Germans, 802; Camp
David meeting with
Bush (1989), 810–11;
and Bush's call for
EC integration, 813;
and MT–Mitterrand
meeting, 815†, 815;
and Bush's turn away
from MT, 816–17;
Chequers seminars on
Germany (1990), 816,
818, 825, 826, 836†,
836; views on post-
Cold War geopolitics,
818; flies to Bonn
(February 1990),
820–21, 821*; and the
Wood telegram, 824*,
824; in Bermuda with
MT (April 1990), 828;
and telephone line to
Moscow, 829†; on
MT's meeting with
Prunskienė, 830*; and
MT–Yeltsin meeting,
831*; on Gorbachev,
833; and Ridley's
resignation, 836; and
poll tax, 840; on MT's
view of Major, 841,
908; Major's paper
on EMU, 851; and
murder of Gow, 853;
and Brooke's report
on IRA, 854; Iraqi
invasion of Kuwait,
856†, 856, 857, 858,
860, 861, 862, 864–5,
866, 871; on Aspen
speech, 860; and Iraq
'War Cabinet' (1990),
862; and Rome Council
(1990), 872–3; and
leadership contest
(November 1990),
885, 891, 892, 893,
896; first ballot result
(20 November 1990),
892, 893; and MT's
resignation as Prime
Minister, 904*; helps
MT pack, 908; stays at
Easton Neston, 914–15;
briefs MT on Desert
Storm, 917; serves MT
after her departure
from office, 918, 935;
on MT's unhappiness
after losing office, 920;
Major's farewell dinner
for, 924; and Balkan
conflict, 931; villa
outside Rome, 950,
959; final visit to MT,
963
Powell, Colin (1937–;
Senior Military
Assistant to US
Secretary of Defense,
1983–6; Deputy
National Security
Advisor,
1986–7; National
Security Advisor,
1987–9; Chairman,
Joint Chiefs of Staff,
1989–93; Secretary of
State, 2001–5), 422*,
424, 568, 860
Powell, J. Enoch
(1912–98; educated
King Edward's,
Birmingham and Trinity
College, Cambridge;
Conservative MP for
Wolverhampton South
West, 1950–74; Ulster
Unionist MP for South
Down, 1974–87;
Secretary of State for
Health, 1960–63):
MT's first recorded
encounter with, 36–7;
resigns from Macmillan
government, 65;
leadership contest
(1965), 81; influence
on MT, 87–8, 753*;
opposes incomes
policies, 87, 105;
'Rivers of Blood'
speech, 87, 163; 'the
enemy within' phrase,
88, 389‡; as Minister
of Health, 88; February
1974 election, 107*,
107; and Northern
Ireland, 252, 253,
258†, 258, 445, 457–8,
460†; and UUP, 252,
253; and Falklands
War, 288, 321
Powell, Jonathan (1956–;
educated King's
School, Canterbury,
University College,
Oxford and University
of Pennsylvania; chief
of staff to Tony Blair,
1997–2007; National
Security Adviser,
2024–), 5, 942, 944
Powell-Brett, Christopher,
956
power workers' strike
(1970), 102
Pravda (Brenton and Hare
play, 1985), 586
Pravda, Alex, 366*
Pre-Retirement Choice
magazine, 119
Press Association, 513, 518,
523, 729, 752*
Price, Carol, 949†
Price, Charles 'Charlie'
(1931–2012; prominent
US businessman,
banker and diplomat;
US Ambassador to
Belgium, 1981–3; to
the United Kingdom,
1983–9), 406, 407,
421, 426‡, 534, 569*,
600, 602, 677, 682,
686, 691, 917*, 949†
Price Commission, 197
Priestley, Clive, 221
Priestley, Joseph, 327
Prime, Geoffrey, 378
Prior, James (1927–2016;
educated Charterhouse
and Pembroke
College, Cambridge;
Conservative MP for
Lowestoft, 1959–83;
for Waveney, 1983–7;
Minister of Agriculture,
1970–72; Leader
of the House of
Commons, 1972–4;

Prior, James – *cont'd*
Secretary of State for
Employment, 1979–81;
for Northern Ireland,
1981–4; created
Lord Prior, 1987):
Heath Shadow
Cabinet, 83; Heath
government, 108;
and party leadership,
114, 126, 127; and
1975 leadership vote,
125*, 125†; enters
second leadership
ballot, 126, 127;
Shadow Employment
spokesman, 129, 146,
151–2, 153, 154–5,
170; as economic critic
of MT, 146, 200, 205,
228, 270, 272; caution
over unions, 151–2,
153, 154, 155, 170,
183, 196, 197, 217–18,
228, 276; MT's views
on, 155; Employment
Secretary, 183, 196,
217, 225; and public
spending control,
202, 203, 228, 272,
278; and monetary
policy, 205, 224,
225, 270; excluded
from economic policy
decisions, 216; first
Employment Bill, 217;
and steel industry,
219; Northern Ireland
Secretary, 262–3,
264–5, 276, 351; and
1981 budget, 270;
and Dry narrative of
economic recovery,
280; and 1985 budget,
492; as Chairman of
GEC, 509*
Private Eye, 321*, 358, 588
privatization, 202, 325, 339,
398–409; underpricing
of assets, 337‡, 769;
asset sales, 337–8, 656;
and Lawson, 337–8,
355†, 355, 400, 401,
402*, 402, 408,
409; and choice of
1983 election date,
337; MT's initial
caution, 337, 338; of
British Telecom (BT),

338–9, 400, 402†,
402–4, 404*, 464; and
monopoly issue, 338,
339, 400, 401, 402†,
402, 403, 405*, 405,
408–9, 413, 768–9,
967–8; Tory manifesto
(1983), 343‡, 343,
400*, 400; and Tebbit,
359; increased salaries
of senior executives,
402–3, 403*, 405;
regulatory bodies,
403, 768–9; of British
Airways (BA), 404–8,
405*, 600; fattening-up
of BA for, 404–8, 405*;
of BG, 408–9, 409*,
409†, 770; failures of
regulation, 409, 769*,
769; success of policy,
412†, 412–13, 600,
602, 768; Macmillan's
'family silver' speech
criticizing, 412;
breaking up of British
Leyland, 527–8; foreign
multinationals and
BL, 527–8; of British
Rail, 758; of electricity
industry, 758, 768,
769–74, 770*, 771*,
784, 889*; in MT's
third term, 758, 768–9;
of water industry, 758,
768*, 768
Proctor, Harvey), 541
Proffitt, Stuart (1961–;
educated Uppingham
and Worcester College,
Oxford; HarperCollins
Publishers
(1982–98; Publisher,
Trade Division,
1992–8); Publishing
Director, Allen Lane/
Penguin Books,
1998–. Editor of this
biography), 923
Profumo affair/scandal, 76‡,
76, 949
Prole, Mrs (Colchester
milliner), 44
proportional representation,
161, 167
protectionism: of Trump, 5;
and EC, 874*, 874, 925
Prunskienė, Kazimira
(1943–; Prime Minister

of Lithuania, 1990–91.
Five days before she
met Mrs Thatcher,
George Bush had
jumped the gun by
publicly referring to her
as 'Prime Minister'),
830*, 830
Public Honours Scrutiny
Committee, 922†
Public Sector Borrowing
Requirement (PSBR),
195, 225, 267–9,
269*, 271*, 355, 399,
491, 542; Labour
government (1974–9),
117, 144‡
public-sector pay, 169, 195,
202, 217–19, 224,
379, 765–6; incomes
policies, 76, 86, 102,
104, 105, 106, 144,
145, 151, 167, 168,
169–71; Macmillan's
'pay pause', 76;
teachers' pay, 100; and
Heath government,
106, 107, 382*; police
pay, 173, 202; Clegg
Commission, 174, 195,
196; comparability
concept, 174, 195, 196;
MPs' pay, 354†, 354;
of executives/managers,
402–3, 405
Pulzer, Peter, 591, 592
Putin, Vladimir, 5, 6, 807†
Pym, Francis (1922–2008;
educated Eton
and Magdalene
College, Cambridge;
Conservative MP
for Cambridgeshire,
1961–83; for
Cambridgeshire South
East, 1983–7; Secretary
of State for Northern
Ireland, 1973–4; for
Defence, 1979–81;
Chancellor of the
Duchy of Lancaster and
Leader of the House
of Commons, 1981–2;
Foreign Secretary,
1982–3; created Lord
Pym, 1987): in Heath
government, 99;
Shadow Agricultural
spokesman, 129,

132, 154, 160–61; supports devolution, 160–61; Military Cross in Second World War, 183*, 289§; Defence Secretary, 183, 283; excluded from economic policy decisions, 216; and public spending control, 228, 272, 278; Leader of the House, 229; and 1981 budget, 270; as putative alternative leader (1981/82), 274, 289; Foreign Secretary, 289§, 289–90, 293, 329, 335–6, 353, 480–1; MT's dislike of, 289–90, 331, 335–6, 344†, 345†; and Falklands War, 291, 293, 298, 299–300, 300*, 306, 307, 310, 312†, 315, 319, 323; in Falklands War Cabinet, 291, 293, 299–300, 300*; and Hong Kong, 329, 331; and 1983 election campaign, 344†; leaves Cabinet, 350; MT steers towards Speakership, 350, 354; Centre Forward grouping, 495

Qaboos bin Said (1940–2020; educated Sandhurst; overthrew his father as Sultan with British support in 1970; Sultan of Oman, 1970–2020), 440
Qatar, 437*
QEII (ocean liner), 314
Quayle, Dan, 864
Queen's College, Oxford, 30, 590
Quinn, Paddy, 262

Raban, Jonathan, 583
race/ethnicity: Powell's 'Rivers of Blood' speech, 87, 163; Rhodesia, 158–9, 160, 192–4; MT's 'swamped' comment, 163–4, 843; Reagan's view of South Africa, 234*, 555; and slavery/slave trade, 327; Declaration on Anti-Semitism, Racism and Xenophobia (Dublin summit), 851†; 'ethnic cleansing' phrase, 931*; *see also* South Africa
Radcliffe Rules, 936
radio, 187†; MT's appearances on, 3, 68, 71, 72, 83–4, 133*, 171, 623, 671; *Any Questions?* (BBC), 68, 71, 83–4, 113–14; *Petticoat Line* (BBC), 92; *Today* programme (BBC), 124, 187†; *Woman's Hour* (BBC), 133*; *Jimmy Young Show* (BBC), 623, 671
Ramphal, Shridath 'Sonny' (1928–2024; educated King's College, London; lawyer; occupied several posts in the government of Guyana in the 1960s and 1970s; Secretary-General of the Commonwealth, 1975–90; knighted, 1970), 546, 549, 554, 556†, 560
Randolph Hotel, Oxford, 32–3, 38*
Rapier missiles, 861*
Ratford, David, 574*
Rawlinson, (Sir) Peter (*later* Lord Rawlinson of Ewell), 707, 708
Rayner, Sir Derek (*later* Baron Rayner), 139*, 221
Reagan, Nancy, 426‡, 426, 688, 690, 691, 921, 940, 949
Reagan, Ronald (1911–2004; Governor, California, 1967–75; President of the United States of America, 1981–9): MT's close relations with, 4, 387†, 387–8, 406, 416, 426, 519, 562, 572*, 676*, 684–91; and Cold War, 5, 238†, 241–9, 364–5, 368, 414–32, 562–9, 614–15, 676, 680–90; and free-market economics, 5; free-trade doctrine, 5; Governor of California, 136; MT first meets, 136; MT's immediate/ early rapport with, 136, 189, 212; congratulates MT on election as Prime Minister, 189; character/temperament, 231–2, 233; economic policy, 231–3, 273; and MT's 1981 visit to US, 231–4, 241–2; MT's economic policy influence on, 232, 655; and apartheid South Africa, 234*, 555; intellectual limitations, 234*, 234, 248, 568, 677, 680†, 685; MT's attitude to intellect of, 234*, 234, 248, 568, 685; MT's foreign policy influence on, 241–3, 246, 368, 423–4, 429, 431–2, 532–3, 562–4, 571–3, 678–9, 684–8; elected President (1980), 241; 'evil empire' phrase, 241; and 'dual track' strategy, 242–3; administration's Cold War hawks, 242; 'zero option' stance, 243*, 243, 563, 566, 576; views on nuclear weapons, 243, 365†, 365, 420, 422, 423, 425–6, 562–7, 600, 601, 923; and Trident missile system, 244†, 244; growing intimacy with MT, 245*, 273; economic aggression against Russians, 245–6, 246†; pipeline sanctions on Soviet Union, 245–6, 247, 248–9, 332; and western Siberia gas pipeline, 245–6, 332; tension with MT over pipeline sanctions, 245, 248–9, 249*; and unrest in Poland, 245; formal visit to Britain (June 1982), 246–8, 319;

Reagan, Ronald – *cont'd*
Royal Gallery speech (1982), 247†, 247–8, 319†, 319; at Versailles G7 summit (June 1982), 247, 248; and Maze hunger strikes, 259*; at G7 summit, Ottawa (July 1981), 273*, 273; assassination attempt (1981), 273; relations with Argentina, 283–4, 284*, 285, 286, 294–6, 303, 314‡, 685–6; British request to over Falklands, 285, 286; and Falklands War, 293–6, 298, 302–3, 306–9, 309*, 310–11, 315–16, 318*, 318, 319, 323; MT's relations with over Falklands War, 307–8, 310–11, 315–16; at G7 Versailles summit (1982), 318, 319; electoral help to MT, 333–4, 600–602, 609*; at G7 Williamsburg summit (1983), 345–6, 490; congratulates MT on 1983 election victory, 364; and SDI, 365–6, 416, 420, 421, 422–3, 425, 427–8, 432, 562; excludes MT over Grenada, 369–76, 372*, 374*, 375*; invasion of Grenada, 369–76; and miners' strike, 387†, 387–8; and lawsuits against BA, 406–7; MT's influences on civil aviation, 406, 407; MT's visit to Camp David (1984), 407, 416, 421–4, 453–4; MT reports meetings with Eastern bloc leaders to, 414–15, 416, 422–3, 684; wins 1984 presidential election, 416; 'Four Points' agreement (Camp David, 1984), 423–4, 427–8, 429†, 429, 432; and MT in Washington (1985), 424–6, 425*; invites Gorbachev to talks, 428; cancer operations, 429; Geneva summit with Gorbachev (November 1985), 429, 431–2, 562; and the Middle East, 434–6, 439†, 439; and MT's Middle East initiative, 434–6; bombing of Libya (1986), 442, 529–31, 530*, 532–4, 533*, 535, 541; and Irish-American lobby, 448, 453–4, 459; visits Irish Republic (1984), 448; aids sterling (January 1985), 490; and Westland affair, 519†, 519; sanctions on Libya, 528–9; gratitude to MT over Libya, 533, 534–5; Reykjavik summit (1986), 562, 565*, 565–9, 566*, 571, 572, 680–81; offensive ballistic weapons proposals, 564–5, 566–9, 570, 571–3; MT's response to Reykjavik, 566–9; MT's visit to Camp David (1986), 568, 570–71, 573, 678; 'Iran-Contra' affair, 569†, 569–70, 572, 575, 676*, 676–7, 678; gratitude to MT over Iran-Contra, 570, 677–8; 'Camp David agreement' with MT (1986), 571–3, 576, 581–2, 678, 680–81, 682–3; and MT's Moscow visit (1987), 575–6; meetings with Kinnock, 600–602; Brandenburg Gate speech (1987), 614–15, 680, 681; congratulates MT on 1987 victory, 614–15; and budget deficit (1987–8), 655; has prostate surgery, 676*; MT's steadfast loyalty to, 677–8; and Gorbachev's 'second zero' proposals (April 1987), 678–9; at G7 Venice summit (1987), 679–80; Washington summit with Gorbachev (December 1987), 682–3, 684*, 684; and Gorbachev's reforms, 684*, 687–8; and Middle East, 685*; ageing/decline of, 685†, 685, 940–41; diagnosed with Alzheimer's disease, 685†, 940–41; Moscow summit with Gorbachev (1988), 687–88; speech at Moscow University (May 1988), 687–8; at special NATO summit (1988), 687; MT's 'farewell' visit to (November 1988), 688–91, 689*, 692; Guildhall speech (June 1988), 688; and southern Africa, 789*, 789; MT's friendship in post-office years, 921, 926†, 940–41; Presidential Library of, 940§, 940; interest in wine, 940‡; death of (5 June 2004), 957–8; funeral of, 957–8, 965; MT's eulogy at funeral, 957

Red Star (Soviet newspaper), 142–3

Redwood, John (1951–; educated Kent College, Canterbury and Magdalen College and St Antony's College, Oxford; Fellow of All Souls College, Oxford, 1972–87, 2003–5, 2007–; head of No. 10 Policy Unit, 1983–5; Conservative MP for Wokingham, 1987–2024; Minister of State, DTI, 1990–92; Environment, 1992–3; Secretary of State for Wales, 1993–5; knighted, 2019): in Policy Unit, 353†; heads No. 10 Policy Unit, 361, 384*, 384, 401; and miners' strike, 384, 387; and

1984 budget, 398, 400; and privatization policy, 401, 402, 403, 408, 769; and stock exchange reform, 411; and poll tax, 465, 468, 469; and local government, 471; on 1985 budget, 491; and ERM question, 492–3; end-of-term advice (1985), 497; stands in 1995 leadership contest, 938; leadership contest (1997), 945–6

Reece, Gordon (1929–2001; educated Ratcliffe College and Downing College, Cambridge; independent television producer and director; joined EMI, 1970; worked for Mrs Thatcher on secondment, 1975; Director of Publicity, Conservative Central Office, 1978–80; returned to CCO for general election of 1983; knighted, 1986), 140, 603, 846; and MT's 1975 party leadership bid, 121, 123, 127*; adviser to MT as Leader of Opposition, 133, 134, 137, 139, 164–5; coaches MT on image/presentation, 134, 165–7; and 'Winter of Discontent', 170†, 170; and 1979 election campaign, 171‡, 171–2, 175; on his importance to MT, 175†; knighthood, 175†, 175; adviser to MT as Prime Minister, 188‡; works in USA, 270; and leadership contest (November 1990), 888*

Rees, Peter (*later* Lord Rees), 496

Referendum Party, 942–3

Regan, Donald 'Don' (1918–2003; Chairman and CEO, Merrill Lynch, 1971–80; US Secretary of the Treasury, 1981–5; White House Chief of Staff, 1985–7), 232, 233

Reichmann, Paul, 632†, 632

Reilly, Elizabeth 'Libbie', 782*

Reilly, William (1940–; President, World Wildlife Fund, 1985–9; Administrator, US Environmental Protection Agency, 1989–93), 781, 782, 785

Reith, John, 1st Baron Reith, 540, 761, 762

RENAMO forces, Mozambique, 789, 791*

Renaud ('the French Bob Dylan'), 585†

Renton, David, 50

Renton, (Ronald) Timothy 'Tim' (1932–2020; educated Eton and Magdalen College, Oxford; Conservative MP for Mid-Sussex, 1974–97; PPS to Geoffrey Howe, 1983–4; Minister of State, FCO, 1985–7; Home Office, 1987–9; Government Chief Whip, 1989–90; Minister of State, Privy Council Office (Minister for the Arts), 1990–92; created Lord Renton of Mount Harry, 1997), 745, 853*, 853, 909; on Wakeham's list after 1987 victory, 616*; Chief Whip, 752, 757, 836, 878, 879, 881, 882; China, 844; and Howe's resignation, 878, 879, 880; resists Tebbit's return, 879; and leadership contest (November 1990), 880*, 880–81, 888, 889, 892, 893, 894, 895–6, 897, 902; gathers reactions to Howe's statement, 884; and 'Catherine Place conspiracy', 894; consults Whitelaw (21 November 1990), 894, 895, 897; and MT's resignation, 904–5; and conspiracy to remove MT, 913

Rentschler, Jim, 213, 214, 294, 295, 298*, 306, 316

Renwick, Robin (1937–2024; educated St Paul's and Jesus College, Cambridge; Rhodesia Department, FCO, 1978–80; Ambassador to South Africa, 1987–91; to the United States, 1991–5; created Lord Renwick of Clifton, 1997), 193, 370, 375, 476, 477, 787*; Ambassador to South Africa, 787, 788–9, 791, 792, 793, 794, 797–8, 798*, 800

Rhodesia (modern Zimbabwe), 80; Smith government, 158–60, 192, 215; 'internal settlement' (March 1978), 159–60, 192–3; British proposals for independence, 193–5, 204; Lancaster House conference/Agreement (1979), 195, 213, 214, 215; British servicemen sent to, 214–15; Mugabe's rule in, 215, 549; trade with apartheid South Africa, 549†; raids on ANC offices (May 1986), 553

Rice, Condoleezza (1954–; Director, Soviet and Eastern European Affairs, NSC, 1989–91; foreign policy adviser to George W. Bush, 2000–2001; US National Security Advisor, 2001–5; Secretary of State, 2005–9), 809, 822

Rich, Marc, 863*

Richardson, Gordon (1915–2010; educated Nottingham High School and Gonville

Richardson, Gordon – *cont'd*
and Caius College, Cambridge; Governor, Bank of England, 1973–83; created Lord Richardson of Duntisbourne, 1983), 147, 198*, 198†, 198, 223, 228, 338*

Richardson, Sir Michael, 139*, 411*, 732*

Rickett, William, 770, 771

Riddell, Peter (1948–; educated Dulwich College and Sidney Sussex College, Cambridge; Political Editor, *Financial Times*, 1981–8; US editor and Washington bureau chief, 1989–91; political columnist, *The Times*, 1991–2010; Commissioner for Public Appointments, 2016–21; knighted, 2022), 656

Ridley, Adam (1942–; educated Eton and Balliol College, Oxford; Deputy Director, Conservative Research Department, 1974–9; special adviser to the Chancellor of the Exchequer, 1979–84; knighted, 1985), 110, 181†, 181

Ridley, Nicholas (1929–93; educated Eton and Balliol College, Oxford; Conservative MP for Cirencester and Tewkesbury, 1959–92; Economic Secretary to the Treasury, 1981–3; Secretary of State for Transport, 1983–7; for the Environment, 1987–9; for Trade and Industry, 1989–90; forced to resign after *Spectator interview*, July 1990; created Lord Ridley of Liddesdale, 1992), 638*; in opposition, 146; junior minister at Foreign Office, 282–3;

Transport Secretary, 359; and the poll tax, 474, 624*, 624, 747; Environment Secretary, 538, 624, 630, 783; and Strategy Group ('A-Team'), 538; character of, 624, 852; and MT's inner city policy, 630–31; and Thyssen collection project, 668; Trade and Industry Secretary, 745; and ERM question, 752, 842, 852; privatization of water industry, 768–9; resigns after *Spectator* interview, 835–6, 852, 855; at MT's farewell lunch, 908†; death of (1993), 939

Rifai, Zaid, 436

Rifkind, Malcolm (1946–; educated George Watson's College and Edinburgh University; Conservative MP for Edinburgh Pentlands, 1974–97; for Kensington and Chelsea, from 2005; Secretary of State for Scotland, 1986–90; for Transport, 1990–92; for Defence, 1992–5; Foreign Secretary, 1995–7; knighted, 1997), 161, 693†; junior Foreign Office minister, 365*, 365, 366*; Scottish Secretary, 474, 619, 839–40, 849–50; and leadership contest (November 1990), 884, 899; and 'Catherine Place conspiracy', 894; individual session with MT (21 November 1990), 899*, 899

'right to buy' (council housing policy), 197, 201–2, 543

Rimington, Stella (1935–; educated Nottingham High School for Girls and Edinburgh University;

Director-General, Security Service, 1992–6; created dame, 1996), 388

riots, inner-city (1985), 501–2

Ripon by-election (1973), 106

Ritz Hotel, London, 1, 962–3, 963*

Roberts, Alfred (MT's father): grocery shops of, 9–10; influence on MT, 9–11, 14, 17, 62, 78, 87, 179, 624; background and education, 9; Methodism of, 9, 10–11, 15, 33, 149; reading and study, 9; sermons of, 9, 11, 87, 291; biographical information, 10; character of, 11†, 15, 16, 33; reputation for sexually inappropriate behaviour, 11†; efforts to advance his daughters, 11–12; feels unthanked/neglected, 11, 51, 72–3; speaking technique, 11; views on Catholicism, 11, 51; Rotarian principles, 14–15; career in local council politics, 14, 15, 61–2; political affiliations of, 14; during Second World War, 14, 15–16; visit of Muriel's penfriend, 15–16; appointed an alderman (1943), 15, 61; as mayor of Grantham, 15; supports appeasement, 15; and KGGS, 22; MT's requests for money, 35–6; on William Cullen, 46; announces Muriel's engagement, 47*; and MT's engagement to Denis, 52; relations with Denis Thatcher, 53; removed as alderman (1952), 61–2; and MT's election to Parliament, 67; MT's familiar address of, 72*; death of first wife, 72–3;

second marriage, 73; death and funeral of, 92†, 92; bible of at 10 Downing Street, 908*
Roberts, Beatrice (née Stephenson; MT's mother), 9; charitable activities, 10; daughters' view of, 11, 12, 13; influence on MT, 12–13; expertise as a seamstress, 12, 597†; character of, 33; and MT's requests for money, 36; relations with Denis Thatcher, 53; death of, 72–3
Roberts, Cissie (Hubbard), 73
Roberts, Harold (MT's uncle), 67, 68
Robinson, Peter (1957–; educated Dartmouth and Christ Church, Oxford; speechwriter to President Reagan, 1983–8), 684
Robinson, Roger, 248–9
Rockefeller, Nelson, 89
Rodgers, Bill (1928–; educated Quarry Bank High School, Liverpool and Magdalen College, Oxford; Labour MP for Stockton-on-Tees, 1962–74; for Teesside, Stockton, 1974–81; founder member of SDP, 1981; SDP MP for Teesside, Stockton, 1981–3; created Lord Rodgers of Quarry Bank, 1992), 227†, 234–5
Rogers, Ginger, 18
Rohan, Mary, 51
Rolls-Royce, 343, 400; insolvency (1971), 102
Romania, 831*, 831
Romberg, Sigmund, *The Desert Song*, 18
Rook, Jean, 133*
Rooke, Denis (1924–2008; educated Westminster City School, Addey, Stanhope School and University College London; Chairman, British Gas plc (formerly the Gas Council, then British Gas Corporation), 1976–89; knighted, 1977; OM 1997), 408*, 408
Rotary movement, 14–15
Rothschild, Lady (Tess), 709*
Rothschild, Nathaniel Mayer Victor (1910–90; 3rd Baron Rothschild, educated Harrow and Trinity College, Cambridge; scientist; Chairman, N. M. Rothschild & Sons Ltd, 1975–6; Director-General, Central Policy Review Staff, Cabinet Office, 1971–4; Chairman, Rothschilds Continuation Ltd, 1976–88), 466†, 712*; and community charge, 466–7, 468, 469, 708; and *Spycatcher* controversy, 707–8, 710–12, 711*, 714–15; and intelligence world, 707–9, 710–11, 714–15
Rothschild, Victoria, 466†
Rothschilds, 411*, 412†, 466†
Royal Air Force, 303–4, 438*, 438, 439, 861*, 952*
Royal Bank of Scotland, 885*
Royal Hospital, Chelsea, 950, 956, 961, 966, 967
Royal Irish Regiment, 454†
Royal Marines, 965*, 965
Royal Navy: MT's defence cuts, 244*, 283, 286; contingency plans for Falklands conflict, 284; *Endurance* despatched for South Georgia, 284; action during Falklands War, 303–6, 313–14, 319–20; and Iraqi invasion of Kuwait, 859, 861*
Royal Society, 590, 778–9, 780, 786
Royal Ulster Constabulary (RUC), 260, 454*, 454, 459‡, 460, 716*; Loughgall barracks attack, 719–20, 854; and British Army, 720, 721, 726–7; and intelligence sharing, 720, 726–7
Ruding, Onno (1939–; Minister of Finance of the Netherlands, 1982–9), 734
Runcie, Robert (1921–2000; MC, 1945; educated Merchant Taylors', Crosby and Brasenose College, Oxford and Westcott House, Cambridge; Archbishop of Canterbury, 1980–91; created Lord Runcie of Cuddesdon, 1991), 503†, 503, 776, 777, 968
Rushdie, Salman (1947–; educated Cathedral School, Bombay, Rugby and King's College, Cambridge; works include *Midnight's Children* (1981) and *The Satanic Verses* (1988), which resulted in Ayatollah Khomeini's issuing a fatwa in 1989 calling for Rushdie's death; blinded in one eye by an Islamist murder attempt, 2022; knighted, 2007), 587, 695–7, 696*, 696†
Russian Orthodox Church, 576†, 576
Russian Social Democratic Labour Party (RSDRP), 418§, 418
Ryan, Patrick, 724–5, 725*
Ryan Jr, Frederick (special assistant to the President and director of appointments and scheduling, 1983–9; publisher and CEO, the *Washington Post*, 2014–23), 921, 940‡, 940
Ryder, Richard (1949–; educated Radley and Magdalene College, Cambridge;

Ryder, Richard – *cont'd*
Conservative MP for Mid-Norfolk, 1983–97; Government Chief Whip, 1990–95; Vice-Chairman, BBC, 2002–4; created Lord Ryder of Wensum, 1997), 595*; political secretary to MT as Leader of Opposition, 130, 150, 155*; runs MT's political office, 185, 201, 595*; runs for Parliament, 270; No Turning Back Group, 496; and Howe, 520, 561, 661, 745, 883; and Meyer's leadership challenge, 756; on Peter Morrison, 852; on Foreign Office Europhiles, 875*; and leadership contest (November 1990), 880*, 885, 900; as Major's Chief Whip, 938
Ryedale by-election, 533, 534, 537

Saatchi, Charles (1943–; educated Christ's Hospital; co-founder, Saatchi & Saatchi, 1970; partner, M&C Saatchi, from 1995; noted collector of contemporary art), 164
Saatchi, Maurice (1946–; educated LSE; co-founder, Saatchi & Saatchi, 1970, Chairman, 1985–94; partner, M&C Saatchi, from 1995; Co-Chairman, Conservative Party, 2003–5; created Lord Saatchi, 1996), 164, 611
Saatchi & Saatchi (advertising agency), 164–5, 166, 539; 'Labour isn't working' poster, 165, 167; and 1979 election campaign, 171–2; and 1983 election campaign, 344*, 347; and 1987 election, 535–7, 603, 609, 610, 611
Saddam Hussein (1937–2006; President of Iraq, 1979–2003; engaged in three wars: the Iran–Iraq War, 1980–88; the invasion of Kuwait, 1990 and the ensuing Gulf War, 1991; the Second Gulf War of 2003–11. Hanged for crimes against humanity in 2006), 434, 785, 856–67, 857*, 908, 917, 931; WMD capability, 870, 871
Saïd, Wafic (1939–; businessman and philanthropist; founder and Chairman, Saïd Foundation; founder, Saïd Business School, Oxford), 437, 958
Sakharov, Andrei, 573, 579, 589, 689‡
Salford Quays, 632
Salmond, Alexander 'Alex' (1954–2024; educated Linlithgow Academy and St Andrews University; Scottish National Party MP for Banff and Buchan, 1987–2010; for Gordon, 2015–17; Leader of the SNP, 1990–2000 and 2004–14; First Minister of Scotland, 2007–14), 659
Saltley coke depot, Birmingham, 103, 152, 218, 382*, 382, 385, 387
Saltwood (Alan Clark's castle in Kent), 887
Sammy and Rosie Get Laid (Frears film, 1987), 586
Sampson, Anthony, 788†
Sampson, Colin, 721
Samuelson, Paul, 89
San Francisco, 89
Sandhurst military academy, 59, 434
Sandinista government, Nicaragua, 569†, 633*
Sands, Bobby, 259–60, 262†
Santa Fe (Argentine submarine), 301
Sarajevo, 932
Sarotte, Mary Elise, 810, 834
Satanic Verses, The (Rushdie novel, 1988), 587
Saud, Prince, 864*
Saudi Arabia, 433, 434; arms sales to, 437*, 437–8, 439–40, 440*; MT's friendship with Bandar, 438†, 438–9, 439*; Iraqi invasion of Kuwait, 857, 858, 859, 861
Saunders Watson, L. M. M. (Michael), 638
Savile, Jimmy, 133*, 133
Savoy Hotel, London, 55
Sawyer, Kate, 958–60
Sayle, Alexei, 586
Scargill, Arthur (1938–; educated White Cross Secondary School and Leeds University; President, Yorkshire National Union of Mineworkers, 1973; President, NUM, 1981–2002; Honorary President from 2002), 171, 230, 968; at Saltley coke depot, 103, 218, 382*, 385, 387; at Hadfields steelworks, 218; elected NUM leader, 279, 380; prediction of coal industry's destruction, 381*, 396; secret 'hit list' allegations, 381*; refusal to call national strike ballot, 381, 383, 384–5, 389–90; at Orgreave, South Yorkshire, 385–6; MT labels as 'the enemy within', 389; receives support from Gaddafi and Eastern bloc, 393, 417‡, 417, 418‡, 418; attitude to violence, 394*, 394
Scarlett, Sir John, 369
Scarman, Leslie, Baron, 153
Schapiro, Leonard, 147†, 237, 246*
Schlesinger, James, 137, 138*, 138

Schloss Freudenberg (near Zug, Switzerland), 14*, 226, 357, 390
Schmidt, Helmut, 135†, 190, 211, 239, 242–3, 332, 665–6
Scholar, Sir Michael, 345, 350, 360*, 464–5
Schöpflin, George, 366*
Schumpeter, Joseph, 147*
Schweitzer, Pierre-Paul, 89
Scoon, Sir Paul, 371
Scotland: waning Tory support in, 160*, 161, 612, 618–19, 619†; devolution issue, 160–62, 171; 1979 general election, 161†, 162; devolution referendum (March 1979), 162*, 162, 171; rating revaluation in, 467–8, 468*, 469, 470, 619, 624; poll tax in, 470, 471–2, 472*, 473, 474, 624, 839–40, 849–50; domestic rates abolished, 474; Scottish party conference (1986), 538*; 1987 general election, 612, 618–19, 619†; Scottish Labour, 619–20; education in, 639–40; legal system, 766–7; MT's misunderstanding of nationalism, 968
Scottish National Party (SNP), 161†, 162, 659
Scowcroft, Brent (1925–2020; educated US Military Academy, Columbia University; Lieutenant General, US Army; Deputy National Security Advisor, 1973–5; National Security Advisor, 1975–7 and 1989–93), 699, 704, 803†, 812, 828; on MT, 137, 692, 701, 871; and SNF negotiations, 702, 703; at Camp David meeting, 810; and MT's view of EC, 813–14; and Gulf crisis, 856†, 856–8, 864, 866,

871; relations with Charles Powell, 864
SDP (Social Democratic Party): Warrington by-election (1981), 273; lead in the polls (1981), 274, 279; and trade union political power, 276, 341–2; wins Crosby by-election, 279; SDP-Liberal Alliance, 341, 342, 346, 348, 600, 603–4, 604*, 606, 612, 615; and 1983 election, 346, 348; opinion polling in 1985, 495; and 1987 election, 603–4, 604*, 606, 612, 615
Second World War: and Grantham, 13–14, 15–16, 17, 21, 31; MT's views shaped by, 21, 28‡, 28, 333, 802, 825, 969; and Oxford University, 27*; Allied victory in the Far East, 29; story of 1940 and MT, 54†, 225, 322; decorated senior Tories, 183*; Katyn massacre, 244‡; Maginot Line, 429*, 429; Irish neutrality, 718*, 718, 969
Secret Intelligence Service (SIS or MI6), 368*, 368, 369, 377, 417†, 417, 706, 725, 726; and GCHQ, 378; exfiltration of Gordievsky, 430–31; secret contacts with ANC, 552; as not 'avowed' (publicly acknowledged), 707*, 716–17; Oldfield as former head, 712†, 712, 716–18; statutory basis for, 715; and Gibraltar shootings, 723; backchannel with IRA, 727
Security Service (MI5), 377, 544, 716*; and miners' strike, 388, 393, 417‡, 417, 418‡, 418; Spycatcher controversy, 706–15,

714*; Duff heads, 706, 713, 715; as not 'avowed' (publicly acknowledged), 707*; and Victor Rothschild, 707, 708–9, 711; lifelong duty of confidentiality, 709–10, 710*, 714; alleged plot against Wilson, 713*, 713; 'formal oversight' suggested for, 713–14; Security Service Act (1989), 714, 715; tracking of IRA operatives, 721
Seitz, Raymond (1940; Executive Assistant to Secretary George Shultz, Washington, 1982–4; Minister and Deputy Chief of Mission, US Embassy, London, 1984–9; Ambassador to the UK, 1991–4), 600, 812
Seldon, Arthur (1916–2005; educated Raine's Foundation School and LSE; founder Editorial Director of the Institute of Economic Affairs, 1957–88; author of numerous books and pamphlets, including *Capitalism* (1990)), 110, 146
Selleck, Tom, 689*
Senter, Sir John, 59, 60
Serbia, 931, 932
Sergeant, John, 892
Seymour, Diana, 950*
Seymour, Sir Julian, 937, 943, 950*, 951, 960; heads MT's post-retirement operation/affairs, 915†, 920, 921†, 921, 936*, 944; on MT and Thatcher Foundation, 922; in Hong Kong with MT, 928, 945; and 1995 leadership contest, 938; and MT's mental decline, 945, 955*, 955; and MT's funeral plans, 961
Shackleton, Edward, Baron, 282*, 282, 321

Shah, Eddie, 382†
Shakespeare, William, 19, 695
Shamir, Yitzhak (1915–2012; born Poland; Foreign Minister, 1980; Leader of the Likud Party, 1983–92; Prime Minister of Israel 1983–4. After the 1984 elections he alternated posts with Shimon Peres of the Labour Party, serving as Foreign Minister, 1984–6 and Prime Minister, 1986–92), 433, 685*
Sharkey, John (1947; joint Managing Director, Saatchi & Saatchi UK, 1986–9; created Lord Sharkey, 2010), 535–6
Sharp, Dame Evelyn, 70
Shattock, Jeanne, Lady, 450†
Shea, Michael, 535, 557, 558, 560
Sheerness steelworks, 218–19
Sheffield, HMS, 305–6, 306*, 307, 317
Shelton, William (1929–2003; educated Radley, Tabor Academy, Marion, Massachusetts and Worcester College, Oxford; Conservative MP for Clapham, 1970–74; for Streatham, 1974–92; knighted, 1989), 121, 123, 125*, 125, 129, 142
Shepherd, Richard (1942–2022; educated Isleworth Grammar School, LSE and Johns Hopkins University; Conservative MP for Aldridge-Brownhills, 1979–2015; knighted, 2013), 943
Sheppard, David (1929–2005; educated Sherborne and Trinity Hall, Cambridge; Bishop of Liverpool, 1975–97; created Lord Sheppard of Liverpool, 1998), 471, 503*
Sherbourne, Stephen (1945–; educated Burnage Grammar School and St Edmund Hall, Oxford; head of the office of Edward Heath MP, 1975–6; political secretary to the Prime Minister, 1983–8; chief of staff to Leader of the Opposition, 2003–5; knighted, 2006; created Baron Sherbourne of Didsbury, 2013), 344, 349, 352, 384‡, 464, 467, 475, 498, 618; on Westland affair, 515, 519; and US bombing of Libya, 533; preparations for 1987 election, 535, 538; on MT's adoration of Young and Bell, 536; and Tebbit–MT conflict, 538, 539; 1987 election campaign, 608, 610; leaves post with MT, 627–8
Sherman, Sir Alfred, 110, 111, 123*, 131, 146, 147†, 221
Shevardnadze, Edvard (1928–2014; member, Politburo, 1985–90; Minister of Foreign Affairs, USSR, 1985–90; Chairman of Supreme Council and head of state, Georgia, 1992–5; President of Georgia, 1995–2003; Hon. GCMG, 2000), 799†, 799, 815
shipbuilding industry, 143–4, 144*, 144†, 173*, 337*, 400*; Type 22 naval frigates, 506
Short, Edward 'Ted' (*later* Baron Glenamara), 96, 98
Short, Sharp Shock, A (Brenton and Howard play, 1980), 585–6
Shultz, George (1920–2021; educated Princeton University; US Secretary of Labor, 1969–70; Director, Office of Management and Budget, 1970–72; Secretary of the Treasury, 1972–4; Secretary of State, 1982–9), 249, 368, 371, 407, 416, 419, 572, 678, 679; at Camp David (December 1984), 422, 424; on Geoffrey Howe, 426*; on Gorbachev, 428, 429; at Reykjavik summit, 566–7; and MT's visit to Reagan (1986), 570, 571; on MT's divergence with Reagan, 681; and Middle East, 685*; and MT's 'farewell' visit to Reagan, 689, 690; and verb 'to handbag', 690; at MT's funeral, 965
Sieff, Sir Marcus (*later* Baron Sieff of Brimpton), 139*, 732*
Sieve, Yvonne, 85
Sikhs, 164*
Sikorsky Aircraft Corporation, 506, 507, 508, 509, 510, 512, 516*, 516, 517, 521
Silvester, Fred (1933–2025; educated Sir George Monoux Grammar School and Sidney Sussex College, Cambridge; Conservative MP for Walthamstow West, 1967–70; for Manchester, Withington, 1974–87; Opposition whip, 1974–6), 116, 118*
Simon, Bill, 137, 138
Sinclair, Sir Jeremy, 165
single currency concept: and Delors, 486–7, 733; German support for, 486–7; ERM designed as forerunner of, 490; Lawson opposes, 490, 662; and Bruges Speech, 673; MT

opposes, 673, 742,
837, 870, 906, 925,
933; Delors' three-
stage process, 733,
742, 872*; Major's
views on, 847, 848†,
848; and 'hard ecu'
idea, 848*, 848, 851,
876, 883, 955; French
policy on, 873‡, 873;
Leon Brittan's views
on, 875†, 875; MT
suggests referendum on,
886*, 886; Major wins
opt-out for Britain,
929; and 1997 election,
943*; referendum
pledges on, 943
Single European Act (SEA,
1986), 481, 487–8,
489, 662, 665, 672,
930, 934, 935
Sinn Fein, 255, 260,
445*, 445, 452,
456; 'Armalite and
ballot box' strategy,
263*, 263, 445*;
broadcast ban on,
726; MT's view of,
727; and King's speech
(November 1988), 728;
interest in ending the
armed struggle, 854
Sir Galahad, HMS, 319–20
Sir Tristram, HMS, 319–20
Skidelsky, Robert, 147*
Skinner, Dennis (1932–;
educated Tupton Hall
Grammar School
and Ruskin College,
Oxford; Labour MP for
Bolsover, 1970–2019;
Chairman, Labour
Party, 1988–9), 906
Skinner, Revd Reuben, 18
Sky Television, 764–5
slavery/slave trade, 327
Sleaford Gazette, 28
Slocock, Caroline (1956–;
educated Talbot Heath
School, Bournemouth
and University College
London; private secretary
(home affairs) to Prime
Minister, 1989–91;
author of *People Like
Us: Margaret Thatcher
and Me* (2018)), 643,
904, 908

Slovenia, 931
Smith, Adam, 147*, 620
Smith, Geoffrey, 562
Smith, Howard (1919–96;
educated Regent Street
Polytechnic and
Sidney Sussex
College, Cambridge;
Ambassador to
Czechoslovakia,
1968–71; Ambassador
to the Soviet Union,
1976–8; Director-
General, MI5,
1978–81; knighted,
1976), 707
Smith, Ian, 158–60, 215
Smith, John (1938–94;
educated Dunoon
Grammar School
and Glasgow
University; Labour
MP for Lanarkshire
North, 1970–83;
for Monklands East,
1983–94; Secretary
of State for Trade,
1978–9; Leader of the
Labour Party and of
the Opposition from
1992 until his death
from a heart attack in
1994), 515, 941
Smith, Lorna, 19, 20, 21
Smithers, Peter (1913–2006;
educated Harrow and
Magdalen College,
Oxford; diplomat and
botanist; Secretary-
General, Council
of Europe, 1964–9;
Conservative MP for
Winchester, 1950–64;
knighted, 1970), 666–7
Soames, Christopher
(1920–87; educated
Eton and Sandhurst.
Son-in-law of
Winston Churchill.
MP for Bedford,
1950–66; Minister of
Agriculture, 1960–64;
Ambassador to France,
1968–72; Vice-
President, European
Commission, 1972–7;
Governor of Southern
Rhodesia, 1979–80;
Leader of the House

of Lords and Lord
President of the
Council, 1979–81;
created Lord Soames,
1978), 130, 136, 183,
228, 276*, 276
Social Democratic and
Labour Party (SDLP),
251, 259, 260, 445*,
445, 452, 455, 457,
460, 718
Social Democratic Party,
German (SPD), 332,
333
Socialist Workers Party, 344
Socrates, 84
Solidarity (Polish trade
union), 245, 693†, 693,
694*, 694
Solzhenitsyn, Alexander
(1918–2008; author of
many works including
*One Day in the Life
of Ivan Denisovich*
(1962), *The First Circle*
(1968) and *The Gulag
Archipelago* (1973);
sentenced to eight years
in the Gulag for anti-
Soviet activities, 1945;
released, 1953; exile
in Siberia, 1953–6;
officially rehabilitated,
1957; expelled from
the Soviet Union, 1974;
Soviet citizenship
restored, 1990; Nobel
Prize in Literature,
1970), 135, 146, 689*
Somerville College, Oxford,
23, 25–6, 27–8, 29–34,
451*, 591–2
Songs of Praise (television
programme), 959, 963
Sorensen, Eric (1942–;
educated Bedford
School and Keele
University; Director,
Merseyside Task
Force, DoE, 1981–4;
Director, Inner Cities
Directorate, DoE,
1984–7; head of Urban
Policy Unit, Cabinet
Office, 1987–8), 630,
632
South Africa, 79, 80, 141,
545–6; Denis Thatcher
recuperates in (1964),

South Africa – *cont'd*
79, 80, 81, 546*, 956;
Denis Thatcher's views
on, 80, 546; Enoch
Powell's views on, 88;
and Rhodesia, 158;
Reagan's view of, 234*,
555; MT opposes
sanctions on, 529, 545,
548, 549–50, 554–61,
559*, 578, 661, 786,
794, 800, 971; British
passport-holders in,
546†; 'Cape Coloureds'
in, 546‡, 546; P. W.
Botha's reforms, 546–7;
MT supports release
of Nelson Mandela,
546, 547†, 547, 553,
554, 786, 789, 798;
MT receives Botha at
Chequers (1984), 547†,
547; Commonwealth
seeks sanctions on,
548–51, 553, 554–9;
international sanctions
on, 548, 559*; states
of emergency in,
548, 553–4; trade of
'Frontline States' with,
549†; MT's desired
settlement, 549, 551,
552*, 552–3; Eminent
Persons Group (EPG)
to, 550–51, 552, 553–4,
556; MT's 'irregulars',
551–2; raids on ANC
offices (May 1986),
553; London 'review
conference' on (August
1986), 554–5, 559,
560, 561; Howe as
EEC emissary to, 554,
555, 556; Renwick
as UK Ambassador,
787, 788–9, 791, 792,
793, 794, 797–8,
798*, 800; Western
hypocrisy over exports
to, 787; MT's high
standing among whites,
788–9, 791, 792;
US Comprehensive
Anti-Apartheid Act,
789*; Kohl as MT's
ally over, 789–90;
MT receives De Klerk
at Chequers, 792–3,
798–9, 799*; Kuala
Lumpur CHOGM
(1989), 793–4; Cold
War analogy, 797;
and sanctions on Iraq,
863*; the Thatchers in
(2003), 956
South Georgia, 307*, 307;
Argentina's occupation
of, 284; repossession
of, 299, 300–301, 302
South Korea, 366–7
South West African
People's Organization
(SWAPO), 791–2
Southall riots (1981), 272
Southerst, Jean, 25
Southwark Council, 629†
Soviet Union: MT's views on/
relations with, 26*, 90,
134–5, 142–3, 191,
236–49, 333,
364–9, 414–32, 572–82,
680–84, 697–700, 968
(*see also under*
Gorbachev, Mikhail);
nuclear weapons, 26*;
MT's first visit (1969),
90; Keith Joseph on,
131; détente, 134–5,
142, 236–42, 968; MT's
major speeches on,
134–5, 142; dissidents/
prisoners of conscience,
135, 238, 547‡, 547,
573, 579, 589, 689‡;
MT's first visit as Prime
Minister, 191, 239;
Cambridge spy ring,
207–8, 706, 708, 714;
Foreign Office view
of, 237–8, 238*, 242,
365*, 366–8, 369, 417*;
human rights abuses,
238, 573, 683, 689‡;
MT's desire to defeat,
238; SALT II, 238, 240;
invades Afghanistan
(1979), 239–41, 240†,
419, 577, 683; Moscow
Olympics (1980), 240;
Katyn massacre, 244‡;
Reagan's pipeline
sanctions on, 245–6,
247, 248–9, 249*, 332;
western Siberia gas
pipeline, 245–6,
248–9, 249*, 332; death
of Brezhnev, 249; and
Falklands War, 296;
economic problems in
1980s, 346; Anti-Ballistic
Missile (ABM) Treaty,
365‡, 365, 422, 563†,
564, 566, 571; Chequers
seminar of experts
(1983), 365, 366*,
366–8, 369, 414; shoots
down KAL 007 airliner,
366–7; fears pre-emptive
strike from West, 369;
walks out of Geneva
negotiations (1983), 376,
414; support for NUM,
393; Orwell's *1984*, 414;
Jews in, 418, 579; MT
attends Chernenko's
funeral, 426§, 426–8;
and Gordievsky row,
431*, 431, 432; MT's
Moscow visit (1987),
565, 573–82, 576‡,
600; Chequers seminar
of experts (1986),
573–4, 574*; Brezhnev
Doctrine, 577†, 577–8,
581; MT's appearances
on Soviet television, 580,
805; withdrawal from
Afghanistan, 686, 687;
nationalities demand
political autonomy,
697, 803, 805; UK's
expulsion of spies
(1989), 699–700, 700*,
803*, 804*, 804; and
German reunification
issue, 804, 805, 807,
808–9, 812–13, 814,
815, 821†, 821, 822–3;
as one of 'Four Powers'
after war, 804, 815*,
821, 822; MT sees
as bulwark against
reunified Germany, 805,
809, 811, 821, 823,
824–5; and biological
weapons, 806–7, 830,
833*, 833†, 833;
Lithuania declares
independence, 829–30;
MT's EC integration
analogy, 873; Moscow
coup (August 1991),
926–7; final crumbling
of, 926
Spain, 309†, 668, 669, 951
Spanish Civil War, 111,
122*, 147

Sparrow, John (1933–2020; educated Stationers' Company's School and LSE; head of Central Policy Review Staff, 1982–3; Chairman, Horserace Betting Levy Board, 1991–8; knighted, 1984), 336
Special Air Service (SAS), 221–2, 719–20, 721–2, 724, 725, 726, 727, 854, 865
Spectator (magazine), 1, 148, 400, 477, 487, 492, 616*, 654, 767, 835–6, 836*, 852, 886†
Spence, Ivan, 66
Spencer, Stuart, 241
Spice, Betty, 25, 26
Spicer, Michael (*later* Lord Spicer), 342
Spiegel, Der, 827
Spigel, L., 348
Spitting Image (television programme), 498–9, 587*, 587, 731
Spring Rice, Cecil, 'I Vow to Thee, my Country', 776, 971
Sprinkel, Beryl, 232*, 232
Srebrenica massacres, 932
St Catharine's College, Cambridge, 827
St John Stevas, Norman (1929–2012; educated Ratcliffe College, Fitzwilliam College, Cambridge and Christ Church, Oxford; barrister, author; Conservative MP for Chelmsford, 1964–87; Parliamentary Under-Secretary, Department of Education and Science, and Minister for the Arts, 1973–4; Leader of the House of Commons and Minister for the Arts, 1979–81; created Lord St John of Fawsley, 1987), 183, 197, 229
St Lawrence Jewry, London, 149
St Paul's Cathedral, London, 961, 965

St Paul's School, London, 97*
St Vincent, M. J., 612
Stahl, Lesley, 678
Stalker, John, 721†, 721
Stanford University (USA), 237
Stanley, John (1942–; educated Repton and Lincoln College, Oxford; Conservative MP for Tonbridge and Malling, 1974–2015; Minister for Housing and Construction, 1979–83; Minister of State for the Armed Forces, 1983–7; Northern Ireland Office, 1987–8; knighted, 1988), 142
Starmer, Sir Keir, 659–60; Blairite influences on, 4, 5
Stechford by-election, 163*
Steel, David (1938–; educated Prince of Wales School, Nairobi, Kenya, George Watson's College, Edinburgh and Edinburgh University; Liberal MP for Roxburgh, Selkirk and Peebles, 1965–83; for Tweeddale, Ettrick and Lauderdale, 1983–97 (Liberal, 1983–8; Liberal Democrat, 1988–97); Liberal Chief Whip, 1970–75; Leader of Liberal Party, 1976–88; co-founder Social and Liberal Democrats, 1988; knighted, 1990 (KT, 2004); created Lord Steel of Aikwood, 1997), 357
steel industry, 217–19
Stephens, Caroline (*later* Lady Ryder of Wensum), 130, 158, 159, 184, 185*, 185, 186, 194†, 227, 549*, 595*, 595
Stephenson, Phoebe, 9
Sterling, Jeffrey (1934–; educated Reigate

Grammar School, Preston Manor County School and Guildhall School of Music; businessman; special adviser to Secretary of State for Industry, later for Trade and Industry, 1982–90; Executive Chairman, P&O, 1983–2005; knighted, 1985; created Lord Sterling of Plaistow, 1991), 398
Stern, Fritz (1926–2016; Professor, Columbia University, 1953–97; author of *Gold and Iron* (1977) and *The Five Germanies I Have Known* (2006)), 826
Stock Exchange: Big Bang (October 1986), 409–10, 412, 655, 768; restrictive practices, 410*, 410†, 410–11; reform of, 410–12; 'Black Monday' (19 October 1987), 655; IRA bombing of, 854
Stockton-on-Tees, 943
Stokes, John (1917–2003; educated Haileybury and the Queen's College, Oxford; Conservative MP for Oldbury and Halesowen, 1970–74; for Halesowen and Stourbridge, 1974–92; knighted, 1988), 839
Stone, Michael, 722
Stone, Norman (1941–2019; educated Glasgow Academy and Gonville and Caius College, Cambridge; Professor of Modern History and Fellow, Worcester College, Oxford, 1984–97; Professor of International Relations, Bilkent University, Ankara, 1997–2007; author of *The Eastern Front, 1914–17* (1975); *Hitler* (1980); *The Atlantic and Its Enemies* (2010)), 826

Stowe, Kenneth (1927–2015; educated County High School, Dagenham and Exeter College, Oxford; principal private secretary to the Prime Minister, 1975–9; Permanent Under-Secretary, Northern Ireland Office, 1979–81; Permanent Secretary, DHSS, 1981–7; knighted, 1980), 173, 180, 202, 255
Straight, Michael, 208*
Strategic Arms Limitation Treaty, 238
Strategic Defense Initiative (SDI, Star Wars): MT's views on, 365–6, 420, 421, 423, 425, 429–30, 571, 572, 579; Reagan announces, 365; Soviet view of, 365, 422–3, 427–8, 563†, 563, 564, 566, 567, 568; research, development and testing, 366, 422–4, 425, 430*, 430, 564; discussed at Camp David (December 1984), 407, 416, 422–4; MT discusses with Gorbachev at Chequers, 420; 'Four Points' agreement (Camp David, 1984), 423–4, 427–8, 432; Howe's speech attacking, 428–9; MT given 'highly restricted' briefing on, 429–30; British research contracts, 430*, 430; Reagan's commitment to, 562, 564*, 564†, 564, 566–7, 568–9, 571, 572; MT discusses with Gorbachev in Moscow, 579
Strathclyde Council, 639–40
Strauss, Johnan, *A Night in Venice*, 33
Strauss, Norman (1936– ; educated Kilburn Grammar School; worked for Unilever, 1961–81; part-time member, Prime Minister's Policy Unit, 1979–82; co-founder, Oxford Strategic Leadership Programme, 1982) 151, 153, 154, 155
Streep, Meryl, 960–61
Strevens, Barry, 306, 480, 539, 732†
Stuart, Keith (1940; educated King George V School, Southport and Gonville and Caius College, Cambridge; Chairman, Associated British Ports Holdings plc, 1983–2002; knighted, 1986), 766
Stuart, Prince Charles Edward (Bonnie Prince Charlie), 266*
Stuart-Black, Lois, 920
Suez crisis (1956), 61, 286, 291
Sukhodrev, Viktor, 428
Sultan, Prince (of Saudi Arabia), 437–8, 439
Sun, 133, 137, 230–31, 359, 436, 522†, 525*, 722, 760; and school milk controversy, 98; circulation surpasses *Daily Mirror*, 166*; importance of for MT, 166*, 166, 189*, 189; 'Crisis? What Crisis?' headline, 169; and 1981 budget, 270; 'Gotcha' headline, 305; on MT's Grenada humiliation, 373
Sunday Dispatch, 70–71
Sunday Express, 116†, 127, 711, 716
Sunday Graphic, 56
Sunday People, 133
Sunday Telegraph, 556, 558–9, 583–4, 621, 886†, 886, 954
Sunday Times, 86*, 375, 393, 504, 525*, 557, 714*, 714, 881*, 881–2; and leadership contest (November 1990), 886†, 886, 888; on Mark Thatcher, 920
Sunday Trading (Shops Bill, 1986), 531–2, 532*, 844

Sununu, John, 781, 785, 891
Swan Court, Chelsea, 57†, 57–9
Swan Hunter, Tyneside, 506
Swift, Jonathan, *Gulliver's Travels*, 591†
Swiss National Bank, 226, 552, 790
Syria, 434, 437*

Taiwan, 363
Tambo, Oliver (1917–93; Deputy President, ANC, 1958–67; led ANC's mission in exile living in London, Tanzania and Zimbabwe, 1960–90; acting President, ANC, 1967–77; President, 1977–91; returned to South Africa, 1990; National Chairman, ANC, 1990–93), 788†, 788, 790, 799
taxation: of working women, 77; Selective Employment Tax (SET), 82–3; income tax rates, 83†, 83, 85–6, 87, 90, 199; discrimination against married women, 83; estate duty, 83; in USA, 90; Capital Transfer Tax introduced, 117; on North Sea oil, 117, 659*, 659; and 1974–9 Labour government, 122–3; capital transfer tax, 122, 124; increases in VAT, 173, 176*, 176, 199; in Tory manifesto (1979), 173; and 1979 election campaign, 176; Howe's first budget, 199; and 1981 budget, 268–9, 269†; and 1982 budget, 280; level of after 1983 election, 355; and Lawson, 360, 398–400, 465–6, 468†, 470, 472, 491–2, 542‡, 542–3, 602, 658–60; in MT's second term, 360, 398–400; and 1984 budget, 398–400;

on unearned income, 399*; MT vetoes VAT on newspapers, 399, 491, 658†; MT's dislike of property taxes, 463; 'progressive'/'regressive' terms, 471*; mortgage interest tax relief, 491, 670*, 838†; inheritance tax, 658*, 658, 947*, 967*; 1988 budget, 658–60, 659†, 668; in MT's third term, 658–60, 659†; as 'Thatcherized', 659–60
Taylor, D. J., 588
Taylor, Edward 'Teddy' (1937–2017; educated Glasgow High School and Glasgow University; Conservative MP for Glasgow Cathcart, 1964–79; for Southend East, 1980–97; for Rochford and Southend East, 1997–2005; knighted, 1991. Despite his Shadow role, Taylor never held office in any of Mrs Thatcher's administrations), 161†, 161
Taylor, Eric, 450†
Teasdale, Anthony, 750, 877, 883
Tebbit, Margaret, 450, 456, 499*, 499, 537, 539, 879†, 951
Tebbit, Norman (1931–2025; educated Edmonton County Grammar School; Conservative MP for Epping, 1970–74; for Chingford, 1974–92; Parliamentary Under-Secretary, Department of Trade, 1979–81; Minister of State, Department of Industry, 1981; Secretary of State for Employment, 1981–3; for Trade and Industry, 1983–5; Chancellor of the Duchy of Lancaster, 1985–7; Chairman, Conservative Party, 1985–7; created Lord Tebbit, 1992): in opposition, 142*; Employment Secretary, 276, 278, 350, 352*, 353; 'on your bike' speech, 277–8; and public spending control, 278; and trade union reform, 278, 341–2; and 1983 election date, 342; friendship/rivalry with Parkinson, 350*, 350; increasingly fractious relations with MT, 350; relations with MT, 353, 358, 359, 498–9, 508*, 533, 536, 538–9, 561, 599, 603†, 603, 604, 606, 611–12; ambition of, 359, 499, 536, 603; and privatization policy, 359, 402; rivalry with Heseltine, 359; Trade and Industry Secretary, 359; and miners' strike, 386; and 1984 budget, 398; and Brighton bombing, 449–50, 456, 499*, 499, 604†, 604; and Anglo-Irish Agreement (1985), 456; supports poll tax, 472; and ERM question, 494; and 1985 reshuffle, 496, 498, 499–500, 506; Spitting Image's depiction of, 498–9; and Heseltine, 499, 506–7, 508*, 508, 514, 845; Party Chairman, 500, 527, 538–9, 541, 543–4; and Westland affair, 506–7, 508*, 508, 514; foreign multinationals and BL, 527, 528; and US bombing of Libya, 533, 534; preparations for 1987 election, 535, 536–7, 538, 602–4; Bell and Young as rivals of, 536–7, 603*, 603–4; and Bell's drug taking, 536; in Strategy Group ('A-Team'), 538; and BBC coverage of raid on Libya, 541; and South Africa, 556; left-wing hatred of, 599; sues Guardian for libel, 599; McAlpine's animosity to, 603†, 603; 1987 election campaign, 606, 609, 610, 611–12; on Labour's defence policy, 609; decision to leave government, 617; and MT's tenth anniversary, 722; and Hong Kong immigration issue, 844–5, 849; refuses return to Cabinet, 879†, 879; and leadership contest (November 1990), 885, 888, 889*, 896–7, 898, 901; alleged meeting with Clarke (20 November 1990), 896*; at MT's farewell lunch, 908†
Teesside Development Corporation, 630
Teicher, Howard, 530, 532–3, 534
television: MT's sparing appearances, 3, 123, 188‡; Reece coaches MT, 134; Weekend World, 153, party political broadcast (January 1979), 170†, 170; and 1979 election campaign, 175, 177; The Granada 500 programme, 176; MT's clothing and make-up, 189, 597, 759, 760; Channel 4, 386‡, 759–60, 764; Spitting Image, 498–9, 587*, 587, 731; ITV (Independent Television), 540–41, 761, 762*, 763, 764*, 764; MT's appearances in Soviet Union, 580, 805; MT's appears on Face the Nation (CBS), 678; Death on the Rock (Thames Television documentary), 723†, 723‡, 723; The

INDEX

television – cont'd
Thatcher Factor, 731;
coverage of Parliament,
758*, 758–61, 970;
MT's Broadcasting
Bill, 762*, 762, 765;
new technologies,
762–3, 764–5; satellite
broadcasting, 764–5;
series based on *The
Downing Street Years*,
936–7
Teltschik, Horst (1940–;
Ministerial Director,
Federal Chancellery,
and head, Directorate-
General for Foreign
and Intra-German
Relations, Development
Policy, External
Security, 1982–90;
Deputy Chief of Staff,
Federal Chancellery,
1983–90), 485–6, 809,
812, 814, 820–21,
821*, 825, 827
Tennyson, Alfreds, Lord,
584, 939, 959
terrorism, 174; Islamist, 5;
as personal threat to
MT, 99*, 106, 141†,
263, 855, 950†, 950;
Irish Republican, 141†,
174*, 174, 207, 252,
447–52, 460*, 499,
671†, 715*, 718‡,
718–27, 853–5, 950†,
950; MT's views on
Rhodesia, 193*, 193,
215; MT's attention
to the victims of, 207,
252*, 252, 854–5;
Iranian embassy siege,
Princes Gate, 221–2,
865; Chelsea Barracks
bombing (1981),
252*; and MT's
views on Middle East,
433, 436; security
of Thatcher family,
442–3; early release
concept in Northern
Ireland, 454, 456;
European Convention
on the Suppression
of Terrorism
(ECST, 1977), 455,
457, 460*, 460,
720–21; Enniskillen

Remembrance Day
bombing, 460*,
720; MT's Carlton
Lecture (November
1984), 466*; Libyan-
sponsored, 528–30,
533*, 534, 535, 720,
724–5; extradition
from US to UK,
534; Loyalist in
Northern Ireland,
718‡, 718, 719*, 722;
MT's comments on
ANC, 787–8, 788†;
releases due to Belfast
Agreement, 951; Al-
Qaeda attacks in USA
(11 September 2001),
954*
Terry, Sir Peter, 854
Terry, Quinlan, 667*, 667
Thailand, 921
Thames Water, 769*
Thatcher, Amanda (MT's
granddaughter), 947–8,
962, 966, 967*
Thatcher, Carol (MT's
daughter): birth and
childhood, 56–8, 57*,
59, 68*, 72; education
of, 58, 94, 97*; on
MT as parent, 58,
94, 141; MT's guilt
over, 58, 443, 594; on
father's breakdown,
79–80; on final illness
of Alfred Roberts, 92;
on MT's predicament
in 1973, 106; training
as a solicitor, 141; and
father's first marriage,
166‡; and 1979
election campaign,
176; Downing Street
flat, 184*; on brother's
disappearance during
motor rally, 280;
and 1983 election
campaign, 345;
mother warns about
'freebies', 440; security
of, 442–3; on *Anyone
for Denis?*, 588;
personal life, 594*,
594, 948*; sacked
by Max Hastings,
594†, 948*; dress
sense, 594; on MT's
female staff, 595†;

and 11 Hambledon
Place, 596–7; and
1987 election, 608; at
Reagan's dinner for
MT in Washington,
689†; and leadership
contest (November
1990), 884, 888*; and
MT's last days at 10
Downing Street, 910;
and MT after her
departure from office,
915, 918–19, 948,
960, 962; and MT's
memoirs, 923; wins
*I'm a Celebrity, Get
Me Out of Here!*, 957;
*A Swim-on Part in the
Goldfish Bowl*, 960;
portrayed in *The Iron
Lady*, 961; announces
death of mother, 964;
at MT's funeral, 965;
and MT's will, 967*
Thatcher, Sir Denis (MT's
husband): and MT's
financial security, 26,
52, 53; first meets MT,
41–2; background of,
41, 71*; character of,
45, 948–9, 956; MT's
first dates with, 45,
46; collapse of first
marriage, 52–3, 54,
166‡, 166; engagement
to MT, 52, 53–4;
acceptance of MT's
political ambitions, 53,
956; liking for alcohol,
53, 64, 79, 171*, 184,
188*, 551†, 588*,
732‡, 937, 942*, 949;
as passport to Home
Counties respectability,
53, 58–9; relations with
MT's parents, 53; war
service of, 54, 292, 314;
marries MT (December
1951), 55–6; and 1951
election, 55; birth of
children, 56–7, 57*;
early married life,
56–9; as not an
involved father, 57,
58*; frequent business
trips, 58*, 63, 64, 70,
73; parenting, 58*; and
move to Farnborough
(1957), 59; and rugby

INDEX

union, 59, 185*, 185, 596; job at Burmah Oil, 79†, 141; nervous breakdown, 79–80; role in relation to his wife's career, 79–80; and 1964 election campaign, 79; recuperates in South Africa (1964), 79, 80, 81, 546*, 956; as golfer, 80, 596, 597*, 793†; and 1966 election, 81; on MT's leadership bid, 118, 956; on first leadership ballot (1975), 126, 956; admires Reagan, 136; on son Mark, 141*, 442; retires, 141; on MT's Christian values, 149*; on Elspeth Howe, 150; and Rhodesia, 160; and MT's appointment at Prime Minister, 179; on Hoskyns and Ridley, 181; Downing Street flat, 184; 'old-fashioned' domestic views, 184; at Chequers, 185–6; at 1980 party conference, 227; in Washington with MT (1981), 233; on Northern Ireland, 250; and Falklands War, 292, 293, 314, 317, 320; as a Cavalier, 327†; in China with MT, 330*; and 1983 election date, 343; finances as separate from MT's, 354‡, 915†; and privatization policy, 401; with MT in Washington (1985), 426; refuses permanent security protection, 443; and Brighton bombing, 448, 449, 450; forbids pet ownership, 539†; views on BBC, 539, 761†, 761; as heavy smoker, 551†, 921, 937, 939, 949; and MT's Moscow visit (1987), 575; portrayed in *Anyone for Denis?*, 588*, 588; and Oxford honorary degree issue, 592; nature of marriage to MT, 594; on 11 Hambledon Place, 596, 597; gifts of jewellery to MT, 597; and 1987 election, 608; and issue of MT's retirement, 625; 'can't buck the markets' phrase, 657*; at Reagan's dinner for MT in Washington, 690–91; on MT's tenth anniversary (1989), 729; broaches possibility of MT stepping down, 732; and Meyer's leadership challenge, 755; in Namibia with MT, 792; views on Germans, 808*, 808; and MT's unpopularity in 1990, 853; and Howe's resignation, 879; and Tebbit's views on immigration, 879; and leadership contest (November 1990), 888*, 888, 892; advises MT (21 November 1990), 896, 901, 903; last visit to Chequers, 908; last days at 10 Downing Street, 909, 910; awarded baronetcy, 910†, 910, 918; leaves Downing Street for last time, 910–11; life after MT's departure from office, 914–15, 915†, 918, 919, 920–21, 948–9, 954–5; stays at Easton Neston, 914–15; purse-strings of as tight, 915†; and MT's memoirs, 923; and Robin Butler, 924*; views on EC, 924; Ruby Wedding celebrated at Claridge's, 929; views on Major, 930, 942*; ill health in old age, 936–7, 956; attitude to food, 949*; lunch companions, 949; church attendance at Royal Hospital, Chelsea, 950; as high Anglican, 950; has aortic valve replacement (2003), 956; death of (26 June 2003), 2, 956; funeral of, 19–20;
Thatcher, Diane (née Burgdorf), 729–30, 732, 947, 948, 956
Thatcher, Margaret (MT) (Baroness), **background, childhood and education**: birth (13 October 1925), 1, 9; childhood, 9–13, 15–17, 18, 19, 20, 969; lower-middle-class origins, 9–13, 42, 67, 81, 969–70; Methodist activity, 10–11, 775–6, 966; ambition to join Indian Civil Service, 10, 39, 327; Oxford entrance exam, 11–12, 23; Cust blood theory, 13*; early political activity, 14; at Kesteven and Grantham Girls' School (KGGS), 16–17, 19, 20–3; relations with father, 17, 72–3; first trip to London, 18; early boyfriends, 19, 31–4, 37–8, 38*, 52, 937†, 937; elocution lessons, 19, 25, 342; poetry recitations, 19, 959; schoolgirl 'autograph book', 19, 912; Sixth Form, 20–23; School Certificate exams, 20; application for Oxford, 22, 23; school reports, 22; at Somerville College, Oxford, 23–6, 27–8, 29–34, 451*, 591–2; Higher Certificate, 23; Latin School Certificate, 23; and OUCA, 24, 27, 29–31, 32–3, 34; politics at Oxford, 24, 27–8; growing interest in the law, 26–7, 35; MT on her

INDEX

Thatcher, Margaret – cont'd
youthful interests, 26–7; chemistry studies at Oxford, 26, 27; overwork at Oxford, 26; second-class degree, 26; campaigns in 1945 election, 28–9; first party conference (Blackpool, 1946), 29–30; male friends at Oxford, 30–34; teaches in Grantham during vacation, 94*, 94†, 94; Irish heritage, 266*, 266
Thatcher, Margaret (MT) (Baroness), **early adulthood and career**: as candidate for Dartford, 14, 39–40, 41, 42–4, 48–50, 53–5, 937; studies for the Bar, 27, 50; as research chemist at BX Plastics, 35–6; tight finances during first job, 35–6; life in Colchester, 35–7, 38, 42; Young Conservatives in Colchester, 36–7; seriousness about a political career (late-1940s), 38–9; courted by William Cullen (future brother-in-law), 40–41, 42, 44–6; first meets Denis, 41–2; matchmakes between Cullen and Muriel, 42, 44, 45–7; life in Dartford, 44–50, 50*; research chemist at J. Lyons and Co., 44; first dates with Denis, 45, 46; relationship with Robert Henderson, 46, 47–8, 50*, 50, 51–2, 53, 937†, 937; and Muriel's wedding, 47; Dartford election result (1950), 49; rents flat in Pimlico, 50–52; only meeting with Churchill (1950), 50; passes driving test, 51*; engagement to Denis, 52, 53–4; qualifies for the Bar, 53, 56, 57, 59; growing stature in Conservative Party, 54; honeymoon, 55–6, 88*, 954; marries Denis (December 1951), 55–6; Dartford election result (1951), 55; as practising barrister, 59–61, 60*, 60†; benefits from rarity of women, 60–61, 63; shifts to tax law, 60; attempted return to political fray (1952), 61, 62; returns to active politics (1956), 62–3; seeks a constituency (1956–8), 62–4; impact of father's removal as alderman, 62; adoption in Finchley, 63–4; enters Parliament (October 1959), 65–6, 67

Thatcher, Margaret (MT) (Baroness), **family life**: parenting, 52†, 57–8, 68*, 71, 72; birth of children, 56–7, 57*; early married life in Chelsea, 56–9; as concerned and conscientious mother, 57–8; children's schooling, 58, 71*, 71; guilt over upbringing of her children, 58, 592, 594; and MT's political ambitions, 58, 62–3; at Dormers, Farnborough, 59, 72–3, 80; Denis's nervous breakdown (1964), 79–80, 956; flat at 34 Westminster Gardens, Marsham Street, 80; The Mount (second home in Kent), 80, 106*, 141; personal crisis (1964–5), 80; properties in Lamberhurst, Kent, 80, 93, 96, 106*, 107, 112, 141; holidays, 88*, 226; flat in Scotney Castle, Lamberhurst, 106*, 141, 169; home in Flood Street, Chelsea, 106*, 121, 141, 596; Downing Street flat, 184*, 184; domestic/ housekeeping duties while PM, 184, 185; at Chequers, 185–6; son missing during motor rally, 280, 920; views on nature of MT's marriage, 594; home at 11 Hambledon Place, Dulwich (from 1986), 596–7, 911, 917; poll tax payments while Prime Minister, 749*, 840*; departure from Downing Street, 907‡; last days at 10 Downing Street, 907–10; accepts of loan flat at 93 Eaton Square, Belgravia, 917; residence at 73 Chester Square, Belgravia, 920–21, 921*, 948, 951, 956–7, 961*; as not always happy in later years, 920, 947, 948–9; Ruby Wedding celebrated at Claridge's, 929; delight in her grandchildren, 947–8; impact of death of Denis, 956–7, 958

Thatcher, Margaret (MT) (Baroness), **early parliamentary career**: backbencher, 67–73; maiden speech, 68–9, 70–71; introduces Private Member's Bill, 68–71; first appearance on *Any Questions?*, 68; appointed to first government post, 73–4; first platform speech at conference (1961), 73–4; Parliamentary Under-Secretary at Ministry of Pensions and National Insurance, 73–4; 1964 general election, 78–9; shadow pensions spokesman, 79, 81; six Shadow posts in Opposition, 79, 81–2; Shadow Minister for Fuel and Power, 81–2, 86; Shadow Transport Minister,

81–2; 1966 election, 81, 83, 84–5; Deputy Treasury Shadow, 81, 82–3; leadership contest (1965), 81; Shadow Education Secretary, 82, 90–92, 93; political position developed in late 1960s, 83–4, 86; public persona developed, 83–4; moral and social issues of 1960s, 84; Conservative Political Centre Lecture (October 1968), 86, 87–8; promoted to Shadow Cabinet, 86; connections with Enoch Powell, 87–8; 1970 general election, 93; Selsdon Park Hotel conference, 93

Thatcher, Margaret (MT) (Baroness), **Education Secretary**: appointed by Heath, 93–4; comprehensivization of secondary schools, 95–6; Circular 10/70, 95; withdraws Labour Circulars, 95; relations with Department, 96–7, 100, 109, 180; teacher unions, 96, 98; budgets and expenditure, 97–8; school milk controversy, 98†, 98–100, 640; saves Open University, 98; BBC *Panorama* documentary (July 1970), 99; 'relaunch' (1972), 100–101; White Paper (1972), 100–101, 101*; Heath supports, 100; school leaving age raised, 100; and Heath's economic policies, 103–5, 107; seat at Heath's Cabinet table, 104*; February 1974 election, 107–8, 109; opposes deal with Liberals (February 1974), 108; MT's farewell party, 109

Thatcher, Margaret (MT) (Baroness), **in opposition 1974–5**: as potential leadership candidate, 109, 112, 115–16, 117–21; Shadow Environment Secretary, 110, 112–17, 339; Vice-Chairman of CPS, 110; supports Joseph's rethink, 111–12; promotes middle-class interests, 112, 113, 124; October 1974 campaign, 113–14, 116; presents election broadcast (October 1974), 113; coded attacks on Heath, 116*, 116†, 116; decides on leadership bid, 117–19, 118*; Shadow Treasury spokesman, 117–21, 122–3, 125, 126; meeting with Heath (November 1974), 118–19; accused of hoarding, 119–20; challenges Heath for party leadership, 121–6, 123*; leadership campaign team, 121; first leadership ballot, 125*, 125†, 125–6; second leadership ballot, 126–7; becomes party leader, 127

Thatcher, Margaret (MT) (Baroness), **Leader of the Opposition**: 'what to do with Heath' question, 128–9; acceptance speeches, 128; entourage/staff, 129–30, 139, 142; first Shadow Cabinet appointed, 129; battle of ideas, 130–31, 150; attitude of party grandees, 130; grandee nicknames for, 130; policy-making, 131–2, 145–6, 150–55, 156; EEC referendum, 132–3, 135†; electoral strategy developed by, 133–4; first major speeches on international situation, 134–5, 142; Reece coaches on image/presentation, 134; trips abroad, 135†, 135, 136–9, 153, 156*, 156–9; visits West Germany, 135†; Kissinger on, 135–6; visits to United States, 135, 136–9, 153, 156–9; meetings with Reagan, 136, 189; 'Let Our Children Grow Tall' speech (1975), 137*, 137; businessmen sympathetic to cause, 139*, 139; conference speech (1975), 140–41; police protection, 141–2; earns sobriquet 'the Iron Lady', 142–3; against Wilson in Commons, 142; against Callaghan in Commons, 143, 144; resignation of Wilson, 143; Shadow Cabinet split over unions, 145–6, 151–5, 159, 167–8, 172; consults economic thinkers, 146–7; 'Intellectuals for Margaret', 147–8, 149; Iain Macleod Memorial Lecture (1977), 149; trade union power question, 151–5; Stepping Stones process, 154–5, 200; first visit to Communist China, 156*; presence on the public stage, 156–7; as skilled party manager, 159; devolution issue, 160–2; party divisions over Europe, 162–3; advertising strategy, 164–7; rhetorical conquest of Labour, 165; cultivation of popular newspapers, 166–7; public split about pay policy, 168–9; 'Winter of Discontent', 169–71; vote of confidence debate (December

Thatcher, Margaret – *cont'd*
1978), 169; party political broadcast (January 1979), 170†, 170; refuses televised debate (1979), 171†, 171‡, 171–2; 1979 election campaign, 171–8; redrafting of manifesto (1979), 172–3; denationalization, 173*, 173; final election broadcast (April 1979), 177*, 177; becomes Prime Minister, 178, 179; Cazenove pays for office, 411*

Thatcher, Margaret (MT) (Baroness), **Prime Minister**: refused honorary degree by Oxford University, 1, 590–91, 970; powerful example to successors, 4–5, 6; close relations with Reagan, 4, 387†, 387–8, 406, 416, 426, 519, 562, 572*, 676*, 684–91; 'There is no such thing as society' comment, 149, 623*, 623–4, 966; fight over EEC budget contribution, 173, 190–91, 208, 209–12, 353–4, 475–8, 477*, 663, 664; arrival in Downing Street, 179–80; approach to bureaucracy, 180†, 180–81; Prime Minister's Questions, 180–81, 760, 883*, 883, 905, 909; visits to departments, 181*, 181; Central Policy Review Staff, 181–2; appoints first Cabinet, 182–3; personal staff, 184–5, 186–7; political office, 184, 185; cosiness of Downing Street operation, 185; 'Garden Room girls', 185, 202, 614; tendency to criticize 'the government', 187; European reaction to election of (1979), 189–90; Reagan congratulates MT on election (1979), 189; first foreign leaders to visit, 190, 251; first journey abroad, 190; at G7 Tokyo summit (1979), 191–2, 239; Rhodesia, 192–5, 204, 213, 214–15; CHOGM in Lusaka (1979), 193, 194; first Queen's Speech, 196–7; right to buy, 197, 201–2, 543; initial objection to interest rate rises, 198–9, 205, 654–5; public spending White Paper (November 1979), 204, 205; 'Wets' and 'Dries', 205–6, 222–3, 223*, 270–74, 276–8; Blunt scandal, 207–8, 706; visits Northern Ireland (August 1979), 207; Cabinet reshuffle (January 1981), 229; visits newly elected Reagan in USA (1981), 231–4, 241–2; foreign policy 'gurus', 236–7, 237*, 239, 240, 365, 366*, 366–8, 369, 414, 573–4, 574*, 577†, 808; US nuclear weapons on British soil, 239, 294; Reagan's visit to Britain (June 1982), 246–8, 319; Maze hunger strikes, 254–6, 259–63, 262*, 265, 727; and direct dealings with Dublin, 254, 256–9, 258‡, 263–4, 445‡, 445–8, 452–61; Dublin summit with Haughey, 256–7; 1981 riots, 259, 271, 272; Cabinet reshuffle (September 1981), 262, 276–7; Anglo-Irish summit, London (November 1981), 263–4, 264*; sense of crisis (summer 1981), 267–75, 276–8; at G7 summit, Ottawa (July 1981), 273*, 273; 1981 public expenditure review, 273–4; Hoskyns' 'blockbuster' memo, 274–6; Lord Mayor's Banquet speech (1981), 278–9; Falklands War Cabinet, 291, 293, 297, 298–301; private account of Falklands conflict, 293*, 293, 947*; Conservative Women's Conference speech (May 1982), 316–17; at G7 Versailles summit (1982), 318, 319; consequences of Falklands War, 321–3, 324, 325–6, 340; addresses UN General Assembly (June 1982), 325; visit to China (1982), 329–30, 330*, 332; operation for varicose veins, 329, 940*; and choice of 1983 election date, 333*, 334, 337, 340–41, 341*, 342–3, 343*; Reagan's electoral help for, 333–4, 600–602, 609*; visit to Berlin (1982), 333; foreign affairs and security policy unit, 335–6, 353; Policy Unit's role enhanced, 335, 353; visits Falkland Islands (1983), 341†, 341; 1983 election campaign, 344–7; at G7 Williamsburg summit (1983), 345†, 345–6, 347, 490; and Parkinson's affair with Keays, 347–8, 357, 358–9, 498, 500, 617–18; scale of 1983 victory, 348, 349*, 349; Cabinet reshuffle (June 1983), 349–53; and Cabinet government theory, 353; salary of, 354‡; signs Solemn Declaration on European Union

(1983), 354, 480–81;
public-spending
Cabinet (21 July 1983),
356; eye operation,
357*, 357, 940*; signs
Joint Declaration
(December 1984),
363–4, 407, 416, 421,
843–4, 844*, 921†,
927, 928; speech to
Winston Churchill
Foundation, 368;
Reagan excludes over
Grenada, 369–76,
372*, 374*, 375*;
rejects Falklands–
Grenada comparisons,
374–5; Mansion House
speech (1983), 376;
GCHQ dispute, 377–9,
396; bombing of the
Grand Hotel, Brighton
(1984), 391–2, 448–51,
450§, 450‡, 452, 466,
499, 589*, 604†, 604,
855, 951; and lawsuits
against BA, 405–7; at
Camp David with
Reagan (1984), 407,
416, 421–4, 453–4;
first meeting with
Gorbachev, 407, 416,
417–21, 422–3; 'Four
Points' agreement
(Camp David, 1984),
423–4, 427–8, 429†,
429, 432; attends
Chernenko's funeral,
426§, 426–8; and
Geneva summit
(November 1985),
431–2, 562; Middle
East policy, 432–9,
685*; promotion of
British trade, 437–42,
441*, 794–7; supports
Reagan's bombing of
Libya, 442, 529–31,
530*, 532–4, 533*,
535, 541; Anglo-Irish
summit (November
1983), 446†, 446–7;
Anglo-Irish summit
(November 1984),
451†, 451–3, 452*;
Anglo-Irish Agreement
(1985), 456, 457–60,
718–19; impact of
Westland affair, 473,
515, 524*, 524–5, 526,
527–9, 543, 564;
secures EU budgetary
rebate, 475–8, 476*,
477*, 663, 664;
Anglo-French summit
(Paris, 1984), 478–9;
Luxembourg IGC
(December 1985),
486–8; refusal to join
ERM, 494–5, 509,
651, 652, 662, 733–5,
847–9, 933–4; 1985 as
bad year for, 495–7;
Cabinet reshuffle
(September 1985), 496,
497†, 497–501, 506;
leak of Solicitor-
General's letter on
Westland, 513, 514,
515–16, 517–19,
520–21, 522–4, 523*,
523†, 768; Westland
Commons debate
speech, 520; Sunday
trading debate, 531–2,
532*, 844, 971; low
popularity in 1985–6
period, 535–6, 536†,
537; preparations for
1987 election, 535–7,
600–605; Cabinet
reshuffle (May 1986),
537–8; Strategy Group
('A-Team'), 538;
broadcasting policy,
539–42, 761–4, 765; at
Nassau CHOGM
(1985), 549–51, 551†;
response to
Gorbachev's nuclear-
free world proposal,
562–4; and Reykjavik
summit (1986), 562,
565*, 565–9, 571, 572,
680–81; response to
Reagan's ballistic
missile proposals,
564–5, 566–9, 570,
571–3; Moscow visit
(1987), 565, 573–82,
576‡, 600; visit to USA
(1986), 568; visits
Reagan at Camp David
(1986), 568, 570–71,
573, 678; and
'Iran-Contra' affair,
570, 572, 676*, 676,
677, 678; 'Camp David
agreement' with
Reagan (1986), 571–3,
576, 581–2, 678,
680–81, 682–3;
meeting about the
Alliance threat (April
1987), 604*; 1987
election campaign,
605–12, 608†; 'going
on and on' comment
(1987), 606; victory in
1987 election, 612–13,
614–15; thoughts of
political mortality after
1987 victory, 613,
615–16, 616*, 625;
first Cabinet of third
term, 617; mission for
her third term, 620;
social reform in third
term, 620, 621, 622,
629–40, 644–50;
'bourgeois
triumphalism'
accusations, 621, 622;
policies on inner cities
in third term, 629–33,
943; northern tour
(September 1987), 630;
AIDS crisis, 640–44,
642†, 643*; anxieties
over Lawson, 646, 652,
654–5, 656–8, 660–62,
669–71, 738–43,
749–52; 'can't buck the
markets' phrase, 657*,
657; post-SEA
approach to EU, 662*,
662–6; special Brussels
Council (February
1988), 663–5, 721;
resentment against
Delors, 664–5, 671,
672, 673–4; and
Thyssen collection
project, 666–9;
renovates 10 Downing
Street (1988), 667*,
667†, 667; Bruges
Speech (September
1988), 671†, 671–5,
672*, 725, 743, 968;
visit to USA (1987),
677–8, 680; at G7
Venice summit (1987),
679–80; receives
Gorbachev's top
officials (1987), 682;
toughens stance with

Thatcher, Margaret – *cont'd*
Gorbachev (1988), 686–7; and post-1982 future of Falkland Islands, 686; and Reagan–Gorbachev Moscow summit (1988), 687–8; at special NATO summit (1988), 687; Reagan's praise at Guildhall (June 1988), 688; relations with Bush, 691–2, 699, 700–701, 704–5, 822–3; increasing difficulties with Kohl, 692, 809–10, 814, 820; and Rushdie affair, 695–7; Gorbachev's visit to UK (April 1989), 697–9; visits Kohl in Deidesheim (April 1989), 701–2; loss of standing with US under Bush, 702–4, 816–17; *Spycatcher* controversy, 706–15, 714*; Oldfield revelations, 715–18; visits Enniskillen (November 1987), 720; Gibraltar shootings (March 1988), 721–2, 723, 724, 727, 854; tenth anniversary (May 1989), 729–30, 731–3; holds meeting on egg crisis, 730–31; thoughts of stepping down, 732; at Madrid summit (June 1989), 741–3, 840; Madrid Conditions on ERM, 742, 840, 842–3, 848, 852, 867–8; July 1989 reshuffle, 744–6, 747–8; impact of Lawson's resignation, 753, 754; Walden interview (October 1989), 754†, 754; Meyer's leadership challenge, 755–7, 810, 813, 838, 880, 913; reform of legal profession, 766–8; speech to Royal Society on climate change, 779, 780; 'Saving the Ozone Layer Conference' (London 1989), 781†, 781; visit to Kenya and Nigeria (1988), 791†; Namibian crisis (1989), 791–2; second African tour, 791–2; Pergau Dam affair, 795–7; relations with free Mandela, 798, 799‡, 799–800; meets Mandela at Downing Street, 800–801; and 'Four Power' framework, 804, 814, 815*, 815, 821, 822; sees Soviet Union as bulwark against reunified Germany, 805, 809, 811, 821, 823, 824–5; at Camp David with Bush (1989), 810–12; at Strasbourg Council (1989), 814†, 814–15, 842; Chequers seminars on Germany (1990), 816, 818–19, 825–7, 836†, 836; *Der Spiegel* interview, 827; meets Yeltsin in Downing Street (April 1990), 830†, 830–31; meets Gorbachev in Moscow (June 1990), 832, 833; at NATO summit (July 1990), 834–5; at G7 in Houston (1990), 835†, 835‡, 835; growing personal unpopularity, 838–9, 846–7, 847*, 878*, 878, 913; speech to Conservative Central Council at Cheltenham, 845–6; Aspen conference (August 1990), 856–61, 859*; Iraqi invasion of Kuwait, 856–67, 862*, 862†, 870–2, 878, 891*, 891, 908; military plans for liberating Kuwait, 861, 866, 870–72, 917; Iraq 'War Cabinet' (1990), 862, 866*; entry to ERM, 868*, 868–9, 869†, 870, 968; Rome Council (1990), 872–6, 873*, 877; and Howe's resignation, 878–80; leadership contest (November 1990), 880–81, 884–92, 891†, 893–903; CSCE summit in Paris (November 1990), 880, 885, 887, 888–9, 891–2, 894–5, 896; speech at Lord Mayor's Banquet (November 1990), 882; Tory establishment conspiracy to remove, 886–7, 890–91, 893–4, 897–8, 900, 901–4, 908–9, 909*, 913–14, 916, 930; first ballot result (20 November 1990), 891–3; sees Cabinet ministers individually (21 November 1990), 897†, 897, 898–901; resignation (22 November 1990), 903†, 903–7, 905‡; resignation statement to Cabinet, 903–5; last days at 10 Downing Street, 907–10; No. 10 farewell lunch, 908–9; last visit to Chequers, 908; awarded Order of Merit (OM), 910‡, 910, 911, 918; leaves Downing Street for last time, 910–11; resignation honours list, 918*, 922†
Thatcher, Margaret (MT) (Baroness), **later life**: cooperation with present biographer, 1–2; archives to Cambridge, 1, 946†, 946–7, 947*, 967*; choice of biographer, 1, 947; conditions set for this biography, 2; decline in mental powers, 2, 945, 952, 953, 955, 958–9, 960–61, 962; increasing Euroscepticism, 6, 924–5, 928–9, 930, 942–3, 952–3; 'backseat driver' comment,

INDEX 1063

908, 916, 924, 946; bewilderment at sudden fall, 912–13, 914, 918; stays at Easton Neston, 914–15; continued close protection officers, 915*; access to classified information revoked, 915–16; salary, 915; receives 'public duty cost allowance', 916*; bitterness at culprits in her downfall, 916, 919–20, 924, 930; initial attitude towards her successor, 916; financial help from friends/admirers, 917–18, 918*; in Commons after her fall, 917, 928–9; kept briefed on Desert Storm, 917; office at Great College Street, 917, 926; behaviour of son Mark, 919, 920; sense of bereavement at loss of office, 919, 920; and Barclay brothers, 920–21, 921*; as not always happy, 920, 947, 948–9; offers of public service, 920; speaking/lecture tours, 921†, 921, 939; advisory role with Philip Morris, 921; friendship with Reagan in post-office years, 921, 926†, 940–41; engagement in current controversies, 924–5, 926–9, 930, 931–4; presidency of the Bruges Group, 924; return to power belief, 924; office at Chesham Place, Belgravia, 925–6; leaves the Commons (1992), 925, 929; takes on Major's government over Europe, 925, 928–9, 930, 932–3, 934–5, 937–8, 942–3; interest in Russia, 926; private trip to China (1991), 927–8; at party conferences, 928; visits to Hong Kong, 928; 1992 election campaign, 929–30; enters Lords as life peer, 930†, 930–31; as Baroness Thatcher of Kesteven, 930–31; *Newsweek* article (1992), 930; interventions in Balkan conflict, 931–2, 945; receives Order of the Garter, 939–40; dental implant operations, 940†, 940; Keith Joseph Memorial Lecture (1996), 942; 1997 election campaign, 943; congratulates Blair on 1997 election win, 944; occasional returns to Downing Street, 945*; and leadership contest (1997), 945–6; meetings with Blair, 945; reliance on friends, 949†, 949–50; as top of PIRA death list, 950†, 950; church attendance at Royal Hospital, Chelsea, 950; friendship with Pinochet, 951, 952; speech at spring conference in Plymouth (2001), 953–4; reaction to 9/11 terrorist attacks, 954*; illness in Madeira (2001), 954–5; 2001 leadership election as last significant intervention, 954; suffers transient ischaemic attacks, 955*, 955, 962; hearing problems by late 1990s, 955–6; withdraws from public life (2002), 955; final years of, 956–62; develops polymyalgia rheumatica, 956, 962; attends Reagan's funeral, 957–8; receives full-time, live-in care, 957, 958–60; celebrates her eightieth birthday, 958; final foreign trips, 959; Streep's portrayal in *The Iron Lady*, 960–61, 961*; plans her funeral, 961‡, 961–2; final weeks of life at Ritz Hotel, 962–3; bladder cancer operation, 962; death of (8 April 2013), 1, 3, 963, 964; funeral of, 965–7, 971; will and probate, 967*

Thatcher, Margaret (MT) (Baroness), **character and characteristics**, 90; stamina and hard work, 1, 26, 68, 99, 356–7, 593, 950, 971; egotism, 2, 185, 947; lack of petty vanity, 2; as rarely introspective, 2, 922, 947, 959; confrontational style of, 4, 142, 150, 171, 396, 508, 593–4, 600, 725*, 964, 968; love of USA, 5, 89–90; disruptive power of, 6; as profoundly respectable, 6; role as woman in politics, 6, 592–3; influence of father, 9–11, 13, 17, 62, 78, 87, 179, 624; appreciation of Methodism, 10–11, 147, 148–9, 389†, 621, 775–6, 950, 966; sacramental aspect of religion, 11*, 51*; admiration for her father, 11†, 13; love of method, 11; relationship with her mother, 11, 12, 13; speaking voice/style, 11, 19, 25, 165–6, 759*, 759, 760; *Who's Who* entry, 11; keen interest in clothing/fashion, 12–13, 14, 18, 22*, 23, 24, 36, 38, 40, 44, 73, 594, 597†, 597–8, 959; love of domestic labour, 12–13; mother's influence, 12–13; preference for urban life, 13; showing of affection and concern, 13; love of

Thatcher, Margaret – *cont'd*
dancing, 14, 18, 31, 32–3, 35, 43, 233; susceptible to elegant clothes, 14, 18, 24, 73–4, 86, 375; taste/preference in men, 14, 30, 31*, 31, 36, 60–61, 150, 198*, 375, 438, 625, 780, 831, 841, 933; literal-mindedness, 16*, 16, 97; powers of concentration, 17, 592; sense of humour, 17, 25, 960; sleep patterns, 17, 188, 608*; strong interest in glamour, 17, 18, 48; fondness for simple moral precepts, 19; love of language, 19, 959; purposefulness, 19, 20–21, 25, 130–31, 592, 593–4, 967; intellect, 21–2, 40, 131, 148, 149–50, 154, 593; ambition, 21, 36, 49–50, 71, 116, 133; competitiveness, 21, 118; earnestness, 21, 110; physical appearance in youth/early adulthood, 21, 24, 25, 31, 32, 42, 43; impresses by elegance and manners, 22*, 22; judgements on other woman, 22, 36, 59†, 117*, 150*; anxiety about her weight, 24*, 24, 175*; impression created at Oxford, 24–5; social/personal insecurity, 24–5, 67, 68, 122, 156, 158, 594, 608, 969–70; honesty, 25; public service, 25; determination, 27, 154, 210, 263, 394, 426, 466, 495, 531, 592, 593, 714, 729; courage and resolution, 28, 122, 126, 131, 207, 322, 593; gifts as a public performer, 28, 82, 112–13, 122, 133, 176, 177, 189, 611, 783, 921, 936, 937, 953–4; impressed by intelligence/intellect, 30, 87, 110, 183, 237, 369, 498, 589–90, 593, 933; hairstyle, 35, 40, 134, 547*, 549*, 597, 959; snobbery, 35; lifelong preference for male company, 45, 46, 47–8, 596; prodigious energy, 56, 150, 175, 195–6, 233, 344, 347, 356, 537, 593, 874†, 919, 971; accuracy and meticulousness, 60, 74, 76, 81*, 299; admiration for ancient institutions, 60, 970–71; force of personality, 61, 235, 326, 438, 477, 508, 606, 677, 760–61, 962; physical appearance in adulthood, 63, 68, 74, 78, 585, 592; admiration for Jewish values, 64–5, 88, 110, 111, 351, 432–3, 434, 504*, 504; lack of complacency, 65; neatness and competence, 67*, 67; treatment of staff, 68, 185–6, 592–4, 595, 913; belief in impact of personal/handwritten letter, 70, 439*, 502*, 572*, 644, 753, 854–5; self-awareness, 71; fainting due to low blood pressure, 72, 158, 645†, 940*; health, 72, 80, 158, 357*, 357, 539*, 539, 560, 645, 732, 813*, 940*, 940, 954–6, 955*, 962; debating abilities, 74–5; as quick learner, 74; heartlessness notion, 75, 621; as non-judgmental on marital/sexual behaviour, 76*, 595; appetite for detail, 76, 82, 122, 967; combative qualities, 76, 82, 87, 113, 123, 142, 197, 208, 391–2, 452, 508, 674, 729, 876, 886; bossiness and hectoring, 78*, 89, 153–4, 159, 211, 325–6, 619, 691–2, 703, 812, 969; as consensus breaker, 78, 87, 113, 131, 172, 175, 225–6, 277, 461, 887; small shopkeeper homilies, 78; dislike of Opposition, 79; antique collecting, 80–81, 81*; porcelain collector, 81, 590, 908; public preaching role, 82, 142, 158, 743–4; lecturing/holding forth, 89, 134, 153–4, 159; elements of self-parody, 97; powers of mental and physical endurance/stamina, 99, 188, 421–2, 424; anger and acidity, 100, 159, 248, 303, 316, 608†, 743, 754, 867, 935–6, 951, 960, 968; excited by ideas, 110, 130–31, 146–50, 593; as not an intellectual, 110, 131, 149, 154, 935; male attraction to, 122, 149, 187*, 237, 577*, 577, 585, 589, 598*; sense of mission, 130–31; caution, 130, 145, 172, 178, 199, 300*, 322, 347, 396, 435, 766, 970; deferential to social systems/proprieties, 130; matters of dress and protocol, 130; as cut off/innocent, 133–4; serious and high-minded, 133–4; hats, 134, 156; jewellery, 134, 186, 597, 959, 967*; professionalism, 134; surprising broadmindedness, 140, 595; admired by some of intelligentsia, 147–8, 149–50, 589; 'use of her femininity', 149, 577, 593, 595; alcohol consumption, 159, 184, 188, 267, 279, 662*, 732, 753, 813*, 919; personal attitude to immigrants, 164*; as

'that bloody woman' (TBW), 164, 535–6, 536*, 606; double entendres, 166†, 626*, 626; as divisive figure, 173–4, 389, 558–9, 941–2, 968; height, 175, 760*; says what she believes, 177–8; ecological/climate concerns, 182*, 192*, 729†, 729, 769, 770, 778–82, 779†, 781‡, 783–6, 880, 920; no gift for organization/ administration, 182, 275, 616–17; as indifferent to what she ate, 184, 701*; earrings, 186*, 186; clothing while Prime Minister, 186†, 186, 575, 594, 597–8, 731, 759, 760, 776, 882, 905; aura of invincibility, 188, 724, 961, 970; appeal to the aspirant working class, 189, 198, 201–2, 588, 599–600; readiness to give in to respected people, 193; permitting a decision but distancing herself from it, 198–9; TINA nickname, 205*; Dunkirk analogies, 225; dislike of holidays, 226, 390; 'The lady's not for turning' catchphrase, 227*, 227; use of 'royal we', 275*; ability to insult and antagonize, 275, 326, 453, 561, 593, 612, 752, 794, 878, 883–4, 913–14, 935–6; ignorance of military matters, 292†, 292–3, 322; choice of pictures and decorations at Downing Street, 326–7, 590, 667; romantic sense of history, 326–7, 743–4; abusive/rude/ unpleasant side of, 326, 375, 593, 793, 837, 878; Cavalier or Roundhead question, 327†, 327; 'Victorian values', 327–8, 328*; hesitation over welfare state reform, 336; romantic, high Tory streak, 351, 622*; as always insecure in PM job, 356–7, 359, 608; lack of small talk, 370, 594; other people's patriotism, 379; leadership during miners' strike, 396–7; as wary of grand strategy, 401; single-mindedness, 407; suffers from Dupuytren's contracture, 539*, 539, 560, 940*; disliked by many writers/ intellectuals, 583–4, 585–8, 590–91; view of as 'philistine', 583–4, 591; as mythological figure, 583, 598, 693*, 694, 832–3, 970; cultural interests, 584†, 584; cultural depictions of, 584–8, 731; handbag, 585, 690, 698, 928, 970; gait, 588; as a 'gay icon', 588; as Gloriana figure, 588, 667; offended by *Anyone for Denis?*, 588; affection for Oxford and Somerville College, 591–2, 970–71; perceived ungenerosity of spirit, 593–4; and sexual fulfilment, 593; as willing to be teased, 593; relationships/ contacts with women, 594–6; ruthlessness, 595; left-wing hatred of, 599; domineering personality view of, 606; tetchiness/bad temper during 1987 campaign, 606, 608*, 608, 610–11; signs of ageing, 608*, 732; suffers tooth abscess, 610; view on homosexuality, 634, 716; dislike of Royal Commissions, 646*, 646; avoidance of word 'I', 730*, 730; physical and mental exhaustion in late 1989, 754, 755; dislike of the telephone, 822; formal writing style, 922; unsuited to detachment, 922; extreme dislike of public disclosure, 923; coat of arms and motto, 930–31; sense of righteousness, 937, 966, 968; hand-written condolence letters, 938–9; faithful attender of funerals and memorial services, 939*, 939†, 939; as singer, 949–50; hostile reaction to after death, 964–5; tributes after death, 964; commonplace book, 967, 969, 971; disdain for Western European nations, 969; liking of binary choices, 969; Christie's sale of clothes and effects (December 2015), 970*, 970; opposes televising of Parliament, 970

Thatcher, Margaret (MT) (Baroness), **political views/beliefs**: free-market philosophy, 5, 82, 110, 138, 329; free-trade doctrine, 5, 41, 874*, 874; unity of English-speaking peoples, 5; as legitimist, 6; supports leaving EU in post-office years, 6, 952–3; sympathy for aspirations of ordinary voters, 6; on Empire, 11, 28, 39, 327; early political allegiance/ views, 14, 27–8, 29; on appeasement in 1930s, 15, 738–9, 739*; value of hard work, 15, 78, 86–7, 138–9, 593; shaped by Second World War, 21, 28‡, 28, 333, 802, 825, 969; anti-Communism, 26*, 48–9, 54, 55, 90,

INDEX

Thatcher, Margaret – *cont'd*
134–5, 138–9, 142–3, 148, 156*, 333, 365, 368, 417–18, 577–8, 968; wartime economy/policy, 27–8; anti-German attitudes, 28‡, 28, 152, 333, 701–2, 755, 802–3, 804, 806, 807–11, 814–18, 823, 835‡, 969; fairness in British character, 28; individual enterprise, 29, 49; British greatness/civilization, 43–4, 48–9, 326–7, 971; English and not British focus, 43, 58; personal responsibility, 43; 'small shopkeepers', 48; on NHS, 50; doctrine of nuclear deterrence, 54, 243, 325, 365, 366, 423, 425–6, 562–5, 569, 834–5; rule of law, 60, 167, 171, 172, 374, 406, 696–7, 723–4, 921, 971; Suez crisis as turning point, 61, 286; 'solvent society' verity, 65; attitude to local government, 69–70, 463–71; attitude to trade union power, 69, 77, 85, 105–6, 151–5, 169, 170, 172–3, 177, 217–18; support for corporal punishment, 71–2, 935*; on taxation, 74, 77, 82–3, 85–6, 87, 127; health and welfare, 75–6; on power/efficacy of the state, 76, 78; financial stringency, 77; free speech, 77; opposes creeping power of the state, 82, 85, 86; 'Thatcherite' ideology develops, 82; hostility to permissive society, 84, 620; 'the enemy within', 88; supports grammar schools, 91–2, 95–6; 'workers not the shirkers' soundbite, 127; rejects pursuit of equality, 137; Christian roots of, 148–9, 158, 620–21, 634, 775–7; on immigration, 163–4; on Nazism, 164†; support for capital punishment, 177, 355; belief in inequality, 178, 199; monetarism as a matter of principle, 216; Chinese regime as evil, 331–2; distaste for monopoly, 338–9, 402–3, 410–11, 762*, 767–70, 771, 773–4, 967–8, 971; desire for wider share ownership, 338, 403–4, 413; patriotism, 345; fear of extreme-left subversion, 388, 389, 392, 465, 466*, 466; Arab–Israeli conflict, 432–7, 439; dislike of property taxes, 463; German reunification issue, 483–4, 802*, 802–3, 804, 805, 806, 807–11, 814–18, 819, 822–3; on inner cities, 502*, 502–3; dislike of economic sanctions, 529; international law, 529, 531; on apartheid, 545–6, 800–801; on women priests, 596; private healthcare, 610, 644, 649; Unionism, 619–20; on education, 638†, 638; on nation's cultural assets, 667; on subsidized art, 667; on farmers, 730; human rights, 743; 'No. No. No.' words on European integration, 875–6, 877, 883; Maastricht referendum idea, 886, 928–9, 934–5; on Blairism, 942; on Belfast Agreement terrorist releases, 951; on multiculturalism, 953‡, 953; revives the creation of hereditary peers, 970

Thatcher, Margaret (MT) (Baroness), **writings**: memoirs, 1, 765*, 835, 920, 922–3, 935–6, 937*, 937–8; 'Wake up, women' article (1952), 56; 'I SAY A WIFE CAN DO TWO JOBS' (*Evening News*), 71; on family and political work (*Liverpool Daily Post*), 72; *Statecraft* (2002), 786, 952–3, 953*, 955; *Wall Street Journal* article, 817, 820; *The Downing Street Years* (first volume of memoirs), 922‡, 922, 935–6, 937*, 937; *The Path to Power* (second volume of memoirs), 937–8

Thatcher, Michael (1989–; son of Mark Thatcher and Diane Burgdorf; educated Texas A&M University), 698†, 730, 781‡, 947–8, 961–2, 967*

Thatcher, Sir Mark (MT's son): circumcision, 52†; birth and childhood, 56–8, 57*, 59, 68*, 72; education of, 58, 71*, 97*, 434, 625; MT's indulgence towards, 141*, 141, 441–2; and father's first marriage, 166‡; at Downing Street, 180*; commercial activities, 184*, 440–42, 682†, missing during motor rally, 280, 920; and conflicts of interest, 440–42; mother warns about 'freebies', 440; and Al-Yamamah deal, 442; leaves Britain for Dallas, 442, 443; and Oxford honorary degree issue, 592; and 11 Hambledon Place, 596–7; gifts of jewellery to MT, 597; at Reagan's dinner for MT in Washington, 689†; and MT's tenth anniversary, 729–30, 732; and leadership contest (November

INDEX 1067

1990), 884, 888*; and
baronetcy, 910; and
MT's last days at 10
Downing Street, 910;
and MT after her
departure from office,
919, 920, 947, 959,
962; office's unease
about interventions
of, 919, 920, 947; and
house at 73 Chester
Square, 921*; and
MT's memoirs, 923;
character of, 947, 959;
end of marriage to
Diane, 948; house in
Constantia, near Cape
Town, 950; father
recuperates with in
South Africa (2003),
956; arrested for
alleged involvement
in 'Equatorial Guinea
coup', 960; portrayed
in *The Iron Lady*, 961;
announces death of
mother, 964; at MT's
funeral, 965; and MT's
will, 967*

Thatcherism concept:
enduring influence of,
4–7, 967–8; and 'New
Labour', 4, 941–2; and
Enoch Powell, 36–7;
as Romantic belief, 49;
as vision/disposition of
mind, 49, 229, 326–8,
359, 935; Joseph as
intellectual driving
force, 131–2, 337;
and Reece, 134; 61
and Walden, 147, 177–8,
199; Howe's role, 150,
400, 733; Peter Jenkins
on, 228, 234; *Changing
Gear* pamphlet on,
277; Tebbit's 'on your
bike' speech, 278; and
Policy Unit, 335, 353,
400, 503, 605, 614;
economic doctrines
of, 350, 359; and
'Cambridge mafia',
351†, 351; Walters on,
359; Lawson's role,
400, 658–60, 659†,
668, 671, 733; and
MT's EC agenda, 480,
672–4; and Centre

Forward group, 495;
No Turning Back
Group, 496*, 496,
893, 899; 'rolling
Thatcherism', 605, 614,
629–31; dominance
of after 1987 election,
613, 615; and
Scotland, 619–20, 640,
775–7; inner-city policy,
629–31; 1988 budget,
658–60, 659†, 668,
671; 20 June Group
of writers opposes,
695–6; applied to
legal profession,
766–8; 'Sermon on the
Mound', 775–7, 961‡,
971; *Newsweek* article
(1992), 930; in MT's
memoirs, 935
Thomas, Harvey, 450
Thomas, Hugh (1931–2017;
educated Sherborne
and Queens' College,
Cambridge; Professor
of History, University
of Reading, 1966–76;
Chairman, Centre
for Policy Studies,
1979–90; author of
The Spanish Civil War
(1961); created Lord
Thomas of Swynnerton,
1981), 147–8, 170*,
237*, 237, 246*; and
Falklands War, 284*;
and Soviet Union,
366*, 574*; and
Grenada crisis, 376
Thomas, Pamela, 61
Thompson, Brigadier Julian,
317, 322, 324
Thorn, Gaston, 481
Thorneycroft, Peter
(1909–94; educated
Eton and Royal
Military Academy,
Woolwich; MP for
Stafford, 1938–45; for
Monmouth, 1945–66;
Chancellor of the
Exchequer, 1957–58;
created Lord
Thorneycroft, 1967;
Chairman, Conservative
Party, 1975–81):
resigns from Macmillan
government, 65;

Party Chairman, 129,
154, 165; and 1979
election campaign, 171,
172; Party Treasurer,
270; and MT's tenth
anniversary, 732; at
MT's farewell lunch,
908†
Thorpe, Jeremy, 108*, 108
Thyssen-Bornemisza,
Carmen Cervera 'Tita'
(1943–; Spanish former
beauty queen who
became Miss Spain,
1961; art dealer and
fifth wife of Hans
Heinrich Thyssen-
Bornemisza, whom
she married in 1985
and from whom she
inherited a £700
million art collection),
668*, 668, 669
Thyssen-Bornemisza de
Kászon, Hans Heinrich
'Heini' (1921–2002; art
collector who inherited
a vast number of old
masters on the death
of his father in 1949),
666–9
Tickell, Crispin
(1930–2022; educated
Westminster and Christ
Church, Oxford;
chef de cabinet to
the President of the
European Commission,
1977–80; Permanent
Secretary of the
Overseas Development
Administration, 1984–7;
British Permanent
Representative, United
Nations, 1987–90;
Warden, Green College,
Oxford, 1990–97;
knighted, 1983), 780,
782, 783, 784
Tilney, Lady (Guinevere),
186†
Times, The, 137, 145,
344, 358, 447, 471,
562, 755–6, 765, 951;
and 1975 leadership
contest, 124, 125;
on Heath, 168; letter
of 364 economists
opposing MT (1981),

Times – cont'd
270–71; on Falklands invasion, 289; and Howe's SDI speech, 429; and Westland affair, 512; and Wapping dispute, 525*, 525; 'We are all Thatcherites now' leader, 615; and *Spycatcher* controversy, 710–11; on Rome Council (1990), 875; and leadership contest (November 1990), 887
Times Educational Supplement, The, 96
Tiplady, John, 63
Tisdell, Ken, 39
Tito, Marshal (Josip Broz), 433*
TNT (freight company), 525
Tocqueville, Alexis de, 147*
Tolstykh, Valentin, 682*
Tomlinson, Albert, 79
Top Girls (Caryl Churchill play, 1982), 586
Top of the Pops (BBC programme), 133
Top Salaries Review Body (TSRB), 496–7
Tornado aircraft, 437, 438, 439, 796, 861*, 862–3, 865
Toronto, Canada, 139
Tottenham riots (1985), 502
Tovey, Sir Brian, 377
Townsend, Sue, 587
Toxteth riots, 272, 630
trade unions: MT's attitude to, 69, 77, 85, 105–6, 151–5, 169, 170, 172–3, 177, 217–18; defeat of Wilson's reforms (1969), 102; and Industrial Relations Act, 102, 105, 146, 151; secondary picketing, 103, 152, 170, 172–3, 197, 218–19, 230, 382; 'Pentonville Five', 105; Keith Joseph on, 131; and *The Right Approach*, 145–6; Shadow Cabinet split over, 145–6, 151–5, 159, 167–8, 172; Heath's view of, 151; closed shop, 152–3, 159, 168, 172–3, 278; Scarman inquiry, 153; Stepping Stones process, 154–5, 200; 'Winter of Discontent', 169–71; legal immunities, 172–3, 217–18, 276, 278; and 1979 election campaign, 177; MT's first Queen's Speech, 197; SDP attitude to, 276, 341–2; political levy, 341–2; GCHQ dispute, 377–9, 396; Shah's union-busting newspapers, 382†; and miners' strike, 387, 394; Murdoch's coup against at Wapping, 516, 525–6, 600, 765; attitude to EEC changes, 672†, 672; MT's liking for in Poland, 693†, 693; at the BBC, 761†; in MT's third term, 765–6; Dock Labour Scheme (DLS), 766; New Labour view of 1970s, 941; *see also* industrial relations
Trades Union Congress (TUC), 105, 107, 394, 672†, 672
Trafalgar House, 440†, 440–41
Trans-Manche, 479
Transport and General Workers' Union, 387, 388
Travers, Tony, 748*
Trend, Sir Burke (*later* Baron Trend), 104*, 707, 708
Trevor-Roper, Hugh (1914–2003; educated Charterhouse and Christ Church, Oxford; Regius Professor of Modern History, Oxford, 1957–80; Master of Peterhouse, Cambridge, 1980–87; author of *The Last Days of Hitler* (1947); created Lord Dacre of Glanton, 1979. Trevor-Roper had become notorious in 1983 when he mistakenly authenticated the Hitler Diaries, for Rupert Murdoch, as being genuine. In fact they were fakes), 826–7
Trident missile system, 244*, 244, 564, 568, 569
Trudeau, Pierre (1919–2000; Prime Minister of Canada, 1968–79 and 1980–84; Leader of the Liberal Party of Canada, 1968–84), 346
Truman, Harry, 317, 676*
Trump, Donald, 4–5, 965‡
Tunis, 436
Turnbull, Andrew (1945–; educated Enfield Grammar School and Christ's College, Cambridge; treasury secretary to the Prime Minister, 1983–5; principal private secretary, 1988–92; Permanent Secretary, Department of the Environment, later Department for Environment, Transport and the Regions, 1994–8; Permanent Secretary, Treasury, 1998–2002; Cabinet Secretary, 2002–5; knighted, 1998; created Lord Turnbull, 2005), 396, 735*, 736, 737*, 737, 741, 743, 901*, 901–2, 917; and miners' strike, 283, 382, 386, 390, 395; and local government, 466, 845; at MT's individual sessions with ministers (21 November 1990), 899*, 899, 900; and MT's resignation as Prime Minister, 903†, 903–4, 905*

Turnbull, Malcolm (1954–; educated Brasenose College, Oxford; Liberal Member, Wentworth, NSW, House of Representatives, 2004–18; Leader of the Liberal Party, Australia, 2015–18; Prime Minister, Australia, 2015–18; wrote *The Spycatcher Trial* (1988)), 710
Turner, Graham, 558, 583–4, 589
Tusmore, Oxfordshire, 958
Tutu, Desmond (1931–2021; Archbishop of Cape Town and Metropolitan of Southern Africa, 1986–96; leading spokesman for black South Africans; winner, Nobel Peace Prize, 1984), 548, 555
TV-am, 764
20 June Group of writers, 696
25 de Mayo (Argentine carrier), 302*, 304
Twinn, Ian (1950–; educated Cambridge Grammar School and University College of Wales, Aberystwyth; Conservative MP for Edmonton, 1983–97; PPS to Minister of State for Energy, 1987–90), 867, 891–2, 893, 908†

Ukraine, 829*, 832; Putin's invasion of, 6
Ulster Defence Association, 726
Ulster Defence Regiment (UDR), 207, 454†, 454, 460, 726
Ulster Unionist Party (UUP), 252, 253, 445, 719
unemployment: White Paper on Employment Policy (1944), 27–8, 75*, 75; in 1930s, 151; in 1970s, 165, 167; 'Labour isn't working'

slogan, 165, 167; in MT's first term, 204, 225*, 225, 227, 234, 271*, 279, 334; and crime, 272; hits 3 million mark (January 1982), 279, 334; Tory manifesto (1983), 343; Youth Training Scheme, 343, 492, 607; in MT's second term, 360, 495, 501, 544*, 544, 602*, 602, 665; and Lord Young, 501; and 1987 election, 607†, 607, 612; Lord Young's employment and training programmes, 630; in MT's third term, 840–41
Union of Democratic Mineworkers (UDM), 396, 772
United Arab Emirates (UAE), 437*, 440
United Nations: Security Council, 213, 290–91, 318–19, 319*, 686, 782, 856–7, 861, 863, 865, 866–7, 871; and Falklands War, 290–91, 301–2, 309–10, 311‡, 311–12, 313, 318–19, 319*, 861; Article 73 of Charter, 311‡; and Palestinian self-determination, 433; and Israel's right to exist, 435*, 435; Article 51 right to self-defence in Charter, 531, 533, 861, 866–7; and climate change, 779, 780, 781, 782, 783–4, 785, 786; MT's address to General Assembly, 783–4; global environmental fund, 785; and southern Africa, 792; Iraqi invasion of Kuwait, 856–7, 859–60, 861–2, 863, 866–7, 871†, 871–2, 891*, 891; MT suggested for Secretary-General, 920*, 920
United States of America: 'Europe, whole and

free' concept, 5; MT's early views on, 55, 61; and Suez crisis (1956), 61, 286; State Department's International Visitor Program, 88†, 88; MT visits (1967), 88–90; MT visits (1969), 89†; MT's citing of American examples, 90, 138–9; MT repairs ties with, 135–6; MT visits (1975), 135, 136–9; MT visits (1977), 153, 156–9; 'special relationship' with UK, 212–13, 535; MT visits (1979), 212–14; MT visits (1981), 231–4, 241–2, 269; struggle over INF deployment in Europe, 238–9, 240, 242, 294, 332, 333, 346, 364, 372, 373, 414, 505; and Falklands War, 247, 284*, 285, 286, 293–300, 302†, 302–3, 305, 306–9, 310–11, 315–16, 318*, 318†, 318–19; MT visits (1982), 248; Irish-American lobby, 251‡, 448, 453–4, 459; and Maze hunger strikes, 259, 262; MT addresses General Assembly (June 1982), 325; Anti-Ballistic Missile (ABM) Treaty, 365‡, 365, 422, 563†, 564, 566, 571; MT visits (1983), 368; Marine barracks bombing, Beirut, 371–2; MT addresses Congress (February 1985), 404, 425, 454; MT visits (February 1985), 404, 424–6, 425*, 454; 'treble-damage provisions', 406–7; MT visits (1984), 407, 416, 421–4, 453–4; Glass–Steagall Act (1933), 411–12, 412*; MT visits (July 1985), 429; Mark Thatcher's security in, 442, 443;

United Nations – *cont'd*
UK's extradition
treaty with, 534;
Comprehensive Anti-
Apartheid Act (1986),
559*; MT visits
(1987), 677–8, 680;
MT's 'farewell' visit
to Reagan (November
1988), 688–91, 689*,
692; conventional
forces in Europe
(CFE), 703; phases
out CFCs, 781†;
and southern Africa,
789*, 789, 793*;
Congressional Black
Caucus, 793*; as one
of 'Four Powers' after
war, 804, 814, 815*,
821, 822; MT visits
(1989), 810–12; public
opinion on Iraq crisis
(1990), 866–7, 872;
lecture tour tradition,
921; Margaret Thatcher
Foundation, 922*; and
Bosnian crisis, 932*,
932; Al-Qaeda attacks
(11 September 2001),
954*; *see also* Bush,
George H. W.; Reagan,
Ronald
United Technologies, 506,
516
University College, Oxford,
591*
University Grants
Committee, 95
Unwin, Brian (1935–;
educated Chesterfield
School and New
College, Oxford;
Treasury, 1968–85;
seconded to the Cabinet
Office, 1981–3; Deputy
Secretary, Cabinet
Office, 1985–7;
knighted, 1990), 472
Upper Clyde Shipbuilders,
102
Urban, George
(1921–97; Hungarian-
born journalist, author
and broadcaster), 826
urban areas: inner-city
riots (1985), 501–2;
policy on inner cities,
502–3, 504, 621,
629–33, 943; *Faith
in the City* (Church
of England report),
503–4, 775; task force
plan, 504; inner cities
in MT's third term,
613, 614, 629–33,
943; MT's inner cities
comment (1987), 613,
629; MT's third term
reform programme,
621; Clarke–Ridley
power struggle over
inner-city policy,
630–31; 'Walk in
the Wilderness'
photograph (1987),
630; and planning
system, 631*; City
Action Teams, 632*;
Urban Development
Corporations, 632*;
Action for Cities
(report, 1988), 632
Urban Priority Areas, 502,
503
Ure, Sir John, 639
Utley, T. E. (Peter)
(1921–88; educated
privately and Corpus
Christi College,
Cambridge; journalist;
leader writer, 1964–80,
and Chief Assistant
Editor, 1980–87, *Daily
Telegraph*; contested
(Unionist) North Antrim,
1974), 123*, 170

Vaizey, John
(1929–84; educated
Colfe's Grammar
School, Lewisham
and Queens' College,
Cambridge; economist
and educationalist;
Professor of Economics,
Brunel University,
1966–82; created Lord
Vaizey of Greenwich,
1976), 149
Vale of Glamorgan by-
election, 733
Van der Post, Laurens
(1906–96; Afrikaner
writer, farmer,
soldier, explorer,
conservationist; friend
of Prince of Wales;
knighted, 1981), 326–7,
551‡, 551–2, 555
Vance, Cyrus, 158
Vassall, John, 129*
Vaughan, Janet, 25
Védrine, Hubert (1947–;
diplomatic adviser to
President Mitterrand,
1981–6; Minister of
Foreign Affairs,
1997–2002), 477, 680,
817
Verity, William, 178
Victor Smith, Paddi (*later*
Lilley), 67*, 67, 68*, 68
Victoria, Queen, 290
Vietnam, 577
Vietnam War, 88, 89, 824†
Vietnamese Boat People, 191
Vincent, John (1937–2021;
educated Bedales
and Christ's College,
Cambridge; Professor
of Modern History,
University of Bristol,
1970–84; Professor of
History, 1984–2002.
He was a columnist for
the *Sun* and *The Times*
in the 1980s), 591
Vinson, Nigel (1931–;
educated Pangbourne
Naval College; founder
and Chairman, Plastic
Coatings Ltd, 1952–72;
pioneer of the idea
of portable pensions;
created Lord Vinson,
1985), 129
Virgin airlines, 946
Vogue magazine, 597
Volcker, Paul (1927–2019;
President, New York
Federal Reserve Bank,
1975–9; Chairman,
American Federal
Reserve Board,
1979–87; Chairman,
President's Economic
Recovery Advisory
Board, from 2008),
232, 689*
Vukovar, 931

Waddington, David
(1929–2017; educated
Sedbergh and Hertford
College, Oxford;
Conservative MP for

Nelson and Colne, 1968–74; for Clitheroe, 1979–83; for Ribble Valley, 1983–90; Chief Whip, 1987–9; Home Secretary, 1989–90; created Lord Waddington, 1990), 617, 746*, 746, 752, 844, 900
Wade-Gery, Sir Robert, 229–30, 257, 258; and Falklands War, 291–2, 313–14
Wadhams, Peter (1948–; educated Palmer's School, Grays, Essex and Churchill College, Cambridge; Director, Scott Polar Research Institute, 1976–2002; Professor of Ocean Physics, Cambridge University, 2003–15; author of *A Farewell to Ice* (2016)), 783*, 783, 784
Waite, Terry, 695*
Wakeham, Alison, 888*, 950*
Wakeham, John (1932–; educated Charterhouse; Conservative MP for Maldon, 1974–83, for Colchester South and Maldon, 1983–92; Government Chief Whip, 1983–7; Lord Privy Seal, 1987–8; Leader of the House of Commons, 1987–9; Lord President of the Council, 1988–9; Secretary of State for Energy, 1989–92; created Lord Wakeham, 1992): Chief Whip, 350, 352*, 510, 538, 616; and Brighton bombing, 449, 450; and ERM question, 493–4; and 1985 reshuffle, 496, 497†, 498, 500; and Westland affair, 510, 512; in Strategy Group ('A-Team'), 538; and South Africa, 556; 1987 election campaign, 606, 608;

advice on first Cabinet of third term, 616, 617; Leader of the House, 617; Energy Secretary, 772–3, 889*; and Iraq 'War Cabinet' (1990), 862; and Major, 867; and leadership contest (November 1990), 888*, 888, 889*, 889, 891–2, 895, 896–8, 897†, 899–900; at MT's farewell lunch, 908†; and conspiracy to remove MT, 913
Wakeham, Roberta, 450†
Waldegrave, William (1946–; educated Eton, Corpus Christi College, Oxford and Harvard University; younger son of 12th Earl Waldegrave; Conservative MP for Bristol West, 1979–97; Secretary of State for Health, 1990–92; Chancellor of the Duchy of Lancaster, 1992–4; Minister of Agriculture, Fisheries and Food, 1994–5; Chief Secretary to the Treasury, 1995–7; created Lord Waldegrave of North Hill, 1999), 106, 125, 467, 471, 542*, 808*, 818; and Blue Chips group, 277; at CPRS, 466†; and local government, 466, 468, 471, 472; as Fellow of All Souls, 468‡, 468; and poll tax, 468, 471, 472; on Wakeham's list after 1987 victory, 616*; in rising generation of Conservative politicians, 645; on Rushdie affair, 696; and German reunification issue, 816; Health Secretary, 880; and 'Catherine Place conspiracy', 894; individual session with

MT (21 November 1990), 899
Walden, Brian (1932–2019; educated West Bromwich Grammar School and the Queen's College, Oxford; Labour MP for Birmingham All Saints, 1964–74; for Birmingham Ladywood, 1974–7; presenter, *Weekend World*, 1977–86), 187*, 519, 537, 759*, 764, 875, 876; as convert from socialism, 147; television interviews with MT, 147, 153, 327–8, 754†, 754; and Thatcherism, 147, 177–8, 199; interview with MT after Lawson's resignation, 754†, 754, 759*
Waldheim, Kurt, 193
Wales, 175; devolution issue, 160; devolution referendum (March 1979), 162*, 162, 171
Wałęsa, Lech (1943–; co-founder and Chairman, Solidarity trade union, 1980–90; President of Polish Republic, 1990–95), 245, 693, 694*, 694, 695
Walker, Jenonne, 932
Walker, Peter (1932–2010; educated Latymer Upper School; Conservative MP for Worcester, 1961–92; Secretary of State for the Environment, 1970–72; for Trade and Industry, 1972–4; Minister of Agriculture, Fisheries and Food, 1979–83; Secretary of State for Energy, 1983–7; for Wales, 1987–90; created Lord Walker of Worcester, 1992), 225; dropped from Shadow Cabinet by MT, 129; Agriculture Secretary,

Walker, Peter – *cont'd*
183, 225; and public spending control, 228, 272, 278; and 1981 budget, 270; leaks CPRS report, 335, 356; Energy Secretary, 351–2, 381*, 381, 383–4; and miners' strike, 383–4, 385, 386, 388, 390, 394, 396, 408–9, 450†; and privatization policy, 401–2, 408–9; opposes poll tax, 473; on unemployment (May 1985), 495; and 1985 reshuffle, 499–500; and South Africa, 556; and MT's first third term Cabinet, 616, 617; Welsh Secretary, 617
Wall, Stephen (1947–; educated Douai and Selwyn College, Cambridge; private secretary to the Foreign Secretary, 1988–90 private secretary to the Prime Minister, 1991–3; Ambassador and UK Permanent Representative to EU, 1995–2000; head of European Secretariat, Cabinet Office, 2000–2004; knighted, 2004), 745, 814*
Wall Street Journal, 136, 764, 817, 820
Wallace, Kenneth, 11†, 31
Wallace, Mary, 11†, 16, 23
Wallis, Allen, 406
Walsh, Shirley (later Ellis), 17, 19, 21, 966–7
Walters, Alan (1926–2009; educated Alderman Newton's School, Leicester, University College, Leicester and Nuffield College, Oxford; Professor of Economics, LSE, 1967–76; chief economic adviser to the Prime Minister, 1981–3 and 1989–90; knighted, 1983): influence on MT, 147*, 147, 269, 651; *Money in Boom and Slump*, 147; as MT's economic adviser, 226–7, 268, 269, 271*, 670, 739, 749–52; on PSBR, 267, 268; and 1981 budget, 268, 269; Falklands plebiscite idea, 309‡; and Lawson, 353, 654, 670‡, 670, 749–52, 753, 754; and public spending control, 356; on Thatcherism, 359; at Chequers meeting (September 1983), 360; and ERM question, 490–91, 652, 653, 662, 670†, 670, 739, 750, 850*, 850; and Delors, 672; resigns as adviser, 752–3, 855; and nuclear power, 772
Walters, Barbara, 137
Wandsworth Council, 847
Warburton, Arabella, 878, 882, 919–20
Ward, Alison, 112, 130, 185, 226, 595
Warnock, (Helen) Mary (1924–2019; educated St Swithun's, Winchester and Lady Margaret Hall, Oxford; headmistress, Oxford High School, 1966–72; Mistress of Girton College, Cambridge, 1985–91; Chairman, Committee of Inquiry into Special Education, 1974–8; Chairman, Committee of Inquiry into Human Fertilization, 1982–4; created Baroness Warnock, 1985), 14*, 14
Warrington by-election (1981), 273
Warry, Peter (1949–; educated Clifton College and Merton College, Oxford; Group Managing Director, Aerospace Engineering plc, 1982–4; special adviser and deputy head, No. 10 Policy Unit, 1984–6; Chief Executive, Nuclear Electric, 1996–8; Chairman, the Royal Mint, 2012), 384*, 400–401, 528
Warsaw Pact, 142, 414, 686, 805, 811*, 811, 832, 834, 835*; countries of after fall of Communism, 922, 925
Washington DC, 137–9, 158–9
Washington Post, 138†, 138, 213, 297–8, 317, 359, 421, 577
Washington Speakers Bureau (WSB), 921
Wass, Douglas (1923–2017; educated Nottingham High School and St John's College, Cambridge; Permanent Secretary, Treasury, 1974–83, and joint head of the Home Civil Service, 1981–3; knighted, 1975), 89*, 225, 268
water industry, 758, 768*, 768–9
Watkin, David, *Morality and Architecture*, 148*
Weatherill, Bernard 'Jack' (1920–2007; educated Malvern College; tailor; Conservative MP for Croydon North East, 1964–92; Deputy Government Chief Whip, 1973–4; Deputy Opposition Chief Whip, 1974–9; Speaker of the House of Commons, 1983–92; created Lord Weatherill, 1992]., 123, 354, 929
Webley, Simon, 110
Weekend World (television programme), 153

Weinberger, Caspar (1917–2006; born in California; lawyer; Director of Finance, California, 1968–69; counsellor to the President, 1973; US Defense Secretary, 1981–7; Hon. GBE, 1988), 294, 298*, 298, 302, 305, 314, 323, 422*, 422, 424, 429–30, 689*
Weinstock, Arnold, Lord, 516
Welch, Colin, 123*
welfare: early welfare state, 10, 27; prevailing postwar consensus, 43; MT at MPNI, 73–6, 76*; women in government posts, 74; Beveridge Report (1942), 75–6; indexing of benefits to inflation, 228; social security benefits, 228, 279, 335; child benefit, 269; one-parent-family benefit, 269; de-indexing of social security payments, 335; fears on abolition of welfare state, 335; suspicions of MT's intentions towards welfare state, 335; MT's hesitation over radical reform, 336; *see also* National Health Service (NHS)
Wellington, Arthur Wellesley, 1st Duke of, 324, 327*, 327, 590
Wells, John (1936–98; educated Eastbourne College and St Edmund Hall, Oxford; writer, actor and director; played title role in *Anyone for Denis?* (as well as writing it, with Richard Ingrams) at Whitehall Theatre, 1981–2), 588
Wesley, John, 147, 389‡, 777
Wesley's Chapel, City Road, London, 55
West, Teddy, 35

West Derbyshire by-election, 537
West Germany, 135†, 190, 238–9, 242–3, 245, 305, 332; MT visits (1982), 333; neutralism in, 333; support for single currency, 486–7; and apartheid South Africa, 548*, 548, 555; independence of central bank, 654†; British troops in, 679, 804; and NATO, 700–701, 736†; and SNF negotiations, 700, 701, 703–4, 736†; and Rome Council (1990), 872 *see also* German reunification
Westland affair, 472, 505–6; Heseltine resigns over, 473, 504, 514*, 514–15, 515*; impact on MT, 473, 515, 524*, 524–5, 526, 527–9, 543, 564; and DTI, 506‡, 506, 507, 508, 510, 517–19, 520, 522–3; and Tebbit, 506–7; American option, 506, 507, 508, 509, 510, 511–12, 516*, 516, 517; 'European solution', 507–8, 509–10, 511, 514–15; Whitehall battle, 507–14; involvement of Law Officers, 511–13, 513*, 515–16, 517–19, 520–21, 522–4, 768; leak of Solicitor-General's letter, 513, 514, 515–16, 517–19, 520–21, 522–4, 523*, 523†, 768; Hanson as 'mystery buyer', 516; House of Commons debate on (27 January 1986), 518–19, 520–21; Sikorsky bid accepted, 521; select committees investigating, 522, 524
Westminster Council, 629†, 748*, 749*, 847
Weston, Garfield, 732*

Weston, John (1938–; educated Sherborne and Worcester College, Oxford; Director of International Security Policy, FCO, 1981–5; UK Permanent Representative to NATO, 1992–5; UK Permanent Representative to UN, 1995–8; knighted, 1992), 287, 430
White, Sir Gordon, 404†
Whitehouse, Mary (1910–2001; educated Chester City Grammar School; freelance journalist and broadcaster; co-founder, 'Clean Up TV Campaign', 1964; Honorary General Secretary, National Viewers' and Listeners' Association, 1965–80; President, 1980–93. Author of two autobiographies: *Who Does She Think She Is?* (1971) and *Quite Contrary* (1993)), 84, 763, 777
Whitelaw, William (1918–99; educated Winchester and Trinity College, Cambridge; served in Scots Guards, 1939–46, awarded the Military Cross; Conservative MP for Penrith and the Border, 1955–83; Secretary of State for Northern Ireland, 1972–3; Secretary of State for Employment, 1973–4; Deputy Leader of Conservative Party, 1975–9; Home Secretary and Deputy Prime Minister, 1979–83; created Viscount Whitelaw, 1983; Leader of the House of Lords and Lord President of the Council, 1983–8): Chief Whip, 83; in

Whitelaw, William – *cont'd*
opposition, 109, 114, 115, 151, 159, 164; and party leadership, 109, 114, 115, 125*, 125, 126†, 126, 127, 731; enters second leadership ballot, 126†, 126, 127, 731; Deputy Leader, 129, 132, 154, 159, 731; on MT's entourage/staff, 129; attitude to MT, 130, 164; and 1979 election campaign, 171; Deputy Prime Minister, 182, 351, 627, 746*, 746; Home Secretary, 182, 218–19, 221–2, 229; importance of in MT's governments, 182, 299, 350–51, 464, 468*, 468, 472, 473, 616, 626–7; Military Cross in Second World War, 183*, 289§; 'Inner Group' on economic policy, 216; Iranian embassy siege, Princes Gate, 221–2; and dinner for the permanent secretaries, 221; and public spending control, 228, 272, 278; chairman of Civil Contingencies Unit, 229; prepares for confrontation with miners, 229; Northern Ireland policy, 252; and 1981 budget, 270; and September 1981 reshuffle, 274; in Falklands War Cabinet, 291, 299, 304; and Falklands War, 306, 307, 308, 320; on CPRS paper, 336; and local government, 339, 340, 464, 468*, 468; and 1983 election date, 342; as Leader of the House of Lords, 350–51, 464; moves to Lords, 350–51, 356; supports poll tax, 472, 629; and ERM question, 493, 494, 652; and 1985 reshuffle, 496, 497†; and Heseltine, 506§, 506–7; and Westland affair, 510–11, 512, 627; on foreign multinationals and BL, 528; preparations for 1987 election, 535; in Strategy Group ('A-Team'), 538; and broadcasting policy, 540, 764; and South Africa, 556; and 1987 election campaign, 610; in MT's third term, 616, 731, 732, 849; ill health and retirement, 626–7, 627†, 746; and AIDS public education, 642; and Oldfield revelations, 715–16; on MT, 731; and MT's tenth anniversary, 731, 732; and Howe-Lawson collaboration, 735; views on BBC, 761; advises on message to MT (21 November 1990), 894, 895, 897; and conspiracy to remove MT, 913

Whitmore, Clive (1935–; educated Sutton Grammar School and Christ's College, Cambridge; principal private secretary to the Prime Minister, 1979–82; Permanent Under-Secretary, MOD, 1983–8; Home Office, 1988–94; knighted, 1983), 215; principal private secretary to MT, 180, 181*, 190, 191, 194*, 227, 274; visit to Soviet Union (1979), 191; on MT's relations with Reagan, 248, 316; and Falklands War, 286, 287, 292, 300, 304, 306, 316, 322, 324; and Mark Thatcher, 441, 442; and Westland affair, 514*, 524; and *Spycatcher* controversy, 707

Whittingdale, John (1959–; educated Winchester and University College, London; Conservative MP for Colchester South and Maldon, 1992–7; for Maldon and East Chelmsford, 1997–2010; for Maldon, 2010–; political secretary to the Prime Minister, 1988–90; private secretary to Margaret Thatcher, 1990–92; Secretary of State for Culture, Media and Sport, 2015–16; knighted, 2022), 517, 523, 524, 604*, 627–8, 628*, 756, 846, 870, 907, 946; and Howe's resignation, 878, 880; and leadership contest (November 1990), 884, 886, 888, 891, 892, 903; serves MT after her departure from office, 918, 934

Wicks, Nigel (1940–; educated Beckenham and Penge Grammar School and Portsmouth College of Technology, London University and Cambridge University; private secretary to the Prime Minister, 1975–8; principal private secretary to the Prime Minister, 1985–8; knighted, 1992), 494, 508, 519, 522, 539, 670, 717, 770, 772, 841

Wilberforce, Richard, Baron, 103

Wilcox, Ella Wheeler, 959

Wilde, Oscar, 921

Wilkie, David, murder of, 394, 417†, 418

Willetts, David (1956–; educated King Edward's School, Birmingham and Christ Church, Oxford; No. 10 Policy Unit, 1984–6; director of studies, Centre for Policy

Studies, 1987–92; Conservative MP for Havant, 1992–2015; Minister of State for Universities and Science, 2010–15; created Lord Willetts, 2015): 268*; in Policy Unit, 353†, 401, 620–21, 621*, 641, 654; and privatization policy, 403; and stock exchange reform, 411–12; and 1987 election campaign, 608†, 610; and AIDS, 641, 642; and NHS 'internal market', 644
Williams, Sir Anthony, 284
Williams, Miss Gladys, 22
Williams, Shirley (1930–2021; educated at eight schools in UK and USA and Somerville College, Oxford; Labour MP for Hitchin, 1964–74, for Hertford and Stevenage, 1974–9; Secretary of State for Prices, 1974–6; for Education, 1976–9. Member of 'Gang of Four' which founded SDP; elected SDP MP for Crosby in by-election, 1981; lost seat, 1983; created Baroness Williams of Crosby, 1983), 119*, 227†, 234–5, 279
Williamson, David (1934–2015; educated Tonbridge and Exeter College, Oxford; Deputy Secretary, Cabinet Office, 1983–7; Secretary-General, European Commission, 1987–97; knighted, 1998; created Lord Williamson of Horton, 1999), 476, 477*, 477, 488, 665
Willink, Rachel, 24
Wilson, Harold (1916–95; educated Wirral Grammar School, Bebington

and Jesus College, Oxford; Prime Minister 1964–70, 1974–6; created Lord Wilson of Rievaulx, 1983): 1964 election victory, 79; 1966 election victory, 81, 83, 84–5; Prime Minister (1964–70), 82–3, 85–6; MT's views on, 82; on 'Selsdon Man', 92; February 1974 election, 107; Policy Unit of, 107; forms third administration, 108; wins October 1974 election, 114; views on MT, 124*; resigns as Prime Minister (1976), 143; alleged MI5 plot against, 713*, 713
Wilson, Marie, 720
Wilson, Richard (1942–; educated Radley and Clare College, Cambridge; Deputy Secretary, Cabinet Office, 1987–90; Deputy Secretary, Treasury, 1990–92; Cabinet Secretary and head, Home Civil Service, 1998–2002; created Lord Wilson of Dinton, 2002): as Cabinet Secretary, 2; at Cabinet Office, 625–6, 631, 644, 645, 766; and green issues, 781*, 782, 784; on MT's susceptibility to younger men, 841; and poll tax, 850; visits MT after her fall, 919
Wimbledon tennis championship, 835†
Windsor, Roger, 393
Winehouse, Amy, 636*
Winning, Norman, 26
Wintour, Anna, 597
Witheridge, John, 503†
Wold, Anne, 957–8
Wolfson, David (1935–2021; educated Clifton College, Trinity College, Cambridge and Stanford

University; chief of staff, Political Office, 10 Downing Street, 1979–85; Chairman, Great Universal Stores, 1996–2000; created Lord Wolfson of Sunningdale, 1991), 950; chief of staff to MT's political office, 184, 224; and 1981 budget, 268, 269; Hoskyns' 'blockbuster' memo, 274–5; and September 1981 reshuffle, 275; and Middle East politics, 434; and Brighton bombing, 449; MT and Denis holiday with (1986), 539; 1987 election campaign, 608†; and NHS crisis, 646; and MT's tenth anniversary, 732*
Wolfson, Susan, 950
Woman's Own magazine, 133*, 596, 623, 624
women: MT's character and achievements as a woman, 1, 3, 6–7, 186, 188, 592–3, 729, 969–70; and home/ family life, 6–7, 57–8, 62–3, 68*, 68; and MT's disruptive power, 6–7; and Oxford Union, 27*, 27; pay gap, 35, 84; Conservative attitude to women in politics, 39, 40, 62–4, 122, 913; MT's housewife analogies, 41, 43, 83, 224; MT on women's patriotism, 44; marriage as ending women's careers, 53–4; MT's 'Wake up, women' article (1952), 56; MT's early parliamentary career, 68, 73–5, 84; and education, 71; MT's first government post, 73–4; equalizing of employment/pension/ taxation rights of women, 74; taxation of working women,

women – cont'd
77, 83; discrimination against married women in taxation, 83; divorced or deserted mothers, 83; *A Fair Share for the Fair Sex* (policy document), 84; MT as Education Secretary, 96–7; attacks on women politicians as more personal, 119–20; MT targets women in Labour-voting households, 133; Callaghan's condescension towards MT, 143; MT's 'use of her femininity', 149, 577, 593, 595; and 1979 election campaign, 172; no women appointed to MT's first Cabinet, 183; only ever woman in MT's Cabinet, 276, 351; women on MT, 594–5; MT's view on women priests, 596; Conservative women MPs after 1987 victory, 617*; MT's 'tigress' image, 729; no women in first Major Cabinet, 916; male remarks on MT's mental health, 955; sexist tropes on female leaders, 964
Women2Win, 959
Wood, Andrew (1940–; educated Ardingly and King's College, Cambridge; Minister, British Embassy, Washington, 1989–92; Ambassador to the Russian Federation, 1995–2000; knighted, 1995), 823–4, 824*
Woodhouse, C. M. 'Monty', 63†, 73
Woodward, Rear Admiral John 'Sandy', 304*, 304, 305*, 311, 313
Woolton, Frederick Marquis, 1st Earl of, 44
Woolwich West by-election, 134
Wootten, Amy, 27†, 27

Worcester College, Oxford, 30
World Trade Organization (WTO), 872†
Worlock, Derek, 471
Worsthorne, Peregrine (1923–2020; educated Stowe and Peterhouse, Cambridge and Magdalen College, Oxford; columnist; Associate Editor, *Sunday Telegraph*, 1976–86; Editor, 1986–9; knighted, 1991), 621
Worth, G. A., 28
Worthington, Mark 920, 930, 939, 942, 943, 945, 955, 956, 961, 965*
Wright, Oliver (1921–2009; educated Solihull School and Christ's College, Cambridge; Ambassador to West Germany, 1975–81; Ambassador to the United States, 1982–6; knighted, 1974), 334, 601*
Wright, Patrick (1931–2020; educated Marlborough and Merton College, Oxford; Ambassador to Syria, 1979–81; Deputy Under-Secretary, FCO, 1982–4; Ambassador to Saudi Arabia, 1984–6; Permanent Under-Secretary and head of Diplomatic Service, 1986–91; created Lord Wright, 1994), 705, 735, 736, 738, 739–40, 807, 813, 836; and Bruges Speech, 672, 673; and MT's views on Germans, 806, 807–8; and MT's health, 813*; at Strasbourg Council (1989), 815; and poll tax, 839–40; Iraqi invasion of Kuwait, 866
Wright, Peter, (1916–95; educated Bishop's Stortford College and St Peter's College,

Oxford; Principal Scientific Officer, MI5, 1955–76; Chairman, Fluency Committee, MI5/MI6, which investigated Soviet penetration, 1964; wrote *Spycatcher*, 1987), 706–15, 714*
Wright, Virginia, 705, 740
Wyatt, Woodrow (1918–97; educated Eastbourne and Worcester College, Oxford; journalist; Labour MP for Aston Division of Birmingham, 1945–55; for Bosworth Division of Leicester, 1959–70; Chairman, Horserace Totalisator Board, 1976–97; created Lord Wyatt of Weeford, 1987), 518*, 529, 534, 551*, 615–16, 629, 732*, 754†, 769, 838, 933, 942*; as convert from socialism, 147; Cavalier or Roundhead question, 327†; and miners' strike, 395–6, 397; closeness to MT, 516†, 683, 846†; diaries, 516†, 846†; and Murdoch, 516†, 526, 605†, 765; and Westland affair, 516–17, 526, 527; and Queen Mother, 556, 846; and leadership contest (November 1990), 886, 907; sits in Lords, 931

Yakovlev, Alexander, 697
Al-Yamamah arms contract, 439–40, 440*, 442
Yeltsin, Boris (1931–2007; President of Russia, 1991–9), 682†, 682, 698*, 830†; MT meets in Downing Street (April 1990), 830†, 830–31; elected Chairman of Russian parliament, 831; and Moscow coup (August 1991), 926–7; MT's phone call to during siege, 926–7; as

President of Russia, 926–7
Yemen, 577, 863
Yeovil, Somerset, 506†, 506
Yom Kippur War, 106
Yorkshire Post, 72
Youde, Edward (1924–86; educated School of Oriental and African Studies, University of London; private secretary to the Prime Minister, 1969–70; Ambassador to People's Republic of China, 1974–8; Governor of Hong Kong, 1982–6; knighted, 1977), 329
Young, David (1932–2022; educated Christ's College, Finchley and University College London; Director, Centre for Policy Studies, 1979–82; special adviser, Department of Industry, 1980–82; Chairman, Manpower Services Commission, 1982–4; Secretary of State for Employment, 1985–7; for Trade and Industry, 1987–9; Deputy Chairman, Conservative Party, 1989–90; created Lord Young of Graffham, 1984): Alan Clark on, 501*; Employment Secretary, 501, 502, 503, 504, 630; and policy on inner cities, 502, 503, 504; and Sunday trading debate, 532; and preparations for 1987 election, 535, 536–7, 603–4, 605*, 605; political ambition of, 536, 603; and Tebbit, 536, 603*, 603–4; 1987 election campaign, 606*, 606, 608, 610–11, 612; Trade and Industry Secretary, 618, 621–2, 630; views on BBC, 761; electricity privatization, 771; resigns from Cabinet, 838

Young, Hugo (1938–2003; educated Ampleforth and Balliol College, Oxford; journalist and author, the *Sunday Times*, 1965–84; political columnist, the *Guardian*, 1984–2003; author of *One of Us*, 1989), 151, 225, 228, 599, 600, 615

Young, Janet (1926–2002; née Baker, married Geoffrey Young, 1950; educated Headington School, Oxford, in America and St Anne's College, Oxford; Leader of House of Lords, 1981–3; Lord Privy Seal, 1982–3; Minister of State, FCO, 1983–7; created Baroness Young, 1971), 276, 351

Young, Jimmy (DJ), 133*, 133, 171, 623, 671

Young, Stuart, 541, 542

Young and Rubicam (advertising firm), 409, 536–7, 537*, 539

Young Conservatives: Colchester, 36–7, 38; Heath's attitude to, 42–3; Dartford, 42; conference in Eastbourne (1975), 127

Young Ones, The (BBC comedy), 586

Younger, George (1931–2003; 4th Viscount Younger of Leckie, educated Winchester and New College, Oxford; Conservative MP for Ayr, 1964–92; Secretary of State for Scotland, 1979–86; for Defence, 1986–9; created life peer, 1992; KCVO, 1993; KT, 1995), 467–8, 469, 496; and poll tax in Scotland, 470, 471–2, 473; Defence Secretary, 514, 720, 795*, 795; and US attack on Libya, 530‡, 530; on MT's ageing, 608*; and Northern Ireland, 720, 721; and Meyer's leadership challenge, 756–7; resigns from Cabinet, 838; and MT's leadership campaign team (1990), 885*, 885, 889–90

Youth Training Scheme, 343, 492, 607

Yugoslavia, former, 931–2, 945

Zagorsk, 576
Zakheim, Dov, 298*
Zambia, 193, 194‡, 194–5, 506*, 553, 788
Zamyatin, Leonid (1922–2019; Soviet Ambassador to the UK, 1986–91), 418‡, 686, 687
Zayed, Sheikh (1918–2004; President of the United Arab Emirates, 1971–2004), 440†, 440
Zelikow, Philip (1954; US Department of State, 1985 9; NSC staff, 1989–91), 803, 818
Zhao Ziyang (1919–2005; Premier of China, 1980–87; General Secretary of the Chinese Communist Party, 1987–9), 329, 331, 927†, 927
Zia, Muhammed, 240†
Zoellick, Robert (1953–; Counselor of the State Department, 1989–92; Deputy Secretary of State, 2005–6; President, World Bank, 2007–12), 692, 703, 803†, 824
Zulus, 551, 552*
Zurich Economic Society, 148, 149